# UTOPIA
## IN
## P☭WER

## THE HISTORY OF THE SOVIET UNION FROM 1917 TO THE PRESENT

BY

# MIKHAIL HELLER

### AND

# ALEKSANDR NEKRICH

*Translated from the Russian by Phyllis B. Carlos*

SUMMIT BOOKS • NEW YORK

Originally published in Russian by Overseas Publications
Interchange Ltd. as *Utopija u vlasti* in 1982. Published in
French by Editions Calmann-Levy as *L'utopie au pouvoir* in
1982, copyright © 1982 by Editions Calmann-Levy. Revised
Russian language manuscript copyright © 1985 by Mikhail
Heller and Aleksandr Nekrich.

English language translation copyright © 1986 by Summit Books,
a Division of Simon & Schuster, Inc.

Chapters 1–6 were written by Mikhail Heller, 7–10 by Aleksandr M.
Nekrich, the others by both authors.

Published by SUMMIT BOOKS
A Division of Simon & Schuster, Inc.
Simon & Schuster Building
1230 Avenue of the Americas
New York, New York 10020

SUMMIT BOOKS and colophon are trademarks of
Simon & Schuster, Inc.

Designed by Irving Perkins Associates

Manufactured in the United States of America

10 9 8 7 6 5 4 3 2
10 9 8 7 6 5 4 3 2    Pbk.

Library of Congress Cataloging-in-Publication Data

Heller [Geller], Mikhail, date.
  Utopia in power.

  Translation of: Utopija u vlasti/Mikhail Geller,
Aleksandr Nekrich.
  Bibliography: p.
  1. Soviet Union—History—1917–      .
I. Nekrich, A. M. (Aleksandr Moiseevich)  II. Title.
DK266.G3713   1986        947.084        86-5792

ISBN: 0-671-46242-3
ISBN: 0-671-64535-8 Pbk.

# CONTENTS

# ACKNOWLEDGMENTS

My contribution to this book was written at the Russian Research Center of Harvard University, where I enjoyed the stimulating conversation and encouragement of an unusually congenial group of colleagues. I would also like to thank the National Endowment for the Humanities, the Ford Foundation, and the American Council of Learned Societies for their support of various portions of this work. Finally, I would like to thank Steven Jones for his valuable contribution in preparing the final version of the English translation.

Aleksandr M. Nekrich

# INTRODUCTION

THE MAN OF THE FUTURE IS THE ONE WHO WILL HAVE
THE LONGEST MEMORY.
——FRIEDRICH NIETZSCHE——

From time immemorial history has been written by the victors. "Woe to the vanquished," said the ancient Romans, by which they implied not only that the vanquished may be exterminated or turned into slaves but that the conquerors write the history of their wars; the victors take possession of the past and establish their control over the collective memory. George Orwell, perhaps the only Western writer who profoundly understood the essence of the Soviet world, devised this precise and pitiless formula: "Whoever controls the past controls the future." Orwell was not the first to say this, though. Mikhail Pokrovsky, the first Soviet Marxist historian, anticipated Orwell when he wrote that history is politics applied to the past.

The history of the Soviet Union is not just another example confirming the general rule. In this case history was placed at the service of the state to the greatest possible extent and in the most conscious, systematic way. After the October revolution not only the means of production were nationalized but all spheres of existence, and above all, memory, history.

Memory makes us human. Without it people are turned into a formless mass that can be shaped into anything the controllers of the past desire. Count Alexander Benckendorff, a Baltic-German nobleman and Russia's first chief of gendarmes under Tsar Nicholas I, advised this approach to history: "Russia's past is admirable; its present more than magnificent; as for its future, it is beyond the grasp of the most daring imagination; it is from this point of view... that Russian history must be conceived and

9

written." The chief of gendarmes was convinced of the correctness of his view. So was Maxim Gorky, the leading Soviet writer under Joseph Stalin, who said: "We must know everything that happened in the past, not in the way it has been written about heretofore; but rather, in the way it appears in the light of the doctrine of Marx-Engels-Lenin-Stalin."

Benckendorff's worthy suggestions seem to have been adopted and grafted onto the Marxist-Leninist-Stalinist doctrine, with the result that the Soviet people were successfully deprived of their social memory. In the decades after the Bolshevik revolution an unparalleled expertise was developed in manipulating the past and controlling history. Not only was the history of the Soviet Union controlled and manipulated; the history of Russia and of the nations which had been part of the Russian empire suffered as well. Soviet textbooks begin the history of the Union of Soviet Socialist Republics, founded in 1922, with the ancient Armenian kingdom of Urartu. Thus, it would seem that the triumphal march to the radiant heights of mature socialism began on the shores of Lake Van in the ninth century B.C.

Many Western historians who verbally reject the official viewpoint of Soviet historiography in fact accept it. They find the sources of the 1917 revolution in the internecine warfare of the Kievan princes, the Tatar yoke, the atrocities of Ivan the Terrible, the cruelties of Peter the Great, the "Conditions" limiting monarchical power that were torn up by Empress Anne in 1730, or the manifesto granting a few liberties to the nobility, signed by the short-lived Tsar Peter III in 1762. Reaching back into the distant past, Soviet historians argue that the dream of socialism was nurtured by the peasants of Yuri Dolgoruky or that Ivan Kalita, the grand duke of Moscow, brought prosperity and prominence to the future capital of the first victorious socialist country in the world. Similarly turning to the distant past, Western historians draw a direct line from Ivan Vasilievich (Ivan the Terrible) to Joseph Vissarionovich (Stalin), or from Malyuta Skuratov, head of Ivan the Terrible's bodyguard and secret police force, to Yuri Andropov, the longtime head of the KGB who recently headed the Soviet state, thus demonstrating that from the time of the Scythians Russia was inexorably heading toward the October revolution and Soviet power. It was inherent in the national character of the Russian people. Nowhere else, these scholars think, would such a thing be possible.

There is no question that historical events affect the lives of nations, not only in the immediate present but over the long term, even for centuries. Clearly in studying history one must take into account many factors: geographical, climatic, and soil conditions, as well as national characteristics and forms of government. Moreover, there are certain similar factors in all modern societies, such as urbanization, industrialization, and demographic cycles.

In studying the history of the Soviet state it is insufficient to consider such factors. One particular characteristic—the total influence of the ruling party on all spheres of existence on a scale never before known—acts as a determining force in all Soviet institutions and on the typical Soviet citizen, Homo Sovieticus. This total influence has distorted the normal processes at work in contemporary societies and has resulted in the emergence of a historically unprecedented society and state.

The transition from pre-October Russia to the USSR, as Aleksandr Solzhenitsyn has said, "was not a continuation of the spinal column, but a disastrous fracture that very nearly caused the nation's total destruction." The history of the Soviet Union is the history of the transformation of Russia—a country no better or worse than any other, one with its own peculiarities to be sure, but a country comparable in all respects to the other countries of Europe—into a phenomenon such as humanity has never known.

On the date of October 25, 1917, under the old Russian calendar (November 7 by the Western calendar), a new era began. The history of Russia ended on that day. It was replaced by the history of the Soviet Union. The new era affected the entire human race, because the whole world felt, and still feels, the consequences of the October revolution. "The history of Homo Sapiens," Arthur Koestler has written, "began with zero." One might add that the history of Homo Sovieticus began the same way.

## LIST OF ACRONYMS AND ABBREVIATIONS

*Agitprop*   Department of Agitation and Propaganda
*ARA*   American Relief Administration
*CCP*   Chinese Communist party
*Cheka*   All-Russia Extraordinary Commission for the Struggle Against Counterrevolution and Sabotage
*CIA*   Central Intelligence Agency
*CPSU*   Communist Party of the Soviet Union
*Dalstroi*   Far Northern Construction Project
*FRG*   Federal Republic of Germany
*GDR*   German Democratic Republic
*Glavlit*   Main Literature and Art Administration
*GOELRO*   State Commission for the Electrification of Russia
*Gosizdat*   State Publishing House
*GPU*   State Political Administration
*GUPV*   Main Frontier Troops Administration
*Gushossdor*   Main Highway Construction Administration
*ICBM*   intercontinental ballistic missile
*IFLI*   Institute of Philosophy, Literature, and History
*Kavburo*   Caucasus Bureau
*KGB*   State Security Committee
*Komsomol*   Young Communist League
*Komuch*   Committee of Members of the Constituent Assembly
*KONR*   Committee for the Liberation of the Peoples of Russia
*KPD*   German Communist party
*LEF*   Left Front of Art
*MGB*   Ministry of State Security

13

| | |
|---|---|
| *MIRV* | mutiple independently targeted reentry vehicle |
| *MRBM* | medium-range ballistic missile |
| *MRC* | Military Revolutionary Committee |
| *MTS* | machine and tractor station |
| *MVD* | Ministry of Internal Affairs |
| *NATO* | North Atlantic Treaty Organization |
| *NELP* | Novocherkassk Electric Locomotive Plant |
| *NEP* | New Economic Policy |
| *NKVD* | People's Commissariat of Internal Affairs |
| *NTS* | National-Labor Alliance of Russian Solidarists |
| *OGPU* | Unified State Political Administration |
| *Orgburo* | Organizational Bureau |
| *ORI* | United Revolutionary Organization |
| *OUN* | Organization of Ukrainian Nationalists |
| *PMO* | Petrograd Military Organization |
| *Polrevkom* | Provisional Polish Revolutionary Committee |
| *Profintern* | Red Trade Union International |
| *Proletkult* | Proletarian Cultural and Educational Organization |
| *PUWP* | Polish United Workers party |
| *RAPP* | Russian Association of Proletarian Writers |
| *ROA* | Russian Liberation Army |
| *RONA* | Russian National Liberation Army |
| *ROVS* | Russian Union of All Military Men |
| *RSDLP* | Russian Social Democratic Labor party |
| *RSFSR* | Russian Soviet Federated Socialist Republic |
| *SMERSH* | military counterintelligence |
| *SMOT* | Free Interprofessional Association of Workers |
| *Sovnarkom* | Council of People's Commissars |
| *SR* | Socialist Revolutionary |
| *Uchraspred* | Department of Records and Assignments |
| *UPA* | Ukrainian Insurgent Army |
| *VSNKH* | Supreme Economic Council |
| *VIKZHEL* | All-Russia Executive Committee of the Railroad Workers' Union |
| *VSKhSON* | All-Russia Social Christian Union for the Liberation of the People |
| *Zakburo* | Transcaucasian Bureau |

# 1

# BEFORE OCTOBER 1917

## WORLD WAR I

The October revolution was a direct consequence of World War I. The decade preceding the war had been one of rapid economic growth. Industrial progress, in general, had begun in Russia in the 1860s after the emancipation of the serfs, but it intensified especially after Japan defeated Russia in 1905. Forced to rebuild its shattered navy and reequip its land forces, the tsarist government allocated large sums for military purposes, from which the industrial sector benefited the most.

Six months before the war started, the French economist Edmond Théry published a book entitled *The Economic Transformation of Russia*, in which he presented some rather eloquent figures. In the five-year period 1908–1912, coal production increased by 79.3 percent over the preceding five years; iron by 24.8 percent; steel and metal products by 45.9 percent.[1] From 1900 to 1913 the output of heavy industry increased by 74.1 percent, even allowing for inflation.[2] The rail network, which covered 24,400 kilometers in 1890, had grown to 61,000 kilometers by 1915.[3] Industrial progress helped to reduce Russia's dependence on foreign capital. Although *The History of the USSR*, a textbook for students of history at Soviet universities and teachers colleges, states that in 1914 the "specific weight" of foreign capital in the Russian economy was 47 percent,[4] another Soviet source, the historian L. M. Spirin, estimates that foreign investments amounted to only about "one-third of total investments."[5] The English writer Norman Stone notes that on the eve of World War I foreign investment in Russia had declined by 50 percent in the period 1904–1905, and amounted to 12.5 percent in 1913.[6]

Edmond Théry emphasized that Russian agriculture had made as much progress as industry. From 1908 to 1912 wheat production rose by 37.5 percent over the preceding five years; rye by 2.4 percent; barley by 62.2 percent; oats by 20.9 percent; and corn by 44.8 percent. Théry commented: "This increase in agricultural production served not only to meet the new needs of the population. . . . It also allowed Russia to expand its foreign markets significantly and, thanks to its earnings from grain exports, to end its unfavorable balance of trade." In good harvest years, such as 1909 and 1910, Russian wheat exports amounted to 40 percent of world wheat exports. Even in bad years, such as 1908 and 1912, they still accounted for 11.5 percent.[7]

The population of the Russian empire, which in 1900 was 135 million, reached 171 million in 1912. Théry, basing himself on the demographic statistics of the beginning of the century, predicted a population of 343.9 million by 1948.[8] The figure cited by Soviet historians for the Russian empire in 1917, based on 1914 borders, is 179,041,100.[9]

The nation's economic progress was accompanied by fundamental social change. In the last fifty years of the empire, the urban population grew from 7 million to 20 million. The hierarchical structure of the state began to crumble. Social barriers fell. The importance of the nobility, the autocracy's traditional base of support, declined. "The class that provided leadership has ceased to fulfill its function; it is obsolete," wrote Vasily Shulgin, a prominent conservative politician (a monarchist) and subsequently one of the most talented chroniclers of the revolution.[10]

Major improvements were initiated in public education. In 1908 a law introducing compulsory primary education was adopted (although its implementation was interrupted by the revolution and delayed until 1930). The increased government spending for education serves as an index of the efforts being made: between 1902 and 1912 such spending rose by 216.2 percent.[11] By 1915, 51 percent of all children between eight and eleven years of age were in school, and 68 percent of all military conscripts knew how to read and write.[12] Certainly Russia still lagged behind the advanced Western countries, but the increased number of schools and greater funding testify to the government's commitment and the considerable success achieved in this area. The first two decades of the twentieth century also saw a remarkable flowering of Russian culture, which is often referred to as Russia's Silver Age.

The governmental system evolved at a much slower pace than the economic, social, and cultural structures. The 1905 revolution, which grew out of the disastrous war with Japan, compelled Tsar Nicholas II to accept a series of reforms and introduce a constitution. Russia became a constitutional monarchy with an elected assembly, the Duma. Freedom of the press, assembly, and association were guaranteed. These rights, and the powers of the Duma, were more limited than in the Western democracies, but they existed nevertheless. In the Duma, highly diverse political trends were represented—from the Bolsheviks on the left to supporters of absolute monarchy on the right. However, the Duma was based on indirect representation (a system of elections passing through several stages) and a limited franchise (allowing only those with certain qualifications to vote).

In 1906 Prime Minister Stolypin introduced a law allowing every head of a peasant family to become the owner of his share of the village's communal land. Trotsky explained clearly and concisely the potential importance of this reform, which was not fully implemented. "If the agrarian problem . . . had been solved by the bourgeoisie, if it could have been solved by them, the Russian proletariat could not possibly have come to power in 1917."[13]

During the brief period between the 1905 revolution and World War I, Russia underwent a political evolution unprecedented in its history. Nevertheless, discontent spread to all strata of the population. Despite major improvements in their condition, the peasants continued to feel intense land hunger and firmly believed that the only solution to their problems was to divide up the large landed estates. Workers' conditions were slowly improving. They had obtained, albeit with certain restrictions, the right to strike over economic issues and, after 1912, both health and accident insurance. Still they demanded a shorter workday and a better standard of living. The young bourgeoisie, seeking a place in the country's political system, demanded an extension of political rights. The intelligentsia dreamed of a revolution that would bring "freedom," and from its ranks came the nuclei of the numerous political parties. Also opposed to the central government were all the heterogeneous peoples included in the Russian empire, the bitterest discontent being found among the Poles, the Finns, and the Jews.

Russia on the eve of World War I served as confirmation of a rule deduced by Alexis de Tocqueville from an analysis of the causes of the French revolution: for a bad government, the most dangerous time is when it begins to reform itself.

The case of Mendel Beilis, a Jew accused of the ritual murder of a Christian child, summed up the situation in a nutshell. Despite the openly expressed desire of the tsarist government and the judges for a conviction, the jury of half-literate Ukrainian peasants acquitted Beilis. The verdict in his favor was a remarkable expression of the weakness of progovernment forces.

Thus, Russia became involved in the world war at a time of rapid economic development, in an era of demolition and new construction, under conditions of universal discontent and rising expectations, with a weak government incapable of winning popular support. On several occasions the dangers posed by an entrance into the European conflict were pointed out. In February 1914, for example, Petr Durnovo, minister of the interior under the Witte government of 1905–06 and subsequently a member of the tsar's Council of State, sent Nicholas II a memorandum that included these prophetic words:

> A war involving all of Europe would be a mortal danger for Russia and Germany, regardless of which was the victor. . . . In the event of defeat, a possibility which cannot be excluded when faced with an enemy such as Germany, social revolution in its most extreme form would be inevitable in our country.

The memorandum was found among the tsar's papers after the revolution, unmarked by any royal notations. It is possible that the tsar did not bother to read it.[14] Even Grigory Rasputin, that evil genius in the bosom of the royal family, whose influence on the destiny of the nation grew steadily after 1906, warned against the dangers of a war.

To this day historians disagree over who was responsible for and what were the actual causes of World War I. It is often forgotten that in the summer of 1914 one sentiment dominated in Europe: that war among civilized nations was impossible.

Europe entered the war after forty-five years of peace, if we count only wars between "white men," the last such being the Franco–Prussian war of 1871. War seemed inconceivable. Nevertheless it broke out. All the participants had prepared for it, yet they were all taken by surprise. For Russia the war became a test of the solidity of the various components of its colossal governmental, economic, and social organism.

The first battle lost by the Russian army, in East Prussia in August 1914, revealed the government's true condition and gave a glimpse of the factors that would bring the regime's downfall in the spring of 1917. Most historians, be they Russian or Soviet, attribute this defeat to the Russian army's unprepared, hence premature offensive, undertaken with the aim of saving France.

As early as August 1911 General Zhilinsky, then head of the Russian

General Staff, promised the French allies he would send an army of 800,000 men against Germany "on the fifteenth day of mobilization."[15] When war was declared the French army launched an immediate offensive, but suffered very heavy casualties. Count Ignatiev, the Russian military attaché in Paris, reported that losses were as high as 50 percent in some French regiments. He added: "It is now clear that the outcome of the war will depend on what we can do to divert the German forces toward outselves."[16] The defeat of France would undoubtedly have meant the defeat of Russia as well. The Russian army was inadequately equipped for this crucial offensive, but that did not become apparent until too late.

The causes of the Russian defeat in East Prussia had to do above all with poor generalship, especially on the level of the General Staff and Field Headquarters (the Stavka). The hopes firmly held by all the belligerents, that the war would not last more than five or six weeks, of course proved false. The embattled nations were obliged to readjust, technically and psychologically, to the reality of prolonged positional warfare.

From the very first the Russian army suffered from a shortage of artillery shells, bullets, and rifles; like the other countries, they had believed the war would not last long. A "master plan" for the development of the Russian arms industry stated clearly that the political and economic situation excluded the possibility of a prolonged war.[17]

In 1915, terribly shaken by its enormous losses on the battlefield, Russia was forced to withdraw from Poland—due in part to the shortage of ammunitions. Thus, a technical problem, munitions supply, became a central issue of state policy. The need to reorganize the economy to meet the demands of the war gave rise to a multitude of economic and political questions touching on the very essence of the tsarist system.

The shortage of shells was neither the sole nor the principal reason for Russia's difficulties, for in 1916, despite an abundance of munitions, amply provided by a reconverted industry, the Russian army was able to achieve success only once—in General Brusilov's offensive against the Austrians in Galicia. The shell "shortage" had been merely a symptom of a serious affliction in the tsarist state organism.

No sooner had the outburst of patriotic enthusiasm faded after the first few weeks of war than a crisis of authority began to develop in the army. By July 1915, 9 million men had been drafted. The number of officers, insufficient even for a peacetime army of 2 million, was sharply reduced by the loss of some 60,000 during the first year of war. This meant that hardly any of the 40,000 officers from before the war remained. The military academies graduated no more than 35,000 officers each year. By September 1915 it was a rare thing to find a front-line regiment (usually numbering

3,000 soldiers) with more than a dozen officers. Not until late 1915 and early 1916 did the practice of promoting the most outstanding rank-and-file soldiers begin on a large scale. The lack of noncommissioned officers was felt even more acutely.

The crisis of authority in the army was the most striking symptom of the general crisis of authority in the country. Shulgin, an important figure in the Duma, expressed his complaints to the tsar: "Goremykin [the prime minister], a senile fool, is in fact incapable of being the head of the government in the midst of a world war. . . . He is organically incapable, because of his age and his hidebound rigidity, of coping with the demands imposed by the war."[18] In January 1916 Nicholas replaced Goremykin with Stürmer. Shulgin had this to say about the new prime minister: "The problem is that Stürmer is a small man, a nonentity, while Russia is involved in a world war. The problem is that all the great powers have mobilized their best forces, while in our case, we have a Santa Claus for a prime minister. . . . That is why the country is in an uproar."[19]

The country was in an uproar because the Russian armies were being beaten. Prices were rising. Food supply to the cities was breaking down, although there was plenty of grain in the countryside. Russia was in an uproar because it was sick of the war. All segments of the population were beginning to see the source of their misfortunes in the tsar, the tsarina, and Rasputin.

The books that have been written about Grigory Rasputin and his inexplicable influence over the empress and, through her, Nicholas II would form an entire library. The correspondence of the imperial couple has provided abundant material for the most diverse interpretations, hypotheses, and speculations: the empress's mysticism; the miraculous powers of "the monk" Rasputin, who on three occasions saved the hemophiliac prince from bleeding to death; hypnosis; even witchcraft. All that is beside the point. As Shulgin wrote: "Who does not know the sentence [attributed to the tsar]: 'Better Rasputin than ten hysterics a day.'" The historian rightly added: "I do not know whether this sentence was actually spoken, but it matters little since all of Russia repeated it."[20]

The myth of Rasputin, the illiterate Siberian muzhik reputed to have cast a spell over the imperial family and to be shamelessly officiating in Petrograd, spread all over Russia despite the lack of modern means of communication. The myth wielded a death blow to the emperor's prestige.

The breach between society and its ruler became final in August 1915, when Nicholas assumed personal command of the army, thus shouldering direct responsibility for all of the country's defeats and disasters. His presence at Field Headquarters in Mogilev removed him from the capital.

One consequence of this became evident in February 1917, when the tsar, as if caught in a trap, was unable even to reach Petrograd. Meanwhile the influence of the tsarina and thus of Rasputin over the political life of the country grew apace.

The country lived its own life and the government lived its—in a vacuum. Despite the war—one might say because of it—rapid industrial growth continued. In 1914 the index of economic growth, taking 1913 as 100, rose to 101.2, in 1915 to 113.7, and in 1916 to 121.5.[21] The extraction of iron ore increased in the same period by 30 percent, and petroleum production by an equal amount. There was major expansion in both the chemical industry and the machine industry. The drastic reduction of imports forced the industrialists to start producing machinery domestically. According to statistics from January 1, 1917, Russian factories in August 1916 were turning out more munitions than the French and twice as much as the British. In 1916 Russia made 20,000 light cannon and imported 5,625. It was 100 percent self-sufficient in the production of howitzers and 75 percent in heavy artillery.[22] Subsequently, the reserves of armaments in imperial Russia proved large enough to last through more than three years of civil war.

In order to harness the turbulent and unplanned process of industrial growth and to eliminate the bottlenecks that developed along the way, some structural transformations, some reforms, were needed. But Nicholas II had only one desire: to keep the country as he had found it upon his ascension to the throne after his father's death. All of the tsar's actions, and all of his inaction, were directed to this end. Shulgin has suggested an eloquent postmortem for the Russia of that time: "An autocracy without an autocrat."[23]

To the tsar's personal inaction was juxtaposed a tumultuous political area. "In 1917 there were political parties for nearly every social class," the Soviet historian Spirin notes—with some perplexity.[24] It should be added that these parties had originated well before 1917 and that most of them functioned legally, with their own representatives in the Duma. The Bolshevik representatives, who openly called for Russia's military defeat, were not arrested until November 1914, and then exiled only after a trial.

By mid-1915 virtually all the parties in the Duma had gone into opposition. The Progressive Bloc, the core of the parliamentary opposition, was formed in August 1915. It included the Constitutional Democrats (Cadets), the Union of October 17 (Octobrists), the Progressives, and the Nationalists. The binding force in this coalition of liberals, centrists, and rightists (except for the extreme right) was the sole liberal party in Russian history: the Cadets. The Cadet program stressed that it was a party of all the people, not of one class, and that its highest loyalty was to Russia and a strong Russian state. The Cadets explained their role in opposition to the tsar by their desire to strengthen the state. To a large degree they defined progress as Russia's ability to defend its international position.

The Cadets proclaimed that "everyone without exception" should be subject to the rule of law and that "fundamental civil rights" should be guaranteed to all citizens. They called for the eight-hour day, trade union rights, and mandatory medical and old age insurance paid for by the state. They advocated distribution of crown lands and monastery lands to the peasantry and expropriation of the large landed estates with indemnification. Categorically opposed to federalism or any change in the political structure that might weaken the empire, they saw as their main task to prepare Russia for "a parliamentary system and the rule of law."[25]

The Cadet party's principal base was among those connected with the zemstvos, the institutions of local government introduced in the reforms of the 1860s. At the beginning of the war two empire-wide organizations, the Union of Zemstvos and the Union of Towns, were founded with the aim of involving the general public in the war effort, in cooperation with the government. The work of these organizations provided considerable scope for the expansion of the Cadets' influence.

The Octobrist and Progressive parties, also members of the Progressive Bloc, held liberal monarchist views. In allying themselves with the parliamentary opposition, they hoped on the one hand to help channel discontent and on the other to persuade Nicholas II to heed the warning voices and change the government, appointing ministers who would "enjoy the confidence of the nation."

The revolutionary parties, the Socialist Revolutionaries (SRs) and Social Democrats (Bolsheviks and Mensheviks), sought to combine revolutionary activity with legal opposition in the Duma. During the early years of the war, revolutionary agitation found little response among the people. Particularly unpopular was the Bolsheviks' slogan for a Russian defeat. The arrest of the participants in a Bolshevik conference in Finland in November 1914, including Lev Kamenev, who was presiding, and the party's other Duma representatives, deprived the Bolsheviks of their leadership inside Russia.

It was extremely difficult to direct a revolutionary party from exile. The Okhrana, the tsarist secret police, had infiltrated these parties with their agents and watched their every move. One agent, Evno Azef, dealt a particularly devastating blow to the SRs after becoming the head of its terrorist wing and a member of its Central Committee. *Agents provocateurs* completely penetrated the Bolshevik party as well. The Old Bolshevik Gusev-Drapkin recalled in his memoirs that in 1908–09 the Bolshevik organization in St. Petersburg was in total disarray.

> At that time, provocation was extremely widespread. Sverdlov was a member of the Leningrad committee, with four others. He suspected one of them of being an agent. Well, after the February revolution, when the archives of the Police Department were opened, it turned out that all four had been agents. Sverdlov had been the only Bolshevik on the committee.[26]

The situation was pretty much the same in the other cities. Roman Malinovsky, a favorite of Lenin's and at one time the head of the Bolshevik group in the Duma and actual leader of the party inside Russia, was one of the Okhrana's most highly prized agents.[27]

The secret police had a special attitude toward the Bolsheviks. Lenin's policy of systematic divisiveness was in perfect accord with the desires of the police: to prevent unification of the different groupings within the Russian Social Democratic Labor party (RSDLP). A Police Department memorandum urged the heads of "all police organizations to give urgent instructions to their secret collaborators that, when participating in party meetings, they must insistently promote, and defend with conviction, the total impossibility of an organic fusion of the disparate tendencies and in particular the impossibility of a reunification between the Bolsheviks and Mensheviks."[28] This had been Lenin's position since 1903.

The police entered so fervidly into the revolutionary spirit that they began to use party jargon. They referred to one of the tendencies in the RSDLP as "inclined toward opportunism." Violation of party discipline equally provoked the ire of the police. On June 24, 1909, police headquarters informed the Okhrana chief in Moscow:

> Some members of the Bolshevik center, Bogdanov, Marat, and Nikitich (Krasin), have begun to criticize the center, have turned toward *otzovizm* and *ultimatumizm*, and after getting hold of a large part of the money stolen at Tiflis, have begun to engage in clandestine agitation against the Bolshevik center in general and some of its members in particular. Thus, they have started a school on the island of Capri, where Gorky lives.[29]

It seems that the police were less concerned about the bank robbery in Tiflis than about *otzovizm*, *ultimatumizm*, and criticism of "the Bolshevik center," that is, of Lenin.

The gendarme general A. Spiridovich, in commenting on the usefulness of secret agents, also noted that their work "very often served the party and hurt the government."[30] And Lenin was certainly right when, as a witness on May 26, 1917, before an examining magistrate of the special commission on the Malinovsky affair, he affirmed that this agent had done more good for the party than harm.[31]


## SPRING 1917

By the end of 1916 the general discontent that was the result of war weariness, military defeats, and high prices was intensified by reductions in food supplies to Petrograd and Moscow. On January 19, 1917, the "Section for the Maintenance of State Security and Public Order in the Capital" reported in a top secret document that "the rising cost of living and the continual failure of government measures aimed at counteracting the scarcity of food products had provoked a violent wave of discontent, even before Christmas."[32]

The food difficulties that began to affect the cities in 1916 stemmed above all from the government's inability to organize the purchase and transportation of agricultural products to the rail terminals. The wartime harvests were even better than those before the war (if the territory occupied by the Germans is not counted). In 1914, 1,413 million centners were harvested. In 1915 the figure was 1,529 million, and in 1916, 1,286 million.[33] It is true that the army consumed more than in peacetime: 28 million centners of food products in 1913–14; 159 million in 1916–17. But at the same time, grain exports fell from 210 million centners in 1913–1914 to 1 million in 1916–17. The food difficulties were tied to the peasants' refusal to sell their grain at prices constantly eroded by inflation.

The government was unable to understand the reasons behind this crisis. Its attempts to control prices often amounted to nothing better than the measures applied by the governor of Tashkent who strolled through the bazaar on Saturdays and ordered a flogging for any merchant whose prices were, in his view, higher than "normal." Every attempt to organize the provisioning of the cities with the help of specially appointed officials resulted in fiasco. Not knowing what to do, the government kept changing its policies. The politicians had no better grasp of the situation. The right explained the crisis as the result of Jewish and German conspiracies; the Union of the Russian People opened its own "Russian bread stores." The left blamed it on conspiracies by the landowners and kulaks. And everybody agreed that delays on the railroads were at fault. In reality, however, there was an adequate rail system. What was lacking was grain; the trains rushed out after the wheat, but there was no rush of wheat to the trains.[34] The top secret police report on the situation in the capital, cited above, concluded that society was longing "to find a way out of an abnormal political situation that is daily becoming more abnormal and strained."[35]

The parliamentary opposition was increasingly taken with the idea that it must obtain a "responsible ministry" from the tsar, one in which representatives of the Progressive Bloc would hold the key posts. A group of Duma deputies headed by Aleksandr Guchkov, a confirmed monarchist and leader of the moderate liberals, began to plot the ouster of Nicholas II in order to save the dynasty.

The revolutionary parties, although their slogans against the war and the tsar were finding a growing response in the country, judged that the time was not yet ripe for revolution. In January 1917 Nikolai Chkheidze, a Menshevik leader, member of the Duma, and supporter of the international socialist antiwar conferences at Zimmerwald and Kienthal, argued: "At this time there can be no hope for a successful revolution. I know that the police are trying to organize some simulated revolutionary outbursts in order to draw the workers into the streets and attack them."[36] Also in January, Lenin, living in Zurich, totally cut off from Russia and receiving infrequent and confused reports, spoke in the same vein as Chkheidze: "We of the older generation may not live to see the decisive battles of this coming revolution."[37] Aleksandr Shlyapnikov, Lenin's representative in Petrograd and head of the Russian Bureau of the Central Committee, wrote, "All of the underground organizations and political groups [at the end of 1916] were opposed to mass actions in the coming months of 1917."[38]

Everyone in the country felt that major changes were imminent and unavoidable—everyone except the revolutionaries. As Shulgin was to say, the revolution was ready but the revolutionaries weren't.

On February 10 Mikhail Rodzyanko, president of the Duma, arrived at the tsar's country palace with a report on the situation and a warning that if the Duma were dissolved, as Nicholas intended, revolution would break out. This revolution, Rodzyanko warned the tsar, "will sweep you away and you will rule no more." "God will provide," answered Russia's last autocrat. In reply he was told: "God will provide nothing. You and your government have made a total mess. Revolution is inevitable."[39]

The disturbances in Petrograd began even earlier than the president of the Duma had anticipated. On February 23 groups began to gather in various parts of Petrograd demanding bread. Workers walked off the job and joined the demonstrators. On February 26 the Fourth Company of the Pavlovsky Regiment opened fire on the mounted police. The soldiers began siding with the demonstrators.

The parliamentary opposition hoped that the situation could be saved through the creation of a "responsible ministry." In a telegram, Rodzyanko told the tsar:

Anarchy rules in the capital. The government is paralyzed. The transportation of food and fuel is completely disorganized. Social unrest is mounting. The streets are the scene of disorderly shooting. Military units are firing on one another. It is necessary to appoint someone who enjoys the nation's confidence to form a new government. Any delay is out of the question; it would mean death. I pray to God that in this hour, the responsibility does not fall on the monarch.

Upon reading the telegram, Nicholas II said to his minister of the court, Count Frederiks: "Once again, this fat-bellied Rodzyanko has written me a lot of nonsense, which I won't even bother to answer."[40] The tsar contented himself by giving the Duma a two-month vacation.

Taken by surprise by the burgeoning, spontaneous movement, the revolutionary opposition did not know what to do and limited itself to discussion. At Kerensky's house, where the representatives of all the revolutionary parties gathered (all Menshevik tendencies, the SRs, the Trudovik, or Labor, group, and the Bolsheviks, represented by Shlyapnikov), the general enthusiasm was soon cooled off by Yurenev, who was close to the Bolsheviks. There is not and there will not be a revolution, he said. The reaction is growing. The soldiers and the workers have different objectives. Preparations must be made for a long period of reaction. We must adopt a wait-and-see attitude.[41] It was evident to all present that Yurenev was articulating the Bolshevik party's point of view. In his memoirs, the Bolshevik worker V. Kayurov, a member of the party's Petrograd Committee, explained how unexpected the events were for the party. He noted that the center had not issued any instructions. The Petrograd Committee had been detained, and Shlyapnikov, the representative of the Central Committee, found himself unable to issue any instructions for the following day. On the evening of February 26 Kayurov had no doubt that the revolution would be crushed. The demonstrators were unarmed; no one would be able to reply to the government when it took energetic measures.[42] The Bolsheviks held fast to a wait-and-see position, for in the autumn of 1916 Lenin had rigorously forbidden Shlyapnikov to collaborate in any way with the other socialist parties.

If revolutionary agitation in the capital was on the rise without any leadership, it was not because the revolution was strong but because its enemy, the tsarist regime, was extremely weak. "The problem," said Shulgin, "was that in this immense city it was impossible to find even a few hundred people who sympathized with the ruler."[43]

By noon on February 27, some 25,000 soldiers—slightly more than 5 percent of all troops and police forces concentrated in Petrograd and its surroundings—had gone over to the side of the demonstrators. But this was enough for the rebellion to become a revolution. It is true that the victors were not yet aware of their victory—no more than the defeated were aware of their defeat. On the evening of February 27, roughly 30,000 soldiers arrived at the Tauride Palace, where the Duma held its sessions, looking for some form of governmental authority. The Duma, which had dreamed of much power, barely had the courage to form a Provisional Committee, which proclaimed that it had assumed the task of restoring order. On February 28 this proclamation was pasted up around the city.

A few hours before the formation of the Duma Committee, a Soviet had been organized in another part of the same Tauride Palace. Addressing itself to the workers of Petrograd, the Soviet asked them to send deputies that same afternoon, on the basis of one deputy per thousand workers. That evening the Soviet elected as its president the Menshevik Chkheidze, and as vice presidents two left-wing deputies from the Duma, Kerensky and Skobelev. The number of Bolsheviks in the Soviet was so small that they were unable to organize themselves as a faction. Shlyapnikov, who was elected to the Soviet's Executive Committee, recalls that its very first meeting heard a report on the food situation in Petrograd. It turned out that the situation was "by no means catastrophic."[44] Thus, the initial cause of the disturbances in the capital leading to the overthrow of the tsar proved to be nonexistent.

While two opposing powers emerged in Petrograd, the Duma Committee and the Soviet, the emperor was traveling from General Headquarters at Mogilev toward the capital. His train was stopped at the station of Dno by insurgent soldiers, and Nicholas was compelled to sign his abdication on March 2, after General Alekseev, supported by the commanders of all five fronts, told him that his abdication was the only possible way to assure the continuation of the war against Germany. Only two corps commanders, Count Keller and Khan Nakhichevansky, spoke on behalf of the tsar. The Duma Committee sent Guchkov and Shulgin, both of them monarchists, to accept the abdication.

Thus, with the agreement of revolutionaries, liberals, and monarchists alike, the monarchy departed. Russia became a democratic republic.

These events unfolded at a very rapid pace, in a way that astounded the participants. And the casualties were very small compared to what they would be later on. In February a total of 169 were killed and less than 1,000 wounded.[45]

From 1916 on, especially in Petrograd, there was constant discussion of plots of one kind or another—revolutionary, liberal, and monarchist— all aimed at rectifying the situation. The only successful plot was the assassination of Rasputin in December 1916. However, this plot can be considered "successful" only in the sense that the "holy father" actually was killed, albeit with difficulty.

When the revolution transferred power to those who were called plotters and who in fact were, consciously or unconsciously, trying to destroy the tsarist regime, it was discovered that none of them had a program.

The Provisional Government created by the Duma Committee was headed by Prince Georgy Lvov, former president of the Union of Zemstvos, and consisted mainly of representatives of the former parliamentary opposition. Its proclaimed purposes were to continue the war and to convoke a Constituent Assembly to decide Russia's future. The socialist parties firmly believed that, in accordance with Marxist doctrine, Russia was on the eve of a bourgeois democratic revolution, so that they did not aspire to power themselves. The bourgeoisie had to fulfill its historic task, they believed; only after that would the socialists have their turn. Lenin, however, distrusted the February revolution. For him, in Zurich, the Petrograd events looked like the result of a "conspiracy of the Anglo-French imperialists."[46] His first orders had a familiar ring: no reconciliation with the other parties.[47]

The Provisional Government's weakness, which was evident from the very first day of its existence, its lack of a clear program, its lack of confidence, allowed the Soviet to become a second power in the country. However, the Soviet did not follow a determined course either. On March 1 it issued the famous Order No. 1, which established elected committees in the Petrograd barracks, with the authority to distribute weapons and to withhold them from officers, and abolished the traditional forms of military discipline. This order was immediately extended to the entire army, despite the Soviet's explanation that it was intended for rear echelon units only. This was a major factor in the army's decomposition. However, the Soviet was relying on the army to continue the war against Germany, particularly since Germany had not responded to proposals for "a peace without annexations or indemnities." The Bolsheviks too were inconsistent on this question. On March 12 three Bolshevik leaders arrived in Petrograd from internal exile—Muranov, a former Duma deputy; Lev Kamenev, a former member of *Pravda*'s editorial board; and Stalin, a member of the Central Committee. They immediately took editorial control of *Pravda*, which on March 15 published an article by Kamenev containing the following sentences: "When one army opposes another, the most absurd policy would be to propose that only one lay down its arms and go home. ... A free people will stand firmly at their posts and will answer bullet for bullet."[48]

On April 3 Lenin arrived in Russia. The leader of the Bolshevik party was amazed that he was not arrested after having returned with the help of the German authorities. Instead, representatives of the new government gave him a ceremonious welcome. Everyone, including members of his own party, was dumbfounded by Lenin's speech, which proclaimed the need to struggle for power.

The controversy about Lenin's relations with Germany during the war and the revolution continues to this day. It started in April 1917. "This method of transportation," wrote Vladimir Bonch-Bruevich, a close aide of Lenin, referring to the so-called sealed train, "drew frantic howls from the infuriated bourgeoisie, with the SRs and Mensheviks joining in the chorus. Even within our party, there were very many who found this procedure unsuitable and incorrect."[49]

Lenin's strength lay in the fact that for him every method was correct and suitable as long as it sped the revolution's victory. It is necessary, he would teach the Bolsheviks, to know how to use "all subterfuges, ruses, and illegal means, to know how to remain silent, to conceal the truth."[50] Lenin understood perfectly well that it was in the Germans' interest to help those Russian revolutionaries who favored the defeat of their own country. Ludendorff wrote after the war that revolution in Russia had always been his passionate desire. "How many times I dreamed that it might come about. ... A constant vision." This vision suddenly became real, a saving miracle. "In April and May 1917," wrote the German general, "despite our victories on the Aisne and in Champagne, only the Russian revolution saved us."[51] Although Lenin's activities were not carried out with this aim in mind, the fact that the Russian revolution saved Germany from defeat in 1917 did not trouble the Bolshevik leader, who yearned for power regardless of the cost.

The April Theses, a program presented by Lenin on April 4 to RSDLP delegates attending an all-Russia conference of soviets, surprised everyone, including the Bolsheviks, by its unexpected character. Perhaps the party members would have been less surprised if they had had the chance to read Lenin's "Letters from Afar," sent from Switzerland. But *Pravda* had published an abridged version of the first letter and suppressed the other three altogether. The editors of *Pravda*, Kamenev and Stalin, had their own plan: to unite with the Mensheviks and collaborate to a certain degree with the Provisional Government. *Pravda* published Lenin's theses in its April 7 issue, but the next day it commented on his views in a statement by the editors: "In regard to Comrade Lenin's general scheme, we find it unacceptable in that it proceeds from the assumption that the bourgeois democratic revolution has been completed and anticipates an immediate transformation of this revolution into a socialist revolution."

One could not find a better articulation of the differences between the editors of *Pravda*, who had been the party's leaders in Lenin's absence, and Lenin himself. For Kamenev, Stalin, and the other Bolsheviks, Marxism was a doctrine from which deviation was not possible, whereas for Lenin there were no dogmatic truths: he was possessed by one idea—power. In the April 4 meeting at which the theses were presented, according to Bonch-Bruevich, an eyewitness, Lenin drew "sarcastic smiles" and "some chuckling" from his audience when he "stated candidly that he had had very little time and little material to base his observations on." With the exception of some brief weeks during 1905, Lenin had not been in Russia since 1900. In April 1917, en route to Petrograd, "I met only one worker on the train," the Bolshevik leader admitted. But that was good enough. "My thoughts," said he, "might be a bit theoretical, but I suggest that on the whole they are correct and correspond to the general political situation in the country."[52]

Lenin could have had worse luck and not run into that worker on the train. But even without him, Lenin grasped what was essential in Russia's political situation: the country had become, according to him, the freest in the world; that is, the government was weak and open to challenge.

The April Theses were both a concrete program and a utopian one. The concrete demands were an end to the imperialist war, fraternization with the enemy, and confiscation of large landholdings and nationalization of all lands, which were then to come under the control of the local soviets. All these demands were directed toward the Provisional Government, which was, as Lenin knew, incapable of satisfying them. Consequently, it would have to be overthrown. The utopian parts of the program—the abolition of the police, the army, and civil service; the election of officials subject to recall at any time, with salaries not to exceed those of an average worker's—these were the promises of a future government. It is true that Lenin's program was one of "unabashed radicalism" and "primitive demagogy," as Sukhanov said.[53] But it took into account the two principal demands of the majority of the population—peace and land.

After the February revolution, the Petrograd Soviet began to receive numerous *nakazy* (mandates), expressing above all the complaints and desires of the peasants and workers. An examination of the first one hundred peasant mandates shows that they called first for the confiscation of the large landed estates and the crown lands and for their distribution to the peasantry and, second, for the prompt conclusion of a "just peace." The first one hundred mandates presented by the workers show that they were less revolutionary-minded than the peasants. The workers sought mainly the improvement of their situation (the eight-hour workday, higher wages, etc.), not a fundamental transformation. For example, 23 percent of the peasant mandates demanded peace, as opposed to only 2 percent of the workers' mandates.[54]

The peasants' demands for peace coincided in part with Lenin's defeatist slogans; their desires for land ran counter to the Bolshevik program. The head of the party instantly forgot the old scholastic disputes over the agrarian question which for many years had created divisions in the Social Democratic party ("municipalization," "socialization," "nationalization"). He simply appropriated the program of the SRs: land to the peasants.

April 1917 may be regarded as the birthdate of Soviet ideology. This was the first manifestation, on a scale affecting the destinies of the state, of an extremely important feature of this ideology, soon to become the dominant one: flexibility, free of all fetters, a capacity to accept instantaneously what it had previously condemned and to condemn what it had previously accepted. Related to this are two essential elements: the leader can decide to make a 180-degree turn; and the party, with some hesitation to be sure, fairly quickly will fall into line.

Lenin, unfettered by any restraints and commanding a party which had 77,000 members in April 1917,[55] confronted a Provisional Government constrained by the fact that it held only half the power, the other half being held by the soviets. The government's hands were also tied by the lack of a state apparatus. The former machinery of state had been dismantled and discarded as a vestige of tsarist rule, and the creation of a new apparatus was delayed by the emergence of dual power everywhere, the local soviets successfully challenging the young administration of the Provisional Government. Lastly, the Provisional Government was hobbled by moral standards and sentiments that would soon be regarded as "survivals of capitalism," such as keeping one's promises, being loyal to one's allies, and having faith in democracy and the people. The representatives of the moderate socialist parties (SRs and Mensheviks), who from the days of the first coalition in May 1917 played a growing role in the Provisional Government, were hampered by their theoretical views concerning history and revolution, by the belief that social classes come to power in a certain sequence, following historic laws. Moreover, the members of the Provisional Government seemed to find power too hot to handle, as if waiting for the moment when they could be rid of it. "On April 20," Shlyapnikov writes, "Kamenev criticized the Provisional Government at a meeting of the Executive Committee of the Soviet: 'The solution is to transfer power to another class.' Some voices came from the ministerial benches: 'Then you take the power.'"[56] In June, at the Congress of Soviets, Tsereteli protested with a certain sadness that at the time there was no political party in Russia willing to say, "Give us the power." Then came Lenin's famous reply: "There is such a party. No party can refuse power, and our party certainly does not." The Provisional Government believed that no one in Russia wanted power. Lenin's words were not taken seriously. History has shown that when such politicians as Lenin, Stalin, and Hitler did tell the truth about their intentions no one believed them.

The weakness of the government left nothing to stand in the way of the revolutionary tide sweeping over Russia. The revolution became a blind revolt, giving vent to popular hatreds that had accumulated over the centuries. The intelligentsia, which for decades had laid the groundwork for revolution, now looked upon it with bewilderment. In his diary Gorky voiced the intellectuals' feelings: "We worshipped the revolution like romantic lovers. But a shameless brute came along and violated our beloved."[57] The Provisional Government, the government of the Russian intelligentsia, was unavoidably drifting to the left, attempting to catch up with the rebelling masses but always lagging behind, because the people, spurred on by Lenin's extremist slogans, dreamed of an end to all government. No one could be expected to outdo Lenin in the field of revolutionary slogans; he preached the expropriation of the expropriators, a phrase which translated into simple language had an irresistibly attractive ring: "Steal back what was stolen."[58]

In June, Kerensky, as minister of war, was able to persuade the army that an offensive was possible. On June 18 the Russian troops went into action, scoring major successes. Rumors concerning a tightening of military discipline sowed alarm among the soldiers of the Petrograd garrison, who feared they might be sent to the front. Demands for the overthrow of the Provisional Government received a favorable hearing, especially with the First Machine Gun Regiment, which was strongly influenced by the Bolsheviks and anarchocommunists.

During the preparations for the armed demonstration of July 4 by Petrograd workers and soldiers joined by 10,000 sailors from Kronstadt, Lenin left the capital to rest at Bonch-Bruevich's country home in Finland. He returned on July 4 and spoke without enthusiasm to the demonstrators from the balcony of Kshesinskaya's palace. It was clear to him that he would not be able to seize power at this time.

To this day historians disagree as to whether this demonstration was the result of a Bolshevik plot or was a spontaneous movement of the workers, soldiers, and sailors. Even the official historians of the Communist Party of the Soviet Union have not come to a definite conclusion. In his *History of the CPSU, Short Course*, Stalin wrote: "The Bolshevik party was opposed to armed action at that time, for it considered that the revolutionary crisis had not yet matured, that the army and the provinces were not yet prepared to support an uprising in the capital."[59] However, the post-Stalin version of the *History* says that the "workers and soldiers of Petrograd would have had enough forces to overthrow the Provisional Government and take power," but that it was still too early for such an action because the "majority of the population was still following the SRs and Mensheviks."[60]

Lenin did not object to the July actions, but he did not insist on their continuation after troops loyal to the government and the Soviet entered Petrograd. For him, the July demonstrations were a rehearsal, a test of the adversary's will to resist. Zinoviev recalled the situation:

> During the July days our entire Central Committee was opposed to an immediate takeover. Lenin thought the same. But when, on July 3, the wave of popular indignation rose high, Comrade Lenin sprang into action. There and then, in the refreshment room on the top floor of the Tauride Palace, a small meeting was held—Trotsky, Lenin, and myself. Laughing, Lenin said to us: "Shouldn't we try for it now?" But he immediately added: "No, we couldn't take power now; it wouldn't work out, because not all the soldiers at the front are with us yet."[61]

Zinoviev is slightly mistaken, because on July 3 Lenin was not in Petrograd. Nevertheless, Zinoviev accurately describes Lenin's attitude toward the demonstration: if it succeeds, we will take power, "laughing"; if it fails, we will try again.

The July rehearsal ended unhappily for the Bolsheviks, mainly because the Petrograd Soviet supported the Provisional Government. Bonch-Bruevich recalls a conversation with Lenin after the July disaster: "'What now?' I asked Vladimir Ilyich. 'Armed insurrection. There's no other way.' 'When?' 'When circumstances allow. But no later than the fall.'"[62] It could be that Bonch-Bruevich, who wrote his memoir after the party's victory, exaggerated Lenin's optimism a bit. On July 5, when Trotsky met with the Bolshevik leader, Lenin was in a panic: "'Now they will shoot us down, one by one,' he said. 'This is the right time for them.' But he overestimated the opponent—not his venom, but his courage and ability to act."[63]

Lenin had good reason to worry. One of the decisive arguments that convinced the troops loyal to the Provisional Government and the Soviet to move against the demonstrators were documents suggesting that Lenin and the Bolsheviks were German spies. In his *History of the Russian Rev-*

*olution*, Trotsky referred to July 1917 as "the month of the most gigantic slander in world history." The accusation that the Bolsheviks had received German money was used to justify the Provisional Government's decision to arrest the Bolshevik leaders. Lenin fled to Finland. The arrested Bolshevik leaders, Kamenev, Kollontai, Lunacharsky, and Trotsky, were soon released.

The controversy over "German money" continues even today. In this argument two different questions have to be distinguished: (1) Was Lenin a German agent? (2) Were the Bolsheviks receiving money from Germany?

First of all, the defeated have always denounced the leaders of victorious revolutions as "agents of foreign powers." This most primitive explanation for their own defeat actually explains very little. The concept of a foreign agent suggests a person carrying out the will of another. There is no question that Lenin was his own man and was pursuing his own aims, which at a certain stage coincided with those of Germany. And within a year many of those who had accused Lenin of collaborating with the Kaiser's Germany availed themselves of German aid in the struggle against Lenin's government.

As to whether or not the Bolsheviks had any German financial support, revolutionary leaders have always been accused—most often, justly—of receiving money from foreign powers. In July 1917 documents were published attesting to links between two Bolsheviks, Hanetsky and Kozlovsky, and the German Social Democrat Parvus, who made no attempt to conceal his links with the German Foreign Ministry. Lenin bitterly denied these accusations, but his denials were strange and not very convincing. For example, he wrote that Hanetsky had only "engaged in business as an employee" of Parvus's firm.[64] The party, Lenin asserted, could not have had any dealings with Parvus because since 1915 Lenin had denounced him as a "German Plekhanov" and a "renegade," "licking Hindenburg's boots."[65] In fact, Lenin stated categorically: "It is an infamous lie that I was in contact with Parvus."[66] Lenin had not had any relations with him; it was his emissaries who were responsible. Despite all the denials of Lenin, Trotsky, and other party leaders, none of them ever explained how it was possible by August 1917 for the party to be publishing, according to Lenin's own figures, "seventeen daily papers, 1,415,000,000 copies weekly altogether, 320,000 daily."[67]

Mark Aldanov, a talented writer of historical novels and an astute historian, who in 1919 wrote the first biography of Lenin, discussed this question in a Russian emigré newspaper in 1935. He recalled one small party that before 1917 had engaged in very little agitational work, published a small paper, and spent about 300,000 rubles a year, a sum obtained from a few wealthy members.[68] Shlyapnikov, whose honesty there is no reason to doubt, informs us that from December 2, 1916, to February 1, 1917, the amount that came into the Bolshevik coffers was 1,117 rubles, 50 kopecks.[69] In March, in a fit of generosity, Gorky donated 3,000 rubles.[70] Trotsky, in denouncing "the most gigantic slander in world history," contends that the money needed for the Bolshevik press was donated by ordinary workers. Nevertheless, it is hard to imagine that in the midst of severe inflation the workers were able to give tens or hundreds of thousands of rubles weekly to a party that was far from the only workers' party and not even the main socialist party. Aldanov speculated in 1935: "The account books kept on the Wilhelmstrasse could prove to be precious documents on the history of the October Revolution, but history will not gain access to them very soon. Moreover, the records in those books are probably quite one-sided. Receipts are not given in such cases."[71] Aldanov was mistaken. History got hold of the "account books" of the German Foreign Ministry only ten years after he had written those lines. It is true that no receipts bearing Lenin's signature were found—but German documents referring to the transfer of funds to the Bolsheviks were.

German money, however, does not explain the success of Bolshevik propaganda. It may have allowed them to conduct their propaganda on a large scale, but the government had no less substantial amounts of money at its disposal. The important thing was knowing how to use it.

The July defeat and the general conviction that the Bolsheviks were German agents marked a delay in Lenin's ascent to power. But the situation in the country became more critical every day: defeats on the front (the German army was threatening Riga and Narva and, to the south, Moldavia and Bessarabia); inflation and unemployment were on the rise; and food supplies were short. The second coalition government, formed in July and headed by Kerensky, put off the most pressing problems until the end of the war, at which time a Constituent Assembly would be convoked. On August 26 Commander-in-Chief Kornilov decided to intervene. He ordered General Krymov's Third Cossack Army Corps to Petrograd. He wanted to put an end to the nation's disintegration, reestablish order, and punish the Bolsheviks, whom he considered responsible for the chaos. However, his action brought the opposite result. A very courageous soldier who had won fame in the world war, Kornilov was a total incompetent in political matters. What was called the Kornilov plot was nothing but a confused blunder. Although he lacked sufficient forces and allies, Kornilov directly challenged the Petrograd Soviet, which, seeing its power threatened, sought help from the Bolsheviks. The moderate socialist Voitinsky, commissar of the Northern Front, assured the Soviet's leaders, "Not one regiment, not one company of the Northern Front will obey Kornilov's orders without the approval of the Army Committee or myself."[72]

Kornilov's troops faded away like ghosts even before reaching Petrograd. Meanwhile the Bolsheviks had been cleared of the accusations brought against them only a few weeks before by the very same Soviet and government that now gave them the seal of approval as good revolutionaries. The Committee of Struggle Against Counterrevolution, formed by the Soviet, included Vladimir Nevsky, the leader of the Bolshevik's Military Organization, which at that time had 26,000 members operating in forty-three groups at the front and seventeen in the rear.[73]

When he learned of Kornilov's military action, Lenin immediately ordered that he be fought, but that Kerensky not be supported, that as many concessions as possible be wrested from him, and that the Bolsheviks make use of the situation to arm the workers. The course of events, he wrote, could bring the Bolsheviks to power this time, "but we must *speak* of this as little as possible in our propaganda."[74] The party began its final sprint on the road to power.

## FALL 1917

The overthrow of the autocracy changed the situation in Russia, but only for the worse. The economy was collapsing, factories shutting down, food supplies dwindling, and the value of the currency plummeting. Meanwhile, the war went on. The only real conquest of the revolution was total freedom of expression. This intoxicating freedom became a powerful weapon in the hands of the Bolsheviks; while they promised everything at once (peace, land, and bread), the other parties suggested waiting for victory, for the Constituent Assembly, for an end to the chaos. Late in the night of August 31 or early in the morning of September 1, the Bolsheviks won a majority in the Petrograd Soviet. On September 25 Trotsky was elected chairman of the Soviet. After returning to Russia from the United States in May 1917, Trotsky had immediately supported Lenin. In July he joined the Bolshevik party and was placed in its leadership. Arrested after the July events, he was released on bail from Kresty prison after the fiasco of Kornilov's attempted coup. As president of the Petrograd Soviet, Trotsky became not only the tribune of the revolution (his speeches drawing overflow crowds to the Modern Circus) but also de facto leader of the insurrection being planned. On September 5 the Bolsheviks won a majority in the Moscow Soviet. This was a signal for Lenin: it convinced him that power was within easy reach. In mid-September, from his hiding place in Finland, he sent two letters stressing the need for an immediate seizure of power. But the Central Committee needed a lot of persuasion. Some of the party's leaders— Kamenev, Zinoviev, and Stalin, in particular—held a much more moderate position than Lenin. They were convinced that the All-Russia Congress of Soviets, scheduled for October 25, would peacefully deliver power to the Bolsheviks. Finding the situation intolerable, Lenin returned to Petrograd. Until now, Soviet historians have been unable to agree on the date of the party leader's return from Finland. According to Stalin's *Short Course*, Lenin returned on October 7.[75] Margarita Fofanova, at whose Petrograd apartment Lenin stayed, attests that he came back on September 22.[76] What is known for certain is that on October 10 he was present at a crucial Central Committee meeting, together with Bubnov, Dzerzhinsky, Zinoviev, Kamenev, Kollontai, Lomov, Sokolnikov, Sverdlov, Stalin, Trotsky, and Uritsky. Lenin had considerable difficulty persuading his comrades of the need to organize an insurrection; however, he had one trump card. As early as September 29 he had sent an ultimatum in the form of a letter, threatening to resign from the Central Committee, while reserving the right to "campaign among the rank and file of the party and at the party congress."[77] In 1921, while Lenin was still alive, Bukharin remembered that the "letter was written with extraordinary force and threatened us with all sorts of punishments. We were all astounded. . . . The Central Committee unanimously decided to burn the letter."[78] Burning a letter in Lenin's absence was one thing. But on October 10, when Lenin demanded in person that a vote on the insurrection be taken, Zinoviev and Kamenev were the only two who had the courage to vote against.

Lenin's argument amounted to these five points: (1) the revolutionary movement was on the rise all over Europe; (2) the imperialists (the Germans and the Allies) were ready to make peace in order to join forces and strangle the Russian revolution; (3) there was undeniable evidence that Kerensky and company were preparing to surrender Petrograd to the Germans; (4) a peasant revolt was developing, and the Bolsheviks already had the people's confidence; and (5) obvious preparations were underway for a second Kornilov attempt. Zinoviev objected: "We are told (1) that the majority of the Russian people are with us and (2) that the majority of the international proletariat are with us. Alas, both assertions are false and that is the heart of the problem."

In fact, that was not the problem. All of Lenin's arguments proved false: (1) his hopes for a world revolution were misplaced; (2) the Germans and the Allies continued the war for another full year; (3) Kerensky had no intention of surrendering Petrograd; (4) the peasants had begun dividing up the land, but this was far from being a "peasant revolt"; (5) and no one was dreaming of a "second Kornilov attempt." Lenin was right about only one thing: power was available for the taking, and no one was willing to defend the government. Kerensky and his ministers persisted in seeing the right as the only enemy, and naturally this eliminated any type of support from the right. The weakness and indecision of the Provisional Government irritated the "moderates" and "centrists." Bukharin proudly remembered that "on the door to my apartment was written 'Bukharin, Bolshevik.' But nobody dared to raise their little finger to me. Of course it was really stupid on the part of the bourgeoisie not to have finished us off at that time."[79] Bukharin was certainly right to call it stupidity, except that in the fall of 1917 power was not in the hands of the bourgeoisie. Power was in the streets and everyone agreed that "things had to change," even if for the worse. Pierre Pascal, a member of the French military mission, noted in his diary in September that the "corps of pages voted for the Bolsheviks," and in October that "yesterday Mr. Putilov told me he had voted for the Bolsheviks."[80]

Lenin found the greatest resistance in the Central Committee of his own party; his comrades feared failure and wondered what they would do upon taking power. He answered them: "The seizure of power is the business of the uprising; its political purpose will become clear after the seizure."[81] He freely quoted Napoleon: "On s'engage et puis—on voit."

For over sixty years Soviet historiography has maintained the legend that the October revolution was a meticulously planned operation, a classic model of "the art of insurrection." This legend is not in keeping with the facts. Moreover, in the legend, the leaders of this perfect operation keep changing. First it was Lenin and Trotsky. On the first anniversary of the revolution, Stalin referred to "the Central Committee of the party, headed by Comrade Lenin," as the inspirer of the insurrection but stressed that "all the work of practical organization of the insurrection proceeded under the direct leadership of the chairman of the Petrograd Soviet, Trotsky."[82] Trotsky himself contributed a good deal to the legend of the splendidly organized insurrection. Later on, in the 1930s, Stalin portrayed himself as the leader of the insurrection, while acknowledging that Lenin had provided some help. Since the mid-1950s, Lenin has been the only recognized leader.

But doubts regarding the reliability of the legend could not be better founded. Suffice it to say that to this day Soviet historians disagree about the date on which the October revolution began. Some suggest it was the morning of October 24; others say the evening of that day; still others argue for October 22, the day the Petrograd Soviet assumed control over all military units in the capital.

On October 10 the Central Committee had voted for insurrection. But at its next meeting, on October 16, everyone insisted it was necessary to wait because delegates from various parts of Petrograd spoke of the lack of combativity, especially in the workers' districts of Vyborg, Narva, and Vasilevsky Island. Krylenko, the representative of the Petrograd Military Organization (PMO), reported indifference among the soldiers. Only Lenin kept urging and arguing, dragging the Central Committee on toward power.

Trotsky seemed to be everywhere, speaking at countless meetings, rousing the workers and soldiers with his revolutionary appeals. The other popular Bolshevik speakers, Lunacharsky, Kollontai, Volodarsky, also kept up an endless round of speeches. The Central Committee was waiting for power to fall into its hands like ripe fruit, but Lenin insisted on the need to seize it, and no later than October 20.

The existing forms of authority were collapsing. The peasant soldiers of the Petrograd garrison wanted one thing: to go home and take part in the distribution of land. The government did not know what it wanted. It did not know which forces were on its side, and above all it did not seem to recognize its enemies. Petrograd was full of rumors about a Bolshevik plot, rumors which reached their peak in October. On October 17 Gorky's newspaper, *Novaya zhizn* (New life), which had a circulation of 10,000 among Petrograd workers and which stood very close to the Bolsheviks,[83] published an editorial warning the Bolshevik party against an uprising that would bring ruin to the party, the working class, and the revolution. On October 18 it published the famous letter from Zinoviev and Kamenev in which Lenin's close comrades declared that an armed insurrection, just a few days before the Second Congress of Soviets, would be an unacceptable action threatening the proletariat and the revolution with catastrophe. Lenin's indignation upon reading this letter is well known; he called its authors traitors and "strike breakers" because they had given away the secret of the insurrection to the bourgeoisie. In reality, it had not been a secret to anyone for a long time. Lenin himself had given it away in articles, letters, and public proclamations printed in the Bolshevik press.

The question of armed insurrection was openly debated in the legal press, but the most typical sign of the decomposition of government machinery was that the authorities did not seem to consider these discussions important. Kerensky refused to call in reinforcements from the front. Out of sheer curiosity a city official called the apartment of Maria Ulyanova, Lenin's sister, and learned that Lenin was in Petrograd, but no one attempted to arrest the leader of the impending insurrection.

In an interview with the American ambassador, David Francis, Foreign Affairs Minister Tereshchenko described the government's state of mind with desperate frankness. The interview took place on October 24. "I expect

a Bolshevik action tonight," said Tereshchenko. "If you can crush it," said
the ambassador, "I hope it happens." "I think we could," Tereshchenko
replied, "but I hope it happens anyway, whether we crush it or not. I'm
tired of this uncertainty and tension."[84]

The Bolsheviks were not sure of their success, but they kept moving
toward power, as though drawn by the collapsing weight of the existing
government. They were coming to power, albeit somewhat more slowly than
Lenin would have liked. The Military Revolutionary Committee (MRC),
created by the Petrograd Soviet, became the main leadership body of the
insurrection. The seizure of power was carried out, not in the name of the
Bolshevik party, but in the name of the Soviet, although the central bureau
of the MRC consisted only of Bolsheviks and Left SRs. In fact, power
passed into the hands of the MRC bureau on October 21, when it issued
an order to stop any weapons from being given out without its authorization
and sent commissars into the military units to make sure that this edict
was enforced. On the morning of October 22, the garrison was notified by
telephone of this decision, which specified among other things that no order
would be valid unless signed by the Military Revolutionary Committee.
Meetings and demonstrations were organized in the capital. Trotsky gave
a fiery speech at the House of the People, promising that the Soviet government would give the poor and the front-line soldiers everything they
would ever want, beginning with bread, land, and peace.

The revolution had already happened, although nobody was aware of it.
Those who filled Petrograd's theaters did not notice. Chaliapin sang Don
Carlos, a part he rarely performed in Russia. Tamara Karsavina danced
for the first time in the operetta The Doll. All kinds of philosophical,
literary, and sociopolitical lectures attracted large audiences. Even the
members of the Provisional Government failed to notice that power had
slipped from their fingers into the hands of the Bolsheviks.

Lenin's behavior during these days is still an enigma. After October 20
he seems to have disappeared. He remained in hiding, but there is no
evidence of his activity in the form of letters, notes, or instructions until
the evening of October 24. The much touted Central Committee meeting
of October 21, where Lenin supposedly uttered the famous words, "Yesterday was too soon, the day after tomorrow will be too late," is only a
legend created by John Reed that no document or witness supports. It is
true, however, that when Lenin read Reed's book, the legend struck him
as so felicitous that he did not correct it.

Lenin stayed underground throughout the day of October 24, as the
Military Revolutionary Committee began sending out commissars and small

armed detachments to secure government buildings. Two unarmed commissars went to the central telegraph office and brought it under Bolshevik control. A detachment from the Izmailovsky Regiment appeared at the Baltic Railway Station and stayed there to "maintain order." Detachments of Red Guards occupied some bridges but left others in the hands of government troops—in cases where the troops refused to withdraw. No one wanted to shoot. But little by little power in the capital changed hands. Meanwhile, as late as 6 PM Lenin did not suspect a thing. He sent out an urgent letter stressing that the situation was extremely critical, that it was necessary to deal a death blow to the government. In the fourth and fifth Russian editions of Lenin's works this letter is entitled "Letter to Central Committee Members." Actually Soviet historians added this title; the letter was addressed to the district committees of the party, through which Lenin meant to exert pressure on the Central Committee. On the evening of October 24, far from Smolny Institute, Lenin still feared the Provisional Government, which was no longer in power, and continued to urge the Central Committee to begin an insurrection that was already practically over.

The enigma of Lenin's absence from leadership between October 20 and 24 is doubled by the mystery of the insurrection leaders' behavior. They refrained from inviting Lenin to Smolny Institute, the seat of the Petrograd Soviet and the Bolshevik Central Committee at that time, the whole day of October 24, while he, no less curiously, awaited their invitation. Stalin wrote, in his commemorative article of November 6, 1918, "On the evening of October 24, Lenin was summoned to Smolny to lead the movement as a whole." However, by the time the Central Committee considered it appropriate to summon their chief, Lenin had already lost patience and was in a streetcar heading for Smolny.

In his *History of the Russian Revolution*, Trotsky says that Lenin, upon his arrival at Smolny, approved the actions of the chairman of the Petrograd Soviet. "Lenin was in rapture, which he expressed by exclaiming, laughing, and rubbing his hands. Afterward he became more silent, reflected a moment and said: 'Oh, well, it can be done that way too. As long as we take power.'"[85] Nikolai Podvoisky, who together with Vladimir Antonov-Ovseenko and Grigory Chudnovsky was in direct command of operations, recalled that after Lenin arrived at Smolny he began showering them with notes: Have the telegraph office and telephone exchange been taken? And the bridges?[86]

Lenin's impatience had little influence on the course of events, however. Slowly but surely the city was passing into the hands of the insurgents, who encountered no resistance. The battle for the city (no one yet realized that it was a battle for the entire country) was waged by 6,000 or 7,000 Bolshevik supporters (2,500 soldiers from the Pavlovsky and Kexholm regiments, 2,500 sailors from Kronstadt, and about 2,000 Red Guards) and 1,500–2,000 defenders of the Provisional Government. The enormous Petrograd garrison declared itself neutral and did not intervene. At 3:30 AM the cruiser *Aurora* dropped anchor near the Nikolaevsky Bridge, and a detachment of sailors chased off the Provisional Government's patrol and occupied the bridge. The Winter Palace, seat of the Provisional Government, was isolated from the rest of the city.

In the morning, the ministers still did not know they had lost power. They could not have learned it from the newspapers, whose articles were hopelessly out of date; *Izvestia* cautioned the Bolsheviks against any "foolish adventure"; *Novaya zhizn* counseled them "not to be the first to fire"; the Menshevik newspaper *Rabochaya gazeta* (Workers' gazette) hoped for a compromise.

By this time Lenin knew that he had won. At about 10 AM he wrote a proclamation "To the Citizens of Russia," announcing, "The Provisional Government has been deposed," and stating, "The cause for which the people have fought, namely, the immediate offer of a democratic peace, the abolition of landed proprietorship, workers' control over production, and the establishment of Soviet power—this cause has been secured." Trotsky recalled that after writing this proclamation Lenin turned around "with a tired smile and said, 'This change—hiding underground from Pereverzev's police one moment, being in power the next . . . *Es schwindelt'* [it makes you dizzy.] He supplemented his words with an eloquent gesture of his hand: round and round his forehead," to show how it made his head spin to have gained power at last.[87] The Winter Palace, it is true, had not yet been taken. But Lenin wanted at all costs to announce victory to the first session of the Congress of Soviets. He began therefore to send notes to the members of the Military Revolutionary Committee demanding an immediate attack. This time the tone was different. He threatened to have the members of the committee shot if the order was not carried out.[88] A new era had begun. Threats of execution and later actual executions were to become essential elements of policy.

The taking of the Winter Palace was a long, drawn out affair. The Red Guards and soldiers were not particularly anxious to launch an attack, especially since the number of defenders was decreasing by the hour. The insurgents entered by ones and twos through the "servants' entrance" of the palace, which was not defended. The *Aurora* fired some blanks, giving the signal to the Peter and Paul Fortress to direct its artillery fire against the Winter Palace; after firing about thirty shells, the gunners succeeded in hitting their target only two or three times. More and more Red Guards were entering the palace. Initially, the officer cadets defending the Provisional Government took the Red Guards prisoner. Then, as the Red Guards' numbers grew, they took the cadets prisoner and disarmed them. Antonov-Ovseenko made his way into the palace and arrested the members of the Provisional Government, then sent a telegram to Lenin: "The Winter Palace was taken at 2:04 AM."

The Congress of Soviets, which by then consisted only of Bolsheviks and Left SRs, the Mensheviks and Right SRs having walked out in protest against the seizure of power, approved the formation of a "provisional workers' and peasants' government." It was called the Council of People's Commissars, or Sovnarkom, and was to rule "until the convocation of the Constituent Assembly." This government was made up entirely of Bolsheviks. Its president was Lenin; Trotsky became people's commissar of foreign affairs; Rykov, internal affairs; Milyutin, agriculture; Lomov, justice; Nogin, commerce and industry; Shlyapnikov, labor; Teodorovich, food; Lunacharsky, education; and Stalin, nationalities. Thus the October revolution was completed.

"In some respects, a revolution is a miracle," Lenin later wrote.[89] And so it must have seemed. For the second time within the year a government, stricken with impotence, was toppled by a flick of the finger. In October, as in February, the government discovered at the critical moment that it had no support. The difference between the two revolutions was that in February the tsarist government was swept aside by an explosion of universal discontent, whereas in October the Provisional Government was overthrown by a party led by a man who knew what he wanted and who was firmly persuaded that he incarnated the laws of history, that he alone had fully assimilated the teachings of Marx and Engels.

Lenin got what he wanted; the Bolshevik party came to the Congress of Soviets with power in its hands. To achieve this goal he had had to overcome the resistance of his comrades, which was far more serious than that of the Provisional Government. The "rightist" enemies of the Provisional Government—generals and officers—were convinced that if the Bolsheviks came to power they could not hold on to it for more than a few weeks and that in the meantime at least Kerensky would have been ousted.

On October 25 the first session of the Congress of Soviets adopted two decrees presented by Lenin, on peace and on land. For the first and last time, the Bolshevik chief kept his word; he gave the country peace and land. Soon a new war would break out, a civil war this time, which would last more than three years. As for the land, it would turn out that the landlords had much less than was believed for the peasants to take, and soon the state would confiscate everything grown on the land anyway. Meanwhile, on October 25 Lenin read aloud the text of the decree on peace, which called upon the peoples and governments of all the belligerent countries to agree to a just and democratic peace without annexations or indemnities and an immediate three-month armistice to allow for peace negotiations. His decree on land stated in part: "All land... shall be confiscated without compensation [in any form] and become the property of the whole people."[90]

Lenin included in the Decree on Land the exact wording of a program drawn up by an SR newspaper. This program was based on 242 "mandates" submitted by local peasant representatives to the All-Russia Congress of Peasant Deputies, held in Petrograd in August 1917. Commenting on the program at that time, Lenin wrote: "The peasants want to keep their small farms. . . . No sensible socialist will differ with the peasant poor over this." He added that as long as "political power is taken over by the proletariat, the rest will come by itself."[91]

Lenin was able to listen calmly to the angry SRs at the Second Congress of Soviets as they denounced him for "stealing their program." "A fine Marxist this is," they said, "who has harassed us for fifteen years from the heights of his Marxist grandeur, for being petit bourgeois and unscientific, but who no sooner seizes power than he implements our program." To which he responded calmly: "A fine party it is which had to be driven from power before its program could be implemented."[92] Lenin was calm because he alone knew that without the support of the peasantry he could not retain power, and that as long as he had power, he could easily take back what he had given and what he had promised.

In the week after the insurrection, a few half-hearted and uncoordinated attempts by the former government to oppose the new one ended in failure. Kerensky, who had left the Winter Palace on the morning of October 25, sought aid at Pskov, the site of Northern Front general headquarters. Only General Krasnov, commander of the Third Cavalry Corps, took up the defense of the Provisional Government, the same Krasnov who under General Krymov's orders had marched on Petrograd in August to overthrow the Kerensky government. Krasnov managed to gather together only 700 cavalrymen, "less than a normal regiment."[93] But these modest forces allowed him nonetheless to occupy Gatchina and then Tsarskoe Selo. On October 30 detachments of the Red Guard, reinforced by sailors, stopped the Cossacks' advance at the hills of Pulkovo outside Petrograd. Trotsky wrote that this victory belonged to a Colonel Valden, who had accepted the command of the Red Guards, "not because he agreed with us," but apparently because "he hated Kerensky so much that this hatred awoke a certain sympathy for us in him."[94] Krasnov ordered a retreat to Gatchina, where he was arrested. Kerensky had time to flee, thus ending his brief passage through Russian history.

While General Krasnov in his strange alliance with the socialist Kerensky led several hundred Cossacks on Petrograd, General Cheremisov, commander of the Northern Front, considered the country's main danger to be the "German of Berlin," against whom the front had to be maintained; as for the Bolsheviks, the "Germans of Petrograd," they would not be able to stay in power anyhow. At the same time, the representatives of the "revolutionary democrats," the Mensheviks and Right SRs, formed a Union for the Salvation of the Homeland and the Revolution. But their struggle against the Bolsheviks remained verbal.

During his first week in power the most serious resistance Lenin ran into came from his closest comrades in the Central Committee and the government. It broke out on two fronts, when the All-Russia Executive Committee of the Railroad Workers' Union, the Vikzhel, demanded on October 29 that a "homogeneous socialist government" including all the socialist parties be formed. Their demand included the threat of a general railroad strike. The poet Alexander Blok was wrong when he wrote, "The Vikzhel has shown the breadth of its black hands." The Vikzhel's "hands" were not "black" (that is to say, reactionary) but pink. During the October days, the neutral position of the union, which refused to allow military trains into Petrograd, had contributed to the Bolshevik victory. And when the union issued its ultimatum, the Central Committee agreed to the "necessity of broadening the base of the government and the possibility of changing its composition." It did this in Lenin's and Trotsky's absence. The former was leading the suppression of a desperate attempt by the officer cadets to start an insurrection in the city; the latter was mobilizing forces against Krasnov. A Central Committee delegation headed by Kamenev went to a meeting called by the Vikzhel and agreed to the proposal of a coalition government made up of eighteen members, five of them Bolsheviks, but excluding Lenin and Trotsky. A delegation of workers from the Putilov Factory declared at this meeting: "We will not allow bloodshed between the revolutionary parties; we will not allow a civil war." One of the workers summarized the opinion of the capital's proletariat in these words: "To hell with Lenin and Chernov [leader of the Right SRs]. Hang them both!"[95]

With Trotsky's support, Lenin rejected the very idea of a coalition. "If you have a majority," he said to the supporters of a coalition government, "take power in the Central Executive Committee and carry on. But we will go to the sailors." In response Kamenev, Rykov, Milyutin, Zinoviev, and Nogin left the Central Committee, and Rykov, Teodorovich, Milyutin, and Nogin left the Council of People's Commissars, the Sovnarkom. In their declaration, they stressed that the only way to maintain a purely Bolshevik government was through "political terror."[96]

As always, Lenin managed to put down the revolt of his troops through blackmail; he threatened to resign and appeal to the "rank and file." Later, Kamenev and his supporters made a full apology and returned to the bosom of the Central Committee and government. Kamenev, the unrecognized father of future "Eurocommunism," proposed more than once while Lenin was still alive that measures be taken to soften Bolshevik rule. But each time he quickly abandoned his proposals. Historians justly reproach him for his weakness and indecision. But this lack of tenacity in defending his ideas is primarily explained by the fact that Kamenev, in every dispute with Lenin, soon realized that a weakening of Bolshevik rule would threaten the very foundations of the party. The Old Bolshevik Kamenev did not want to change the party's character.

In rejecting all attempts at compromise and all claims by the other socialist parties to even the sightest share of power, Lenin only confirmed what had been stated in *Pravda* the day after the seizure of the Winter Palace:

> We are taking power alone, relying on the country's voice and counting on the friendly support of the European proletariat. But having taken power, we will punish with an iron hand the enemies of the revolution and the saboteurs. . . . They dreamed of a Kornilov dictatorship. . . . We will give them the dictatorship of the proletariat.[97]

For Lenin, the dictatorship of the proletariat meant the dictatorship of the Bolshevik party.

Soviet power spread over the country with no serious resistance. Only in Moscow, where Lenin had said victory would be sure and there would be nobody to fight,[98] did the resistance last for eight days.[99] In general, local garrisons and armed workers' detachments easily dealt with any attempts to stop the Bolsheviks from taking power. The assassination of General Dukhonin, the commander-in-chief at Mogilev, by the Red Guards of the new commander-in-chief, Ensign Krylenko, completed the annihilation of the old army.

The consolidation of Soviet power could not be considered complete until the problem of the Constituent Assembly was resolved. The decision to convene the assembly, freely elected by the citizens to determine the future political regime in Russia, had been made by the Provisional Government. "All the best people of Russia," wrote Gorky, "for nearly a hundred years had lived by the idea of a Constituent Assembly."[100] Among the slogans the Bolsheviks had used to campaign against the Provisional Government was the immediate convocation of a Constituent Assembly. They accused the government of preventing the people, "the true master of the Russian soul, from pronouncing its sovereign word." On April 4 Lenin, who had barely arrived in Russia, said with indignation, "I am accused of harboring views in opposition to the quickest possible convening of the Constituent Assembly! I would call these charges delirious raving if decades of political struggle had not taught me to view honesty in an opponent as a rare exception."[101]

The elections to the Constituent Assembly, the freest elections in the history of Russia, took place after the October revolution. The composition of the assembly (SRs, 40.4 percent; Bolsheviks, 24 percent; Cadets, 4.7 percent; Mensheviks, 2.7 percent)[102] determined the ruling party's attitude toward it, an attitude which was violently negative. Nevertheless, on January 5, 1918, the Constituent Assembly met. Bonch-Bruevich, head of the Sovnarkom's administrative service, a friend of Lenin, and head of "Room 75," the embryo of the Soviet repressive agencies, recalls a "humorous conversation" in the halls of the Tauride Palace the day before the first session of the Constituent Assembly. Lenin's laughing reply to a comrade who impatiently insisted on knowing when the Constituent Assembly was finally going to begin its deliberations was this: "Since we made the mistake of promising the world that this talk shop would meet, we have to open it up today, but history has not yet said a word about when we will shut it down."[103] In order to teach the deputies to the Russian parliament where power lay, Bonch-Bruevich brought a "detachment of the most reliable sailors" to the Tauride Palace—200 sailors, or about one armed sailor for every two deputies, which was ample compensation for the absence of a Bolshevik majority. "I noticed," wrote Bonch-Bruevich, who was in the room with his sailors, "that two of them, surrounded by their comrades, were aiming their guns at Chernov." Bonch-Bruevich persuaded them not to kill the president of the assembly, adding that Lenin would not allow it. "Okay, since the Little Father doesn't want it, but it's too bad," said one sailor, speaking for everyone. At that time the "Little Father," as the sailors affectionately called Lenin, felt that it would be enough to disperse the Constituent Assembly. He gathered the members of the government and after a quick exchange of opinions, the unanimous conclusion was reached that the talk shop was useless. . . . It was decided not to interrupt the proceedings, to give them a chance to jabber to their heart's content for a day, but not to allow the next day's session to take place, to announce that the assembly was dissolved, and to urge the deputies to return to their homes.[104]

Lenin lost all interest in the Constituent Assembly after it refused to acknowledge the primacy of the Bolshevik government and the decisions of the Soviet Congress. The historic announcement by the sailor Zheleznyakov, "The guard is tired," ended the brief history of the Russian parliament. The guard's wishes became the fundamental law.

The left SRs, a splinter from the Socialist Revolutionary party, played an important role in the dissolution of the Constituent Assembly and the consolidation of Bolshevik power. For a short time after the October revolution the Left SRs, led by Maria Spiridonova, Boris Kamkov, and Vladimir Karelin, maintained an attitude of friendly neutrality toward the new seat of authority. In November they entered the government and were given three ministerial posts, which allowed Lenin's government to present itself as a pluralistic one. At the Constituent Assembly the Left SRs blocked with the Bolsheviks.

On the eve of the gathering of the Constituent Assembly, Lenin played the role of judge, jury, and executioner for the first time. Bonch-Bruevich brought him "the first reports of sabotage," compiled by Room 75. Lenin read it all, verified it, checked the sources of the documents, compared handwriting, and arrived at the conclusion "that the sabotage movement really exists, that it is mainly directed from one center, and that this center is the Cadet party." He therefore decided to outlaw the party and brand its members "enemies of the people."[105] A few days later, as president of the Sovnarkom, Lenin signed a decree to that effect. After chasing the Cadets out of the Constituent Assembly with the help of the Left SRs, Lenin was able to dissolve the parliament with little effort. A by-product of the decree outlawing the Cadet party was the murder in a hospital of two of the party's leaders, Shingarev and Kokoshkin, deputies to the Constituent Assembly.

After the dissolution of the Constituent Assembly, a demonstration took place in Petrograd which encountered the bullets of the Red Guards.

The workers of the Obukhov Factory, the cartridge factory, and other factories took part in the demonstration. Under the red flag of the Russian Social Democratic Labor party, the workers of Vasilevsky Island, Vyborg, and other districts marched to the Tauride Palace. It was exactly these workers who were shot, and for all of *Pravda*'s lies, it cannot conceal this shameful fact.[106]

Gorky wrote this in an article entitled "January 9—January 5," which drew a parallel between the shooting of workers by the tsar's troops on January 9, 1905, and the shooting of workers by the Red Guard on January 5, 1918.

# 2

# FROM THE REALM OF NECESSITY TO THE REALM OF FREEDOM, 1918–1920

## THE SHAMEFUL PEACE

Nikolai Berdyaev was wrong in believing that of all tendencies, bolshevism was "the least utopian and the most realistic," that it best corresponded to the situation existing in Russia in 1917.[1] The Bolsheviks had an easy victory because they promised utopia: everything for everyone, right away. "The face of truth is terrible," wrote the Spanish philosopher Miguel de Unamuno. "The people need myths and illusions; they need to be lied to. Truth is frightening, insupportable, deadly." The Bolsheviks offered the illusion of peace, land, and bread. The reality, however, was a new war, forced grain requisitioning, famine, and unprecedented terror.

Shortly before the October revolution, at his retreat in Finland, Lenin put down in writing his plan for transforming Russia. He called his utopia *State and Revolution*. He considered this work so important that in a note to Kamenev he requested that if the author were killed the pamphlet be published at all costs. Basing himself on the doctrine of Marx and Engels and taking as a living model the Paris Commune, Lenin outlined the communist state which would emerge after the proletarian revolution. In this state there would no longer be an army or police, all officials would be elected, and the functions of administering the state would be so simple that anyone, even a cook or housekeeper, could learn them. Government officials would earn no more than skilled workers; Lenin gave great importance to this concept. The author of *State and Revolution* recognized that the victory of the proletariat would not immediately give birth to a communist society; a period of transition would be necessary, during which the dictatorship of the proletariat would replace the dictatorship of the bourgeoisie. "The proletariat needs the state," Lenin quoted Engels, "not in the interests of freedom, but in order to hold down its adversaries." The dictatorship of the proletariat had two basic functions: to suppress the exploiters' resistance, and to provide leadership for the masses of the population. The first function seemed simple to him, since the repression of an insignificant minority would be the work of the overwhelming majority of the population, the working class. The second function presented no major problems either; people should submit to the "armed vanguard" until everyone could "become accustomed to observing the elementary rules of social intercourse... without coercion, without subordination."[2]

Immediately upon taking power Lenin ran into harsh reality, which put his utopia to the test. First of all, the new government had to resolve the war problem, which had been fatal to the Provisional Government. Negotiations with Germany began at Brest-Litovsk in December. Prince Max von Baden described in his memoirs some of the peculiarities of these talks. His cousin, Prince Ernst von Hohenlohe, a member of the German delegation, was placed next to a Madame Bitsenko at the dinner table: "She earned this distinction by having murdered a minister." Anastasia Bitsenko had committed this act in 1905. The veteran terrorist represented the Left SRs in the delegation. The encounter at the dinner table between Hohenlohe and Bitsenko, and at the negotiating table between Leon Trotsky and General Hoffmann, was a confrontation between utopia and reality. The majority of the Bolshevik Central Committee thought that if they simply announced the war was over they could calmly proceed to the building of communism. The Germans demanded reality, that is to say, territory: Poland, Lithuania, parts of Latvia and Byelorussia.

Bukharin, the spokesman for the Left Communists, an important grouping within the Central Committee, rejected in principle any compromise with the imperialists and preached a "revolutionary war" against Germany, explaining that it would ignite a "worldwide conflagration." Trotsky proposed the celebrated formula, "neither war nor peace," which was supported by the majority of the Central Committee. The Soviet government announced, through Trotsky, that it would withdraw from the war but not sign a peace treaty. Lenin, in the minority, argued the realities of the situation: we have no army, we are helpless, we must sign a treaty. His comrades and disciples had been blinded by utopia. They failed to understand what was obvious to Lenin: utopia could not be realized unless power was maintained. This last argument was Lenin's most important, convincing, and decisive one. When the Germans, taking advantage of Trotsky's announcement, began a new offensive and issued an ultimatum, Lenin demanded that it be accepted immediately. He explained, "If the Germans said that they wanted to overthrow Bolshevik power, we would naturally have to fight."[3] In other words, power was worth fighting for, but not territory or other such "outmoded" concepts. In discussing Trotsky's refusal to sign the peace treaty, Bonch-Bruevich asks, "How can such a nonsensical attitude be explained?" He answers:

> Generally it has been said that pseudo-patriotic and nationalistic prejudices played bad tricks on the negotiating commission; none of its members, including Trotsky, wanted to take upon himself the woeful responsibility of placing his signature on this humiliating peace treaty, which ignorant loudmouths might interpret as "betrayal of the homeland," a direct blow to Russia as a state.[4]

Lenin's fanatical self-assurance and belief in his utopia allowed him to disregard such "pseudo-patriotic and nationalistic prejudices."

On March 3, 1918, the Soviet delegation signed a peace treaty at Brest-Litovsk, "a shameful peace," as Lenin put it, agreeing to German occupation of the Baltic states, parts of Byelorussia, and all of the Ukraine. The Soviet Republic agreed to pay an enormous indemnity to the Germans in the form of provisions, raw materials, and gold. But Lenin still held power. "The Brest-Litovsk peace," the *Small Soviet Encyclopedia* observes, "fulfilled the essential task of preserving the dictatorship of the proletariat."[5]

The Left SRs resigned from the government to protest the treaty, but they continued to support the Bolsheviks. Some officers and generals refused to recognize the unilateral peace, but the soldiers and peasants were opposed to war. Their support allowed Lenin to stay in power. The shameful peace did not, however, solve any internal problems. All existing conflicts were exacerbated.

On April 8, in a conversation with Lunacharsky, the people's commissar of education, Lenin presented an idea he "had been toying with for some time." In Campanella's *City of the Sun* the fronts of the houses were covered with frescoes that served to educate and instruct the citizens of that utopian city. Lenin proposed that Lunacharsky select some slogans for a similar "monumental form of propaganda." Later Lenin picked his favorites from among the suggested slogans. He was especially fond of one: "The golden age is coming; people will live without laws or punishment, doing of their own free will what is good and just." Perhaps these words of Ovid had haunted Lenin as he wrote his *State and Revolution*. But the golden age did not come after the October revolution. Certainly, men began to live without laws, but nothing they did of their own free will was good or just.

## THE SPIRIT OF DESTRUCTION

The first task Lenin assigned to the proletarian revolution was the destruction of the state—the smashing of the old state machinery, in Marxist terminology. This had begun before the revolution, for the army had already fallen apart. After October the judicial system was abolished and replaced by revolutionary tribunals, which railroaded people to prison on the basis of "proletarian conscience and revolutionary duty." Pillaging, looting of wine cellars, and murders were daily occurrences in the revolutionary capital; they found an indignant chronicler in the person of Maxim Gorky. Until the newspaper *Novaya zhizn* was shut down in July 1918, in a column called "Untimely Thoughts," Gorky constantly and indignantly presented the facts and castigated the people's commissars who, in their efforts to prove their "devotion to the people," did not hesitate to "shoot, assassinate, and arrest those who did not think like them, did not hesitate to lie and slander their enemies."[6] As an example, Gorky mentioned the case of the sailor Zheleznyakov, who, "translating the ferocious speeches of his leaders into the simple language of a man of the people, said that for the good of the Russian people, it would be all right to kill a million" opponents.[7] Bonch-Bruevich, who after October 1917 was in charge of security in Petrograd, remembered that "to maintain public order in the city, from the end of October until February 1918, at a time when drunkenness and brawling were at their peak, the only reliable forces we had were the Latvian riflemen at Smolny, some soldiers of the Chasseurs, Preobrazhenzky, and Semenovsky regiments, who were guarding the State Bank, and some units from the Second Fleet."[8] A few pages later, Bonch-Bruevich tells of his visit to the "loyal sailors" of the Second Fleet. They were commanded by two "politically conscious anarchists," the same Anatoly Zheleznyakov who closed down the Constituent Assembly and who, according to Gorky, was willing to kill a million people, and his brother, an alcoholic and a murderer. Bonch-Bruevich narrates the monstrous exploits of these sailors, "the pride and joy of the Russian revolution," with a bit of fear perhaps, but also with obvious satisfaction at knowing they were on "our side." One of the sailors described how he had put forty-three officers in front of a firing squad.[9] When the Zheleznyakov brothers began to pillage and kill on a level unheard of even in revolutionary Petrograd, they were disarmed and sent to the front to defend Soviet power. Disarming them required "a strong detachment of Bolshevik Latvians." Also, "just in case, we alerted the Volynsky and Chasseurs regiments, who at that time had distinguished themselves by their sobriety, or rather, their tolerable degree of drunkenness."[10]

Clearing the city of anarchists, whether "conscious," "spontaneous," or "pure," did not mean an end to arbitrary justice. The suppression of the enemy took on an organized character. Room 75 was too weak to defend the government, though it had done its best. At a meeting of the Petrograd Soviet, Bonch-Bruevich explained that he had obtained confessions from detainees by threatening to shoot them.[11] (The death penalty had been abolished just a few days before.) Room 75 was only the forerunner of the true political police. On December 7, five weeks after the revolution, it was replaced by a new body that became a key instrument of Soviet power, the All-Russia Extraordinary Commission for the Struggle Against Counterrevolution and Sabotage—the Cheka. The idea for such an agency had come to Lenin in the aftermath of October. He searched for the right man to head it up: "Is it impossible to find among us a Fouquier-Tinville to tame our wild counterrevolutionaries?"[12] At the beginning of December a man was found who actually did resemble the bloody public prosecutor of the French revolution, whose standard sentence had been the guillotine. At a meeting of the Sovnarkom, this man, Felix Dzerzhinsky, recited his creed: "Do not believe that I seek revolutionary forms of justice. We don't need justice at this point. We are engaged today in hand-to-hand combat, to the death, to the end! I propose, I demand, the organization of revolutionary annihilation against all active counterrevolutionaries."[13]

The new organ of "revolutionary annihilation," directly under the authority of the Sovnarkom and its president, Lenin, gave priority to the struggle against "sabotage."

From its inception, the new government showed a complete mastery of vocabulary. A new art was born, the art of propaganda, of changing the meaning of things by changing their name. After the proletarian revolution, strikes, the weapon of the proletariat, lost their justification; so they were renamed. When, as we shall see, a general strike of civil servants began, it was denounced as "sabotage," a sinister term implying the need for severe punishment. Power was in the hands of the Bolsheviks, as the nation, and above all the intelligentsia, would learn all too quickly.

Among the ideas of Engels that are still relevant today are these prophetic words: "Nations that have boasted of making a revolution have always discovered on the day after that they had no idea what was happening, that the completed revolution had nothing to do with the one they wanted." In Russia the first to discover this truth "the day after" were the intellectuals. For over a century they had lived for the revolution, longed for it, worked for it. The more the monarchy weakened, the more active they became. As early as the turn of the century they had felt the underground tremors of impending disaster, had hailed the coming onslaught of the "new Huns," had called down fire from heaven, and had agreed to be trampled into the dust for the sake of Russia's regeneration. The February revolution, which brought freedom and lent a voice to the "great silent mass" of the people, at first seemed to be their dream come true. But the people bore little resemblance to the icon worshiped by the intellectuals, who although they controlled the Provisional Government, had no clear idea what to do with their power. Gorky noted in his diary the lament of an anonymous intellectual reflecting the sentiments of most of his kind: "I feel terrible, like a Christopher Columbus who has finally reached the shores of America but is disgusted by it."

The intellectuals did, however, find the strength to fight against the "shameless brute" who had violated their beloved. A strike of civil servants and municipal employees broke out first in Petrograd, then in Moscow, and spread to other cities as well. Urban transit systems and power plants shut down. Moscow's teachers went on strike (for three months), as did those of Petrograd, Ekaterinburg, Astrakhan, and Ufa. Doctors, health workers, nurses, and pharmacists followed suit. University professors refused to recognize the new government. Many technicians also resisted, expressing their ideas mainly through the All-Russia Union of Engineers. One week after the October insurrection, the Central Executive Committee of the Soviets invited the "creative intelligentsia" of Petrograd to a meeting at Smolny. Aside from two Bolsheviks, Rurik Ivnev and Larissa Reissner, only three intellectuals showed up, Vladimir Mayakovsky, Vsevolod Meyerhold, and Alexander Blok. Mayakovsky, who in March 1917 had proclaimed, "Long live art free of politics," and Meyerhold, director of a spectacular show, *The Masked Ball*, at the Imperial Alexandrinsky Theater, represented the new revolutionary art.

The hopes of these artistic innovators were described years later by the modernist theatrical director Aleksandr Tairov: "What was our reasoning?

The revolution was destroying the old forms of social life. We would destroy the old forms of art. Consequently, we too were revolutionaries and could march in step with the revolution."[14] These revolutionary artists were sadly mistaken to expect any lasting sympathy from the political revolutionaries. Nevertheless, for a while the new government made use of these "destructive elements." Evgeny Zamyatin described them as "the slippery school of con man art," who "knew when to wear the red cap and when to take it off, when to sing the glories of the tsar and when to sing the hammer and sickle." With the exception of one real poet, Mayakovsky, Zamyatin noted, "the Futurists were the slipperiest of all; without losing one second, they announced that the official artists of the new regime would, of course, be they."[15]

At Smolny, Alexander Blok was an alien presence—he who had seen the revolution as Russia's purifying fire, who when he closed his eyes could hear "the music of revolutions." It was also with his eyes closed that he wrote "The Twelve" and "The Scythians." He came to his senses rather quickly and with quite a shock: "When the Red Army and socialist construction began, I couldn't take it any more," he wrote in his diary.

The disenchantment of the overwhelming majority of the intellectuals did not surprise Lenin; he preached that only the intelligentsia could bring "revolutionary consciousness" to the working class but had always been suspicious and ill disposed toward them. What he did not expect, however, was the disenchantment of the working class, in whose name and for whose sake the revolution had been carried out.

Of the three slogans that had allowed the Bolsheviks to take power, peace and land reflected above all the interests of the peasantry. The third slogan, bread, expressed the interests of the working class but its exact meaning was a good deal less clear. Also unclear was the meaning of "workers' control of production." Moreover, it was symptomatic that the decree on workers' control was not adopted on October 25 along with the other two, but twenty days later, on November 14, 1917.

This decree provided for "workers' control of production, of the purchase, sale, and storage of raw materials and finished products, and of the financial aspects of the enterprise."[16] What could be simpler than this at first glance? The workers would control everything, and all economic problems would be solved by the producers themselves. In January 1918 Lenin encouraged the proletariat: "You are the government, do as you wish, take what you need, we will support you. . . . You will make mistakes, but you will learn."[17] This monumental experiment, involving the entire Russian economy, soon has its effect. The workers often interpreted the vague concept of "workers' control" in a very simple way. "I came to the factory and began to put workers' control into effect," a Communist worker related. "I broke open the safe to count the money, but there wasn't any."[18] The organ of the Central Council of Trade Unions, *Vestnik truda* (Labor herald), complained that the workers regarded "the factories that have been placed in their hands as an inexhaustible ocean from which unlimited quantities of goods can be taken without doing any harm."[19]

Governmental measures completely disorganized the functioning of industry. In May 1918 Tomsky, president of the Central Council of Trade Unions, said, "Current labor productivity has dropped to a point that threatens us with total disorganization and collapse."[20] The decline in labor productivity was one expression of growing discontent among the workers. A. Volsky (Jan Waclaw Machaiski) made this comment in the magazine *Rabochaya revolyutsiya* (Workers' revolution), whose only issue appeared in June–July 1918: "After the bourgeois revolution of February, workers' wages were substantially increased, and the eight-hour day was won; after the proletarian revolution of October, the workers didn't get anything."[21] There was another difference between the two revolutions: after the proletarian revolution, the working class lost the possibility of fighting for its rights. "Control of production" proved to be a fantasy; the destruction of the management system existing in industry brutally aggravated the workers' plight.

In March 1918 an emergency convention of delegates from local plants and factories was held in Petrograd. It stated:

> The unions have lost their independence and no longer serve to organize the defense of workers' rights. The Soviets of Workers' and Soldiers' Deputies seem to fear the workers. They do not allow new elections, but have entrenched themselves; they have become government bodies and no longer express the opinions of the working masses.[22]

A declaration adopted by delegates from the largest factories in Petrograd and from the railroad workshops, power plants, and printing houses appealed to the All-Russia Congress of Soviets. It summed up the results of the first months of the revolution as follows:

> On October 25, 1917, the Bolshevik party, allied with the Left SRs and supported by armed soldiers and sailors, overthrew the Provisional Government and seized power. We, the workers of Petrograd, have in our majority accepted this change of government, made in our name but without our knowlege or participation. . . . Moreover, the workers have supported the new government, which declared itself a workers' and peasants' government and promised to carry out our wishes and respect our interests. All our organizations were placed at its service. Our sons and brothers have shed their

blood for it. We have patiently endured famine and adversity. In our name all those whom the new government has designated its enemies have been cruelly repressed. Hoping that the promises it gave would be kept, we resigned ourselves to the eradication of our liberty and our rights. But four months have gone by already, and we see that our trust has been cruelly abused, that our hopes have been brutally stamped out.[23]

The delegates' movement, expressing the disenchantment of the working class, began to spread to other cities. In Moscow an organizing committee was established for an All-Russia Conference of Factory Delegates. The movement was labeled Menshevik, Right SR, counterrevolutionary, and broken up.

The workers voted against "proletarian power" with their hands—production fell off tremendously—and with their feet—they abandoned the disorganized and ruined factories. In May 1918, at the first congress of local economic councils, Aleksei Gastev discussed the workers' refusal to work: "In fact, we are faced with an enormous sabotage in which millions participate. I laugh when I am told of bourgeois sabotage, when the terrified bourgeois is singled out as if he were the saboteur. We are dealing with national, popular, proletarian sabotage."[24]

The collapse of industry soon had repercussions on agriculture. The Bolshevik party had won the support of the peasants by "borrowing" the agrarian program of the SRs. Lenin did not try to hide this fact: "At least until the summer of 1918, we maintained power because we had the support of the peasantry as a whole."[25] In October 1917 the peasants had supported the Bolsheviks, but disenchantment quickly set in. A popular song in the first years of the revolution had this line: "Our engine runs full steam ahead. Last stop is the commune." The Russian peasants didn't want to go that far; they wanted to get off at the first stop, the distribution of the landed estates.

Radical agrarian reform, of which the peasants had dreamed for centuries and the intellectuals for a hundred years, swept the country like wildfire, but with unexpected results. In the overwhelming majority of regions, those who had tilled the soil from time immemorial received on the average half a desyatina, or 1.35 acres, of additional land.[26] Workers, artisans, and household servants who had fled the cities also demanded—and received— a plot of land. However, this was not the main reason for the peasants' disillusionment. Each had obtained a bit of land, and the large estates had at last been abolished. Dissatisfaction over the new government began the moment it started demanding agricultural produce from the peasants without providing anything in return. Inflation had stripped money of its value, and industry no longer produced for the countryside's needs. Peasant "sabotage" was now added to that of the intelligentsia and the proletariat. In November 1917, 641,000 tons of grain were stored; in December 1917 136,000; in January 1918, 46,000; in April 1918, 38,000; in May 1918, 3,000; in June 1918, 2,000.[27] The cities were starving. The famished workers further reduced their already low output or simply fled to the countryside.

The Bolshevik government created discontent among those who had supported it. But Lenin's disappointment with the proletariat was just as strong. (He had always been unhappy with the peasantry.) Within a few months after the revolution, the Russian working class, whose "political maturity" Lenin had praised, proved itself in his eyes to be immature, not proletarian enough, and lacking in the training necessary to run the country.

The utopian dreams of *State and Revolution*, written on the eve of October, evaporated upon contact with reality. In March 1918 Lenin wrote a new utopian program, an article called "The Immediate Tasks of the Soviet Government," in which he spelled out the most important features of "communism" (which later came to be called war communism, after its failure became apparent). The "task of suppressing the resistance of the exploiters," Lenin wrote, had been fulfilled for the most part. "Now we must administer Russia." This second task was as easy as the first, in the author's view. It could be accomplished simply by establishing "nationwide accounting and control of the production and distribution of goods."[28]

In October 1921 Lenin described his 1918 program more fully:

> At the beginning of 1918 we made the mistake of deciding to go over directly to communist production and distribution. We thought that under the surplus food appropriation system the peasants would provide us with the required quantity of grain, which we could distribute among the factories and thus achieve communist production and distribution. I cannot say that we pictured this plan as definitely and clearly as that; but we acted approximately on those lines.[29]

It was precisely at the beginning of 1918 that Lenin, according to Trotsky, then his closest comrade-in-arms, constantly repeated at Sovnarkom meetings: "In six months we will have built socialism." Ten years later, Andrei Platonov would write *The Strange Herbs of Chevengur*, a novel about some revolutionary dreamers who decide to build socialism "at one blow," using "the fighting methods of revolutionary conscience and compulsory labor service."

Unlike Platonov's characters, Lenin had vast resources at his disposal for realizing his communist utopia. In industry, "control of production" gave way to nationalizations. Private trade, the foundation of the capitalist system, was banned. And compulsory labor service was introduced. "We ought to begin," Lenin wrote, "by introducing compulsory labor service for the rich."[30] Later these principles would gradually be extended to the majority, the workers and peasants. The example of wartime Germany served as confirmation to Lenin that such a scheme could succeed. "German imperialism . . . displayed its economically advanced position by the fact that it went over, earlier than any of the other warring powers, to a system of compulsory labor service."[31] Lenin's plan had the simplicity of genius: the Kaiser's Germany plus Soviet power equals communism.

Compulsory service was applied to the peasants in the form of government decrees in May and June 1918 instituting grain requisitioning. Under the so-called surplus food appropriation system (*prodrazverstka*) peasants were obliged to sell the state all their surplus, at fixed prices. This requisitioning of grain, Lenin said, "must become our fundamental activity" and "must be pursued to the end. Only when this problem is resolved will we have the socialist foundations on which to build the glorious structure of socialism."[32]

The ban on private trade and the absence of any state trading system brought famine to the cities, an outcome that must have seemed incomprehensible to a population which had revolted because of food shortages. Lenin formulated his scheme for building the "glorious structure" in the following manner: "There are two ways to fight hunger, a capitalist one and a socialist one. The first consists of free trade. . . . Our path is that of the grain monopoly."[33] And so the battle for grain began. In order to confiscate grain, the government organized "food detachments," a measure Lenin described as the "first and most momentous step toward the socialist revolution in the countryside."[34] Poor peasants' committees were established by decree on June 11, 1918, to help bring the "revolution to the countryside." Part of the grain discovered and confiscated by these committees was to be distributed to the poor peasants themselves, as a "material incentive."

Bonch-Bruevich offers these recollections of the period of "war communism":

> The onrush of revolutionary events . . . changed our social relations to such an extent that we considered it best to nationalize absolutely everything, from the biggest factories down to the last hairdressing shop run by one hairdresser owning a clipper and two razors, or down to the last carrot in a grocery store. Roadblocks and checkpoints were put up everywhere so that no one could get through with food [smuggled from the countryside]. Everyone was put on government rations.[35]

Bonch-Bruevich does not explain that the rations varied considerably and that certain categories of the population did not get any at all or that only "speculation by bag traders," who smuggled foodstuffs past the roadblocks, saved the urban population of the Soviet Republic from death. In 1918 and 1919 city dwellers obtained 60 percent of their food from the black market. The grain monopoly and the government's food policy contributed greatly to the demoralization of citizens by forcing them to resort to illegal measures, fostering crime on a huge scale and giving birth to an extremely powerful black market. The grain monopoly and the ban on private trade trained people to think that commerce, in and of itself, was a counterrevolutionary activity or at best an unworthy occupation. The grain monopoly, like all the acts of the Soviet government, had not only a concrete goal but also an "educational" function, undermining both the administrative structures of the old society and its moral foundations as well.

On January 13, 1918, a decree on the separation of church and state deprived the church of all its property and legal rights, in effect outlawing it. In September a decree on the family and marriage and one on the schools were adopted almost simultaneously. Marriage (only civil marriage was recognized; religious marriage was abolished) and divorce were made freely available. Alexandra Kollontai declared the family's obsolescence, both to the state, because it prevents women from doing work useful to society, and to family members themselves, because the state would gradually take over childbearing.

However, the state could not afford to assume this task immediately after the revolution, although articles were inserted in the legal code making it possible in the future. The government's intentions were made clear at a national educational conference in remarks by Zlata Lilina, Zinoviev's wife and the director of public education in Petrograd, who called for the "nationalization" of all children, to remove them from the oppressive influences of their families, because children, "like wax, are highly impressionable" and because "good, true Communists" could be made out of them.

Schools became coeducational, tuition was abolished, and tests were done away with, along with homework. While supporting school reform, the All-Russia Union of Schoolteachers spoke out against the subordination of schools to the state.

The destruction of the prerevolutionary social fabric (the army, the legal system, administration, the family, the church, schools, political parties, the economy) did not frighten Lenin. He was convinced he had the key to building a new world, a pure utopia, on a bare, newly cleared surface. The key was the dictatorship of the proletariat.

## BIRTH OF A DICTATORSHIP

The dictatorship of the proletariat was part of the Russian Social Democratic Labor party's program from its inception. To Lenin, the model for such a dictatorship, as discussed by Marx, was the Paris Commune. In *State and Revolution* Lenin said that only a complete ignoramus or bourgeois swindler could argue that the workers as a class are incapable of directly administering the state. After taking power, however, he changed his tune. Clemenceau liked to say that war was too serious a matter to be left to the generals. Lenin soon reached the conclusion that dictatorship of the proletariat was too serious a matter to be left to the proletariat.

Lenin defined the dictatorship of the proletariat first of all as a system that rejected parliamentarism, with its separation of legislative and executive powers. The dictatorship of the proletariat would fuse the executive and legislative functions.[36] This meant that the holders of power could pass laws strengthening their own authority without any checks or balances. Lest there be any misunderstanding, Lenin gave this clear explanation: "The scientific definition of dictatorship is a power that is not limited by any laws, not bound by any rules, and based directly on force."[37]

Since the proletariat showed itself incapable of exercising such a dictatorship, the vanguard of the working class, the party, had to assume the task. Lenin did not conceal his views: "When we are reproached for exercising the dictatorship of a party ... we say, 'Yes, the dictatorship of a party! We stand by it and cannot do without it.'"[38] Even before taking power, he had scorned the bourgeois concept of "the will of the majority." "What is needed," he wrote, is "a strength which at the decisive moment and place will crush the enemy's strength."[39]

Lenin's first contact with the practical reality of power persuaded him of the need for a dictatorship of the party and beyond that—this was a new contribution to Marxism—the dictatorship of a single leader. In March 1918 he justified such a dictatorship by the needs of the modern economy.

> Large-scale machine industry—which is precisely the material source, the productive source, the foundation of socialism—calls for absolute and strict unity of will. ... But how can strict unity of will be ensured? By thousands subordinating their will to the will of one. Given ideal class consciousness and discipline on the part of those participating in the common work, the subordination would be something like the mild leadership of a conductor of an orchestra. It may [also] assume the sharp forms of a dictatorship. ... Be that as it may, unquestioning subordination to a single will is absolutely necessary.[40]

Four months after the revolution, in March 1918, Lenin spoke of the need for a one-person dictatorship for economic reasons. In March 1919, in a eulogy for Yakov Sverdlov, he stressed the need for personal dictatorship for political reasons. "In this time of violent struggle, as we exercise the workers' dictatorship, we must advance the principle of personal authority, the moral authority of one man [like Sverdlov] whose decisions are accepted by everybody without lengthy discussions."[41] Firm authority was a concept Lenin had been attached to for a long time. Trotsky in his pamphlet *The Second Congress of the RSDLP: Report of the Siberian Delegation* (published in Geneva in 1903) described Lenin's plans.

> The state of siege [in the party], on which Lenin insists so energetically, requires the party to have a strong central authority. The practical experience of organized distrust [toward the leadership] requires an iron hand; Lenin makes a mental rollcall of the party's personnel and comes to the conclusion that he and only he has that iron hand.

Lenin did not hide his intentions; Trotsky did not have to guess at them. According to the stenographic record of the Second Congress, when a delegate named Popov referred in his remarks to the omnipresent and all-penetrating spirit of the Central Committee, Lenin raised his fist in the air and called out: "The fist." The power of the fist, which Lenin had established within his party, was extended to the country as a whole. Thus was born the twentieth-century "philosophy of power."

Upon discovering that reality did not bear the slightest resemblance to his previous conception, Lenin decided to change it by force, first of all by changing other people's conception of it. It is significant that the first decree of the Council of People's Commissars was a decree on the press putting censorship into effect and outlawing magazines and newspapers guilty of a critical attitude toward the new government. Bonch-Bruevich admits that for some, "even some of the Old Bolsheviks," it was hard to accept the fact that "our old program" from before the revolution had called for "freedom of the press," but after the seizure of power this freedom was immediately abolished. Bonch-Bruevich formulates the "new demands of October" this way: "During a revolution there should be only a revolutionary press and no other."[42]

A good pupil of Lenin and Stalin, Hitler pointed out that the bourgeoisie's weakness in relation to revolutionary Marxism stemmed primarily from a separation between spirit and force, between ideology and terror. In Marxism, said the Führer, "spirit and brute force are harmoniously blended." He added, "National socialism is what Marxism could have become, if it had broken its absurd ties with the democratic order."[43] Lenin was the first to discover the secret of blending "spirit and brute force," the practical use of force to carry out a utopian program, and the use of a utopian program as camouflage for brute force.

Essential to Lenin's policy, which sought to maintain a minority in power, was splitting the majority, atomizing society.

One of the government's first actions was to wipe out all the ranks, titles, and "social estates" that had existed in old Russia. Unlike the bourgeois revolutions, which had introduced the formal equality of all citizens under the law, the proletarian revolution established inequality as a principle. This was done by the Soviet constitution, adopted in July 1918. One section of the population was completely stripped of its rights. The Russian language was enriched by the word *lishenets*, "disfranchised person." The *lishentsy* were people whose income came from a source other than their own labor: individual tradesmen, religious officials, former police collaborators, members of the imperial household, but also "persons who hire labor with the aim of extracting a profit." This referred primarily to peasants who hired others, even if this meant one worker in the spring or fall to help work the land. No less than 5 million people fell into this category. Deprivation of rights affected all family members. For the children this meant above all being prohibited from studying at the university level and having only limited access to secondary school, depending on the number of openings. All peasants had their electoral rights curtailed: in elections to the soviets the vote of one worker had the value of five peasant votes.

The peasantry was divided into many categories: rural proletarians, poor peasants, middle peasants, and kulaks. Since there were no specific criteria for determining the category to which any one peasant belonged, arbitrariness became the rule. In the system created, the possession of one or two cattle or one or two horses determined one's position in society and the future of one's children. "Social status" became a permanent scar. The revolution forbade social mobility to those individuals whose social origins were undesirable. These could not be changed any more than could racial origins.

A concrete example of "disenfranchisement" was the decision by the Petrograd Commissariat of Food Supply in June 1918 to put into effect a "class-based rationing for the various groups of the working or nonworking population." Initially, four categories were created: (1) industrial workers performing heavy physical labor; (2) all other workers and salaried employees; (3) those in the liberal professions; and (4) nonworking elements.[44] This decision stemmed from Lenin's orders of December 1917 on "the need to distribute food rations according to a class principle."[45] On September 27, 1918, *Pravda* reported: "The Commissariat of Social Security has confirmed the necessity of stripping all kulaks and bourgeois elements, both rural and urban, of their rations. The surplus thus obtained will be used to increase the rations of the rural and urban poor." Having divided society into categories, the government assumed the right to sentence part of the population, the lower castes, to starvation, for the preservation of the upper castes.

An essential instrument of Lenin's policy was the Cheka, which functioned in fact as a special organ of the Bolshevik party, directly under Lenin's control. According to Krupskaya, what Lenin feared most of all from the very first days in power was the softness of his own comrades. He was infuriated by a resolution of the Second Congress of Soviets abolishing the death penalty, passed on October 25, 1917, on a motion by Kamenev. The February revolution had abolished the death penalty, and when Kerensky attempted to restore it to punish deserters, the Bolsheviks had strenuously objected. Now Lenin angrily repeated: "Nonsense. How can one make a revolution without firing squads?" According to Trotsky, Lenin insisted this was a big mistake, "a pacifist illusion." After the death penalty was abolished, the Bolshevik government, under pressure from Lenin, decided in spite of the decree to "have recourse to a firing squad when it becomes obvious that there is no other way."[46]

A network of "extraordinary commissions" (local Cheka units) covered the entire Soviet Republic. They were set up in major cities, county seats, and provincial capitals, on the railroads, in the ports, and in the army. Very soon the Cheka was granted unlimited power. It was, according to one of its leaders, "an organ that employs in its struggle the methods of investigating commissions, the courts, and the armed forces."[47] The extraordinary commissions themselves made arrests, conducted investigations, held trials, handed down sentences, and carried them out.

On August 30, 1918, in Petrograd, the student Leonid Kanegisser assassinated Uritsky, the chairman of the Petrograd Cheka, and in Moscow, the Socialist Revolutionary Fanny Kaplan wounded Lenin. This day marked a turning point in the history of the Cheka. It was ordered to carry out a "merciless mass terror." The Sovnarkom published a decree on September 5 authorizing the Red Terror. That same day Fanny Kaplan was shot without trial by the Cheka.[48] A wave of executions ensued. "The number of executed," said Yakov Peters, deputy chairman of the Cheka, "has been greatly exaggerated. In no way does the total exceed 600."[49] In Peters' view, this was not excessive, since it was in retaliation for the assassination attempt on the party's leader. Grigory Petrovsky, people's commissar of internal affairs, issued a special order expressing indignation "at the insignificant number of serious acts of repression and mass executions of White Guards and bourgeoisie" and requiring that "substantial numbers of hostages be taken."[50] Dzerzhinsky, chairman of the Cheka, explained in a memorandum what a hostage was: "Hostages must be taken from among... people of high social position, large landowners, factory owners, prominent officials and academics, close relatives of people formerly in power, etc." This was because "nobody will intercede or give anything" for some "rural teacher, forester, miller, or small shopkeeper."[51]

The hostage system, unknown in prerevolutionary Russia, was supplemented by another instrument of repression new to the country—the concentration camp. The notoriety stemming from its use by Hitler should not obscure the fact that the Soviet state was the initiator of this institution. Trotsky had the honor of being first to use the term. In his order of June 4, 1918, he demanded that all Czechoslovaks who refused to lay down their arms be detained in concentration camps.[52] On June 26 Trotsky sent a memorandum to the Sovnarkom proposing that all former officers who refused to join the Red Army be considered part of the bourgeoisie and placed in "concentration camps."[53] On August 8 Trotsky substantially enlarged the category of those subject to detention and ordered camps established in Murom, Arzamas, and Sviyazhsk for holding "reactionary agitators, counterrevolutionary officers, saboteurs, parasites, and speculators."[54] On August 9 Lenin, troubled by the extent of the peasant insurrection in Penza province, sent a telegraph to the Penza Executive Committee urging it to carry out "ruthless mass terror against the kulaks, priests, and White Guards; confine all suspicious elements in a concentration camp outside the city."[55]

The concentration camp became a universal instrument of terror against "suspicious elements." On September 5, 1918, after this method of repression had already been widely employed, it was legalized by a decree of the Sovnarkom: "It is necessary to protect the Soviet Republic from class enemies by isolating them in concentration camps." The next point in this decree states: "All persons implicated in the activities of White Guard organizations, conspiracies, or uprisings are subject to being shot."[56]

As a punitive measure the concentration camp was second in severity to the death penalty, which was restored officially on February 21, 1918, by a decree of the Sovnarkom granting the Cheka the "right to take immediate reprisals against active counterrevolutionaries."[57] This category included "enemy agents, profiteers, marauders, hooligans, counterrevolutionary agitators, and German spies." All were to be "shot on the spot," in other words, without investigation or trial.[58] The Cheka expanded this list, in its "proclamation" of February 22, to include "saboteurs and other parasites." On June 16 the People's Commissariat of Justice informed the revolutionary tribunals that they were not under any "constraints" in selecting "the methods of struggle against counterrevolution, sabotage, etc."[59]

The exact number of people shot during the first year of the revolution is unknown. According to Latsis, only twenty-two people were shot by the Cheka during the first half of 1918, but during the second half of that year "more than 6,000 were shot."[60] Aside from the fact that Latsis's figures are open to question, the number of people shot by agencies other than the Cheka, such as the revolutionary tribunals and local soviets, is not known. It should suffice to note that the official announcement of the execution of "former Tsar Nicholas Romanov" states that on July 16, 1918, the sentence handed down by the Presidium of the Urals Regional Soviet was carried out. It added: "The wife and son of Nicholas Romanov have been sent to a safe place."[61] In fact, the tsar, his wife, son, and four daughters, a doctor, a cook, a footman, and a maidservant were all shot. If Latsis, the first historian of the Cheka, always counted one when eleven people were shot, his statistics can hardly be considered reliable.

From the very first days of the regime, dictatorship was for Lenin a panacea for all problems, be they political, economic, or social. In 1902, in his notes on Plekhanov's draft program for the RSDRP, Lenin wrote that if the peasants did not adopt the proletarian standpoint, "We will say, under the 'dictatorship': there is no point in wasting words when the use of power is required." After reading this remark, Vera Zasulich wrote in the margin, "Against millions! That's easily said." For Zasulich, a terrorist who had been willing to shoot an official of the autocracy, a dictatorship imposed on millions seemed unthinkable. For Lenin, who was against individual acts of terrorism, mass terror was an indispensable method for building a socialist society. This meant mass terror against the peasants. (A resolution of the Council of Workers' and Peasants' Defense of February 15, 1919, said, "hostages must be taken among the peasantry, so that if the snow is not cleared away, they will be shot."[62]) It meant mass terror against the workers. (All workers discontented with the new government were declared "nonworkers," not "pure proletarians"; they had been contaminated by the petit bourgeois mentality; meanwhile, the concentration camps were baptized "schools of labor."[63]) And it meant mass terror against all other classes as well.

In September 1918 all the regional Chekas received the following order from Dzerzhinsky: "In its activities, the Cheka is completely independent; it carries out searches, arrests, and executions, and reports afterward to the Sovnarkom and the Central Executive Committee."[64] Besides these unlimited powers, the Cheka was granted "infallibility." Criticism was forbidden of "this organ, whose work proceeds under extremely difficult circumstances."[65]

During the first months following the revolution a new state was born, a totalitarian state. It was not so much the severity of its laws as their complete arbitrariness that became their distinguishing feature. The constitution had deprived a substantial section of the population of its rights and placed it outside the law. But this was not unique to the Soviet system. In Old Russia certain categories had had limited rights. Even after the reform of 1861 this was true of the peasantry. Jews were also denied many civil rights. But these limitations were defined by law, which also allowed for the possibility of passage from a more restricted "social estate" to another that enjoyed all rights. After the revolution, even the categories that, according to the constitution, had all rights were in fact deprived of them.

In 1922 Lenin demanded that an article be included in the penal code giving heavy sentences to those who "objectively aid or might aid" the world bourgeoisie. This concept of "objective" (or "unintentional") aid meant that the state, in the person of its leaders, could define or choose whomever it wished as an opponent. And the Cheka would take appropriate measures, against which there was no appeal.

Former tsarist officers became one category of active or potential enemies, but when military specialists were needed to help organize the Red Army, they were transferred to the category of "useful citizens." During the summer of 1918, when the civil war was brought to the countryside through the formation of poor peasants' committees, the only useful peasant was the poor one or the agricultural laborer. When evidence showed that this policy tended to unite all the peasantry against Soviet power, the "middle peasant" was added to the category of "useful," and by the end of 1918 the poor peasants' committee were phased out.

In the preface to the *Red Book of the Cheka*, the situation in postrevolutionary Russia was defined in a precise and vivid manner: "The new dictator who had replaced the landowners and the bourgeoisie found himself in splendid isolation as he undertook to build anew."[66] But this "splendid isolation" had been chosen by the dictator himself.

The isolation of Lenin's party became complete with the resignation of the Left SRs in March 1918. Later, in July, the Left SRs carried out a number of armed actions and were charged with attempting to overthrow the Bolshevik government. "In leaving the government," said the closing argument of the Bolshevik prosecutor, "the Left SR party freed the government from a useless burden that was restraining its activities, but it did not pass immediately into the enemy camp."[67] The Left SRs had walked out of the government to protest the signing of the Brest-Litovsk treaty, but they had remained in the Central Executive Committee and other Soviet institutions, including the Cheka. On July 6, 1918, two Left SRs, Blymkin and Andreev, assassinated German Ambassador Mirbach. Soviet historians interpret that act as a signal for a general Left SR uprising. However, a resolution of the Left SR Central Committee stated that the action was "directed against the current policy of the Sovnarkom and not at all against the Bolsheviks."[68]

The armed "demonstration of discontent" against Bolshevik policy that the Left SRs organized showed that Lenin's power rested on very fragile foundations. A handful of Black Sea sailors who were part of a Cheka detachment commanded by Popov nearly toppled the government. Joachim Vatsetis, a former tsarist army colonel who had crossed over to the Soviet side and who commanded a division of Latvian fusiliers, became the man on whom Lenin's power depended. The situation in Moscow on July 6 closely resembled that in Petrograd on October 25, 1917. Most of the garrison remained neutral, and the outcome was decided by a few armed units. The Latvian rifles (2,750 soldiers) and some students at a military academy (eighty of them) were the only forces that defended Lenin's government against the Left SRs, who were not seeking to take power in the first place. The rebellious Popov detachment did not have more than 600 people and had only two batteries.[69] Vatsetis was instructed to crush the "uprising," whose leaders had gone to the Fifth Congress of Soviets, then in session, to explain their aims. Four commissars were sent to "supervise" Vatsetis, who commanded the only unit capable of fighting. At the Kremlin, where he was to receive instructions, the commander of the Latvian division found a disturbed and frightened Lenin: "He came over to me with short, rapid strides and asked me very quietly: 'Comrade, can we hold out until tomorrow?'"[70] Lenin understood very well that the "rebel" action was directed against him personally.

A few rounds of artillery directed against the Cheka building, where Popov's men had positioned themselves, were enough to discourage the Left SRs, who were only protesting against the treaty with Germany (and against Lenin, who insisted on the treaty). In all other matters they agreed with the Bolsheviks. Blymkin, who later gave himself up to the Cheka in the Ukraine, stressed in his testimony that there had not been an insurrection and that shots had been fired only as "acts of self-defense by revolutionaries."[71] The verdict of the revolutionary tribunal was a confirmation of Blymkin's words: twelve men from the Popov detachment were shot by a firing squad, along with Aleksandrovich, a Left SR who had been Dzerzhinsky's deputy and had attempted to use the Cheka to serve his party's interests. Left SR leaders Maria Spiridonova, Boris Kamkov, Vladimir Karelin, and Yuri Sablin were given symbolic prison sentences and later set free. Blumkin was pardoned and given a job with the Cheka.

The events of July 1918 allowed the Bolsheviks to rid themselves of a "burden" (the Left SRs in the government) and showed once more that the Cheka and loyal military units were the key to retaining power. The Left SRs, erstwhile friends and comrades-in-arms of the Bolsheviks, suddenly found themselves tagged with a label that was to become standard practice: "agents of the Russian bourgeoisie and of Anglo-French imperialism."[72]

## UP TO AND INCLUDING INDEPENDENCE

"What is our Russian empire?" asked Andrei Bely in his novel *Petersburg*. "Our Russian empire," he answered, "is a geographical entity; that is to say, a piece of a well-known planet. And the Russian empire includes, first and foremost, Great Russia, Little Russia, White Russia, and Ruthenian Russia; secondly, the kingdoms of Georgia, Poland, Kazan, and Astrakhan; thirdly, it includes oh, et cetera, et cetera, et cetera."[73] In the 1897 census, the first systematic census in the empire, the population was 122,666,500, of which 44.32 percent were Russian. In short, the Russian state was multinational.

From the time of Peter the Great until the coronation of Alexander III, the nationalities policy of the Russian empire was distinguished by its relative tolerance toward the national traits of the various peoples contained within it. Only the Poles, whose state had been crushed and whose territory had been partitioned by Prussia, Austria, and Russia, continued their fight for national independence. Alexander III introduced a new chauvinistic policy of Russification, which aroused great discontent among the non-Russian peoples, and which Nicholas II continued.

The 1905 constitution allowed the nationalities of the empire to present their demands and express their aspirations, and it soon became evident, at least before 1917, that there were no major separatist tendencies. The inhabitants of the Russian empire wanted reforms, democratization, equality of rights for all citizens, but not the fragmentation of the state. Among the first acts of the Provisional Government was the nullification of tsarist laws restricting the rights of national minorities and the proclamation of full equality for all citizens of the Russian Republic, regardless of religion, race, or national origin.[74] The foundations were also laid for local self-rule. The governors of Transcaucasia and Turkestan were replaced by special committees, consisting mainly of Duma deputies who were natives of those regions. Administration of the southwestern provinces was placed in the hands of Ukrainians, and in the summer of 1917 the Ukraine was recognized as a separate administrative unit.

In 1917 nationalist movements developed with unexpected vigor, fed by the same sources as other revolutionary movements. There was a difference, though. In the "borderlands" the peasant discontent caused by the postponement of agrarian reform was not directed against the landowners but against the Russian settlers; it took on a nationalist, anti-Russian character.

The October revolution hastened the decomposition of the empire; even the peoples that a short time before had not even dreamed of autonomy began to demand independence. The Soviet government recognized full independence for Poland. This did not require very much effort, since Poland had been occupied by the Germans and the Provisional Government had already promised it independence. Independence was likewise granted to Finland. However, People's Commissar of Nationalities Stalin, speaking at the congress of the Social Democratic party of Finland on November 14, 1917, called on the Finnish Bolsheviks to take power, adding: "And if you require our help, we will give it to you, fraternally extending our hand to you. You can be sure of that."[75] In January 1918, when the local Bolsheviks in Finland attempted to take power, Soviet troops stationed there at the time did indeed aid the insurgents.

Before coming to power, Lenin often referred to Poland, Finland, and the Ukraine as nations whose right to independence was being frustrated by the Provisional Government. In June 1917 he expressed indignation at the Provisional Government's refusal to carry out its "elementary democratic duty" to declare itself in favor of autonomy for the Ukraine and its right to secede freely. After October his attitude on this issue changed. The Ukrainian nationalist movement had assumed vast dimensions after the February revolution. One of its leaders, professor Mikhail Hrushevsky, whose *History of the Ukraine* provided a historical and literary basis for the movement, declared in March 1917: "There is no longer a Ukrainian problem. There is the great and free Ukrainian people, who are creating their own future under new conditions of liberty."[76] Hrushevsky was elected president of the Central Rada, which represented the revolutionary parties and national minorities.

Gradually the Rada became the highest expression of the will of the Ukrainian people. On June 13 it published its first universal declaration. "Henceforth," it stated, "the Ukraine will be the Ukrainian People's Republic. Without seceding from the Russian republic, without endangering its unity, we shall take a firm stand upon our land, so that we can help all of Russia with all our strength, so that the entire Russian republic can become a federation of free and equal peoples." This document also delineated the boundaries of the new republic: "The territory of the Ukrainian People's Republic includes all territories inhabited by a majority of Ukrainians."[77]

The Bolsheviks, who had criticized the Provisional Government for being slow to grant Ukrainian demands for independence, were themselves opposed to independence for the Ukraine. Yuri Pyatakov, head of the Ukrainian Bolsheviks, said after the universal declaration was published, "We should not support the Ukrainians, because their movement bodes no good for the proletariat. Russia cannot exist without the Ukrainian sugar industry; the same can be said about coal (the Donets basin), wheat, and so forth."[78] But the Bolsheviks' weakness in the Ukraine (in August 1917 they had 22,303 members there, with 15,818 in the Donbass, Kharkov, and Ekaterinoslav)[79] forced them to ally with the Rada as the Provisional Government. On the eve of the October revolution, the Rada supported the Bolsheviks, believing that they were even weaker than the Provisional Government. In Kiev their combined efforts put an end to the power of the Provisional Government on October 29. Soon after the victory, these momentary allies came into conflict. The Rada refused to recognize the all-Bolshevik Sovnarkom as the legitimate government of Russia and demanded that it be replaced by a more representative socialist body. On December 4 the Soviet government issued an ultimatum to the Rada: while recognizing the right of the Ukraine to independence, it demanded that the soviets and Soviet power in the Ukraine be recognized, or else there would be war.

Two days before the ultimatum, the Soviet government had issued the Declaration of Rights of the Peoples of Russia, which solemnly proclaimed: (1) the equality and sovereignty of all peoples; (2) the right of nations to self-determination, up to and including separation and the formation of nation-states; (3) the liquidation of all national and national-religious privileges and restrictions; (4) the free development of national minorities and ethnic groups inhabiting the territory of Russia.[80]

A congress of soviets, convened in Kiev, gave a majority to the supporters of the Rada. The Bolsheviks walked out and organized their own congress in Kharkov. The central executive committee elected in Kharkov declared itself the sole legal government of the Ukraine and sent a telegram to Moscow announcing its total subordination to the Soviet government. On December 12 the Bolsheviks in Kharkov expelled all other socialist parties from the central executive committee and became the sole ruling party. War with the Rada began. In January 1918 units of the Red Guard occupied Kiev.

The nationalist movement in Byelorussia was in an embryonic stage in

1917. The Byelorussian peasants did not display any awareness of their ethnic differences from the Russians. Political life in Byelorussia centered around the Russian and Jewish socialist organizations. In March a Byelorussian National Committee consisting of representatives of all ethnic groups and social classes was founded. It called for autonomy and federation with Russia. Gradually a Byelorussian socialist party, the Gromada, became the main force in the committee. In July a Byelorussian rada was created on the Ukrainian model. At the same time Bolshevik influence grew, especially among the soldiers, who were impatiently waiting for peace to come. The Gromada refused to accept the October revolution and in December convened a Byelorussian national congress, which on the night of December 17 declared Byelorussia independent.

As for the 16 million Muslims inhabiting the Russian empire, their First All-Russia Congress began in Moscow on May 1, 1917, attended by about a thousand delegates. The congress passed a resolution granting equal rights to women, in a break from longstanding Islamic tradition. It also assumed the right of religious self-determination, the right to select the religious leader of Russia's Muslims, the mufti, who was previously appointed by the tsar. The national question provoked a heated debate. A group of delegates, headed by Volga Tatars, advocated the preservation of a unitary Russian state with national-cultural autonomy. The Azerbaijani delegation, supported by the Bashkirs and Crimean Tatars, demanded a federation and territorial self-rule for all peoples. By a majority vote, the congress passed a federalist resolution. On July 21 a second congress met in Kazan and decided, in view of the weakening of the central government, to begin organizing autonomous Muslin cultural institutions without delay. On November 20 a national assembly met in Ufa and elected three ministers—for religion, education, and finance. Their task was to take concrete steps to assert the cultural and national autonomy of all Muslims in Russia.

By October 1917, then, the Muslims of Russia had laid the foundations for their own religious and cultural administration. Events during the next few months, however, broke all links between the various Muslim regions, and each group went its own way in trying to cope with the problem of incipient civil war.

A political party of the Kazakhs and Kirghiz, the so-called Alash-Orda, was founded in the summer of 1917 at a congress in Orenburg. Its goal was the unification of all the nomadic tribes of the steppes into an autonomous "Kirghiz state." The Bashkir delegates in the First All-Russia Muslim Congress had also demanded autonomy. But after the congress rejected their demand for a Greater Bashkiria, which would have united all the Tatars and Bashkirs of the Ural and Volga regions, as well as their demand for a Lesser Bashkiria, which would have included only the territories inhabited by Bashkirs, they walked out of the congress. They then attended the Orenburg meeting, opting for territorial autonomy together with the Turkic tribes of the steppe lands and Turkestan. During the spring and fall of 1917 there were frequent clashes between Muslins and Russian settlers. In September the Provisional Government declared martial law in the entire Semirechie region in Central Asia, to stop interracial strife.

In December, the Bashkirs, Kazakhs, and Kirghiz declared their autonomy in Orenburg and established relations with the Cossacks of that region. Thus an anti-Bolshevik movement was created, led by Dutov, the ataman of the Orenburg Cossacks, and supported by Muslim political leaders.

The Bolshevik forces in the steppes of Kirghizia and Kazakhstan were insignificant. "In October 1917 there were fewer than thirty Bolsheviks in Ashkhabad, and in Kazakhstan there were about a hundred. In Verny, there was no Bolshevik organization at all before the October revolution. Until mid-1918 only a few isolated groups of pro-Bolshevik soldiers and workers functioned in certain towns of Kirghizia."[81] Bolshevik slogans found support among the soldiers, the railworkers, and the settlers. These elements saw the dictatorship of the proletariat as a *Russian* dictatorship. Since the Bolsheviks proclaimed a power of the soviets of workers, soldiers, and peasants, and since there were no workers, soldiers, or peasants among the Kazakhs and Kirghiz, the Muslim tribesmen also perceived Bolshevik power as Russian power.

The political movement in Turkestan was composed of a conservative religious current and a liberal, pro-Western one. Initially enemies, they drew closer toward the end of 1917 because they both called for autonomy, which the Russian government refused to grant. The Muslim socialist movement, close to the Left SRs, was much less influential, but it played a decisive role in the October events. In Turkestan, as in the rest of Central Asia, the Bolsheviks could be counted on one hand. On October 25 railworkers opened fire on a Cossack club in Tashkent. Within two days the soviet, controlled by the Bolsheviks and supported by the Left SRs, had taken over the city. On November 15 the Third Regional Congress of Soviets met and proclaimed the victory of Soviet power throughout Turkestan. The congress rejected Muslim demands for autonomy, since it might weaken Russia's authority, and declared itself against Muslim participation in the Soviet government in Central Asia. According to the resolution, this was because of the "uncertain" attitude of the local population toward the soviet and because the native population had no proletarian organizations, which the Bolsheviks would have welcomed into the government.[82]

The Crimean Tatar National party, founded in July 1917, came into conflict almost immediately with the Provisional Government because the government refused to place Muslim schools under Tatar control or to allow the formation of an exclusively Tatar military unit. The main strength of the Bolshevik organization in the Crimea, established in June 1917, was in Sevastopol. The Left SRs and Mensheviks held a majority in the Sevastopol Soviet, which condemned the October seizure of power. The first conference of Crimean Bolsheviks did likewise. A delegation of Baltic sailors sent to Sevastopol by the Bolshevik Central Committee soon straightened out the situation. The Bolsheviks loyal to Lenin walked out of the soviet and created a revolutionary committee (*revkom*), which organized a massacre of Black Sea naval officers, dispersed the soviet, and had its Menshevik and Left SR leaders shot. Tatar nationalists convened a constituent assembly, the Kurultai, in Bakhchisarai, which proclaimed itself the sole legal authority in matters concerning Crimean Tatars. The Kurultai adopted a constitution based on Western democratic models and installed a national directory, which functioned as a de facto Tatar government of the Crimea and refused to recognize the legitimacy of Bolshevik power.

In 1916 the population of the Caucasus region was approximately 12 million, including 4 million Russians, Ukrainians, and Byelorussians, nearly 2.5 million Azerbaijanis, less than 2 million Armenians and about the same number of Georgians, and 1.5 million "mountain peoples," as the ethnically variegated native inhabitants of the Caucasus Mountains were called.[83]

The three main political parties in Transcaucasia—the Azerbaijani Muslim Democratic party (Mussavat), the Armenian Federation (Dashnaktsutiun), and the Georgian Social Democratic party (the Georgian Mensheviks)— had all been founded before World War I. All three supported the Provisional Government after the February revolution, favored autonomy within the framework of a Russian federation, and enjoyed mass support from their respective national constituencies.

The October revolution, the first signs of decomposition in the Russian Army of the Caucasus, and Turkish advances into Transcaucasia began to change the situation. On November 11 the Mussavat, Dashnaktsutsiun, and Georgian Mensheviks established their own local provisional government, the Transcaucasian Commissariat, whose purpose was to maintain order in the region until the All-Russia Constituent Assembly elected a government for the Russian state as a whole. After the Constituent Assembly dissolved by the Bolsheviks, the Transcaucasian delegates returned to their home region and organized a legislative body, the Transcaucasian Seim (or Diet). Lacking influence among the masses, the Bolsheviks directed their propaganda at the soldiers. In the elections for the Constituent Assembly in the Transcaucasian region the Bolsheviks received only 4.6 percent of the vote.[84] Even in Baku, their stronghold in the region, roughly 80 percent of the Bolshevik vote came from the soldiers. The Bolsheviks tried to use their support among the soldiers to take power in Tiflis in November 1917, but Georgian workers thwarted the attempt.

In April 1918 the Turks, who had taken Batum and Kars, issued an ultimatum to Transcaucasia: it would be occupied unless it declared its independence. On April 22 the Transcaucasian Federation, which included the ruling Mensheviks of Georgia, the Dashnak government of Armenia, and the Azerbaijani Mussavat, proclaimed the independence of the Transcaucasian Federal Republic.[85]

On the western borders of the old Russian empire, independent states were formed with no difficulty, since these territories were under German occupation. In December 1917 Finland, Lithuania, and Latvia proclaimed their independence. In February 1918 Estonia did the same.

By the beginning of 1918 the Russian state had disintegrated. The developing civil war was a contest not only between the supporters of different political and social systems but also between advocates of differing national conceptions about the future state. Both the Reds and the Whites fought for unification of the Russian state, but each side presented its version of this same program differently.

The Bolshevik program on the national question was authentically Marxist in the sense that it embraced two mutually contradictory principles: the self-determination of nations, and the centralized state. Lenin favored a centralized party and extended the centralist principle to the state. For him, the nationalities problem was above all a problem of political power. He considered the national minorities of the Russian empire his allies in the struggle for power. In 1915 he glorified treason: "Whoever argues against treason and against the disintegration of the Russian state . . . has adopted the bourgeois, and not the proletarian standpoint."[86] From October 25, 1917, he championed and defended a strong, centralized state, seeing it as "a tremendous historical step forward . . . toward the future socialist unity of the whole world."[87]

Lenin's wish for a strong, centralized state was inspired not by patriotism but by his desire for a powerful weapon in the fight for world revolution, which was for him the principal purpose of the October revolution. This is why Lenin's policies had a "dialectical" character. In his telegram to the Congress of Soviets of Tashkent, he wrote, "The Council of People's Commissars will support autonomy for your region based on Soviet principles."[88] Lenin was for independence, on the condition that it was subordinated to "Moscow's point of view," that is, the views of the Central Committee.

Lenin was forced to fight against those Bolsheviks who did not understand the subtleties of the party's nationalities policy. Pyatakov, Dzerzhinsky, and Bukharin argued that the proletarian revolution was going to eliminate social classes and would likewise put an end to the very concept of nations. They demanded that all references to independence and autonomy be abandoned, on the grounds that these were bourgeois categories. The people's commissar of nationalities, Stalin, was, like Lenin, a strong defender of centralized power. In May 1918 Stalin formulated his commissariat's policy, explaining that Soviet power would recognize autonomy as long as it was under Moscow's leadership and control. Autonomy was not granted to the nation but to the working class and the toiling peasantry, and only if they supported Soviet power.[89]

Lenin opposed the "national nihilism" of some of his comrades because of tactical considerations, understanding better than anyone the strong appeal of "self-determination" as a slogan.

When Confucius was asked how he would rule, the wise man answered: I would start by giving words their true meaning. As Lenin began his rule the first thing he did was to strip words of their meaning. He would give them meanings depending on the need of the moment and modify them depending on the audience. The Bolshevik party entered the civil war with a program defending the right of nations to self-determination "up to and including independence," while at the same time insisting that "the principle of self-determination must be an instrument in the struggle for socialism and must be subordinated to the principles of socialism."[90]

## REDS AND WHITES

The October revolution, which was supposed to bring peace to Russia, plunged it instead into a civil war of the most terrible kind. The first volleys were fired in the south of Russia, in the Cossack regions. In February 1917 the Cossacks had refused to support the tsarist regime; until then they had been regarded as its strongest bulwark. They had likewise refused to support the Provisional Government, declaring their neutrality toward the Bolshevik seizure of power.

Of the two main Bolshevik slogans, peace and land, the Cossacks unquestionably supported the first; they wanted to go home. On the question of land, they differed radically from the rest of the Russian peasants. They wanted, not more land, but the preservation of what they had. It was the traditional privilege of a Cossack male to be granted thirty desyatinas, about eighty acres, of land in exchange for military service until age thirty-six. At the turn of the century the Don Cossack region, the largest of the eleven Cossack territories (all located in the outlying parts of the empire), had a population of 1,022,086 Cossacks and 1,200,669 non-Cossacks.[91] Sverdlov announced that the most important task of Soviet policy was to divide the Russian villages into two enemy camps, to turn the poorest peasants against the "kulak elements." Only if we can split the countryside, he said, will we obtain the same results in the villages that we have in the cities.[92] These attempts to foster divisions were not successful, and the government was forced to abandon them by dissolving the poor peasants' committees at the end of 1918, six months after they had been formed. In the Cossack regions the campaign to turn non-Cossacks against Cossacks resulted in fierce hostilities between them.

The enemies of the revolution converged on the Don region, hoping for support from the Cossacks. But the Cossaks did not want the restoration of the monarchy. They wanted simply to take advantage of the revolution to obtain greater autonomy, while preserving their privileges. General Alekseev, the last chief of staff of the tsarist army, did not find the help or the support he was hoping for on the Don.

Alekseev's plan was to organize a "volunteer army" to fight the Soviet government. His work went slowly. His army grew from about 300 in November 1917 to approximately 3,000 in January 1918, staffed mainly by former officers, officer cadets, and private school students. Alekseev and General Kornilov, the de facto commander of the Volunteer Army, had high hopes for a great influx of volunteers, especially from among former officers (of which there had been 133,000 in May 1917). Their hopes were in vain. The officers did not wish, any more than the soldiers, to keep on fighting; they considered the war over. General Kaledin, ataman of the Don Cossacks, declared on January 29, 1918: "Our situation is hopeless. Not only does the population not support us; it is hostile to us." He committed suicide the same day.

Red forces, 10,000 strong, led by Rudolf Sivers, had entered Don Cossack territory in mid-January. By January 23 Rostov—the region's main city—was taken. The Volunteer Army, burdened with wagon trains full of politicians, journalists, professors, and wives of officers and soldiers, fled into the steppes. There began what was known as the Icy March. Each soldier of the Volunteer Army had only a few hundred cartridges, and for each of its eight artillery pieces there were 600–700 shells. Through severe difficulties, surrounded on all sides by the enemy, the Volunteer Army reached the Kuban region, hoping to find what it had not found on the Don. On April 17, at Ekaterinodar, General Kornilov was killed in battle. His death was an irreparable loss for the future White Army. General Denikin assumed command. He abandoned the siege of Ekaterinodar and led the army back to the Stavropol region, between the Don and the Kuban, from whence the Icy March had begun. During those eighty days of constant combat, from January to April, the situation had changed radically in southern Russia. The Germans had occupied the Ukraine, and the Don Cossacks had abandoned their neutrality. The establishment of Soviet power had been accompanied by mass executions. Under Sivers' orders, all captured "volunteers" had been executed, and there were many executions for other reasons. For example, General Renenkampf was shot for refusing to serve in the Red Army. The church was persecuted, and a draconian system of grain requisitioning was put into effect. On April 10, 1918, the Cossacks rebelled. General Krasnov was elected ataman, and he organized the Army of the Don.

Another center of struggle against Soviet power arose in the east. Thousands of Czechoslovak prisoners of war were being transported by train to Vladivostok to be shipped to France to join the war against Germany and Austria. On May 17, 1918, they revolted and took Chelyabinsk. Moscow ordered all soviets from Penza to Omsk to disarm the members of the so-called Czech Legion, but the legionnaires rejected the demand. On May 25, the Czechs took Mariinsk and by June 8 they held Novonikolaevsk (now Novosibirsk), Penza, Syzran, Petropavlovsk, Kurgan, Omsk, and Samara.[93]

During World War I the Czechs and Slovaks had refused to defend the Austro-Hungarian monarchy and had surrendered to the Russians en masse. By the end of the war there were close to 200,000 Czechoslovak prisoners in Russia. The Czech Legion had reached the strength of 50,000 soldiers and officers. Under the terms of the Brest-Litovsk treaty, the Soviet government was required to disarm the legion. The Czechs gave up some of their arms but hid the rest.

The Czech revolt gave a powerful impetus to the anti-Bolshevik movement east of the Volga. On August 6 Kazan fell. The Czechoslovaks needed only to cross the Volga and the road to Moscow would have been open to them. For the first time since the October revolution, the Soviet government was threatened by a truly dangerous foe. The creation of a regular army became a necessity. Until then, scattered uprisings by disparate opponents of the Bolshevik party in the borderlands of the old Russian empire had been crushed by semiguerrilla Red Guard detachments and units of the Red Army still affected by a revolutionary zeal which did not readily accept authority. The forces of the Cheka had sufficed to crush a number of peasant revolts. The Soviet newspapers of spring 1918 are full of information about this.[94] The extent of repression can be judged from documents published by the Soviet authorities concerning the executions that followed the crushing of the July 1918 uprising in Yaroslavl. After the city was retaken "fifty-seven people were shot on the spot." Then a "special investigating commission" subjected hundreds of people to "an exhaustive interrogation" after which it was "discovered" that 350 people "were the ringleaders of the conspiracy and had had relations with the Czechoslovaks." The entire "gang of 350" was shot "by order of the commission." Ten more were executed after a further investigation conducted by the Cheka of Yaroslavl. The *Red Book of the Cheka* gives a very candid account of the suppression of the Yaroslavl insurrection, which lasted from April 6 to April 21. Latsis relates that 106 of the conspirators, and an armored division that went over to their side with two armored cars, held off the assaults of the First Soviet Regiment of the International Detachment and a Left SR unit for a long time. The suppression of the Left SRs in Moscow, it should be noted, did not stop them from supporting the Soviet side in Yaroslavl. After an artillery barrage, with an armored train from Moscow taking part, "a large part of the city was consumed in flames." Then the city was subjected to air bombardment with "bombs of the highest destructive power." The following ultimatum was presented to the besieged city: all its inhabitants must leave or "it would be subjected to a merciless hurricane of fire by heavy artillery, and also chemical shells."[95] Such methods of warfare were not successful when the well-trained and disciplined Czechoslovak troops appeared, however.

The Central Executive Committee proclaimed the republic in danger. Trotsky, appointed people's commissar of war, took on the task of creating a regular army. Earlier than the other party leaders, including Lenin, Trotsky understood that dreams of "the people in arms" or of the army being replaced by the militia were nothing but utopia. He based the new army on two principles: the employment of military specialists, and terror. It was obvious that an army could not function without professionals and equally obvious that the officers of the tsarist army had no desire to serve the Bolsheviks. Trotsky ordered the mobilization of former officers and NCOs. Refusal to join the army meant internment in a concentration camp; in addition, the families of officers were taken hostage. Fear had an important role in Trotsky's theoretical system. "Intimidation," he wrote, "is a powerful [instrument] of policy, both internationally and internally. War, like revolution, is founded upon intimidation. A victorious war, generally speaking, destroys only an insignificant part of the conquered army, intimidating the remainder and breaking their will. The revolution works in the same way: it kills individuals, and intimidates thousands."[96] Trotsky's terms *individuals* and *thousands* were merely figures of speech: in reality it was a matter of millions and tens of millions. Nevertheless this passage can be accepted as a clear statement of the concept of terror on which the Soviet Republic was founded. It was necessary to kill some in order to shatter the will of the rest.

After the fall of Kazan, Trotsky left for the front and signed an order with the following warning: no mercy for the enemies of the people, the agents of imperialism, or the lackeys of the bourgeoisie. He warned that in the train of the people's commissar of war, where the order was drafted, there was a standing revolutionary tribunal with full powers and that in Murom, Arzamas, and Sviyazhsk, concentration camps had been set up. Having reached Sviyazhsk, on the west bank of the Volga across from Kazan, Trotsky reorganized the Fifth Army. Showing his fist of steel, he ordered the commander and the commissar of a regiment shot because they had retreated without orders. The execution of the commander did not produce any commentary; that of the commissar (a man named Panteleev) was a real sacrilege in the eyes of the Communists because one of their own had been shot. The incident was discussed throughout the civil war; later it was used to demonstrate Trotsky's "Bonapartist aims."

Trotsky's pitiless feat yielded the desired results. On September 10 Kazan was retaken. By the beginning of October all of the Volga region was in the hands of the Red Army, which at this point numbered more than half a million men. By the end of the year, the figure had passed one million. The army's character also changed. Commanders were no longer elected, they were appointed. Soldiers and commanders took an oath written by Trotsky. It began, "I, a son of the working people," and ended, "If I violate this oath, may the merciless hand of revolutionary law punish me." The creation of this mass professional army took place under the slogan of world peace. "The objectives of socialism," wrote Trotsky in the preface to his plan for the creation of the army, "is total disarmament, perpetual peace, and fraternal collaboration among all of the earth's people's."[97]

A mass professional army could not function, much less fight, without military specialists. Trotsky created a revolutionary army with the same officers who the day before had been denounced as enemies of the revolution. Only a small number of officers and generals willingly served the Soviet government. One of the first to join the Red Army was General Mikhail Bonch-Bruevich, who had commanded the Northern Front and was the brother of Vladimir Bonch-Bruevich, the administrator of the Council of People's Commissars. Trotsky gave him the task of organizing a general staff. General N. M. Potapov, who had crossed over to the Bolshevik side even before the October revolution, was appointed second in command of the army and put in charge of Field Headquarters, the Stavka.[98]

The overwhelming majority of officers were mobilized and forced to serve the Soviet regime. Trotsky's policy of using military specialists ran into stubborn resistance from other Bolshevik leaders. He had to confront a coalition led by Lashevich, head of the military section of the Central Committee; Zinoviev, president of the Northern Commune and boss of Petrograd; and Stalin, representative of the Central Committee on the Southern Front. Trotsky's adversaries did not question the principle of using military specialists; they stressed that they should be employed only as "aides de camp" and, when they were no longer needed, "thrown away like a squeezed lemon."[99] General Novitsky, who had volunteered to join the Red Army, protested in an open letter to Trotsky. Trotsky replied with assurances that officers "who work conscientiously in the present difficult conditions deserve respect."[100] Lenin was leaning toward Trotsky's adversaries. In March 1919 he advised the commissar of war to purge the army of old officers and to name Lashevich commander-in-chief. He was extremely surprised to hear that over 30,000 officers were serving in the Red Army and that it would not be able to survive without them.[101] A realist, Lenin at once grasped the correctness of Trotsky's policy and publicly expressed his enthusiasm for this original method of building socialism with bricks from the old regime. Even General Denikin praised the cleverness of the Soviet policy.[102]

Trotsky made massive use of military specialists, placing them under the constant surveillance of political commissars. "For the first time, the commissar came onto the scene in the role of Soviet enforcer."[103] Every command by an officer had to bear the commissar's signature. The commissars had the right to demote the unit's "commander" (the officer in charge, in the vocabulary of 1918) or even to arrest him. With his characteristic pomposity Trotsky declared that the commissars were the "new Communist order of samurai, in which the members have no caste privileges, know how to die, and teach others how to die for the cause of the working class."[104] The commissars might die and teach others to die, but their main task was to act as "the eyes of the proletariat," controlling the military specialists and, in a sense, "conquering the elements," riding the whirlwind of revolution. Like the samurai, however, the commissar must above all be loyal.

The German occupation of the Ukraine enabled the White generals to form major military units. By mid-1918 the most important anti-Bolshevik force was General Krasnov's Army of the Don. The White Cossacks took Novocherkassk and after that abandoned their interest in Moscow and Russia. Their main wish was to subdue the local non-Cossack population. By the summer of 1918 the Volunteer Army had between 8,000 and 9,000 soldiers. The two anti-Bolshevik armies were caught up in constant political and strategic disputes. While Krasnov launched an offensive against Tsaritsyn, Denikin began a second campaign in the Kuban. In the fall of 1918 Denikin defeated the Eleventh Army of the Northern Caucasus, at the same time that the Red Army was victorious on the eastern front. In January 1919 the Don Cossacks abandoned their siege of Tsaritsyn. Denikin ordered a mobilization of all officers under forty in the territories occupied by the Volunteer Army. The White Army became stronger, but it was no longer a volunteer army, and it lost its homogeneity. On January 8, 1919, after an agreement with the atamans of the Don and Kuban Cossacks, General Denikin became commander-in-chief of all the armed forces in the south of Russia. For the first time an army with a national objective, liberating the country from Bolshevik power, was created.

The metaphor so widely used by Soviet historians (the counterrevolution as a "ring of fire") is not an accurate description of the civil war. The fire that broke out the day after the October revolution blazed everywhere in the country, to one degree or another. The universal dissatisfaction with Lenin's policies developed into major bonfires, however, only in the southern, northern, eastern, and western outlands, and these did not merge into one general anti-Bolshevik conflagration because they lacked a single leader and a single unifying idea.

The fact that the main centers of counterrevolutionary strength were on the periphery gave the Soviet government major strategical advantages. "Our central position," wrote Trotsky, "made it possible for us to act along internal operational lines and reduce our strategy to one simple idea: the consecutive liquidation of fronts depending on their relative importance."[105] The course of military operations in 1919 was convincing proof of the advantages the Soviet government derived from its central position, controlling the main rail lines and junctions.

In the summer of 1919 several focal points of anti-Bolshevik strength appeared in the eastern part of Russia. In the Volga region a Committee of Members of the Constituent Assembly (the Komuch) established its sway, the SRs being the moving spirit in this formation. After the taking of Ekaterinburg by the Czechs, a Urals Regional Government was formed. Likewise, a so-called Siberian Government made Omsk its capital. Orenburg Province was under the rule of the Cossack Ataman Dutov, who professed formal loyalty to the Komuch but in fact acted independently. Disputes and conflicts arose between these governments because of their differing, often diametrically opposed views on fundamental questions: what attitude to take toward the revolution and the changes it had made and toward the peasants and the workers, and what kind of structure to advocate for the future Russian state. Robert Bruce Lockhart, a British agent in

Russia, recalled a letter he received from General Alekseev in the summer of 1918. The right-wing general stated that he would rather collaborate with Lenin and Trotsky than with Savinkov and Kerensky.[106] Similar sentiments were expressed by members of the Siberian Government, who were obliged to collaborate with SRs from the Komuch. In September a conference at Ufa established a directorate whose aim was to provide overall leadership for all anti-Bolshevik forces in the east of Russia. A council of ministers was chosen, with the army and navy portfolios going to Admiral Kolchak. On November 18, 1918, the SR members of the directorate were arrested, and Admiral Kolchak was named "supreme ruler." He proclaimed himself "commander-in-chief of all the land and sea forces of Russia."

In March 1919 Kolchak launched a drive toward the Volga along a broad front. The Red Army, weakened by the transfer of its best units to the south, could not hold its ground. By the end of April, however, the commander of the Soviet eastern front, a former colonel of the tsarist General Staff, Sergei S. Kamenev, inflicted a stunning defeat on Kolchak's army, driving it back to the Urals and pursuing it into Siberia. No sooner had Kolchak's army begun to retreat than Denikin launched an offensive from the south. His troops took the Ukraine, then Kursk, Voronezh, and Orel, after which they directly threatened Moscow by way of Tula. At the same time, independently of Denikin, General Yudenich started a drive against Petrograd from the Baltic region. Trotsky was sent to Petrograd to cope with the emergency and in a few days organized a successful defense of the city. At the end of October Yudenich's army retreated in disorder. The commissar of war warned the Baltic republics that the Red Army would march on them if they did not disarm Yudenich. He threatened Finland in similar fashion, vowing to send his Bashkir divisions against Helsinki if necessary. Meanwhile the Red Army defeated Denikin north of Orel and soon drove him south to the Black Sea. At the end of 1919 the victory of the Red Army on all fronts was assured.

General Denikin, in his *Sketches of the Russian Turmoil* (*Ocherki russkoi smuty*), spoke with blunt honesty about the causes of the White defeat. He cited the moral decomposition of the army, the looting and pogroms, which corrupted officers and soldiers alike and undermined discipline. But that was not the main problem. Denikin noted with perplexity that after his troops had liberated an immense territory, "we expected all elements hostile to the Soviet government to rise up. But there was no uprising."[107] The commander of the White Army correctly reduced the entire problem of the civil war to what he called "one question": Are the mass of the people sick of Bolshevism and will they rally to our side?[108] These were really two separate questions. To the first the answer was yes; to the second, no.

The main reason for the defeat of the counterrevolution in Russia was that its leaders failed to understand the political essence of a civil war. The revolution was led by people with political experience, but the counterrevolution was led by soldiers who had never concerned themselves with political and social questions. In mid-May 1918 Denikin and Alekseev drafted a program entitled "The Objectives of the Army," which said that the Volunteer Army was fighting to save Russia by (1) forming a strong, disciplined, patriotic army; (2) waging a war to the death against bolshevism; and (3) restoring order and unity to the country. On December 4 the constitution of the Volunteer Army was published. It recognized the laws in effect on Russian territory before October 25, 1917; that is, it recognized the February revolution, and it guaranteed freedom of religion, the press, and assembly and the inviolability of private property. On November 18, 1918, Admiral Kolchak declared in his first appeal to the population that his main aim was "the creation of an effective army, the defeat of bolshevism, and the establishment of law and order so that the people can freely choose the form of government they desire and put into effect the great ideas of liberty that are now being proclaimed throughout the world."[109]

The primary objective of both Denikin and Kolchak was to create an effective fighting force. Their other objectives were vague and ill defined. The lack of a clear-cut program left an opening for the Red propagandists to attribute whatever they wished to the White generals.

The prime objective in a civil war must be to win the support of the population. The Bolsheviks came to power because they promised peace and land. The first promise was not kept, but the blame for that was laid on the counterrevolution. As for the land, it remained in the peasants' hands, although the "surplus food appropriation system" subjected whatever the peasants grew to confiscation. Life became much harder, especially in the cities. Hunger, cold, and terror reigned. Nevertheless the new government kept one of its promises: the old ruling classes lost all their privileges. Not only did they live worse than before; they lived worse than the proletariat. Although the workers did not have any material satisfaction, at least they had a psychological one. The promise voiced in the workers' hymn, the Internationale, "We have been naught; we shall be all," was realized in inverted form: those that had been all became naught. This was a verifiable, undeniable accomplishment of the October revolution.

Popular support for the government at that time depended on two key questions: the future of the nationalities inhabiting the former Russian empire, and the future of the land that the peasants had taken. The Whites openly proclaimed their goal of restoring "Russia one and indivisible." Their Russian nationalism clashed with the irresistible growth of local nationalism in the outlying regions of the Russian state, the same regions in which the anti-Bolshevik forces were concentrated. The Bolshevik party concealed its true centralizing aims beneath the slogan of self-determination. (Thus it came out ahead in the competition for popular support on the national question.)

The programs of the White governments dealt with the land question in an ambiguous way. The clause in the constitution of the Volunteer Army referring to the "inviolability of property" could be interpreted as a repudiation of the agrarian reform. On territory occupied by the Whites the land was frequently returned to the large landowners. On Soviet territory, peasant discontent was aroused by government requisitions and the formation of state farms and communes on former estate land, which the peasants thought should be divided up among themselves. A wave of peasant revolts in the Ukraine in 1919 was the direct result of a decree placing "all the large, cultivated holdings formerly belonging to the big landowners" in government hands so that state farms could be organized.[110] Such decrees reflected the government's utopian goal of creating "grain, meat, milk, and fodder factories that would emancipate the socialist system economically from [dependence on] the small proprietor."[111] Despite such grievances, when the peasants compared them to the White policy of returning the land to the former landlords, the Bolshevik government came out the lesser evil. The population viewed the White program as a return to the past. The program of the revolution seemed to promise hope. For the majority an unknown future was preferable to the discredited past.

The revolution had a single leader whose authority was recognized by all revolutionaries, and this was one of its greatest assets. The leaders of the Soviet government quarreled among themselves no less than the White leaders and there were no fewer animosities among the members of the Revolutionary Military Council and the Red generals than among the White generals. To the clashes of ambition common to all armies and all wars was added a special rivalry, between the political and the military leaders of the Red Army. "The constant and unending dissension and quarreling among the political leaders about the so-called question of command do us great harm," wrote Commander-in-Chief Vatsetis to Lenin in January 1919. "Some party members, overcome with ambition, seek to occupy high positions of command despite their lack of military training for such duties and their total inability to function successfully as commanders."[112] As chairman of the Council of People's Commissars, president of the Council of Labor and Defense, and head of the party, Lenin had unlimited power and unchallenged authority, which allowed him to act as the final arbiter in all disputes. To maintain a balance between hostile groups, Lenin would often support one side against the other for a while, then reverse himself and support the side he had opposed. In July 1919, for example, over Trotsky's objections, Lenin had Vatsetis removed as commander-in-chief, replacing him with Sergei Kamenev. To console Trotsky, Lenin gave him a blank piece of paper with his signature as chairman of the Council of People's Commissars at the bottom, approving in advance any order the commissar of war might issue.[113] The White movement had neither an uncontested leader like Lenin nor an astute strategist who knew how to maneuver, as he did, in the political shoals of civil war without losing sight of the main objective.

Another decisive factor in the Bolshevik victory was terror. Ghastly episodes of White terror are known from many accounts. But terror in the White-occupied areas was always a matter of individual acts by sadistic or fanatical generals, such as Mai-Maevsky or Slashchov. The Red Terror was sponsored by the state. It was not directed against individuals or even political parties but against entire social groups, entire classes, and in some phases of the civil war against the majority of the population. The intimidation that Trotsky viewed as a powerful instrument of policy, both internationally and domestically, was applied on a scale of which the Whites had no idea. It was in the civil war that Stalin first revealed his talents. "Be assured that our hand will not tremble," he wrote to Lenin, who had sent him as a special emissary to Tsaritsyn and telegraphed him to be "ruthless."[114] Stalin immediately passed Lenin's message along to Shaumyan in Baku: "We must be especially ruthless toward the bandits in Dagestan and elsewhere who are preventing trains from moving through the Northern Caucasus; a certain number of auls [mountaineers' settlements] must be burned to the ground to teach them not to attack trains in the future."[115]

On January 24, 1919, the Organizational Bureau (Orgburo) of the Bolshevik Central Committee stated that, "in view of the experience with the Cossacks in the civil war," the only correct procedure was "to wage the most ruthless possible war against all the Cossack upper elements, exterminating them to the last man." The Orgburo document called for "total extermination" of the wealthy Cossacks and "ruthless mass terror against all Cossacks who have taken part directly or indirectly in the struggle against the Soviet government."[116] The suppression of the Don Cossack revolt of the spring and summer of 1919 took the form of genocide. One historian has estimated that approximately 70 percent of the Don Cossacks were physically eliminated.[117]

This deliberate and systematic terror, embracing the entire population, was also applied in the army. After destroying the old army and beginning to build another "on new foundations," the Bolsheviks soon returned to the conception of a regular standing army, but this time with a discipline more rigorous than the tsarist troops had known. "In the Red Army," Vatsetis wrote to Lenin,

> discipline is based on harsh punishments, particularly executions. . . . Through these punishments and executions we have struck terror in the hearts of everyone, soldiers, commanders, and commissars alike. . . . The death penalty . . . is utilized so often at the front, for all possible reasons and on all possible occasions, that the discipline of the Red Army could be called sanguinary in the full sense of the word.[118]

Vatsetis was wrong in assuming that Lenin did not know what discipline was like in the Red Army. The chairman of the Council of People's Commissars explicitly discussed Red Army discipline on October 17, 1921: "Strict, stern measures were adopted, including capital punishment, measures that even the former government did not apply. Philistines wrote and howled, 'The Bolsheviks have introduced capital punishment,' Our reply is, 'Yes, we have introduced it, and have done so deliberately.'"[119]

Terror and the promise of utopia. "I am a simple man, you know," the chairman of the Cheka in Poltava confessed to the old Russian writer Vladimir Korolenko. "To tell you the truth, I haven't read anything about communism. But I know what it's about—that there shouldn't be any money. And you see, there isn't any money in Russia anymore. . . . Every worker gets a card telling how many hours he's worked. . . . He needs a coat. He goes to a store and hands in his card. They give him a coat worth so many hours work. . . . Nowadays," the Cheka official admitted, "we're obliged to commit many cruelties. But after we triumph . . ."[120] The conversation took place on July 10, 1919.

This mixture of utopian promises and ruthless mass terror produced an explosive compound enabling the Bolshevik party to blast its way to victory in the civil war. A crucial factor in this process was the presence of a leader who knew how much of each component to put into the mix, depending on the needs of the moment.


## FOREIGN INTERVENTION

The intervention of foreign powers in the Russian civil war did not substantially alter the balance of forces in that war. Soviet historians have made much of Winston Churchill's reference to a "campaign by fourteen nations." Churchill, one of the few Western leaders who advocated intervention, mistook his wish for reality.

In the years 1918–1920 there was not one general intervention in Russia but a number of unrelated campaigns, whose objectives varied or, sometimes, remained totally unclear. For the intervening powers the interests of Russia were always secondary, and few among them understood what was going on in postrevolutionary Russia.

The first phase of intervention, from the summer of 1918 to November of that year, was for the Allies simply part of the war against Germany. After the February revolution, the countries of the Entente feared a separate peace between Germany and Russia. Their fears were justified; if the Provisional Government had withdrawn from the war, its outcome might have been quite different. The German army, transferred to the western front before the arrival of the Americans, might have won the second Battle of the Marne.

The Allies began to plan an intervention in Russia immediately after the October revolution. They had no doubt that the revolution was the work of the Germans because the benefits to Germany were so obvious. The struggle against bolshevism was seen as an extension of the struggle against Germany.

Before making peace with Germany, the Soviet government maintained contact with the Allies. In early 1918, when the port of Murmansk was threatened by a German–Finnish offensive, Trotsky, who had just been named people's commissar of war, ordered the Murmansk Soviet to collaborate with Allied troops. In March the British landed 2,000 men. After the signing of the Brest-Litovsk treaty the Germans demanded that the Soviet government order the evacuation of Allied troops from Murmansk. Germany regarded their presence as a *casus belli*. The Allies' refusal to comply and the landing of additional troops—with the agreement of the Murmansk Soviet—gave the Bolshevik government a pretext to initiate military action against the "interventionists." The fighting began on June 28. This area in the north of Russia remained under Allied control until the fall of 1919, when it was evacuated.

The successful German offensive on the Eastern Front in March 1918 increased the Allies' concern. They were afraid that German troops might quickly extend their control as far as the Urals. In London on March 16, 1918, the Supreme Allied War Council adopted Clemenceau's proposal to land Japanese troops in Russia's Far Eastern region. The first Japanese units reached Vladivostok on April 5. In August American troops arrived. By the end of September 1918 the Allied expeditionary corps in the Far

Eastern region had 44,000 men: 28,000 Japanese, 7,500 American, 1,000 Canadians, 2,000 Italians, 1,500 British, and 1,000 French. The number of Japanese troops was increased to 75,000. They occupied several rail centers along the Amur River and the Sino—Russian border, reaching the shores of Lake Baikal. The other Allied troops remained in Vladivostok.

The Czech Legion, formally under Allied command, was the only foreign military unit that regularly took part in operations against the Red Army. After Kolchak's coup in November 1918, the Czechoslovaks ceased their military activities and concentrated on trying to find a way out of Russia. On January 15, 1920, to improve their bargaining position, they turned Kolchak over to the Political Center, an SR-dominated body which had assumed power in Irkutsk. A week later, the Center transferred power to a Bolshevik revolutionary military committee. On February 7, 1920, Admiral Kolchak was shot by a firing squad.

The main arena of British intervention was the Caucasus and Transcaucasia. In August 1918, invited by the Transcaucasian government, the British entered Baku, but they were soon forced to retreat under pressure from Turkish forces, which had also entered the region. Meanwhile, in the Trans-Caspian territory the rail workers of Ashkhabad, enraged by local commissar Frolov's bloody reign of terror, overthrew Bolshevik rule on July 13, 1918. A locomotive engineer named Funtikov became head of the Trans-Caspian Government, the only government in revolutionary Russia actually composed of workers. None of the ministers in this government had more than a high school education except the minister of foreign affairs, a teacher named Zimin. Funtikov's government asked the British for aid. In response, General Malleson sent 2,000 troops from Baluchistan, who helped occupy the rail line from Ashkhabad through Merv to Krasnovodsk on the Caspian.

After the capitulation of Turkey, Austria-Hungary, and Germany in October and November 1918, the Allied forces in Russia openly proclaimed their anti-Bolshevik (not merely anti-German) aims. As before, however, they were unable to develop a unified strategy. Frequently the various Allied powers pursued contradictory policies. France and England, for example, expressed a desire to help General Denikin but at the same time supported nationalist movements in the Ukraine and the Caucasus opposed by Denikin. In May 1919 the Allied Supreme Council promised aid to Admiral Kolchak on the condition that "the Allied Governments will have proofs that they are really helping the Russian people to achieve freedom, self-government, and peace." The Allies demanded that Kolchak convene a Constituent Assembly, restore a republic rather than a monarchy, and guarantee independence for Poland and Finland and autonomy for the Baltic states, the Caucasus, and the Trans-Caspian territory. Meanwhile, one of the Allied powers, Japan, refused to aid Kolchak and supported, instead, its own protégés, the Cossack atamans Semenov and Kalmykov.

Churchill, British war minister, strongly supported intervention, while Lloyd George, British premier, repeatedly sought to come to terms with the Soviet government. The British military representatives inside Russia opposed the policies of both ministers and were, in turn, condemned by British public opinion. French policy was equally hesitant and ambivalent. Besides all this, the Allied powers competed with one another in pursuit of spheres of influence on Russian territory, each placing its own self-interest above the common cause.

The fighting capacity of the Allied troops sent to Russia was extremely low. Having survived the terrible battles of the world war, they did not wish to die in a strange land. Antimilitarist sentiment spread throughout Europe and, especially in the defeated countries, contributed to revolutionary outbreaks—in Germany, Austria, and Hungary in particular. Bolshevik slogans fell on fertile ground in France, Britain, and the United States as well.

Fears that the Allied troops in Russia might become demoralized and refuse to fight contributed to their evacuation. On September 27, 1919, the Allies withdrew from Murmansk and Arkhangelsk. The evacuation of Siberia began at about the same time. Only the Japanese remained, hoping to keep their bases in the Russian Far East. In August 1919 the British completed their withdrawal from Central Asia. They left the Caucasus at the same time, except for Batum, which they held until March 1921. (Under the Brest-Litovsk treaty, it was supposed to be returned to Turkey.) From Batum they watched the Red Army invade Georgia, Azerbaijan, and Armenia, areas the British had evacuated on the grounds that "the situation in the Caucasian republics had been stabilized." French intervention was equally ineffective. On December 17 and 18, 1918, a French naval squadron landed units of the French Eastern Army in Odessa, approximately 45,000 strong. They occupied areas around Tiraspol, Nikolaev, and Kherson. After four months of idleness they were hastily evacuated on April 5 and 6, 1919.

The nations of the Entente gave the White armies substantial aid in the form of money, arms, and supplies. However, the presence of foreign troops on the territory of the former Russian empire in support of those who advocated a "Russia one and indivisible" gave a formidable weapon to the Soviet propagandists. It allowed the Bolsheviks to pose as defenders of the country's national interests.

In fact, the number of foreigners fighting on the side of the Red Army greatly exceeded the number of foreign "interventionists." Until the fall of 1918, Latvian, Polish, Chinese, Czech, and Finnish "internationalists," who as a rule were experienced soldiers, constituted the main fighting forces of the growing Red Army. In the fall of 1918 their number exceeded 50,000. By the summer of 1920, the international units numbered nearly 250,000.[121] The international units were among the most self-sacrificing of the Red forces; their members were inspired by the concept that their only land was the land of the soviets. The foreigners who served in the Red Army were called internationalists, rather than interventionists, to suggest that they were the incarnation of a progressive idea and consequently had the historical right to fight alongside the Bolsheviks. This form of intervention was euphemistically called "fraternal aid in building a new world."

## "GIVE US WARSAW"

In a history of the civil war the Polish–Soviet war of 1920 requires separate consideration. Soviet historians nevertheless continue to describe it as "the third campaign of the Entente" against the Soviet Republic.

Adam Mickiewicz, the Polish national poet, told of a prophetic vision in which he saw an independent Poland reborn out of the collapse of the three empires which had partitioned his land. The prophecy came true in 1917–1918: however the resurrected nation soon came into conflict with the hereditary enemy on its eastern border. Clashes between Polish and Soviet troops began in early 1919, in areas of the Ukraine, Byelorussia, and Lithuania. In August 1919 the Polish army took advantage of the weakness of the Soviet forces engaged on the fronts of the civil war to establish a battle line extending from Vilna through Minsk to Lvov. Secret negotiations then began between the governments of Lenin and Pilsudski.

The first meeting between Moscow's envoy, the Polish Communist Julian Marchlewski, and Warsaw's representatives took place on October 11, the day that Denikin's army reached Orel, its point of farthest advance toward Moscow. The White forces took Orel on October 13. Pilsudski's representative told Marchlewski that the Poles were not interested in helping Denikin and therefore had not attacked Mozyr. Such an attack, coinciding with Denikin's offensive at Orel, could have shattered the entire southern front of the Red Army. As conditions for an armistice, Pilsudski proposed recognition of the existing battle line as the Polish–Soviet border, an end to Communist agitation in the Polish army, and an end to Soviet military operations against Petlyura.[122] With the exception of the last point, Lenin agreed. But on December 14 Marchlewski returned to Moscow and the talks were broken off. By then Orel had been retaken by the Red Army, Moscow was no longer threatened, and Denikin was in retreat.

Jozef Pilsudski, who assumed the leadership of the Polish state in November 1918, had for many years been a socialist, but as he put it, he got off the socialist train at the stop marked "independence." The leaders of the White armies were strong advocates of a "Russia one and indivisible," and did nothing to calm Polish fears about their future in the event of victory. In June 1919 Kolchak deeply offended the Poles by announcing that, after his victory, a Constituent Assembly would reexamine the question of the border with Poland. Denikin's attitude was the same as Kolchak's. Pilsudski's hope was that a Soviet Russia would be weaker than a republican Russia. His strategic aim was to establish a federation including Poland, Byelorussia, Lithuania, and the Ukraine, which would support all breakaway tendencies in the former Russian empire, from Finland to the Caucasus, thus solidifying a buffer region between Poland and Russia.

Lenin believed that the spark of the Russian revolution would ignite the fire of world revolution. In his view, conflict with Poland, a potential "Red bridge" to the West, was inevitable. None of the Bolsheviks doubted the necessity of "forcing the Polish bridge"; the only question was when and how to do it. Trotsky, who had said, "The road to London and Paris goes through Calcutta," declared at the end of 1919: "When we have finished off Denikin, we will throw all the strength of our reserves against the Polish front."[123] Poland interested the Soviet government less for its own sake than as a means of breaking through to Europe, above all to Germany.

Pilsudski decided to strike first. On April 17, 1920, he ordered an offensive against Kiev. On April 21 he signed a treaty with Petlyura, recognizing his directorate as the supreme authority in the Ukrainian People's Republic and proclaiming the total independence of the Ukraine.

Kiev fell on May 7. The Soviet troops, aware of their weakness, withdrew without offering any serious resistance. It proved easier to conquer the Ukraine, however, than to govern it. The Poles, who wished to appear as liberators, were regarded as invaders. The Ukrainians did not want the kind of independence that was imposed from abroad. Petlyura proved incapable of establishing any stable political structures.

On June 12 the Soviet army, strengthened by fresh reserves, reoccupied Kiev. The speed of Poland's initial victory was now matched by the speed of its defeat. Pilsudski's armies withdrew in haste to the boundaries of ethnographic Poland.

The Polish invasion gave rise to a new political phenomenon in the Soviet Republic, a burst of government-sanctioned patriotism. Patriotism, which

Lenin had denounced at the beginning of the world war as a bourgeois concept and which after the revolution was persecuted and ridiculed, suddenly became part of the Communist party arsenal. On April 29 the party's Central Committee appealed not only to the workers and peasants but to "the respected citizens of Russia" to defend the Soviet Republic. This marked the resurrection of a concept of Russia that had been discredited by the revolution. The Central Committee referred to age-old enmities between Poland and Russia and recalled earlier invasions of Russia, in 1612, 1812, and 1914. It expressed certainty that "the respected citizens" would not allow the Polish "pans" (landlords) to impose their will on the Russian people. The Ukrainian Communists, who for three years had fought ruthlessly against Ukrainian nationalism, called on the Ukrainian people as a whole to rise up in defense of their homeland.

The appeal to Russian patriotic feeling produced immediate results. General Brusilov, former commander of tsarist armies in the world war, published a statement in *Pravda* calling on his fellow generals and officers to forget their grievances and do their patriotic duty—defend their beloved Russia from the foreign yoke, even at the cost of their lives.

This excess of patriotism disturbed the Soviet leaders, and measures were taken to curb it. The newspapers published a spate of articles emphasizing the class character of the Polish–Soviet war. Trotsky temporarily closed down the magazine of the General Staff, which had carried an article contrasting "the inherent Jesuitism of the *lyakhs*" (an insulting term for Poles) to "the honest and open souls of the Great Russians."[124]

Karl Radek discovered a formula which was typical of the way dialectics is used to reconcile the irreconcilable. "Since Russia is the only country where the working class has taken power, from now on the workers of the world must become Russian patriots."[125]

A concrete result of this use of patriotic slogans was a successful mobilization of former officers and NCOs. By August 15, 1920, there were 314,180 of them in the Red Army.[126]

After the Polish withdrawal from Kiev, the Soviet Republic concentrated the bulk of its forces on a single front and made ready, for the first time in its history, to invade another country. In command of the offensive was Mikhail Tukhachevsky, a twenty-seven-year-old former tsarist officer. All the army commanders under him—Kork, Lazarevich, Sologub, and Sergeev—had been colonels in the tsarist army.

The question of whether to cross the Polish border was discussed in the Politburo. The opinions of the Polish Communists, the "experts," were divided. Karl Radek warned of the dangers of such an action, which he said most Poles would perceive above all as an invasion by Russians. The majority of the Polish Communist leaders, however, warmly supported the plan to Communize Poland with the help of the Red Army. Most importantly, Lenin was resolutely in favor of invasion.

On Lenin's insistence the Politburo voted to invade and rejected an armistice proposal from British Foreign Minister Curzon, although Trotsky supported it. For Lenin, the fact that in March 1920 a general strike in Germany had foiled a right-wing attempt to seize power (the Kapp putsch) was irrefutable proof that the German working class was ready for revolution. By crossing Poland the Red Army would be able to lend a fraternal hand to the German proletariat. The miracle of the October revolution would be repeated as the miracle of the world revolution. Tukhachevsky, in his marching orders for the western front signed on July 2, proclaimed: "On our bayonets we will bring peace and happiness to toiling humanity. Forward, to the West!"

On July 23 a Provisional Polish Revolutionary Committee (the Polrevkom) was organized in Moscow, with Marchlewski as titular head. Its real leader was Dzerzhinsky. The Polrevkom was the first attempt to use foreign Communists living in Moscow to staff a Soviet government that would be installed beyond the borders of the Soviet Republic. Experience in this field was still lacking, and the activities of the Polrevkom were improvised following the Moscow model. Stalin, however, foresaw that the Polish experiment could be repeated. On June 16 he wrote Lenin a letter presenting theoretical arguments for a proposed confederation of such future Soviet states as Poland, Germany, and Hungary. These populations, he argued, could not be treated like Bashkirs or Ukrainians and simply included in a federation of Soviet republics. [127]

Bialystok, the first major Polish city to be taken, fell on July 28. The Red Army offensive rolled on, even though negotiations between Polish and Soviet representatives were proceeding in a desultory way and despite the fact that the last of the White armies, the army of Wrangel, had begun military operations aimed at breaking out of confinement on the Crimean peninsula. Lenin swept aside the fears of Central Committee members who suggested a halt in the Polish offensive in order to deal with Wrangel. Lenin knew that the Whites and the Poles would not coordinate their actions. During the negotiations with Marchlewski, Pilsudski's personal representative had stated clearly that it was central to Pilsudski's policy "not to allow the Russian reactionaries to triumph in Russia." [128] Wrangel by himself did not pose a serious danger.

On August 6 Tukhachevsky was named commander of the entire Polish front, combining the western and southwestern fronts. On August 14 Trotsky signed an order that ended: "Red armies, forward. Onward, heroes. On to

Warsaw!"[129] Soviet troops were expected to enter Warsaw on August 16. Along with the war cry, "Give us Warsaw," another now was heard: "Give us Berlin!" By mid-August Gai's cavalry corps was only ten days' march from Berlin. The delegates to the Second Congress of the Comintern, held in Moscow July 19 to August 7, could follow the progress of the Red Army on the map hanging at the front of the hall. The world revolution was coming to Europe on the points of swords and bayonets. Lenin was categorical in his conversations with the French delegates: "Yes, Soviet troops are in Warsaw. Soon Germany will be ours. We will reconquer Hungary. The Balkans will rise against capitalism. Italy will tremble. Bourgeois Europe is cracking at all its seams in this storm!"[130]

At the end of the congress, on August 7, small red flags surrounded Warsaw on the map. But the Soviet offensive was stopped on the outskirts of Warsaw. After its stunning defeat on the banks of the Vistula, the Red Army was forced into a rapid retreat.

The two sides in the war, and many military historians since then, have meticulously analyzed the military operations in search of the causes for the Red Army's success and defeat. Trotsky and Tukhachevsky charged that defeat was the result of Stalin's behavior. They said that Stalin, a member of the Revolutionary Military Council of the southwestern front, had disobeyed orders. Stalin later blamed the "traitors" Trotsky and Tukhachevsky.

On a military level, the causes of the Red Army's defeat are evident: insufficient coordination of the two fronts, "underestimation of the enemy's forces, and overestimation of our own troops' successes."[131] On the political level, things are even clearer: Lenin repeated Pilsudski's mistake. Pilsudski had imagined it was possible to bring independence to another nation on the point of a bayonet. Lenin was convinced that communism could be implanted the same way. But as a Soviet historian has put it, "The Polish bourgeoisie and Catholic clergy succeeded in contaminating the minds of the Polish peasants and small handicraft producers, as well as some of the workers, with the poison of bourgeois nationalism."[132] The Soviet commander-in-chief, Sergei Kamenev, commented that the Red Army had reached out its hand to the Polish proletariat but "did not find that proletariat's hand reaching out in response. Undoubtedly, the more powerful hand of the Polish bourgeoisie held that hand down and kept it deeply, deeply hidden."[133]

Great Britain and France had done their best to stop the initial Polish invasion of Russia. By granting Poland modest assistance in the form of money and arms, they exerted pressure for an armistice.[134] After January 1920 the Entente's policy in regard to Russia was based mainly on Lloyd

George's views. While rejecting the Soviet system, as all other Allied leaders did, Lloyd George strongly opposed intervention in Russia's affairs, considering it a waste of time and money. On April 16, 1919, he declared he would rather see a Bolshevik Russia than a bankrupt Great Britain.

Lloyd George formulated the principles of a policy that was to become standard for the West vis-à-vis the Soviet Union: to smother bolshevism with generosity. He declared that trade with the Soviet Republic would allow Russia's economy to revive, put an end to its chaotic state, and help surmount the difficulties that had given rise to bolshevism. When Lev Kamenev arrived in London on August 4, 1920, to hold talks with the British, "he was given such a courteous reception by Lloyd George that it would not have been any better had he been sent by the bloodthirsty tsar and not by Russian proletarian democracy."[135] Lloyd George was hoping to persuade the Soviet representative to accept peace on the basis of the Curzon line (the roughly ethnographic eastern frontier of Poland proposed at the Versailles peace conference in 1919). Unable to obtain any concessions from Moscow, which expected Warsaw to fall at any time, he set out to tame the Poles. An inter-Allied mission headed by British diplomat Lord D'Abernon left for Poland. France was represented by Ambassador Jusserand and General Weygand. British diplomat Maurice Hankey, a member of the mission who left Warsaw after six days of talks, announced in his report that Poland could not be saved. He suggested that "suitable conditions" be obtained for Poland through a peace agreement and that Allied efforts be concentrated on trying to improve relations with Germany and, through it, with Russia.[136] When Lloyd George, seeking to learn the real intentions of the French government, told Marshal Foch that Great Britain was ready to send its troops to Poland if France would do so as well, the marshal answered bluntly: "There aren't any troops."[137]

General Weygand, refuting the legend that he was the "father of the victory" on the Vistula, wrote in his memoirs: "The victory was Polish, the plan was Polish, the army was Polish."[138]

The Riga peace treaty, signed on March 18, 1921, was satisfactory to both parties. The Poles obtained a border much farther east than the one proposed by Curzon in July. The Soviet government, fearing worse conditions, was forced to accept the proposal. The Allies were particularly pleased. With Poland's help and at little cost to themselves the Bolshevik advance into Europe had been stopped.

In his diary Lord D'Abernon quoted Gibbon's historical observation that if Charles Martel had not stopped the Moors at Crécy, the Koran would have been taught at Oxford. D'Abernon added: "It is possible that the battle of Warsaw saved Central Europe and part of Western Europe from a more perfidious danger: the fanatical tyranny of the Soviets."[139] Historians today might modify this remark: the Polish victory on the Vistula postponed the Marxism-Leninism requirement in Eastern European schools for one generation.

The signing of the peace with Poland allowed the Soviet command to concentrate its efforts on Wrangel. By mid-October "a political and military" agreement had been reached between the Soviet government of the Ukraine and the Ukrainian Insurgent Army of Makhno.[140] By then the Soviet army outnumbered Wrangel's by "more than four to one in infantry and almost three to one in cavalry."[141] A few military successes by the Whites during the summer of 1920 could not alter the outcome of the struggle, nor did a few political reforms which Wrangel decided to institute. Wrangel, a conservative, found himself obliged to agree to reforms that even the liberal Denikin had rejected, but it was too late. During the first half of November, Soviet troops occupied the Crimea. The remnants of Wrangel's army boarded ships and sailed into exile. For the White movement defeat had come.

## THE PEASANT WAR

The war between Reds and Whites, between the regular Red Army and the regular White armies, was only one aspect of the civil war. The other was the peasant war. Peasant wars had figured prominently in Russian history—especially those led by Stepan Razin in the seventeenth century and by Emelyan Pugachev in the eighteenth. The peasant war of the twentieth century surpassed both of those in area and numbers involved. The Decree on Land, adopted on October 26, 1917, legalized the peasants' seizure of the great landed estates, which were abolished without compensation. The peasants, having gained what they wanted, considered the revolution over. The party of the proletariat, however, having taken power, insisted that the peasants provide grain and soldiers for a revolution the peasants no longer wanted. Conflict was inevitable.

During the summer of 1918 revolts broke out in many cities. Among the rebels were not only supporters of the old regime but also some of the most politically conscious members of the working class—rail workers, printers, and metalworkers. These anti-Bolshevik outbreaks were especially widespread in the Urals region, an important industrial center. "The Left SRs stirred up the backward elements of the working class against us in the factories of Kushva, Rudyansk, Shaitansk, Yugovsk, Setkino, Kaslino, and elsewhere," a Soviet historian acknowledges.[142] In elections to the Izhevsk

Soviet at the end of May 1918, the Bolsheviks won only 22 seats out of 170. As always in such cases, they walked out of the soviet "in protest" and declared it "anti-Soviet." In August a rebellion broke out in Izhevsk. "The immediate pretext for the revolt," writes the historian Spirin, "was the worsening of the food situation in the city and *some* improper actions of certain *individual* leaders of party and government bodies" [emphasis added—M. H.]. But the main reason, in Spirin's opinion, was "social." "A large number of workers in Izhevsk, as is well known, were contaminated by a petit bourgeois mentality."[143] The workers of neighboring Votkinsk joined the insurgent Izhevsk workers. Together they formed the People's Army of Izhevsk, more than 30,000 strong. Defeated after a hundred days of fighting near Izhevsk and Votkinsk, the soldiers of this army retreated eastward with their families and became one of Kolchak's toughest fighting units.

The "petit bourgeois mentality" contaminating these insurgent workers was expressed in their opposition to living in hunger, to petty tyranny by "certain individual leaders," to the loss of rights they had enjoyed before the revolution, and in general to conditions that were worse than before the proletarian party took power.

The "petit bourgeois mentality" of the peasants was expressed in their desire to work the land freely, to dispose of the fruits of their labor as they pleased, and not to go back to war. The bloody conflict between the peasants and the Bolsheviks was not the result of grain requisitioning alone. The peasants believed that the revolution would bring them freedom. The ideal of liberty embodied in the ancient Russian word *volya*, implying total lack of constraints, stirred the vast peasant mass. The soviets were seen as a form of self-government for the countryside that would free it from the burdensome rule of city people. The countryside wanted to live without the cities. In response the cities declared war on the countryside. A "food army" was organized to requisition grain, and draconian measures were employed to suppress peasant unrest. "To break the kulak resistance, the dictatorship of the proletariat used extraordinary measures: trials before revolutionary tribunals, imprisonment, confiscation of property, the taking of hostages, and even the shooting of people on the spot in cases of armed resistance."[144]

Any opposition to the Soviet government, any expression of discontent with Bolshevik policies among the peasants, was declared the work of "kulaks." But the term *kulak* had never been clearly defined. The purported number of kulak households in rural Russia at the time of the revolution and civil war varies depending on the date of the source. In 1924 a Soviet historian wrote: "Under existing conditions in our country, only by stretching the figures could one say that kulak households account for 2 or 3 percent, and for even these households it has not yet been demonstrated clearly enough that they function as kulak households."[145] In 1964 a Soviet historian asserted, "The kulaks represented 15 percent of all peasant households."[146] In August 1918 Lenin placed the number of kulak families at 2 million, out of 15 million peasant families.[147] But in April 1920, at the Ninth Party Congress, he spoke of only "1 million" rural families engaged in "exploiting the labor of others."[148] This figure was insignificant in a country whose population in 1920 was 130.5 million, with 110.8 million living in the countryside.

"The kulak is the enemy" was a formula that made little sense, the definition of kulak being so unclear and the officially acknowledged number of kulaks being so insignificant. Therefore the phrase was turned around: "Any enemy must be a kulak." An initial wave of peasant revolts swept the country in 1918. According to the official figures of the Cheka, between July and November 108 "kulak rebellions" broke out in the Soviet Republic. For the entire year there were "245 major anti-Soviet uprisings in the twenty provinces of Central Russia alone."[149]

Mikhail Kalinin, president of the Central Executive Committee, who played the role of peasants' representative in the heart of the proletarian party, stated in May 1919: "I believe that unrest among the peasants can only be the result of a misunderstanding, because no better government could be imagined for the peasants than the Soviet government."[150] But the peasants were able to imagine a better one quite easily—one without Communists. The peasant revolts rarely put forward explicit political programs, but there were three common demands: an end to grain requisitioning; removal of Communists from the soviets; and an end to Communist terror. One of the most moving documents of the period was a letter of July 31, 1919, to Lenin from Filipp Mironov, commander of a Cossack corps of the Red Army, expressing the grievances primarily of the Cossacks but also of the Russian peasantry as a whole. Mironov objected first of all, in the name of the peasantry, to any immediate leap into communism, the forcing of peasants into communes. "I think," he wrote, "that the Communist system is a lengthy process requiring much patience; it must come from the heart and not by force." Mironov sharply protested the monstrous cruelty that accompanied the establishment of Soviet power in the Don region: "Vladimir Ilyich, it is impossible—I don't have enough time and paper—to describe the horrors of 'Communist construction' on the Don. And in other rural areas it is no better." Mironov rejected what he called "the diabolical plan to exterminate the Cossacks, after which of course would come the turn of the middle peasants." He warned Lenin that if the bloodthirsty policy of the Communist party was not changed it would be necessary to stop fighting Krasnov and start fighting the Communists.[151] A former lieutenant colonel in the tsarist army, Mironov had sided with the Bolsheviks immediately after the October revolution and became a celebrated commander of the Red Army. Nevertheless he was executed by the Cheka in Moscow's Butyrki prison in 1921.

The reason for the large number of peasant revolts in Central Russia was that it was within close reach of the urban power centers and was therefore exploited with particular intensity by the requisitioning units. But as the requisitions spread to other regions, the peasants rebelled there, too.

The Cossack regions rose up against the Communists, and so did the Ukraine. A Soviet historian notes, "In the Ukraine by mid-1919 the entire peasantry, all sections of it, were opposed to Soviet power."[152] A party official admitted in 1920: "In the Makhno movement it is hard to tell where the poor peasant leaves off and where the kulak begins. It was a mass peasant movement."[153]

In March 1919 a Red Army brigade that had been sent to Byelorussia rebelled. The insurgents took Gomel and Rechitsa. The brigade consisted mainly of peasant soldiers from Tula, who made common cause with the local insurgent committee of Polesye, which represented the Byelorussian peasantry. In an appeal to the peasants the new commander of this "First Army of the People's Republic," an ensign named Strekopytov, announced the formation of a "new people's power," the abolition of grain requisitioning and emergency taxes, and an end to the war. The slogans of the insurrection were: (1) all power to the Constituent Assembly; (2) a mixture of private and governmental initiative in commerce and industry; (3) strict laws protecting the interests of labor; (4) respect for civil liberties in practice; (5) land to the people; and (6) entry into the League of Nations by the Russian Republic.[154]

In early 1919 a peasant revolt broke out in the middle Volga region— the so-called *chapan* revolt.[155] Intensified grain requisitioning in the Volga region was accompanied by

a series of additional obligations: delivery of carts to the army; provision of firewood for the cities and the railroad; compulsory hauling of goods for the army; and commandeering of horses. . . . At the same time the disrupted transport system and the priority given military shipments prevented manufactured goods and other supplies from being delivered in return for the grain sent to the cities.[156]

The insurgents captured several towns and nearly reached Syzran.

In the Fergana region of Central Asia in the summer of 1919 the Peasant Army, organized to protect the Russian population from armed units of Muslim peasants, reversed itself and reached an agreement with the anti-Bolshevik Muslims. The Peasant Army, under the command of K. I. Monstrov, agreed to joint operations with the Muslim peasants of Madamin-bek.[157] As in other regions, the spark that set off the insurrection was requisitioning and the "grain monopoly," which came to Turkestan that summer.

The entire peasantry of Russia was resisting. Besides the major revolts, countless minor ones broke out. From 1918 to 1920 the reality of the peasant war was concealed beneath the war between Reds and Whites. Yet all along the peasants were fighting on two fronts. A peasant song of the time included these words:

> Hey, little apple tree,
> Color so ripe,
> On the left we fight the Reds,
> On the right the Whites.

By the end of 1920 the civil war was actually over. The Red Army had won. Soviet power had completed its "triumphal march," begun in October 1917 but interrupted by the war. The danger that the large landowners would return was now past. The peasants considered the land theirs for good. Resistance to the requisitions and to the party's policy in the countryside intensified. The Soviet authorities responded more harshly than ever.

From 1920 to 1921 the civil war became a peasant war. Mikhail Pokrovsky, the first Russian Marxist historian, wrote that in 1921 "the heartland of the Russian Republic was almost completely surrounded by peasant uprisings, from Makhno on the Dnepr to Antonov on the Volga."[158] But the dimensions of the war were far greater than indicated by Pokrovsky. The Red Army was battling the peasantry in Byelorussia, in the southeast of European Russia, in eastern and western Siberia, in Karelia, and in Central Asia.

Just as the peasant revolt spread geographically, it grew numerically, becoming a genuine mass movement. Entire armies appeared. By the end of 1920 Makhno's army in the Ukraine was 40,000–50,000 strong. The peasant army led by Antonov in the Tambov and Voronezh regions numbered 50,000 in January 1921. An informational report from the Bolshevik party's regional committee in the Kuban area spoke of the formation of "full-scale rebel armies" there in the spring of 1921. In western Siberia, the Ishim District (*uezd*) alone had 60,000 peasant rebels, and there were peasants fighting throughout the region, in the provinces of Chelyabinsk, Ekaterinburg, Tyumen, Tobolsk, and elsewhere. The "First Army of Justice," led by Sapozhkov, active along the Volga, had 1,800 bayonets, 900 sabers, 10 machine guns, and 4 artillery pieces.[159] By comparison, the White armies in the period of February 1–15, 1919, had 85,000 men on the southern front, 140,000 on the eastern front, 104,000 on the western front, 12,500 in northern Russia, and 7,500 in the Northern Caucasus.[160]

The tactics of the peasant fighters varied according to local conditions, their material resources, and the talents of their commanders. Makhno and Antonov favored guerrilla warfare, sudden attacks and speedy retreats. Perfect knowledge of the terrain and, above all, the support of most of the peasants allowed the rebels to "swim like fish in the sea" and assured the success of these tactics. The enemy was furious and denounced the guerrillas because they would not "engage in open battle, face to face, but resorted instead to sneak attacks, like bandits and thieves."[161] In other areas the peasant armies did engage in open combat, laying siege to cities and taking many. In February 1921 peasant units in the lower Volga region took Kamyshin, and in March Khvalynsk.[162] At the same time Siberian peasant armies took Tobolsk and Kokchetav and occupied all seven districts of Tyumen Province, four districts of Omsk Province and Kurgan District in Chelyabinsk Province. They laid siege to Ishim, Yalutorovsk, and Kurgan and reached the approaches of Akmolinsk and Agbasar.[163]

Operational command of the campaigns against the peasants went to the most prominent military leaders of the Red Army, including the commander-in-chief, Sergei Kamenev, two commanders of fronts, Tukhachevsky and Frunze, and such commanders of armies as Budyonny, Yakir, Fedko, Tyulenev, and Uborevich. Just as under Catherine the Great the best-known generals were sent in pursuit of Pugachev, in 1921 the Red commanders who had won the greatest fame in battle with the Whites were assigned to hunt down Antonov, Makhno, Sapozhkov, and the other peasant chieftains.

Tukhachevsky, who a moment before had been knocking at the gates of Western Europe, took charge of operations against the Antonov rebellion. In May 1921 he had under his command 35,000 bayonets, 10,000 swords, several hundred machine guns, and 60 cannon. The latest in military technology was available for his use: armored cars and airplanes. Tukhachevsky was issued orders that said: "The task of eradicating these bands must not be thought of as a more or less prolonged operation, but as a serious and urgent military mission, a campaign, even a war."[164]

Antonov's comrades did not leave behind a history of their movement written from their own point of view. All the leaders of the movement were killed. All that is known of the rebellion comes from official Soviet sources.

Antonov himself, a Socialist Revolutionary from Tambov, had spent many years in prison before the revolution. He first came out against Bolshevik policies in August 1918. In the spring of 1919 he began a systematic struggle against the local authorities in the Tambov region. In 1920 the Tambov peasants refused to accept the policy of confiscation any longer, a policy enforced by the cruelest methods. Its harshness can be guessed from the following tactful admissions in a circular addressed to all provincial food supply committees by the Central Executive Committee of the Soviets: "Requisitions, which are a burdensome obligation to the state, are carried out by persuasion and by force. But there are many cases in which force has been applied in illegal and unacceptable ways." The circular, dated February 23, 1921, added that "violations of revolutionary legality" had by that time become a regular part of "the work of the food supply system."[165] Rebelling against this system, the peasants joined Antonov. "In the Tambov District the following percentages of the population have joined the bandits: in the village of Aleksandrovka, 25 percent; the village of Afanasyevka, 30 percent; Khitrovo and Pavlodarovo, 40 percent. . . . In some villages of Kirsanov District more than 80 percent of the male population belong to the outlaw bands."[166]

No Soviet historian has yet claimed that the number of kulaks in Tambov Province ever reached 80 percent, or even 25 percent. Antonov's was an army of peasants, not kulaks. The full military might of the Soviet Republic was thrown against this army. A Central Interdepartmental Commission for the Struggle Against Banditry was formed, including representatives from the party's Central Committee, the government's Council of Labor and Defense, the Cheka, even the Commissariat of Posts and Telegraph. The head of the commission was Efraim Sklyansky, deputy chairman of the Revolutionary Military Council of the Republic.[167]

In the war against the peasants not only were regular military units used, the rebel movements were widely infiltrated by agents. A retired Chekist has described how Antonov's command staff was penetrated this way.[168] No less important, however, were the "administrative measures." First of all, hostages were taken—people who would be shot if any rebel units appeared in the given area. Anyone who "harbored bandits" or their families would also be shot.[169] After March 1921 the families of "bandits" began to be deported from Tambov Province. In June the commission to combat banditry found it necessary, "although most of the bands in Tambov Province have been smashed and the kulaks have come to understand the power of the

Soviet government," to deport from the province "all persons who were involved in any way with banditry, including some rail workers." In 1929, Kalinin recalled the Antonov rebellion. It had been necessary, he said, to deport to the north of Russia "the villages most seriously infected with banditism." In other words, entire villages were deported. "Many peasants in Tambov and Voronezh provinces," Kalinin recalled, "took part in that struggle between Soviet power and the old world."[170] It was not by accident, incidentally, that Kalinin was discussing the subject of mass repression against the peasants in 1929. That year a new phase began in "the struggle between Soviet power and the old world"—forced collectivization and "de-kulakization."

Tukhachevsky, commander of the Tambov punitive expedition, summed up the experience of pacification as follows:

> The Sovietization of the centers of rebellion in Tambov Province followed a definite progression, district by district. After troops were brought into a given district, we would concentrate maximum force there—the army, the Cheka, and the party and Soviet apparatuses. While the military units were busy wiping out the bands based in the district and establishing revolutionary committees, the Cheka was catching any surviving bandits. After Soviet power was consolidated in one district, all our forces were transferred to the next.[171]

The most important element in pacification "Tambov style" was not the destruction of the armed rebel units but the eradication of the "spirit of rebellion" after armed resistance had been overcome. This task was entrusted to the Cheka, which worked hand in glove with the party committees. On April 4, 1921, the Central Committee sent a letter to the party province committees with the following instructions: "The province committees of the party and the Cheka units in each province must constitute a single whole in the work of preventing or suppressing counterrevolutionary outbreaks in the affected area."[172] It may be assumed that the idea of fusing the Cheka and the party committees into "a single whole" was a development of Lenin's thought that "a good Communist has the qualities of a good member of the Cheka."[173]

The outbreak of peasant war was explained away very simply: it had been instigated by White Guards and Anglo-French imperialists. On September 8, 1921, *Pravda* reported that Antonov had "received his orders from abroad, from the Central Committee of the Cadet party." The Cheka reported to the Council of People's Commissars: "It has now become clear that in Ryazan, Tula, Kaluga, Smolensk, Tambov, and Tver provinces, uprisings were organized according to a general plan with the cooperation of Anglo-French capital."[174] An awareness of the aims and demands of the peasant rebels, however, is sufficient grounds for rejecting this conspiracy theory out of hand. In May 1920 a congress of the working peasants of Tambov Province adopted an insurrectional program calling for: the overthrow of Soviet power and destruction of the Communist party; the convening of a Constituent Assembly on the basis of universal, equal, direct suffrage and a secret ballot; the establishment of a provisional government, composed of representatives of the parties and associations that had fought the Bolsheviks, to rule until the Constituent Assembly was held; the land to go to those who work it; both Russian and foreign capital to be allowed to help revive the country's economy.[175]

The peasant rebels east of the Volga also called for the replacement of Soviet power by a Constituent Assembly, universal suffrage, denationalization of the land, an end to grain requisitioning, free trade, abolition of collective farms, the transfer of power on the local level to "councils of three" or "councils of five" elected by general assemblies. They demanded recognition for all parties except the monarchist Black Hundreds and the dissolution of all institutions of the Bolshevik party as "harmful to the working people."[176]

In western Siberia the peasants demanded the institution of "genuine popular sovereignty"—peasant dictatorship, convening of the Constituent Assembly, denationalization of industry (for "the nationalization of factories and plants at base destroys the country's economic life"), and egalitarian land tenure. An appeal by the Tobolsk Command of March 6, 1921, proclaimed: "The Communists say that there can be no Soviet power without Communists. Why? Can't we elect nonparty members to the soviets? Long live popular Soviet power! Down with the Communists! Long live the complete freedom of the people!"[177]

The best known and most fully worked out program of peasant revolt was that of the Makhno movement. Many of its participants, including Makhno himself, wrote their memoirs, and a history of the movement by one of its members exists.

Kubanin, an authority on the Makhno movement, describes the reasoning of the Ukrainian peasants as follows:

> Soviet power gave the land to the peasants and raised the slogan, "Steal back what was stolen." This was the work of the Bolsheviks. But the government that carried out grain requisitioning, that refused to give all of the large landholdings to the peasants, and that organized state farms and communes—that is the government of "the commune," the government not of the Bolsheviks but of the Communists.

The peasants frequently expressed this attitude with the formula: "We're for the Bolsheviks, but against the Communists."[178]

In June 1918 Makhno had a long talk with Lenin and tried to explain to him the attitude of the Ukrainian peasants. The peasant masses, Makhno said, saw the revolution as "a way of freeing themselves from the yoke of the landlord and the wealthy kulak but also from the servants of the rich, the political and administrative functionaries who rule from the top down." In his memoirs Makhno writes: "Lenin asked me the same question three times and was amazed each time at the answer," because the way the peasants understood the slogan "power to the local soviets" was not the way the Bolshevik leader understood it. For the peasants it meant that "the entire government must correspond in all ways directly to the will and consciousness of the working people themselves." Lenin objected: "The peasants of your area are infected with anarchism."[179]

The political label Lenin sought to paste over this reality missed the main point: the peasants were willing to follow anyone, be it the SR Antonov, the "anarchocommunist" Makhno, the peasant chiefs who belonged to no party, or the Bolsheviks themselves when they gave the peasants the land and said "Steal back what was stolen." They would follow anyone if they thought it would lead to land and liberty.

The peasants accepted the revolution, interpreting it their own way, but refused to accept the Bolshevik regime.

## FROM PEASANT WAR TO KRONSTADT

To Lenin, the innumerable peasant uprisings engulfing the country did not seem reason enough for a change of policy, for abandoning the attempt to build communism immediately. The peasant war did not threaten the urban centers. Its isolated hotbeds could be extinguished one by one. It was not a serious threat to the government. But the revolt of the Kronstadt sailors, as Lenin put it, lit up reality like a flash of lightning.

In late 1920 the workers, whose living conditions were growing constantly worse, began to express their discontent more and more loudly. Strikes broke out in Moscow and other industrial centers, but in Petrograd, the "cradle of the revolution," they assumed especially large dimensions. The strikers were declared not to be workers, since real workers would not go on strike against a "workers' state." "Do you really think these are workers striking?" asked a member of the Petrograd Executive Committee. "There are no real workers left in Petrograd: they are at the front, or in food supply work, and so on. These people are scum, self-seekers, shopkeepers hiding away in the factories while the war is on."[180]

A decree of January 22, 1921, reducing the bread ration for workers by one third, was the straw that broke the camel's back.[181] The strikes and demonstrations that began involved the workers of the Trubochny Metals Factory, the Patronny and Baltic plants, and giant Putilov Factory, and many other Petrograd factories. The demonstrations were dispersed by Communist officer cadets (*kursanty*), because regular units were no longer considered reliable. The situation in Petrograd in February 1921 was remarkably similar to that of February 1917. Red Army soldiers were not issued boots for fear that if they left their barracks they would join the protesters. On February 24 the party's Petrograd Committee announced the formation of an emergency Defense Council. The city was placed under martial law, and mass arrests began. At the same time extra rations were distributed to workers and soldiers: one tin of preserved meat and one pound of bread daily.[182]

The disturbances in Petrograd spread to Kronstadt. The most active elements in the movement there were the sailors of the battleships *Petropavlovsk* and *Sevastopol*, who with the crew of the battleship *Respublika* had been mainstays of support for the Bolsheviks in 1917. On March 1 a mass meeting of the garrison and civilian population of Kronstadt endorsed a resolution drafted by the *Petropavlovsk* sailors. Among its demands were: new elections to the soviets by secret ballot, because "the present soviets do not express the will of the workers and peasants"; freedom of speech and the press for "workers and peasants, anarchists and left socialist parties"; the release of all "political prisoners of socialist parties"; a review of the cases of those being held in prisons and concentration camps; removal of the roadblock detachments (whose purpose was to prevent illegal trading in grain and other foodstuffs between town and country); and "full freedom of action in regard to the land," as well as the right to raise livestock, for peasants who did not employ hired labor.[183]

A delegation from Kronstadt, sent to Petrograd to acquaint the workers with this resolution, was arrested. In reply Kronstadt formed a Provisional Revolutionary Committee, consisting of sailors and workers. Stepan Petrichenko, a senior clerk on the *Petropavlovsk*, was elected chairman. On March 2 Lenin and Trotsky signed an order outlawing the Kronstadt movement, charging that it had been organized by "French counterintellegence" and branding the rebels' resolution an "SR–Black Hundred" document. It charged that the movement was led by a former tsarist general, Kozlovsky, and announced that martial law was extended to all of Petrograd Province.[184]

Aleksandr N. Kozlovsky, commander of artillery at Kronstadt, was one of tens of thousands of military specialists serving in the Red Army. He played no part in organizing or leading the rebellion (although he and other specialists did give military advice to the rebels). He was singled out by official Soviet propaganda because, as the only former tsarist general at Kronstadt, he was indispensable for the myth of a "White Guard conspiracy." His family was arrested, as were the families of all the Kronstadt rebels.

On March 5 Trotsky ordered the insurgents to surrender. "Only those who surrender unconditionally," he declared, "can count on the mercy of the Soviet Repubic."[185] Trotsky, who in 1917 had called the Kronstadt sailors the "pride and glory of the revolution," began preparations to take the island fortress by storm.

The Kronstadt rebellion, Lenin told the Tenth Party Congress in March 1921, was more dangerous to the Bolshevik government than Denikin, Kolchak, and Yudenich combined. It was so dangerous because of the proximity of Kronstadt to Petrograd and the fact that the rebels were military professionals with a powerful arsenal under their control. But there was a special danger in the anti-Bolshevik but revolutionary slogans of the Kronstadt sailors: "All power to the soviets but not the parties"; "Down with counterrevolution from the left and from the right"; "The power of the soviets will free the working peasantry from the Communist yoke." These appeals reflected the moods of the peasants but also of the workers. "Here in Kronstadt," a rebel proclamation said,

> has been laid the first stone of the third revolution. . . . This new revolution will also rouse the laboring masses of the East and of the West, by serving as an example of the new socialist construction as opposed to the bureaucratic Communist "creativity." The laboring masses abroad will see with their own eyes that everything created here until now by the will of the workers and peasants was not socialism.[186]

The slogan of a "third revolution" directed against the "commissarocracy" could not fail to stir Lenin's worst fears. On March 7, artillery bombardment of Kronstadt and its outlying forts began.

To direct operations, Commander-in-Chief Sergei Kamenev and Commander of the Western Front Tukhachevsky were brought to Petrograd. Direct command of the forces gathered to suppress the rebellion was placed in Tukhachevsky's hands. Lenin, Trotsky, and the other Soviet leaders, who never stopped denouncing the "White general" Kozlovsky, were not at all troubled by the fact that former tsarist officers, colonels and generals, directed the operations against Kronstadt. An overwhelming force was concentrated to crush the rebels. Against the 3,000–5,500 sailors who were defending Kronstadt,[187] approximately 50,000 troops attacked across the ice from the coasts north and south of the island fortress. The Red forces broke through the Kronstadt defenses during the night of March 17–18. On March 18 all the Soviet newspapers carried front-page articles commemorating the fiftieth anniversary of the Paris Commune and denouncing Thiers and Galliffet, the "bloody butchers" who had suppressed the Communards and executed them *en masse*. In 1919 a bulletin of the Kiev Cheka, *Krasny mech* (Red sword), had given voice to the kind of thinking that in 1921 allowed bloody butchery against the workers and sailors of Kronstadt: "To us everything is permitted, because we were the first in the world to take up the sword not for the purpose of enslavement and repression but in the name of universal liberty and emancipation from slavery."[188]

The rebel sailors had done no more than arrest local Communists who refused to join them. The Communists, by contrast, took severe reprisals. Immediately after the suppression of the revolt thirteen Kronstadt sailors were shot. Executions continued in the prisons of Petrograd. A large number of Kronstadt sailors were sent to the Pertominsk concentration camp on the White Sea, where many of them died. Petrichenko, who fled to Finland, lived there until 1945, when he was turned over to the Soviet government; he died in a camp.[189] Later Soviet historians, not content with repeating the charges about "the White general Kozlovsky" and "French intelligence," added another culprit to share the blame for the uprising—Trotsky and the Trotskyists.[190]

The most important thing about Kronstadt was that it made Lenin realize that his policy of building communism posthaste had suffered a defeat.

# 3

# THE SEARCH FOR A "GENERAL LINE," 1921–1925

## A STEP BACKWARD

In a letter to Maxim Gorky, Mikhail Pokrovsky described a proposed history of the civil war whose chronological framework would stretch from the February revolution to Kronstadt and the Antonov revolt. Thus, for the chief official Soviet historian the suppression in 1921 of the Kronstadt revolt and of the peasant movement in Tambov Province marked the end of the civil war.

Earlier, in 1920, Soviet power had been established in Siberia, Turkestan, and the Ukraine. In some areas it was impossible for various reasons to install a Soviet regime directly. There, transitional forms were introduced: the Far Eastern Republic, which lasted from April 1920 until the fall of 1922, when the Japanese left the region once and for all; the People's Republic of Khorezm, founded in February 1920; and the People's Republic of Bukhara, founded in September 1920.

The formation of the People's Republic of Bukhara was preceded by the emergence of a pro-Communist left wing in the Young Bukhara party. That party then organized an uprising in Chardzhou and asked for help from the Red Army, located nearby. Red Army units under the command of Frunze immediately lent a fraternal hand. Despite stubborn resistance by troops loyal to the emir of Bukhara, the city and its subject territory were taken. The emir fled, and the People's Republic was proclaimed.

The Sovietization of the Caucasus followed a similar scenario. In April 1920 the Central Committee of the Bolshevik party formed a special Caucasus Bureau, the Kavburo, and placed it under the command staff of the Eleventh Red Army, operating in the Northern Caucasus. The Kavburo did the thinking, and the Eleventh Army carried out the plan. In late January 1920 Chicherin, the commissar of foreign affairs, sent a note to the Azerbaijan government demanding cooperation in the fight against Denikin and promising in return to recognize the independence of Azerbaijan. But as early as April 17 Lenin secretly named his own representative to be director of the future Soviet oil industry in Baku. The Kavburo urged the Baku Communists to launch an uprising on April 27. The Azerbaijan Communists, with whom the Musavatist government was conducting negotiations (despite the fact that the Communists were officially illegal), issued an ultimatum demanding that the government surrender power to the Soviets. Before the twelve-hour ultimatum could expire, on April 28 an armored train carrying Ordzhonikidze and Kirov arrived in Baku. With them Soviet power came to Azerbaijan. Ordzhonikidze, as head of the Kavburo, directed a massive wave of repression, aimed primarily at the leaders of the nationalist movement. Soon the Azerbaijan Communist party announced the appearance of a new star on the horizon of the world revolution. The Baku newspaper *Kommunist* welcomed the arrival of an important visitor in November 1920 with these words: "Arriving on a visit to Baku [today] is Comrade Stalin—a working-class leader of exceptional energy, firmness, and self-denial, the only recognized authority on questions of revolutionary tactics, and leader of the proletarian revolution, in the East and the Caucasus."[1]

The absence of any Communist organization in Armenia, the result of the pro-Turkish policies of the Russian Communist party, delayed the Sovietization of that republic. An attempt by Armenian Communists living outside Armenia to organize a coup did not succeed. A war with Turkey which broke out in September 1920 ended quickly with the defeat of the Armenian army. On November 27 Stalin, after arriving in Baku, ordered Ordzhonikidze to begin operations against Armenia. On the same day Ordzhonikidze received instructions from Lenin[2] to issue an ultimatum to the Armenian government: surrender power to the "Revolutionary Committee of the Soviet Socialist Republic," positioned nearby on Azerbaijan soil.

Without waiting for the deadline to expire, the Eleventh Army entered Armenian territory. On December 6 the Revolutionary Committee arrived in Erevan. A coalition government of Communists and Dashnaks was formed. On December 21, 1920, all laws of the Russian Republic (RSFSR) were made binding for Armenia. The Dashnaks were expelled from the government and repressed.

Georgia, the largest of the Transcaucasian republics, with a government enjoying popular support and a fairly strong army, was seen by Lenin as a serious opponent. When Ordzhonikidze, intoxicated by his success in Baku, asked for permission to invade Georgia, it was denied. The war with Poland had just begun, and Moscow did not want to fight on two fronts. On May 7, 1920, a treaty was signed in Moscow with the ambassador from Georgia. In the first clause the RSFSR recognized the independence and sovereignty of the Georgian state and renounced all former Russian privileges. In a secret clause Georgia pledged to legalize the Communist party and allow it to carry on its activities openly. Kirov, vice-president of the Kavburo, was appointed Soviet ambassador to Tiflis. "It was no secret to anyone," recalled the Georgian Communist leader Makharadze, "that under the circumstances of the time (1920) the activities of the Communist party consisted exclusively of preparing for armed insurrection against the existing government."[3] After Soviet power had been established in Azerbaijan and Armenia, Georgia found itself surrounded on three sides. Still Lenin considered the occupation of Georgia premature. Sergei Kamenev, the Red Army commander-in-chief, had reported to Lenin three times that an invasion of Georgia could lead to war on a large scale in the Caucasus.[4] Occupation of Georgia might also cause the collapse of talks then underway with Britain. Although Leonid Krasin, the Soviet representative in London, reported that Lloyd George had made a statement recognizing that the Caucasus was within the Soviet sphere of influence, Lenin's fears were not dispelled.

Sovietization of the Caucasus was considered necessary for economic and strategic reasons by all the Bolshevik leaders, despite differences over tactics. In January 1921 the Politburo passed a resolution to overthrow the Georgian government, but Lenin urged that the action be given the appearance of an insurrection to which the Red Army would offer support. Georgian Communists were instructed to organize an uprising.[5] On February 16 the Eleventh Army crossed the border to lend a "fraternal hand" to a Military Revolutionary Committee formed in the tiny village of Shulaveri two days earlier. The Georgian army was short of weapons. "The most essential thing was to obtain rifles and cartridges. We sent telegrams everywhere. No one could promise us anything. Only from London came a categorical reply, a refusal."⁶ On March 18 the Georgian government surrendered. Lenin, fearing a popular resistance movement if the methods used in Azerbaijan were repeated in Georgia, urged Ordzhonikidze to employ milder tactics. Ordzhonikidze scorned Lenin's suggestion and set about the work of Sovietizing Georgia, using the same methods tested out in the other Caucasian republics (and for the preceding three years in the Russian Republic).

The Kronstadt rebellion had finally forced Lenin to reexamine his policy toward the peasantry. As late as the beginning of 1921 he still rejected all proposals to alleviate or alter the surplus grain appropriation system, the *prodrazverstka*. Kronstadt convinced him that, with the overwhelming majority of the population opposed to the government's policy, the position of an occupying power in one's own country could no longer be maintained.

Lenin realized that he had made a mistake. In a conversation with Clara Zetkin at the end of 1920, he admitted he had been wrong to believe that the invasion of Poland would set off a revolution. The German Communist Zetkin recalled that as Lenin spoke his face had a look of inexpressible suffering. Lenin's face at that moment reminded the art lover Zetkin of the crucified Christ of Grunewald. Unfortunately no one was present to paint Lenin's face when he admitted his mistake in believing that communism could be built overnight in Russia: "We thought that under the surplus food appropriation system the peasants would provide us with the required quantity of grain, which we could distribute among the factories and thus achieve communist production and distribution." With less than full sincerity he added: "A not very lengthy experience convinced us that that line was wrong."⁷ The experience had lasted four years, from October 25, 1917, to October 17, 1921, when Lenin made this confession of error. It was indeed a lengthy experience, and very costly in human life. But by "admitting his error" Lenin made an important contribution to the art of ruling the Soviet Union: self-criticism by the Leader eliminates the mistake at once, as though it had never existed, and the Leader remains infallible.

On March 15, 1921, at the Tenth Party Congress, Lenin presented the New Economic Policy. The congress approved it. The era of NEP began.

The NEP was first and foremost an agrarian policy. "The peasantry is dissatisfied with the form of its relations with us," Lenin explained to the Tenth Congress. "It does not want relations of this type and will not continue to live this way.... The peasantry has expressed its will in this respect definitely enough. It is the will of the vast masses of the working population."⁸ At his suggestion the congress changed the type of relations "between them and us." The surplus grain appropriation system (*prodrazverstka*) was replaced by the "tax in kind" (*prodnalog*).

For the year 1921–22 the tax in kind was set at 240 million poods (2.5 million centners) of grain, approximately one third of the amount previously set for requisitioning during that year. One might conclude that this was a substantial easing of the burden on the peasantry—except for the fact that about 240 million poods had actually been requisitioned during 1920–21. The "easing of the burden" can be judged more precisely if the tax in kind is compared to the direct taxes imposed before 1914: the tax in kind was 399 percent of the 1914 tax.[9] The significance of the policy change was not that it eased the tax burden but that it limited arbitrary action by the state. On March 8, 1921, the peasants of Panfilov Township (*volost*), in the Gryazevetsk District of Vologda Province addressed a letter to "our beloved leader and great genius, Comrade Lenin." They informed him:

> At the present time practically everything has been taken from the peasants of our township—bread, grain, livestock, hay, raw materials. . . . In 1920 because of the drought the yield relative to seed grain was only four to one, but the agents of the food supply committee did their requisitioning on the basis of a six-to-one yield.

The Vologda peasants, begging not to be considered "pernicious elements" but on the contrary "citizens wishing to do fruitful work to strengthen the liberty of the workers and peasants," proposed that requisitioning be replaced by a tax in kind, so that the peasants "would know how much tax was owed and when it was due."[10] The decree on the tax in kind regularized both matters.

The new policy could not be limited to the tax change. It implied that the peasants could increase agricultural production without fear of confiscation. But it made no sense to allow this surplus unless it could be sold legally. Up to the last Lenin did not wish to abandon his dream of an immediate leap into communism. At the Tenth Party Congress Trotsky recalled that a year earlier, in February 1920, he himself had suggested that a tax in kind be substituted for requisitioning. At the Eighth Congress of Soviets, in December 1920, the Mensheviks and SRs—the last time they were allowed to participate openly in a discussion—urged that grain requisitioning be abandoned. Lenin rejected all these proposals as constituting a return to capitalism. In his conception commerce and capitalism were the same thing; consequently, freedom to trade meant a step back toward capitalism. At the end of 1920 a decree was passed declaring that all food products held by the state would thenceforth be given out free of charge. Actually there was hardly any food, but the Bolshevik leaders still thought that communism was just around the corner.

In abandoning grain requisitioning, Lenin clung compulsively to the

hope that he could avoid granting freedom of trade, that he would not have
to allow the market to sully the purity of communist relations. Under his
plan, exchange between peasant producers would remain strictly a local
phenomenon (with products being transported by horsedrawn vehicles only,
not over the rails). This trade would be more like barter than buying and
selling. Utopianism died hard. But reality proved stronger. In the fall of
1921 the leader of the revolution was forced to admit: "[The] system of
commodity exchange has broken down. . . . Nothing has come of commodity
exchange; the private market has proved too strong for us; and instead of
the exchange of commodities we have gotten ordinary buying and selling,
trade."[11] The New Economic Policy likewise marked a 180-degree turn in
industry. Small private businesses were authorized, individuals were allowed to rent large enterprises, and foreigners were allowed to lease some
factories and mining operations as concessions. Even more important was
the change in attitude toward labor. Workers had taken part in all protests
against the Communist regime, but their discontent was most vividly expressed in the sharp decline of labor productivity. "In the years 1919–
1920 the average output annually of a worker was only 45 percent of the
quantity of products that resulted from his labor before the war."[12] The
plan for a "great leap forward" into communism based itself on the need
to force the workers to work. Just as Dzerzhinsky had proclaimed the
concentration camps to be "schools of labor," Trotsky advocated the "militarization of labor" and the formation of "labor armies."[13] The people's
commissar of war questioned the notion that slave labor was unproductive.
"Is it true that compulsory labor is always unproductive? We have to reply
that is the most pitiful and worthless liberal prejudice."[14] Human beings
do not want to work, Trotsky argued, but social organization forces them
to, driving them to it with a whip. If it were true that compulsory labor
was unproductive, he argued, "our entire socialist economy would be doomed
to failure. For we can have no way to socialism except by the authoritative
regulation of the economic forces and resources of the country, and the
centralized distribution of labor power in harmony with the general state
plan."[15] The NEP constituted an admission that forced labor was unproductive after all. It was an attempt to find "another road to socialism." The
principle of concentration, the amalgamation of enterprises into "trusts,"
was introduced, along with that of *khozraschet* (the requirement that an
enterprise be financially self-sustaining, rather than dependent on central
state funds). On January 1, 1922, the principle of self-financing was extended to the forced labor camps. *Pravda* wrote on August 30, 1922: "The
experience of the first few months during which the compulsory labor camps
have operated on the basis of self-financing have produced positive results."

In 1921, after all the horrors of world war, revolution, and civil war, one more calamity befell Russia: a famine of such severity as the country had never known.

The threat of famine became evident early in the summer of 1921. At first the government sought to minimize the extent of the disaster. On August 6, in an appeal to the world proletariat, Lenin announced that "several provinces" of Russia were affected by a famine no less terrible than the famine of 1891. The population of the famine-struck Volga region in 1891 was 964,627. In 1921 the count was in the millions: no less than 20 percent of the country's population and more than 25 percent of the rural population starved.[16] The famine was grisly. The writer Mikhail Osorgin, editor of the newsletter *Pomoshch* (Relief), the organ of the All-Russia Famine Relief Committee, knew the situation in the areas of famine from the hundreds of letters the committee received. He wrote about the cannibalism that became an everyday occurrence: "People mainly ate members of their own families as they died, feeding on the older children, but not sparing newborn infants either, those who had hardly had the chance to live, despite the fact that there wasn't much to them. People ate off to themselves, not sitting together at a table, and no one talked about it."[17] The famine was a test of the capabilities of the new system. For the first time it confronted a task that could not be solved by force. The success of the October revolution and the victory in the civil war had created a mentality of omnipotence among the Bolsheviks, the conviction that everything could be solved by a soldier's rifle or a Chekist's pistol. Ekaterina Kuskova recalled an account by Bonch-Bruevich of a visit to the Kremlin by Maxim Gorky in 1919.

> We entered an office and found Lenin bent over some documents in deep concentration. "What are you doing?" Gorky asked. "I'm thinking about the best way to cut the throats of all the kulaks who won't give bread to the people." "Now that's an original occupation!" Gorky exclaimed. "Yes, we are taking them head on in the fight for bread, the most elementary question of human existence."[18]

To Lenin the struggle for the existence of some was inseparable from the extermination of others. The best way to obtain bread was to "cut the throats of all the kulaks." But in 1921 throat cutting could accomplish nothing. The peasantry had no grain stocks left. Even seed grain had been confiscated. All the leaders of the Soviet government blamed the famine on the drought. In 1891 Lenin had had a different kind of explanation: "The government bore sole responsibility for the famine and 'the general ruin.'"[19] But in 1921 the famine was the result of drought and civil war. At the Tenth Party Congress Trotsky briefly summarized the results of the war:

"We have destroyed the country in order to defeat the Whites." The main cause of the famine, however, was the requisitioning policy, the policy of an immediate leap into communism.

The absence of food reserves, the spread of the famine to the cities (unlike in 1891), the ruined transport system, the peasant revolts, and the unrest among the workers—all these created a critical situation. Only the capitalist countries were in a position to provide immediate assistance, more exactly, only the United States, because Western Europe was exhausted by the war and was barely able to feed itself. The Soviet government, however, would not ask the capitalists for help, assuming that they would automatically reject such a request. To Lenin it seemed only natural that the capitalist countries would refuse to help a government whose openly proclaimed goal was world revolution. Nevertheless, the impossible situation finally forced Lenin, after long hesitation, to agree to the formation of a nongovernmental organization, the All-Russia Famine Relief Committee. On July 21, 1921, Mikhail Kalinin signed the decree of the Central Executive Committee authorizing formation of the committee, which included some of the most prominent Russian scientists, literary and cultural figures, and political personalities of the prerevolutionary era. Many of them hesitated a long time before agreeing to collaborate with the Soviet government.

Lenin set precise limits on this never to be repeated experiment in cooperation on an equal basis between the Soviet government and the Russian intelligentsia:

Today's directive to the Politburo: Kuskova must be rendered strictly harmless. You are in the "Communist cell" [of the Famine Relief Committee] and will have to be on your toes, keeping a strict watch over everything. We shall get Kuskova to give us her name, her signature, and a couple of carloads [of food] from those who sympathize with her (and others of her stripe). Not a thing more. (Lenin's emphasis—M. H.)[20]

Ekaterina Kuskova, a journalist who had been prominent in the early Russian Social Democratic movement, later a liberal, was one of the initiators of the committee. She explained to Kamenev: "Help can come only from abroad. It will not come by itself. They will think their aid will go to you and the Red Army rather than to those who are starving."[21] A guarantee was necessary. The All-Russia Famine Relief Committee served as that guarantee. Gorky, a member of the committee, appealed to world public opinion to send aid, as did the committee as a whole.

During this period Lenin's prime concern was to assure food supplies to the industrial centers, above all to Moscow and Petrograd. Every day he sent telegrams to the southern and eastern parts of the country calling for bread. "In view of the extremely grave food supply situation at the center," he said in a telegram to Rakovsky, chairman of the Ukrainian Council of People's Commissars, "I propose: three quarters to be brought here, one quarter to be left for the cities and workers of the Ukraine. . . . But bear in mind that the food crisis here is desperate and downright dangerous."[22] In a telegram of May 4 he ordered the Siberian Revolutionary Committee to send 3 million poods (1 million centners) of wheat to the center during the month of May. His telegram of July 12, 1921, to Turkestan said: "With the same speed required in urgent military matters, it is of major political importance that you immediately load and send freight cars, express, to Moscow with 250,000 poods [82,000 centners] of wheat."[23] The lessons of the February crisis that produced Kronstadt were still fresh. Grain was confiscated from any possible source to prevent food riots in the working-class centers. A "shameful peace" was made with the intelligentsia, and Lenin bided his time, waiting for the New Economic Policy to produce results. But before these results materialized, who should come to the rescue but the imperialists.

On August 21, 1921, Maxim Litvinov, representing the Soviet Union, signed an agreement in Riga with a representative of the American Relief Administration (ARA), headed by Herbert Hoover. When N. Kutler, a member of the All-Russia Famine Relief Committee, heard about this agreement, he said: "Well, it's time for us to go home. . . . Our job is done. Now only 35 percent of the population in the areas of the famine will die, instead of 50 or 70 percent."[24] Kutler was only partly right. The help from abroad did save millions, but it was not time for the committee members "to go home." Most of them were arrested right after the agreement with the ARA was signed, that is, as soon as they were no longer needed.

The August 31 *Pravda* reported on a special meeting of the Moscow Soviet at which its president, Lev Kamenev, "noted with satisfaction that an agreement had been reached between the Soviet government and Herbert Hoover's organization, an agreement that has already brought tangible results." Kamenev reported that the first ship "loaded with food for the children" had arrived in Petrograd that day and that regular shipments would be coming from then on.

A man named Eiduk, a veteran agent of the Cheka who was attached to the ARA as the Soviet government's representative, writing in *Pravda*, May 25, 1922, gave the following summary of the work of the ARA and other relief organizations. As of May 1922, the ARA had fed 7,099,574 persons;

the American Friends Service Committee, 265,000; the International Child Relief Association, 250,751; the Nansen Committee, 138,000; the Swedish Red Cross, 87,000; the German Red Cross, 7,000; the British trade unions, 92,000; and the International Red Aid organization, 78,011. The article on the ARA in the 1926 edition of the *Great Soviet Encyclopedia* provides further information: The ARA was active in Russia from October 1, 1921, to June 1, 1923; at the height of its activity it fed approximately 10 million people; it spent nearly 137 million gold rubles during its operations, while the Soviet government spent approximately 15 million gold rubles in connection with the ARA. By 1930 the official Soviet reference works had changed their tone in regard to the ARA. The *Small Soviet Encyclopedia* of 1930 stated that "under the pretext of charity" the ARA had "helped to reduce the severity of the economic crisis in America by finding outlets for American goods." In 1950 the second edition of the *Great Soviet Encyclopedia* asserted that the ARA "took advantage of the fact that it was allowed to organize its own apparatus on Soviet territory to engage in espionage and subversion and support counterrevolutionary elements. The counterrevolutionary actions of the ARA were energetically protested by the broad masses of the working people." The encyclopedia did not bother to explain why the ARA was allowed to operate on Soviet soil or what work it did other than "espionage and subversion." The first volume of the most recent edition of the *Great Soviet Encyclopedia* now admits that the ARA was "of some help in fighting the famine," but it still contends that "the ruling circles of the United States tried to use it to support counterrevolutionary elements, espionage, and subversion, to fight the revolutionary movement, and to strengthen the position of American imperialism in Europe."[25] According to the figures of the Central Statistical Bureau of the USSR, 5,053,000 lives were lost because of the famine of 1921–1922.[26] These losses should be added to the 10,180,000 killed in the civil war of 1918–1920. Altogether, from 1918 to 1922, the country lost more than 14 million people, approximately 10 percent of the population. The Soviet demographer B. Ts. Urlanis gave the following estimates for the percentages of populations lost in other major civil wars: Spain, 1936–1939, 1.8 percent; the United States, 1861–1865, 1.6 percent. These figures help to illustrate the monstrous dimensions of the bloodletting in the Russian civil war. If we add to this the nearly 2 million lives Russia lost in World War I and the nearly 1 million persons lost to emigration after the revolution, we can understand how much the population diminished from 1914 to 1922.[27] The famine was a major test for the young Soviet government. All the unique features of the system were displayed: cruelty, vengefulness, and obstinacy. Lenin was willing to sacrifice a substantial section of the peasantry as long as the industrial centers were kept in food. Gorky, who was pressured by Lenin into leaving the Soviet Republic late in 1921, expressed his attitude toward the peasantry in a Berlin interview with Western journalists, an attitude that undoubtedly reflected the views of Lenin and the other Bolsheviks. "I assume that most of the 35 million affected by the famine will die."[28] The great humanist was optimistic about the future: "The half-savage, stupid, difficult people of the Russian villages will die out . . . and their place will be taken by a new tribe of the literate, the intelligent, the vigorous."[29] This dream, or at least its first part, was realized ten years later. Those who hindered its immediate realization, especially those active in the All-Russia Famine Relief Committee, paid the price. Many of them, including Kuskova, were expelled from the Soviet Republic in 1922; others were arrested and sent into internal exile. The history of the committee and of relations with the ARA set the pattern for the Soviet government's dealing with those who tried to help it while maintaining their own independence: (1) make concessions, if there is no alternative; (2) renounce all concessions when the need for them is past; and (3) take revenge.

The famine showed the new government's stability, the determining factor behind which was the party, its ranks hardened by the awareness of their total isolation within the country, by the elitist character of their organization, and by a feeling of total omnipotence. If the party was the skeleton of the state, the Cheka gave it muscle. The party was the source of the Idea: that everything is permitted because the party is doing the work of History. The Cheka provided the hands to put this great, all-permitting Idea into practice. Gorky made the categorical assertion that "the cruelty of the forms taken by the revolution is explained, in my opinion, by the exceptional cruelty of the Russian people."[30] He called the charges of brutality against the leaders of the revolution "lies and slander." In this he expressed the naiveté common to many of his contemporaries, who failed to understand the true nature of the system then coming into existence, a system in which the repressive bodies played a vital role. Their omnipresence and omnipotence created a paralyzing atmosphere of fear in Soviet society. Along with fear, the enticements of hope contributed in a very important way to stability. The New Economic Policy embodied a promise of improvement in the situation. Soviet citizens began to assume—as they would many times thereafter—that since things couldn't get worse, they were bound to get better. Finally, the absence of any alternative contributed to stability. The program of the Whites had been defeated, and the socialist opponents of bolshevism were robbed of their arguments by the introduction of the NEP. The people had nothing left but to hope for the future.

Leonid Krasin, invited to London by Lloyd George to discuss the normalization of Anglo-Soviet relations, gave an interview to the London *Observer*, which was printed with the headline, "How the Famine Is Helping the Soviet Government." The attitude of the West toward starving Russia seems to have opened Lenin's eyes. He saw that the capitalist world did not understand the goals of the revolution. Ignorant of the danger, the capitalists preferred to make their profits today rather than think about tomorrow.

The lifting of the blockade by the Allies in January 1920 meant the end of their war against Soviet Russia. This action was followed by peace treaties between the Soviet Republic and three neighboring countries, Estonia, Latvia, and Lithuania. In May 1920 Krasin began negotiations for a trade treaty. In July the Soviet government accepted Britain's three conditions: an end to hostilities and to propaganda warfare; repatriation of prisoners of war; and recognition in principle of debts to private individuals. At the height of the Polish–Soviet war the trade treaty was signed. Upon his return home, Krasin told the Communists of Petrograd how he had applied pressure to the British government:

> We did everything we could to attract the British business community. When the honest burghers of the commercial establishment declined, we turned to the semi-speculator elements. We signed an agreement with the Armstrong Gun Factory for the repair of 1,500 locomotives. Armstrong put pressure on his workers, who in turn pressured Lloyd George by pointing out that orders from Russia would reduce unemployment. The British bourgeoisie began to have apprehensions about competition from Germany, and the trade agreement was signed.

Krasin also announced forthcoming agreements with Norway and Italy. Around the same time Sweden agreed to accept Soviet gold, the first country to do so. "At present," the people's commissar of foreign trade boasted, "we are very close to obtaining a major loan, and this big loan will be given by none other than France."[31] When Lenin was warned in the summer of 1921 by opponents of his harsh policy toward the Famine Relief Committee that the arrest of its members might affect relations with France, formerly the chief supporter of the White movement, Lenin replied with full self-assurance: "Our policy will not undercut [trade] relations with France; it will speed them up. . . . We are on the way to achieving trade talks with France."[32] The agreement with the ARA convinced Lenin once and for all that it was possible to establish normal trade and diplomatic relations with the capitalist world by using the industrial and commercial interests against the diplomats and, conversely, using the diplomats against the industrial and commercial interests. Above all, the Soviet leaders concluded that it was possible to have normal relations with the capitalists without abandoning the goal of world revolution.


## A BI-LEVEL FOREIGN POLICY

In the spring of 1919 an unofficial diplomatic mission sent by Lloyd George and Woodrow Wilson and headed by the American William Bullitt arrived in Moscow. Bullitt inquired into the Bolsheviks' attitude toward a possible armistice between the Red and White armies, but in his detailed reports from Moscow he failed to mention the First Congress of the Third, or Communist, International (the Comintern). The congress was in session in the Soviet Republic's capital during Bullitt's visit and *Pravda* wrote about it at length, but the news seemed to have no interest for the Allied representative.

Of the thirty-four "delegates" to the First Congress of the Comintern, thirty lived in Moscow and worked for the People's Commissariat of Foreign Affairs, two were chance visitors (from Norway and Sweden, where there were no Communist parties), and only two were actually mandated by foreign Communist parties. One of them, Hugo Eberlein, represented the German Communist party (KPD), which had been founded two months earlier. He had come to Moscow to express his party's disagreement with the idea of founding the Comintern. Rosa Luxemburg, the moving spirit behind the KPD, was opposed to the formation of a new international as long as "the relative backwardness of the Western revolutionary parties leaves all the initiative in the hands of the Bolsheviks." Despite Eberlein's objections, Lenin insisted that the birth of the Third International be proclaimed in March 1919.

The new international organization, with its headquarters in Moscow and the expenses of its founding paid for by the Bolshevik party was awash in the glow of victorious revolution. It disdained to conceal its aims. In the first issue of the magazine *Kommunisticheskii internatsional* (Communist international) Grigory Zinoviev published an article, "The Prospects for Proletarian Revolution," in which he made this prediction: "Civil war has flared up throughout Europe. The victory of communism in Germany is absolutely inevitable. In a year Europe will have forgotten about the fight for communism, because all of Europe will be Communist. Then the struggle for communism in America will begin, and possibly in Asia and other continents."

The Second Congress of the Comintern, in the summer of 1920, laid the basis for a bi-level foreign policy. The congress adopted the famous "twenty-one conditions" that had to be met by any party wishing to join the Comintern, to become a section of the Third International. The standard pattern for a Communist party was established. It would be a detachment of an international army engaged in the struggle for power. Among the conditions for admission to the Comintern were the following: the obligation to help the Soviet Republic in its struggle against counterrevolution, employing all legal and illegal means to this end (condition 13); the obligation to combine legal and illegal methods in fighting against the government of one's own country (condition 3); and the obligation to form an underground organization (condition 4).

The classic example of a bi-level foreign policy—aboveboard through the Commissariat of Foreign Affairs and secretly through the Comintern—was Soviet policy toward Germany. The certainty of a revolution in Germany was one of the main arguments Lenin had used to justify the October revolution. The events of November 1918, when Germany might have become Communist but failed to do so, discouraged the Bolsheviks, but they did not give up hope. The Soviet government began to cooperate on the official level with the Weimar Republic, but activity aimed at the Sovietization of Germany never ceased. This activity increased sharply after the founding of the Comintern. A number of "specialists" on revolution—Radek, Zinoviev, Bela Kun, Matyas Rakosi—made preparations for the seizure of power by the German Communists. In April 1922 Germany and Soviet Russia signed a peace treaty in the Italian city of Rapallo. It provided for mutual renunciation of demands for war reparations, the establishment of diplomatic relations, and economic collaboration, including joint Soviet–German industrial and commercial firms. The Rapallo treaty broke the unity of the capitalist countries vis-à-vis Soviet Russia and freed both Germany and the Soviet Republic from diplomatic isolation. The obvious advantages of the Soviet–German treaty, the result of the Soviet government's own initiatives, did not prevent the Soviet leaders from continuing to use the Comintern and the KPD to foment revolution. In the fall of 1923, in fact, it seemed that nothing would stop the mighty forward stride of history.

"At the beginning of September 1923," a former Soviet diplomat wrote,

I passed through Moscow on my way to Warsaw. In Moscow everyone seemed fired up. The revolutionary movement in Germany was growing faster and faster. . . . Comintern work was going ahead full steam. The future members of the Soviet government of Germany were being appointed. From among Soviet Russian leaders a solid group was chosen to become the nucleus of the future German Council of People's Commissars. The group included economic experts ... military men ... Comintern figures ... and several highly placed GPU officials.[33]

At that time *Pravda* published some verses about Germany in flames: "A cry in the wind: It is time! In the swirling snow, a slogan: Fire!" During this time official relations between the Soviet and German governments remained impeccable.

Relations with England provide another example of the Soviet dual policy. England began to seek a rapprochement with Soviet Russia in 1920. Trade talks began. Some trade was already underway "through various neutral countries that had established trade relations with Soviet Russia."[34] Karl Radek noted that this situation helped Russia to grow stronger. The same Radek, at the Baku Congress of the Peoples of the East in September 1920, called on the workers and peasants of Persia, Turkey, and India to rise up against British imperialism, promising in the name of the Soviet government to provide arms "for our common battles and common victories."[35] Likewise at the Baku Congress Zinoviev, chairman of the Comintern, called for a jihad, a holy war, against Great Britain. Zinoviev was a member of the Politburo, the top executive body of the Soviet state. "It is no secret to anyone," Lev Kamenev, another member of the Politburo, admitted, "that the Central Committee and the Politburo of our party direct the Comintern."[36]

The foreign policy of the young Soviet state was based on a principle enunciated by Lenin in December 1920: as long as capitalism and socialism exist they cannot live in peace.[37] At the height of the debates over the Brest-Litovsk treaty, Lenin presented a resolution to the Seventh Party Congress. It stated that the Congress authorized the Central Committee to break any and all peace treaties and to declare war against any imperialist government or against the entire world if the Central Committee considered the moment ripe.[38] The resolution was meant to placate the opponents of the Brest-Litovsk treaty, but it expressed the essence of Lenin's foreign policy. The proletarian state, the embodiment of progress, was always right in its relations with capitalist states, which were the embodiment of reaction. Whatever the Soviet state did was in accordance with the laws of history and therefore was entirely and completely justified.

## THE RED TURNS RUSTY

The "step backward" Lenin took in March 1921 with the introduction of the NEP was conceived as a maneuver, a forced retreat. It was carried out on a moment's notice, a complete surprise to the ranks of the Bolshevik party. Stalin suggested that the maneuver was a little late in coming: "Didn't we wait too long to abolish grain requisitioning? Did we really need such events as Kronstadt and Tambov to make us realize we could not go on living under war communism?"[39]

The realization that it was impossible to live under war communism forced the government to change its policy, to abandon utopia temporarily and return to reality. But utopia was not rejected altogether; hope for the miracle of world revolution was kept alive. It was necessary to arrange a certain coexistence between reality and fantasy, the belief that tomorrow or the day after it would again be possible to take two, three, many more steps toward the final goal of communism. The coexistence of reality and fantasy gave a special quality to Soviet life in the early 1920s. As one Soviet poet described it, "The color of the times has changed. No longer Red, but rusty."[40]

For the second time in a few years a drastic reevaluation of values took place. Revolutionary ideas, which had reigned unchallenged since October 1917, sweeping aside all compromise or deviation from the ideal, suddenly seemed old-fashioned and out of place. The right to exist was restored to concepts that before March 1921 had been considered extinct or worthy of extinction.

The New Economic Policy removed the tourniquets that had totally cut off the country's blood supply. Denationalization of small businesses and of some medium-sized industries, legalization of private trade, and the beginnings of trade with foreign countries quickly restored circulation. People at the time commented on the miraculous opening of stores and the appearance in them of things people had once known but had forgotten even the look of. The hero of the novel *Chevengur* returns to his hometown:

> At first he thought the Whites had taken [it]. There was a buffet at the train station where gray rolls were sold without a line and without ration cards. Near the station . . . there was a gray sign whose letters dripped because of the poor quality of the paint. The sign announced primitively and briefly:

> **Everything on Sale, To All Citizens! Prewar Bread!**
> **Prewar Fish! Fresh Meat! Our Own Preserves!**

> . . . In the store the owner explained in a very concise and sensible way, to an old woman who had just come in, the meaning of these changes: "We've lived to see the day. Lenin tooketh away, and now Lenin giveth."[41]

The NEP opened the door to certain capitalist economic forms which coexisted with the socialist forms. It was possible to compare and make choices. The result was competition. The 1923 census revealed that 77 percent of wholesale trade was conducted by the state, 8 percent by co-operatives, and 15 percent by private individuals. In contrast, 83 percent of retail trade was in private hands and only 7 percent was state-controlled.[42] The consumer could choose whether to buy from the government or from a private trader.

Money, which had lost all value during the revolution and civil war, reappeared on the scene. In principle it was supposed to have withered away. Besides, everyone had been issuing currency: the Soviet government, the White generals, municipalities, even factories. A numismatic catalog published in 1927 listed 2,181 types of currency that had circulated during the civil war. Mikhail Bulgakov wrote about "trillionaires," people owning trillions of rubles, in Moscow in late 1921.[43] When the possibility arose of using this money actually to buy goods, it suddenly became a serious factor. On February 15, 1924, a series of monetary reforms ended with the intro-duction of a new unit, a ruble with fixed value. It was called the *chervonets* and was worth ten prewar gold rubles. Backed by government gold, it also had historical tradition behind it. A unit of currency of the same name had existed under Peter the Great.

The times became "rusty" because, alongside the hierarchy of values created by the revolution, old values were restored. For example, a class of capitalists was now sanctioned by the Soviet government, although they were allowed no political power. These were the so-called Nepmen. They lived like people on the slope of a volcano, never knowing what the morrow might bring. But they had money, for the moment, and with it the opportunity to buy anything they wished. In the cities gambling houses and cabarets opened for business; luxury cars and coaches, furs and jewelry made their appearance.

The NEP inevitably provoked discontent within the ruling Communist party. It seemed a complete betrayal of revolutionary ideals. The hurt and angry question, Is this what we fought for? began to be heard. Before and after October 1917 the debates among the party's leaders had been about how to take power and how to hold it. Now a new question arose: What should we do with the power? This immediately led to another: Who in fact was exercising power?

The simplest answer was the proletariat. That was the official answer. Lenin had another answer: the dictatorship of the party, the vanguard of the proletariat. There was a problem, though. Ever since the civil war had ended, the proletariat had expressed its discontent more and more insis-tently. Radek quoted with indignation the words of an independent worker in reply to a Communist agitator: "No, we are not trying to get freedom for the capitalists and landowners. We want freedom for ourselves, the workers and peasants, freedom to buy what we need, freedom to travel from one city to another, to go from the factories to the villages—that's the kind of freedom we need."[44]

The Bolshevik party was the master of the country. The party had been conceived and built as an army of professional revolutionaries. After it had achieved its aim of taking power, it did not wish to limit itself, to surrender part of its power to non-Communist government officials. The party wanted to be the government. Lev Kamenev, speaking at the Twelfth Party Congress in 1923, dotted all the i's.

> Those who speak against the party, who demand a separation of functions between the party and the government, want to impose on us the same division of powers that exists in other states. . . . Let the Soviet government apparatus govern, they say, and let the party occupy itself with propaganda, with raising the level of Communist consciousness, etc. No, comrades, that would be too great an occasion for rejoicing for our enemies.[45]

The party did not wish the Soviet state to be like "other states." It wanted all the power in its own hands.

Certainly the party had all the power. "We have quite enough political power," Lenin said in a speech to the Eleventh Party Congress in March 1922. "The economic power in the hands of the proletarian state is quite adequate to ensure the transition to communism. What then is lacking?" By the time the Eleventh Congress took place, the party had been thoroughly purged as a result of a decision of the Tenth Congress a year earlier; in the intervening year 23.3 percent of the membership had been expelled. Still the party's leader was dissatisfied with the organization, even in its purged form. Lenin scolded the Communists for their lack of sophistication and questioned whether they were actually directing the machinery of state or being directed by it. He cited the lessons of history: "If the conquering nation is more sophisticated than the vanquished nation, the former imposes its culture upon the latter; but if the opposite is the case, the vanquished nation imposes its culture upon the conqueror." Lenin feared that his barbarians, having conquered Russia, were adopting the culture of those they had vanquished. He assailed the Communists for their lack of "sophistication," by which he meant knowledge of administrative methods for running the state and the economy.[46]

According to Lenin, during the year from the Tenth to the Eleventh Congress, "we showed quite clearly that we cannot run the economy." The reason for poor management, in Lenin's opinion, was "Communist conceit" (komchvanstvo).[47] Communist conceit was the arrogance of conquerors who were sure that everything they did was right and that all problems could be solved by force. This kind of arrogance was a sin in Lenin's eyes because it undermined party discipline. The heroes of the civil war wanted their reward; each behaved like a prince in his own domain. Former front-line comrades formed cliques and challenged the authority of the Central Committee. Lenin's tactic was to use one clique against the other, seeking to weaken them all and strengthen the Central Committee.

Aleksei Rykov described the situation to Liberman, a prominent specialist in the prerevolutionary lumber industry, who was invited to take charge of the nationalized Soviet lumber industry:

> Here I am in charge of socialist construction at the head of the Supreme Economic Council. Lenin trusts me—yet it's so hard working with him! You can never rely on him 100 percent. I go see him, we talk things over, we come to an agreement, he tells me: "Take the floor and I'll support you." But the moment he senses that the majority is against your proposal, he will betray you. . . . Vladimir Ilyich will betray anyone, abandon anything, but all in the name of the revolution and socialism, remaining loyal only to the fundamental idea—socialism, communism.[48]

For Lenin the fundamental idea was embodied in the party, to which he was always loyal. His struggle against the Workers' Opposition, an intra-party grouping which opposed his policies at the Tenth Party Congress, was carried out under the banner of party unity. The mortal sin of the Workers' Opposition was that it objected to the idea of equating the party with the working class and to the party's claim to dictatorial power in the name of the "proletarian vanguard." The Workers' Opposition complained that the working class was the only class "dragging out a miserable existence doing convict labor."[49] It called for the trade unions to defend the interests of the workers and for the management of the economy to be turned over to the unions. This was an infringement on the "fundamental idea," the party's monopoly of power.

The monopoly of power did not mean a monopoly by all the members of the party. Lenin was displeased with the membership. In his speech to the Eleventh Party Congress he said: "It must be admitted, and we must not be afraid to admit, that in ninety-nine cases out of one hundred the responsible Communists are not in the jobs they are now fit for, that they are unable to perform their duties, and that they must settle down to learn."[50]

In 1919 Trotsky had referred to the military commissars as a new order of samurai.[51] In 1921 Stalin, following his usual practice, borrowed this idea from his rival, but made it less grandiloquent, more precise and detailed. Stalin described the Communist party as "an order of Teutonic knights within the Soviet state who direct the bodies of the state and inspire their activities."[52] Both Trotsky and Stalin saw the party as an elite order inspired by a particular idea (Trotsky's commissars were the party's "best elements"), but each chose his metaphor according to his own taste. The fundamental difference between the samurai and the Teutonic knights was that the "dog knights," as Marx called them, forcibly converted the people of an occupied country to the true faith, whereas the samurai lived in their own country.

Developing the parallel between the Communist party and the Knights of the Sword, Stalin emphasized the "importance of the old guard within this mighty order." But he also noted that the old guard had been reinforced since 1917 by new leaders who had been "steeled in the struggle." Thus we see that a year before he was elected general secretary of the Central Committee, Stalin envisaged the party as a conquering order in an occupied country structured along rigorously hierarchical lines.

Soviet society was a hierarchical pyramid with the ruling party at the top. At the bottom was the peasantry; a bit higher, the useful intelligentsia; higher still, the working class; and at the very top, the party boss. In one of the earliest Soviet novels, *The Week*, written by the Communist novelist Yuri Libedinsky, a Cheka official named Klimin describes an argument he had had with a certain intellectual "over the question of special dining facilities for responsible officials." The intellectual had argued that such facilities should be closed.

> His line was that the revolution requires us to stay within the limits of the average ration, even in the case of qualified personnel. But my reasoning is this: We are the revolution; we, who at our meetings call ourselves the leading vanguard. If each of us, besides the pain and work we have to bear, had to go hungry, it would weaken us and put a strain on us, and in that case our vanguard wouldn't last very long. It's pretty simple after all. For them, for revolutionaries, the revolution is something apart from themselves, an idol demanding sacrifices, but as for me . . . I can say, the way some king did once, "I am the state."[53]

The same Cheka philosopher had a discussion with a young Communist woman who suggested that words rather than force be used to explain the party's policies to the peasants. This was his response to her:

> Talk with them? . . . They wouldn't understand. As if these hardworking peasants hadn't killed plenty of our propagandists and political activists for no reason except that they preached communism too openly. They don't read our books; they use our newspapers to roll their cigarettes. No, Anyuta, things are much more complicated. We have to reshape their lives. They

are savages; they live alongside us but they're still in the Middle Ages; they believe in sorcerers, and to them we're just some special kind of sorcerer. [54]

. This young Communist woman, who had not yet been "steeled in the struggle," needed this kind of ideological working over because she had been to Moscow and had seen a stairway in a railway station there

> a big set of stairs, full of people from top to bottom. Men, women, children, lying on the stairs surrounded by their miserable filthy things. . . . And down this awful stairway, stepping disgustedly and carefully, mostly disgustedly, came an ever so elegant commissar, and his commissar's star was shining on his chest, and ever so carefully among these filthy, tired bodies he placed the tips of his shiny lacquered boots. [55]

This stairway was realistically described by a proletarian writer. It had not yet dawned on him that he should not and must not write this way. The scene on the stairs could serve as a symbol of the young Soviet state.

The party, an order of knights in a conquered country, of sorcerers among savages, could not carry out its functions as master in the land unless it was solidly united, unless it was a docile instrument in the hands of its leaders. The need for unity seemed especially obvious to Lenin during the transition to the NEP. An army requires discipline more than ever when it is retreating. The Tenth Party Congress passed a resolution against the "anarchist and syndicalist deviation," meaning the Workers' Opposition, and another "On Party Unity," which banned factional activity on pain of expulsion.

The resolution on party unity opened a new chapter in the history of the Bolshevik party. It is significant that this resolution, voted in the absence of approximately 200 delegates, who had left the congress to help suppress the Kronstadt revolt and the Antonov movement, remained secret for several years. The authors of the resolution, and all those who voted for it, felt unconsciously that the character of the party was changing. Only Radek, with a sense of foreboding, warned the delegates that one day they might feel its effects on their own necks; but this did not stop him from voting for it. The resolution eliminated the last remnants of the socialist movement's traditional democratic principles. The Bolshevik party became a totalitarian party in which loyalty to ideas became intolerable. The sole requirement of members was loyalty to the top leadership, which made all the decisions. The abrupt turn to the NEP became a test of such loyalty. Those who persisted in believing in ideas, who would not accept the "rusty color of the times," were expelled from the party, left it on their own, or committed suicide. On May 20, 1922, *Pravda* published an obituary for a seventeen-year-old Young Communist who had committed suicide: "He was often heard to say that first of all one must be a Communist and only after that a human being." The young man apparently had not been able to withstand the conflict. The Communist in his soul had not been able to defeat the human being and so killed him. But for many the victory over human feeling came easily.

Two weeks after the October revolution Maxim Gorky wrote: "Lenin, Trotsky, and their comrades have already been affected by the vile poison of power, a fact attested by their shameful attitude toward freedom of speech, individual freedoms, and all those rights for whose triumph democrats have always fought."[56] Two and a half years later, in early 1921, Aron Solts, a man known as the "conscience of the party," had this to say:

> Being in power for a long time in the era of the dictatorship of the proletariat has had a corrupting effect on a significant number of veteran party activists. This is the source of their bureaucratism, their extremely haughty attitude toward rank-and-file party members and toward the unaffiliated mass of workers; this is the source of their extraordinary abuse of their privileged position for their own material advancement. A Communist hierarchical caste has been created and entrenched.[57]

To party official Solts this "Communist hierarchical caste"—or, as Stalin put it, "order of knights"—had developed and taken shape as a result of being in power for a long time. Bukharin, the eminent party theoretician, saw deeper causes: "A certain stratum of Communist cadre could degenerate on the basis of their being the sole authority. . . . Our form of government is a dictatorship; our party is the party that dominates the country."[58]

Zinoviev, not having the power of clairvoyance, proclaimed with pride at the Eleventh Congress:

> We have a monopoly on legality. We have denied political freedom to our opponents. We do not permit legal existence to those who aspire to become our rivals. . . . The dictatorship of the proletariat, as Comrade Lenin has said, is a very harsh thing. In order to assure the victory of the proletarian dictatorship there is no other way than to break the back of all opposition to this dictatorship. . . . No one can foresee a time when we will be able to revise our opinion on this question.

The party's unlimited dictatorial power was the main cause of its degeneration. It transformed revolutionaries into veritable feudal lords, and it invited an influx of careerists and fortune hunters. In impotent rage Lenin demanded that corrupt Communists be "tried on the spot and shot, unconditionally." But it was precisely such people—without any ideals or convictions—who did best as members of a dictatorial party with a monopoly on power. Rosa Luxemburg's predictions were realized to the letter. A few months after the October revolution she had written:

> [With] the repression of political life in the land as a whole, life in the Soviets must also become more and more crippled. Without general elections, without unrestricted freedom of press and assembly, without a free struggle of opinion, life dies out in every public institution, becomes a mere semblance of life in which only the bureaucracy remains as the active element. . . . A few dozen party leaders of inexhaustible energy and boundless experience direct and rule. Among them, in reality only a dozen outstanding heads do the leading and an elite of the working class is invited from time to time to meetings where they are to applaud the speeches of the leaders, and to approve proposed resolutions unanimously—at bottom, then, a clique affair—a dictatorship, to be sure, not the dictatorship of the proletariat, however, but only the dictatorship of a handful of politicians.[59]

One year after the introduction of the NEP, at the Eleventh Party Congress, Lenin made a surprising admission. He said the Soviet state was "like a car that was going not in the direction the driver desired, but in the direction someone else desired; as if it were being driven by some mysterious, lawless hand, God knows whose. . . . The car is not going in the direction the man at the wheel wanted it to go."[60] These were the tragic words of a man who believed he had discovered the laws governing the motion of the vehicle of state, who thought he knew the direction in which it was going, but who suddenly discovered that the machine was out of his control. His response was to strengthen the hand at the wheel.

On Lenin's suggestion, the Central Committee that convened after the Eleventh Congress elected Joseph Stalin to a newly created position, that of general secretary. Lenin was confident of Stalin's abilities as a "driver." They had been thoroughly tested during the civil war.

In 1920, in his pamphlet *Left-Wing Communism, an Infantile Disorder*, Lenin ridiculed the debates then going on about the dictatorial character of the Soviet state. To him it was "ridiculous and childish nonsense" to discuss whether there was a dictatorship of the party or of the working class, a dictatorship of the leaders or of the masses. This, he said, was "like discussing whether a man's left leg or right arm is of greater use to him."[61] But he was dissimulating. He knew perfectly well that the right arm was more important and he said as much: "To object to the necessity of a strong central power, dictatorship, and unity of will ... has become impossible."[62]

The need for a strong right arm was felt especially after the civil war, when the struggles against the countless enemies of the revolution broke out with renewed force. The liberalization of the economy was accompanied by a new wave of terror. This was another "rusty" aspect of the times. *In the Land of the NEP and the Cheka* was the title of memoirs written by Boris Cederholm, an inmate of the Solovki labor camp and one of the first to escape to the West and tell about it. The NEP and the Cheka were two sides of the same coin in Soviet Russia in the first half of the 1920s.

One initial result of the NEP was a worsening of the situation for the working class, the class with hegemony, as the propagandists loved to say. The workers went on strike out of prerevolutionary habits which had not yet been broken. They demanded better conditions. On December 2, 1923, in a speech to Moscow Communists, Stalin referred to a "wave of strikes and unrest that spread through several regions of our republic in August of this year."[63] But workers had also gone on strike in 1921 and 1922. The Smolensk Archive contains numerous reports by GPU agents on the workers' discontent over their miserable wages, late wage payments, food shortages, and the high cost of living, as well as reports on strikes at factories and workshops and on the railroads.[64] The Smolensk GPU blamed the strikes on anarchist agitation. In Moscow the Mensheviks were blamed.

At the Eleventh Party Congress Aleksandr Shlyapnikov recalled that strikes by workers in Zlatoust and Bryansk had been denounced as the "work of monarchists." Everyone was blamed for strikes—anarchists, Mensheviks, monarchists—but worst of all, the workers themselves. At the Eleventh Congress Lenin laid the theoretical basis for blaming the Russian proletariat. He said that since "large-scale capitalist industry had been destroyed and the factories and shops had ceased to function, the proletariat had disappeared." Lenin did not hesitate to revise Marx. It was true that Marx had written that those employed at factories and plants constituted the real proletariat and that this had been true of capitalism as a whole for 500 years, but "for Russia today this is not true." In response to this argument Shlyapnikov taunted Lenin: "Allow me to congratulate you on being the vanguard of a nonexistent class."

In June 1953, when the workers of East Berlin went on strike and poured into the streets to protest low wages and high prices, the East German Communist party announced that the people had not justified the confidence placed in them by the party. Bertolt Brecht wrote a poem advising the party to dissolve the people and elect a new one. The Soviet leaders had employed this formula long before Brecht. Having led a revolution in the name of a class that did not exist, they set about creating the kind of class they needed. Contempt for the interests of those who are "not real proletarians" has become a Communist virtue and has been justified "theoretically." Soviet historians have come to the conclusion that the prerevolutionary Russian worker was not a "pure proletarian."[65]

During the discussion of the situation in the party which was permitted for a short time at the end of 1923, many participants complained, "In the eyes of the workers the party cells and many party members always act as defenders of management, of increased production quotas and all kinds of deductions or layoffs. All the Communist party members seem to think it is their duty at all costs to justify every injustice, even the most obvious, to the workers."[66] If on the other hand certain individual Communists protested against management along with the workers, "our higher party bodies think that such Communists are not reliable."[67]

The most widely used word in official parlance during the NEP was *smychka*, the "bond" or alliance between the workers and the peasants. The workers supposedly played the leading role in this alliance; they were the embodiment of the dictatorship and of all progress. And yet their conditions deteriorated drastically during this time.

If the workers played the leading role, the peasants played the role of the led. Although they represented the "anarchic petit bourgeois element," their situation began to improve quickly, for agricultural products became the basis of the country's economic revival. Anastas Mikoyan wrote in his memoirs: "1922 was the first year after the revolution when not only the domestic requirement for grain was satisfied but grain began to be exported in substantial quantities."[68] Mikoyan did not mention that these exports began at a time when the ARA was still feeding millions of starving people, but there is no question that the export of grain (and lumber) in the early 1920s was the only source of foreign currency, which the Soviet republic required in order to engage in foreign trade. The peasantry was the most important economic force in the country, although its political rights were restricted. Posters began to go up appealing to the peasants: "Turn in your savings for a government loan, backed by gold, and after a while you'll be rich." But the peasants remained second-class citizens, as they were well aware. The Smolensk GPU recorded the moods among the peasantry, for example, a report covering the period May 15–31, 1922:

> Among the peasants there are no limits to the grumbling against the Soviet government and the Communists. In the conversation of every middle peasant and poor peasant, not to speak even of the kulak, the following is heard: "They aren't planning freedom for us but serfdom. The time of Boris Godunov has already begun, when the peasants were attached to the landowners. Now we [are attached] to the Jewish bourgeoisie like Modkowski, Aronson, etc."[69]

## ASSAULT ON THE HUMAN SPIRIT

Peasant discontent with the Soviet government and the policies of the Communist party increased as persecution of the church intensified. "Strange as it may seem," the religious historian Nikita Struve wrote, "the church was better prepared for revolution than the state."[70] The process of preparing the church for reform, underway since 1905, culminated in the Holy Synod of 1917, which on November 5 elected Tikhon, the metropolitan of Moscow, to be the new head, or patriarch, of the Russian Orthodox church.

Conflict between the church and the Soviet state was inevitable because the Communist party, after taking power, undertook not only to transform the country economically, socially, and politically but to create a new kind of human being, the "new man." It sought spiritual power. A decree of January 23, 1918, proclaimed the separation of church and state, the confiscation of church property, and the suppression of its legal rights. In effect the church was outlawed. In reply Patriarch Tikhon pronounced an anathema against the open and secret enemies and persecutors of the church and called on the faithful to defend the church. In March 1918 the patriarch emphatically condemned the Brest-Litovsk treaty as a betrayal of commitments given to the Russian people and the Allies. On the first anniversary of the October revolution he sent a letter to the Council of People's Commissars listing the crimes of the new government and calling for the release of prisoners and an end to violence, bloodshed, and the persecution of the faith.

The difficult position the Soviet government found itself in at the time obliged it to modify its anticlerical policy. A December 1918 memorandum by the people's commissar of justice listed certain things that should not be done, although they were being done everywhere, for example, the arbitrary closing of churches, confiscation of religious objects for revolutionary use, police raids during church services, the arrest of priests, and the drafting of priests for compulsory labor. Local soviets were urged not to offend the feelings of religious people.[71] This moderation did not last long. In March 1919 the commissar of justice suggested that local authorities "launch a war against superstition," invade the sanctuaries, take inventories, and subject all relics to scientific examination.

During the civil war Patriarch Tikhon withheld support from either side. Although he granted autonomy to bishops in areas under White control, he refused to place the authority of the church on the side of the Whites.

The famine of 1921 became the occasion for a harsh blow at the church. In August Patriarch Tikhon appealed to the heads of all Christian churches to aid the victims of the famine. A Church Famine Relief Committee was founded, and collections were taken at all churches. The government denied authorization for the church committee and ordered it dissolved. Kuskova recalled the patriarch's "tremendous energy," which "inspired all the faithful in Russia and abroad to come to the rescue." This display of energy greatly alarmed the Bolsheviks, she believed. In their eyes "the efforts of the patriarch and of our committee were nothing but an attempt to organize counterrevolution."[72]

On February 19, 1922, the patriarch urged the diocesan councils to turn over all church valuables, with the exception of sacred objects, to a fund for famine relief. On February 26 a government decree confiscated all church valuables, including sacred objects. The faithful tried to oppose this confiscation. In the three months that followed, 1,414 bloody clashes between church people and government troops were recorded.[73]

Resistance by church people in Shuya resulted in the death of four and the wounding of ten. Lenin used this occasion to send a top secret letter to the Politburo demanding total suppression of any further resistance. "This crowd [publika] must now be taught a lesson so that they won't dare even dream of resisting again for years to come."[74] Lenin gave orders to arrest as many "representatives of the reactionary bourgeoisie and reactionary clergy" as possible, to hold a public trial, and have "a very large number" shot.[75] The trial was held in Moscow in April–May 1922; eleven defendants were sentenced to death. Five were actually executed. Patriarch Tikhon was subpoenaed as a witness and later was named a defendant. He was placed under house arrest and prevented from carrying out his church duties. A related trial in Petrograd in July 1922 involved eighty-six defendants, ten of whom were sentenced to death and four executed, including Metropolitan Veniamin. During 1922 a total of 8,100 priests, monks, and nuns were executed.

"Antireligious work" continued unabated, in particular the "exposure of superstition." Items such as the following one in *Pravda*, August 5, 1922, were common: "Petrograd—On August 2 the investigator for important civil cases, in the presence of clergy and experts, including professors from the Petrograd Medical Institute, examined the relics of [Saint] Alexander Nevsky. Instead of relics the shrine turned out to contain fragments of bone mingled with rubbish."

The campaign against the church was greatly facilitated by a schism within it. A group of Petrograd clergy, headed by Aleksandr Vvedensky, visited the detained patriarch at his home and asked that they be placed in charge of the patriarchal offices, so that the church "would not be left without a directing body." The patriarch delegated his authority to Metropolitan Agafangel of Yaroslavl, but entrusted the patriarchal offices to Vvedensky and his supporters until Agafangel arrived. On May 18, 1922, they carried out a coup, announcing the abolition of the patriarchate and the formation of a "supreme" executive body of the church. This marked the birth of the Living Church, "to which the Soviet government gave its moral, material, and especially political support."[76] Great hopes were placed in the Living Church. Zinoviev told Vvedensky it seemed to him that "your group could be the starting point for a great movement on an international scale."[77] The head of the Comintern, who in 1921 had helped to found an international trade union organization, the Profintern (or Red Trade Union International), may have had in mind the formation of a religious international under the leadership of the Bolshevik party. While offering support to the Living Church and holding radiant international prospects up to its leaders, the Soviet authorities reminded them of the other side of the coin. The confirmation of death sentences for five of those condemned in the Moscow trial "was meant not only to sober up the hot-headed counter-revolutionary priests but also to give a lesson in the political ABCs to the new 'supreme' executive body of the church."[78]

From the first day of the revolution, Lenin saw the intelligentsia as the main enemy, a force that would not submit "without lengthy discussions" to the "authority of one man" (as he had said in reference to Sverdlov). There was no need to explain action against members of the intelligentsia who opposed the Soviet government. What needed explanation was persecution of the neutral strata, which were dangerous because of their instinctive kindness, their humane impulses, their compassion for all who were persecuted. In reply to a letter from Gorky objecting to mass arrests in Petrograd, Lenin set forth his credo on November 15, 1919: "In general the arrest of the Cadet public (and those sympathetic to them) is correct and necessary. . . . You have spoken unjust and angry words to me. About what? About the fact that a few dozen (or maybe a few hundred) Cadet gentlemen and Cadet sympathizers have to sit in prison for a few days in order to head off conspiracies."[79] Three days after his letter to Gorky, Lenin repeated his argument almost word for word—after all it was such a good argument—in a letter to Maria Andreeva, Gorky's one-time companion: "In order to head off conspiracies it is impossible not to arrest the entire Cadet and Cadet-sympathetic public. This entire crowd is capable of helping the conspirators. It would be criminal not to arrest them."[80] In this case Lenin had recourse to the terminology of the Slavophiles, who distinguished between the "people" and the "public," that is, the intelligentsia.

Lenin's term *Cadet sympathizer* made it possible to disregard the party membership of those who were arrested. The entire Russian intelligentsia as such was subject to accusation. The fact that many of the arrested intellectuals had helped the Bolsheviks before the revolution only compounded their guilt. If they had been so kind-hearted before, who could guarantee they would not be again—toward the Bolsheviks' enemies? Lenin came up with a very significant innovation: it was necessary to arrest not only conspirators but those "capable of helping" conspirators. In his view, the entire intelligentsia fell into that category.

One more in a series of blows against the intelligentsia fell in August 1922. On August 28 *Izvestia* simultaneously published a decree of the Central Executive Committee dissolving the All-Russia Famine Relief Committee and several sensational reports about the discovery of a plot by the so-called Petrograd Military Organization (PMO). "More than 200 people" were arrested in this case.[81] The Cheka lumped together a group of Kronstadt sailors, a group of naval officers, and a group of professors. There is every reason to believe that the PMO affair was fabricated from beginning to end. Even Soviet historians have been unable to reach a consensus on the exact "crimes" of the accused.[82] Lenin personally directed the preparations for the trial and the trial itself. A large number of Russian scientists and cultural figures were arrested, including the geography professor Tagantsev and the poet Nikolai Gumilev. A number of geologists, together with the Russian Physics and Chemistry Society, petitioned for the release of the detainees. Among those shot in the case, in addition to the "leaders of the conspiracy" and "the most dangerous conspirators," were the chemistry professor M. Tikhvinsky and Gumilev. Appeals to Lenin in behalf of these two were especially strong, because Tikhvinsky, a particularly outstanding chemist, had been a Bolshevik before the revolution, and Gumilev was one of Russia's greatest poets.

After the two were executed certain legends grew up about Lenin's alleged attempt to intercede in their behalf, that his orders to spare them arrived too late, that the Cheka agents had acted on their own. Liberman reports that Leonid Krasin was horrified when he learned that Tikhvinsky had been shot: "'They killed him in spite of Lenin's promise,' Krasin exclaimed. 'It can't be. Or maybe he knew everything. . . . Maybe it's that the revolution has its own inalterable laws. But if that is it, where will it all end? Because, you know, Vladimir Ilyich was very fond of Tikhvinsky, was on a first-name basis with him.'"[83] Krasin, who knew Lenin very well, suspected him of knowing everything. Lenin's posthumously published letters include his "resolution" on the Tikhvinsky case: "Tikhvinsky wasn't arrested by accident. Chemistry and counterrevolution are not mutually exclusive."[84] When someone approached Dzerzhinsky to ask that Gumilev be pardoned ("Were we entitled to shoot one of Russia's two or three poets of the first order?"), the head of the Cheka replied: "Are we entitled to make an exception of a poet and still shoot the others?"[85] Chemistry and counterrevolution were not mutually exclusive; neither were poetry and counterrevolution. In fact, both chemistry and poetry seemed counterrevolutionary in and of themselves. Science, poetry, the intelligentsia—all added up to counterrevolution.

The trial of the PMO was the last major trial organized by the Cheka. A decree of February 6, 1922, dissolved the Cheka and transferred its functions to the State Political Administration, better known by its Russian initials GPU. This organization was made part of the People's Commissariat of Internal Affairs (NKVD) of Soviet Russia. After the formation of the Soviet Union, the GPU became the Unified State Political Administration— OGPU. In one of his novels Ilya Ehrenburg described what two Russian letters pronounced "che" and "ka" had meant:

> For any citizen who lived during the revolution, these two syllables which children learned before they learned the word "Mama"—because they were used to frighten children even in the cradle, the way the word bogeyman had once been—two syllables that accompanied the unlucky to their death and even after, to the mass grave; two simple little letters that no one could ever forget.[86]

The two letters pronounced "che-ka" were replaced by three pronounced "gay-pay-oo." Soon these three letters would inspire no less fear than the first two. The appointment of the Cheka head Dzerzhinsky to be head of the GPU and later of the OGPU stressed the unchanging nature and role of the "organs" of repression.

The first big show trial organized by the GPU was the trial of the SRs, which began in June 1922. To Gorky, then living in the West, the trial of the SRs was an act of war against the intelligentsia. Gorky, in a letter to Rykov, which Lenin was to call "Gorky's disgusting letter," described the trial as one in a series aimed at "exterminating the intelligentsia in our illiterate country." The SR trial began just at the time when the verdict in the case of the "concealment of church treasures" was upheld. All of the charges against the SRs had to do with their activities before 1919, for which an amnesty had been declared on February 27, 1919. Twelve of the defendants were sentenced to death, but the sentences were "suspended."

Political trials were only one aspect of the war against the intelligentsia, a battle that was increasing in fury. The Central Committee announced: "In the first months of 1922 a revival of activity has become evident on the part of the former bourgeois intelligentsia."[87] The reactivation of "bourgeois ideology" could be seen in the founding of a number of privately owned publishing houses, as permitted by Soviet law, and the reappearance of such magazines as *Byloe* (The past), *Golos minuvshego* (Voice of bygone times), *Ekonomist*, and *Pravo i zhizn* (Law and life).

"Harmful tendencies" were also evident at a conference of agronomists in March 1922. These professors of agronomy and economics passed a resolution favoring "abstract legality, above classes." People's Commissar of Health Semashko informed Lenin that at a congress of physicians the doctors had "praised the liberal zemstvo tradition in medicine and called for democracy and the right to print a publication of their own." A historian of the Cheka and the GPU states that during this period "anti-Soviet organizations, operating through the intelligentsia (professors, specialists, writers) carried on work among the student youth and among petit bourgeois and philistine elements, establishing bases of support in higher educational institutions, in the press, in literary circles, and in the cooperatives."[88]

In March 1922 Lenin wrote an article "On the Significance of Militant Materialism," in which he said that the "first and foremost duty of a Communist" is to declare "a systematic offensive against bourgeois ideology, philosophical reaction, and all forms of idealism and mysticism." In a letter to GPU head Dzerzhinsky, dated May 19, 1922, Lenin translated these philosophical terms into everyday language. He referred to the intellectuals, the "professors and writers," as "patent counterrevolutionaries, accomplices of the Entente, . . . spies and corrupters of the student youth."[89] Some "professors and writers" were arrested, tried, and shot; others died of hunger. One researcher noted, "In the history of the Russian Academy of Sciences three fatal epidemics seem to have occurred: 1918–1923, 1929–1931, 1936–1938."[90] A unique feature of the first period was that many prominent Russian scientists and academicians froze or starved to death during that time. The historian cites obituaries published in the newsletter of the Russian Academy of Sciences. The obituary for the historian Lappo-Danilevsky, who died on February 7, 1919, noted: "He is the seventh victim torn from the ranks of full members of the academy since the end of May 1918." That the academy had slightly more than forty members at the time points up the extent of the catastrophe. Prominent scientists and academics continued to die, among them V. A. Zhukovsky, the founder of hydrodynamics and aerodynamics, the respected Orientalist B. A. Turaev, the great mathematician A. M. Lyapunov, the linguist A. A. Shakhmatov, and the theologian I. S. Palmov. In 1921 Lenin signed a decree on the "creation of favorable conditions for scientific work." Its aim was to save the life of Academician Ivan Pavlov, Russia's only Nobel laureate. The need for such a decree was eloquent testimony to the tragic situation in which Russian science found itself.

Lenin, in his May 19 letter to Dzerzhinsky, urged "thorough preparation" for a new method of repression aimed at the intelligentsia: the deportation of "the writers and professors helping the counterrevolution."[91]

In May 1922 Lenin also read the draft for the first Soviet penal code. He insisted that it was necessary to "put forward publicly a thesis that is correct in principle and politically correct (not just a narrow juridical thesis) that would explain the essence of terror, its necessity and limits, and the justification for it. The courts must not ban terror—to promise that would be deception or self-deception—but must formulate the motives underlying it, legalize it as a principle plainly, without any make-believe."[92] He urged that "the application of the death sentence be extended . . . to all forms of activity by the Mensheviks, SRs, and so on."[93] But his main contribution to the science of jurisprudence was the way he formulated the clause on "propaganda or agitation":

> Propaganda or agitation . . . which objectively assists that section of the international bourgeoisie which refuses to recognize the rights of the Communist system of ownership that has superseded capitalism, that section which is striving to overthrow the Communist system by violence, either by means of foreign intervention, blockade, or by espionage, financing the press, and similar means, is an offense punishable by death, which, if mitigating circumstances are proved, may be commuted to deprivation of liberty, or deportation.[94]

Lenin introduced the concept of objectively aiding the international bourgeoisie. In this way, as the Polish philosopher Leszek Kolakowski put it, Lenin "laid the foundations for the system of law characteristic of totalitarianism, as opposed to the laws of a despotic system."[95] In despotism the characteristic feature is the severity of the law. What is characteristic in a totalitarian system is the fictitious nature of the law. Lenin's contribution—the death penalty for views which might "objectively aid" the bourgeoisie—meant that the government could kill anyone it wished, anyone it disliked. Or if there were extenuating circumstances, it could send such persons to prison or labor camps or deport them. In reality, then, the law did not exist, nor did the penal code.

The first experiment in applying the new formula was the deportation of a large group of scientists, writers, doctors, and agronomists. On August 31, 1922, *Pravda* published an article entitled "A First Warning." Noting that "certain strata of the bourgeois intelligentsia have not accepted Soviet power," the newspaper reported that the "most active counterrevolutionary elements" among these strata had been arrested and sent into internal exile "in the northern provinces and some deported from the country" by a decree of the GPU. The deported professionals represented a very broad spectrum ("160 of the most active bourgeois ideologists").[96] From the few available documents and memoirs it may be gathered that the Politburo decided to strike this blow at the intelligentsia on Lenin's initiative after singling out the most important centers of independent thought which in their opinion had to be paralyzed. Some names were provided (the list of philosophers was drawn up almost entirely by Lenin himself), but for the rest the initiative was left to the GPU and to influential party leaders and their retainers who might have personal scores to settle. The list of the proscribed was drawn up with one central aim in mind: to give the intelligentsia a warning, expelling the main troublemakers and intimidating the rest. This is why the list included some people against whom no complaint had ever been made and left out others who seemed to be prime candidates for deportation.

## CHANGING LANDMARKS

Deportation from the country was a drastic measure, but compared to a death penalty handed down at a show trial, it was benign. The Soviet government could not, in 1922, risk shooting one or two hundred of the best-known Russian intellectuals; that might make too unfavorable an impression abroad. Another obstacle to mass execution was the shortage of skilled scientific and cultural personnel, whom the state needed, despite their unreliability.

In July 1921 there occurred an event which opened up new possibilities for the Communist party "on the ideological front" in relation to such skilled personnel. An anthology entitled *Smena vekh* (Changing landmarks) was published in Prague, giving distinctive shape to a movement that had first begun in the Soviet Republic, gained the active support of the Communist party—because to its members the party was coming to lose its bolshevist substance and to take on a nationalist character—then spread to the emigré community.

After the October revolution more than a million people left Russia. The exact number of emigrés remains unknown. Lenin spoke of "emigrés numbering probably from 1,500,000 to 2,000,000."[97] An emigré Russian historian refers to approximately a million.[98] A recent Soviet historian gives the figure 860,000.[99] According to statistics published by the League of Nations in 1926, 1,160,000 people left Russia after the revolution. Approximately one fourth were officers and soldiers of the White armies, including about 100,000 in Wrangel's army evacuated from the Crimea to Constantinople. Civilian emigrés came from all classes and professions, but especially from those the Soviet government considered inimical. A substantial number of the emigrés were from the intelligentsia. All political parties were represented, from the extreme right to the extreme left, from the monarchists to the Socialist Revolutionaries and anarchists. The varied political complexion of the emigré community was convincing proof that political life inside Soviet Russia had been stifled. All political parties other than the Communist party ended up in the anti-Soviet camp, some willingly, others driven to that position by the one-party dictatorship.

The emigrés had been dispersed to all parts of the world (Czechoslovakia, Yugoslavia, Bulgaria, Poland, Germany, Latvia, France, China). A great many believed they would soon return to their homeland, that the Bolsheviks were on the verge of collapse. However, defeatist tendencies also arose among the emigrés and were reinforced from within Soviet Russia. "The 'changing landmarks' trend [smenovekhovstvo] began to appear among the old intelligentsia inside the Soviet Republic as early as 1918," one Soviet historian has noted.[100] There are many similarities between the policies of the Soviet government toward priests who were willing to risk a schism in order to collaborate with the regime and its policies toward those members of the intelligentsia who were willing to make peace with the conquerors.

In the spring of 1920, after the Polish invasion of the Soviet Republic, patriotism became respectable again and provided the basis for the initial conception of "a change of landmarks" (that is, a reorientation). That summer a certain Professor Gredeskul, a former leader of the Cadet party and a noted legal expert, went on a nationwide speaking tour, with the approval and support of the authorities. He then wrote a series of articles for *Izvestia* based on his lectures. His main argument was as follows:

> It becomes clearer every day that we are not facing a dead end of history or an accidental episode but a broad, smooth, well-lighted road down which the historical process is moving. And this process, which is being guided this time by the conscious efforts of far-sighted leaders, is taking us toward the greatest transformation ever seen in human history.[101]

The idea of a change of orientation arose spontaneously among the emigrés as well as being influenced by Gredeskul and his supporters. It was also in the spring of 1920 that E. A. Efimovsky, the editor of *Slavyanskaya zarya* (Slavic dawn), an emigré newspaper published in Prague, voiced the opinion that the Bolsheviks were defending the national interest of the Russian state. In one of his articles he spoke of an inevitable conflict between Europe and Soviet Russia. "In this conflict we will be on the side of Soviet Russia. Not because it is Soviet but because it is Russia."[102] In

Paris a dramatist named Klyuchnikov gave a reading of his play *Ediny kust* (which might be rendered "From a Single Bush"). Among the guests were a number of leading Russian writers: Ivan Bunin, Aleksandr Kuprin, Aleksei Tolstoy, Mark Aldanov, and Ilya Ehrenburg, who had recently fled from the Crimea.[103] They all agreed on the play's deficiencies. Kuprin said it was dull as khaki; Tolstoy, that it was mediocre as a rusty nail. But the important thing, said Tolstoy, was the idea behind it. The theme of the play was that "the motherland is all one bush, and its many shoots, including those that grow crooked or off to the side, are fed by the same vital juices." Tolstoy drew a conclusion: "Back there in Russia the harsh wind of rejection is blowing, but here in the West there is nothing but decay, hopeless, narrow-minded materialism, and total demoralization."[104]

In the fall of 1920 a collection of articles was published in Harbin, a center of Russian emigration in Manchuria. Its author was Nikolai Ustryalov and it was entitled *The Struggle for Russia*. This book contained the essence of what was to be the changing landmarks ideology. When the anthology bearing that title actually appeared in Prague in July 1921, it provided a name for the movement but introduced nothing essentially new in comparison to Ustryalov's contributions of 1920.

Nikolai Ustryalov, a talented writer who emerged as the chief ideologist of the new movement, dedicated *The Struggle for Russia* "to General Brusilov, a courageous and loyal servant of Great Russia, both in its hour of glory and in its troubled times of suffering and misfortune." On May 30, 1920, during the Polish invasion, Brusilov had published an appeal in *Pravda* urging his readers to forget "selfish feelings of class struggle" and to remember instead "their own native Russian people" and their homeland "Mother Russia." To Ustryalov Brusilov's action seemed the model of genuine patriotism.

Ustryalov argued in his book that the defeat of the White armies had to be recognized. It was time for the defeated to make their obeisance, to go to Canossa. He called on Wrangel, who was still holding out in the Crimea, to "convert" voluntarily, to accept "the other faith" and hail the example of Brusilov.[105] The Russian intelligentsia, Ustryalov held, fought against bolshevism for many reasons, but its nationalist motives were the main ones.[106] The intelligentsia had opposed the revolution because it was destroying the state, causing the army to fall apart and bringing humiliation to the motherland. Without this nationalist inspiration, Ustryalov felt, the struggle against the Bolsheviks would have been senseless and would not have occurred.

The defeat of the White armies, said Ustryalov, had opened his eyes.

He confessed that, along with most of the Russian intelligentsia, he had misjudged bolshevism. Ustryalov's new outlook could be reduced to three points. First, the Russian revolution had in essence been a nationalist one. Its roots went back to the Slavophiles, the pessimism of Chaadaev, Herzen's revolutionary romanticism, and Pisarev's utilitarianism. Among its ancestors were Chernyshevsky, the Jacobinism of Tkachev, Dostoevsky, the Russian Marxism of the 1890s, "which was led by those whom today we consider the exponents of the authentic Russian idea—Bulgakov, Berdyaev, and Peter Struve,"[107] Maxim Gorky, the followers of Vladimir Soloviev, Andrei Bely, and Alexander Blok. This nationalist revolution had "been fueled by a quintessentially Russian 'blind revolt, senseless and merciless.'" Ustryalov saw a certain justice in this elemental outbreak but suggested that the revolution had done its job and it was time to stop. Only bolshevism, "despite all its shortcomings, its painful and somber practices," was able to do what the old Russian nationalist theoretician Konstantin Leontiev had advocated: "to freeze the disintegrating power of the revolutionary floodwaters."[108]

It was Ustryalov's belief that the Soviet government had now frozen the revolution and was proceeding to carry out the country's national tasks. This was the second point in his new theory. The Bolsheviks had turned out not to be anarchists, as everyone feared, but statists, supporters and builders of a strong state. Only the Bolsheviks, said Ustryalov, as the third point in his program, "are capable of restoring Russia as a great power."[109] By this he meant restoring the Russian empire. Ustryalov was an unconditional supporter of "Russia one and indivisible." He was convinced that "Bolshevik centralism" was tainted only on the surface with the demagogy of "free self-determination for the peoples."[110] It was in the interest of this revived Russian state that the struggle against bolshevism cease. In the name of empire Ustryalov condemned the peasant revolts, "the blindly destructive anarchistic wave," which if victorious could transform "great Russia into a hodgepodge of 'liberated nationalities'—an 'independent Siberia' in the east, a 'self-governing Ukraine' and a 'free Caucasus' in the south, a 'greater Poland' and a dozen 'lesser' nationalities in the west."[111]

The national destiny of the Russian revolution was so evident to Ustryalov that he categorically denied any foreign inspiration:

Even if it were mathematically proven that 90 percent of the Russian revolutionaries were foreigners, mainly Jews, that would not in the least disprove the purely Russian character of the movement. Even if alien hands lent themselves to the cause, the soul of the revolution, its inner nature, for better or for worse, remains authentically Russian, proceeding from the ideas of the intelligentsia and refracted through the psyche of the people.[112]

Ustryalov displayed great perspicacity. In the Soviet state of Lenin's time he detected many traits that later would become characteristic of the Stalinist Soviet Union. He saw what many of the Bolshevik leaders did not. The source of his clairvoyance was his certainty of an exact parallel between the Russian and French revolutions. "The transition from a revolutionary situation to a normal statesmanlike condition will occur not in spite of or in opposition to the revolution but through it."[113] He was convinced that in Russia the evolution from radicalism to empire that had been seen in France would inevitably recur. To him the summer of 1920 was the coming of the Consulate, and the battles with Poland were like Napoleon's victories at Arcole and Marengo. The next step in the process would be the naming of an emperor.

Ustryalov's method of historical analogy enabled him to foresee certain features of the rising Soviet state. At the same time it led him into gross error. He saw the revolution as an invigorating and renewing force (and predicted a rebirth of Russian literary and cultural achievements that never came).[114]

Vasily Shulgin, in concluding a book on the defeat of the Whites and the White exodus from Russia, expressed a self-consoling thought that in many respects coincided with Ustryalov's views:

> Our ideas have crossed the front lines and conquered our enemies' consciousness. . . . Let us suppose that the Reds only think they are fighting for the glory of the International . . . and in fact are shedding their blood, however unconsciously, for nothing other than the restoration of the "Divinely Protected Sovereign State of Russia." . . . If this is the case, it means that the "White idea," having crossed the battlelines, has conquered their subconscious minds. . . . We have foreced them to serve the White cause with Red hands. . . . We have triumphed. . . . the White idea has been victorious.[115]

The changing landmarks movement arose among the right-wing, conservative sectors of the Russian intelligentsia. Efimovsky was a monarchist, Ustryalov and Klyuchnikov supporters of Kolchak, Shulgin a monarchist, and Gredeskul a right-wing Cadet. They all "changed their landmarks" when they came to the conclusion that the White cause was being served by Red hands. The ideologists of this movement were adherents of such conservative thinkers as Konstantin Leontiev and Joseph de Maistre. They accepted bolshevism because the idea of liberty, so crucial to the left-wing intelligentsia, was a secondary matter to them.

The turn to the New Economic Policy seemed to be a confirmation of the changing landmarks point of view. In November 1921 Ustryalov wrote: "Before our very eyes the tactical 'degeneration of bolshevism' is occurring as we have consistently predicted for more than a year and a half."[116] To Ustryalov and his supporters there was no question that bolshevism was degenerating. In an article entitled "The Radish" he argued that Soviet Russia was "Red on the outside, White on the inside." Symbols of this "radishness" were the "Red flag waving on top of the Winter Palace and notes of the Internationale being played on the bells of the Kremlin towers."[117] The changing landmarks supporters took up the term national bolshevism, which had originated in 1919 in Germany, suggested as an ideology for the Russian intelligentsia after the "elimination of the White movement in its only serious and promising form from the point of view of the state (Kolchak and Denikin)."[118] The liberal theorist Peter Struve had polemicized against the advocates of national bolshevism. Struve's fundamental error, as Ustryalov saw it, was that he confused bolshevism and communism. Bolshevism was a Russian phenomenon; communism was internationalist and therefore alien to Russia. The changing landmarks supporters hoped that the revolution would adapt to the national interests of Russia and accomplish what the weak tsarist regime had been unable to. It seemed to them that events confirmed their hopes.

"The ideology of reconciliation has become a firmly established part of the history of the Russian revolution," Ustryalov asserted.[119] In the early 1920s the changing landmarks ideology of reconciliation was sharply criticized in emigré circles and often indignantly condemned as treason. But it had an effect. According to official data, from 1921 to 1931, 181,432 emigrés returned to Russia, between 10 and 12 percent of all who had left. In 1921 alone 121,843 returned.[120] In other words, the overwhelming majority were repatriated during the first year of the NEP, which was also the first year of the openly proclaimed changing landmarks movement. The chief practical significance of that movement for the Soviet government, however, lay elsewhere: it divided the intelligentsia, the greater part of which had either actively opposed the October revolution or passively refused to accept it. The changing landmarks movement was the equivalent among the intelligentsia of the Living Church. In both movements sincere individuals worked alongside direct Soviet government agents, believing that they were acting in Russia's interest, that the Kremlin towers would digest and expel the Red flags waving above them, or, as Ustryalov said, "The Red flag will blossom forth in the national colors."[121]

The Soviet press greeted *Changing Landmarks* enthusiastically. *Izvestia* discussed it in an article entitled "A Psychological Breakthrough": "The essence of all the articles in the anthology comes down to the acceptance of the October revolution and the renunciation of all struggle against its results."[122] *Izvestia* was surprised at the extent to which "people who just yesterday were fighting against toiling Russia, arms in hand, have now managed to understand its spirit and historic mission." *Pravda* greeted the anthology with an editorial entitled "A Sign of the Times."[123] The anthology was reprinted on Soviet presses. Lenin talked about it. Trotsky at the Second Congress of Political Educators in October 1921 insisted: "Every province must have at least one copy of this book." The topic was also discussed at the Eleventh and Twelfth congresses of the Soviet Communist party.

The changing landmarks tendency was used above all to disrupt the emigration. For many years, the Soviet authorities would consider the mere existence of an organized and hostile emigration a serious danger. The struggle against the emigration would be waged with the help of the GPU and ideology. Having created the provocateur "Trest monarchist organization," the GPU would play a successful game from 1921 to 1927, creating dissension first of all within the monarchist emigré organizations and leading foreign intelligence services by the nose. The changing landmarks ideas penetrated broad segments of the emigration; they later became an important component of the ideology of "return to the homeland" and a basic element in the Eurasian movement.

Ustryalov was rather disconcerted by *Pravda*'s compliments and in reply to "A Sign of the Times" wrote that the authors of *Changing Landmarks* were by no means "five minutes from being Communists."[124] Nevertheless, the logic of reconciliation forced the changing landmarks supporters, who believed that they could become a loyal opposition, equal partners in a dialog with the Bolsheviks, to do such things as approve the terror, approve the deportation of "thinking people" from the country, and welcome the birth of the GPU. The GPU was welcomed because it was replacing the "notorious Cheka." Terror was welcomed because "it was necessary to freeze hearts with fear in order to paralyze the enemy's will and restore discipline in the army and among the unbridled masses. To this end all means are good and all hands acceptable."[125] Deportation was justified because "at the present time a purely organic process is underway in Russia, in which the tissues of the state are being reconstituted. The country's 'brain' must not interfere in any way with this process during this period of time (which cannot by necessity last very long)."[126]

Perhaps the most important practical result of the changing landmarks movement was that it provided an ideology for the intelligentsia remaining in the country and for the bureaucratic apparatus, which was growing with spectacular speed. When Lenin returned to work in 1922 after several months' illness he discovered with horror that the Council of People's Commissars in his absence had created 120 committees. In his estimation 16 would have been enough. The nationalization of industry and the system of requisitioning and distributing food had led to a vast increase in the number of officials. Since most of them were totally untrained, it was necessary to staff each post with several persons, swelling the apparatus still further. In 1917 there were nearly 1 million functionaries; in 1925, 2.5 million. The transportation system employed 815,000 people in 1913; in 1921 the number had grown to 1,229,000, although utilization of the system had declined to one fifth of its 1913 volume. In 1913 civil servants were only 6.4 percent of the work force; in 1920 they were 13.5 percent. For the most part people went to work in Soviet government offices out of necessity, in order to receive a ration. The changing landmarks movement provided them with an ideological rationalization.

In September 1922 *Pravda* published the results of a statistical survey among 230 engineers and staff members of Soviet government offices and industrial "trusts." To the question, "What is your attitude toward the Soviet government?" the answer of 12 was "hostile" and of 46 "indifferent"; 34 gave no answer; 28 said "sympathetic"; and 110 said they were changing landmarks supporters. Their answer to the second question helps to explain the appeal of the changing landmarks ideology. The question had to do with the future prospects of the Soviet Republic: 34 had no definite opinion; another 34 did not answer; 68 answered that the consolidation of state capitalism would lead to the victory of communism; and 94 foresaw the collapse of state capitalism and a return to the previous capitalist system. [127] That was how the changing landmarks message was understood, that the Bolshevik government would reestablish a strong state and then remove itself from the scene or be transformed.

The changing landmarks movement gave new legitimacy to the Bolsheviks by presenting them as authentic heirs of the Russian historical tradition. This justified the methods used by the new government. In commemoration of the seventh anniversary of the October revolution, Ustryalov commented approvingly: "Across the limitless plains of Russia an idea is spreading far and wide—Konstantin Leontiev's slogan, dormant until now: 'We must rule without shame.'"[128] Although the changing landmarks ideology legitimized the Bolshevik nationalities policy, it did so too openly, too much "without shame." When Ustryalov wrote, "The Soviet government will naturally try as quickly as possible to incorporate into the 'proletarian revolution' those petty states which have now erupted like a rash upon the body of the former Russian empire," this was certain to cause indignation among the Communist leaders of the national minorities. At the Eleventh Party Congress in 1922 the Ukrainian Communist Nikolai Skrypnik demanded that the changing landmarks supporters within the government apparatus be given a firm official rebuff: "Russia one and indivisible, the past slogan of Denikin and Wrangel, is now the slogan of all these changing landmarks people. Professor Ustryalov is also an advocate of this slogan." At the Twelfth Party Congress Stalin complained that the "great power ideas of the changing landmarks people are filtering all through the party," that the party was falling under the hypnotic spell of "Great Russian chauvinism."[129]

The penetration of these ideas into the government apparatus and into the party was particularly harmful, from Lenin's point of view, for in 1921 and 1922 a debate was on within the party leadership over the future form and structure of the Soviet state.

## AN INDISSOLUBLE UNION

After the civil war it became necessary to establish a constitutional basis for normal relations between the various Soviet republics. The Russian Republic, the RSFSR, occupied 92 percent of the territory and was inhabited by 70 percent of the population of the future Union of Soviet Socialist Republics. The remaining territory was occupied by the Union republics: the Ukraine, Byelorussia, Azerbaijan, Georgia, Armenia, the Far Eastern Republic, with its capital at Chita, and the two "people's republics" of Khorezm and Bukhara.

On September 20, 1920, the RSFSR and Azerbaijan signed a treaty which became the prototype for all future treaties between the RSFSR and other Soviet republics. The two sides agreed to a close military, financial, and economic union. The treaty provided for the unification in the shortest possible time of the armed forces and the military commands of both republics, as well as the agencies in charge of foreign trade, the domestic economy, supply, rail and water transport, postal and telegraph services, and finance. Azerbaijan was the weakest and poorest of the Soviet republics. The Ukraine, on the other hand, was the strongest and the most stubborn defender of its sovereign rights. The treaty signed with the Ukraine in December 1920 left substantially greater powers in its hands. The Ukrainian Republic's commissariats of war, foreign trade, finance, labor, and posts and telegraph and its Supreme Economic Council were merged with the central government of the new union, but the Ukraine retained a number of commissariats, in particular a commissariat of foreign affairs, which had the right to enter into diplomatic relations with other countries.

The treaties between the RSFSR and the other Soviet republics created a paradoxical situation. Each republic had the formal right to conduct its own foreign policy but in practice was denied the right to pursue an independent domestic policy. Moscow constantly violated the treaties by intervening unceremoniously in the internal affairs of the republics. The Communists of the Ukraine and Georgia sharply protested these intrusions. Moscow's constant conflicts with Kiev and Tiflis clearly showed the inadequacies of the system of bilateral treaties among the Soviet republics. Soviet Russia's full emergence upon the international scene (in connection with the Genoa conference in the spring of 1922) made it more necessary than ever that relations between the center and the outlying regions be normalized, and in August 1922 the Central Committee established a commission to draft a new Soviet constitution, in part to resolve these issues.

The only anti-Soviet nationalist movement that had not been crushed during the civil war was the Basmachi movement of Central Asia (then called Turkestan). This movement gained new strength in the aftermath of the Red Army takeover of Bukhara in September 1920. After a brief period of collaboration with the Communists, the Young Bukhara movement turned against them. In the fall of 1921 the situation in Turkestan was further complicated by the appearance of Enver Pasha. Formerly a leader of the Young Turks in Turkey, Enver had been minister of war under Sultan Abdul Hamid during World War I. After Kemal Ataturk came to power in Turkey (in 1920), Enver declared himself a supporter of the Communists, as did a number of other Young Turk leaders. He drafted a memorandum for the Congress of the Peoples of the East, held in Baku in September 1920, offering his services in the fight against "Western imperialism."

In the fall of 1921 the Soviet authorities sent Enver to Central Asia. Their aim was to exploit his popularity among the Muslims to help suppress the Basmachi movement. After arriving in Bukhara, Enver decided to turn against the Communists, join the native rebels, and attempt to unite them under his leadership. After some initial successes in combat against Red Army units he sent an ultimatum to Moscow in May 1922 demanding the withdrawal of Russian troops from Turkestan and promising in return to support Communist activities in the Middle East. Enver's death in battle in August 1922, the rivalries among the various Basmachi groups, and the reforms carried out in 1922 by the Turkestan Bureau of the Central Committee (the return of waqf lands, lands held in usufruct, to the Muslim clergy, permission to reopen Muslim religious schools, and recognition of Islamic religious law, the *sharia*) were all instrumental in suppressing the Basmachi movement.

Once the civil war was over, nationalist movements in the Soviet republics took on the new form of Communist nationalism.

The organizational structure and centralist principles of the Communist party required a centralized state. When Skrypnik complained at the Eleventh Party Congress about the changing landmarks elements in the party who dreamed of restoring "Russia one and indivisible," one of the delegates shouted from the floor: "The party, one and indivisible." Indeed, it could be said that the primary goal of the party's founder was exactly that: a party, one and indivisible. The party mission was, in Lenin's view, to express class interests, not national interests. But after the party came to power it unavoidably began to express the interests of the Russian state above all. Lenin assumed that Russia would be a torch to light the fire of world revolution. The larger and more powerful the torch, the hotter it would burn and the quicker the flames would spread.

The Russian Communist party was itself multinational, but its composition did not reflect exactly the country's ethnic diversity. In 1922 it had 375,901 members, of which 270,409 were Russian, that is, 72 percent. In addition there were 22,078 Ukrainians, 19,564 Jews, 9,512 Latvians, 7,378 Georgians, 6,534 Tatars, 5,649 Poles, 5,534 Byelorussians, 4,964 Kirghiz, 3,828 Armenians, 2,217 Germans, 2,043 Uzbeks, 1,964 Estonians, 1,699 Ossetians, and 12,528 of other nationalities.[130] What is most striking about these figures is the overwhelming predominance of Russians in the party. Besides that, the substantial number of Jews is noteworthy. In February 1917 Jews were granted equal rights, and during the revolution and civil war they were active in large numbers on both the Red side and the White. All this resulted in a new explosion of anti-Semitism. Pogroms against Jews were a common feature of the civil war. No less than 100,000 Jews were killed in these pogroms.

On the nationality question the Jewish, Latvian, Polish, and Estonian Communists were usually the most extreme advocates of centralism and the most ardent defenders of a "Russia one and indivisible." Lenin remarked that "people of other nationalities who have become Russified" (a reference to the Georgians Stalin and Ordzhonikidze and the Pole Dzerzhinsky) always "overdo it with respect to the 'truly Russian' frame of mind."[131] The Communists of the smaller republics became the chief opponents of renascent "Great Russian chauvinism." The stronger the national Communist party, the greater its resistance to this reviving trend. Moreover, the Ukrainian and Georgian Communist parties were acting as Communist parties normally do, that is, demanding total power for themselves.

National Communist views were expressed most strongly by Nikolai Skrypnik. A Ukrainian, he had joined the Marxist movement in 1897 and after 1903 sided with Lenin. From 1900 on he had lived in St. Petersburg and Siberia. It was not until 1918 that he returned to the Ukraine, on Lenin's insistence: "We don't need just any Ukrainian; what we need is Skrypnik."[132] Lenin was convinced that this veteran Bolshevik would defend Moscow's views against both the local nationalists and the "nihilists" who denied the importance of nationality. Skrypnik justified Lenin's confidence, working first with the Cheka and then, in 1920, assuming the post of Ukrainian commissar of internal affairs.

During 1922 and 1923 Skrypnik became one of the sharpest critics of the Russian party's nationalities policy. Particularly noteworthy was his criticism of Stalin's views on the national question in June 1923 at the Fourth Conference of the Central Committee with Responsible Officials of the National Republics and Regions. He spoke of the party's failure to carry out its nationalities program, citing in particular its inability or reluctance to combat the rise of Great Russian chauvinism within its own party apparatus as well as among government officials.

The June 1923 conference on nationality issues was held specifically to deal with the question of "Sultan-Galievism," the first "national deviation" to be suppressed by the party. A Tatar from the Volga region, Sultan-Galiev had joined the Bolsheviks before the revolution. In 1918 he became a member of the leading body (collegium) of the People's Commissariat of Nationalities, headed by Stalin. Sultan-Galiev dealt with matters concerning the Muslim peoples and was in charge of the Central Muslim Military Collegium. He played a major role in Bolshevik efforts to win over the Muslims of the former Russian empire, in particular helping to organize a "Muslim Socialist Army," to whose Red banners Lenin and Trotsky urged all Muslims rally.

Sultan-Galiev viewed the October revolution as an opportunity for the Tatars to realize their national aspirations. He dreamed of a Tatar-Bashkir Republic and the unification of all the Muslim peoples of the former tsarist empire into a new, powerful state of their own. In the fall of 1919 he published a series of articles in the magazine *Zhizn natsionalnostei* (The life of the nationalities), organ of the Commissariat of Nationalities, presenting his concept of world revolution. The weak link in the capitalist chain was not the West but the East, and the Communists should direct their efforts accordingly. But the Eastern peoples did not have an industrial proletariat; therefore different methods would have to be employed to arouse their revolutionary enthusiasm. Above all, Muslim activists should be utilized to spread communism in the East.

For Sultan-Galiev the transition to the NEP and the rise of the changing landmarks ideology were signs that his hopes had been misplaced. He came to the conclusion that the "German model" of Marxism could not meet the needs of the colonial peoples. He wrote a series of articles prefiguring the ideology of Islamic socialism. He advocated the formation of a "Colonial International" independent of the Comintern and based on an alliance of the workers and peasants in each colonial country with the native petit bourgeoisie and even progressive elements of the grand bourgeoisie.

Sultan-Galiev foresaw five stages in the realization of his ideas: (1) the formation of a Muslim Communist state in the central Volga region; (2) the incorporation into this state of all the Turkish peoples, followed by (3) all the other Muslim peoples of the former Russian empire; (4) the creation at first of an Asian International and then of an international embracing all the colonial peoples; and finally (5) the establishment of the political hegemony of the colonial and semicolonial countries over the industrialized metropolitan centers.

Sultan-Galiev was arrested in the spring of 1923. For the first time the political police were brought into a dispute among Communists, and for the first time a prominent party figure was arrested for his views. At the June 1923 conference on nationality questions Stalin explained the reasons for the arrest of his former associate in the Commissariat of Nationalities. The GPU had allegedly intercepted secret, seditious correspondence by Sultan-Galiev.[133] The Tatar dissident was freed not long after his first arrest but was rearrested in 1929. He died in the 1930s at a time and place unknown. The term *Sultan-Galievism* continued to be used as a weapon against all nationalist deviations and was among the charges brought against the defendants in the Moscow trials of 1936–1938. The arrest of Sultan-Galiev and the condemnation of Sultan-Galievism in the summer of 1923 was for Stalin a way of avenging a defeat he had suffered earlier on the question of the draft constitution for the Union of Soviet Socialist Republics.

In August 1922 the commission assigned by the Central Committee to draft a constitution for a union of the Soviet republics and headed by Stalin came up with a draft proposing the "autonomization" of the other Soviet republics; that is, they should all become part of the RSFSR but retain their "autonomy" within it. The first clause in this "Draft Resolution on Relations Between the RSFSR and the Independent Republics" proposed: "That a treaty be concluded between the Soviet republics of the Ukraine, Byelorussia, Azerbaijan, Georgia, Armenia, and the RSFSR concerning the formal incorporation of the former into the RSFSR, leaving open the question of Bukhara, Khorezm, and the Far Eastern Republic."[134]

Lenin categorically opposed Stalin's "autonomization" plan. He regarded it as a crude and undisguised violation of the party's nationalities policy and of its central principle, the right of nationals to self-determination. In his view it would provoke major conflicts that could only weaken the Soviet cause. On October 6, 1922, the Central Committee approved a new draft rewritten along lines favored by Lenin, entitled, "On the Relations Between the Sovereign United Republics." Its first clause stated: "It is deemed necessary that a treaty be concluded between the Ukraine, Byelorussia, the Federation of Transcaucasian Republics, and the RSFSR unifying them into a single Union of Socialist Soviet Republics while reserving to each the right to secede freely from this Union."[135]

Lenin's "federalization" plan won out over Stalin's "autonomization." But in the meantime Stalin had succeeded in partially neutralizing the Caucasian republics, especially Georgia, by pushing through the formation of the Transcaucasian Federation, which was placed under the authority of the Transcaucasian Bureau (Zakburo) of the party, headed by Ordzhonikidze, the conqueror of Georgia and one of Stalin's cronies. The discussion that followed the Central Committee's approval of Lenin's plan showed that even "federalization" did not receive support everywhere, because it did not guarantee genuine sovereignty. While the constitution of the USSR was being worked out, the Central Committee's position was frequently criticized.[136]

The nationality question was discussed freely for the last time at the Twelfth Party Congress in April 1923. Lenin had been impaired by illness through much of 1922. Nevertheless, at the end of 1922 and the beginning of 1923 he made preparations for an open attack on Stalin and his henchmen at the upcoming party congress, intending to call for a sharp condemnation of their actions. To Lenin, Ordzhonikidze's behavior in Georgia was evidence of a severe crisis in the party over the nationality question. In the heat of an argument Ordzhonikidze, the representative of the Russian party's Central Committee, had slapped a member of the Central Committee of the Georgian Communist party. Lenin did not wish to look at the real reason for the failure of the party's nationalities policy, it being the inevitable result of a state where autocratic power was in the hands of a dictatorially centralized party.

For Lenin the "intrigues of the class enemy" were behind the conflict, the "bourgeois elements" that were filling up and defiling the state apparatus. The countermeasures that Lenin wished to present to the Twelfth Party Congress amounted to nothing more than the strengthening of the party's control over the machinery of state and government officialdom. However, Ordzhonikidze himself was a leading member of the party's institutions of control. Lenin intended to propose other measures as well, including a "code of conduct" for Communists assigned to work in areas populated by minority nationalities. All of these measures were aimed directly against Stalin, but Lenin's illness prevented him from speaking at the congress. He entrusted all his materials on the nationality question to

Trotsky, asking him to speak against Stalin in defense of the Georgian Communists and to present Lenin's view.

Trotsky could not make up his mind to speak at the congress. It was Rakovsky, one of Trotsky's closest collaborators, who spoke against Stalin's policy. He warned that unless the necessary corrections were made, the mishandling of the nationality question could lead to a civil war. Stalin refuted the arguments of all his critics with little effort. As ever, he stood firmly on Marxist principles. He defended a strong, centralized state and the leading role of the party in all spheres of life. He pointed out that the political base of the proletarian dictatorship was necessarily located in the central industrial regions, not in the outlying areas, with their predominantly peasant population. In other words, the Russian Republic had to have primacy over the national republics. Stalin supported his arguments with numerous quotations from Lenin. He questioned Lenin's argument that it was better to be overly indulgent toward the national minorities than to overdo things in the opposite direction. Stalin argued that it was never good to overdo.

On July 6, 1923, the Central Executive Committee formally approved the Constitution of the USSR. On January 31, 1924, ten days after Lenin's death, the constitution was ratified by the Eleventh Congress of Soviets.

In September 1924 the people's republics of Khorezm and Bukhara "dissolved themselves" and were absorbed by the Uzbek, Turkmen, and Tadzhik republics. Earlier, in November 1922, the Far Eastern Republic had "dissolved itself" to join the RSFSR.

The Constitution of the USSR did not go into effect until 1924, but the fundamental principles of Soviet nationalities policy, the principles of the centralized Soviet state, had been laid down long before. Zinoviev expressed them clearly and concisely as early as 1919, when he proclaimed the natural resources of the non-Russian republics—Azerbaijani cotton and Turkestani cotton, for example—indispensable to the new state. Unlike their predecessors, however, the Soviets would be imparting civilization when they came.

## LENIN'S MANTLE

On May 25–26, 1922, Lenin suffered a stroke. His right side was paralyzed and he lost the power of speech. Not until October 2 did he gradually begin to resume work. On December 13 a second stroke put him almost entirely out of commission. From then until March 9, 1923, when a third stroke turned him into a living corpse (that survived for another eleven months), Lenin could do nothing more than think, dictate his thoughts for a few minutes each day, and hope that his advice would be taken by his cohorts and disciples.

Lenin used those last weeks of conscious life for a desperate effort to work out some formulas that he hoped would cure the serious disorders he had discovered in the party and the state after he had fallen ill. When he saw that his own death was imminent and inevitable, he offered his last advice on how he should be replaced as head of the party and the state. The struggle for Lenin's mantle, to use the expression common at the time, began with the first signs of his illness. The structure of the party's governing bodies limited the number of candidates. Formally speaking, the highest body of the party was its congress, which was held once a year every year from 1917 through 1925. Between congresses the party was led by the Central Committee. In 1919 a Political Bureau (better known by its short form, Politburo) was elected for the first time. Power within the party was concentrated in the Politburo. At the same time there existed a Secretariat, in charge of day-to-day affairs, and an Organization Bureau, the Orgburo, which handled organizational matters.

On April 3, 1922, in the aftermath of the Eleventh Party Congress, a new Politburo was elected, consisting of Lenin, Kamenev, Trotsky, Stalin, Zinoviev, Rykov, and Tomsky. Bukharin, Molotov, and Kalinin were elected as alternate members of this top leadership body. The youngest of them all, Bukharin, was thirty-four. Stalin was forty-three and Trotsky forty-two. The dying Lenin had just turned fifty-two.

A Soviet poet, Nikolai Aseev celebrated October with the words: "Long live the revolution that has thrown down the power of the old." The old rulers who had been "thrown down" were really not that old; the century was still young. The leaders of the Bolshevik party, on the other hand, were middle-aged men who expected to live for a long time.

Lenin himself limited the number of those who aspired to his mantle or to a share of it. In his "Letter to the Congress," which he dictated from December 23 to December 25, 1922, and which is commonly called Lenin's Testament, he wrote: "I would strongly urge that at this congress [the Twelfth Congress—M. H.] a number of changes be made in our political structure."[137] For Lenin "an increase in the number of Central Committee members to a few dozen or even a hundred represented a significant change in the political structure. He placed such an increase "at the head of the list." The Central Committee elected at the Eleventh Congress had twenty-seven full members and nineteen alternates. If we add to that the Control

Commission, with five full members and two alternates, we get a total of fifty-three. That is, the central leadership already consisted of "several dozen." To increase it to a hundred would have meant doubling its size. The new members were to come, as Lenin advised, from among the rank-and-file workers in the party. However, he himself had written a little earlier, "Is it really true that every worker knows how to run the state? People working in the practical sphere know that this is a fairy tale."[138]

Enlarging the Central Committee was intended to heighten its authority and improve the machinery of party and state in general. If we keep in mind the fact that Lenin was recommending the election of workers from the factory floor to the Central Committee, that is, people completely unfamiliar with the administrative work of the party, the absurdity of the advice becomes clear, despite its author's conviction that this measure could work a miraculous cure.

The miracle cure was supposed to transform the "political structure" of the party. Lenin knew perfectly well that he was the real leader of the party. He tried to lead like the conductor of an orchestra and avoid brutal repressive measures against his comrades. If necessary, when controversies became too sharp, he used the weapon of his personal authority as the party's founder and leader, the man who had made the revolution against the advice of many of his lieutenants and whose far-sightedness had been confirmed by the Brest-Litovsk treaty. At the Ninth Party Congress in March–April 1920 a group of Old Bolsheviks called for a broadening of party democracy. These democratic centralists reproached Lenin for the fact that "a tiny handful of party oligarchs decide everything" and that the Central Committee had imposed a system of "bureaucratic centralism." Lenin replied with a theoretical explanation of the necessity for one-man dictatorship: "Soviet socialist democracy and individual management and dictatorship are in no way contradictory. . . . The will of a class may sometimes be carried out by a dictator, who sometimes does more alone and is frequently more necessary."[139]

In 1920 Lenin had spoken in favor of a dictator, but in the last weeks of his conscious life in 1922–23 he was in despair because he saw several candidates for dictator. A conflict among them meant the danger of a split in the party. This was something Lenin feared greatly. He who had never hesitated to split if he was not obeyed unquestioningly now feared the deadly consequences of a split after his death.

In his Testament, Lenin gave his assessment of the six leading figures in the Central Committee. In Gogol's *Dead Souls* Sobakevich gave Chichikov the following brief description of the inhabitants of their provincial capital:

"The only decent man in town is the prosecutor, and he too is a swine." This was the immortal model Lenin followed in characterizing his associates on the Central Committee.

First Lenin took up the "two outstanding leaders of the present Central Committee," Stalin and Trotsky. He regarded the possibility of a clash between these two potential dictators as "the greater part of the danger of a split." Lenin continued: "Comrade Stalin, having become general secretary, has unlimited authority concentrated in his hands, and I am not sure whether he will always be capable of using that authority with sufficient caution." On the other hand, Trotsky "is distinguished not only by outstanding ability. He is personally perhaps the most capable man in the present Central Committee. But he has displayed excessive self-assurance and shown excessive preoccupation with the purely administrative side of the work." Then came Zinoviev and Kamenev, Lenin's closest comrades in the prerevolutionary days of exile. He commented meaningfully that "the October episode with Zinoviev and Kamenev [that is, their opposition to the October revolution] was, of course, no accident, but neither can the blame for it be laid upon them personally, any more than nonbolshevism can upon Trotsky." The Testament then devoted a "few words" to Bukharin and Pyatakov, "the most outstanding figures among the younger party members." Of Bukharin, Lenin said, "[He] is not only a major and most valuable party theorist; he is also rightly considered the favorite of the whole party, but his theoretical views can be classified as fully Marxist only with great reserve." As for Pyatakov, "he is unquestionably a man of outstanding will and outstanding ability, but he shows too much zeal for administration and the administrative side of the work to be relied upon in a serious political matter."

Ten days later Lenin dictated an "Addition to the Letter," stating in part:

> Stalin is too rude, and this defect, although quite tolerable in our midst and in dealings among us Communists, becomes intolerable in a general secretary. That is why I suggest the comrades think about a way of removing Stalin from that post and appointing another man in his stead who in all other respects differs from Comrade Stalin in having only one advantage, namely, that of being more tolerant, more loyal, more polite, more considerate to the comrades, less capricious, etc.

The direction of Lenin's thinking is obvious. Not one of the "outstanding members of the Central Committee" was worthy of succeeding him; none of them had the necessary abilities to act as dictator, to exercise one-man rule over the party. Lenin disqualified the two most outstanding leaders,

Stalin and Trotsky, because one had concentrated unlimited authority in his hands and might not always be capable of using it with sufficient caution while the other displayed excessive self-assurance and was excessively preoccupied with the purely administrative side of things. (The recollection that Trotsky had had a Communist commissar, Panteleev, shot was also very much alive among the Old Bolsheviks.) Besides, the author of the Testament did not fail to mention Trotsky's non-Bolshevik past. To be sure, he urged that Trotsky not be blamed for that any more than Zinoviev and Kamenev for their opposition to the October revolution, but it is unclear what Lenin meant when he suggested they should not be blamed personally for those errors. What is clear is that Lenin never forgot anything about anyone. In regard to Bukharin, although Lenin called him a major theoretician of the party, he also reproached him for theoretical views that were not fully Marxist, rather a serious defect for a major theoretician of a Marxist party. Pyatakov, too, had outstanding abilities but could not be relied on in serious political questions, another contradiction that Lenin did not explain.

Lenin's Testament was not read at the Twelfth Congress, although heads of delegations were allowed to see it. Later there arose a legend that Stalin had concealed the letter from the party by not allowing it to be read to the Congress. It is true that within a few years the Testament became an illegal document, possession of which was punished by prison or a labor camp. But there is no question that in 1923 the "outstanding members of the Central Committee" had no desire to see it published. For several years even Trotsky denied the existence of Lenin's Testament—until Max Eastman published it in the United States in October 1926. Boris Souvarine likewise published it in France.

The message of the Testament leaves no room for doubt. Lenin was urging insistently that he be replaced by a collective leadership. Only then would the deficiencies of each member of the leadership be compensated for by the merits of the others. It is true that none of them had very great merits, but the leader of the party had no one but himself to blame for that. He had raised and trained those who were to replace him and in the process had gotten rid of any who showed the least bit of independence.

In 1920 at the Ninth Congress one of the democratic centralists, Valerian Osinsky, spoke of the dictatorship that was threatening the party and named three potential candidates for supreme dictator: Lenin, Trotsky, and Stalin. During the revolution and civil war the Soviet government was identified with two names by its supporters and enemies alike, Lenin and Trotsky.

Chairman of the Petrograd Soviet, leader of the October insurrection, first people's commissar of foreign affairs, who issued inflammatory manifestos ("To All, to All, to All") calling for world revolution, the first representative of the "new world" to engage in talks with the imperialists (at Brest-Litovsk), organizer of the Red Army, and brilliant orator, Leon Trotsky was considered by many the natural successor to Lenin. He too considered himself such. This conviction was one of the main reasons for his defeat as the battle for Lenin's mantle began.

General secretary of the Central Committee, member of the Politburo and the Orgburo, people's commissar of nationalities, and people's commissar of the Workers' and Peasants' Inspectorate, Joseph Stalin was known only to the narrow circles of the party and military leadership. He rarely spoke at meetings. His articles did not sparkle with professional craftsmanship. John Reed did not even mention him in *Ten Days That Shook the World*, Reed's chronicle of the October revolution. But at the beginning of 1918, when Lenin became fed up with the endless discussions in the Central Committee and sought to have a special bureau created "for solving urgent questions," it consisted of four men: Lenin, Trotsky, Sverdlov, and Stalin. Stalin was also a member of the editorial board of *Pravda*, along with Trotsky, Bukharin, and Sokolnikov.

Lenin had complete confidence in Stalin and indulged all his caprices, while Stalin, aware of his importance, behaved like a prima donna. When at the Eleventh Party Congress Preobrazhensky listed all of Stalin's duties and questioned whether it was possible for one man to handle this vast amount of work on the Politburo, the Orgburo, two commissariats, and a dozen subcommittees of the Central Committee, Lenin immediately spoke up in Stalin's defense, calling him irreplaceable as commissar of nationalities and adding: "The same thing applies to the Workers' and Peasants' Inspectorate. This is a vast business; but to be able to handle investigations we must have at the head of it a man who enjoys high prestige."[140] After the Eleventh Congress (March–April 1922), Lenin proposed Stalin for the post of general secretary, only to complain eight months later, as though he had forgotten what he had done, that Stalin had concentrated too much authority in his hands. Lenin also made the sudden discovery that there were major defects in the functioning of the Workers' and Peasants' Inspectorate and that Stalin was the main source of the monstrous growth of bureaucracy.

Stalin did not make himself general secretary. Lenin did. Lenin had been his mentor, protector, and constant model. According to Boris Souvarine, Victor Adler once chided Plekhanov jokingly, "Lenin's your son." Plekhanov retorted, "If he's my son, he's an illegitimate one." Souvarine adds: "Lenin might have said the same about Stalin."[141] The question of whether Lenin was the legitimate or illegitimate son of Plekhanov and Marx continues to stir debate among philosophers, historians, and specialists in family law, but the question of whether Stalin was Lenin's son is disputed less and less. Stalin was not only his legitimate heir but his only one. The fact that the father, at the end of his life, got angry at his son and tried to disinherit him is nothing unusual.

Many reasons are given to explain Stalin's rise to power. The main reason was that he was Lenin's legitimate heir. The majority of the party perceived the situation that way. This was a necessary condition for his success, but as the logicians say, it was not by itself sufficient reason.

Stalin displayed brilliant strategy in the struggle for power. First of all, he pretended not to want the power and formed an alliance with two other hopefuls, Zinoviev and Kamenev, letting them act as senior partners in a triumvirate. Trotsky, on the other hand, tended to alienate all who were not his loyal allies.

The Bolsheviks, who looked at themselves in the mirror of the French revolution, saw in Trotsky, the commissar of war and chairman of the Revolutionary Military Council, a potential Bonaparte. Trotsky knew this and yet in a pamphlet entitled *Lessons of October*, which he published after Lenin's death, he wrote: "Robespierre never had the chance to acquaint himself with the Plekhanovian philosophical idea. He violated all the laws of sociology and instead of exchanging handshakes with the Girondists he cut off their heads."[142] Trotsky committed an irreparable error in threatening to use the guillotine when he was unable to make good his threat. By bringing up the question of Zinoviev's and Kamenev's conduct in October 1917, Trotsky seemes to have forced the triumvirs to drag up his own non-Bolshevik past.

On October 8, 1923, Trotsky sent a letter to the Central Committee. Lest he be accused of factionalism, he signed it alone. A week later the Central Committee received the so-called Platform of the Forty-Six, which discussed the same issues Trotsky had brought up. Among the signers were Preobrazhensky, Pyatakov, Antonov-Ovseenko, Vladimir Kosior, and Osinsky. Both letters sharply criticized "the policies of the majority of the Politburo."

The first part of the Platform of the Forty-Six spoke of a grave economic crisis: strikes, growing unemployment, production breakdowns, and the inefficiency of most of heavy industry. The blame for the catastrophic situation was laid on the majority faction in the Politburo. The second part of the platform spoke of a crisis within the party: "We observe the ever increasing, and scarcely concealed, division of the party between a secretarial hierarchy and 'the quiet folk,' between professional party officials recruited from above and the general mass of the party, which does not participate in party life."[143] The Platform of the Forty-Six made the same arguments as Trotsky's letter. Both asserted that the source of the party crisis lay in the system by which all secretaries of local party organizations were appointed from above rather than elected by the organization.

Trotsky and his associates were absolutely correct. The appointment system was Stalin's most effective instrument in conquering power. Although he did not invent it, he perfected it. Boris Souvarine, in his analysis of the structure of the state, singled out the two chief concentrations of central power—the Secretariat, which worked in close association with the Org-buro; and the Central Control Commission, with its local control commissions, introduced in 1920 to register all complaints against officialdom but very quickly transformed into a weapon for combatting all criticism and maintaining the strictest discipline.

The importance of the Secretariat was that it handled all questions relating to personnel assignments and leadership posts in local organizations. In 1920 a Department of Records and Assignments, the Uchraspred, was established within the Secretariat, with the initial task of organizing emergency mobilizations of party members. It set the mobilization quotas for each local organization. After the civil war, when major mobilizations of party members ended, the Uchraspred took over the job of assigning personnel to party posts. Under the party's rules, members were always totally at the disposal of the Central Committee. After the civil war this meant at the disposal of the Uchraspred. By the beginning of 1923 all party posts down to the district level came under its jurisdiction. At the Twelfth Party Congress in 1923 the report on the work of the Uchraspred stated that during 1922 it had assigned "more than 10,000 party members, about half of whom were 'responsible officials.'"[144]

The party congress elected the Central Committee, which in turn elected the Politburo, Orgburo, and Secretariat. The Secretariat, through the Uchraspred, chose all the regional and district secretaries of party committees. They in turn selected the delegates to the congress, which elected the Secretariat. By 1923 this system, in which the Secretariat in effect elected itself, had been perfected. Stalin had the party machinery in his hands.

Trotsky and his associates justly criticized the system of appointments from above, but they were criticizing a system that Lenin had created and were thereby violating Lenin's precepts. More importantly, they were criticizing a system created with their consent and participation. They voiced their opposition to the system after the Twelfth Congress, when it began to turn against them. Despite the sharp polemics between the supporters of Trotsky and Stalin, they agreed on one decisive point: the party should run the entire life of the country, not only its political life, but social, economic, and cultural matters as well. Their agreement on this point showed that the struggle between Stalin and Trotsky was in the last analysis only a struggle for power.

Lenin had often stressed the all-encompassing role of the party. In 1918 the non-Communist specialist S. Liberman discovered intolerable practices among those in charge of the lumber industry. Lenin listened to Liberman's complaints, agreed with him, then warned: "The rectification of our errors must always come from above, not from specialists. That is why if you have any proposals, you should call me on the phone, and I myself will make the necessary changes."[145] At the end of his life Lenin was to say: "We must know and remember that the entire constitution of the Soviet Republic, both in legal terms and practical matters, is based on the fact that the party does everything, planning, building, and straightening out errors, according to one single principle."[146] That principle was the autocratic rule of the party.

In the early 1920s Gabriel Myasnikov and the Workers' Group, which he organized among industrial workers in Petrograd and the Urals, put forward some slogans that were quite unusual for Communists. After the Tenth Party Congress, Myasnikov sent a letter to the Central Committee with the following proposal: "Now that we have smashed the resistance of the exploiters and constituted ourselves the sole power in the land, we must proclaim freedom of speech and the press of a kind that no one in the world has had before—for everyone, from the monarchists to the anarchists." Myasnikov was expelled from the party and arrested. After escaping from the Soviet Union in 1928, he acknowledged that he had remained alive thanks only to his "heroic past"—the murder of Grand Duke Mikhail Romanov.

On January 16, 1924, five days before Lenin died, the Thirteenth Party Conference decided to make public the entire resolution on party unity passed on Lenin's urging by the Tenth Party Congress in 1921. The conference reminded all who criticized the "Politburo majority" that they were fighting against Leninist ideas. In May 1924 at the Thirteenth Party Congress, the first after Lenin's death, Trotsky made clear once again that his entire past and future opposition to Stalin was nothing more than a struggle for power: "I have never recognized freedom for groupings inside the party, nor do I now recognize it, because under the present historical conditions groupings are merely another name for factions." Then Trotsky uttered words that in effect constituted a death sentence for all who criticized Stalin from the point of view of "true Leninism":

In the last analysis, the party is always right, because the party is the sole historical instrument the working class possesses for the solution of its fundamental tasks. . . . I know that no one can be right against the party. It is only possible to be right with the party and through it since history has not created any other way to determine the correct position.[147]

If the party is always right, if one cannot oppose it, if there can be no doubt that it alone will carry out the mission assigned to it by history, the only alternative is to try to seize power within the party.

On January 21, 1924, Lenin died. Stalin organized the funeral in his own manner. Despite the protests of many Old Bolsheviks and of Lenin's widow, Lenin's corpse was embalmed and placed in a glass coffin inside a mausoleum built of wood upon Red Square. On January 30, Krupskaya asked in *Pravda* that Lenin not be mourned with "public worship of him." She asked that statues of him not be erected nor cities named after him. "If you wish to honor Vladimir Ilyich's name, build child care centers, kindergartens, houses, schools, and so on." The opposite was done. Gigantic funeral ceremonies were organized, as were pilgrimages to the mausoleum. Petrograd was renamed Leningrad. Cities like Lenino, Leninsk, and Ulyanovsk appeared on the map.

The deification of Lenin was particularly necessary for his heirs, each of whom tried to tear off a piece of his halo. They felt themselves to be lesser deities. Along with Leningrad other new names for towns and cities appeared: Zinovievsk, Trotsk, and Stalingrad. And all the while Stalin was operating for the most part in the background, pushing Zinoviev to the fore. On January 26, Stalin spoke very modestly in the Hall of Columns at the Central Trade Union Building in Moscow. His modest speech, which Soviet schoolchildren would later be required to learn by heart for decades thereafter, was entitled "A Pledge." *Pravda* published only short excerpts.

The spectacular funeral for Lenin showed convincingly that Stalin was Lenin's most outstanding disciple. The Politburo, after placing Lenin's body in the mausoleum, thus encasing the relics of the new saint, at the same time submitted their teacher's brain to scientific examination. A German professor by the name of Vogt undertook the task and soon discovered "important peculiarities in the structure of the so-called pyramidal cells of the third layer." The journalists of the time reported that these special characteristics of Lenin's brain were "the reason for his ingenious ideas and the ingenious tactics that Lenin devised at the most difficult stages of the revolution when many others felt the ground slip from under their feet and lost all perspective."[148] The deification of the leader proceeded, fully in accordance with the doctrine of Marx: the mausoleum represented the cultural-ideological superstructure; the pyramidal cells, the material base.

## THE YEARS OF WAITING

Saltykov-Shchedrin, the Russian satirist, told the story of the people of Glupov (Dumbville), who under one of their governors had a holiday in the spring to commemorate the ills of the past and one in the fall to prepare for the evils to come. The people of the Soviet Union celebrated the years 1923–1926 as a time of hope and expectation. It was one of the calmest periods in Soviet history, despite continued rumblings of discontent. The country was slowly convalescing, gradually getting back on its feet, remembering with horror the ills of the past, mourning its millions of dead, and hoping for better things to come.

One of the rare personal diaries that has come down to us from the 1920s has the following entry for December 17, 1923:

> Policies have changed. Free trade is permitted now, and theaters, streetcars, newspapers, etc., cost money. But Lenin has preserved an oasis of socialism in Russia—the government agencies and their staffs—while he allows the rest of the country to live the capitalist way. So far as anyone can foresee, the second stage of our revolution will come down to a struggle between these two principles, the socialist and the capitalist. [149]

Mostly it was the rural areas that began to "live the capitalist way." Nowhere was the return to normalcy painless, however. Industry was seized with a sudden passion for profit making and raised its prices drastically. A widening gap, or "scissors," to use Trotsky's term, appeared between prices for manufactured goods and those for agricultural products. In 1924 the "scissors" began to close again as the party took up a new slogan, "Face the Countryside." The "link" (*smychka*), the bond between the workers and the peasants, was declared to be fundamental to all government policy. Land area under cultivation quickly increased, reaching 80 percent of the prewar total. In 1925 Bukharin issued his famous call to the peasantry: "Enrich yourselves. Develop your plots of land. Don't be afraid of restrictions." [150] On the eighth anniversary of the revolution Stalin declared, "At present our task is to forge a solid alliance with the middle peasantry."

Industry also revived, although the process was slower than in agriculture. The introduction of material incentives in industry and the formation of conglomerates that were given the capitalist name *trusts* and that operated on the basis of profitability helped to hasten the recovery of industry. This was especially true of small industry, which produced for the peasant market. It did not require large outlays of capital and provided a quick return on investment. The expansion of the domestic market made possible a fairly rapid revival of plants producing consumer goods. Heavy industry recovered at a slower pace.

Industrial recovery based on the profit principle had one adverse effect, unemployment. In October 1921 there were 150,000 unemployed; at the beginning of 1924, 240,000. This increase was in part the result of layoffs by factories seeking to increase profits by reducing payrolls but also the result of an influx from the countryside. Together with unemployment there was a severe shortage of skilled labor.

Demands for higher productivity, which was obtained "through the intensification of labor and only to a small degree through improved organization of production and modernization of equipment,"[151] caused much unrest among the workers, especially since increased productivity was not accompanied by wage increases. In the spring of 1925 a wave of strikes swept the main industrial areas, particularly Moscow and Ivanovo. Sokolnikov, the commissar of finance, admitted in 1925 that "in the eighth year of Soviet power" the wages of metalworkers, miners, and rail workers had barely reached the prewar level. The average wage in 1925 was 40 chervonets. M. Larsons wrote that in 1923 a people's commissar received 210 chervonets as well as an apartment.[152]

A new class of capitalists, the Nepmen, came into existence with the introduction of the NEP, a social group that seemed to exist beyond the pale of Soviet society. They did not have the right to vote, they could not form professional associations or be members of trade unions, and their children could not study at the university level. They owed their existence to a policy reversal by the Soviet government, and they understood that at any time a change of policy could sign their death warrant. The Nepmen were necessary for NEP, but they were treated with repugnance. Private businessmen never lost the feeling of precariousness, that their existence was only temporary. That was why private enterprise attracted mainly adventurers and speculators, whose hope it was to make some fast money and spend it as quickly as possible while keeping out of sight of the ever watchful GPU. Due to the hostility of the Soviet system toward private enterprise and the reluctance of private businessmen to invest in any long-term industrial projects, throughout the NEP period the share of private business in overall industrial production remained quite small: 3.8 percent in 1925.[153]

The fact that the social organism contained an alien presence in the form of capitalists contributed to the special atmosphere of this era in Soviet history. The Nepmen were accused, for example, of corrupting the Communists and were blamed for the massive spread of alcoholism.

The question of whether to legalize the production of alcohol in the land of the radiant future provided lengthy debate among the Bolsheviks. Before the revolution they had fiercely criticized the tsarist government for profiting from drunkenness. Now they had to choose whether to continue or revoke prohibition, which had been introduced by Nicholas II at the beginning of World War I.

Those who favored legalizing alcohol production, with a state monopoly on vodka, argued that illegal production was very widespread and that large revenues for the state could be obtained by legalization. In 1922 *Pravda* published a ringing declaration by an Old Bolshevik, A. Yakovlev, with the headline, "It Shall Not Pass." Yakovlev sharply denounced a certain Professor Ozerov, who favored government sale of vodka, promising that it would bring 250 million gold rubles per year into the state coffers. Ozerov proposed charging twice the price before the revolution. Yakovlev replied:

> Soviet power, which exists for the people and for the national economy, . . . cannot take this suicidal road for the sole reason that in the pursuit of these imaginary 250 million, or even a real sum of that size, the national economy would suffer such losses and such destruction that even billions of rubles would not make up for it.[154]

The ranks of the party and the Central Committee were against a revival of the state monopoly on the sale of alcohol. Nevertheless, the Politburo insisted on the measure. The debate continued until 1924. Stalin ended the discussion when he introduced a statement at a Central Committee plenum, signed by six other Central Committee members, solemnly stating that Lenin had told him and the other six in the summer and fall of 1922 that the vodka monopoly had to be introduced. In so doing Stalin annulled "all of Lenin's earlier statements on this question" found in his collected works. In 1927 Stalin recalled their discussions:

> What's better, the bondage of foreign capital or the introduction of liquor? That was the issue before us. Clearly, we settled on vodka because we felt— and still feel—that if we, for the sake of the victory of the workers and peasants, have to soil ourselves a little bit, then we will agree to even those extreme means in the interest of our cause.[155]

The vodka monopoly introduced in January 1923 was a compromise. The production of vodka was legalized at only half its normal strength—that is, 40 proof. This was immediately called Rykov vodka, or *rykovka*, in honor of the party leader who signed the decree and who himself was no enemy of the bottle. The power and attraction of alcohol was explained this way by Aron Solts, the Old Bolshevik known as the "conscience of the party":

When life is hard, when you don't have the strength or hope to change it, you wish you could picture it or imagine it to be different. To do this you have to put reason to sleep and dull the power of critical thought, which you can do with alcohol. When you drink you forget all your sorrows, all your troubles disappear, and all your problems fade away.[156]

This comment, which ends up sounding rather favorable toward alcohol, may provide a clue to some of the thinking behind the steady increase in vodka production, aside from the desire for larger state revenues. The initial plan for vodka production for the year 1929–30 provided for 41 million *vedra* (406 million liters), but this was increased to 46 million (456 million liters).[157] In those days sorrows, troubles, and problems were multiplying by the thousands.

Public Prosecutor Ivan Kondurushkin gave this summary of NEP's results:

As of 1927 we have accomplished the following: (1) restored industry to the prewar level of production; (2) restored the transportation system, which is now working smoothly; (3) stabilized the currency; (4) revived and organized the working class, which numbers 300,000 more than in 1922; and (5) revived agriculture, fully restoring the area previously under cultivation.[158]

The economic success of the policy begun in March 1921 was undeniable. It enabled the economy to return more or less to its prewar condition. But that was not the goal of the Bolshevik party, which had made a revolution in order to create a new society and a new kind of human being.

During the "years of waiting" between the end of the civil war and the beginning of the Stalin revolution the old society was under attack on every front. The first Soviet legal code on the family and marriage was adopted on September 18, 1918. Its aim was to "revolutionize" the family and the four main provisions of this code did indeed make it a revolutionary document for its time: only civil (not religious) marriage was recognized; there was no requirement for consent by any third party to a marriage; divorce was permitted without restrictions—if only one member of the couple wanted it, the divorce went through a court, but in cases of mutual consent, divorces were granted by the marital registry office; and the legal concept of illegitimacy pertaining to children was abolished.

The chief expression of this revolution in the family was the destruction of the "old bourgeois morality." The ideas of Alexandra Kollontai, commissar of social welfare and a prominent party member, were very widely accepted. Clara Zetkin in her *Recollections of Lenin* described his attitude toward Kollontai's ideas: "No doubt you have heard the famous theory that in communist society satisfying sexual desire and the craving for love will be as simple and trivial as 'drinking a glass of water.' A section of our youth has gone mad, absolutely mad, over this 'glass of water.'"[159]

It was true that the "glass of water" theory became very popular in a society where the family had suffered heavy losses continuously for seven years of war and revolution. According to the 1897 census, women constituted 50.3 percent of the population, and men 49.7 percent, roughly equal proportions. According to the census of 1926, there were 5 million fewer men than women in the Soviet Republic. It was under these conditions that the party waged its fight against the "bourgeois family." Lenin expressed his indignation over "free love" theories in private to Zetkin and others, but he never spoke about it publicly. Instead he preached the "new revolutionary morality." The hero of a novel about free love that was popular in the 1920s quoted Lenin almost word for word: "Komsomol morality does exist. . . . Our morality is entirely subordinated to the interests of the proletarian class struggle! Komsomol morality is a system that serves the working people in its struggle against exploitation of every kind. Whatever is useful to the revolution is moral; whatever is harmful to it is immoral and intolerable."[160] Morality as a weapon in the class struggle was a theme constantly reiterated by party theoreticians. Preobrazhensky dedicated his book, *The Moral and Class Norms of Bolshevism*, to that paragon of Bolshevik morality, GPU leader Felix Dzerzhinsky.

The party's policy toward children also contributed to the breakup of the family. In the *ABCs of Communism*, Bukharin and Preobrazhensky, the authors of this most popular 1920s guidebook for the "new Soviet man," wrote: "Children belong to the society into which they are born, not to their parents."[161] A prominent Soviet legal authority, one of the drafters of the new code on marriage and the family, expressed the same idea even more succinctly: "The family must be replaced by the Communist party."[162]

On September 30, 1918, at virtually the same time that the new family code was adopted, the All-Russia Central Executive Committee approved a resolution establishing schools that would combine learning with labor. The school was revolutionized. Everything outdated was thrown away: desks, daily lessons, homework, textbooks, grades, tests. All education was made free of charge and coeducational. In working out a model for the new Soviet school, the Bolsheviks drew upon the most advanced pedagogical ideas of Russian educators, in particular, Konstantin Ventsel, as well as those of progressive Western educators, such as John Dewey.

The new Soviet school was "self-administered" by a collective consisting of all pupils and all employees, from the teachers to the janitors. The very word *teacher* was abolished and replaced by the term *shkrab*, short for *shkolny rabotnik*, school employee.

During the civil war the Soviet government was unable to carry out its utopian dreams for this new type of school. Only at the end of 1923 was a plan adopted for reorganizing the school system, which was to be oriented toward the training of skilled specialists who would have a Marxist, working-class view of the world. One thing had been accomplished during the initial, utopian phase: teachers' resistance to the politicization of the school had been broken. Lenin insisted that the bourgeoisie be fought in the schools as well, that education cannot proceed apart from politics. The chief slogan in the second phase of the Soviet school system was, "We do not need literacy without communism." As a result, communism was included everywhere, even in arithmetic. For example, students were asked to solve the following problem: "The insurrection in which the Parisian proletariat took power occurred on March 18 in 1871. The Paris commune fell on May 22 the same year. How long did it last?" The politicization of education was facilitated by the use of new methods comprehensively conceived with long-term aims. Or, as the *Small Soviet Encyclopedia* said, "in the Soviet Union for the first time in history, schools took up the task of combatting religion; the school became an antireligious institution."[163]

Education was unabashedly made a class privilege. When children started school, they were immediately and bluntly made aware of their class origins. Among the first lessons they learned was that people were divided into two categories, the higher category of working people and the lower category of nonworkers.

One of the main aims of the class-oriented school was to train internationalists, as V. N. Shulgin, an influential Marxist educator explained: "Our goal is not to turn out a Russian child, a child of the Russian state, but a citizen of the world, an internationalist, a child who will fully understand the interests of the working class and who is capable of fighting for the world revolution. . . . We educate our children, not for the defense of the motherland but for worldwide ideals."[164]

This education of children in the spirit of universal ideals meant first of all the extirpation of their national roots. "We realized a little too late," Mikhail Pokrovsky admitted in a self-criticism at the First Conference of Marxist Historians, "that the term *Russian history* is a counterrevolutionary term." Schools taught the history of the revolutionary movement. Civic history was eliminated. The manipulation of social memory began. Simultaneously war was declared on classical Russian literature. In 1930 a proletarian literary critic objected that "the terms 'Russian literature' and 'the history of Russian literature' have not yet been denied their civil rights as part of the school curriculum, of textbooks, and of teaching aids."[165] Many classical writers were removed from the curriculum and others were studied only from a special angle. For example, the works of Pushkin, Griboedov, and Lermontov were analyzed as models of "the literary style of the Russian nobility during the rise of commercial-industrial capitalism."

One of the most tragic consequences of war and revolution were the homeless children, the *besprizorniki*. Hundreds of thousands of children lost their parents in the war zones, and millions lost them during the 1921 famine. Government statistics spoke of 7 million homeless children in 1922.[166] The officially encouraged breakup of the family only increased the problem. Krupskaya admitted in 1925: "I myself have written in the past that the problem of homeless children was a legacy of the war and economic dislocation, but after observing these children, I can see that we must stop speaking in those terms. We must say that the roots of the problem lie not only in the past but also in the present."[167]

In 1921, at the height of the famine, a civic organization, the Save the Children League, was suppressed. It had functioned since 1918 and included former members of the Cadet party, SRs, and Mensheviks, as well as unaffiliated activists. The Commissariat of Education had insisted that the League be abolished on the grounds that representatives of the bourgeoisie could not be allowed to rescue proletarian children and then miseducate them. A Commission to Improve the Lives of Children was organized and placed under the direction of Dzerzhinsky, head of the Cheka. Thus, concern for children became the task of the organs of repression.

Two months after the revolution a new law was passed under which all cases involving children or adolescents under eighteen were transferred from the common courts to "special commissions for cases involving minors, these commissions having purely pedagogical and medical aims." It was forbidden to refer to minors as criminals; they were delinquents. In 1920 a new decree allowed the special commissions to refer cases involving minors above fourteen back to the regular courts.

A policy of harsh punishment became one way of dealing with the problem of homeless children. They were imprisoned or sent to concentration camps. Another solution was to place them in what were called children's homes or in a special category of such institutions—vocational-agricultural labor colonies. Among Communist educators one theory gained a special currency: namely, that these children without parents or families could serve as splendid material for breeding the "new Soviet man." Many of the children's homes and labor colonies were placed under GPU jurisdiction. Finally, there was a third way of dealing with the problem—leaving the homeless children to their fate. Delinquents for whom vacancies could be found were sent for reeducation to the children's homes; the rest were left on the streets.

Toward the end of the 1920s, the economic revival and improved material conditions brought about a reduction in the number of homeless children. The Stalin revolution in the 1930s would throw new millions of children without parents into the streets.

One of the chief tasks undertaken by the Soviet government was the elimination of illiteracy. In 1855, 93 percent of all Russians were illiterate; in 1897 the figure was approximately 77 percent. The American scholar Daniel Lerner, basing himself on information drawn from twenty-two countries, has demonstrated a very close link between urbanization and literacy. In the mid-nineteenth century only two Russian cities had more than 100,000 inhabitants. In the early twentieth century, when Russia's industrial growth rate became one of the fastest in Europe, the literacy rate rose rapidly. The tsarist government, however, is not usually given credit for this rise in the literacy rate.

Immediately after the October revolution the "anti-illiteracy front" was opened, alongside the military front and the economic front. The goal was not so much to teach illiterates how to read and write as to teach them to think correctly. "The illiterate," Lenin explained, "remains outside of politics, and that is why he must be taught the alphabet. Without this there can be no politics."[168] Bogdanov, the ideologist of proletarian culture, held the view that illiteracy would be eliminated and education provided to the people spontaneously through a kind of natural process. Lenin's view was the exact opposite. A decree of the Council of People's Commissars on the elimination of illiteracy, which Lenin signed on December 26, 1919, said in the preamble:

> With the aim of providing the entire population of the republic the opportunity of conscious participation in the political life of the country the Council of People's Commissars hereby decrees: All inhabitants of the republic between the ages of eight and fifty who do not know how to read or write must take part in the literacy campaign.

The workday for illiterates was reduced by two hours with no cut in pay. However, article 8 specified that "those who seek to avoid the obligations put into effect by this decree . . . will be subject to prosecution."[169] Learning to read and write became a duty, a kind of tax required by the government, and refusal to fulfill this obligation was made a crime.

In 1926, when the first census was taken under Soviet rule, it was determined that 5 million people had overcome illiteracy. This indicates that after the revolution the population acquired literacy at approximately the same rate as before, despite all the noisy propaganda and intimidating decrees. In the early 1930s the literacy rate would rise much more quickly, with intensified industrialization and urbanization.

A new family and marriage code adopted in 1928 completed the stage of revolutionary upheavals in the realm of family law. Under the new code registered and unregistered marriages were recognized as equally valid. Either husband or wife could dissolve the marriage without even informing the other. All he or she had to do was make a written statement. A postcard to the registry office was sufficient. "A divorce now costs three rubles," wrote Mikhail Koltsov in *Pravda*. "No more formalities, no papers, no summons, not even the need to inform in advance the person you are divorcing. Subscribing to a magazine is harder. . . . For three rubles why not indulge yourself?"[170]

The new legal code was meant to strike a mortal blow at the family and to tear apart the social ties which had begun to reassert themselves under NEP. The struggle against the intelligentsia and the destruction of the family and the old morality were meant to clear the ground for the new society. Since the state felt itself to be insufficiently powerful as yet, it sought to disrupt all ties between individuals, leaving each isolated in relation to the state.

Despite all this, the countryside—where the majority of the people lived—remained a bulwark of the old forms of authority and old morality. It was through the cells of the Young Communist League (the Komsomol), and especially in the form of "free love," that the new morality reached the countryside, although its influence remained marginal during this period.

Religion did not wither away despite the bitter fight against it. Churches were torn down, members of the clergy arrested, and antireligious propaganda constantly intensified. The publishing house Atheist began operations in 1922. A newspaper by the same name began to come out once every five days in 1923, along with a monthly magazine *Bezbozhnik u stanka* (The godless at the workplace), which published caricatures prefiguring the crude anti-Semitic cartoons of the Nazi era. On February 17, 1923, Emelyan Yaroslavsky, director of antireligious propaganda, announced the formation of the League of Militant Atheists, which published the mass distribution magazine *Bezbozhnik* (The godless).

The struggle against the Orthodox church was made easier by the schism that persisted within it and by certain improprieties disclosed at the higher levels of the patriarchate. In December 1926, Metropolitan Sergii, executing the duties of the patriarch, was arrested. He was released in March 1927 and in July published a declaration which, to quote a historian, "transformed the church into an active ally of the Soviet government."[171] The majority of the clergy and the faithful, this historian continues, understood that "this sin was necessary to save the church from destruction." A number of bishops were sent to penal exile on the Solovetsky Islands, and although they did not endorse Metropolitan Sergii's declaration per se, they urged that the unity of the church be maintained. In spite of this "spiritual and moral catastrophe for the Russian church,"[172] religion continued to serve as a barrier to the degradation of society and the creation of the "new human being" the Soviet authorities wanted. Religion remained a traditional model, whose existence alongside the model of the new Soviet man allowed comparisons and a choice. But the party did not lay down its arms. "Have we suppressed the reactionary clergy?" asked Comrade Stalin in 1927. He answered: "Yes, we have suppressed them. The only trouble is that we have not yet eliminated them completely. Antireligious propaganda is the means that must bring to completion the job of eliminating the reactionary clergy."[173] Stalin was explaining the situation to a delegation of American workers, but he failed to add that besides propaganda the job of elimination was being speeded along with the help of the GPU.

## THE EMIGRÉS

During the "years of waiting" there was the other possibility for comparison. The window to the West remained open. Beginning at the end of 1922 trips abroad for a limited period of time became quite common. Soviet engineers, foreign trade officials, and Nepmen went abroad on business, and writers and artists went for professional reasons. It also became a common form of punishment to send party leaders who were out of favor on foreign assignments, commercial or diplomatic. For Russians the West had always been both attractive and repulsive. In the 1920s it seemed much more like home because of the large Russian emigré community.

The Soviet authorities even tried to influence the emigrés, encouraging the changing landmarks tendency among them. This policy was symbolized by the founding of the newspaper *Nakanune* (On the eve), with editorial offices in both Moscow and Berlin. Soviet writers were allowed to publish their books in Berlin, Prague, and Riga as well as Moscow. It was not expressly forbidden to meet with emigrés, and Soviet citizens who did so were not punished after returning home. Film rental agencies in the Soviet Union, seeking profits, went so far as to print pinup shots of Asta Nielsen and Mary Pickford in *Pravda*. Scenes of bourgeois decadence in the West, especially of sleazy Russian emigré taverns, were regularly featured in Soviet films. Theater audiences viewed with delight the scenes of corruption and splendor from the outside world.

Soviet party leaders engaged in lively polemics with emigré politicians, and Soviet literary critics reviewed the books of emigré writers. The tone was nasty, sarcastic, malicious; the victors were mocking the vanquished. Still, in a certain sense the emigré community remained a part of Soviet life. It was insulted and ridiculed but also feared to some extent. In turn the emigré community eagerly followed all developments inside Russia. The emigrés were influenced by Soviet ideas, but they too influenced Soviet ideology.

The emigré community was a faithful reflection of prerevolutionary Russian life, with its countless political parties and groupings and schools of religion, philosophy, and literature. Revolution and civil war, defeat and forced exile strengthened dogmatic and intolerant attitudes. One of the principal lessons of the civil war was never absorbed—that the defeat of the anti-Bolshevik camp was largely the result of lack of unity. In exile the politicians continued the struggle, but mostly among themselves, one party against another.

The church set the example. In the fall of 1921 a council of the church in exile convened in Karlovci, Yugoslavia. The monarchists sought to have the council proclaim a legitimate tsar from the house of Romanov. Others at the council protested that this would be "interfering in politics, which was inadmissable at a church gathering."[174] In 1922 Patriarch Tikhon condemned the Karlovci council for its political activities and named Metropolitan Eulogius the head of the church abroad. The majority of emigrés felt that the church in exile should be linked with the Patriarchate in Moscow. In 1926 and 1927 a split took place. Most of the bishoprics (eparchies) in Western Europe recognized the authority of Metropolitan Eulogius, but the bishoprics in the Balkans, the Middle East, and the Far East accepted the authority of Metropolitan Antonius, a supporter of the Karlovci council. The monarchist movement was torn by inner dissension, especially between absolutist and constitutionalist tendencies and two rival pretenders: Nikolai Nikolaevich, the uncle of Tsar Nicholas II; and Kirill Vladimirovich, a grandson of Tsar Alexander II and a cousin of the last tsar.

In August 1922 Kirill Vladimirovich proclaimed himself the true heir to the throne, but the majority of the monarchists chose Nikolai Nikolaevich as their leader, although it was left open who would actually ascend the throne. That was to be decided after the monarchy's return to power in

Russia. The monarchist program essentially called for the formation of a new Volunteer Army to invade Russia. The key to success was financial aid, and possibly military aid, from abroad.

Pavel Milyukov, chief organizer and ideologist of what was called the Republican-Democratic Alliance, categorically rejected foreign aid. "I do not know how we will return to Russia," he said in 1925, "but I do know how we will not return." That is, it would be impossible to return in the wake of a foreign army.[175] During the NEP Milyukov came to the conclusion that a certain evolution was underway in Russia as a result of the long-term policies of the Soviet government, which was being forced to shift from destruction to reconstruction of Russia's productive forces. Milyukov proposed no plan of action but placed his hopes on a historical process that would lead the Russian people themselves to overthrow the regime that oppressed them.

Petr Struve, the spokesman for conservative liberalism, was attacked by both left and right. For the left he was a monarchist who wanted to rehabilitate the tsarist regime. For the right he was a liberal who, horror of horrors, had been a Marxist in the past. He called for a strong state that would restore order in Russia and defend property rights while respecting the legitimate freedoms of the people.

The numerous parties of the left, People's Socialists, Left and Right Socialist Revolutionaries, Social Democrats, Mensheviks, and anarchists, debated the pros and cons of dictatorship by a party or by a class and argued over whether the Bolsheviks were socialists or not. In 1921 the Mensheviks began to publish *Sotsialistichesky vestnik* (Socialist herald) in Berlin. It provided a wealth of information about events in the Soviet Union.

Alongside the traditional parties new movements and organizations arose in exile. For example, an anthology was published in Sofia in 1921 entitled *Exodus to the East*, with the subtitle "Forebodings and Accomplishments: A Profession of Faith by the Eurasians." It set forth the main tenets of "Eurasianism." "We honor the past and present of Western European culture, but we do not see it as the future," said the foreword to the anthology.[176] The authors felt, as Herzen had, that "history is now knocking at our door." In the article "A Turn Toward the East," Professor Savitsky asked rhetorically, "Are there many people in Russia in whose veins the blood of Khazars, Polovtsians, Tatars, or Bashkirs does not flow?"[177] Russia was not only the West but the East, not only Europe but Asia as well. In fact it was not Europe at all but Eurasia.[178] The anthology advocated Russian nationalism as its main secular idea. Its authors warned, however, that they did not want to restrict nationalism to the framework of national chauvinism.[179] The Eurasians went further than the Slavophiles, who had spoken not only of the Russian people but of all the Slavic peoples; the Eurasians appealed to "the entire range of peoples of the Eurasian world, among whom the Russian people occupy a special position."[180]

A split occurred in the ranks of the Eurasians in 1929, marking the beginning of the end for this movement. Its ideas nevertheless inspired a broad range of political currents among Russian emigrés. The idea that because of its geopolitical situation and national character Russia could never become a democracy drew a section of emigrés with Eurasian views into collaboration with the Soviet government in the 1930s.

In 1923 a General Congress of Nationally Minded Russian Youth was held in Munich. It founded the League of Young Russians, electing A. L. Kazem-Bek as its president. This later became the Young Russia party, which advocated restoration of the monarchy in Russia with a legitimate heir from the house of the Romanovs to be placed on the throne. The congress passed a declaration that stated in part, "The development of antinationalist, liberal, and democratic schools of thought undermined the state and cleared the way for aggressive socialism and its logical culmination, modern communism." The declaration singled out as the "most negative factors in modern life" what it called "freemasonry and international capital, which is concentrated mostly in the hands of the Jews."[181]

The Young Russia movement sought to combine monarchism with "young nationalist ideas," which were said to be on the rise in all countries. This meant, above all the ideas of Italian fascism. Their infatuation with nazism was to come later. (The Young Russians wore blue shirts and greeted their leader Kazem-Bek with shouts that were the equivalent of "Heil Hitler.") Varshavsky, the historian of this second generation of emigré youth, the "unnoticed generation," observed that the social orientation of the Young Russians and other Russian nationalist youth groups—expressed in the slogan "a monarchy above classes, a monarchy of the working people"— was related not only to the influence of fascism and national socialism but also to their personal experience. The harsh conditions of emigré life deepened their suspicion and hostility toward democracy. Fascism seemed to provide a program combining the ideas of national and social rebirth.

One of the paradoxes of emigré life was that the right-wing parties and movements which had been conservative in Russia engaged in revolutionary activity abroad, while parties with revolutionary pasts became passive. The activism of the right-wing parties, their training of cadres for a future army and infiltration of agitators and terrorists into the Soviet Union, made them easy prey for the GPU. Soviet agents and provocateurs penetrated all the emigré organizations, but those favoring close ties with their homeland were especially vulnerable to GPU tricks and subterfuge.

All the parties and movements whose programs called for the restoration of a strong Russian state, nationalism, and opposition to democracy evolved in the same direction. The changing landmarks group, the Eurasians, and the Young Russians found more and more attractive features in the Soviet system and concluded that "there was no need to exaggerate the differences between the 'ideological' measures of the Communists and the real needs of the people."[182] Ultimately they agreed to collaborate with the Communist authorities. The "cunning dialectic of revolution"[183] allowed them to close their eyes to all unpleasant features.

Only a small number of Russian emigrés belonged to political parties, but the vast majority belonged to military, social, professional, and literary associations of one kind or another. Until the mid-1920s Germany was the center of Russian emigré life, especially Berlin, where there were at least forty Russian publishing houses, each of which brought out more than a thousand titles, and where three daily Russian papers were published, as well as numerous magazines, with views ranging from monarchist to anarchist. There too a Russian-language theater was able to survive. In the mid-1920s Paris became the center of Russian emigration, with as many as 300 emigré organizations. In Paris alone there were seven Russian newspapers and many magazines.

The tragedy of separation from the homeland, the difficulties and misfortunes of life in exile, the petty problems of everyday life, the perennial dissatisfaction with everything Western prevented the Russian emigrés from seeing the enormous amount that they actually accomplished, their tremendous contribution to Russian culture. The creative work of major Russian writers in exile such as Ivan Bunin and Marina Tsvetaeva, and of historians, philosophers, theologians, naturalists, engineers, artists, and painters are an inseparable part of the Russian heritage. But to this day no history of the Russian emigrés has been written. Very few understood that there was another side to the tragedy of emigré life. This was best expressed by Vladimir Nabokov, who became a great writer in exile. On the tenth anniversary of the October revolution he wrote:

> Above all we must celebrate ten years of freedom. The freedom that we enjoy, I believe, is not known in any country in the world. In the unique and special Russia that invisibly surrounds us, enlivens and supports us, feeds our souls, and colors our dreams, there is no law but the law of love of Russia and no power other than our own consciences. . . . Some day we will thank the blind Clio for allowing us to taste this freedom and enabling us to understand and cultivate in exile our profound feeling for our native land. . . . Let us not curse our exile. Let us repeat in our day the words of

Plutarch's ancient warrior: "Late at night in a savage land far from Rome I pitched my tent and my tent became Rome for me."[184]

Nabokov composed this paean to inner freedom just at the time when the years of waiting were coming to an end in the Soviet Union.

## WHO WILL PREVAIL?

The Thirteenth Party Congress marked the victory of a triumvirate, three leaders who had agreed to assume Lenin's mantle collectively. Kamenev chaired the congress, Zinoviev gave the report for the Central Committee, and Stalin organized the congress. Trotsky admitted defeat. But no sooner had the congress ended than Stalin began to undermine the position of his fellow triumvirs. Thus began the inexorable rise to power of Joseph Stalin.

A debate has gone on among historians for the past half century: Did Stalin create the apparatus or did the apparatus create Stalin? The desire to portray Stalin as the creator of the apparatus, the bureaucratic machine and system, is understandable. This conception allows one to divide Soviet history into the pre-Stalin, Stalin, and post-Stalin periods. But there is no doubt that the apparatus existed before Stalin, just as there is no doubt that he perfected it and used it to consolidate his power—just as his rivals tried unsuccessfully to do. "To be a leader and organizer," Stalin wrote in 1924, "means first of all to know your party cadres, to be able to grasp their strengths and weaknesses . . . and second to know how to assign them."[185] Stalin's technique was quite simple, but effective. He especially knew the weaknesses of the party members he assigned to one or another post, and in making assignments his aim was above all to punish some and reward others. One of the delegates to the Fourteenth Party Congress in December 1925 made this revealing observation: "The comrades are living and eating well right now, and so not everyone will raise his hand to vote against something, only to be sent to Murmansk or Turkestan for that."[186]

The party apparatus, Stalin's instrument for taking power, was an outgrowth of the party, but the character of the party had been shaped by Lenin more than anyone else. In 1926 Stalin's opponents—Trotsky, Zinoviev, Kamenev, Krupskaya, Pyatakov, and others—formed the United Opposition. In July they addressed a letter to the joint plenum of the Central Committee and the Central Control Commission. They denounced the situation in which "all discussion is from the top down and the ranks below merely listen, thinking for themselves only in isolated cases and on the sly. Those who are dissatisfied, have doubts, or disagree are afraid to raise their voices at party meetings. . . . Party members are afraid."[187]

The United Opposition sought to portray all this as the result of Stalin's policies. However, during the discussion held on the pages of *Pravda* in 1923, when the Oppositionists were still in power, the situation was the same. "Party members have forgotten how to think for themselves. They are afraid to 'yap' about anything until orders come from above. They wait for ready-made decisions to be handed down and even for the ready-made explanations for those decisions."[188] "There is self-seeking, sycophancy, and fear of expressing one's own opinion. . . . Everyone is pretty much preoccupied with the question of assignments and transfers."[189] "Under the system of command from above there is no party life for the ranks. The bureaucratic atmosphere, with official circulars setting the tone, pushes the ranks out of the picture. . . . Tale bearing, informing, and bootlicking are increasing, and careerism thrives on this soil."[190] "Some party officials use 'comrade' only in addressing someone of lower rank. They invariably address their superiors (ingratiatingly) by their first and middle names."[191] All of this was printed in the pages of *Pravda* during a brief moment of freedom for party members when a discussion was allowed by the top brass. They were talking about Lenin's party.

At the Fourteenth Congress in 1925 a member of the oppositional Leningrad delegation complained about the widespread practice of informing, which had taken "such forms and such characteristics that a comrade cannot tell his friend his most intimate thoughts."[192] The complaining comrade was justly reprimanded by Sergei Gusev: "You're faking, Bakaich, you're faking, believe me. In the past Lenin taught us that every member of the party has to be an agent of the Cheka; in other words, keep his eyes open and act as an informer. . . . I think that every party member must report on others. If we have a problem, it is not informing but the lack of informing."[193] Ten years later both of these men were able to return to the question of informing because both the complainer and the reprimander were in Lubyanka prison. But Gusev was absolutely right to accuse Ivan Bakaev (familiarly called Bakaich) of faking. It was hardly appropriate for Bakaev, one-time head of the Petrograd Cheka, to complain about informing. And Gusev was a hundred times right to recall that informing became a party norm under Lenin.

Stalin did not invent the party; he inherited it from Lenin. But he perfected it and embellished upon it in his own way, discarding everything extraneous or incidental. He enlarged the Central Committee to sixty-three full members and forty-two alternate members in 1925, thereby carrying out Lenin's recommendation that a struggle between Stalin and Trotsky could be prevented in this way. He carried out what was called the Lenin enrollment, bringing 203,000 new members into the party from February to August 1924, increasing the membership by 50 percent. Earlier, at the end of 1923, the question of holding a "party week" for the recruitment of 100,000 new members was discussed. The prevailing opinion at that time was that "our cadres are not equipped to integrate such a large number of new recruits. Our Martin ovens, the party cells, don't have the capacity to refine and temper this quantity of youthful raw material."[194] Yet within a few months 200,000 members were admitted. The party underwent a drastic change. Its new members were ignorant of the extraneous or incidental traditions which Stalin was energetically uprooting. The aim of the Lenin enrollment was to bring workers from the factory floor into the party. But the flood of new recruits mainly consisted of privilege seekers. "Many of them," a party member complained in *Pravda*, December 8, 1924, "view the party as some sort of pancake covered with sour cream." The new recruits were looking for jobs and got them. Workers from the factory floor became workers with briefcases, and party members from the countryside were promoted just as readily. But they had to pay for these privileges. The members of the party became vassals. They forfeited even those minimal liberties which Soviet citizens still enjoyed at the time.

The party, despite this rejuvenation, was led by the so-called Old Guard, the veteran party members. In January 1924 the Old Guard of those who had joined before 1917, those with experience in the tsarist underground, numbered only 8,249. The total party membership was 401,481, 56.6 percent of whom had joined between 1920 and 1924.[195]

The struggle for power was waged among the numerically insignificant number of former underground activists. It was in those circles that the political combinations, coalitions, and blocs were formed. It was there that Stalin showed his remarkable abilities at political maneuvering, employing others to do his dirty work. The main burden of the assault on Trotsky in 1923–1924 was eagerly assumed by Zinoviev and Kamenev. Later, in fighting those two, Stalin used Bukharin and enjoyed the benevolent neutrality of Trotsky. Unlike Trotsky, who referred darkly to the guillotine, or Zinoviev, who demanded Trotsky's arrest for publishing his article "Lessons of October," Stalin wore the mask of moderation. Recalling that his fellow triumvirs had demanded the arrest and expulsion of Trotsky, he uttered these remarkable words:

> We did not agree with Zinoviev and Kamenev because we knew that a policy of amputation is fraught with grave dangers for the party, that the method of amputation and of bloodletting—for they demanded blood—is dangerous

and contagious. Today you cut off one member of the party, tomorrow another, the next day a third, and soon what will be left of our party?[196]

Stalin fought his opponents with deeds, not words. Many years later the phrase "salami tactics" became famous. Stalin deprived his opponents of power little by little, cutting off tiny slices, one at a time. In January 1925 Trotsky was removed as commissar of war, after which he lost the support of the army apparatus, especially with the removal of his close ally Antonov-Ovseenko as head of the Political Directorate of the Red Army. Similarly, Kamenev was removed as head of the Moscow party organization at the end of 1925.

But Stalin also used words to fight his enemies. He had no trouble showing that they were unprincipled politicians, that at one time they had supported and defended Stalin only to turn against him later and say, as Kamenev did at the Fourteenth Congress: "We are against the creation of a 'Leader.' . . . I suggest that our general secretary is not a figure who can unite the Old Bolshevik general staff around himself." In reply to demands for party democracy, Mikoyan defended Stalin with the acid comment that when the Oppositionists were in power they were against democracy, but when they went into opposition they suddenly became its champions. Stalin himself did not hesitate to remind those who called for democracy of their own past.

> In the ranks of the Opposition there are people like Beloborodov whose "democratism" is still remembered by the workers of Rostov; Rozengolts, whose "democratism" was visited upon our water and rail transport workers; Pyatakov, whose "democratism" made the Donbass region not only yell but scream; . . . and Byk, whose "democratism" still makes Khorezm scream.[197]

During the power struggle of the 1920s a method of debating developed in which Stalin showed himself a past master. This system, essentially a semantic one, was an extremely important factor in enabling Stalin to defeat his opponents. Lenin deserves credit for developing this semantic system in 1903, when he called his group the Bolsheviks (majority supporters) when in fact they were in the minority on all but one question at the Second Party Congress. In the polemics that constantly shook the party from 1903 to 1917 (and after), Lenin always sought to pin a discrediting label on his opponents rather than defeat them by argument.

In the debates of 1923–1928 the adversaries constantly juggled labels and special terms such as "leftist," "rightist," "centrist," and "general line." Stalin demonstrated great virtuosity in this semantic game. The opponents of the "general line," which was constantly changing, could be accused of leftist views with rightist deviations or of a right deviation with leftist tendencies. Two new concepts were also created: "Leninism," a system of views that were always correct; and "Trotskyism," a system of views that was always hostile to Leninism. Any inappropriate phrase spoken by chance or out of carelessness became a crime. Stalin's first shot fired against his fellow triumvirs, a month after the Thirteenth Congress, was an attack on Kamenev, who had spoken of Nepman's Russia rather than NEP Russia. "Does Kamenev understand the principled difference here?" Stalin asked in his comradely way. "Of course he understands it. Why then did he put forward this strange slogan? Because of his characteristic disregard for theory and precise theoretical definitions."[198]

Every line was put through a strainer. Every word uttered by an opponent was reinterpreted, distorted, and falsified.

The best exammple of the semantic game Stalin played was his reduction of the dispute with Trotsky to a question of two slogans: "socialism in one country" and "permanent revolution." Lenin and all the other leaders had believed that the sparks of the Russian revolution would touch off a worldwide conflagration. After that would come the building of the radiant future. On March 12, 1919, Lenin said exactly that: "The tasks of construction depend entirely on how swiftly the revolution wins out in the main European countries. Only after that victory will we be able to undertake the tasks of construction in a serious way."[199] On November 6, 1920, he was even more categorical: "In one country it is impossible to achieve such a task as the socialist revolution."[200]

After the failure of the revolution in Europe, especially the fumbled attempts to start a revolutionary fire in Germany in 1923, all of the Bolsheviks understood that they had to build something in Russia. In late 1924, on the basis of a single sentence found in a 1915 article by Lenin, Stalin declared that it was possible and necessary to "build socialism in a single country," the Soviet Union. It was not enough, however, to formulate this positive program; he contrasted it to a negative program, which he called "the Trotskyist theory of permanent revolution." Long before the 1917 revolution Trotsky had put forward the theory that the Russian revolution would inevitably "pass over" from a bourgeois democratic to a socialist revolution and that its ultimate fate would depend on the world revolution, which was also inevitable. In full agreement with Lenin, Trotsky believed that only assistance from the victorious world proletariat would make it possible to consolidate the victory of the Russian proletariat.

In 1924 the question of the transition from bourgeois democratic to socialist revolution was purely of historical interest. But Stalin used the old formula of "permanent revolution" to construct the demon theory of Trotskyism, which allegedly denied the possibility of building socialism in the Soviet Union.

The debate between Stalin and Trotsky took place on two different levels. Trotsky argued theoretically in the traditional style of Marxist scholasticism. He agreed that the process of building socialism could begin in the Soviet Union, but he thought it impossible for the process to be completed within a single country. Stalin, for his part, avoided the fine points of theory, arguing in practical terms. He defended "Leninism" against "Trotskyism." He defended the honor of the Russian proletariat against Trotsky, who supposedly had no faith in its capacities. He made it clear that the policy of "building socialism in one country" meant a peaceful, constructive life, while "permanent revolution" would mean new wars and revolutions. Trotsky's defeat was inevitable. Bled white by its suffering, the country longed for peace.

This debate was typical of all the internal disputes in the party from 1923 to 1928. There were no clear differences of principle, as can be seen from the content of the discussions and the ease with which the adversaries changed their minds and shifted from one camp to another. The real difference between Stalin and all of his opponents was the way they debated and their attitude toward dogma. Many factors contributed to Stalin's victory, but the most important was the inner weakness of his opponents, unable as they were to free themselves of the dogmas by which they were bound. This was especially true of Trotsky, the most outstanding of Stalin's rivals, but none of them were able to overcome the prejudices of old fashioned Marxism. Stalin, Lenin's best disciple, was a Marxist of a new type, a Marxist of the twentieth century, possibly even the twenty-first.

In many respects Trotsky and Stalin were twins. Their attitude toward party democracy was the same. Trotsky wrote in November 1930: "What we mean by the restoration of party democracy is that the real, revolutionary, proletarian core of the party must win the right to curb the bureaucracy and to carry out a genuine purge of the party."[201] He went on to specify all the elements that had to be purged, quite a long list. Trotsky's and Lenin's attitudes toward democracy in society were also the same. Trotsky wrote in November 1932:

> The regime of the proletarian dictatorship cannot and does not wish to hold back from infringing the principles and formal rules of democracy. It has to be judged from the standpoint of its capacity to ensure the transition to a new society. A bourgeois democratic regime, on the other hand, must be judged from the standpoint of the extent to which it allows the class struggle to develop within the framework of democracy.[202]

The dictatorship of the proletariat was not bound by any "formal rules of democracy," but the democratic regime must allow its enemies to fight against it.

In principle Trotsky's attitude toward culture was also the same as Stalin's. Writing in exile in June 1933, Trotsky granted that "the party is obliged to permit a very extensive liberty in the field of art," but he added, "eliminating pitilessly only that which is directed against the revolutionary tasks of the proletariat."[203] Lastly, their attitude toward morality was the same. "The means can only be justified by the end," Trotsky wrote. "But the end must also be justified. From the point of view of Marxism, which expresses the historical interests of the proletariat, the end is justified if it increases humanity's power over nature and contributes to eliminating the power of man over man."[204] From the standpoint of this morality (if it can be called that), Trotsky justified the murder of the tsar's children but condemned the murder of his own children by Stalin, because Stalin was not a true representative of the proletariat.[205]

Trotsky was hopelessly outpaced by Stalin because Trotsky continued to believe in certain unshakable truths, for example, that the proletariat was a class with a historical mission to perform and that there were certain invariable historical laws that would specifically ensure the victory of Trotsky, who represented the true interests of the proletariat. He also believed in the party as the only instrument history had provided for the proletariat. His faith in these eternal truths bound Trotsky and the entire Opposition hand and foot and prevented them from using all the means at their disposal for fighting Stalin. To them, Stalin in the last analysis represented the party, and thus the proletariat and the laws of history. Stalin did not have any such complexes. He knew that he was right because he had the power, and that meant that anything was permitted.

A central topic of debate was the NEP. The question under discussion was this: What economic levers could the state use to obtain the resources necessary for industrial development when agriculture remained almost entirely in private hands? Until 1925 all the party leaders had agreed with the policy of *smychka*, the alliance with the peasantry. As a British historian noted, "If anyone in January 1925 had been acute enough to predict an imminent break between Stalin and Zinoviev on this issue, he would almost certainly have seen in Zinoviev the prospective champion of a peasant policy and Stalin and its opponent."[206] Even Trotsky in the fall of 1925 acknowledged that there was nothing threatening about the economic processes underway in the countryside, and he denounced any policy of "dekulakization" at that time.[207]

Bukharin was the chief ideologist of the NEP and he defended it against the attacks, first Trotsky's, then Zinoviev's and Kamenev's. But he was not opposed in principle to violence and exploitation. In 1920 Bukharin had advocated nationalization of all economic activities, militarization of labor, and rationing for everyone—in short, the universal use of force in regulating the economy.

Just as Stalin had "construed" Trotsky's political program in his own way, by reducing it to the slogan of permanent revolution and investing his own, Stalinist, meaning in that slogan, so too an economic program was devised for the United Opposition. A report by Preobrazhensky, "The Fundamental Law of Socialist Accumulation," was said to be the essence of the Opposition's economic point of view. Preobrazhensky argued that the October revolution was premature in the sense that Russia had not yet reached the necessary level of capitalist development, that what Marx called the stage of "primitive accumulation of capital" had not been completed. In other words, Russia did not yet have the industrial base necessary for material goods to be distributed "to each according to his needs." The capitalists had accomplished their primitive accumulation through the exploitation of colonies. According to Preobrazhensky, primitive socialist accumulation, which was necessary for the building of a socialist industry, would have to take place at the expense of the lower forms of economic life, in particular that "internal colony," the peasantry.[208]

Preobrazhensky's ties with Trotsky provided a splendid opportunity for Stalin to attribute the primitive accumulation theory to the Opposition as a whole. Growing numbers of Oppositionists leaned toward such extreme views, especially those like Kamanev and Zinoviev who based themselves in Leningrad and Moscow, where the workers were discontented with the social inequities produced by the NEP. They were inclined in this direction also because of the moderate position of Stalin and his associates, who argued for a program of "civil peace," as Bukharin did at the Fourteenth Party Congress.[209] Even Stalin asked whether there was any need for class warfare "now that we have the dictatorship of the proletariat and now that the party and trade union organizations function with full freedom." The general secretary answered his own question. "Of course not."[210]

Bukharin's program, supported by Stalin, stated that war against the peasantry would be fraught with fatal consequences, both political and economic, for the Soviet state. That was why economic development had to be based on an alliance with the peasants, providing them the opportunity to increase their productivity, organize cooperatives, and develop forms of exchange through the market. On April 17, 1925, Bukharin uttered the famous words: "We must tell the peasants, all the peasants, enrich yourselves. Develop your plots of land and don't be concerned about being pressured."[211] Later when Stalin began manufacturing a "right deviation," he chose these words of Bukharin's as the essence of the deviationists' program.

Bukharin's words provoked indignation among Oppositionists. Among the peasants they aroused hope. One man, a keen observer who considered himself the unofficial "loyal opposition," greeted them enthusiastically. This was Nikolai Ustryalov, whom Stalin called the "spokesman for the bourgeois specialists in our country."[212]

Ustryalov had no doubt that a new period in Soviet history had begun, one more step toward the emancipation of Russia from alien internationalist ideas. He also had no doubt that this period was crucially linked with the name of Stalin, whom Ustryalov regarded as Lenin's true disciple, he who had grasped Lenin's doctrine "dynamically," as befits the teachings of a master dialectician. Ustryalov proclaimed the "twilight of the Leninist Old Guard," noting that the former "masters and favorites of the revolution, the October guard, the stalwarts of the iron cohort, the pride and glory of the proletarian vanguard," had been dethroned.[213] In October 1926 Ustryalov declared, "Not only are we now 'Against Zinoviev'; we are definitely 'For Stalin.'"[214] Ustryalov did not delude himself about his new hero; he quoted the "wise words" of Konstantin Leontiev: "Good people are not infrequently worse than bad people. It is known to happen. Personal honesty may be pleasing on the personal level and may inspire respect, but there is nothing political or organizational about these fragile qualities. Very good people sometimes do terrible damage to the state."[215] From his peaceful nineteenth-century vantage point, Leontiev could not of course have imagined what terrible damage the bad people would do.

Ustryalov hailed Stalin's victory because he saw him as Lenin's true disciple. As early as 1923 Ustryalov had described Lenin and Mussolini as two equally important figures who "for all their political polarity... mark a new stage in the evolution of modern Europe."[216] In 1926 Stalin too was marking a new stage in European history as he marched inexorably toward full personal power within the party—and consequently within the state.

The Fourteenth Party Congress, in December 1925, brought an end to the interregnum, the period of "collective leadership." Three years earlier, Lenin's appearance before the Fourteenth Comintern Congress was described this way: "The applause is joyful and stormy because it has seemed a very long wait.... The entire auditorium sings the Internationale—because the applause, the ovation, seemed insufficient to express the boundless love for the leader and the limitless faith in him."[217] In December 1925 Stalin's speech to the party congress was greeted by "applause swelling to an ovation; all the delegates rose and sang the Internationale."

Stalin began consolidating his power at once. Kamenev and Zinoviev were removed from their posts in the Moscow and Leningrad party organizations, and Kamenev was demoted from full to alternate member of the Politburo. After the congress Kirov was sent to Leningrad to "restore order" there. In 1926 Zinoviev, Trotsky, and Kamenev were removed from the Politburo.

Stalin made use of every means to consolidate his power, including the art of medicine. In October 1925, by order of the Politburo, Commissar of War Frunze underwent an operation. (An ally of Zinoviev's, Frunze had replaced Trotsky as commissar of war a few months earlier.) The surgeons discovered that the ulcer they were ordered to remove had scarred over. The surgery was unnecessary, but the patient never rose from the operating table. He was replaced as commissar of war by Stalin's crony Voroshilov. At Frunze's funeral Stalin pronounced these mysterious words: "Perhaps this is the way, just this easily and simply, that all the old comrades should be lowered into their graves."[218]

Zinoviev and Kamenev, forced out of all their posts, proposed an alliance to their old enemy Trotsky. The United Opposition of 1926–1927 criticized Stalin for making concessions to the kulaks, refusing to industrialize the country, and bureaucratizing the state apparatus. This criticism of Stalin's policies, however, could not save the Opposition because it suffered from an inherent weakness.

The Fifteenth Party Congress, entirely dominated by the Stalinists, was held in December 1927 after a two-year interval, the first time that a congress had not been held once a year since the party had come to power. At the congress Kamenev gave a speech of repentance in which he said there were only two possible roads. One was the creation of a second party. "This road, under the conditions of proletarian dictatorship, would be disastrous for the revolution. . . . This road is closed to us, forbidden, ruled out by our entire system of ideas, by all of Lenin's teachings on the dictatorship of the proletariat." The other road was "to submit wholly and entirely to the party." "We have chosen this road," said Kamenev, "because we are deeply convinced that a correct Leninist policy can triumph only within our party and through it, not outside it or against it."[219] Trotsky himself, even after being deported from the Soviet Union in February 1929, held the same position, that the Soviet state was still the historical instrument of the working class.

Capitulation did not save the Oppositionists. Kamenev and 121 other

Opposition leaders were expelled from the party by the Fifteenth Congress. Some had already been arrested. Rykov concluded a speech at the congress with these words: "I don't think we can guarantee that the prison population will not have to be increased somewhat in the near future."[220] Ten years later, while sitting in prison, he may have regretted those words.

To the Opposition's objections that Stalin was using terror against party members, the general secretary replied: "Yes, we are arresting them and we will continue to. . . . Some say that in the history of our party such incidents have never been seen before. Untrue. What about the Myasnikov group? And the Workers' Truth group? Who does not know that the members of those groups were arrested with the full agreement of Zinoviev, Trotsky, and Kamenev?"[221]

The Fifteenth Congress ended the dispute over the succession to Lenin and definitively answered the question, Who will prevail? Over a period of five years Stalin had carried out what Boris Souvarine called his "molecular *coup d'état*."[222] He assumed the mantle of Lenin.

## WHAT TO DO ABOUT CULTURE?

In April 1918 some representatives of the newly organized Union of Activists in the Arts gathered at the home of Maxim Gorky for a meeting with the commissar of education, Anatoly Lunacharsky, an occasional dramatist and literary critic in his own right. They proposed that the executive committee of their union be placed in charge of the arts instead of the existing collegium, or board, of the Commissariat of Education. In other words, they wanted artists to administer the arts. Lunacharsky responded: "We were against the Constituent Assembly in the political arena. We are all the more opposed to a Constituent Assembly in the arts."[223]

The party announced its intention to administer art and culture directly. This involved two elements: (1) what artists should not write, paint, sculpt, etc.; and (2) what they should. The first part of this program was easy to carry out. Press censorship was introduced immediately after the revolution, in November 1917. Then after the civil war, on June 8, 1922, the Council of People's Commissars announced the formation of a Main Press Committee, whose purpose was to "unify all existing forms of censorship in Russia." Two months later a government decree established the Main Literature and Art Administration (Glavnoe Upravlenie po Delam Literatury i Iskusstva), which became famous under the acronym Glavlit as the main Soviet censorship agency over the years and which exists to this day. The duties of Glavlit, according to its founding decree, included "prior examination of all literary works, periodical and nonperiodical publications, maps, etc., intended for publication and distribution." In addition, Glavlit was to "issue all official authorizations for printed works of any kind, prepare lists of banned books, and work out provisions governing printing establishments, libraries, and the book trade."[224]

The second part of the program was harder to implement. Practical experience with ways of pressuring artists into doing what the party required had not yet accumulated.

First of all, the party had to assert its inalienable right to act as the sole authority in cultural matters. A challenger to this right was a group that called itself Proletkult, short for Proletarian Cultural and Educational Organization. Its leader, the ex-Bolshevik Aleksandr Bogdanov, had worked out the theory of an autonomous proletarian culture even before the revolution. He held that the "organizational principle of the bourgeoisie" was individualism and that therefore bourgeois culture was individualistic. The organizational principle of the proletariat was collectivism. The proletariat had to reexamine all previously existing culture from this point of view, reevaluate it, and take control of it. The proletariat would then transform all old science and scholarship and create a new "universal organizational science," which would enable it to "organize all human existence in a harmonious and complete fashion." After the February revolution, the supporters of Proletkult announced themselves as an independent worker's organization—independent, that is, of the Provisional Government's Ministry of Education. After the October revolution numerous Proletkult circles, studios, and laboratories were organized for industrial workers who wanted to paint, write poetry, or take to the stage. Proletkult published books and pamphlets, held conferences, and opened what it called the Proletarian University in Moscow. The work of "creating a proletarian culture" had begun.

Lenin declared war on Proletkult. Bad enough that it was led by his former friend Bogdanov, who had become a dangerous enemy, a man whose philosophical writings Lenin never ceased to denounce; in addition, Proletkult was seeking "to wall itself off from the party's leadership."[225] Bogdanov held that "Proletkult was the class organization of the proletariat for culture and the creative arts just as the workers' party was its political organization and the trade union was its economic organization." Lenin answered that the proletariat has only one organization, the party, which "guides and directs not only in politics but also in economics and culture."[226] In 1919 the Proletarian University in Moscow was closed down, particularly because a course in Bogdanov's "organizational science" had been given there. In its place a so-called Communist University was founded. In October 1920 the Politburo took up the question of Proletkult three times. At the session on October 9, Lenin spoke nine times on the question; so did another expert on culture, Stalin.[227]

On December 1, 1920, *Pravda* published a letter by the Central Committee on the subject of Proletkult. This was the first in an endless series of Central Committee pronouncements on cultural questions. Proletkult was stripped of its autonomy, and Communist party members were removed from the central committee of Proletkult and obliged to acknowledge the guiding role of their party and its leadership in this sphere. The letter expressed the Central Committee's views on other cultural questions as well: for example, that futurism reflected "perverse and absurd tastes." Soon after the publication of this letter Proletkult renounced its former ties with the futurists and passed a resolution stating that "futurism and comm-futurism are ideological currents characteristic of the final phase of bourgeois culture in the age of imperialism" and therefore must be recognized as "hostile to the proletariat as a class."[228]

The death of Alexander Blok marked the end of an era, the collapse of faith in the revolution on the part of the intelligentsia, the demise of hope. "Life has changed," Blok wrote in his diary on April 17, 1921. Earlier he had written "The Twelve," a poem in which Christ led the revolutionaries into the future. Now he wrote, "Throughout the world, the louse has conquered and everything will go a different way now, not the way we used to live, the way we loved."[229] At his last public appearance, a meeting in honor of the eighty-fourth anniversary of Pushkin's death, Blok spoke of the poet's mission: "They also take away peace and liberty . . . not outward peace, but the inner calm of creativity. Not juvenile libertinism . . . but creative freedom, a secret inner liberty. And the poet dies because he can no longer breathe; life has lost its meaning."[230] Within a few months Blok himself died, and his death was quite symbolic. On May 29, 1921, Gorky addressed a letter to Lunacharsky: "Would you please ask the Politburo as quickly as possible to give permission for Blok to leave for Finland." Twelve days later Lunacharsky passed on the request in behalf of Blok, who was seriously ill. The next day the Politburo discussed the question and passed a resolution to "improve the food situation for Alexander Blok." Blok's condition worsened. On July 23 the Politburo agreed to allow the poet to leave the country but would not give permission for his wife to accompany him. The poet was in no condition to travel by himself. On July 29 Gorky sent a telegram to the Kremlin addressed to Lunacharsky: "Urgent. Condition extremely serious. Immediate departure for Finland indispensable."

On August 1 Lunacharsky again raised the question with the Central Committee. This time the authorization was granted.[231]

On August 7 Blok died at the age of forty. Weeks had passed since Gorky's initial letter. It is common knowledge that it was Lenin who decided questions involving departure from the Soviet Republic by people prominent in science and culture.

Neither the fact that most intellectuals protested against the October revolution nor that numerous cultural figures went into exile stopped the progress in the arts that had been going on in Russia since the turn of the century. Not even the lack of essential materials, such as paints and canvas for artists, marble for sculptors and architects, and paper for writers, stopped this powerful creative impulse. Andrei Bely wrote: "In its most difficult days Russia became like a garden of nightingales. Poets sprang up as never before. People barely had the strength to live but they were all singing."[232] However, as Lenin explained to Clara Zetkin, the task of the party was to direct this spontaneous artistic and cultural outpouring into a constructive channel serving the state and to bring it under the control of party institutions.[233] Viktor Shklovsky jotted down this note at the time: "Art must move organically, like the heart in the human breast, but they want to regulate it like a train."[234]

The task of regulating art fell to party members who were connected with one or another artistic endeavor. Proletarian writers and proletarian artists became cultural leaders. The magazine of the proletarian writers, appropriately enough, was named *On Guard* (*Na postu*).

In 1923 Trotsky coined a phrase for designating nonproletarian writers and artists who wanted to live and work in the Soviet Republic but were not fully qualified to do so (in the eyes of the party); he called them fellow travelers (*poputchiki*). Those writers and artists who were not classed as outright enemies could be granted the designation *poputchik*, but there was a thin line between "enemy" and "fellow traveler." Maxim Gorky, who had left the country and who was regarded with hostility by the proletarian writers, was classed as a fellow traveler. So was Mayakovsky, although one of *Pravda*'s leading journalists, Lev Sosnovsky, denounced Mayakovsky in 1921 for having dared to take "our very old comrade Svortsov-Stepanov" to court because he had "refused in his capacity as director of the State Publishing House, Gosizdat, to pay royalties on some futurist nonsense published in a theatrical journal." The article concluded unequivocally, "So you want to fool around, Messieurs Futurists? We will see that your inappropriate and costly fooling comes to an end."[235]

This was not the first warning to the fellow travelers. They had been warned by the shooting of Gumilev, the death of Blok, and the deportation of many leading intellectuals from the country; and they had been threatened repeatedly with the "stern whip of the dictatorship" in newspaper and magazine articles. On February 27, 1922, the Orgburo passed a resolution "on the struggle against petit bourgeois ideology in the field of literature and publishing."[236] This was the second Central Committee pronouncement on cultural questions. It indicated what should and should not be published. In particular it authorized the printing of works by a group of young writers who had formed the first literary association after the revolution, the Se-rapion Brothers, but only on the condition that "the latter do not contribute to any reactionary publications." Which publications were reactionary, of course, was decided solely by the party.

The danger to culture and free creative activity was first pointed out by Evgeny Zamyatin, who was also the first to disclose the real nature of the October revolution as the beginning of a new era. "We have lived through the epoch of suppression of the masses," he wrote in 1920. "We are living in an epoch of suppression of the individual in the name of the masses."[237] With the foresight of genius he wrote the novel *We*, in which he described the Only State, the state of the future, in which there is only one individual, the Benefactor, and in which the citizens are mere numbers. In this state, where the citizens' capacity to fantasize has been surgically removed so that they can become just like machines, the fate of literature, art, and culture is foreordained. "How is it possible," asks the hero of the novel, "that the ancients did not see as plain as day the total absurdity of their literature and poetry? The grand and majestic power of the written word was spent for nothing. It was simply ridiculous. Everyone wrote whatever came to mind."[238] In Zamyatin's negative utopia, literature is a branch of the civil service. Ten or fifteen years later Zamyatin's terrible prophecy became a reality. Today it seems like a commonplace, but in 1920 the idea of a "state literature" was an entirely new concept.

Zamyatin was the most consistent and fearless defender of creative free-dom. He issued his warning about the threat to culture not in *We*, whose publication was banned, but in an article entitled "I Am Afraid," in which he said,

> True literature can exist only where it is created, not by diligent and trust-worthy officials, but by madmen, misfits, heretics, dreamers, rebels, and skeptics. But when a writer must be sensible and rigidly orthodox, ... there can be no literature cast in bronze, there can be only a paper literature, a newspaper literature, which is read today and used for wrapping soap to-morrow.[239]

Zamyatin was not alone. The painter Kazimir Malevich, one of the world's first abstract artists, insisted on the independence of the arts.

> All social and economic relations do violence to art. . . . Whether a portrait is being painted of some socialist or some emperor, whether a mansion is being built for a businessman or a humble dwelling for a worker—these differences cannot be taken as the starting point for art. . . . It is about time we understood at last that the problems of art and the problems of the belly are extremely remote from one another.[240]

The old Russian writer Vikenty Veresaev also complained: "Our creative work is being done more and more on two levels—one that we write for ourselves, the other for publication."[241] Even Aleksandr Zharov, the bard of the Young Communist League, who was more devoted to the party than anyone, expressed regret: "I'm not allowed to sing sad songs. A mark would go against me on my party card."

By the the mid-1920s voices of protest became less frequent and more discreet. It was harder for them to break into print, but the voices praising the policies of the party and the shackling of literature grew louder and more triumphant. At his last public appearance, Alexander Blok, still very hesitantly, pointed to a phenomenon he found astonishing. He contrasted the youthful volubility of the radical critic Belinsky, who continued Pushkin's rebellious tradition in Russian literature, to the polite restraint of Chief of Gendarmes Count Benckendorff, who on behalf of Tsar Nicholas I helped harass Pushkin and drive him to his grave. Blok said that he always believed the Belinskys were totally opposed and totally hostile to the Benckendorffs and it would be terribly painful if that turned out not to be so.[242] But Blok was not mistaken. The Soviet Belinskys were turning into Soviet Benckendorffs, and although they did not have the polite voice of the chief of gendarmes, they outstripped him by far in the techniques of repression.

A leading Soviet literary critic of the early 1920s, Petr Kogan, declared:

> For a long time to come the revolution must forget about the end for the sake of the means, must get rid of the dream of freedom so that discipline will not be weakened. A splendid yoke, not of gold but of steel, solid and organized—that is the new element the revolution has brought in for now. Instead of a yoke of gold a yoke of steel. Whoever does not understand that this is the only road to emancipation does not understand anything about current events.[243]

Kogan sang the glories of the yoke of steel in full seriousness, not knowing that Zamyatin had already predicted such things in his novel *We*. The Only State had launched a spaceship with the following assignment: "Your mission is to subject to the beneficial yoke of reason all unknown beings in inhabiting other planets, beings perhaps still living in the wild state of freedom. If they fail to understand that we bring them mathematically infallible happiness, our duty will be to force them to be happy."[244] Petr Kogan is the same literary critic who noted with approval the "exceptional interest the imaginative literature of today is showing in the Cheka and the Chekists," that is, the security police agencies and their agents.[245] "The Chekist," Kogan said, "is a symbol of an almost inhuman decisiveness, a being who does not have the right to normal human feelings, such as pity, love, and doubt. He is an instrument of steel in the hands of history."[246] With this instrument of steel a party could carry out its historical task— forcing people to be happy.

The year 1925, which was marked by the death of another writer, the suicide of Sergei Esenin, was the high point of the NEP in culture as well as politics and economics. Through the force of inertia the powerful wave of innovation in the arts begun at the turn of the century continued. Besides that, social cataclysms have always been fertile ground for literature, and it would be difficult to imagine greater cataclysms than the combination of war and revolution from 1914 to 1922. Another factor favorable to the arts was the internal dispute in the party, which occupied the attention of the leaders and diverted them from working out a single clear line for bringing culture to heel.

The conjunction of all these factors created opportunities for development in the figurative arts, theater, the cinema, and literature that were never to occur again. The experiments in form, language, and subject matter of the writers Andrei Bely and Velemir Khlebnikov and the renovation of the literary language carried out by Remizov and Zamyatin, in combination with numerous topics not dealt with before in literature, produced such remarkable prose writers as Boris Pilnyak, Isaac Babel, and Vsevolod Ivanov, and such poets as Osip Mandelstam, Anna Akhmatova, Boris Pasternak, and Marina Tsvetaeva. In the theater this was the age of Meyerhold, the herald of an October-style revolution in the theater; Tairov, the proponent of what he called chamber theater; and Forreger, the film experimentalist, and his protégé, Sergei Eisenstein. Likewise, Lev Kuleshov and Dziga Vertov created a new kind of poetics for a new medium, the cinema.

After 1925 Stalin's position as top leader of the party was no longer in doubt. More attention was now paid to literature, and a general line was proclaimed in cultural matters. In February 1925 the Moscow Committee of the party called a conference to take up the question of the intelligentsia. This was the last occasion on which members of the intelligentsia were able to express their views publicly and have an exchange of opinion with the party leadership. Lunacharsky and Bukharin represented the party, and the intelligentsia was represented by Academician Pavel Sakulin, a renowned literary historian, and Yuri Klyuchnikov, a writer and supporter of the changing landmarks point of view. The fate of the intelligentsia and freedom of thought were the topic for discussion. Lunacharsky presented the main report and indicated that the party had "no fixed and final, indisputable, ready-made opinion on the fate of the intelligentsia."[247] The party had a goal, "to persuade or to force" the intelligentsia to work with the proletariat. Lunacharsky quoted Lenin, "If persuasion does not work, force must be used."[248]

Academician Sakulin responded first of all that the better part of the Russian intelligentsia could never regard the revolution as alien because the intelligentsia itself had "nurtured the dream of political freedom and social equality."[249] Secondly, he hoped that "during the time when war communism was dominant, before it was terminated by the course of events, the position of the intelligentsia was very difficult."[250] By this he did not mean their material situation but the ideological and methodological dictatorship which the Central Committee had proclaimed over education and scientific research.[251] Addressing the party and the government, Sakulin then presented the main demand of those intellectuals who wanted to work with the revolutionary authorities: "There should be no claim to a monopoly on the truth. . . . The essence of the truth is that it requires freedom in education and research, and competing schools of scientific thought."[252]

Klyuchnikov presented a different position, the changing landmarks view: "Since the Soviet government is fighting for its ideals under conditions of tremendously hostile encirclement and since it can transform ruined Russia into a mighty power only if its ideals are victorious," the intellectual outside the party has "no alternative but to recognize that his fate must be to submit."[253] Klyuchnikov contended that for the intellectual to do creative work he must be placed in an appropriate environment enabling him to be creative. But political freedom was not necessary. "To give that to us intellectuals outside the party, even those who are marching firmly in step with the Soviet authorities, would be dangerous. We would just shoot off our mouths."[254] The stenographic record at this point records applause. The intellectuals present in the great hall of the Moscow Conservatory apparently agreed that they would all just shoot off their mouths if they were given political freedom.

Bukharin's speech at this conference showed that the Soviet government had no intention of granting any freedom. The man whom Lenin had called the "favorite of the party" and who at that time was acting as chief theorist for the Stalinist majority, was frank and open. "Freedom in education is a sophism," he said.[255] Such categories as the people, good, and freedom were mere verbal badges, empty shells.[256] The party had come to power "by marching over corpses. For this it had to have not only nerves of steel but also a knowledge of the road history had marked out for us, based on Marxist analysis."[257] The party's victory had confirmed the accuracy and correctness of Marxist ideology. The party would not renounce the hegemony of Marxism because "it is the most powerful weapon in our hands, allowing us to build what we want."[258] "In particular," Bukharin declared, "it is essential to us that intellectual cadres be trained in an ideologically precise way. Yes, we will produce standardized intellectuals, produce them as though in a factory."[259]

A few months after this conference the Central Committee's press department held a conference on party policies in regard to literature. Thus the Central Committee was proceeding from a definition of the general line to a specific application of its policy toward the most important section of the intelligentsia, the writers.

There was no single, unified point of view. The proletarian writers, who had formed the so-called October Group and had published the magazine *On Guard* since 1923, called for a big stick policy in relation to the fellow travelers. The fellow travelers were mainly published in a magazine called *Red Virgin Soil* (*Krasnaya nov*), run by the Old Bolshevik Aleksandr Voronsky. It was revealed by Vardin, a leader of the *On Guard* group, that "in 1921 Comrade Voronsky was given certain directives and certain resources in order to keep a certain group of writers in Soviet Russia. ... At the time we had to be careful that the Pilnyaks would not defect to the Whites."[260] Voronsky's view was that since proletarian literature did not exist, the party had to give the fellow travelers "a moral working-over," to paraphrase Lenin. This line had Trotsky's support as well. He did not think proletarian literature would have time to come into existence because the period of proletarian dictatorship would be too short. Bukharin on the other hand upheld the theory of socialism in one country and favored the development of proletarian literature. He believed it was necessary to reeducate some of the fellow travelers and get rid of the others.

At the Central Committee conference of July 1925 two different policies were advanced. Voronsky proposed that the party abstain from adopting the viewpoint of any one literary current and instead aid all the revolutionary groupings while prudently seeking to orient them. Vardin proposed that the party install the dictatorship of the party in literature and that the Russian Association of Proletarian Writers (RAPP) be the instrument of that dictatorship. As to the fellow travelers, he favored the establishment of a "literary Cheka." A letter signed by thirty-seven prominent Soviet writers was read to the conference. Among the signers were Aleksei Tolstoy, Isaac Babel, Mikhail Zoshchenko, and Sergei Esenin. The writers spoke of their close ties with post-October Soviet Russia, confessed their own errors, but at the same time complained about the attacks upon them by the *On Guard* group, which was presenting its views as though they were the views of the party as a whole. This letter was a totally new phenomenon. Writers were asking the party for protection, addressing it as a supreme arbiter.

The resolution of the Central Committee combined both points of view on how to control literature. Everyone agreed on the main thing, that it was up to the party to identify without fail the "social and class essence of all literary currents" and to exercise its authority over them.[261] The only disagreement was over what kind of sauce to cook the fellow travelers in.

The majority of Soviet writers who felt that they were suffering under the tutelage of the *On Guard* group accepted the Central Committee resolution as a charter of liberties for the writer. Only a few understood its real meaning. Pasternak commented that the country was not going through a cultural revolution but a "cultural reaction."[262] Osip Mandelstam, as his widow Nadezhda tells us in her memoir *Hope Against Hope*, understood that the noose would be tightened more and more around the neck of literature. There were even some who found the idea of a "literary Cheka" entrancing. Mayakovsky spoke on October 2, 1926, during a discussion on the Soviet government's theatrical policy. He called for legal reprisals against Mikhail Bulgakov for his play *The Days of the Turbins*, which depicted the Whites rather favorably. It had been staged by the Moscow Art Theater. "Accidentally, and to the great joy of the bourgeois, we gave Bulgakov a chance to whine and squeal—and whine he did, but we won't let him again."[263] Mayakovsky totally identified himself with those who would decide whether or not to allow writers to whine and squeal. The former rebel poet had become a hunter of heretics.

After the Central Committee resolution, power in the fields of literature, art, and theater gradually passed into the hands of the *On Guard* group, to those who were commonly called "the frenzied zealots."

# 4

# IN PURSUIT OF CONFLICT, 1926–1928

## THE DEATH OF NEP

Historians disagree on exactly when the NEP ended, but it began to die out in late 1926. The "grain procurement crises" of 1927 and 1928—sharp reductions in peasant deliveries of grain to the state—were the visible symptoms of NEP's mortal illness. But sooner or later, one way or another, the NEP was doomed. The Soviet system was not suited to, indeed had not been created for, the resolution of problems through normal, traditional methods under peaceful conditions.

The system had been created by a revolution to carry out a "great leap forward" into utopia. Under Lenin, during the civil war, primitive but effective forms of government had been worked out: intimidation, open terror, and rule by decree. But they were effective only under crisis conditions. Crisis alone permitted the authorities to demand—and obtain— total submission and all necessary sacrifices from its citizens. The system needed sacrifices and sacrificial victims for the good of the cause and the happiness of future generations. Crises enabled the system in this way to build a bridge from the fictional world of utopian programs to the world of reality.

In the second half of 1926, the NEP began gasping for breath. The restoration of the economy had, for the most part, been accomplished. It became necessary at that point to decide what direction further economic development should take, especially in regard to heavy industry. Bukharin's program, embodied in the slogan, "Enrich yourselves," represented a peaceful, traditional model of development.

During the NEP years N. Valentinov (whose real name was Nikolai Volsky) edited the *Commercial-Industrial Gazette*, organ of the Supreme Economic Council, the VSNKH. A Bolshevik until 1905, then a Menshevik, Valentinov-Volsky knew Lenin and the other Bolshevik leaders well. In his opinion the "right-wing Communists were following a program parallel to Stolypin's."[1] In other words, Bukharin's program, supported by Stalin in 1925, was similar to the Stolypin land reform, with the difference that Nicholas II's prime minister believed in the permanence of his reform, whereas the 1925 program only temporarily sanctioned private farming on nationalized land.

Bukharin's program had a positive impact on agriculture. As Valentinov-Volsky put it, "The year 1925 and the first half of 1926 were indeed happy times for the peasantry."[2] But this period can be called happy only in relative terms: it was better than the preceding one and immeasurably better than the one that followed. Even in this "happy" period the peasants were squeezed by taxes and uncertain what the future would bring. On an income of 250 rubles, a peasant paid as much in taxes as a small businessman or merchant paid on 1,200 rubles or a worker on 3,800.[3] For 16.4 kilos of rye in 1913 a peasant could buy 5.48 meters of cloth; for the same amount of rye in June–July 1927 he could buy only 2.55 meters of cloth. The corresponding figures for malt were 103 and 61.9; for sugar, 8.24 and 3.93 pounds.[4]

Still, the peasants were much better off than the workers. Unemployment was increasing, but wages were not. "Nine years after the October revolution the workers in the main branches of our industry do not even dare to dream of their prewar wages."[5] Discontent over a policy that allowed the peasants to live better than the workers was quite natural. Among rank-and-file party members and lower-level party officials nostalgia for the lost paradise of war communism was felt more and more strongly. "Once there were some brothers named Wright," recalls the hero (one of a group of "the last real Communists," who have gathered in a cave) of "Mahogany," a story by Boris Pilnyak. "These brothers decided to fly into the sky, and they perished, smashed to the ground, after falling from the sky. . . . Comrade Lenin has perished, like the Wright brothers. . . . What kind of ideas he had no one remembers any more, comrades, except us." Such was the lament of a "Communist called up under war communism, demobilized in 1921."[6]

In 1928 Artem Vesely published a "demi-short story" called "The Barefoot Truth." Some Communists from the Kuban, heroes of the civil war, were writing a letter of complaint to their former commander, Mikhail Vasilievich: "The truth must be spoken plainly—there's more bad in our life than good." They complained of their poverty and the scornful attitude of the Soviet authorities, the bureacratic apparatus, toward them. "The old saying isn't wrong," the veterans complained, bitterly recalled their wartime exploits against the Whites. "As long as the watchdog barked, he was needed. When he got old, he was chased away." They asked a key question: "What did we fight for, Mikhail Vasilievich? For government bureaus or workers' committees?"[7] The heroes of Vesely's story were not the only ones asking this question or voicing these complaints, as is shown by the fact that the party's Central Committee passed a special resolution on May 8, 1929—the first of its kind—"sharply reprimanding" the editors of the magazine *Molodaya gvardiya* (Young guard) for publishing "The Barefoot Truth," "a one-sided, tendentious depiction of Soviet reality, essentially a caricature that is objectively beneficial only to our enemies."[8] For the heroes of "The Barefoot Truth" the main source of misfortune, the death of the revolution, lay in the fact that "committees were replaced by bureaus"—that is, by the bureaucratic apparatus.

The Soviet apparatus—in the government, the state economy, and the party—never stopped growing. By 1928 functionaries numbered 4 million. But this gigantic apparatus, controlled from the center, was incapable of administering the country under normal conditions. "A big fuss is made about the apparatus," wrote Demyan Bedny, the leading "proletarian" poet, in its defense. "But it has to make a devilish effort to get the proletarian steamshhip moving." What's more, this steamship was "towing behind it a huge barge, the peasantry, which is reluctant, sluggish, and intractable."[9] In fact, the apparatus itself was sluggish and incapable of independent action, consisting as it did of two incompatible elements: unskilled, often illiterate Communist leaders; and the civil servants under them, who trembled with fear—a fear the leaders cultivated perennially and systematically.

The only efficient organ of Soviet power was the Cheka-GPU. Whenever something had to be done quickly an "extraordinary commission" was created. This combination of words—it was assumed—could produce results just by itself. For example, Mikoyan relates that in December 1922, when it was necessary to obtain boots and warm clothing, the Council of Labor and Defense established an extraordinary commission for the procurement of felt boots (*valenki*), bast shoes (*lapti*), and sheepskin coats (*polushubki*), abbreviated Chekvalap.[10] When an extra effort had to be exerted and a special committee was set up for that purpose, Feliks Dzerzhinsky, head of the Cheka-GPU, was invariably placed in charge. He directed the rail system, the aid program for homeless children, the Main Labor Committee, and the Extraordinary Commission for the Struggle Against Snowdrifts. When a mass society of Friends of the Soviet Cinema was organized, Dzerzhinsky was chosen its chairman.[11] Again, in 1924, when the Society for the Study of Interplanetary Communications was founded, the head of the GPU was not forgotten.[12] This was how they carried out the will of Lenin, who proclaimed that "the Cheka must become an instrument of discipline such as we succeeded in creating in the Red Army."[13]

On January 31, 1924, Dzerzhinsky was nominated chairman of the Supreme Economic Council, the VSNKH, the body that directed the Soviet economy. "Dzerzhinsky brought the GPU apparatus closer than ever to the tasks of economic construction," his biographer tells us.[14] Valentinov-Volsky, in his memoirs about work at the Vesenkha, portrays Dzerzhinsky as a calm, sober-minded director. The quality that Valentinov valued most in the head of the GPU at the Vesenkha was Dzerzinsky's awareness that he should not frighten those who worked under him. After his death in July 1926 the functionaries at Vesenkha sincerely mourned him. "What a shame that Dzerzhinsky's gone. It was easy to work with him. He appreciated and defended us specialists. Under him we could sleep in peace without fear that the Black Maria would come for us."[15] These lamentations effectively convey the atmosphere in the "peaceful years" of the NEP. Dzerzhinsky's reasonableness was akin to that of the intelligent slavemaster, who knows that slaves represent material value. Nevertheless, the head of the GPU made clear where he stood: "I was named to the Supreme Economic Council. . . . I introduced the principle of planning with an iron hand. Some people know very well that I have a very heavy hand which can strike strong blows. I will not permit work to be done as it has been up to now, that is, anarchically."[16]

The most important characteristic of the system of rule created by the Communist party was that all problems were considered solely from the point of view of political utility. This applied to the economy as much as to other problems. In the latter part of the NEP the handling of economic problems, as with all questions of "the general line," ran into difficulties that had not existed during war communism, when Lenin's authority swept all disagreements or objections aside, difficulties that would not exist after 1929 either, when Stalin's power would likewise sweep all objections aside.

The difficulties in 1926–1927 consisted mainly in the fact that the United Opposition existed. Trotsky was easily beaten, but his slogans and his criticism of Stalin and Bukharin as "defenders of the kulaks" found an echo in the party, among those who were asking, "Is this what we fought for?"—among those who remembered the ideals of communism, among workers discontented with their conditions, and among the almost 2 million unemployed.[17] Trotsky's criticisms were reinforced when his former opponents Zinoviev and Kamenev joined him. The oppositionists, although excluded from the party apparatus, were still able to air their views in the "Discussion Bulletin" supplement to *Pravda*, published from time to time during precongress discussions, and to circulate them privately in manuscript form by the method later called *samizdat*. Within the party it was known not only that Ustryalov praised the policies of Stalin and Bukharin but also that the Mensheviks criticized them sharply from a Marxist viewpoint, on the grounds that they were leading the country not to communism but "from the old landlord-capitalist economy to a new peasant-capitalist economy."[18]

During the entire period of internal struggle in the party only once was a totally new idea proposed. A worker named Yakov Ossovsky, a Communist since 1918, proposed the formation of a second party in the Soviet Union, the creation of a two-party system. As an orthodox Marxist, he believed that the presence of two economic sectors (one private, the other state) made two parties necessary: "As long as we hold to the principle that ours is the only party and that it requires absolute unity," Ossovsky wrote, "a free exchange of opinions in our organizations and party press is not permitted, despite the fact that within the party a difference of opinion does exist, owing to the diversity in the economy."[19] Ossovsky was censured by the Central Control Commission and expelled from the party.[20] Bukharin declared that open discussion, such as Ossovsky proposed, was impermissible "because it would shake the very foundations of the proletarian dictatorship, the unity of our party and its dominant position in our country, because it would bring grist to the mill of the groups and splinter groups that are yearning for political democracy."[21] Even the oppositionists condemned Ossovsky's proposal. There had never been two parties in the Soviet Union. Nevertheless, in the years 1923–1928, the views of the opposition did have an effect on the "general line."

In the fall of 1926 the peasants sharply reduced the sale of grain and other products to the state. Ante Ciliga, a Yugoslav Communist who had arrived in Moscow in 1926 to represent his party, wrote in his memoirs: "The autumn of 1927 was marked by an occurrence new to me: in the stores there was no meat, no cheese, no milk. Then there began to be interruptions in the sale of bread."[22] The crisis in grain deliveries and the attendant difficulties in food supply were taken by Stalin as an occasion to strike a new blow at the opposition. In October 1927, Trotsky and Zinoviev were expelled from the Central Committee. After their attempt to organize a counterdemonstration on November 7, the tenth anniversary of the Bolshevik revolution, they and dozens of others were expelled from the party.

Having driven the Opposition leaders out of the party, Stalin began to take over their program and follow their suggestions. To overcome the crisis he resorted to "extraordinary measures." Thirty thousand party members were sent into the countryside to wring grain out of the peasantry. Party leaders, too, traveled into the field. On January 15, 1928, Stalin left Moscow for the Urals and western Siberia. It was the last time he was to travel through the country in that way. Stalin issued some drastic orders to local party officials: in the case of peasants who refused to sell their grain, he told them, article 107 should be applied. This article (added to the Criminal Code in 1927) stipulated imprisonment for one year, with possible confiscation of property, for anyone who "concealed goods." Poor peasants were invited to join in the search for hidden grain, with 25 percent of the confiscated grain to be distributed to them at a discount or on credit. Stalin's method of collecting grain, the so-called Urals-Siberia method, was extended to the entire country.

The peasants said, "1919 has returned." The roofs of peasant huts were torn off for insufficient deliveries. Military units were sent into the villages to search for hidden grain. It was officially declared that the kulak was to blame for everything. But not long before, Kalinin had written, "The kulak is a bugbear, a ghost of the old world. This is not a social layer or a group, not even a handful. It's a matter of a few individuals, and they are dying out."[23] Rykov complained: "God only knows what we're doing. To please Trotsky, Pyatakov, and Zinoviev we use the term *kulak* for the genuine middle peasant who, entirely in accordance with the law, wants to be prosperous."[24] In July 1928 Stalin proudly told the Central Committee plenum: "We will press down and gradually squeeze the capitalist elements in the countryside, even if in some cases it brings them to ruin."[25]

The situation in the Russian countryside at the end of the NEP was neatly summed up by Boris Pilnyak:

The peasants at that time were perplexed by the following problematical dilemma, completely incomprehensible to them. . . . Fifty percent of the peasants got up at three in the morning and went to bed at eleven at night, and everyone in the household worked without letup, from the smallest to the largest. . . . Their huts were in good shape, and so were their wagons. Their cattle were well fed and well cared for. They themselves were well fed and up to their ears in work. They conscientiously paid their tax in kind and other obligations to the state. But the authorities were afraid of them and considered them enemies of the revolution, no more, no less. The other 50 percent of the peasants each had a hut open to the wind, one skinny cow, one mangy sheep, and that was all. . . . The state exempted them from the tax in kind, reimbursed them for the cost of sowing, and regarded them as friends of the revolution. The "enemy" peasants maintained that 35 percent of the "friendlies" were drunks, . . . 5 percent were unlucky, . . . and 60 percent were good-for-nothings, windbags, philosophizers, goof-offs, stumblebums, and clods. The village "enemies" were pressured in every way to become "friendlies," and thus lose the capacity to pay their taxes and let their homes get torn open by the wind.[26]

Neither Pilnyak nor the peasants he described imagined what would be done to the peasants and their villages when the NEP was over.

On July 11, 1928, a secret meeting took place between Kamenev, representing the no longer united opposition, and Bukharin, leader of the "right wing." After collaborating with Stalin closely for several years, Bukharin suddenly informed Kamenev: "We consider Stalin's line disastrous for the revolution as a whole. . . . Our differences with Stalin are many times more serious than all the differences we had with you." Suddenly Bukharin discovered that Stalin was "an unprincipled intriguer who subordinates everything to the preservation of his own power. He changes his theories depending on whom he wants to get rid of at any particular moment." Kamenev's notes of this conversation with Bukharin fell into the hands of the Trotskyists, who took perverse pleasure in publishing them in early 1929. For Stalin this was one more piece of ammunition in the battle he was undertaking against the right wing. He readily accepted support from the "left" in his struggle against the "right." Many former Left Oppositionists, who had been sent into internal exile or confined in special prisons for political opponents ("polit-isolators"), took this occasion to announce their capitulation, their agreement with Stalin's new policy, which they were convinced was actually their policy. According to Ciliga, Preobrazhensky's book on primitive socialist accumulation was reprinted, and Stalin even tried to win Preobrazhensky over. In response to doubts Preobrazhensky expressed, his suspicions that the Central Committee still favored right-wing policies, Stalin assured him: "If necessary, I shall have the entire Central Committee arrested, but I shall carry out the five-year plan."[27] The arrest of almost the entire Central Committee did not come about until 1935–1938. For the time being, Stalin merely deported Trotsky to Turkey in February 1929, after having him forcibly removed from Moscow on January 17, 1928, and confining him to Alma-Ata in Central Asia for a year.

Stalin officially announced the end of the NEP in December 1929, but as early as April 1928 he terminated "civil peace" as the prevailing condition. "We have internal enemies. We have external enemies. This, comrades, must not be forgotten for one moment."[28] The Shakhty trial was the signal for the war against society to begin. In March 1928 the authorities announced the discovery of a "counterrevolutionary plot." Fifty-three engineers, technicians, and directors of the coal industry at the Shakhty mines in the Donbass (Donets basin) were arrested and accused of wrecking and espionage. A sensational six-week trial followed, from May to July, with still more revelations later in the year. This was the first in a series of "wreckers' trials" that went on into 1931. The word *wrecker* (*vreditel*) in fact became one of the most widely used terms in Soviet officialese.

The Shakhty trial was the first public show trial since that of the SRs in 1922. The respite of the NEP had intervened. Robert Conquest, author of the most complete history of the Great Terror (aside from Solzhenitsyn's *Gulag Archipelago*), suggests that the Shakhty affair was initiated by Evgeny Evdokimov, the GPU official in charge of the region where Shakhty was located.[29] Without discounting the individual initiative of Evdokimov, a former criminal who made a brilliant career in the "organs" during the civil war and who became one of Stalin's boon companions,[30] we may conclude that the Shakhty defendants were deliberately selected at a higher level.

Among the accused were three German engineers. In this way the Shakhty trial was designed to accomplish foreign policy aims as well as domestic ones. Moreover, it was a test model for the show trials to come. The defendants were accused of sabotage and spying for the benefit of a foreign power with whom relations at the moment were bad. Some of the defendants signed confessions, which constituted the main evidence against all of them. (Two of the Shakhty defendants never appeared in court, undoubtedly because they refused to sign or died under interrogation. Several disputed the charges presented by the prosecutor, Nikolai Krylenko.) The indignation of the Soviet people was aroused throughout the affair. Twenty years later George Orwell's *1984* described a state in which "two minutes of hatred" were held every day. Citizens would gather in front of television sets; the image of Goldstein, the enemy of the people, would appear on the screen, and everyone would hate him. In the Soviet Union in the 1920s there were no television sets. There were newspapers instead. The first experiment in organized hatred was carried out at Lenin's instigation in the SR trial. During the Shakhty trial, hatred was organized on a significantly broader scale.

An investigation took place in Ekaterinburg in the summer of 1920 into the murder of a group of "specialists," technicians working at the Egorshinsky mines. The specialists had been killed by "local party comrades," who considered them counterrevolutionaries. Witnesses questioned by the court testified that they knew of no counterrevolutionary actions by the murdered technicians. The murderers were defended by N. V. Kommodov, who argued: "Healthy blood flows in their veins. They have experienced all the burdens of social inequality and have learned to hate their class enemies. It was this feeling that guided their actions."[31]

Eight years later an editorial in *Pravda* entitled, "A Class Trial," said: "Today in the Hall of Columns at the House of Trade Unions before the Supreme Court of the USSR there appeared the constellation of 'heroes' of Shakhty.... They were firmly guaranteed the deadly class hatred of the workers and toiling people of the whole world."[32] Kommodov, who acted as attorney for one of the defendants, could find no convincing arguments for his client, in whose veins flowed the "diseased blood" of a specialist. The hate campaign whipped up by the press included a statement by the twelve-year-old son of one defendant, asking that his father be shot.

A new era had begun.

## FOREIGN POLICY

The Treaty of Rapallo opened up a period of normal diplomatic relations with the capitalist world; 1924 became the year of the Soviet Republic's "recognition"—by Great Britain in February, followed by Italy, Norway, Austria, Greece, Sweden, China, Denmark, and in October, France. But Soviet foreign policy had two levels: traditional diplomatic relations on one level and, on the other, the activity of the Comintern. After hopes for a revolution in Germany were dashed, the principal task of the Communist parties was to support the foreign policy aims of the Soviet Republic. At the end of 1924, S. Medvedev and A. Shlyapnikov, representatives of the "workers' opposition," wrote in an open letter to the *Baku Worker* that the entire activity of the Comintern amounted to

> artificially creating materially sick Comintern sections and supporting them at the expense of the masses of Russian workers, who had paid for their property with blood and sacrifices but who were unable to use it for themselves under the present circumstances; in reality, hordes of petit bourgeois servants supported by Russian gold have been created."[33]

While it may be true that the Comintern sections lived off of "Russian gold," it is difficult to agree that their only activity was to collect their pay. The Comintern sections actively, though blindly, carried out orders from Moscow. In cases where there was discontent with disobedient leaders, they were immediately replaced by obedient ones. The foreign Communist parties surrounded themselves with a cloud of pro-Communist mass organizations, societies, and clubs that sympathized either secretly or openly with the party and mobilized world public opinion for the defense of the Soviet Union. The German Communist Willy Munzenberg became a master of the new methods of propaganda: he organized and directed the International Organization for Aid to Revolutionaries, the League of Struggle Against Imperialism, and a pro-Communist (that is to say, pro-Soviet) press group in Germany and conducted worldwide campaigns for the defense of the victims of capitalism (the German anarchist Max Hoelz, the Hungarian Communist Matyas Rakosi, and the American anarchists Sacco and Vanzetti).

Quite often the two levels of foreign policy functioned together and it was difficult to determine where one ended and the other began. Walter Krivitsky, who was head of the Soviet military intelligence network in Western Europe and who in 1937 refused to return to Moscow (where he knew he would be shot), recounts in his memoirs that in 1923, when the French occupied the Ruhr, the Soviet government expected a revolution at any moment. Krivitsky and five other officers were sent to Germany to create within the heart of the Communist party the core of the future German Red Army and the future German Cheka, as well as special detachments of propagandists whose mission it was to undermine morale in the bourgeois army and reserves.[34] By autumn 1924, the situation in Germany had stabilized itself, but Zinoviev, the chairman of the Comintern, declared that a revolutionary situation had arisen in Estonia. Berzin, head of military intelligence, received an order from Zinoviev to back up the revolution: sixty officers were sent immediately to Estonia. On December 1, 1924, a "revolution" broke out in Revel. The Soviet agents and local Communists received no support at all from the population, and the putsch ended in a bloodbath.[35]

In the fall of 1927 Stalin (who by this time was directing the Comintern) was offended by the reproaches of the Trotskyists, who accused him of betraying the world revolution; he decided that a revolutionary situation had arisen in China. Stalin sent the German Communist Heinz Neumann and the Soviet Communist Besso Lominadze to Canton. In December 1927 Stalin's agents stirred up a rebellion in Canton that was immediately crushed. In Revel, more than 150 people were shot. In Canton, more than 5,000 were executed.

The lack of separation between traditional diplomatic activity and the innovative moves of the Comintern was indicated by the fact that quite often Soviet diplomatic representatives abroad were at the same time officials of the Comintern. G. S. Agabekov, a top GPU official and a dip-lomatic resident in the Near East, related that "in 1926, the Soviet consul in Meshed (Persia) was also a representative of the Third International, just as in 1924–25 the Soviet plenipotentiary in Afghanistan (Stark) was also the Comintern's secret representative in Afghanistan and the northern provinces of India."[36]

In the 1920s the Soviet Union concentrated its attention on three coun-tries: Germany, England, and China.

Excellent relations with Germany had developed in the realm of tradi-tional diplomacy; at the same time, the German Communist party gained support, while relations on a third level (economic) continued to develop and strengthen. Economic relations were not limited to trade; they also included the all-around technical aid that Germany accorded to the Soviet Union. More than 2,000 German engineers and technicians arrived in the Soviet Union after the signing of the Rapallo treaty.[37] They actively assisted in renewing Soviet industry. German–Soviet military cooperation was pro-vided for in a secret clause of the Rapallo treaty. The Treaty of Versailles prohibited the German army, 100,000 strong, from having modern arma-ments, particularly aircraft and tanks. By the middle of 1923, Junkers was able to build airplanes in Fili, near Moscow. In 1924 a center for training German pilots was opened in Lipetsk. Russian and German chemists ex-perimented together to produce poison gases. Krupp built artillery factories in Soviet Central Asia.[38] Reports of German–Soviet military collaboration were published in due course and denied by both Soviets and Germans, but they were fully confirmed by documents found in the German archives after World War II. Again the question arises, which of the two sides won in the process of this cooperation? General von Seeckt was able to rebuild the German army, getting around the Versailles treaty, and he was able to arm it with the latest weaponry, built and tested on Soviet territory. The Red Army certainly profited: military men received training in Germany, industry obtained modern technology. However, since Stalin eventually exterminated all the officers and generals who had been in Germany or had had dealings with German officers, it could be said that only the German side profited.

Robert Conquest suggests, not without reason, that at the time of the Shakhty trial, the inclusion of German engineers among the accused was explained by the fact that in 1927 German technical aid had become predominant and the number of German engineers and technicians had grown too great. It was decided to teach them a lesson. The Shakhty trial implicated three German engineers, but thirty-two others were arrested at the same time. The very number of those arrested indicates the numerical significance of German personnel in the Soviet Union. After the trial, the Soviet government turned to the Americans for technical aid. In mid-1929 the Soviet Union had technical agreements with twenty-seven German firms and fifteen American firms. By the end of 1929, forty American firms were cooperating with the Soviet Union.[39]

After Great Britain's recognition of the Soviet Union, Anglo–Soviet relations were normalized, but Moscow regarded England as its principal adversary, particularly in Asia (Afghanistan and China). In 1924 the Soviet Union tried to take advantage of the fact that for the first time in British history the Labour party won at the polls. It was the newly formed Labour government that recognized the Soviet Union. An attempt was made to turn the British Communist party into a mass organization and to penetrate the trade unions. But in October 1924 the Labour party was defeated. One of the principal causes of this defeat was a document which the English press published as "Zinoviev's Secret Letter." The controversy surrounding the authenticity of this letter, which gave directives to English Communists, is still going on. Even if the letter was a fake, it contains nothing that Zinoviev could not have written. The directive that particularly roused the indignation of English public opinion (to conduct an operation to undermine the army) was one of the twenty-one conditions necessary for all Communist parties for admission to the Comintern. During the general strike in 1926, a collection was taken up in the Soviet Union for use by English strikers. An Anglo–Russian trade union committee was created.

The treaty with China, signed in 1924, provided for the preservation of the Soviet Union's rights to the Chinese Eastern Railway (the part of the main Trans-Siberian rail line, built by the tsarist government in 1903, that passed through Manchuria for a distance of 1,481 kilometers, with a 240-kilometer spur to Harbin) and for the Soviet Union to maintain a protectorate over Outer Mongolia, which had declared itself a people's republic. At the same time, the Soviet Union supplied aid to the Chinese nationalist party, the Kuomintang, led by Sun Yat-sen. Soviet military advisers, directed by Galen-Blyukher, were operating in China. The tiny Chinese Communist party, acting under orders from Moscow, joined the Kuomintang. Soviet policy in China became one of the major themes of the controversy between Stalin and Trotsky. Trotsky insisted on the necessity of stirring up the revolutionary struggle in China, under the leadership of the Communist party; Stalin defended the policy of supporting the Kuomintang and Chiang Kai-shek, who led the party after Sun Yat-sen's death. Stalin and Bukharin believed that the Kuomintang played an "objectively progressive role." Chiang cooperated with Moscow but did not want the Communists in his party. In 1926 the Communists were expelled from the Kuomintang and arrested. In April 1927 Chiang Kai-shek organized a massacre of Communists in Shanghai. Soon after, Stalin, hoping to exonerate himself, sent Neumann and Lominadze to Canton. He termed the failure of the Cantonese insurrection a "victorious rear-guard battle."

The Soviet Union's foreign policy for this period was guided by three central precepts: (1) the Soviet Union was the most important factor of world revolution and thus its strengthening, combined with an equivalent strengthening of the world revolutionary movement for the sake of Soviet interests, was the revolutionary task of Communist parties in other countries; (2) conflict between the Soviet Union and the capitalist countries was inevitable, and the revolutionary movement in the capitalist countries was a reserve force that could help Moscow; (3) the nature of capitalist countries was such that subversive revolutionary activity conducted against them did not exclude the possibility of carrying on normal diplomatic and trade relations with them.

The full extent of Western economic and technological aid to the Soviet Union will not be known until the Soviet archives are opened up. The Western firms that collaborated with Moscow have concealed the information almost as carefully as their Soviet partners. Nevertheless, the American historian Anthony Sutton has come to the conclusion, on the basis of German and English archives, that 95 percent of Soviet industrial enterprises received Western aid in the form of machines, technology, and direct technical aid.[40]

The Soviet Union made skillful use of the competition among capitalist firms. "In the realm of technical assistance," wrote *Economicheskaya zhizn* (Economic life), "we have neither an English, nor a German, nor an American orientation. We maintain a Soviet orientation. . . . When we need to modernize our oil, automobile or tractor industries, we turn to the United States because it is the leading country in these industries. When we speak about chemistry, we approach Germany."[41] It was also able to turn for help to Germany, England, and the United States, even though Germany and England recognized the Soviet Union in 1924, while U.S. recognition did not come until 1933. The capitalist firms, who were competing bitterly with each other, rushed to offer their services: they gained concessions, supplied the latest equipment and technology, sent engineers and technicians, and took on Soviet trainees. The myth about a "blockade," "economic isolation," and the hostile attitude of the capitalist "sharks" toward "the socialist homeland" falls apart in the face of the facts. In the 1920s only aid from the West permitted the Soviet authorities to restore the economy rapidly, including transportation, all branches of industry, and the extraction of useful minerals. This aid was given in spite of the Soviet government's policy, which put all sorts of obstacles in the way of the capitalist firms and ended the concessions as soon as Soviet specialists had assimilated Western technology. The capitalist firms were always in a weak position; they had never before encountered a partner as powerful as a government, and they were thirsty for profits. Along with the Comintern and pro-Communist organizations, these firms played the role of organizers of public opinion in favor of the Soviet Union. When Standard Oil decided to build an oil refinery in Batum, a top public relations expert was sent to persuade public opinion that a socialist country was a state like any other. Without knowing a word of Russian, this representative of Rockefeller's knew everything after several days: The Russians (he always talked about the Russians, not the Soviets) are okay! That's why the United States ought to recognize the Soviet Union and extend credit to it.[42]

One of the important factors in the development of Soviet–capitalist relations was the activity of certain individual foreigners. First in line is Armand Hammer, son of Dr. Julius Hammer, one of the founders of the American Communist party. Young Armand Hammer arrived in Moscow in 1921 with a recommendation from Martens, the unofficial Soviet trade representative in the United States. He had brought with him a freightcar full of drugs and medicines as a gift to the Soviet government. He met with Lenin, who was drawn to the enterprising young American. Lenin advised him to assume management of the Alapaevsky asbestos mines on a concessionary basis, and he personally organized the immediate formation of this concession, which ordinarily would have taken months. Hammer did not limit himself to the first million he earned from the asbestos concession. Until 1930 he lived with several members of his family (his wife, mother, brothers, and uncle) in Moscow. Hundreds of pages, the best of which are by Mikhail Bulgakov, have been written about the housing crisis in Moscow. Hammer rented a twenty-four-room house in Moscow and converted it into the unofficial embassy of the United States. He took out a concession on the production of pencils and pens. In 1926 his factory produced 100 million pencils and made enormous profits, which he used to buy Russian works of art. Unlike all the other concessionaires, Hammer was able to convert his revenues to dollars. His example was infectious. He served as an intermediary in the conclusion of an agreement between the Soviet government and Henry Ford, an ardent enemy of the Communists. The American Consolidated Company (50 percent of the capital was Hammer's; the other 50 percent was the Soviet government's) conducted the affairs of "three dozen American firms" trading with the Soviet Union.[43] The phenomenal successes of Armand Hammer, who made millions in the Soviet Union, could not fail to entice other capitalists.

The most convincing proof of the nonexistence of "aggressive capitalist plans" was the fact that the Red Army, which in 1929 numbered 1.2 million men, was equipped with prewar Russian and foreign armaments. Soviet industry was still in no condition to produce the necessary weaponry, so it was supplied by the Germans, English, Americans, and French: for example, heavy machine guns, like the Maxim and Colt; light machine guns, like the Browning and Lewis; artillery on a par with the American 76-inch howitzer; and Renault tanks, built in Fili with the help of the Germans.

The first five-year plan was not implemented until after the contracts on plant construction and technical aid were signed with the Western firms.

Soviet foreign policy successes on the third, economic level, however much they were concealed and disclaimed, did not impede the "pursuit of conflict" on the first two levels. The crisis in Anglo–Soviet relations, brought on by the meddling of Soviet trade unions ("independent from the state") in English affairs during the general strike of 1926, led, after a raid by London police on Soviet trade offices, to a break in diplomatic relations which lasted from 1927 to 1929. Also in 1927, France demanded the recall of Soviet Ambassador Rakovsky, a Trotskyist who had declared in a letter to the Central Committee that in the event of war with the imperialists he would urge the soldiers of the imperialist armies to desert. The French considered such promises incompatible with diplomatic status. Meanwhile, a Russian emigré assassinated the Soviet ambassador to Warsaw, Voikov, who had taken part in the murder of the tsar's family in 1918, and in December the putsch in Canton, conceived by Stalin, ended in defeat.

The Soviet government presented all these separate events as elements in a single plot that was sure to end in an inevitable—and imminent— war: an attack by imperialist forces. This episode in history comes under the heading, "The 1927 War Scare." Historians still debate whether or not the Soviet leaders, primarily Stalin, actually believed in the inevitability of an attack on the Soviet Union. After all, 1927 was the calmest year in the world since the end of World War I. Economic relations with the West were developing. But the "war scare" gave Stalin an additional argument to use in favor of the rapid liquidation of the Opposition, which was undermining unity in the face of imperialist intervention. In 1929, Chicherin, who was nominally still deputy commissar of foreign affairs but who in fact had been removed from things for a long time, made a frank disclosure to the American journalist Louis Fischer, whom he met in Wiesbaden while receiving treatment: "In June 1927 I returned from Western Europe. Everyone in Moscow was talking about war. I did my best to dissuade them: 'No one is planning to attack us,' I insisted. Then I was enlightened by a colleague. He told me: 'Hush, we know that. But we need this for the struggle against Trotsky.'"[44]

The Sixth Congress of the Comintern, which gathered in Moscow in July 1928, decided on a new policy line for the second level of Soviet foreign policy. (This turned out to be the Comintern's next-to-last congress. The last would meet in 1934, and in 1943 Stalin would dissolve the Third International by a stroke of the pen.) The sessions of the Sixth Congress were not held in the Kremlin, as before, but in the House of Trade Unions. The Congress stressed the need to strengthen discipline within the Communist parties, to subordinate local interests to the interests of the international Communist movement—that is, to Moscow—and to comply unconditionally with all Comintern decisions. According to the old Bolshevik tradition, the new line provided an opponent: the "rightist" Bukharin, who was opposing the extremely left-wing Trotskyist line, then being supported by Stalin. The Communist parties received a directive to regard the socialist parties, labeled "social fascists," as the principal enemy. Marxist scientific analysis enabled Stalin to conclude that the West had entered a period of world stabilization; therefore the task of the Communists was to tear the working class away from the influence of the "social fascists." Then, when the epoch of crises and wars arrived, which was inevitable in view of the growing contradictions among the principal capitalist countries, particularly between England and the United States, the Communists would be able to try to seize power.

In January 1928 Trotsky and his comrades addressed a letter to the Comintern complaining of the repression they were under. They admitted that repression can play an extremely positive role if it supports a just line and contributes to the liquidation of reactionary groups. The Trotskyists stressed that, as Bolsheviks, they were quite familiar with the use of repression and had repeatedly used repressive measures themselves against the bourgeoisie, the Mensheviks, and so on. They declared that even in the future they had no intention at all of renouncing repression against the enemies of the proletariat. They believed only that the use of repression against them was unjust and that repression against Bolsheviks had always been ineffective. For he who supports a political line that is just will be victorious.

This Trotskyist logic was brilliantly confirmed by Stalin's victory in all his endeavors and Trotsky's defeat. Trotsky must have taken some consolation, however, in the fact that Stalin had adopted his line.

## THE DAWN OF A NEW CIVILIZATION

In 1928 the "rusty times" came to an end. After the Shakhty trial, which culminated in five executions, things got redder and redder.

During the years of the NEP the worst of the war-inflicted wounds were healed, the economy was restored despite the many difficulties, and life assumed a semblance of normality. But these accomplishments were paid for dearly. The population lived in uncertainty, fearful of breaking the law, afraid of what was to come. Paradoxically, those who were considered the victors (the workers) lived in poverty, although without fear, while those who knew they were the vanquished (the middle peasants, Nepmen, intellectuals) enjoyed material comfort, but lived in fear.

Existence under the NEP was measured by various yardsticks. On the one hand, the party knew what the ultimate goal was, but its leaders were locked in bitter internecine warfare over the right to lead the country to that goal by each leader's "only correct path." Meanwhile, on another level, the United States became a universal model and object of adoration. Stalin spoke of combining "American efficiency with Russian revolutionary scope." Aleksei Gastev, a proletarian poet and founder of the League of Time, issued this call: "Let us take the hurricane of revolution, the USSR; add the pulse of America; and we will do the job as steadily as a chronometer." Lev Sosnovsky, a writer for *Pravda* and a Left Oppositionist, announced a search for "Russian Americans," people who would know "how to work with a rhythm, an ardor, and a doggedness, the likes of which old Russia never knew." The peasant poet Petr Oreshin exclaimed: "And every rural cottage dreams a wondrous dream—a New York of steel." The writer N. Smirnov turned out a popular novel, *Jack Vosmerkin the American*, about a Russian-American who returned to his homeland to transplant American know-how onto Soviet Russian soil. The peasants of the village where Jack Vosmerkin settled regarded him with hostility, not only because the peasant is a backward type but also because as soon as the peasant begins to apply progressive methods—however admirably American they are—he begins to grow rich. And immediately becomes an enemy of the Soviet government.

Although life seemed to be returning to normal, a mounting antireligious campaign was cause for concern. For example, a peculiar hybrid—the "Red" church service, along with "Red" baptisms and "Red" Easters— was introduced. Non-Christian names were recommended. The civil registry offices hung up lists with such suggestions for girls' names as Atlantide, Brunhilda, Industriya, Octobrina, Februarida, Idea, Kommuna, and Mayina, and for boys, Chervonets, Spartak (Spartacus), Textile, Styag (Banner), and Plamenny Vladilen ("Fiery Vladimir Lenin"). On the back page of *Izvestia* a certain Demyan Kasyanovich Mironov announced he was changing his name to Dekamiron. In the rural areas, however, most marriages were still held in churches and children's names were chosen from the Christian calendar of saints.

Schools were expected to wither away, along with the family, but a German historian visiting the Soviet Union made this observation: "The Bolsheviks have organized public education in such a way that no one can exceed the limits of the officially authorized level of knowledge and education, so that the proletarian state will not be threatened by a superfluous exchange of information which would transform the citizens into 'subversive elements.'"[45] The American writer Theodore Dreiser, who spent seventy-seven days in the Soviet Union in 1927, said much the same thing to Bukharin: "You take a child and you drum limited concepts into his head. He does not know anything more than what you teach him, and he will never know anything—you just watch. The success of your revolution, then, depends on the education of the children, does it not? 'In part, yes,' agreed Bukharin."[46]

From 1921 to 1928 Soviet literature flourished, but a peculiar kind of writer, unknown before then, appeared on the scene. It seemed that Bukharin's idea of standardizing the intellectuals, turning them out "as though from a factory," was being taken literally. Writers became increasingly aware that the traditional calling of Russian literature, the defense of the humble and the abandoned, did not correspond to the new reality. The writers themselves began to plead with the authorities, as Ilya Selvinsky did: "Comrade! . . . Do our thinking for us, switch on our nerves, and get us going, just like a factory." Mayakovsky declared a *fait accompli*: "I feel I'm a Soviet factory." To the population, Stalin was still a chief like any other, much less famous than Trotsky. But having taken the party apparatus in hand long before and having involved himself more and more in the economy and foreign affairs, he began to express his views on literature as well. This took the form at first of personal letters, but these were circulated in all literary, editorial, and censorship circles and were looked upon as directives. For example, Sholokhov, whom a number of "proletarian" writers accused of being a plagiarist and a champion of the White Cossacks, was declared by Stalin to be an "illustrious writer of our time."[47]

Revolutionary slogans were still alive, as were hopes for a world revolution, the advent of a classless society, and the withering away of the state once all class enemies had been defeated. But the newspapers dealt with more mundane topics as well. They made much of the search for the mysterious Tungus meteorite by the courageous Soviet geologist Leonid

Kulik. Universal attention was paid to the daring Arctic explorations of the Norwegian Amundsen and the Italian Nobile, but of course the Soviet Arctic explorers on the icebreaker *Krasin* and the Soviet Arctic fliers who saved them from certain death on the polar ice received the most attention of all. These were the first Soviet heroes not connected with war or revolution.

Soviet justice came into being as a form of revolutionary class justice. It was not ashamed of terror, for it was clearing the way for a better future. In a separate room of the Moscow Museum of the Revolution, relics of tsarist "hard labor" were assembled, including instruments of torture and models of the torture chambers. "Prisons have existed and still exist," Bukharin explained, "and a system of coercion exists, but these are directed at new and different goals." "We have merely turned the concept of 'freedom' inside out," he added.[48] He meant that freedom had been for landowners and capitalists, but now it was for workers and peasants. But according to official data, no less than 40 percent of the Soviet prison population was made up of workers and peasants, and their numbers continued to increase. A simple comparison of the figures shows that ten years after the revolution the number of those in Soviet prisons exceeded the largest number of prisoners at any time in the tsarist era. In 1925, 144,000 persons were serving sentences in Soviet prisons; in 1926, the figure was 149,000; and in 1927, 185,000.[49] In 1912 the population of the tsarist prisons was 183,864. Then the number dropped steadily, reaching 142,399 in 1916.[50] The population of Soviet prisons and camps would later grow at rates no one could have imagined.

Lenin's indignant words were to come true:

> Scarcely at any time in the past has there been such a degree of overcrowding of prisoners: they have been placed in fortresses and in castles as well as prisons and given special accommodations at police stations. Even private homes and apartments have been temporarily converted into prisons. There is no place to accommodate all those who have been seized, no way of sending the exiles to Siberia in the usual "transports" without organizing special convoy forces.[51]

Lenin's indignation over the inhumanity of the tsarist regime was expressed in 1902, when there were 89,889 people in prisons.

After the October revolution prisons were abolished. They became known as houses of detention. Convict labor (*katorga*) was eliminated until 1943: it was replaced by the "corrective labor camp." Even the word *punishment* was struck from the law dictionary and replaced by the expression "measures of social defense." And there was no punishment: people who broke revolutionary law were to be annihilated, isolated, or, in the case of "socially friendly" workers and peasants influenced by "survivals of the accursed past," reeducated. Advanced Western methods were used for "reeducation." Political prisoners (members of other socialist parties or Communist oppositionists) enjoyed almost the same rights they had had under the tsars. Marxist legal experts spoke of the impending "withering away" of the law, which would lead to the "liquidation" of the system of coercion, prisons, and so forth.

After 1926 the GPU's prerogatives began to expand. Quite a few hopes were aroused by the disappearance of the Cheka. The GPU, reported one German traveler, "is more refined and elegant than the Cheka. Its agents are extremely courteous, charming, and obliging; they wish to erase the memory of the Cheka."[52] Foreigners who came to know the "work of the GPU" directly, as clients of that institution, had a different opinion. One of the first foreign accounts of the Solovetsky concentration camps was entitled, as we have noted before, *In the Land of the NEP and the Cheka*, by the Finnish writer Boris Cederholm.[53] Technically, the title was wrong; it should have said GPU not Cheka, but Cederholm saw no difference between them. Neither did the American journalist George Popov, who entitled his memoirs about his time in Lubyanka prison in 1924 simply *The Cheka*.[54] The GPU inherited its main residence, the Lubyanka, whose very name inspired horror, from the Cheka: "Shake someone awake at night and say the word 'Lubyanka' and he will stare at his bare feet, say goodbye to everybody, and even if he's young, and healthy as an ox, he'll break down and cry like a baby."[55] And of course the GPU inherited Dzerzhinsky, its chairman, from the Cheka.

During the early years of NEP some indecisive attempts were made "to reinforce a very important democratic principle, according to which only judicial bodies should have the right to mete out punishment."[56] But these attempts ended quickly. In October 1922 the GPU acquired the right to apply "extrajudicial" measures of repression, including execution, to "bandits." Its pool of clients quickly widened. On May 6, 1926, for example, the central newspapers reported the GPU's execution of three officials of the Commissariat of Finance "for speculation in gold, foreign currency, and government bonds."

From the Cheka the GPU inherited its own places of detention, including Solovki, the prison camp on the Solovetsky Islands. Until the appearance of Hitler's camps, the Solovki served as a symbol of arbitrariness, cruelty, and tyrannical power. "Here, we don't have Soviet power; we have Solovetsky power." That was how the head of the camp greeted the prisoners. "Solovetsky power" was the power of the GPU, but after all, that was the quintessence of Soviet power.

From 1927 on, the GPU took a more and more active part in the struggle unfolding within the party, although it had been involved since 1923. To commemorate the tenth anniversary of the "organs" in December 1927, *Pravda* saluted their successes and declared that the GPU was vital in the struggle against the class enemy and in maintaining law and order.[57] Throughout 1927, the GPU's prerogatives continued to expand. After the assassination of Voikov in July, the GPU was "obliged" to take decisive measures in order to defend the country against foreign spies, provocateurs, and assassins, as well as from their monarchist allies and the White Guard.[58] After an explosion at a party club in Leningrad (perhaps a provocation), the GPU announced the execution of ten former monarchists, who were charged with espionage. The repression broadened and intensified. The humanitarian penitentiary system was denounced as a manifestation of bourgeois humanism, an anti-Marxist deviation.

In 1928 Bukharin, who already knew what Stalin was, declared: "We are creating and will create a civilization in comparison with which capitalist civilization will seem like a vulgar street dance compared with the heroic symphonies of Beethoven."[59] In fact, a new civilization was being born. Its unusual nature was understood by one of the rare foreigners who visited the Soviet Union in 1927, Alfred Fabre-Luce, who declared that it existed only "in the future, that is, in the realm of the impossible." "I feel like some hero of Einstein's relativity concept," he wrote in his conclusion, "who returns to his native planet, gray-haired after a ten-minute voyage."[60]

Osip Mandelstam defined the dawning civilization less poetically and more precisely: "They think," he said to his wife regarding the people of Moscow, busily going about their affairs, "they think that everything is normal just because the streetcars are running."

CHAPTER

# 5

# THE
# GREAT RUPTURE,
# 1929–1934

## FIVE IN FOUR

The dream of a planned economy along the lines of Germany's war economy had preoccupied Lenin as early as 1918. In 1920 the first long-term plan was drawn up by GOELRO, the State Commission for the Electrification of Russia. This plan initially provided for the construction of one hundred power plants. Lenin proclaimed electrification as the key to communism. But in January 1921, Zinoviev spoke of no more than twenty-seven power plants. In the end, the GOELRO plan remained on paper.

In 1927 Soviet economists began drafting the first five-year plan—a comprehensive plan providing for the development of every region, using every resource for the industrialization of the country. It was supposed to go into effect in October 1928, but was not even submitted for approval until the Sixteenth Party Conference in April 1929.

Just as an experienced boxer prepares his opponent for a knockout by "softening him up" with blows to the liver, stomach, kidneys, and heart, Stalin softened up the country before hitting it with the Great Change. The softening up of the party was brought to completion with the elimination of the "right wing." In February 1929, at a joint session of the Politburo and the Central Control Commission, Bukharin was censured for his "unprincipled behavior" in conducting talks with Kamenev. Rykov, chairman of the Council of People's Commissars, and Tomsky, leader of the trade unions, were also censured. In April 1929 the Central Committee removed Bukharin from his posts as editor of *Pravda* and president of the Comintern and Tomsky from his post as chairman of the All-Union Central Council of Trade Unions. Bukharin's supporter Uglanov lost his positions as secretary of the Moscow Committee, secretary of the Central Committee, and candidate member of the Politburo. In November 1929, Bukharin was expelled from the Politburo. "Right deviation" had become a crime.

In April 1929 the Sixteenth Party Conference passed a resolution calling for a second general purge (the first was in 1921): anyone who at any time (from 1921 to 1929) had voted against Stalin or supported an opposition platform—no matter which one—was purged. The conference decided to extend the purge to include nonparty officials working in Soviet institutions. All Soviet functionaries were subject to the purge—or, one might say, passed through purgatory. Broad strata of "worker activists" were enlisted to help in checking over the biographies, service records, conduct, and loyalty of these functionaries. Special "light cavalry" units were set up, consisting of Komsomol members, while trade union officials and shock-workers acted as judges. Thus the party involved broad sections of the population in repressive activity.

Instructions from the Commissariat of Workers' and Peasants' Inspection divided all those "purged" from the Soviet apparatus into three categories. Those in the "first category" were deprived of their rights to all benefits, pensions, and jobs and were evicted from their apartments. Those in the "second category" were allowed to find work in government organizations other than the kind presently employing them or in another district. Those in the "third category" were demoted, and the demotion was placed on their record. The grounds for purging someone under one category or another were so broad (including "corrupt elements who have perverted Soviet laws or linked up with the kulaks and Nepmen... embezzlers, bribe takers, saboteurs, wreckers, and parasites")[1] and so ambiguous that the entire population was intimidated, especially considering the hundreds of thousands of watchful eyes of the "people's purifiers." Besides, the Shakhty trial was still fresh in people's memories.

One of the results of the new policy was the flight of highly placed officials from the Soviet Union and the refusal of some Soviet diplomatic, commercial, and intelligence personnel abroad, where the purge was also conducted, to return to their country. Early in 1928 Boris Bazhanov, who had worked as one of Stalin's assistants since 1923, fled to Persia. Agabekov, head of the Eastern sector of the OGPU's foreign department, immediately received the order to kill Bazhanov. While the assassination was being planned, "a telegram arrived from Moscow canceling the 'liquidation' order. . . . It turned out that Bazhanov, in his work in Moscow, had not been privy to any important secrets."[2] Several months later Agabekov himself fled. Soviet diplomats Bessedovsky, Barmin, Dmitrievsky, and many others stayed in the West.

An important part of the "softening up" process was the new offensive against the church. On April 8, 1929, a law was passed that strengthened the state's control over the parishes. On May 22 an amendment was made to article 13 of the Soviet constitution, which until then had provided for freedom of religion and of antireligious propaganda. Propagation of religion now became a crime against the state. Priests and their families were deprived of civil rights. As "disenfranchised persons" they did not have the right to ration cards, medical aid, or communal apartments. The children of priests were not allowed to attend schools or higher educational institutions. Thus they were forced to renounce their fathers in order to obtain an education or simply to live.

Hundreds of churches were destroyed, including many that were historical monuments. The churches that survived had their bells removed, ostensibly so that their ringing "would not disturb the workers." On August 27 a "continuous work week" was introduced; the seven-day week was abolished and replaced by a new system—four days of work followed by one day of rest. "Utopia has become a reality," exclaimed one enraptured writer. "The continuous-production week has knocked our time out of its calendar saddle. With the elimination of that sleepy interval, the seventh day, Sunday, the country has entered a state of permanent waking."[3] Industry was not really ready for the continuous work week, but the system did have the advantage of eliminating Sunday. The "continuous week" lasted until 1940, when the Soviet government, of its own good will, granted the workers Sunday as a day of rest.

Among the factors that helped create the particular atmosphere of the five-year-plan era and helped forge the new Soviet consciousness, a special place belongs to the "control figures."

The drafting of a detailed five-year plan to transform the economy "required much more information about interindustry links than could be available in the existing state of information and statistics."[4] Nevertheless, the plan was drafted in two versions, an initial variant and an optimal variant. Even the initial version was very optimistic. "Miracles seldom occur in economic life," writes one English historian, "and in the absence of divine intervention it is hard to imagine how one would expect simultaneous increases of investment and consumption, not to speak of the output of industry, agriculture, and labor productivity, by such trememdous percentages."[5] But scarcely had the optimal figures been adopted than Stalin raised them to a new, unprecedented level. In 1926 Stalin had ridiculed Trotsky's "fantastic" projects, his desire for "super-industrialization," his idea of building a giant electric power plant on the Dnepr. The Dneprostroi project, observed the general secretary at one time, would require enormous resources, several hundred million rubles. This would be, said Stalin, using his own brand of humor, like "the peasant who after saving a few kopeks, instead of repairing his plow, went out and bought a Gramophone."[6] By early 1930 Trotsky's figures seemed "shabby" to Stalin. Mensheviks, right-wing Communists, and nonparty members were thrown out of the statistical, economic, and scientific research institutes as "wreckers." Those who replaced them furnished the new figures required of them—and they were astronomical.

The optimal plan provided for coal production to double, from 35 million tons in 1927–28 to 75 million tons in 1932. Stalin's figure was 105 million tons. The corresponding figures for oil were 11.7 million, 21.7 million, and 55 million tons; for iron, 3.2 million, 10 million and 16 million tons. Similar leaps were made in all the control figures for the five-year plan.[7] But this was still not enough. In December 1929, a gathering of "shockworkers" (udarniki) called for the fulfillment of the five-year plan in four years. "Five in Four" became the slogan of the day. But this, too, was not enough. Stalin announced that "tempos decide everything." On February 4, 1931, he mentioned the possibility—hence the necessity—of fulfilling the plan in the decisive sectors of industry in three years.

The figures intoxicated not only the formulators of the plans but also those who carried them out, the citizens of the country. It seemed that one more effort, one more factory built, one more dam constructed—and happiness would be there, right around the corner. With one more step they would "catch up with and surpass" the capitalist countries. Mayakovsky added his urgings: "Forward, time!" Stalin warned: "If in ten years we do not cover the distance that other countries took fifty or a hundred years to traverse, we will be crushed." In a popular play of the early 1930s, Fear by Aleksandr Afinogenov, the old professor Borodin, reactionary but re-educated by the GPU, asserts that "the general motivation for the behavior of 80 percent of all those I have investigated [Soviet citizens—M. H.] is fear." The other 20 percent, explains the professor, are the workers, newly risen to a position of responsibility. "They have nothing to fear; they are the country's masters." But, adds the learned expert, "their mind is afraid for them... the mind of the manual laborer fears excessive strain and develops a persecution complex. They strive constantly to catch up and surpass. And gasping for breath in this endless race, the mind loses its sanity and slowly becomes degraded."

The figures ceased to mean anything; they became a mere symbol of the desire to race forward. Like a balloon they carried the country away into a nonexistent world.

But the country could not ignore reality. An army of workers and technicians was thrown into fulfilling the senseless plans. It seemed that the ideas of Trotsky and Bukharin on the militarization of labor, rejected in the early 1920s, were being revived. The only quota that was met far ahead of time was the employment index. The expectation was that the state economy would employ 14.7 million, but by 1932 22.9 million were employed. The shortage of qualified workers was compensated for with quantity. Just as masses of soldiers are thrown into battle when firepower is lacking, millions of former peasants, undisciplined, ignorant of the tools and machinery, were mobilized to carry out the five-year plan.

The rapid growth of the urban population led to a catastrophic worsening of the housing situation. Food supplies in the cities were severely strained. Strumilin, future academician and one of the authors of Stalin's version of the five-year plan, wrote in *Essays on Soviet Economics* in 1927 that the rate of accumulation, "given our long experience of consumer asceticism, could exceed all known records." All records for "consumer asceticism" were indeed surpassed during those years in the villages, which literally starved to death. But even in the cities the situation was extremely critical. In April 1929 bread was rationed. By the end of the year, rationing was extended to all foodstuffs, then to manufactured goods. In 1931 additional "coupons" were issued, for it was impossible to obtain one's allotment even with ration cards.

The real situation for workers in this period can be seen from the reports by GPU agents that survived in the Smolensk archives. In 1929 (and the situation only worsened after that) a worker received 600 grams of bread a day, plus 300 grams for each member of his family; between 200 grams and 1 liter of vegetable oil a month; 1 kilogram of sugar a month; and for clothing, 30–36 meters of cotton a year.[8] A significant number of workers ate in the factory canteens. A novel by Fedor Gladkov described one such canteen at the Dneprostroi dam project: "I go to the factory kitchen and am sickened by the very sight of the vile poison being made there. I go to the work sites, where the food is delivered in thermoses. The bluish swill stinks like a corpse and a cesspool. The workers prefer plain bread and water."[9] One GPU agent reported the complaints of the workers who ate in Canteen No. 7: "In the so-called soup it is hard to find pieces of anything.

It is not soup, but vegetable water; there is no fat, and the meat is not always washed sufficiently. . . . [In some cases] little worms were found in the lunch."[10]

In the summer of 1931 Stalin declared war on "egalitarianism." Equality was said to be a petit bourgeois notion. A pejorative term was used for it: *uravnilovka*, "leveling." Inequality officially became a socialist virtue. A new system of wage scales was introduced, with payment depending on output (piece rate) as well as on one's job category. The workers were to be stimulated from then on by material incentives. Certain nonmaterial incentives, awards and honorific titles, were also introduced, but material benefits always came with them. Their recipients obtained promotions, special rations, and so on. There were at least six different prices for the same merchandise: (1) government prices for goods purchased with ration cards; (2) "commercial" prices, significantly higher, for goods purchased without ration cards; (3) "moderately increased prices" for goods sold exclusively in working-class districts (these were lower than "commercial" but higher than government prices); (4) prices in "model stores," general stores where prices were higher than "commercial" prices; (5) prices at the *torgsin*, a store where goods were sold only in exchange for gold or foreign currency; and (6) market prices.

Prices never stopped climbing, wages rose only nominally, and production quotas constantly increased. To accelerate the pace of the work, the "shockworkers' movement" and the system of "socialist emulation" were utilized.

This period saw the rise of special stores and special dining halls for the various categories of leaders. And hierarchical precedence was strictly respected. The wife of a member of the Politburo of the German Communist party, who was in Moscow in 1931, recalls how, one fine day, a section of the dining room of the Hotel Luxe, reserved for the Comintern, was marked off. It was thenceforth set aside for the highest-ranking officials only, and the food they were served was better than that given to second- or third-class Comintern officials.[11]

GPU agents in Smolensk reported the reaction of the workers to these new perquisites for officialdom.[12] Similarly, Ante Ciliga related what an old Leningrad worker told him: "We live worse now than at the time of the capitalists. If we had had to face such starvation, if our salaries had been so low in the days of our old masters, we would have gone on strike a thousand times."[13] In fact, the workers did go on strike: there are GPU reports to this effect in the Smolensk archives. But it was very difficult to strike, for many reasons: workers were fired, which resulted in the loss of ration cards, eviction from factory housing, even arrest; the trade unions "worked together as one" with management;[14] and the official propaganda never stopped assuring the workers that Soviet power was their power, that if only they went one step further, the happy days of communism would begin. Besides, the wreckers were responsible for all the difficulties.

In April 1929, when work on the first five-year plan was just starting, Stalin was already preparing his scapegoats. Wreckers like those in the Shakhty trial, he declared, "are sitting now in all the branches of our industry."[15] Wrecking and sabotage, he said, had occurred and will continue to occur.[16] Arrests and trials confirmed the general secretary's words. The first five-year plan period was also a time of major show trials. In August 1930 a number of bacteriologists "under the leadership" of Professor Karatygin were arrested and tried in closed session for allegedly bringing on an epidemic among horses. The Indian writer Rabindranath Tagore, then traveling around the Soviet Union, chose that moment to comment approvingly, in numerous interviews, on everything he had seen in the land of the victorious proletariat.

In September 1930 it was announced that forty-eight figures prominent in the food industry, headed by a Professor Ryazanov, had been shot for creating difficulties in the food supply system.

In November–December 1930 the second full-scale show trial after Shakhty was organized in Moscow, the trial of the so-called Industrial party. The indictment alleged that the clandestine Industrial party had no fewer than 2,000 members. Eight of them were placed on trial. The Shakhty trial had proven that too large a number of defendants detracted from the spectacle. That experience was taken into account. The accused were charged with wrecking activities carried out on orders from French President Raymond Poincaré, Lawrence of Arabia, and the Dutch oil magnate Henri Deterding. Except for those arrested, there were no witnesses and no material evidence at all. They all confessed their guilt, especially Professor Ramzin, the "head" of the party. Ramzin had been a Bolshevik in 1905–1907, but had left the party and devoted himself to a career in engineering. After the revolution he had loyally cooperated with the Soviet authorities. Suddenly he was the head of an anti-Soviet "clandestine organization." The defendants confessed to everything: to being in league with the capitalist emigré Ryabushinsky, who gave them their instructions, and to having planned to install a former tsarist minister, Vyshegradsky, as minister of finance after the overthrow of Soviet power. In the course of the trial it came out that both Ryabushinsky and Vyshegradsky were dead, but that did not affect the outcome of the trial. Five of the accused were sentenced to be shot, but were pardoned. Ramzin was released very quickly.[17] The use of provocateurs was necessary in all the trials staged by the GPU "organs."

Repression continued after the Industrial party trial. Preparations began for a trial of the so-called Toiling Peasants' party. Judging by the massive arrests of agrarian economists, agronomists, other agricultural specialists, and cooperative members, the "organs" intended to fabricate an under-ground organization with tens of thousands of members. This was logical. In a peasant country a "peasant party" had to be proportionately larger than an Industrial party. The "organs" selected Professor Kondratiev as the leader of the Toiling Peasants' party. Professor Chayanov's fantastic novel, *My Brother Aleksei's Journey to the Land of Peasant Utopia* (published in 1920 under the pseudonym Ivan Kremnev), which predicted that in 1984 (Chayanov was the first to choose this date, long before Orwell) Russia would be a free peasant country, was designated as the organization's secret program. Yaroslavsky, writing in *Pravda*, made a point for the benefit of the investigator in the case: "Now, after the exposure of this clandestine organization of bourgeois restorationists, this kulak manifesto takes on a special significance."[18] The newspapers pointed to a direct link between the "kulak conspirators" and the party's right wing: "All the sympathies of the Kondratievites were on the side of the rights in their struggle against the party leadership. The rights were smashed. And now, thanks to the vigilance of the dictatorship of the proletariat, the leaders of the Kondra-tievites have been placed on GPU rations."[19] For reasons unknown, the trial of the Toiling Peasants' party never took place. Those arrested, in-cluding Kondratiev and Chayanov, perished in prisons or in camps.

In March 1931, a trial of Mensheviks was held in Moscow. The majority of the accused worked in the planning agencies; they were accused of wrecking activities "in the planning sphere"—of raising or lowering figures so as to prevent fulfillment of the plans. This trial is of particular interest to historians because one of the defendants, Mikhail Yakubovich, who spent twenty-two years in prisons and camps, survived. In 1967, in a letter addressed to the prosecutor general of the USSR, Yakubovich described how the trial was rigged.

Massive arrests and some trials of "wreckers" continued. The arrests were not limited to the "technical" intelligentsia—engineers, technicians, planners, and managers—but included even rank-and-file workers. "The class enemy," said one article on the reasons behind the poor functioning of the rail system, "the White Guards and the kulaks, still have the potential to infiltrate the railways by taking 'modest' and inconspicuous jobs as 'oilers.'"[20] Oilers, switchmen, and yardmen, not to mention engineers and firemen, went off to prison and the camps, along with milling machine operators, metalworkers, and others blamed for breakdowns in production and failure to fulfill unfulfillable plans. They swelled the ranks of the monstrously enlarged army of prisoners, which occupied a more and more important place in the program for building communism. A significant number of the major objectives of the first five-year plan were brought to completion with the help of prison labor. The Baltic–White Sea canal was built entirely by prisoners. Approximately 500,000 prisoners[21] over a period of twenty months cut their way through the Karelian granite, by manual labor, without machinery, to build a canal that proved unnecessary.[22]

But the race continued, and in Stalin's words: "The party whipped the country on, rushing it forward at full speed."[23]

In 1932 the summing up began. By juggling figures (making calculations with percentages, in rubles whose value was fixed at will by the planning organs, and using 1913 as the base year for comparisons), it was possible to claim that the "main indices" of the plan had been fulfilled. Where it was not fulfilled, wreckers were to blame. Of course, some indices could be checked. The plan had called for an increase of 15–20 percent in the buying power of the ruble. But the reality of inflation was obvious to all Soviet citizens. The plan promised the "elimination of the shortage of manufactured goods by the end of the planning period," an increase of 69 percent in real wages, and "for a number of the most important consumer goods, a doubling of the norms of consumption."[24] The waiting lines for goods bought with ration cards, including bread, were hours long and left no doubt that these promises had not been kept. Nevertheless, in an unusually short time gigantic industrial projects were completed in the Urals, the Kuznetsk basin, the Volga region, and the Ukraine. Factories were built in Moscow and Leningrad, textile mills in Central Asia, and so on. The Turkestan–Siberia Railway, built before the revolution, was extended and a branch added to Karaganda. In all, 5,500 kilometers of rail were laid. (The plan called for 16,000.)

A great deal was accomplished. Stalin had a right to ask at the Seventeenth Party Congress in 1934: "Is this not a miracle?"[25] But it was not. The plan was realized primarily through "domestic accumulation," which was obtained thanks to the "consumer asceticism" Strumilin had written about—that is, the ruthless exploitation of the population. The country was exporting raw materials, including foodstuffs—grain, meat, sugar— for which there was a severe need at home. At the same time, the importing of vitally needed goods, such as wool, cotton, rice, and leather, was stopped. Timber was exported at dumping prices: "We must cut down not only the amount of timber that grows in a year, but much more; in essence, our task is not to utilize the forests, but to obliterate them."[26] Production was expanding, in oil and gold, which were also exported, the increased amounts of gold and timber obtained largely through prisoner labor. Even certain treasures from Russian museums were sold, and gold was extorted from the citizenry by every possible means. According to Walter Krivitsky, Stalin decided to revive the customs of the good old days by resorting to the simplest means of acquiring foreign currency: manufacturing dollars in the cellars of the GPU. In 1908 Stalin had directed the "expropriations" from the state treasury at Tiflis; a quarter of a century later he gave the order to begin manufacturing $100 bills in Moscow, in the Lubyanka.[27]

The five-year plan could not have been implemented without foreign assistance. In 1928 a group of Soviet engineers arrived in Detroit and requested that Albert Kahn and Company, an eminent firm of industrial architects in the United States, design plans for industrial buildings worth $2 billion.[28] Close to a dozen designs were to be made in Detroit, the rest in the Soviet Union. According to an agreement with the Supreme Economic Council of the USSR, the American firm agreed to design all aspects of Soviet industry, heavy and light. Foreign designers, technicians, engineers, and skilled workers built the industrial units of the first five-year plan. Primarily they were Americans, who pushed the Germans out of first place after 1928; after them came the Germans, British, Italians, and French. The dam on the Dnepr was built by the firm of Colonel Hugh Cooper, a prominent American hydraulic engineer; the majority of the largest Soviet power plants were equipped by the British firm Metropolitan-Vickers; Western companies designed, built, and equipped Magnitogorsk and Kuznetsk, the Urals Machinery Works, the Kaganovich Ball Bearing Plant in Moscow, an automobile plant in Nizhny Novgorod, and a truck plant in Yaroslavl, among others. Ordzhonikidze, the commissar of heavy industry, was able to state with full justification: "Our factories, our mines, our mills are now equipped with excellent technology that cannot be found in any one country. ... How did we get it? We bought the most highly perfected machinery, the very latest technology in the world, from the Americans, Germans, French, and English, and with that we equipped our enterprises." And he added caustically, "Meanwhile, many of their factories and mines still have machinery dating from the nineteenth century, or the early part of the twentieth."[29]

Lest the foreign participants in socialist construction begin to feel too independent, or Soviet citizens forget who the enemy was, a few foreigners were arrested from time to time. In April 1933 one more "wreckers" trial was staged, featuring five British engineers from Metropolitan-Vickers among the eighteen defendants. The fact that the British firm, which had been equipping Soviet power plants since 1923, was virtually in a monopoly position was undoubtedly a factor behind these indictments. In spite of many hours of interrogation, the Britishers refused to plead guilty and got off with light sentences. Thornton, the leader of the group, was sentenced to three years, Cushny to two, two were deported, and the other acquitted. The Soviet citizens in the case received sentences ranging from eighteen months to ten years.

It is impossible to sum up the results of the first five-year plan strictly in terms of industrial successes (or failures). From 1928 to 1932 significant strides were made in the industrialization of the country. But the main arena of the "Great Rupture," or the "great backbreaking," as Solzhenitsyn called it, was agriculture. The main object of this all-out offensive—and its main victim—was the peasantry, that is, the overwhelming majority of the population.

## FULL STEAM AHEAD—INTO THE SWAMP

Stalin's article "A Year of Great Change" appeared in *Pravda* on November 7, 1928. It spoke of "the radical change that has taken place in the development of our agriculture from small, backward individual farming to large-scale advanced collective agriculture."[30] The article ended: "We are advancing full steam ahead along the path of industrialization." This might have seemed just a metaphor, but within seven weeks it became reality.

Stalin announced the start of a new revolution on December 27, 1929, at a conference of "Marxist students of the agrarian question." The Soviet Union had just celebrated Stalin's fiftieth birthday, December 21. The country discovered for the first time that Stalin had been its Great Leader (*Veliky Vozhd*) all along, organizer of the October revolution, creator of the Red Army, victorious commander against the Whites and foreign invaders, guardian of Lenin's "general line" and vanquisher of all its opponents, leader of the world proletariat, and great strategist of the five-year plan. Portraits of the Leader were printed in unbelievable numbers, his bust appeared in all prominent places, and a pamphlet containing "birthday materials" about him was circulated everywhere. The most enthusiastic article, which set forth the main lines for the future cult of Stalin, was written by Karl Radek. Since 1921 the National Socialists in Germany had been on a campaign to build up a cult around Hitler. By 1929 they had accumulated considerable experience. This was the model Radek drew on for his trend-setting article. Stalin responded to all the homage paid him on his birthday by pledging to shed "all of his blood, to the last drop if necessary," for the cause, and he gave the credit for all his accomplishments to "the great party of the working class, which nurtured me and reared me in its image."[31] Using a figure of speech from the as yet unforgotten Bible, Stalin described his origins with astonishing accuracy. The party had made Stalin what he was, but as sometimes happens, the child turned against its parent, killed it, and in turn sired a new offspring, a party fashioned in Stalin's image.

On December 27 the Leader announced the end of NEP and the start of a new era. The problem was as follows, he declared: "Either we go backward to capitalism or forward to socialism."[32] In exact conformity with Bolshevik tradition, the problem was presented so as to allow only one response. It was necessary to go on the offensive. "What does this mean?" Stalin asked, and answered himself: "It means that after a policy that consisted in limiting the exploitative tendencies of the kulaks, we have switched to a policy of eliminating the kulaks as a class."[33] The path forward was the path of "complete collectivization." To those who questioned whether dekulakization was necessary for complete collectivization, Stalin replied: "The question is absurd!" A great lover of Russian proverbs, he added, "When the head is cut off, why cry over a few hairs?"[34]

The next sixty-five days shook the country more than the ten days in October 1917 that "shook the world." Those nine weeks convulsed the lives of the Soviet Union's more than 130 million peasants, transformed the country's economy, and changed the very nature of the state.

Two processes went on simultaneously: the creation of collective farms (kolkhozes), and the liquidation of the kulaks. Above all, dekulakization was necessary to provide the "material base" for the collective farms. From the end of 1929 to the middle of 1930,

> more than 320,000 kulak faramers were dekulakized. Their property (worth more than 175 million rubles) was transferred to the indivisible funds of the kolkhozes and used for the entrance fees of poor peasants and unpropertied farmhands. Former kulak property amounted to more than 34 percent of the total value of the indivisible funds of all the kolkhozes taken together.[35]

The liquidation of the kulaks deprived the countryside of the most enterprising and independent-minded peasants and broke the spirit of resistance. Moreover, the fate of "dekulakized persons," deportation to Siberia or the north of Russia, served as an example for anyone who thought of not joining the kolkhoz. It was necessary to join immediately. A commission of the Politburo formed on December 8, 1929, under the direction of Yakov Yakovlev, commissar of agriculture, proposed that "complete collectivization" be carried out in the lower Volga region by autumn 1930, the central Black Earth region and the Ukrainian steppes by autumn 1931, the left bank of the Ukraine by spring 1932, and the north and Siberia by 1933.

Stalin and his "close comrade-in-arms" Molotov insisted that the pace be even faster. On December 10 the Kolkhoztsentr, the central office established to administer all kolkhozes, sent a directive by telegraph to local organizations in the regions slated for complete collectivization: "Implement 100 percent collectivization of draft animals and cattle, 80 percent of hogs, and 60 percent of sheep and poultry."[36] Joining the kolkhoz meant surrendering your property, all of it, to the collective.

Party members (25,000 of them) were sent to the villages to force the peasants to join kolkhozes. It was announced that whoever did not join would be considered an enemy of the Soviet state. On July 1, 1928, only 1.7 percent of the peasantry belonged to kolkhozes; by November 1929 the figure had risen to 7.6 percent; in March 1930 it was 58 percent.

There had not been a final decision on the exact form the kolkhoz should take, whether all land, implements, and animals should be collectivized or some left in individual hands. There was still a lack of personnel capable of administering collective farms. The necessary tractors and other machinery were not available. Lenin, who never stopped hoping for miracles, once said: "If tomorrow we could supply 100,000 first-class tractors—you know very well that at present this is sheer fantasy—the middle peasant would say, 'I am for the *kommuniya*' (i.e., for communism)."[37] Stalin fully shared Lenin's steadfast faith in the direct and inseparable connection between the material base and the spiritual superstructure (100,000 tractors equals "I am for communism"), but he acknowledged that he did not have the tractors. He promised 60,000 by the spring of 1930 and the magical 100,000 for the following year. In 1928, according to official Soviet figures, there were only 26,700 tractors.

Unfazed by such problems, Stalin simply cracked the whip harder at the local party officials, who in turn drove the rank-and-file activists (the "twenty-five-thousanders") harder. The number of collective farmers steadily increased, and the number of kulaks dwindled. The term *kulak* had never been defined. Anyone who employed hired labor was considered a kulak, but so was anyone who owned two horses or two cows or a nice house. Since there was no clear notion of what a kulak was, overall quotas for dekulakization and collectivization were assigned for each region. The quota for collectivization was the same everywhere, 100 percent. The dekulakization quota varied, averaging 5–7 percent.

Many of the peasants who had previously been regarded as middle or prosperous peasants were now listed as kulaks and made subject to dekulakization. In addition, many less prosperous middle peasants and even some
poor peasants were deported, after being labeled—to make repression against
them easier—with the absurd term *kulak henchmen (podkulachniki)*. . . . In
some regions 15–20 percent of the peasants were deported; for every kulak
deported three or four middle or poor peasants were arrested.[38]

That is how a *History of the USSR* published in Moscow thirty years after
the events described the situation in the countryside in 1930. In a fit of
inexplicable frankness it admitted that the concept "kulak henchman" was
absurd. Yet the leadership had used that term to justify the harshest measures against the peasantry.

On the basis of resolutions passed by the Central Committee of the party,
the government's Central Executive Committee, and the Council of People's
Commissars on January 3 and February 1, 1930, as well as special instructions dated February 4, all kulaks and *podkulachniki* were divided
into three categories.

Organizers and perpetrators of terrorist acts, and those engaged in active
anti-Soviet work, were isolated and sent to concentration camps. Kulaks who
demonstrated the slightest active resistance were deported to remote regions
of the country, where they were put to work cutting down the forests, doing
farm labor, etc. The other kulaks remained where they were, but they could
not have any land allotments from within the bounds of the kolkhozes.[39]

Moreover, "during the autumn and winter of 1930–31 additional deportations were carried out affecting the expropriated kulak households."[40]

Kulaks and their "henchmen" were deported with all of their families,
including infants and old people. Hundreds of thousands were shipped in
unheated boxcars thousands of kilometers away to remote parts of the Urals,
Siberia, and Kazakhstan. Many died en route; many others died after their
arrival, for as a rule they were deported to uninhabitable locations in the
forests, mountains, or steppes. In 1937 Walter Krivitsky recalled what he
had seen by chance at a railroad station in Kursk in the winter of 1934:
"I will never forget what I saw. In the waiting area there were nearly six
hundred peasants—men, women, and children—being driven from one
camp to another like cattle. . . . Many were lying down, almost naked, on
the cold floor. Others were obviously dying of typhoid fever. Hunger, tor-
ment, and despair were written on every face."[41] A quarter of a century
later, during the brief period of the Thaw, a number of Soviet writers
confirmed what the "defector" Krivitsky had written.

The full story of this first socialist genocide has yet to be written. Chronologically, the first genocide of the twentieth century was that of the Armenians by the Turks. The massacre of Don Cossacks by the Bolsheviks during the civil war likewise approached genocidal proportions. The Turks destroyed a population of a different faith and nationality; the Cossacks suffered during a fratricidal civil war. The genocide against the peasants in the Soviet Union was unique not only for its monstrous scale; it was directed against an indigenous population by a government of the same nationality, and in time of peace.

In 1945, after the defeat of Nazi Germany and the public disclosure of all its crimes, jurists, sociologists, psychologists, historians, and journalists began the inevitable controversy over whether the German people had known about the Nazi crimes or not. There is no question that the Soviet city people knew about the massacre in the countryside. In fact, no one tried to conceal it. Stalin spoke openly about the "liquidation of the kulaks as a class," and all his lieutenants echoed him. At the railroad stations, city dwellers could see the thousands of women and children who had fled from the villages and were dying of hunger. Kulaks, "dekulakized persons," and "kulak henchmen" died alike. They were not considered human. Society spat them out, just as the "disenfranchised persons" and "has-beens" were after October 1917, just as the Jews were in Nazi Germany.

The great proletarian humanist Maxim Gorky invented a formula to justify this genocide: "If the enemy does not surrender, he must be destroyed." Gorky's article containing this formula was printed simultaneously in *Pravda* and *Izvestia* on November 15, 1930, then publicized in speeches and lectures, in newspapers and magazines, and over the radio. "We are opposed by everything that has outlived the time set for it by history, and this gives us the right to consider ourselves again in a state of civil war. The conclusion naturally follows that if the enemy does not surrender, he must be destroyed."[42]

Official sources note forty-five instances of hostile action against collectivization in Central Asia in early March 1930, involving 17,400 persons, and "rebellions and disturbances in other regions."[43] This is a ridiculous understatement of the peasantry's resistance to the kolkhoz: collectivization provoked hostility among the peasants in the Ukraine, Siberia, Central Asia, the Caucasus, the Kuban, and the Don region. The detailed documentary evidence presumably resides in the KGB archives. Scattered bits of testimony allow us nevertheless to deduce the breadth of the resistance. In the Northern Caucasus and in a number of regions in the Ukraine regular units of the Red Army, backed by air power, were thrown against the peasantry. Frinovsky, commander of the frontier forces of the NKVD, who directed the suppression of the peasant rebellions, reported to a meeting of the Politburo that the rivers of the Northern Caucasus were carrying thousands of corpses to the sea. In some areas Red Army men refused to fire on the peasants and were shot immediately; in other cases small units went over to the rebels.

Once war was declared on the peasantry, the Soviet propaganda machine indignantly denounced cases of resistance, especially the murder of "twenty-five thousanders," the activists assigned to driving the peasants into the kolkhozes.

Passive resistance became the universal form of resistance. The peasants refused to join kolkhozes as long as they had sufficient strength not to yield to threats and force, and they destroyed their livestock as a sign of protest. Livestock transferred to the kolkhoz died from lack of shelter, fodder, and care.

The statistics demonstrate the disaster that struck the Soviet livestock herd. In 1928 there were 33.5 million horses in the country; in 1932, 19.6 million. For cattle the figures were, respectively, 70.5 million and 40.7 million; for pigs, 26 million and 11.6 million; for sheep and goats, 146 million and 52.1 million.[44] In Kazakhstan the number of sheep and goats fell from 19.2 million in 1930 to only 2.6 million in 1935.[45] From 1929 to 1934 a total of 149.4 million head of livestock were destroyed. The value of these animals and their products (milk, butter, wool, etc.) far exceeded the value of the giant factories built during the same period. The destruction of horses meant a loss of 8.8 million horsepower. In 1935, when there were already 379,500 tractors, the available horsepower was still 2.2 million less than in 1928, when there were only 26,700 tractors.

Passive resistance was suppressed just as fiercely as the active variety. In Voronezh in the summer of 1930 a show trial was held featuring sixteen leaders of the "Fedorovite" religious sect. This movement, headed by a peasant named Fedorov, had arisen in the early years of the NEP in what had been Voronezh Province. The main tenet of their faith was "nonresistance to evil," and they sought by every means possible to "avoid evil temptation" or "participation in evil deeds." During the NEP the Fedorovites, and other sects such as the Dukhobors, Molokane, and Baptists, were spared persecution by the Soviet authorities, who hoped to use them against the Orthodox church. When the Fedorovites refused to join the kolkhozes, however, they were immediately branded enemies, conspirators, and kulaks. Fifteen of their leaders were sentenced to death (and immediately shot). The sixteenth was condemned to lifelong confinement in a psychiatric hospital. Nearly 2,000 Fedorovites were deported to the taiga and tundra, to meet a slow but certain death. For three months the regions infected with the idea of nonresistance to evil were "combed out." The peasants, praying and appealing to their tormentors, offered no resistance to arrest.

The peasants' passive resistance, the destruction of livestock, the complete disorganization of work in the kolkhozes, and the general ruin caused by continued dekulakization and deportations all led in 1932–33 to a famine that surpassed even the famine of 1921–22 in its geographical extent and the number of its victims. On this occasion, however, the government took no measures against the famine and in fact contributed to tis spread, using it as a weapon in the civil war against the peasantry.

The difference between the two famines was not limited just to the larger scale of that brought on by collectivization. Another difference was that the government denied the existence of the later one. Even to mention it was a crime against the state. In 1921 the Soviet government, however reluctantly, had allowed independent figures to seek help from abroad. In the 1930s nothing was said about the famine, and grain continued to be exported throughout this period. In 1928 grain exports amounted to only 1 million centners; in 1929, 13 million; in 1930, 48.3 million; in 1931, 51.8 million; and in 1932, 18.1 million.

When Terekhov, a secretary of the Ukrainian party's Central Committee, asked at a Moscow conference that grain be sent to save the starving collective farmers of the Kharkov region, Stalin cut him off: "I see that you are a good storyteller. You have invented this tale about a famine, hoping to frighten us, but it won't work!"[46] It was impossible to frighten Stalin with "tales" of a famine. If he did not want to save the people dying of hunger, it was not because grain was lacking (the export of grain was evidence to the contrary) but because the famine and the havoc it wreaked vitiated the peasantry as a political force and broke the last vestiges of its resistance.

"For Stalin the peasants were scum," Khrushchev recalled much later in his memoirs. "He had no respect for the peasants or their work. He thought the only way to get farmers to produce was to put pressure on them. Under Stalin, state procurements were forcibly requisitioned for the countryside to feed the cities."[47]

In the cities the workers were not starving; they merely lived from hand to mouth. The leaders, however, denied themselves nothing. Dmitrievsky, the former Soviet diplomat, described how he had been fed at a sanatorium for "higher-ups" in the Crimea: "The usual menu abounded in tasty dishes, with everything in which Russia is rich. Breakfast at eight, with eggs, ham, cheese, cocoa, tea, and milk. At eleven, yogurt. Then a four-course midday meal: soup, fish, meat, dessert, and fruit. During the afternoon, tea and pastries. In the evening, a two-course supper."[48] Walter Krivitsky, who vacationed in similar conditions during the famine, at the former estate of the Baryatinsky princes near Kursk, recounted the self-justifications of the luxuriating Soviet elite: "We are traveling a difficult road to socialism. Many have fallen along the way. We must eat well and relax after our labors, enjoying for a few weeks of the year the comforts that are still not accessible to others, for it is we who are building the happy life of the future."[49]

The completion of the first five-year plan gave Stalin the opportunity to play benefactor, announcing the great achievements and benefits to the people. Since the very first days of the revolution the party had deceived the workers and poor peasants, in whose name it ruled, by promising them that paradise on earth was imminent. In the late 1920s the deception, both conscious and unconscious, became a lie. During the first five-year plan it became the Great Lie. The Great Terror was preceded by—and is invariably accompanied by—the Great Lie. As a British humorist once said, there are three kinds of lies: a lie, a barefaced lie, and statistics. He was unaware of a fourth kind, Stalinist statistics, and a fifth, the Stalinist lie.

In summing up the achievements of the First Five-Year Plan, Stalin was not ashamed to announce that workers' wages had risen by 67 percent and that the material conditions of the workers and peasants had improved from year to year. In a popular Moscow anecdote of the period a tourist guide at a zoo points to a crocodile recently brought to the capital and explains that from tail to head it is five meters long but from head to tail it is six. "How could that be?" asks a tourist. "You don't believe it? Measure it yourself," the guide answers. "You'll see." Stalin had roughly the same answer for anyone who wanted to check his figures. Only "sworn enemies of the Soviet system" could have any doubts about the improvement of the workers' and peasants' conditions in the Soviet Union, he declared.[50]

Fifteen years after the revolution Pravda proclaimed, "For a Communist there is no task more noble than the improvement of the workers' conditions."[51] In the fall of 1932, when those words were written, famine and collectivization were at their height. Seventeen years after the revolution Stalin declared: "There would have been no use in overthrowing capitalism in November 1917 and building socialism all these years if we were not going to secure a life of plenty for our people. Socialism does not mean destitution and privation."[52]

For all of Stalin's lies, however, collectivization never went smoothly. In late February 1930 it became obvious even to Stalin that the mad dash to collectivize everything, which he himself had ordered at the end of 1929, threatened to end in disaster. Discontent began to penetrate the army, which was composed of the sons of peasants. So Stalin took a step backward, as though intending to retreat. On March 2, 1930, Pravda published his article, "Dizzy with Success," in which he placed all the blame on those who were following orders, the local party activists. The peasants who had been driven into the kolkhozes read this as the abandonment of collectivization. After all, had he not written, "Who benefits by these distortions, this bureaucratic decreeing of a collective farm movement, these unseemly threats against the peasants? Nobody but our enemies!" After the publication of this article the kolkhozes collapsed like a house of cards. In the central Black Earth region, where 82 percent of the individual farms had been collectivized by March, only 18 percent remained collectivized in May. To the peasants Stalin had become the good and just ruler supreme. All the trouble had been caused by local misrulers.

A step backward had been taken, however, only to prepare the way for ten new steps forward. By September 1931 nearly 60 percent of the farms had been collectivized again; in 1934, 75 percent. Repression against the peasants did not end with the establishment of the kolkhoz system. The aim of collectivization was to "solve the grain problem." The kolkhozes were formed for the convenience of the state, but the appropriate methods for controlling the kolkhozes were not found immediately.

First, a system of obligatory deliveries to the state was introduced (and meeting these obligations became "the first commandment of the collective farmer"). The kolkhozes were obliged to surrender between 25 and 33 percent of their products at fixed prices established by the state. Second, the kolkhozes were stripped of all agricultural machinery, that is, of the very tractors that were supposed to make the peasants say, "I am for communism." The kolkhozes had the land and the labor force, but the machinery was held by state-run machine and tractor stations (MTSs) established by a decree of June 5, 1929. In return for its services the MTS took another 20 percent of the harvest, and it was impossible to conceal the harvest from the MTS personnel, since they actually worked the kolkhoz fields. Thus, control was established over kolkhoz production. In addition, "political departments" attached to the MTSs were introduced in January 1933, with the task of monitoring the collective farmers from the political point of view. The head of each political department was flanked by a GPU representative, who could instantly turn word into deed by arresting errant peasants. In January 1933 Stalin spoke ironically about those who believed that after the liquidation of the kulaks there would be no more enemies. He pointed out that storehouse personnel, accountants, and managers could be enemies, too. Immediately 34.4 percent of all employees at storage facilities were arrested and charged with sabotage; the same with 25 percent of all bookkeepers, and so forth.[53]

Among the more eloquent documents of the period is a secret letter of

May 8, 1933, to all party and government workers and all organs of the GPU, the courts, and the procuracy. This letter, marked "secret, not for publication," was found in the Smolensk archives. It provides a good summary of what happened during collectivization, especially the forms and methods used to carry it out. The letter, signed by Molotov as president of the Sovnarkom and Stalin as general secretary of the party's Central Committee, consisted of two parts: "Regularization of Arrest Procedures"; and "Reduction of Overloading [i.e., an excessive number of prisoners] at Places of Confinement." The instructions under the first part were "to prevent arrests by persons not authorized by law—chairmen of district soviet executive committees, district and regional plenipotentiaries, chairmen of village soviets, chairmen of kolkhozes and associations of kolkhozes, secretaries of party cells, etc." The "etc." was particularly significant. It meant that until then virtually anyone had been able to arrest peasants. The letter put an end to this situation, except for "the Far Eastern Territory, Central Asia, and Kazakhstan," where the continuation of these practices was authorized for another six months.

The second part of the letter showed the results of such mass arrests and indiscriminate power to arrest. The letter stipulated that no more than 400,000 people should be held in places of confinement—other than labor camps and penal colonies. As of May 8, twice that number were being held, because the letter instructed the GPU, the commissariats of justice of the Soviet republics, and the procuracy of the USSR to "undertake immediately to relieve the overloading at places of detention and within a two-month period reduce the number of prisoners from 800,000 to 400,000."[54]

If the overloading of the prisons was relieved, that did not mean that the prisoners were freed, but only that they were dispatched to the camps more quickly. Room was made in the prisons, and the work force in the camps was swelled. The Western journalist William Henry Chamberlin, who was a correspondent in Moscow in the 1930s, had the following to report about the camps: "I was informed by a reliable source that in the concentration camps in Siberia alone there were close to 300,000 prisoners. The number of Soviet citizens who were deprived of their liberty without the slightest hint of a trial during the years of the five-year plan must be estimated at no less than 2 million."[55] The official figure of 800,000 in the prisons alone as of May 8, 1933, suggests that the total number must have been far more than 2 million.

The economic results of collectivization were deplorable. During the first four years of the five-year plan the total harvest of grain diminished, according to official calculations, from 733.3 million centners in 1928 to

696.7 million in 1931–1932. The yield per hectare in 1932 was 5.7 centners. In 1913 it had been 8.2 centners.[56] In 1928 the total output for
agriculture was 124 percent of the amount in 1913. In 1929 this dropped
to 121 percent; in 1930, 117 percent; in 1932, 107 percent; and in 1933,
101 percent. Livestock production in 1933 was only 65 percent of production in 1913.[57] Yet in summing up the results of collectivization on
January 7, 1933, Stalin was satisfied: "The party has succeeded in creating
conditions which enable it to obtain 1,200–1,400 million poods [394–460
million centners] of marketable grain annually, instead of 500–600 million
poods [164–197 million centners], as was the case when individual peasant
farming predominated."[58]

This success was paid for primarily with millions of human lives. The
demographic results of collectivization were tragic. The number of victims
has never been, and will never be, determined exactly. (The losses of
livestock were calculated, on the other hand, down to the last sheep.)
Population figures and the data on the birth rate and mortality rate were
no longer published after 1932. Stalin took personal charge of statistics.
In January 1934, at the Seventeenth Party Congress, the "Congress of
Victors," he reported "an increase in the population of the Soviet Union
from 160,500,000 at the end of 1930 to 168,000,000 at the end of 1933."
Ten years later he would tell Churchill that "the poor peasants" had taken
reprisals against "10 million kulaks," of whom the "vast majority" were
annihilated, the rest being sent to Siberia.[59] In 1935 Molotov reported that
in 1928 the kulaks and well-to-do peasants had numbered 5,618,000, but
as of January 1, 1935, only 149,000 were left.[60] Aleksandr Orlov reports
that foreign journalists, including those who praised Stalin's policies, estimated the number of victims of the famine at 5–7 million. The GPU gave
Stalin an estimate of 3.3–3.5 million.[61] The Soviet demographer Boris
Urlanis notes a population loss of 7.5 million between the end of 1932 and
the end of 1933.[62]

After considering all the estimates and accounts, Robert Conquest arrived
at the cautious figure of "over 5 million deaths from hunger and the diseases
of hunger."[63] In a *samizdat* essay written in the period 1976–1978, I. G.
Dyadkin estimated the population loss from 1929 to 1936 at 15.2 million.[64]
The authorities expressed their opinion of Dyadkin's figures by arresting
him.

The monstrous dimensions of this bloodletting become more apparent if
we recall the angry indictment Bakunin hurled at the tsarist autocracy: "In
the course of some 200 years the tsarist system had destroyed more than
a million victims as a result of its brutish contempt for human rights and
human life."[65] Bakunin included in his total for the "tsarist system" victims

of war, epidemics, and other natural disasters that occurred in the course of those 200 years. A comparison of the number of victims in these two periods, 200 years of tsarist rule and a few years of Stalinist collectivization, shows the difference between autocracy and totalitarianism, between an unhurried historical existence and an insane rush toward "progress."

With amazing insight, as early as 1919, Ivan Bunin uncovered "the Bolsheviks' diabolical secret." They wanted to kill human sensibility. "People live by a certain measure," Bunin wrote in his diary,

> Even imagination and sensibility are measured. And so you go beyond this limit. As with the price of bread or beef. "What? Three rubles a pound!" (That is still within your frame of reference.) But if the price is raised to a thousand rubles, there will be no more shouts or amazement, only numbed insensibility. "What's that, seven?" "No, my dear, seven hundred." Then you really feel stunned, paralyzed. Because if seven people are hanged, you can still imagine it, but try to imagine seven hundred, or even seventy.[66]

Bunin still measured sensibility by nineteenth-century standards. It never occurred to him, of course, that the number of people hanged, shot, tortured to death, and so on would be measured, not in the hundreds, but in the millions.

One of the most important aspects of collectivization was its sociological shock effect. The post-October tremor did not touch the deeper strata of society, but the shock of collectivization reached the very foundations of rural society. It destroyed the old peasantry and in its place produced a new social type—the collective farmer, a being who very quickly lost all interest in working the land. In the latter half of the 1920s such writers as Konstantin Fedin, Vsevolod Ivanov, and Leonid Leonov had written about postrevolutionary rural Russia. The revolution had not affected it at all, they said; it continued to live in the sixteenth century or at best the seventeenth. They portrayed Russia as a kind of antediluvian beast, a brontosaurus with a huge, inert body (the countryside) and a tiny brain (the city). Collectivization killed the brontosaurus.

The best works about collectivization were left to us by Andrei Platonov: *The Foundation Pit (Kotlovan)*, which was never printed in the Soviet Union; and the short novel *Vprok* (meaning "pointless, for no good reason"), whose very title aroused immediate and angry criticism from Stalin. In these works Platonov in effect was asking, Does the country really need this insane attempt to reach socialism on paper? The entire subsequent history of the Soviet Union demonstrates that collectivization left the economy with a gaping wound that has never healed.

In *Doctor Zhivago*, Boris Pasternak very accurately described the consequences of collectivization. Through terror people were broken of the habit of thinking; an illusory world was created for them, which they were required to accept as real. Pasternak was wrong, though, when he said the authorities could not admit that collectivization had been a mistake. For Stalin collectivization was not a mistake but a great victory.

Politically, collectivization was a brilliant success. From Stalin's point of view it was absolutely necessary. S. Dmitrievsky, the Soviet diplomat who defected while in Stockholm in 1930, published a biography of Stalin in 1931 that may be considered the first apologia for the Leader to appear in the West and the first statement of certain ideas that the Leader could not express openly at home.

> The edifice of Stalin's dictatorship can be maintained and his plans carried out only if political and economic power is fully monopolized by Stalin. Political power has been in his hands for a long time. But up until now he had not had full economic power. That is possible only on the basis of a monopolistic state capitalism encompassing the country's entire economic life without exception. [67]

Dmitrievsky noted a threat to Stalin's dictatorship from the peasant quarter. "The victory of the peasantry within the country would be a victory for the West, for its fundamental conception of individualism and liberalism in political life."[68]

Dmitrievsky wrote his biography of Stalin just when collectivization was in full swing. When that campaign was over, the entire economic life of the country was indeed in Stalin's hands. The entire citizenry became completely dependent on the state, both politically and economically. Simultaneously, monopoly control was exerted over another part of people's lives, the spiritual aspect.

## THE INEXORABLE RISE OF JOSEPH STALIN

This is how Dmitrievsky described a Politburo meeting in 1930: "Rudzutak, steady and impassive, usually chairs the meeting. But the central, the decisive presence, despite his customary silence, even because of it, is Stalin. All eyes are on him. Many at the meeting dislike him, some even hate him, but for the moment he is nothing less than the autocrat of the Russian state."[69]

The American journalist Louis Fischer concluded his account of the Sixteenth Party Congress, held in June–July 1930, with these words:

A good comrade should advise Stalin to stop the orgy of glorification of his person. . . . Every day hundreds and thousands of telegrams full of compliments in exalted, exaggerated Oriental style—"You are the very greatest Leader," "the most faithful disciple of Lenin," etc.—are addressed to him. Three cities are named after him, along with countless villages, collective farms, schools, factories, and institutions. . . . Though Stalin may not be responsible for this state of affairs, he tolerates it. He could put an end to it just by pressing a button.[70]

Fischer later learned that when this passage was translated for Stalin, the Leader's response was brief and to the point: "Scum!"

Robert C. Tucker, the American biographer of Stalin, argues that the real cult, the deification, of Stalin began at the end of 1931 with an article in which the general secretary presented himself as the only legitimate interpreter of Marx. It is true that in 1929–1930 Stalin had not yet assumed all the attributes of the Supreme Leader and Teacher, whose every word became law for all of progressive mankind. Nevertheless, by then he not only possessed vast power but had already become the object of a cult, as Louis Fischer described. In those first years of the five-year plan he was not universally worshiped, as he soon would be. Evidence of reluctance to make a god of him could be seen in two attempts to challenge his authority in the early 1930s. They were made, not by veteran oppositionists, but by Bolsheviks of the younger generation.

In November 1930 a plot was uncovered, the "Syrtsov plot" as Dmitrievsky called it, or the "right-ultraleft bloc" in the official terminology, which considered the combination of such mutually exclusive concepts perfectly acceptable. A few months earlier Sergei Syrtsov had begun a meteoric rise, becoming chairman of the Council of People's Commissars of the RSFSR in 1929 and an alternate member of the Politburo after the Sixteenth Party Congress, in July 1930. His fall was every bit as sudden as his rise. Dmitrievsky, who gives the fullest account of the "plot," says that Syrtsov, a favorite of Stalin's, along with a number of other "high party and government officials, came to the conclusion that the most decisive measures had to be taken to change the policies of the government to which they themselves belonged."[71] Dmitrievsky stresses that Syrtsov, in all his articles and speeches, "remained what he was, a devoted adherent to the Stalinist system of ideas." What he was dissatisfied with was the administrative mess, the incredible bureaucracy of the machine of state. His "purely practical, nonideological platform"[72] was endorsed by Besso Lominadze, who at one time had been sent by Stalin to attempt a revolution in Canton, and by Lazar Shatskin, a leader of the Komsomol. What is more, Dmitrievsky states, "there were rumors that Stalin himself was somehow mixed up in this plot, hoping to use it to carry through a number of radical changes."[73] Knowing Stalin, we cannot reject even such fantastic rumors. Would he really have refrained from playing the provocateur if that suited his ends? The "conspirators" were arrested and removed from their posts, but only mild sanctions were taken against them. It was the last time that criticism of the party line was viewed simply as a political matter, rather than "treason" or "terrorism."

The summer of 1932 saw the second challenge to Stalin's authority in this period. Mikhail Ryutin, a former Bukharin supporter and one-time secretary of the party's Moscow committee, circulated a 160-page program containing three main demands: (1) economic retreat (a slower pace of industrialization and an end to forced collectivization); (2) democracy within the party; and (3) removal of Stalin. An entire chapter of the program dealt with Stalin, whom Ryutin called "the evil genius of the party and the revolution," "the gravedigger of the revolution," and a "provocateur."[74]

Charges were brought not only against Ryutin but also against Uglanov, formerly first secretary of the Moscow committee, and against Tolmachev and Eismont, formerly people's commissars and Central Committee members. All were accused of trying to form a "counterrevolutionary bourgeois-kulak organization" whose purpose was to "restore capitalism in the USSR." Ryutin had once been an editor of the military newspaper *Red Star*. Now he was charged with attempting to organize a terrorist group among student officers at the Military School of the All-Union Central Executive Committee, with the aim of assassinating Stalin. For the first time party members were accused of plotting terrorist acts when all they had done was express oppositional views. For the first time Stalin demanded the death penalty for the "plotters." However, the Politburo refused to authorize the execution of Ryutin. According to Krivitsky, Kirov opposed the death penalty in this case and rallied the majority of the Politburo behind him.[75] Stalin would recall the Ryutin platform with a vengeance four years later, and within a year and a half he made Kirov pay for his conduct.

Ryutin circulated his program at the height of the famine, in the midst of collectivization and the mad rush to complete "five in four." Meanwhile the Left Opposition, i.e., Trotsky, supported Stalin.

The Trotskyists welcomed the decision to collectivize agriculture, although Trotsky did reproach Stalin for his theoretical illiteracy, for not even considering the second volume of *Capital* in his policy of collectivization.[76] (Trotsky wrote this in his *Bulletin of the Opposition*, which he began to publish after being expelled from the Soviet Union in 1929.) Sometimes it

is possible to find in Trotsky's *Bulletin* letters from the Soviet Union criticizing collectivization for not being radical enough. "In place of the dis-
possessed and deported kulaks," a certain A. T. complains in a letter dated
June 12, 1930, "in the soil fertilized by centrist illusions, we see the
sprouting of new capitalist shoots."[77] In a 1931 pamphlet, *Problems of the
Development of the USSR*, Trotsky called collectivization "a new epoch in
the development of humanity, the beginning of the liquidation of the 'idiocy
of rural life.'" Ante Ciliga, who in 1930 was in Stalin's prisons and camps,
told of the unenviable position of the imprisoned Trotskyists when they
received instructions from their leader to defend the view that the Soviet
Union was a "workers' state." It is true that Trotsky wrote, "The Soviet
Union has not entered into socialism, as the ruling Stalinist faction teaches."
Instead, Trotsky argued, it had entered "only into the first stage of development in the direction of socialism." In a letter to his son in October
1932 he wrote that it would be wrong to raise the slogan "Down with Stalin"
as a war cry at that moment because "at present Milyukov, the Mensheviks,
and Thermidorians of all sorts... will willingly echo the cry.... It may
happen within a few months," this great strategist of the revolution continued, "that Stalin may have to defend himself against Thermidorian pressure, and that we temporarily may have to support him."[78] With enemies
like these, Stalin didn't need friends.

The years of the First Five-Year Plan were the years of Stalin's inexorable
rise. He concentrated all power, material and spiritual, in his hands. He
was praised and glorified without restraint. A single word from him could
stop or start the entire country. He would utter brief slogans and entire
policies would change: "Technology decides everything," "Tempos decide
everything," "Cadres decide everything." He devastated the countryside
and killed millions of peasants, then blamed his subordinates. He imposed
a regime of virtual slavery on the workers, then declared: "Of all the greatest
treasures in the world, human beings, cadres, are the most precious and
the most decisive." He announced that "life has become more joyous,"
and the country, bathed in blood and tears, was compelled to rejoice.

Hundreds of books have been written about Stalin in an attempt to
penetrate the mystery of his success, the cult that surrounded him, his
seemingly inexorable rise to greater and greater heights and unlimited
power. He himself revealed the secret of his success in a simple formula:
"If you are backward, if you are weak, that means you are wrong and
can be beaten and enslaved. If you are mighty, that means you are right,
and people have to beware of you."[79] Stalin was referring to the might and
power of the state, to the idea that might makes right in both foreign and

domestic policy, but his formula also applied to the individual in a political power struggle.

For decades Trotsky's views decisively influenced most biographers of Stalin, "the irreplaceable general secretary," as Souvarine called him. Stalin was portrayed as a mediocrity, "a gray blur," borrowing the expression first used by Sukhanov. He was a liar, a scoundrel, and a good-for-nothing who had accidentally usurped the position that rightfully belonged to Trotsky, the brilliant organizer, writer, theoretician, and practical leader. After Stalin's death many biographers seemed inclined to depict him as a devil who had been plotting virtually since childhood to seize total power. The personality traits of the mature Stalin, whose monstrous power unbalanced his mind, were projected back to an earlier period onto the Stalin who was fighting for power and who won because he understood the true nature of the Bolshevik party better than his opponents and who best understood the weaknesses of his rivals.

We can safely assume that his plans for the kind of state and society he wanted did not crystalize in his mind until the late 1920s, when his victory over his rivals, Trotsky, Zinoviev, and Bukharin, was no longer in doubt. We can obtain a fairly clear picture of Stalin's plans, ideas, and aspirations from Dmitrievsky's books, although most biographers of Stalin disregard him completely.

Dmitrievsky was unquestionably a follower of Ustryalov, and he carried the changing landmarks ideology a step further, portraying Stalin as the embodiment of Russian national communism. Dmitrievsky's book on Stalin (1931) and his *Soviet Portraits* (1932) were aimed at winning the emigré community over to Stalin's side. What he wrote then seemed strange and unbelievable, but today it deserves special attention, because Stalin soon embarked on the road Dmitrievsky predicted.

A certain process had been underway in Russia, Dmitrievsky argued: "People who with full sincerity considered themselves at first to be nothing but Communists have now become National Communists, and many of them are already standing on the threshold of pure Russian nationalism."[80] The future of Russia was to be a national, or people's, empire, and the general secretary was the man leading the country to that state. "Could it be that only a thick-headed battering ram like Stalin can break through the door to Russia's future?" Dmitrievsky asked rhetorically.[81] To him, Stalin's dictatorship was in many respects already a national, people's dictatorship. At any rate, it was "far more closely linked with the masses than any so-called democracy."[82] The strength of the Stalinist system lay "not only in its bayonets" but in these links with the nation.[83]

Stalin's program consisted of several points, according to Dmitrievsky. First, to follow a "policy of applying maximum pressure, both in the party and the state apparatus, until everything and everyone is about to burst." Then would come the time when the idea of a "Red, proletarian, Russo-Asiatic imperialism" could be put into effect. The world had been divided into two camps—imperialism and its opponents. At the head of those fed up with imperialism and willing to fight to the death against it would stand the Soviet Union. That was how Stalin summed up his views, according to Dmitrievsky.[84] But the struggle against imperialism meant a struggle against the West. "It is necessary to catch up with and surpass the hated West, to bring it down, to break its arrogant power. For the sake of this objective, he is ready to sacrifice not only the small nation to which he was born but every generation now alive."[85]

This enemy of democracy and of the West, this implacable despot "who has no doubts about anything, who feels no pity for anyone," was building a national, people's empire. Russia was "gradually and ever more thoroughly ridding itself of the buzzing fly of Marxism, and advancing farther and farther along the road to a national system. Stalin's victory was the first step on this road, because it broke the back of the main force fighting Marxism in this country."[86]

In 1932, when Dmitrievsky wrote those lines, Trotsky still believed that Stalin was a Marxist, insufficiently grounded in theory and inclined to violate the letter and the spirit of the doctrine, but a Marxist nevertheless. To Dmitrievsky Stalin was already a fighter against Marxism. Both observers were right, each in a certain sense. Stalin was a Marxist as long as he found it helpful and an anti-Marxist whenever its dogmas became a constraint upon him. This was also true of nationalism, which also contained too much dogma for Stalin. He would regard Russia as the motherland only so long as the power in Russia was "ours, the workers' power, Stalinist power," as Dmitrievsky rightly observed.[87]

Nationalism, Marxism, whatever—anything was used as building material to consolidate the power Stalin had inherited from Lenin. Dmitrievsky saw Stalin as the predecessor of a future Russian Caesar, the builder of a future nationalist-led Russia. In fact, Stalin was a Caesar serving his own ends and building his own, purely Stalinist state.

Stalin's triumph was celebrated at the Seventeenth Party Congress in January 1934. This was his apotheosis. The achievements of industrialization were visible, collectivization had been completed, the spiritual life of Soviet society had been firmly taken in hand, and new laws had been passed that chained the citizenry down in all possible ways. In five years the country had changed beyond recognition. No one would dare any longer to challenge Stalin's autocratic rule.

Kirov, who had less than a year to live, called it the Congress of Victors. In September 1934, Hitler told his National Socialists, gathered at Nuremburg, that they were the real congress of victors.

In his speech to the Seventeenth Party Congress Stalin promised peace and tranquility:

> At the Fifteenth Congress it was still necessary to prove that the party line was correct and to wage a struggle against certain anti-Leninist groups; and at the Sixteenth Party Congress we had to deal the final blow to the last adherents of these groups. At this congress, however, there is nothing more to prove and, it seems, no one to fight. Everyone now sees that the line of the party has triumphed.[88]

The stenographic record at this point records "thunderous applause." Of the applauding delegates, who numbered 1,966, only 59 were to take part in the next congress, the Eighteenth, in 1939. Nearly two-thirds of the delegates to the Congress of Victors were arrested in the intervening five years. Of those, only a very few survived.

The first official biography of Stalin was published in 1935 in a great many languages. Stalin had always hoped Gorky would write it, but the father of proletarian literature never got around to it, and "the social demand" had to be met by Henri Barbusse. It was rumored that the biography was actually written by Alfred Kurella, a German Communist writer, and that Barbusse merely put his name to it. Be that as it may, Barbusse's book, *Stalin: A New World Seen Through One Man*, was soon banned in the Soviet Union, for nearly all the Leader's friends and comrades-in-arms mentioned in the book had become enemies of the people. Nevertheless this "biography" provided the promoters of Stalin's cult with a splendid model to follow. Consider this paean to Stalin, for example: "Although you do not know him, he knows you and is thinking of you. Whoever you may be, you have need of this benefactor. Whoever you may be, the finest part of your destiny is in the hands of that other man, who also watches you, and who works for you."[89]

Of course there was also Dmitrievsky's portrait:

> Calm, immovable, Stalin sits there, with the stony face of an antediluvian lizard, in which only the eyes are alive. All thoughts, desires, plans converge upon him. He listens, reads, considers, thinking intently. Confidently, without any haste, he issues his orders. He weaves his web of intrigue. Elevates his own people and crushes the others. Buys and sells bodies and souls.[90]

Barbusse is more flattering about the Benefactor's outer appearance. He is a "man with a scholar's mind, a workman's face, and the dress of a simple soldier."[91]

The ultimate assessment was given by Kirov at the Seventeenth Congress. He called Stalin "the greatest man of all ages and nations." Stalin had reached the heights of power. The next stage would begin with Kirov's murder.

## ALL QUIET ON EVERY FRONT

Tranquility on the Soviet Union's borders was an essential condition for the success of Stalin's "revolution from above." Soviet diplomacy—the "ground floor" of Soviet foreign policy—sought to ensure such tranquility during the First Five-Year Plan.

Only one incident seriously disrupted the calm, but it gave the Red Army the opportunity to show itself in battle for the first time since the civil war. There had been no diplomatic relations between China and Moscow since 1928. In the summer of 1929, Chiang Kai-shek's government provoked the Soviet Union: the consulate staffs in Manchuria and northern China were arrested. (The consulates in Harbin and Mukden had continued to function despite the break in diplomatic relations.) The civilian employees of the Soviet-owned Chinese Eastern Railway were also arrested. Then the railroad was seized. When China refused to release the Soviet citizens and return the railroad, Soviet forces intervened and defeated the Chinese army after several battles. The Special Red Army of the Far East was commanded by Vasily Blyukher, who in 1924–1927 had been a military adviser to the Kuomintang. In December 1929 the status quo was restored on the Soviet–Chinese border. Chiang Kai-shek had miscalculated, underestimating the strength and determination of the Soviet government. Although the Stalin regime feared serious international complications, it would try to use to its own advantage any situation that arose.

At the end of the 1920s, Moscow intervened in a civil war in Afghanistan in support of King Amanullah, who was threatened by a major rebellion. Agabekov, in his account of this episode, stated that the decision was made to support Amanullah because he based himself on the southern Afghan tribes, the "natural enemies" of the British, rather than Bacho Sakao, who based himself on the population of northern Afghanistan and therefore might try to "extend his influence into Soviet Turkestan." A "strike force" under the command of Primakov, former Soviet military attaché in Kabul and a hero of the civil war, was sent to Afghanistan to support Amanullah. After a series of successful engagements with Bacho Sakao's troops, the Soviet military unit was recalled, for Amanullah had given up the struggle against the insurgents.[92]

Relations with Germany were at the center of Soviet foreign policy interests during the First Five-Year Plan. Only at the end of this period was a longstanding aim of Soviet diplomacy achieved, that is, the signing of nonaggression pacts with France (in 1931) and, over Germany's objections, with Poland (in 1932). In 1926 and 1931, Germany and the Soviet Union renewed and amplified the terms of the Treaty of Rapallo. The privileged relations between the two countries, as opponents of the Versailles system, included not only diplomatic and economic but especially military cooperation. The German foreign policy line had developed out of the struggle between German "Westernizers" and "Easternizers," between supporters of close ties with the Soviet Union and advocates of a Western orientation. Among those favoring the Eastern orientation were the Reichswehr, conservative politicians, and some industrialists; the Westernizers were primarily Social Democrats.

It is easy to understand why Stalin's dislike for the Social Democrats— for socialists in general—was particularly keen with regard to the German Social Democrats. Stalin's leaning toward the conservative elements in Germany can be explained not only by their support for a pro-Soviet orientation but also by the general secretary's partiality for anyone who favored firm, authoritarian rule. The Soviet Union's relations with Fascist Italy, for example, were excellent from the moment Mussolini came to power. Aleksandr Barmin writes that in 1924 the Soviet ambassador to Italy, Yurenev, invited Mussolini to dinner. The day before the dinner, Giacomo Matteotti, a socialist and leader of the opposition, was kidnapped (and subsequently killed) by the Fascists. Italian Communists and liberals demanded that Yurenev withdraw his invitation. The Soviet ambassador refused to do this and ceremoniously received Il Duce.[93] During the First Five-Year Plan, Italy received huge orders from the Soviet Union for industrial equipment, and Italian industrialists in turn offered the Soviet Union long-term credits guaranteed by their government.[94]

The "second-floor" aspect of Soviet foreign policy—involving the Comintern—centered on one main task, the implementation of the decisions of the Sixth Comintern Congress, held in the summer of 1928, especially the decision that the main enemy was "the social fascists." This phrase, first put into circulation by Zinoviev in 1922, referred to the Social Democrats and implied not only that they were the main enemies of the working class but also that the real fascists were not a great danger. Moscow viewed the growing power of the Nazis (who won 6.5 million votes in Germany in 1930) as a rather positive phenomenon. It showed, according to the Comintern leaders, that the masses were losing their illusions about parliament and democracy. Besides, the Nazis were enemies of the Western democracies and, as Stalin saw it, would not be able to maintain a pro-Western orientation. In 1931 Stalin asked Heinz Neumann, a leader of the German Communist party (KPD), "Don't you think that if the nationalists came to power in Germany they would occupy themselves solely with the West, so that we would be able to build socialism freely here?"[95] The KPD was given orders from Moscow to wage a relentless struggle against the Social Democrats, particularly against the left wing. In submitting to these orders, the Communists not infrequently joined forces with the Nazis to fight the socialists. This meant an abrupt change of tactics for the German Communists. Just the day before, the party had still followed Neumann's slogan: "Hit the fascists wherever you meet them." Stalin, who had decided on this change of policy, summoned three members of the German leadership to Moscow, Thaelmann, Neumann, and Remmele. After their return, they announced the new orders: the Social Democrats are the enemy.

Many historians have accepted the view that in paving the way for Hitler's victory Stalin was following the formula: a victory for Hitler today means victory for the Communists tomorrow. This notion was widely accepted in Communist circles in Germany in the early 1930s. Actually Stalin's policy with regard to Germany was shaped by three factors. The first was hatred for the Social Democrats. But this feeling was not a personal phobia. All the Bolsheviks shared it, including Trotsky. True, he opposed the term *social fascist*, but at the same time he opposed any alliance with parties and organizations that refused to break with reformism or wanted to revive social democracy.

The attitude of Stalin and Trotsky toward social democracy and nazism in the 1930s clearly shows the difference between the two heirs of Lenin and no less clearly shows that Stalin was the genuine Leninist. From 1931 to 1941, without any shame or hesitation, Stalin carried out at least four 180-degree turns in foreign policy, guided solely by his own interests. In June 1933, after Hitler had come to power, the magazine *Communist International* ridiculed a suggestion by the "Austro-Marxists" (as the Social Democrats of Austria were called):

The Austro-Marxists suggest that the USSR make an alliance with the "great democracies" on an international scale in order to fight fascism. ... The social fascists advise the Soviet proletariat to enter into an alliance with "democratic" France and its vassals against German and Italian fascism. The social fascists seem to have forgotten the existence of French, British, and American imperialism.[96]

Within less than a year the "Soviet proletariat" did precisely what the Austro-Marxists had advised. But Trotsky stuck to the old position. Even in 1938 he argued:

What in fact would a bloc of the imperialist democracies against Hitler mean? The shackles and leg irons of Versailles in a new form, but even heavier, bloodier, more difficult to bear. . . . To be allied with imperialism in a struggle against fascism is the same as being allied with the devil against his horns and claws.[97]

By 1938 Stalin was an ally of the democracies and Trotsky criticized him unmercifully for betraying the cause of the proletariat and the world revolution. In June 1940 Trotsky still insisted on his position: "A socialist who advocates defense of the capitalist 'homeland' plays a role just as reactionary as the peasants of the Vendée who fought to defend the feudal order, that is, their very own chains."[98] This time Trotsky found himself in the same camp with Stalin, who had managed to change camps again by concluding an alliance with Hitler in 1939. Trotsky gave the impression of a clock that had stopped working in 1917 and Stalin one of a clock that runs in whatever direction its owner wishes. Each claimed, of course, that his was the only correct time, since it corresponded to the laws of history.

Hostility toward the Social Democrats was the first element of Stalin's policy vis-à-vis Germany. The second element was the conviction that the Nazis were nationalists whose main concern was to oppose the Versailles system. In 1923 Karl Radek had tried to use the rising Nazi party as a force to help destroy the Weimar Republic and thereby contribute to a Communist revolution. Radek gave the Nazis their first hero, Schlageter, who was shot by the French in the occupied Ruhr, by making a famous funeral speech in his honor, a speech approved by Stalin and Zinoviev. Radek expressed the conviction of the leaders of the Comintern that the "vast majority of the nationally minded masses will belong not to the capitalist camp but to the workers' camp," that "hundreds of Schlageters" would come over to the camp of the revolution.[99] Hitler, in turn, expressed the belief to his comrades that a Communist could always make a good Nazi, but a Social Democrat never could.

Finally, the third element was fear of seeing the Communists come to power in Germany. At the Fourth Congress of the Comintern, Zinoviev said:

"We know very well that in only a few years, many of the industrial countries will outdistance us and occupy first place in the Comintern and then, as Comrade Lenin said, we will become a backward Soviet country among developed Soviet countries." Zinoviev apparently had nothing against this prospect. Stalin was categorically opposed. He had no intention of yielding first place in the Comintern.

In the 1930s a new and important factor appeared on the world political scene: pro-Soviet public opinion. The cultivation of Western public opinion began right after the October revolution. Its effects were described by the American journalist George Popov in his book *The Cheka*, which tells of his arrest in 1922: "One of the greatest political successes of the Moscow despots is to have conditioned world opinion in such a way that anyone who dares to discuss the shortcomings of the Soviet state, even though they are undeniable, is declared 'anti-Bolshevik' and accused of lacking objectivity."[100]

In the eyes of the Western intelligentsia, the world economic crisis transformed the Soviet Union, the land of the five-year plan, into a paradise on earth. Arthur Koestler, who visited the Soviet Union in 1932–33 and wrote about it with the same enthusiasm as all the other Western writers, journalists, and businessmen, made the following remark much later, when he was settling his scores with the past in his autobiography: "If history itself had been a supporter of communism, it would not have been able to synchronize so perfectly the gravest crisis of the Western world and the first phase of the Russian industrial revolution. The contrast was so strong that it inevitably led to this conclusion: they are the future, we are the past."[101] Soviet planning was contrasted to the chaos of the Western economy, and the absence of unemployment in the Soviet Union to the millions of unemployed in the West.

The term *iron curtain* came into general use after Churchill's speech in Fulton, Missouri, in 1946. Goebbels had used it before Churchill, but the first to do so was the Russian writer Vasily Rozanov in 1917: "With a clank, a squeal, and a groan, an iron curtain has descended over Russian history. The show is over. The audience has risen from its seats. It is time for people to put on their coats and go home. They look around. There are no more coats and no more homes."[102] To Rozanov, the iron curtain was the revolution, which interrupted the course of Russian history. The term was used in the same sense in 1921 by an emigré writer named Polyakov.

Soviet propagandists also used the term, but in a different sense. In 1930, an article entitled "The Iron Curtain" appeared in *Literaturnaya gazeta*. Its author, Lev Nikulin, began with these words:

When there is a fire on the stage, the stage is separated from the auditorium by an iron curtain. From the point of view of the bourgeoisie, there is a conflagration in Soviet Russia that has lasted for twelve years in a row. Pulling on the ropes with all their might, they have tried to lower the curtain little by little, so that the fire does not spread to the orchestra pit.[103]

A fire had indeed been raging in the Soviet Union. By 1930 it had devoured millions of people, but the West knew nothing about it—the West did not want to know. The end of the NEP and the coming of the "Great Change" meant, in particular, the end of all connections with the outside world that were not totally monitored by the authorities. Unsupervised contacts had still been possible in the latter half of the 1920s.

The Soviet Union's isolation from the rest of the world was possible only through the complicity of the West. It was not difficult to isolate the Soviet people: the strictest censorship, no more individual trips abroad, no correspondence with foreigners or conversations with them, and incessant propaganda. Koestler was rather surprised by the questions he, a German Communist, was asked by the Soviet people concerning the situation in the West:

> "When you left the bourgeois Press was your ration card withdrawn and were you kicked out at once from your room?" "What is the average number per day of French working class families starving to death (a) in rural areas, (b) in the towns?" "By what means have our comrades in the West succeeded in temporarily staving off the war of intervention which the finance-capitalists are preparing with the aid of the Social Fascist traitors?"[104]

Koestler added that these questions were always asked, the same ones in every town he visited, and that they were asked in neo-Russian, "Dzhugashvilian" language (Stalin's original name was Dzhugashvili).

The ignorance of the Soviet people was the result of the combined efforts of the "organs" and the propaganda machine. But the scores of books, the hundreds and hundreds of articles written about the Soviet Union by French, German, English, and American democrats, liberals, and conservatives who had been authorized to travel in the land that was building socialism reinforced the iron curtain from the Western side by not allowing people in the West to learn the truth about the Soviet Union.

Journalists who had lived for a long time in the Soviet Union, such as Walter Duranty, the *New York Times* correspondent in Moscow, participated in the deception. Their reasons varied widely: a desire not to offend the Soviet authorities, fear of being considered "unobjective," a desire to promote their own government's policies. Western correspondents concealed, distorted, and interpreted the facts falsely. It was with their help that the monstrous extent of the famine of 1931–1933 was concealed from the world.

Many Western intellectuals saw the October revolution as the dawn of a new era. To them the Great Depression of the 1930s signaled the end of Western civilization. They believed that the Soviet Union represented a joyous tomorrow for all mankind. "I have seen the future and it works," declared Lincoln Steffens, an influential American journalist and true friend of the Soviet Union. The eminent British Fabians Sydney and Beatrice Webb published a book entitled *Soviet Communism: A New Civilization?* They answered the question in no uncertain terms. It was a new civilization.[105] "I have never eaten so well as during my trip to the Soviet Union," announced the famous master of paradox Bernard Shaw, who visited the country of the future at the height of the famine. On the eve of his departure he entered the following in the visitor's book at Moscow's Metropol Hotel: "Tomorrow I leave this land of hope and return to our Western countries of despair."[106] Ella Winter, an American who was in the Soviet Union in 1932, spoke of certain momentary "difficulties" in terms of labor pains: "Is a woman happy bearing the long-awaited child? They are giving birth to a new world, a new world outlook, and in this process questions of personal gratification become secondary."[107] After traveling in the Soviet Union in 1934, the Labourite Harold Laski announced: "Never in history has man attained the same level of perfection as in the Soviet regime."[108]

Arthur Koestler explained the thought process he went through on his visit to the Soviet Union to gather materials for an enthusiastic book about the land of socialism. He reasoned dialectically. The standard of living was low, but it had been lower under the tsars. The workers lived better in the capitalist countries, but their situation was growing worse, while in the Soviet Union workers' conditions were improving.

The main argument in the minds of all Western devotees of the new society was that things would be different when the revolution came in their own country. This was the reasoning of French, English, and Americans alike. Edmund Wilson, the influential American literary critic, even proposed in an "Appeal to Progressives" that they "take communism out of the hands of the Communists" in order to build it themselves.[109] In the Soviet Union, he wrote, "I felt as though I was in a moral sanctuary, where the light never stops shining."[110]

The enthusiastic international campaign by intellectual "friends of the Soviet Union" rendered enormous practical service to Stalin's country. Public opinion was won over. A New York travel bureau recruited workers for the Soviet Union with publicity like this: "Come to Soviet Russia. Intellectuals and workers of every profession, both men and women, are cordially invited to Soviet Russia... where the greatest social experiment in the world is taking place, amidst a myriad of colorful nationalities, marvelous scenery, splendid architecture, and exotic civilizations."[111] Largely influenced by public opinion, the United States recognized the Soviet Union in 1933, after establishing close economic and cultural ties with it.

A highly characteristic trait of the pro-Soviet campaign was its language. All the books written in this period about the Soviet Union, whether in German, French, or English, by professional hack writers like Anna Louise Strong or refined aesthetes like Edmund Wilson, seem to have been written in the same "Dzhugashvilian" Soviet language. The lies that were being purveyed, whether consciously or unconsciously, lent a similar tone and color to all such works. The virus of the lie and the instrument of its contagion (the Russian language) spread through the entire world. And it seemed normal, after the Reichstag fire, when the Gestapo began hunting down all political opponents, that the leadership of the German Communist party should declare: "The proletariat has not lost the battle. It has not been defeated. . . . This is only a temporary retreat."[112]

The few Western intellectuals who tried to poke a hole in the iron curtain, to expose the conspiracy of lies about the Soviet Union and write the truth about it, were pitilessly ostracized from the camp of progressive humanity. This is what happened to the Romanian writer Panait Istrati in the early 1930s, for example, as it had to the American Max Eastman in the late 1920s.

Apologists for the Soviet Union submissively accepted all the twists and turns of Stalinist foreign policy, explaining them in the first half of the 1930s as a necessity for undermining imperialist and social fascist plots; in the second half of the 1930s and thereafter—as Stalin's wisdom. They glorified his genius even more shamelessly, if it is possible, than did those in the Soviet Union. A noted English biologist warmly recited a story about how Stalin personally had gone at night to a railroad freight station in Moscow with the sole purpose of helping the stevedores.[113] Heinrich Mann maintained that for Stalin, *Geist* (spirit) is more important than *Macht* (physical might), and on and on.

## "LIFE HAS BECOME MORE JOYOUS"

When Panait Istrati, a Romanian novelist, vagabond, and revolutionary, during his 1927–28 stay in the Soviet Union, expressed his disillusion with things in the land of socialism, he was told, "One can't make an omelette without breaking eggs." He retorted: "I can see the broken eggs. [But] where's this omelette of yours?"[114]

The eggs were broken relentlessly, and after the building-and-wrecking machine of collectivization and industrialization had been at work for a while one could begin to see the outline of the "omelette." On December 13, 1931, Stalin gave an interview to the German writer Emil Ludwig, the biographer of great men. "The task to which I have devoted my life . . . is the strengthening of the socialist state, and that means the international state."[115] The word was spoken: the strengthening of the state, which was a revision of all the theories of that time that were considered orthodox Marxist. At the root of these theories was an army of quotations from Marx asserting that the state would soon wither away. Stalin still used the adjective *international*, but the main part was the noun *state* and the verb *to strengthen*. The cement for this state was to be fear. Emil Ludwig asked Stalin: "It seems to me that a large part of the Soviet population is experiencing terror, fear in the face of Soviet power, and that to a certain extent the stability of Soviet power is based on this fear."[116] Stalin answered: "You are mistaken . . . Do you really think that it would be possible to retain power for fourteen years and to have the backing of the masses, millions of people, owing to methods of intimidation and fear? No, that is impossible." But, he added: "There is a small portion of the population who really fear Soviet authority and fight it. . . . But here it is a question not only of a policy intended to intimidate these groups, which really do exist. Everyone knows that we Bolsheviks do not limit ourselves to intimidation; we go much farther, to the point of liquidating this bourgeois segment."[117] Stalin corrected the German writer: not intimidation but liquidation of part of the population— the "bourgeois segment." It is doubtful however, that this correction could calm the part of the population that was considered beyond the pale and destined for liquidation.

During the First Five-Year Plan, a series of laws aimed at strengthening the government was passed. Some tightened up labor discipline: hundreds of thousands of peasants who had arrived in the cities and factories were to be "reeducated," turned into proletarians through forcible administrative measures.

A September 1929 resolution of the Central Committee made the director of an enterprise its master, its individual boss. Up to this time, an enterprise was headed by a "triangle": the director, the party secretary, and the president of the trade union committee. Now the director had the right to make all decisions autonomously: he could fire workers without notifying the trade unions, which in 1933 were formally dissolved and merged with the Commissariat of Labor. (The resolution said that the trade unions were being dissolved at their own request.) For an unauthorized absence from work (even for a single day) a worker could be prosecuted. But the director, who had broad rights, also lived under a threat. If the enterprise did not fulfill the plan or if the quality of production was poor, the director could be prosecuted. "The labor code not only did not advance the norms and decrees of the first years of the dictatorship of the proletariat, on a number of points it actually retreated."[118]

In August 1932 the cruelest of a series of laws aimed at "strengthening state discipline" was adopted. It was a resolution "guarding the property of state enterprises, kolkhozes, and cooperatives and reinforcing public socialist ownership." Since everything in the Soviet Union was public property, the law applied to all government employees, including collective farmers (who in fact were the main targets of this law). A peculiar feature of this law was its "application of legal repression" by means of only one punishment: "the supreme measure of social defense: execution by shooting, with confiscation of all property." In the case of extenuating circumstances, execution was replaced by "deprivation of freedom for a period of not less than ten years, with confiscation of all property."[119] This law was soon extended "by analogy" to "a broad range of crimes ... including speculation, sabotage by state farm workers, theft of seed, etc."[120] Today Soviet historians admit, "The law of August 7 was excessively severe and insufficiently worked out from the legal point of view. Malicious embezzlers and those who committed utterly insignificant misdemeanors alike came under its provisions."[121] But it was precisely its maximum cruelty, its universality, that made this law one of the most essential instruments in "strengthening the state."

No less important was the law adopted at the end of 1932 that introduced the system of internal passports. Just two years earlier such passports had been called "the most effective instrument of police pressure and of extortionist policies in so-called police states."[122] Now they became the latest achievement on the road to socialism. The passports limited citizens' freedom of movement and facilitated control over them. Above all, since the passports were issued only to city dwellers, the system tied collective farmers to the land. The prohibition against unauthorized resignation from an enterprise and the right of the Commissariat of Labor to transfer skilled workers and specialists to other locations or branches of industry in a sense also tied city inhabitants "to the land." All citizens became servants of the state, which assigned them their place of work and prohibited them from quitting, on pain of severe punishment.

Another law, enacted on June 8, 1934, crowned the system by which the population was now enslaved: "betrayal of the homeland" became punishable by death. This law definitively rehabilitated the notion of "home-land." That term now referred to the Soviet state—which by party and state decree was projected retroactively into Russian history. The law also revived the term *punishment*, which had not been used since 1924. Similarly, the state abandoned the earlier concept of "reeducating" transgressors and instead announced its strict intention to punish them. In the decade following the revolution, the prevailing view was the Marxist notion that being determines consciousness. Consequently, by altering being, that is, the economic conditions of one's environment, the state could alter consciousness. With the exception of those who should be exterminated as incurable, it was possible to correct, to reeducate, the rest. But in 1934 it was decreed that the individual, not society, was responsible. It was his fault if he could not overcome the "birthmarks of capitalism," the "remnants of the past," and he ought to be punished, for although his being had changed, his consciousness remained unaltered.

Finally, the law of June 8, 1934, rehabilitated the family: its members became collectively responsible for any flagrantly criminal deed committed by one of them. Members of the family who knew of the intentions of a "traitor to the homeland" could be sentenced to prison camp for a period of two to five years, while those who did not know could be exiled for five years. (The last measure was not repealed until 1960.) This notion of collective responsibility demonstrated that the state was interested in reviving a strong family. A new family and marriage code would be adopted in 1936, but as early as 1934 the change in attitude was evident. The restoration of the destroyed family had begun, but on a new basis. Each Soviet family had to accept a new member, the Soviet state.

At the end of the First Five-Year Plan, a sword of Damocles hung over every Soviet citizen: they were all equal, for they were all on the brink of a precipice and they were all afraid. Stalin had explained to Emil Ludwig very well how the system of terror works: if a group of the population is destined to be liquidated, it is completely natural for a hierarchy of fear to arise. Everyone is afraid, but to different degrees, and the fear involves different punishments. Moreover, everyone recalls the existence of those destined for liquidation and is even more afraid of falling into this category. At the same conference of Marxist students of the agrarian question in December 1929 at which Stalin gave the signal for the "liquidation of the kulaks as a class," Yuri Larin explained that this liquidation did not mean that all kulaks would be shot immediately. It sufficed to execute some of the condemned and let the others wait.

During the First Five-Year Plan, the specific features of Stalin's policy were definitively developed. He would draw the string taut, and at the last moment, when it was at the breaking point, he would relax the tension, only to tighten it again with still greater force. He often drew it tight and relaxed it almost simultaneously. Some American historians call the last year or two of the First Five-Year Plan "the great retreat." That was precisely the impression Stalin wished to give: after the insane figures of the first Stalin five-year plan, even a step backward to figures that were just as unrealizable but more modest seemed like a victory for common sense.

In 1932 collective farmers were allowed to cultivate private plots once again, but that was the same year that the law of August 7 was passed. The Soviet press sounded the alarm: in the giant factories, the shops, the sovkhozes (state, as opposed to collective, farms), the lunchrooms, "the individual had been forgotten." *Pravda* was indignant: "It is time to put an end to the bureaucratic, manor lord disdain for questions of public catering and to understand finally that there is no task more noble for a Communist than improving the condition of the workers."[123] Such an appeal in the fifteenth year of the proletarian revolution might seem strange had it not been launched at the very moment when conditions for the working class were worse than at any time since the civil war.

In 1928 the Central Committee had passed a special resolution that branded the technical intelligentsia a class enemy. In 1931 a secret directive called for improving the attitude toward the technical intelligentsia as well as their material situation; but in 1933 a new resolution demanded a redoubled effort against "wreckers."

In the course of the First Five-Year Plan, an intricate hierarchical system of privileges took shape. During war communism, only a norrow segment of leaders enjoyed privileges; during the NEP, some privileges of a material kind slipped out of the party's control. Money opened the way to the good life, independent of the party and the state (if you did not, of course, take into account the permanent fear that nagged at the Nepmen). During the five-year plan, the stratum of leaders was broadened considerably, and the party, that is to say, Stalin, became the exclusive dispenser of all privileges. But he granted privileges not only to the leaders but to all the citizens. His article, "Dizzy with Success," was an authorization for peasants to leave the collective farms (if only for a few months). His declaration, "Life has become more joyous, comrades; life has become gayer" (at the most acute period of the famine) was a directive for everyone to "be merry." After receiving this directive, Komsomol leader Kosarev tried to persuade young people: "It is wrong to think that we are against personal well-being, against comfortably furnished rooms, tidiness, fashionable clothes and shoes, that we crush any aspiration for individual desires. . . . We are not against music, we are not against love, we are not against flowers."[124]

Everyone who was forbidden to do anything was forbidden at the request of the workers; everyone who was authorized to do something was authorized to do so by the party, that is, Stalin. The struggle against asceticism, declared in 1932, became the next weapon for strengthening the state. Ascetics had nothing to lose but their ideas. If Stalin granted material benefits to those who appreciated them, he could also take them away. Those who lost favor with Stalin could lose their apartments, positions, and the "special rations" that went with a favored position. In 1932, Isaac Babel, who was in Paris, had a conversation with Boris Souvarine. The author of *Red Cavalry* portrayed Stalin in colorful terms in the early 1930s, just the way his contemporaries, people close to the "court," saw him. Babel described how Stalin summoned an executive of the Commissariat of Nationalities whom the Politburo had decided to punish for some infraction. Stalin announced his punishment, seized his identification cards one by one for every establishment the man had worked for, confiscated his party card, and when the demoted man was about to leave called him back: "Hand over your pass to the Kremlin dining hall."[125]

During the First Five-Year Plan a state was built up on the basis of a very complicated system of privileges and fear of their loss. This system was sound, for famine and poverty reigned; therefore, everything became a privilege. Everyone depended on a higher benefactor, just as in the feudal system vassals depended on their suzerain. One need only give a nudge to one "benefactor" to nudge an endless series of favor seekers and favor granters.

The Stalinist state needed a Stalinist society. The revolution had destroyed the old order, and a kind of hybrid society, the not quite dead remnants of the old order and the beginnings of the new postrevolutionary society, had survived under the NEP; during the First Five-Year Plan the society of the NEP era was destroyed. Out of the debris of the prerevolutionary and NEP societies, a new society was formed according to the specifications of the Great Builder, as Radek called Stalin. This society had no need at all for ascetics or for the followers of any ideas, including Marxists: it needed doers.

In 1931 the Central Committee passed a resolution on schools. The schools returned to the old methods, courses, lessons, and themes condemned by the revolution. Commissar of Education Lunacharsky, the former symbol of the revolutionary school, was replaced by Andrei Bubnov, who had served for many years as the head of the Political Directorate of the Red Army. Three hundred fifty "experienced party functionaries" and one hundred Komsomol members were sent into the schools, which had been overwhelmed by an "alien element," as the Central Committee resolution put it. In 1932 all experiments in the realm of education were branded "leftist deviations" and "latent Trotskyism." "Firm schedules," "firm discipline," and a whole gamut of punishments, right up to expulsion, were introduced in the schools.

The role of the school as an "educational," "civilizing" factor was assigned to the prison system and the concentration camps, which developed very rapidly during the First Five-Year Plan, which included prisoner labor. In 1928 criminal legislation was reviewed and adapted to the expanding system of camps, which became necessary as a result of the sharp increase in the number of prisoners. In 1930 the task of protecting society against "particularly dangerous social offenders by means of isolation combined with socially useful labor, and by adapting them to the conditions of a working community" was entrusted to the "corrective labor" camps. [126] As early as 1929 all the camps had been placed under the direction of the OGPU, which for years had directed the archetypal camp at Solovki. The OGPU became the country's largest construction company. With a virtually limitless supply of unskilled labor at its disposal, the OGPU conducted massive arrests of engineers and technicians to manage the unskilled laborers. A new, purely Soviet institution arose, the *sharashka*: a prison in which engineers, scholars, and researchers worked in their fields of specialization for the interests of the state. At the large-scale building sites, in the "super-factories," the specialists were monitored by armed guards. The largest construction site of the First Five-Year Plan, the Baltic–White Sea Canal, was built by prisoners under the leadership of "engineer-wreckers." Trotsky's dream of "militarized labor" became a reality under Stalin in the form of the "penalization of labor." The gates of the camps were adorned with Stalin's words: "In the Soviet Union labor is a matter of honor, prowess, and heroism."

The prisoners constituted the bottom of Soviet society; at the summit was the Leader, the Boss. In 1933, Afinogenov, after the success of *The Fear*, wrote a new play, *The Lie*. Aware of the explosiveness of his subject, he sent the text to Comrade Stalin in person. Stalin worked on the play for a long time, making corrections, cutting out parts, adding to it. Then, for lack of time, he returned the manuscript without adding the finishing touches, with the following note: "Comrade Afinogenov! The point of your play is rich in its conception, but its execution was poor." [127] It cannot be ruled out that, for Stalin, the point of the play was expressed by one of its characters: "One had to be a boss to think." [128] Several years later, at an all-union conference for the wives of Red Army commanders, one of the wives recounted her conversation in the Far East with a Gold, a representative of the indigenous population. The man was seated in a boat and his wife was rowing. "Why aren't you rowing?" the lady asked him. "I am thinking," he answered. When she saw them a second time, the man was rowing while his wife sat behind him. "Now," he explained, "Stalin is doing the thinking about how I should live, so I am free to work."[129]

The restructuring of society's material base was accompanied by a complete alteration of its superstructure. Society's spiritual life was harnessed to the state's chariot to an extent that would have seemed impossible not long before. Krylenko, the commissar of justice, renowned prosecutor, and amateur chessmaster, declared in 1932: "We must once and for all put an end to neutrality in chess. We must condemn once and for all the formula 'chess for chess's sake,' just as we do 'art for art's sake.' We must organize shock units of chess players and immediately begin to fulfill a five-year plan for chess."

The chess five-year plan was an innocent game in comparison to the "antireligion five year plan" announced on May 15, 1932. Under this plan, "by the first of May 1937 not a single house of prayer will be needed any longer in any territory of the Soviet Union, and the very notion of God will be expunged as a survival of the Middle Ages and an instrument for holding down the working masses."

All of science came under attack as well. "The philosophical, natural, and mathematical sciences," declared the journal *Marxism and the Natural Sciences*, "have the same political character as the historical sciences." In 1929 the number of academicians doubled. In the elections for three Marxists—the philosopher Deborin, the historian Lukin, and the literary critic Friche—nine academicians, including Ivan Pavlov, voted against them in a last stand in defense of scientific freedom. After a second ballot, the Marxists were elected to the Academy. Aleksei Krylov, a mathematician and naval architect, quoting Pushkin, exhorted the resisters: "What does it matter, sir? Go ahead and kiss the villain's hand."[130]

The housebreaking of the Academy of Sciences went beyond the election of Marxists. In 1930 the Academy was assigned a new task, formulated as follows: "to assist in developing a unitary scientific method based on the materialist world view, consistently orienting the entire system of scientific knowledge toward the satisfaction of the needs of the socialist reconstruction of the country and the further development of socialist society."[131]

In December 1930 Stalin gave an interview to a group of philosophers at the Institute of Red Professors. He called for a struggle against the "Menshevizing idealism" of Deborin and the Menshevik views of Plekhanov and urged them to pay no attention to the modesty of Lenin, who did not consider himself a professional philosopher; on the contrary, they should give the leader of the October revolution the place he deserved—that of the head of Russian Marxism, the greatest Russian Marxist philosopher, one of Marxism's leading lights together with Marx and Engels. The hint was well taken. In September 1931 *Bolshevik*, the organ of the Central Committee, published an article that unmasked the "Menshevizing idealism" of Deborin and his school (whatever that meant) and indicated that "it was necessary to develop materialist dialectics... on the basis of the works of Marx, Engels, Lenin, and Stalin." Thus Stalin was elevated to the rank of a classic writer of Marxist philosophy, on a par with the other three. On the fiftieth anniversary of Marx's death *Pravda* explained that Marx should be studied "in accordance with" Stalin's works. The publication figures for the Marxist "classics" presented in January 1934 at the Seventeenth Party Congress eloquently demonstrated that all the classics were equal, but one was more equal than the others. Marx and Engels had a circulation of 7 million, Lenin 14 million, Stalin 60.5 million. American correspondent Eugene Lyons, who was walking around Moscow on November 7, 1933, counted all the portraits of Lenin and Stalin in the windows of the houses along Gorky Street. The count was 103 to 52 in favor of Stalin. The "four-headed portrait" soon gained great popularity: the four profiles of Marx, Engels, Lenin, and Stalin looking to the future. Goebbels saw in this portrait an excellent propaganda device and immediately prepared a similar one for Germany; true, it had only three profiles: Frederick the Great, Bismarck, and Hitler. This trinity also looked resolutely to the future.

Philosophical expertise was, and is, an indispensable attribute of the Leader of the Communist party, Supreme Guardian of the Doctrine, but of perhaps even greater significance is history. The conquest of history was somewhat more difficult for Stalin than it was to proclaim himself "coryphaeus of Marxism," for history consists, in addition to theory, of facts. In October 1931 the magazines *Proletarskaya revolyutsiya* and *Bolshevik* published Stalin's article (in the form of a letter to the editor), "Some Questions Concerning the History of Bolshevism." Stalin used as a pretext an article by A. Slutsky on Lenin's views on the internal party struggle among German Social Democrats on the eve of World War I. This was certainly not a burning issue at the end of 1931, but the historical importance of this article cannot be denied. It marked the establishment of Stalin's ideological autocracy.

Stalin dictated to historians what they must do and how they must work. Their first mission was to alter the history of the party, then the history of Russia. The core of the new history of the party was the absolute infallibility of Lenin and the existence of two party leaders. Robert Tucker has observed that, in a certain sense, Lenin evolved after his death. He continued to be infallible, but "attached to his successor like a Siamese twin, he became inevitably smaller in many areas. Only the facets of his life and activities that were connected with Stalin were idealized on a grand scale."[132] As for methodology, Stalin announced that only "archive rats" and "hopeless bureaucrats" could research documents and facts. The main point was a correct purpose. Interpreting Stalin's speeches in an address to the Institute of Red Professors, Kaganovich emphasized that in creating the history of the party the key task was to employ "flexible Leninist tactics." It is not important what an "authentic Bolshevik" has or has not done in his time: facts and documents must be interpreted from the point of view of the present moment.[133] Stalin "interpreted" Trotsky from the point of view of the present. "Trotskyism," he wrote, "is the vanguard of the counter-revolutionary bourgeoisie"; consequently, Trotsky always was an agent of the counterrevolution.

The doctrine became firmly established, distinguishing itself in both versatility and cruelty. It could change instantaneously, switching to its antithesis, but in the interval between the changes it remained immobile. The doctrine could be expressed only in the exact words of the Leader, without even a comma changed. Stalin's letter to *Proletarskaya revolyutsiya* (and this was the first of many such occasions) was immediately echoed in all areas of Soviet life. The journal *Proletarian Music* (January 1932) dedicated an editorial to it with the headline: "Our Tasks on the Music Front," while a lead article in the journal *For Soviet Accounting* (February 1932) bore the title "For Bolshevik Vigilance on the Bookkeeping Front," and the *Journal of Neuropathology and Psychiatry* (February 1932) published an article "For a Bolshevik Offensive on the Neuropathology Front." Stalin's letter was studied by economists, naturalists, and technicians. Maxim Gorky added his voice to the chorus: "It is vital that we know everything that has happened in the past, not as it has already been recounted, but in the light of the doctrine of Marx-Engels-Lenin-Stalin."[134]

From Gorky to workers on the bookkeeping front, everyone responded the same way (in public, at least), not only in the territories of the Soviet Union, where Stalin's power had become absolute, but also wherever Communist parties, sections of the Comintern, existed. Arthur Koestler relates that in January 1935, when the Saar was preparing to vote on a referendum that would decide whether it would remain under French administration or become part of the German Reich, the Communist party ordered people to vote for "a Red Saar in a Soviet Germany."

"But there is no Soviet Germany as yet, so what do we stand for?" a miner asked the leader of a Communist cell in despair. "We stand, comrade," the latter answered, "for a Red Saar in a Soviet Germany." "But there is no Soviet Germany, so do you mean we should vote for Hitler?" "The Central Committee," objected the secretary of the cell, "did not say you should vote for Hitler. It said you should vote for a Red Saar in a Soviet Germany." "But, comrade, until there is a Soviet Germany, would it not be best to vote for the status quo?" "By voting for the status quo," explained the secretary, "you would align yourself with the social fascist agents of French imperialism." "Then who the bleeding hell are we to vote for?" cried the miner. "You are putting the question in a mechanistic manner," the secretary reproached him. "The only correct revolutionary policy is to fight for a Red Saar in a Soviet Germany."[135]

After the elections, in which Hitler received more than 90 percent of the vote, the organ of the Saarland Communists bore this front-page headline: "Defeat of Hitler in the Saar." According to the laws of Marxist-Stalinist dialectics, the Hitlerities, who had expected 98 percent, had suffered a defeat.

The letter to *Proletarskaya revolyutsiya* marked a turning point in the official attitude toward Russian history. Stalin pointed out that a history of European Marxism should be written from the point of view of the Russian Bolsheviks. They were, as Lenin had predicted in 1902, the vanguard of the international proletarian movement. The Russian revolution was the beginning of the world revolution, and it was not for the Western Marxists to give lessons to their Russian comrades, but vice versa.

On February 4, 1931, Stalin presented his view of Russian history: "The history of old Russia," said Stalin, consisted, among other things, in her constantly being beaten for her backwardness. "She was beaten by the Mongol khans. She was beaten by the Turkish beys. She was beaten by the Swedish feudal lords. She was beaten by the Polish-Lithuanian pans. She was beaten by the Anglo-French capitalists. She was beaten by the Japanese barons. She was beaten by everyone because of her backwardness."[136] This interpretation of Russian history was still partly in accordance with the (until then) orthodox Marxist views of Pokrovsky. On May 15, 1934, a resolution "On the Teaching of the Nation's History in Soviet Schools" marked a break with the old policy regarding Russian history and the beginning of a new policy. In 1936 the Soviet press published a letter by Stalin, Zhdanov, and Kirov which was a critique of projected textbooks on the history of the Soviet Union and gave new instructions for teaching Russian history.

In 1934 Stalin, the victor, the creator of collectivization and industrialization, state builder, and Supreme Ideologue, took up the weapon of

Russian nationalism. In a certain sense this confirmed the predictions of Ustryalov and Dmitrievsky, but only in a certain sense. Stalin used Russian nationalism as he had used a great number of other bricks for building his empire. He needed Russian nationalism to legitimize his authority. He could not, and probably did not want to, stress continuity with the revolution and the destructive elements of the past while he was in the process of building a new state and social system. That is why he chose a new line of ancestors, the Russian princes and tsars, the builders of a mighty state. After 1934 Stalin—and all Soviet historians after him—stopped saying that "everyone had beaten" Russia. They began to say that Russia had beaten everyone. The signal was given to crush Pokrovsky's historical school. The history of Russia, which after 1917 had been revised from the point of view of the class struggle, was being revised in light of the struggle for the creation of a strong state. The people remained at the center, but for the Pokrovsky school the people wanted liberty, whereas for the Stalin school they wanted strong authority.

One of the key aspects on the "ideological front" was literature. In the first year of the First Five-Year Plan, its situation reflected, with a certain belatedness, the complex twists and turns of the intraparty struggle. Representatives of leftist views, supporters of Trotsky, were still present on the staffs of literary journals and in literary associations, and adherents of the "right" still held important posts. Bukharin, who was a specialist on the intelligentsia, was subjected to increasingly violent attacks, and Stalin began to express his own literary views more and more frequently. RAPP, the Association of Russian Proletarian Writers, assumed greater and greater control over literary life. In the summer of 1928 the Central Committee issued a new resolution on cultural questions. In its opening sentences, its most soothing passage, it cited the resolution of 1925, but further on it declared war on any "backsliding from a class position, eclecticism, or benign attitude toward an alien ideology." The resolution declared that literature, theater, the cinema, painting, music, and radio had to take part "in the struggle . . . against bourgeois and petit bourgeois ideology, against vodka and philistinism," as well as against "the revival of bourgeois ideology under new labels and the servile imitation of bourgeois culture."[137]

The cultural revolution had begun. "Industrial and financial plans" for literature were announced, and the call went out for "shock troops" in literature, which became a very important matter—one that could not be entrusted to mere writers. "We must reexamine our list of coryphaei," wrote *Literaturnaya gazeta*. "It is essential to conduct a thorough purge. Along with the slogan of a cultural revolution, the task of creating a literature of the masses has taken on urgent meaning." But, explained *Literaturnaya gazeta*, "the good writers, the coryphaei, are incomprehensible to the masses; their style is too complicated. (The mediocrities have a much simpler style.)" Hence, "more attention to mediocre writers!"[138]

Writers began to search for ways to liquidate literature. RAPP announced that art was "the most powerful weapon in the class struggle." Mayakovsky urged that writers meet society's demands. S. Tretyakov, a member of LEF (Left Front of Art) declared: "We cannot wait forever while the professional writer tosses and turns in his bed, giving birth at last to something useful and comprehensible only to himself." Tretyakov called for the creation of workshops to which literary workers would bring materials (travel diaries, biographies, etc.). Others would arrange them, and still others would cast them in a language easily understood by the masses. Marxist literary critic V. Pereverzev considered even this measure insufficient:

> The creator [the working class—M. H.] does his work himself; he does not contract it out to others.... He commands others.... We do not contract work out to the men of LEF, nor to the men of RAPP; as the ruling power, we simply give the order to sing to anyone who knows how to sing the songs we need, and the order not to to those who do not know.[139]

In January 1929 Voronsky, the principal advocate of the policy of utilizing fellow travelers in Soviet literature, was arrested for "Trotskyism." In the fall of 1929 a campaign of denunciation against Boris Pilnyak and Evgeny Zamyatin began. They were condemned for having published their books abroad (Pilnyak's *Mahogany* and Zamyatin's *We*). This was only a pretext, for until then Soviet writers had regularly published their books abroad. Pilnyak explained that the Soviet magazine *Krasnaya nov* was about to publish *Mahogany*, and Zamyatin explained that *We* had appeared in the West years earlier, in 1926. Actually, the two men were chosen in order to intimidate other nonparty writers in the unaffiliated professional organization, the Writers' Union. Pilnyak was the head of the Moscow branch of that organization, and Zamyatin headed the Leningrad branch.

The authorities had other grievances against both men. Pilnyak had committed a grave sin by publishing his "Tale of the Unextinguished Moon," which told about the strange death of Red Army Commander Gavrilov on the operating table, where he had been placed by order of "Number One." It was easy to identify Commissar of War Frunze as the model for Gavrilov and Stalin as the model for "Number One." Zamyatin's sins included *We* and the article "I Am Afraid." Besides that, his uncompromising honesty, which he considered a necessary condition for true literature, was particularly unforgivable.

*Literaturnaya gazeta* devoted its whole front page to the disgraced writers:

> The conception of a Soviet writer is not geographical; it is social. Only the person who links himself and his work with the socialist system in the present period of reconstruction, a period in which the proletariat is attacking the remnants of capitalism, a period of fierce resistance by the class enemy, only this person can call himself a Soviet writer.[140]

The newspapers devoted much space to indignant telegrams and resolutions condemning Zamyatin's and Pilnyak's "shameless conduct." This was the first time such a campaign had been conducted. Many organizations and individuals in the world of Soviet culture (people who had never read the condemned books) wrote statements with headlines like "Traitors to the Revolution," "Fraternization with the White Guards," "Literary Sabotage," and "Treason at the Front." Pilnyak surrendered, asked for permission to revise his book, and wrote a new novel, *The Volga Flows to the Caspian*, under the literary tutelage of Nikolai Ezhov, then a secretary of the Central Committee, who was to become famous later in areas other than literature. Zamyatin, for his part, wrote to Stalin saying it was impossible for him to be a writer in the Soviet Union. He requested (and with Gorky's help obtained) permission to leave the country.

At the end of 1929 a Central Committee resolution announced that the literary policies of RAPP were closest to those of the party and called for all literary forces to unite around RAPP. Mayakovsky joined RAPP and within the year committed suicide. In his work *The Bathhouse* (1929) he put the new credo of Soviet literature in the mouth of Pobedonosikov: "I beg you, in the name of all the workers and peasants, don't get me worked up. . . . You should soothe my ears and rest my eyes, not get me worked up. . . . We want to relax after all our state and civic responsibilities. Back to the classics! Learn from the great geniuses of our accursed past." Even in "stepping on the throat of his own song," Mayakovsky still got people worked up, and that was useless and harmful. If Demyan Bedny could say, "I'm not an organ grinder whom you can just order to play another tune," how much more difficult it was to tell Mayakovsky to change his tune. Yet the officially required theme songs changed daily. Trotsky, in commenting on Demyan Bedny's fall from grace (in 1932), remarked that Bedny had been able to sell himself wholesale but found it hard to do so retail, that is, to follow every minute change of orders, every political zigzag. How much harder for Mayakovsky to "sell himself retail." His suicide allowed him to enter the pantheon nonetheless. Stalin killed him a second time by naming him (in a resolution to Comrade Ezhov) "the best and most talented poet of our Soviet epoch."[141]

In 1932 a new Central Committee resolution abolished all literary schools, trends, and associations, including RAPP. This decision was like a bolt from the blue. Averbakh and his henchmen, the leaders of RAPP, had terrorized all of Soviet literature for years; now at a stroke of the pen they had been thrown from their pedestal. When Boris Souvarine asked who had influenced Stalin in this decision, Babel answered that no one had. "Stalin decides everything for himself, on his own. For two weeks he invited in and listened to Averbakh, Bezymensky, and *tutti quanti*. Then he decided: we'll get nowhere with these fellows. In the Politburo he suddenly proposed his resolution. No one batted an eye."[142]

Perhaps Babel oversimplified things. Stalin's decision might have been prompted in part by his desire to win over Gorky, who detested the men of RAPP. In 1932 Stalin was a frequent guest at Gorky's house, where he met other writers as well. It was during one of these meetings that Stalin bestowed the noble title "engineers of human souls" on Soviet writers. Undoubtedly, it was at that time, after his letter to *Proletarskaya revolutsiya*, that Stalin decided to take personal charge of literature, as he had of philosophy and history. He needed efficient and dependable types to serve as "transmission belts," not Marxist ideologues like Averbakh. They "worked people up" too much. Instead of proletarian writers, Stalin decided to rely on fellow travelers, but only those who were ready, as Pereverzev put it, "to sing the songs we need" on command. Stalin counted heavily on Gorky's help to carry out his plan for the final subjugation of literature, and culture in general, to the party.

In 1928 Gorky, who was living on Capri, began receiving numerous letters and telegrams from Soviet institutions and individuals—writers, workers, members of the Pioneer youth organization, and so on—urging him to return to his homeland. The flood of requests, regulated by GPU head Genrikh Yagoda, reached such proportions that Gorky was unable to refuse. Other factors undoubtedly played a part: nostalgia for his homeland, the tempting prospect of assuming first place in Russian culture, and the persuasive arguments of his secretary Kryuchkov, a GPU agent.

At the end of 1928 Gorky returned to Moscow. There is no doubt that many in the Soviet Union looked forward to his return, for his authority as a great writer, a great humanist, and a defender of the oppressed was undeniable. Moreover, he was not a party member. Until 1933 Gorky made occasional visits to the Soviet Union, where he had at his disposal a sumptuous house in Moscow and two luxurious villas (one outside Moscow, the other in the Crimea) and where many factories, schools, even corrective labor camps, and an entire city had been named after him. In 1933 he was refused a visa to leave for Italy and remained in the Soviet Union until his death in July 1936. In 1932 Souvarine asked Babel about Gorky. Babel told him that whenever Stalin left Moscow for one of his country places, his responsibilities were assumed by Kaganovich, but on a more general plane, Gorky was "the number two man."

Civic responsibilities changed Gorky. He continued as before to stigmatize injustice, hunger, and poverty, but only when they occurred in the West. For his homeland he had only praise and approval. In 1930, on the first day of the "Industrial party" trial, he wrote an article that began: "In Moscow the Supreme Court of the workers and peasants of the Union of Socialist Soviets is trying a group of people who organized a counterrevolutionary plot against workers' and peasants' power."[143] The great writer could have waited for the end of the trial to make his pronouncement, but no, he already knew that "a counterrevolutionary plot" had been organized. Just two weeks later, *Pravda* and *Izvestia* published a new article by Gorky, "To the Humanists." The proletarian humanist fell upon the bourgeois humanists, particularly "Professor Albert Einstein and Mr. Thomas Mann," for having signed a protest statement by the German League for Human Rights against what Gorky called "the execution of forty-eight criminals, organizers of the famine in the Soviet Union."[144] The Gorky who had protested the death penalty in the Bolshevik-organized trial of SR leaders in 1922 and who had railed unceasingly against the monstrous cruelty of bourgeois justice had disappeared. Forty-eight directors of the Soviet food industry were shot after a secret trial—or without a trail, but Gorky said, "I know very well the indescribable vileness of the actions of those forty-eight."[145]

Aleksandr Orlov, once a highly placed Chekist, wrote that after hearing about the execution of the forty-eight Gorky became hysterical and accused Yagoda of killing innocent people in order to dump the blame for the famine on them.[146] If this is true it puts Gorky in a worse light still, for in 1931 he returned to Capri for a vacation from "building socialism" and could have publicly condemned the executions then. Instead, he spoke out against a new group of defendants in another one of Stalin's show trials. This time it was the trial of a group of Mensheviks, which took place March 1–8, 1931. Gorky not only agreed with the verdict ("all of these criminals" had been involved in "wrecking activity over the course of several years"); he also believed that not all of them had been caught and that the hunt should continue.[147] One peculiarity of the Menshevik trial and Gorky's article about it was that among the accused were people he knew well, including a close friend, Nikolai Sukhanov, author of a seven-volume history of the Russian revolution. Gorky did not forgo the opportunity to mock Sukhanov, calling him a "conceited scholar."[148]

In his assertion of the need for "the consoling lie," the lovely mirage, as the best means of educating the people, Gorky displayed such zeal that he earned a gentle rebuke from Stalin himself. In one of the most tragicomic episodes in the history of Soviet culture, Gorky called for the prohibition of self-criticism in the Soviet Union. Stalin admonished him: "We cannot do without self-criticism. We really cannot, Aleksei Maksimovich."[149]

In his speeches, articles, and letters to foreign friends, Gorky denounced the "legends" about forced labor and terror, collectivization and famine in the Soviet Union. He denied the "very vulgar fable that there is an individual dictator in the Soviet Union."[150]

After abolishing all literary trends and associations, Stalin wanted to see the establishment of a single writers' organization under the firm control of the party and state. It was partly to accomplish this task that he placed Gorky in charge of all Soviet culture. At the First Congress of Soviet Writers in the summer of 1934, Gorky coped marvelously with his task. He introduced a new obligatory literary style, an "artistic method" that soon became obligatory in all cultural fields: "socialist realism." This was the method of the consoling lie, which Gorky said was necessary to create a "new reality."[151] The writers' congress enthusiastically adopted this new ethic for all "engineers of human souls" and builders of the "new reality." From the platform of the congress Viktor Shklovsky denounced Dostoevsky: "If Fedor Mikhailovich were here, we would have to judge him as the heirs of humanity, as people who are judging a traitor. Dostoevsky cannot be understood outside of the revolution, nor can he be understood as anything but a traitor."[152] Dostoevsky had done his time and did not need to fear for the future, but the delegates to the writers' congress engaged in more contemporary denunciations: they denounced each other.[153] They also reported with satisfaction that "in our kolkhoz fields ... Pioneer children catch their fathers, accomplices of the class enemy, in the act of stealing socialist property and bring them before the revolutionary tribunals."[154] The writers reported with equal pride their trip to the Baltic–White Sea Canal, a trip that produced the most disgraceful book in the history of literature, a glorification of the concentration camp.[155]

Last but not least, the congress sang the praises of Stalin. Everyone said as much as their literary talents would permit. "Comrade Stalin is a mighty genius of the working class," said one delegate.[156] Another called him "the most beloved of all leaders of any epoch and any people."[157] Here too Gorky set the tone. "Leaderism," he said, "is a sickness of our century. Internally, it was the result of decadence, impotence, and the poverty of individualism;

externally, it was manifested in the form of such purulent abscesses as, for example, Ebert, Noske, Hitler, and similar heroes of capitalist reality. Here, where we have created a socialist reality, such abscesses are of course impossible."[158] He concluded with, "Long live the party of Lenin, the leader of the proletariat. Long live the leader of the party, Joseph Stalin."[159]

The First Soviet Writers' Congress completed the process of nationalizing literature, begun after the October revolution. The congress approved the Central Committee's decision to establish a single organization for all writers, the Soviet Writers' Union, under the direction of a representative of the Central Committee, Aleksandr Shcherbakov. One could count on the fingers of one hand the writers who did not take the oath of loyalty to the party: Bulgakov, Platonov, Mandelstam, and Akhmatova. Congresses in other cultural spheres were held on the model of the writers' congress. They too established single unions for everyone in their field and took a loyalty oath. Stalin paid special attention to the cinema, which Lenin had called the most important of the arts. As far back as 1928 a group of directors, including Eisenstein, Pudovkin, Kozintsev, and Trauberg, had asked for a "firm ideological dictatorship in the field of the cinema."[160] In January 1935 they greeted this dictatorship. Aleksandr Dovzhenko declared: "The artists of the Soviet Union have created an art founded on 'yes,' on the conception: I uplift, I inspire, I educate."[161]

By 1934 collectivization had been completed, industrialization begun, and the superstructure nationalized. The country's spiritual life, with the active help of the "creative intelligentsia," the "masters of thought," was placed entirely at the service of the state, that is, of Stalin.

Gorky held "the traitor Dmitrievsky" up to shame for having written, "We are slaves. We need teachers, leaders, prophets." This was only true under capitalism, Gorky harangued. "They willingly crawl after any leader, expecting exactly the same thing from each of them: perhaps the Boss will expand the limits of 'philistine good fortune' under capitalism."[162] He urged people not to follow "just any leader," but only the ones who were building a "new, socialist reality" in the "land illuminated by Lenin's genius, in the land where Joseph Stalin's iron will works tirelessly and miraculously."[163]

The enormity of Gorky's activity in his final years has not yet been adequately judged. It was primarily with his help that the spiritual enslavement of the Soviet people was made possible. He called on the people to follow "that single guiding idea which does not exist anywhere else in the world, the idea that has been soundly formulated in Stalin's six conditions."[164] Abusing his prestige as a great writer and humanist, Gorky never stopped trying to pound into the heads of Soviet citizens the notion that the GPU was the country's most important cultural force. He maintained that "the work of the Chekists in the camps clearly demonstrates the humanism of the proletariat."[165] In January 1936 he dreamed: "In fifty years, when things will be a little calmer and the first half of the century will seem like a splendid tragedy, a proletarian epic, it is probable that art as well as history will then be able to do justice to the wonderful cultural work of the rank-and-file Chekists in the camps."[166] His dream was realized much sooner: Aleksandr Solzhenitsyn, an artist and historian, did justice to the cultural work of the Chekists in *Gulag Archipelago*.

Among the most shameful pages of Gorky's prose, his letter "To the Women Shockworkers at the Building Site of the Moscow–Volga Canal" takes first place. Gorky, the defender of women, who for decades had bemoaned their fate in tsarist Russia, addressed the women prisoners who were being killed off by inhumanly hard labor in a Soviet "corrective labor camp": "Your labor once again demonstrates to the world what a healthy effect work can have on people, work that has been given meaning by the great truth of bolshevism, and it demonstrates how splendidly the Lenin–Stalin cause has done in organizing women."[167]

Thanks to such spiritual teachers Stalin was able by 1934 to assert unlimited power over the country and the people. He was right when he told Emil Ludwig that he could not hold power by fear alone. He needed lies as well. The "spiritual teachers" created a mirage that they tried to make people believe by claiming that the mirage was more real than reality, that it was reality.

Having completed the base and the superstructure, Stalin moved on to the next task, to the final on the road to socialism. On December 1, 1934, at Smolny in Leningrad, Sergei Kirov was killed.

CHAPTER

# 6

# SOCIALISM "ACHIEVED AND WON," 1935–1938

## THE KIROV ASSASSINATION

Khrushchev in his "secret speech" to the Twentieth Party Congress in 1956 hinted at what had been known outside the Soviet Union for many years— that Stalin masterminded the Kirov assassination. Walter Krivitsky, who had headed Soviet intelligence in Western Europe, wrote about Stalin's role in 1939, as did Aleksandr Orlov in 1953. (Orlov had also served as a foreign agent for Stalin, particularly in Spain.) Elisabeth Lermolo, perhaps the only firsthand witness to reach the West, wrote about this as well in 1955.[1] The wife of a former tsarist officer, Lermolo was serving a ten-year sentence in exile in Siberia when she chanced to meet Leonid Nikolaev, Kirov's future assassin, while he was visiting his aunt, an acquaintance of Lermolo's. After the assassination Lermolo's name was found in Nikolaev's notebook and she was dragged into the affair, being interrogated by Stalin himself. During her six years in prison she had occasion to meet and speak with members of Nikolaev's family, including his wife, Milda.

Today the course of events leading to Kirov's death is more or less well known. Nikolaev, a young member of the Communist party who had some sort of grievance against Kirov, fell into the hands of an agent of Stalin's, Viktor Zaporozhets, deputy chief of the Leningrad NKVD. Zaporozhets arranged things so that Nikolaev had the opportunity to shoot Kirov. The details of the murder plot, as it has now been reconstructed, were actually given by one of the conspirators himself, Genrikh Yagoda, former head of the NKVD, during the Moscow trial of 1938. Only the "chief organizer" of the plot, Stalin, was of course not named.

Why did Stalin kill Kirov? The controversy over this question still goes on. Boris Nicolaevsky, a sharp-eyed Menshevik historian who knew many of the Bolsheviks quite well, had a chance to talk with Bukharin in Paris in February 1936. He suggested that Kirov represented a new political line, distinct from Stalin's. This point of view, presented in the Menshevik publication *Sotsialistichesky vestnik* (Socialist herald) in 1956, was picked up by some Soviet historians in 1964, at the height of the struggle against the "cult of personality." They tried to show that the Seventeenth Party Congress had been discontented with Stalin and his policies and that it had even hoped to replace him with Kirov. Hence the assassination and the purge.

It is easy to understand the aims of these historians. How could they explain that the party and its "highest body," the party congress, had marched to Stalin's sacrificial altar without a murmur? The myth of resistance to Stalin by the "best Communists," the authentic Leninists, removes the need for such explanation. But this myth raises other questions. How is it that the dedicated oppositionists were unable to pose a viable alternative to Stalin, and yet the loyal Stalinist Kirov was able to? And when did he do so? After Stalin had succeeded on all battlefronts? Kirov's conduct as Leningrad party boss was no better and no worse than any of Stalin's other governors. His speeches show not the slightest trace of an alternative program.

It is highly plausible that Stalin saw Kirov as a rival. Young, energetic, firm, a relentless enemy of all opposition, and a Russian to boot, Kirov may well have seemed a dangerous competitor. Moreover, Leningrad, the cradle of the revolution, functioned as a second power center, which might under certain circumstances challenge Moscow's primacy. These considerations do not really explain why Stalin decided to kill Kirov, however. A more illuminating approach is to ask what Stalin sought to gain by the assassination.

Walter Krivitsky was in Moscow in the summer of 1934. On the night of June 30 he prepared reports on the situation in Germany for a special session of the Politburo, which was to discuss the "night of the long knives," when Hitler murdered Ernst Roehm and his other former comrades of the SA. Among those included in the Politburo discussion was an intelligence official named Berzin. Krivitsky passes along Berzin's account of the Politburo discussion. After listening to those who considered the murder of Roehm and the others a sign that Hitler's power was weakening, Stalin rejected their view and presented his own summary conclusions: "The events in Germany do not in any way mean that nazism is about to collapse. On the contrary, they will surely lead to a consolidation of the regime and the strengthening of Hitler's personal power."[2]

The "consolidation" of Stalin's power began the day Kirov was assassinated. On December 1 a law calling for speedy trials in political cases was ratified. It also provided that sentences involving capital punishment should be carried out immediately. Robert Conquest has written that the Kirov assassination could easily be called the "crime of the century."[3] In the years that followed, millions of Soviet citizens, accused of the most diverse, and imaginary, crimes, were put to death. The "Kirov affair" started the earthquake known as the Great Terror. Immediately after the murder, thirty-seven "White Guards" were put to death in Leningrad, followed by thirty-three in Moscow and twenty-eight in Kiev.[4] Elisabeth Lermolo reports that executions took place at NKVD headquarters in Leningrad for nights on end; each morning there would be a pile of some 200 corpses in the basement.[5]

A confidential letter from the Central Committee to all party organizations drew "the lessons of the events linked to the cowardly murder of Comrade Kirov." Trotskyists were sought and found all over the country. In Leningrad 30,000 or 40,000 people were arrested. Ante Ciliga met some of them in exile in Siberia. On December 22 *Pravda* announced that the real culprits in the murder of Kirov had been found, the members of the Zinovievist "Leningrad center." Ciliga in his memoirs recalls the Verkhne-Uralsk prison, where he witnessed the arrival of Zinoviev, Kamenev, and other Zinovievists not long after their trial in the Kirov affair. Others arrived as well, Shlyapnikov and Medvedev, former leaders of the Workers' Opposition, Timofei Sapronov, leader of the Democratic Centralists, and so on. Half the occupants of the Kremlin from the years 1917–1927, Ciliga remarks ironically, had moved to Verkhne-Uralsk.[6]

A purge of the party, underway since 1933, was scheduled to end in 1935, but the Central Committee decided to review the status of all full and candidate members immediately. On February 1, 1935, a new exchange of party cards began. (Members had to hand in their old cards and received new ones only if they had been checked and approved.) The membership, already under pressure since 1933, felt more intimidated than ever; those in charge of the review seemed to be examining them under a microscope, trying to peer into their very souls.

Between 1924 and 1933 the party had grown to colossal size, from

470,000 to 3,555,000, but from January 1931 to January 1933 more than a million members had been purged. Now more were to go. In these conditions new members learned how to behave so as not to be expelled—flatter their superiors, speak only in the most guarded way, keep an eye on their fellow members, and choose friends with the greatest caution. A party card admitted the bearer to the privileged stratum of society, but its loss cast him into the pit. He became a pariah, worse off than someone who had never been in the party. Every expelled member immediately came under the scrutiny of the "organs" of state security.

In July 1934 the official name of the "organs" had been changed again. The GPU became the People's Commissariat of Internal Affairs, or NKVD, and the "chief of security" became a "people's commissar." As in 1922, when the Cheka became the GPU, this transformation gave rise to high hopes, which were encouraged by promises that the jurisdiction of the "organs" would be circumscribed.

Stalin used the Kirov assassination to reverse this trend, to create an atmosphere of tension and conflict in which the "organs" would be called upon to use force to resolve problems. The main blow was aimed at the party itself, which was said to be in great danger. The opposition, which willingly approved the harshest use of terror against other strata of the population, considered the party sacrosanct and could never imagine the use of terror against it. Stalin had no such qualms. He acted according to Machiavelli's dictum: No one can strengthen his own power by relying on those who helped him win it. In 1935 Stalin dissolved two organizations that reminded him of those who had helped him win power, the Society of Old Bolsheviks and the Society of Former Hard Labor Convicts, that is, political prisoners under the tsars. The second organization included some former terrorists of the People's Will, but terrorism had become the most horrendous crime against the state. The displays at the Museum of the Revolution were also changed. The terrorists who had assassinated Tsar Alexander II were no longer there to remind people that bombs can be used to change the government. Their pictures were stored in the cellars. These two societies were also dissolved simply because they were organizations. Soon all organizations would be dissolved, whether they had to do with philately, Esperanto, or anything else.

In August 1929 *Pravda* had published an article entitled "What Will the USSR Be Like in Fifteen Years?" The author, Yuri Larin, concluded on the following note: "Our generation will be able to see socialism with its own eyes."[7] The prophecy came true much sooner than expected. In August 1935 Dmitry Manuilsky, Stalin's representative at the Seventh Congress of the Comintern, declared: "Between the sixth and seventh congresses of the Communist International a major event in the lives of the people has taken place: the definite, irreversible victory of socialism in the USSR."[8] That was how the Soviet people learned that they had finally reached their longed-for destination.

True, one year later, in reporting to the Congress of Soviets on the proposed new constitution, Stalin warned that although "our Soviet society has already, in the main, succeeded in achieving socialism," that was only "what Marxists call the first, or lower, phase of communism." This meant that the march was not yet over; in fact, conditions were becoming increasingly difficult—the closer they came to the ultimate goal, the greater would be the resistance of the class enemy. In other words, the better things get, the worse they get.

Nevertheless, Stalin asserted, "for the USSR socialism is something already achieved and won."[9] Most important of all, though, socialism has already been built. American press magnate Roy Howard, who interviewed Stalin in March 1936, asked him whether it wouldn't be correct to call what exists in the Soviet Union "state socialism." Stalin categorically rejected such a definition: Our society is socialist, a genuinely socialist society "because private ownership of factories, plants, the land, banks, means of transportation has been abolished and replaced by public ownership."[10]

The year of the decisive attack upon the party—1935—was also the year of the "turn toward man." The main slogans of the day were "Man is the most valuable capital" and "Cadres decide everything." This was socialism with a human face, but the face was Stalin's. Along with the new orientation came an attempt to "humanize" him, too. To the standard epithets ("wise," "ingenious," "made of steel") new ones were added: "beloved," "dear," "kind," "good," "great humanist." During the May Day parade in 1935, Pravda reported, the demonstrators carried "thousands of portraits of him. There were also carvings and statues of the leader, and his name, repeated a million times that morning, was cast in metal, embroidered on transparent gauze, and spelled out in chrysanthemums, roses, and asters."[11]

Flowers were back in favor, along with the fox trot and tango, and parks for culture and recreation were opened. A carnival was held for the people of socialism's capital in 1935, at Moscow's new Central Park of Culture, and on Red Square in July of that year a parade of gymnasts was organized. It was strikingly similar to the mammoth spectacles in Nazi Germany, with the difference that instead of storm troopers marching to military strains, the marchers in Moscow were athletes and smiling children. The parade was led by children, 5,000 Pioneers carrying slogans fashioned of fresh flowers: "Greetings to Comrade Stalin, the Pioneers' best friend." "Thank you, Comrade Stalin, for our happy life" fluttered above a column of Pioneers from the Dzerzhinsky District.[12] A devoted Maxim Gorky responded to the athletes' parade: "Long live Joseph Stalin," he wrote, "a man of enormous heart and mind, a man whom yesterday our young people thanked so touchingly for their 'joyful youth'!"[13] Since 1935 Stalin had been children's best friend. Newspapers published a photograph of the most humane of men with his daughter Svetlana, then with other little girls giving him flowers. Especially popular (the poster circulated in the millions) was a photograph of Stalin with a dark-eyed, high-cheekboned little girl named Gelya Markizova, taken in January 27, 1936, in the Kremlin at a "reception for the workers of the Buryat-Mongolian ASSR." The poster continued to give pleasure to Soviet citizens for a long time, even though Gelya's father was shot as an "enemy of the people" and her mother was arrested and later committed suicide.

Since January 1, 1935, food ration cards had been rescinded, and the statistics on the fulfillment of the Second Five-Year Plan, which began in 1933, had stirred hopes for a better life. On August 30, 1935, an ordinary, nonparty Soviet miner, Aleksei Stakhanov, mined 102 tons of coal, instead of the usual 7, in a single shift. Stakhanov's "spontaneous initiative" was taken up by other miners and spread to other industries. In December the Central Committee approved the workers' initiative, and production quotas were increased by anywhere from 15 to 50 percent throughout industry. The Soviet press launched a furious campaign against "pseudo-specialists," who were trying to hold back the Stakhanovite movement with arguments about "scientifically based" production quotas. Cartoons showed giant workers sweeping the specialists aside.

In real life, the workers understood that the record-breaking achievements were falsified, that entire work teams had prepared the site for Stakhanov's feat of labor, that the whole purpose was to increase production quotas. They responded by beating up Stakhanovites and killing some. These actions were denounced as terrorism and punished accordingly. Bernard Shaw reported his conversation with a "shock worker" (through an interpreter, of course) and commented on the man's popularity among his fellow workers. In backward England, Shaw explained, a worker who produced so much would soon be discouraged by his fellow workers, with a brick to the head, but in the Soviet Union things were different.[14]

In 1935, the eighteenth year of the revolution, the overwhelming majority of the population lived in worse conditions than before the revolution. Strumilin calculated that in 1935 the average monthly consumption of basic agricultural products was 21.8 kilograms of bread, 15.9 kilograms of potatoes, and 4.07 kilograms of milk and dairy products. Strumilin was pleased with these figures and boasted that workers in the Soviet Union were consuming bread in quantities that would "undoubtedly be envied by many workers in fascist countries."[15] Of course, the workers in the land of socialism had no way of comparing. How could they find out the actual bread consumption in fascist countries? But they could compare their situation to that of agricultural laborers in the Saratov region of tsarist Russia in 1892, because Lenin had calculated the average annual consumption of cereal products of such workers—419.3 kilograms. Lenin also mentioned that the agricultural laborer ate 13.3 kilograms of bacon yearly. Strumilin said nothing about bacon.[16]

A 1934 survey of 83,200 kolkhozes in the Russian Republic, the Ukraine, and Byelorussia showed that the collective farmers were paid in kind, on an average yearly basis, 1.30 centners of grain in 1932, 2.33 in 1933, and 2.59 in 1934.[17] In old Russia the minimum adequate food intake was considered to be 2.5 centners per person per year. It should be kept in mind that Soviet peasants had to save part of their grain for their animals. After February 1935, when they were given permission to tend their own plots of land around their houses, their situation began to improve. The kolkhoz charter was also modified to allow each household to keep one cow, two calves, one sow with piglets, and ten sheep. At the same time, individual households began to deliver goods to the market.

The end of food rationing did not improve the situation for the workers, however. So-called commercial prices were abolished and new, standardized prices were introduced, but these were considerably higher than the prices workers had paid with ration cards. For example, the price for rationed bread in 1933 had been sixty kopeks per kilogram, the commercial price had been three rubles, but the new, standardized price was one ruble.[18] The Russian emigré economist Bazilli estimated that in 1913 the average monthly wage enabled a worker to buy 333 kilograms of rye bread, but only 241 kilograms in 1936. The corresponding figures for butter were 21 and 18; for meat, 53 and 19; for sugar, 83 and 56.[19] During the NEP a worker spent about 50 percent of his earnings on food; in 1935, 67.3 percent.[20]

In late 1936 a French miner, Kléber Legay, went to the Soviet Union as part of a workers' delegation. Determined not to let himself be fooled, he decided to make careful notes, writing down all facts and figures and checking on them directly. These were the prices he recorded for various items: white bread, 1.2 rubles per kilogram; meat, 5–9 rubles; potatoes, 40 kopeks; lard, 18 rubles; men's shoes, 290 rubles; men's boots, 315 rubles; women's shoes, 280 rubles; a man's overcoat, 350 rubles; a child's suit, 288 rubles; a man's shirt, 39–60 rubles. The average worker's wage was 150–200 rubles a month, and pension payments were 25–50 rubles.[21] There were twelve paid holidays. Workers had to contribute to a government loan fund the equivalent of from two to four weeks' wages a year. They paid very low rents, but the housing situation was abominable. From 1929 to 1932 the urban population had increased from 28 million to 40 million, whereas living space had increased only 22 million square meters, less than 2 square meters per person. As a rule, workers lived in communal apartments with no or very few amenities.

The Stakhanovites enjoyed substantial privileges. A special decree of the All-Union Central Trade Union Council gave Stakhanovites priority in the allocation of union-operated vacation homes and resort areas. In 1935 their earnings varied from 700 to 2,000 rubles a month, and in 1936 they rose to as high as 4,000 [22] They were also awarded various decorations, which in effect made them part of the social elite. The Stakhanovites were said to be a new "nobility," a new set of "notables" or "celebrities" (znatnye lyudi). The Soviet vocabulary was soon enriched by other despised words from the prerevolutionary past. In September 1935 new military titles were introduced: lieutenant, captain, major, colonel, marshal. The purpose, Pravda said, was "to heighten further the role, importance, and authority of the command staffs of the Red Army."[23] Even among artists a hierarchy was established, with the invention of the title "people's artist of the USSR."

Trotsky wrote in his Bulletin of the Opposition:

> Never has the Soviet Union known such inequality as now, almost two decades after the October revolution. Wages of 100 rubles a month for some, and of 800 to 1,000 for others. Some live in barracks and their shoes are worn out; others ride in luxurious cars and live in magnificent apartments. Some struggle to feed themselves and their families; others, besides their cars, have servants, a dacha near Moscow, a villa in the Caucasus, and so on.[24]

This accurate assessment did not provent Trotsky from continuing to say that since factories and land were nationalized in the Soviet Union, the working class was still exercising its dictatorship, although it had no rights and lived a miserable existence.

The Marxist Bukharin totally disagreed with the Marxist Trotsky. Bukharin claimed that the Soviet government, the dictatorship of the proletariat, was

> entering a stage of very fast growth for proletarian democracy. Countless forms of mass initiative are developing, with the most varied systems for the selection of the best, the leaders, the shock workers, the Stakhanovites, the heroes of Soviet labor; the barriers that derived from a different array of

social forces are now falling. This is the consistent and logical development of Soviet democracy itself.[25]

Bukharin spoke of two tremendous conquests of "genuine democracy, not the falsified bourgeois version," the All-Union Conference of Stakhanovites and the Congress of Kolkhoz Shock Workers.[26] It was in the same vein that kolkhoz shock worker Evdokiya Fedotova, after chairing one of the sessions of the congress and having the honor of being noticed by Stalin, wrote in *Pravda*, "I ran down the stairs like a young girl, full of joy and pride that he had seen how I worked and had liked it."

Some barriers had indeed fallen, as Bukharin mentioned. In 1935 the children of *lishentsy* were admitted to schools without further restrictions. In May 1936 it was forbidden any longer to deny jobs to people on the grounds of bourgeois origin. Other new restrictions appeared, however. On April 8, 1935, a special law extended all penalties under the criminal code, including capital punishment, to children of twelve and older. It was at this point that Stalin began to have his picture taken with children in his arms.

The "law on children" pursued several aims at once. It was one of a series of measures geared to strengthening the family and parental authority. The head of the family became the representative of the state within the household. In a sense this law was also a supplement to the law on treason to the fatherland passed in 1934, in that twelve year olds would be held responsible from then on for failure to denounce treason on the part of parents. Thus, the children were included in the system of collective responsibility. The law on children seemed so typically Soviet that when the Nazis adopted a similar law in 1944, Himmler felt obliged to justify it in the following terms: "We are instituting absolute responsibility on the part of all members of the clan. . . . And let no one say that this is bolshevism. . . . It is a return to the most ancient traditions of our ancestors."[27] There were other practical objectives behind the new law. It made a final solution possible to the problem of the homeless children, and it handed investigators a splendid tool for putting pressure on defendants.

The process of transforming the Soviet family into a fully "socialist" one seemed to move in two contradictory directions. On the one hand, all earlier theories of the family were pronounced bourgeois prejudices or undertakings of the enemy. On the other hand, *Pravda* insisted: "The family is the most serious thing in life."[28] In 1936 a new marriage and family code was adopted. It made divorce much more difficult, which was logical, since in a country stripped of rights, free divorce seemed sacrilegious. Abortion, which had been legalized for the benefit of women since November 18, 1920, was banned again on June 27, 1936, with the justification that "only under socialism, where the exploitation of some by others no longer exists and where women are full members of society, . . . can the struggle against abortion be seriously posed." Many years later, on November 23, 1955, the right to abortion would be restored "owing to the uninterrupted growth of women's level of consciousness and culture."

Stepping forward as the new apostle of the socialist family was Makarenko, an educator who had worked in the correction colonies of the GPU and NKVD for many years. He proposed that his experience in training young criminals and delinquents be made the universal pedagogical method in the Soviet Union. He also recommended two institutions as the model context for training children: the corrective labor colony and the army.

Makarenko's theory became the official theory of Soviet education. The child should be educated as a member of a collective organized along semimilitary lines and should be instilled with respect for the authority of the collective and of the person chosen to lead it. Postrevolutionary pedagogy had stated that punishment taught people to be slaves. Makarenko objected: "Punishment may produce slaves but it may also produce those who are good and free and proud."[29] Makarenko's theory could not have been more appropriate for this time, when all of society was being punished for "indiscipline." In 1937 he wrote *The Parents' Book*, in which he applied his general ideas to the family. The family, he said, is also a collective, and the interests of the collective are primary. They are expressed, of course, by the person in authority, who represents the family. Thus a nicely finished system of education was worked out: the child is raised in an authoritarian family, a microcosm of the state, then in an authoritarian school, the same kind of microcosm, and at last enters adult life—in the authoritarian state itself.

The subordination of the family to the interests of the state was a constant theme in literature, the cinema, and every form of art. The family is an important form of the collective, so the argument ran, but the state is an incomparably more important one. That is why, in the 1936 movie *Party Card*, the wife denounces the husband to the security organs. That is why the hero of Soviet children was twelve-year-old Pavlik Morozov, who had turned in his father, a "kulak." Gorky called on Soviet writers to glorify this adolescent who, "by overcoming blood kinship, discovered spiritual kinship."[30] In the novel *Skutarevsky*, Leonid Leonov portrayed a great scientist, one of the old intelligentsia, nobly betraying his own son. This call for the betrayal of one's kin was directed to all family members without distinction; in that respect full equality reigned.

## "STALINIST AND DEMOCRATIC"

The year 1936 was marked by two events, the adoption of the constitution and the publication of official "comments" by Stalin, Kirov, and Zhdanov on a proposed textbook of Soviet history. The two events might not seem of equal importance, but to the historian they were factors of equal weight in the formation of the socialist state. The constitution institutionalized the new society; the "comments" announced the "nationalization" of history, the social memory.

The decision to modify the Soviet constitution was taken "on the initiative of Comrade Stalin" at the Seventh Congress of Soviets on February 6, 1935, only a few weeks after the Kirov assassination. Bukharin, during his trip to Paris in early 1936, told Boris Nicolaevsky that he had written virtually the entire constitution. He was very proud of it, because it introduced not only universal and equal suffrage but also the equality of all citizens before the law. He thought it would lay the basis for a transition from the dictatorship of a single party to a genuine people's democracy.[31]

The 1936 constitution, the Stalin constitution, as it was immediately baptized, did assure democratic rights to all citizens: freedom of speech, association, and the press, freedom to demonstrate, freedom to propagate both religious and antireligious ideas, and inviolability of privacy in the home and in one's correspondence. Freedom of movement was not mentioned, but all citizens were given the right to vote (none were disenfranchised any longer), and elections were to be secret and direct. The Stalin constitution was proclaimed "the most democratic in the world."

As Solzhenitsyn was to say, the constitution never went into effect, not for a single day. Stalin gave his report on its draft form in August 1936, as the force of the Great Terror was mounting daily. In 1937, when the first elections under the new constitution were held, the terror reached its peak. Not that nonimplementation of the document was any great surprise. Previous constitutions had also assured freedom of association, assembly, and the press, but only "in the interests of the workers." The 1936 constitution had the qualifying phrase "in accordance with the interests of the workers and for the purpose of strengthening the socialist system." One thing was made absolutely clear: "Whoever seeks to weaken the socialist system is an enemy of the people."[32]

The new constitution granted equality to all in the sense that all were equally unequal. Stalin explained that the dictatorship of the working class remained in force, as did "the present leading role of the Communist party."[33] This constitution added a step. In previous ones the Communist party's leading role was only implied. The 1936 constitution spelled it out plainly and unmistakably.

The official proclamation of the party's right to represent everyone, to lead everyone and decide everything, at the same time that equality was granted to all, marked the consecration of the totalitarian state, which had received its finishing touches during the first half of the 1930s. At the time another totalitarian state existed, Nazi Germany. According to Nicolaevsky, Bukharin had given a lot of thought to nazism, in which he saw the accelerated decomposition of the capitalist system. He was concerned to prevent a similar decomposition in the Soviet Union and favored building an international movement to fight fascism. Above all, the ideas of nazism had to be fought with better ideas. Nazism's central concept, as Bukharin saw it, was violence. We have to fight violence, he said, under the banner of our new humanism, proletarian humanism.[34]

Bukharin's remarks to Nicolaevsky in Paris in February 1936 had a pathetic ring. Here was one of the leaders of the October revolution, one who had contributed the most to Stalin's rise, dreaming in a confused and vacillating way about a possible "second party" of intellectuals who could advise "the first party." He had been searching in Marx's papers for some profound observations that other researchers might have missed, some guide to what should be done. "Ah, Karlusha Karlusha," he sighed about an unfinished article of Marx's, "why didn't you finish? . . . [How] you would have helped us!"[35] Notwithstanding his Marxist education—perhaps because of it—Bukharin never understood that he had drafted the constitution of a totalitarian state. It was true there was a difference between this state and Nazi Germany. It could be boiled down to two slogans. Whereas Hitler said, "If necessary we will be inhuman," Stalin said, "Man is the most valuable capital."

The Soviet state relied on total terror, as did the Nazi state, and both relied on the Big Lie. The finishing touch was placed on Soviet totalitarianism with Stalin's proclamation of a "democratic" constitution. Under Lenin, terror was still called terror, and bureaucracy was called by that name, as was any uprising against Bolshevik rule. Under Stalin, as Kolakowski has written in his thoroughgoing analysis of the Soviet state, "the party was still being attacked by its enemies, but it no longer made mistakes, never. The Soviet state was irreproachable and the people's love for it was boundless." Having eliminated all means of public control over the government, the state justified its power with the argument that "in principle" it embodied the interests, needs, and desires of the workers. The state claimed legitimacy on an ideological basis. Kolakowski adds that the omnipotence of the Big Lie was not the result of Stalin's evil nature. It was the only possible way to legitimize power based on Leninist principles.[36]

The universality of the Big Lie helped Stalin in his claim that the 1936 constitution was a "document proving that the past and present dreams of millions of honest people in the capitalist countries have been realized in the USSR." As paradoxical as it may sound, in this case Stalin was telling the truth, for millions of people in capitalist countries belived that the "dreams of humanity" had come true in the Soviet Union.

Many were unable to see the truth, but many were willingly deceived. Yuri Pyatakov, who was expelled from the party at its Fifteenth Congress, then "exiled" to the Soviet Foreign Trade Office in Paris after capitulating to Stalin, and finally executed by Stalin in 1938, gave Valentinov-Volsky the following explanation in 1928, at the time of his capitulation:

> Since you do not believe that people's convictions cannot change in a short period of time, you conclude that our statements [of capitulation] . . . are insincere, that they are lies. . . . I agree that people who are not Bolsheviks, the category of ordinary people in general, cannot make an instant change, a turn, amputating their own convictions. . . . We are not like other people. We are a party of people who make the impossible possible. . . . And if the party demands it, if it is necessary or important for the party, we will be able by an act of will to expel from our brains in twenty-four hours ideas that we have held for years. . . . Yes, I will see black where I thought I saw white, or may still see it, because for me there is no life outside the party or apart from agreement with it.

A real Bolshevik, Pyatakov was ready for anything. The specter of revolution was haunting the world, he said, "and do you really think I am not going to be part of it? Do you really think that in this great worldwide transformation, in which our party will play a decisive role, I will remain on the sidelines?"[37]

Eight years later, and once again in Paris (a city that seemed to inspire such reflections), Bukharin told Nicolaevsky: "It is difficult for us to live. . . . But one is saved by a faith that development is always going forward. It is like a stream that is running to the shore. If one steps out of the stream, one is ejected completely."[38]

Party members closed their eyes to Stalin's machinations and willingly accepted black as white in order to stay in "the stream of history." Their thinking might have been voiced by the Negro spiritual: "O Lord, I want to be in that number/When the saints go marching in."

Some Western intellectuals also wanted "to be in that number." Others saw nothing special about Soviet totalitarianism because they considered that kind of thing natural to Russia. They portrayed Stalin as the direct heir of Nicholas I and Ivan the Terrible. Western Marxists consoled themselves with the thought that Stalin's socialism had nothing in common with authentic socialism, and non-Marxists assumed that nothing like that could happen in countries that had been spared "Russia's accursed past."

The year of the Stalin constitution, 1936, was notable for another crushing blow to the "superstructure," that is, to the intellectual and spiritual forces of Soviet society. *Pravda* indicated the connection: "The draft of the Stalin constitution reflects a fact of exceptional importance, the full equality of rights enjoyed by the intelligentsia." In the same breath *Pravda* recalled Ivan Pavlov's warning to young scientists: "Don't ever think that you know everything."[39] The implication was that only the party and its Leader know everything. Viktor Shklovsky, with the native talent for aphorisms he had as a young man, once observed: There is no truth about flowers; there is only the science of botany. In the late 1920s the Soviet government began to insist that there was a truth about flowers, about animals, about humans, about the universe. That truth was Marxism, and only the party and its Leader knew it for certain. The purpose of this campaign was to make the educated public more manageable, to make science manageable, as Mark Popovsky put it in his book on Soviet science.[40]

An effort to intimidate scientists began. They were arrested one by one at first, then in groups. In 1929 a group of historians, including Sergei Platonov and Evgeny Tarle, were arrested; in 1930 it was a group of microbiologists; then it was agronomists, physiologists, aircraft designers, and so forth. Some were killed, others broken in spirit. In 1934 Professor S. Pisarev was forced to sign a denunciation of his friend Academician Vavilov; otherwise, he was threatened, his children would be killed, his wife tortured, and he himself killed as well.[41] Academician Ukhtomsky was forced to renounce his brother, a bishop already under arrest, and some of his students, also under arrest.[42] Vavilov, the great botanist, who died of starvation in Saratov prison, said that a process of selection was taking place in the scientific field, to produce a strain of people "lacking the gene of honesty." This was the same Vavilov who in the name of science and "for the good of the cause" went to Afghanistan in 1924 and, in return for Soviet permission to go there for his research on strains of wheat, agreed to take photos of a fortress on the India–Afghanistan border; the same Vavilov who during the worst years of the famine, in 1931–1933, went abroad "to praise the achievements of Soviet agriculture and the Soviet government."[43] Later he agreed to lead Trofim Lysenko by the hand into the domain of science, only to be sent to his own painful death by Lysenko.

In a 1924 polemic with the famous psychologist and physiologist Ivan

Pavlov, Bukharin declared that he himself followed "neither Kant's categorical imperative nor the commandments of Christian morality, but revolutionary expediency."[44] In 1936, in his conversations with Nicolaevsky, Bukharin spoke at length about "humanizing" Communist theory. Nicolaevsky pointed out, "What you are now saying is nothing other than a return to the Ten Commandments." Bukharin replied: "Do you think the Commandments of Moses are obsolete?"[45] It may be that Bukharin was reminded of the Ten Commandments because he had encountered the Devil. He told the Menshevik leader Fedor Dan, "He is a petty, malicious man. Not even a man. A devil." He was talking about Stalin.[46]

By 1936 the devil and his numerous assistants, including those who quietly regretted it, had accomplished their task: science was under control. The Academy of Sciences passed a resolution stating, "We will resolve all problems that arise before us with the only scientific method, the method of Marx, Engels, Lenin, and Stalin."[47]

On July 4, 1936, the Central Committee conducted an utterly astounding experiment in the liquidation of an entire science by the mere stroke of the pen, by a single decree. Liquidated was "so-called pedology," for it was based on "pseudo-scientific, anti-Marxist assumptions."[48] Only a few years before pedology had been the "science of development for the new socialist individual," "a unified, independent science built on the foundation of dialectical materialism."[49] The abolition of pedology was followed by the closing down of other sciences: genetics, sociology, psychoanalysis, cybernetics, and so forth. Pedology was the first in a long line.

The problem with pedology was that it tried to be an exact science, studying the child with the aid of what the decree called "senseless and harmful questionnaires, texts, and so on." As long as official ideology proceeded from the assumption that existence determines consciousness, pedology was useful because it showed that poor conditions, a poor environment, has a negative influence on the child. In 1936 it was proclaimed that socialism had been built, but the "senseless and harmful questionnaires, texts, and so on" were demonstrating that children still lived in poor conditions. When a pedologist studying Chuvash children came to the conclusion that they studied poorly due to poor conditions, the journal *Pedology* (which was liquidated along with the science and the pedologists) immediately responded: What kind of poor conditions did the researcher uncover? Conditions created by the Soviet government and the Communist party? At the first—and last—pedological conference, in 1928, A. Zalkind, in the main presentation, defined pedology's tasks as follows: "Pedology had to respond, clearly and unambiguously, as to whether from the pedological standpoint the new socialist environment was a proper one for the creation of the new mass individual." Two years later that question sounded suspicious, and in 1936 downright counterrevolutionary.

In the cultural field, 1936 began with an article in *Pravda* on January 28, "Some Chaos Instead of Music," a devastating blast at Shostakovich's opera *Katerina Izmailova*. The fact that *Pravda* took an interest in musical questions was a sign that the process of "taming the arts" was nearing completion. Up until then party directives passed through professional channels. For example, the magazine *Worker and Theater* (*Rabochii i teatr*) complained in 1932, "Instead of calling on composers to master the method of dialectical materialism, the magazine *Proletarian Musician* urges them to this day to master the creative method of Beethoven."[50] Now the Central Committee was intervening directly in cultural matters, without delegating its authority to anyone. The article in *Pravda* was unsigned, meaning it voiced the official opinion, and it referred to Soviet culture as a whole: "This ultraleft deformity in opera derives from the same source as ultraleft deformity in painting, poetry, pedology, and science." The article warned, "This playing around with unintelligible things could end badly."[51]

On February 6 *Pravda* published another article against Shostakovich, this time taking up his ballet *The Clear Stream*. On February 20 it was the architects' turn, with an article headlined, "The Cacophony in Architecture"; on March 1 painters were taken to task in "Daubers, Not Painters"; on March 20 the theater and theatrical writing were attacked in "Outward Glitter, Inner Falsity" (specifically against Bulgakov's play *Molière*, put on by the Moscow Art Theater).

Writers, artists, musicians, actors organized meetings at which they approved the articles in *Pravda* and went on to denounce one another and recant. Arkady Belinkov, whose books on Tynyanov and Olesha are the first true histories of Soviet culture, once wrote: "Art is the dynamometer of the vileness of a tyrannical regime. The degree of vileness can be measured by the speed with which art is turned to dust."[52]

The second great event of 1936 was the publication in *Pravda* on January 27 of the "comments" by Stalin, Kirov, and Zhdanov on a "proposed textbook of Soviet history" as well as on a "proposed textbook on modern world history." Written in June 1934, the "comments" were published a year and a half later (after the assassination of one of the authors) to complete the process of nationalization of spiritual life. Memory became state property.

In Soviet ideology history occupies a central place. The teleological nature of this ideology makes history a legitimizing factor. History validates the firm hand that leads men toward the great goal. "With every major historical zigzag of policy, [the bureaucratic policy makers] are compelled to revamp history all over again. Thus far we have had three large-scale alterations."[53] Trotsky wrote those words in reference to the period 1923–1931. The alterations of the history of the party and the revolution took place only a few years after the events themselves, before the eyes of living witnesses. Facts were deleted, reworked, falsified, but party members went along with it all because history gave legitimacy to the leaders and the party as a whole.

In publishing his "comments," Stalin proclaimed himself historian-in-chief, displacing Mikhail Pokrovsky as the head of the school of Soviet Marxist history. An editorial in *Pravda* was blunt about it: Pokrovsky's scheme was oversimplified; he did not see "shifts and transitions within the framework of a single formula." Pokrovsky himself admitted that his approach was not scientific, from which *Pravda* concluded, "That which is not scientific can only be anti-Leninist."[54] An official document with the title, "On the Battlefront of Historical Science," and the subtitle, "At the Council of People's Commissars and the Central Committee of the Party," stated that the "erroneous historical views typical of the so-called Pokrovsky school of history" had led to a situation in which there had taken root among historians, "especially Soviet historians," certain "anti-Marxist, anti-Leninist, essentially liquidationist, antiscientific views in regard to historical science."

In 1936 André Gide, a faithful friend of the Soviet Union, visited the land of socialism by invitation from the highest quarters. His travel notes, *Retour de l'URSS*, contained quite a few critical remarks, although his impressions of the country on the whole were favorable. This led to a scandal among "progressives" around the world and especially in the Soviet Union. Gide was branded forever an enemy of socialism. He had observed quite rightly that "in the USSR everyone knows ahead of time that there is only one opinion on any question, once and for all.... Every morning *Pravda* instructs Soviet citizens in what they should know, think, and believe."[55] Gide failed to understand the main thing, though; *Pravda* had a far more important task—to make Soviet citizens remember differently and think differently than they had been made to do the day before.

Stalin's "comments" on historical questions stressed above all that a history of Russia should be written together with a history of the other peoples that had joined the Soviet federation. A famous formula was changed: instead of "Russia, a prisonhouse of nations," it was necessary now to say "tsarism, a prisonhouse of nations." Among *Pravda*'s articles on cultural questions in 1936, it printed a special resolution by the Central Committee on a production of Borodin's comic opera *Bogatyri* (Epic heroes), updated with a new text by Demyan Bedny. The farce had been received favorably in 1932: "The play makes some daring incursions into the present day, which heightens its political effectiveness," said a review in *Worker and Theater*.[56] By 1936 everything had changed.

> The production . . . (a) attempts to glorify banditry in Kievan Russia as if it were a positive revolutionary element, which contradicts real history and is completely false in its political implications; (b) it gratuitously slanders the heroes of Russia's folk epics, when in the eyes of the people the most important of those heroes represent the best features of the Russian people themselves; (c) it gives an antihistorical and contemptuous picture of Russia's conversion to Christianity, which in reality was a positive step in the history of the Russian people.[57]

A decree of the Central Committee and the Sovnarkom was published together with the "comments" announcing the formation of a commission "to review, improve, and where necessary, rework already written history textbooks." On March 3, 1936, a contest began for "the best elementary school textbook presenting a basic course on the history of the USSR, with brief reference to world history." The results were announced in August 1937. Besides announcing the "best textbook," oddly enough the jury subjected all the views presented in the "comments" to scathing criticism, not naming the authors, of course, but only certain persons "active in historical science." This criticism was not purely academic; nine of the ten jurors were arrested in 1937–1938. The tenth was Zhdanov, who had served as chairman of the jury.

From 1934 to 1936 the past was nationalized and totally relativized. Facts only existed to the degree that Stalin mentioned them, and only in the interpretation he gave them. If he said, "The barbarians and the slaves overthrew the Roman empire with a crash," any professor who dared to tell his students that the empire had lasted another 550 years after the Spartacus revolt would go straight to jail. Once when he casually remarked that the Azerbaijani people must have descended from the Medes, the result was that linguists searched for fifteen years to find words of Median origin in the Azeri language, "although the 'Median language' existed only in myth."[58]

"The past, starting from yesterday, has been actually abolished," George Orwell wrote in his account of a society without memory.

> Every record has been destroyed or falsified, every book has been rewritten, every picture has been repainted, every statue and tree and building has been renamed, every date has been altered. And that process is continuing day by day and minute by minute. History has stopped. Nothing exists except an endless present in which the Party is always right.[59]

"Marxist-Leninist history" was the sole "truth about the past," said *Pravda* on January 27, 1936. "History in the hands of the Bolsheviks must be a concrete science, the objective truth, and thereby serve as a tremendous weapon in the struggle for socialism," *Pravda* repeated on August 22, 1937. In a similar vein Adolf Hitler wrote in *Mein Kampf*: "History is not studied to learn what happened in the past but to learn what behavior will be necessary in the future to fight for the existence of our people."[60]

In order to assume the role of supreme historian, Stalin had to discredit and destroy the Pokrovsky school. That was one of the reasons why Stalin revived Russian nationalism and patriotism. Pokrovsky had ardently exposed and denounced Russian imperialism and colonialism and the Russian autocracy. For him, "Muscovite imperialism" began in the sixteenth century, when "the southern part of the river route from Europe to Asia, from Kazan to Astrakhan, was seized" by Moscow and when it began its effort "to seize the northern part as well, the outlet to the Baltic Sea."[61] Likewise the conquest of the Caucasus and Central Asia were criminal colonial wars: "Making Asians tremble at the Russian name was not achieved easily or cheaply. . . . Entire villages were burned to the ground in retaliation for one Russian body found in the vicinity."[62] Pokrovsky publicized little-known vices of the "great" Russian tsars, that Peter the Great had been a syphilitic, that the monster Ivan the Terrible "brazenly asserted he was not a Russian at all, but a German, and the entire boyar nobility of his time, imitating their tsar, began to trace their ancestries back to some foreign notable."[63]

Having completed the edifice of his state, Stalin needed some ideological cement to help hold it in place, something that orthodox Marxism, with its promise of "the withering away of the state" could not provide. The cement he found was patriotism, which he called Soviet, although it sounded more and more like plain old Russian patriotism. What counted most for Stalin was that Russian patriotism had deep roots among the people. Also, Russian history contained useful examples for training his subjects in such virtues as loyalty to the state, and to the ruler, and military courage. Stalin chose what he found useful out of the Russian past: heroes, worthy character traits, enemies to hate, friends to love.

Soviet history, as cooked to taste by Stalin, took the form of a monstrous mixture of nationalism and Marxism. The history textbook was allowed to mention the coming of Christianity to Russia, but only because it represented "progress compared to pagan barbarism," and to assert that the monasteries had played "a progressive role in the first few centuries after Russia's conversion" because they taught people to read and write and served as "bases for colonization."[64] The building of a strong Muscovite state and the drive to reach an outlet to the sea were also labeled progressive, as were certain grand dukes and tsars, through whom the laws of history operated, and if certain movements among the people hampered the "progressive" actions of the tsars, the former became "reactionary." The people were progressive when they supported a good tsar and, incidentally, usually did support him, especially against reactionary feudal lords. That was how orthodox Marxist schematism was ingeniously intertwined with schematic orthodox nationalism.

Aleksei Tolstoy apparently foresaw the changing attitude of the party, that is, Stalin, toward the Russian past. His novel *Peter the Great* first appeared in 1930, with a second part in 1934. The critics in RAPP denounced it as "ideologically alien." In 1931 Emil Ludwig asked Stalin, "Do you consider yourself a continuator of the work of Peter the Great?" Stalin answered categorically: "Not at all. Historical parallels are always risky. This one is absurd,"[65] In 1937 *Pravda* showed the change of attitude: "Owing to the baneful influence of Pokrovsky, many of our historians have taken a terribly contemptuous approach to the figure of Tsar Peter I." That was wrong. "Peter was a great political figure and a great reformer for his time, an outstanding personality, colorful and picturesque." *Pravda* went on the explain that "the age of Peter I was one of the most progressive periods in Russian history."[66]

Another great progressive was born in 1937, Prince Alexander Nevsky. The resurrection of Saint Alexander, whose remains had at one time been scornfully ejected from the Alexander Nevsky Monastery in Petrograd by the Bolshevik scientific atheists, had become necessary owing to foreign policy considerations. An enemy of the Germans, and a victor over them, was needed.

The first volume of the *Small Soviet Encyclopedia*, which was also the first Soviet encyclopedia, had taken a dim view of Alexander Nevsky.

> As prince of Novgorod, he rendered valuable service to the capitalists of Novgorod, successfully holding onto the shores of the Gulf of Finland for their sake. In 1252 he obtained the yarlyk from the Golden Horde, making him a grand duke. Alexander skillfully smoothed over the conflicts between the Russian feudal lords and the Tatar khan and suppressed disturbances among the Russian population protesting the heavy tribute being paid to the Tatars.

All of this changed in 1937. Suddenly Alexander Nevsky was proclaimed a great patriot, a great warrior who had stopped the German Drang nach Osten, and a great statesman, who had tried to achieve centralization and the unification of the Russian principalities under "one strong arm." On Stalin's orders, Sergei Eisenstein made a film showing that the main enemy was the Germans. "We can wait to deal with the Mongols. There is an enemy more dangerous than the Tatar. . . . Closer, more vicious. One you can't buy him off by paying tribute—the German."[67] In 1937 when this screenplay was written by Eisenstein and Petr Pavlenko, and in 1938 when the film came out, these words sounded almost like an article from *Pravda* on foreign policy, with the Mongol (Japan) on one side and the German (Hitler) on the other. Nine months after the film's appearance, in August 1939, the foreign policy lineup had changed, the film had lost its topicality, and it was withdrawn from Soviet movie theaters. The German was no longer the enemy; he had been bought off with tribute.

*Alexander Nevsky* also had a message for the domestic political scene; it showed the harmful influence of the *veche* (the elected popular assembly in Novgorod) and the benefits of a single ruler toward whom the boundless devotion of the people is directed. Stalin personally revised the screenplay, editing out the scene of Alexander's death. He preferred the movie to end with Alexander's triumphal entry into Pskov. After all, "Such a good prince must not die!"[68] In an Aleksei Tolstoy screenplay, another "good prince," Tsar Peter, is made to say: "I was very harsh with you, my children. Not for my own sake, but because Russia was so dear to me."

Aleksandr Dovzhenko, speaking in 1940 at a conference on the historical film, took note of one of its peculiar features:

> In the films on Peter the Great, on Alexander Nevsky, on Minin and Pozharsky, and on Bogdan Khmelnitsky . . . there is a kind of servile desire to bring history closer to our time and even to put lines in the heroes' mouths that are virtually taken from the current speeches of our leaders. The result is that Alexander Nevsky could be appointed secretary of the regional party committee in Pskov, and something along the same lines with Peter and the others.[69]

Dovzhenko's remarks, not published until 1964, were amazingly bold. He knew very well that Peter and Alexander Nevsky were speaking with the voice not of some regional secretary but of the general secretary of the Central Committee and that the general secretary had appointed himself the new Peter, the new Alexander Nevsky—and later, the new Ivan the Terrible.

Petr Pavlenko, Stalin's favorite scriptwriter, was working on a novel at the same time as the screenplay for *Alexander Nevsky*. It was about the coming war. In it he imaginatively portrayed how Stalin would parade through Moscow on the night the war began, and he described the scene in the same terms he had used for Alexander Nevsky's triumphal entry into Pskov.

The crowd roared. It chanted, "Stalin, Stalin, Stalin." It was a battle cry of strength and honor. 'Forward," it seemed to say. At the height of its aroused fury the crowd was calling for its leader, and at two o'clock in the morning he came from the Kremlin to the Bolshoi Theater to be with Moscow in its time of peril. . . . His calm figure, dressed in a soldier's greatcoat buttoned to the neck, with a soldier's cap on his head, was modest enough to make you cry. There was nothing superfluous or accidental about his person. His face was stern. He strode along at a rapid pace, turning often to the members of the Politburo and the government who surrounded him to say something to them, holding his hand up all the while to the crowds of people.[70]

Four years later, when war actually broke out, Stalin did anything but come out to greet the people. He went into hiding at his dacha outside Moscow.

Films and novels about "history," promoting Stalin's current policies and his shifting, utilitarian conceptions of the past, of course had the purpose of inducing "the desired psychological state" in the citizenry, as a historian of Nazi films put it in reference to the analogous process in Germany. Soviet and Nazi movies strikingly resembled each other. The Nazi movie *The Old King and the Young* (1935) dramatized the conflict between the Prussian king, Frederick Wilhelm I, and his son, the future Frederick II, with the father demanding unconditional obedience as commander-in-chief of the army and head of state. This scenario was repeated almost word for word in the conflict between Peter the Great and Tsarevich Aleksei (in the screen version of Aleksei Tolstoy's *Peter the Great*). The only difference was that Peter saw he could not make a great ruler out of his son, and so killed him. "All of Hitler's actions became acceptable," writes a historian of the Nazi cinema, "because ever since the time of Frederick Wilhelm II people supposedly had said, 'The country will collapse if it is not guided by a strong will.'"[71]

The elimination of the "Marxist historical school" untied Stalin's hands. Pokrovsky's schematism had certain fixed points of reference, such as classes, the role of the proletariat. In keeping with orthodox Marxism, Pokrovsky argued that semifeudal Russia could not have been more progressive than capitalist England. Stalin swept aside all these "Talmudic subtleties," while retaining Marxist phraseology and Marxism's unlimited possibilities for "dialectical" self-refutation. Stalin himself would decide what Marxism was. He made clear that it was unnecessary for others to read Marx; he had done the reading for them.

This "turn on the historical front" had important practical consequences, especially in relation to the non-Russian nationalities.

The first period in the history of the national republics, from the adoption of the 1922 constitution to the beginning of the First Five-Year Plan, passed under the aegis of the slogan "indigenization" (*korenizatsiya*), meaning the training and development of "indigenous cadres" and reliance on the native population, rather than Russian or Russified elements. The term first appeared in party resolutions at the Tenth Congress, in 1921. The Soviet authorities could not get by in that early period without the help of the native intelligentsia and was forced to try to win them over. The national republics at that time enjoyed fairly broad powers in domestic political, economic, and especially cultural affairs. Each republic was not only allowed but obliged to have its own language. Every national group, even the smallest, acquired its own alphabet. There was another aspect, however, to the imposition of an obligatory national language in areas where several languages were spoken, as in Byelorussia and especially Transcaucasia. It prevented the unification of several nationalities around one major non-Russian language. Administrative fragmentation, especially in Central Asia, served the same purpose.

The policy of encouraging indigenous populations bore some fruit, especially on the cultural level. In the Ukraine, for example, a real cultural renaissance took place. There was a negative side, however. Native "cadres" were inclined toward independence from the center, toward cultural autonomy and "national communism." An attempt to combine communist ideas with national traditions emerged in the non-Russian republics as well as at the center of power. These national communist trends contained an element of discontent over the centralizing habits of "Soviet colonialism." Stalin sent up a danger signal about this as early as 1926 in a letter to Kaganovich and other members of the Ukrainian Politburo.[72]

From the late 1920s to the mid-1930s, as a Soviet historian admits, "fundamental changes occurred in relations between the central government and the republics. The powers of the central institutions were considerably expanded, and the centralization of the unified state was intensified."[73] In this second period of relations between the republics and the center, Moscow stripped the national republics of all their rights. "The economic autonomy of the republics was narrowed down more and more." In addition, "centralization was carried out in a number of cases with violations of Leninist principles, expressed in the form of a downgrading or diminution of the sovereign rights of the union republics."[74]

Arrests took place in all the national republics. Purges began in 1929 and continued without interruption for ten years, hitting the native cadres particularly hard. In 1933 Pavel Postyshev was sent to the Ukraine by Moscow with a special assignment to "knock some people in the head as a lesson to others."[75] His main target was Nikolai Skrypnik, the Old Bolshevik and Ukrainian commissar of education, who was an ardent supporter of Ukrainization. In 1928 he had approved a new Ukrainian orthography. In 1933 he was accused, among other things, of attempting to "separate the Ukrainian language from Russian" and "sell it" to Polish, German, and other Western languages.[76] On July 7, 1933, Skrypnik committed suicide. Half a year later Stalin spoke of Skrypnik's "falling into sin."[77]

In Tadzhikistan the premier, Khodzhibaev, was expelled from the party, along with the president of the republic's Central Soviet Executive Committee, Maksum, and other leaders.[78] The leaderships of Byelorussia, Kirghizia, and other republics were also purged. A 1932 Central Committee resolution calling for the dissolution of all literary tendencies, groupings, and associations made national cultures all the more dependent on Moscow.

The Stalinist interpretation of history furnished the central government with a new and powerful weapon in its struggle against all forms of national independence. Stalin's "comments" called for a history not just of Russia but of the Soviet Union as a whole, and sure enough, when a history textbook appeared in 1937, *A Short Course in the History of the USSR*, under the editorship of one Professor Shestakov, it began with the history of the kingdom of Urartu. Thus the history of the Union of Soviet Socialist Republics began on the shores of Lake Van, nine centuries before Christ. The ruling of the jury in the contest for the best textbook on the history of the Soviet Union went even further. Reconsidering the main thesis of the Pokrovsky school, that annexation of other nations by the Russian empire had been an absolute evil, the jury recommended that such annexation be viewed as "a lesser evil." A few years later historians were advised to regard unification with Russia as an absolute good. To this day, Soviet historians invariably refer to the incorporation of the Ukraine (under Bogdan Khmelnitsky) into Russia as the "unification of two great sister peoples." Earlier, in 1931, the *Small Soviet Encyclopedia* had criticized Khmelnitsky for betraying the Ukrainian "peasants' revolution to the Moscow serf owners." In 1940 the same historical event was described as "a lesser evil than annexation by the Poland of the landed gentry or the sultan's Turkey."[79]

The new conception of history, which was completely ahistorical and allowed facts, dates, events, individuals to be juggled freely in accordance with the latest resolutions of the Central Committee, opened up tremendous practical possibilities. For example, in 1940, when Molotov explained the reasons for the annexation of the Baltic republics (in the post-Stalin era this was always called "the victory of the socialist revolution in the Baltic states,"[80] he indicated that these nations had been "part of the USSR" in the past.[81]

Until 1930 it was commonly said that the revolution had opened the way to friendship among the peoples of the Soviet Union. After the 1934–1936 period this friendship was said to be "eternal," these nations had always been friends, from the time of Kievan Rus and the grand dukes of Moscow, and their friendship would live forever. It became a crime to question this idea. Under the slogan of eternal friendship a brutal, massive repression was carried out in the union republics—during the Great Terror. The totalitarian state, which had achieved unification in all spheres of life, wished to fuse the varied Soviet peoples into a single socialist people, with a common past but no memory.

## ORDINARY TERROR

The Kirov assassination inaugurated an era that is often called the Great Terror. This period is particularly interesting because of the prominence of the victims: leaders of the party, the government, the military, and the economy. In fact, the party seemed to be bent on its own destruction. Nevertheless, the breadth of repression in 1936–1938 was not on a par with the genocide against the peasants in 1930–1934. The Great Terror, if we are to use the term, was unique in its universality. Preceding waves of repression had targeted specific social groups, but the terror that began in 1935 was directed against society as a whole.

The enigma of the Great Terror has never ceased to fascinate historians, sociologists, psychologists. Nikita Khrushchev, in his memoirs, asks: "Why did Stalin commit these crimes? Was he deceived? If he was deceived, then by whom? And with how many victims did we pay for this deception?"[82] The question, What were the causes of the Great Terror? has evoked numerous and varied answers, ranging from the need to replace an aging generation of leaders to Stalin's madness. All of them may fit as parts of the puzzle—with the exception of madness. There are substantial indications that after the war Stalin became mentally unbalanced,[83] but the same cannot be said of the period 1935–1938. To be sure, the obvious pleasure he took in torturing and killing people was no sign of perfect mental health. In 1937 he suggested that all leading officials train at least two deputies capable of replacing them. Four times he assigned people to the post of commissar of posts and telegraph before destroying them. This was how he displayed his "sense of humor," which Churchill so greatly appreciated.

Some writers have seen in Stalin a personality similar to that of Joseph Fouché, the French revolutionist who went on to become minister of police under the Consulate and Napoleon, and who also served Louis XVIII after the restoration. Stalin, for his part, spoke highly of Fouché: "He tricked them all; he made a fool of everyone." Boris Souvarine noted the "curious similarity in temperament and psychology" between Stalin and Fouché, adding that both had been seminarians in their youth.[84] The difference was of course that Fouché never became emperor. It may be that after reading Stefan Zweig's book *Joseph Fouché*, which was a great success in Moscow in the 1930s, Stalin began to fear that there was a Fouché around him. Ezhov, in fact, accused Yagoda, after replacing him as people's commissar of internal affairs, of "conducting a policy à la Fouché."[85]

Stalin pursued a different kind of policy. In building a socialist state, that is, a totalitarian one (the terms may not be synonymous in theory, but in practice they have been identical), Stalin needed a monolithic party, one that would "obey him like a corpse," to borrow the excellent German expression. By 1935 the party had penetrated every cell of the social organism, so that a blow against the party affected every part of the state. That is why the terror became total. When one strand was pulled, the whole ball of string came along: the governmental, military, economic, and cultural apparatuses.

The enemy was everywhere. The country was in the throes of madness. On March 3 and 5, 1937, Stalin gave his most candid speeches, at the notorious "February–March Plenum" of the Central Committee, which was entirely devoted to implementing the terror. Stalin warned that since the enemy was everywhere, he who carried a party card was the most dangerous. This line of thought was developed in numerous pamphlets all with the same title: "Certain Perfidious Practices of Foreign Intelligence Agencies in Their Recruitment Work." One of the authors explained, "In order to carry out their spy missions, they find all means are good, being an 'active militant,' being a Stakhanovite at work . . . or even constantly marrying and divorcing as a way of finding a suitable informant."[86] The enemy was everywhere, the "former people" (those who had held positions under the old regime), the wreckers, the kulaks, and now the spies. No one could be trusted. The newspapers hammered away at that theme, and so did the movies. Pavlenko's novel about the coming war included a Chinese Communist, broken by torture, who escaped while being taken out to be shot. In the movie version of the book, this Communist confesses to being a spy. In another movie the hero and the spy resemble one another exactly. The message was constantly stressed: anyone could be a spy. In a terrible joke of the period, a man looks at himself in the mirror and says, "It's either you or me."

The patron–protégé system on which the party apparatus was based meant that when an important leader was arrested a geometric progression of arrests ensued. On March 5, 1937, Stalin cited the case of a Central Committee secretary named Mirzoyan who, when assigned to Kazakhstan, gathered up thirty or forty of "his own people" from Azerbaijan and the Urals, where he had previously worked, and "entrusted them with the responsible posts" in his new location. Mirzoyan, said Stalin, had an entire "workshop" that he took around with him. Obviously things did not go well for this crew when its foreman was arrested.

There were other grounds for arrest, though. Stalin observed that there were comrades who had always "fought against Trotskyism but nevertheless maintained personal relations with certain Trotskyists." Personal links with enemies of the people was sufficient reason to arrest someone. According to Khrushchev, Beria warned him, after becoming head of the NKVD, that his relations with former NKVD boss Ezhov had been too friendly.

Arrests in this period were not limited to friends and acquaintances of those arrested earlier, however. They were based on regional and district quotas. Planning applied to this industry, too. Vladimir Petrov, who worked in the cryptography division of the NKVD in Moscow, recalls the texts of some telegrams sent out at the time: "Frunze. NKVD. You are charged with exterminating 10,000 enemies of the people. Report results by signal. Ezhov." The telegram to Sverdlovsk ordered that 15,000 be wiped out.[87]

"The party began to lose its authority and become subordinated to the NKVD," Khrushchev reports. Certainly all the arrests and executions were carried out by the NKVD, which was also in charge of the camps, but it and its personnel were just as defenseless as other Soviet institutions and citizens. On September 25, 1936, Stalin sent a telegram from Sochi to Moscow, addressed to Kaganovich, Molotov, and the other members of the Politburo. (It was cosigned by Zhdanov.)

> We consider it absolutely necessary and urgent that comrade Ezhov be appointed to the post of people's commissar of internal affairs. Yagoda has definitely proved himself to be incapable of unmasking the Trotskyite–Zinovievite bloc. The GPU lagged behind for four years in this matter. This has been noted by all party activists and by most representatives of the NKVD.

(The reference to a four-year lag was Stalin's way of reminding the others of the Ryutin affair, in which he had asked for the death penalty to no avail.) That telegram was sufficient to put an end to Yagoda, although he had been Stalin's most loyal henchman since 1933 and controlled the "all-powerful" machinery of the NKVD. He went like a lamb to the slaughter, exactly like the millions of Soviet citizens he himself had victimized.

On March 18, 1937, Ezhov spoke to a gathering of the senior officers of the NKVD in their clubroom at the Lubyanka, NKVD headquarters. He announced that their former boss, Yagoda, had been an agent of the tsarist Okhrana since 1907 (at which time he would have been ten years old), that he was a German spy, and that his closest collaborators had also been German spies. Nobody blinked an eye.[88] Thus the Cheka officials of "the Yagoda enrollment" went to their deaths as submissively as their chief. In July 1938 Stalin repeated the operation. He appointed Beria to be Ezhov's deputy, then in December Beria replaced Ezhov, and the "Ezhov enrollment" was liquidated without the slightest resistance.

The mad wave of terror was speeded along more madly than ever by the bloody Moscow trials. In August 1936 Zinoviev, Kamenev, and fourteen "coconspirators" were tried. A year and a half earlier they had been convicted as "morally responsible" for the Kirov assassination, a charge they admitted. Now they were tried for the assassination itself, and for planning to kill Stalin, spying for foreign intelligence, and so forth. In January 1937 came the turn of Pyatakov, Radek, and fifeen "coconspirators" accused of essentially the same crimes.

On June 13, 1937, Commissar of Defense Voroshilov published an announcement concerning the arrest of a group of top military commanders, who had confessed to "treason, sabotage, and espionage." *Pravda* reported that they had all been shot after being sentenced by a military court. Among them were Deputy Commissar of Defense Tukhachevsky; Yakir, commander of the Kiev Military District; Uborevich, commander of the Byelorussian Military District; Primakov, deputy commander of the Leningrad Military district; Putna, the Soviet military attaché in London; corps commanders Eideman and Feldman; and army commander Kork. Another traitor was said to have shot himself—Yan Gamarnik, also a deputy commissar of defense and head of the army's political directorate.

The Red Army was decapitated. Its best senior commanders were destroyed. In 1932 Boris Souvarine had asked Isaac Babel if there was any change in the Soviet Union. Babel had a one-word answer: war. In the event of war, who would lead the army? Souvarine asked. Babel, who knew the army's top commanders very well, answered without hesitation: Putna.[89] Vitovt Putna, who had served in the same guards regiment as Tukhachevsky before the revolution, was among the first to be executed.

From May 1937 to September 1938 the victims of repression [in the military] included nearly half the regimental commanders, nearly all brigade commanders, and all commanders of army corps and military districts, as well as members of military councils and heads of political directorates in the military districts, the majority of political commissars in army corps, divisions, and brigades, almost one-third of the regimental commissars, and many instructors at military academies.[90]

In reality the army's losses were even more devastating than the above admission in an official publication. Because of the purge in the military the army was totally unprepared at the outbreak of war, entirely lacking a well-trained command staff.

One of the side effects of the terror was a new wave of defections. One defector, Walter Krivitsky, had a chance to reveal some of Stalin's secrets before being murdered by a Soviet agent. In particular, he revealed that Stalin had given orders to the NKVD to collaborate with the Gestapo in falsifying all the documents that later served as the main evidence against Tukhachevsky and the other murdered generals. After the war a Gestapo agent named Alfred Naujocks, who had directed the doctoring of these documents, confirmed Krivitsky's allegations. The only difference was that Naujocks believed the idea had been masterminded not by Stalin but by Heydrich, the head of the Gestapo, who said that "if this affair is successful, it will be Russia's greatest disaster since the revolution."[91] Neither Heydrich nor Hitler (who gave the green light for the operation) knew that Stalin had dreamed up the whole elaborate scheme. Stalin oversaw all the details of this purge in person. At the Twenty-Second Party Congress in 1961 it was revealed that there had been no trial of the leaders of the Red Army. The Politburo had simply voted for their execution, then afterward the press accounts told of an imaginary military tribunal, sentences and so on.

Stalin's work in personally supervising the terror consisted essentially in signing lists that were brought to him, lists authorizing the arrest or execution of tens of thousands of leaders of the party, the government, and the economy. He also directly oversaw some of the interrogations, making insertions or deletions in the "confessions" certain victims were expected to sign, including the names of others Stalin might want to be incriminated. Aleksandr Orlov, who held a responsible post at the NKVD in Moscow during the preparations for the first Moscow trial, said that Stalin personally deleted the name of Molotov from a list of "beloved leaders of our party" against whom terror had allegedly been planned by purge victims. *Pravda* published the list without Molotov's name. There were Stalin, Ordzhonikidze, Voroshilov, Kaganovich, Kosior, Postyshev, and Zhdanov.[92] Why wasn't Molotov among them? people wondered. "For six weeks Stalin held Molotov between life and death, then spared him."[93] In other words, he finally ordered Molotov's name included as one of the "beloved leaders" targeted by the "terrorists" whose confessions were being prepared for trial.

Stalin personally insisted on the use of torture. Orlov recalls a conversation he had with an NKVD official named Mironov, one of Yagoda's closest collaborators, who was in charge of preparations for the first big show trial. When Mironov had reported to Stalin that Kamenev did not want to confess to crimes he had not committed, the Leader asked the NKVD man, "How much does our state weigh, including all our factories, machines, army, and navy?" The baffled Mironov said he had no idea. Stalin insisted. "Well, it would have to be some astronomical figure," Mironov guessed. "Exactly," Stalin concluded. "Now, could Kamenev or anyone else bear up under such astronomical weight? Don't come back to see me without Kamenev's confession in your briefcase."[94]

The exact number of victims of the Great Terror is not likely ever to be known. Robert Conquest, who analyzed all available data up to 1971 (for the second edition of his book, *The Great Terror*) arrived at the extremely guarded estimate that in January 1937 the prisons and camps held about 5 million people and that between January 1937 and December 1938 approximately 7 million more were arrested. Conquest did not include common criminals in this figure, since he did not think they could be regarded as victims of Stalin's terror. Actually, a large number of children of "enemies of the people" were classed among the "common criminals." Conquest estimated that under Ezhov (that is, from January 1937 to December 1938) approximately 1 million were shot and 2 million died in prison.[95] Solzhenitsyn's estimate is larger—1,700,000 shot by January 1, 1939.[96]

In *The Great Terror*, Conquest wrote that up to 1950 in the camps of the Kolyma region alone at least 2 million prisoners died. In his later book *Kolyma* he cites an objective and impartial source, *Lloyd's Register*, for all the ships carrying prisoners to Kolyma were insured by Lloyd's, and comes to the conclusion that no less than 3 million must have died in those camps. The British author added that from 1938 on Kolyma held at least twice as many prisoners as all the prisons of tsarist Russia in 1912 (when there were 183,249 prisoners, the highest number in Russian history up to that point) and that in one camp on the Serpantinka River alone more prisoners were shot in 1938 than in the last hundred years under the tsars.[97] Solzhenitsyn, in explaining how difficult it was to imagine the monstrous scale of this empire of prison camps, said that the prisoners themselves gave the exaggerated figure of 20–30 million, "when in fact there were only between 12 million and 15 million."

The first socialist totalitarian state had been built, containing an empire of camps such as history had never seen. Hitler was offended by criticism of the Nazi death camps: "If I had the vast spaces of Siberia, I wouldn't need concentration camps."[98] Stalin made use of the vast spaces of the entire Soviet Union and far outdid Hitler in the number of prisoners he held. The empire of the camps, the Gulag Archipelago, as Solzhenitsyn was to call it, played an important economic and psychological role. In a country where the number of political prisoners was counted in the millions, the inhabitants could not help feeling a constant daily, hourly pressure crushing their spirit, forcing them to obey, conform, fulfill the quotas, do the work.

The monstrous terror of the Ezhov era (the "Ezhovshchina") shook the country to its depths once more, stunning it with horror, eliminating finally all those who might still show some initiative, have faith in moral values, believe in revolution or in anything other than Stalin. Yes, Stalin had built socialism and created the kind of party he had dreamed of, an order of Knights of the Sword. This party was also Lenin's dream come true, a combat party, a party of a new type. On March 3, 1937, Stalin had referred to the "leading cadres of our party." The top command consisted of 3,000–4,000 officials; below them was an officer corps of 30,000–40,000; then a stratum of noncommissioned officers numbering 100,000–150,000. The remaining millions of party members were merely the rank and file, a gray herd, to be driven or used as the leaders chose.

Stalin was the commander-in-chief and the high priest. His power knew no bounds. In 1937 the Polish poet Antoni Slonimski, a lover of practical jokes, published a "letter from Moscow" in a Warsaw literary magazine reporting on the coronation of Stalin. Many readers believed him. Undoubtedly, had Stalin wished to be crowned, he could have easily become the first socialist monarch. The party was willing to accept anything from him. Khrushchev, who in 1937 was one of the party's top "generals," says that when Stalin showed him and the other "leading cadres" the confessions of Tukhachevsky, Yakir, and the others, he did not question their authenticity, not even the statement of a close friend of Khrushchev's, "confessing" that during the civil war he had killed his commander, Nikolai Shchors, in order to replace him in his post.[99] Aleksandr Fadeev, a "proletarian" writer who never lost faith in Stalin, wrote a message a few hours before committing suicide in May 1956: in it he grieved over the many Soviet writers "destroyed by the enemy hands of Ezhov and Beria."[100] The men Stalin chose to lead the party, and to be his servants in every sphere, including literature, were well described by Arthur Koestler: "They believed whatever they could prove and proved whatever they believed." The only thing Koestler forgot to add was that any forgery served them as "proof."

Stalin had complete control of the machinery of terror. Anthony Eden, an admirer of Stalin's, told of a conversation in December 1941 (after Hitler had invaded the USSR) in which Stalin commented that Hitler was an exceptional genius who had been able, in a short time, to turn a divided and bankrupt nation into a world power and to make the German people obey him blindly. "But Hitler has shown that he has a fatal weakness," Stalin added. "He does not know when to stop." Eden could not hold back a smile. Stalin had been speaking seriously. He paused and asked what Eden found so amusing. Before he could answer, Stalin went on: "I understand why you're smiling, Mr. Eden. You're wondering if I will know when to stop. I assure you that I will."[101]

In 1938 Stalin showed he was capable of stopping. In July, Ezhov was transferred to the Commissariat of Water Transport (one of Stalin's jokes), and in December the "liberal" Beria took over the NKVD. Beria's advent was meant to signal a drawing back, a liberalization, but even Khrushchev admitted that, far from coming to an end, the terror simply became more subtle and discriminating.[102]

The totalitarian socialist state's most characteristic feature was its denial of the existence of terror. In 1918 Soviet power proclaimed the Red Terror openly, to all the world. In 1930 and after, the genocide against the peasantry was carried out under the somewhat veiled, but still sufficiently clear slogan: liquidation of the kulaks as a class. The mass terror in the second half of the 1930s proceeded under the slogan of "expanding democracy." Speaking at the Eighteenth Party Congress in 1939, Stalin himself described the close connection between the terror and the expansion of democracy:

> In 1937 Tukhachevsky, Yakir, Uborevich, and other fiends were sentenced to be shot. After that, the elections to the Supreme Soviet of the USSR were held. In these elections, 98.6 percent of the total vote was cast for the Soviet government. At the beginning of 1938 Rosengolts, Rykov, Bukharin, and other monsters were sentenced to be shot. After that, the elections to the supreme soviets of the union republics were held. In these elections 99.4 percent of the total vote was cast for the Soviet government.[103]

Socialism had been built, according to the official dogma. In fact, what had been formed was a society that took the Leader's words for reality and rejected the reality it lived in. A French song was very popular in 1937, "Tout va très bien, Madame la Marquise" ("Everything's just fine, Madame Marquesse"). Written in 1935, it penetrated the Soviet Union with extraordinary rapidity. The Soviet authorities undoubtedly thought it reflected conditions in the land of socialism quite well. Another popular song of the time, which virtually became a second national anthem, contained these lines: "I know no other country/ Where people breathe so freely."

## ON THE ROAD TO WAR

During the second half of the 1930s the international situation was marked by the emergence of several states that made no secret of their aggressive designs. In 1935 Fascist Italy invaded Abyssinia. In 1936 Germany occupied the demilitarized Rhineland, driving the final nail in the coffin of the Versailles system. In 1937 Japan, which had taken Manchuria in 1931 and turned it into the puppet state of Manchukuo, began a new war against China.

Stalin directed Soviet foreign policy, but from the shadows, rarely granting interviews to the foreign press and never meeting foreign diplomats. It was not until a few years later that he acquired the taste for such meetings. "Stalin does not hold any government office," Litvinov explained to the British ambassador, who wanted to meet the party's all-powerful general secretary. "He does not like to meet foreigners and has entrusted that task to me."[104] The only exception Stalin made was for the American ambassador, William Bullitt, and for his successor, Joseph Davies.

On questions of foreign policy Stalin did not take a complicated approach. (This can be illustrated by a comparison of Stalin's views with those of Harry S. Truman.) In 1941 the Soviet press indignantly denounced the senator from Missouri for saying that the United States should wait and see which side was winning the war, Germany or Britain and France, and then support the winner. Unknowingly Truman was repeating a position Stalin had taken as early as 1925, although Stalin's words were not published until after the war, in 1947: "If war breaks out, we cannot stand aside with folded arms. We must enter in, but we will be the last to do so. And we will step in to throw a decisive weight on the scales, a weight that may tip the balance in our favor."[105]

The two main considerations in Stalin's foreign policy were Germany and Japan. In its relations with Japan the Soviet Union sought on the one hand to solve all conflict peaceably (for example, by selling the Chinese Eastern Railway, a source of tensions, to Manchukuo in 1935) and on the other hand to try to divert Japan into a war with China. Stalin had hoped that after 1933 the American president, Franklin D. Roosevelt, would more actively oppose Japan over China, but in that hope he was soon deceived. As for Germany, Stalin wished to base relations on the same kind of collaboration that had existed before Hitler's accession to power. Ideological differences did not seem to him to be an obstacle. On May 7, 1939, Boris Souvarine warned of the possibility of a Stalin-Hitler pact, one of the only voices in the West to foresee that. Why should Stalin take fascism and nazism more seriously than he did bolshevism? Souvarine asked. What was important to Stalin was strength.[106] Germany was the strongest world power, Ezhov explained to Krivitsky in 1936, echoing Stalin. "We must come to an agreement with the great power that is Nazi Germany."[107]

The Soviet approach toward Germany had a dual aspect. On the public level, the Soviet Union joined the League of Nations on November 19, 1934 (before that the League had been scornfully dismissed as a band of robbers), signed a mutual assistance pact with France on May 2, 1935, and introduced a "popular front" policy (favoring the Western democracies against fascism) to be carried out by the Communist parties and the Comintern. But Stalin had no real love for the "democracies" and no confidence in their power. The same Comintern congress that adopted the "popular front" policy, the seventh and last congress of the Comintern, held in Moscow in August 1935, stated in one of its resolutions that "the main contradiction in the imperialist camp" was, strangely enough, "the Anglo–American antagonism."[108] The democratic countries were portrayed as being torn apart by internal contradictions, which the Communist parties were urged to intensify. These parties were instructed to fight against military spending and the "militarization of youth." An exception was made for France, however, since it had become an ally of the Soviet Union.

The Soviet attitude toward Japan and Germany was not consistent. The Japanese aggressors should be fought by all possible means, said a Comintern directive to the Chinese Communists. By contrast, the German Communists were advised to join Nazi organizations, such as the Arbeiterfront, and fight there for higher wages and better conditions.

Commissar of Foreign Affairs Litvinov represented the public line of Soviet policy, with his calls for "collective security" and resistance to aggression. The behind-the-scenes policy was indicated by Molotov, the Soviet premier and Stalin's close collaborator, in a speech on foreign policy in 1935 which dealt mainly with Soviet–German relations. The documents of the German Foreign Ministry, captured by the Allies at the end of World War II and published in London during the 1950s, show that secret negotiations between Stalin's agents and the Hitler government began as early as 1933. Evgeny Gnedin, a counselor at the Soviet embassy in Berlin in 1935–1936 and after that a journalist and head of the press department at the Moscow Commissariat of Foreign Affairs, states that Stalin's confidential spokesman in secret talks with the German ambassador to Moscow was none other than Karl Radek.[109] Gustav Hilger, a German diplomat who had worked in Moscow since the revolution, referred to the 1934–1935 period this way: "We noticed in many Soviet leaders a deep and unchanging nostalgia for the olden days of Soviet–German collaboration."[110]

In the summer of 1935, in talks with the German economic minister, Hjalmar Schacht, the Soviet trade representative in Berlin, David Kandelaki, began to explore the terrain, under Stalin's direction, for a possible Soviet–German agreement. In 1936 Kandelaki was able to meet with Goering. After Germany and Japan signed the anti-Comintern pact in September 1936, Stalin again assigned Kandelaki to probe the possibilities for an agreement. Krivitsky wrote that Stalin at that time reported to the Politburo: "In the near future a pact with Germany will be signed."[111] However, two and a half years passed before Stalin's prediction came true.

On July 18, 1936, General Francisco Franco led a rebellion in Spain against the Republican government. Stalin waited until October 4 before sending a telegram to Spanish Communists expressing support for the Spanish Republic. The Soviet Union gave limited support to the Republican side in Spain and pursued cooperation with the "democracies" in a moderate way. More than ever Soviet policy functioned on two levels. All aid to Spain was channeled through the Comintern; on the official level a low profile was maintained. Germany and Italy openly sent regular units to support Franco, while the Soviet Union sent only a few advisers. The recruitment of volunteers for the International Brigades went on among Communists and antifascists all over the world, but not in the Soviet Union. On the other hand, the NKVD operated extensively in Spain. From 1937 on the main enemy in Spain bore the name "Trotskyites" or "Trotskyite accomplices." The practice of eliminating foreign Communists, which had begun among those living in the Soviet Union, was extended to Spain. Those who thought they had escaped the terror in Moscow found their executioners had caught up with them. Stalin had no need for revolution, nor was he interested in such things as "the emancipation of the working class." His own kind of revolution was all that interested him, one which placed people in power who would be as obedient to him "as a corpse."

The terror, the "meat grinder," as Khrushchev called it, dealt a serious blow to Soviet foreign policy. An astounded world looked on as one after another leading government figure was sentenced to death in the Moscow trials. People concluded that the Soviet state was afflicted with an incurable illness. The decapitation of the Red Army gave rise to serious doubts about its fighting capacity. Among the reasons for Anglo–French "appeasement" in relation to Hitler was lack of confidence that the Soviet army would be able to fight.

The changes that took place in the Soviet Union during the 1930s, along with the victories of the fascist states, had a curious effect on the Russian emigré "diaspora." Above all, the emigrés were forced to acknowledge the undeniable: their hopes for a collapse of the Bolshevik regime were in vain. The West had no desire to intervene, and no internal force had been able to overthrow the regime, nor had it collapsed as a result of the disputes inside the party or the economic disasters. The recognition of these facts logically led a section of the emigré community to accept the Soviet government. The ideas of the changing landmarks tendency and the Eurasians took the form of a movement for a "return to the homeland."

The arguments of the emigrés who wished to return to the Soviet Union (the "returners," *vozvrashchentsy*, as they were called) were described as follows by I. Bunakov-Fondaminsky, one of the founders and editors of the emigré publication *Sovremennye zapiski* (Contemporary notes) and coeditor with Georgy Fedotov of *Novy grad* (New city). Soviet foreign policy was becoming more nationalistic, that is, protective of national interests; the army was acquiring discipline; individual landownership was becoming stronger (a reference to the private plots peasants were allowed to have around their homes); the school system was being reorganized; and respect for the family and for one's country was being encouraged among the youth. Bunakov summarized the thinking of the "returners" this way: "Underneath the Red flag, the USSR is becoming nationalist Russia—we must return to the homeland."[112]

Bunakov, for his part, argued against the "return to the homeland" movement. It made no sense, he said, because a new wave of emigration was soon going to start, of those who would want to think for themselves. "By educating the people, the Bolshevik government is unavoidably laying the groundwork for its own destruction." The youth, when it had developed and matured, would ask "even more important questions, about the individual, about freedom, about God. At that point the conflict with Bolshevik ideology will become inevitable." The new wave of emigrés, Bunakov predicted, would want to "think about things they had never thought through before, give shape to their new realizations, and set up a radio station to send waves of free thought back to the homeland from abroad."[113]

The emigrés reacted in contrasting ways to the successes scored by the fascist states. Some were attracted to national socialist and fascist ideas: a corporatist state, a strong leader, hostility toward democracy, anti-Semitism, and chauvinism. The realization, however, that Nazi Germany represented a danger to Russia split the emigrés into "defensists," who believed that in the event of war they should support Stalin, and "defeatists," who believed that the overthrow of the Soviet government, even with Hitler's help, would be the lesser evil.

The NKVD played a sinister role in emigré political life, continuing the worthy tradition of the Cheka and GPU. Walter Krivitsky recalled meeting a man named Furmanov, the head of Soviet counterintelligence work connected with the White emigrés.[114] In any future history of the Russian emigré community, Furmanov should have a prominent place, along with his predecessors and successors. Operation Trust dealt a terrible blow to the monarchist wing of the Russian emigration, in particular to the association of former officers, the Russian Union of All Military Men, or ROVS (Rossiisky Obshche-Voinsky Soyuz). The "organs" of the Soviet security police paid special attention to those organizations which "actively" engaged in anti-Soviet work, especially those which sent agents into the Soviet Union. This "activism," which Georgy Fedotov called the "senseless heroism of the blind," ended in the virtual destruction of the ROVS, and it caused heavy losses to another organization, the National Union of Russian Youth, formed at a congress of youth and student organizations in 1930, which later became the NTS (Natsionalno-Trudovoi Soyuz), or National-Labor Alliance of Russian Solidarists.

In 1930, GPU agents in Paris kidnapped General Kutepov, the president of ROVS. Thirty-five years later, *Krasnaya zvezda* (Red star) published an article praising S. V. Puzitsky, a "pupil of Dzerzhinsky's," for his brilliant leadership of the "operation to arrest Kutepov."[115] In 1937, Kutepov's successor, General Miller, was likewise kidnapped in Paris. It then became evident that an assistant to Kutepov and Miller, a much-heralded White general named Skoblin, was an NKVD agent. Skoblin managed to escape from France, but his wife, a famous singer of Russian folk songs, Nadezhda Plevitskaya, was arrested and ended her days in a French prison. Much later, it became known that she too had worked for the "organs." A Moscow theatrical figure recalled in his memoirs that in the mid-1920s, through her booking agent, Plevitskaya had asked for permission to come to Russia, but Dzerzhinsky would not grant such permission; he wanted his agent to stay at her post. "Dzerzhinsky knew something her manager didn't know," writes the memoirist.[116] Plevitskaya continued to pierce the hearts of emigrés with her plaintive songs: "Ah, Mother Russia, you are covered deep in snow. . . ."

The "meat grinder" of the late 1930s forced the emigrés to define their attitude toward the homeland. This period saw a deepening rift between those for whom the question of Russia was seen from a moral angle and those who looked at it from a purely political viewpoint. Georgy Fedotov wrote,

We will never forgive the Bolshevik regime for the profound and terrible way in which it has deformed the soul of the people. This loss of moral sense stems not so much from the materialist and atheist propaganda and the destruction of the family as from the universal necessity to lie and betray, from the penetration of the political police into people's most private affairs. You have to lie to live, betray for a piece of bread.[117]

Among politically minded emigrés there were a few small groups, mostly right-wing, who regarded the Stalinist terror as positive, since it rid the country of many Communists and Jews. The "returners," on the other hand, saw Soviet successes as proof of a renaissance of Russia and the terror as necessary to counteract the enemy. The Union for Repatriation (Soyuz Vozvrashcheniya), which functioned in Paris under the tutelage of the Soviet embassy, attracted many young emigrés.

After 1929–1930 the iron curtain hid the Soviet Union completely from the eyes of young emigrés. Trips abroad by Soviet citizens (and thus the chance for emigrés to meet them) virtually came to an end. The Soviet press stopped mentioning emigré writers and literature altogether. Only after Stalin's death, for example, would people in the Soviet Union hear of a world famous Russian emigré writer, Vladimir Nabokov. The young emigrés who came to the Union for Repatriation wanting to go back to their roots, of which they knew so little, were told they had to earn the right to repatriation. Some were asked to fight in Spain, others to perform missions of a different kind. Sergei Efron, husband of the poet Marina Tsvetaeva, sent one of his acquaintances to Spain, "to Comrade Orlov," who was the chief NKVD operative there.[118]

In 1937, Ignace Reiss, a man highly placed in the Soviet intelligence network, broke with Stalin and called for a "return to Lenin." Paris received orders to eliminate the traitor. Sergei Efron and several other aspiring "returners" were given the assignment. Reiss's bullet-riddled corpse was found near Lausanne, and Efron returned to Russia, where prison and death awaited him. [119]

In 1938–1939 the emigrés made their choice between Hitler and Stalin. Most chose Stalin because Hitler seemed worse and Stalin embodied Russia. Some who chose Hitler, however, discovered after the war how similar the two totalitarian systems were and unhesitatingly passed from the Nazi camp to the Communist fatherland. Some went to Moscow, where they were greeted warmly. Konstantin Rodzaevsky, head of the Russian Fascist party, who turned himself in to the Soviet authorities in Harbin in 1945, repented in a letter to Stalin filled with boundless ingenuousness:

The erroneous principle of the liberation of the motherland from Jewish communism at all costs was the source of my fatal error and of the wrong general line of the Russian Fascist party during the Soviet–German war. . . . I issued a call for an "unknown leader," appealing to the strong elements in the USSR to save millions of Russian lives by selecting a Commander X, an unknown leader capable of overturning the Jewish government and creating a new Russia. I failed to see that, by the will of fate, of his own genius, and of millions of toilers, Comrade J. V. Stalin, the leader of the peoples, had become this unknown leader. [120]

Historians have not finished trying to decipher by whose "will" Stalin became the "leader of the peoples." But they all agree that by the end of the 1930s socialism had been built in the Soviet Union.

In February 1938 the third and last major show trial took place in Moscow, bringing to an end the Ezhovshchina and the building of socialism. This was the most notorious of the three trials, with Bukharin, "the favorite of the whole party," the last of Lenin's comrades-in-arms, on the stand, along with Yagoda, Stalin's loyal hatchetman, who knew too many secrets. Then socialism began to flower. In September 1938 the new epoch was blessed with the publication of the *History of the Communist Party of the Soviet Union: Short Course*, more commonly referred to simply as the *Short Course*. With this publication the totalitarian state received its bible.

Thus was achieved a society in which the individual depended entirely on the state. The state gave him his daily bread, both material and spiritual, and he better not ask for any other. With the appearance and sanctification of the *Short Course*, the only permissible version of history, memory was taken away. History became an essential tool in the process of dehumanization.

In December 1938, Beria replaced Ezhov as commissar of internal affairs, a signal that the latest application of the shock treatment was nearly over. A "liberal" would replace the blood-stained executioner, and life would become peaceful. Meanwhile, the country was heading full steam ahead toward war.

CHAPTER

7

# ON THE BRINK, 1939–1941

### READY TO REPEL THE FOE?

According to the 1939 census, the population of the Soviet Union, as of January 17, was 170.6 million (on a territory of 21.7 million square kilometers). Two-thirds of the population, or 114.5 million (67.1 percent), lived in the countryside, and only one-third, or 56.1 million (32.9 percent), lived in the cities. An estimated 8 million Soviet citizens, or 9 percent of the total adult population, were in concentration camps.[1]

The Soviet Union is a land of great riches, with vast mineral reserves, including oil, coal, and precious metals. Numerous rivers and seas provide an important energy source. The diversity of climate, soil type, and terrain provides remarkable possibilities for grain production, livestock raising, fruit and vegetable growing, fishing, and forestry. These natural resources would have sufficed to meet the needs of many generations, had they been utilized in a rational way.

Forced industrialization was carried out in a very short time, mainly at the expense of agriculture, which was brought to ruin, and of consumer goods industry, which was largely neglected. As we have seen, industrialization and collectivization meant the destruction of the most productive strata of the rural population (the so-called kulaks and well-to-do middle peasants) and the transformation of a significant part of the peasant population into a cross between wage workers and paupers, reduced to servitude and tied to their particular localities. Compulsory deliveries of farm products to the state in inordinate quantities and at extremely low prices debased the value of the collective farmer's labor and prevented most kolkhozes from breaking out of perpetual poverty and de facto servitude to the state. Millions of people who were driven from the rural areas on the basis of "class criteria" or who fled to the cities before the internal passport system was introduced in 1932, and hundreds of thousands recruited for work in the cities, swelled the ranks of the industrial working class, which together with the scientists and engineers built an industrial base during the 1930s that provided the basis for the defense industry.

On the eve of World War II the Soviet Union held first place in the world for extraction of manganese ore and production of synthetic rubber. It was the number one oil producer in Europe, number two in the world; the same for gross output of machine tools and tractors. In electric power, steel, cast iron, and aluminum it was the second largest producer in Europe and the third largest in the world.[2] In coal and cement production it held third place in Europe and fourth place in the world. Altogether the USSR accounted for 10 percent of world industrial production.[3]

It is not enough to evaluate overall productivity, however. One must also take into account the size of investments, the productivity of labor, the quality of production, and the state of production relations.

Let us look, for example, at the ferrous metallurgy industry, a key sector, and one of the most powerful in the Soviet economy. The statistics are fairly impressive: 99 blast furnaces, 391 open hearth furnaces, 207 electric furnaces, 227 rolling mills, and 139 batteries of coke ovens.[4] At the same time, starting in 1937, at the height of the terror, and continuing through the first half of 1940, this sector of industry regularly failed to fulfill the plan. The official figures on increases in production, themselves very much open to question, claim only a 3 percent increase in the smelting of cast iron and steel from 1938 to 1941 and only a 1.1 percent increase in sheet iron production. The average output of steel per square meter of open hearth furnace was less in 1940 than in 1937.[5] Production also decreased from 1937 to 1940 in the motor vehicle industry, electrical engineering, transport, road building, the paper industry, and construction machinery.[6]

One reason for these decreases was that the targets set by the Third Five-Year-Plan (1938–1942) did not correspond to the economic realities. Another no less important reason was the mass terror carried out by Stalin.

Repression not only stripped industry of managers, chief engineers, and scientific and technical personnel; it also sowed fear and uncertainty. The spy phobia artificially created by the party leaders intensified the general atmosphere of suspicion. Very broad prospects opened up for careerists and climbers of all sorts, for informers, slanderers, slackers, and self-seekers—in short, the cream of the new ruling class. Newly appointed managers often preferred not to make technological improvements, whose benefits might not be evident immediately, out of fear of being charged with "wrecking activity" by members of this new elite.

Right up to the outbreak of war, ferrous metallurgy, the foundation for all processing and machine industries, remained one of the weakest links in the Soviet economy. This especially affected the arms industry.

During the ten years preceding the war, arms spending increased fivefold, according to the official budget figures, from 5.4 percent of the total budget during the First Five-Year Plan to an average of 25.4 percent during the first three years of the Third Five-Year Plan.[7] The projection for 1941 was that 43.4 percent of the budget would go for defense.[8] The USSR was far behind schedule in introducing mass production of new types of weapons, particularly fighter planes, tanks and artillery. At the outbreak of war the arms industry was still in the process of retooling, although its infrastructure had been significantly expanded.

As in the Soviet economy generally, the decisive role in the arms industry was not played by economic or technological considerations but by the frequently incompetent opinions of the party leadership, especially those of Stalin and Zhdanov, the Central Committee secretary in charge of the army and defense industry. Their conceptions of war, military technology, and strategy and tactics had not advanced beyond the experiences of the civil war. For example, Stalin suggested that tanks produced at one Leningrad factory be equipped with 107mm cannon, because such cannon had made a very good showing in the civil war.[9]

Stalin had no idea that the field artillery he was talking about was a completely different weapons system from the kind of cannons mounted on tanks. As a result of similar ignorance, a decision was made on the eve of the war to stop production of the most urgently needed types of antitank guns, the 45mm and the 76mm.[10] This went on despite the objections of Boris Vannikov, people's commissar of the armaments industry, who bluntly told Zhdanov during a meeting of a commission of the Central Committee, "You are disarming the army on the eve of war." Vannikov was arrested at the beginning of June 1941.[11] Similarly, Professor V. I. Zaslavsky, a talented tank designer, fell victim to repression, and B. I. Shavyrin, a designer of mortars, was accused of slowing down the output of mortars, although he had nothing to do with the production process.[12] In general, a search went on everywhere for people to blame for alleged disruption of war preparations, but those truly responsible, the top leaders of the party and government, were never touched. The situation was no better with the production of anti-aircraft guns, antitank weapons, and machine guns.

At the beginning of 1939 the great wave of terror ebbed. The blood-stained dwarf Ezhov was replaced at the NKVD by Beria, who had arrived from Georgia. Under Beria repression took on more routine forms. Beria used his position in the NKVD not only to strengthen his influence within the party leadership but also to exploit more systematically the labor of prisoners and internal exiles as well as the "free" work force in the NKVD's employ.

Since the Soviet government does not publish statistics on the number of prisoners, approximate figures must be used. The most cautious and conservative estimates made by Western researchers place the number in the camps at the beginning of the war with Germany at 6.5 million (in 1940), down from 8 million in 1939.[13] The reason for this decline was the high death rate. Most of those arrested in 1937 and 1938 were unable to survive the harsh conditions in the camps for more than two or three years. It is true that the Soviet concentration camps did not have gas chambers or crematoriums like the Nazi death camps. Mass extermination was organized in a more primitive way, due to technical backwardness. People were simply shot, starved to death, or killed off by disease, brutal treatment, or unendurably demanding labor.

The Gulag described by Solzhenitsyn and other writers both Soviet and foreign was only one part, though certainly the most important part, of the monstrous state within a state that was the NKVD. In addition to the camps the NKVD had special research laboratory prisons (sharashkas), industrial enterprises, and separate administrative divisions for the construction of canals, tunnels, roads, and railroads.

The NKVD played an important part in the Soviet economy. With the most inexpensive labor supply in the world, the prison and camp population, the NKVD functioned as a cornerstone of the economic system, as is shown by official Soviet documents. According to the "State Plan for the Economic Development of the USSR in 1941,"[14] the NKVD was responsible for 50 percent of the lumber production and export in the Far East and in the Karelian and Komi autonomous republics, more than one-third in Arkhangelsk and Murmansk provinces, and between one-fifth and one-fourth in Yaroslavl, Gorky, Molotovsk, and Sverdlovsk provinces and in the Krasnoyarsk Territory. The NKVD was also involved in hauling, delivering, and exporting timber in thirty-two other provinces, autonomous republics, and union republics. [15]

NKVD enterprises produced bricks in the Khabarovsk Territory and oil on the Ukhta River (250,000 tons according to the 1941 plan). [16] Its prisoner labor brought in 40 percent of the chrome ore extracted in the Soviet Union as a whole for the same year (150,000 tons out of a total of 370,000). [17] NKVD economic components likewise produced cement, lumber for construction and other commercial uses, steam-powered tugboats, motor launches, barges, tractor trailers, scrapers, heavy graders, steamrollers, farming equipment, furniture, knitted fabric for underwear, socks and stockings, shoes, and so on. [18] From other sources we know that prison labor was also used for uranium, coal, and gold mining. [19]

The fullest picture of the NKVD's place in the Soviet economy may be derived from the plan for capital construction in 1941. The total sum to be allocated for such construction was 37,650 million rubles (not including the amounts for the commissariats of defense, the navy, and roads). The NKVD was allotted 6,810 million rubles, that is, 18 percent, much more than any other commissariat. As for installations that were expected to begin operations in 1941, their total value was 31,165 million rubles, of which the NKVD accounted for 3,860 million rubles' worth, or more than 12 percent. [20]

In view of the fact that the capital equipment (tools and machinery) available to prisoners was on a level incomparably lower than that used by free workers, we can state with assurance that on the eve of the war with Germany forced labor constituted more than 20 percent of all labor in the Soviet Union. The scanty information that we have concerning wages in one of the divisions of the NKVD, the Main Highway Construction Administration (Gushossdor), indicates that the average yearly wage in this division was half of that for industrial workers in other commissariats (2,424 rubles as opposed to 4,700). [21]

According to figures that are far from complete, the deployment of this slave labor force in 1941 was as follows: mining, 1 million; hired out to various state enterprises, 1 million; general construction, 3.5 million; construction and maintenance of camps and manufacture of camp necessities, 600,000; logging, 400,000; agriculture, 200,000. [22] An unprecedented economic and administrative power was thus concentrated in the hands of the NKVD. Even the party apparatus, not to mention the state, was to one degree or another under its control.

In "free" enterprises, events proceeded in their own way. "Storming" (*shturmovshchina*) flourished. When the plan could not be met during the initial weeks, efforts were made to meet it "by storm" during the last ten days. Many Soviet firms still practice this rush job method today. Very often factories had to stop work because the prerequisite raw materials or semifinished goods were not delivered on time. In Leningrad in 1940, for example, in the heavy machinery industry, 1.5 million work hours were lost for this reason.

There was a constant search for scapegoats, a completely sterile task, because no particular Comrade X or Y was to blame; the fault lay with the defective planning system and party leadership as a whole.

Unable to cope by normal methods with the existing inefficiency and waste or with such plagues as *shturmovshchina*, absenteeism, and drunkenness, the government decreed a number of harsh new labor laws in June– July 1940. A system of "work books" (*trudovye knizhki*) had been introduced in 1938, in effect tying the worker to a particular enterprise, where this book containing his work record was kept. Without it he could not take a new job. Then on June 26, 1940, a new law changed the workday from six or seven to eight hours and the work week from six to seven days. Workers were now denied the right to change jobs without a permit. Absenteeism and lateness became criminal offenses, with penalties ranging from a fine to outright imprisonment. In July 1940 tractor and combine drivers were forbidden by law to leave their jobs without authorization.[23] In October 1940 a system of "state labor reserves" was established, including young people from the age of fourteen up. Children who ran away from factory schools (to which they were assigned) could be punished with up to six months' imprisonment.

In 1936 Stalin had announced to the world that socialism had essentially been built in the USSR. Then the party announced that a new kind of human being had emerged in the process—Soviet man. At the same time the party and state decreed a return to the most archaic social relations in production, long since left behind by all of the more advanced countries— that is, the binding of the worker to the place of production. This was not a very surprising development, however, because the overwhelming majority of the population, the peasantry, had been tied to the kolkhoz since collectivization and to the local village since the internal passport system was introduced in 1932.

Now workers and peasants became equals, as it were, in their social rights relative to production. Both classes found themselves in absolute subservience to the state, the only employer. The new labor laws created a situation highly reminiscent of war communism, with its compulsory labor service and other draconian measures.

One of the main arguments for introducing such drastic laws in industry was the need for iron discipline in view of the war threat, an argument used throughout Soviet history. The siege mentality created by repeated war scares, in 1927, again in 1931, again in 1937, and so on, allowed the party leadership to justify its arbitrary and repressive acts as necessary against foreign agents, who were "everywhere."

Throughout the mid-1930s no government in the world was actually in a position to launch a major war, even if one had wanted to. It is well known that Nazi Germany, despite its great military-industrial potential, the intensely chauvinist atmosphere prevailing within it, and the favorable international situation it enjoyed, still required six years before it was ready to attack Poland. The real danger of war for the USSR began with Nazi aggression in Europe.

## ON THE WAY TO THE MOSCOW–BERLIN AXIS

The entire second half of the 1930s was overshadowed by constantly accumulating military and political conflicts. Events were moving swiftly toward a new world war.

In 1935 Germany repudiated the military provisions of the Versailles treaty and introduced the draft. To this measure Stalin responded with understanding, even approval. At the end of March 1935 he told Anthony Eden: "Sooner or later the German people are bound to free themselves from the chains of Versailles. . . . I repeat, a great people like the Germans are bound to break loose from the Versailles chains." And he added, "The Germans are a great and courageous people. We never forget that."[24] What impressed Stalin about the Germans was not their cultural achievements but their "greatness" and "courage." Little did it matter that the Germany he was talking about was Nazi.

There was a certain logic in Stalin's position. He had long dreamed of an alliance with Germany. Now that the Versailles system had collapsed, its two opponents, Russia and Germany, could work together openly. The fact is that Stalin repeatedly expressed his desire for a general political accord with Nazi Germany, as an examination of the events leading up to the Stalin–Hitler pact of August 23, 1939, demonstrates.

"Stalin has been obsessed with the idea of an agreement with Germany since 1933," a Soviet diplomat named Gelfand, who defected to the United States from a post as counselor at the Soviet embassy in Rome, told a British diplomat, N. Butler, in a confidential interview.[25]

Hitler became chancellor in January 1933. Three months later, in the first half of May, a group of senior officers headed by General von Bock-elsberg visited Moscow. Defense Commissar Voroshilov, in his speech welcoming the German military delegation, stressed the Red Army's desire to continue its longstanding friendly relations with the Reichswehr.[26]

At about the same time Stalin read the Russian translation of *Mein Kampf*. Although he might not have been completely convinced from this reading that Hitler harbored anti-Soviet intentions, since a goodly share of Hitler's remarks might have been dismissed as propaganda, Stalin nevertheless felt obliged to take some measures. The special relationship with the Reichswehr was ended, and its installations on Soviet territory were closed down.[27]

Still the question of future relations between Germany and the Soviet Union remained undecided. The Soviet leadership continued to hope that after an initial period of tension during the Nazi consolidation of power it would be possible to reestablish the previous rapport between the two countries. On August 16, 1933, Abel Enukidze, secretary of the USSR Central Executive Committee, expressed this view openly to the German ambassador, von Dirksen. "The National Socialist reshaping [of Germany]," he said, "could have favorable consequences for German–Soviet relations." Enukidze was quite blatant in his attempt to point out common lines of development and analogous traits between German national socialism and Soviet communism.[28]

In late 1933 and early 1934, that is, right when the Soviet government was deciding to orient its foreign policy toward "collective security," it made persistent overtures to Germany, one after another, urging a renewal of friendly relations.

On November 6, 1933, Deputy Defense Commissar Tukhachevsky said to von Twardowsky, counselor at the German embassy in Moscow, "In the Soviet Union the Rapallo policy remains the most popular." It would never be forgotten, he added, that the Reichswehr had helped to train the Red Army in very difficult times. The Red Army would heartily welcome the renewal of such collaboration. All that was needed was to dispel the fears of a hostile policy by the new German government toward the Soviet Union. [29]

In a meeting with Mussolini on December 4, 1933, Litvinov said, "We want to have the best possible relations with Germany. However, the USSR fears an alliance between Germany and France and seeks to parry such a move by making its own rapprochement with France."[30]

On December 13 Litvinov reiterated this to Nadolny, the German ambassador in Moscow: "We will not instigate anything against Germany. . . . We have no intention of intriguing against her."[31] This theme was developed by both Litvinov and Molotov in speeches before a session of the Central

Executive committee of the USSR on December 29, 1933.[32] The session was held shortly after the Central Committee of the party had passed a resolution favoring a policy of collective security in Europe.[33]

Although in 1934 the Soviet Union made an official turnabout in foreign policy, even joining the League of Nations in September and becoming a very active member, Stalin secretly continued the old orientation toward Germany. Defense Commissar Voroshilov and Chief of Staff Egorov, in conversation with German officials in January 1934, repeatedly stressed the Soviet desire for the best possible relations with Germany.[34]

Stalin pursued the same line in his report to the Seventeenth Party Congress in February 1934. He was quite cautious in his assessment of the situation in Germany. He noted that "fascism of the German type... is wrongly called national socialism—wrongly because the most searching examination will fail to reveal even an atom of socialism in it."[35] As to the first part of the name, suggesting nationalism, Stalin had no comment. Instead he began to revise the party's traditionally unfavorable attitude toward nationalism in general, including Russian nationalism. It was not long after this that the "comments" by Stalin, Kirov, and Zhdanov on Soviet history textbooks were written. This shift in attitude toward the historical past occurred simultaneously with the beginning of a revised attitude toward fascism, particularly the German type.

Stalin considered the Nazi party an instrument of the big industrialists and the Reichswehr. He did not grasp the relatively autonomous character of the fascist movement. Believing that the Reichswehr had complete control of the situation, and being intent on a renewal of military collaboration with Germany, he never understood the danger nazism represented.

"We are far from being enthusiastic about the fascist regime in Germany," he said to the Seventeenth Party Congress. *"But fascism is not the issue here*, if only for the reason that fascism in Italy has not prevented the USSR from establishing the best relations with that country."[36] The door remained open for an entente with Germany.

According to Walter Krivitsky, head of Soviet military intelligence in Western Europe, Stalin regarded the events of June 30, 1934, in Germany (the "Night of the Long Knives," when Hitler murdered his former cohorts, among them Ernst Roehm) as the end of the "party period" and the beginning of the "state period" of the Nazi regime.[37] Shortly after June 30, Krivitsky reports, "the Politburo decided at all costs to induce Hitler to make a deal with the Soviet government." After the Night of the Long Knives, Stalin concluded that "Hitler represented the organized state power standing above the nation," the kind of organized power Stalin valued so highly. Only one problem remained—to convince Hitler that Russia was Germany's logical ally.[38]

Although the Soviet press had been carrying on a campaign in favor of collective security and against the aggressive, expansionist aims of the Nazis, Radek, himself the director of the press campaign, explained with cynical candor to Krivitsky: "Only fools can imagine we would ever break with Germany. What I am writing here is one thing—the realities are something else. No one can give us what Germany has given us. For us to break with Germany is simply impossible."[39]

Radek was probably referring not only to military collaboration with Germany but also to the important technical and economic assistance received from that country during the First Five-Year-Plan. It is certainly true that foreign economic assistance, including German, played a decisive role in Soviet industrialization.

The Soviet Union began presenting proposals to Germany, one after the other—for example, that the two powers provide joint guarantees to the Baltic states; that they join together in an "Eastern Pact" that would guarantee the security of all participating countries; and so on. Hitler rejected all these proposals.

At the same time, the policy of collective security, that is, rapprochement with France and England, was pursued more intensively. Stalin's new hope was that fear of encirclement would prompt Germany to improve relations with the Soviet Union.

Kalinin, the official head of state (president of the Central Executive Committee of Soviets), told the new German ambassador, Schulenburg: "The outcries in the press should not be given too much importance. The German and Soviet peoples are linked by many different ties and depend on one other in many ways."[40]

During Anthony Eden's visit to Moscow in March 1935, Stalin tried to give him the same impression, to frighten him with the prospect of a Soviet–German alliance in order to dissuade Britain from seeking an agreement with Germany at the expense of the USSR. He told Eden that Soviet talks with Germany for loans and credits had included the question of "certain products" that did not bear mention out loud, in other words, armaments, chemicals, and the like.

> Eden (agitated): What? Surely the German government hasn't contracted to deliver arms to your Red Army?
>
> Stalin: Yes, they have, and in the next few days we will probably sign a credits agreement.[41]

The stakes were high. If Stalin could persuade the British that Hitler was not to be trusted, the danger of an Anglo–German accord directed against the Soviet Union would be eliminated. Then Hitler would have no choice but to seek an agreement with the Soviet Union.

Three and a half months after Eden's trip to Moscow, in July 1935, Stalin ordered his confidant, David Kandelaki, Soviet trade representative in Berlin, to initiate talks aimed at the improvement of political relations between Germany and the USSR. Kandelaki was in charge of economic negotiations underway at the time with the president of the Reichsbank, Hjalmar Schacht, who had close ties with top industrial and financial circles. By Stalin's logic, the big industrialists were the real power behind Hitler; thus talking with Schacht meant talking directly to the boss. Kandelaki also met with Goering, whom the Soviet leaders considered to be the link between the industrialists and the German government. Schacht advised Kandelaki to pursue the matter through diplomatic rather than commercial channels. For his part, he promised to inform the German Foreign Ministry of the Soviet inquiry.[42]

The "Kandelaki initiative" was backed up by Surits, the Soviet ambassador in Berlin, by Bessonov, a counselor at the Berlin embassy, and by others who persistently called for improved Soviet–German relations. In a visit to the German Foreign Ministry on December 21, 1935, for example, Bessonov stated bluntly that it would be desirable to supplement the 1926 neutrality pact between the two countries with a "mutual nonaggression pact."[43]

Evgeny Gnedin, a prominent Soviet journalist and diplomat who served at the Berlin embassy in 1935–1936, has confirmed that a serious reappraisal of attitude toward nazism was being made in Moscow at the time. "I remember," Gnedin writes,

> that we members of the Berlin embassy staff were rather taken aback when Eliava, the deputy commissar for foreign trade, who was passing through Berlin (in 1936, as I recall) and who had access to Stalin because of long-standing personal ties, gave us to understand that "at the top" Hitler was viewed "differently" than he was in the Soviet press or by the Soviet embassy staff in Berlin.[44]

During 1935 and 1936 Stalin continued to hope for an agreement with Hitler despite warnings from the international section of the NKVD that "all of the Soviet attempts to appease and conciliate Hitler are doomed. The main obstacle to an understanding with Moscow is Hitler himself."[45]

When, in May 1936, Germany did grant the Soviet Union substantial credits as a result of the talks in 1935–1936, Stalin read the action as a desire for a general political agreement. At a Politburo meeting Stalin took issue with the NKVD: "Well, now, how can Hitler make war on us when he has granted us such credits? It's impossible. The business circles in Germany are too powerful, and they are in the saddle."[46]

During 1936 neither the confrontation with Germany in Spain nor the signing of the "anti-Comintern pact" between Germany and Japan dissuaded Stalin from the conviction that it was possible to reach an agreement with Germany. At the end of May 1936, Kandelaki and his deputy Friedrichsohn met with Goering, who was not only very interested in an improvement in German–Soviet relations but also promised to take the matter up with Hitler.[47] In July Bessonov had a meeting with Hencke, a high-ranking official in the German Foreign Ministry. Bessonov listed the concrete conditions necessary to reach a nonaggression pact. Hencke explained that, in the German government's view, nonaggression pacts were possible only between states sharing a common border, and that was not the case with the Soviet Union and Germany.[48]

This statement was of crucial importance for the future of Soviet–German relations. In December 1936 and February 1937 Schacht met again with Kandelaki and Friedrichsohn. He explained that trade relations could be expanded on the condition that the Soviet government renounce all further Communist agitation outside its borders. According to Schacht's notes, Kandelaki expressed "sympathy and understanding." Kandelaki revealed that he had been entrusted by Stalin and Molotov to make known their views, which he had with him in written form. He then read the statement, which said that the Soviet government had never placed obstacles in the way of political talks with Germany, that Soviet policies were not in any way directed against German interests, and that the Soviet government was ready to enter into negotiations concerning the improvement of German–Soviet relations. Schacht urged Kandelaki to have this communication presented officially by the Soviet ambassador in Berlin.[49]

After the conclusion of the economic agreement between the Soviet Union and Germany in May 1936, Stalin was convinced that the talks with Hitler were on the right track. "In the immediate future we shall consummate an agreement with Germany," he told Ezhov, according to Krivitsky. And in December 1936 Krivitsky himself was ordered to "throttle down" intelligence work in Germany.[50]

On February 11, 1937, however, the German foreign minister, von Neurath, informed Schacht that the Soviet proposals had been rejected because of the Franco–Soviet mutual assistance pact and the activities of the Comintern. At the same time, Neurath explained that if events inside the Soviet Union continued to evolve in the direction of an absolute despotism, more and more dependent on the army, Germany might reconsider its policy toward the USSR.[51]

Hitler was guided by a number of considerations in rejecting Stalin's overture at that time—not only domestic instability and the anti-German policy of collective security but also the weak response by France and England to Hitler's remilitarization of the Rhineland and unilateral denunciation of the Locarno pact (in March 1936). To Hitler this meant that an expansionist Germany need not fear any serious resistance from the Western powers. He decided that for the moment it was more advantageous to play the anti-Soviet card.

Hitler used the Soviet overtures to try to frighten Britain with the prospects of a Soviet–German rapprochement. At the beginning of 1936 British military and diplomatic circles were taking this threat very seriously. Baron Geyer, the German military attaché in London, in a conversation with British Chief of Staff Dill, spoke of strong pro-Russian tendencies in the German army and suggested that a Soviet–German pact could well become a reality if Britain and Germany did not come to an agreement themselves.

In London it was believed that the policy of rapprochement between Germany and the Soviet Union enjoyed the support of the Reichswehr, Schacht, an important group of industrialists interested in business dealings with Russia, and even a section of the Nazi party. But Hitler was thought to be adamantly opposed to any improvement in relations other than on the level of trade.[52] There was a mistaken assumption in British political circles that the Germans had taken the initiative in this policy.[53] The Foreign Office feared that if the system of collective security collapsed, a German–Soviet rapprochement would be inevitable. Only the collective security policy could prevent a Soviet–German pact.[54]

In the Soviet Union the situation began to deteriorate rapidly. An unheard of reign of terror was setting in. Radek, at the Moscow trial of January 1937, playing the double role of defendant and chief witness for the prosecution, confessed to treason and spying in behalf of Germany. (These lies about himself and others did not save his life for long. He was sentenced to ten years in prison, but died in a labor camp, apparently in 1940.)

In the spring of 1937 rumors of an imminent agreement between the USSR and Germany circulated in Western foreign ministries and the Western press. The Soviet Union issued a formal denial of these rumors, but only in April 1937, two months after Hitler's categorical rejection of the Soviet proposals.[55]

In March 1938 Germany annexed Austria. On September 30, 1938, the Munich agreement was signed, under which Great Britain and France acceded to the separation of the Sudetenland from Czechoslovakia and its incorporation in Germany. The Munich agreement, however, was aimed not only at Czechoslovakia but also at the Soviet Union. After Munich and the Anglo–German declaration of nonaggression an analogous Franco–German declaration soon followed.[56] Moscow's nervousness increased when a pro-Nazi puppet government was established in the Transcarpathian Ukraine, a former part of the Russian empire which had gone to Czechoslovakia but was now detached from that country. Rumors spread that the Germans were reviving one of their old projects, a formally independent, German vassal state in the Ukraine.

Under these conditions Stalin decided to resort once again to his favorite tactic, the double-cross. In his report to the Eighteenth Party Congress on March 10, 1939, he warned Great Britain and France that their "nonintervention" policy was bound to fail and hinted at a possible reversal of Soviet foreign policy.[57]

Several months later, on August 23, after the signing of the Soviet–German nonagression pact, during an evening reception to celebrate the occasion, Molotov "raised his glass to toast Stalin, commenting that it was Stalin with his speech in March 1939, which had been correctly understood in Germany, who achieved the turnabout in political relations [between the USSR and Germany]."[58] A week after that celebration Molotov told the deputies to the Supreme Soviet of the USSR that it had been Stalin who at the Eighteenth Party Congress had predicted an agreement between the USSR and Germany. "It is evident now," Molotov added, "that in Germany on the whole they understood this statement of Comrade Stalin's correctly and drew practical conclusions from it. (Laughter.)...The historical foresight of Comrade Stalin was brilliantly confirmed. (Stormy applause in honor of Comrade Stalin.)"[59]

Five days after Stalin's speech Germany occupied Czechoslovakia and installed on its territory the German protectorate of Bohemia-Moravia and an "independent" Slovakia under the tutelage of the Third Reich. These events radically changed political opinion in Britain. In response to new German pressure on Poland (demands for the annexation of Danzig and the Polish corridor), Britain adopted a "policy of guarantees." From March to May 1939 Britain gave commitments of direct military aid to Poland, Romania, Greece, and Turkey in the event of unprovoked aggression.[60] The draft was reintroduced in Britain for the first time since World War I. Chamberlain's government asked the Soviet Union to clarify what its policy would be in the event that Poland and Romania were threatened with aggression.[61] At the same time, Chamberlain began to probe the possibility of an agreement with the Germans that would guarantee British security.[62]

The Soviet Union, for its part, began to play its own kind of double game. In mid-April 1939 it initiated talks with Britain and France on the question of a military alliance. On the other hand, energetic soundings were resumed in Berlin on the possibility of a broad political agreement between the USSR and Germany against Britain and France.

On April 15 the British government urged the USSR to declare publicly that in the event of aggression against any European neighbor of the USSR, as long as that country itself resisted the aggression, it could count on Soviet assistance.[63] On April 17 the Soviet Union proposed a mutual assistance pact to England and France, to last from five to ten years, with guarantees of assistance to any Eastern European country bordering on the Soviet Union between the Baltic and Black seas that fell victim to aggression. The Soviet proposal provided for the signing of a military convention.[64]

Ten days before this, however, Peter Kleist, a German Foreign Ministry official, heard Georgy Astakhov, the Soviet chargé d'affaires in Berlin, say that it made no sense for Germany and the USSR to engage in ideological warfare when they could coordinate their policies.[65] And on the same day that the Soviet proposal was delivered to Britain, Aleksei Merekalov, the Soviet ambassador in Berlin, told Weizsaecker, the German deputy foreign minister, that the Soviet Union would like to have normal relations with Germany, relations that "might become better and better, " and that ideological differences should not be an obstacle.[66]

On May 3 Maxim Litvinov, who during the 1930s had come to symbolize the policy of collective security, was dismissed as commissar of foreign affairs. The dismissal of this Jew, who had often been a target of Nazi propaganda, and his replacement by Molotov produced a very favorable impression in Berlin. A German diplomatic courier stressed that Molotov's appointment "apparently guarantees that Soviet foreign policy will be conducted in strict accordance with the conceptions of Stalin."[67]

On May 5 Astakhov was informed that armaments which the Soviet Union had ordered from the Skoda factories in German-occupied Czechoslovakia would be delivered.

During May, the exchange of proposals and further discussion through diplomatic channels continued between England and France, on the one hand, and the Soviet Union, on the other. The essential point for the USSR was a guarantee that the Baltic states (Latvia, Lithuania, and Estonia) would not somehow fall to the Germans and that, in the event of war with Germany, Soviet troops would be allowed to pass through Polish and Romanian territory unimpeded. This meant, in effect, that the Soviet Union was asking England and France's approval for the annexation of the Baltic nations. The governments of Poland and Romania rejected the request for free passage of Soviet troops on their territory because they feared, not without reason, that this would result in irreversible social and political changes.

On May 20, in the midst of these negotiations with England and France, Molotov called in the German ambassador, Schulenburg. The ambassador was amazed by one of Molotov's remarks: that both governments should seriously think about ways of placing their relations on a better political foundation.[68] In Berlin this statement was seen as a very promising opening, but a decision was made to wait until Molotov became more explicit. The Nazis suspected the Soviet government of using the German government's willingness to improve relations as a way of pressuring Britain and France into making greater concessions. In one of his memorandums to Hitler, the German foreign minister noted, however, that the USSR no longer aggressively promoted world revolution and that a gradual normalization of German–Soviet relations was possible.[69] The German Foreign Ministry began an intensive study of the prospects of a German–Soviet rapprochement and its possible effects on Germany's alliance with Japan and Italy. During June and July, Stalin and Hitler refrained from any decisive moves. At the same time intensive Soviet–German trade talks continued.

At the end of May 1939 the Far East became the scene of major battles between Japanese forces, on one side, and Soviet Mongolian troops, on the other. The deterioration of Soviet–Japanese relations increased the Soviet government's anxiety and its fear of being drawn into a war on two fronts, west and east.

Hitler was preoccupied with a similar concern. His generals clearly stated their opposition to a two-front war. The overall strategy of Nazi Germany was to defeat its adversaries one at a time, while seeking to prevent a political or military alliance among them. The worsening of Polish–German relations and the relative military weakness of Britain and France made Hitler more receptive to the idea of a rapprochement with the Soviet Union.

In the middle of June Stalin decided to try talking with the Germans again, but to be more explicit this time. On June 15 Astakhov met with Draganov, the Bulgarian envoy to Berlin, and explained to him that the Soviet Union had to choose among three possibilities: a pact with France and Britain; prolongation of the Anglo–Franco–Soviet talks; or an agreement with Germany. The latter possibility would correspond most closely with Soviet wishes, he said, and he proceeded to outline for Draganov the substance of a Soviet–German agreement. He noted in particular that the Soviet Union refused to recognize Romanian sovereignty over Bessarabia; in other words, he made it clear that one of the bases for a future agreement would be the "return" of Bessarabia to the Soviet Union. He also said that the one obstacle to an agreement was the Soviet fear of a German attack through the Baltic countries or Romania. If Germany were to declare that it would not attack the Soviet Union or would agree to a nonaggression pact, the USSR would probably refrain from making a pact with Britain. However, Astakhov continued, since the Soviet Union did not know Germany's real intentions, there was much to say in favor of prolonging the talks with Britain, in order to maintain a free hand. Draganov, as Astakhov surely expected, informed the German Foreign Ministry of this conversation without delay. [70]

On June 15, while Astakhov was meeting with Draganov, the British and French governments were conveying to the Soviet government their responses to its proposals. They agreed to a mutual assistance pact but refused to sign a military convention simultaneously because the time period was too short. They suggested instead that there be consultations between the three countries' general staffs. [71]

The British government wished to prolong the negotiations because at that point it was making a deep probe of German intentions. Henderson, the British ambassador in Berlin, saw Goering on June 9 and told him that if Germany wanted to initiate peace talks with Britain, it would meet with a "not unfriendly response." [72] From June to August 1939, British–German talks of an unofficial character began, were broken off, and began again several times. [73] However, Germany's demands, especially the demand that the Near East be viewed as its "natural economic sphere," were absolutely unacceptable to Britain. The positions of Germany and Britain were irreconcilable in another respect: the Nazis aspired to unrestricted supremacy on the European continent.

Stalin did not understand that this was a favorable moment for the Soviet Union, although he constantly harped on the theme, derived from Lenin's theory of imperialism, that the contradictions between the rival capitalist powers were irreconcilable.

It was thus that in the summer of 1939 both Britain and the Soviet Union found themselves interested in prolonging negotiations on a mutual assistance pact. In so doing, they left the key decisions on the fate of the world in the hands of Hitler's Germany, which desired the outbreak of war as quickly as possible.

On June 28 Molotov again made the point to Schulenburg that the normalization of political relations with Germany was possible and desirable. [74] Schulenburg replied that Germany would welcome such normalization. Molotov expressed his satisfaction; he was particularly pleased that Germany regarded the 1926 neutrality pact between the two countries as still in effect. [75]

On July 22 commercial talks between Germany and the Soviet Union started again, with a high-ranking German official, Julius Schnurre, in attendance. The next day, the Soviet government suggested to Britain and France that talks be held in Moscow between representatives of the armed forces of the three countries. Britain and France accepted the proposal on July 25. The government of Neville Chamberlain nevertheless attempted to stall the talks. The British military mission did not arrive in Moscow until August 11, and it came with instructions not to make any specific commitments that might under certain circumstances tie the hands of the British government. The delegation was instructed in particular not to discuss the Baltic states or the positions of Poland and Romania.[76] So unencouraging were the instructions from the British government to its military mission, in fact, that the British ambassador in Moscow wrote to Lord Halifax to inquire whether his government actually desired progress in the negotiations.[77]

Stalin's mistrust of Britain's intentions deepened. Probably by this time Soviet intelligence already knew that Germany had set August 26 as the date for the attack on Poland.

Hitler, for his part, was worried about the military talks in Moscow. So was the German high command, whose strategic conception was to subdue Poland with a blitzkrieg, limiting the fighting to that one front.

On July 27, Schnurre stated clearly to Astakhov and Babarin, the head of the Soviet delegation at the trade talks, that a gradual normalization of political relations between Germany and the Soviet Union was possible and desirable. Astakhov objected to this gradual approach; the matter was urgent, and the Soviet Union felt an imminent threat from the direction of Germany, all the way from the Baltic to Romania. Astakhov wanted to know whether Germany had long-range political aims in regard to the Baltic states, and he underscored the seriousness of the Romanian question. He also stated outright, the first time for a Soviet diplomat, that Danzig should be returned to Germany and that the question of the Polish corridor should be resolved in Germany's favor.[78] In this conversation the main outlines of the future Soviet–German pact began to emerge.

On July 29, Schulenburg received orders from Berlin to meet with Molotov to confirm Astakhov's and Babarin's statements. The telegram especially underlined the point that *no matter how* the Polish question might be resolved, by peaceful means or otherwise, Germany was ready to ensure Soviet interests and to reach an agreement with the Soviet government.[79]

On August 3, Ribbentrop met with Astakhov in Berlin.[80] The same day Molotov met with Schulenburg in Moscow. Both sides sought to clarify exactly what their respective obligations would be under the indicated agreement. Schulenburg told Molotov that from the Baltic to the Black Sea there were no conflicts of interest between the Soviet Union and Germany, that the anti-Comintern pact was not directed against the Soviet Union, any more than Germany's nonaggression pacts with the Baltic states, and that Germany's demands on Poland did not affect Soviet interests. Molotov restated what the Soviet side wanted from Germany and expressed his distrust of Germany's intentions, but more importantly, he left no doubt that the Soviet government was ready for a new relationship with Germany.[81]

It was thus that at the beginning of August, on the eve of talks between the military missions of the Soviet Union, Britain, and France, the situation was such that the Soviet Union was able to choose among three possibilities: to ally itself with Britain and France against the fascist aggressor, Nazi Germany, which was preparing to attack Poland; to guarantee its own interests by reaching an agreement with Germany and thereby open the door to a German attack on Poland and hence a general war; or to stay clear of any and all agreements and thereby hope to keep out of war.

Later assertions by the Soviet government that it had no choice in making its pact with Germany do not correspond to historical reality. In fact, Stalin was inclined toward an agreement with Germany for many reasons. Above all, he hoped to obtain from Germany the Baltic region, eastern Poland, and Bessarabia. Also, as an absolute despot, he was extremely hostile toward any form of democracy. He easily understood the psychology of his fellow dictator, Hitler. After all, the two had so much in common. They had learned a great deal from one another; they used analogous methods against their real or imagined political opponents; and there was a striking similarity between Soviet and Nazi propaganda.

On August 10, one day before the British military delegation arrived in Moscow, Astakhov met with Schnurre again and informed him that instructions he had received from Moscow stressed the Soviet government's desire to improve its relations with Germany. Astakhov explained that the USSR had entered into military talks with France and Britain, not with any special enthusiasm, but simply out of the necessity to protect itself from the German threat, which had forced the Soviet government to seek help wherever it could find it. The situation had changed once talks with Germany had begun. The outcome of the talks with Britain and France was uncertain, and it was quite likely that the question of alliances was completely open from the standpoint of the Soviet government. Astakhov's own meeting with Schnurre was undoubtedly an indication of this. At the heart of the discussion was the question of Poland, but neither participant wished to be candid on the subject; each sought only to present his government's position.[82]

The military talks with Britain and France began the next day in Moscow. During the most intensive phase of the negotiations, on August 14, Astakhov informed Schnurre over the phone that he had been instructed by Molotov to say that the Soviet Union was interested in discussing not only economic problems but also such matters as the press, cultural cooperation, the Polish question, and past Soviet–German political relations. Moscow was suggested as the site of the negotiations. [83]

Thus, by mid-August the Soviet Union had decided in principle to make an agreement with Germany. In effect, the terms had already been formulated by Molotov and made known to the German government: the Baltic states, including Lithuania, were consigned to the Soviet sphere of interest, along with Bessarabia; and the Polish question to be solved "in Germany's favor." All that remained was to hear the German reply.

Astakhov left Schnurre on August 14, at about 2 PM. Seven hours later, Ribbentrop sent Schulenburg a telegram, telling him to communicate the following message to Molotov: First, the period when Nazi Germany and Soviet Russia were in hostile camps was past. A new future was coming into existence. Second, there were no real conflicts of interest between Germany and the USSR. Germany did not harbor any aggressive designs toward the Soviet Union. In the area between the Baltic and the Black Sea there were no problems that could not be solved to the mutual satisfaction of the two great powers, in particular those of the Baltic states, Poland, southeastern Europe, and so forth. Ribbentrop announced a turning point in German–Soviet relations. He was ready to travel to Moscow at once to meet with Stalin and explain to him Hitler's view. He did not exclude the possibility of establishing a basis for further improvement in their relations.[84]

On August 16, Schulenburg communicated this information to Molotov, whose reaction was very encouraging. The Soviet government, he said, welcomed the German desire to improve relations and believed in the sincerity of Germany's intentions. He raised the idea of a nonaggression pact being signed during Ribbentrop's visit. He restated the Soviet demands: a nonaggression pact; German pressure on Japan to improve relations with the Soviet Union and put an end to the border conflict; and mutual guarantees in regard to the Baltic states.[85]

At that point the governments of Germany and the Soviet Union were in a hurry. They knew that ten days later Germany would invade Poland. Hitler needed support from the USSR, which shared a long border with

Poland. Stalin was eager to obtain what he wanted from Germany before the attack on Poland. In the Kremlin the draft of a nonaggression pact was hastily prepared.

On August 16, Ribbentrop sent Schulenburg a new telegram to deliver to Molotov. Germany would be willing to sign a twenty-five-year nonaggression pact with the USSR and jointly to guarantee the Baltic states. At the same time it would use its influence to help normalize Soviet–Japanese relations. Since a serious incident with Poland might occur at any moment, the telegram said, a rapid and thorough clarification of Soviet–German relations was desirable. The German foreign minister would be ready to go to Moscow at any time after August 18.[86]

On August 17, Molotov informed Schulenburg that the Soviet government was willing to forget the past and improve its relations with Germany. First, however, economic and credit agreements should be signed, with a nonaggression pact to be concluded shortly thereafter. In any event—and this was the most important part of Molotov's reply—a protocol should also be signed in which, among other things, the German statements of August 15 would be included. While agreeing in principle to Ribbentrop's visit, Molotov specified that a certain amount of time would be necessary to prepare for his arrival.[87]

The Soviets needed this delay to find a convenient pretext for breaking off the talks with the French and British military delegations. The pretext was furnished by the British, who, on the one hand, did not have formal authorization to sign an agreement and, on the other, had not been able to persuade the Polish and Romanian governments to allow Soviet troops to pass through their territories in the event of war with Germany. These could be used as grounds for breaking off the talks. However, had the Soviet government sincerely wished to reach an agreement with Britain and France, it could have waited a few days longer to learn the results of the French and British diplomatic efforts in Warsaw.

Such patience was no longer consistent with Stalin's plans. He had decided upon an alliance with Germany. The idea had long been ripening in his mind, and the time to realize it had come.

On August 17, a four-day suspension of the Anglo–Franco–Soviet talks was announced.

On August 19, the Soviet government formally agreed to Ribbentrop's visit to Moscow, to occur during the week after the signing of the Soviet–German economic agreement. At the same time Molotov delivered to Schulenburg the Soviet draft of a nonaggression pact.[88] It included a special clause: the treaty would go into effect only if a secret protocol were signed on foreign policy questions of interest to both parties.

The trade pact was signed on August 20. The next day *Pravda* noted in its lead story that the agreement "could be a serious step toward a further improvement of relations, not only economic but also political, between the USSR and Germany."[89]

At 3 PM on August 21, Schulenburg delivered a telegram to Molotov in which Hitler announced his agreement in principle with the Soviet draft treaty and the secret protocol. Hitler warned that a crisis in German–Polish relations could break out at any time and insisted that Stalin meet with Ribbentrop on August 22 or 23 at the latest.[90]

Stalin's reply was positive. He agreed to meet with Ribbentrop on August 23. In his answer to Hitler he expressed the hope of seeing the establishment of peace and cooperation between the USSR and Germany.[91]

The same day, August 21, after the British and French delegations announced that they had received no replies from their respective governments, Voroshilov, who was chairing the talks, announced their adjournment for an unspecified period, until Paris and London produced their answers. But all this mattered very little. Stalin had made up his mind. The double game was at an end.

Neville Chamberlain's game of double-cross also came to an end. For him, it ended in defeat, for at that point Britain faced the certainty of war with Germany.

On the evening of August 23, at the Kremlin, the Soviet–German non-aggression pact was signed. Hitler did not accede to all of Stalin's demands; nevertheless, the pact went further than the usual promises to renounce aggression and resolve differences through peaceful means. The two parties also agreed (in article 4) not to participate in any alliance aimed directly or indirectly against the other signatory. Treaties of friendship or alliance often include such clauses.

Germany promised to try to persuade its ally Japan to normalize its relations with the Soviet Union. The USSR agreed to supply Germany with food and strategic raw materials in return for industrial equipment.

The additional secret document signed at the same time as the non-aggression pact left no doubt that this ten-year treaty was a political alliance, establishing the two powers' spheres of influence in Europe.

The preamble to the agreement stated that in strictly confidential conversations the representatives of the two states had discussed "the question of the boundary of their respective spheres of influence in Eastern Europe." The Soviet Union and Germany agreed that in the event of political and territorial "rearrangement" in the Baltic region (Finland, Estonia, Latvia, Lithuania), the northern border of Lithuania would be considered the border between the spheres of German and Soviet influence. In that case Vilnius would be returned to Lithuania. In the event of changes in the Polish state, the border between the two spheres would go along the Narew, Vistula, and San rivers. This meant that the Baltic states and eastern Poland would be in the Soviet sphere. Germany also stated that it had no interest in Bessarabia, meaning that it would go to the Soviet Union.[92]

This secret agreement, never published in the Soviet Union, became known only at the Nuremberg trials. Even now the Soviet government conceals from its people the real nature of the Stalin–Hitler pact. This was the first but not the last secret agreement to be reached between Germany and the USSR in 1939–1941.

On the evening of August 23 a party was held in the Kremlin to celebrate the signing of the pact. As the German guests were leaving, Stalin addressed Ribbentrop "with words to this effect," according to Hencke, one of the Nazi officials present: "The Soviet government takes the new pact very seriously. He [Stalin] could guarantee on his word of honor that the Soviet Union would not betray its partner."[93]

Stalin also warned the Germans against underestimating the strength of their adversaries, England and France. "England," he told Ribbentrop, "despite its weakness, would wage war craftily and stubbornly," and he expressed the opinion that the French army was a factor to take into serious account.[94]

For Stalin, the pact with Germany was the culmination of many years of effort. In an August 31, 1939, report to the Supreme Soviet on the reasons for the nonaggression pact, Molotov said first of all that Russia and Germany had suffered the most from World War I. He stressed that the Soviet government had long desired to improve its political relations with Germany. Recalling that Hitler had extended the 1926 neutrality pact in 1933, he added: "*Even before this* the Soviet government considered it desirable that a major step be taken on the path of improved relations with Germany, but circumstances were such that this did not become possible until now." These words clearly expressed Molotov's regrets that the pact had not been reached earlier (and remind us of the Kandelaki initiative). Molotov also regretted that the Soviet–German agreement was limited to a nonaggression pact.

> *It is true* that in the present case this is not a mutual assistance pact, as was discussed in the talks with France and Britain, *but only* a nonaggression pact. *Nevertheless*, given the present circumstances, it is difficult to overestimate the international importance of the Soviet–German pact. . . . It is a turning point in the history of Europe, and not only of Europe.[94] (Emphasis added.)[95]

It truly was a turning point in the history of Europe and of the world. By signing the pact with Germany, the Soviet Union opened the door to war. It was no coincidence that the same session of the Supreme Soviet passed a law on compulsory conscription, replacing the previous law on universal military service.[96] The very name of the new law testified to the fact that a qualitative change had occurred in the Soviet government's attitude toward war and peace. The time had come when a war in Europe would be beneficial to Soviet interests, just as the policy of collective security, buttressed by the Comintern's popular front tactic, had served those interests until then.

With the conclusion of the secret agreement with the Soviet Union, Germany was protected against a major conflict on its eastern front. The way was clear for an attack on Poland.

On August 24, *Pravda* called the Soviet–German pact an "act of peace," which would undoubtedly contribute to "an easing of tensions in the present international situation." A week later, on September 1, Germany invaded Poland and World War II began.

On September 3, Ribbentrop asked Molotov whether the Soviet Union would not find it desirable to move against the Polish army and occupy the Soviet sphere of influence. Stalin did not want the Soviet Union to be identified with the German aggression. He preferred to wait and present to the Soviet people and the world the Red Army's entry into Poland as an action intended to protect the Ukrainian and Byelorussian population from German aggression. This was why Molotov said in his reply that the Soviet Union agreed with Germany that the right moment was absolutely necessary for taking concrete action, but that moment had not yet arrived. Hasty action could only "hurt *our* cause," he said, and contribute to the unification of "*our*" adversaries." The text of this document is very important, for in speaking of "our adversaries" and "our cause" Molotov implied—the first time for the Soviet Union—that the Soviet government had the same adversaries and objectives as Nazi Germany.[97]

At that point Stalin felt the time was right for Soviet troops to enter Poland. All reservists up to the age of forty-five, especially technicians and medical personnel, were called up. Hospitals were improvised in school buildings, many goods disappeared from the stores, and rumors spread that rationing was about to begin.[98] The Soviet population, particularly in the western regions, felt the winds of war.

The swift advance of German troops through Poland took the Soviet government by surprise. It had expected military operations to last longer. This was a major lesson in modern military strategy. Future events were to show that it was a lesson the Soviet leadership never fully grasped.

In Berlin the Soviet delay in entering Polish territory was viewed with growing concern. Such action represented the only way of testing the practical value of the German–Soviet pact. The German press agency distributed a statement by General von Brauchitsch, commander-in-chief of German land forces, implying that an armistice between Germany and Poland would be signed at once and that therefore military action on Poland's eastern border would be unnecessary. This statement sought to prod the Soviets into action. Meanwhile, the Soviet government was seeking to justify a move against Poland in the eyes of the Soviet people. On September 10 Molotov told Schulenburg with undisguised cynicism that "the Soviet government wants to use the continuing advance of German troops to explain that Poland has fallen and that, consequently, the Soviet Union is forced to come to the aid of the Ukrainians and Byelorussians 'threatened' by Germany." This action would provide respectability in the eyes of the masses and would remove the impression that the Soviet Union was acting as an aggressor.[99]

Needless to say, this approach was not to the liking of the Germans, who suggested instead a joint communiqué justifying military action in Poland on the grounds that order needed to be restored on the former Polish territory.[100] This proposal was rejected; Stalin feared such close identification with Hitler.[101] A convenient formula was soon found. Without mentioning Germany, it spoke nebulously of third parties that might attempt to take advantage of the chaos in Poland. Molotov asked the Nazis to understand that there was no other way of justifying the Soviet intervention to the masses.[102]

On September 17 the Red Army crossed the Polish border. It was a treacherous stab in the back of the Polish army, which kept up its desperate resistance for another two weeks.

Pressed by Germany, Stalin was finally forced to agree to a joint communiqué. The original draft proposed by the Germans was far too candid in Stalin's opinion. Eventually, the Soviet draft was accepted, but even that was fairly revealing. The presence of German and Soviet troops in Poland, it said, was not in contradiction to the interests of the two states, as defined in the Soviet–German pact.[103] A protocol signed in Moscow on September 20, 1939, by representatives of the Soviet and German armed forces (with Voroshilov, the people's commissar of war, and Shaposhnikov, chief of the general staff, signing for the Soviet side) contained a paragraph on the willingness of the Soviet command to place the necessary troops at the Germans' disposal in order to destroy Polish military units or "bands" if it turned out that the German command did not have sufficient forces at hand. To the Soviet population and the rest of the world, the Soviet intervention was presented as a liberating crusade. The full truth about the facts and events connected with the Stalin–Hitler pact have been carefully hidden from the Soviet people.

The Soviet–German aggression against Poland culminated in a joint parade of Soviet and German troops at Brest-Litovsk.[104] The Soviet press, as was to be expected, did not say a word about it.

On September 27 Ribbentrop made a second visit to Moscow. The next day a Friendship and Border treaty was signed. It established the border between the German and Soviet spheres of influence, a border passing through Polish territory. At the same time another confidential protocol was signed. It authorized the departure of German nationals from the territories occupied by the Soviets, as well as of Ukrainians and Byelorussians from the German-occupied territories. A special additional secret protocol provided that Lithuania would be in the Soviet sphere, while the province of Lublin and part of Warsaw Province would be in the German sphere.

In another secret agreement Germany and the Soviet Union stated that neither would allow, on its territory, "Polish agitation" directed against the other party, that they would nip all such activities in the bud and would keep one another informed, so that the necessary measures could be taken. Thus Nazi Germany and the socialist Soviet Union joined hands against the Polish Resistance.[105] In a joint statement on the signing of the friendship pact, the German and Soviet governments announced that the pact had resolved all problems arising from the collapse of the Polish state and had laid the basis for a lasting peace in Eastern Europe. They likewise stated their desire for an end to the war between Germany, England, and France. If Britain and France refused to stop the war, Germany and the USSR would engage in mutual consultations in regard to necessary measures. "It is not only absurd, it is criminal," Molotov said, "to wage a war to 'smash Hitlerism,' under the false slogan of a war for democracy."[106] Eighteen months later, Stalin would speak of the need to smash Hitlerism and would raise high the banner of the defense of democracy.

The partitioning of Poland between Germany and the USSR, and the secret agreements between the two powers, radically changed the situation in Europe. For the Soviet government it was very important to show that the Red Army had taken as much a part as the Wehrmacht in the war against Poland. Germany had to remember that the USSR provided military as well as political help. At the session of the Supreme Soviet on October 31, Molotov bragged about the military partnership with Germany: "It proved enough for Poland to be dealt one swift blow, first by the German army *and then* by the Red Army, to wipe out all remains of this misshapen offspring of the Versailles treaty" (emphasis added).[107]

Answering Ribbentrop's congratulations on the occasion of his sixtieth birthday, Stalin made a special point: "I thank you, Herr Minister. The friendship of the peoples of Germany and the Soviet Union *forged in blood* has every reason to be lasting and solid" (emphasis added).[108]

In Moscow people joked cynically: the friendship was forged in blood all right, Polish blood.

The Soviet leadership did its best to present the backstabbing of Poland by the Red Army as an attempt to save the Ukrainian and Byelorussian populations from the sorry situation they had been brought to by the senseless policies of the old Polish government. It is characteristic of the attitude of the Soviet and German governments that no document of the period refers to the Polish population: it was treated as though it had never existed. Three million Poles lived in the areas annexed by the Soviet Union. Special NKVD troops were rushed into eastern Poland, under the leadership of General Ivan Serov, with the mission of finding, arresting, and deporting "socially alien elements." These troops were accompanied by party functionaries whose role was to prepare the 12 million inhabitants of eastern Poland to "freely choose" fusion with the Ukrainian and Byelorussian Soviet socialist republics.

The secret agreement provided for Soviet occupation of the Baltic states. In the fall of 1939 the governments of Latvia, Lithuania, and Estonia, under heavy Soviet pressure, signed mutual assistance pacts with the USSR. Then, in 1940, under the false pretext of anti-Soviet activities on their territories, Soviet troops were brought in. Again, the populations of these countries were organized to "freely choose" absorption into the Soviet Union, on the basis of a schedule carefully worked out in Moscow. From June 17 to June 21, 1940, in Lithuania and Latvia, "people's governments" were formed, then elections to popular assemblies held. On July 14 and 15 similar elections were held to the State Council in Estonia. On July 21, 1940, Soviet power was established simultaneously in all three countries.[109]

Two weeks later the Supreme Soviet admitted the three Baltic republics to membership in the USSR. The new Soviet republics were immediately flooded with NKVD troops, and preparations for mass deportations to Siberia of suspicious persons or elements hostile to Soviet power soon followed. General Serov was in charge of all these operations.

Bessarabia had been occupied by Romanian troops and annexed to Romania in 1918. The Soviet government had never recognized this action.

In July 1940, assured of support by Nazi Germany, the USSR demanded the immediate return of Bessarabia, and the Romanian government was forced to comply. In August Bessarabia merged with the autonomous republic of Moldavia to form the Moldavian SSR.

Whereas the Soviet Union might have had some arguable legal right to Bessarabia, the occupation of northern Bukovina, which had been part of the old Austro-Hungarian empire, was a simple annexation. It was not even provided for in the secret Soviet–German agreements of 1939. Molotov, in reply to the question of the German ambassador in Moscow, explained that Bukovina was "the last missing component of a reunified Ukraine."[110]

Hitler had used similar arguments to justify the occupation of Austria, the Sudetenland, Klaipeda (Memel), and so on. He was simply including in the Reich all areas with German-speaking populations. Stalin sympathized with this approach.

Finland, under the secret protocol of August 23, 1939, was included in the Soviet sphere of influence. On October 2, when the Finnish ambassador to Germany, Wuorimaa, tried to find out the intentions of Germany and the Soviet Union toward his country, German deputy foreign minister Weizsaecker made it clear that Germany would not interfere in relations between Finland and the Soviet Union.[111]

Annexation was not initially part of the Soviet plan; Stalin hoped to bring Finland into his orbit through political pressure alone. He had no intention of going to war against a country that would have the support of Britain, possibly Germany, the Scandinavian countries, and the United States as well. Essentially his aim was to move the border, which ran across the Karelian isthmus only thirty-two kilometers from Leningrad, farther to the north, away from this Soviet industrial center. The city was too easily exposed to heavy artillery fire. He also wished to block access to Leningrad from the Gulf of Finland and to guarantee the security of the rail line from Murmansk. Of course, Finland itself was not a threat to the Soviet Union.

On October 5 the Soviet government presented its demands to Finland. If Finland would cede the Karelian isthmus, the USSR would in exchange give it a vast territory, twice the size of the isthmus, from Soviet Karelia, along the Finnish border. (The Soviet territory was sparsely populated and of very little value.) In addition, the Soviet Union demanded the right to lease the Finnish peninsula of Hanko (Hango), at the entrance to the Gulf of Finland, and the ice-free port of Petsamo on the northern coast west of Murmansk, in order to build Soviet naval and air bases. The Finns were naturally reluctant to give up Hanko, since this could mean placing Finland's fate in the hands of its powerful neighbor. No resolution of the issue could be found, and talks between the two countries were broken off on November 13. Both sides began to mobilize their forces and strengthen their defenses.

The Finns had the well-equipped Mannerheim Line of fortifications stretching across the Karelian isthmus for about 125 kilometers, quite a strong position, although not the very last word in military technology. In his haste to wring the desired concessions from Finland, Stalin organized a provocation. He ordered the military command in Leningrad to shell the Soviet village of Mainila, about 800 meters from the Finnish border, then blamed it on the Finns. The Soviet press was immediately filled with calls for retaliation: "Wipe out the Wretched Gang" was one.[112]

Stalin's hope that he could intimidate Finland into accepting the Soviet terms and thus avoid an armed conflict was not borne out. Finland would not yield its territory and compromise its independence. The Finnish people wholeheartedly supported their government, which was led by the Social Democrat Wajno Tanner. Stalin, infuriated, ordered that Finland be issued an ultimatum and, if it did not accept, that shelling of its border positions begin. On November 28 the Soviet Union tore up its nonaggression pact with Finland. Stalin was confident that the artillery attack would be enough to force Finland to capitulate and accept his conditions. However, just in case, he ordered the formation of a puppet government headed by Otto Kuusinen, a Comintern leader and veteran of the Finnish Communist party. A so-called people's government of the (nonexistent) Finnish Democratic Republic was established at Terioki, and the Soviet government immediately concluded a friendship and mutual assistance treaty with this fictional entity.[113] He planned to create a Karelo-Finnish Soviet Republic as part of the USSR, by merging Finland with the existing Karelian Autonomous Republic.

Events, however, did not conform with Stalin's expectations. The Finns were not intimidated by his ultimatum. Advancing Soviet divisions encountered fierce resistance, and it soon turned out that the Soviet troops were not at all ready for a war under winter conditions. They were not trained to fight on skis; there were shortages of automatic weapons; many did not have winter uniforms; and cases of frostbite were numerous. Surprise attacks by elite Finnish sharpshooters inflicted heavy casualties. In an attempt to overcome the Red Army's deficiences, Soviet professional skiers were inducted, and many met inglorious deaths. Soviet transport equipment was likewise unfit for the harsh winter. All attempts to crack the Finnish defenses by a frontal assault on the Mannerheim Line were repelled, with heavy casualties.[114] The Red Army leaders in charge of the Finnish operations proved incompetent. General G. M. Shtern had to be called from the Far East, and General Meretskov, head of the Leningrad military command, was replaced by Marshal Timoshenko. To raise morale, volunteers from the Communist youth of Leningrad and Moscow were brought in. Many of them had only rudimentary military training. Hastily thrown into battle, they suffered enormous losses. The two largest Soviet cities, Moscow and Leningrad, were soon suffering from food shortages. The particularly cold winter of 1939–40 caused chaos in transportation. For the people the war against tiny Finland proved a terrible bloodletting. Only in February 1940, after twenty-seven divisions and thousands of guns and tanks were concentrated, did the troops under Marshal Timoshenko manage to break through the Mannerheim Line. At that point Finland's only recourse was to call for a truce.[115]

During this ignominious campaign, the Soviet Union's military weakness was glaringly revealed. To this day the Soviet government has not told its people the truth about the losses suffered in that war. According to recent Finnish figures, 100,000 Soviet soldiers were killed, while the Finns lost 20,000.

The war with Finland cost the Soviet Union more than just physical losses. It was discredited internationally. The League of Nations formally condemned the USSR for aggression in December 1939, expelling it from the organization. Three other states had been branded aggressors by the League of Nations: militarist Japan, Fascist Italy, and Nazi Germany. Now the socialist Soviet Union joined the list.

The British and French governments were preparing to take advantage of the indignation of world public opinion to shift the center of military activity from Western to Northeastern Europe. An expeditionary corps of 50,000 volunteers was quickly organized, but the Finnish government chose not to let its territory become a testing ground for the great powers, as Spain had been. It decided, after some hesitation, to sign a peace treaty with the USSR. The agreement was signed in Moscow on March 12. The Soviet Union received the Karelian isthmus, including Vyborg (Viipuri) and the Gulf of Vyborg with its islands, the western and northern shores of Lake Ladoga, including the towns of Keksholm, Sortavala, and Suojarvi, a number of islands in the Gulf of Finland, some territory east of Merkjarvi, including the town of Kuolajarvi, and the western parts of the Rybachy and Sredny peninsulas. It was also granted the right to lease the Hanko peninsula and surrounding islands to install naval and air bases and garrisons.[116]

The so-called people's government was never supported by the people of Finland; it disappeared as quickly as it had arisen. Kuusinen, the head of this rump government, soon became the president of the Presidium of the Supreme Soviet of the Karelo-Finnish Soviet Republic, a new component of the USSR made up of the former autonomous republic of Karelia and the new regions acquired from Finland under the 1940 agreement. The new republic reminded freedom-loving Finns that their country could be annexed at any time. Only in 1956, when the Soviet government became convinced that Finland was firmly under its influence, did the Karelo-Finnish Republic once again become the Karelian autonomous republic within the RSFSR.

One negative result of the war with Finland was that it further convinced Germany that, in military respects, the Soviet Union was a colossus with feet of clay, that it could easily be defeated.

The war exposed serious shortcomings in the Soviet military organization, especially in the Commissariat of Defense. It was revealed, for example, that information from Soviet intelligence on the positions of gun emplacements in the Mannerheim Line had not been marked on the field maps of front-line units, resulting in needlessly heavy Soviet losses inflicted by the Finnish batteries.

"In our war against the Finns," said Khrushchev,

we had an opportunity to choose the time and the place. We outnumbered our enemy, and we had all the time in the world to prepare for our operation. Yet even in these most favorable conditions it was only after great difficulty and enormous losses that we were finally able to win. A victory at such a cost was actually a moral defeat.

Our people never knew that we had suffered a moral defeat, of course, because they were never told the truth.[117]

The top leaders of the party and government, Stalin, Molotov, and the other Politburo members, could not help but see that the war with Finland was a sharp warning of danger ahead. Although Voroshilov was removed as people's commissar of defense, he remained a member of the Politburo, when he should have been tried by a military tribunal. The top leadership knew that for years he had neglected his duties as head of the armed forces. His subordinates (Tukhachevsky among them), while still alive, had taken care of all administrative functions; Voroshilov himself had not the slightest idea of the real condition of the Red Army.

Voroshilov was replaced as people's commissar of defense by Marshal Timoshenko, the former commander of the Kiev Military District. There were other changes, too, but none of them could fundamentally alter the sorry state of affairs in the army's high command, since the best generals had been liquidated or sent to prisons and concentration camps. General Shtern, one of the ablest Soviet military leaders, was shot in April 1941, after his successful part in the Finnish campaign. The officers promoted to the highest positions lacked experience in commanding large units. Officers on the middle and lower levels also left much to be desired. As of May 1, 1940, Soviet infantry units lacked as many as one-fifth the officers they required. Officer training at the military academies was of very poor quality. At company and squad level, 68 percent of the commanders had only five months of military training for the rank of second lieutenant.[118]

At the beginning of the war with Germany, only 7 percent of the officers had higher military education, and 37 percent had not completed their secondary education. Approximately 75 percent of the commanders and 70 percent of the political commissars had less than one year's experience in the positions they then held.[119] In mid-1940 the Soviet government suffered serious arms shortages. By mid-1940 the Soviet government was fairly well aware of seriously neglected aspects of the country's preparations for war, despite the practically unlimited spending for military purposes (in 1941, for example, allocations for defense alone amounted to 43.4 percent of the state budget). Industry, for example, was not producing enough modern weapons, and mass production of up-to-date military aircraft was only in the preparatory stages.

In the 1930s the Soviet government proceeded from the assumption that sooner or later the USSR would be drawn into a world war. Soviet military doctrine, and with it the official propaganda machine, told the population that any future war would be fought on enemy soil and would not be costly in human lives. The war would inevitably be an offensive, not a defensive one. That was why, in negotiating with the French and British, the Soviet side repeatedly sought free passage for the Red Army through Polish and Romanian territory in the event of war with Germany. The absence of a common border with a potential enemy as dangerous as Nazi Germany had been a positive factor of prime importance, for it meant that a surprise attack by Germany from the west was ruled out. The Soviet Union was separated from Germany, let us recall, by Poland, the Baltic countries, and Romania. The Soviet leadership had often denounced these states as a *cordon sanitaire* erected by the west against the Bolshevik revolution. This assertion contained an element of truth, but the *cordon sanitaire* also worked in reverse. It was impossible to launch a surprise attack on the Soviet Union since it was necessary, first, to pass through these intermediate states.

After Stalin's "ingenious" conclusion of his pact with Hitler, the situation changed. Now Germany had a common border with the Soviet Union. All the immediate advantages the USSR obtained from the Stalin–Hitler pact were minor compared to this negative consequence. With the partition of Poland and the Soviet occupation of the Baltic states, Stalin placed himself on a 3,000-kilometer border with a potential aggressor, every point on which was vulnerable. This was a fatal mistake.

Soviet historians do not say a word about this, of course, and for good reason. To acknowledge this error would lead to further acknowledgments. Thus far the official position has been that the refusal of France and Britain to sign a mutual assistance pact with the Soviet Union left it with no choice: it was obliged to sign a nonaggression pact with Germany and stay out of the war; otherwise, it would have been drawn into a war on two fronts, against Germany in the west and Japan in the east.[120]

Let us take a closer look at these arguments.

One reason the British and French hesitated to conclude a military alliance with the USSR during the talks in the summer of 1939 was that they had doubts about the military capacity of the Soviet army, which had been weakened by the mass extermination of its officers in the 1930s. The Soviet government, for its part, had little confidence in Chamberlain, author of the Munich accord. But did Hitler, who violated the Munich agreement and invaded Czechoslovakia, inspire greater confidence as a political partner?

Official Soviet historians contend that if the USSR had failed to sign the nonaggression pact with Germany, the German army would have marched into the Soviet Union after occupying Poland, with the blessing, perhaps even the support, of England and France. This does not correspond to reality. Without the Stalin–Hitler pact, it is highly unlikely that Germany would have dared to invade Poland, since it would have risked confronting a coalition of Britain, France, and the Soviet Union. Even the belated conclusion of an alliance between Britain and Poland on August 25 disconcerted Hitler enough to make him postpone his attack until September 1.[121] Thus, within days of the Soviet–German agreement, Hitler was questioning the correctness of his calculations.

It is a myth that the Soviet government had only one alternative in August 1939. As we have seen, Astakhov himself, in his converstion with the Bulgarian envoy Draganov, outlined three possibilities facing the Soviet Union: agreement with Britain and France; agreement with Germany; no agreement of any sort with anyone, that is, a policy of waiting, of delaying, in short, a policy of neutrality.[122] This means that the Soviet leadership had considered the policy of neutrality. (Astakhov certainly did not raise it on his own initiative.) Indeed neutrality, staying out of the European conflict altogether, could have been the best course for the Soviet Union.

Let us suppose, however, that Hitler the adventurist had decided to settle accounts with Poland, despite the lack of an agreement with the Soviet Union, on the assumption that Britain and France would not stir in Poland's behalf any more than they had for Czechoslovakia in March 1939. Still, if the Soviet Union had backed Poland, would Hitler have risked a war? At that point it was impossible. Germany lacked the human and material resources for such a war. A simple comparison of Germany in 1939 with Germany in 1941 proves the point.

Against Poland Hitler was able to marshal a force of fifty-seven divisions (to Poland's forty-seven divisions and brigades), 2,000 tanks (to Poland's 166), and 1,800 planes (to Poland's 771). In addition, Germany had thirty-three understrength divisions in the west, to counter any attack by France and Britain.[123] We should add that Germany's war industry was only beginning to develop and was suffering from major shortages of oil and other strategic raw materials.

According to Marshal Shaposhnikov, head of the Soviet General Staff, in his remarks to the British and French military delegations in Moscow in August 1939, the Soviet Union could at that time have mobilized against Germany 120 infantry and 6 cavalry divisions, 5,000 pieces of medium and heavy artillery, 9,000–10,000 tanks, and 5,000–5,500 bombers and fighter planes.[124]

Given this unfavorable relationship of forces for Germany, the Soviet thesis of an immediate danger from Germany after its attack on Poland does not stand up.

Another official thesis of Soviet historiography is true, however: Germany was able to go to war against the Soviet Union only after taking over most of continental Europe and adapting the economic resources thus acquired to the German war effort.[125] But this refutes the thesis of a German threat in 1939. In September 1939, even if Germany had waged war against Poland under conditions of political isolation, there was no danger that it would have gone on to attack the Soviet Union at that time.

The official Soviet argument suffers from another weakness: at the time of the Stalin–Hitler pact there was no real danger of war with Japan. As we have seen, there were major clashes with Japan on the Mongolian border in the summer of 1939. But Japan got the worse of the encounter and chose to reconsider its "grand strategy," turning its eyes instead to the Asian and southern Pacific colonies of the European powers. Even in 1941, when the Soviet Union found itself in serious difficulties, Japan concentrated its attention on southern Asia and the Pacific, so that the Soviet government decided to withdraw entire divisions from the Far East to the Soviet–German front.

The official Soviet argument insists on the danger of a two-front war.[126]

One reason for this is that for nearly ten years the Soviet leadership was hypnotized by the idea that war with Japan was likely—in view of Japanese expansionism in Manchuria and China.[127] (Japan's policy reversal in 1939 apparently did not register, and so the preconception remained unaltered.)

The truth is that all of the rationalizations for Stalin's decision to make a pact with Hitler were invented after the fact to justify Soviet policy and whitewash the military-political leadership.

The Soviet–German pact actually was motivated in part by the idea of setting the capitalist powers against one another. The Leninist doctrine that contradictions between capitalist states should be exploited to further the cause of socialism made any policy justifiable as long as it promoted war between the imperialist powers.

Which side to choose to try to achieve this end? Germany offered certain long-term advantages, and of more immediate importance, it offered eastern Poland, the Baltic states, and Bessarabia.

Another consideration drew Stalin to the pact with Hitler.

Stalin was sure that Germany would not risk attacking France and Britain unless it felt safe on its eastern front. In signing the pact with Hitler, Stalin knew quite well that war in Europe would inevitably follow. In his report to the Supreme Soviet on August 1, 1940, Molotov said with satisfaction: "This agreement, which our government will abide by scrupulously, has eliminated all possibility of friction in Soviet–German relations while Soviet measures are taken along our western border, and at the same time it has provided Germany with a calm certainty in the east."[128]

The official press echoed these words: "This agreement and the economic and practical pacts between the USSR and Germany which followed it have provided Germany with *a calm certainty in the east.* They also provide it with substantial assistance in solving the economic problems it faces" (emphasis added—A. N.).[129] This undoubtedly referred to the agreed-upon Soviet deliveries of food and strategic raw materials.

Stalin needed a war in Western Europe for one other reason. Despite his boasts about the strength of the Red Army, he knew the situation was very serious. The best military cadres had been eliminated, the arms industry was not yet producing up-to-date weapons, agriculture was still in crisis, and civilian industry was functioning by fits and starts. The Soviet Union needed time to prepare for a major war. Stalin assumed that the pact with Germany would buy time, that Germany would be bogged down in positional warfare on the western front, as it had in World War I, that bloody battles like those of the Marne and Verdun would weaken France, Britain, and Germany alike. Then the Soviet Union's moment would come. Soviet policy during 1939–1941 flowed from this perspective. Military production targets were scheduled to ensure readiness for war no earlier than 1942.

Contrary to the predictions of Hitler's strategists, the war in Poland lasted six weeks, not two. Despite its lack of modern armament, its isolation, and the inertia of its French and British allies, the Polish army, fought the invader with extraordinary courage. Hitler's armies were not able to take Warsaw completely until September 28. Even after the Red Army's treacherous attack in their rear, the Poles fought on for another two weeks, with battalions of workers coming to the aid of the regular Polish army. The last center of resistance, on the Hela peninsula, held out until the early part of October. Then a reign of terror settled over Poland.

Shortly after this victory Hitler launched a "peace offensive" toward Britain and France. His condition for making peace was the recognition of German hegemony over Europe; in effect he was asking for the capitulation of the Western powers. The Soviet Union supported this "peace offensive." Stalin and Molotov declared that Britain and France were the aggressors, that Germany was only defending itself. A campaign was launched in the Soviet press to persuade the United States not to intervene in Europe and not to support Britain and France.

In April 1940 the German army occupied Denmark and Norway. On May 10, 1940, it launched its offensive on the western front. The same day, Molotov told the German ambassador that he had no doubt of Germany's success. [130]

The campaign in Western Europe ended a month and a half later with the capitulation of France, the evacuation of the British expeditionary force from Dunkirk to the British Isles and the occupation of Belgium, the Netherlands, and Luxembourg by German troops. The entire western part of the continent was in German hands. Britain alone continued the war against Germany, but its situation was extremely grave.

The speed with which France was defeated came as a total surprise to government leaders around the world, including Stalin. His expectation of protracted positional warfare in the West turned out to be wrong, and his conception of World War II as a repetition of the "first imperialist war" proved hopelessly outmoded.

Molotov conveyed to the German ambassador in Moscow the Soviet government's warmest congratulations on his army's "brilliant successes" in France. [131] But the real mood in the Kremlin was anything but cheerful. A decision was made to incorporate the Baltic states and Bessarabia into the USSR without delay. This was done during June and July 1940. Stalin's haste reflected his uncertainty over Germany's next move. The fall of France had decisively shifted the balance of forces. The international position of

the Soviet Union had worsened considerably, and the Soviet–German accords of 1939 were no guarantee against German attack.

In late June and early July 1940, the new British government of Winston
Churchill made several moves in the direction of improving relations with
the USSR, but no positive response came from the Soviet government,
mesmerized as it was by the German victories. [132]

After the Soviet occupation of Bessarabia and Northern Bukovina, Germany began to intervene in Romania and the Balkans, while Italy began
making moves against Yugoslavia and Greece.

On September 27, 1940, Germany, Italy, and Japan signed a military
alliance, the Tripartite Pact. Although it contained a proviso that the relations of the signatories with the USSR would not be affected, the Soviet
government correctly interpreted the pact as a step toward widening the
war.

In the midst of these difficulties and complications, Stalin had a chance
to rejoice. On August 20, 1940, his agents finally succeeded in killing his
mortal enemy, Trotsky. They had pursued the exiled revolutionary for years,
killing one of his secretaries, Erwin Wolf, in Spain in 1937; then his older
son, Leon Sedov, in 1938; and finally, Trotsky himself. His murderer,
Ramon Mercader, drove an iceax into Trotsky's head. Stalin rejoiced over
the way his rival was killed—like a mad dog—as much as over the fact
of his death. On August 24, 1940, *Pravda* celebrated the event in characteristic fashion: an editorial entitled "Death of an International Spy."

Mercader, who was sentenced to twenty years in prison, refused to name
those who had guided his hand. He was awarded the title Hero of the Soviet
Union. (He was fated to receive his Hero's gold star more than twenty years
later in Moscow—not from Stalin or Beria, who would no longer be on the
scene, but from someone with Politburo authorization. At that time Mercader would change his name to Lopez and apply for membership in the
Communist Party of the Soviet Union, but his application would be rejected
on formal grounds, the real reason being that the post-Stalin Soviet leaders
would prefer not to be further associated with Trotsky's assassin. Despite
everything, these leaders sometimes do consider the judgment of history.
The rejected Mercader-Lopez, in anger, would tear the gold star from his
chest. Nevertheless, to the end of his days he remained a member of the
fraternal Spanish Communist party.)

In autumn 1940 the Axis powers intensified their moves into Southeastern
Europe, threatening British as well as Soviet interests. Hungary and Romania were by then virtual satellites of Germany, German military influence
in Bulgaria was increasing, and at the end of October Italy invaded Greece.

Under these circumstances, in the late autumn of 1940 Britain again tried to open talks with the Soviet Union, but the attempt failed. Moscow's attitude toward Britain and the United States had undergone a certain change: it was evident that Britain would not capitulate to Germany and was waging war more and more stubbornly; it was also evident that the expansion of Germany and Italy into the Balkans was a direct threat to the security of the USSR. The Soviet leadership chose to adopt a more active approach, lest it find itself completely isolated. The stupid Soviet press campaign against U.S. entry into the war was stopped. On August 6, 1940, a Soviet–U.S. trade agreement was renewed. At the end of January 1941 the United States made a conciliatory gesture, lifting a "moral embargo" that had been in effect since December 1939, when because of the Soviet attack on Finland the U.S. government advised American companies not to trade with the Soviet Union. In March 1941 Congress rejected an amendment seeking to exclude the USSR from aid under the lend-lease program. But matters did not reach the point of rapprochement with Britain and the United States, primarily because the Soviet Union continued to respect scrupulously its agreements with Germany and wished not to give Hitler any pretext for violating those agreements. Fear of provoking Germany was the key to Soviet policy in this period.

In 1940 and 1941 the Soviet Union conscientiously abided by the terms of its agreement to supply Germany with strategic raw materials, in particular oil and grain. In this way the Soviet Union contributed significantly to the German preparations for war against—the Soviet Union itself.

Soviet–German economic relations had been defined by the agreements of August 19, 1939, and February 10, 1940. Germany needed strategic raw materials. At the beginning of World War II the German economy depended to a great extent on imports, such as tin (90 percent imported), rubber (over 85 percent), raw materials for textiles (approximately 70 percent), bauxite (99 percent).[133]

During the seventeen months from the Stalin–Hitler pact to the German invasion, the Soviet Union supplied Germany with 865,000 tons of oil, 140,000 tons of manganese ore, 14,000 tons of copper, 3,000 tons of nickel, 101,000 tons of raw cotton, over 1 million tons of lumber, 11,000 tons of flax, 26,000 tons of chrome ore, 15,000 tons of asbestos, 184,000 tons of phosphates, 2,736 kilograms of platinum, and 1,462,000 tons of grain.[134]

The Soviet side honored its commitments with exceptional care and punctuality. The last train of goods crossed the Soviet border heading for Germany a few hours before the German attack in the early hours of June 22, 1941.

It was not only through direct Soviet deliveries that Germany received assistance in building up its military might; deliveries from other countries were also able to reach Germany through Soviet territory. Under the Soviet–German agreement the USSR purchased strategic raw materials in Germany's behalf in the Far East, the Middle East, Latin America, and so on. The Soviet Union also bought nonferrous metals for Germany. Great quantities of rubber, bought by Japan, moved over the Trans-Siberian Railway to Germany, which urgently needed them, since it had reserves sufficient only for two months. On one occasion in 1941 the Soviet government went to the extreme of making up one entire freight train loaded with rubber for Germany. Graphite from Madagascar, tungsten and rubber from French Indochina, crude oil, dairy products, fats, soybeans—all these products reached Germany by Soviet rail. The Germans assessed the Soviet economic aid and the USSR's role as an intermediary as "of the utmost importance."[135] It is entirely possible that without this help Germany would not have been able to go to war against the USSR. Hitler was to a considerable extent justified in telling his council of war on August 22, 1939, that Germany had nothing to fear from a blockade, in the event of war, because the East would provide everything it needed.

In return the Soviet Union was supposed to receive weapons from Germany for the Soviet navy, including fully equipped cruisers and other armaments. Germany actually did provide the cruiser *Lutsev*, equipment for submarines, artillery systems, and so on. The *Lutsev*, delivered to Kronstadt in June 1940 at a price of 100 million Reichsmarks, was not completely finished or equipped. Part of its equipment was never delivered. Germany also agreed to send advisers to the USSR to train the *Lutsev* crew.[136]

Germany did not completely fulfill its commitments under the economic agreements. At the time of Germany's invasion of the USSR it still owed 229 million Reichsmarks' worth of goods. The Nazis got the best of the deal. They obtained substantial economic aid which helped them prepare their attacks on France and the Balkans and, after that, on their supplier, the Soviet Union.

The Soviet government's assistance was not confined merely to supplying strategic materials to Germany. Some six weeks after the Stalin–Hitler pact, at the beginning of October 1939, the Soviet government proposed that the Germans build a naval base for themselves thirty-five miles northwest of Murmansk, for fueling and repairing its submarines and warships. The Germans used "Basis Nord," as it was called, during their campaign in Norway, abandoning it only in September 1940, when they had no more use for it. Admiral Raeder, commander-in-chief of the German navy, sent a letter thanking the Soviet government, which replied that it was glad to have been of service.

German auxiliary cruisers, involved in operations against the British, were allowed to take on fuel and food at Murmansk. For this Admiral Raeder and the German government expressed their thanks to the Soviet naval command.[137] Admiral Kuznetsov, commissar of the Soviet navy, promised to respond to these thanks "not with empty words but with deeds."[138]

The Soviet government also authorized German naval vessels to seek refuge in the port of Murmansk. When war began in September 1939, the Soviets held British and other Allied naval vessels in Murmansk, to allow German ships to travel safely back to their bases in Germany. Later, when the battleship *Bremen* tried to break the British blockade and return to Germany, the Soviet authorities held all British and Allied ships at Murmansk until the *Bremen* had reached home safely.[139]

Stalin's government likewise made its icebreakers available to help German commerce raiders, camouflaged as merchant ships, pass through the northern Arctic route to the Pacific. On August 12, 1940, the raider *Schiff-45* was helped through the Bering Strait by a Soviet icebreaker and reached the Pacific on September 5.[140] Together with another German raider, *Schiff-45* was responsible for sinking a number of Allied vessels with a total tonnage of 64,000.

The Germans, for their part, limited the movement of their ships in the Baltic and Black seas during the Soviet–Finnish war. Abusing its formal neutrality, the USSR sent its ships out to obtain weather information for the Germans. This was used by the Luftwaffe in the bombing of British cities.

In its desire to appease Hitler, the Soviet government went to the extent of handing over to the German authorities approximately 800 anti-Nazi German and Austrian activists, including former Comintern functionaries who had been held in Soviet prison camps. The formal pretext for this action was the clause in the Stalin–Hitler pact providing for the liberation of German and Austrian citizens detained in the Soviet Union on charges of "espionage for Germany." They were handed over to the Nazis. It is easy to imagine the joy of the Gestapo at the delivery of, among others, Franz Korichoner, founder of the Austrian Communist party. There was nothing unusual about all this. The core of the Comintern had been eliminated in the USSR during the Great Terror of the 1930s. The Gestapo took care to eliminate the rest. "*I deshevo i milo* (Cheap and sweet)," as Stalin used to say.

The very organization of the Comintern had been placed at the disposal

of the short-term foreign policy interest of the Soviet state. At the beginning
of the war many Western Communist parties, following Moscow's orders,
declared the democratic states (Britain and France) to be the aggressors.

As Germany occupied Denmark, Norway, Belgium, the Netherlands, and
other countries, the Soviet government closed the Moscow embassies of
each victim of aggression and denied support to the populations of those
countries in their resistance against the German occupation. This situation
lasted until the Soviet Union itself became the victim of German attack.

Shortly after the capitulation of France, Germany began a propaganda
offensive, with Soviet support, urging Britain to make peace.[141] At the same
time the German air force began its terroristic bombing raids on British
cities. But the British refused to surrender. Hitler was in a hurry. He
wanted to establish German hegemony over all of Europe as quickly as
possible, and he became convinced that Britain would not give in as long
as the Soviet Union existed. In July 1940 Hitler and the German high
command began a discussion of the problems connected with waging war
against the Soviet Union.[142] On July 31 the German General Staff received
orders to draw up a plan for such a war. This was to become Plan Barbarossa.[143]

Hitler then began his war preparations on the diplomatic level. First he
needed to consolidate the forces of the totalitarian states (Germany, Italy,
and Japan), who wished to divide the world among themselves. Hence the
Tripartite Pact of September 27, 1940, under which Germany was assigned
the "Euro-African space," Italy the "Mediterranean area," and Japan "the
East Asia space." Soon after, Germany sent a military mission nearly
the size of a division to Romania. The mission's real task was to prepare
the Romanian army for the attack on the Soviet Union. Also in September,
Germany sent troops to Finland, which it considered a prospective ally.

The German military-industrial base was strengthened. At the end of
1940 Germany's "Lebensraum" consisted of 4 million square kilometers,
with a population of 333 million. From the summer of 1940 on, the Germans
began to make systematic use of the economies of the occupied or satellite
countries for the war effort. Foreign workers were brought in as labor for
German industry, freeing a significant number of Germans for military
service. Industrial production soon experienced major growth.

As the German Reich grew larger and stronger, conflicts with the Soviet
Union became more and more frequent. The Reich no longer needed Soviet
assistance to the same degree as it had in the first months of war.

For its part, the Soviet government sought to use the period of peaceful
relations with Germany to increase its own territory and strengthen its

position, wherever possible. On April 9, 1940, Molotov told Schulenburg that the Soviet Union was interested in the continued neutrality of Sweden. Germany was forced to take this into account.

Lithuania also became a source of friction between the Soviet Union and Germany. Under the secret protocol of 1939, the Lithuanian region of Mariampol was to remain in the German sphere of influence, and the Soviet Union had agreed to stay out of the area. Yet on August 3, 1940, Soviet troops occupied this territory.

The dispute over Lithuania was resolved later, on January 10, 1941, when the two powers signed another secret agreement, under which the Soviet Union agreed to pay Germany $7.5 million, one-eighth of which would be paid immediately in the form of nonferrous metals, the remainder to be paid in gold.[144]

Earlier in 1940, during the German offensive in Norway, the USSR had slowed down its deliveries of strategic goods, fearing that the German move into Scandinavia might have a bearing on the Baltic states within the Soviet sphere of influence. Once it was convinced that the German offensive would be limited to Norway, deliveries were resumed. But the incident left its mark on relations between the two powers, making Germany particularly sensitive to its dependence on Soviet supplies.

In August and September 1940 new frictions developed in the wake of the Soviet annexation of Bessarabia and Northern Bukovina. Germany gave Romania a unilateral guarantee and, acting as a mediator, awarded Transylvania to Hungary. For the Soviet Union, this was a violation of article 3 of the nonaggression pact, which called for discussions between the two powers on problems affecting their common interests. Economic negotiations between the two states likewise produced friction. In addition, the Soviet Union objected to the fact that it had not been notified of the Tripartite Pact until the eve of its being signed.

In October 1940 Germany explained to the Soviet Union that it was sending its military mission to Romania at Romania's request and supposedly, to protect Germany's interest in Romania's oil.[145] Serious tensions between the Soviet Union and Germany were also developing over Bulgaria and the rest of the Balkans.

It was under these circumstances in the fall of 1940 that the question arose as to whether it was possible and desirable to continue collaboration, or whether Soviet and German interests had become irreconcilable. On October 13, Ribbentrop sent Stalin a letter that began with an analysis of the relations between the two countries and ended with an invitation to the USSR to join the Tripartite Pact and thus share in the division of the world into spheres of influence. Ribbentrop invited Molotov to Berlin to discuss these questions and said that he was ready to come to Moscow with representatives of Japan and Italy to pursue this proposal, which he emphasized "would be *practically* beneficial to all of us."[146]

Molotov arrived in Berlin on November 12. He listened quietly to the speeches of Ribbentrop and Hitler, who explained that Britain had been defeated and would never set foot on the European continent again. Molotov agreed with Hitler that both powers had greatly benefited from their collaboration. He stressed that Germany had been protected on its eastern flank and that this had been a major factor in the victories of the Reich in the first year of war. He added, however, that not all problems had yet been solved, in particular the questions of Finland, Bulgaria, Romania, and Turkey. The German minutes of the meeting (the Soviet version has never been published) state that Molotov agreed with the Führer's observations on the role of America and England. "Soviet adherence to the Tripartite Pact," he said, "seemed *perfectly acceptable in principle*, as long as it participated as an equal partner, not just a passive object." If this condition were accepted, he saw no obstacle to Soviet participation "in this joint effort" (emphasis added—A. N.).[147] But he asked for further clarification, particularly of the Asian area.

Molotov reproached the Germans for not responding to Stalin, who had asked that Southern Bukovina be added to the Soviet sphere. He further insisted on the withdrawal of German troops from Finland and cessation of anti-Soviet propaganda in that country. Hitler promised all of this but at the same time warned Molotov to avoid another war with Finland. Molotov asked German agreement to a Soviet guarantee of the integrity of Bulgaria, such as the German one given to Romania. Hitler had no objection, as long as Bulgaria itself asked for such a thing. He also said that he shared the Soviet point of view on the need to change the agreement to include the Turkish straits and to authorize free passage of Soviet warships from the Black Sea to the Mediterranean.

Molotov listened without commenting when the proposed agreement on the division of the world into four spheres of influence was outlined. On November 14 he returned to Moscow. Twelve days later the Soviet answer was sent to Hitler. The USSR accepted the German proposal to divide the world into spheres of influence but with certain changes: the Soviet sphere should extend south of Baku and Batum, that is across Turkish territory, into northern Iran and Iraq. The USSR should have the right to establish a military base on the straits, Turkey should be invited to join the Tripartite Pact, and territorial guarantees should be given to Turkey jointly by Germany, Italy, and the Soviet Union. If Turkey refused, the three powers would take appropriate military and diplomatic measures to safeguard their interests.

In addition, the Soviet government, while agreeing to respect German economic interests in Finland, insisted that Germany immediately withdraw its troops from that country. It also asked that Japan renounce its claims to coal and oil deposits on the northern Sakhalin island and that Bulgaria become part of the Soviet sphere and sign a mutual assistance pact with the Soviet Union.[148]

These were the conditions the socialist Soviet Union proposed for agreeing to the Nazi plan to divide up the world. Later official claims that the Soviet government had rejected the Nazi proposals do not hold water. Molotov wrote to the Germans several times after that, asking for their answer to the Soviet counterproposals. All in vain. Hitler had decided on war against the USSR. On December 18, 1940, Plan Barbarossa was adopted in its final form.

A month earlier King Boris of Bulgaria had arrived in Berlin to discuss Bulgaria's adherence to the Tripartite Pact. (It formally joined on March 2, 1941.) On November 20, 1940, Hungary joined the pact. On November 23 Romania followed suit, as did Slovakia on November 24. Hitler had obviously decided to disregard Soviet views on such matters. Soviet protests were never answered. The irritation in Moscow over these developments took the form of erratic behavior. For example, the Soviet government spoke out against a rapprochement between Finland and Sweden (which could have had the beneficial effect of ensuring Finnish neutrality in the event of a Soviet–German war). It warned Finland that an agreement of this kind would annul the peace treaty it had signed with the Soviet Union. In other words, it threatened Finland with a new war. The result was that inside Finland the supporters of a rapprochement with Germany gained ground against the moderates.

Nazi Germany was clearly preparing for a new war, this time against the Soviet Union. But it decided first to take the Balkans and in that way isolate its two enemies, Britain and the Soviet Union.

In fact, the Balkan war was started by Italy, which on its own initiative, without consulting Germany, invaded Greece on October 28, 1940. In March 1941 Germany attacked Greece, saving Italy from a military disaster. The Reich then demanded that Yugoslavia join the Tripartite Pact. The Yugoslav premier agreed, but on March 27 he was overthrown in a popular revolt.

It was at this late hour, on April 5, 1941, that the Soviet Union signed a friendship treaty with Yugoslavia, which gave no practical aid to the besieged Yugoslavs but served as a kind of Soviet protest against Nazi expansion in the Balkans. The next day, April 6, Germany attacked Yugoslavia and quickly defeated its army. The Soviet Union did not lift a finger to help its "friend."

On June 18 Turkey signed a nonaggression pact with Germany. By this time Germany had completed its military buildup in Poland and Romania along the Soviet border. On June 20 German paratroops finished their operations in Crete against the British, who were forced to withdraw to Egypt.

The normalization of Soviet–Japanese relations was the only major success for Soviet foreign policy during this period. The fighting along the Mongolian border had ended in mid-September 1939, after the signing of the Stalin–Hitler pact. Germany's pact with the Soviet Union, the fall of France, the occupation of the Low Countries, the beleaguering of Britain— all this supported the views of the militarists in Japan, who advocated expansion to the south against the French, British, and Dutch colonies, not to the north and west, against the Soviet Union. Industrial and commercial sectors in Japan, interested in trade relations with the Soviet Union, especially those in the fishing industry, urged their government to sign a new fishing treaty with the Soviets. The old one had expired in 1939. Germany was also interested in seeing Japan expand southward, since this would distract the United States from Europe and force the British to disperse their forces to protect their empire.

The fishing pact was extended through 1942. On April 13, 1941, Japanese Foreign Minister Matsuoka, on a visit to Moscow, signed a neutrality pact. This normalization of relations was very important for the Soviets at a time when relations with Germany were increasingly strained. The agreement was signed by the Japanese in spite of direct pressure on Matsuoka by Hitler and Ribbentrop, who hinted to him quite clearly that war against the Soviet Union was not far away. But since Japan had already chosen to expand southward, Matsuoka chose to guarantee its northern flank by signing the treaty. Thus the danger of a two-front war, both for Japan and for the Soviet Union, was greatly reduced.


## DECEPTION AND SELF-DECEPTION

The Soviet government had a vast international intelligence network at its disposal. Classified information on military and political matters found its way to Moscow through various channels: the Commissariat of Foreign Affairs, the Commissariat of Internal Affairs (NKVD), the Commissariat of Defense, and the Comintern. The Soviet intelligence operations in Europe and Asia were among the best in the world, not only because they were staffed by steeled professionals, such as Richard Sorge, Lev Manevich, Rado, and Trepper, but also because they had a fairly broad base of support among Western Communists, antifascists, and left intellectuals, whose devotion to communist ideals and to the first socialist country in the world led them to assist the Soviet intelligence effort. As a result, Soviet information was exceptionally reliable.

Nevertheless, during the Stalin terror of the 1930s, nearly every Soviet intelligence operative outside the country became suspect. Many of them, after returning to Moscow, were arrested in the late 1930s, along with their families, accused of high treason, and shot. Despite the enormous damage the Soviet government did in this way to its own intelligence service, it maintained a core of reliable agents.

As early as the fall of 1940 Moscow received word from Switzerland that a plan for an attack on the Soviet Union, Plan Barbarossa, was being drafted. The source of this information was an officer on the German General Staff. In early 1941 more detailed information on Plan Barbarossa reached Moscow.

Confirmation of such reports from Bern, Berlin, and Paris came from Tokyo from Sorge, whose sources had access to the most confidential documents in the Japanese government's possession. For six years Sorge had transmitted absolutely reliable information to Moscow. On several occasions he had assured the Soviet government correctly that despite the armed clashes between Japanese and Soviet forces in Mongolia, Japan would go to war against the United States, not Russia.

In early May 1941 Sorge provided Moscow with the substance of a conversation between Hitler and the Japanese ambassador in Berlin, in which Hitler revealed his intention of attacking the Soviet Union. On May 12 Sorge reported that 150 German divisions were being massed along the Soviet border and that the proposed date for the invasion was June 20. In his next report, May 15, Sorge corrected the date to June 22 and provided a rough outline of the planned operations. At the height of the German offensive against Moscow, in October 1941, Sorge informed his superiors that the Japanese government intended to attack the British and Dutch colonial possessions in Southeast Asia. On October 18, 1941, Sorge was arrested; three years later, on November 7, 1944, the Japanese government executed him by hanging. The Soviet government did not lift a finger to save him. Stalin had no desire to save the life of this or any other firsthand witness to his mistakes and crimes. Sorge's wife was arrested by the Soviet authorities and sent to a camp. Likewise, nothing was done to save Manevich, who was arrested in Italy. No wonder that a number of Soviet intelligence agents chose not to return to their homeland. Those who did were either shot or spent many years in confinement.

On March 1 and March 20, 1941, official warnings about the coming German attack were also delivered to the Soviet government by Sumner Welles, the U.S. undersecretary of state.[149]

On April 2 Churchill instructed Ambassador Stafford Cripps to meet with Stalin to give him certain vital information concerning the movement of German troops in Poland and to warn him of an imminent German invasion. Stalin and Molotov avoided meeting with the British ambassador, however.[150] Only on April 19 did Cripps succeed in relaying his information to the Commissariat of Foreign Affairs.[151]

Stalin treated all reports with distrust, suspecting British intelligence of fabricating them in order to provoke a war between the Soviet Union and Germany. To please Stalin, Filipp Golikov, head of Soviet army intelligence, told him that the possibility was not excluded that the British were inventing false reports about an imminent German attack. Nevertheless, these reports were so numerous and so consistent that it must have been hard not to conclude that the Germans actually were preparing to attack.

The Soviet border patrol likewise systematically informed the Central Committee and the government of the situation along the border. The number of "enemy spies" killed or detained while on reconnaissance on Soviet territory rose during the first quarter of 1941 to a figure fifteen to twenty times greater than in the first quarter of 1940, and during the second quarter of 1941 the figure was twenty-five to thirty times greater than in the same period of 1940.[152] In 1940 there had been 235 incidents on the Soviet western border, and several groups of German commandos wearing Red Army uniforms had been discovered. Starting in the summer of 1940, both the number and depth of penetrations into Soviet air space increased. From January to June 1941 there were 152 such incidents.[153]

On April 20, 1941, the Ukrainian frontier military district reported increased military preparations on the German side all along the border and on Hungarian territory. On June 5 the Main Frontier Troops Administration (GUPV) reported that during the months of April and May the Germans had concentrated between eighty and eighty-eight infantry divisions, thirteen to fifteen motorized divisions, seven tank divisions, sixty-five artillery regiments, and other forces along the Soviet border.

On June 6 the GUPV reported that approximately 4 million German troops had been concentrated near the Soviet border. Stalin was personally informed of this on the same day. On June 11 Stalin was informed that since June 9 the German embassy in Moscow had been burning its papers and that its personnel had been instructed to prepare for evacuation in a week's time.

On June 10 and 13 the Soviet ambassador in London, Ivan Maisky, was invited to the British Foreign Office and informed that Germany was about to launch an invasion of the Soviet Union. In the event of such an attack, Foreign Minister Anthony Eden said, Great Britain was ready to aid the Soviet Union. Similar warnings were sent to Moscow by Soviet diplomats assigned to the Vichy government in France.

Groups of anti-Nazi fighters warned the Soviet Union of the concentration of troops in Poland, Romania, and Hungary and military construction activities and other preparations for war on those territories. Among inhabitants of the regions on both sides of the border rumors that the Germans were about to attack circulated widely, and the Soviet command was fully aware of these rumors.

Nevertheless, in spite of abundant information, as well as the urgent requests by the military authorities of the border regions that at least minimal precautions be taken in case of an attack, no orders came from Moscow. Some commanders chose to act on their own authority. On June 18 Lieutenant General Bogdanov, commander of the frontier troops in the Baltic region, ordered the evacuation of the families of all military personnel and on June 20 took additional measures to strengthen border defenses.

The German ambassador, Schulenburg, returned to Moscow toward the end of April after reporting to Hitler in Berlin. He came away from his meeting with Hitler with the impression that the attack on the Soviet Union would occur in the very near future. Risking arrest on treason charges, he tried to warn the Soviet ambassador in Berlin, Dekanozov (who was also deputy commissar of foreign affairs and a confidant of Beria). Dekanozov dismissed Schulenburg's warning with the greatest suspicion, considering it a provocation.[154] (In 1944 Schulenburg took part in the plot against Hitler and was executed.)

On August 22 and 23, 1939, there had been total surprise when the Soviet press reported Ribbentrop's arrival and simultaneously printed an account of the Nazi party congress in Nuremberg, Germany. For many long years the German fascists had been denounced in the Soviet press as the most hated enemies of the Soviet Union. Now it suddenly turned out they were not fascists but National Socialists—that is, socialists of some kind. Ribbentrop, who to the Soviet press had been a warmonger, was greeted ceremoniously at the Moscow airport, which was decked with flags bearing the iron cross as well as the hammer and sickle. The newspapers showed

Ribbentrop next to Stalin, who was smiling and looking pleased. The population of course knew nothing of what went on at the meetings with Ribbentrop.

The strongest emotional reactions against Soviet–German rapprochement came from Soviet youth. At Moscow University those who presented the official account of the new development, the teachers of Marxism-Leninism, encountered angry and sarcastic questions and comments. Their confused explanations provoked outbursts of laughter.

Thousands of propagandists were sent to offices and enterprises to explain that the rapprochement was not a tactical maneuver but a change of policy of historical significance. A two-volume edition of Bismarck's memoirs was hastily prepared. He had been a strong proponent of a German–Russian alliance. Professor A. S. Jerusalimsky, the best Soviet expert on German history, was assigned to write an introduction. Stalin himself read the proofs of the introduction and made a number of changes. The main idea was summed up in these words, clearly intended for Hitler: "Bismarck saw the main danger for Germany in a conflict with Russia. ... His policy was based on an understanding of the strength and invincibility of the Russian people."[155]

On government orders, Sergei Eisenstein produced a Wagner opera at the Bolshoi Theater. Before then the German composer had not been regarded with favor, to say the least. The periodicals were filled with articles about the traditional friendship between the Russians and Germans. Forgotten were the "dog knights" whom Eisenstein himself had caricatured in *Alexander Nevsky*.

All this was far from being mere facade. In all institutions connected with foreign affairs the dismissal of people of Jewish origin began—in the commissariats of foreign affairs and foreign trade, the navy, the press agency TASS, and the main Soviet publications. Foreign diplomats and correspondents in Moscow took note of this. Jews were also removed from positions of authority in international ports, airlines, and railways. For the first time since the founding of the Soviet state anti-Semitism was becoming official policy; until then it had been camouflaged by talk about internationalism.

On some occasions official approval of the Hitler government's anti-Semitic policy was openly expressed on the local level, especially in the Ukraine and Crimea. Anti-Semitism also increased in the personnel directorates of the Red Army.

An objective analysis of the events preceding the war totally shatters the myth of a well thought out foreign and domestic policy led by the party and the Soviet government. In reality the leadership floundered helplessly, revealing a total inability to assess developments in the complicated international situation.

We have already mentioned Stalin's mistaken assumptions on how the war between Germany and the Allies would proceed. Another major error was made in regard to the Balkans in the spring of 1941—the USSR overestimated the military capacity of Yugoslavia. Stalin signed a friendship and nonaggression treaty with Yugoslavia on the eve of Germany's invasion of that country, thus repeating his error in regard to Western Europe. He counted on a prolonged war between Germany and Yugoslavia. Under the treaty, if one of the parties was attacked, the other would nevertheless maintain "a policy of friendly relations." But Yugoslavia was defeated after a very short campaign. The Soviet Union did not provide any assistance and could not have done so, for the Soviet government was fully aware of its own unpreparedness for war, and it was badly frightened by Germany's quick defeat of Yugoslavia. The uncertainty of Soviet policy reflected this fear of Germany. The government did its best not to irritate the Germans, going out of its way to show them it was ready to make additional concessions if Germany demanded them.

To the mounting concern of the Soviet government, Germany made no new demands. In April the USSR said it was ready to agree to a final line of demarcation with Germany, extending from the Igorka River to the Baltic Sea. The Soviet government also accepted the proposals made by the Germans on this question.[156] It continued to deliver raw materials and foodstuffs to Germany in the most scrupulous way, delaying its own buildup of strategic materials. German reconnaissance flights over Soviet border territory became more and more frequent, but orders were given not to fire on them. The Soviet side limited itself to diplomatic protests. In some instances German planes which landed on Soviet territory were immediately returned to the Germans even though rolls of reconnaissance film were found on board.[157]

According to memoirs of Soviet military leaders, Stalin still hoped at that late date to maintain peace with Hitler but feared some provocation by the German generals. Like Hitler, he was extremely suspicious of generals. He continued to regard all warnings from British and American sources as machinations aimed at starting a Soviet–German conflagration, at which the Western powers would warm their hands.

Stalin chose the occasion of Japanese ambassador Matsuoka's departure from Moscow to praise publicly Soviet–German "friendship." He appeared unexpectedly at the departure ceremony and greeted Schulenburg warmly: "We must remain friends and you must do everything for that." To Colonel

Krebs, the German military attaché, he said: "We must remain friends, no matter what happens."[158]

On May 5, 1941, Stalin was named chairman of the Council of People's Commissars (a position equivalent to prime minister in Western countries). This appointment put Stalin in a position to negotiate with that other premier, Chancellor Hitler, or at least that is one possible interpretation. That hypothesis is strengthened by the increasingly friendly gestures made toward Germany, such as the closing of the Moscow embassies of Belgium, Norway, and Yugoslavia (countries occupied by Germany) and the establishment of diplomatic relations with Iraq, where a profascist coup had recently occurred.

Stalin had made no public speeches since March 1939. He was obliged to show his face at last, to try to raise the morale of the Red Army commanders, who were discouraged by the events of the preceding few years (the arrests of Red Army leaders, friendship with Nazi Germany, the poor showing in the war with Finland). On May 5 he addressed the graduates of the Red Army military academies. In a forty-minute speech he called for greater mastery of the art of war and an enhanced capability to repel aggression.

Soviet willingness to make further concessions to Germany was understood by certain high-ranking officials of the Reich. Schnurre, head of the foreign trade department, expressed the opinion in a confidential memo that the Soviet Union would respond to new economic demands by Germany, thus enabling the Germans to meet their strategic needs for additional food and raw materials.[159]

Hitler continued to ignore these overtures, and the disarray in the Soviet government increased, especially after Rudolf Hess's flight to Great Britain on May 10, 1941. Stalin was convinced that this flight was part of a plan Hitler had to reach an understanding with Britain against the Soviet Union. In reality Hess took his action without Hitler's knowledge. For Britain Hess's flight was confirmation that Hitler was determined to invade the Soviet Union but feared having to fight a two-front war. Hess suggested that Europe be divided into two spheres of influence, one for Britain, one for Germany, and that Soviet territory as far as the Urals should go to Germany. Knowing Germany's intentions and understanding that Hess spoke for no one but himself, Britain chose to inform the Soviets of the Hess affair. For Stalin this was one more confirmation of his suspicion that Britain and Germany were intriguing against the USSR; to him the British warnings were nothing but attempts by the British imperialists to provoke a war with Germany.

It was impossible to ignore the real situation, however. Germany was building up its troop concentrations on the Soviet border, as was widely reported by the world press and attested to daily by the commanders of the military districts along the border.

Little by little Stalin was losing hope that Hitler would suggest new talks, and his alarm over the Soviet lack of preparedness for war mounted accordingly. It was under these conditions that on June 14 TASS issued a communiqué referring to foreign rumors that Germany had made new demands on the Soviet Union, that talks were underway aimed at reaching a new and more solid agreement, and that both countries had built up their troops along their common border. TASS denied that Germany had made new demands; hence new talks could not have occurred. The Soviet side had respected the nonaggression pact and would continue to do so. The rumors concerning Soviet preparations for war with Germany were "false and provocative."[160] This communiqué seemed to be an overture to Germany to clarify its intentions and initiate new talks, but again there was no German reaction. The TASS communiqué had a demoralizing effect on the Soviet military, since it seemed to deny that there was any danger of war.

On June 18 a German sergeant crossed over to the Soviet side with the warning that at 4 AM on June 22 German troops would go on the offensive all along the Soviet border. The next day, as if in mockery of this warning, *Pravda* published an editorial entitled "Summer Vacation for the Toilers."

Stalin was still hoping that Berlin would invite him to the negotiating table. Even as late as the evening of June 21, when more and more alarming reports were coming in, Stalin told Defense Commissar Timoshenko: "We are starting a panic over nothing."

On June 21, at 11 PM another German, Private Alfred Liskof, defected to the Soviet side and warned that his army would attack at four the next morning. At the same time Soviet military intelligence received one more report from Berlin that the invasion was set for June 22. According to some estimates, the Soviet government received as many as eighty-four advance warnings of the German attack.[161]

Despite the immense resources invested in building fortifications on the western border, these works were in total disarray when the Soviet–German war began. The construction of fortifications along the old border (the one predating September 17, 1939) had begun in 1929 and went on until 1935, creating fortified lines of reinforced concrete to a depth of two to three kilometers. To give an idea of how outdated these fortifications were, it should suffice to say that they were built with redoubts armed with nothing more than machine guns and provided no protection against 155mm or 210mm artillery fire. In 1938 the modernization of these installations and their armaments, which had begun, was postponed in accordance with a decision to alter the entire system of fortified districts and lines of fortifications. No sooner had construction of new fortifications begun than the border was moved westward. Orders were issued to stop work on the fortification along the old border. Work began on fortified districts on the new border, but it soon turned out that the most important considerations—the potential strength of the enemy and of Soviet defenses in the fortified districts—had not been taken into account. More time was lost in drawing up new designs and specifications. Then the main effort was put into fortifying the Baltic Military District. The Soviet command wrongly assumed that the main enemy blow would come from East Prussia, aiming at the Baltic region. At the end of March 1941, when it turned out that a major concentration of German troops was concentrated south of Polesye, it was decided to fortify the Kiev Military District. At that point the necessary materials and equipment to strengthen the Kiev district were lacking. Of the 2,500 fortifications built along the new border, only 1,000 were fully equipped with artillery. The rest had machine guns only. The armaments had been removed from the fortifications on the old border and the installations turned into—storage sites for the local kolkhozes. The old border, along which Soviet troops could have established a second line of defense in the event of a retreat, was left bare, while the new border was insufficiently fortified and armed.

Matters were no better in regard to the building of new airfields or new airstrips at existing fields, or new railroads and terminals. A. Zaporozhets, head of the main political directorate of the Red Army, reported to Timoshenko: "The majority of the fortified districts along our western border are for the most part inoperative."

Official Soviet historians generally justify these grave shortcomings with the argument that the Soviet Union did not have enough time to prepare for the war. Such statements do not correspond to reality. For many years the officially stated policy was to keep the country in a state of permanent mobilization. The population had been taught for years that it should be ready to make any and all sacrifices in order to strengthen the nation's defenses, and real sacrifices had been made. The Soviet government did have both the time and the resources to prepare the country for war, but owing to the incompetence of the leadership the enormous resources extracted from the population were uselessly squandered and the gigantic investments failed to produce the results they should have.

In 1940 and early 1941 the government issued several decrees on the army's lack of preparedness and the inadequacies in the construction of fortifications and provision of arms and equipment. Only 50 percent of the armored formations and motorized units had new arms and equipment; for the air force in the border districts the figure was only 22 percent.[162]

The military high command also committed serious errors in its assessment of how the enemy forces were deployed and what their plans and intentions were. As Marshal Zhukov, the man who became chief of the General Staff in February 1941, later admitted in his memoirs, "The most dangerous situation strategically was in the Southwestern Direction, that is, the Ukraine, and the Western Direction, that is, Byelorussia, for in June 1941 the Nazi command had concentrated its most important land and air forces in those areas."[163]

The Soviet high command wrongly believed that the main blow would come from East Prussia and would strike at Riga, Kaunas (Polotsk), and Minsk, and from the Brest region, along the Baranovichi–Minsk line. In reality the German high command had decided to strike its main blow just north of the Polesye region in Byelorussia. The Soviet command expected an offensive south of the Polesye. One must conclude that the Soviet leadership totally disregarded all of the information provided by its intelligence network, which had provided thoroughgoing details of the German plans.

The defense plan for the western border also had serious flaws. It envisaged an immediate counteroffensive as soon as the Germans struck. It did not foresee that the enemy would be able to penetrate deep into Soviet territory; yet the high command was well aware of the weakness of its border defense lines. Maneuvers in January 1941 had shown clearly, for example, that Soviet forces would find themselves in great danger if the enemy penetrated as far as Bialystok and Lvov.

In addition to all this, when fighting actually broke out, the commanders of the military districts on the border were paralyzed and deprived of all initiative when orders were issued not to fight back, so as to avoid giving any pretext for armed action by the Germans.

# 8

# THE WAR, 1941–1945

## TO THE BRINK OF DEFEAT

To the very last, Stalin expected a sign from Hitler. On the evening of June 21, when he heard about the defector Liskof, Stalin reacted in his usual manner. "Haven't the German generals sent this defector over to provoke a conflict?" he asked Timoshenko, the commissar of defense.[1] Stalin apparently could not imagine that Hitler would start a war against the Soviet Union. He preferred to believe that the German generals, intoxicated with their military successes, wanted to provoke such a war. Besides, Stalin knew only too well that his country was not ready, that Soviet military plans were geared to the year 1942. Also, Stalin was simply afraid. He grew indecisive; it seems that he desperately yearned to postpone the inevitable. Possibly he was hoping for a miracle.

What about his "comrades-in-arms," the other members of the Politburo? Zhukov states in his memoirs that Stalin briefly informed them of the situation and asked, "'What shall we do?' No answer was forthcoming."[2] Finally, Timoshenko suggested that an order be issued immediately, placing all troops on full military alert. The draft of the order was read, but Stalin rejected it. He suggested that perhaps everything could still be settled peacefully.

Nevertheless the intelligence information received by the Soviet government and military proved to be correct: on June 22 at four in the morning,

Germany and its allies, Romania, Hungary, and Slovakia, went on the offensive along the entire German–Soviet border.

From the first hours of the invasion, the commanders of the border regions, disoriented by Moscow's orders, began to lose contact with their troops. It was not until the night of June 21, at 12:30 AM, that they received Timoshenko's order warning them of a possible German offensive on June 22 or 23 along the southwestern and western borders. The order began with the following strange formulation: "The task of our troops is to resist any provocation which could lead to major complications."

This meant that the Kremlin at that point was still hoping for a miracle to avert the war. The commanders of the border regions were to place their troops on a state of full alert, ready to meet any possible offensive by the Germans or their allies, and for this purpose, were to occupy quietly the firing positions in the fortified areas along the borders, order a state of alert for the anti-aircraft defenses, camouflage and disperse aircraft and troops, put the air defense forces on a state of alert, and take measures to black out cities and other targets. The last point of the order said: "No other measures are to be taken without special orders."[3]

Marshal Malinovsky reported that when he asked whether to open fire on the enemy if he invaded Soviet territory, the answer was, "Do not give in to any provocations and do not open fire."[4] Once the German offensive had started, Timoshenko warned General Boldin, the deputy commander of the Western Military District, "I am informing you and asking you to inform Pavlov [the district commander] that comrade Stalin has not authorized artillery fire against the Germans." Boldin started to shout into the telephone: "How can that be! Our troops are being forced to retreat. Cities are burning and people are dying." He insisted that mechanized units be called into action immediately, as well as artillery and anti-aircraft guns. Timoshenko answered: "Do not take any measures other than reconnaissance missions into enemy territory, to a depth of no more than sixty kilometers."[5]

It was not until the evening of June 22, when the situation became critical because of the deep penetration by German tanks, that the front-line commanders were issued orders to launch "heavy counterattacks to destroy the enemy's main forces and drive operations back onto enemy territory."[6] This surrealistic order reflected a complete misunderstanding of the real situation and a total disregard, or ignorance, of the facts on the part of the Soviet military and political leadership.

The facts were as follows: The concentration of German forces and their allies numbered 190 divisions, or 4.6 million soldiers, including 17 tank divisions and 13 motorized divisions, 50,000 cannons and mortars, some

5,000 aircraft, and more than 3,700 tanks. Of these divisions, 153 were German, constituting more than 70 percent of the German army. Counting reinforcement units, the German troop strength alone amounted to 3.3 million.[7]

At the beginning of the war the Soviet armed forces numbered 5 million,[8] and 170 divisions and 2 brigades were concentrated in the western border regions—that is, 54 percent of the entire Red Army, or about 2.9 million men. The first line of defense consisted of 56 divisions and 2 brigades, dispersed over a depth of up to 50 kilometers from the border. The second line of defense was positioned 50–100 kilometers inside Soviet territory, and the reserves 150–400 kilometers from the border.[9]

In the zones where the Germans concentrated their most devastating blows, their superiority in numbers was considerable, from 1.8 to 2.2 times the Soviet troop strength. Soviet forces had at their disposal 1,800 late model tanks, some 34,700 cannon, 1,540 late model airplanes, and a large number of obsolete aircraft and tanks.[10]

Thus, the German army enjoyed an absolute advantage both in number of troops and in armaments. It also had considerable experience in modern warfare and a well-trained officer corps.

At 4:15 AM, when Germany launched its offensive, its air force made devastating bombing raids on all Soviet airfields near the border. On the first day of the war, 1,200 Soviet planes were destroyed,[11] the vast majority of them not even having a chance to take off. Railroad terminals and lines of communication were put out of commission, arms and ammunition dumps seized or destroyed: for some unknown reasons, these depots were located too close to the border.

While isolating centers of resistance by Soviet troops, the German command developed its offensive toward the east. Toward the end of the first day, the German tanks had advanced as many as sixty kilometers toward Brest and had occupied Kobrin.[12]

On the evening of June 22 Timoshenko ordered the Northwestern, Western, and Southwestern fronts to go on the offensive in all main directions, to smash the enemy, and to drive operations back onto enemy territory. Besides not corresponding to the real situation at the front, this order was truly criminal because it forced the commanders to send their troops into certain encirclement, under murderous fire. Similar orders were issued to the troops in the Baltic Military District by their commanding general, F. F. Kuznetsov. Tens of thousands of casualties and hundreds of thousands of prisoners were the price the Soviet people paid for the disarray and incompetence of the military high command, the Politburo, and Stalin himself.

It was not until the fourth day that Soviet General Headquarters (Stavka Glavnogo Komandovaniya) understood the unrealistic nature of its orders to counterattack. At that point, German troops had already penetrated between 130 and 150 kilometers into Soviet territory. On June 28, one week after the war began, Minsk, the capital of Byelorussia, fell, and 319,000 prisoners and huge stocks of armaments fell into enemy hands.

On the Northwestern Front, scattered Red Army units, completely deprived of command, hastily withdrew toward the Western Dvina. But this natural border could not be held: the columns of German tanks crossed the Western Dvina, took Daugavpils, and on July 9 took Pskov without even stopping.

It was only in the Lutsk-Brody and Rovno region, at the junction of the Southwestern and Southern fronts, that Soviet troops inflicted heavy casualties on the Germans in a bloody tank battle; this delayed the German advance for a week, but Soviet forces soon had to pull back to the old border, to the Korosten, Novograd-Volynsky, and Proskurov regions.

On the Western Front, after bitter clashes, Soviet troops were forced to withdraw to the Dnepr. And on the Southwestern Front, in early July, the Germans had taken Berdichev and Zhitomir.

After three weeks of fighting, the German army had penetrated a distance of 300–600 kilometers into Soviet territory. It had occupied Latvia, Lithuania, Byelorussia, the Ukraine up to the right bank of the Dnepr, and almost the whole of Moldavia. Russia had not experienced such a disaster since the time of Napoleon. During World War I the Russian generals, whom Soviet historians accuse of incompetence, never suffered such devastating blows.

The German army's losses were heavy: from June 22 to July 13, they reached approximately 92,000, or 3.68 percent of the German troops on the Soviet front.[13] But these losses were nothing compared to those of the Red Army.

Through the middle of July a vast and hard-fought battle raged along a front 1,400 kilometers long, between the Polesye region and the mouth of the Danube. On August 8 the Germans succeeded in crossing the Dnepr between Kiev and Kremenchug. Stubborn resistance continued for a month and a half. Budenny, commander of the Southwestern Direction (in Soviet terms, a "direction" included several "fronts," whereas a Soviet "front" was the equivalent of an "army group" in Western military terminology), requested authorization from General Headquarters to abandon Kiev and its fortified region and withdraw his troops from the Dnepr to the Psel river. General Headquarters refused. As a result, the Germans encircled four Soviet armies, most of whose many soldiers were killed or taken prisoner.

According to one account, General M. P. Kirponos, commander of the Southwestern Front, committed suicide, as did some of the members of his headquarters staff.[14]

Upon taking Kiev, the German Army Group South launched an offensive aimed at Kharkov, the Donbass, and the Crimea. East of Kiev, the Germans headed toward Bryansk and Orel, with the objective of taking Moscow. By the end of September 1941 the situation was truly critical.

## THE GOVERNMENT, THE PEOPLE, AND THE WAR

Eight hours after the German invasion began, at noon on June 22, 1941, Molotov, the deputy premier, went on the radio to inform the Soviet people of the treacherous German attack. Stalin chose not to speak. He had reason enough for that decision, for his policies were now exposed as total failures, in particular his friendship and collaboration with Germany and his failure to prepare the country for war. He was in the habit of associating his name with all Soviet victories and achievements, and he certainly did not want his name identified with defeat. For several days Stalin seems to have been in shock. He secluded himself in his dacha at Kuntsevo outside Moscow and in effect withdrew from the affairs of state. Not until a number of days had passed, and after other members of the Politburo had pressured him (as was made known at the Twentieth Party Congress in 1956) did he return to his duties.

It took another week before the Soviet leadership sent its first directive to party and government organizations in the front-line areas and another five days before Stalin went on the radio to announce this program of action to the population, on July 3, 1941. He was obliged to tell the people that the enemy had made deep inroads into the Soviet Union. At this moment of crisis Stalin, who had deprived millions of their homes, property, and rights during collectivization, who had created a system of slave labor camps, who had executed the best military leaders and the cream of the intelligentsia, who had shot or imprisoned millions of Soviet citizens, issued a pleading call to his "brothers and sisters."[15]

In this difficult hour the best and noblest instincts were aroused among the people: the spirit of self-sacrifice, the feeling of responsibility for the country, and a sense of patriotic duty. In the threatened areas, entire divisions of popular militia (*opolchenie*) were formed, as well as special units to guard against German paratroops, and labor battalions to build new lines of fortifications. The recruitment stations were flooded with volunteers.

In Leningrad alone ten divisions of popular militia were formed; together with other volunteer formations, they totaled 159,000.[16] In Moscow there were twelve divisions, totaling about 120,000. In Kiev 29,000 joined. It was not only the industrial workers who entered these units, but the intellectuals as well—teachers, students, artists, musicians, writers, scientists. Most of them had no military training, and there was neither the time nor the necessary weapons and supplies to provide it.

To understand better the situation in which the country found itself by fall of 1941, let us hear the testimony of a major witness, Nikita Khrushchev, who was then the first secretary of the Central Committee of the Ukrainian Communist party:

> The situation quickly turned very bad, mostly because there was so little help forthcoming from Moscow. Shortly after the war started, during the German advance on Kiev, there was a great awakening of patriotism among the people. The workers from the "Lenin Forge" and other factories around Kiev came to the Central Committee in droves asking for rifles so that they could fight back against the invaders. I phoned Moscow to arrange for a shipment of weapons with which to arm these citizens who wanted to join the Front in support of Red Power. The only person I could get through to was Malenkov. "Tell me," I said, "where can we get rifles? We've got factory workers here who want to join the ranks of the Red Army to fight the Germans, and we don't have anything to arm them with." "You'd better give up any thought of getting rifles from us. The rifles in the civil defense organization here have all been sent to Leningrad." "Then what are we supposed to fight with?" "I don't know—pikes, swords, homemade weapons, anything you can make in your own factories." "You mean we should fight tanks with spears?" "You'll have to do the best you can. You can make fire bombs out of bottles of gasoline or kerosene and throw them at the tanks."
>
> You can imagine my dismay and indignation when I heard Malenkov talking this way. Here we were, trying to hold back an invasion without rifles and machine guns, not to mention artillery or mechanized weapons! I didn't dare tell anyone what Malenkov had said to me. Who knows what the reaction would have been. I certainly couldn't tell the people how bad the situation was. But the people must have figured out on their own how woefully underequipped we were. And why were we so badly armed? Because of complacency in the Commissariat of Defense and demoralization and defeatism in the leadership. These factors had kept us from building up our munitions industry and fortifying our borders. And now it was too late.[17]

(Naturally Khrushchev did not say a word about the fact that in the Ukraine, particularly in the western region, in certain instances the population actually welcomed the Germans as liberators.)

Initially the mobilization affected all men born between 1905 and 1918 and capable of bearing arms; in the last year or two of the war the draft was extended to those born through 1927.

In the regions west of the Yaroslavl–Ryazan–Rostov-on-the-Don line, martial law was decreed and the organizing of popular militias and anti-paratroop units began.

On December 26, 1941, a law decreed the mobilization of all industrial and office workers in the war industry who had not been drafted. Unauthorized departure from a job in any of these enterprises was equivalent to desertion. Forced overtime was instituted; all holidays were suspended for the duration of the war. The workday was increased to between ten and twelve hours, and in the cities where a state of emergency existed, such as Leningrad and Tula, the workday had no end. Transportation workers and office workers were also mobilized.

The country's human resources were sharply reduced at the very beginning of the war, because a significant portion of the Soviet Union was quickly occupied by the enemy. Moreover, in the first few months of war millions of Soviet soldiers were either killed, wounded, or captured.

With a large percentage of the male population called off to war, they were replaced on the job by women aged sixteen to fifty-five, who had to take over the heavy work of men: stoking furnaces, handling hot metal, operating heavy machinery. People over sixty and adolescents of fourteen and older were also brought into the factories.

On June 30, 1941, the State Committee for Defense was formed, an emergency body, which concentrated all power in its hands. Stalin was its chairman, Molotov its vice-chairman, Voroshilov and Malenkov initially its other two members. Later, the committee was filled out with Beria, Bulganin, Voznesensky, Kaganovich, and Mikoyan. Local defense committees were also created, each consisting of the first secretary of the local party organization, the chairman of the local soviet, and representatives of the local army and state security units.[18]

In the threatened regions, the evacuation of factories and specialists to the eastern parts of the Soviet Union began. Thus, 1,500 factories were relocated to the Volga region, the Urals, Siberia, Kazakhstan, and Central Asia. Some estimates put the evacuated population at 10 million. But the great mass fled eastward without waiting, leaving homes and belongings. In areas farther from the front, evacuation was better organized. The factories moved to the east began producing for the front rather quickly. Workers and engineers toiled under the harshest conditions. The construction of industrial sites took place during the fall of 1941 and the winter of 1941–42, which was very severe. The factories were reconstructed with great speed: four months after being dismantled, many were already producing at full capacity. The workday was from twelve to fourteen hours long. Workers lived under the most unimaginable conditions, often in mud huts or tents. Food was in short supply.

The reconversion of the economy was basically completed during the first year of war. This was a particularly difficult time. Industrial production was 2.1 times lower than before the war. During the first six months of the war the output of ferrous metals decreased by a factor of 3.1 and that of nonferrous metals by a factor of 430(!). Ball bearing production was twenty-one times less than before the war.[19]

Airplane production also dropped sharply. In the last quarter of 1941, it was less than half that of the third quarter. In December 1941, only 35 percent of the plan for aircraft production was completed. At that point, four-fifths of the aeronautics industry was being transferred to the east. The plan for tank production for the second half of 1941 was completed by 61.7 percent. Ammunition production reached only 50–60 percent of that foreseen in the plan.[20]

During the war, the standard of living of the urban population was very low. The rationing system barely provided the minimum. People had to turn to the black market, where prices were astronomical. Many city dwellers went out into the rural areas regularly to exchange clothing or utensils for food. Practically all the earnings of the city dwellers went for food or rent. Industrial workers, especially those in heavy industry, received "first category" rations: 800 to 1,000 or 1,200 grams of bread per day (bread being the staple of the diet). Workers in other branches of industry were assigned to the second category: 500 grams. Office workers were allotted between 400 and 450; children up to twelve years of age, housewives, and other dependents received 300–400 grams. The usual monthly allowances of meat or fish were 1,800 grams; fats, 400 grams; macaroni or groats, 1,300 grams; sugar or sweets, 400 grams. There were also the categories of "higher rations" and "special higher" rations. Many industrial and office workers turned their ration cards over to the dining halls at their places of employment and had all their meals there. The privileged stratum (the party and government officials) had their own system of provisioning, which was very different from that of ordinary mortals, both qualitatively and quantitatively.

Many offices and firms were assigned collective farm lands as subsidiary enterprises that could be drawn upon to help feed their staffs. Industrial and office workers in the cities had received small private plots, to grow potatoes and other vegetables for their personal needs. During the war these gardens became the primary source of food for hundreds of thousands of families. Basic items like shoes, clothing, and textiles also became rare luxuries during the war. From time to time, some factories paid their workers with coupons usable for the purchase of shoes and clothing; these coupons, as well as the items they were supposed to buy, became the object of black market speculation.

The already critical housing situation was greatly complicated by the war, especially in Kazakhstan, Kirghizia, Uzbekistan, and the other Central Asian republics, where many evacuees went. The refugees concentrated in cities and regions where they could find industrial work and public services. The situation for those who did not find work in their field and were forced to perform agricultural tasks was even worse. Unfamiliar with the work, their productivity was far below that of the collective farmers; their earnings and living standards were accordingly quite low.

Almost half the cultivated land in the Soviet Union fell to the Germans, who soon controlled areas that had produced more than half the country's grain and animal products. The Germans were able to seize crops that had been harvested but not yet shipped, as well as tractors, combines, and other agricultural machinery. In the areas not reached by the Germans, livestock were removed, and tractors, trucks, and horses were mobilized for the war effort. Agriculture was thus deprived of hauling power. Almost all able-bodied men were either at the front, in German captivity, or in Soviet prison camps. Only the very young or the very old, the women, and the sick remained in the villages. Cows were used to till the land, and when there were none, women would harness themselves to the plow. Many farming tasks were done by hand. Virtually the entire harvest was turned over to the state in the form of obligatory deliveries. The amount to be delivered was frequently determined on the basis not of the actual harvest but of an imaginary "projected harvest," approximately 25 percent higher. Failure to meet these obligations was severely punished; people could even be sent to jail, as though they had been found guilty of sabotage. Often no seed grain was left for the next season's planting. The situation was particularly bad in Central Russia, where even before the war the peasants had had trouble making ends meet. The war put the finishing touches on the ruination of the collective farmers. The only hope was the small private plot each peasant household was allowed to cultivate. The produce from this could be used for personal consumption or profitably sold to city dwellers or exchanged for needed items. The peasants in the warmer regions of Transcaucasia and Central Asia, where they had some livestock, vegetables, fruit crops, and oil-producing crops, were better off.

All around the country, collections were taken for the Red Army. Objects of value, money, jewels, government bonds, all poured into the national defense fund. Money was also raised for particular projects, such as tank columns or airplanes. Often, in areas far from the front, enormous sums were contributed by individual "collective farmers" (100,000, 200,000 rubles). Where did this money come from? From the astronomical prices charged for food on the black market, where speculators built up enormous fortunes during the war. They contributed a tiny portion of their gains to the national defense fund. Thus, a part of the money cruelly extorted from the population, especially the evacuees, was placed at the disposal of the state. These donors were trumpeted as exemplary patriots, written about in the newspapers, and extolled over the radio.

No sooner had the war begun than the system of "socialist national relations" began to shake apart. The first fissures appeared in the newly acquired regions, the Baltic states and the western parts of Byelorussia and the Ukraine. The policy of "purges" and deportations of nationals, among the first measures carried out by the new Soviet authorities in 1939–1940, had aroused sufficient fear and hatred among the population for them to welcome the Germans as liberators. The situation was not much better in the regions of the interior, a fact which can be blamed on the regime, with its policy of repression.

In August 1941 the autonomous republic of the Volga Germans was abolished. These were German settlers who had come to the Volga region two centuries earlier. The Volga Germans were accused of collaborating with Nazi Germany, when in fact they were among the most loyal inhabitants of Russia. They were deported to the East and the Far North.

Thus, the first blows against harmonious relations among nationalities in the Soviet Union were dealt by the Soviet state itself, not the invading enemy.

In late 1943 and early 1944, several nationalities of the Northern Caucasus region were deported, also on charges of collaborating with the enemy: the Chechens, Ingush, Balkars, and Karachai. They were followed soon after by the Kalmyks and Crimean Tatars. At the same time, other non-Russian peoples were removed from the shores of the Black Sea: Greeks, Bulgarians, and Krymchaks. Their fate was soon shared by the Kurds and the Khemshins. Plans were made to deport the Abkhazians, too. In all cases where a deported nationality had its own autonomous region, that administrative structure was abolished. The deportations affected over 1 million people, most of them Muslims.[21] They were crowded into cattlecars and shipped off to Siberia, the Urals, and Central Asia. The aim of the deportations was essentially to have a more "reliable" (i.e., Russian) population along the Soviet borders and in areas where there was tension.

Russians and Ukrainians were brought in to replace the deported populations in the towns and villages of the Northern Caucasus, the Stavropol region, and the Crimea.

The deportees lived under very crowded conditions and in great deprivation. Tens of thousands died of starvation and disease while being deported or in the first years of adjustment to their new status and location. They were restricted to "special settlements," where they existed under constant close surveillance, not allowed to move about as they pleased. No books, magazines, or newspapers in their native languages were published, and teaching the mother tongue in the schools was forbidden. They no longer had access to university education.

In Transcaucasia, despite the fact that German troops reached the Greater Caucasus Range in the fall of 1942, the situation was relatively stable among the non-Russian nationalities, although in the mountains there were armed groups hostile to Soviet rule. The large concentration of NKVD troops and Red Army units in the region was one of the most powerful arguments against any attempt to revolt. Moreover, the nationalities of Transcaucasia saw no practical way to protect themselves other than by loyal support to the Soviet state. The entry of Soviet troops into Iran at the beginning of the war, the alliance between the USSR, England, and the United States, and the traditional enmity toward Turkey (especially on the part of Armenians) were also contributing factors.

In the republics of Central Asia, the nationalities situation during the war was complicated by the influx of refugees, evacuees, and deportees. The war effort required the creation of a new economic infrastructure in the region, an increase in the production of cotton and nonferrous metals, exploration for and exploitation of new sources of raw materials, and the exploitation of such sources when found. The influx of Russians, Ukrainians, and others substantially changed the economy and culture of Central Asia, particularly in relation to urban growth and development, for it was in the cities that the bulk of the new Russian population concentrated. According to an Uzbek demographer,

> Before the 1950s, and particularly in the years before and during the Great Patriotic War, the industrialization of the peripheral national regions, including the republics of Central Asia, and the strong migration of Russians into these regions (as well as Ukrainians, Byelorussians, and some other nationalities), brought as a consequence a noticeable decrease in the proportion of the population constituted by the nationalities originally inhabiting the union republics of Central Asia, as well as the autonomous republics and regions of the area.[22]

The weight and influence of Russians in the local administration and, above all, in local industry rose in proportion to the influx of Russians, while the Russian language and Soviet Russian culture penetrated more deeply into the native milieu. This had the political side effect of heightening the interdependence of the local elite and the "all-union" bureaucracy.

During the war, the population of the Gulag was sharply increased by the deportees from the Baltic states, western Poland, Moldavia, and the Caucasus, as well as by Crimean Tatars, Volga Germans, "defeatist elements," "*okruzhentsy*" (troops who had been encircled by the Germans), and other unfortunates. The detainees were put to work building airports, landing strips, and roads in the Far North. It was they, not enthusiastic Communist youth, as tourist guides today claim, who built Magadan, the capital of the Kolyma region. It was also they who built the underground hangars near Kuibyshev and the airports and landing strips at Soroka, Onega, Kargopol, on the northern Dvina, and in the northern Urals and Pechora regions. The slave labor of prisoners was used in war plants, the expansion of port facilities on the Arctic Ocean, and the construction of roads in Siberia and Transcaucasia. Prisoners died by the thousands from undernourishment and fatigue and from the inhuman treatment meted out by the guards and administrators, by the entire NKVD system, which was aimed at breaking and destroying the human personality. The loss of life among camp inmates proceeded at a preplanned rate. Those assigned to heavy labor lived no more than three years as a rule. New prisoners were brought in to replace the dead; and the process went on without end.

As we have said, the camps were swelled with the victims of the "purges" in the newly annexed territories of western Poland, Lithuania, Latvia, Estonia, Bessarabia, and Northern Bukovina. From 1939 to 1941, 1,060,000 Polish citizens were deported to Siberia and the Urals. This deportation began with the Soviet–German pact ushering in a new partition of Poland.[23]

Estimates vary on the number of Poles sent to "corrective labor camps." According to information at the time, there were 200,000; but more recent information compiled by Robert Conquest suggests there were 440,000 in the labor camps; the remaining 620,000 were sent either to prisoner of war camps or enforced settlements in remote areas.

Two hundred thousand people were deported from the Baltic countries, that is, 4 percent of the combined total population of 5 million. Of these, between 50,000 and 60,000 ended up in the labor camps. Two hundred thousand were also deported from Bessarabia. Many Volga Germans, representatives of an "enemy nationality," likewise were sent to the camps;

later some of the Crimean Tatars, Kalmyks, and peoples of the Northern Caucausus deported in 1943–1944 also ended up in the camps.

The slave labor force was also replenished with inmates convicted under a law prohibiting theft of state property, which dated from August 1932. Usually this meant the culprit had stolen a loaf of bread or a pair of shoes, or, often, had picked some leftover potatoes or ears of grain from an already harvested field.

There were new categories as well: those convicted of "spreading rumors" or "sowing panic," and those who had failed to bring in their radios. (At the beginning of the war a government decree ordered that all citizens surrender their radio sets to be kept in state storage until the end of the war.) By the late summer of 1941, the *okruzhentsy* began to arrive in the camps, soldiers who had been encircled by the Germans because of the errors of their commanders or the conditions of war and who had miraculously escaped. As a general rule, all these categories were sentenced to ten years in the camps. After the Battle of Moscow, those suspected of having stayed in the city, rather than fleeing or being evacuated, were rounded up. It was said they had planned to welcome the Germans in Moscow.

Later additions to the camps were those who had collaborated with the enemy: the German-appointed *Bürgermeisters* and village elders, those who had served in the German-sponsored police in occupied areas (the so-called Polizei), members of nationalist organizations, "Vlasovites" (supporters of General Vlasov, discussed later in this chapter), and German and Japanese war criminals. A 1943 law providing for death by hanging or condemnation to hard labor was applied to the last several categories.[24]

Prisoners in all these categories were sent to Mine No. 17 at Vorkuta, later to Norilsk and Dzhezkazgan. These in effect were death camps where existence was so dreadful that many preferred to throw themselves under the wheels of the railcars carrying ore or coal.

Researchers estimate that between 1939 and 1941 alone, 1.8 million prisoners died in the camps.

Stalin, who was interested in creating the impression in the West that the Soviet Union was a humanitarian state, authorized a visit to Magadan in 1944 by the American vice-president, Henry Wallace, who was accompanied by Owen Lattimore, the noted Far Eastern expert. Wallace was very enthusiastic about what he saw. And he was shown very impressive things: a dairy farm, greenhouses where vegetables were grown, needlework produced by prisoners. Under orders from Moscow, the notoriously cruel Nikishov, director of Dalstroi (the Far Northern Construction Project, the euphemistic official name for the vast and deadly prison labor system in the Kolyma region), gave his important visitors a grand reception. Prisoners were shut up in their barracks; watch towers were taken down; male and female NKVD personnel masqueraded as prisoners, impressing the Americans with their health and vigor. On their return to the United States, Wallace and Lattimore wrote quite favorably about Nikishov, the NKVD, and the Soviet system.[25] Later, when Wallace ran against Truman in the presidential elections, the Soviet press spoke of Wallace in glowing terms.

## VICTORY AT MOSCOW

On September 24, 1941, the German high command adopted a new plan for an offensive aimed at Moscow; it was given the code name Typhoon. The German strategic idea was to launch an uninterrupted offensive from Smolensk to Moscow and take the capital by storm. The operation was entrusted to Army Group Center, under the command of General von Bock. At his disposal he had over 1 million soldiers: 44 infantry divisions, 8 motorized infantry divisions, 24 tank divisions (1,700 tanks), over 14,000 guns and mortars, and 950 fighter planes. The Soviet forces in front of Moscow had 95 divisions, 6,800 guns and mortars, 780 tanks, and 545 planes. Thus, the Germans had twice as many tanks and guns as the Russians, and almost twice as many planes.[26]

The German offensive began on September 30 and by October 2 had broken through Soviet lines at several places. As a result the main forces of the Soviet Western Front and "Reserve Front" were encircled in the Vyazma region. "At the moment when the German tank units pierced the Vyazma defense lines, no intermediate lines of defense were left between Vyazma and the Mozhaisk line, nor were there any troops capable of slowing the enemy tank units in their rush toward Moscow," says the official Soviet history of the war.[27]

By October 14 resistance by Soviet troops in the Vyazma pocket had been broken. The cream of the Moscow intelligentsia, who had volunteered for the people's militia divisions (opolchenie), were killed in this battle. Many had not even learned how to fire a rifle. It was not a battle but a slaughter. The fate of Jewish volunteers who were taken prisoner was particularly tragic; almost all of them were exterminated. The destruction of the Moscow volunteer corps, which went into battle totally untrained, sent by the command to ward off the blow of the professional German army, remains one of the most tragic pages in the history of the Nazi–Soviet war.

According to German statistics (Soviet sources do not mention the losses), the German army captured 663,000 prisoners, 1,242 tanks, and 5,412 guns at Vyazma.[28]

During the morning of October 15, rumors of the defeat at Vyazma spread through Moscow. Orders were given for the immediate evacuation of offices and staffs, both military and civilian. It was considered possible that the Germans might reach Moscow within twenty-four hours. Train stations were filled with people being evacuated to accompany their enterprises to new locations in the East. But there was also an "unorganized" population fleeing from the Germans. All roads east were crowded with vehicles and pedestrians. Many took nothing but a few possessions in knapsacks on their backs. It was a veritable exodus. The authorities in Moscow seemed paralyzed. Here and there, looting occurred in the suburbs. The panic reached its climax on October 16. There were cases of military personnel hastily changing into civilian clothes. Religious people prayed. Some people were convinced that all was lost, that the end of human civilization had come. Not until twenty-five years after the war, however, was acknowledgment made in an official publication that Moscow had been seized with panic.[29] Nevertheless, the majority did not lose faith in the nation's ability to resist. During those difficult October days tens of thousands of Muscovites went out to build defense lines, and many of them were killed.

On October 19 a state of siege was declared in Moscow. The defense of the capital was entrusted to General Zhukov, commander of the Western Front. On the eve of the renewed German thrust Zhukov hastily brought reserves to the capital. The attack began on November 15–16. The forces of the German army maintained their superiority over the Soviet army in terms of artillery (2.5 to 1) and tanks (1.5 to 1), but this time, the Soviet air force outnumbered the German (1.5 to 1). The British and Americans had sent a large number of airplanes, tanks, and other arms.

Extremely bitter fighting ensued. In spite of their heavy losses, the Germans kept advancing toward Moscow. The Soviet troops fought tenaciously, defending every inch of soil. An example of the heroism of those defending the approaches to Moscow was the feat of thirty-three soldiers of General Panfilov's division who stopped the advance of German tanks at the Dubosekovo crossroads at the price of their lives.

Soon the German offensive showed signs of running out of steam. Tula, one of Russia's most important industrial centers, 182 kilometers southwest of Moscow, was encircled, but did not fall. Nevertheless, the main German tank forces were stopped only 29 kilometers from Moscow. Reconnaissance elements of some German tank units reached Moscow's western outskirts. But by then the German offensive had petered out. German losses had been heavy: 155,000 killed, wounded, or frozen; 800 tanks and 300 heavy guns lost.[30]

The German high command did not have enough reserves to continue the offensive. The freezing weather also helped to bring the Germans to a stop.

During those first six months of war, the Soviet armed forces and their leadership had acquired considerable military expertise; for the first time the Germans encountered serious opposition. The Soviet soldiers were fighting for their homeland, and that gave them added strength.

On December 5–6 the Soviet army launched a counteroffensive in the western strategic sector. The operation lasted one month, but it failed to reach its objectives, because of insufficient strength. Nevertheless, Soviet troops did advance westward some 100–250 kilometers from Moscow, relieving the capital of any immediate danger. On December 8 Hitler signed orders placing the German eastern front on the defensive.[31]

The Battle of Moscow was a major event. For two years the German armies had gone from victory to victory, conquering all of Europe. Now for the first time they had been stopped and made to suffer heavy losses. Their hopes for a quick and easy victory had been shattered. The rulers of the Third Reich had to face the prospect of a protracted war on two fronts. The victory at Moscow completely eliminated the danger of a German invasion of Britain, gave renewed strength to the European resistance, and fostered a crisis in the coalition of fascist powers.

The beginning of the Soviet offensive coincided with two other events of major importance. On December 7, 1941, Japan attacked the United States; and on December 11, Germany declared war on the United States.

In December 1941 and January 1942, Hitler removed thirty-five of his generals, among them von Brauchitsch, commander of all land forces, von Rundstedt, and Guderian. A number of SS divisions were sent to the eastern front.

At the beginning of the Soviet counteroffensive, Stalin hoped that it would develop into a victorious general offensive on all fronts. But his hopes were soon deceived.


## LOST BATTLES AND LOST LIVES

The Battle of Moscow brought the total liberation of three provinces (oblasts)—those of Moscow, Tula, and Ryazan—while those of Leningrad, Kalinin, Smolensk, Orel, Kursk, Kharkov, and Stalingrad were partially cleared. Heroic resistance continued at Sevastopol.

Despite heavy German losses at Moscow (almost fifty divisions), the German high command managed to reorganize its forces in a brief period and immediately began preparations for a new offensive.

The Soviet high command had overestimated the capacities of its own forces and had launched incautious offensives in different directions, with the result that by April 1942 its strength had run out. All the painstakingly accumulated reserves were expended. Stalin did not appraise the new strategic situation correctly. In his orders to the military councils of the various fronts, he said it would be possible to drive the Germans westward without stopping and force them to exhaust their reserves before the spring of 1942, "in this way assuring the total destruction of Hitler's armies in 1942." This assessment drew no objections from the Stavka or the General Staff, but Stalin's predictions proved unfounded.[32]

One of the first defeats of the Red Army in 1942 was its attempt to break the blockade of Leningrad. The armies on the Leningrad and Volkhov fronts were to pierce the German lines from opposite directions and link up after making a breakthrough. The attempt was doomed from the start—because of delays in the concentration of a sufficient number of troops, inadequate training, and shortages of supplies and material. At the request of Meretskov, commander of the Volkhov Front, who realized that his troops were not prepared for the offensive, the Stavka (Stalin and Vassilevsky) authorized a postponement, but only for a short time, when in Meretskov's words, "at a minimum . . . fifteen to twenty more days were needed."[33] German intelligence detected the preparations for the offensive and determined fairly accurately where the blow would fall, so that the German high command was prepared to repel the attack. According to Meretskov, the forces of the Volkhov Front, which had been given orders to advance, had been severely weakened in previous combat and had not been properly reinforced, certain divisions having only two-thirds or half of their regular strength. Artillery, mortars, and automatic weapons were also lacking. The Second Shock Army, for example, had the troops of a regular army corps.

"The only reserves the front had," Meretskov reports, "were two very weak cavalry divisions and four ski battalions. The front did not even have a second line of defense. We did not have the means to build on an initial successful attack so as to expand in the enemy's rear and deal him a final blow."[34] The front commander was gambling on the promise from General Headquarters that reserves would be sent as soon as the army crossed the Volkhov.

The offensive was begun several times, but each time it foundered. The Second Shock Army found its progress slowed by the forests and marshes on the right bank of the Volkhov and was unable to reach its objective,

Lyuban. The troops from the Leningrad Front were also unable to fulfill their mission of breaking the German encirclement from the inside. These exhausting battles, which went on for four months, led to the needless loss of tens of thousands of Soviet soldiers, achieving nothing. During these operations the Stavka repeatedly made unconsidered decisions, abolishing the Volkhov Front at one moment and restoring it again at the next. As a result of the incompetence and poor leadership of the Stavka, in demanding the continuation of this senseless offensive, and of M. S. Khozin, the commander of the Leningrad Front, the Second Shock Army was literally driven into a trap. Not until the middle of June did the Soviet side manage, after fierce fighting, to break a hole in the German encirclement through which a few units and individual officers and soldiers of the Second Shock Army were able to escape.

The Northwestern Front also suffered heavy losses. Not only were the Soviets unable to smash the German troops they had encircled in the Demyansk region; in the end they were defeated in their attempt to stop the Germans from breaking through the Soviet encirclement to relieve the German Sixteenth Army in the Demyansk salient and reunite it with the main German forces in that area.

But the situation in the German-held Rzhevsk–Vyazma salient was even worse. Here a trap was laid for the Soviet forces. They were allowed to break through the German defenses only to have the trap sprung and find themselves encircled. They were forced to fight their way back, with terrible losses. Entire Soviet divisions and corps perished.

The calculations of the Soviet high command were in error—they assumed it was possible to remain on the defensive and simultaneously go on the offensive in several directions. This defective approach had been proposed by the General Staff and approved by Stalin in March 1942.

The Soviet command made several attempts to retake the Crimea by amphibious landings at Theodosia and Eupatoria. Each time they were repelled with heavy losses, in spite of Soviet superiority in troop strength (2 to 1) and equipment (1.5 to 1). These defeats were due to the incompetence of the local commanders, Lieutenant General Kozlov and Lev Mekhlis, the Stavka representative. The enemy's strength and intentions were not discovered in time; thus the German offensive against Kerch, on May 8, 1942, was a disaster for the Soviets, whose troops beat a disorderly retreat across the Kerch straits to the Taman peninsula. According to Soviet sources, 176,000 were killed.[35] According to German figures, 150,000 Soviet troops were captured, along with great quantities of equipment.[36] Kozlov and Mekhlis were merely given a slap on the wrist, in the form of a demotion.

Stalin and his generals did not have a clear understanding of their army's capabilities. They made an adventurist decision to launch an offensive in the Kharkov region, with troops of the Southwestern and Southern fronts. Their objective was to destroy the German army in the southern sector of the Soviet–German front. The General Staff had some objections to the plan of operations, which involved heavy risks, because the Germans outnumbered the Soviets on both flanks, threatening to encircle them. Stalin, however, ordered the General Staff not to interfere, and he approved the plan submitted by Timoshenko, commander of the Southwestern Direction.[37]

The offensive started on May 12, with Timoshenko commanding the Southwestern Front and Malinovsky the Southern. The Soviets had the advantage in terms of men, tanks, and aircraft. The Germans had superiority in artillery.

At first the Soviet forces made a successful breakthrough toward Barvenkovo, but by May 17 it was obvious that the offensive of the Southwestern Front had to be stopped immediately, so that troops could be shifted to the Kramatorsk region to stop the threat from German forces that had broken through the defenses of the Southern front. Stalin decided to continue the offensive regardless.[38]

During the evening of May 18 Khrushchev, who was a member of the Southwestern Front's Military Council, reported to the head of the General Staff, Vassilevsky, that the situation had worsened in the Barvenkovo bulge and that Stalin had refused the request of the Southwestern Front that the offensive be broken off. He asked Vassilevsky to present the Southwestern Front's request again to Stalin. Vassilevsky says he advised Khrushchev to speak with Stalin directly.[39] According to Khrushchev, Vassilevsky, fearing Stalin's rage, refused to intercede. Stalin refused even to discuss the subject with Khrushchev. He had Malenkov pass on the message that the operation must proceed.[40] Zhukov gives a different version of these events. According to him, on May 18 Khrushchev still himself favored continuing the campaign.[41]

Catastrophe was becoming more and more unavoidable. German divisions attacking from the north and south had joined forces south of Balakleia. The concentrations of Soviet troops were surrounded and destroyed. Between May 24 and 29, according to German sources, 240,000 Soviet soldiers and officers were taken prisoner.[42] Tens of thousands of others lost their lives. The Soviet Informburo, however, announced only that there had been 5,000 killed and 70,000 missing in action. It was thus that the command attempted to hide the slaughter at Kharkov from the people.

During the initial six months of war, the Red Army suffered staggering losses, in terms of soldiers killed and captured, and the figures increased as the Germany army advanced eastward. At the end of June and the beginning of July 1941, the Germans captured 329,000 soldiers at Bialystok and Minsk. At the end of July they captured 310,000 in Smolensk; at the beginning of August, 103,000 at Uman. But it was not until the last ten days of September that the number of casualties reached its all-time high, with 665,000 taken prisoner in the vicinity of Kiev, this being followed in mid-October by the capture of 663,000 near Bryansk and Vyazma.[43] At the end of the first seven months of war the total number of Soviet prisoners in German hands had reached 3.9 million.[44]

A sorry fate awaited them. A month before the attack on the Soviet Union, the high command of the German land forces had issued a directive under which all captured Red Army political commissars were to be executed immediately; it likewise authorized the shooting of Red Army prisoners "without any formalities." German soldiers and officers were not to be held responsible in cases of the murder of Soviet prisoners. Often they were killed as a pastime.

An order from the German army dated October 1941 instructed that prisoners and the civilian population in the occupied regions be left to starve and no supplies be given to them at the expense of the German army. K. Kromiadi, who later became a collaborator of General Vlasov, described the situation of the Soviet prisoners in the fall of 1941 as follows:

> The prisoners were half-naked, dirty, exhausted; none had shaved for a long time; worst of all, they were in the throes of utter despair. Nobody cared about them; their government had placed them outside the law. . . . And conditions in the camps were unimaginable. Prisoners were dying. The way these people—half-insane from their situation—were treated by the camp administration was revolting. Brutality, including the use of weapons, was a daily occurrence. But most terrible of all was the fact that the feeding of the prisoners was merely a "formality." The people had reached the point of complete exhaustion and were barely able to stand on their feet. . . . That winter, 80 percent of them starved to death or froze.[45]

Given these conditions, the prisoners were ready to do anything to escape from the death camps. Their situation was made even more tragic by the fact that their government had abandoned them. Many of them were labeled traitors to the homeland simply because they had been taken prisoner. Although in November 1941 the Soviet government protested the mistreatment of the prisoners, it rejected the services of the International Red Cross, which had proposed to exchange lists of prisoners of war between Germany and the Soviet Union. Theoretically, this would have given some guarantee of security to the one and the other. The Red Cross also wanted to help provide material aid to the prisoners. The Soviet government consistently rejected such proposals. It is not very likely that the Red Cross would have succeeded in stopping Hitler, who had sanctioned the extermination of Soviet prisoners, but it was no less criminal for the Soviet government to neglect any possibility of saving its citizens' lives.

For the Soviet government these prisoners did not exist. They had already been scratched off the list, erased from official memory. For example, at the Teheran conference in 1943 Stalin confided to Churchill that in the Soviet Union all soldiers wished to become heroes; those who did not had been killed.

All hope lost, they died by the hundreds of thousands. According to official German documents of May 1, 1944, 5,754,000 Soviet soldiers had been captured since June 1941. At least 3,220,000 of them died. As to those who survived, a sad fate awaited them on their return to the Soviet Union, as will be seen later. Beginning in the middle of 1942 the strongest and most skilled were forcibly employed in German industry. In December 1944 over 630,000 Soviet prisoners of war were doing forced labor for the Germans.[46]

## THE DRIVE TO THE VOLGA

The Soviet winter offensive lasted on various fronts until April 1942. Three months later, the Germans launched a new offensive which was very well prepared. Their goal was to smash the Soviet forces in Central Russia. They were hoping to reach the Volga, take the Caucasus, and force a Soviet surrender.

On the German–Soviet front in the summer of 1942, the Germans had an advantage over the Soviets in terms of men (6,200,000 to 5,500,000) and in fighter planes (3,400 to 3,160). The Soviets had more artillery (43,640 guns and mortars and 1,220 katyusha rocket launchers to 43,000 guns and mortars) and tanks (4,065 to 3,230 tanks and motorized howitzers).[47]

The Soviet high command presumed that the main thrust would be directed at the center of the front. Kursk-Voronezh was the direction thought second most likely to fall under German attack, with the same aim—outflanking Moscow, but from the southeast. In fact, the German high command had decided to make its main thrust to the south.

The offensive began on June 28, 1942, from the area east of Kursk. At the same time, Voronezh was attacked from Volchansk. Five German armies and three from its allies—Italy, Hungary, and Romania—took part in the attack. Their objective was to surround and destroy the Soviet forces of the Bryansk Front, commanded by F. I. Golikov, and later those of the South-western and Southern fronts, thereby gaining free access to the Volga and the Caucasus. On July 2 the German armies broke through the Soviet defenses at the junction of the Bryansk and Southwestern fronts, to a depth of eighty kilometers. On July 7 the fighting reached the outskirts of Voronezh. Rokossovsky replaced Golikov at the command of the Bryansk Front, and Vatutin was named commander of the new Voronezh Front. The Soviet command threw its reserves into the battle, but these reinforcements arrived too late. The Germans continued their offensive.

On July 15 the Soviet defenses were breached between the Don and the northern Donets rivers. At that point the German offensive extended along a front 500–600 kilometers long. Soviet troops abandoned Rostov on July 24 and crossed the Don in retreat. By July 27 fighting was taking place in the direction of Stalingrad.

One consequence of the Soviet defeats was a severe erosion of discipline, with an increasing incidence of desertion to the enemy and unauthorized withdrawal. Many units were retreating in disorder, abandoning arms, ammunition, and equipment. The number of self-inflicted wounds was on the rise, especially among soldiers of non-Russian nationality. Cases of indiscipline, cowardice, and panic reached such proportions that the high command was greatly alarmed. Punitive and disciplinary units were strengthened: their orders were to fire at will on all units or soldiers withdrawing without proper orders. On July 28 Stalin issued Order No. 227, which stated the following: "It is time to put an end to retreats. . . . Not a single step backwards! . . . Each position, each meter of Soviet territory must be stubbornly defended, to the last drop of blood. We must cling to every inch of Soviet soil and defend it to the end!"[48]

This order also condemned the widespread belief that Russia after all was a huge country and there was plenty of room to retreat, and it stressed the need to reestablish iron discipline in the army, to punish without pity all who displayed cowardice or committed acts of indiscipline. The political directors of the Red Army were given especially great authority. Measures were also taken to strengthen military counterintelligence (SMERSH). Commanders and commissars of retreating units were threatened with demotion and court martial.

By August 19 the fighting had reached the outskirts of Stalingrad. Meanwhile on the Southern Front, after breaking through Soviet defenses in the Tsimlyansk region on July 29, the Germans drove toward the Caucasus. On August 5 they took Stavropol, and on August 11, Krasnodar. They reached the gates of Maikop and occupied Beloreshenskaya, but were unable to break through to Tuapse. Meanwhile, south of Rostov, they reached Mozdok on August 8 and Pyatigorsk the following day. Continuing their offensive, the German vanguard units reached the Greater Caucasus Range and occupied several mountain passes, reaching as far as the pass on Mount Klukhori. On August 21, 1942, the iron cross was waving from the peak of Mount Elbruz. It was not removed by Soviet soldiers until February 17, 1943. Near Grozny, the eastward drive of the Germans was stopped, and they were forced to assume defensive positions. They were also unable to reach Transcaucasia.

Thus, by the fall of 1942 the German armies had penetrated deeper into Russia than any invading army from the west had ever done.

In the Caucasus the Germans were able to create a local government with the assistance of collaborators, including many former emigrés such as Ali-Khan Kantemir and the Dagestani General Bicherakhov. In Berlin, at the Ministry for the Eastern Countries, a National Committee of the Northern Caucasus was set up. Kantemir was formally in charge, but the Germans actually controlled it. It proclaimed its willingness to collaborate with Germany, having as its objective the separation of the Caucasus from the Soviet Union. The committee recruited Soviet prisoners of war from the Northern Caucasus into the armies of the Reich, mainly the Caucasian Legion. The German government, however, was no less alien to the mountain peoples of the Caucasus than the Soviet government. If the Caucasians had a dream, it was to free themselves of both governments, not replace one with the other.

Armed groups had been active in the mountains since the collectivization of agriculture in the 1930s, and their activities increased as the German offensive approached. Major Soviet units were withdrawn from the front and used against these groups. The bulk of the population, however, remained loyal to the Soviet government.

The German offensive in the summer of 1942 spurred a new wave of evacuations of urban populations. Once again Central Russia and the Volga region were covered with hundreds of thousands of refugees, many of them heading for Central Asia. Trains followed trains, filled with machinery, engines, raw materials, and fuels. Huge amounts of industrial equipment fell to the invaders, but the Soviets managed in spite of everything to save some equipment. New factories arose in the eastern part of the country, in Central Asia and Siberia, but on the whole industrial production decreased during the second half of 1942.

In 1941 and 1942, during the German offensive, many towns and villages were abandoned to their fate by the local authorities, both party and government. In some cases, the Germans would arrive only a few days after the officials' departure. They would find and take factories, stores, agricultural and industrial products, livestock, and fuel. And also important archives, such as those of Smolensk, which afterward came into the hands of the United States and still serve as an invaluable source of knowledge of the history of the Soviet Union during the 1920s and 1930s.

The local authorities never failed, however, to execute political prisoners before the arrival of the Germans. From June 28 on, mass arrests began in the Baltic nations and eastern Poland. NKVD troops arrested and shot people in the cells and yards of the prisons of Lvov, Rovno, and Tallin. In Tartu 192 corpses were thrown into a pit. Prisoners were also killed during evacuation at prisons in Minsk, Smolensk, Kiev, Kharkov, Zaporozhye, Dnepropetrovsk, and Orel. At a molybdenum mining complex near Nalchik, where prison inmates were working, all prisoners were executed by machine gun fire. As the Germans neared the Olginskaya camp, the NKVD released those who had been condemned to less than five years; all the rest (thousands upon thousands) were shot on October 31, 1941.[49] These were not isolated incidents: the full history of the executions of prisoners during the Soviet retreat has yet to be written.

## THE GERMAN OCCUPATION

In 1941 and 1942 the German armies occupied 1,926,000 square kilometers of Soviet territory: the Baltic states, Byelorussia, the Ukraine, a significant part of Russia, the Crimea, the Caucasus, and Moldavia. These regions were economically the most highly developed in the USSR; before the war their populations had reached 85 million, that is, 40 percent of the total Soviet population.[50] This area produced 63 percent of the country's coal, 68 percent of its cast iron, 58 percent of its steel, 60 percent of its aluminum, 38 percent of its grain, and 84 percent of its sugar. This was also one of the principal centers of livestock breeding in the Soviet Union (38 percent of its sheep and 60 percent of its hogs). Moreover, hundreds of military plants and facilities were located in the occupied areas.[51]

The Nazi leadership had worked out a set policy toward the inhabitants of the USSR well in advance of the invasion. As official German documents make clear, the extermination of a major part of the population was planned for Poland and European Russia. Plan Ost called for the deportation of 31 million people from these territories, with colonization by German settlers over a thirty-year period. The plan called for the starvation of millions of Poles and Russians. Goering, speaking in August 1942 at a conference of

Reich representatives in the occupied eastern territories, cynically declared: "In the past, this was called robbery.... Still, I'm ready for some robbing, some efficient robbing."[52] Alfred Rosenberg, one of the original Nazi theoreticians and later the Reich's minister of the occupied eastern territories, predicted that "very difficult years certainly lie ahead for the Russians."[53]

The Nazis wanted to destroy all state structures in the occupied territories and enslave the population at the lowest possible cultural level. "Our guiding principle," said Hitler, "is that the existence of these people is justified only by their economic exploitation for our benefit."[54]

The Soviet-occupied territories were divided into two main Reich commissariats: Ostland and "Ukraina." Ostland comprised Estonia, Latvia, Lithuania, and Byelorussia. "Ukraina" included the regions of Volynia and Podolia (with Rovno as regional center), Zhitomir, Kiev, Nikolaev, Dnepropetrovsk, and Taurida (with Melitopol as the center). These territories were under "civilian" administration. All other occupied territories were under direct military rule as combat zones. In the southwest the region between the Dniestr and the Bug and to the north of Odessa was placed under Romanian rule and called Transniestria. Each major administrative unit was divided into smaller units (Kriegsgebiete, Stadtskomissare, etc.). In rural zones volosts, the prerevolutionary administrative units, were reinstituted. In the cities nominal authority was exercised by *Bürgermeisters*, appointed by the Germans; in the villages they appointed "elders" (*starosty*). Everywhere, collaborators were recruited to serve in local police bodies; they were feared and hated by the population, who called them Polizei.

The Nazis' main aims were first to exploit the occupied territories economically and second to guarantee a secure rear area and safe lines of communication for the troops advancing into Central Russia and the foothills of the Caucasus. The Nazis' entire policy was subordinated to these ends, and the methods they used corresponded to them: extermination of all Jews and members of other "inferior" nationalities; elimination of Communists and their families; pillage of the occupied territories; pitiless exploitation of the population; and elimination of the few rights they had enjoyed under the Soviet regime.

On the eve of the invasion Hitler had ordered the formation of *Einsatzgruppen*, special detachments under Himmler's command, whose purpose was to seek out and destroy all Jews, Communists, and other "antisocial" elements. These units were later reinforced by units of Ukrainians and Balts, who served as rural and urban police. The extermination of Jews began immediately after the invasion and continued throughout the occupation. More than 7,000 Jews were killed in Lvov immediately after it was taken by German troops. Criminal elements among the "Banderaite" Ukrainian nationalists participated in hunting down and murdering Jews.[55] Ghettoes were established for the Jews in many Ukrainian and Byelorussian cities, and afterward those who had been driven into the ghettoes were pitilessly annihilated. No mercy was shown to anyone—neither women nor children nor the elderly. They were shot, buried alive, burned alive, or killed in gas chambers. Tens of thousands of Jews, including Soviet citizens, were liquidated by the Nazis in such death camps as Auschwitz, Maidanek, and Treblinka. According to the estimates of a special Anglo–American committee in 1946, the Germans killed 1,050,000 Soviet Jews.[56]

Very unhappy with the Soviet regime after twenty years, part of the population undoubtedly had some illusions concerning improvements in their conditions under the Germans. In certain parts of the Ukraine the German army was welcomed with flowers. These illusions were soon shattered. The German government was even more brutal than its Soviet counterpart. In other words, however bad it was, the Soviet government was their own, whereas the Germans were strangers who despised the population and not only robbed them but humiliated them at every turn.

On the other hand, almost all families in the occupied territories had children, fathers, or brothers in the Red Army. Patriotism, the feeling of belonging to a common land and a common cause, a sentiment that had been lost or completely uprooted, was reborn as a reaction to the invaders' cruelty. This was fertile ground for active and passive resistance toward the invaders. The Germans deported 4,258,000 Soviet citizens to Germany to work in industry and agriculture.[57] Most of them were mistreated and exploited mercilessly. They had to wear special badges that said *Ostarbeiter* (worker from the East) and were segregated from Western workers. Any contact with the local population was strictly forbidden.

An exception was made to this general policy in the case of the Kuban Cossacks. In mid-April 1942 Hitler authorized the formation of Cossack volunteer units to be used against the Red Army and the partisans. Hitler had been informed that the Kuban Cossacks constituted an independent nation whose ancestry was traceable to the Ostgoths. They were therefore counted as friends of the Reich. They were allowed to set up an autonomous government and granted freedom of religion, culture, and education. On October 1, 1942, a Cossack district consisting of six subdivisions was formed with a population of 160,000 inhabitants. The Cossacks were authorized to return to private landownership, under the condition that they serve in the German army. The Germans expected to increase their Cossack legions to 25,000. Nevertheless, the Germans had to withdraw from these areas in January 1943, and the main cities of the region, Rostov and

Novocherkassk, were retaken by the Red Army. Over 20,000 Cossacks joined the German army in its retreat. They were commanded by the German general von Pannowitz.

The Germans pursued a "special" policy in the Northern Caucasus, where they succeeded in forming several units of local mountaineers. The reason for this policy was their desire to use the Caucasus to supply their needs for oil. Their plans called for the formation of a General Commissariat of the Caucasus, which was to include the Northern Caucasus and Transcaucasia.

The occupied parts of the Caucasus were put under military rule. Unlike the rest of the occupied territories, where kolkhozes had been maintained as useful economic units to provide the food and raw materials Germany needed, the Caucasian mountain tribes were allowed to dissolve theirs if they so desired. Nevertheless, whenever the needs of the German army were at stake, the invaders acted just as harshly as in the other occupied regions, imposing forced requisitions, severe punishments, and collective responsibility for any sabotage against the German army.

The policy of employing non-Russians in the war against the Soviet Union was also used in the case of the Crimean Tatars, who were allowed to set up their own national institutions, and the Kalmyks, who were encouraged by the Germans to revive their nomadic traditions. But everywhere the Germans would crush the slightest attempt to attain any real national independence. The nationalist organizations were always strictly controlled by the authorities. Thus, the Germans suppressed attempts by the Crimean Tatars to use Muslim committees to create a national movement. Punitive expeditions by the Germans against partisans in the Crimea did not spare the Tatar villages, many of which were burned down.

Part of the population in the Caucasus, in the Crimea, and in Kalmykia collaborated with the Germans—on a very small scale. Some were guilty of atrocities and war crimes. We lack detailed information on this topic, since Soviet sources remain silent. According to some Western researchers, of the 134,000 Kalmyks who lived in the Soviet Union in 1939, 5,000 became active collaborators.[58] For the Crimean Tatars, the figure was between 12,000 and 20,000 collaborators out of a population estimated at 250,000 in 1939.[59]

The German political and military command set itself three tasks when it planned the war against the Soviet Union: to eliminate bolshevism; to destroy any trace of a non-German state on Soviet territory; and to exploit the population and transform the occupied zones into German colonies. These objectives were based on the theory of the inferiority of the Slavic race and the superiority of the Aryan race over all others. The German political doctrine rejected in advance all collaboration with the peoples of the Soviet Union. The only relations it permitted were those of slavemaster to slave. This point of view, often expressed by Hitler, determined all policies in the occupied territories and even governed attitudes toward the anti-Communist forces willing to collaborate with the Germans.

Those forces included various Russian emigrés, Ukrainian, Byelorussian, Polish, and Caucasian nationalists, as well as members of various anti-Soviet organizations. The German authorities used them as interpreters, technical personnel, sometimes as advisers, but never granted them political representation of any kind. The emigré organizations were torn by internal conflicts, each rival group seeking to win Germany's exclusive support, and they were hampered by the vagueness or absurdity of their political programs. As long as Germany held the initiative in the war, the Nazi leaders kept a tight rein on the anti-Soviet organizations, cutting short all their attempts at political action in the occupied territories.

For example, in the Ukraine, when the Organization of Ukrainian Nationalists (OUN) proclaimed the creation of a Ukrainian state in Lvov on June 30, 1941, their leaders Stetsko and Bandera were simply arrested by the German authorities, along with many of their supporters. Likewise, when another leader, Melnik, attempted to set up a government in Kiev, he was also arrested. This policy of repression led to a declaration of war on two fronts by the OUN, against the Red Army and against the Germans, but in reality they never attacked the Germans. In 1944 Bandera and Melnik were freed and allowed to lead the armed struggle of the Ukrainian nationalists against the Red Army, which at that time was on the offensive. Many exiled Ukrainian nationalists served in the SS Galichina division and in the Nachtigall regiment.

Erich Koch, *Gauleiter* of the occupied Ukraine, said in August 1942: "The attitude of the Germans in the [Ukraine] must be governed by the fact that we are dealing with a people which is inferior in every respect. ... No social contact whatsoever with the Ukrainians. ... This people must be governed by iron force, so as to help us win the war now."[60]

The same policy was implemented with minor deviations in Byelorussia. In mid-1942, when Byelorussia became the scene of a massive partisan movement, the Germans attempted to change tactics and tried to use western Byelorussian emigrés. In October 1941 the legal existence of the nationalist organization Samopomoshch was authorized. Ivan Ermachenko, its leader, an exile who had fought in Wrangel's army, was named to head a Council on Byelorussian Affairs, working under the general commissar of Byelorussia, Wilhelm Kube. But the Byelorussian population refused to collaborate with this organization, seeing it as a German puppet.

As the military situation on the battlefronts deteriorated, Kube attempted more and more to use the Byelorussian nationalists against the partisans, who had the support of the population. The Byelorussian resistance at that point had over 100,000 men. In June 1943 the Germans set up a "Trust Rada" (Rada Doveriya), an advisory body with which the general commissar was to consult on local matters. But the population remained hostile. At the beginning of September 1943 the resistance blew up a German office in Minsk. In reprisal the SD (Security Service) shot 300 people without regard for age or sex. On September 24, 1943, Kube was killed when a bomb, planted by a partisan, exploded in his house. On the eve of the recapture of Minsk by the Red Army the Germans held a "congress" of Byelorussian nationalists, who declared themselves the heirs of the Byelorussian Rada of 1918. But this was the sole action the congress took, for its leaders hastily fled to Berlin to escape the advancing Red Army.

From about the fall of 1941 on, groups of partisans sprang up in many places. Their nuclei were Red Army soldiers who had successfully broken out of German encirclement, local party and government officials, and a small number of local inhabitants. At first there was no central unified command, and many of the groups operated on their own, attempting to reach the front lines. Later, diversionary units especially trained for guerrilla warfare were sent behind German lines, equipped with weapons and radios. Legend has it that from the beginning the partisan units were led by the Central Committee and the underground local party leaderships. But the reality was different. The partisan war, largely spontaneous, was an outgrowth of the repression and atrocities of the invaders. It was only after the first Red Army counteroffensives and the stabilization of the situation that scattered groups began to unite to form regular detachments which later developed into large military formations. At various Red Army field headquarters, special sections were set up to communicate with the partisan units and direct them. A central headquarters of the partisan movement was established in Moscow.

This movement was especially widespread wherever the Nazis earned the hatred of major parts of the population because of the atrocities they committed. The extermination of the Jews in Byelorussia horrified the local population and was one of the reasons for the growth of the partisan movement. By the middle of 1942 almost the whole of Byelorussia, including its capital Minsk, had been won by the resistance, a movement that at the time had as many as 100,000 members. The partisans were also very popular in the Ukraine, in the Leningrad and Novgorod regions, and in the Crimea. By the end of 1942, the movement was linked in a number of regions to urban underground organizations. Large groups of partisans came into existence, such as those led by Kovpak, Fedorov, and Kozlov.

The German command had to divert as much as 10 percent of its ground forces on the Soviet front to the struggle against the partisans. In 1943, according to Soviet figures, twenty-five divisions of regular German troops, not including reserves, special units, police, and so on, were used for this purpose. A partisan movement of these dimensions could exist only with the support of the local population.

The partisans caused trouble in the rear of the German army, hitting its lines of communication, blowing up military targets, derailing convoys, and killing high-ranking officers. They also took reprisals against collaborators and thereby reduced the Germans' room for maneuver in their efforts to manipulate the local population. Often they tried and executed anyone even suspected of collaborating with the enemy, in many cases on the basis of rumor alone. In the Crimea, for example, the partisan command ordered the burning of Tatar villages, allowed partisans to rob the native population, and deliberately misinformed Moscow, alleging that the Tatars had generally collaborated with the invaders. Similar situations occurred in Kalmykia and the Northern Caucasus.[61]

According to official Soviet figures, which are probably considerably inflated, almost 1 million armed partisans fought in the resistance movement against the Germans between 1941 and 1945.[62] In 1943 and 1944 they coordinated their operations with the advancing Red Army. It is estimated that the number of partisans in the 1944 offensive was 250,000.[63]

## STALINGRAD

On July 17, 1942, the Battle of Stalingrad began, as fighting reached the city's outer suburbs. It ended with a Soviet victory on February 2, 1943. For the Red Army the defensive stage of the battle lasted until November 19, 1942.

The Soviet troops who retreated, after heavy fighting, into Stalingrad were a badly battered force. At the beginning of the battle, only eighteen of the thirty-eight divisions which formed the Stalingrad Front were fully equipped. Fourteen were completely unfit for combat (they had between 300 and 1,000 fighters), and six had no more than 25–40 percent of their regulars.

During the months of August and September, the German forces continued to advance. Soviet soldiers engaged in stubborn and courageous street fighting and house-to-house combat. Incidents like the defense of the Stalingrad Tractor Factory and the fighting for Mamai Kurgan and the Pavlov house were inscribed forever in the annals of the war.

The Soviet high command correctly saw in Stalingrad the turning point of the war against Germany. At that point it was quite clear that in spite of the immense Russian spaces east of the Volga, it was not possible to withdraw any farther. A Soviet defeat at Stalingrad would have allowed the Germans to establish a solid border on the Volga, to call an end to the war, and probably to set up a Russian collaborationist government. Zhukov, who had been named deputy supreme commander, was sent to Stalingrad to coordinate and lead all operations of the Stalingrad and Don fronts. He had saved Russia in the Battle of Moscow in 1941. Now he was to save Stalingrad.

The fighting in Stalingrad showed once again that the incompetent meddling of political commissars in military operations often led to gross errors and created difficulties for the military commanders. On October 9, 1942, the institution of commissars was abolished again, and a united command was reinstated. Reserves, ammunition, and armaments were rushed to the Stalingrad area and deliveries were kept up continuously. Behind the lines, well-equipped armies were hastily put together. The desperate resistance by Soviet troops prevented the Germans from taking all of the city. The German advance stalled. By mid-October the German command was forced to issue orders to go over to the defensive.

The Soviet Union found itself in an increasingly favorable position. Military production was rapidly increasing. In the second half of 1942, 15,800 fighter planes were produced (as against 9,600 during the first half), 13,600 tanks (as against 11,000), 15,600 artillery systems (as against 14,000).

By mid-November some 2 million soldiers were taking part in the Battle of Stalingrad, almost equally divided between the two sides. The Soviets held an advantage in armament: 1.4 to 1 in tanks and motorized artillery, 1.3 to 1 in field guns and mortars, 1.1 to 1 in fighter planes.

The plan of the Soviet command was to use the forces of three fronts, the Southwestern, the Stalingrad, and the Don, to encircle the German armies between the Volga and the Don, and then destroy them.

The Soviet offensive began on November 19, 1942. By November 23 a German army group numbering 330,000 was surrounded in the Stalingrad area. Its commander, General von Paulus, was unable to obtain Hitler's permission to break out of the encirclement. He was ordered to organize the defense and await assistance from the troops of Field Marshal von Manstein. But fresh Soviet troops blocked Manstein's attempt to break the blockade of Paulus's group. On December 16 the Soviet forces on the outer ring of the Stalingrad "pocket" counterattacked and Manstein was forced to withdraw in haste. Initially, Paulus rejected all offers to surrender; Hitler had forbidden him to yield. The Soviet forces began the systematic destruction of the encircled Germans. At last, on February 2, 1943, Paulus surrendered. Ninety thousand soldiers, including twenty-four generals and Field Marshal von Paulus himself, were taken prisoner.

The German defeat at Stalingrad was a boost to the morale of the Soviet troops and the home front. It increased the prestige of the military and political command and Stalin's personal authority. The fact that victory had been achieved in the ruins of the city that bore his name led mystics and believers to see in this success an act of providence or fate. The propaganda machine used the victory to praise the party's organizational genius. Silence was maintained about the war's first twenty months and the responsibilities of the leadership. Finally, the Stalingrad victory increased the Soviet Union's international prestige.

Stalingrad was a major blow to the Reich. It created trouble and gave rise to doubts among Germany's allies, adding vigor to the resistance in Europe and strengthening the positions of the neutral states. The victory at Stalingrad was facilitated by the British victory in North Africa, at El Alamein, and the landing of American troops in Algeria in the fall of 1942. Those operations diverted a substantial part of the German air force from the Soviet front.

The Soviet offensive at Stalingrad soon developed into a general advance along an enormous front ranging from Leningrad to the Caucasus. The Caucasus, the North Caucasus, Rostov-on-the-Don, and part of the Donets Basin were liberated. In late January 1943 Voronezh was retaken, followed by Kharkov, Belgorod, and Kursk. However, the German command retook the city of Kharkov and the northeastern part of the Donets Basin. This counteroffensive took the Soviet front-line commanders and the general staff completely by surprise. They had believed that in this region the adversary had been routed and was in full retreat. On March 18 the Germans took Belgorod. The Red Army was forced once again onto the defensive. In the northwest, Demyansk was retaken and Rzhev liberated. On the western front, the Soviet offensive stopped at the approaches to Smolensk. By then the front was 270–300 kilometers from Moscow.

In January 1943 Soviet troops partly broke the blockade of Leningrad. The city had suffered terribly. In December 1941 Hitler had named Colonel General Küchler commander of the newly formed Army Group North. His assignment had been to wipe Leningrad from the face of the earth. For almost 900 days this city of 2.5 million was subjected to endless artillery shellings. Residential electric power and water supply were disrupted. In 1942 alone the city was shelled by artillery for 254 days. In spite of the indescribable suffering of the population, the factories in Leningrad continued to turn out weapons. Workers, engineers, and technicians remained at their posts. Many died of hunger and fatigue on the job. Eight hundred thousand residents died in the siege, but the city held out. Several times Soviet troops launched very costly offensives seeking to break the siege, but they all failed. The only access to the city, called the "road of life," was over the frozen Lake Ladoga. Not until January 1943 did Soviet forces manage to open a ten-kilometer-wide corridor providing a land link with the rest of the country. From that time on, the situation in Leningrad began to improve. But the blockade was not completely lifted until 1944.

## KURSK: THE TURNING POINT OF THE WAR

In the spring of 1943 the German–Soviet front, from Leningrad to the Black Sea, was stabilized. As the German military historian General Tippelskirch has said, the Soviet military command showed increasing flexibility in attaining its strategic objectives, but in questions of tactics, the German army maintained its supremacy.

The number of regulars in the Red army and navy had increased from 2.9 million men in 1941 to 6 million in 1943.[64] The Soviet war industry had greatly increased its production and, supplemented by American deliveries of matériel and foodstuffs, was meeting the needs of the armed forces.

Despite defeats, the German high command decided in the summer of 1943 to try to regain the strategic initiative and deal a decisive blow to the Soviets, one that would put an end to the war. The new offensive began on July 5, 1943, in the Kursk-Belgorod region. This gigantic battle mobilized almost 2.25 million people on both sides, 6,000 tanks and over 4,500 planes. The Soviet army was far larger than the German one, not only in terms of troops (1,337,000 men against 900,000) but also in armaments.

On July 23 the German offensive was contained. On August 3 the Soviets counterattacked along the Orel-Kursk-Belgorod line. On August 23 they retook Kharkov, this time for good. The Battle of Kursk, which lasted fifty days, was won by the Red Army. The power of the German army was shattered.

The Battle of Kursk developed into a major strategic offensive, from Velikie Luki in the northwest to the Black Sea in the south. All of the

Ukraine east of the Dnepr, including its capital, Kiev, was liberated; bridge-heads were established on the right bank of the Dnepr, and many parts of Central Russia and a part of Byelorussia were liberated. In the south, the Germans were expelled from the Taman peninsula, including Kerch.

In the midst of the Kursk-Belgorod battle, on July 25, the landing of American and British forces in Italy began. In September, Mussolini's Fascist regime was overthrown and Italy surrendered. Nevertheless, the Germans invaded northern Italy, and the war there took on a prolonged character.

## THE KATYN TRAGEDY

The Allied victories in Africa, at Stalingrad, and at Kursk and the events in Italy helped strengthen the resistance in the nations occupied by the Germans. Growing discontent in Europe boded ill for Hitler, with his predictions of a thousand-year reign for the "Great German Reich."

The Soviet attitude toward the resistance and the national liberation movements in Europe was two-sided. On the one hand, the USSR helped them with money, arms, and men when the resistance organizations were led by Communists who sought not only to expel the invader but also to set up their own political system. On the other hand, it felt obliged to support the legal governments in exile, with which the United States and Great Britain had diplomatic relations.

The touchiest aspect of this policy was in the area of Soviet–Polish relations. After the division of Poland in 1939, a Polish government in exile was formed abroad and recognized by Britain, the United States, and other countries. In 1941, at Britain's request, the Soviet Union and the Polish exile government restored diplomatic ties. Many Polish citizens, among them many prisoners of war in Soviet camps, were freed, and the formation of Polish units on Soviet territory began. At that point, there were almost 250,000 Polish prisoners of war. Moreover, after the Soviet annexation of the western Ukraine and western Byelorussia, a large part of the Polish population had been deported to Siberia and Central Asia: approximately 1,200,000 people.

When Polish General Wladyslaw Anders, formerly a prisoner of war of the Soviets, was allowed to start organizing Polish troops in the USSR, it was discovered that many men on the Polish army's officer lists had disappeared. Of the 14 generals taken prisoner by the Red Army, only 2 could be found, and only 6 out of 300 higher-ranking officers. The Polish command began an investigation, questioning Poles who had been prisoners of the Soviets. It was established that the 15,000 missing officers had been held in three camps, Kozelsk, Ostashkovo, and Starobelsk, and that they were known to have been there up until the spring of 1940. After that all trace of them was lost. The Soviet authorities claimed total ignorance on the matter. The Polish command set up a special commission to investigate the disappearance of the 15,000. It was discovered that the camps had been evacuated in April 1940 and that the Polish prisoners had been taken to nearby train stations and shipped to a place west of Smolensk.

Anders and the diplomatic representatives of the Polish government in Moscow tried to obtain an answer from official Soviet sources as to the fate of the missing officers. At a meeting with Stalin on December 3, 1941, General Sikorski, head of the Polish government in exile, asked about them again. The answer was unexpected: "They fled." Stalin was then asked where 15,000 men could have fled to. His answer was plainly absurd: "To Manchuria."[65] The Polish government in exile continued to search through official Soviet channels for the missing men, with the help of Britain and the United States, but to no avail.

In February 1943 the Germans announced they had discovered in the Katyn forest, near Smolensk, the buried corpses of thousands of Polish officers. Each one of them had been shot in the back of the neck with a German bullet.

On April 16, 1943, the Sovinformburo announced that the crime of the Katyn forest had been the work of the Nazis.[66] The Germans responded with the creation of an international commission under their leadership. It said that the Polish prisoners had been executed by the NKVD in April 1940, that is, one and a half years before the Germans took Smolensk. The Germans authorized Polish physicians living in occupied Poland to hold an independent investigation. The doctors concluded that the Katyn murders had taken place in 1940. Nevertheless, the Germans failed in their attempt to obtain an anti-Soviet statement from them. The Poles did not want the NKVD crimes exploited by their sworn enemies, the Nazis.

The Polish government in London asked the Red Cross to investigate the matter. The Soviet Union categorically refused to cooperate with the Red Cross in such an investigation.

The discovery of the Katyn massacre and the furor raised over it led Stalin to break relations with the Sikorski government on April 25, 1943.[67] Churchill had urged Sikorski to keep the matter quiet, to preserve the anti-German coalition.[68] The Soviet government took advantage of the situation to organize a Union of Polish Patriots, which Stalin hoped would become the future Polish government.[69] At the same time, a Polish division was organized on Soviet territory. It was thus that the Katyn controversy unexpectedly came to serve the long-term political objectives of the Soviet government.

Immediately after the liberation of Smolensk by Soviet troops, a Soviet commission investigated the massacre and, of course, found it had been the work of the Germans in the fall of 1941, not of the NKVD in April 1940.[70] Its findings did not even mention such important details as the material of the ropes used to tie the victims' hands, the origins of the square wounds produced by bayonet stabbings, and the character of the vegetation on the graves. The commission also named the guilty, among them a certain Colonel Arens. He, to the surprise of all parties, turned himself in at the Nuremberg trial. At Soviet request, the Katyn affair was included in the indictment. But when it was established that Arens had been away from Smolensk in the fall of 1941 and that the Soviet testimony was very cloudy, a decision was made not to include Katyn in the final judgment of the Nuremberg tribunal. Later, Churchill was to write in his memoirs: "It was decided by the victorious Governments concerned that the issue should be avoided, and the crime of Katyn was never probed in detail."[71]

For years a number of organizations and individuals laboriously gathered facts and testimony to establish what happened to the 15,570 Polish prisoners who had been in the Soviet camps of Ostashkovo, Kozelsk, and Starobelsk between September 1939 and April 1940. In 1952 the U.S. Congress set up a special commission of inquiry. All the facts and testimony were summarized, leaving no doubt about who committed the crime and when.

Among the prisoners were a large number of reservists, including 1,000 lawyers, hundreds of schoolteachers, university professors, journalists, artists, over 300 medical doctors, and a number of priests. Here was the cream of the Polish intelligentsia, equally hated by the Nazis and the Soviet Communists. Officers on active duty numbered between 8,300 and 8,400.

The corpses of 4,443 Polish prisoners of war were found in the Katyn forest.[72] They were identified as those who had been held in the Kozelsk camp. Some of the younger ones had offered resistance and had been beaten; some showed wounds from bayonets of the type used in the Red Army. The bullets were made in Germany prior to 1939. Bullets of this type had been sold before the war in Poland, the Soviet Union, and the Baltic countries.

The last letters received by the families of the prisoners were dated April 1940. In the personal diaries which by some miracle survived, the last date written was April 9. It was also discovered that the prisoners had written on the walls of the railroad cars in which they were shipped. All the inscriptions said the same thing: the trains were heading northwest and being unloaded at Gnezdovo. People were treated with utter brutality. At

Gnezdovo the road from the railroad station to the forest was lined with NKVD men. Prisoners were unloaded and forced to board buses, which disappeared into the forest and returned empty for the next load.

Those who remained in the camp at Kozelsk kept a count of those who were taken. The lists of victims were given to the Polish resistance and thus survived. A total of twelve shipments from Kozelsk, 50–300 each, was thus recorded. The following are excerpts from one diary, whose author left the Kozelsk camp on April 8, 1940, with a group of 277.

> April 8,
> We were loaded at the station into a prison-train under heavy guard. . . .
> We are moving in the direction of Smolensk. . . .
> April 9,
> Tuesday—Today weather like that during the winter. . . . Snow on the fields. . . . It is impossible to deduce the direction of our motion. . . . Treatment is rough. . . . Nothing is allowed. . . . 2:30 PM we are arriving at Smolensk. . . . Evening, we arrived at the station Gniazdowo [Polish spelling]. It appears that we shall get off . . . a lot of military men around. Since yesterday we have had only a piece of bread and a sip of water.[73]

Finally, living witnesses of the massacre were found. They said that the crime had been carried out by personnel from the Smolensk and Minsk divisions of the NKVD.

The Katyn massacre took place in April 1940, over a year before the German occupation of the Smolensk region. As was shown by an independent commission of inquiry, three-year-old vegetation was found on the graves discovered in 1943: in other words, the crime was committed in 1940 and not in 1941.

What happened to the other 10,000 Polish prisoners detained in the Ostashkovo and Starobelsk camps? All trace of those held at Ostashkovo disappear at the Bologoe and Vyazma train stations; the traces of those from Starobelsk are lost in the Kharkov region. Nothing more has been found about either group.

But 448 prisoners from the Kozelsk camp survived. They were considered possible collaborators of the Soviet government, a judgment made by the NKVD officials who operated in the camps under the command of a General Zarubin. They were transferred to the Pavelich Bor camp between the end of April and the end of May 1940. In early June 1941 they were moved to the Gratsovets camp.

The chairman of the Soviet commission of inquiry into the Katyn crime, which was set up immediately after the liberation of Smolensk, was Academician Nikolai Burdenko, a surgeon and a prominent figure in Soviet medicine. It was he who signed the official finding of the commission stating that the crime had been committed by the Germans in 1941. After the war, in 1946, when Burdenko was seriously ill and had retired, he confessed to a friend, Dr. Olshansky:

> There is no question that these "Katyns" have happened and will happen. If you begin to dig around in the soil of our mother Russia, you will surely come across a goodly number of similar archeological discoveries.... We were obliged to totally refute the widespread German accusations against us. Under Stalin's personal orders, I went to the place the bodies were discovered. An examination was made, and it was found that all the bodies had been there for four years. Death had occurred in 1940. ... In fact, for me as a physician, that question is incontestable and there is no need for discussion on the topic. Our NKVD comrades committed a major mistake.[74]

Stalin knew the truth about Katyn; the extermination plan had been worked out by the NKVD and approved by Beria. Among others implicated in the affair, to various degrees, were Beria's assistant Merkulov (both he and Beria were shot in 1953) and NKVD Generals Zarubin and Reikhman.

The Katyn massacre was entirely in keeping with Stalin's political aims— to purge Poland of all patriotic elements, to wipe out the intelligentsia, and thus to clear the ground for a pro-Soviet regime. This was the policy he later pursued, at the time of the Warsaw uprising in 1944 and after that, when the Red Army was extending its control over all of Polish territory.


## THE STATE AND THE CHURCH

The influence of the Russian Orthodox church and the number of its practicing members had been greatly reduced by the socioeconomic transformations in the Soviet Union and by government persecution. Of the 50,000 priests and 163 bishops before the revolution, only slightly more than 100 priests and 7 bishops remained at the outbreak of war. One thousand monasteries and sixty seminaries had been closed.[75] In response to government persecution, all sorts of sects and communities, a kind of "church of the catacombs," came into being.

On the eve of World War II the religious policies of the party and the state began to change: the party understood the need to revive and exploit patriotic feelings. In the fall of 1939, after the annexation of the western Ukraine and Byelorussia, and again in the summer of 1940, after the occupation of the Baltic states, the patriarch of Moscow sent his bishops to these regions. The government was hoping in this way to win the complete submission of its new subjects. The Moscow Patriarchate willingly carried out this mission, since its own interests were being served as well.

The church was not left floundering by the German invasion. On June 22, 1941, the vicar general, Metropolitan Sergii, issued an appeal to the church and the people, calling on them to defend the country, and he condemned those priests who refused to heed his call. At the other extreme, in Berlin, Metropolitan Seraphim urged the Orthodox faithful to rise up against bolshevism under Hitler's leadership.[76] During the first two years of the war, Sergii issued twenty-three epistles praying for victory. On his initiative, collections were taken up to finance the formation of the Dmitry Donskoi tank column.[77] Stalin was generous enough to accept this gift from the church.

The German invasion awakened a tide of religious feelings among the population.[78] In the occupied territories the Germans authorized the resumption of religious worship. For Hitler, the function of the church was to help the occupation authorities keep the population submissive. The religious aspect of the matter was of little interest; in Germany itself the Nazis did little more than tolerate the church. One of their objectives was to prevent any unification of the Russian Orthodox church and the antonomous Ukrainian church. The law on religious tolerance published in Berlin on June 19, 1942, was in fact a measure designed to regulate religion. All religious organizations were ordered to register with the German district commissar. The commissar had the right to remove any priest suspected of political unreliability. Religious organizations, and their local and central officials, had to limit their activities to strictly religious matters or else face penalties ranging from fines up to the dissolution of the church community.[79] Shortly before the promulgation of this law, Hitler told his inner circle: "The formation of unitary churches for larger parts of the Russian territory is . . . to be prevented. It can [only be] in our interest if each village has its own sect which develops its own image of God."[80]

The special units, *Einsatzgruppen*, which were in charge of exterminating Jews and other "undesirables," were also given the power to control the activities of the church, up to and including the arrest and execution of priests.

The main objective of Nazi policy vis-à-vis religion was to use the religious sentiments of the population to Germany's advantage. As one German document stated: "All the resources of the churches, mysticism, religion, and propaganda must be . . . employed to this end: 'Hitler against Stalin!'— or 'God against the Devil.'"[81]

Sometimes German commanders supported the resumption of religious activities on the territory under their control.[82] Their aim was purely pragmatic: to ensure a secure rear area for the German army and safe communication lines by placating the local population. However, such commanders were severely reprimanded in Berlin. For example, following the celebration of a mass in the Smolensk Cathedral in August 1941, Hitler ordered the Wehrmacht not to help the church in the occupied territories.[83]

The clergy's attitude toward the German occupation varied widely: from open support to the organization of resistance. In this respect, the story of Metropolitan Sergii Voskresensky is instructive. Sent to Riga as bishop in 1940, he refused to return to Moscow after the outbreak of the war. The Gestapo arrested and later released him, and he began preaching in favor of a German victory. At the same time he revived religious life in the Baltic region. By 1943 he had organized approximately 200 parishes, religious education was underway, and the church was publishing its own magazine. Such was Sergii's religious influence in the Pskov region that the Germans ordered his transfer to Vilnius. This was the beginning of a series of conflicts between Sergii and the Germans. He was assassinated on April 28, 1944, on the road from Vilnius to Riga, presumably by the Germans.[84]

Naturally, the mass of believers did not have the slightest idea of what the Germans were plotting behind the scenes in regard to the church. What mattered to them was the right to express their religious beliefs openly, without fear of persecution. They never suspected that the Germans not only reviewed sermons for proper subject matter but also censored the texts.

On September 4, 1943, Stalin met with Metropolitan Sergii and two other high church officials. He approved the patriotic activities of the Orthodox clergy and faithful and authorized election of a "patriarch of Moscow and all Russia" and the gathering of a Holy Synod.[85] In a special appeal to the priests of the occupied regions, Metropolitan Sergii of the Moscow Patriarchate warned against any collaboration with the enemy, which would be an act of "treason against the church and the motherland." He condemned Bishop Polikarp of Kiev for collaboration with the Germans.[86]

Thus, not only was the state reconciled with the church; it also acknowledged de facto that the church would be considered (when needed) an integral part of the regime. On September 8, Sergii was elected patriarch by a Council of Bishops, which adopted a major document entitled "Condemnation of the Traitors to the Faith and to the Motherland." It stressed that "every person guilty of treason to the cause of the church and who has gone over to the camp of fascism will be excommunicated as an enemy of the Cross, and if he is a bishop or other clergyman, will be defrocked."[87] The war against Nazi Germany was thus proclaimed one of the goals of the Orthodox church.

Soon afterward, a theological institute with a two-year course of study was opened in Moscow, and one-year theology courses were authorized in the dioceses.[88] Prayers for Stalin's health were organized in all churches. The metropolitan of Kiev and Galicia wrote fervently in the church magazine: "The faithful see in our leader . . . the incarnation of all that is best and brightest, all that constitutes the sacred spiritual heritage of the Russian people, the legacy of their ancestors."[89]

This official reconciliation between Stalin and the church also meant that, from then on, the Soviet regime would support the patriarch and the authorities in their struggle against deviations from the Orthodox line, a kind of "general line" of the church. Soon afterward, many leaders of the New Church repented and were accepted back into the fold of the Orthodox church. The state now intensified its struggle against unauthorized sects all over the country, supporting the official church in every region, such as the Georgian and Armenian Orthodox churches.

As in the past, all church nominations had to be approved by state agencies. As far as privileges went, the high clergy were placed on the same footing as high state and party officials. When the first decorations were issued after the war, among the recipients were bishops of the Russian Orthodox church.

## THE SOVIET UNION AND THE WESTERN ALLIES

From the first hours of the German–Soviet war it became apparent that Hitler's hopes for the political isolation of the Soviet Union were unfounded. Turkish Foreign Minister Saracoglu was the only neutral to speak of it favorably. On hearing of the invasion, he said: "This is not a war, but a crusade."[90] Yet even Turkey remained neutral and stayed out of the war.

The British reaction was different from that of the United States. In 1940–1941, the British empire had suffered defeat after defeat in its outlying regions: General Wavell's Near Eastern offensive failed and was followed by the pro-German coup in Iraq. The British were defeated in Greece and Crete, and a Spanish attack on Gibraltar seemed inevitable. In the naval war the British merchant fleet was suffering enormous losses, particularly in the Atlantic. It became much more difficult for Britain to supply itself with the raw materials and food it needed to survive.[91] For the British, this was one of the worst periods of the war.

In the middle of 1941 both the Soviet Union and Britain inevitably had to face the choice of whether to make an alliance or not—the Soviet Union because of the threat of a German attack; Great Britain because of the very difficult situation in which it found itself after two years of war. A public opinion survey taken in Britain in April 1941 showed that almost 70 percent of those polled favored friendly relations with the Soviet Union. (In March 1939 it had been 84 percent.[92]) The British government had already shown its willingness to form an alliance with the USSR—by its warnings to the Soviet government on the impending German attack, by its attitude in the Hess affair, and by its agreement with the United States on measures to take in support of the USSR in the event of a German–Soviet war. Immediately after the attack of June 22, 1941, Churchill announced that Britain considered itself the ally of the Soviet Union and would render it all possible aid, stressing at the same time that he had been and still was an opponent of communism.[93] His position was far different from that of the British military specialists, who believed that the Soviet Union would be defeated in a matter of ten days.[94]

On July 12, 1941, an agreement was signed in Moscow between Britain and the Soviet Union, both sides undertaking not to make a separate peace with Germany.[95] On August 2 a military and economic pact was signed between the Soviet Union and the United States.[96] And in October a tripartite agreement was concluded on the delivery of arms, military equipment, and strategic materials to the USSR.[97] The flow of supplies soon began, and Allied tanks and airplanes played their part in the Battle of Moscow. Assistance to the Soviet Union was very important in late 1941 and early 1942, when the Germans had reached the outskirts of Moscow and Leningrad and were advancing steadily in the Russian southwest. The Soviet war industry, part of which had fallen into the hands of the Germans and the rest transferred to the east, was virtually paralyzed. U.S. and British arms deliveries were shipped through the dangerous waters of the Arctic Ocean, where German warships sent many Allied ships to the bottom. Allied seamen showed great courage in regularly bringing supplies through to Murmansk. A British air force unit was stationed there to carry out air reconnaissance and to protect the convoys as they approached Soviet shores.

From September 1941 to mid-June 1942 sixteen convoys were sent to the Soviet Union; they delivered over 3,000 planes, 4,000 tanks, 30,000 motor vehicles, and large quantities of other materials.[98] In mid-June these deliveries were suspended because of heavy British losses from attacks by German warships. During the entire war the Allies sent the USSR 18,700 planes, 10,800 tanks, 9,600 guns, 401,400 motor vehicles, 44,600 machine tools, 2,599,000 tons of petroleum products, 517,500 tons of nonferrous metals, 172,100 tons of wire and cable, 1,860 locomotives, and 11,300 flatcars. These contributions amounted to 12 percent of the armament produced in the USSR for use against the Germans.[99] The Allies also sent foodstuffs, clothing, and so on, to the USSR, and American trucks rendered the Soviet army mobile.

On the political level, the U.S.–Soviet–British alliance, formally concluded in 1942, focused on the question of a second front in Western Europe—that is, an Allied landing in France.[100] The political maneuvering over the question of the second front involved not only the exchange of opinions, demands, and promises between the leaders of the three countries but also well-organized public opinion campaigns in Britain and the United States calling for the immediate opening of a second front.

On the military level this was impossible. In 1941–1942 the Allies lacked both the necessary forces and the experience for a gigantic landing of this type. Also, the prevailing British strategic doctrine, which the Americans for a long time accepted, differed radically from that of the Soviets, who were willing to accept higher risks. The Soviet Union especially insisted that its military burden be lightened, and indeed that burden was far heavier than what the Allies bore.

In the summer of 1941, 70 percent of the German armed forces were concentrated on the German–Soviet front. In the first half of 1944, on the eve of the Allied landing, the figure was 63 percent and even after the opening of the second front, it was between 55 and 57 percent.[101] The absence of a second front in Europe meant even greater Soviet military losses, and these were already monumental for many reasons—the general hazards of war, the criminal negligence, mistakes, and oversights of the Soviet government and high command, and the lack of combat experience. From mid-1943 on the Red Army's losses decreased significantly.

In 1943 a second front in France instead of an Allied landing in Italy was perhaps possible. But this time, political considerations came into play, particularly the desire to prevent the USSR from reaching the Balkans, a region which Britain still considered vital to its interests. The landing in Italy could have led to a successful Allied offensive in the Balkans, but this did not come about. At the same time a new question confronted the Allies: Had the USSR built up enough strength to win the war on its own without their assistance? This possibility could not be ruled out and had ominous implications for Britain and the United States.

In November 1943 the Soviets officially announced their peace program. The main points were as follows: liberation of the European peoples from Nazi occupation; assistance to them in restoring their independence; free choice of government for the liberated peoples; severe punishment of those responsible for the war; implementation of the necessary measures to prevent any new German aggression; lasting economic, political, and cultural collaboration among the European peoples.[102] No doubt the program was very appealing. The problem was knowing how to guarantee free elections in practice.

Starting in mid-1943 the foreign and domestic policies of the Soviet Union seemed to pursue more clearly defined goals. Inside the country an effort was made to strengthen the prewar system and reestablish the authority the party had lost since the beginning of the war. The techniques of propaganda and repression needed to achieve this end were brought to bear. In terms of foreign policy, the Soviet Union skillfully took advantage of President Roosevelt's suspicious attitude toward British imperial policy. Roosevelt was counting on firm and lasting collaboration with Stalin. American politicians and experts avidly sought the least sign of what was being called in the West the transformation of communism into Russian nationalism. These hopes increased after May 1943, when Stalin ordered the dissolution of the Communist International, which for a long time had been a rump organization. At the same time the Soviet Union began to strengthen its contacts with the resistance and national liberation movements, especially in Southeastern Europe, cleverly exploiting the natural desire of the Eastern European peoples for a change in the previously existing systems, which had turned their countries into satellites of Germany. This extremely skillful maneuver on Stalin's part provided the Soviet Union with immense possibilities for expansion in the postwar period.

Great Britain and the United States, on the contrary, supported parties and political figures linked in one way or another to the collaborationist regimes or the remnants of the old cliques. Neither the British nor the Americans made timely efforts to find and consolidate centrist and liberal forces in the countries about to be freed from the Germans. This stemmed, on the one hand, from a total lack of understanding of the nature of the Soviet regime and an organic inability by the Western statesmen to assess correctly the thinking of the Soviet leadership and, on the other, from their inability to understand and accept the fact that change was unavoidable, since it was the outgrowth of the struggle against totalitarian nazism.

The American leaders understood the problems of India and the Near East better because the latter involved oil and the former the dismemberment of the British empire, which, as they saw it, would open the doors of the British possessions to American business. Lastly, the Americans, concerned with their war against Japan, overestimated their need for the

Soviet Union in the war. In general, they did not quite understand Europe; its spirit was foreign to them and its problems too complex, dangerous, and irritating.

As a rule, therefore, the United States and Britain continued to support the conservative elements in Eastern and Southeastern Europe, thus playing into the hands of the Communist parties, which were often controlled and led by the Soviet Union. The Communists did what Britain and the United States had been unable to do: from the start they put forward a program of national renewal, by which they won support not only from the working class but from the urban and rural middle classes as well. The policies of the Western Allies were vulnerable: they lacked a concrete, positive program to present to the liberated peoples of Europe. The Communist parties soon filled the void with their programs for action.

Starting in 1943 the Soviet government began to play a leading role in the policies of the anti-German coalition. Stalin himself attended the Teheran conference, held November 28 to December 1, 1943. Cleverly playing on the differences between the United States and Britain, he obtained a firm promise that a second front would be opened in France no later than May 1, 1944. Churchill's plan for another front in the Balkans was rejected. Stalin's second victory at Teheran, which would be confirmed and reinforced at the Yalta conference in February 1945, was the official recognition by the Allies of the Curzon line as Poland's future eastern border. His third victory was the recognition of his claim to Koenigsberg, which historically had never belonged to Russia. For his part, Roosevelt also won a victory with Stalin's agreement to declare war on Japan no later than three months after the end of the war in Europe.

By the end of 1943 the world political and military situation had changed radically. The Allies had settled the great strategic and political questions in Teheran. Intensive preparations for the landing in France began, and in Germany a plot against Hitler by senior officers was ripening. On the German–Soviet front, the Soviet command firmly held the strategic initiative. The Soviet armed forces outnumbered the Germans by 1,259,000 (6,165,000 to 4,906,000). The USSR had 2.5 times as many planes (8,500 to 3,000) and 1.4 times as much artillery (90,000 batteries to 54,000), and so on.[103]

In January 1944 a new Soviet offensive began, resulting in the final breaking of the Leningrad blockade on January 27, 1944, after a siege of 870 days. Novgorod was likewise liberated. Thus the front was moved westward between 150 and 280 kilometers from Leningrad. On the Southwestern Front in the spring of 1944 all of the Ukraine west of the Dnepr was liberated, including Krivoi Rog, Nikopol, Nikolaev, and Odessa. In

April and May came the Crimea's turn. In the south, Soviet troops reached the prewar border along a front 400 kilometers long.

On June 6, 1944, Allied troops landed in Normandy. Germany was caught in the pincers of a two-front war.

On June 10, Soviet troops began a second offensive on the Leningrad Front, occupying Vyborg and reaching the Soviet–Finnish border. On June 23, an offensive on three fronts started toward the west. On July 3, Minsk was liberated, and the next day Soviet troops crossed the old Polish border. During the summer of 1944 most of the territory of the Baltic states was cleared of Germans.

In July and August the Red Army entered Poland and occupied almost one-fourth of its territory, with a population of 5 million. The Soviets were accompanied by Polish troops organized in the USSR. A Polish National Liberation Committee was formed in Lublin in opposition to the Polish government in exile. It had the advantage of being in Poland and of enjoying full military and political support from the Soviet Union. The government in exile was far away, in London, but it had the trust of the overwhelming majority of the country's population.

At the beginning of August 1944 Stanislaw Mikolajczyk, prime minister of the Polish government in exile, arrived in Moscow to hold discussions with Stalin. The talks collapsed. Stalin wanted a government in Poland which recognized the new border and would bow unconditionally to Moscow's political aims. As for the government in exile, it hoped to reestablish an independent Poland whose eastern border would be the same as before September 17, 1939; Britain and the United States helped resolve this dispute in the USSR's favor.

The Soviets set as a condition for settling the Polish question the disarmament and dissolution of all formations of the Home Army, which was loyal to the government in exile. In August Soviet troops occupied the Praga suburb of Warsaw on the right bank of the Vistula. The Polish capital was on the left bank, several hundred meters away. The offensive was cut short because, according to a later official version, it was necessary to reorganize and regroup after a very rapid advance.

The Polish government in exile decided to call for an insurrection in Warsaw to liberate it before the arrival of Soviet troops. On August 1, 1944, underground units of the Home Army, under the command of General Bor-Komarowski, began an insurrection which was joined by many of Warsaw's inhabitants. The Polish command in Warsaw counted on support from the Soviet troops. According to one version of the events, a Captain Kalugin from Soviet field headquarters reached Warsaw and established links with the Polish command. However, his report to his superiors that a Soviet landing on the western bank of the Vistula was possible received no reply. What became of Kalugin after that is not known.

The British and American governments begged Stalin to support the insurgents. Stalin refused, arguing that the insurrection had begun without any prior coordination with the Soviet command and that it was an adventure for which the London Poles were to blame.[104]

On October 2 the insurgents capitulated. Hitler ordered the population removed from the city, the insurgents disarmed and taken prisoner, and most of Warsaw destroyed.

The Warsaw uprising was in the last analysis beneficial to Stalin's political goals. Its failure proved to be fundamentally detrimental to the Polish government in exile. A new trip by Mikolajczyk to Moscow, at a time when Churchill was also there, was futile. Churchill had often warned Mikolajczyk that he would not support him unless he made concessions to Soviet demands.[105] Roosevelt, who had never really involved himself in Polish affairs, stated that he would defer to the Soviet and British governments on the question.He told Mikolajczyk that if a mutual satisfactory agreement would be reached, American government "would offer no objection."[106]

Meanwhile, the Polish armed forces under Soviet command had reached the size of 286,000. On December 31 the Polish National Liberation Committee became a provisional government and was immediately recognized by Moscow. On November 24 Mikolajczyk resigned and a new government was established in London, headed by Tomasz Arciszewski, a leader of the Polish Socialist party and a stubborn opponent of any concessions to Moscow.

This was the situation when Stalin, Roosevelt, and Churchill met once more, this time on Soviet territory, at Yalta.


## YALTA: THE BLESSING OF THE SOVIET EMPIRE

After the Normandy invasion in June 1944 and the attempt on Hitler's life in July, it was clear that the end was only a matter of time, making a summit meeting inevitable.

In the summer and fall of 1944, Soviet armies knocked Finland out of the war, occupied Bulgaria, Romania, Yugoslavia, and a large part of Hungary, and approached Warsaw. They played a major role in deposing governments that had collaborated with Germany and Italy.

In October 1944 Churchill, trying to secure the flanks of the British empire, made a "gentleman's agreement" with Stalin, with Roosevelt's consent, to apportion the influence of Great Britain and the Soviet Union in the Balkans and Eastern Europe. (To this day the Soviet side has denied the authenticity of this agreement.) According to Churchill, Britain recognized that Romania and Bulgaria were in "the sphere of natural Soviet interests" and that "Great Britain will fully respect Russian action." Soviet influence in Hungary was also recognized.[107] Later, in the last days of the war, Churchill tried to snatch Czechoslovakia and urged Eisenhower to occupy Prague before the Soviet army. Eisenhower's refusal, backed by Truman, thwarted Churchill.[108] Only in Greece did the Soviet Union recognize the primacy of British interests. The United States, of its own accord, virtually withdrew from the affairs of Central and Eastern Europe, maintaining an interest only in Poland and of course in Germany and Austria.

Several months before the Yalta conference, the Soviet Union already controlled the fate of Eastern Europe and the Balkans and to a significant degree that of Central Europe. The presence of 6.5 million Soviet soldiers buttressed Soviet claims. This was simply a fact of life, which both Roosevelt and Churchill understood and accepted.

At the end of 1944 and beginning of 1945, Soviet military production had reached its highest point, accounting for 51.3 percent of total industrial production in the USSR.

By October 1944 all the territory of the prewar Soviet Union, except for part of Latvia, had been liberated. The Red Army entered non-Soviet Europe. Romania and Bulgaria were soon out of the war. Bucharest and Sofia fell as the Red Army marched into the Balkans.

Well before their entrance into Europe, Soviet authorities had trained foreign Communist cadres to lead the new pro-Soviet regimes in the nations of Southeastern Europe, where the arrival of the Red Army was soon followed by radical social and economic change. Many of these new government leaders had been officials in the Comintern; others had taken part in the underground Communist movements in their respective countries during the war. The Soviet leadership preferred those who had served in the Comintern, survivors of the purges, whose servility was beyond question. The same tactic was applied everywhere: first of all, unification of all opponents of the old regime, including representatives of the old ruling classes; then the gradual, systematic elimination of all opponents of the Communist party in the given country, all sympathizers of the Communists being recruited to the new regime, all others being suppressed; and finally, an open takeover by the Communists, backed by the armed forces and secret police. In the first stage, the industrial workers and farm workers and part of the peasantry tended to support the program of social reforms put forward by the Communists because it promised to rid the nation of corrupt government and exploitation by capitalist and feudalistic landowners and to give power to the people. Once they realized the new power was worse than the old, it was too late.

In Bucharest on August 23, two days after the beginning of the Soviet offensive, King Michael reached an agreement with the Romanian Communists to oust the dictator, Antonescou. On August 24 Communist units took over all strategic points in the capital. On August 31 Soviet tanks entered the city. King Michael was awarded the highest military honor, the Soviet Order of Victory. Soon afterward he was forced to flee because the Soviet government had decided to put an end to the masquerade and place its cronies in power.

Things went well for the Soviets in Bulgaria from the start, undoubtedly because the revolution had been led by veterans of the Comintern. On September 9 the Communist-led Patriotic Front came to power. Several hundred politicians and parliamentarians were executed; others either fled or pledged allegiance to the new government. Veteran Comintern leader Georgy Dimitrov returned to Sofia.

In Yugoslavia the government was practically in the hands of the Communists, headed by Josip Broz Tito. His was the only party that had led a continuous armed struggle against the invaders from July 1941 on, creating a huge insurrectional army. Final victory was obtained with help from the Red Army, which participated in the taking of Belgrade.

Things went differently in Slovakia, where on August 29, 1944, a popular insurrection broke out when the Germans entered Slovakian territory invited by the puppet government of Monsignor Tiso. The insurrection continued to the end of October 1944 before it was suppressed. The Red Army was unable to break through the German defenses in the Carpathians to help the insurgents.

At the beginning of October 1944 the Soviet army entered Hungarian territory. Horthy announced his break with Germany and asked the anti-Nazi Western powers for a cease-fire. But he was overthrown by Szalasi, the leader of the Hungarian fascists, which greatly prolonged the battle for Hungary. Several times the Soviets launched very costly offensives which did not bring the desired results. Military operations on Hungarian territory ended only with the German withdrawal in March 1945. Power passed to a coalition government supported by Moscow. After some time, the allies of the Communists and the fellow travelers were kicked out of the government and forced to flee the country; others in fact joined the Communist party. Rakosi, an old Cominternist, was placed at the helm. That he had spent twenty years in Hungarian prisons and his way of thinking had not changed since the 1920s had fatal consequences for Hungary.

On July 20, 1944, the German generals' plot against Hitler, long in the planning stages, was finally carried out. But the bomb that went off at Wehrmacht headquarters missed him. All the people involved in the plot were executed. Thus was lost the last hope of those officers who would have liked to reach an understanding with the Allies after Hitler's fall.

By the autumn of 1944 the Germans had successfully stabilized their front in western Prussia, along the Vistula, and in the Warsaw region.

In December 1944 the British and Americans, stopped by the German counteroffensive in the Ardennes (the Battle of the Bulge), appealed to Stalin to divert the Germans and begin the invasion of East Prussia ahead of schedule. By the end of January 1945, one week before the Yalta conference, Soviet forces had reached the Oder–Niesse line, were approaching Frankfurt-am-Oder and Kustrin (Kostrzyn), and had taken Schneidemühl (Pita). The Red Army was only sixty-five kilometers from Berlin.

Selecting a meeting place for the Allied leaders was hardly the minor problem it might seem at first glance. While Roosevelt and Churchill corresponded about the site of their future meeting with Stalin, the latter had already made his decision.

Military action had ended in the Crimea in the middle of May 1944. The palaces in Livadia, Oreanda, and Alupka were renovated and the grounds cleared of debris. Airports, roads, bridges, and railways were quickly put in order. At the same time the native population of the Crimea was also cleared out: the Crimean Tatars were accused en masse, every man, woman, and child, of collaboration with the Germans and deported to Siberia and Central Asia. Whether or not Roosevelt and Churchill knew about these deportations, they constituted a violation of human rights bordering on genocide, a bad omen for the impending conference.

Churchill categorically opposed Stalin's proposal to hold the meeting at Yalta, fearing that it would give Stalin a great advantage. But Roosevelt insisted that they still had to reckon with the most important factor: in the Soviet Union all decisions were made by one man, Stalin. The future of the world would depend on his participation in the conference. The American president believed that if the Allies were patient and understanding, the USSR would take part in the new world organization of nations (the United Nations) and become a constructive force in world affairs.[109] If on the other hand the wartime alliance against the Axis powers were to break up and the world were divided into two armed camps, the Soviet Union could become a disruptive force.

Roosevelt also had other, more practical, considerations. He was incurably ill, and several urgent matters remained unfinished: the utter defeat of Nazi Germany and the establishment of a future world order. He realized that the USSR remained the decisive Allied force in the European theater. Another important task was ending the war in the Far East. Japan still had an army of 4 million, a significant part of which (the Kwantung army) was inaccessible in Manchuria. Putting it out of action, potentially the most important part of the final stage of the war, could be done only by the Soviet Union. Roosevelt's military advisers gloomily predicted that without the Soviet army's help it would take another eighteen months after the end of the war in Europe before Japan could be brought to its knees. They calculated that a landing on the Japanese islands would cost 1 million American lives. This was a weighty argument. The president also knew that a test of the atomic bomb could be conducted no earlier than in five months, in July 1945.

At Roosevelt's insistence Churchill grudgingly accepted Stalin's proposal to hold the conference in the Crimea. From this time on Stalin was in complete psychological control of the situation. His political skill had never attained such heights, nor would it ever again after the conference. True, it was impressively buttressed by the bayonets of the Soviet army, then inundating Europe.

Under the unique conditions of the wartime alliance, a confrontation between two diametrically opposed systems of political thoughts, or more precisely, a clash of two worlds—the Soviet and the free world—took place at Yalta. However, something completely unexpected happened: a convergence not only of viewpoints but also of ways of thinking.

The Soviet world had tremendous advantages, first and foremost its military strength. Its ignorance of the Western world also worked in its favor. Moreover, the West as a whole, not only its leaders, recognized the Soviet Union's decisive role in smashing the German war machine; thus, the Soviet world also had Western sympathy for the sacrifices borne by the Soviet people and the desire to make compensation for them.

There were also more practical considerations. Roosevelt probably hoped—and this was his mistake—that a war in the Far East would divert the Soviet forces from Europe, thus weakening Soviet pressure. The mistake is almost incomprehensible, since the Soviet Union had promised it would declare war on Japan after the conclusion of the war in Europe, when the European theater of operations would no longer require many troops.

It was very easy for Stalin to satisfy Roosevelt. The American president was overwhelmed by Stalin's willingness to collaborate with Chiang Kai-shek, rather than with the Chinese Communists. Roosevelt was also satisfied that Stalin had agreed to join the United Nations under the conditions stipulated by the United States. How could the USSR have refused? It was granted three votes, since the Ukraine and Byelorussia were allowed to join the UN as independent members.

At the time of the Yalta conference, February 4–11, 1945, Soviet prestige in the West was at its peak.

The Western statesmen were concerned most of all over the situation in Poland, which was under Soviet control. Its future was in Stalin's hands. Both the American president and the British prime minister tried to coax what they could out of Stalin. But for Stalin the Polish question had essentially been decided. During the preliminary meeting of foreign ministers to discuss the agenda of the conference, Molotov suggested to Eden that the most important thing was not to interfere with the Poles because Poland was already liberated.[110] Herein lay the essence of the Soviet position: the West should not interfere. Indeed, the Soviet Union was even prepared to make a few concessions, for example, the inclusion of several Polish leaders residing in the West as members of the Polish government which had been organized in the USSR and a promise to hold free elections (a promise never kept). The British requested permission to station British observers in Poland, with a guarantee of their freedom of movement. Stalin was magnanimous. Why observers? Let England and the United States send *ambassadors* to Warsaw. Churchill was grateful. Of course he understood that Poland's fate was in Stalin's hands and sought to mollify him. Still there was a ticklish ethical problem. England had entered the war to defend its ally Poland, invaded by Germany. Poland was a "question of honor for England."[111] Stalin understood that, but explained that for the USSR it was not only a question of honor but of security. Churchill no longer insisted on the return of Lvov to Poland and even recognized the Curzon line as the border between the Soviet Union and Poland. Moreover, Churchill himself provided a justification: "[After] all Russia has suffered in fighting Germany and after all her efforts in liberating Poland, her claim [to Lvov and the Curzon line] is one founded not on force but on right."[112]

Churchill's declaration about the right of the USSR to Lvov was a crucial turning point in the conference. It signified Britain's willingness to sanction the changes in the Soviet–Polish border made when Poland was divided by the Nazi–Soviet pacts of August 23 and September 28, 1939.

Still, Churchill wanted to get Stalin's pledge about the future Polish government. The most important thing, as he saw it, was not the territory but the form of government to be established on it. He was right, of course, in principle. But at this conference everything was important, both territory and power. Churchill proposed the creation of a Polish government without delay, right there at Yalta. Stalin feigned indignation: "I am called a dictator and not a democrat, but I have enough democratic feeling to refuse to create a government without the participation of the Poles themselves."[113] Even the worldly Churchill was flabbergasted. In fact, Stalin and Churchill each made use of the ideological Achilles' heel and the particular language of his opponent. Roosevelt stood, as it were, above the battle. Juggling the very same terms and concepts, while each of the participants at the conference tossed in his own idea, was one of the methods of the political game at Yalta.

However, there was always the danger of "becoming too absorbed." For example, Churchill moved heaven and earth in order to get a more acceptable agreement about Poland from Stalin. Obliquely he tried to show Stalin that he was not hostile to communism. He recalled, for example, that despite his former conflicts with Gallagher, a Communist member of Parliament, he, Churchill, had sent condolences when Gallagher's two adopted children died. Churchill also explained to Stalin that opposition to communism in England was not based on disagreement over the principle of the relation between the individual and the state. During the war the interests of the individual were subordinated to those of the government. One needed only to add, "exactly as in the USSR." The apotheosis of Churchill's display of a benign attitude toward communism was his toast "to the proletarian masses of the world."[114]

In the end the Soviet point of view on the Polish question was the one adopted. It was decided that the London Poles would join the provisional government already existing in Poland, to form a national unity government. The Curzon line was recognized as Poland's eastern border, and the question of the western border was postponed until the following peace conference. The Poles agreed to hold elections as soon as possible, after which the Allies would establish diplomatic relations with the new government.

In the meantime, at the end of March 1945, the Soviet military authorities lured the chiefs of the Polish resistance into an ambush, making them believe that the Soviets wanted to negotiate. They were arrested, taken to Moscow, and tried (the so-called Trial of the Sixteen) in June 1945. They were sentenced to prison terms of various lengths, which they served in Soviet camps, three of them dying there, including General Leon Okulicki, head of the Home Army; one man who was not sentenced was later released to the authorities in the Polish People's Republic, where he died.

The historical meaning of the dispute over the future borders of Poland was understood and exposed by the Mensheviks in exile. An editorial of the party's organ observed the following, based on the example of what happened to Polish territory.

What was being decided and drawn up in advance was the fate of the future world order. Which one will set the precedent: annexation and invasion, or democratic peace? Will the most important Eurasian state, which claims to lead the international working-class movement and to be the bearer of the ideals of the future, successfully pass the test not only of strength (which it has already passed) but also of law and justice, at least in international relations? This is a problem of worldwide importance.[115]

Expansionist by nature, the Soviet system failed this second test.

The conference decided that Germany would be occupied by the Allied troops and the nation would be demilitarized, de-Nazified, and democratized. These measures called for abolition of the armed forces, destruction of the German military machine, an end to Nazi influence in political life, and punishment of all war criminals.

The conference also stated that the Allies had no intention of harming the German people. This was an important declaration because the Nazis presented the Allied demands for an unconditional surrender as meaning the destruction of the German people in the event of defeat and used this prospect to frighten the population into continuing the war. Hitler's last hope was the outbreak of a conflict between the Soviet Union and its Western allies in the final stages of the war.

At Yalta a convergence of the ways of thinking, if not the ideologies, of Stalin and the Western leaders clearly took place. For example, in the discussion of Poland's western borders, there arose the question of where the Germans of East Prussia would go. According to Churchill, the issue was the forced resettlement of millions of people. Personally, Churchill said, he was not terribly shocked by such a prospect, but many in England would be. Giving East Prussia to Poland would mean resettling 6 million Germans. It could be done, Churchill admitted, but still there were persuasive arguments against it. Stalin solved the problem very simply: "When our soldiers arrive all the Germans will flee, and not one German will be left." Churchill responded that the problem then would be how to handle those who fled to Germany, adding: "Of course we have already killed six or seven million Germans and most likely will kill another million before the war is over."

Stalin: "One? Or two?"

Churchill: "Oh, I'm not proposing any limitation. So there should be room in Germany for some who will need to fill the vacancy. I am not afraid of the problem of the transfer of populations as long as it is in proportion to what the Poles can manage and what can be put in the place of the dead in Germany."[116]

The three leaders repeatedly expressed their commitment to Allied unity.

The very thought that one of them would try to attain world supremacy was dismissed as preposterous.[117] All three favored a better and more stable world. Roosevelt was moved to liken the relationship among the allies to the relations among members of a family.[118]

But what was each of them really thinking? Stalin knew that events would take a different turn after the war. Indeed, he did not hide this. Therefore he tried to accomplish everything he could at Yalta while he had the chance. The issue of the future of Germany quite probably bothered him most; after all, Eastern and Southeastern Europe were virtually recognized as in the Soviet sphere. However, a solution to the German problem did not depend on Stalin alone. Although he agreed in principle with the American and English proposal to dismember Germany, in actuality that solution contradicted his concept of a Soviet–German alliance and, more specifically, his plan to exploit German material and human resources for the restoration and development of the Soviet economy.

Reparations became a subject of heated discussion. Britain and the United States, recalling the experience with reparations after World War I, were extremely reluctant to open discussion of the problem. Churchill jokingly suggested solving the problem of reparations according to the principle, "To each country according to its needs, from Germany according to its ability." But Stalin rejected this allusion to the principle of communism. He had a different maxim: "To each according to his worth."[119] Churchill explained frankly that England did not oppose confiscation of German factories by the Soviet Union, as long as England could still get German exports. Stalin calmly reassured him, "Of course the Russians will confiscate German factories as soon as they reach them."[120]

How Stalin really envisioned the future Germany would become clear only four years later, when the German Democratic Republic was established. At Yalta Stalin confined himself to the telling prediction that, indeed, Germany did have a future.[121] Time would show that Stalin envisioned this future to be in a Sovietized Europe.

In reading the Yalta documents on the rights of small nations, one is struck by the actual similarity of what appear to be different viewpoints on the part of Stalin and the Western leaders. Stalin made it perfectly clear that he would never agree to submit any action of the great powers to the judgment of the small nations: "Do you want Albania to have the same status as the United States? What has Albania done in this war to merit such a standing? We three have to decide how to keep the peace of the world, and it will not be kept unless we three decide to do it."[122] Somehow, Stalin complained, certain liberated countries had gotten it into their heads that although the great powers had shed blood for their liberation, they could accuse the great powers of not taking the rights of small countries into account. (One wonders whether Enver Hoxha, who wrote a heart-felt book about Stalin, ever read the papers of the Yalta conference.)

Roosevelt agreed that the great powers bore the greater responsibility and that *"the peace terms should be written by the three powers represented at Yalta"* (emphasis added—A. N.).[123] Churchill observed conciliatorily: "The eagle should permit the small birds to sing, and care not whereof they sing."[124] But the "Mountain Eagle," as Stalin was sometimes called in the USSR, having just deported entire lesser nationalities, wanted the "small birds" to keep silent altogether. Andrei Vyshinsky, no doubt on Stalin's orders, warned Charles Bohlen (Roosevelt's interpreter at Yalta and later ambassador to Moscow) that the Soviet Union would never agree to the right of the small powers to judge an act of the great powers. When Bohlen observed that the U.S. delegation at the conference always had to keep in mind the concern of the American people that the rights of smaller nations be protected, the former public prosecutor snapped, "The American people should learn to obey their leaders." Bohlen sarcastically retorted that if Vyshinsky were to visit the United States, he, Bohlen, would like to see him tell that to the American people.[125] A little while later Vyshinsky, the "prosecutor of death" in the purge trials, would go to New York as the Soviet delegate to the United Nations and would tell the American people and the "small birds" that chirped there what they needed to know. And the American press would sing the praises of Vyshinsky's mind, energy, and wit.

A frank exchange, as it were, between the democratic and Soviet experience of rule took place at Yalta. Several times during the conference Churchill, seeking a concession from Stalin, reminded him that general elections were soon to take place in England and that if a satisfactory outcome were not reached at Yalta he could be removed from power. After all, the Soviet Union had no better friends than he and Eden. Stalin consoled his "comrade-in-arms" with the thought, "Victors are never kicked out," and added for the British prime minister's edification: "People will understand that they need a leader, and who could be a better leader than the one who won the war?" Churchill tried to explain that England had two parties and that he belonged to one of them. "Stalin has a much easier task since he was only one party to deal with." Stalin weighed the situation: "One party is much better," he said profoundly.[126]

Who would know better than Stalin?

The United States and Great Britain gave de facto recognition at Yalta to the formation of the Soviet empire, whose European borders stretched from the Baltic in the north to the Adriatic in the south and in the west to the Elbe and the Werra. In the Far East, in exchange for joining the war against Japan, the USSR received Southern Sakhalin and the Kurile islands, so that its borders almost reached the Japanese island of Hokkaido. Only a small strip of water would now separate the USSR from Japan.

The signing of the agreement which stipulated the conditions for the Soviet entry into the war against Japan crowned the Soviet empire. The president of the United States and the prime minister of Great Britain became this empire's godfathers, but these godfathers were hardly being altruistic. They obtained what they felt was most vital for their respective countries at the time when the war was coming to an end in Europe: agreement on a general policy regarding defeated Germany, recognition (albeit only verbal on the Soviet side) of the dissemination of democratic principles in the liberated countries of Europe; approval of the new world organization of nations; and Soviet agreement to enter the war against Japan. Given the domestic political situations in the United States and Britain, the prevailing pro-Soviet sentiment in the West, and finally the actual military situation at the time, it is unlikely that the United States and Britain could have achieved anything more.

## THE CAPITULATION OF GERMANY

The final Soviet offensive, operation Vistula-Oder, began on January 12, 1945. On two fronts (the First Byelorussian and First Ukrainian) the command had concentrated 45 percent of its regulars, 70 percent of its tanks, 43 percent of its guns and mortars, and its entire air force. At that point, the Soviet forces were twice the size of Germany's in soldiers, three times in artillery, and seven times in aircraft.[127]

From January 12 to January 17, the German defenses were breached along a wide front. At the beginning of February the Soviets took Silesia, reached the Oder, and established a bridgehead on the river's left bank. The German army suffered enormous losses: thirty-five divisions were completely destroyed, and twenty-five lost between 60 and 70 percent of their regulars.[128] According to Soviet figures, the Germans suffered half a million casualties, killed, wounded, or captured. The Red Army also took many guns and airplanes. At that point, Soviet troops were between 80 and 160 kilometers from Berlin.

On April 25 American and Soviet troops met in the vicinity of Torgau, on the Elbe. On April 26 the war entered its final stage. On April 30 Hitler committed suicide. On May 1 Soviet soldiers raised the victory flag in Berlin. The day after, the fight for Berlin was over. On May 7 the Soviets reached the Elbe along a wide front. On May 8 Germany signed an unconditional surrender in Karlshorst, a suburb of Berlin, Zhukov signing for the Soviet Union.

The war that had started on September 1, 1939, was over.

## A CHALLENGE TO THE REGIME

Among the most complex problems of the World War II period in Soviet history, and one that Soviet historians are not allowed to study, is the question of collaboration on the part of some Soviet citizens. The Soviet literature on this subject endlessly repeats the same stereotyped formulas about the traitor Vlasov, the general who defected to the Germans, and the just retribution that came to him. Yet it was not just a question of Vlasov.

At the end of the war the Wehrmacht had in its ranks over 1 million Soviet citizens of various nationalities, including several hundred thousand Russians. These people came from many different backgrounds and had chosen to collaborate with the Germans for a variety of reasons. Many prisoners of war, having been abandoned by their government, signed up with Vlasov as a means of surviving in the German camps. They probably hoped to cross over to the Red Army at the first opportunity. Others hoped to sit things out until the war ended. There were those, however, who joined the Nazis of their own free will, out of political conviction or simple hatred of the Soviet government, which they wished to overthrow and replace with one more to their liking.

One of them later wrote that the German occupation allowed anti-Soviet attitudes to come to the fore:

> If all of Russia had been occupied, it is very possible that the entire country would have become anti-Soviet. Under Soviet rule, these people remained docile and did not reveal their revolutionary inclination, something that requires a great effort of will. At the beginning of the war, the conviction that the Soviet government would soon collapse lent courage to even the most passive elements.[129]

Among Soviet prisoners of war, anti-Soviet ideologists made their appearance. Of these, special mention should be made of Milety Aleksandrovich Zykov (probably a pseudonym), who claimed to have been an assistant to the editor of *Izvestia* from 1931 to 1935, to have been arrested in the purges, and then to have been released in March 1942. After being taken prisoner by the Germans, he drafted a memorandum calling for the creation of a new Russian government and army, headed by some Soviet general among the prisoners of war. This government would make a defensive alliance with Germany.

Another ideologist was Georgy Nikolaevich Zhilenkov, former secretary of the party in the Rostokino District of Moscow and later a member of the military council of the Twenty-fourth Army. In the fall of 1942, while in German captivity, he was appointed commander of the Central Experimental Unit, the "Ossinotorf Brigade," consisting of Russians and used against the Red Army. With Colonel Vladimir Boyarsky, excommander of the Soviet Forty-first Guards Division, Zhilenkov wrote several memoranda in which he called on the German government to form a Russian National Committee and a Russian army of 50,000–80,000 men, launch a war of national liberation against the Stalinist regime, and promise the Russian people an independent development in the framework of the "new order" in Europe. These memoranda were seasoned with a good dose of anti-Semitism. [130]

In mid-August 1942, Colonel Mikhail Shapovalov, former commander of a Soviet artillery corps, who was taken prisoner at Maikop, drafted a similar document.

It seems that Soviet officers who were prisoners of the Germans discussed the future of the Soviet Union intensively. All sorts of tendencies appeared, and many different proposals were made. One of them was that a "Committee for the Implementation of the 1936 Constitution" be formed.

To Hitler, however, the idea of having Russian, Slavic, allies seemed atrocious. He categorically forbade the arming of anyone in the occupied territories. "Only Germans shall have the right to bear arms," he ruled. [131]

As early as 1941 some German officers, who kept their distance from Nazi racial theories and were concerned only with military considerations, began to use Soviet prisoners as auxiliary personnel: interpreters, drivers, railroad police, and so on, and even as support troops. Later, with the development of the partisan movement, Russian units were formed against them. For example, in the Lokot District of the Bryansk Region a Russian brigade, 20,000 strong, was organized to fight the partisans. It was called the Russian National Liberation Army (Rossiiskaya Osvoboditelnaya Natsionalnaya Armiya—RONA), although it had police functions only. It was headed by Bronislav Kaminsky, an adventurer notorious for his cruelty. He enjoyed the absolute trust of the German authorities and was in effect the master of the district; he had been granted full power to police the area. By virtue of his service in the struggle against the partisans, Kaminsky was promoted to brigadier general by the Germans, and his "army" became an SS division. In the summer of 1944, this division was assigned to help crush the insurgents in Warsaw. Later the German commander ordered Kaminsky shot for the atrocities committed by his troops. [132]

In July 1941, on the initiative of Colonel von Tresckow, the chief of operations for the staff of the German Army Group Center who later participated in the 1944 plot against Hitler, a Russian brigade was formed under a Colonel Sakharov. In the same army group a Cossack unit was formed, headed by a former Red Army major and regimental commander named Kononov, a member of the Communist party since 1927. Kononov defected to the Germans on August 22, 1941.[133]

At the end of December 1941, with Hitler's blessing, the organization of "national legions" of non-Russian Soviet prisoners began. In total numbers these units were not very large: 110,000 from the Caucasus; between 110,000 and 170,000 from Central Asia and Kazakhstan; 20,000 Crimean Tatars; and 5,000 Kalmyks. On average, 15 percent of each unit consisted of Germans.[134]

Some former Soviet prisoners of war even became officers or noncommissioned officers in the national legions, but they did not have the right to issue orders to German soldiers. A very important fact that must be borne in mind is that many of the legionnaires were precisely exprisoners of war, rather than men who had deliberately crossed over to the German side. The fighting capacity of these units was not very high, and between 2.5 and 10 percent of the legionnaires deserted.

In 1943 70–80 percent of the national legions were sent west. Sometimes the legionnaires made contact with local resistance groups and went over to them.[135] There were cases of open rebellion against the Germans, like the one in April 1944 by a Georgian battalion on Texel Island in Holland. It is probable that if the Soviet government had not abandoned its soldiers who were prisoners of the Germans, such cases of rebellion and of legionnaires joining the Resistance or crossing over to the Red Army would have been more numerous. But having lived in the Soviet Union, they knew only too well how vindictive the Soviet government could be. Nevertheless, in 1944 an SS regiment commanded by G. Alimov and made up of soldiers from Turkestan joined the uprising in Slovakia.

Such instances were not always the rule, however. For example, the Nazis used legionnaires and Cossack units against the resistance movements in Western Europe and the Balkans and in the suppressions of the Warsaw uprising in 1944. Also, in the Saint Donat massacre in the Drome region of France they used troops from the "national legions" (called Mongols by the local French population).[136]

It is important to understand the reasons that led individuals or groups to collaborate with the Germans. As a general rule, persecution by the Soviet government, particularly harsh during the period of collectivization, was responsible, as were the massive repression of the later 1930s and the chauvinist policies toward non-Russian minorities. It is not surprising that instances of collaboration with the enemy, including combat on the German side, were more frequent in both relative and absolute terms among non-Russian nationals than among Russians.

One can only speculate about the course events might have taken if, instead of implementing a policy of genocide, repression, and violation of human and national sensibilities, the Nazis had adopted a more moderate attitude, one more acceptable to the population, Russian or otherwise. Such a policy was impossible, however; the Nazis would have stopped being Nazis, and World War II would probably not have taken place. Hitler's Germany sought total subjection and partial extermination of the peoples of the Soviet Union, Poland, and other Eastern European states. Whatever the differences of opinion within the Nazi leadership over tactical questions, their goal remained unchanged: to enslave the Slavic peoples and make permanent the Reich's hegemony over Europe. This explains why the enemies of the Stalinist dictatorship in the Soviet Union had no choice but to fight the merciless invader of their country. They did so, however, with the secret hope that after victory things would improve.

After the German defeat at Moscow, some German experts on Soviet affairs, as well as some officials of the Reich, began to feel more and more convinced that Germany could win only if the Russian national anti-Stalinist forces could be rallied. [137] But this project ran counter to the official doctrine of the master race and the subhumans. The German experts in charge of psychological warfare against the USSR thought that if a "Russian de Gaulle," a Soviet general, could be found, the Red Army's anti-Stalinist forces would rally around him.

A search for such a general started in the prison camps. That was how Vlasov was found. He had commanded the Second Shock Army and had been captured on the Volkhov Front in July 1942. Vlasov was reputed to be one of the most capable Soviet generals. In 1942 he turned forty-two. He had served in the Red Army since 1919 and was a party member. His peasant background and excellent army record gave him impeccable credentials. At one time he had commanded the Ninety-ninth Infantry Division, which was considered the finest in the Kiev Military District before the war. During the defense of Kiev he had commanded the Thirty-seventh Army and, during the Battle of Moscow, the Twentieth Army. Then he had served as deputy commander of the Volkhov Front and finally as commander of the Second Shock Army. Those were Vlasov's outstanding credentials. [138] For a while, Stalin himself had wanted to assign him to command the Stalingrad Front. [139] Vlasov enjoyed an excellent reputation in the army because on three occasions he had extricated his troops from German encirclement. He was also distinguished by great personal courage.

What led him to accept the Nazi offer? To judge from documents that survived and accounts by his contemporaries, Vlasov was deeply disillusioned with the Stalin regime. He had witnessed all the prewar purges in the army. Also, he had been one of those who had to bear the bitter burden of defeat during the first year of war. The incompetence, brutality, and irresponsibility of the top leadership caused him to rebel inwardly. This inner break with the Stalinist system ripened under the tragic conditions of captivity. Vlasov became involved in the Germans' game, hoping to come out of it with an independent Russian national army allied with Germany. One cannot help but wonder at his political naiveté. From the start he made a fatal mistake: nothing but destruction awaited Russia upon Hitler's victory. There was no reason whatsoever to expect help from Germany in the struggle against Stalin. Hitler's war was directed, not against Stalin personally or bolshevism alone, but against the very existence of Russia as a nation.

The Soviet Union was part of a coalition that included the Western democracies, the United States and Great Britain, and the resistance movements. Nazi Germany was a deadly threat to all of them. Vlasov enjoyed a certain sympathy from some Wehrmacht officers, who had been assigned to use him and his reputation for propaganda purposes and who invested considerable effort in supporting him as the aspiring leader of an independent anti-Stalinist movement.

Undoubtedly, although Vlasov genuinely expected to benefit from his alliance with the Germans in his struggle against Stalin, the Germans never considered him an ally. He was a veteran Soviet general and, in his own fashion, a Russian patriot. And that was precisely what aroused the Nazis' mistrust of him. For the Nazis he could be nothing more than a means to help them attain their ends. As in the case of the national legions, it was only the exigencies of war that led the Germans to authorize the formation of the Russian Liberation Army, the ROA. The Nazis trusted neither of these formations. They used some of them to fight partisans in the occupied Soviet territories and the resistance movements in the West. But as a general rule the Nazis feared using these units against the Red Army, considering their defection likely.

Whether Vlasov had read *Mein Kampf* or merely heard of it, German cruelty to Soviet prisoners of war and "Eastern workers" should have led him to question the morality of being in league with the Nazi racists. It is true that no such scruples had prevented Stalin from signing the German–Soviet pact and later waging a joint struggle with the Nazis against the

Polish resistance. There was another historical precedent. During World War I the Bolsheviks had openly favored the defeat of tsarist Russia in the war with Germany, employing the slogan "Turn the imperialist war into a civil war." Moreover, they had accepted financial aid from the German General Staff. But when Vlasov decided to lead a struggle against Stalin, his choice of allies was no less important than the struggle itself. In fact, it was not he who made the choice: the German officers, concerned with the outcome of the war, chose him from among dozens of Soviet generals in German captivity. They made the selection at their own risk, hoping that the Nazi leaders would understand Vlasov's value in rallying the Russian army against the Soviet regime.

From his first leaflet, drafted by German propaganda specialists and signed by him on September 10, 1942, at the Vinnitsa prisoner of war camp, a leaflet calling on the Soviet intelligentsia to join forces in the struggle against Stalin and his clique, Vlasov allowed himself to be used for Nazi propaganda aims. Contrary to the facts, he said that the executions of Soviet prisoners and brutality toward them by the Germans were nothing but "false propaganda." In this "open letter," he called for an alliance with Germany, which was highly misleading, of course, for Germany had no intention of allying itself with Vlasov. It is true, however, that the German officers had told Vlasov otherwise.

At the end of 1942 the Germans authorized and helped in the formation of a Russian National Committee, but they hid the fact that they only needed the organization for propaganda purposes. Among the several dozen Soviet generals held prisoner, only a few agreed to participate in the committee, among them Major General V. F. Malyshkin, former head of the general staff of the Nineteenth Army, taken prisoner in the Battle of Vyazma; Major General F. I. Trukhin, former head of the operations section of the general staff of the Baltic Military District; and Major General Ivan Blagoveshchensky, commander of a coastal artillery unit. The propaganda section of the committee was entrusted to M. A. Zykov, and foreign relations to G. N. Zhilenkov.

On December 27, 1942, the Russian National Committee published its program, the so-called Smolensk Manifesto.[140] It had thirteen points, including the following demands: abolition of the kolkhozes and transfer of the land to the peasants; reinstitution of private trade and professions; an end to forced labor; freedom of speech, assembly, and religion; and release of all political prisoners. The manifesto called on Red Army soldiers and officers to join the ranks of the Russian Liberation Army, "which is fighting shoulder to shoulder with the Germans." It also referred to Germany as a nation which, under Hitler's leadership, sought to create a new order in

Europe, free of Bolsheviks and capitalists. Although this manifesto was named after the city of Smolensk, it was actually written in Berlin.[141] Soon after the publication of the manifesto, Vlasov was allowed to speak in several occupied cities. At a public meeting in Mogilev he demanded that the Germans make known their intentions concerning Russia. He also said, "The Russian people lives, has lived, and will live. It can never be turned into a colonized people." Hitler forbade any more public speeches by Vlasov in occupied Soviet territory. In a memorandum, the Führer defined Vlasov's movement as solely an instrument of German propaganda. The overwhelming majority of "Eastern soldiers" were sent west.

How deeply disappointed Vlasov and his collaborators were over German policy may be seen from some of their public statements. Malyshkin complained to an audience of 5,000 Russian emigrés gathered in the Wagram Hall in Paris: "The German command has not succeeded in persuading the Russian people that the German army is only fighting against bolshevism and not against the Russian people itself." Malyshkin called on the Germans to change their policies and asserted that Russia had never been and would never be a colony. He added: "Russia can be defeated only by Russia."[142] This sentence, borrowed from Schiller's *Demetrius*, became the trademark of all Vlasovite propaganda.

In the summer of 1944, shortly after the attempt on Hitler's life, Himmler, who had been one of the principal opponents of the Russian Liberation Army, had the idea of using Vlasov's movement to serve the interests of Germany, which at that point was heading toward defeat. On September 16 he met with Vlasov; as a result of this meeting the idea of a Russian political movement fighting alongside the Germans against the Stalin regime was revived. The decision was made to create a Committee for the Liberation of the Peoples of Russia (KONR). Vlasov was assigned to bring into this committee all the "national committees" already established under German auspices. Himmler promised that the KONR would be recognized as a provisional government once the German army had reconquered Soviet territory. Naturally, Himmler could easily promise anything he wanted. For him the main thing, of course, in view of the horrendous losses Germany had incurred, was to deploy additional military forces against the Red Army—be they Russian, Turkic, or anything else, as long as they would fight for the Reich. In addition, the KONR could be used for propaganda purposes. The KONR was under the direct control of Himmler's secret police apparatus, which in June 1944 had kidnapped and murdered the ideologist of Vlasov's movement, Zykov.

On November 14, 1944, the KONR met in Prague and adopted the so-called Prague Manifesto, which called for the overthrow of Stalin's tyranny, liberation of the peoples of Russia from the Bolshevik system, and restoration of the rights won in the "popular revolution of 1917." Included among the manifesto's goals were an end to the war and an honorable peace with Germany. The future regime was portrayed as a free state of all the people, "without Bolsheviks or exploiters."[143]

The KONR program curiously combined recognition of the necessity for, and legitimacy of, the 1917 revolution with condemnation of the Bolshevik betrayal of revolutionary ideals. That point of view was a seductive one for many Russian and Soviet intellectuals, who favored ideas of socialism but rejected the excesses of the Stalinist dictatorship. The future social and political order in Russia was presented as a strong centralized state (national labor) which would carry out tasks typical of a welfare state, providing social justice, equality, and a guaranteed standard of living. Specific to the Soviet situation was the demand for dissolution of the kolkhozes and a return to private enterprise.

In the opinion of Boris Nicolaevsky, a well-known political writer and Menshevik leader, the central idea of the Vlasov movement "was not the formation of an army to lead an armed struggle against Stalin's dictatorship but an attempt at creating an anti-Bolshevik program on the basis of a democratic program, not narrowly nationalist or separatist, but federalist, oriented toward Russia as a whole."[144]

Vlasov's movement was a very complex phenomenon, born under exceedingly unfavorable historical conditions, a fact that left an indelible mark upon it. Its complexity can be seen, for example, in the documents of the movement and the speeches of its leaders. Having decided to become allies of the Nazis, they were forced to abide by certain rules and pay tribute to Hitler's policies. This is not, however, the only reason for the anti-Semitic views of several prominent leaders, such as Zhilenkov and Malyshkin.[145] The curriculum of the ROA propaganda schools included a special anti-Semitic segment which repeated Nazi propaganda word for word.[146] However, in drafting the Prague Manifesto, Vlasov and others firmly resisted all pressure to include anti-Semitic slogans in the program.[147] It would seem that Nicolaevsky was right that the KONR's call for an end to the "criminal war" led by the Soviet Union and British and American plutocrats against Germany amounted to nothing but the parroting of Nazi propaganda. It has been argued that without such wording the manifesto could never have been published.[148]

Should Vlasov be considered an anti-Stalinist and the head of a political movement? There can be no unequivocal answer. Probably Vlasov, the Soviet generals who rallied to his cause, and the majority of his closest collaborators were convinced anti-Stalinists. This hypothesis is supported by the fact that there was some freedom of choice for the Soviet generals in German captivity. General M. F. Lukin, former commander of the Nineteenth Army, was offered the leadership of the future "Russian army" by the Germans. Lukin countered with an offer he knew to be unacceptable to the Nazis, and they did not approach him again. He survived the war, then spent a number of years in Soviet prison. But General Karbyshev, who also refused to collaborate with the Germans, was frozen to death at Mauthausen.

It is difficult to avoid the impression that the program of social reforms camouflages the most important fact of the time when it was conceived: Vlasov had no chance whatsoever of freeing himself from the Germans, who wanted to use him, the ROA, and the KONR solely for their own purposes. Vlasov understood that the moment had passed, that Germany had lost the war. But he harbored naive hope, encouraged by the "Solidarists" of the NTS (National Labor Alliance of Russian Solidarists), that a conflict was inevitable between the Soviet Union and its Western allies. These illusions, incidentally, were shared and supported by the entire Nazi leadership. Vlasov counted on reaching an understanding with Great Britain and the United States, but his hopes were doomed.

At the end of January 1945 the KONR armed forces were formed. At Hitler's request, Vlasov was named commander. He never succeeded in bringing under its banners all the "Eastern troops" and other German formations in which Soviet citizens and emigrés were serving (numbering approximately 1 million all together). How many men did Vlasov's army have? Estimates vary: it is probable that at most he had between 50,000 and 60,000 men. In any event, at the end of April 1945 the First Division had 20,000 men; the army consisted of two divisions, neither fully equipped, plus reinforcement units.

The composition of the divisions was heterogenous. The First Division, according to an American researcher, consisted of a certain number of soldiers from the Kaminsky Brigade who had taken part in the suppression of the Warsaw uprising and some SS men from Byelorussian units of the Siegling division who had fought against the Allies in the West.[149] The Vlasovites deny this allegation. The majority, however, had served in "Eastern units" of the German army or had been Soviet *Ostarbeiter*, prisoners of war, or refugees from the USSR. The Second Division, which was only in the process of formation, consisted of "Eastern battalions" from Norway, and former prisoners of war and *Ostarbeiter*. Among ROA troops there were some war criminals. But it would be unfair to label the whole army as such.

The Vlasovite command made great efforts to recruit to their army among the *Ostarbeiter*, but the task was not an easy one. Colonel Koreisky of the ROA, who attended a meeting in Sosnowiec (Upper Silesia) to celebrate the publication of the Prague Manifesto, later recalled:

> The *Ostarbeiter* would walk in front of us, barefoot, dirty, with tears in their eyes. Colonel Kromiadi could not bear it and began to cry. These slaves of the Germans, our sons and brothers, went silently by, every now and then giving us a glance full of revulsion. A young girl yelled at us, "Traitors."...
>
> The prisoners of war and *Ostarbeiter* would join the Polish underground units or organize their own. In battle they fought better than anyone. They had no other choice: victory or death.[150]

Few knew at that time, and few in the Soviet Union know even today, the full extent of military collaboration with the Germans by Soviet citizens. Many Soviet families lost members during the war; for this reason for a long time they considered those who fought on the German side to be traitors pure and simple. In 1945 people in the Soviet Union had other concerns. The masses had gone from a state of desperation in 1941 to a feeling of certain victory in 1943, to a feeling of pride over the total defeat of the despicable enemy in late 1944 and in 1945. Even if some might have wondered where the Vlasovites came from, what prompted them to turn traitor, they preferred to keep their thoughts to themselves. It was only after the 1955 amnesty, when the surviving Vlasovites returned to their homes, that they began to be regarded less harshly and some references appeared in Soviet literary works to the sad plight of the Soviet soldiers who were taken prisoner by the Germans, among them the Vlasovites. After the publication of the first volume of Solzhenitsyn's *Gulag Archipelago*, a polemic arose among the Soviet intelligentsia over the proper attitude to take toward Vlasov. The discussion continues to this day.

History willed, however, that Vlasov's troops should finally take part in the war not on the side of the Nazis but against them. Under the pressure of strategic circumstances, the First Division of the ROA, led by General Bunyachenko, and a unit that had joined it, led by Colonel Sakharov—a total of 20,000 troops—left Germany. On April 28 they entered Czechoslovakia. There Bunyachenko refused to join the German army group led by Schörner: he wanted to safeguard his division for a future that did not seem very clear. The division dug in fifty kilometers from Prague. Vlasov was with it. By that time Soviet and American troops had also entered Czechoslovakia, but Prague was still in the hands of SS units. The Czech National Council placed its hopes on the arrival of the Allies. Unaware of an Allied agreement that Prague was to be occupied by Soviet troops, while the Americans would stop at a line west of Prague, the National Council called for an armed popular uprising.

On May 5 the SS units began an unrestrained massacre of the people of Prague, who had risen up against them. Seeing that no help was on the way, the Czech National Council asked Bunyachenko for assistance. On the morning of May 7, after bloody fighting, Bunyachenko's division defeated the SS troops. But the Czechs then proposed that the ROA division either wait for the Red Army and surrender to it or abandon Prague. Bunyachenko chose the latter course: the division started its last march to surrender to American forces. One may agree with the American author who said that Prague would have been liberated in the following days, regardless of whether Vlasov's division took part in the fighting.[151] It should be added, however, that this would have been done at the cost of Prague's destruction by the SS and the deaths of thousands of Czechs.

Toward the end of the war, Vlasov and his entourage increasingly hoped to see a conflict break out between the Western allies and the Soviet Union. That was why Bunyachenko tried to avoid the deployment of his division on the German side. He expected that the Allies would soon need his troops in a new war against the Stalinist regime. The Second Division also kept moving and avoided taking part in combat on the German side. The Prague uprising was an unexpected opportunity for the Vlasovites to cleanse their record of the blot of collaboration with the Nazis, and Bunyachenko seized that opportunity.

The Vlasovites were quickly disarmed by the Americans, and partly by Soviet troops. Some Vlasovite units managed to escape to the West, thanks in part to the assistance of certain U.S. army commanders.

The American command turned Vlasov over to the Soviets. On August 2, 1946, *Pravda* announced the verdict of the Military Collegium of the Supreme Soviet in the trial of Vlasov and others. The list of accusations was stereotypical: agents of German intelligence, espionage, diversionary activities, and terrorism against the Soviet Union. The *Pravda* announcement indicated that all the defendants had pleaded guilty. Petr Grigorenko in his memoirs states that he was told by a friend from before the war, a Soviet army officer who had been "planted" by the investigative agencies in a prison cell with one of the Vlasovite defendants, that "our one assignment was to persuade Vlasov and his companions to confess to treason without saying anything against Stalin. For such a confession they were promised life. A few of them wavered, but most, including Vlasov and Trukhin, did not."[152]

There were rumors that at least one of them, Major General Trukhin, refused to plead guilty and declared he had been and remained a confirmed anti-Stalinist. To all efforts at persuasion Trukhin replied that he had "not been a traitor and would not confess to treason. Stalin I hate. I consider him a tyrant and will say so in court." As for Vlasov, he responded to threats that he would be tortured to death as follows: "I know. And it frightens me. But it is even more frightening to blacken my own name. Anyhow, our sufferings will not be in vain. The time will come when the people will speak well of us." According to this account, there was no open trial. The defendants were tortured for a long time, then hanged when they were half dead.[153] In fact, it is impossible to determine whether there actually was a trial or if, at the end of the interrogations, the death sentences were simply read and carried out, as had often happened before.

All the accused were hanged: Bunyachenko was not saved by his rescue of Prague from the SS. On the contrary, it worked to his disadvantage, since his action deprived the Red Army of the glory of liberating the city. It is also true that this page of history was immediately rewritten in all Soviet and Eastern European histories and textbooks, which simply state that Prague was liberated by Soviet troops on May 9, 1945.

## POTSDAM, THE WAR AGAINST JAPAN, AND THE BOMB

On July 17, two and a half months after the conclusion of the war in Europe, in Postdam, a suburb of the German capital, the last conference of heads of state of Great Britain, the Soviet Union, and the United States began its work. It lasted until August 2. Roosevelt, who had died in April, was replaced by his vice-president, Harry Truman. During the conference, changes also took place in the British government. Labour won in the general elections at the end of July and Churchill was replaced in the midst of the conference by Clement Attlee, leader of the Labour party. Ernest Bevin, the new British foreign minister, also appeared at the conference. Stalin was thus the only survivor of the wartime Big Three, which gave him specific moral and practical advantages in the Potsdam discussions. But the Soviet Union's biggest asset was the fact that during the course of the war it had become the principal force in the destruction of Nazi Germany. Soviet troops were throughout Europe. By the end of the war Soviet armed forces numbered 11 million.

The Allies were in agreement on the need to disband the Nazi party and to eliminate Germany's armed forces and military potential. Their policy toward the defeated country was expressed in the principles of demilitarization, denazification, decartelization, and democratization. Berlin and the rest of Germany were divided into occupation zones.

By the time of the conference the Soviet Union had already placed the German territories east of the Oder–Neisse line under Polish control. The Soviet position on this question prevailed after some dispute. Great Britain and the United States had no alternative but to acknowledge the *fait accompli*. From then on, Poland's western border was the Oder–Neisse line (that is, a line running south from the Baltic Sea along the Oder and Neisse rivers all the way to the Czechoslovak border). Königsberg and its environs were given to the Soviet Union, as had been agreed at the Teheran conference. The Potsdam conference decided to prepare drafts of peace treaties with Germany's former satellites Finland, Bulgaria, Romania, Hungary, and Italy. To this end a Council of Foreign Ministers was established on a permanent basis, consisting of the ministers of Britain, China, the Soviet Union, France, and the United States.

At Potsdam, the Soviet Union reaffirmed its promise to declare war on Japan.[154] Potsdam marked not only the end of the war in Europe but also the beginning of a new era for humanity, the atomic age. The first tests of the atomic bomb had taken place in the United States on the eve of the conference. Churchill and Truman were excited. According to Field Marshal Alanbrooke, Churchill

> was already seeing himself capable of eliminating all the Russian centers of industry and population without taking into account any of the connected problems, such as delivery of the bomb, production of bombs, the possibility of Russians also possessing such bombs, etc. He had at once painted a wonderful picture of himself as the sole possessor of these bombs and capable of dumping them where he wished, thus all-powerful and capable of dictating to Stalin.[155]

Both Truman and Churchill were surprised by Stalin's indifference toward the news of the detonation of an A-bomb. It was said that either he did not understand or he underestimated the importance of the new weapon. In reality, Stalin was fully aware of what had taken place but was clever enough to hide his feelings.

Two years before the tests in New Mexico, the Soviets had already begun to investigate thermonuclear reactions. At the end of 1942 Georgy Flerov, one of the most capable Soviet physicists, along with his colleague K. A. Petrzhak, had discovered the spontaneous disintegration of plutonium. He explained his findings in a letter to Abram Ioffe, the father of Soviet nuclear physics, and to the State Defense Committee, urging them to focus attention immediately on the problem of harnessing atomic energy and developing an atomic weapon. At more or less the same time another Soviet physicist, Igor Kurchatov, was summoned to Moscow to meet with a group preparing a report on the subject to the Central Committee. The report was given a favorable hearing, and a special bureau was established under Kurchatov. It was not until Stalin returned from Potsdam, however, that special attention was accorded to the atomic project. Beria, the head of state security, was placed in charge of the project, and enormous resources were allocated to it. Soviet intelligence was ordered to devote its efforts to obtaining atomic secrets, and it succeeded in obtaining a great deal. By December 1946 the first Soviet atomic reactor was built.

This example shows quite instructively how history works, how events in one field have an immediate effect on other fields. In Stalin's first postwar policy statement, made in connection with the elections to the Supreme Soviet on February 9, 1946, he stressed that it was essential to encourage scientific research.[156] Scientists' salaries were doubled or tripled, housing was built for them, and they were provided with better medical care than the rest of the population. It was at this point that the higher strata of the scientific community became an integral part of the top bureaucracy.

In April 1941 the Soviet Union had signed a neutrality pact with Japan. This pact served the Soviet Union well during the difficult first two years of war. Thanks to this pact, the Soviet command had been able to risk weakening the Far East and transfer significant military contingents west. The forty divisions stationed in the Far East were far from full strength. From many divisions entire regiments were transferred to the German front, leaving only their numbers as camouflage to confuse the command of the Japanese Kwantung army.

At the beginning of 1942 Japan had definitely abandoned all plans for war against the Soviet Union. After Germany's surrender the Japanese government sought several times to induce the Soviet Union to act as a mediator to end the war between Japan and the Western allies. One purpose of these overtures was to discourage Soviet entry into the war against Japan.

During the Potsdam conference the Japanese government offered to send Prince Konoye to Moscow to initiate talks. Stalin informed Truman and Churchill of the Japanese proposal, explaining that since the Japanese had not expressed willingness to surrender unconditionally, as the Allies insisted, the Soviet government had stated that it could not give a concrete reply to an inquiry made in such general terms.

At Potsdam Truman formally suggested that the Soviet government break its neutrality pact with Japan and enter the war against it, citing the Soviet

Union's obligations as a member of the United Nations. Both Truman and Stalin deliberately disregarded the fact that the UN charter had not yet been ratified; ratification came only on August 20, 1945, eleven days after the Soviet Union declared war on Japan.

But all these were mere legal arguments. Immediately after the end of the war with Germany, four Soviet armies had been hastily transferred to the Far East. Marshal Vassilevsky had been sent there as commander-in-chief, along with Marshals Malinovsky and Meretskov to direct operations. For Stalin, the question of war against Japan had long been decided. This issue had several aspects. On the military level, an offensive in the Far East and the destruction of the Japanese Kwantung army would give the Soviet Union the immense territory of Manchuria and enable it to establish strong points to the southeast of the existing Soviet borders. In the context of continuing civil war in China, the Soviet Union could become an influential force on the continent of Asia, capable of intervening in the affairs of China, Indochina, and Korea. Furthermore, Stalin thought of himself with pride as the man who had regained the lost lands conquered by imperial Russia. From this point of view, to defeat Japan in the Far East would be to avenge the defeat of Russia in the war of 1904. In addition, by participating in the war against Japan, the Soviet Union would acquire the legal and moral right to have a voice in all matters involving the Pacific region.

By the end of July the Soviet command had concentrated 1,500,000 men in the Far East (to the Japanese 1,040,000), 26,000 guns (against 5,360 for the Japanese), 5,500 tanks (against 1,155), and 3,900 planes (against 1,800).[157] Soviet superiority was overwhelming, and the Soviets planned to break Japanese resistance in a very short time, before Japan's capitulation to the United States.

On August 6, the United States dropped the first atomic bomb on Hiroshima. Japan offered to surrender on the one condition that the rights of the emperor be respected. Demanding an unconditional surrender, the United States dropped a second bomb on Nagasaki. When news reached Moscow of the frightening consequences of the first bomb, the Soviet government, not wanting to be late to the "feast of the victors," declared war on Japan. This was officially announced on August 8. The next day the Soviet offensive in Manchuria began.

On August 14 Japan surrendered, in utter shock from the effects of the atomic blasts. Later, Soviet official historiography would say that the surrender was the result of the offensive in Manchuria. In reality, military operations in Manchuria continued until August 19—that is, five days after the unconditional Japanese surrender—when the commander of the Kwantung army, General Yamada, signed a statement of capitulation at Marshal

Vassilevsky's headquarters. The Soviet troops continued their offensive nevertheless, hoping to take as much Manchurian territory as possible and occupy all key points in Manchuria. The troops of the First Far Eastern Front entered Korea and reached the thirty-eighth parallel, the demarcation line agreed on by the American and Soviet armies.

On August 20, the troops of the Trans-Baikal Front occupied Port Arthur and reached the sea between Peking and Mukden. Troops of the Second Far Eastern Front occupied the southern part of Sakhalin Island and also the Kurile islands.

On August 23, the war in the Far East ended.

According to Soviet figures, some 84,000 Japanese troops were killed in these operations. (Japanese sources indicate a figure four times smaller—21,000.) Approximately 600,000 Japanese were captured, including 148 generals. Red Army losses, according to Soviet sources, were insignificant: 32,000 dead and wounded. [158]

On August 14, the day of Japan's surrender, at the height of the Soviet offensive in Manchuria, a Sino–Soviet friendship treaty and other supplementary pacts were signed. One of these turned Port Arthur into a Soviet naval base, although formal civil administration remained in the hands of the Chinese. Port Dalny (Dairen) became a "free city," with a special zone for Soviet piers and depots. An agreement was also signed for joint utilization of the Chinese Eastern Railway. All these agreements were concluded for a thirty-year period. China agreed to recognize the independence of the People's Republic of Mongolia after a plebiscite, which was to be organized. [159] Through the war the Soviet Union was able to realize its military and political designs in the Far East to the fullest.

On September 2, the commander-in-chief of Allied troops in the Pacific theater, General Douglas MacArthur, accepted Japan's formal surrender aboard the aircraft carrier USS *Missouri*.

September 3, the day of victory against Japan, was declared an official holiday in the Soviet Union.

World War II had ended.

## THE BALANCE SHEET

With the war over, the situation in the world changed radically. Millions of Allied soldiers had inundated Europe, but demobilization had begun and thousands were returning home. It was a happy time as families were reunited. A time of joy, a time of sorrow. A time of grief and remembrance. A time of hope and rebirth. A time to give life to new generations. In the

Soviet Union there was scarcely a family that had not lost someone in the war.

Of all the participants in World War II, the Soviet Union suffered the greatest losses. Figures differ on how great those losses were. According to Soviet sources, they amounted to 10 million soldiers and an equal number of civilians, a total of 20 million people.[160] In 1973, the figures were given for the Russian Republic (RSFSR), the Ukrainian SSR, the Byelorussian SSR, and the Karelo-Finish SSR. Under the rubric "killed and tortured to death," 6,844,551 civilian casualties were cited, along with 3,932,256 prisoners of war.[161] The figures for the republics of Transcaucasia, Kazakhstan, and Central Asia remain unknown. Western historians have produced slightly different figures: 13,600,000 Soviet soldiers killed and 7,700,000 civilian casualties, a total of 21,300,000 victims, or 11 percent of the Soviet population in 1941.

In the six-year war, from 1939 to 1945, Germany lost 3,250,000 soldiers and 3,810,000 civilians, a third of the losses of the Soviet Union. In the same period Great Britain and the Commonwealth lost 452,000 soldiers and 60,000 civilians, or forty-two times less than the Soviet Union. Between December 1941 and September 1945 the United States lost 295,000 men, seventy-two times less than the Soviet Union. Poland suffered very heavy losses: 5,300,000 people (mainly Jews) exterminated in the Nazi death camps, and 120,000 soldiers killed. These losses amounted to 20 percent of Poland's prewar population. Yugoslavia lost 1,300,000 civilians and 300,000 soldiers. The countries of the antifascist coalition lost 18,587,000 soldiers and 25,140,000 civilians, for a total of 43,727,000 people. The countries of the fascist bloc lost only one-fourth as many: 5,930,000 soldiers and 5,087,000 civilians, a total of 11,017,000.

The total number of deaths in World War II was 55,014,000, or 6.4 times the number of World War I (8,634,000).[162] Military actions had brought ruin to many European countries.

The Soviet losses amounted to 38 percent of the total losses in World War II.

For one thing, the war was fought on Soviet territory for three and a half years. The Nazis sought the physical eradication of the Russians and many other nationalities of the USSR. In addition to those killed in military operations, many Soviet citizens were exterminated in mass executions, in prisoner of war camps, as well as in the Nazi death camps. On the other hand, the unprecedented Soviet losses were also a direct result of criminal negligence on the part of the leadership, Stalin and the members of the Politburo, the Central Committee, and the government, in failing to prepare adequately for war. The policy of entente with Nazi Germany, from 1939 to 1941, also had extremely grave consequences. The elimination during the years of terror of almost all the upper echelons of the military command left the Soviet army in the hands of officers whose knowledge and military experience dated from World War I and the Russian civil war or who had been hastily trained and lacked experience.

In spite of its demagogic slogan, "People are the most valuable capital," the Soviet government showed total disregard for human life.

The Soviet command often sought to win a battle at any cost, rather than to win it without suffering unnecessary losses. The history of the Soviet— German war offers numerous examples of soldiers openly sent to their slaughter by order of the high command, of men killed because of the vanity and carelessness of their superiors, of ill-prepared offensives that lacked the necessary logistical support and ended in retreats and enormous losses. Even experienced commanders like Zhukov, Vassilevsky, Kirponos, Timoshenko, and Meretskov lacked the courage to oppose the adventuristic and erroneous orders of the supreme commander-in-chief, Generalissimo Stalin.

In the most difficult and dangerous sectors of the front, penal battalions were used. It was here that, according to the official account, military personnel served sentences for criminal or military offenses.[163] However, it was easy to end up in a penal battalion because of an incautious word, criticism of the actions of the command, or a joke. Those in penal battalions were stripped of their military ranks and decorations. Few of the great number who served in penal units survived. How many perished? The official statistics are silent about this, but it is certainly a matter of many thousands.

During the war Stalin, with the knowledge and blessing of the Politburo, ordered the deportation to Siberia of tens of thousands of inhabitants of the annexed territories, many of whom died of hunger and disease. Over 1 million people were deported from the Crimea and the Caucasus in 1943 and 1944. Tens of thousands of lives were lost as a result. No one knows the number of victims arrested by the state security agencies as "enemies of the people" or "German spies"—except of course those agencies themselves. It is very likely that the vast majority of those arrested were not guilty of such offenses. But the work of the security police was judged in terms of the number of "hostile agents" rendered harmless, and the number was constantly increased. Thousands of Soviet soldiers who had the misfortune of becoming prisoners of the Germans but who miraculously survived turned up later in Soviet correction camps as traitors to the homeland.

For this reason, blame for the losses suffered by the Soviet people belongs not only to the Nazis and their satellites and collaborators and to the hazards of war. The Soviet leaders were also to blame, but not one of them was ever tried for these crimes.

Examples of heroism on the part of Soviet soldiers are numerous. In his unpublished memoirs, Colonel Novobranets describes the fierce hand-to-hand night combat the men of the Soviet Sixth Army engaged in as they broke out of encirclement in the first weeks of the war. In the border regions, the border guard units and the regular army troops that took part in the initial battles of the German invasion fought desperately. The resistance by the garrison of the Brest fortress was heroic, despite the fact that the command had abandoned it. The fortress was besieged on all sides by the Germans but continued to resist for twenty-eight days. The few survivors, after unprecedented suffering at the hands of the Germans, ended up in Soviet prison camp in Kolyma as "traitors to the homeland." They were not rehabilitated until many years after the war.

There were also many cases in which Soviet pilots flew directly into enemy targets. When captured by the Germans, partisans also bore themselves courageously. As a rule, they were executed after terrible torture. Such was the fate of Zoya Kosmodemyanskaya, a female partisan fighter captured by the Germans near Moscow. General Karbyshev refused to join the Germans and was transformed into an ice block, frozen alive in the Mauthausen camp.

As in any event of these dimensions, the war gave birth to myths and legends whereby soldiers were endowed with miraculous strength. Words were attributed to them which later became part of the history of the war. Such mythology is inevitable and has always been part of wars. For example, many Soviet books on the war attribute the following words to the political officer Klochkov, who allegedly said to a handful of soldiers of General Panfilov's division, near Moscow: "Russia is huge, but we cannot retreat any further, for behind us is Moscow." Who could have reported these words, when Klochkov and all his men but one were killed, and the one survivor was mortally wounded and unable to speak coherently? A journalist named Aleksandr Krivitsky took this mission upon himself; he was the first to write about the heroic feat of Klochkov and the other "Panfilov men." Asked by Shcherbakov, director of the Red Army's Main Political Directorate, how he knew Klochkov had said those words, Krivitsky replied, "That's what he must have said."

The Soviet victory in the war was not the result of Stalin's wise and infallible leadership, nor that of the State Defense Committee and the high command. The Soviet Union won the war *despite* the party leadership's colossal errors, through the combined efforts of the people, the army, and those same leaders.

Before the war the adventuristic and dangerous policies of the government led to the creation of a common border between the Soviet Union and the principal military force in Europe, Nazi Germany. The dismantling of the pre-1939 border defenses and the absence of adequate fortifications at the new border gave the enemy a considerable advantage at the beginning of the war and permitted enormous gains in time and territory. These mistakes alone (not to mention the senseless orders for offensive operations in the first days of the war, which resulted in the encirclement and ruin of entire armies) caused incalculable damage to the Soviet war effort. During the first days of the war, the Soviet Union lost a territory equal in size to the parts of Western Europe occupied by Germany in 1939–1940. Only the vastness of Soviet territory and the existence of a very distant rear area with an industrial base rich in raw materials (the Urals, Siberia, Transcaucasia, and the Far East), together with Hitler's political and strategic blunders, saved the Soviet Union from total defeat in 1941. In spite of everything, its resources sufficed finally to exceed Germany's strength, both in numbers of divisions and in volume of military production. If the Soviet Union had been the size of France or Germany, the mistakes of the Communist party and its leaders would have brought the country to defeat. It suffices to recall that during the first three weeks of the war, the German armies advanced faster into Soviet territory than they had into Poland.

For example, this is what Artillery Chief Marshal Nikolai Voronov wrote:

If the fascist invaders, who treacherously attacked us at dawn on June 22, 1941, had met an organized resistance on the part of our troops, starting from lines of defense prepared in advance, if our aircraft, moved in time and dispersed to forward airfields, had dealt hard blows to the enemy, if the manner of advancing our troops had corresponded to the situation, during the initial months we would not have suffered such great human and material losses. We would not have given the enemy vast amounts of Soviet territory, and the people would not have had to endure such sufferings and ordeals.[164]

Another military leader, Marshal Grechko, wrote: "Sadly, it must be admitted that one of the chief causes of the setbacks at the beginning of the war had its roots in the errors of the top military leadership."[165]

In 1941 the Soviet armies had vast territories behind them and they were able to withdraw to Leningrad in the northwest, Moscow in the west, and Rostov-on-the-Don and the Crimea in the south. In 1942 they also had room for withdrawal and retreated to Stalingrad and the Greater Caucasus Range.

Stalin's famous order No. 227, known as the Not One Step Back order, denounced the apparently widespread idea that it was always possible to retreat farther. But this idea reflected an objective reality: the immensity of Soviet territory, which allowed it time to prepare a counteroffensive. The fact of so much territory in reserve compensated to a certain degree for the mistakes of the Communist party politicians and the military leadership.

The Soviet Union had a stable rear, solidified, on the one hand, by the patriotism of the people and, on the other, by the cruelty of the Germans who left the population no other choice but to fight to the end. The Soviet system proved solid enough to withstand the terrible blow dealt by Hitler's Germany. Aid from the United States and Britain also played a major role.

The experiences of the war demonstrated that totalitarian regimes, which base themselves on unlimited violence, imposing a state of constant fear and an ideology of moral or racial superiority, have a certain stability. It took the combined efforts of the states of the anti-Hitler coalition and the occupation of the capital of the Reich through the fierce struggle of the Soviet armed forces to smash the Nazi system. Also necessary was a military program unifying the members of the coalition, a program which had at its base the ideals of liberty and democracy. The Nazi regime put up a desperate resistance until it was physically destroyed. In carrying the fight through to the end, the Soviet Union and its allies showed a tremendous will to achieve victory.

For a quarter of a century, with the exception of the brief NEP interim, before collectivization, the Soviet population had known very difficult times. It had grown used to privations, malnutrition, lack of sleep, and poor housing. For this reason, it was able to endure wartime hardship that people of Western culture would probably have been unable to endure.

The Soviet leadership was able to recover after the initial blows of the enemy. The Soviet Communist party, having at its disposal devoted and loyal political cadres, a powerful state security organization, and years of experience in subjugating and governing the masses, soon reestablished its control everywhere it had been lost or weakened. Identifying its interests with those of the people, it led and took the credit for the upsurge of patriotism.

The government even succeeded in presenting its mistakes and crimes as proofs of foresight and as correct defensive measures. For example, the terror of the 1930s, which had eliminated the most competent military commanders, industrial leaders, and so forth, was portrayed as the timely destruction of a "fifth column," of "German spies" and "enemies of the people." This explanation was taken up enthusiastically by the Communist parties abroad and circulated by the liberal antifascist intelligentsia in the

West. The disorganized retreats and defeats of 1941 and 1942 were portrayed as a wise strategy of "mobile defense" and the like.

For a long time victory overshadowed the privations, difficulties, and pain. Soldiers returned to their homes with hope for improvement in their lives. The war was over. But nostalgia for the past, and regret over the unrealized dreams of German–Soviet hegemony in Europe, haunted Stalin for years to come.

Even at the height of the war, five months after the German invasion, on November 6, 1941, Stalin still sought to justify his policy of 1939–1941. He still described the Nazis with sneaking sympathy. "As long as the Hitlerites were engaged in the recovery of German lands, reuniting the Rhineland, Austria, etc., with Germany, they could be considered nationalists with some justification."[166] This was a strange pronouncement coming from a man who claimed to be the main theoretician of "proletarian internationalism." It sounded like understanding, if not approval, of the Nazis' actions. In fact, Stalin himself recovered some former lands of the Romanov empire with Hitler's assistance—the Baltic states, western Byelorussia, and the western Ukraine—at the time acquiring some "lands" formerly belonging to the Habsburg monarchy—Northern Bukovina and the Transcarpathian Ukraine.

Stalin also struck a nostalgic note in a completely different historical context. In a telegram congratulating Pieck and Grotewohl, on October 13, 1949, on the occasion of the founding of the German Democratic Republic, he wrote: "The experience of the last war has shown that the greatest sacrifices were borne by the German and Soviet peoples, and that, in Europe, *these two peoples have the greatest potential for carrying out major actions of worldwide significance*" (emphasis added—A. N.).[167]

Woe unto the other European peoples, who did not have such great potential!

Stalin's daughter, Svetlana Alliluyeva, has made clear what Stalin meant by "actions of worldwide significance."

> He had not guessed or foreseen that the pact of 1939, which he had considered the outcome of his own great cunning, would be broken by an enemy more cunning than himself. This was the real reason for his deep depression at the start of the war. It was his immense political miscalculation. Even after the war was over he was in the habit of repeating, *"Ech, together with the Germans we would have been invincible!"* But he never admitted his mistakes. (Emphasis added—A.N.)[168]

Stalin nevertheless did learn a few lessons from his mistakes. The main practical conclusion, which he drew after the war, was to avoid sharing a common border with Germany. In 1941, a common border had left the Soviet Union open to German attack on a large front. After World War II, Stalin reverted to the idea of a *cordon sanitaire*, in a unique and modified form. This time, instead of the prewar *cordon*, a buffer zone of "fraternal socialist countries" separated the Soviet Union from Germany. Most likely Stalin thought that Germany would eventually reunite. Thus he returned to an ancient geopolitical concept: do not share a border with a powerful neighbor.

Twenty million human lives—such was the cost of Stalin's miscalculation.

CHAPTER

9

# THE TWILIGHT OF THE STALIN ERA, 1945–1953

## REPATRIATION

The war was over. Troop trains full of demobilized Soviet soldiers headed east from Germany, Austria, Czechoslovakia, Hungary, Poland, and Bulgaria. Soviet civilians came out to meet them at all the railroad stations wearing their best clothes, which had somehow been preserved despite the war and were often in tatters. Those who had taken Berlin and Budapest danced gallantly on the platforms, dragging out their war booty accordions.

There were other troop trains heading east as well, but these had sealed doors and barred windows. They too carried Soviet soldiers, but no music or singing came from these tightly locked cattlecars. No one met them at railroad stations. These trains kept traveling day and night. There were also troop ships that pulled up to deserted wharfs to unload former Soviet prisoners of war returning from the Nazi camps. They touched foot on their native soil under heavy guard. Also being returned were those who willingly or otherwise had aided the Germans or had worked for them. Among them were some who had never lived in postrevolutionary Russia but whom the British, American, or French allies had considered Soviet citizens. They were turned over to the Soviet government, to deal with as it saw fit, without trial of any kind.

At the end of the war more than 5 million Soviet citizens were in Germany and other countries of Western Europe, including former prisoners of war, workers and peasants who had been transported to Germany for forced labor (the so-called *Ostarbeiter*), and people who had left the Soviet Union at the time of the German retreat.

Under the Yalta agreement, Soviet citizens wishing to return to their homeland were to be repatriated. The agreement also provided for forced repatriation; it extended to those wearing German uniforms at the time of capture and to those who had belonged to the Soviet armed forces after June 22, 1941, had not been released from their duties, and on the basis of reliable information were thought to have collaborated with the enemy.[1] In practice this agreement opened the way for forcible repatriation of anyone, indiscriminately, without distinction, even including people who were not Soviet citizens.

First the British government and then the United States responded in a most obliging way to the Soviet government's intention to regain as its subjects all who had turned up in the West during the war, regardless of their personal desires.[2] The Soviet government was anxious not only to prevent the formation of a new political emigration in the West but also to disrupt or destroy the old emigré community.

The forced repatriation began soon after the end of the war and was largely completed by 1947. Some of the former Soviet prisoners of war, delivered to the ports of Murmansk and Odessa by British ships, were shot by NKVD troops right on the docks where they were landed. Among those being forcibly repatriated many attempted suicide. The Soviet officers in charge of this operation did not hide from their British counterparts that death awaited many upon their return to the Soviet Union.[3]

The British authorities also delivered former White emigrés who had never been Soviet citizens. Even the NKVD officers receiving the repatriots, who had seen much in their lives, were amazed at this unexpected gift from the British. Merkulov, the Soviet minister of state security, said the following of the British: "They don't even know that we have them trapped in a corner on a chess board and now we'll make them dance to our tune like the last pawn on the board."[4]

In Paris the NKVD conducted virtually a public manhunt for Soviet citizens who did not want to return to the USSR.[5] In the Beauregard detention camp, where those subject to repatriation were held, the Soviet authorities behaved just as they did in the concentration camps on Soviet territory. It was only two years after the war, in 1947, that under the pressure of public opinion the French police raided the Beauregard camp and found stores of weapons. Only then was the camp closed.[6]

Altogether 2,272,000 Soviet citizens—prisoners of war and those of "equivalent status"—were repatriated to the Soviet Union with the help of the British and American authorities. What was their fate? The overwhelming majority were accused of treason. They were not tried individually. Special three-men boards (troikas) handed down group sentences. Twenty percent were given death sentences or twenty-five years in camps; 15–20 percent were condemned to terms between five and ten years; 10 percent were exiled to remote parts of Siberia for periods of no less than six years; 15 percent were assigned to forced labor detachments rebuilding areas destroyed by the war; and only 15–20 percent were allowed to return to their homes. Of the 15–20 percent remaining, some were undoubtedly killed or died in passage and some escaped.[7] The Allied governments knew that many of the forced repatriates faced certain death, but those governments were not particularly concerned, guided as they were by pragmatic considerations and the wish to assure themselves of Soviet cooperation in the postwar world.

The forced repatriation of non-Soviet citizens who had been born in prerevolutionary Russia helped to intimidate many Soviet citizens who wished to settle in the West.

Even after the war the Allied military administration continued to return Red Army personnel who fled to Western occupation zones in Germany. However, despite all obstacles, between 13,000 and 14,000 Soviet citizens fled to the West during the first four postwar years.[8] Only in 1951 did the United States officially change its policy and grant the right of asylum to refugees from the Soviet Union. The Soviet government never released the official data on the number of defectors. In individual cases Soviet propaganda denounced them as spies or hirelings of imperialism. The horrors of the Nazi camps—where up to 11 million people were killed during World War II—had provoked such a wave of legitimate rage that no one even wanted to give a serious thought to the victims of the other totalitarian regime, the war's victor.

In addition to former prisoners of war and those of "equivalent status," there were 3.2 million Soviet citizens in Western Europe after the war. Almost all of them returned to the Soviet Union or were forcibly repatriated. According to an official report of the Soviet Central Administration for Repatriation Affairs, as of January 1, 1953, the number of Soviet citizens who had returned to their homeland was 5,457,856. As of the same date, 4,059,736 foreign citizens had been returned to their countries from the Soviet Union, including former prisoners of war from the countries that had been defeated in the war.[9]

## THE INSURRECTIONAL MOVEMENT

The war was over, but not for everyone. Insurrectional movements in opposition to Soviet rule continued in the western Ukraine and the Baltic nations, the result of strong aspirations for independence and a reaction against the Soviet purges of 1939–1941, collectivization, and the danger of new deportations.

In 1939 a purge had taken place in the western Ukraine after it was annexed. All opponents or suspected opponents of the Soviet government had been arrested and deported to the eastern parts of the Soviet Union. Some were shot. Ukrainian and Polish organizations and institutions had been banned, but at the same time the schools had been completely "Ukrainized." Legal Ukrainian parties ceased to exist. The Uniate church was spared in 1939–1941, but priests were given special passports and churches became subject to heavy taxation.[10]

At the time of the Red Army's retreat in 1941, mass arrests were carried out among the western Ukrainian population. In the majority of prisons, NKVD troops shot all inmates who had been sentenced to more than three years. In some towns the NKVD burned prisons with all their inmates. According to Ukrainian sources, 10,000 prisoners were shot in Lvov, Zolochevo, Rovno, Dubno, Lutsk, and other cities.[11]

During the brief Soviet period in the territory, from 1939 to 1941, a relatively powerful underground organization, the Organization of Ukrainian Nationalists (OUN) had survived. After the arrival of the Germans in the Ukraine, the OUN leaders attempted to set up independent Ukrainian governments in Lvov and Kiev, but these bodies were dispersed by the Germans and their leaders jailed.[12] Many Ukrainian nationalists sought to collaborate with the Germans. Some joined SS units (such as the Galichina division); others fought the Red Army and helped the Germans hunt down Communists and Jews. Once it became evident that the German authorities did not have the slightest intention of allowing the formation of an independent Ukrainian state, the OUN declared war on two fronts: "against Stalin and against Hitler." Their main efforts, however, were directed as before against the Red Army.

In July 1944, when the Red Army entered the western Ukraine, the OUN set up a Supreme Council for the Liberation of the Ukraine. OUN leader Roman Shukhevich became the commander of the Ukrainian Insurgent Army (UPA), under the pseudonym General Taras Chuprinka (nicknamed "Tur").

The chiefs of the OUN hoped for the weakening of both Germany and the Soviet Union and expected that Britain—especially since Churchill was prime minister—would actively oppose the hegemonic designs of the USSR in Europe. They foresaw a general popular insurrection, which would be supported by the peoples of the other territories occupied by the Red Army. But this proved an empty dream. The OUN had to confine its military operations to those of its own forces. Its main objective was to defend the western Ukrainian population from the threat of a new wave of terror and mass deportations. In the western Ukrainian rural areas the population supported the UPA, allowing it to wage an armed struggle even for many years after the end of World War II.

When the Red Army entered the territory of the western Ukraine, the Soviet command and the government of the Ukrainian Soviet Socialist Republic called on the insurgents to lay down their arms, promising an amnesty. This appeal brought no tangible results. From 1944 to 1947 there were six such offers, extending the period of amnesty further each time. [13] In 1945 the principal agricultural regions of the western Ukraine, deep in the country, were controlled by the insurgents. In February 1946 the majority of the population boycotted the first elections to the Supreme Soviet, while official communiqués stated, as usual, that the population had voted "unanimously" for the only candidates.

The OUN program underwent major changes with the years. In 1950 the OUN called for the total dissolution of the kolkhozes but opposed a return of the landowners and capitalists. It advocated that the land be freely turned over to the peasants and become family property. The OUN also called for freedom for social and political organizations. According to Ukrainian sources, the ideology of the OUN was gradually evolving toward liberal democracy.

Besides waging an armed struggle, the insurgents widely disseminated leaflets, even organizing propaganda raids into Slovakia, the eastern part of Ukraine, Byelorussia, and Romania. While pitilessly killing every NKVD officer or soldier and every party or Soviet activist who fell into their hands, the insurgents sometimes spared regular army soldiers, feeding them and giving them OUN literature. Such instances, however, were not numerous. Cruelty was the rule on both sides. The UPA, which was fighting for independence, attacked the Poles, killing 3,000 of them in the Ukraine, and likewise attacked the Jews. The UPA theater of operations spread through Poland (beyond the Curzon line) and Czechoslovakia (in the mountains of Slovakia).

After the German defeat, UPA detachments were divided into smaller units, which also made forays into the eastern Ukraine. Soviet sources are silent about the strength of the insurgents. According to Polish sources, as many as 6,000 insurgents operated in Polish territory alone, in the zone immediately adjacent to the Soviet border. Ukrainian sources claim that UPA forces had attained 20,000 fighters in the fall of 1944, that is, when the Soviet troops entered the western Ukraine.[14] The magnitude of the movement may be judged by the fact that the local population generally aided the insurgents and that in May 1947 an agreement was signed between the Soviet Union, Poland, and Czechoslovakia for joint military action against the Ukrainian insurgents, who naturally were labeled bandits.

In June 1945 three Polish divisions were deployed against the insurgents, but the results were minimal. In an effort to separate the insurgents from their base of support, the Polish government relocated its Ukrainian population to the northwest of Poland. Polish sources noted that the Ukrainian rebellion was not defeated until the insurgents were physically crushed and the Ukrainian population deported.[15]

The 1947–48 famine forced tens of thousands of peasants in the eastern Ukraine to flee to the western part, where they became a reserve force for the insurgent movement.

All means were used against the insurgents—military operations, mass deportations to Siberia, relocation of entire villages from areas controlled by the insurgents to eastern regions of the Ukraine, and collectivization of the land. Ukrainian educators were sent from the eastern Ukraine to "re-educate" the population in the western part, and the Uniate church was banned.

The technique used to accomplish this last measure should be examined more closely. After the death of Metropolitan Shcheptitsky, head of the Uniate church in the western Ukraine, in November 1944, this church was invited to fuse with the Orthodox church. An intensive press campaign against the Uniates ensued. A resolute man, the new Metropolitan Slipoy was arrested along with his bishops and sentenced for allegedly collaborating with the Nazis during the war. Slowly, using various methods, including the murder of Bishop Romsha of Transcarpathia in 1951,[16] the Uniate church was virtually destroyed, and its legal existence came to an end.

This was a major blow to the Ukrainian nationalists, but not a fatal one. The tenacity of the western Ukrainian movement can be judged by a document of the Ukrainian Ministry of Internal Affairs, Order No. 312, dated December 30, 1949, which again announced an amnesty for all those who voluntarily laid down their arms. This order also gives us an idea of the social composition of the insurrection movement because it includes among the other categories of "bandits" youths who had fled the factories, the Donets mines, and vocational schools.[17] The armed struggle, on a smaller scale than before, continued during the first half of the 1950s.

From 1946 to 1950, some 300,000 people were deported, exiled, or arrested in the western Ukraine. Included in this figure are former collaborators with the German SS, former members of the Galichina SS division, among them criminals who had committed many murders and taken part in the mass execution of Jews in the Ukraine. But most of the deported were innocent peasants. The western Ukraine underwent collectivization and forced industrialization, which required the massive shipment into the area of specialists from the eastern Ukraine and Russia. The composition of the population changed and the rebellion withered away. Some nationalist leaders like Shukhevich died in the struggle; others like Okhrimovich were captured and executed. The final blows to the OUN came with the assassination by Soviet agents of Lev Rebet in 1957 and Stepan Bandera in 1959. Both were then living in West Germany.

Thus the period of armed struggle by Ukrainian nationalists came to an end. A new stage would unfold in the post-Stalin era—the peaceful struggle of the Ukrainian intelligentsia for their right to a national culture.

## THE COLD WAR AT HOME AND ABROAD

After the war the international position of the Soviet Union changed radically. Soviet troops were in Central, Eastern, and Southeastern Europe, in the northeast of China, on the Kurile islands, and on the island of Sakhalin.

The allies of the Soviet Union from the days of the anti-Hitler coalition silently accepted these changes because they were powerless to impede them. Ill-prepared for peace, they suffered an unprecedented, major defeat on the international arena. At that point, Finland, Poland, Czechoslovakia, Romania, Bulgaria, and Hungary entered the Soviet sphere of interest. The Soviet Union also had great influence in the Balkans, in Yugoslavia and Albania. It had troops in Vienna and Berlin. Communism was making great strides everywhere in Europe. Greece was plunged into civil war. The local Communist parties were growing in France and Italy.

In Asia powerful independence movements were developing in Indochina, Korea, Burma, the Philippines, Indonesia, and India. In China a civil war was underway in which the Communists had the clear advantage. The Soviet Union had never before been so popular in the East.

Everything seemed to favor the USSR. Of the six major Western powers before the war, only two maintained their positions: Great Britain, albeit badly shaken, having witnessed the collapse of its colonial empire and entered a period of cardinal change in world status; and the United States, which had emerged from the war powerful as never before.

During World War II the United States became aware of the full extent of its interdependence with Europe. Seeking to help the European states overcome their financial straits as quickly as possible, so that they could oppose the advance of communism, the Americans offered economic assistance for reconstruction—the Marshall Plan.[18] American leaders also announced their intention to oppose the further spread of communism (the Truman Doctrine).[19] The U.S. government proposed that the Soviet Union and other Eastern European states participate in the reconstruction plans, but the former and, under its pressure the latter, too, rejected the offer.[20]

The Soviet government had no desire whatsoever to join with those nations in efforts toward a speedy recovery of the world economy. It wanted to create its own political and economic sphere, independent of the West, whose center would be the Soviet Union, surrounded by satellite states. In fact, during the first years after the war, the economies of these countries became increasingly dependent on the Soviet Union, tending to become only auxiliary.

It was expected that another means for reviving and strengthening the Soviet economy would be the reparations to be paid by the defeated nations and the industrial machinery transferred from those countries to the USSR as "spoils of war." However, because of inefficiency and mismanagement Soviet industry was unable to use a major part of this equipment, which simply sat and rusted.

In 1947 peace treaties were signed with Germany's former European allies, Italy in particular.[21] The Soviet Union attempted to obtain a trusteeship over Libya, a former Italian colony, thereby causing great commotion in the West.[22] Seeking to gain a foothold in Africa and the Middle East, it recognized the state of Israel, founded in 1948.[23] But the USSR's first attempt to establish itself in the Middle East was thwarted by the Western powers, and the Soviet Union focused all its attention on Eastern Europe.

Soviet policy sought to make satellites of the Eastern European countries, recently liberated from the Germans. It was a simple, even primitive policy, but it was effective. Relying on the Soviet divisions that controlled the territories of those states, the Communist parties, which initially had taken part in coalitions of democratic antifascist parties, led military coups and came to power in each one of these countries. The technique was always the same, with only slight variations. During the first three or four years after the war, the bloc of Communist states of Eastern and Southeastern Europe took shape. These regimes called themselves people's democracies. A world socialist system was born.

In October 1949 the German Democratic Republic was proclaimed.[24] That same year, the Chinese Communists came to power after many years of civil war, establishing the People's Republic of China. The Communist victory in China was not a source of great joy for Stalin, as was erroneously assumed in the West. Secretary of State Dean Rusk declared, for example, that China had become a "Slavic Manchukuo," a Soviet colony.[25] Such superficial statements, the result of appraising the policies of these states on the basis of their common ideology, were typical of both sides in that era.

In place of a divided China, torn by civil war, the USSR witnessed the birth on its borders of an enormous, centralized Chinese state, with a population greater than three times its own. To stress its position as the "older brother" and Stalin's position as Mao's senior in the international Communist movement, Stalin made Mao wait several days before receiving him during his visit to Moscow in 1950. On the other hand, the victory of communism in China confirmed to Stalin the value of one of Lenin's postulates—that the capitalist world would steadily shrink.

The newly created socialist states wanted to be independent. Some of their leaders attempted to escape from subjection to Moscow and the necessity always to act in accordance with Soviet interests. This happened in the case of Tito, who had seemed likely to be Stalin's strongest ally.[26] Tito was secretly supported by Georgy Dimitrov, the former Comintern general secretary.[27]

Stalin threatened to destroy Tito,[28] and he excommunicated the heretic by expelling the Yugoslav Communist party from the Cominform, the new international Communist organization that was founded in 1946,[29] replacing the Comintern, which had been dissolved in 1943. These measures did not break the Yugoslavs. The disintegration of the socialist system started at the same time it was born: a fact of major historical importance. It proved that the so-called socialist camp was not in fact a voluntary association of states sharing a uniform social system and ideology, but a forced agglomeration of totalitarian states with socialist characteristics.

Lenin's dictum, "We seek a voluntary union of nations, a union which does not admit any coercion by one nation against another, a union based on total trust, the clear understanding of fraternal unity, a perfectly voluntary pact,"[30] twenty-five years later sounded exceedingly cynical.

• • •

On March 5, 1946, former British Prime Minister Winston Churchill gave a speech at Fulton, Missouri, with President Harry S. Truman in attendance. Churchill noted with alarm an indisputable fact: an iron curtain had been lowered from the Baltic to the Adriatic.[31] A furious arms race began, and the danger of atomic war became a central fact of life in the modern world. Since then each side has sought to maintain military superiority, so that attempts at arms limitation or a ban on nuclear weapons have constantly been forced into dead ends or been blocked by insurmountable technical and political difficulties.

The Soviet Union mobilized its enormous resources to develop first the atomic bomb and then the hydrogen bomb. It soon caught up with the United States as far as nuclear weapons were concerned.

The arms race, the divergence of opinion over virtually all major questions of international relations, the "anticosmopolitan" campaign in the USSR and anticommunist hysteria in the United States, poisoned the international atmosphere, creating tense and dangerous situations and setting the stage for armed confrontation.

In April 1949 the North Atlantic Treaty Organization (NATO) was born. This military bloc consisted of the United States, Great Britain, France, Italy, Canada, Belgium, the Netherlands, Portugal, Denmark, Norway, Iceland, and Luxembourg. Later, in 1952, Greece and Turkey joined, and in 1955 the Federal Republic of Germany.

The creation of NATO was in large part the result of the threat of Soviet military action against Turkey and Iran. After the war the Soviet Union launched a campaign against Turkey, demanded a renegotiation of the Montreux pact on the Straits and the return to Soviet Georgia and Armenia of lands annexed by Turkey following World War I.[32] Military hysteria was on the rise in Armenia and Georgia.

In Iran, the Soviet Union refused to withdraw the troops it had sent there in 1941, under an agreement with Britain against the German threat. It also supported Azerbaijani separatists in northern Iran, who had rebelled against the central government.[33]

In Europe, the Soviet government started a crisis over Berlin when, in violation of international agreements, it attempted to block access to the city by the Western powers.[34] The United States, however, successfully carried out the Berlin airlift, breaking the blockade and forcing the Soviet Union to back down.

Nevertheless, in all the cases just mentioned, the USSR and the United

States had enough sense to keep the conflict from becoming a "hot war," although at times it seemed as if peace hung only by a thread. The danger of another world war was especially great during the Berlin crisis, and again during the Korean war.

One of the consequences of the Japanese defeat was the liberation of Korea, which had been occupied by Japan since 1910. Korea was about to become a free nation, but instead an agreement between the Soviet Union and the United States established the thirty-eighth parallel as a temporary dividing line for military operations by the two powers in the Far East, and as a result Korea was cut in half. In 1945 the Soviets withdrew their troops from North Korea, after having installed a loyal Communist government headed by Kim Il Sung. The Korean Democratic People's Republic was founded in the north. In the south, a pro-American government was formed under Syngman Rhee, the Republic of Korea. Each government claimed to represent the entire Korean people.

On the thirty-eighth parallel, violent clashes started by North Korea on June 25, 1950, led to a war between the two Koreas. Soviet historiography claims to this day that it was South Korea which started the war.[35] Nevertheless, Khrushchev's memoirs provide testimony that confirms the facts generally known before then. His account is essentially as follows.

The war was started at the initiative of Kim Il Sung, with the support of Mao and Stalin. Kim arrived in Moscow at the end of 1949 and suggested launching a military attack against the South, so that the people would rise up and establish a people's government (Communist). Stalin hesitated, fearing American intervention. In the end, he offered Kim Il Sung the opportunity to give more consideration to the situation and return with a concrete plan. "Naturally," wrote Khrushchev,

> Stalin couldn't oppose this idea. It appealed to his convictions as a Communist all the more because the struggle would be an internal matter which the Koreans would be settling among themselves. The North Koreans wanted to give a helping hand to their brethren who were under the heel of Syngman Rhee. . . . Stalin, of course, didn't try to dissuade him.

What Khrushchev wrote further is extremely revealing of the ways of thinking of Soviet leaders, who always claim to defend world peace. "In my opinion, no real Communist would have tried to dissuade Kim Il Sung from his compelling desire to liberate South Korea from Syngman Rhee and from reactionary American influence. *To have done so would have contradicted the Communist view of the world.* I don't condemn Stalin for encouraging Kim. On the contrary, I would have made the same decision"[36] [emphasis added—A. N.].

Stalin solicited Mao's advice. The Chinese leader approved Kim's proposal. Soviet leaders and Kim Il Sung celebrated the beginning of the undertaking at Stalin's dacha. Shipments of Soviet arms to Korea began. Soviet airforce units were put into place near Pyen Yan.

This is how Khrushchev described the ensuing events:

> The attack was launched successfully. The North Koreans swept south swiftly. But what Kim Il Sung had predicted—an internal uprising... unfortunately failed to materialize.... [There] weren't enough internal forces for a Communist insurrection in South Korea. Apparently the Party's preparatory organizational work had been inadequate. Kim had believed that South Korea was blanketed with Party organizations and that the people would rise up in revolt when the Party gave the signal. But this never happened.[37]

For Khrushchev, the North Korean offensive was justified because this was not a conflict between two peoples, but a war between classes.[38]

On June 27, 1950, the UN Security Council met to discuss the situation resulting from the North Korean invasion of South Korea. On the agenda was the condemnation of aggression and a proposal to aid the Korean Republic. Curiously, the Soviet delegate was absent from the meeting. He said he was protesting the fact that China was represented by a delegate from Formosa. The Soviet Union abstained from using its veto power in the Security Council and allowed the body to recommend that all members provide South Korea with assistance, "which is necessary to repel international aggression and bring peace and security to the region."[39] Later, the USSR called the resolution illegal. Stalin was convinced that the North Korean offensive together with the Communist resurrection in the South would bring total victory to the North before any foreign military intervention took place. But his hopes proved false. The United Nations asked for troops to restore Korean peace and the United States sent troops stationed in Japan. A bloody war began which lasted three years.

At first the scales tipped toward North Korea, whose troops reached Pusan in the far south by mid-September. The offensive was cut short when 50,000 Americans landed in the South. Then China sent its own divisions to assist North Korea. At the end of November 1950 the South Koreans and the Americans, commanded by General MacArthur, carried out a successful offensive, pushing the North Korean and Chinese troops back north of the thirty-eighth parallel.

The Soviet Union, which had sanctioned the original North Korean military action and provided material assistance, found itself in a tight situation. Soviet advisers were present in Korea, and some airborne divisions had been deployed to the provinces of northeast China.[40] According to an official Soviet publication, "In case of deterioration of the situation, the USSR was prepared to send five divisions into Korea to help the Democratic People's Republic push back American aggression."[41] In reality, when the North Korean troops found themselves isolated in the South, Stalin issued orders for the immediate recall of Soviet advisers, fearing they might be taken prisoner and constitute proof of Soviet involvement in the war.

The situation in Korea was saved for the Communist side by the intervention of China, which Stalin approved. The joint offensive by UN and South Korean forces ran out of steam, and they withdrew to positions along the thirty-eighth parallel. On November 30 Truman threatened to use the atomic bomb.[42] The danger of military confrontation between the USSR and the United States was very real; it would have led to World War III. Both sides felt they had gone too far. As a result, in mid-1951 the front was stabilized, but the fire of war was not extinguished for quite a long time.

## FROM WAR TO PEACE

What was the population of the USSR at the end of World War II? Official statistics do not furnish any figures for 1945, but we do have figures for 1950: 178.5 million people, 15.6 million less than before the war.[43]

After the war the birth rate began to decline. During the 1950s it was no more than 25 per 1,000; the corresponding figure before the war had been 30 per 1,000. During the first years after the war, this decline stemmed from the fact that entire age groups of adult males had been decimated. But the decline continued during the 1960s, and even increased. It is necessary therefore to take into account the unfavorable economic and social factors contributing to the decrease in the birth rate, such as low salaries, the deep-rooted housing crisis, and the constant increase in employment of female labor in production.

In 1971–72, there were half as many births per 1,000 women between the ages of fifteen and forty-nine as there had been in 1938–39.[44] During the first postwar years, the working-age population was also significantly smaller than before the war.

The Soviet economy, particularly in the occupied areas, had been seriously impaired by war. The concentration of effort on war production had led to a major reduction of population resources and a decrease in the production of consumer goods. During the war, construction of housing units, which were already inadequate, was sharply curtailed—at a time when housing suffered great destruction.

The transition period from war to peace was relatively short. On September 4, 1945, the State Defense Committee was dissolved and its functions transferred to the Council of People's Commissars (Sovnarkom).[45] Departments of the arms industry were reorganized. Tanks and artillery production was reconverted to the production of tractors and transportation machinery.

The regions destroyed by the war required major capital investments. According to Soviet official figures, 1,710 towns and cities had been partially or totally destroyed, as were approximately 70,000 villages, 32,000 industrial enterprises, 65,000 kilometers of railroad. In addition, some 25 million people had lost their homes.[46] The Fourth Five-Year Plan allocated 40 percent of all capital investments—115 billion rubles—to parts of the economy either destroyed or damaged by the war.[47]

The return to normalcy took place under difficult circumstances. The population was reduced to a state of misery. A famine devastated the southern part of the country, and armed movements persisted in the regions newly annexed to the Soviet Union.

In September 1946 uniform prices replaced the system of double pricing: commercial prices, on the one hand; and those charged under the rationing system, on the other. The result was increased prices for basic foodstuffs for the bulk of the urban population. The price of a kilogram of rye bread went from 1 to 3.4 rubles, a kilogram of meat from 14 to 30 rubles, sugar from 5.5 to 15 rubles, butter from 26 to 66 rubles, milk from 2.5 to 8 rubles.

At the same time that uniform state prices were established, lower-paid workers were granted a "bread supplement" of 110 rubles per month (in old rubles), and all those paid less than 900 rubles a month received salary increases. At that point, the minimum monthly salary was 300 rubles. The average salary was 475 rubles in 1946, and 550 in 1947.

During the war and the first postwar years prices rose sharply because of the devaluation of the ruble, shortages of goods and foodstuffs, and the existence of several widely disparate price levels.

At the end of 1947 a monetary reform—the revaluation of the ruble— was introduced. The old bank notes were exchanged for new ones, at a rate of ten to one. People with deposits in savings banks were given a more favorable rate than those who had kept their savings at home. The inhabitants of rural areas suffered most from the reform, followed in part by those speculators who had enormous sums in their possession. Undoubtedly, this reform had a revitalizing effect on the Soviet economy.

The war economy had given a boost to some branches of production, such as aircraft, motor vehicles (tanks and tractors), and special steels, and new oil fields had been opened in the eastern part of the country. But on the whole, industrial production was in trouble.

At the end of the war, metal production was approximately on the level of 1933–1935,[48] while that of tractors was on the 1930 level.[49] With the transition to a peacetime economy, total production reached no higher than 92 percent of its prewar level.[50] By as early as 1948, however, industrial production was 18 percent higher than before the war, and it continued to grow.[51]

At the end of World War II the Soviet Union had an enormous army of more than 11 million. After demobilization, it was reduced to less than one-third that size. In 1948 the Soviet armed forces numbered 2,483,000. Seven years later, however, that figure had doubled.

The Soviet Union hastened to develop its own atomic bomb, seeking to end the U.S. monopoly in that area. For this purpose, the best scientists were mobilized both inside the USSR and among foreign sympathizers. Soviet intelligence launched a mass recruitment drive for agents who could obtain any information concerning atomic energy. Several specialized institutes, restricted towns, and experimental sites were established. Beria, the head of state security, was personally put in charge of the project. A special Ministry of Medium Machine Building was set up; it was in reality a ministry for the development and use of atomic energy.

In 1949 the USSR officially announced it had the atomic bomb[52] and in 1953 the hydrogen bomb.[53] Stalin could be completely satisfied with himself: The Soviet Union had become an atomic power.

In 1950 the USSR started the first postwar stage of the arms race. Direct military spending in 1952, on the eve of Stalin's death, accounted for nearly one-fourth of the total annual budget.[54] The restoration of heavy industry was largely complete at the end of 1950. Production of steel, rolled iron, and petroleum increased substantially over prewar levels.[55] New metallurgical plants were built in the Baltic states, Transcaucasia, Central Asia, and Kazakhstan.

In contrast, the production of consumer goods at the end of the Fourth Five-Year Plan still had not reached the prewar level. As before, the population suffered from shortages of basic necessities and the severe housing crisis. In Moscow, however, investments were being made, in skyscrapers, giant structures meant to immortalize the Stalin era, and the Soviet government generously distributed gifts among its Eastern satellites, such as universities, institutes, and hospitals.

The state invested major sums in the development of health care in this period. Preventive medicine was improved in the cities, but the hospital situation was always dismal. There were shortages of beds, staff, and essential medicine. Medical personnel, doctors and nurses—to say nothing of technicians—remained among the lowest-paid categories.

The nation's economic development limped along, hampered as before by the perennial problems of the Soviet system. All economic questions, regardless of their size, were decided by the central government, while initiative by local economic agencies was kept to a minimum. Moscow set the plan for each enterprise, often without any realistic assessment of its capabilities. Each factory inevitably depended on other sectors of industry for the supply of raw materials and related enterprises. The transportation system was constantly late with deliveries. The absurdity of this supercentralized system was such that thousands of kilometers existed between suppliers, producers, and related enterprises. It was not unusual to have raw materials produced in the Far East delivered to central Russia when the same material could have been found close at hand, but in the possession of some other agency or department. Bad management and chaos engendered interruptions of production, "storming" at the end of the planning period, and enormous material waste.

The concentration of decision making at the center also led to a swelling of the bureaucratic apparatus. A multitude of unnecessary central inspection operations were instituted. Industries were caving in under the avalanche of commissions, inquests, and investigations. A huge army of "fixers" (*tolkachi*), employees especially charged with procuring raw materials and hard-to-get items, motors and the like, invaded factories, offices, and ministries. Bribery became the accepted way of doing business. The government attempted to fight corruption but could accomplish nothing because corruption had become an integral part of the system.

Another pillar of the system was "*pokazukha*," the practice of deliberately deceiving the higher authority about the rate of production and the fulfillment of plan targets. Plant managers were often afraid to tell the truth concerning the state of production and preferred to submit triumphant-sounding reports claiming fulfillment or overfulfillment of the plan or higher labor productivity. They would scheme endlessly to avoid being ranked among the "delayers." For this reason, official statistics must be viewed with great caution; many statistics, as was later officially admitted, were simply false.

The lie became a way of life. Enterprises deceived ministries. District party committees misled regional committees, which in turn provided false information to the Central Committee. As for the Central Committee members, especially the top leaders, they in turn lied to the people, to themselves, and to all humanity.

During the 1950s construction projects for hydroelectric complexes on the Dnepr and the Volga began. In 1952, with prison camp labor, the 101-kilometer Volga–Don Canal was completed, linking the White, Baltic, Caspian, Azov, and Black seas into a single water transport system.

The canals, the power plants, the factories using their power, and man-made "seas" of artificial lakes were built, as a rule, without the least regard for the ecology. Rivers passing through large populated areas were polluted with industrial waste. Animal life in the rivers began to die off. Fishing on the Volga and its tributaries, which had long been the pride of all Russia, was endangered. Valuable forested areas and lowlands were flooded and adjacent land turned into marshes—for example, in the area of the "Sea of Rybinsk."[56] Scientists, local authorities, and ordinary people tried to stop this pitiless destruction of natural resources, but in vain. Once a plan had been approved by the central government, it could not be changed.

After the war, administrative reforms were frequently introduced and the nature and functions of specific economic bodies changed, but no essential change in economic planning and management resulted.

On March 15, 1946, the title *people's commissar* was changed back to the old term, *minister.* In its own way this underlined the autonomous power of the state, which had long since ceased to depend on "the people." On Stalin's orders, the employees of many ministries—waterworks, justice, foreign affairs—began wearing the same uniforms as military personnel, police, agents of state security, and railroad employees. Civilian as well as military ranks and titles were also introduced in all areas.[57]

Evidence of the deep reaction that came over the Soviet Union in these years was the 1947 law forbidding marriages between Soviet citizens and foreigners.

The terror of the 1930s had undermined the basic social unit, the family. Ideological divisions and the informer system shook the foundations of the urban family, already unstable after the revolution. As for the rural family, it was disintegrating under the impact of forced collectivization, impoverishment, and the flight to the cities. The loss of an important part of the male population during the war had thrown millions of families into difficult, often dire conditions. Families with single mothers constituted a category numbering in the millions.

The code of family law in effect before and during the war, with its simple procedures for divorce and the right of abortion (but only on the basis of medical necessity), reflected the Marxist concepts of equality between the sexes and free love and had played an important part in the development of the Soviet society at its early stage. In and of itself, the law was commendable: it proclaimed total equality between men and women. But legal equality in all fields, including production, and the verbal assurance of free access for women to all jobs and professions, was not backed up by economic and social conditions guaranteeing real equality. A woman had to face the dual obligation of materially supporting her family and performing the domestic tasks connected with childrearing. True, in all major industrial centers the state assumed the obligation of setting up child care centers, nurseries, and kindergartens, but their numbers were insufficient. The problem was solved to some extent by the age-old institution known as grandmother.

At the end of the war, the state returned to the old "bourgeois" concept of the family as the basic unit of society. Stalin understood that a stable family would make the job of controlling the people much easier. Unregistered marriages and free love ran counter to the aims and practices of the Soviet state, with its policies of limiting movement and monitoring the lives of citizens through the internal passport system.

In 1944 a new family law was put into effect.[58] Thenceforth the state would recognize only registered marriages. The notion of illegitimate children was revived. Although these children received no such official designation, a dash was entered in the "father" space on their birth certificates. Divorce procedures were made more difficult: mutual consent became necessary, and the state charged a rather large sum. The state also stressed the responsibility of the family to raise children in a Communist (i.e., conformist) spirit. The long-term objective of the law was to increase the population. Abortion was prohibited. Single mothers received government aid, and special government awards and honors were introduced for mothers of large families.

The 1944 law on the family reflected the social transformations the society had undergone. Present-day Soviet society, with its conformism and its deep longing for tranquility after long years of trials and sufferings was coming into being. If the first postrevolutionary generation wanted to break free of the constraints of the "old ways," the survivors of the 1920s and 1930s dreamed of stable family lives, perhaps even a return to the mythical "good old days." But the wishes of the population clashed sharply with the policies of the state. The family as the base unit of this unique form of society, which was absorbed by the state, could also become a source of resistance. For many, it was a shelter and a defense against the party's "all-seeing eyes" and the government's "all-hearing ears."

Schools continued to be separate for each sex, a practice put into effect during the war. This segregated education of schoolchildren had very negative psychological consequences. Schoolboys wore military-type uniforms and caps reminiscent of those in the lycées of tsarist times. Putting uniforms on civil servants and schoolchildren was a way of regimenting society typical of Stalin's last years. There is rumored to have been a plan to introduce uniforms for full and corresponding members of the Academy of Sciences, but the number of stars for academicians' shoulder patches could not be decided upon.

The uniform dress codes in civilian life symbolized the essential features of Soviet society in the later Stalin years.

### Agriculture

In 1947 famine struck a major part of the European territory of the country. The areas that had been occupied by the Germans, and pillaged by Germans and Soviets alike, were especially affected. The famine resulted from serious droughts, which struck the breadbasket of European Russia: a significant portion of the Ukraine, Moldavia, the lower Volga regions, central Russia, and the Crimea. During the preceding years the state had forced the kolkhozes to turn over to the state excessive amounts of grain, sometimes not even leaving enough for seed. Thus, the country had exhausted its grain reserves. Still the state demanded that the peasants, who had been completely robbed of grain, deliver millions of tons of grain. For example, in 1946, in the midst of the drought, Ukrainian collective farmers were forced to deliver 400 million poods (131 million centners). This figure, like most of the other plan targets, had been arbitrarily determined; it did not correspond in any way to the real capacities of Ukrainian agriculture.

In desperation the peasants wrote letters to the Ukrainian government in Kiev and the central government in Moscow, imploring them to intercede and save them from death. Khrushchev, who at the time was first party secretary in the Ukraine, after long hesitation and fearing that he would be accused of sabotage, decided to write a letter to Stalin asking for authorization to set up a temporary rationing system and retain some agricultural produce to feed the rural population.[59] Stalin crudely rejected the request in a reply sent by telegram. After that, hunger and death inevitably awaited the Ukrainian peasants. They began to die by the thousands. Cases of cannibalism were even reported. In his memoirs, Khrushchev quoted a letter sent to him by A. I. Kirichenko, first party secretary of the Odessa Region, who had visited a kolkhoz in the winter of 1946–47: "I found a scene of horror," said he. "The woman had the corpse of her own child on the table and was cutting it up. She was chattering away as she worked, 'We've already eaten Manechka. Now we'll salt down Vanechka. This will keep us for some time.' Can you imagine? This woman had gone crazy with hunger and butchered her own children."[60]

But Stalin and his close assistants did not wish to acknowledge this terrible reality. The merciless Kaganovich was sent to the Ukraine as the party's first secretary. Khrushchev fell temporarily into disgrace and was transferred to the post of chairman of the Ukrainian Council of People's Commissars. But no mere reshuffling of personnel could save the situation. The famine continued and took nearly a million lives.

After the end of the war, energetic measures were taken to assimilate the newly annexed western parts of Ukraine, Byelorussia, and Moldavia into the political and economic system existing in the rest of the country. Several methods were used, including deportations, agrarian reform, "de-kulakization," collectivization, and the importation of settlers from the old parts of the Soviet Union.

First came a new deportation of "politically unreliable" and "alien class" elements. In the countryside, property was confiscated from the rich land-owners, and in the initial stages land was divided among the poor and landless peasants. But very soon, as early as 1947, collectivization began, meeting resistance from the peasantry. Two years after the beginning of collectivization, for example, in the summer of 1949, despite all means of coercion, pressure, deportation, and intimidation, 30 percent of all peasant households in Estonia remained in individual hands.

In Latvia the stage of agrarian reform was rapidly concluded. The official history of the Latvian Soviet Socialist Republic says that the party, following tradition, "went from a policy of limiting the kulaks to eliminating them as a class. In forming kolkhozes, the peasants would vote not to include kulaks in them." But as was to be expected, "wreckers" soon made their appearance. "Active saboteurs," the book tells us, "were brought to justice; other kulaks were expelled from the country [i.e., deported to Siberia— A. N.] and their lands annexed to the kolkhozes."[61] Mass arrests in the Baltic countries did not spare even deputies to the Supreme Soviet. In Lithuania, when one of the victims said, "What are you doing? I am a deputy!" the MVD (Ministry of Internal Affairs) arresting officer replied calmly, "No matter, there is a need for deputies in Siberia, too."

The authors of the textbook *History of the USSR: The Epoch of Socialism*, published in 1974, wrote:

The Central Committee of the All-Union Communist party, with its resolution of May 21, 1947, on the formation of kolkhozes in the Baltic countries, warned the local authorities that in this important question they should not be hasty and recommended that kolkhozes be created on a fully voluntary basis with modern machinery and well-equipped machine and tractor stations (MTSs) available. In preparing for collectivization, the most basic forms of peasant cooperation played an important role.[62]

The textbook accurately reported the wording of the resolution but significantly said nothing about the actual events. The following excerpts from a 1958 *History of the Latvian SSR* do.

There was no attempt, it reports, to "use existing forms of agricultural cooperation . . . as a point of departure. The large network of agricultural cooperatives, which embraced nearly three-quarters of the small farms in Latvia, was dismantled. . . . Collectivization of the bulk of the peasantry was carried out in the spring of 1949 at a forced pace which, in a number of cases, led to a violation of the voluntary principle."[63] The disparity between these two versions of history is immense. The first falsifies the situation; the second addresses what actually took place. The first does not mention that forced collectivization was a cause of the outbreak of armed resistance in the Latvian countryside, which was followed by mass repression. The second version makes it clear: "The Soviet government was forced to isolate a portion of the kulaks and other hostile elements."[64]

The armed resistance to forced collectivization continued in Lithuania for several years. In September 1952, at the Seventh Congress of the Lithuanian Communist party, great attention was paid to the struggle against the "bandit underground of bourgeois nationalists" and against "surviving elements of bourgeois nationalist ideology and religious superstition."[65]

Throughout the 1940s the Baltic countries were the scene of sometimes bitter armed struggle against the Soviet government. Collectivization also spurred armed resistance in the western regions of Byelorussia.[66]

During the first five years after the war, extensive industrialization of the Baltic countries was carried out, based on reconstructing the old and creating a new power system. Three years after the end of the war industrial development had already surpassed prewar levels.

The volume of industrial production in Estonia, especially in the chemical and engineering industries, had grown by 1950 to over 3.4 times its prewar level.[67] Also by 1950 the number of blue collar and white collar workers in the Baltic countries had increased by 40 percent since 1940.[68] In Latvia industrial production in 1950 was three times the prewar level; for the same period in Lithuania it was twice the prewar level.[69]

The industrialization of the Baltic states destroyed the old social structure. The ethnic composition of the population changed rapidly, especially in Latvia and Estonia, which were more developed industrially. Many Russians and Ukrainians were settled in the cities, and many were appointed to important positions. Many naval personnel appeared in Baltic ports. The Soviet government's principal objective was to alter the national composition of the population in the Baltic states and to create a solid base of support out of non-Baltic elements.

The difficulties in agriculture in the first postwar years throughout the Soviet Union were intensified by the enormous damage done by the war. The German invaders had devastated 98,000 kolkhozes and 1,876 sovkhozes,[70] confiscated and slaughtered millions of head of livestock, and deprived the rural localities almost completely of their draft animals in the occupied territories. In agricultural areas the active population was reduced by almost one-third.

The sharp reduction of the human resources in the countryside was also a result of the natural process of urban growth. On the average, as many as 2 million people left the rural areas each year.[71] The difficult conditions in the countryside led young people especially to migrate to the cities. Many demobilized soldiers also chose to settle in the cities rather than return to agriculture.

During the war large tracts of land belonging to the kolkhozes had been transferred to enterprises or municipalities or illegally appropriated by them. In other areas land had become an object of commerce. A 1939 resolution of the Central Committee and the Sovnarkom adopted measures against selling off kolkhoz lands. From the point of view of the "revolution from above," which was being carried out in the countryside, this tendency toward a return to private property exposed the fact that regardless of how much the state sought to hide it, no abrupt psychological change had ever taken place within the peasantry. To the peasants, revolution had been an act of oppression rather than justice, since land confiscated from the old owners had not been divided among the peasantry but turned over to the kolkhozes, that is, by the government. Then, during the war, land had been strong-armed by factories and municipal authorities.

The Soviet government was fully aware of what these occurrences meant. In a new decree against selling off kolkhoz lands, on September 19, 1946, the Council of Ministers and Central Committee called these "deviations" in the countryside "deeply damaging to the work of the kolkhozes and extremely dangerous to the overall process of socialist construction in our country."[72]

By the beginning of 1947, over 2,225,000 cases of unauthorized appropriation or use of land had been discovered, affecting a total of 4.7 million hectares. Between 1947 and May 1949, the misuse of an additional 5.9 million hectares came to light.[73] Government bodies—from the local to the republic level—were shamelessly robbing the kolkhozes, using all sorts of pretexts to impose what amounted to payment in kind. In September 1946 the standing debt owed to the kolkhozes by various agencies and organizations reached 383 million rubles.[74] In 1947, in the Akmolinsk Region of Kazakhstan, the authorities took from the kolkhozes 1,500 head of cattle and 3,000 centners of grain and other foodstuffs, for a total value of 2 million rubles. The thieves, who included high-ranking party and government officials, never had to answer for their actions.[75]

The misuse of kolkhoz land and goods aroused widespread indignation among the collective farm peasantry (kolkhozniks). Many kolkhoz chairmen were voted out, but the new kolkhoz heads were unable to change government policies, and the situation remained at an impasse.

After the war, tractor and agricultural machinery production increased rapidly. Despite this improvement, however, the situation in agriculture remained catastrophic. The state continued its policy of investing very little in agriculture—only 16 percent of the budget during the first postwar five-year plan. Crops sown on cultivated land in 1946 were only 76 percent of the amount sown in 1940. Drought and other natural disasters reduced the 1946 harvest below the level of the previous year, when the country had still been at war. "In terms of grain production, our country remained for a long time at the same level as the Russia of the old regime," Khrushchev acknowledged.[77] Between 1910 and 1914 grain harvests comprised 267 million kilograms; the figure was 302 million for the period 1949–1953.[78] Grain yields were below the 1913 level, despite mechanization, fertilization, and other improvements.

| Grain Yield | (in centners per hectare) |
|---|---|
| 1913 | 8.2 |
| 1925–1926 | 8.5 |
| 1926–1932 | 7.5 |
| 1933–1937 | 7.1 |
| 1949–1953 | 7.7 |

The per capita output of agricultural products was correspondingly lower. If the two years before collectivization (1928–1929) are taken as 100, agricultural production in 1913 was 90.3, but in 1930–1932 it was 86.8; in 1938–1940, 90.0; and in 1950–1953, 94.0.[79] The grain situation became acute despite reductions in grain exports (which fell from 1913 to

1938 by a factor of 4.5) and the reduced number of livestock and the consequent reduction in the amount of grain used as cattle feed. From 1928 to 1935, for example, the number of horses fell by 25 million, which meant a saving of more than 10 million tons of grain, or 10–15 percent of the total grain harvest in that period.[80]

In 1916 Russia had within its territory 58,380,000 head of horned cattle. As of January 1, 1941, the figure was 54,510,000, and in 1951 57,090,000, which was lower than the 1916 level.[81] Not until 1955 was the 1916 level exceeded.[82] According to official Soviet statistics (adjusted for inflation), between 1940 and 1952 overall agricultural production increased by only 10 percent.[83]

The February 1947 Central Committee plenum called for more centralization of agricultural production, taking from the kolkhozes the decision not only of how much but of what to plant. Political sections were reestablished at the MTSs. Propaganda was to substitute for food for the utterly starved and impoverished collective farmers. In addition to their deliveries to the state, the kolkhozes had to contribute to the seed fund and allocate a portion of the harvest to the "indivisible fund," a kind of capital fund. It was not until these obligations were met that the collective farmers could be paid for their workdays (*trudodni*). Quotas for deliveries to the state were set by the central government. Projected crop yields were estimated carelessly, and actual harvests were often below plan targets. The first commandment for collective farmers was to hand over to the state its quota. Local party and government bodies would often force the more efficient kolkhozes to fill in their poorer neighbors' unmet quotas, which ultimately led to the impoverishment of all. The peasants fed themselves for the most part with the produce they grew on their minuscule private plots. To be able to take these goods to the market, however, they were required to have a certificate stating that they had met their obligations to the state; otherwise they were branded as speculators or "deserters" and faced fines or even prison sentences. Taxes on private plots were increased and had to be paid in kind, often in goods that the kolkhozniks did not produce. For this reason, producers were forced to obtain goods at market price and deliver them to the state free of charge. Rural Russia had not seen such horrible conditions even under the Mongol yoke.

In 1952 state prices for grain deliveries were lower than in 1940. The price the state paid for potatoes was less than the cost of transportation. Kolkhozes were receiving an average of 8.63 rubles per centner for grain, while sovkhozes were getting 27.90 rubles. A collective farmer had to put in sixty workdays to purchase one kilogram of butter, and to clothe himself modestly required one year's income.[84]

In the early 1950s the central authorities' continuous arbitrary decisions on what and how to plant resulted in extremely poor harvests in most kolkhozes and sovkhozes, even in such favorable areas as the Volga region, the central black earth region, and Kazakhstan. Foolish orders from on high and shortages of machinery did not explain everything, however. Poor harvests were also the result of the fact that, over the course of many years, little by little, the peasants' love of working the land had been destroyed. In the past the earth had repaid their toil and devotion, sometimes generously, sometimes less so. But this stimulus, falsely labeled by the authorities the "stimulus of material interest," no longer existed. Working the land was turning into forced labor, with little or no compensation.

Many collective farmers went hungry; others suffered from malnutrition. Their private plots were their only salvation. The situation was particularly harsh in European Russia. Things were better in Central Asia because of price increases, particularly for cotton, the main crop. They were also better in the south, which specialized in vegetables, fruits, and wine.

In 1950 a campaign of consolidation and amalgamation of kolkhozes was initiated. By 1953 the number of kolkhozes had decreased from 237,000 to 93,000.[85] This reform could also have strengthened them economically, but lack of investments, forced deliveries to the state at fixed low prices, the lack of sufficient trained technicians and specialists, and finally, the limitations imposed by the state on the use of private plots deprived the collective farmers of incentive and destroyed any hope of extricating themselves from their dire situation.

In 1951 Khrushchev proposed that the Gordian knot strangling agriculture be cut by the creation of "agrocities"—that is, large-scale agricultural enterprises to replace the numerous and weak kolkhozes. He was sharply criticized for this proposal in the press, which was quite unusual, keeping in mind Khrushchev's status as a Politburo member. Such a move would have amounted to an admission that the party's agricultural policies had been a fiasco for many years. Khrushchev's idea recalled Stolypin's agrarian reform shortly before the revolution, which aimed at creating large peasant farms producing for the market. Khrushchev, at mid-century, was advocating profitable agricultural enterprises based on the transformation of collective farmers into agricultural workers. The material basis for an effective implementation of Khrushchev's plan, however, was lacking.

The government continued to trumpet success, openly lying to the Russian people and the world about the achievements of the "socialist" state. At the Nineteenth Party Congress, in the political report, Malenkov announced without batting an eye that the Soviet Union's grain problems had been solved and 8 million poods (2.6 million centners) of grain had been harvested.[86] Two years later, after Stalin's death, it was officially announced that all figures relating to agricultural production had been inflated.

The 33 million collective farmers, whose labor was feeding a population of 200 million, constituted, with the exception of prisoners, the poorest and most downtrodden sector of society.

## The Working Class and Urban Population

One of the first measures adopted by the Provisional Government after the February 1917 revolution was the introduction of the eight-hour workday. Previously the workday had lasted from ten to twelve hours. For the peasants the workday was irregular, as is always true in agriculture. In 1927 the seven-hour working day was introduced for the urban population. This important social advance lasted until 1940, when the eight-hour day was reimposed. Antilabor legislation, already discussed in Chapter 7, was implemented the same year. Those laws remained on the books until 1956.

According to official Soviet statistics, the average wage of a Soviet worker increased more than 1,100 percent between the beginning of industrialization in 1928 and the end of the Stalin era in 1954.[87] But this does not give us any idea of real wages. Soviet sources provide fantastic figures which do not correspond to reality. Estimates by Western researchers suggest that, in the best of cases, the cost of living increased by a factor of between nine and ten from 1928 to 1954. At the same time, however, the Soviet worker enjoyed numerous benefits, including free medical care and education.

According to Janet Chapman, an American expert on the Soviet economy, benefits paid to blue collar and white collar workers in addition to wages amounted to the following percentages (adjusted for price changes): in 1928, 15.8 percent; in 1937, 22.1 percent; in 1940, 20.7 percent; in 1948, 29.6 percent; in 1952, 22.2 percent; and in 1954, 21.5 percent.[88]

Taking 1928 as a base of 100, the cost of living underwent the following changes during the same period (1928 = 100):

| 1937 | 1940 | 1944 | 1948 | 1952 | 1954 |
|------|------|------|------|------|------|
| 478  | 679  | 952  | 1565 | 1053 | 900  |

Thus, at the end of the Stalin era the cost of living had increased by a factor of nine to ten over the period before collectivization.[89]

If taxes and obligatory loans to the government (purchases of bonds) are excluded and the value of social benefits included, the change in real wages for the same period was as follows:[90]

| 1928 | 1937 | 1940 | 1944 | 1948 | 1952 | 1954 |
|------|------|------|------|------|------|------|
| 100  | 86   | 78   | 64   | 59   | 94   | 119  |

This table demonstrates that the increase in wages and salaries was less than the increase in the cost of living. By 1948, for example, wages were twice those of 1937, but the cost of living was three times higher. The lowering of real wages was also the result of increases in taxes and obligatory purchases of government bonds (in effect, loans to the state out of workers' wages). By 1952 there was a significant rise in real wages, but they were still lower than in 1928, although they had exceeded the 1937 and 1940 levels.

To form a clearer picture of the situation the Soviet worker faced compared to his Western counterpart, let us examine the quantity of produce each could buy with one hour's wages. If the Soviet worker's wages are taken as a base of 100, we get the following picture:[91]

| Country | 1928 | 1936–1938 | 1950 | 1951–1952 |
|---------|------|-----------|------|-----------|
| Soviet Union | 100 | 100 | 100 | 100 |
| Austria | 90 | 158 | 200 | 167 |
| Czechoslovakia | 94 | 142 | 329 | — |
| France | 112 | 283 | 221 | 200 |
| Germany | 142 | 213 | 271 | 233 |
| Great Britain | 200 | 192 | 443 | 361 |
| United States | 370 | 417 | 714 | 556 |

This table speaks for itself: in 1952, for the same amount of work, a British worker could buy 3.5 times more produce than a Soviet worker and an American 5.5 times more.

Soviet citizens, especially of the older generation, are generally convinced that under Stalin prices decreased every year, whereas under Khrushchev and his later successors they have constantly risen. This explains the existence of a certain nostalgia for the Stalin era.

The mystery of those price decreases is exceptionally simple. First, prices registered a tremendous leap after the beginning of collectivization. The price of rye bread increased 950 percent between 1928 and 1937, and almost 1,800 percent between 1928 and 1952. During the same period the price of prime beef went up 950 percent and 1,600 percent; of pork, 950 and 1,950. The price of herring had increased 1,500 percent by 1952.

Sugar prices had increased 900 percent by 1937 and 1,500 percent by 1952; sunflower oil, 2,700 percent and 3,300 percent; eggs, 1,050 percent and 1,830 percent; and potatoes, 400 percent and 1,000 percent.[92] After raising prices between 1,500 and 2,000 percent, it was fairly easy to put on the charade of a yearly price drop.

Second, price decreases occurred at the expense of the kolkhozes; that is, the state paid extraordinarily low fixed prices for agricultural products. In 1953 government procurement prices in Moscow and Leningrad provinces were as low as 2.5 to 3 kopeks for a kilogram of potatoes.[93]

Lastly, the majority of the population never noticed any differences in prices because supplies were short, and in many regions meat, fats, and other goods never reached the stores.

This was the "secret" of the price drops of the Stalin era. Twenty-five years after the revolution, the Soviet worker had a poorer diet than the Western worker.

The housing crisis also grew worse. By comparison with prerevolutionary times, when there were serious housing problems in densely populated cities (in 1913, seven square meters per person), the crisis reached disastrous proportions in the years after the revolution, especially during collectivization. Masses of rural inhabitants poured into the cities to escape famine or in search of work. During the Stalin era civilian housing construction was tightly limited. Only high-ranking party and government officials received apartments in the cities. In Moscow, for example, in the early 1930s an enormous housing complex arose in Bersenevskaya Embarkment near the Stone Bridge. It was called Government House and had spacious and comfortable apartments. Some hundred meters from it another complex was located, a former poorhouse converted into communal apartments, each inhabited by between twenty and thirty persons, with one kitchen and one or two bathrooms each.

Before the revolution, most of the workers lived in barracks next to their factories; after the revolution the barracks were renamed. They were called "communal dwellings" (obshchezhitiya). The larger enterprises built new homes for managerial personnel and engineers, but the housing problem remained unsolved because the lion's share of the budget was allocated to industry, especially the war industry, and energy production.

For the vast majority of the urban population during the Stalin era housing conditions grew worse every year: population growth generally exceeded the pace of civilian housing construction. In 1928 there were 5.8 square meters per inhabitant; in 1932, 4.9; in 1937, 4.6. The First Five-Year Plan called for the construction of 62.5 million square meters of new housing, but only 23.5 million were built. The Second Five-Year Plan called for 72.5 million square meters; only 26.8 million were built.[94] In 1940 the average per capita living space had fallen to 4.5 square meters.

Two years after Stalin's death, when the mass construction of buildings began, each city dweller had 5.1 square meters. For a better idea of the crowded living conditions, we should recall that the officially prescribed Soviet standard is 9 square meters per person (in Czechoslovakia the standard was 17 square meters). Many families had only 6 square meters. Entire clans, two or three generations each, shared a single room.

The example of Mrs. A, a cleaning lady at a large Moscow enterprise, is indicative. She was part of a clan of thirteen people, living in one room of twenty square meters. The room had seven beds. The six other people, adults or children, slept on the floor. Sexual relations took place virtually in the open. People had become accustomed to it and paid no attention after a while. For fifteen years the three families that lived in that room asked in vain to be relocated. They were not able to move until the early 1960s.

These were the conditions of hundreds of thousands, if not millions, of city dwellers. In 1975 in Moscow the housing bureaus still refused to handle requests from people who had more than five square meters per person. Such was the legacy of the Stalin era.

Low labor productivity was and remained the Achilles' heel of the Soviet economy, even though attempts were made to raise it through a complex system of incentives and bonuses. Between 1928 and 1955 production increased at an average of 100 percent for the Soviet economy as a whole. If the plan was fulfilled or overfulfilled, a bonus was paid. As a general rule, bonuses were higher for engineers and technicians than for industrial workers.[95]

In theory, the working class was the driving force of society, but its real political impact declined steadily as the bureaucratic elite grew in number and as its role in the state expanded. The identification of the interests of the elite with those of the entire people found its reflection in basic party documents, as well as in the rules and programs of the CPSU. At the end of the Stalin era, the formula that the party is the organized vanguard of the working class in the Soviet Union (Seventeenth Party Congress, 1934) was replaced by the formula that it is a "voluntary militant union of Communists who share the same ideas" (Nineteenth Party Congress, 1959). This shift not only signified a transition from the concept of the "dictatorship of the proletariat" to that of the "whole peoples' state," it was also an admission of the reduced role played by the working class in spite of the leadership's continued proclamations of its role as a driving force.

## The Party

During the last two or three years of the war a policy was adopted of drastically increasing the number the Soviet Communist party members in the army and the reserves. The party's authority was restored in accordance with success on the battlefield, as is shown by the following figures.

On January 1, 1941, the party had 3,872,000 members. During the war more than 3 million were killed.[96] Nevertheless, by January 1946 party membership had reached 5,511,000.[97] Growth was particularly rapid from the second half of 1942 to the end of the war. In the second half of 1941, 343,500 new members (full and candidate members) joined the party; during the second half of 1942, 1,147,000 joined; in 1942, 2,794,000; and in 1944, 2,416,000.[98]

Inside the army, joining the party was made easier by a special resolution reducing the probation period for candidate members from one year to six months in the case of those who had distinguished themselves in battle. During the war many joined the party out of conviction, seeing it as the organizer of the struggle against the Nazi invader. No special privileges were gained by joining. In fact, one was likely to be killed in battle sooner than others. "Communists, forward!" was not only a slogan; it was an everyday reality of life at the front. Naturally the political officers singled out certain individuals, urging them to join, and given conditions at the front, it was often impossible to refuse. In the rear, if many joined out of patriotic conviction, as many joined as a way of furthering their careers.

Statistics on the social composition of the party might be useful in corroborating the declining role of the working class in the Soviet Union, but no such statistics have been published in the USSR since the Seventeenth Party Congress in 1934, when 60 percent of the membership were workers, or rather had come from the working class, because the percentage of members working in production was much smaller, 9.3 percent. According to party tradition, functionaries of the party apparatus were and still are assigned to the working class category. Peasants constituted 8 percent of the membership in 1934, and white collar workers 32 percent.[99]

Western researchers, using information about the educational level of delegates to party congresses and statistics derived from local party conferences and other sources, estimate that by the Nineteenth Party Congress in 1952 (the last under Stalin) workers constituted only 7.6 percent of the delegates and peasants 7.8 percent.[100]

Despite the increased influx of workers and peasants during the war, the CPSU was actually transformed into a party of functionaries, specialists in various fields, and intellectuals in the service of the organization.[101] Membership for most of them was above all a means of advancing their careers. Politically the party's composition also changed radically. Most of the Old Bolsheviks had been killed in the terror of the 1930s, and the second generation of Communists suffered heavy losses during the war.

Similar changes affected the social composition of the soviets, from the local level up to the supreme soviets of the republics and the USSR. The higher the institution, the fewer the workers or peasants that were still "linked with production." And even those described in the statistics as active producers were in reality part of the new, power-corrupted labor or kolkhoz aristocracies. In 1937, of the deputies to the Supreme Soviet of the USSR, 42 percent were listed as workers, 29.5 percent as peasants, and 28.5 percent as intelligentsia. In 1950 the corresponding figures were 31.8 percent, 20.4 percent, and 47.8 percent.[102]

With grim determination the party continued to increase its influence, neglecting neither the material, the spiritual, nor the moral aspect of life for the "new Soviet man." Local party organizations were required to monitor the moral behavior of members and their families more rigorously. Informing the authorities about "amoral" behavior became common practice. Party bureaus at enterprises and offices, local trade union committees, and even higher party and government agencies were swamped by denunciations and complaints of all sorts. In the late Stalin era hypocrisy and sycophancy became a central characteristic of Soviet society.

The war accelerated the crystallization of the present-day form of modern Soviet society. However, completion of the process was continually impeded by arbitrariness and terror, which constantly threatened all levels of society, including the most highly placed in the bureaucracy.

During the war major shifts occurred in the structure of the bureaucracy. Its military wing acquired more weight, its numbers grew, and its castelike tendencies became more evident. During the terror of the 1930s the corps of generals had been almost completely annihilated. Those who had been spared were reduced to automatons who faithfully followed the orders of the party leadership. But the conditions of war were such that in spite of all the restrictions imposed by the high command, generals in the field had to make their own decisions. This revived their sense of responsibility and self-esteem, not only in their own eyes but in the eyes of the population as well. For a short time the marshals and generals enjoyed popularity. It is true that they were subjected to constant surveillance by State Security. Their adjutants, drivers, and mistresses often served as informers for the security agencies and more than one paid dearly for a carelessly spoken word. Soon after the end of the war, the most popular marshals began to be sent off to the provinces. Zhukov, the most famous of all, was sent to Odessa to command the military district. Others were assigned to occupation duties in Germany and Eastern Europe, some retired or were transferred to the reserves, and a few were sent to prison.

In an attempt to keep the officers in a state of perfect obedience, the government at first showered those returning from the front with considerable privileges. Senior officers were given land to build homes on, generals were given larger lots. The top generals and marshals received government dachas fully equipped with the most modern conveniences on favorable terms. Exclusive stores and tailor's shops were established for all generals, where they and their families could purchase higher quality goods at very low prices.

During the war another wing of the bureaucracy acquired new size and strength: the managers of the big enterprises engaged in military production and construction.

The importance of the state security organs was also enhanced. The number of state security agents grew enormously. The officers of SMERSH (military counterintelligence) became the backbone of the security apparatus. The head of SMERSH became the head of state security for the entire country.

After the war the agencies of the judiciary, the procuracy, and the police were filled with demobilized officers. Often demobilized officers of peasant background were unable to find positions in the postwar army or in cities and became kolkhoz chairmen, but directing a kolkhoz could prove to be more difficult than commanding a battalion or even a company.

With the war over, people expected improvements in their situation. Instead, they were called upon for further sacrifices. The abstract idea of building socialism could no longer inspire enthusiasm in the exhausted population. The party then resorted to the proven method of frightening the population with the threat of imperialist aggression. Newspapers wrote that it was necessary to resist the offensive of the Western powers, who allegedly wished to steal the fruits of the victory over fascism from the Soviet people. This new enemy—Western imperialism—was very abstract, nebulous, elusive. It was a lot more practical to find an "enemy" inside. Then it could be identified. The "enemy" thus chosen was the intellectual, the "rootless cosmopolitan" whose name did not sound very Russian. This the population could understand easily. And for those who were not entirely sure, the press, lecturers, university professors, and experts in Marxism-Leninism (whose number grew constantly in the postwar years) explained the matter authoritatively and at great length.

The party's need to exploit patriotic sentiment was great. Stalin well understood that in the first postwar years patriotism was a very powerful ideological weapon. As was the case with all the formulas he used, Stalin's definition of patriotism was extremely simple: it was, he declared in his report on the twenty-seventh anniversary of the October revolution, "the deep devotion and the deep faith of the people toward its Soviet homeland and the fraternal friendship of the workers of all the nationalities in our country."[103]

This notion also included awareness of the total superiority of Soviet society over all others and pride in being a part of it. The "new Soviet man," Homo Sovieticus, was encouraged to develop a feeling of special importance of his mission and of a special destiny. Such a superiority complex is the most dangerous attitude any society can have. It fosters the conviction that anything is permissible in the name of a greater goal. How great this goal actually is, however, depends entirely on the leadership that interprets it.

Soviet patriotism was, for the government, a means of forcing the people again to accept a hard existence and the new "temporary difficulties."

In another of his speeches, Stalin called the Soviet people "little screws" in a great machine.[104] Everyone knows about screws; they can be screwed in or out at will, and sometimes when treated roughly their heads fly off. The day after Stalin's speech members of the staff of one of the laboratories at the Aerodynamics Institute in Moscow lined up in the hallways and marched down the halls chanting, "We are little screws; we are nuts and bolts."

## Lysenko, Lysenkoism, and Soviet Science

One of the most striking indications of the crisis of the Soviet system under Stalin was Lysenkoism.

The agrobiologist Trofim Lysenko successfully caught Stalin's attention by a very simple method. With the aim of winning an important position in science, he made a speech at the second congress of collective farmers with exemplary work records in February 1935, in which he asserted that while in the countryside the kulaks were fighting the Soviet government, in the city, the "kulaks of science" were doing the same. Stalin was the first to applaud, calling out, "Bravo, Comrade Lysenko. Bravo." This was the beginning of Lysenko's rise. Soon he became president of the Lenin All-Union Academy of Agricultural Sciences and used his position to drive out the true geneticists, his scientific adversaries, and even saw to it that some were imprisoned. In 1940 the noted Russian botanist and geneticist Nikolai Ivanovich Vavilov was arrested. He died in prison in 1943. Other leading scientists in the fields of biology and agronomy were arrested.[105]

Lysenko's name is linked with a general social phenomenon, "Lysenkoism," similar to the Rasputin phenomenon in tsarist Russia. Rasputin promised the tsarina the salvation of Orthodox Russia. Lysenko promised the Central Committee, and Comrade Stalin personally, the creation, in a short time, of an abundance of agricultural products. Both Stalin and the Romanov family had hoped for a miracle, but the miracle Stalin and the Central Committee expected was "scientifically based."

Unlimited possibilities were made available to Lysenko in his effort to organize abundance, including the moral and physical right to destroy his opponents. The destruction of agrobiology and of geneticists and biologists, which had begun on the eve of the war, was started with renewed vigor soon after the war was over.

In the summer of 1948 Lysenko called for a public debate with his opponents, who supported the theory of heredity in the origin of species. They accepted the challenge, not even suspecting that Lysenko's report to the August 1948 session of the Lenin All-Union Academy of Agricultural Sciences had been approved beforehand by the Central Committee. Lysenko's basic argument had been concealed until a convenient moment arose. The concluding act in the play came when the geneticists expressed themselves publicly, whereupon Lysenko told them that the Central Committee had approved his theory, which denied the existence of genes and the theory of heredity. After Lysenko's acknowledgment, the geneticists, who were defending the right to have more than one scientific theory, again asked for the floor in order to announce their "repentence."[106]

The August 1948 session of the academy gave the signal for repressive measures against geneticists. As a result, all scientific work in the field was halted, and hundreds of genuine researchers and experimental agronomists lost their jobs. Lysenko's pseudo-science became established throughout the country, dealing Soviet agriculture yet another blow after collectivization and the war. Even today the Soviet economy has not completely overcome these three catastrophes.

The August 1948 session was also the point of departure for a party offensive in the ideological field. The philosopher Prezent became Lysenko's closest assistant; he was assigned the task of giving a philosophical explanation for the new method. The session was presented to other fields as an example of the defense of Marxism-Leninism.

Genetics was effectively banned throughout the Soviet Union. Professor Nuzhdin, one of Lysenko's helpers, wrote shortly after the conclusion of the academy's session that "Mendelism-Morganism has been condemned. It has no place in Soviet science."[107] Nevertheless, in spite of harsh repression, some centers of genetics were able to survive. For example, Academician N. N. Semenov, director of the Institute of Chemical Physics of the USSR Academy of Sciences and a future Nobel laureate, put a laboratory at the disposal of Professor Rapoport, a noted geneticist, without requiring any detailed reports on the nature of his research.

But Lysenkoism was not limited to the rise of Lysenko and his cronies to key positions in science and thereby in the Soviet bureaucracy. It also expressed the party's fundamental policy in regard to science. Like a cancer, Lysenkoism rapidly spread and metastasized.

In the summer of 1950 a joint session of the USSR Academy of Sciences and the USSR Academy of Medical Sciences announced that Academician K. M. Bykov and his disciples were the sole defenders of Pavlov's physiological theories. All other schools were declared hostile, and their activities came to an end. Bykov was well liked in the party because of his servility, the positions he had taken in favor of Russian science and in opposition to any links with foreign science. Almost all Soviet biologists who had gained any recognition were declared apostates between 1948 and 1950: Academicians I. I. Shmalgauzen, A. R. Zhebrak, P. M. Zhukovsky. N. P. Dubinin, L. A. Orbeli and his school, and A. D. Speransky and his students. The least serious accusation was brought against Professor Anokhin—carelessness in methodology.[108]

The main targets of these campaigns were Jewish scientists, for example, Academician Lina Shtern, a biologist, and her students, who were denounced for "the perfidious Zionist character" of their school. The physicist D. Biryukov wrote in *Culture and Life* that "the rotten methodology of this 'school' was supported by the arrant cosmopolitanism which had come to flourish within it."[109] The school of Georgian Academician I. Beritashvili was declared idealist and "openly hostile to the doctrines of Pavlov."[110] The publishers responsible for the appearance of a translation of *What's Life from the Standpoint of Physics*, by the famous Austrian scientist E. Schrödinger, were also dragged through the mud.[111]

The highpoint in the campaign to claim priority for Russian over Western science was a session of the USSR Academy of Sciences held in Leningrad January 5–10, 1949, and dedicated to the two hundred twenty-fifth anniversary of the founding of the Russian Imperial Academy of Sciences. In his introductory remarks the president of the academy, S. I. Vavilov (the brother of Lysenko's victim), stressed the need for a struggle to affirm Russian science's primacy in discoveries. Among the claims to "firsts" advanced during the campaign of the years 1946–1950 were inventions in the fields of radio, electric lighting, the electric transformer, electrical transmission with direct and alternating current, electric-powered and diesel-powered ships, the airplane, the parachute, and the stratoplane. The discovery of the law of conservation of energy was attributed to Lomonosov. These are but a few examples of the claim, some of them so absurd that they inspired satirical sayings: "Soviet watches are the fastest in the world" and "Russia is the elephant's natural habitat."

The 1949 Academy of Sciences session in Leningrad marked a deliberate break with Western science. Three foreign members of the Academy were removed—the British scientist Dale, an honorary full member, and the American Muller and the Norwegian Brock, who were corresponding members. It is true that the first two had already announced their resignation from the Academy to protest the persecution of scientists in the USSR. Brock was expelled because of his articles on the situation of science in the Soviet Union and Eastern Europe.[112]

These campaigns of ideological purification were used by some to settle old grievances. The active participants of these pogroms would later hold the positions of the scientists accused of "cosmopolitanism" or "bourgeois liberalism." The research institutes of the academy and the universities were filled with graduates from the Academy of Social Sciences, which was under the party's Central Committee, and from the party's higher schools. Competence was no longer the criterion for selecting doctoral candidates; instead it was loyalty to the party and willingness to participate in any and all ideological pogroms.

During Stalin's last years, the level of Soviet research in the social sciences, already low, declined sharply, largely thanks to Stalin's new theoretical works, *Marxism and Problems of Linguistics* and *Economic Problems of Socialism in the USSR*. As soon as they were printed, they became the object of universal study. The whole of social science was reduced to commentary on the Leader's new "works of genius." When Stalin issued a negative judgment on the linguistic theories of N. Marr, a new ideological crusade began, this time against "Marrism" and its defenders. An avalanche of denunciations descended upon Soviet linguists, archeologists, and ethnographers, many of whom had shared Marr's theories on the evolution of language, theories which the party had previously supported. Stalin's writings on the economy managed to confuse economists totally and were used as a pretext for new polemics and persecutions of scholars.

Physics was the only domain where the party's obscurantists were never able to rally scientists in the "struggle against hostile manifestations." True, the magazine *Problems of Philosophy* published inflammatory articles containing accusations of philosophic idealism and kowtowing to Western physics, but they were dealing with a touchy subject. The desire to develop atomic weapons weighed far more heavily than the desire to conduct a pogrom against the physicists. During a meeting called to discuss the struggle against "rootless cosmopolitanism," Academician A. F. Ioffe, the leading atomic researcher, presented the representatives of the Central Committee who chaired the meeting with the following choice: scientists could either work in their laboratories or they could waste their time in useless meetings. If the latter choice was made, the organizers of the meetings would have to replace the scientists in the laboratory. Disarmed, the apparatchiki were forced to report that the meeting had taken place, and nothing more was heard of it. Shortly before, Academician Petr Kapitsa had categorically refused to take part in the atomic bomb project. The authorities did not want to risk alienating other physicists. Ioffe's remarks, like Kapitsa's attitude, were acts of resistance against the government, which in this instance felt powerless to take direct reprisals. Instead, it chose revenge. For many years, under both Stalin and Khrushchev, Kapitsa was denied permission to go abroad to attend international scientific meetings.[113]

One of the principal characteristics of the Soviet regime is continuous ideological struggle. It is unimportant against whom or what this struggle is directed; rather, it is the very process of struggle that is significant—a struggle into which the masses may be drawn, making them accomplices.

During the period of late Stalinism the main focus of ideological struggle was the affirmation of Soviet Russian patriotism. Given the specific conditions of the time, this form of nationalism took on a distinctly anti-Semitic coloration. The anti-Semitic policies of the Soviet government, which can be traced back to the 1920s, developed especially rapidly during the Nazi–Soviet rapprochement, when the government apparatus, mainly in the foreign affairs and state security agencies, was purged of Jews (as was described in Chapter 7).

In 1941 Erlich and Alter, two Polish socialists of Jewish origin who had fled to the Soviet Union, were executed on "espionage" charges. The accusation, which was a complete fabrication, was an extreme expression of official Soviet anti-Semitism.[114] In 1943 all Jews began to be systematically removed from the army's political apparatus and replaced by Russians. After the war the same policy was applied to Jews who held command posts.

The flames of anti-Semitism, ignited by the Nazis in the occupied territories, were further fanned by the authorities after those areas were liberated. In the Soviet army and in the rear, rumors intentionally were spread about cowardice and desertion on the part of Jews. Those who miraculously escaped mass extermination by the Nazis often were accused by the Soviet authorities of having been agents of the Germans; otherwise, how could they have survived? After the war Soviet Jews began to be depicted as agents of "American imperialism."

The campaign to rid Soviet society of "antipatriotic" elements began a few months after a speech by Stalin at a gathering of voters on February 9, 1946. He did not make any special references to socialism or communism; instead, the state, the Soviet social system, and the greatness of "the motherland" were the main themes of his speech.[115]

On June 28, 1946, *Culture and Life*, a new party publication, appeared. It was to be issued every ten days by the Central Committee's Directorate of Agitation and Propaganda, "Agitprop." Agitprop had been simply a department (*otdel*) of the Central Committee; the fact that it had been transformed into a "directorate" (*upravlenie*) indicated that the role of ideology in the party-government system was being reinforced. Soon a far-reaching offensive began against "ideological deviations" in all fields of science and culture.

The party's control was particularly strict over literature and history, which had a tremendous influence in the shaping of individual personality. This was particularly true in Russia, where reading was a mass phenomenon. It is likely that all prewar generations were raised on the Russian classics, and the literary tastes of the majority were therefore firmly conservative, despite the many attempts to create a new proletarian culture, with such works as Gladkov's *Cement* and Serafimovich's *Iron Flood*. The party leadership finally understood that its best interest lay in maintaining the people's conservative tastes and encouraging those young writers who followed classical models, albeit with new content that glorified the revolution, socialism, and Soviet patriotism. After the war a novel by one of these writers, *The Young Guard*, by Aleksandr Fadeev, described the Young Communist heroes who had resisted German occupation in the mining town of Krasnodon. These Young Communists were fully in the tradition of the classical heroes of Soviet literature. However, Fadeev, the secretary of the Writers Union and a Central Committee member, "had forgotten" to stress the party's leading role in organizing the anti-Nazi resistance. Thus in 1947 he became the target of party criticism. As a true son of the party, and under its guidance, he rewrote the novel, making it much worse.

The war provided a new generation of heroes—authentic for the most part—who appeared in the works of such writers as Vasily Grossman, Viktor Nekrasov, Boris Polevoi, and Konstantin Simonov. The war became the principal theme of Soviet literature for many years.

But there was a need for a new kind of hero, a shining example for the period of reconstruction and socialist emulation. He was born in the form of the *Cavalier of the Golden Star,* a novel by Semen Babaevsky. This book, and others like it, were printed in the millions. Critics praised them, and the authors received the Stalin prize. But readers shied away from them; they were too primitive and full of lies.

At the same time a new danger appeared, presented by a young generation of writers and poets who had matured and become seasoned by their wartime experience. They sought to rethink the world in which they lived. In the eyes of the party, however, any such rethinking was sedition of the worst kind. "New winds" were blowing in all areas of cultural life. The party ideologists, who saw in this trend an erosion of ideology and, consequently, harm to the Soviet regime, rose to meet this danger. The party launched a campaign that did not overlook any field of cultural endeavor. Volunteers willing to judge and condemn their colleagues were found everywhere. With a zeal as great as their lack of talent, they were then and are still the party's main reserve force. The party had only to give the signal and point out the channel down which the streams of mud were to flow, and the rest took care of itself.

Initially, from 1946 to 1948, this ideological campaign was headed by Zhdanov, a secretary of the Central Committee. After his death it was headed by Mikhail Suslov, also a secretary of the Central Committee. Unlike Zhdanov, who loved to show off in front of huge auditoriums, Suslov preferred to operate from behind the scene, letting his subordinates do the dirty work.

In his speeches of 1946–1948, Zhdanov demanded that the influence of Western culture be totally rooted out. Whether he spoke to the Leningrad writers, philosophers, or composers, he insisted on emphatic condemnation of all deviations from Marxism-Leninism and from the party's cultural line. He was very shrewd in his choice of targets for destructive criticism. In literature he attacked Mikhail Zoshchenko, whose satires were very popular among all strata of the population. In one of Zoshchenko's works, *Adventures of a Monkey*, a primate escaped from the zoo, lived under normal Soviet conditions, and reached the conclusion that there was no difference between the two types of existence.[116] Zhdanov denounced Zoshchenko for this.[117] His second victim was a poet very respected and dear to the Russian intelligentsia, Anna Akhmatova. In music, Dmitry Shostakovich was attacked. As a rule party leaders selected the most talented representatives of the arts for defamation; independent talent has always presented and will ever present a threat to any totalitarian regime, and the Soviet regime is no exception.

In August 1946 the leadership of the Soviet Writers' Union was changed on orders from the party's Central Committee. Fadeev replaced Tikhonov as secretary general of the union; Tikhonov became a mere undersecretary, as were three newcomers, Vishnevsky, Korneichuk, and Simonov. That same month the Central Committee passed decrees denouncing the magazines *Zvezda* (Star) and *Leningrad* and the repertories of Soviet theaters, and in September denounced the film *A Great Life*.

Similar ideological campaigns were soon orchestrated in the republics and regions. The leaderships of the Writers' Union and other professional associations such as the Composers' Union were now obliged to do what previously the local party organizations alone had done—to watch over the ideological state of affairs in their respective fields and to give timely warnings of any deviations. Special plenary sessions were conducted both in Moscow and locally.

During one of these sessions, a plenum of the Writers' Union in Moscow in December 1948, the secretaries of the local unions engaged in "self-criticism." They repented their sins: idealizing the past of their respective nationalities; forgetting the class struggle; lacking the skill to create works on socialist construction; and lastly, failing to monitor the work of other writers. The representatives of the union's leadership, Simonov, Gorbatov, and Surkov, also pointed to other "negative phenomena," such as formalism, aestheticism, bourgeois liberalism, the inability to use the method of socialist realism, and being under the influence of Western writers. Kazakh writers were accused of not being able to distinguish between the oppressive nature of tsarism and the liberating role of Soviet Russia.[118] These obviously political charges marked the opening of a campaign against the folk epics of the Central Asian nationalities, especially those descended from the Mongols. This campaign reached its zenith in 1951.[119]

At the 1948 Writers' Union plenum, Shcherbina, the vice-minister of culture, and Bolshakov, minister of cinematography, explained to the writers what was expected of them: glorification of the heroic labor of the workers, collective farmers, and intellectuals. In accordance with the Central Committee's directives, it was explained that writers could make fun of everything that is "not part of our concept of morality and the Soviet way of life," in particular, it was all right to ridicule "kowtowing to bourgeois culture." Special attention was to be directed to the necessity of combatting American culture. As an example, Shcherbina referred to the American movie *The Iron Curtain* and called on Soviet filmmakers to answer blow for blow.[120] Such was soon forthcoming from Ilya Ehrenburg, who was always in the right place at the right time. In an article in *Culture and Life* he denounced the film using the full range of unflattering epithets so typical of the style of the Stalin era.[121]

The Soviet Composers' Union experienced pretty much the same things. Its head, Tikhon Khrennikov, was notorious for having been able to adapt, like Mikoyan, to every official twist and turn. This time Sergei Prokofiev was subject to an attack. The desperate Prokofiev recanted in a letter to the Central Committee. Khachaturian, Muradeli, and Myaskovsky were also attacked for being "sluggish" about reorienting themselves; on the other hand, Shostakovich was praised ever so slightly for his musical score for the film version of Fadeev's revised *Young Guard*.[122] But although the composers voted docilely in favor of any condemnation and denunciation they were asked to, their works continued to be somewhat out of harmony with "the glorious achievements of the Soviet people." This was their way of resisting the government.

During the first half of 1949 the war against "rootless cosmopolitans" reached its height. No field was spared. *Pravda* added fuel to the fire by publishing an editorial condemning an "antipatriotic" group of theater critics.[123] The editorial differed from other press commentary directed against "cosmopolitans" in its exceptional vulgarity, boorishness and insolence, undisguised anti-Semitism, and—what is of no less importance—the charges it leveled at the "rootless cosmopolitans." According to Soviet law these charges could be interpreted as premeditated crimes. Soon afterward Simonov, at a meeting of Moscow critics, revealed the conspiratorial nature of the "rootless cosmopolitans."[124]

Others, such as Anatoly Sofronov, echoed these attacks. He accused the drama critics of having taken lessons from clandestine anti-Soviet organizations. Some of the victims in desperation denounced themselves, confessing to a desire to hurt the image of Soviet drama, deliberately conspiring for that purpose, and so on. Writers' real names were printed alongside their pseudonyms to eliminate any shadow of doubt concerning their Jewish origins. This method had been widely used in Nazi Germany.

One of the results of the war against Germany was intensified repression against various nationalities in the border regions of the Soviet Union. The mass deportations of Caucasian peoples and Crimean Tatars in 1943–44 were followed after the war by new deportations of Balts, Greeks, and Turks. Plans were made to deport the Abkhazians, but they were not carried out.

Further, a reassessment of the national liberation struggles by non-Russian nationalities within the tsarist empire was also begun. In 1947 a discussion arose about the character of the resistance movement led by Shamil in the Caucasus in the first half of the nineteenth century.[125] The discussion originated in the recesses of the USSR Academy of Science's Institute of History, but it gradually developed into an ideological crusade against the orthodox Marxist point of view, according to which Shamil's struggle had been progressive. At the end of the discussion, which lasted for nearly five years, Shamil was branded an agent of British intelligence and his movement was pronounced reactionary. This reassessment of tsarist colonial policy in the Caucasus, and later, in Central Asia, led to the conclusion that virtually all anticolonial movements in territories seized by tsarist Russia had been reactionary. At the same time, the national epics of these peoples were proclaimed reactionary as well. An entire group of historians and literary critics in Kazakhstan, Azerbaijan, Kirghizia, Yakutia, and Dagestan were expelled from the party, removed from their jobs, and stripped of their academic degrees; some were even arrested.[126]

The discussion gradually transformed into an ideological pogrom, which rapidly assumed an anti-Semitic taint. Academician I. I. Mints and his students were accused of cosmopolitanism and "wrecking," although it would have been hard to find a historian more devoted to the party than Mints. Throughout his scholarly career he was in the foremost ranks of party ideological forces, and his contribution to the falsification of the history of the USSR was by no means insignificant. The campaign against cosmopolitanism, against "bourgeois objectivism," the "whitewashing of American imperialism," and so forth, continued through almost all of the postwar years, nearly until Stalin's death in March 1953.

Similar campaigns were launched among philosophers, economists, legal specialists, linguists, and literary historians. One of the most glaring examples was the persecution of Academician Evgeny Varga, director of the USSR Academy of Sciences Institute of World Economy. For decades he had been among the highest party and Comintern authorities on world economic matters. An orthodox Marxist, he had always predicted the decay of the capitalist economy, each crisis being followed by a worse one. He defended the Marxist thesis of the absolute and relative impoverishment of the working class under capitalism. But the new world economic situation which had come about after World War II forced Varga to examine his position. He published a book on the changes which had affected the capitalist economy after the war and spoke of the possibility that these changes might enable the capitalist system to survive a new crisis. Varga was accused of deviation from Marxism-Leninism and was relieved of his duties as director of the institute. The institute was reorganized. Some of Varga's colleagues were forced from their jobs, and some persecuted; several people were arrested. At a meeting of the institute, Varga was publicly denounced, having "the blood of the Russian people" on his hands. This was said about a man whose only son had been killed in the war. Varga's was not an isolated case. At Moscow University in 1947–1949 the persecution of scholars and scientists took on a mass character. Often students as well as faculty members participated in the humiliation of professors.

## THE EMPIRE OF THE CAMPS

In the early 1940s the overwhelming majority of those arrested during the previous decade had already died, and the NKVD was facing labor shortages at a time when there were many production plans to meet. They did not have to wait long to replenish their labor supply. At the end of the war and afterward, many new categories of prisoners appeared: soldiers from Vlasov's army, members of nationalist formations who had fought on the German side, Soviet workers who had been taken to Germany (they were called *ostovtsy*, from the German word *Ostarbeiter*—"Eastern worker"), former Soviet prisoners of war, and so-called enemy elements from the Baltic nations, Poland, East Germany, Romania, and Hungary. (The Soviet Union generously agreed to organize an all-socialist-countries penal servitude system [*katorga*] on its territory.)

Among the detained were many German and Japanese prisoners of war who had simply been transferred from the prisoner of war camps to the labor camps. Their crimes had been to make "anti-Soviet" statements— that is, they had complained about prison conditions, such as denial of permission to correspond with their families. Also sent to the camps were Soviet citizens who had nurtured unrealistic hopes of improvement and relaxation of the Stalinist regime in the wake of the victory over German nazism.

In addition, there was a greater influx of Baptists and members of various other religious persuasions. Their crime consisted in wishing to believe in God in their own fashion and not according to the dogma of the state-approved church and church communities. Also sent to the camps were those who had "conspired" in the anti-Soviet plots newly invented by the KGB. If there really had been as many conspirators as were found in the camps, Soviet power would hardly have survived.

The last category of permanent camp and prison inmates consisted of those sentenced for common crimes. The largest category was that of inmates sentenced for collaborating with the enemy during the occupation, among them not only real collaborators but also those who had not actively opposed the Germans. This category totaled up to 3 million, including those who had been soldiers in the German security service (SD) and Gestapo collaborators, many of them guilty of monstrous crimes. But there were also innocent people, and their numbers were not small.

How many prisoners were there after the war? The figures are contradictory. The lowest of the figures suggested by Western scholars (because the USSR has not said a word on the question) is 8 million;[127] the highest, 15 million.[128] According to estimates by the British government presented at a session of the UN Economic and Social Council on August 15, 1950, 10 million were performing forced labor.[129]

How many camps were there after the war? Western sources have named 165 camps and groups of camps.[130] More precisely they might be termed slave empires. Let us comment on some of them.

*Abez-Inta*, a group of camps in the Komi Autonomous Republic. In 1948 these seven camps held some 14,000 prisoners, half of them arrested on political grounds or on trumped up charges.[131]

*Osoblag Vaigach* (the Vaigach "special camp" was located on Vaigach Island). People given death sentences were forced to work in the lead mines. Between 3,000 and 4,000 people fit this category. Between 1,200 and 1,300 new inmates arrived each year. The annual mortality rate was nearly 50 percent.[132]

*Vorkuta*. In 1953 this camp complex held approximately 130,000 inmates. It was here that one of the most famous prisoner rebellions took place in 1953.[133]

*Potma* (in Mordovia), with 40,000 inmates in 1942.[134]

*Taishet-Bratsk*. Between 25,000 and 30,000 prisoners.[135]

*Bamlag* (the Baikal-Amur railroad camp complex). Thirty separate camps were located on its vast territory in 1953, containing between 350,000 and 500,000 prisoners.[136]

*Sevvostlag* (the Northeast camp complex), whose center was the city of Magadan. This group of camps had a radius of 1,000 kilometers. It was located in the huge expanse between Yakutsk, the Bay of Nagaev, and the mouth of the Kolyma River. Data for 1940 show that it held more than 3 million prisoners; other sources put the number up to 5 million.[137]

*Karlag* (a complex near Karaganda). According to information for 1941, it contained as many as 100,000 prisoners. In the summer 350 branches of the camp operated, but the number dropped to 180 in the winter. It covered nearly 1.5 million hectares of land, 500,000 of which were cultivated. The empire had 250,000 head of livestock. The Karlag complex was sometimes described as a "vacation resort," because it included a special camp for handicapped inmates, at Spassk.[138]

Conditions for camp inmates were particularly severe in 1946–1948 and in 1950. The majority of them had been put in the camps following German captivity or debilitating labor in German factories. Sapped of their physical strength, they never produced more than 40 percent of the quotas stipulated for the Soviet camps.[139] Such failure was punishable by reduced food rations, which in turn led to death.

In 1950, upon orders from the Main Directorate of the Corrective Labor Camps, the Gulag, mass executions took place in all camps: according to directives, 5 percent of all inmates were to be eliminated.[140] The country needed coal, uranium, tungsten, gold, platinum, and timber, however, and the labor force had been manifestly reduced as a result of war. Consequently a new order was issued to exploit the prisoners more profitably, improving their nutrition and living conditions to keep them from dropping like flies. In 1950 the average ration for those in the camps who met their work quotas was 800 grams of bread, 20 of fat, 120 of semolina, 30 of meat or 75 of fish, and 27 of sugar. Only bread was issued directly to prisoners; the rest went straight to the camp kitchen for the preparation of hot meals (two a day, morning and evening).[141] To get an idea of the horrible situation of these people even after conditions had been improved, suffice it to say that they were awakened at 4 AM and "lights out" was at 10 PM. The workday lasted ten to twelve hours, not counting the time spent going from camp to worksite and back.[142] Those who did not meet their quotas were allotted only 400 grams of bread daily and thin soup twice a day. Inmates being punished were given only 200 grams of bread.[143]

To encourage "shock workers," they were given a bonus of 10 rubles and tobacco. The prisoner could use this money to buy food in the camp commissary. But what could he buy with 10 or 20 rubles per month?[144] During those years, the Soviet press often spoke of the exploitation of blacks by whites in South Africa and indignantly referred to the fact that the salaries of black workers were four to eight times lower than those of their white counterparts. The Soviet prisoner, the zek, doing hard labor earned twenty to thirty times less than a free Soviet worker. It might be argued that these were criminals. Indeed, there were criminals among them, but they constituted only about 25 percent of the cases. The majority, besides the "politicals," were workers, men and women sentenced for such offenses as arriving twenty minutes late to work, being absent without a valid excuse, or committing petty larceny (stealing a piece of bread, for example), or for collecting grain left lying in the field after the harvest.

In the Nazi camps, an indelible tattoo was made on each victim's arm: his number. Prisoners were also marked in Soviet camps; they had to wear a number on their clothing.

In 1948 "special regime" camps were created for "Vlasovites" and others who had collaborated with the Germans, and of course for counterrevolutionaries. Conditions there were much harsher than in the regular corrective labor camps. Baptists too—martyrs of their faith—were sent: between 1948 and 1950 belonging to a Baptist community could mean twenty to twenty-five years in a camp.[145]

The prisoners' moral situation was atrocious. Besides the humiliation of wearing a number and having barred windows in their barracks, they were subject to the ill temper of the guards, who often opened fire without warning.[146] In the special camps the censors, (MVD officials), too lazy to inspect letters addressed to the inmates, simply burned them.[147]

Nevertheless, the war substantially transformed the camp population's state of mind. They were now filled with people who had fought for or against the Soviet government. The majority of them had already borne arms and knew how to use them. They could defend themselves from the pressures of common criminals, who were the camp administration's guards and who were especially deployed against the "enemies of the people." Common criminals were officially called "the socially close" (that is, to the Soviet regime, to be distinguished from the "socially dangerous," those who had been sentenced for "counterrevolutionary activity"). The new inmates had different life experiences than did the "enemies of the people." They had not been stupefied by propaganda about the alleged building of socialism. Those imprisoned during the 1930s, especially the former party and government officials, considered their arrests to be cases of misunderstanding, of governmental error. The newcomers cared not one bit about building communism. They despised the system, which in their eyes was no better than the Nazi regime. The Nazis at least hadn't butchered their own people, only others. This hatred was simmering, ready to blow up at any time.

According to information that is far from complete, rebellions took place in the following camps in the years after the war: 1946, Kolyma; 1947, Ust-Vym (Komi ASSR), Dzhezkazgan (Karaganda); 1950, Salekhard, Taishet; 1951, Dzhezkazgan; 1952, Vozhel (Komi), Molotov, Krasnoyarsk region; 1953, Vorkuta, Norilsk, Karaganda, Kolyma; 1954, Revda (Sverdlovsk), Karabash (in the Urals), Taishet, Reshoty, Dzhezkazgan, Kengir, Sherubai Nura, Balkhash, Sakhalin; 1955, Vorkuta, Solikamsk, Potma.[148]

During Stalin's last years, the special camps, instituted in 1948, became the centers of political resistance. It was there that prisoners sentenced under article 58 of the penal code were sent, for "anti-Soviet" or "counterrevolutionary" activity. The idea was advancing slowly that unity was needed to obtain their rights.[149] The prisoners began by eliminating the informers and then went on to defend their comrades whom the administration wanted to transfer for misconduct. Strikes, protests, and armed revolts began to break out in the camps in the late 1940s and early 1950s. The ball was rolling. "And we, liberated from indecency, freed from surveillance and eavesdropping, turned around with our eyes wide open and saw . . . that there were thousands of us! That we were *political*! And that we could *resist*!" wrote Solzhenitsyn.

In the Vorkuta camps, small underground groups constituting a veritable "resistance" movement sprang up. "The existence of numerous clandestine organizations in the special Vorkuta camps and their activities," wrote a veteran of that camp, "were perhaps the most astonishing phenomenon of all for the Europeans." (The writer, Joseph Schomler, was a German prisoner, one of many allowed to return to the West after Stalin's death.[150])

The head of one resistance group described by Schomler was a former Soviet officer who had been a prisoner of the Germans and who was sentenced, after repatriation, to ten years in the camps. His group consisted of former Red Army officers. They perceived their liberation to be contingent upon a war between the USSR and the Western powers, and they were preparing for the decisive moment when, as in 1941, the camp authorities would start preventive executions of prisoners. The overwhelming majority of the participants supported the social and economic principles of the Soviet system, but opposed the dictatorship and wanted reforms in agriculture. The most indomitable were the OUN members from the Western Ukraine.

The prison authorities zealously fanned national conflicts and antagonisms and encouraged anti-Semitism. For example, Ukrainians from German auxiliary forces who hunted and murdered Jews during the war were designated foremen in brigades that included Jewish prisoners.[151] Schomler reported the following conversation with a certain Katchenko.

> When I asked him why he had been arrested, he answered:
> "I killed eighty-four Jews."
> "By yourself?"
> "Yes, with my own revolver. And they gave me twenty-five years for that. It isn't fair, is it?"

"During the war," Schomler continued, "such creatures had all worked either for the *Sicherheitsdienst* or the Gestapo. Now they are mostly in privileged positions working for the NKVD. Katchenko, for example, was in charge of one of the building projects in the town."[152]

Everywhere the causes of the strikes and revolts were the same: the trampling of human dignity, persecution by the prison authorities, murders of inmates by the guards. Gradually, the spontaneous protest movements took on a political character.

The revolt in the Pechora camp in 1948 was led by Boris Mekhtiev, a former colonel in the Soviet army. The insurgents' plan was to liberate the camps one at a time and then capture the city of Vorkuta. However, the insurgents were intercepted by fighter planes a hundred kilometers from the city and dispersed. Some of them went in small groups to the Ural mountains to become partisans. Mekhtiev was captured and sentenced to twenty-five years' imprisonment.[153]

That same year, a revolt took place at Construction Site No. 501 during work on the Sivaya Maska–Salekhard Railway, led by a former colonel named Voronin (or Voronov?) and Sakurenko, a former lieutenant in an armored tank division.[154] A second insurrection, in 1950 was led by one Belyaev, a former general who had been sentenced to twenty-five years for "counterrevolutionary" activity.[155] An insurrection also took place at Kengir in 1954. It lasted forty-two days and was led by a former colonel named Kuznetsov.[156] In all probability, former military personnel from the Nizhni Aturyakh division also led the Berlag revolt.[157]

The outbreaks by inmates of the camps had more and more clearly defined objectives. The Salekhard insurgents under the command of Colonel Voronin liberated not only their "brigade" but others as well. They opened the gates of the camp compound, took the neighboring camp by assault, and began a march on Vorkuta, some fifty kilometers away.[158] What were their objectives? According to certain sources, the insurgents wanted to capture the radio station and call on the civilized world for help and on the inmates in other camps to rise up.[159]

In January 1952 a strike broke out in Ekibastuz which soon grew into an uprising. For the first time in the history of the Soviet camps, several thousand inmates joined efforts to protest the senseless murder of one of their comrades by a guard. They refused to work and went on a hunger strike for three days. The strike terrified the Gulag authorities. A commission was sent to the camp, supposedly to investigate the complaints. The prisoners courageously presented their claims and demands.[160] After the commission left, arrests and transfers to other camps began. Many were sent to the Kengir camp, where they were forced to work wearing handcuffs.

Agitation became particularly widespread in the camps after Stalin's death and Beria's elimination, that is, during the spring and summer of 1953 and again in 1954. At this time the movement began to take on an openly political character.

## CRISIS IN THE REGIME

One of the most glaring signs of the crisis the regime faced at the end of the Stalin era was the intensifying power struggle among Stalin's closest associates. After the war, and to a large degree because of Stalin's poor health, the Politburo began to splinter into several rival groups. Gradually Stalin's former close associates, those who had helped him rise to power after Lenin's death and during collectivization, were pushed into the background. Younger and more ambitious men took their places—Zhdanov, Malenkov, Beria, and Nikolai Voznesensky.

The Zdhanov grouping dealt the cards during the first two years after the war. The group's influence derived from the key economic posts it held. It consisted of Voznesensky, president of the State Planning Commission and a Politburo member, Aleksei Kosygin, an alternate member of the Politburo, Aleksei A. Kuznetsov, Central Committee secretary in charge of party control over the army and the state security agencies, and lastly, Zhdanov himself, a Central Committee secretary in charge of policy and ideology, and the group's driving force. Stalin gave Zhdanov the most crucial assignments. It was Zhdanov who inspired and led the campaign for the "ideological" purification of Soviet society and the campaign to establish the "primacy" of Soviet science. He also headed the struggle against heretics (such as Tito) in the international Communist movement. For a while his influence on Stalin was exceptional. The dictator even urged his daughter, Svetlana, to marry Zhdanov's son. Zhdanov was also the instigator of a new policy aimed at strengthening the party by luring intellectuals and veterans of the war against Germany into its ranks.

Zhdanov's relentlessness and aggressiveness, however, wore out with time. The ambitions of his group were frustrated by Zhdanov's death in August 1948, after which Georgy Malenkov's star began to rise. A careful and intelligent operator, Malenkov in fact directed the Central Commitee apparatus, which he had helped to organize.

For several years Malenkov had served in Stalin's personal secretariat, which was led by Poskrebyshev. There he had mastered the arts of party apparatus intrigue, which makes Machiavellianism look like child's play. He rose during the terror of the 1930s, and in 1939, at the age of thirty-seven, became a Central Committee secretary and member of the Orgburo in charge of party personnel. He had the support of Beria, who came to Moscow in 1939. Formerly a secretary of the Georgian Central Committee, Beria was named commissar of internal affairs when Ezhov was removed.

Malenkov and Beria formed a bloc and worked together. Both of them became members of the Politburo in 1946.

Stalin adroitly manipulated the rival groupings, now advancing one, now pushing it back, without ever letting go of the reins of power himself. In reserve he kept Nikita Khrushchev, whom he trusted because he did not consider him a pretender to the throne.

Both rival groups, for their part, tried to use Stalin's suspicions and mistrust to consolidate their own positions. Zhdanov took advantage of the conflict with Yugoslavia to incite a pathological hatred of Tito in Stalin. In 1947 Zhdanov's rise led to the temporary eclipse of Malenkov, who was sent to Uzbekistan and was replaced for a short time by Aleksei Kuznetsov, a former secretary of the Leningrad provincial party committee. Malenkov returned to Moscow after Zhdanov's death. Along with Beria he fabricated the "Leningrad affair," in which the Leningrad grouping was accused of trying to seize power in order to stifle the influence of the Zhdanov group once and for all. Voznesensky, Kuznetsov, N. N. Rodionov, the chairman of the council of Ministers of the RSFSR, and many other ranking state and party officials originally from Leningrad were accused of antiparty and antistate activities and destroyed. In the ensuing witchhunt in Leningrad itself, hundreds upon hundreds of people were victimized.

According to Khrushchev's account, the strengthening of the Malenkov–Beria group caused Stalin himself some alarm. In the years 1947–1949 Stalin had several strokes. He became more acutely mistrustful and suspicious. In 1949 he summoned Khrushchev from Kiev and named him secretary of the Moscow party committee and a secretary of the Central Committee, probably hoping in this way to balance the forces in the Politburo and to use Khrushchev to conduct the upcoming purge. Stalin's old cohorts, Molotov, Voroshilov, Andreev, and Mikoyan receded more and more into the background. In 1949 Vyshinsky replaced Molotov as minister of foreign affairs, although Molotov did remain as deputy chairman of the USSR Council of Ministers. Voroshilov and Andreev had been mere figureheads for a long time. Other Politburo members continued to carry out their respective duties, while taking great care not to be kicked off the team. In the last years of his life Stalin began to believe, or pretended to believe, that Voroshilov was a British agent and Molotov an American one.[161] Molotov's wife was arrested, which did not stop Molotov from continuing to serve Stalin with utter loyalty.

Malenkov and Beria, seeking to clear the road to power, began to rid themselves of all secondary figures who occupied important posts in the party but upon whom they could not rely. They did this by skillfully exploiting Stalin's fears. He saw plots everywhere. It was thus that a number of prominent figures were arrested, among them A. I. Shakhurin, minister of the aeronautic industry, A. A. Novikov, a marshal of the air force, N. D. Yakovlev, marshal of the artillery, Academician Grigoriev, and Academician Ivan Maisky, a former ambassador to London.[162]

Stalin was afflicted more and more by paranoia, the occupational disease of tyrants. Secondary figures, mainly in the state security service, used him to further their own careers, for example, S. D. Ignatiev, who was minister of state security during Stalin's last few years. Growing numbers of people were being accused of counterrevolutionary and conspiratorial activities. The political atmosphere was reminiscent of the period just before the terror of the 1930s.

The idea that a new purge was necessary steadily ripened in Stalin's mind. His intention to carry out a "changing of the guard" became evident when a party congress was finally held, thirteen years after the Eighteenth Congress: the Nineteenth Party Congress, October 5–15, 1952.

The congress established a new body to replace the Politburo and the Orgburo, to be called the Presidium of the Central Committee and consisting of twenty-five full members and eleven alternates. Sitting on this new body were ten Central Committee secretaries, thirteen deputies to the chairman of the USSR Council of Ministers, the first secretaries of the Central Committees of the Byelorussian and Ukrainian Communist parties, the minister of state security, the foreign minister, and leaders of the trade unions, the Communist youth organization, and the party's control commission. In effect this meant that there was a replacement at hand for each of the old Politburo members. Stalin's intention to remove the entire old leadership could not have been clearer. The Central Committee was significantly enlarged, but more than 60 percent of the outgoing Central Committee was reelected.[163] This indicated that the process of forming a stable power elite was close to completion. The regional party secretaries, who in 1952 constituted half of the Central Committee (at the Eighteenth Congress they represented only one-fifth), had become the backbone of the party and state apparatus. Their role in deciding leadership questions would soon grow immensely.

The congress stressed the Soviet nationwide character of the party. Its name was changed from the All-Union Communist Party (Bolshevik) to the Communist Party of the Soviet Union. In both names the idea of one state was predominant. As for the dropping of the old name "Bolshevik," almost all Mensheviks, with the exception of those who had fled abroad, had been destroyed. The same was true of the Bolsheviks. Thus the word no longer served any purpose. While preparing for a major purge in the Soviet Union, Stalin ordered one in the satellite countries. Everywhere—in Bulgaria,

Czechoslovakia, Hungary, Poland, and Romania—trials were staged of Communist leaders who, according to Moscow, were too independent or else contaminated by "Titoism." Bulgarian and Czechoslovakian Communists were tortured in the presence of Soviet advisers. All except the Bulgarian Troicho Kostov confessed to having links with Zionism, U.S. imperialism, and Yugoslav intelligence. They were either executed or sentenced to long prison terms. In Poland and East Germany arrests also took place, but no executions.

The struggle against imaginary plotters became Stalin's main preoccupation. He told Khrushchev, who had been recently called from Kiev:

> We need you here. Things aren't going very well. Plots have been uncovered. You are to take charge of the Moscow organization so that the Central Committee can be sure to count on the local party structure for support in the struggle against the conspirators. So far, we've exposed a conspiracy in Leningrad, and Moscow, too, is teeming with antiparty elements. We want to make the city a bastion for the Central Committee.[164]

A "conspiracy" was soon discovered at the Stalin (now Likhachev) Automobile Factory in Moscow. The talented chief designer Feinzimmer and a group of Jewish employees were accused of sabotage on behalf of the Zionists and the United States.[165] Malenkov named a former investigator from the party control commission to the post of Central Committee party organizer at the factory.

Soviet foreign policy failures in Korea, Berlin, and Yugoslavia and domestic economic difficulties led Stalin to reapply an already tested method for combatting the growing discontent among the population: whipping up national hysteria, especially anti-Semitism. Manifestations of Stalin's anti-Semitic attitude had appeared on numerous occasions since the time of his struggle for power. Many of his political opponents were of Jewish origin. Anti-Semitism had increased in the USSR, mainly in the southern regions, under the impact of Soviet–Nazi friendship in 1939–1941 and during the Nazi occupation. Stalin's anti-Semitism was also intensified by U.S.–Soviet antagonism and U.S. support to the Jewish victims of genocide and the Zionists who were establishing the state of Israel.

The new leadership in the Ukraine installed when Khrushchev was transferred to Moscow—L. G. Melnikov, first secretary of the Ukrainian Central Committee, and Korotchenko, chairman of the Ukrainian Council of Ministers—initiated openly anti-Semitic policies in that republic.[166] The newspapers were filled with Jewish names, people accused of all sorts of mistakes, crimes, and sins. Jews were arrested, forced from their jobs, insulted, and beaten in the streets. Cases of pogroms were reported in Kiev, Kharkov, and elsewhere in the Ukraine. Secret quotas were set limiting employment for Jews as well as access to higher education.

Anti-Semitism was also building in other parts of the country. In Moscow, Stalin himself ordered Khrushchev to organize a pogrom at the Thirtieth Aviation Factory, where there was discontent over working conditions. He suggested that clubs be distributed to the workers to beat up the Jews after work.[167]

In his memoirs, Khrushchev bears witness to Stalin's openly anti-Semitic statements at Politburo meetings. It was not even beyond him to imitate a Jewish accent,[168] fully aware that none of the Politburo members would dare to criticize or even mention his anti-Semitism. Stalin's anti-Semitism became more evident with the affair of the Jewish Antifascist Committee.

The committee, created during the war, had tried to organize financial and material aid for the Soviet Union through Jewish organizations in the United States and to distribute anti-Nazi, pro-Soviet propaganda. Led by Solomon Lozovsky, head of Informburo and a member of the Central Committee, and Solomon Mikhoels, a famous Jewish actor, the committee included several prominent personalities of Jewish origin who were active in the Soviet cultural world. In 1943, Mikhoels and the poet Isaak Fefer had been sent to the United States for several months, to mobilize public opinion and raise funds. The tour had been a major success for the Soviet Union.[169]

In 1944 the Antifascist Committee sent Stalin a letter asking that an autonomous Jewish republic be established in the Crimea, which had been partly depopulated because of the deportation of the Tatars.[170] Stalin later presented this letter as a Zionist attempt to create a bulwark of American imperialism on Soviet territory. In 1948 the committee's members were arrested on Stalin's instructions. They were tortured and in 1952 were shot, including Lozovsky. Before their arrest, Mikhoels had been murdered— on January 13, 1948, on a street in Minsk, by state security agents. After the killing, a truck was driven over his corpse to give the impression it had been an accident. "They killed him like beasts," wrote Khrushchev.[171] Mikhoels's remains were transferred to Moscow, where a solemn funeral was arranged.

More or less at the same time, the secret police began to prepare an attempt on the life of Maxim Litvinov, the former people's commissar of foreign affairs. The crime was ordered by Stalin himself, who suspected Litvinov of collaborating with the United States. But Litvinov died of natural causes in 1951.

The last anti-Semitic provocation, which was not carried out because Stalin died, was the so-called doctors' plot. The affair came about at the initiative of ranking officials of the Ministry of State Security, who were fully aware of Stalin's anti-Semitism and were interpreting his wishes. Among those arrested were prominent Kremlin physicians whose patients were Stalin and other top party and army officials. The doctors included Professor Miron Vovsy, Mikhoels's brother, and Professor Egorov, a head of the medical department of the Kremlin. As a pretext an accusation was drafted by Lidiya Timashuk, a radiologist at the Kremlin hospital, who was a secret police informer. Under atrocious tortures, the accused doctors confessed to having taken part in a plot to murder army, party, and government leaders through the conscious use of incorrect medical treatment. The accusations were so unbelievable that even Abakumov, the seasoned minister of state security, expressed doubts about the "confessions" signed by the unfortunate doctors. The case was reported to Stalin, who ordered that it be prosecuted and that the arrested men be beaten until full confessions were extracted. On January 13, 1953, the newspapers carried stories about the discovery of a plot by Jewish physicians and their impending trial.[172] A week later, on the anniversary of Lenin's death, the *provocateur* Timashuk was awarded the Order of Lenin.[173] Meetings were organized all over the country to express outrage and denounce the "doctor-murderers." In this orgy of anti-Semitism, writers, scientists, and other figures from the Soviet cultural world did what they could to contribute to this orgy. *Literaturnaya gazeta*, whose chief editor was Konstantin Simonov, published a vicious article entitled "Murderers in White Coats."[174] At the party meeting in the presidium of the USSR Academy of Sciences, respectable academicians demanded the death penalty for the doctors.[175] The reactions of the common people were more direct: Jews were insulted, attacked, and often beaten. Patients refused to accept treatment from Jewish doctors, contending that they would be poisoned; some put their denunciations in writing. Many Jewish doctors were chased out of hospitals and clinics. Personnel departments in institutions began to compile lists of Jewish employees.

Stalin was personally in charge of the "doctors' plot." His scenario consisted of several acts: Act One, sentencing after full confessions; Act Two, execution by hanging (it is said that this execution would have taken place in Red Square, in Moscow, as in days of yore); Act Three, pogroms throughout the country; Act Four, Jewish personalities from the world of culture would turn to Stalin, asking that he protect the Jews from pogroms and give them permission to leave the big cities and go back to the land; Act Five, mass deportation of Jews, "at their own request," to the country's eastern territories. The philosopher D. Chesnokov, a member of the Presidium of the Central Committee, had written a book explaining the reasons for the deportation of the Jews. The book had been printed, and the signal was being awaited for its distribution to top party and government circles. As for the appeal by the country's leading Jews, not only had it been written: it had already been signed.

The country lived in anticipation of a new wave of terror such as it had never seen. Where would it have led? This is a key point in Stalin's biography. Success in the implementation of this great design would have been the crowning achievement of the Leader's career.

Stalin's assessment of the world situation led him to the conclusion that the beginning of the 1950s was the most favorable moment for dealing a final blow to capitalist Europe and implanting the socialist system. Created in 1947, the Cominform, which replaced the Comintern, dissolved in 1943, was to consolidate the forces of the international Communist movement and coordinate the efforts of the Communist parties in a struggle for power. Jules Moch, the French minister of the interior, testified in his memoirs that the French Communist party had plans for taking power in 1947.

The peace movement directed from Moscow was another tool in the consolidation of the Communist movement. The movement enabled the Soviet regime's real intentions to remain hidden, while it lured liberal intellectuals in the West who wanted to defend peace in the world. They were ignorant of the fact that the Soviet government had a different concept of peace than did the Western intelligentsia. Yet their goals were spelled out in the name of the Cominform's publication, *For Lasting Peace, for People's Democracy*, which was being printed in Belgrade. The idea was simple enough: only people's democracy could bring lasting peace.

The Soviet Union also benefited from the anti-Communist hysteria sweeping the United States (McCarthyism), which drove prominent American liberals into the Soviet camp and put many intellectuals who had been critical of the Soviet Union on the spot. They feared being taken as supporters of the "cold war" and the McCarthyites.

From 1946 on the USSR was preparing a massive purge, similar to those of the 1930s. The late 1940s and early 1950s were marked by the arrests and trials in the nations of Eastern Europe; the accusations were always the same: spying for the West, plotting, and so forth.

In January 1951, some six months after the beginning of the Korean war, a conference of leaders of the socialist countries was convened in Moscow, at the Kremlin. Stalin and Molotov represented the Soviet Union. Information about the conference proceedings was later produced by Czechoslovak historians who had access to the secret archives of the Central Committee of the Czechoslovak Communist party.[176] These archives contained transcripts from the conference, whose climax was Stalin's speech.

The "Leader of Progressive Humanity" explained to the participants that the time was ripe for an offensive against capitalist Europe. Korea had shown the weakness of the U.S. armed forces. The Soviet camp had achieved military superiority over the United States, but this advantage was only temporary; it would last only four years. Thus, the key task of the socialist camp was to mobilize, within three to four years, and consolidate its military, economic, and political forces to deal the decisive blow against Western Europe. The domestic and foreign policies of all the socialist countries were to be subordinated to this end. Stalin stressed that this was a unique opportunity to establish socialism in all of Europe.

After the January 1951 conference, military spending in the USSR and the other socialist countries rose dramatically, particularly unbudgeted spending, in some countries amounting to 40 percent of total spending. The Soviet Union was swiftly completing its hydrogen bomb project.

Stalin's speech at the Nineteenth Party Congress, on October 14, 1952, was the ideological basis for the offensive against Western Europe. This was an unusual speech for Stalin. He addressed himself exclusively to workers abroad and to Communist parties, explaining to them their immediate tasks and how to accomplish them. He repeated the word *peace* endlessly, but this meant he was talking not about peace but something quite different. Stalin was fairly candid, nevertheless. He praised the foreign Communist parties for their confidence in the Soviet party, that is, for their faithful service, emphasizing that their trust signified their "readiness to support our party in its struggle for a bright future for all peoples."[177] Stalin equated a policy of support for the Soviet Union by the Communist parties with the interests of the people. The concept was crude, but functional: whoever supported the Soviet Union was therefore defending the interests of his people. He also praised Thorez and Togliatti, who assured their listeners that the Italians and French would never fight the USSR. For his part, Stalin promised the foreign Communist parties that the CPSU, which "could not remain in debt to the fraternal parties, would in turn render them support."[178] Stalin promised support not only to the Communist parties but also to "people struggling for their liberation."[179] But from whom were these people to be liberated? Fascism had been shattered, and the "new order" in Europe had been destroyed.

Stalin did not give a direct answer. He recalled the "real measures" the Soviet Communist party had implemented to "eliminate capitalist oppression and that of the landowners." These actions had allowed the Soviet Union to become the "shock brigade" of the international workers and the revolutionary movement. Many "shock brigades" had come into being, however, Stalin emphasized, and it had become easier for foreign Communists to function than it had been.[180] He predicted that the Communists in capitalist countries would come to power and formulated the slogans under which they should advance. Like Lenin, Stalin was masterful at borrowing the slogans and programs of others and adapting them to the needs of the Soviet regime. This time he borrowed from the bourgeoisie the slogans of defense of democracy, national independence, and sovereignty. He did not conceal that the slogans were borrowed. Stalin explained that the "banner of democratic liberties" had been thrown overboard[181] by the bourgeoisie and that there was no one other than the representatives of Communist and democratic parties to pick it up and carry it. "If you want to rally the majority of people around you, . . . if you want to become the nation's vanguard," he added significantly.[182] He had no doubt that the program he had outlined would be realized, and "consequently there is every reason to expect success and victory for fraternal parties in the countries where capital rules."[183]

Stalin wanted to see a Soviet Europe in his lifetime. A new war was in the offing. But at this moment History intervened.

## STALIN'S DEATH

At the end of February 1953, when preparations for the doctors' trial were in full swing, Stalin suddenly suffered a stroke. He died on March 5.

His closest collaborators breathed a sigh of relief. During the dictator's final years, each one of them had felt himself to be in danger.[184] It seemed that even the all-powerful and omnipotent Beria, long the Politburo member in charge of the Ministries of State Security and Internal Affairs, feared for his life. After 1951 he had virtually lost control over state security, when the former regional party secretary of Bashkiria, S. D. Ignatiev, was named minister of state security. Some thought Ignatiev was a front man for Malenkov; others, for Khrushchev.

A few years after Stalin's death, stories began to circulate, especially in the West, to the effect that his death might have been helped along. Particular stress was placed on the fact that Stalin's death saved Beria from his inevitable demise, for Stalin feared him and was planning to eliminate him. Khrushchev's testimony, according to which Beria expressed joy over Stalin's death, was seen as direct or indirect proof that he had played a part in it. This version, very enticing for a novelist, is not supported by any real evidence. Neither Beria nor the other Politburo members who served the dictator with word and deed had enough courage to do away with him. Above all, they feared for themselves and were concerned with nothing else; Beria was no exception. Despised by the rest of the Politburo, Beria had to be even more cautious than the rest.

Stalin died a natural death.

The coffin with Stalin's corpse lay in state at the House of Trade Unions in Moscow. Four days of mourning were proclaimed (one day less than for Lenin), from March 6 to March 9. Thousands of Soviet citizens paraded in front of Stalin's body. Even he had proved to be a mere mortal, this man of many titles: Leader and Teacher of the Workers of the World; Father of the Peoples; Wise and Intelligent Chief of the Soviet People; the Greatest Genius of All Times and Peoples; the Greatest Military Leader of All Times and Peoples; Coryphaeus of the sciences; Faithful Comrade-in-Arms of Lenin; Devoted Continuor of Lenin's Cause; the Lenin of Today; as well as Mountain Eagle and Best Friend of all Children.

Reactions varied. Those who owed their rise to Stalin feared for their future. Others quietly rejoiced and hoped for a better life.

The newspapers immediately began to glorify the members of the old Politburo. In his article, "At Stalin's Coffin," the poet Aleksei Surkov wrote:

> Standing in the honor guard of Stalin's coffin were the members of the Central Committee of the CPSU and the government: comrades Malenkov, Beria, Molotov, Voroshilov, Khrushchev, Bulganin, Kaganovich, and Mikoyan. With proud respect, Soviet citizens looked on as the glorious comrades-in-arms of the great leader paid their last respects to their brilliant mentor.
>
> Our adored chief had placed in those hands, steeled by Herculean labors, the battle flag of the radiant ideas of Lenin and Stalin. He had left to their valiant hearts a precious feeling of responsibility for the fate of the people, for the glorious cause of bringing about communism.[185]

These words were far from the truth. The people possessed no "proud admiration" for those comrades-in-arms, nor had their hands been "steeled by Herculean labors." There were, however, hands not cleansed of the blood of compatriots who had been starved and killed in the camps during Stalin's time. There were no courageous hearts, but there were the hearts of those aspiring to power, who were rejoicing over the death of their mentor. Surkov had been right about at least one thing: they had indeed been reared by Stalin.

The struggle for power began even at the dying leader's bedside, when the Politburo members decided who was to keep the vigil by his side. Malenkov and Beria kept vigil together; Khrushchev with Bulganin.[186] The others were left out. Khrushchev was the one to open the March 9 funeral gathering on Red Square, but the speeches were given by the members of the first post-Stalin triumvirate: Malenkov, Beria, and Molotov.[187] Molotov was brought into the team to function as an intermediate link: after Stalin, he was the figure most familiar to the population.

Malenkov became first secretary of the Central Committee and chairman of the Council of Ministers. Beria became minister of internal affairs, and Molotov foreign minister. Khrushchev remained Central Committee secretary. In his hands he had concentrated all the visible and invisible power of the party apparatus and was preparing himself for the struggle for power, which was approaching by leaps and bounds.

The day after Stalin died his former "close comrades-in-arms" quickly agreed to rearrange the organization of power created by Stalin at the Nineteenth Party Congress, that is, to remove all newcomers from the leadership. On this question, the members of the old Politburo were 100 percent unanimous. Now the Presidium of the Central Committee was reduced to ten members and four alternates.[188]

Stalin's comrades-in-arms feared the reactions of the people, from whom they had been cut off for so long they no longer knew what to expect. For this reason, the government's communiqué on the reorganization of the Presidium included a sentence to the effect that no "panic or disorder" should be allowed.[189] The only real panic, however, was among the funeral organizers. Because of it, unimaginable chaos developed on the streets of Moscow on the last day Stalin lay in state. Over 500 people were suffocated or trampled to death in the crush. Human blood accompanied the Father of the Peoples to the grave.

With Stalin's death came the end of the period of unlimited terroristic dictatorship in Soviet history. At the same time, however, it had been a period of growth, of the formation and ripening of the Soviet society whose principles had been laid down by Lenin in the first years of the Soviet regime. The revolution from above, led by Stalin in the 1930s, had been the logical conclusion of the October revolution and the Leninist strategy. In this sense, Stalin's historic claim to being Lenin's most faithful and consistent pupil is justifiable enough.

The Stalinist dictatorship was the realization of the dreams of all tyrants: absolute control over men's bodies and souls. The system put together in the USSR was more complete and solid than German nazism or any other variety of fascism. It attempted not only to control the souls of the people but to pour them into a new mold—that of the "new Soviet man," Homo Sovieticus. This grand design could not be accomplished by terror alone, although the use of terror as the primary tool for the creation of the new world was of enormous significance. It was also necessary to carry out successive cleansing operations in Russian society, radically transforming the structure of society by political and ideological means.

Wholesale extermination of the representatives of Russia's ruling classes and its intelligentsia followed after the October revolution and during the civil war. At the same time the peasant population was also decimated during the suppression of numerous peasant uprisings that resulted from the extortion and terroristic policies of the new regime. From the point of view of the Soviet regime, the peasant was completely unsuitable material for the creation of a new world. From 1917 to 1922 it was not a matter of thousands, nor even of tens of thousands, but of millions who perished or were forced to flee the country. The regime used the period of the New Economic Policy (1921–1928) to consolidate its power. It was precisely during this time that the dictatorial regime of Stalin, the front man of the new elite—the party bureaucracy—was in the final stages of completion. Now terror was aimed not only against the remaining bourgeois intelligentsia, those who had loyally cooperated with the Soviet regime and the former members of the old "bourgeois" parties; it was also directed against the Socialist Revolutionary party, and even Marxist parties (the Mensheviks and Bundists). The foundations for the slave empire of the Gulag were being laid.

The revolution from above, carried out by the Stalinist dictatorship during the 1930s, whose echoes lasted into the 1940s, marked a new period in the formation of present-day Soviet society and Soviet man. Collectivization had destroyed the most productive strata of the peasantry. It had led to the creation of an enormous army of virtually unpaid labor, and thus was in a sense a physical revolution: millions had died so that other tens of millions could become convenient material from which the dictatorship could forge the "new man." One of the essential traits of the regime was in fact its mass character. The "new man" was created not only by physically eliminating the brightest, most dynamic, and best-educated members of society; it was also created by educating the people within a definite framework, according to a fixed ideology.

At the time of Stalin's death, the Communist Party of the Soviet Union had about 7 million members. At the other end of society, in the Gulag camps, there were 8 million people. The entire system balanced between these two extremes.

The 1939 party announcement that the construction of socialism had been essentially completed in the Soviet Union corresponded to reality. By then the basic socioeconomic structure of the society was established, and it has persisted to this day. The USSR had been industrialized to a considerable extent, had made its appearance on the international arena, and had taken the first steps toward expansion. At the same time in 1939, the great purge came to an end, a purge that affected not only the minority, those opposed to Stalin's policies who were criticized by the party, but also the majority of party functionaries, who agreed with Stalin on everything. It eliminated the majority of those who had any links to the revolution's past and could have kept alive historical memories, or who might have shown some independent initiative—a synonym for potential danger in the eyes of the dictatorship.

The purge of the 1930s was in reality more colossal than the most recent accounts by historians, political scientists, and sociologists suggest. In terms of numbers, fewer party, state, and army officials were eliminated than collective farmers and workers, blue collar and white collar, and their families. Every region was obliged to fill a quota of "enemies of the people." The entire hidden meaning of the terror of the 1930s, one perhaps not even fully realized by the dictatorship itself, was to accomplish a repeated purge of Soviet society as it came into being. The previous purges during the civil war and collectivization certainly had had an impact on people's consciousness, but in the purge of the late 1930s the dictatorship achieved what it had sought for twenty years—mass support for terror by a population that was either seething with zeal or trembling with fear. These people were the necessary raw material for making the "new Soviet man."

The war with Nazi Germany very nearly brought the end of the dictatorship, but the country withstood the German attack, precisely because the Stalinist regime had not had the time to complete its task of creating the "new man." In the exceptional conditions of the war, the best of human feelings and love for the motherland resurfaced. But in defending their country the Soviet people were also saving and defending the dictatorship. The war interrupted the formation of Soviet society, yet at the same time it cleared the path for its completion, since among the millions of victims were many members of the generation born in the first years of Soviet power, who had grown up before the Great Terror of the 1930s. In these people, curiously enough, dreams of world revolution—echoes from their confused childhoods—existed side by side with loyal obedience to the Stalinist dictatorship. Just as they could die on the battlefield with the word *Stalin* on their lips, they could survive with great dreams of liberty. Only a few of those born during the 1920s returned home whole and unharmed. But those who survived were certainly not appropriate material for the creation of the "new man." A new purge became inevitable, especially since the war had awakened the people's collective memory. It had awakened their genuine memory, however, which the regime had assiduously been trying to eradicate, on the one hand by eliminating the bearers of the real one, and on the other by creating an artificial collective memory using the *Short Course on the History of the Soviet Communist Party*, the *Biography of J. V. Stalin*, and numerous other falsifications produced by historians, writers, artists, actors, and poets.

During the last years of Stalin's dictatorship, often referred to as the period of mature Stalinism, its essential traits became more sharply visible, as in the case of older people, whose good and bad sides become more pronounced with age. A similar process occurs in societies. Postwar Stalinist society had many symptoms of premature senility: ideological decomposition; government arbitrariness; complete control by the secret police over all aspects of social life; a vast system of informers among the masses; brutal incursions of the party-state into all aspects of human relations; tension among the nationalities; growing expansionist tendencies; domestic xenophobia; chauvinism; and anti-Semitism. All this against a background of rapid growth of the state's military potential and an increasingly rapid deterioration in economic conditions, especially among the rural population.

The absence of a sense of security, so indispensable to any society, became an obstacle impeding the completion of the formation of Soviet society. All social strata, without exception, suffered from a sense of insecurity and its own powerlessness. The party bureaucracy was more affected than others, since even the power and privileges possessed by the members of this caste disappeared suddenly, unexpectedly, as could the members themselves. The bureaucracy was tired of one-man rule. It dreamed of a different kind of dictatorship, one without a dictator, but it also feared the possible consequences of Stalin's death.

Many works, largely in the West, have been dedicated to the study of the Stalin era, or Stalinism, as it is often called. Interesting points of view have been put forward on Stalinism as a social phenomenon.[190] Some have attempted to judge the Soviet experience from the viewpoint of the interests of man, of human society as a whole. Thus they discovered that during this period of building the "radiant future" tens of millions of people had died, some starved to death, others killed. Some estimates put the number of victims at 25 million, others at 40 million. Solzhenitsyn asserts that during the Soviet period the human losses reached 60 million. Whatever the figure, there is no question that a real demographic catastrophe occurred, such as Russia had never known in all its many centuries of history. It was also a great moral catastrophe for the survivors. How were they to deal with the legacy of the Stalin era? That was the historical dilemma posed in March 1953.

# 10

# CONFUSION AND
# HOPE, 1953–1964

## THE FIRST TRIUMVIRATE

After Stalin's death, Malenkov seemed to be the natural successor, having become the main political figure in the party during Stalin's last years. At the Nineteenth Party Congress in 1952, for the first time since the Fourteenth Party Congress of 1925, someone other than Stalin gave the Central Committee main report. It was Malenkov. A photograph of Malenkov with Stalin and Mao Tse-tung appeared in every newspaper on March 12, 1953, next to Mao's article, which said: "We profoundly believe that the Central Committee of the Communist Party of the Soviet Union and the Soviet government with Comrade Malenkov at its head will undoubtedly be able to continue the work of Comrade Stalin."[1] This was tantamount to an assertion of Malenkov's right to the succession.

Malenkov offhandedly brushed aside Khrushchev's proposal that they meet to discuss how and by whom affairs would be conducted in the future. "We'll all get together and then we'll talk," he retorted, departing from Stalin's dacha after the physicians had certified Stalin's death.[2] Khrushchev said nothing but took his own measures: he removed some important archives to his own offices at the Central Committee and began to prepare for the decisive battle for power.

512

At the joint session of the Central Committee and the leading government bodies on March 6, 1953, Khrushchev gained his first important victory: he was released from his duties as secretary of the Moscow Committee with the recommendation that he concentrate on work at the Secretariat of the Central Committee. Neither Malenkov nor Beria, who had become allies since the time of the "Leningrad affair," saw in Khrushchev a serious rival. Both were directing their thoughts toward seizing control over the state apparatus. Both committed a serious error when they overestimated the significance of their respective posts as head of government and head of the secret police and underestimated the importance of possessing control over the party apparatus. It was the personality of the head of government— not the post of chairman of the Council of Ministers—that was important for holding power. As chairman of the Council of Ministers, Stalin remained the all-powerful dictator. Malenkov occupied this post, but he was not a dictator—he was only the prime minister.

Khrushchev did not try to contend for the premiership. Contrary to his nature, this time he was patient enough to wait. As far as he was concerned, Malenkov was no danger to him. The danger lay in an alliance between Malenkov and Beria. Khrushchev was the embodiment of the party apparatus and understood perfectly well the mood of the regional secretaries, who had now become the real power locally. They wanted to be free from fear and from surveillance by the chiefs of local state security agencies. They were loyal, but they desired greater independence in deciding local matters and a guarantee of personal security. For them, as for Khrushchev, the most dangerous man was Beria, whom the majority of party leaders and the military bureaucracy hated.

After Stalin's death, Khrushchev very rapidly managed to separate the power of the party and the power of the government. On March 14, 1953, Malenkov at his own request was released from his duties as secretary of the Central Committee, but he remained chairman of the Council of Ministers. Khrushchev in effect became first secretary of the Central Committee.[3] This office, abolished after the Nineteenth Party Congress, was officially reinstated in September 1953.

On March 15, 1953, the fourth session of the Supreme Soviet of the USSR confirmed the new government leadership. Voroshilov was elected to the nominal, yet honorary post of chairman of the Presidium of the Supreme Soviet of the USSR. Malenkov was named chairman of the Council of Ministers; Beria, Molotov, and Kaganovich became his first deputies, and Bulganin and Mikoyan were made deputies. The first "triumvirate"— Malenkov, Beria, and Molotov—had come to power, although Molotov was actually shunted aside to the realm of foreign policy.

The new government needed the support of the people, who were still uneasy after the departure of the Omniscient and Omnipresent. The government promised to devote effort to the people's welfare and declared its readiness to improve relations with the United States immediately.[4] On April 1, in accordance with tradition, it announced a new reduction in retail prices for food, clothing, gasoline, and building materials.[5]

Where to begin? This has always been and remains the most important question upon any change in leadership, and so it was for the new leadership. The answer was complicated and far from unequivocal: during Stalin's last years severe tensions had arisen in literally every area of the country's economic and cultural life. The international situation was also fraught with danger; any crisis could escalate into World War III.

As is evident from his first actions, Malenkov understood that it was necessary to give the people the material relief they had been denied for so long. The triumvirate's program was concisely set forth in Malenkov's first official report at the fourth session of the Supreme Soviet on March 15, 1953—one week after Stalin's body was placed in the mausoleum: "The duty of unfailing concern for the welfare of the people, for the maximum satisfaction of their material and cultural needs, is a law for our government."[6] This became a kind of motto for the new leadership.

A campaign began in the press to increase production of consumer goods and foodstuffs. Several months later, at the sixth session of the Supreme Soviet, Malenkov, noting the poor state of affairs in agriculture, made the following appeal: "In the next two to three years we must achieve abundance in food supplies for our population and raw materials for our light industry."[7] The new premier also called for a change in attitude toward the private plots of collective farmers, increased housing construction, and the development of commodity circulation and retail trade.[8] Capital investment in light industry and in the food and fishing industries was increased substantially. The first measures of the new leadership—lowering the taxes on the peasantry—gained it wide popularity. It was Malenkov, not Khrushchev, who was the most popular figure among the population during this period.

One of the most deplorable consequences of Stalin's dictatorship was the decline of agriculture. Stalin's successors were faced with making important decisions, which would not only determine the fates of tens of millions of collective farmers but would also affect the entire economy for decades to come. Of course, none of the new leaders thought of such a radical solution as the abolition of the quasi-feudal system of agriculture. They did, however, seek ways to lessen somewhat the burden on the collective farmers and to increase the profitability of agricultural production.

For many years the collective farmers had barely managed to make ends meet, particularly in central and northwestern Russia. Families maintained their existence not by the ephemeral income of the collective farms, which was trumpeted by the press, but by their Lilliputian personal plots and single cow which nourished each family, as they had since time immemorial. After the war, money taxes and taxes in kind on the private farmers increased unbelievably. With the famine of 1946–47, these new extortions led to the demise of hundreds of thousands of peasants and the complete impoverishment of millions. Taxes were assessed not on the basis of overall value but according to each unit of produce, livestock, or poultry. In order to avoid paying these taxes, the peasants were forced to forgo variety in their farming and raise only those crops that were taxed lightly or that were absolutely indispensable to keep their families from starving to death.

One of the first measures of the "triumvirate" was to reduce the agricultural tax on the private plots, to replace the tax in kind with a monetary tax, and to increase the purchase price on surplus agricultural production. Debts for agricultural taxes in arrears from previous years were canceled entirely. The tax levied in accordance with the law of August 1953 was in effect lowered by an average of 50 percent for each kolkhoznik's household.[9]

An editorial in the first issue for 1953 of *Kommunist*, the Communist party's central theoretical magazine, announced triumphantly: "The grain problem, which previously was considered the most acute problem, has been resolved firmly and conclusively."[10] But the tenth issue of the same magazine published the proceedings of the September plenum of the Central Committee, which was devoted to conditions in agriculture. By the thirteenth issue, not a trace of the optimistic tone remained.[11]

Khrushchev admitted that all the resounding declarations that the grain problem had been solved were untrue. The taxes on the private plots of the collective famers were lowered once more, and the owners of cows received some exemptions. It was decided that in the future small-scale farming by blue collar and white collar workers would be encouraged—the breeding of hogs, poultry, and dairy cattle. This was tantamount to an admission that the private plots in small provincial towns were not only the principal source of their owners' livelihood but also a major source of agricultural supply for a significant part of the population as a whole.[12] But in 1953 one-fourth of the 20 million peasant families had no cows.

In 1954 the tax on cows and pigs was abolished. By this time the tax on the private plot had decreased by some 60 percent as compared to 1952. The effect of these measures was staggering: the countryside and the cities located close to rural areas ceased to experience acute food shortages, although the situation remained grave enough. But above all, the peasants once again began to believe in the government and in the possibility of an improvement in their bleak existence.

It is easy to imagine what the results of a total restructuring of agriculture might have been if granting relative freedom in the use of the private plot, which represented only 2 percent of all cultivated land in the Soviet Union, changed conditions so quickly.[13]

On April 4, 1953, a report was published, without any commentary, by the Ministry of Internal Affairs: the "doctors' plot" had been concocted as a provocation by the former leadership of the former Ministry of State Security, and the accused were innocent of any crimes.[14] This was an astonishing announcement, for Ignatiev, the former chief of state security, had been made a secretary of the Central Committee immediately after Stalin's death. He could not have been elected to the Secretariat of the Central Committee without Khrushchev's consent. But Ignatiev bore direct responsibility for the preparation of the doctors' trial. Did Khrushchev have anything to do with this affair? The question is all the more justified, because Ignatiev was never called to account for his actions, and after he was relieved of his duties as secretary of the Central Committee he was named first party secretary of Bashkiria. Be that as it may, the MVD's April 4 announcement had enormous political significance as a declaration of a break with the previous practice of lawlessness and terror. Many families of those arrested as "enemies of the people" saw the potential for obtaining a review of the accusations and convictions of their relatives. The procuracy of the USSR and party agencies were deluged with hundreds of thousands of individual petitions to review the cases of people who had been convicted.

Later, after Beria's arrest, it was contended in party circles that Beria had not submitted this communiqué to the Secretariat of the Central Committee for approval; otherwise, it would have been published under the name of the entire government—not just the Ministry of Internal Affairs—and it would have been formulated differently. Indeed, that was probably the case. The MVD communiqué created a new, immense, and rather undesirable problem for the new leadership: the rehabilitation of hundreds of thousands, perhaps even millions, of people who disappeared during the Stalin terror. There was probably not one major party or government figure who was not involved, either directly or indirectly, in the massive crimes of the Soviet regime or, at a minimum, who had not derived some profit for himself during the terror of the 1930s and 1940s. Now the number of Beria's enemies in the leadership had increased substantially, since many were in danger of being exposed. In the meantime, Beria gave the order to free the families of members of the leadership who had been arrested and sent to the camps during the last years of Stalin's life. Beria personally officiated when Molotov was reunited with his wife, P. S. Zhemchuzhina, who had been sent to a camp just before Stalin's death.[15] At the same time, he gave the order to free the former minister of state security, Abakumov, who had landed in prison as a result of the "doctors' plot." N. D. Yakovlev, a marshal of the artillery, and his son, as well as aviation Marshal Novikov, who was arrested after having been denounced by Vasily Stalin, were also released from prison.[16]

For a short while, Beria's name became fairly popular among the intelligentsia and the urban population in connection with the April 4 communiqué. Beria and the "triumvirate" made a clever move in combining the Ministry of Internal Affairs with the Ministry of State Security to create a reconstituted Ministry of Internal Affairs. The frightening words *state security* disappeared in a short time, creating the illusion of change and causing a storm of applause among leftist intellectuals in the West.

But these hopes were premature, as evidenced by the decree of the Supreme Soviet on the amnesty of March 27, 1953.[17] This decree, incorrectly called the Voroshilov amnesty (Voroshilov signed it as chairman of the Supreme Soviet Presidium, but it had been drawn up with Beria's active participation), released from prison all those who had received sentences up to five years, sometimes up to eight years, as well as certain categories of invalids, minors, and women. The amnesty did not affect political prisoners.

In the summer of 1953 masses of criminals who had been freed from the camps by the March decree filled the cities. Even in Moscow it became dangerous to go out at night because one could easily be robbed or killed. Ministry of Internal Affairs troops were brought into Moscow and mounted patrols appeared. Later, after his removal, Beria was accused, among other crimes, of intending to use criminals released from prison to seize power.

Beria became popular in the non-Russian republics. His name symbolized a turning point in nationalities policy, toward granting more rights to the union republics. The central committee plenums of each of the republics condemned the Great Russian policy. At the Ukrainian Central Committee "grave distortions" in nationalities policy were discussed. Melnikov, chief of the Ukrainian Communist party, was reproached in particular for the fact that workers from other provinces of the Ukraine had been sent to work in supervisory capacities in the western Ukraine and because, to all intents and purposes, education in the Russian language had been introduced at all institutions of higher learning in the western Ukraine. A similar discussion took place at the plenum of the Lithuanian Central Committee: the inadequate promotion of Lithuanian nationals to supervisory positions was criticized.[18] During this time open protests against Russification could be heard without exception at every non-Russian national party's central committee plenum.

Beria proposed a project to the Presidium of the Central Committee concerning the ethnic composition of the top leadership in the Ukraine. His idea was to name Ukrainian cadres to local leadership positions and not to move them to Moscow. The Presidium relieved Melnikov of his duties as first secretary of the Ukraine and named the Ukrainian Kirichenko in his place. There is no doubt that these changes were made with Khrushchev's consent, since Kirichenko was his protégé. The writer Korneichuk became a member of the Central Committee Presidium of the Ukraine Communist party. Similar changes were made in the Baltic countries and in Byelorussia. As Khrushchev attested in his memoirs, the Presidium of the Central Committee decided that the post of first secretary in each republic should be given to a local leader, not a Russian sent from Moscow.[19] Khrushchev admitted that Beria's plan to reduce the preponderance of Russians in the top leadership of the republics coincided with the Central Committee's opinion. Khrushchev's accusation against Beria, that he was seeking to aggravate tensions between Russians and non-Russians in the union republics as well as between the central leadership in Moscow and the leaderships of the republics,[20] does not stand up to criticism. If Beria really were aspiring to seize power, such a method would have been completely out of keeping with its objective. Whether Beria had a program on the nationalities question and whether he really wanted to reinforce the national character of each republic and, if so, to what end, remain open questions. But immediately after Beria's arrest, plenums and meetings were once again convened in the non-Russian republics, where he was condemned for his attempts to turn the nationalities of the Soviet Union against one another "under the false pretext of struggling against violations of the party's nationalities policy."[21] However, that was all in the usual order of things.

Beria, who was guilty of a multitude of crimes against humanity, was the driving force in the first "triumvirate," as can be concluded from the charges leveled against him in the letter by the Central Committee, addressed to members of the party organizations and to them alone, which followed Beria's arrest. It turns out that it was Beria who defended the idea of international detente, the reunification and neutralization of Germany, reconciliation with Yugoslavia, the granting of further rights to the republics, an end to russification in the cultural arena, and the advancement of members of non-Russian nationalities to local leadership posts. The Central Committee letter also pointed to the extraordinary activity of Beria, who had inundated the Presidium of the Central Committee with all sorts of projects.

Molotov, the third member of the triumvirate, was made minister of foreign affairs, as we have said. An expert in cold war tactics, he now had to normalize relations between the Soviet Union and the Western nations, particularly the United States: these relations had become severely strained over the Korean war and the German question. The new government's program was revealed as early as Malenkov's speech of March 15, 1953. Besides the usual assurances of the USSR's peaceful intentions, the speech contained an indirect appeal to the United States, inviting it to reevaluate U.S.–Soviet relations.[22]

The U.S. government reacted without equivocation, although without haste. In a speech on April 16, 1953, which contrary to the usual practice was published in its entirety in the Soviet Union ten days later, President Eisenhower affirmed: "We welcome every honest act of peace. We care nothing for mere rhetoric."[23] More concretely, he proposed the following: to make peace with honor in Korea; to conclude an agreement on Austria; and to create a broad European association which would include a reunified Germany. He also pressed for the complete independence of the Eastern European states, arms limitation, and the international control of atomic energy.[24] *Pravda*'s commentary on April 25, 1953 ("On the speech of President Eisenhower"), was very mild in tone. The *Times* of London praised *Pravda*'s article: "The article as a whole represents the calmest, clearest, and most rational statement of Soviet policy that has appeared for many a long month."[26] The reaction of the British government, too, was positive. Prime Minister Churchill declared, "We have been encouraged by a series of amicable gestures on the part of the new Soviet government," and proposed to convene a summit conference.[27]

The results of this shift in Soviet foreign policy were not slow in coming. On July 27, 1953, the armistice was signed in Korea and the war was over.

The echoes of Stalin's death, Beria's arrest, and the press campaign in defense of legality reached the ears of millions of prisoners languishing in Soviet concentration camps. They began to go on strike and revolt everywhere: in the Komi republic (Vorkuta), the Urals, Siberia, Central Asia, and Kazakhstan. The most important was the uprising at Kengir in the spring and summer of 1954,[28] in which 9,000 male prisoners and 4,000 female prisoners took part.

An attempt by the Kengir camp administration to provoke the common criminals against the politicals unexpectedly set off a general strike and an uprising by both categories of prisoners. The revolt continued for forty-two days. The prisoners presented demands of a political and social nature, including a call for review of all sentences and a general amnesty, implementation of an eight-hour workday, conversion of "special regime" camps into regular ones, removal of prison numbers from clothing, and improvement of living conditions. They also demanded a meeting with a representative of the Central Committee. Their slogan was: "Long live the Soviet constitution." Several years later, a human rights movement adopted the same slogan.

On Moscow orders, 3,000 soldiers with tanks were sent against the Kengir prisoners. The unequal battle, which began at dawn on June 26, 1954, lasted for more than four hours. The prisoners put up a desperate resistance, hurling Molotov cocktails at the tanks. Their strength won out, however. The prisoners were defeated by the overwhelmingly superior force of the state. The most active rebels were arrested, convicted, and sent to Kolyma.

During this revolt, a solidarity strike was declared on June 10 at the Dzhezkazgan camp. After June 26 the punitive detachment with its tanks turned to Dzhezkazgan. The 20,000 prisoners there were not prepared to do battle; they surrendered.

However, the forty-two days of revolt at Kengir were not in vain. There were changes in the lives of the prisoners: now they began to work at 8 AM, instead of 6, and they worked until 5 PM. The bars on the windows of the barracks, torn off during the revolt, were not replaced. Numbers were removed from prisoners' clothing. Some imprisoned invalids and juveniles were released, and others had their sentences reduced.

Two years before the revolution in Hungary, Soviet prisoners revolted in the camps. At the time their heroic feat went unnoticed by the rest of the world, but theirs was a historic deed, for they partially defeated the terrorism, the exploitation of prisoners, and the arbitrariness that had been rampant in the camps for years. The Resistance movement of prisoners in the Soviet camps also helped make possible the dramatic developments at the Twentieth Congress of the CPSU.

Stalin's death and the first steps toward liberalization undertaken by the new Soviet leadership found an immediate echo in the Soviet Union's satellites in Eastern and Southeastern Europe. Disturbances began everywhere, and the struggle between the old Stalinist leadership and the anti-Stalinists intensified sharply. Only Albania, Romania, and Bulgaria remained more or less calm. In Albania, Enver Hoxha, a staunch Stalinist, had already dealt with all likely and unlikely opposition beforehand. In Romania and Bulgaria, too, the Stalinists held the reins of government firmly in hand. It was only later, after the Twentieth Party Congress, that the anti-Stalinist forces were activated in those countries.

The first serious disturbance in the socialist bloc occurred in Czechoslovakia in early June 1953. Its immediate cause was the monetary reform of May 30, 1953, which seriously affected the workers' already low standard of living. On June 1 disturbances broke out at Plzen; at the same time a general strike was called in the coal mines of Moravska Ostrava. In Plzen 5,000 demonstrators burst into the town hall and ripped down the portraits of Stalin and Gottwald. Troops summoned to the scene refused to fire on the demonstrators. Demands were made for free elections, and the names Masaryk, Beneš, and Eisenhower drew strong applause. No one, however, called for the overthrow of the government. The movement was spontaneous and had no leaders. There was not even any bloodshed: after the troops refused to open fire, special police forces were called in, but they met with no resistance.[29] The unrest in Czechoslovakia was an indication of the discontent brewing against the policies of the Communist party that had seized power in February 1948.

Agitation against the government's economic policy was also the cause of an uprising in East Germany in June 1953. The industrialization and forced collectivization carried out by the East German government led to a massive flight of the population from East to West Germany. The government's response was to increase obligatory deliveries of produce from the peasant households and to force payment of taxes in arrears. In April 1953 distribution of ration cards for foodstuffs to "alien class elements" or to inhabitants of East Berlin employed in the Western sector of the city were terminated. At the same time pressure was put on the workers to increase labor productivity. At the end of May 1953 the Council of Ministers of the GDR issued a decree increasing production norms by 10 percent.[30] Population flow to the West increased. During the first five months of 1953 190,000 people left East Germany for West Germany, as opposed to 182,000 during all of 1952.[31]

At exactly the same time, Moscow received word that the situation in Hungary was deteriorating. The new Soviet leaders insistently advised their satellites to change economic policies immediately, to cease pressuring the workers, peasants, and middle strata of society, and to renounce their costly and unjustifiable programs of industrialization. During the Stalin era the satellites had tried to copy "big brother" in every possible way, utterly ignoring the economic realities of their countries.

Under pressure from Moscow, the Central Committee of the East German Communist party adopted a resolution condemning their former economic policy, admitting serious errors, and revoking all the unpopular measures of the previous months. On the list of errors committed and measures for their rectification, however, no mention was made of the increased production quotas. The resolution was followed by the announcement that these quotas would go into effect precisely on June 30, 1953. On June 16 the workers of East Berlin responded with an immediate work stoppage and mass demonstrations. Thousands of workers converged on the main government building in East Berlin, demanding that the new quotas be withdrawn and prices lowered. They presented political demands as well: the dismissal of Walter Ulbricht, leader of the party, and the reunification of Germany, followed by free elections. The next day, a general strike began in East Germany, and disturbances broke out in a number of other cities, including Leipzig, Dresden, and Magdeburg.[32] Workers in these cities attacked police stations and prisons, freeing political prisoners. As many as 100,000 people took part in these actions.

In order to suppress the incipient general insurrection in the GDR, the Soviet authorities brought in tanks. The Soviet troops were aided by the GDR police.[33] According to some sources, nearly 500 people were killed.[34] The Soviet government portrayed this bloody suppression of a workers' uprising in the GDR as the liquidation of an attempted fascist rebellion. Even more than thirty years later, the Soviet people still do not know what happened in East Germany in June 1953.

The new Soviet leadership observed events developing in Hungary with great uneasiness. The leader of the Hungarian Communist party, Matyas Rakosi, was conceivably the most devoted to the Soviet Union of all the leaders of the socialist countries. He sought to imitate Soviet policies in every respect. As a result, by the early 1950s Hungary was in a disastrous situation economically and politically.

Rakosi and the other Hungarian leaders were summoned to Moscow in the spring of 1953. The Soviet leaders demanded from Rakosi an end to the unwarranted, adventuristic course of superindustrialization and forced collectivization. Moscow insisted on a reorganization of the leadership, the resignation of Rakosi as prime minister, along with the ministers of heavy industry and defense, and the condemnation of past errors.[35] Imre Nagy, an old Comintern member, was named to take Rakosi's place as the head of government; Nagy was considered a moderate and in fact had opposed Rakosi's policies. The Hungarian Politburo accepted the resolution forced upon it but kept its contents secret, getting away with publishing a nebulous communiqué. But Nagy, who had been placed at the head of the government, embarked on a policy similar to the NEP.[36]

Rakosi remained at the head of the party, and soon a bitter struggle developed in the Hungarian leadership. Nagy was accused of rightist deviation and removed from his post as prime minister in April 1955.[37] But at the same time the rehabilitation of the victims of the Rakosi regime had begun, paralleling developments in the Soviet Union. In Hungary, unlike in the Soviet Union, many were restored to their positions in the Communist party. Hungary became the scene of a broad movement for liberalization, which won the support of the entire intelligentsia, from students to writers. Social organizations and circles of various kinds made their appearance, as did magazines and anthologies by writers and artists of a liberal bent. Works that developed a point of view critical of the situation in socialist Hungary were published.[38] A spiritual revolution had begun in Hungary.

On July 10, 1953, Soviet newspapers announced Beria's arrest. The groundwork for Beria's removal had been laid by Khrushchev, in a deal with the other members of the Presidium of the Central Committee. The arrest was carried out by the military group, headed by Marshal Zhukov and assisted by Ivan Serov. Beria's fall brought the end of the first triumvirate. The prestige and influence of Khrushchev, the organizer of the plot against Beria, increased significantly. Malenkov, without Beria's support, came to depend all the more on Khrushchev, who very quickly assumed control of the party apparatus. Khrushchev was not yet able to dictate his own decisions, but even Malenkov could no longer act without Khrushchev's consent; each still needed the other's support. Khrushchev controlled not only the party apparatus; the army, which he had used to eliminate Beria, was also behind him. Zhukov, Konev, Moskalenko, who had directly executed the logistics of Beria's arrest, as well as Marshal Bulganin, who was utterly devoted to Khrushchev, were assigned to the most important political and strategic area—the Moscow Military District.[39]

The official trial of Beria and his accomplices was held in December 1953. (Beria was already dead, although the people did not know this.) Among other things, he was accused of organizing "a group of anti-Soviet conspirators whose aim was to seize power and to restore the rule of the bourgeoisie."[40] It is doubtful, however, that Beria would have sought to restore power to the bourgeoisie rather than for his own dictatorship.

At the same time Beria was declared to have been an agent of British intelligence since 1918. He was tried and sentenced to death along with several other high-ranking members of state security, including some former ministers and their aides. In 1954 Ryumin, the man personally responsible for the "doctors' plot," was tried and shot.[41] The same fate later befell the former minister of state security, Abakumov, who was found guilty, among a multitude of crimes, of fabricating the Leningrad affair.[42]

After Beria's removal, the state security establishment was reorganized.

A majority, though not all, of the high-ranking leaders were removed or replaced. They received first-rate pensions. The Ministry of State Security (MGB) was replaced by State Security Committee (KGB), attached to the USSR Council of Ministers. Its diminished significance in the structure of state power was thus emphasized. In the provinces local KGB chiefs were henceforth subordinate to the first secretaries of the party, who became the veritable masters of their regions. The special sections of the MGB in various institutions, including the one in the Central Committee, were dismantled. The all-powerful "special boards"—the secret tribunals that handed out severe sentences without appeal in trials mainly involving "counterrevolutionary" activities, anti-Soviet agitation, and so on—were also abolished. One of Beria's former deputies, General Serov, who played a key role in the elimination of his boss, was named head of the KGB. Serov was notorious for his "services" in the deportation of the Balts and the inhabitants of the western Ukraine and western Byelorussia in 1939 and 1940. It was under his guidance, too, that the peoples of the Northern Caucusus and the Crimean Tatars had been deported in 1943–44. He also headed the main state security office in the Soviet zone of Germany. And so on. But his personal devotion to Khrushchev, tested during their years as colleagues in the Ukraine, and his lack of political ambition played their roles. These qualities were well suited to the reason for reorganization of the state security agencies: to reduce them to the level of mere instruments. The Central Committee once again assumed full responsibility for the terror apparatus—diminished and limited, yet retained as an indispensable component of the Soviet social system.

As before, the primary reserve of cadres for the KGB was the Komsomol. Many state security employees had previously been Komsomol members of various ranks. After Serov, Shelepin, the former first secretary of the Komsomol's Central Committee, was named head of the KGB. Later, when Shelepin became a member of the Politburo, he was replaced as chairman of the KGB by a Komsomol Central Committee secretary, Semichastny. The preservation of the state security organs confirmed that the basis of the system created by Lenin and perfected by Stalin remained unchanged. But in 1953 all this had not yet become clear.

One week after the rehabilitation of the doctors, the CPSU Central Committee passed a resolution "On the Violation of Laws by the Organs of State Security." The significance of this resolution extended beyond the particular matter of the "doctors' plot": it was the first formal party resolution condemning the state security agencies, which had previously been above both the party and the state.

After the publication of the announcement on the rehabilitation of the doctors, and particularly after the elimination of Beria, a completely spontaneous movement arose in all levels of society against arbitrariness, whether that of the KGB, the police, heads of enterprises, or directors of apartment buildings. This movement took a form that is typical under Soviet conditions. The Central newspapers received thousands of letters with complaints about the arbitrariness of local leaders. The families of the "enemies of the people," either killed or languishing in concentration camps and prisons, had been aroused. For many years they had been the pariahs of society; the party and state had taken every opportunity to remind them that it was official magnanimity alone that permitted them to live and find work and allowed their children to go to school.

As a rule, these letters began with words of thanks to the party, which had unmasked the "despicable traitor" Beria. Then they demanded or requested that the trials of their fathers, mothers, or other relatives be reviewed. The agencies of the procuracy, as well as the party leaders themselves, were confused. They realized that they were in the midst of a wave of popular indignation that could sweep them away. First in one camp, then in another—Kolyma, Kazakhstan, and other islands of the Gulag—strikes and riots flared up and ended in bloody repression. Outside the camps, people openly discussed the crimes that had been committed. Local leaders suddenly became polite and accessible to the population. Citizens made use of the demagogy in the newspapers, where the arbitrariness and violations of the law were condemned, and began earnestly to demand that their civil rights be observed. At the end of 1953 and the beginning of 1954 this movement, which no one had organized, began to widen and grow, exerting considerable psychological pressure on the new leaders.

Is it true or not that the new leadership had no idea of the number of people who had been subjected to repression and were sent to the camps and prisons? This has been a rather controversial question. The governmental economic plans always indicated which ministries were responsible for particular construction projects as well as what funds and human resources each ministry had at its disposal; in many cases, the Ministry of Internal Affairs was named. Therefore it would have been quite easy to guess the size of this secret empire which at any one time had a slave population of 8–9 million people.[43] It is highly unlikely that the top leaders were unaware of this.

After the MVD's communiqué of April 4, 1953, the demand for legality became universal. It concerned not only political prisoners but all areas of social life, for everywhere arbitrariness had taken the place of the law, and the law only expressed this arbitrariness. All the top Soviet and party bodies—not only the courts, the procuracy, the judicial agencies, and the

Ministry of Internal Affairs—were inundated with demands, requests, and complaints. And those very officials who were guilty of the abuses did their best to respond to these complaints.

However, when the question arose of rehabilitating those guilty of "counterrevolutionary crimes," nothing could be done without a general resolution on a government-wide scale. In 1953 some 4,000 people were released.[44] According to the most cautious estimates, there were 8–9 million prisoners in the camps.[45] Although from 1953 through 1955 prison conditions were eased, the problem remained unsolved. The release of prisoners continued, but during 1954 and 1955 only 12,000 people were released and rehabilitated.[46] In 1955 amnesty was declared for those who had collaborated with the Germans in 1941–1944.[47] German prisoners were liberated the same year, in connection with West German chancellor Adenauer's visit to the Soviet Union. In 1956 the Japanese prisoners of war were freed.

After the Twentieth Party Congress, rehabilitation took on a massive character. Special rehabilitation commissions were created endowed with the power to liberate prisoners on the spot, in the camps themselves. The overwhelming majority of surviving prisoners were freed in 1956, the year of the congress; many were rehabilitated posthumously, but this process continued for many long years. The problem was particularly difficult with regard to those who had participated in opposition groups. No opposition leaders were rehabilitated, although, gradually many of the victims of the trials of 1936–1938 were posthumously cleared of the charges against them. Bukharin, Rykov, Zinoviev, Kamenev, and some others remained "guilty," although their innocence of the crimes they were accused of, such as plotting to assassinate Lenin in 1918 (Bukharin), espionage and organizing terrorist activities (Zinoviev, Kamenev, and Bukharin), and sabotage (all of them, plus Rykov), was absolutely clear and was confirmed by the rehabilitation of their "accomplices."

The rehabilitation was necessary not only to those directly affected and their families. It also had enormous significance for the population as a whole. The moral conscience of society was awakened. Candidates for elections to party committees and trade unions were recommended on the basis of their moral values.

The survivors, raised from the dead, rehabilitated and returned to their lives and families, played a major role in exposing the lawless nature of the Soviet state and the immorality of its social system. But was this true only of the Soviet system? The events in Eastern Europe demonstrated that the problem was significantly larger: it was a matter of the socialist system in general and the legitimacy of its existence. In the fall of 1954 facts concerning the tortures used by Polish state security received wide publicity. At the same time, Wladislaw Gomulka, one of the most prominent Polish Communists, was released from prison. In January 1955 the state security agencies in Poland were abolished, and those guilty of torture were brought to trial.[48]

We have already mentioned that the Leningrad affair was fabricated by Malenkov and Beria. Khrushchev reported in his memoirs that even Stalin hesitated before making a final decision, but in the end he decided to leave the matter in their hands.[49] It is typical, however, that in the enumeration of Beria's crimes, the Leningrad affair was passed over in silence. It was only much later, in December 1954, that Beria was charged for this crime. By then however, the question of Malenkov's departure from the post of chairman of the USSR Council of Ministers had already been decided.

During this time Khrushchev climbed steadily higher. At the Central Committee plenum in September 1953, where he gave the main report on the agricultural situation, Khrushchev was formally appointed first secretary of the Central Committee, which confirmed his leading position in the party. He immediately replaced Mikhailov, Malenkov's protégé, with Kapitonov as the head of the Moscow Committee of the party. Khrushchev was also the main reporter at all the Central Committee plenums of 1953 and 1954. His proposal for opening up the "virgin lands" (previously untilled areas in Siberia and Kazakhstan) met with a rather cool reception from the other members of the Central Committee Presidium. Malenkov was inclined to the more intensive exploitation of land already under cultivation.

In July 1954 came the trial of Ryumin, the former deputy minister of state security, who was not, apparently, the initiator of the "doctors' plot" but who had been in charge of the investigation. His trial was an obvious warning to Malenkov to speed up his resignation. Still in store was the trial of Abakumov, the former minister of state security, who had been the principal figure responsible for the investigation into the Leningrad affair. Malenkov's situation became hopeless. Khrushchev proved to be a very skillful intriguer in this instance. But for the first time in many years a high-ranking member of the state was faced with the possibility of leaving his post not only voluntarily, but with honor as well.

At the Central Committee session of January 1955, Malenkov was criticized for giving priority to light, not heavy industry and for his errors in directing agriculture in the early 1950s. In February 1955 Malenkov submitted his formal resignation from his post as prime minister. In it, making a public "self-criticism," he admitted his mistakes and explained that he had not been trained adequately for a role as a government leader.[50] Bulganin, an old friend of Khrushchev's, became the new chairman of the

Council of Ministers. He was not well known as a political figure but, as was asserted at the time, was an able administrator. Malenkov became one of Bulganin's deputies and retained his position as a member of the Central Committee Presidium. During 1955 government personnel underwent various replacements and transfers, bearing testimony to the increase in Khrushchev's influence. Several former ministers were sent as ambassadors to different countries, which thereafter became a common practice. Henceforth career diplomats lost their monopoly on ambassadorial posts. The role of the minister of foreign affairs—Molotov, at the time—became less important.

After Malenkov's departure, Molotov was not only the sole remaining member of the first triumvirate, he was also the main link with the past, the Stalin era, and the cold war. Gradually Khrushchev began his attack on Molotov. Molotov was vulnerable to many serious charges, beginning with his part in the terror and the nonaggression pact and friendship treaties with Nazi Germany in 1939, and ending with the break with Yugoslavia. He was not included in the delegation headed by Khrushchev that departed for Belgrade for a reconciliation with Tito in May 1955. He no longer participated in the conferences of the Warsaw Pact countries. At the July plenum in 1955, Molotov was the only member of the Presidium to maintain his former position with regard to Yugoslavia. Molotov was considered the party's principal theoretician after Stalin. Many dissertations had been written at the USSR Academy of Science on his "theoretical," "philosophical," and other views. He was once elected an honorary member of the USSR Academy of Sciences. (Khrushchev's education consisted of parochial school,* followed by years at the Industrial Academy.) The party leadership used against Molotov his statement of February 1955, that the USSR had just completed the foundations of a socialist society—Molotov had apparently forgotten the party's 1939 announcement that socialism was already constructed.

Thus, gradually disposing of the direct heirs of the Stalin era, Khrushchev approached the Twentieth Party Congress, scheduled for February 1956. His struggle against these rivals unavoidably compelled him to proceed rather hastily with the unmasking of the crimes of the Stalin period and with the rehabilitation of the victims of the Stalinist terror. Having used the Leningrad affair against Malenkov, Khrushchev found himself pressured by demands for further rehabilitations from the families of prominent po-

*The Russian initials for this church school are Ts Psh. Some people have mistakenly thought that these letters stand for Central Party School(!).

litical and military officials who had suffered in the 1930s and 1940s. Khrushchev now had to consider the fates of the former members of the Politburo and Central Committee. This in turn forced him to make some explanation of the role of Stalin and his closest comrades—Molotov, Voroshilov, and Kaganovich—in the annihilation of party cadres. This was a dangerous path for Khrushchev himself: he had been the secretary of the Moscow Committee during the years of the terror, then the leader of the Ukrainian party and the man in charge of the purges in the western parts of the Ukraine, Byelorussia, and the Baltic states in 1939–40, and the suppression of insurgents in the western Ukraine after World War II. The fact that Khrushchev chose to expose the crimes of the Stalin era—despite the risks such a course would pose to his own fate—showed Khrushchev to be a cut above the other Soviet leaders, both as a man and as a political figure. It cannot be ruled out, however, that Khrushchev embarked on this path without being fully conscious of the political consequences of his action and counting on his ability to maintain control over future events.

A special commission was created at the Central Committee under Pospelov, the party's principal theoretician, who had prepared the famous *Short Course*, the falsified history of the Soviet Communist party and, later, the *Biography of J. V. Stalin*, based on it. It was hard to expect a profound and impartial analysis of the past from this commission; however, even the creation of such a committee was an enormous step forward for the still intact Stalinist regime.

"For three years," Khrushchev wrote, "we were unable to break with the past, unable to muster the courage and the determination to lift the curtain and see what had been hidden from us about the arrests, the trials, the arbitrary rule, the executions, and everything else that had happened during Stalin's reign."[51]

## THE TWENTIETH CONGRESS OF THE CPSU

Once in forced retirement, Khrushchev turned to the past and wrote in his memoirs: "Criminal acts had been committed by Stalin, acts which would be punishable in any state in the world except in fascist states like Hitler's and Mussolini's."[52] It was the first time that a Soviet political leader had drawn a parallel between the Soviet socialist state and fascist states. This is one more indication of Khrushchev's exceptional personality.

The establishment of a commission of inquiry, even under Pospelov's chairmanship, was greeted without any enthusiasm by the Stalinist old guard: Molotov, Voroshilov, and Kaganovich. Mikoyan did not object to the commission, but neither did he actively support Khrushchev.[53]

The report for the Central Committee given by Khrushchev on February 14, 1956, at the Twentieth Party Congress, was rather reserved. On the one hand, Khrushchev made several critical remarks about Stalin, Molotov, and Malenkov without actually naming them.[54] On the other hand, he noted Stalin's services in crushing the "enemies of the people."[55] Mikoyan's attack on the "cult of personality" made in his speech on February 16 was much sharper. He specifically referred to Kosior and Antonov-Ovseenko as people who had been wrongly declared enemies of the people.[56]

It was during the congress itself that Khrushchev secured a decision from the Central Committee Presidium to announce at a closed session the results of the investigation conducted by Pospelov's commission. This decision was passed after a stormy session of the Presidium in which Voroshilov shouted that Khrushchev did not understand what he was doing. These sentiments were supported by Molotov and Kaganovich. Voroshilov and Kaganovich did not conceal the fact that they feared being held personally responsible.[57] Khrushchev responded frankly that the members of the Presidium were responsible to varying degrees, depending on each one's participation. He declared his own readiness to accept his share of the responsibility.[58] In this way, Khrushchev undermined one of the foundations of the Communist manner of government: the system of mutual protection and coverup that thrives not only among the party leadership but in every institution, everywhere. In fact, until very shortly before that time all members of the Politburo had jointly ratified death sentences, by signing one after the other.

After long debate it was decided that Khrushchev would present a second report at a closed session—on Stalin's crimes. Of course, the report had been prepared in advance. Without a doubt Khrushchev was confident that the majority of the Presidium would support him; they had no alternative.

Khrushchev decided to limit himself to the crimes committed against party members who had supported Stalin and the general line of the party, avoiding the question of the victims of the "show trials," the left and right oppositionists, and so forth. Meanwhile, on the eve of his secret speech, Khrushchev had already heard from the lips of Prosecutor General Rudenko that, "from the standpoint of judicial norms, there was no evidence whatsoever for condemning, or even trying those men." The entire cases against them "had been based on personal confessions beaten out of them under physical and psychological torture."[59]

Nevertheless, it was decided not to refer to the leaders of the oppositions so as not to embarrass the representatives of the fraternal parties present at the congress who had previously defended the Moscow trials of the 1930s. Later, Khrushchev admitted that this decision had been a mistake. He did not mention the principal victims of the regime: the millions of ordinary Soviet citizens.

Despite these limitations, the secret speech was a bombshell.[60] Khrushchev revealed the mechanism of terror and denounced the system of arbitrariness that had dominated the country for thirty years. To the degree possible, he tried to limit his exposure of Stalin's crimes solely to those against the party elite and its best-known representatives, but the documents he read aloud were sufficient to indicate the brutal and massive nature of the terror. Such was the case with the letter by Eikhe, an alternate member of the Politburo, whose spine was broken by his interrogator; the letter by Rudzutak, chairman of the Central Control Commission, also tortured cruelly; the note from Red Army Commander Iona Yakir, addressed to Stalin; the letter from a former member of the Cheka collegium, Mikhail Kedrov (who was himself guilty of a number of crimes of the Cheka), as well as the numbers of Seventeenth Congress delegates who had been annihilated. Finally, Khrushchev gave the delegates of the congress to understand that the Kirov assassination had been carried out on Stalin's orders, and he promised that a full investigation would be conducted.

An important part of Khrushchev's report took up the question of Stalin's responsibility for the Soviet Union's lack of preparedness for the attack by Hitler's Germany. Khrushchev did not dare go so far as to condemn the Soviet–German pact of August 23, 1939, and the partition of Poland, but this question hung in the air. Another important issue discussed in the report was the lawless mass deportation of non-Russian peoples during the war with Germany. Here again Khrushchev stopped short of the full truth.[61] Finally, Khrushchev spoke of Stalin's other errors and crimes: the break with Yugoslavia, the Mingrelian affair, the Doctors' plot, and the suicide of Ordzhonikidze.

In fact, Khrushchev showed that the entire history of the party when Stalin was at its head had consisted of criminal acts, lawlessness, mass murder, and incompetent leadership. He touched briefly on the systematic falsification of history written by Stalin himself or at his direction. However, he spoke approvingly of Stalin's struggle against the oppositions. This was understandable: after all, something had to be preserved from the inventory of services of Stalin and the party he had led, even though every step they had taken had been bloody.

By his denunciation of the "cult of personality" (an expression borrowed from a well-known letter of Marx's), Khrushchev committed a great historic act: he made it possible for many to understand that the Soviet system was the most inhuman system that had ever existed.

Although Khrushchev's report was theoretically secret, its contents became known widely throughout the country shortly after the conclusion of the closed session of the congress. Accompanied by speeches from delegates who had been at the congress, the report was read out in full to every party organization in the country and followed by stormy discussions.[62] The subject of the heated and impassioned debates was not only Stalin and his crimes but also the Soviet system, the entire social order and the way of life of its citizens. The overwhelming majority of the participants in these meetings approved of what had been expressed at the Twentieth Congress. Assemblies of office workers, industrial workers, and collective farmers were also held to hear a diluted version of Khrushchev's speech. The mystical aura that surrounded Stalin and the refined system of psychological and physical terror began to dissipate. A miracle happened before everyone's eyes. Things began to change because someone had dared to speak out. This was something new and very dangerous for the authorities.

Khrushchev's speech came at the very moment when much in the country was in a state of change: life in the rural areas was improving; legality began little by little to replace the years-old practice of lawlessness; and the people were beginning to recover their self-respect and to demand respect from the authorities. But the sprouts from the seeds sown by the Twentieth Congress of the CPSU were still fragile and weak and needed constant support or they risked being destroyed by forces which, despite their retreat in confusion, still possessed adequate strength. These forces had been tempered by the system of mutual support and coverup and years of experience under the terrorist dictatorship.

The movement for democracy experienced a sudden surge. It was still weak, disorganized, often amorphous, but it was growing. And there was great hope in this.

Very rapidly—evidently, on the orders of Khrushchev himself—the secret speech reached the outside world and spread. As in the Soviet Union, foreign reactions varied. Confusion reigned particularly in the most conservative, Stalinist Communist parties, such as those in the United States, Great Britain, and France. Reactions were varied in the Eastern European countries which during the war had been under fascist rule or occupation and later became Soviet satellites. At the time the ruling elite of these countries were Stalinists who, under the control of Soviet advisers, had conducted the same policy of terror as in the Soviet Union. In 1948–1952 several waves of purges had swept through Eastern Europe (as in the USSR in the 1930s), accompanied by public political trials of former Communist leaders who had confessed to accusations extracted under torture.[63] The leaders of Communist parties, particularly in China and Albania, were alarmed and insulted that Khrushchev did not forewarn them of the secret speech, putting them in a difficult position within their parties. In the Eastern European Communist parties, the ferment that had begun soon after Stalin's death intensified. Long suppressed anti-Soviet (or anti-Russian) feelings came out into the open, and dealing with them was no easy matter. Demands for changes in leadership began to be voiced.

In the Soviet Union itself, the Stalinists recovered rather quickly after the first blow and began an offensive against the Khrushchev line, insisting that the decisions of the Twentieth Congress condemning the cult of personality be reconsidered. For the Stalinist old guard, it was essential on the one hand to blunt the impact of revelations made at the congress and to minimize the extent of the accusations and, on the other, to protect themselves from any possible charges of complicity in Stalin's crimes. The united efforts of the Soviet and foreign Stalinists had their effect. The CPSU Central Committee session of June 30, 1956, adopted a resolution, "On Overcoming the Cult of Personality and Its Consequences." In this resolution, Stalin was called "an extraordinary theoretician and organizer" and given credit for his struggle against the oppositions and for assuring "the victory of socialism" in the Soviet Union, as well as for developing the Communist and national liberation movements around the world. He was accused only of abusing his power, which, as stated in the resolution, was the result of his personal defects. The resolution emphasized that although the cult of personality had slowed the progress of Soviet society, it had not been able to alter that society's fundamental nature. The policy of the CPSU was just, since it expressed the interests of the people.[64] The resolution of June 30, 1956, was in fact substituted for the decisions of the Twentieth Congress and became the principal ideological basis for post-Stalin conformism.

The new Soviet government inherited a rather difficult situation in the realm of national relations. During the war entire populations of Volga Germans, Chechens, Ingush, Karachievtsi, Crimean Tatars, Kalmyks, and others—1.5 million people—had been forcibly removed from locations they had inhabited and deported to Siberia, the Urals, Central Asia, and Kazakhstan. This was accompanied by the confiscation and outright pillaging of their property by NKVD troops. The exiles were subjected to a special regime, that is, they were restricted in their movements and the kinds of jobs they could take, not to mention education. They were subject to special controls and were regulated by special passes. The local NKVD commandant was lord and master of the unfortunates, upon whom they depended for everything, even permission to marry. Any complaint addressed to higher bodies was considered a counterrevolutionary act. An appeal to Stalin resulted at best in "brainwashing" talks with the authorities, at worst—a prison term. Escape attempts were punishable by twenty-five years of hard labor.[65]

After Stalin's death, there arose among these deported peoples, greatly decimated by starvation and an inability to adapt to the new conditions of life, a strong movement to return to their homelands and to obtain compensation from the state for the injustice they had suffered. The Chechens and Ingush began to return on their own to the Caucasus, but often with bloody tragedies. In 1954–1955 the USSR Council of Ministers issued a series of measures to ease restrictions in the special settlements. Certain categories of people were totally removed from the special registry.[66]

These palliative measures, however, could not solve the problems, which had become more and more complex with time. The deported populations demanded their return to their homelands and the restoration of all their rights, including autonomy. The authorities feared the consequences if these people withdrew from the economies of the republics and regions to which they had been sent; they also feared severe ethnic conflicts and economic difficulties in the areas from which the people had originally been deported. These were the costs of the politics of arbitrariness and violence conducted by the Soviet regime. It followed that this price had to be paid and the deported populations immediately returned to their homelands. In his secret report at the Twentieth Party Congress, Khrushchev expressed his indignation at the wartime mass deportations of the Karachai, Balkars, and Kalmyks, but did not even mention the other deported populations: the Volga Germans and the Crimean Tatars. The pre- and postwar deportations of Balts, Poles, Ukrainians, Byelorussians, and others likewise went unmentioned. Still, the mere fact that such deportations were condemned in principle from the speaker's platform of a party congress cannot be overestimated.

Nevertheless, the removal of the special restrictions on the deportees, which followed Khrushchev's condemnation, did not resolve the main problem: the peoples' desire to return to their homelands.

At that point, the victimized populations decided to take their fate into their own hands. Together the Chechens and Ingush comprised 500,000 people united by a desperate determination to return to their native lands. Thousands of Chechen and Ingush families gathered on the main railroad lines leading into Russia. They were refused tickets, admonished, and threatened. But despite all this, during 1956 25,000–30,000 Chechens and Ingush returned, unauthorized, to their homeland. And the authorities wavered. The Chechens and Ingush were included in the resolution of November 24, 1956, that restored national autonomy to certain populations.[67] The resolution also applied to the Kalmyks, Karachai, and Balkars. Their autonomy was reestablished in January 1957. The Crimean Tatars, Volga Germans, and others were left out. But they have continued their struggle to the present day (1985).

Why did Khrushchev pass over the Crimean Tatars in silence? The answer is simple: in 1954, on Khrushchev's initiative, a present had been made to the Ukrainian SSR on the occasion of the three hundredth anniversary of the reunification of Russia and the Ukraine. The present was the Crimea, which was transferred from the RSFSR and joined to the Ukrainian SSR. In his struggle for power, Khrushchev needed the support of the Ukrainian party leaders, who were categorically opposed to the return of the Crimean Tatars. They began a massive resettlement of coastal Crimea with Ukrainians. Even today, there is ample room to accommodate the Crimean Tatars in the Crimea without dislocating anyone.

Unfortunately for the Crimean Tatars, they were not as well organized or united in 1956 as the Chechens and Ingush. Undoubtedly, had they begun to return en masse to the Crimea, they would have won their demands. In November 1956, in connection with the events in Hungary and other countries of Eastern Europe, the Soviet government greatly feared complications in its own country and probably would have been forced to grant concessions to the Crimean Tatars. But this did not happen, and the Crimean Tatars missed their historical opportunity.

The populations of the Crimea and Caucusus were decimated in the course of their deportation. There are conflicting statistics in this regard. Documents of the Crimean Tatar movement indicate that in the first year and a half of deportation, 46.2 percent of the deported population—some 200,000 people—died.[68] However, it is known that on the eve of World War II the Crimean Tatars constituted one-fourth of the total population of the Crimea, which was 1,127,000 people.[69] On May 17 and 18, 1944, 194,000 Crimean Tatars were deported from the Crimea.[70] According to rough figures, close to 18 percent of these died within the first year and a half of deportation. This enormous number testifies to the policy of genocide carried out by the Soviet government.

This genocide was further confirmed by the figures on the losses in population of other deported peoples between the two countrywide census takings of 1939 and 1959. The Chechens lost 22 percent of their population, the Ingush 9 percent, the Kalmyks close to 15 percent, the Karachai 30 percent, and the Balkars 26.5 percent.[71] Data on the losses suffered by other deported peoples remain unavailable; it can be assumed, however, that the figures were not minute.

In the first years after the return of the deported populations to the Caucusus, race relations were rather strained, particularly between the Russians and the Chechen-Ingush. In August 1958 a race riot broke out in the city of Grozny which lasted three days. The pretext was a murder of jealousy committed by an Ingush against a Russian. The victim's funeral turned into a pogrom against the Chechen-Ingush people. This was one of the most serious racial clashes in the Soviet Union since World War II. The disturbances occurred amid slogans calling for the expulsion of the Chechens and Ingush and the formation of a purely Russian local government. The Russian public, including Communists, wore red ribbons so as not to be taken for Chechens. The Chechens of Grozny displayed exceptional restraint and did not respond to these provocations. The local authorities, of course, disappeared immediately. On the third day, looting began. Troops were called in. Moscow sent M. A. Yasnov, chairman of the Presidium of the Supreme Soviet of the RSFSR, and N. K. Ignatov, a CPSU Central Committee secretary, to the scene of the disturbance. General Pliev, commander of the Northern Caucusus military district, arrived to direct the suppression of the riot. In typical fashion, none of the individuals who participated in the pogrom was called to account. One year later, A. J. Yakovlev, regional secretary of the party, was transferred to work in the CPSU Central Committee apparatus as an inspector.[72]

The disturbances of 1958 gave impetus to other, less severe national conflicts in the Chechen-Ingush region, which continued to flare up into the early 1970s. One of the causes of conflict and disturbance was the problem of the Prigorodny region, an ancestral area of inhabitation by the Ingush people which after their deportation had been annexed to Northern Ossetia. Hostility from at least part of the local Russian population was also encountered by the Kalmyks after their return to their native region.[73]

## THE BLOODY AUTUMN OF 1956

The official admission of the crimes of the Stalin regime made at the Twentieth Party Congress evoked a strong reaction not only in Polish political and intellectual circles but also and primarily among Polish workers, whose economic situation left much to be desired. On June 28, 1956, the workers in the Poznan automobile factory CISPO rebelled. They were soon joined by workers from other factories. The movement began with a peaceful demonstration, but clashes developed.[74] The workers attacked the local police headquarters, seized their weapons, and distributed them among themselves. The demands of the rebels were: "Bread" and "Soviet Troops out of Poland." The soldiers in the regular units that had been summoned to disperse the workers not only refused to fire on the workers but joined them. The government declared a state of emergency, called in Ministry of Internal Affairs tank units, and suppressed the uprising. According to official Polish sources, 38 were killed and 270 wounded.

The Central Committee of the Polish United Workers party (PUWP) became the scene of a bitter struggle. The party leadership had been compelled, as was the case everywhere, to rehabilitate party and government members victimized by the purges. One of them, Komarz, was named commander of the internal security troops. Gomulka proposed a program to ease the burdens on the peasantry and to normalize relations with the Soviet Union which was supported by many peasants, workers, intellectuals, and a significant portion of the PUWP. However, a section of the Politburo called the Natolin group opposed the reforms and began to prepare for a coup, timed for the Central Committee plenum in October, which was to elect a new Politburo.

It was in this very complex and confused situation that a Soviet government delegation consisting of Khrushchev, Mikoyan, Molotov, and Kaganovich suddenly arrived to participate in the session of the PUWP Central Committee. The delegation also included Marshal Konev, commander of the Warsaw Pact troops, whose presence signaled that the Soviet leadership was prepared to use force if necessary. In fact the use of force was advised by Polish defense minister Marshal Rokossovsky, who had been sent to Poland and made a member of the PUWP's Politburo on Stalin's order after the war (he was of Polish origin). Rokossovsky met separately with the Soviet delegation. According to Khrushchev's account: "He told us that anti-Soviet, nationalistic, and reactionary forces were growing in strength, and that if it were necessary to arrest [their] growth by force of arms, he was at our disposal."[75]

The idea of putting down the rebellion in Poland with Polish arms was tempting, but after more careful consideration the Soviet leaders concluded that they probably could not rely on the Polish army. The other alternative, using Soviet troops against the traditionally anti-Russian Poles, even at a moment of acute political crisis, was in fact rather somber. Nevertheless, the Soviet leaders were prepared to use force.[76] Konev was ordered to begin moving troops toward Warsaw. Gomulka, who had been elected the new first secretary of the PUWP Central Committee, demanded that Khrushchev immediately stop the movement of Soviet troops advancing toward Warsaw and order them back to their bases.[77] At this point a shameful scene developed: Khrushchev began to lie, claiming that Gomulka had received false information about the Soviet troops' movements. Gomulka repeated his demands and warned of possible serious consequences if the Soviet troops continued to move. Khrushchev ordered the Soviet tanks to halt and wait, without returning to their bases. The Warsaw city party committee gave the order to distribute arms to the workers, who were ready to resist the Soviet troops should they enter Warsaw. But it was only after assurances from Gomulka that not only would he not conduct an anti-Soviet policy but, on the contrary, would cultivate friendship with the Soviet Union that Khrushchev and his entourage returned to Moscow and the Soviet troops to their bases.[78]

The disturbances in Poland did not develop into a general uprising for many reasons. One of the most significant was that in Stalin's time the repression of the moderate elements in Poland had not taken the form of executions and massive bloody purges of the party and state apparatus. On October 21, 1956, when Gomulka came to power, the majority of the party apparatus supported him. The most pro-Soviet elements—Zenon Novak and Marshal Rokossovsky—were removed from the Politburo. The latter soon left Poland for the Soviet Union.

Events turned out differently in Hungary, where emotions ran much higher than in Poland. Events in Hungary had been heating toward the boiling point for three and a half years. Returning to Budapest from Moscow after the Twentieth Party Congress, Rakosi said to his friends: "In a few months, Khrushchev will be the traitor and everything will be back to normal."[79]

Meanwhile, the internal political struggle in Hungary became increasingly intense. Rakosi was forced to promise an investigation into the trials of Rajk and other Communist leaders whose executions had been Rakosi's doing. At all levels of power, including the organs of state security, the most hated institution in Hungary, Rakosi's dismissal was being demanded. He was openly called a murderer. In mid-July 1956 Mikoyan arrived in Budapest to obtain Rakosi's resignation.[80] Rakosi was forced to submit and left for the Soviet Union, where he finally ended his days, cursed and forgotten by his own people and despised by the Soviet leaders as well. Rakosi's removal was followed by the arrest of former leaders of state security who had been responsible for the trials and executions. The public reburial on October 6, 1956, of the victims of the regime (Laszlo Rajk and others) turned into a powerful demonstration in which 200,000 residents of Budapest participated.[81]

Under these circumstances, the Soviet leadership once again decided to call Nagy to power. At the same time, a new ambassador was sent to Hungary: Yuri Andropov, the future head of the KGB and of the Soviet Communist party and state.

The people's hatred was directed against some members of the state security police who symbolized the most despicable aspects of the Rakosi regime. They were caught and killed. There were not, however, persecutions or murders of Communists in general, contrary to the claims of Soviet propaganda. Events in Hungary assumed the character of a genuine popular revolution, and this is precisely what terrified the Soviet leaders. Not only intellectuals but factory workers as well were drawn into the movement: the largest factories of Budapest became the backbone of the revolt. A significant portion of Hungary's youth also participated in the movement, leaving a discernible imprint on its character. The political direction came from the tail-end of the movement, the grass roots, not from its head, as in Poland.

The crucial question was the presence of Soviet troops in Eastern Europe, in effect occupying them.

Although increasingly anxious, Khrushchev withdrew calmly to Moscow, for Gomulka had managed to convince him that Poland was still in the socialist camp and that it did not even object to the Soviet troops stationed on bases in its territory. The new Soviet leadership preferred to avoid bloodshed but was prepared for it should the issue at stake become the loss of the Soviet Union's satellites, even if their status were one of declared neutrality and nonalliance. Such a precedent could lead to the disintegration of the entire socialist system. Yugoslavia's great fortune was that it did not have a common border with the Soviet Union but it did have an impressive army, which had proven its worth in World War II. And the Soviet leaders had been raised on respect for strength. Hungary was not Poland, and Imre Nagy was not Gomulka. The three-year ferment made itself felt. On October 22 demonstrations began in Budapest, demanding a new government led by Nagy. On October 23 Nagy became prime minister and issued an appeal to the people to lay down their arms. However, Soviet tanks were in Budapest and had evoked great tension in the population.

An enormous demonstration took place, mostly of students and young workers. They were joined by army deserters and ordinary passersby. The demonstrators set out for the statue of General Bem, hero of the revolution of 1848. A crowd of 200,000 gathered in front of the Parliament building. The statue of Stalin was toppled. Armed detachments formed, calling themselves freedom fighters; they numbered about 20,000.[82] Among them were former political prisoners liberated by the population. They occupied various sections of the capital, established a central command with Pal Maleter as its chief, and proclaimed themselves the National Guard.

Workers councils—the seeds of the new regime—were forming in enterprises in the Hungarian capital. They presented their own social and political demands, one of which aroused the fury of the Soviet leadership: the removal of Soviet troops from Budapest and from all Hungarian territory. The second event that frightened the Soviet government was the reestablishment of the Hungarian Social Democratic party, followed by the formation of a multiparty government.

Although Nagy had been made prime minister, the new, predominantly Stalinist party leadership, with Gero at its head, attempted to isolate him and in this way aggravated the situation all the more.

On October 24, Mikoyan and Suslov arrived in Budapest. They recommended that first secretary Gero be immediately replaced by Janos Kadar, who had recently been freed from prison. Meanwhile, an armed clash with Soviet troops took place at the Parliament building on October 25. Nagy announced his intention to insist on the withdrawal of Soviet troops and ordered a cease-fire.[83] But clashes continued. The insurgent population demanded the removal of Soviet troops and the formation of a new government of national unity in which other parties would be represented.

On October 26, after Kadar had been named first secretary of the Central Committee and Gero had resigned, Mikoyan and Suslov returned to Moscow. They went to the airport aboard a tank after lengthy and detailed discussions with the new leadership. One wonders if they really believed that reconciliation was possible in Hungary on the same basis that had been attained in Poland five days earlier: the preservation of Hungary as an ally and member of the Warsaw Pact; the redefinition of Soviet–Hungarian commercial agreements in Hungary's favor; the liberalization of the regime, taking into account the specific characteristics of Hungarian life; and the withdrawal of Soviet troops as soon as the situation stabilized.[84] In all probability, they had their doubts.

On October 28, while fighting continued in Budapest, the Hungarian government ordered a cease-fire and the return of armed detachments to their quarters to await instructions. In his radio address, Imre Nagy announced that the Hungarian and Soviet governments had come to an agreement concerning the immediate withdrawal of Soviet troops from Budapest and the inclusion of armed detachments of Hungarian workers and youth in the regular Hungarian army.[85] The announcement of the withdrawal of

Soviet troops was greeted with great delight and regarded as the end of Soviet occupation.

On October 30 the government abolished the system of obligatory delivery of agricultural products. The provinces supported the capital. The workers decided to stop working until the end of the fighting in Budapest and the withdrawal of Soviet troops. A delegation from the workers council of the industrial region of Miklos presented a demand to Imre Nagy that Soviet troops be removed from Hungary by the end of the year.[86]

The report from Mikoyan and Suslov to the Presidium of the CPSU Central Committee regarding the situation in Hungary appeared to indicate, as evidenced by an editorial in *Pravda* on October 28, that the Soviets had accepted the program for democratization, provided that the program preserved Communist party rule and that Hungary remain in the Warsaw Pact alliance.[87] In reality, this article was merely camouflage, as was the order for Soviet troops to leave Budapest. The Soviet government sought to gain time in order to prepare a reprisal not only in the name of the members of the Warsaw Pact but in that of Yugoslavia and China as well. The Soviet interventionist forces in Hungary were to represent the entire socialist camp, so that the responsibility would be shared by all.

Soviet troops were removed from Budapest but concentrated nearby, at the airfield outside the city.[88] The Soviet ambassador, Andropov, continuously informed the Kremlin of the developing situation.

Khrushchev states in his memoirs that on October 30, while Mikoyan and Suslov were in Budapest, the Presidium of the CPSU Central Committee unanimously adopted a resolution for an armed suppression of the Hungarian revolution—stated, of course, in the customary Stalinist terminology. It would be inexcusable, the resolution stated, for the Soviet Union to remain neutral and "not to help the working class of Hungary in its struggle against the counterrevolution."[89] On the same day, a declaration was adopted on the equality of all Communist parties: in reality, this was just more camouflage. Khrushchev states plainly that the Soviet leaders feared the effect of the Hungarian events on other Eastern European countries.[90]

At the request of the Presidium of the CPSU Central Committee, a Chinese delegation led by Liu Shao-chi arrived in Moscow for an advisory conference. At first, according to Khrushchev, Liu declared that the Soviet troops should withdraw from Hungary and allow the Hungarian working class to "put down the counterrevolution by itself." After reluctantly consenting, however, Khrushchev, who was unsatisfied with the Chinese response, repeatedly proposed that the question of intervention be discussed further. After consulting by phone with Mao, Liu confirmed the Chinese position. Since this completely contradicted the decision of the Presidium to intervene, which had in effect already been accepted by the CPSU Central Committee, Khrushchev reported the Chinese response and insisted on the immediate commencement of military operations. Marshal Konev, who had been summoned to the Presidium session, declared that his troops needed three days to put down the "counterrevolution" in Hungary. He was ordered to get his troops prepared for action.[91] This order was given behind the back of Liu, who was leaving that day for Peking, fully convinced that there would be no Soviet intervention. It was decided to inform Liu at the moment of his departure from Vnukovo airport. In order to make a bigger impression on Liu, the Presidium showed up at Vnukovo in full strength. After more hypocritical discussions about "the well-being of the Hungarian working class," Liu finally gave in: Chinese support was assured.[92]

Subsequently, Khrushchev, Malenkov, and Molotov set out in succession for Warsaw and Budapest, where they readily received consent for intervention. The last stage of their journey was Yugoslavia. They had already obtained consent to suppress the revolution in Hungary from the other socialist countries. The Soviet delegates anticipated serious resistance from Tito, but Khrushchev reports, "We were pleasantly surprised. . . . Tito said we were absolutely right and that we should send our soldiers into action as quickly as possible. . . . We had been ready for resistance, but instead we received his wholehearted support. I would even say he went further than we did in urging a speedy and decisive resolution of the problem."[93]

Thus the fate of the Hungarian revolution was sealed. On November 1 Soviet troops began a massive invasion of Hungary. In response to the protests of Imre Nagy, Andropov declared that the Soviet divisions were only replacing troops already stationed in Hungary. Three thousand Soviet tanks crossed the Hungarian border from the Transcarpathian Ukraine and Romania. Summoned once again by Nagy, the Soviet ambassador was warned that Hungary, as a sign of protest against the violation of the Warsaw Pact (the entry of troops requires the consent of the government concerned), was withdrawing from the alliance. That same night, the Hungarian government announced Hungary's withdrawal from the Warsaw Pact, declared itself neutral, and appealed to the United Nations to oppose the Soviet invasion.

None of this worried the Soviets. The Anglo-French-Israeli invasion of Egypt had distracted world attention from the events in Hungary. The U.S. government had condemned the actions of England, France and Israel. The division in the Western camp was thus obvious. There was nothing to indicate that the Western powers would come to the aid of Hungary. The international situation was extremely favorable for Soviet intervention. Soviet propaganda lumped together the war in the Middle East and the events in Hungary, presenting them as one and the same imperialist plot against the "camp of peace and democracy." This explanation, together with the allegations that Communists were being killed in Hungary and that a counterrevolutionary rebellion aimed at restoring capitalism was underway there, had its effect on the Soviet population. They greeted the suppression of the revolution in Hungary either with indifference or with relief that the unpleasantness, thank God, was over.

By the evening of November 1 Soviet troops had occupied all Hungarian airports. The next day Andropov, camouflaging the military preparations, proposed that the Hungarian government name two delegations, one political and one military, to discuss the withdrawal of Soviet troops from Hungary as well as the political problems relating to the Warsaw Pact.[94] The negotiations were to begin the next day. The Hungarian government, not wanting complications, accepted. Meanwhile, Soviet troops continued to be deployed.

At the same time, the Presidium of the CPSU Central Committee began to prepare a new Hungarian government that would replace Nagy's "counterrevolutionary" regime. Janos Kadar, first secretary of the Hungarian Communist party, agreed to be the future prime minister. A Soviet military plane delivered him to Uzhgorod, where the new government was created on November 3. Not until two years later was it known that the Kadar government had been formed on the territory of the USSR. Officially its formation was announced at dawn on November 4, as Soviet tanks burst into the Hungarian capital.[95]

The previous evening a coalition government headed by Imre Nagy had been formed in Budapest. It included representatives of the Communist party, the small landholders party, the Social Democrats, and the Petofi party. An independent, General Pal Maleter, had become a defense minister. All the parties agreed that Hungary should join no military alliances whatsoever and would remain a neutral country.

Meanwhile in Budapest on November 1, official negotiations between the Soviet and Hungarian delegations began. The operation to mislead Nagy's government had been prepared in detail. The Soviet delegation headed by General Malinin pretended to haggle over the date for the withdrawal of Soviet troops. (The Hungarians proposed December 15, 1956, while the Soviets insisted on January 15, 1957.) A continuation of the negotiations was set for 10 PM. Meanwhile, the Soviets announced to the United Nations Security Council, which was to convene at 9 AM, that negotiations on troop withdrawal were already in progress between Hungary and the Soviet Union. The Security Council session was postponed. As soon as it reconvened, the Soviet Union vetoed a resolution on Soviet intervention in Hungary. (Later on, after numerous resolutions were adopted in the General Assembly calling on the Soviet Union to withdraw its troops immediately from Hungary, the General Assembly strongly condemned the Soviet Union for suppressing the rights of the Hungarians with military force. On December 12 fifty-five nations voted for this resolution, including many countries of Asia and Africa.[96])

By the evening of November 3 eleven Soviet divisions were already on Hungarian soil. The Hungarian military delegation led by Maleter, which arrived at Soviet headquarters in the evening to continue the negotiations, was treacherously arrested by General Serov, head of the KGB. It was only when Nagy was unable to make telephone contact with his military delegation that he realized that the Soviet government had deceived him, but he still refused to give the order to open fire.[97]

On November 4 at 5 AM Soviet artillery began to bombard the Hungarian capital. Half an hour later, Nagy informed the population over the radio.

It was an unequal battle. The Soviet armed forces were superior to those of the Hungarian revolution in every respect—manpower, weaponry, and military tactics. Nevertheless, the Hungarians fought heroically. For three days, Soviet troops hammered at the capital. Armed resistance in the provinces lasted until November 14. No one came to Hungary's aid. The Hungarian revolution was crushed by the treads of Soviet tanks and the indifference of the Western nations.

After suppressing the revolution, the Soviet military administration, aided by the state security agencies, launched a repression of Hungarian citizens: massive arrests and deportations to the Soviet Union began.

Imre Nagy and his closest collaborators found refuge in the Yugoslavian embassy. Tito, who had given his consent to the destruction of the Hungarian revolution, did not want to be tainted by association with the murder of legitimate Hungarian leaders. After two weeks of protracted negotiations, the new prime minister, Kadar, gave a written guarantee that Nagy and his comrades would not be persecuted for their actions and declared that they could leave the Yugoslavian embassy and return home with their families. But the bus that was transporting Nagy in the company of two Yugoslav diplomats was intercepted by Soviet officers, who arrested Nagy and then transported him to Romania. The Soviet government paid no attention to Yugoslav protests. Victors trouble themselves about neither the vanquished, nor the fellow travelers, and Tito was a fellow traveler. Later Imre Nagy, who refused to recant, was convicted in a secret session and shot. The news was announced on June 16, 1958.[98] The same fate befell General Pal Maleter.

In his memoirs written fifteen years after the events in Hungary, Khrushchev expressed not the slightest regret. Evidently, it never occurred to him that both he and the Soviet government had behaved despicably and treacherously. Such a notion simply did not exist for a consistent Leninist.

## ATTEMPTS AT IMPROVING THE SOVIET SYSTEM

At first, the new leadership attempted to reorganize the economy on a more stable and realistic basis, to modernize it and introduce more flexible management. The September 1953 plenum of the CPSU Central Committee opened with the question of agriculture.

The economic inefficiency of the kolkhoz system was quite obvious, but to speak of it, even in a whisper, was equivalent to admitting that the very idea of building socialism in the Soviet Union was absurd. Instead, the new leadership chose to try easing the pressure on the rural population: the collective farmers and the inhabitants of the agrarian and semi-agrarian towns and settlements. In 1953–54, quotas were reduced for compulsory deliveries of animal products to the state by collective farmers and by blue collar and white collar workers who were allowed to raise livestock. Permanent mechanics were assigned to the MTSs (machine and tractor stations), and the practice of planting crops on orders "from above" was ended: now the districts (though not the collective farmers themselves) decided what to plant.

Simultaneously, the policy of strengthening and consolidating the collective farms into larger units went on at a fairly steady pace. From 1950 to 1955 the number of collective farms decreased from 123,700 to 87,500; by the end of the "Khrushchev era," in 1964, the number had fallen further to 37,600. The collective farms were gradually being transformed into state farms, and the peasant collective farmers into wage workers. This was evident from the growing number of state farms, which increased from 4,857 in 1953 to 10,078 in 1964, that is, more than doubled.[99] All the newly created farms in the "virgin lands" were sovkhozes.

Other measures were adopted. The practice of estimating the size of the grain harvest and appraising it in terms of total output was abolished, along with the obligatory use of the grass rotation system.[100]

In 1954–55 agricultural investments totaled 34.4 billion rubles, 38 percent more than for the entire Fourth Five-Year Plan.[101] Agricultural "specialists," comfortably ensconced in various offices, were sent out into the fields. Agricultural equipment, tractors, combines, and motor vehicles were also sent to the countryside in significant numbers.

In 1954–55 virgin and fallow lands began to be opened up in Kazakhstan,

Siberia, and the Urals.[102] The first to open up the virgin lands were the prisoners of concentration camps, followed by thousands of young people sent by the Komsomol.

By the middle of 1956, 33 million hectares had been cleared and planted.[103] But poor management reigned everywhere, and undercut the effectiveness of this new beginning. Grain silos were not built in time; the grain rotted in the rain or was blown away by the wind. Every year during the harvest machinery and mechanics had to be sent from other parts of the country, where the harvesting had already been completed, to the virgin lands in Kazakhstan. Naturally, all of this was frightfully expensive, and the results did not warrant the expenditure and effect. As always, there were not enough accommodations for people.

A great deal depended on climatic conditions as well as the organization of production. These new regions could have served as a "reserve bread basket" only if there were a stable grain supply in general. Under a rational economic system, the varied climates in different parts of the country would have made it possible to avoid major fluctuations in the grain supply, even in years of poor harvest. However, every failure, such as the experiments with maize, with the virgin lands, and with the MTSs, compelled the leadership to return to its old ways.

The enthusiasm for the virgin lands led to the mobilization of all the country's resources and technology. For a while the traditional grain-producing regions found themselves in the position of outcasts, while the country fell into dependence on the harvests from the virgin lands. Those harvests depended in turn on the caprices of the weather and were hurt badly by soil erosion, which rendered millions of hectares of plowed land useless. Erosion and bad weather greatly reduced the virgin lands harvest several times in the 1950s and 1960s. The area was hit by particularly bad sandstorms in 1963 and again in 1965.

Nonetheless, ultimately the opening up of the virgin lands was not a vain endeavor as the table below shows;[104] even now they serve as one of the country's sources of grain.

### Cereal Production in the Virgin and Fallow Lands, 1954–1964
#### (millions of tons)

| Year | Total USSR Production | Total Fallow and Virgin Land Production | Total Kazakhstan Production |
|------|-----------------------|-----------------------------------------|-----------------------------|
| 1954 | 85.5                  | 37.2                                    | 7.6                         |
| 1955 | 103.7                 | 37.5                                    | 4.7                         |
| 1956 | 125.0                 | 63.2                                    | 23.8                        |

| Year | Total USSR Production | Total Fallow and Virgin Land Production | Total Kazakhstan Production |
|---|---|---|---|
| 1957 | 102.6 | 63.5 | 10.5 |
| 1958 | 134.7 | 38.4 | 21.9 |
| 1959 | 119.5 | 58.5 | 14.3 |
| 1960 | 125.5 | 58.7 | 12.9 |
| 1961 | 130.8 | 50.6 | 10.3 |
| 1962 | 140.2 | 55.8 | 10.1 |
| 1963 | 107.5 | 37.9 | — |
| 1964 | 152.1 | 66.4 | — |

There were two major defects in the virgin lands project in Kazakhstan, however. First, the crop yield there was lower than elsewhere; second, the production cost of grain there from 1954 to 1964 was 20 percent higher than in the Soviet Union as a whole.[105]

Beginning in 1955 the collective farms were supposed to plan agricultural work jointly with the MTSs.[106] This positive initiative was never carried out. The collective farms, state farms, and MTSs were dominated by a monstrous party-state apparatus in the form of the regional party committees and district soviet executive committees, which themselves were dominated by higher bureaucratic bodies. This apparatus interfered endlessly, dictating decisions and demanding reports, changes, and corrections. It punished and encouraged, reported and released directives, intruded in the affairs of the collective farms, and significantly reduced the positive effect of the new system. Khrushchev himself provided the example. He demanded that maize, the "queen of crops," be planted everywhere,[107] thus disrupting the new system for agricultural planning and management before it had even been fully established. "Maize and only maize is capable of solving the problem of increasing the production of meat, milk, and other dairy products," Khrushchev declared.[108] Once again, the orders had begun to come "from above." In 1955 the bad harvest was not compensated for either by the virgin lands or by maize. Khrushchev's position as first secretary of the CPSU Central Committee was badly shaken. His opponents in the Presidium, Molotov, Kaganovich, and Malenkov, considered the opening up of the lands to be a risky adventure and the widespread planting of maize a caprice, and they openly criticized Khrushchev at sessions of the Central Committee Presidium. His savior was a good harvest in the virgin lands in 1956, which provided almost exactly half the country's total harvest: 63.2 million out of 125 million tons.[109]

In May 1957, encouraged by this success, Khrushchev insisted on catching up with the United States in the production of meat, butter, and milk within three to five years. In other words, by 1960–1962, the production of meat was to be increased 3.2 times.[110]

The fact that Khrushchev's proposal was divorced from reality was evident, particularly in the area of meat production. In 1956 the United States produced 16 million tons, the USSR 7.5 million.[111] But it wasn't simply a matter of this wide lead; the prerequisites for Khrushchev's great leap forward did not exist in the Soviet Union. Cattle raising depends above all on the production of grain for feed, and that was clearly insufficient.[112] Khrushchev's new plan required significant investments, but they were not available. Finally, was it really necessary to surpass the United States in levels of production and consumption? Slogans of this sort had stimulated a certain enthusiasm in the 1930s ("catch up with and surpass America"), for hardly anyone understood what the American economy was, how it worked, or its tremendous productive capacity. Those who did understand either were eliminated or kept their mouths shut. The slogan was designed to galvanize the enthusiasm of the masses. Khrushchev himself proposed the new goal in complete earnestness, but his idea of America did not correspond to reality.

Khrushchev's impatience to obtain immediate results led him to an adventuristic policy that caused a veritable chain reaction: local leaders wishing to get into the good graces of the first secretary, to earn rewards or advancement, created an outward appearance of success in precisely those areas where Khrushchev wanted them. This system, however, had come into being under Stalin. The policy of rapid industrialization had given rise to Stakhanovism, which, in the end, degenerated into pure showmanship (pokazukha) and rivalry among the directors of various enterprises to have the best organization on record. The same was true in agriculture. Each region had its own model collective farm or state farm, equipped with the best machinery and specialists, that served as the showcase for the region.

A sharp rise in livestock production could not be assured for a variety of economic, technical, and technological reasons. During the first year of "competition" with the American meat and dairy industry, 1958, the production of meat was increased by only 301,000 tons; two years later, in 1960, by another 1,007,000 tons.[113]

Once again, as in the Stalin era, bluffing, lying, and deception came into their own. The initiator this time was the party committee of the Ryazan Region, which in 1959 pledged to increase its production of meat four to five times. The risky nature of this unrealistic pledge was beyond all doubt. Nonetheless, Khrushchev personally supported the pledge of the Ryazan

Region and its first party secretary A. M. Larionov, producing a chain reaction in the other regions, where the pledges began to climb higher and higher. It was impossible to provide the amount of meat that had been promised, despite the fact that blue and white collar workers and collective farmers were forced to sell their personal cattle. Often they were paid, not with money, but with promissory notes. The region's businesses and even schools were forced to pay a kind of tax in meat. Special "procurement" agents were sent to buy meat in other regions. All the livestock in the region were slaughtered. But at the Central Committee plenum in December 1959, Larionov was able to report that the production of meat in his region had multiplied four times and that the state had bought 100,000 tons of meat from him;[114] consequently, he assumed a new obligation to sell the state 180,000–200,000 tons of meat in 1960. An enthusiastic Khrushchev, who badly needed a success like this one, made Larionov a Hero of Socialist Labor. Finally, however, rumors of the total ruin of agriculture in Ryazan reached Moscow. But only at the end of 1960 did a special commission of the CPSU Central Committee conclude its investigation with the distressing report that the Ryazan miracle was a sham.[115] Larionov was "advised" to withdraw from the scene, and he shot himself.

Thus ended Soviet–American competition in the realm of meat and dairy production. In 1964 meat production in the Soviet Union reached only 8.3 million tons.[116]

Khrushchev's maize program did not even stand a chance. Introduced in regions of the country where climatic conditions were unfavorable, it ended, as was to be expected, in fiasco.

Other irrational decisions affected agriculture, for example, the elimination of millions of hectares of fallow land, which ultimately hurt grain production substantially. Instead of the anticipated steady progress, agriculture essentially marked time. After a significant increase in the harvest in 1958 (1,110 kilograms per hectare in 1959 as opposed to 790 kilograms in 1950), productivity dropped to 1,090 in 1960, 1961, and 1962, then to 830 in 1963. Only in 1964 did it begin to increase, reaching 1,140 kilograms.[117]

Khrushchev soon began a search for scapegoats. He changed agricultural ministers one after the other, limited their responsibilities, moved agrobiological research institutes into the countryside, and so on. But an indisputable reality remained. Agriculture refused to budge on orders from above.

Khrushchev's intention to change the situation fundamentally led to the liquidation of the MTSs in February of 1958. Their equipment was sold to the enlarged, amalgamated collective farms.[118] In less than a year this operation too was terminated. Many of the collective farms were in a difficult financial state, for the machines they were forced to buy had been sold to them at the current wholesale prices, which considerably exceeded what the MTSs originally paid for them.[119] In addition, many of the MTS workers did not wish to enter the collective farms, preferring instead to seek work at government enterprises. Agriculture lost half its mechanics. Manufacturers of agricultural machinery, deprived of the steady internal market of the MTSs, found themselves with excess production and were forced to cut back. The use of machinery by the collective farms deteriorated sharply as a result of the lack of qualified maintenance.[120] In 1961 the debts of the collective farms to the banks for agricultural machinery reached more than 2 billion rubles.

In the years that followed, the state attempted to improve the grave situation of the collective farms with agricultural machinery and equipment, motor vehicles, spare parts, and gasoline and to ensure timely maintenance of the machinery by creating a special organization, the Selkhoztekhnika, and service stations. These efforts did not bring about any substantive change in the situation.

At first, after the improvements of 1953, and particularly after the agricultural reforms of 1954–55, the situation of the collective farmers, workers, and employees who had their own private plots improved significantly. In 1964 approximately 7 million hectares were in private use, compared with 482.7 million hectares of collective farm land and 571.1 million hectares of state farm and government land.[121] But the productivity of the private plots was quite high. Permission to own a cow and a certain number of domestic animals and poultry was not only materially beneficial to individual owners, kolkhozniks, and those living in small cities and towns; it also improved food supplies in the large industrial centers. From 1959 to 1965 (all figures being given as of January 1 each year), privately owned cattle constituted an average of 42–55 percent of the total number in the USSR; privately owned hogs, 27–31 percent; and privately owned sheep, 20–22 percent.[122] From this it is clear what an important role individual farming played in the production of meat in the Soviet Union.

The country's agricultural population had scarcely begun to get on its feet when their privileges were abruptly revoked. In 1959 city dwellers lost the right to own cows; they were forced to sell them to collective and state farms. The sale and stocking up of fodder for private plots was restricted. A campaign was launched against "parasites" in the collective farms and "speculators" at the kolkhoz's markets. There was an attempt to convince the population that all the misunderstandings and difficulties with food sprang from the negligence of collective farmers and the machinations of speculators at the markets. Here again the economic methods of the Stalin era were revived.

Khrushchev and the other "collective leaders" were often drawn to the methods of the past. The Soviet leaders refused to admit—either openly or to themselves—that all the failures of the economy were tied to the nature of the Soviet regime and were the inevitable concomitants of the Soviet social system; further, they were organic components of the system. The Soviet leaders preferred to find victims to blame for the failures and to retract many of the useful reforms introduced in the first years after Stalin's death. Of the 22 million privately owned cows in the Soviet Union in 1958, no more than 10 million remained at the end of 1962.[123] As for the collective farms which had acquired the cows, they were unable to provide them with fodder.

In 1963, a bad harvest year, it became clear that the government had not managed to accumulate the reserves of grain required in the event of natural calamity. There were bread shortages in many parts of the country. Once again, as in the 1930s and in 1947, long lines formed and bread sales were rationed. The southern parts of the country suffered especially, areas such as the Northern Caucasus and southern Ukraine.

The government began massive purchases of grain from abroad at the expense of the available gold reserve. More than 13 million tons of grain were bought. Later Khrushchev was reproached for this; whereas in Stalin's time the people would simply have been left to swell up and die of hunger, in Khrushchev's it was decided to exchange gold for bread. This illustrates the tremendous qualitative difference between these two periods in Soviet history.

Khrushchev's last desperate attempt to find a way out of the agricultural impasse was connected with the drought and the bad harvest of 1963. His hopes for the extensive development of agriculture through the use of the new lands, particularly in Kazakhstan and Siberia, had not been justified.

The entire agricultural system had to be transformed. Even for a country as large as the Soviet Union, agriculture had to be intensive. The example of the United States, where 3.5 percent of the population produces enough not only to feed the country but to export huge quantities of food, is convincing enough. Khrushchev wanted to duplicate the American experience, but he did so mechanically, without taking into account the differences in economic, political, and social systems of the two countries.

The land needed fertilizing, rest, and renewal. These elementary principles that every Russian peasant knew from birth were rather difficult to put into practice in a state where decisions were based on the demands of the moment, on political expediency, and without regard to the consequences. At the end of his ten years of rule Khrushchev understood the necessity for large investments and fertilization of the land. As hastily as he made his other decisions, Khrushchev in 1963 proposed a new, absolutely unrealistic program to apply the use of chemicals to farming. "Chemicalization" it was called.[124] The program envisaged increasing the production of mineral fertilizers to 80 million tons of mineral fertilizer by 1970, and to 150–170 million tons by 1980. The fantastic nature of this plan is evident from the following figures: in 1963, the USSR produced less than 20 million tons of chemical fertilizer; in 1970, 53.4 million tons; in 1977, 96.8 million tons.[125]

The results of the "shake-up" of agriculture in the post-Stalin years were extremely discouraging. In the course of the seven-year plan (1959–1965), gross output was supposed to increase 70 percent: in fact it increased only 10 percent. In the period of 1960–1964, the average harvest yield grew by an average of only 0.8 percent. The rate of growth of the cattle herd declined 50 percent in comparison to the preceding five years. The yield of milk averaged only 370 kilograms a year per cow. The collective farms were heavily in debt. Such was the picture painted by Brezhnev, the new head of the party, in March 1965.[126]

This was merely one more confirmation that the Soviet economy rests on an unsound basis, that no semi-reforms, reorganizations, decrees, or resolutions will correct it. As long as the economy depends on political decisions that change on one pretext or another, there is no hope for the country to escape its economic impasse.

This is also demonstrated by the innumerable fruitless attempts to improve the structure of the state apparatus by endowing the ministers, main directorates, and enterprise managers with new rights or, on the contrary, limiting these rights, or by dividing the planning organs and creating new ones, and the like. There were a great many such "reforms" in the Khrushchev era, but they achieved no real improvements in the economy. The quicksands of Soviet bureaucracy engulfed everything.

In February 1956 the Twentieth Party Congress approved the Sixth Five-Year Plan. By December of the same year, it was clear that the plan would not work. A temporary transitional plan for one or two years was hastily formulated, followed by a new plan—this time a seven-year plan—for the period 1959–1965. This leapfrogging of plans was due in part to the intensified power struggle that led in 1957 to the complete removal of Malenkov, Molotov, and Kaganovich, along with two key figures in economic planning, Pervukhin and Saburov. At that point it was very easy to blame all errors in planning on the "opposition" and to require a longer period (seven years instead of five) to correct the mistakes they had purportedly made.

Khrushchev wanted the firm support of the local authorities. His personal experience in the Ukraine prompted him to give initiative to local officials and directors to solve local and regional problems. As a result, the ministry of the petroleum industry in Azerbaijan, the ministry of nonferrous metals in Kazakhstan, and a number of other such specialized ministries were formed in the Ukraine. [127]

Toward the end of 1956 the clashes between Khrushchev and the majority of the Central Committee Presidium became sharper. Although the pretext was disagreement over the economic management of the country, the real basis of the clashes were the recent events in Hungary, where the workers councils seemed to be the embryo of a new power. For the Stalinist old guard, the policy of decentralization and relative autonomy seemed to be a reverberation of events in Hungary.

The CPSU Central Committee session of December 1956 criticized the weak control exercised by the central ministries over the ministries of the republics and individual enterprises. Although the plenum recognized the need to broaden the rights of republics in industry, it decided at the same time that the work of the central ministries in regions where particular branches of the national economy were located should be strengthened. [128] Khrushchev, however, soon took his revenge: at the Central Committee plenum of February 1957 a resolution was adopted in favor of an industrial leadership based on the territorial principle and organized by region. [129]

In May 1957 a law was passed to create regional economic councils (*sovnarkhozy*), which were required to manage the economy of their respective regions and to develop local resources and industries as had been done by the *sovnarkhozy* of the 1920s. [130] A total of 105 *sovnarkhozy* were created, of which 70 were in the RSFSR, 9 in Kazakhstan, 11 in the Ukraine, and 4 in Uzbekistan. Each of the remaining republics was organized as a single *sovnarkhoz* directed by the chairman of the given republic's council of ministers. Now Gosplan had to answer only for general planning and plan coordination of the plans, and for allocation of principal resources among the republics. The State Economic Commission was abolished, but the central ministries that managed the armament industries retained all their powers.

The organization of the *sovnarkhozy* encountered blatant disapproval from the bureaucrats in the capital, who were accustomed not only to power but also to the advantages of living in Moscow. Many were forced to leave comfortable positions they had held for a long time and move to the provinces. At first the local bureaucrats supported the creation of the *sovnarkhozy* although they surmised that they could make do without the "bosses" sent from Moscow. Khrushchev's prestige was strongly shaken at the center, but thereby improved in the provinces. This temporary shift in the balance of forces was a decisive factor in the consolidation of his power.

The differences of opinion that divided the top men in power touched on a number of important problems. Khrushchev's adversaries argued that the leadership should maintain total control over and coordination of the work of the ministries. They were also at variance with him on the solution to the constant difficulties involving food and on a number of foreign policy issues.

The creation of the *sovnarkhozy*, which affected the interests of the powerful Moscow bureaucracy, stimulated the formation of a wide opposition to Khrushchev in the party leadership. This opposition arose immediately after Malenkov's resignation from his post as chairman of the Council of Ministers and especially after the Twentieth Party Congress. The events of the summer and fall of 1956 in Eastern Europe fortified the ranks of the opposition, which began to charge Khrushchev with adventurism. The signal for the offensive against Khrushchev was his speech at a meeting in Leningrad in May 1957, in which he advanced his fantastic plan to overtake and surpass America in the production of meat, milk, and wool.

At the Central Committee plenum of June 1957 Khrushchev clashed with an organized opposition. The overwhelming majority of the Presidium was opposed to his policy. Molotov, Malenkov, Kaganovich, Pervukhin, and Saburov opposed him openly. They were joined by Shepilov, a secretary of the Central Committee. Bulganin and Voroshilov also voted with the opposition for Khrushchev's removal from the post of first secretary. The opposition won seven to four.

Khrushchev, however, decided to do battle. With the help of Kapitonov, a devoted supporter in the party apparatus who was later made a secretary of the Central Committee, Defense Minister Marshal Zhukov, and KGB head Ivan Serov, members of the CPSU Central Committee were hastily flown into Moscow from the provinces by military aircraft. They demanded that a Central Committee session be convened. A week of discussion (June 22–29, 1957) brought victory to Khrushchev. His principal adversaries— Malenkov, Molotov, and Kaganovich, as well as Shepilov—were stripped of their posts for constituting an "antiparty opposition."[131]

As usually happens in history, the victor made haste to rid himself of his most powerful ally, who in this case was Marshal Zhukov. As a reward for his part in crushing the "antiparty opposition," Zhukov was made a full member of the Presidium, but his popularity with the population, who believed he had saved Russia from the Germans, made Khrushchev extremely uneasy. He could not forget that during the skirmishes at the plenum of the CPSU Central Committee, in response to Malenkov's angry retort: "Perhaps you intend to move your tanks against us?" Zhukov answered with assurance: "The tanks will move only at my order." These were extremely thoughtless words from the defender of Moscow and the conqueror of Berlin. If he had been more sophisticated politically he would have said: "The tanks will move only on the order of the Central Committee." Thus, Zhukov himself provided the pretext for the later accusation of "Bonapartism." However, if he had not uttered those ill-fated words, another pretext would have been found. Many of the marshals envied Zhukov's glory, and Khrushchev made use of this envy. One cartoon published in a Western European newspaper hastened the denouement. It showed Khrushchev marching ahead, followed at a short distance by a very confident-looking Zhukov. Under it was the caption: "Turn around, Nikita, look who's behind you."

Nikita did turn around. He knew that Zhukov had not the slightest wish to become dictator, but he could not tolerate the marshal's popularity, which was eclipsing his own. As long as Zhukov and Khrushchev were harnessed together, the possibility of reminding the people of Khrushchev's service during the war was closed. It was no accident that several years later the first volume of *The History of the Great Patriotic War Against Hitlerite Germany, 1941–45*, presented Zhukov in a negative light, as the chief of the General Staff who had failed to take timely measures to forestall Germany's "surprise" attack. In all the succeeding volumes, Zhukov's military talents were never once given their due.

In October 1957, while Zhukov was on a trip abroad, Khrushchev convened the Presidium of the Central Committee to discuss the Bonapartist danger Zhukov represented. In response to the doubts of those who proposed to wait for his return to Moscow, Khrushchev answered cynically: "Seven do not wait for one." Zhukov was not only removed from the Central Committee; he also lost his post as minister of defense and was retired.[132]

The results of Khrushchev's struggle for the position of Leader soon became apparent. In March 1958 Bulganin was relieved of his duties as chairman of the Council of Ministers of the USSR. He was replaced by Khrushchev himself, who concentrated in his own hands—just as Stalin had, and for a short time Malenkov as well—the two key posts in the state: party leader and prime minister.

For the first time in the history of the Soviet Union the removal of leaders from top party posts was not followed by their arrest. This was something new in Soviet life and a sign of the stabilization of the uppermost bureaucracy and its resolve not to permit a revival of the practices of the Stalin era, while at the same time retaining the succession of power.

In the final analysis, the traditional gravitational pull of the center was swift to be felt. The regional *sovnarkhozy* were preoccupied mainly with local industries instead of directing the overall development of the region. Very rapidly—already in 1959—a process similar to the amalgamation of the collective and state farms was set in motion: the "weaker" *sovnarkhozy* began to be merged with the more powerful ones. The previous economic hierarchy was quickly restored, but in a form even more misshapen than before.

During the period 1953–1964, power supply sources in the Soviet Union were developed considerably. Big new hydroelectric plants were erected at Kuibyshev (1958), Stalingrad (1960), and Bratsk (1961–1964). New sources of energy rapidly began to be utilized, including Markovo oil in Siberia (1962) and oil and natural gas in the Tyumen Region (1963). New industries were created such as those for natural gas and diamonds. Electric power production grew from 150.6 billion kilowatts in 1954[133] to 507.7 billion in 1965.[134] In the same period the extraction of oil increased from 52.7 million tons[135] to 347.3 million;[136] the smelting of steel from 41.4 million tons[137] to 91 million;[138] and coal production from 347.1 million tons[139] to 577.7 million.[140]

One of the most serious problems of the 1950s and 1960s was how to restructure industrial production in accordance with the demands of the new technical revolution. In one of his speeches, the prominent scientist Academician Petr Kapitsa compared Soviet industry to an ichthyosaur, a prehistoric beast with a long enormous body and a tiny head; that is, a huge industrial apparatus in which science played an extremely insignificant role.

In Stalin's time the scientific and technical achievements of the capitalist world had been furiously refuted and trivialized and declared to be ideological diversions and idealism. Now the Soviet leadership suddenly recognized such achievements as cybernetics. In keeping with these changed attitudes and policies, enormous sums were allocated to science. New research institutions were created. Basic scientific research, which had become almost nonexistent, was revived and expanded. The needs of the state, always tied to the strengthening of its military capacity, required more highly refined technology, more sophisticated weapons.

Since the Soviet state remained and remains the sole employer, the sole unchecked master of revenue and expenditure, the most promising scientific branches were given huge subsidies. That is what made possible, for example, the breakthroughs of Soviet science and technology in missile production, which in turn led to dramatic Soviet achievements in space, the launching of Sputnik, the first earth satellite in 1957, and Yuri Gagarin's space flight on April 18, 1961.

But the lopsided development of Soviet industry led to a chronic shortage of consumer goods and extremely poor quality for many goods and services. Despite all the efforts and reforms, agriculture was unable to cope with its one and only problem: how to feed the population.

In the 1950s and 1960s, the increased role of science, the introduction of more modern technology into industry, and the scientific-technical revolution in a number of areas raised the problem of training highly qualified personnel for industry. The difficulty was that the Soviet system had gradually produced a disdainful attitude toward labor. The children of workers did not want to go to the factories; their parents wanted them to become engineers or professors.

The school system prepared students to enter institutions of higher learning, but those institutions could not accept all applicants. Moreover, under the admissions system in effect, applicants to institutions of higher learning received priority very often in accordance with their parents' positions. Admissions committees received direct orders on which candidates to accept and which to refuse. Those who were excluded preferred any work as long as it was not in a factory. Institutions of higher learning, night schools, and so on, were created to permit education without draining labor forces from production. Nevertheless, many students went to factories only because they were forced to work in order to survive. An attempt was made to solve such problems through educational reform. In December 1958 the ten-year school and general compulsory seven-year education were replaced by a compulsory eight-year program, after which students were required to work in factories or in agriculture for three years. At the same time, three additional (nine to eleven) optional years with professional training were also introduced. For admission to institutions of higher learning, preference was given to those who had already worked and had a good political and professional record.[141]

This reform aroused discontent at almost every level of the population: in the upper reaches of society the privileged parents had already planned a successful climb up the ladder of power or science for their children; at the lower levels, particularly in the cities, parents wanted their children to have access to higher education. Finally, for rural youth who dreamed of leaving the village to study in the city, the new law raised an insurmountable obstacle. Of course, as an alternative one could join in the building of communism in Siberia or Central Asia or go to the virgin lands.

The entire country was mobilized in a systematic campaign for combining "school with life," "science with life," and so on. The Komsomol mobilized thousands of young people for the virgin lands and for construction projects at Bratsk, at Krasnoyarsk, on the Volga, and elsewhere.

Like all Soviet mass campaigns, the campaign for "closer ties with real life" was taken to an absurdity. Scholars and physicians were forced to do uncompensated and unproductive work to the detriment of their professional activity. In Moscow, for example, research fellows at the institutes of the USSR Academy of Sciences were sent to wash floors and staircases and collect garbage at new housing projects. Refusal to do such work was considered an antisocial act.

Another measure which tore thousands of people from their work and disrupted the transportation and commerce systems was the greeting of guests of honor arriving in Moscow. By order of the district party committees, thousands of people were assembled along the main streets leading from the airports to the center of the capital in order to create the impression of enthusiasm for such guests as Nasser and Tito. In other instances, such as the arrival of the American President Nixon, access to the main roads on which he traveled was closed and the streets remained empty.

In the years 1955–1961 a number of laws were passed that improved the legal position of the urban populations, primarily of industrial workers. On April 25, 1956, the antiworker law of 1940, which bound the worker to his job and imposed harsh penalties for absenteeism and tardiness, was repealed. The Soviet worker once again became "free," in the sense that the right to change jobs was restored.[142] A decree of September 8 the same year established a minimum wage.[143]

Changes in the pension laws affected the lives of millions. In July 1956, a new system was introduced providing for significantly larger monthly pensions. They were based on age and seniority on the job and ranged from 300 to 1,200 rubles. The qualifying age for a full pension was set at sixty for men with twenty-five years' seniority and fifty-five for women with twenty years.[144] This was much lower than the qualifying age for pensions in the West. In July 1964 a pension system was introduced for collective farmers, who were given the right to retire at sixty-five in the case of men and sixty for women,[145] but only on the condition that they continue to live on the collective farm. This law, however, avoided the vital question of automatic retirement on pension at a certain age. The absence of such a rule allowed high government officials to hold onto their positions, regardless of their age, sometimes even for life. Furthermore, in connection with the interests of high officials, the system of special pensions for especially important services to the state was not only preserved but broadened. These special pensions were accompanied by other privileges, in particular a 50 percent reduction in rent, free use of public transportation, free annual stays at vacation homes and sanatoriums, and other quite substantial advantages. Special pension systems were retained for scientific researchers, the military, and agents of state security.

Laws were also passed that shortened the work week by two hours[146] and extended maternity leave to 112 days (the latter having been shortened to 70 days in 1940).[147]

The construction of urban housing complexes, which began in the last years of Stalin's life, was expanded greatly.[148] An objective was set "to end the country's housing shortage within ten to twelve years."[149] The government began to encourage the construction of cooperative apartments under conditions that were extremely favorable to the population: the initial payment, at the start of construction, was 15–30 percent of the price of the apartment, with a fifteen-year installment system at 0.5 percent annual interest. At the same time, the construction of apartment complexes by city authorities, enterprises, and ministries increased significantly. The scope of the construction that took place from 1953 to 1964 is evident from the following data: in 1950, there were 513 million square meters of housing space in the entire country; in 1955, 640 million; in 1960, 958 million; and in 1964, 1,182 million.[150] Although improved housing conditions affected the lot of many thousands of families, the housing problem had still not been completely solved even as of the mid-1980s.

The government used this acute problem as yet another way to pressure the population. An apartment could be obtained more quickly if one's political record was impeccable. Any criticism of the authorities cost someone waiting in line for an apartment very dearly. In the best of cases, the wait simply became longer; in the worst, the offender was deprived of the right to receive any housing space at all; a pretext was always easy to find.

In 1958 the leadership instituted a twenty-year moratorium on payments to the owners of government bonds. Such payments had become a heavy burden on the state. At the same time, the issuing of bonds was discontinued, with the exception of "domestic bonds," which could be bought and sold freely. This measure aroused mixed feelings in the population. Millions of Soviet citizens had accumulated these bonds for years, and the payments added significantly to their incomes. On the other hand, the end of obligatory subscriptions to government bond issues through withholding from wages and salaries meant a saving of two to three weeks' wages each year. In 1975 the right of citizens to cash in their government bonds was restored.

The rate of inflation led to a new monetary reform in 1961. Formally, it consisted of exchanging old bills for new at the rate of ten to one, with a corresponding adjustment of prices and wages.[151] Little by little, the buying power of the new money diminished as inflationary tendencies continued.

In 1957 direct taxes on those in low-paid categories were reduced.[152] Even earlier, in 1954, the 6 percent tax on bachelors (imposed during the war) had been dropped.[153] This reduction in taxes occurred against a background of growth in industrial production and increased government revenues, thanks to the "turnover tax" (essentially a sales tax on consumer goods) and to higher prices on food and basic consumer durables. Price increases were systematic, paralleling the rise in gross wages and the cost of public utilities. The latter made up an insignificant part of the budget of the urban family, whose principal expenses were food and clothing. Food alone usually took up more than half of the monthly wage. Family income also increased with the elimination of the tuition charges for secondary schools and higher education, which had been introduced in 1940.

Allowances to families with many children also increased, along with compensation for the temporarily disabled.[154] The minimum wage rose from thirty new rubles a month to sixty. However, the wage differential between the lowest and highest paid personnel remained enormous. Teachers, doctors, and medical personnel—providers of the most essential social services—remained among the lowest paid.

There is no doubt that Khrushchev sincerely wanted the people to have better lives, but his idea of what was good and what was bad did not generally go beyond the accepted framework of Communist ideology, although his thinking contained certain egalitarian features. For example, the party program of 1961 promised to introduce a number of free goods and services by 1980.

Khrushchev made an effort to combat the omnipresent embezzling and bribetaking; in this campaign he used both legal and illegal methods. At his insistence, an article was introduced into the legislature instituting the death penalty for such crimes as the embezzlement of funds and currency speculation. This article was immediately applied to a crime committed before the law went into effect (the Rokotov affair). This was a gross violation of one of the most elementary legal principles: that laws should not be applied retroactively.

In 1957 a campaign was launched against "parasites," a category that included speculators, alcoholics, and hooligans, who by their actions disturbed public order and peace. It became clear very soon that the primary targets of this campaign were people in more or less unregulated professions, such as writers and poets. Many of them were not members of the official artists' and writers' unions and therefore had "no social status." They rapidly became victims of moral terror at the hands of their neighbors, who were spurred on by the authorities. The "parasites" were arrested, convicted, and sent to live in remote regions of the Soviet Union, where, it was thought, they could not possibly "leech" on anyone. A notorious instance was the use of the "parasite" law against the poet Joseph Brodsky in Leningrad in 1964.[155]

The campaign against "parasitism" became another form of political repression. Similarly, the campaign against speculators and bribetakers became a form of anti-Semitism. The overwhelming majority of those condemned to death on these charges were of Jewish origin. Khrushchev, who was no stranger to anti-Semitism, spoke more than once in his speeches about "good" and "bad" Jews, but never about "good" and "bad" citizens. For example, he cited Army General Kreiser as being one of the "good" Jews.

The so-called *druzhiny*, or "people's guards," whose creation was authorized by a decree of the Supreme Soviet in 1959, took an active part in the struggle against parasitism. They were given the right to supervise public order and were released for this purpose from their factories or office jobs by the "collectives" themselves. In many cities the *druzhiny* degenerated quickly into bands that terrorized and blackmailed the population. Local authorities often used the *druzhiny* for violence against undesirables. Later they were used against exhibitions of paintings by unauthorized artists, for intimidating dissidents, and for a variety of other tasks.

Trials by "comrades' courts" were used in a similar way to invade brazenly the personal lives of Soviet citizens.

This is how Khrushchev's regime, which renounced mass terror and arrests in principle, established social control over its subjects' lives. One could say that Khrushchev tried to establish the full sovereignty of the people in Soviet society—by endowing hundreds of thousands of people with a little bit of power over their peers. The massive growth of the party and the Komsomol served the same end. The era of the "new Soviet man" was close at hand.

## COEXISTENCE AND EXPANSION

From Malenkov's first steps in foreign policy, it was evident that the new Soviet leadership was seeking to extinguish the "hotbeds of war" in Korea and elsewhere and to ease relations with the capitalist countries.

The outcome of World War II had been extremely favorable for the Soviet Union and would have been more so but for Stalin's megalomania. His military adventurism and policy of force so distinctly displayed in the Korean war and during the Berlin crisis had in fact failed. It had been Mao, who, by committing his troops in Korea, had saved the situation for the rest of the Communist world.

Between 1953 and 1955 the Soviet Union sought to make peace in many areas. After the end of the Korean war in 1953, the USSR also helped to end the war in Indochina.[156] In 1955 a peace treaty was finally signed with Austria, something the Soviet Union had prevented for ten years by artificially linking such a treaty to concessions by the Western powers on other questions. Later, the CPSU Central Committee laid the blame for this delay and for the worsening of Soviet–Yugoslav relations on Molotov personally.[157]

In 1955 Khrushchev also appeared in Belgrade heading a Soviet delegation and conveyed official apologies to Tito for the Soviet Union's policy toward Yugoslavia after the war. Khrushchev laid responsibility for the policy on Beria, but the Yugoslav leaders viewed this explanation with irony. The Soviet delegation was received coolly. The Yugoslavs were expecting an honest apology, especially for the assertion that Yugoslavia was a capitalist, not a socialist country. For this reason, the following phrase was inserted in a resolution of the Twentieth Party Congress: "Important achievements in the construction of socialism have also been made in Yugoslavia."[158]

The Soviet delegates were not psychologically prepared for this encounter, Khrushchev admitted later. "We still hadn't freed ourselves from our slavish dependence on Stalin."[159] Tito was ready to improve relations between the two states, but he declined the Soviet proposal for restoring close relations between the two Communist parties, assuming correctly that the CPSU had by no means abandoned its claim to the leading role among the world Communist parties. For this reason, the Yugoslav Communist party later refused to endorse the resolutions of two international conferences of Communist and workers parties, held in Moscow in 1957 and 1960.

The new Soviet leadership judged the situation that had developed realistically. The experience of the first three years of its active international policy demonstrated that in the existing situation this policy ("peaceful coexistence") was the most advantageous. At the Twentieth Party Congress this thesis was elaborated in some detail. The congress recognized the existence of two different social systems in the contemporary world (capitalist and socialist), which were economic and cultural rivals. Sooner or later the victory of the socialist system was inevitable, but this victory would be attained through the development of internal contradictions in the capitalist camp and a class struggle, not by "exporting revolution." The possibility of a nonviolent transition to socialism existed in a number of capitalist countries. That was why, under modern circumstances, wars were not inevitable and could be averted. The danger of a new war had not been totally excluded, however: as long as imperialism existed, the breeding ground for war would exist.[160]

This, in short, was the international policy formulated at the Twentieth Party Congress. As we have noted, this program was based on a belief in the inevitable victory of the Soviet Union (the socialist camp) over the entire world. In presenting this program, the CPSU by no means renounced this other part of its policy. First of all, it intended to develop and intensify the ideological struggle against the capitalist nations. This activity could be either enlarged or narrowed, depending on the demands of the moment. Secondly, the thesis of the impossibility of maintaining a status quo and the inevitability of changes in the world was preserved intact. Finally, the Soviet doctrine continued to affirm that the Soviet Union had not only the right but the obligation to aid national liberation movements around the world. The means and forms of this aid were in no way outlined or defined. These three theses in fact provided the basis for constant expansion by the Soviet Union and the other socialist countries.

Soviet foreign policy in the post-Stalin era was based, as Adam Ulam has described it, on expansion and peaceful coexistence;[161] more precisely, it should be formulated as coexistence through expansion. The principles underlying this policy were crude and primitive, but in that lay its strength. The most virulent Western critics characterized it as follows: "What is ours is ours; the rest is negotiable." But they are mistaken; "What's ours is ours; what's yours will be ours" would better correspond to their real view. Soviet leaders were right in contending that their foreign policy, as opposed to the policies of Western leaders, was consistent. The practice of Soviet foreign policy was and is a combination of the principles of coexistence and expansion: it uses the first to camouflage the second.

After Malenkov left his post as prime minister, Soviet foreign policy became noticeably more active, with Khrushchev the driving force behind it. In 1955 a summit meeting with President Eisenhower took place in Geneva. It in no way influenced the situation in Europe, however, where the primary question was still Germany. After the formation of the Warsaw Pact in 1955, the German problem was more clearly defined. Neither the Western powers nor the Soviet Union seriously contemplated a reunification of Germany, despite declarations to the contrary. All the drafts, meetings, and discussions on the German question were more a tribute to established custom and public opinion than real measures taken to solve the problem. There was no solution. The reality was that there were two Germany's: one of them belonged to the Western alliance, the other to the Soviet bloc.

Soviet troops were stationed in the GDR. Everything indicated that the overwhelming majority of the East Germany population gravitated toward the West. The flow of emigration from east to west was quite substantial and threatened to undermine the economic and social structure of the GDR in the very near future. More radical measures were adopted. During a summit meeting with President Kennedy in Vienna in June 1961, Khrushchev tried in vain to persuade him to recognize the GDR. The USSR then tried once again to close access to West Berlin to the Western powers. The 1961 Berlin crisis lasted several months, but the attempt to isolate West Berlin failed. The government of the GDR solved the problem in an original way: in agreement with the Soviet government, the Berlin Wall was built in August 1961 separating the eastern part of Berlin from the western part.[162] Structures like these existed before only in concentration camps, except for the Great Wall of China, whose function had been quite different. Maintaining the Berlin Wall became the principal preoccupation of the East German armed forces. In time, the approaches to the wall were equipped with special electronic gear that automatically opened fire on anyone who attempted to cross to the other side. On June 12, 1964, the USSR and the GDR concluded a treaty of friendship, mutual aid, and cooperation. The Soviet Union formally assumed the task of defending East German territory in case of necessity.[163]

In the 1950s Soviet foreign policy gradually assumed a more and more aggressive character. Wherever the local situation was changing or unstable, the Soviets were very active. If in 1947–48 the Soviet Union supported Israel as a force to weaken Great Britain in the Middle East, then in the mid-1950s Soviet policy was reoriented in favor of closer relations with the Arab world. The causes of this change were the Egyptian revolution of 1952 and the growing conviction that Israel was no more than a satellite of the United States. Relations between the Soviet Union and Israel were severed shortly before Stalin's death, as part of his anti-Semitic policy, and were restored only afterward, in July 1953. From then on Israel was considered part of the enemy camp.

In July 1955 Shepilov, editor-in-chief of *Pravda* and a future secretary of the CPSU Central Committee, was sent to Egypt. From that moment, Soviet expansion in the Middle East increased. Egyptian president Nasser needed arms, which he soon began to receive from a Soviet satellite— Czechoslovakia. Later, the Soviet Union began supplying Egypt directly with tanks and aircraft, MIG fighters, for example, as well as artillery systems.

The conflict over the Suez Canal, in 1956, and the war against Egypt by England, France, and Israel, contributed greatly to the strengthening of Soviet–Egyptian ties. In June 1956 Shepilov replaced Molotov as minister of foreign affairs.[164] In early November "spontaneous" mass demonstrations broke out in Moscow and in other Soviet cities with the slogan: "Hands off Egypt!" Registration of volunteers for participation in the war on the side of Egypt began. At this very moment, Soviet tanks were crushing the Hungarian revolution, but no one in the Soviet Union protested or demonstrated for "Hands off Hungary!" The uproar over the war in the Middle East muffled the moans of Hungarians perishing under the tanks.

Under Khrushchev, Soviet foreign policy was able very quickly to fill the vacuum created by a weakening in the positions of the great Western powers by exploiting the traditional hostility of the populations in the former colonies toward their former rulers. Such was the case, for example, in the Syrian crisis in the summer of 1957. In 1958 there was a new crisis in the Middle East, involving Lebanon, Syria, Iraq, and Jordan. The Soviet Union used this crisis to improve its own position in Syria and Iraq. In the 1960s the Soviet Union gained a solid foothold in Egypt by taking part in the construction of the Aswan Dam and sending in large numbers of military advisers and arms. In 1962 the Soviet Union backed the revolution in Yemen, and two years later a Soviet–Yemeni friendship treaty was signed. The Soviet Union supplied military, economic, and technical aid to all these states. In Africa, Asia, and the Indian Ocean, the Soviet Union steadily provided support to countries opposing the Western powers. But by and large, as soon as the Soviet leaders believed they were firmly established in a country, they began to impose their own conception of international policy and to interfere crudely in internal and foreign policy. That is why there is not a single "ally" with which the USSR has not had conflicts, beginning with Egypt and ending with Indonesia.

Particularly complex, however, were the Soviet Union's relations with its "brother," China.

## THE TWO BIG BROTHERS

During the first several years after the founding of the People's Republic of China, Sino–Soviet relations blossomed, becoming especially close during the Korean war, when the Soviet Union supplied arms to Chinese divisions in Korea.

From 1950 to 1962 the Soviet Union granted China long-term credits of 1.82 billion rubles.[165] China used them to pay for arms bought from the Soviet Union and to aid North Korea.[166] The Soviet Union gave China 790 million rubles in merchandise and gifts.[167] Dividing this amount by twelve years, however, makes it obvious that Soviet aid was not very great. In 1962 China received only 13 percent of the total aid granted by the Soviet Union to socialist countries and only 8 percent of the total of all credits granted to other countries as economic aid.[168] The "Chinese share" was completely disproportionate to the size of its population. According to official Soviet sources, the Soviet Union aided in the construction of 256 enterprises of various types in China. This aid took the form of technical documentation, railroad construction, and the provision of experts. However, it was by no means free of charge. In twelve years, close to 11,000 Soviet advisers and experts traveled to China, receiving an amount equivalent to some 30,000 annual salaries.[169] China paid for all the services provided: freight, construction of railroads, and the training of Chinese students in the Soviet Union.[170] For its part, by the end of 1962 China had supplied the Soviet Union with 2.1 billion rubles in merchandise, food, and raw materials.[171]

Sino–Soviet relations worsened at the very moment that China was attempting to carry out a very ambitious economic program (the "Great Leap Forward"). In 1962 the Soviet Union unexpectedly recalled 1,390 experts, broke 343 contracts that would have employed Soviet experts in China, and ceased work on 257 projects of scientific and technical cooperation, placing the Chinese economic program in serious straits.[172]

The sources of the Sino–Soviet conflict have their roots deep in the past. They are probably related to the territorial annexations and unfair economic agreements imposed on China by tsarist Russia. They can also be traced to Soviet policy in the 1920s and 1930s toward the Kuomintang and the Communist-controlled "Soviet regions" in China. Stalin did not believe a victory by the Chinese Communist party (CCP) was possible; his policy therefore was to collaborate with Chiang Kai-shek. After 1949 the Soviet Union implemented the same policy vis-à-vis China as it had in regard to the socialist countries of Eastern Europe: the subordination of their interests to the interests of their "elder brother," the USSR. On the economic plane, the Soviet Union established joint Sino–Soviet companies on Chinese territory, striving to exploit Chinese resources under the direction and in the interests of the Soviet Union. For example, in the border province of Sinkiang, a joint company was formed to extract minerals. The company in fact enjoyed extraterritorial rights. Between 1949 and 1953 Stalin suggested to Mao more than once that directly controlled Soviet enterprises be established on Chinese territory, thereby offending and humiliating the Chinese leader.[173] The historical experience of thousands of years had taught the Chinese leaders to regard with suspicion any suggestion by foreign governments to use Chinese territory for any reason. The Twentieth Party

Congress formally condemned the practice of "joint companies," and they were liquidated. Like Stalin, however, his heirs were not psychologically prepared to understand the Chinese way of thinking. Consequently, Chinese leaders were offended by Zhukov, then Soviet minister of defense and a member of the CPSU Central Committee Presidium, when he promised that the Soviet Union would immediately come to the aid of any socialist country attacked by "imperialists." They announced that China would not ask the Soviet Union for such aid.[174]

Khrushchev's proposal to Mao in 1959 that the Soviet Union be allowed to build a submarine base for refueling and repair and a radio station in China in return for similar facilities at Murmansk was rejected with indignation. Mao reminded him meaningfully that the Chinese had always assimilated their conquerors.[175]

The condemnation of the cult of Stalin in the Soviet Union provoked first concealed and then open dissatisfaction in China. The Chinese had their own "cult"—Mao's. The cult of personality is, in any event, an indispensable feature of any totalitarian regime—whether in the socialist Soviet Union, Hitler's Germany, Mao's China, or Enver Hoxha's Albania. By this time, Mao's speeches and articles had been declared the Asian form of Marxism-Leninism.[176] While Stalin was alive, Mao remained in the shadows; after Stalin's death, he became the "great theoretician" of the period. In the words of a Russian proverb, "A holy place never stays empty." What disturbed the Maoists was not so much the deglorification of Stalin as its consequences for China and the international Communist movement, which the CCP desired to lead as much as the CPSU. The practical (and not purely verbal) position of the Chinese leadership was clearly shown in 1956 and 1957, when the CCP supported the bloody suppression of the Hungarian revolution by Soviet troops and in 1958, when it was the only Communist party in the world openly to applaud the execution of Imre Nagy.[177]

Sino–Soviet relations were complicated by the existence of a common ideology. For many years the vocabulary of these relations, and of relations in the international Communist movement generally, consisted of mutual accusations such as: deviation from Marxist-Leninist orthodoxy; revisionism; dogmatism; leftist phrasemongering; right-opportunism; adventurism; aspirations to hegemony ("hegemonism"); subversive activities; Trotskyism; servility toward American imperialism; nationalism; capitulation to the bourgeoisie; peasant ideology. Each camp claimed hegemony within the world Communist movement. Relations between China and the Soviet Union, or more precisely, between the CPSU and CCP, were so full of rigidity, hostility, and suspicion that in comparison their relations with the capitalist countries seemed idyllic.

Mao attacked the CPSU's line that war was no longer a fated inevitability. He not only prophesied a worldwide atomic war but hailed it as an opportunity "to do away with imperialism." For example, in a 1958 conversation with Soviet Foreign Minister Gromyko, he argued that in the next war China might lose 300 million people, but when the stocks of nuclear weapons had been exhausted, China would use conventional arms to liquidate the remnants of capitalism and establish socialism throughout the world.[178] In another conversation, Mao called the atomic bomb a "paper tiger" and said that even if one-third of mankind (i.e., 900 million people) or even one-half (1.35 billion) perished in the next war, the other half would survive, imperialism would be swept away, and socialism would reign everywhere. After fifty or a hundred years, the population would more than double.[179] A book published in China in 1960 included the following: "On the ruins of imperialism, the victorious people will extremely quickly build a civilization on a level a thousand times higher than in the capitalist era; they will build their own genuinely beautiful future."[180]

Mao's position on war had an effect exactly opposite to what he had intended. The overwhelming majority of Communist parties supported the Soviet thesis that war was not a fated inevitability. Although in many of its public announcements and statements the CPSU had acknowledged each country's right to determine its own path to socialism, Soviet leaders in fact conducted both an open and a covert struggle against any attempts to establish an unapproved or independent policy on the part of other Communist parties or socialist countries. At the same time, the Soviet Union did not intend to be philanthropic. The "little brothers" had to pay for what they got in one form or another. In early 1961 China turned to the Soviet Union with a request for grain following a bad harvest. The Soviet Union loaned China 500,000 tons of sugar it had received from Cuba. The Chinese had no choice but to buy 6 million tons of wheat from the world capitalist market.[181] Of course the Soviet Union did not have enough grain reserves to feed its own population: two years later, the USSR was forced to buy 13 million tons of grain from the West. In 1958–1960, profiting from the Vietnam insurgency, China increased its support to revolutionary movements on the Asian continent, trying to make them subordinate and to use them to spread China's influence. Chinese and Soviet interests began to clash. Their struggle for hegemony spread to Africa and the Indian Ocean.

Sino–Soviet relations had by 1960 deteriorated to such an extent that in Bucharest, at a conference of Communist parties, a very sharp exchange took place openly between Khrushchev and the Chinese representative.

The ideological disputes between the CPSU and the CCP in fact concealed the conflicting interests of the Soviet Union and China. By the late

1950s and early 1960s China lagged far behind the Soviet Union economically and technologically. In general, China was simply not part of the
modern world. The Soviet Union and the United States were superpowers.
China wanted to bridge this gap as quickly as possible. This gave rise to
Mao's "Great Leap Forward" policy domestically and to an aggressive policy
abroad, the desire to have the atomic bomb at any cost and then the hydrogen
bomb, which in our time is considered the calling card of a great power.

Mao had once hoped to obtain atomic weapons from the Soviet Union.
It cannot be ruled out that at one time or another he received some sort of
half-promise from the post-Stalin Soviet leadership. In any case, the Soviet
Union helped China build a 5,000-kilowatt atomic reactor in 1957–1959.
Later, Chinese engineers perfected it and increased its power to 10,000
kilowatts.[182] Chinese scientists worked at the Atomic Energy Institute in
Dubna (near Moscow) until June 1965.[183]

China's atomic ambitions were in opposition to the interests of both the
Soviets and the Americans, who wanted to limit admission to the "atomic
club." Their reasons were weighty enough: the more nuclear powers there
were in the world, the greater the danger of nuclear war and the more
difficult it would be to maintain peace and secure arms limitation agreements. The USSR also favored such limitation because the arms race placed
a heavy burden on its economy. For China, signing any treaty on nonproliferation of nuclear weapons meant dooming it to remain a second-class
power, in spite of the fact that for the first time in centuries it had appeared
on the international scene as a unified and consolidated state.

The Soviet Union had no desire for a neighbor like China, with a population of 700 million at the end of the 1950s—and growing quickly—to
become a strong military power.

A particularly unfavorable aspect of Sino–Soviet relations, once a powerful centralized Chinese state had been created, was the existence of a
5,000-mile common border. Any deterioration in relations necessarily led
to tension along this border, with all the predictable consequences.

China took advantage of the border problem in its conflict with the Soviet
Union. It accused the Soviet Union of an imperialist policy, particularly
because the Soviet Union still adhered to the unjust treaties imposed by
tsarist Russia on China during a period when China was fragmented and
weak. China suggested that while the status quo could be maintained
temporarily, negotiations to change the border should begin.[184] In the polemics over the border both sides used fairly casuistical arguments. The
Soviet Union admitted that the treaties were unfair,[185] but at the same time
pointed out that the Chinese emperors had annexed the territories of their
weaker neighbors. Therefore, it would be preferable to preserve the his-

torically formed borders and not create new sources of misunderstanding and conflict. But this reasonable point of view was accompanied by the demagogic arguments that in China, as in the Soviet Union, the working class was in power, that "their common goal was to build communism," and that under communism international borders did not have their former importance.[186] This meant in effect that the Soviet Union wanted to postpone any discussion of the border until the advent of communism. Of course, this did not satisfy the Chinese. After all, the Soviet leaders could not give an exact date for the joyous coming of mankind's future. In the mid-1960s bloody conflicts erupted on the Sino–Soviet border, which revived rumors in the Soviet Union of an imminent war with China. It is possible that there were discussions in top Soviet circles of a preventive war.[187]

Khrushchev recalled in his memoirs:

Later the Chinese press took Mao's lead and started to claim that Vladivostok was on Chinese territory. They wrote that the Russians had stolen it from China. It's true at one point in history the Chinese ruled in that part of Siberia before our tsars expanded into the area. We consented to negotiate with the Chinese about our borders. They sent us their version of how the map should read. We took one look at it, and it was so outrageous that we threw it away in disgust.[188]

But it was not only the border problem and nuclear arms that disturbed the Soviet leadership. In the late 1950s and early 1960s China was in that stage of development when, encouraged and directed first by the leaders, then spontaneously, the masses began the "cultural revolution," that is, a pogrom conducted against the intelligentsia and all moderate elements, declaring war on the bureaucracy and spreading egalitarian ideology. It did not limit itself to ideology, however. At the same time, peasant communes began to be created on a particularly egalitarian basis. Chinese literature about the struggle against the bureaucracy and for social and economic equality appeared in the Soviet border regions and even in Siberia. Khrushchev grew alarmed and announced to the CPSU Presidium: "This must stop immediately. The slogans of the Chinese reforms are very alluring. You're mistaken if you don't think the seeds of these ideas will find fertile soil in our country."[189] Khrushchev was not mistaken. There was ferment throughout the immense territory of the Soviet Union.

Despite threatening noises and the occasional crises that erupted in relations with the Western powers, Khrushchev's foreign policy as a whole was oriented toward enlarging contact and cooperation with the Western powers, particularly the United States. For Khrushchev, obsessed with the idea of comparing the Soviet Union to the United States in every area, from meat and corn production to state-of-the-art technology, the policy of co-existence with the West was not merely an empty phrase. Suffering from a kind of Marxist-Stalinist inferiority complex, he tried constantly to be the propagandist of socialism, wanting to prove the superiority of the Soviet Union over the capitalist world and, worse still, to predict on any suitable occasion the inevitable end of capitalism. In 1959, at Eisenhower's invitation, Khrushchev toured the United States with great fanfare and not without a certain success.[190] He provoked a storm of indignation, however, when he declared at a diplomatic reception shortly before his departure: "We will bury you."[191]

During his trip through the United States Khrushchev arranged with President Eisenhower to convene a summit conference for the following year (1960) on the German problem and other matters. He hoped to win the West's recognition of the GDR. China met this news with apprehension and displeasure. Mao was afraid that Khrushchev would go behind his back to Eisenhower on the question of "two Chinas."[192] Mao viewed the prospect of a Soviet–American agreement on nuclear weapons with great alarm. Indeed, as we have seen, the Soviet Union had no desire to share its nuclear secrets with China.

China feared that a Soviet–American accord on atomic weapons would make the superpowers the supreme arbiters of the world. Shortly before the Khrushchev–Eisenhower meeting in Paris, the Chinese declared that they would not feel bound by any disarmament treaty in which China had not taken part.[193] The usefulness of any agreement with Eisenhower suddenly became problematic. A pretext had to be found to pull out. Shortly before the meeting in Paris, an American U-2 spy plane was knocked down by a Soviet missile. The official Soviet declaration announced that the plane had been downed but did not mention that the pilot had been taken prisoner. Only after the publication of the rather muddled U.S. explanation did Khrushchev reveal that the pilot, Captain Gary Powers, was in Soviet hands. Khrushchev held Eisenhower responsible for the reconnaissance flights over Soviet territory, probably hoping this would make Eisenhower more amenable to Soviet demands on the German question. Arriving in Paris, Khrushchev played the game of indignation, declaring that he would not return to the negotiating table unless Eisenhower apologized. Eisenhower refused and the summit meeting was off. Khrushchev virtually capitulated to the Chinese leaders, but at the same time he was forced to abandon discussion of the German problem.

The last years of Khrushchev's rule did not bring a single improvement in Soviet–American relations. Khrushchev had an astonishing ability to lose quickly the advantages he gained on the international scene. Instead of calm, contemplated diplomacy, he preferred "storm and stress" tactics, hoping to frighten and confuse his partners or adversaries. His failures, instead of prompting him to change his tactics, however, drove him to further extremes.

Objectively, the main aim of Khrushchev's foreign policy was to establish a balance of power with the United States and to eliminate the "hot spots" in their relations (West Berlin, Cuba, the arms race) on conditions favorable to the USSR. He sought to achieve this by completely eliminating the rights and influence of the Western powers in these places. At the same time, Khrushchev, like other Soviet leaders, was prepared to use any favorable occasion to constrain "capitalism" within its own sphere. His impatience in conducting international affairs was evident in the autumn of 1960 during the Congo crisis, when he arrived in New York to take part in a session of the UN General Assembly. Khrushchev used his presence to raise questions about the effectiveness of the United Nations and to undermine its prestige. It should be noted that none of his proposals was supported by the representatives of the African or Asian countries, on whom he had been counting. He received no support in his condemnation of UN Secretary-General Dag Hammarskjold, nor for his proposal to institute a "troika" to replace the secretary-general's office, nor in his openly anti-American proposal to transfer UN headquarters to Europe. Khrushchev gave vent to his affected indignation by taking off his shoe and beating it on his desk during British Prime Minister Macmillan's speech, much to the amusement of the delegates and journalists. [194]

In June 1961 Khrushchev met with John F. Kennedy, the new American president in Vienna, at the latter's suggestion. Khrushchev attempted to probe Kennedy for weak spots. He demanded the removal of the Western powers from West Berlin and repeated his proposal for a troika in the UN. Naturally, nothing came of this meeting. The Soviet Union then began to increase the tension over Berlin, which resulted not in the capitulation of the United States and other Western powers, as Khrushchev had hoped, but in the defeat of the Soviet Union and the construction of the Berlin Wall. The USSR soon tested a thermonuclear bomb in the atmosphere.

After discovering that the United States could not be intimidated and that its European allies remained calm on the whole, Khrushchev decided to change his tactics. This decision was also due to the sharp deterioration in Sino–Soviet relations, which became publicly visible during the Twenty-Second Party Congress. Although he never said so, the fear that China would acquire thermonuclear weapons dominated Khrushchev's policy. That is why he strove for agreement with the United States on limiting the proliferation of nuclear arms. Professor Adam Ulam suggests that this striving was what lay behind the Cuban missile crisis that developed in the fall of 1962.[195]

## MISSILES IN CUBA

In January 1959 Cuban dictator Batista's government was overthrown and replaced by a revolutionary government led by Fidel Castro, who had directed the anti-Batista insurrection. Relations between Cuba and the United States soon became extremely strained. The United States had been leasing a military base at Guantanamo Bay in Cuba and the Cuban government tried a number of times to blockade the base in order to force the Americans to abandon it.

Groups of Cuban emigrés formed on U.S. territory in Florida and conducted raids into Cuban territory, supported by the CIA. In 1960 the tension between the two countries resulted in a nearly total ban on the import of Cuban sugar into the United States. The Cuban economy depended on these sales. On January 2, 1961, the United States severed diplomatic and consular relations with Cuba.[196]

On April 17, 1961, Cuban emigrés undertook a major landing operation at the Bay of Pigs. A general mobilization was announced in Cuba. In the course of seventy-two hours of continuous battle the landing was crushed. Many prisoners—Cubans who had earlier fled the country—and a considerable number of weapons of American manufacture were captured.[197]

The tension between the United States and Cuba led to the rapid development of Soviet–Cuban relations. At first much was unclear and things went far from smoothly between the Soviets and Cubans because of the vagueness of Fidel Castro's ideological position and his strained relations with the leaders of the Cuban Communist party. Gradually the conflict was resolved. The Cuban Communist party leader was eliminated politically, and Castro became first secretary of the national leadership of a new organization, the United Revolutionary Organizations, the ORI.[198] An ideological rapprochement between Castro and the CPSU had occurred, and the Soviet leadership took energetic measures to reinforce Soviet influence in Cuba and to use Cuban territory to establish a bridgehead in the Western hemisphere. For the Soviet leadership, such a prospect was too attractive to refuse. The U.S. government, by its clumsy effort to blockade Cuba politically and economically and by its military aid to the anti-Castro Cubans, contributed greatly to the success of Soviet policy.

During 1961 and 1962 the Soviet Union took a series of measures meant to pave the way for military agreements with Cuba. The Lenin Peace prize was awarded to Castro, Soviet cosmonaut Yuri Gagarin toured Cuba in July 1961, government delegations were exchanged, and a number of economic agreements were signed.

From the moment of Castro's election as first secretary of the ORI on March 22, 1962, a new stage began in Soviet–Cuban relations. In July–August 1962, there were talks in Moscow about the delivery of Soviet arms to Cuba and, on August 27, a corresponding agreement was signed.[199]

Beginning in late July 1962, Soviet arms deliveries to Cuba increased considerably. Out of thirty-seven Soviet merchant ships arriving in Cuba in August 1962, twenty were carrying arms. From the end of July to the middle of October, more than one hundred Soviet ships bearing arms arrived in Cuba. The unloading took place at night in strict secrecy. Nevertheless, American intelligence managed to establish that among the weapons delivered were 42 medium-range ballistic missiles (MRBMs); 12 intermediate-type ballistic missiles; 42 IL-28 fighter bombers; 144 surface-to-air missile (SAM) anti-aircraft installations, each equipped with 4 SAM missiles; 42 MIG-21 fighters; other types of missiles; and patrol boats armed with missiles. In addition, 22,000 Soviet servicemen were sent.[200] In September the Soviet Union assured the U.S. government several times that it had no intention of creating a threat to the United States in Cuba and that under no circumstances would offensive surface-to-surface missiles be sent to Cuba.[201]

On October 15 an American U-2 plane in a regular flight over Cuba obtained photographs that fully disproved the Soviet assurances. In the words of Attorney General Robert F. Kennedy, those assurances "had all been lies, one gigantic fabric of lies."[202] The photographs clearly showed Soviet surface-to-surface missiles capable of carrying nuclear warheads. These missiles were installed in the region of San Cristobal, fifty miles southwest of Havana.[203] Their range was 1,000 miles—in other words, they could reach interior regions of the United States. This discovery was a complete surprise to the U.S. government.[204] Further study of the photographs and calculations performed by American experts showed that the intercontinental ballistic missiles deployed in Cuba were equivalent in destructive capacity to nearly one-half that of all ICBMs existing in the USSR at that time.[205] It was discovered that the missiles were aimed at certain American cities and that, within minutes after launching, 80 million Americans would have died.[206] This point was confirmed later by Khrushchev.[207]

Opinions on what to do were sharply divided. Members of the Joint

Chiefs of Staff insisted on immediate military action. Others preferred to limit action to a naval blockade of Cuba as a warning measure. Kennedy was undecided, for he was afraid that events in Cuba would immediately find an echo in the Berlin situation and provoke a world crisis.[208]

In planning the installation of missiles in Cuba, the Soviet government proceeded on the assumption that a direct nuclear threat to U.S. territory would dissuade the Americans from further attempts to overthrow the Castro regime. The Soviet government, as Khrushchev wrote later, wanted not only to "protect Cuba's existence as a socialist country" but also to provide an "example to the other countries of Latin America."[209] He linked the prestige of the Soviet Union to these goals. If Cuba fell, the other countries of Latin America would reject the Soviet Union. That is why the Soviet leadership (Khrushchev emphasized several times that all the decisions concerning Cuba were made collectively) was looking for a confrontation with the United States. They decided to do this by installing missiles in Cuba that were directed at the United States. Khrushchev assumed that once the U.S. government discovered them it would think twice before striking at the missile installations: "If a quarter or even a tenth of our missiles survived—even if only one or two big ones were left—we could still hit New York and there wouldn't be much of New York left."[210] In his memoirs he asserts repeatedly: "We hadn't had time to deliver all our shipments to Cuba, but we had installed enough missiles already to destroy New York, Chicago, and the other huge industrial cities, not to mention a little village like Washington. I don't think America had ever faced such a *real* threat of destruction" (emphasis added—A. N.).[211] It has never been definitely established whether the warheads had been installed in the Soviet missiles or not.

We can believe Khrushchev's statement that the Soviet government only wanted to shift the balance of power in the world by threatening the United States directly. But adventurism was a dominant element, for the entire plan was founded on two dubious hypotheses: first, installations of Soviet missiles in Cuba could be kept secret; and second, the United States would be frightened by the prospect of war and would make concessions. These two calculations proved false. On the contrary, the Soviet Union suddenly found itself facing the threat of its own destruction.

Before the Cuban crisis and during the thirteen days it lasted, the Soviet government tried to deceive the U.S. government as to its real intentions. Thus on October 18, 1962, Soviet Foreign Minister Gromyko, on Khrushchev's instructions, assured President Kennedy that the only aid the Soviet Union was supplying to Cuba was for agriculture and land development, plus a small number of defensive weapons. Gromyko stressed that the Soviet Union would never supply Cuba with offensive weapons.[212] Gromyko did not know, however, that the president already had irrefutable proof of the presence of Soviet offensive missiles in Cuba. The conversation with Gromyko once again confirmed that the Soviet government was consciously misleading the United States. On October 22 Kennedy addressed the American people on television and, after outlining the situation and calling Gromyko's assurances a lie, warned the Soviets that the United States would not tolerate conscious deception.[213]

The president declared a naval blockade of Cuba as a preliminary measure and ordered inspection of all ships heading for Cuba. Kennedy also warned that any missile fired from Cuba against any nation in the Western hemisphere would be considered an attack by the Soviet Union on the United States and would provoke immediate retaliation. After enumerating a series of other military and diplomatic measures, Kennedy called on Khrushchev to cease the provocations that threatened international peace, to give up the quest for world hegemony, and to seek a peaceful resolution of the crisis. He also warned the Soviet government against the danger of any new attempts to cut off access to West Berlin.[214]

Kennedy's order concerning the monitoring of arms deliveries to Cuba took effect on October 24.[215] Soviet arms shipments, meanwhile, continued on their way to Cuba, as did the installation of missiles in Cuba itself.[216] Kennedy acted cautiously and skillfully. The first inspection was made on a non-Soviet ship in order to demonstrate to the Soviet leaders that the examinations would be carried out, but at the same time providing another opportunity for the Soviet leaders to contemplate the consequences of an open confrontation. The United States simultaneously turned to the United Nations.[217]

The president's brother, Robert Kennedy, met several times with the Soviet ambassador, Anatoly Dobrynin, in order to explain to him that the Soviet Union's actions were bringing the world to the brink of war. It is probable that Dobrynin had not been fully informed of the Soviet government's plans, and it cannot be ruled out that he, too, had been misled.

On October 26 Khrushchev sent Kennedy a long letter in which he insisted on assurances from the United States that it would not attack Cuba. He did not, however, offer to dismantle the surface-to-surface missile installations. That same day, an American television journalist, John Scali, was invited to an unofficial discussion by A. Fomin at the Soviet embassy in Washington. Fomin stated that the missiles would be removed if the United States would pledge not to attack Cuba.

The next day, however, October 27, a second letter bearing Khrushchev's signature arrived from Moscow. It was distinctly different from the first, which had been received on October 26. It announced rather harshly that the Soviet Union would remove its missiles from Cuba if the United States would remove its missiles from Turkey. The Soviet Union would pledge not to attack Turkey and not to intervene in its internal affairs, and the United States would give a similar pledge regarding Cuba.[218]

Meanwhile, the situation was aggravated when an American U-2 reconnaissance plane was shot down over Cuba by a Soviet missile and the pilot killed. The American military demanded an immediate retaliatory strike. Never since World War II had the world been so close to the brink of war.

Kennedy decided to ignore Khrushchev's second, more aggressive letter and sent an answer to the first one on October 27, which was conciliatory in tone, expressing the U.S. desire for a permanent resolution of the Cuban problem. The United States was prepared to guarantee that it was not its intention to attack Cuba. For its part, the Soviet Union would immediately have to cease all attempts to construct launching installations for offensive missiles in Cuba.[219]

Robert Kennedy then gave the necessary elucidation to Dobrynin: the president did not want an armed conflict and would do everything possible to avoid military conflict with Cuba and the Soviet Union. But the Soviets were forcing him to it. "The Soviet Union," Robert Kennedy continued,

> had secretly established missile bases in Cuba while at the same time proclaiming privately and publicly that this would never be done. We had to have a commitment by tomorrow that those bases would be removed. I was not giving them an ultimatum but a statement of fact. He should understand that if they did not remove those bases, we would remove them. President Kennedy had great respect for the Ambassador's country and the courage of its people. Perhaps his country might feel it necessary to take retaliatory action; but before that was over, there would be not only dead Americans but dead Russians as well.[220]

The next day, October 28, Moscow agreed to dismantle the missile installations and remove them and to permit the United States to verify this.[221]

A peaceful solution was found to the Cuban crisis, but it could have ended in catastrophe. This, for example, is how the Soviet authors of *A History of Soviet Foreign Policy* described it: "a crisis which in its severity has had no equal in the postwar period, which directly confronted humanity with the threat of worldwide nuclear catastrophe."[222] According to these authors, the responsibility for the crisis rested with the U.S. government. The truth is that the United States was responsible—but for preventing a war. We must give some credit to Khrushchev, however. Having brought the world to the brink of disaster, he had enough sense in the end to take the helping hand Kennedy offered him.

The removal of the Soviet missiles from Cuba caused a cooling in Soviet–Cuban relations for some time, since Castro had hoped to use the missiles as a "big stick" against the United States and as backing for the revolutionary movement in Latin America.

One year after the Cuban crisis, on August 5, 1963, after long and difficult negotiations in Moscow, the Soviet Union, the United States, and Great Britain signed a treaty banning nuclear tests in the atmosphere, under water, and in space. The test ban treaty went into effect on October 10. Later it was signed by more than one hundred nations.[223] China, however, refused to sign, condemning the treaty in a series of communiqués from July to September 1963 as a bargain between imperialists.[224]

## THE WELLSPRINGS OF SPIRITUAL REBIRTH

We have already mentioned that the war forced Stalin to appeal to Russian patriotism to save his regime. The call for patriotism, heroism, and sacrifice evoked a sense of individual responsibility, which had nearly died—not one's responsibility to the party, the government, or the people, but to one's own conscience.

This in turn resulted in the awakening of the collective historical memory, which the regime had mutilated and suppressed. Just as Stalin's *Short Course of the History of the CPSU* was intended to replace the real history of the country and its peoples, official Soviet patriotism was to become the only approved version of patriotism.

The sense of civic responsibility for the fate of one's own country had made the victories of Stalingrad, Kursk, and Berlin possible. The war gave rise to a fresh interest in the past, which led in turn to a partial revival of the collective historical memory among the people.

By the end of the war the military tribunals were no longer trying soldiers for self-mutilation or desertion but for making indiscreet comments comparing life in the Soviet Union with life in other countries the soldiers had seen, for expressing cautious hopes for improvements in Soviet life (a view equated with anti-Soviet propaganda), and for attempting to defect to the West. A new, large-scale purge that Stalin had planned right before he died was intended to "pull up the last roots," that is, to get rid of members of the generations of the 1920s and 1930s who had accidentally survived and still carried fragments of the banned historical memory and who were therefore potentially dangerous to the regime. The purge had already started with the Leningrad affair, the Mingrelian affair, and the Doctor's plot. The only reason it did not turn into a nationwide bloodbath was that Stalin died.

Stalin's death, the ouster of Beria, the reorganization of the state security agencies, the first releases of political prisoners, and the amnesties for certain categories of prisoners created a favorable atmosphere for the restoration of a more or less accurate picture of the past. The desire to reinterpret the history of the Soviet Union led as early as one year after Stalin's death to the publication of such works as Vladimir Pomerantsev's essay "On Sincerity in Literature,"[225] Ilya Ehrenburg's novel *The Thaw*,[226] Vladimir Dudintsev's novel *Not by Bread Alone*,[227] the play *Did Ivan Ivanovich Ever Exist?* by the Turkish poet and revolutionary Nazym Khikmet[228] and essays on the February and October revolutions by Eduard Burdzhalov in the journal *Problems of History*.[229]

The Stalinists, who held posts at every level of the party and government apparatus, had grown quiet after the Twentieth Party Congress. They again took heart after the suppression of the Hungarian revolution and began to use any pretext to hinder the development of more humane and liberal ideas in Soviet society.

In 1958 the entire world witnessed the hounding and humiliation of the poet and writer Boris Pasternak. During his life Pasternak had been the object of fierce criticism and slander campaigns on several occasions. In 1955 he had completed *Doctor Zhivago*, a novel about the fate of the Russian intelligentsia and the revolution in Russia. In the summer of 1956 he submitted the manuscript to the editorial boards of several Moscow magazines and publishing houses. One copy was also sent to Feltrinelli, an Italian publisher with strong procommunist sympathies. After the Hungarian events, as the political climate in the USSR became much more wintry, the leaders of the Soviet Writers' Union saw to it that the novel would not be published in the USSR. Pasternak was forced to send a wire to the Italian publisher asking him to send the novel back for rewriting. Nevertheless *Doctor Zhivago* was published in November 1957 in Italy in two languages, Italian and Russian. Over the next two years it was translated into twenty-four languages.[230] Although the publication of the novel outside the Soviet Union was not officially a crime, it was viewed as a challenge to an unwritten canon of Soviet life. A new campaign against the writer began. All the celebrities of Soviet literature—Konstantin Fedin, Konstantin Simonov, Sergei Smirnov, Aleksei Surkov, Valentin Kataev, and many others—took part in it.

On October 23, 1958, Pasternak was awarded the Nobel Prize for Literature. After that the campaign against Pasternak became totally unrestrained. The Writers' Union, the Komsomol, and party officials of various ranks proceeded against him in unison. At the Gorky Institute of Literature students began to organize a demonstration—on orders from above, of course—demanding that Pasternak be expelled from the country.[231] Despite heavy pressure, however, only a few dozen of the 300 students at the institute took part. The demonstrators marched to the House of Writers carrying slogans saying, "Throw the Judas out of the USSR" and a caricature of Pasternak reaching out with crooked, grasping fingers for a sack of dollars. But the students were only puppets, manipulated by the authorities.

The entire Soviet press immediately joined in on the campaign. The secretary of the Komsomol Central Committee, Semichastny (later the head of the KGB, who was to betray Khrushchev in 1964), gave a speech to a crowd of 14,000 at the Luzhniki Stadium in Moscow. He tore into the poet, using gutter language and demanding Pasternak's expulsion from the country. Among those present were Khrushchev and the other party bosses.

On October 27 the writers gathered to condemn Pasternak. The person who chaired the meeting and set the tone was Sergei Smirnov, known to Soviet readers for his book *The Brest Fortress*. The writers conducted themselves in an unbelievably vile manner.[232] They asked the government to deprive Pasternak of Soviet citizenship.[233]

Hounded unmercifully, Pasternak feared he would be exiled from the country. First he declined the Nobel Prize, and then, in a letter to Khrushchev, asked not to be deported.[234] But the campaign continued. The "wrath of the people" that the party had organized ended up looking infantile and feeble. After all, none of the irate letter writers had read *Doctor Zhivago*, but that did not stop them. Some things had changed since Stalin's death, however. While the Soviet press and fellow writers slung mud at the poet, Pasternak received quite a few letters of sympathy and encouragement. Something like public opinion was coming into existence in the Soviet Union.

Finally Pasternak was forced to write a letter of recantation to *Pravda*. This letter contained some rather curious but revealing lines: "It does indeed appear," wrote Pasternak, "as if I maintain the following erroneous propositions [in the novel]. I seem to be saying that every revolution is a historically illegitimate occurrence, of which the October revolution is an example, and that it has brought misfortunes on Russia, and led to the demise of the traditional Russian intelligentsia."[235] Although Pasternak called these propositions "erroneous," these lines surely must have made some *Pravda* readers think.

Later on Pasternak wrote a poem about the awarding of the Nobel Prize, which included the following lines: "I am caught like a beast at bay./

Somewhere are people, freedom, light,/ But all I hear is the baying of the pack./ There is no way out for me./ . . . /How dare I write such stuff/—I, scoundrel and evildoer,/ Who made the whole world weep/ At the beauty of my native land."[236]

Pasternak died shortly afterward. If it is true that cancer is an affliction of sorrow, then that is what caused the poet's death. He passed away on May 30, 1960. Hundreds of people gathered for his funeral in Peredelkino, near Moscow. They had come to bid farewell to a writer who had been hounded to death by the state.[237]

The Pasternak affair showed that the Soviet regime, after having returned to "Leninist norms," could be just as cruel and unfeeling as it had been under Stalin. But now its fits of anger were directed at more specific targets. It no longer struck indiscriminately.

This affair roused indignation in liberal circles in the Soviet Union and the West, as the many sympathetic letters the writer received show. For the first time after long years of dictatorship in the Soviet Union a kind of public opinion began to awaken. The political prisoners who had returned from the camps played a not insignificant role in this awakening. Some of them took an active part in the struggle for the democratization of society, for example, Aleksei V. Snegov, a former party functionary who had served seventeen years in the camps. Snegov, whose survival was almost a miracle, was released soon after Stalin's death and was named deputy chief of the political department of the Gulag thanks to Mikoyan's influence. It was to a great degree because of Snegov's energetic efforts that the release of political prisoners, their rehabilitation, and their return to normal life went relatively quickly. Snegov also took an active part in the discussions on party history which occurred in those years. After Khrushchev's resignation Snegov continued the struggle for the restoration of the historical truth. His speech during the discussion of the book *June 22, 1941* by the historian Aleksandr Nekrich at the Institute of Marxism-Leninism in February of 1967 was used as a pretext to charge Snegov officially with antiparty activity, which led to Snegov's expulsion from the CPSU.

Snegov was a Communist and a follower of Lenin. He believed that the return to "Leninist norms" would bring about the regeneration of the CPSU. This misconception was typical of many Communists of the older generation. Some of them honestly believed in such a possibility; others tried to talk themselves into believing it, for otherwise their entire life in the service of the Communist party would have seemed a senseless sacrifice. Still others thought that everything was in order, including the arrests of the "enemies of the people," the purpose of which was theoretically to purge the country of its "fifth column." Only one mistake had been made in this process—their own arrest. Their understanding of events had not advanced one bit since the day of that arrest. The CPSU made skillful use of some of those who had been rehabilitated, placing them in various advisory boards of district party committees or charging them with leading salutary talks with the generation that was coming of age.

Some old Communists, who had devoted their entire life to building communism, developed a certain guilt complex. They decided to dedicate their remaining days to the struggle against lawlessness and against any revival of Stalinism. But this was a thorny path. Symptomatic was the story of Fedor Shults, a party member since 1919 who had been arrested in 1937 for criticizing the cult of personality and who spent a total of nineteen years in the camps and in penal exile. Fully rehabilitated in 1956, he was again arrested in December of the same year because of a letter he sent to *Pravda*. In this letter Shults cited specific cases to refute Khrushchev's statement that there were no more political prisoners in the Soviet Union. Among other things he pointed out that a 106-year-old Socialist Revolutionary named Preobrazhenskaya was still in prison in Mariinsk. The court committed Shults to a special psychiatric hospital in Leningrad for compulsory treatment. He remained there until April 1958, and it was not until June 1964 that the case against him was finally dismissed for lack of evidence.[238]

The writer Aleksei Y. Kosterin (1896–1968) became well known as a defender of the Chechens, the Ingush, and the Crimean Tatars, who had been unjustly deported from their native lands. Kosterin was an Old Bolshevik from the Northern Caucasus who had spent seventeen years in Stalin's prisons. His forthright and uncompromising position regarding the crimes committed by the Soviet government finally led to his expulsion from the party and the Writers' Union. His funeral on November 14, 1968, turned into a public act of condemnation of the totalitarian Soviet regime.

There were other honest and fearless members of the older generation who considered themselves Marxist-Leninists, such as S. P. Pisarev.

In the late 1950s and early 1960s Petr Yakir, son of the Red Army commander Iona Yakir, who had been executed in 1937, did much to publicize the truth about the crimes of the Stalin regime. He had spent his childhood and youth in prisons and camps of the Gulag and in exile. A historian by education, Petr Yakir lectured before large audiences at enterprises and institutions until the authorities prohibited his appearances. A group of young intellectuals who advocated the defense of constitutional rights gathered around Yakir. He and his friends Ilya Gabay, Yuli Kim, and others for many years supported the struggle of the Crimean Tatars for full rehabilitation and the right to their historical homeland.

Major General Petr Grigorenko, a department head at the Frunze Military Academy, dared to express his opinions on September 7, 1961, at a party conference of Moscow's Lenin District during a discussion on the new party program, which was to be approved by the Twenty-second Party Congress. In his speech Grigorenko warned of the danger of the emergence of a new cult of personality and suggested a series of measures as safeguards, such as the abolition of high salaries for functionaries in the party and state apparatus as well as the possibility of their removal by vote. The conference participants applauded Grigorenko. They rejected the demand of the shocked party apparatchiks that his mandate as a delegate be withdrawn. During a break in the proceedings, however, the delegates were subjected to some "brainwashing" and subsequently, with the same unanimity, voted to denounce Grigorenko's speech as "politically immature."[239] Grigorenko was removed from his post at the academy and transferred to the Far East.

There he founded the League of Struggle for the Revival of Leninism on November 7, 1963, the anniversary of the October revolution. Its aim was "to do away with all distortions of Lenin's doctrine, to restore Leninist norms in party life, and to give real power back to the Soviets of toilers' deputies." Grigorenko also sought curbs on the power of the bureaucracy and police, free elections, popular control over the authorities, and the possibility of replacing government officials and functionaries. Grigorenko wrote leaflets describing the suppression of the mass movements which had erupted and been suppressed between 1958 and 1963 at Temir-Tau, Novocherkassk, and other places. One of the leaflets was entitled, "Why Is There No Bread?" The members of the organization were arrested. After four months of "psychiatric treatment," they recanted and were released.[240] On the basis of a statement made by a group of medical experts at the Serbsky Psychiatric Institute in Moscow, Grigorenko was sent to a special psychiatric hospital—a prison hospital.[241] Before that he was stripped of his general's rank and discharged from the army without the right to a pension. So began Grigorenko's sufferings.

Some young people reacted with particular anger to the disclosure of Stalin's crimes because they felt deceived and cheated. They responded by forming societies and clandestine youth circles, organizations where heated discussions about the past took place and naive plans were devised for changing Soviet society.[242] Many dissidents who later took part in the Soviet democratic and human rights movement came from these groups.

For young people this was a time of fearless search for truth, of growing maturity and disillusionment, of rejection and of reconciliation with reality. In the late 1950s and early 1960s many young people joined expeditions and went to the Urals, Siberia, and the Far East. They often expressed their emotion and unconscious drive to break away from the usual truisms and attain freedom of self-expression in verses and songs, in which lyricism and politics, protest and hopes, were combined often in the most curious way.

There have always been youth circles. Those which came into existence right after Stalin's death were most interested in reexamining recent history. One such group, which called itself the Union of Patriots of Russia, appeared in 1958 at Moscow University. It was led by L. N. Krasnopevtsev, a graduate student in the Department of the History of the CPSU who had previously majored in history at Moscow University. The nine members of the group were graduate students and young scholars from Moscow University and the USSR Academy of Sciences. They wanted to work out a new ideology, distinct from the official party ideology. They also sought to spread their views among other illegal youth circles. A significant impetus was given to this group and to other future dissidents by the International Youth Festival held in Moscow in 1957. There contacts were made and discussions held; Krasnopevtsev, for example, chaired a discussion club at Moscow University. The group established contacts with the Polish magazine *Po prostu*, the chief editor of which was Liasota, a member of the Polish parliament. The group wrote and distributed a number of leaflets. According to unconfirmed reports, the members of the organization wrote a new history of the CPSU or at least planned to do so, but no manuscript has ever been found. The group's participants were soon arrested, put on trial, and sentenced to camp and prison terms of varying lengths. Three members—Krasnopevtsev himself, Vladimir Menshikov, a junior researcher at the Oriental Institute of the Academy of Sciences, and Leonid Rendel—were sentenced to ten years.[243]

In 1956 an illegal student group calling itself Freedom of Speech was founded in Siberia; all its members were arrested the very same year. Among them was Leonid Borodin (see Chapter 11). In November 1958 another group of Moscow University students was arrested and charged with forming an anti-Soviet organization and attempting to establish an underground printshop. In Leningrad some Social Democrats (Trofimov, Golikov, and others) formed a group. They were also arrested and sentenced.[244]

At Mayakovsky Square in Moscow a monument to the poet Vladimir Mayakovsky was set up in the summer of 1958. Soon lovers of poetry began to gather there regularly to recite Mayakovsky's verses, their own works, or other poets' writings. The Komsomol leadership, instructed to keep a watchful eye on the gatherings at the Mayakovsky monument, at first was pleased by the opportunity to direct the youths' endeavors along the usual channel of Communist "romanticism." In those years the party and Komsomol leaderships expended tremendous effort to make the Komsomol more attractive. Poetry readings at Mayakovsky Square, youth clubs, and amateur theatrical and musical groups, all were to serve the same basic purpose: to maintain the party's influence over the young generation, which was restless and rebellious. But soon the recitation of poems was joined by heated disputes and discussions. And the content of the poetry began to differ completely from that stipulated in the plans of the Komsomol leadership.

At the end of 1958 the KGB was headed by Aleksandr Shelepin, former chief of the Komsomol. Many Komsomol leaders were advanced at that time into the agencies of state security. Shelepin had graduated from the Institute of Philosophy, Literature, and History (IFLI), a famous university which had produced many poets, writers, philosophers, and historians. He knew quite well what the events at Mayakovsky Square meant. Police raids began. The young people who gathered at the monument on Saturdays and Sundays were subjected to provocations, and beatings, along with searches of their homes and confiscation of their books and manuscripts. In some cases students were expelled from universities. The press joined the crusade, calling the young people at Mayakovsky Square "sluggards" and "idlers," stirring up the hatred of narrow-minded Soviet citizens. In May 1961, during the reading of a poem dedicated to the thirtieth anniversary of Mayakovsky's suicide, the KGB provoked a fight during which a number of young people were beaten up.[245] On the eve of the Twenty-second Party Congress, the most active participants in the readings were arrested: Vladimir Bukovsky, Eduard Kuznetsov, Ilya Bakshtein, and Vladimir Osipov. All were put on trial for "anti-Soviet agitation and propaganda," and convicted.

Between 1959 and 1961 the first uncensored magazines were circulated in manuscript form. One of them was the Moscow magazine *Syntax*, which contained writings by such already established authors as Bella Akhmadulina, N. Glazkov, N. Nekrasov, Bulat Okudzhava, and Boris Slutsky.[246] One of the magazine's editors was future dissident Aleksandr Ginzburg, at that time still a student at Moscow University. In all, three issues of *Syntax* were produced. In 1960 Ginzburg was expelled from the university and then sentenced to two years in a camp. In 1961 Yuri Galanskov, a former student at the Historical Archive Institute, published the typewritten magazine *Phoenix '61*. The non-Russian republics also had their share of circles and organizations.

In 1961 there was a series of arrests in the Ukraine after an allegedly underground organization, the Ukrainian Workers' and Peasants' Union, was discovered in Lvov. The members of the group, Lev Lukyanenko, Ivan Kandyba, Stepan Virun, and others, denied that their organization was illegal. In a programmatic document the group had criticized the Soviet government's policy toward the Ukraine from an orthodox Leninist point of view. The members of the organization intended to separate the Ukraine from the USSR as an independent socialist state, applying the constitutional right to self-determination. The group's leader, Lukyanenko, asserted that his group represented Ukrainian public opinion and was in accordance with the constitution. All members of the group were convicted of anti-Soviet activity in May 1961. Lukyanenko and Kandyba were sentenced to death, but this penalty was later reduced to fifteen years' imprisonment. [247]

Lukyanenko's trial showed that the Soviet leaders feared nothing so much as the peoples' struggle for self-determination and that they did not hesitate to suppress such tendencies most ruthlessly. The members of a similar group, the Baltic Federation—an "illegal, anti-Soviet, nationalist organization," as it was termed in the indictment—were arrested in 1962. Among them was the journalist Viktor Kalnish, who had graduated from the Moscow Pedagogical Institute. His sentence was ten years in the camps.

In 1963 two Leningrad engineers, Valery Ronkin and Sergei Khakhaev, wrote a book entitled *From the Dictatorship of the Bureaucracy to the Dictatorship of the Proletariat,* which they wrote from the perspective of "true Marxism." They and several others (among them S. Mashkov) published two issues of a typewritten magazine *Kolokol (The Bell).* In June 1965 the members of the group were arrested and sentenced to varying terms of confinement in labor camps. In 1964 a similar organization was discovered in Moldavia. It called itself the Democratic League of Socialists. Among those arrested were the teacher Nikolai Tarnavsky and Ivan Cherdyntsev. They were sentenced to six years in the camps. Another member of the League, Nikolai Dragosh, author of the pamphlet "The Truth for the People," was sentenced to seven years in a strict regime labor camp.

The authorities reacted very nervously to any manifestation of nationalist feelings in the republics. This was true first of all in regard to the western Ukraine, where popular resistance to Soviet rule had been suppressed only in the early 1950s. One method used to combat "nationalism" was to destroy national cultural treasures and archives. On May 24, 1964, a fire broke out at the library of the Ukrainian Academy of Sciences. The cause, according to the official report, was arson committed by a library employee named Pogruzhalsky for personal motives, but an unofficial investigation showed that the arson was arranged by the KGB and was aimed at destroying Ukrainian cultural treasures: among the items destroyed in the fire were the archives of the Ukrainian Central Rada and a number of works of native folklore, literature, and history. Two months earlier a stained glass window placed in the entrance hall of Kiev University to mark the one hundred fiftieth anniversary of Taras Shevchenko's birth had been removed and destroyed. In May of the same year unauthorized celebrations in honor of Shevchenko, the Ukrainian national poet, were officially prohibited.[248]

Topics such as the search for freedom, love of the Ukraine, and justice found their way into the writings of the Ukrainian poets Lina Kostenko, Ivan Drach, Mykola Vinhranovsky, and Vitali Korotych. The poet Vasyl Symonenko, who died of cancer in 1963 at the age of twenty-eight, became a hero of Ukrainian youth. In a certain sense Symonenko had carried on the tradition of Shevchenko.[249]

Pasternak, by sending his manuscript outside of the Soviet Union, had broken a taboo and set a precedent. Other authors followed in his footsteps, for example, Valery Tarsis, who had a number of writings printed in the West, in particular *Ward Number Seven*, in which he criticized and ridiculed the Soviet way of life. The young poet Evgeny Evtushenko likewise published his *Precocious Autobiography* in the French magazine *L'Express*. Finally, an entire pleiad of authors who lived in the Soviet Union began to publish their writings under their own names in the West. Publishing in foreign countries gradually became more or less permissible legally in spite of all the obstacles, reprisals, and persecution.

For Soviet literature the first decade after Stalin's death was a time when lost values were revived. The liberation from Stalin's legacy, the attempts to uncover the roots of the unhappy past, and the desire to arrive at a clear understanding of present-day Soviet society created an entirely new kind of literature. Khrushchev was anxious to use the anti-Stalinist attitudes held by the most talented writers in the struggle against his enemies on the Presidium of the Central Committee. That was why it was possible for Evtushenko's famous poem, "The Heirs of Stalin," which warned against the danger of a revival of Stalinism, to be printed in *Pravda*.[250] During those same years Evtushenko composed the poem "Babi Yar," in which he fiercely attacked anti-Semitism. The writer Aleksandr Tvardovsky, author of the narrative poem "Vasily Terkin," popular during the war, returned to the editorial board of the magazine *Novy mir*. In 1963 *Izvestia* published Tvardovsky's poem "Terkin in the Other World," a blatant satire of contemporary Soviet society.[251] Under Tvardovsky, *Novy mir* became a center for nonconformist writers. The magazine kept publishing novels and stories through which criticism of Soviet reality ran like an unbroken thread. In 1962 *Novy mir* published *Silence*, a novel by Yuri Bondarev about the fate of a war veteran who has an encounter with the Soviet machinery of terror.[252]

In the same periodical Ilya Ehrenburg's memoirs were printed, in which he tried to reconstruct the real history of Russian literature. Yet he too sought to justify Stalin's misdeeds and the path the Soviet Union had taken.

But *Novy Mir*'s greatest accomplishment of those years was the 1962 publication of *One Day in the Life of Ivan Denisovich*, by Aleksandr Solzhenitsyn.[253] This book about one typical day of a Soviet prisoner, written by a former camp inmate, became a milestone not only in the history of Russian literature but in Russian history itself. The novel was printed as a result of Khrushchev's personal authorization and only after a heated struggle. It was Tvardovsky as chief editor of *Novy mir* who introduced Solzhenitsyn to Russian readers. The mere fact that a labor camp prisoner appeared as the main character in a work of official Soviet literature was indeed a revolutionary act. The publication of *Ivan Denisovich* aroused enthusiasm among the noncomformist sectors of society and hatred among the Stalinists. Thereafter several short works by Solzhenitsyn—"The Incident at Krechetovka Station," "Matryona's Home," "For the Good of the Cause"—appeared in *Novy mir*.[254] The nomination of Solzhenitsyn for the Lenin Prize for Literature in 1963 marked the turning point from official praise and recognition for Solzhenitsyn, the member of the Soviet Writers' Union, to official persecution of Solzhenitsyn, the symbol of reawakening Russian realism. His attempts to publish the novels *Cancer Ward* and *The First Circle* met with resistance from the "partocracy," which mobilized the concentrated power of the party and state, and all the reserves of narrow-minded Soviet philistinism, for the struggle against the great writer. Both novels were printed only outside the Soviet Union, as were all his subsequent works.

The Stalinists and their enemies understood very well that literature had posed a central question: the question of spiritual values and especially freedom of expression in all its forms. Was a renewed commitment to human values possible in Soviet society? After all, each and every significant literary work of the post-Stalin era basically dealt with the ancient yearning for freedom, the hatred of violence and oppression. There was good reason for the authorities to meet with shock and fear, and later to sharply condemn, Vasily Grossman's novel *For the Right Cause*, because of its powerful denunciation of injustice.[255] The KGB confiscated the manuscript of the second part.[256]

In this period some timid attempts were also made to vary the standard theatrical repertoire, which consisted of either ephemeral works echoing official propaganda or the same old classical Russian plays, which had been staged repeatedly, year after year, ever since the pogrom against "rootless cosmopolitanism." Now young actors formed new ensembles, and theater groups not burdened with a Stalinist history and tradition were founded, in particular the Sovremennik Theater in Moscow. Similarly in Leningrad the Theater of Drama and Comedy directed by N. Akimov attained great popularity. Other theaters offered a substantively different repertoire than before. *Did Ivan Ivanovich Ever Exist?* by Nazym Khikmet and Tvardovsky's *Terkin in the Other World* were presented, both biting satires of contemporary Soviet society.

There was also some movement in the pseudo-classical fine arts. At an exhibition at Moscow's Manege Hall, painting and sculpture by young artists appeared, in particular the sculptures of Ernst Neizvestny. These represented a daring challenge to the pompous official school of Soviet classicism. During a tour of the exhibition Khrushchev and his staff were disgusted by the abstract works; they simply did not understand them. The prime minister and Neizvestny had a heated argument. The sculptor declared that being prime minister was not enough to understand art. Khrushchev left angrily, and the head of the KGB and former Komsomol leader Shelepin threatened Neizvestny in a whisper: "Someday you'll rot in a camp." But despite all obstacles, threats, persecution, and the banning of nonofficial exhibitions, new trends in the arts forced their way through.

By the end of the 1950s *samizdat* had developed. This was the term for literature circulated privately in handwritten copies or typewritten manuscripts. The first works to be publicized through the *samizdat* network were *Journey Into the Whirlwind* by Evgeniya Ginzburg and *Kolyma Tales* by Varlam Shalamov. These books were never printed in the Soviet Union, but they received wide recognition in the West, where they were also published in Russian. Ginzburg and Shalamov had gone the painful route of the Soviet concentration camps. They described the inhuman sufferings of millions of people, the victims of the terrorist Soviet regime.

To "rot" in the camps became slightly more difficult—but still possible— since the regime, though it had become less strict, had not changed its nature. The new penal code of the RSFSR, introduced in 1961, and later on some new statutes on the corrective labor camps despite their severity at least set certain limits to despotism. Khrushchev and Voroshilov announced to the entire world that there were no more political prisoners in the Soviet Union. This was not surprising, for political prisoners had been reduced to the status of common criminals. Under article 190–1 of the Penal Code of the RSFSR, the "dissemination of fabrications discrediting the Soviet state and social system" is treated as a crime. It was not difficult to bring charges under this article against anyone who expressed dissent. There was an even worse punishment for the most obstinate resisters:

confinement in a mental hospital, either a "special," i.e., prison facility (*psikhushka*) or an ordinary psychiatric institution. This meant in reality that anyone could be institutionalized on the basis of a doctor's "expert testimony" for openly questioning the correctness of a political decision— let alone calling for the overthrow of Soviet power. Soviet psychiatrists, who are completely under state control, have even invented a special disease, the existence of which is hard to prove but just as hard to disprove: "creeping schizophrenia." In other cases the formula "reformist complex" is used. As time went on confinement to mental hospitals became one of the most widely used methods in the struggle against dissidents. Soviet power had always used this method—under Lenin as well as Stalin—but never to such an extent as in the post-Stalin era under Khrushchev and Brezhnev.[257] For example, while Khrushchev was prime minister, Bukovsky, Grigorenko, Alexander Esenin-Volpin, and D. Ya. Boss were confined in mental hospitals for purely political reasons.

Despite such reprisals the movement for civil rights continued throughout the Soviet Union. Only a relatively small number were involved—dozens, perhaps hundreds—but the state itself continued to provoke dissent.

In 1958, in response to a reawakening of religious interest among the younger generation, an antireligious campaign was started by order of the CPSU Central Committee. The campaign was accompanied by scandalous "disclosures" about the secrets of Christian community life. But the atheist crusade had an unforeseen effect. The struggles within the churches escalated and led to a split in the Baptist church in 1961, to the forming of a new community by the Evangelical Baptist Christians, and then to a nationwide mass persecution of these people, including trials, children being taken away from their parents, and so on.

In the same year the Russian Orthodox church was reorganized. Now it was no longer the general meeting of all members of the community that decided on issues of concern to the parish community but a "council of twenty"—twenty chosen representatives heading the church as "elders," but these elders had to be approved by the local government authorities. Thus the vast majority of church members were prevented from taking part in church affairs.

This reform went along with the state's drive to limit religious activities and to keep them under total control. The officially approved Russian Orthodox church also experienced protests and unrest. A number of clerics wrote open letters and appeals. The most famous were by Father Gleb Yakunin, Father Nikolai Eshliman, Anatoly Krasnov-Levitin, and Boris Talantov. By order of the patriarch the archbishop of Kaluga Germogen was removed from his post because in 1966–1967 he supported the rebellious priests in their protests against violations of the law of 1929, which said that the church affairs of a community were to be decided upon by the general meeting. In the mid-1960s religious dissidents drew increasingly closer to the democratic movement because of the struggle for democratization and for civil rights.

By the beginning of the 1960s the civil rights movement was born. Its founder was Alexander Esenin-Volpin, a talented mathematician, a son of the famous Russian poet Sergei Esenin. Volpin put forth a very simple concept: in the Soviet state—no matter what kind of state it was—laws and a constitution did exist. The misfortune of the society was that the citizens did not believe in the laws, did not know the laws, and therefore could not defend their rights. Violations of rights and laws by party and state functionaries should necessarily be countered by a struggle for compliance with Soviet laws, for compliance with the constitution. This idea, which was the same advocated by Valery Chalidze, received more and more support from nonconformists and liberals, among whom the human rights movement developed in the mid-1960s. In this way, from the beginning most of these activists rejected conspiratorial activity and took the path of open struggle for official compliance with the Soviet constitution, which contained the basic civil rights. Their aim was to ensure that the rights guaranteed by the constitution would be put into effect in daily life.[258]

In this period a feeling of civic responsibility for the domestic and foreign policy of the Soviet regime reawakened. Scientists who took part in developing atomic and thermonuclear weapons for the Soviet Union became aware of the catastrophic consequences of the use of such weapons. Their concern took various forms. In 1956 two physicists at the Thermotechnical Institute (now the Institute of Theoretical and Experimental Physics)—Yuri Orlov and a man named Goldin—raised the demand that those guilty of crimes in the Stalin era should be held personally responsible. Both were expelled from the CPSU, and Orlov was dismissed from the institute.

In 1957, three years after the first testing of a hydrogen bomb, Academician Andrei Sakharov, influenced by the writings of Albert Schweitzer, Linus Pauling, and others, joined the struggle to end the tests. In 1958 Sakharov pointed out in internal memoranda that if the testing of hydrogen bombs continued there would be a danger of radioactive contamination. He asked Academician Kurchatov, chief of the Soviet atomic project, to intervene. Kurchatov flew to the Crimea, where Khrushchev was vacationing. But nothing came of it. In October 1958 tests were conducted.[259] In 1961, at a meeting between Khrushchev and some atomic scientists, it became known that the Soviet leadership had decided to underscore the pressure it was exerting on the German question with a new series of thermonuclear weapon tests. Sakharov wrote to Khrushchev to warn him against this step: "To resume tests after a three-year moratorium would undermine the talks on banning tests and on disarmament and would lead to a new round in the arms race, especially in the sphere of intercontinental missiles and antimissile defense." Khrushchev's response, in an off-the-cuff speech at the same meeting, was frank and cynical. "We can't say aloud that we are carrying out our policy from a position of strength, but that's the way it must be," Khrushchev went on. "I would be a slob, and not chairman of the Council of Ministers, if I listened to the likes of Sakharov."[260]

The Ministry of Middle Machine Building, pursuing its own narrow interests, ordered another test in 1962 which was technically quite unnecessary. Sakharov reports: "The explosion was to be powerful, so that the number of anticipated victims [of the fallout] was colossal."[261] Realizing the criminal nature of this plan, Sakharov tried to stop it by threatening to resign, but to no avail. Then he pleaded with Khrushchev in a phone conversation to stop the tests—in vain. Why would the Soviet leadership worry about the victims of radioactivity when the purpose was to intimidate the United States and the rest of the world with Soviet military strength? Sakharov writes: "The feeling of impotence and fright that seized me on that day has remained in my memory ever since, and it has worked much change in me as I moved toward my present attitude."[262]

The search for freedom, the movement for a liberalization of society, and the revival of individual responsibility for the fate of the country and the people constituted the begining of a spiritual renewal.

This renewal developed in an atmosphere of growing dissatisfaction among the population because of food shortages and the low standard of living.

In Novocherkassk the workers finally exploded in anger.

## THE SHOOTING AT NOVOCHERKASSK

The immediate reason for the disturbance at Novocherkassk was that on June 1, 1962, a decree was published raising prices 30 percent for meat and 25 percent for butter.[263] As is customary in such cases, the Soviet newspapers reported that the people as a whole had approved the new "social advance" of the party and government.[264]

On the very same day—the authorities had overlooked this coincidence—the wages for workers at the Novocherkassk Electric Locomotive

Plant (NELP) were lowered as much as 30 percent. Early in the morning the workers at the foundry began a heated discussion of these developments.

The background to the Novocherkassk events is as follows. Because of the CPSU Central Committee was not able to raise labor productivity by normal means, by making the plan correspond to the productive capacity of the enterprises and real wages, it had decided to organize a new campaign to reduce production costs. Extraordinary efforts were made by the Rostov regional party committee, and not for the first time.

In 1960 a campaign for additional work on a voluntary basis had begun "on the initiative of doctors" in Rostov. This means in reality that the doctors pledged to work a few more hours voluntarily and without pay after an exhausting day. The "initiative" was approved by party organizations in other cities, who seized on it and developed it further. If we recall that at that time doctors (mostly women) belonged to one of the lowest wage groups in the Soviet Union, it is easy to imagine how desperate their situation was. After a while the doctors' "voluntary" work came to a halt and was forgotten, but the idea—which, by the way, was not at all new—of overcoming the weaknesses in the Soviet economy at the expense of the working population received further development in Rostov.

In April 1962 the workers of the Rostov Agricultural Machinery Plant appealed to the workers of other enterprises to reduce costs of production.[265] As is customary, the initiative immediately received a positive response. Among those who responded were enterprises in Novocherkassk. Besides the NELP, the Nikolsk Mining Equipment Plant, the Novocherkassk Electric Power Plant, and a number of others joined the campaign to reduce costs of production. The Novocherkassk city party committee later summarized the commitment as follows: "to save 100 rubles per worker in one year."[266] This meant in practice a wage cut of about 10 percent.[267]

The workers who gathered at the locomotive plant the morning of June 1 posed a question, "What are we going to live on now?" They were answered mockingly by plant director Kurochkin: "You're used to wolfing down meat pies—put jam in them instead." The infuriated workers chased Kurochkin out of the plant; a strike became inevitable, and at about noon 11,000 employees of the NELP stopped work.[268] Although delegates of the plant were sent to other factories, workers there could not be persuaded to join the strike.

A group of workers began dismantling the rails on the nearby rail line to Moscow and building barriers. Women also sat down on the tracks to stop the trains. Slogans appeared on the walls at the factory buildings: "Down with Khrushchev" and "Use Khrushchev for sausage."[269]

On the evening of June 1, soldiers and militia were concentrated at the

NELP and its workers' settlement, which were located a few kilometers outside of Novocherkassk across the Tuzlov River. Tanks were stationed on the Tuzlov bridge. Traffic was stopped. At night about thirty workers were arrested as "ringleaders" of the strike.[270]

On the morning of June 2, the strikers at the NELP were joined by workers from other factories. Novocherkassk also had a rather large number of students—about 16,000 enrolled at the Polytechnical Institute. There had long been unrest among the students because of assignment to undesirable workplaces. It is hard to tell how many students were involved in the uprising. Solzhenitsyn, for example, claims that students were locked up in their dormitories and university buildings on the morning of June 2.[271] According to information published in the West, students did take part in the uprising.[272]

Workers from the NELP, numbering about 300, including women and children, crossed the Tuzlov bridge and headed toward the center of Novocherkassk. They were carrying portraits of Lenin. The demonstration was completely peaceful. Once in the city, the procession grew quickly. Spontaneous mass meetings took place, with speeches given from the backs of trucks. On Moskovskaya Street the demonstrators tried to break down the doors of the municipal police station, hoping to free their imprisoned comrades, but they were met with gunfire and withdrew. Thus the first shots fired in Novocherkassk were by the police. The demonstrators marched on to the building of the city party committee, but it had been vacated. From the balcony of this building the workers gave speeches. Meanwhile, soldiers had arrived and occupied the post office, the bank, and the radio station. Novocherkassk was sealed off by troops, all roads into the city being blocked. Soldiers entered the city party committee, while outside submachine gunners started to push the demonstrators back. Judging by some accounts, the first line of soldiers was soon replaced because the officer in charge committed suicide in front of the soldiers unit so as not to have to fire on the populace. When the soldiers opened fire, they first shot over the heads of the crowd, by accident killing some boys who had climbed into nearby trees. The crowd was enraged. Then the troops fired directly into the crowd—with dumdum bullets.

It was said that there were many soldiers of non-Russian nationality among the troops, who had been transferred to Novocherkassk especially for this mission by order of General Pliev, commander-in-chief of the Northern Caucasus Military District.[273]

The crowd began to flee but the killing continued: the soldiers were shooting people in the back. The streets and squares emptied. The dead and wounded were loaded onto trucks.

According to Western sources, several hundred people lost their lives at Novocherkassk. Solzhenitsyn comes to the conclusion that about seventy or eighty were killed, forty-seven of them by dumdum bullets, a brutal weapon that had previously been used to suppress the prison revolt at Kengir.[274]

After a while the crowd poured into the city's central square once again, and again they were fired upon.

The soldiers who had fired on the crowd the first and second times had already been replaced by others, so when the returning people appealed to their consciences and cursed at them, they answered that they had just arrived. To remove the murderers immediately, to cover up the traces of the crime—such were the tactics of the military and political leadership. Basov, secretary of the Novocherkassk city party committee, had fled to Rostov as soon as the first news of disturbances came in. A CPSU Central Committee team headed by Mikoyan and Kozlov flew in to Novocherkassk to take charge. The crowd demanded that Mikoyan come to the scene of the shooting. After all, the blood of the people was still fresh on the trees and benches of the square and in pools on the pavement. "Let Mikoyan come down here! Let him see all this blood," the crowd demanded. Mikoyan and Kozlov promised a delegation of young workers that the affair would be thoroughly investigated and that those responsible would be severely punished. They insisted, however, that the demonstrators go home and put an end to the revolt. But the crowd would not disperse. By the evening of June 2 tanks with Tommy gunners had been brought in to disperse the crowd. As tracer bullets flew through the air, the crowd slowly dispersed.[275]

The next day, June 3, Mikoyan and Kozlov spoke on the local radio station. They went through the usual litany. The events had been provoked by "enemies" of Soviet power. These enemies would be punished. The army had not used dumdum bullets, they had been fired by "enemies." Actually, Mikoyan was not mistaken. The order to shoot at the people had been given by its enemy—by the top leadership of the party bureaucracy in Moscow. Whether Khrushchev was personally involved in the events or not, as the head of the party and government he was certainly responsible for the bloodbath in Novocherkassk. The people of Novocherkassk were punished. None of those who had been injured and taken to the hospitals returned to their homes; their families were banished to Siberia. Many participants in the events were arrested. (KGB agents had taken photos during the demonstration.) A series of closed trials was held, followed by two public show trials. Nine men were sentenced to death and two women to fifteen years in the labor camps.[276] Not one of the murderers was punished.

Nonetheless the price increases for food were postponed for a while in Novocherkassk. The previously empty shelves of the food stores were suddenly filled with a variety of goods—a method commonly used by the Soviet authorities whenever dissatisfied citizens have had to be quieted for a while until all the troublemakers have been tracked down and arrested. In August 1962 Politburo member Kirilenko came to speak at a plenum of the Rostov regional party committee. The first and second secretaries of the Novocherkassk city party committee were not "reelected" to the new regional committee.[277] This was the extent of the punishment of those responsible.

Novocherkassk was not the only city where disturbances occurred; there were also revolts in Kemerovo in the same summer, provoked by food shortages. Demonstrations and the looting of food stores also took place there.[278]

The leadership did not ignore these events by any means. A secret decree of the USSR Council of Ministers of August 10, 1962, demanded that more concern be shown for industrial workers and that they be treated more tactfully. The decree also referred to another reason for the dissatisfaction of the workers: the illegal refusal by enterprise administrations to hand out work books to workers who wanted to quit.[279] Without a work book, it was impossible to start work anywhere at another factory. One of the usual press campaigns began, this one calling for more attention to the needs of the workers.

At the same time, further preventive measures were taken. In many republics the ministry of internal affairs was reorganized as the ministry of the defense of public order, and the militia (police) were armed. New punishments for political crimes, defined as "anti-Soviet propaganda," were introduced (in article 70 of the RSFSR penal code). Trials involving such charges were held in many cities, in 1963, in Minsk, Omsk, and Leningrad.[280]

In 1963 the food situation worsened due to a drought. Many cities experienced a shortage of bread, and people waited in lines in front of stores. In a number of cities there were strikes and disturbances.

As is often the case, a minor incident or chance occurrence would spark a major disturbance. One day in June 1963 a policeman and a soldier got into an argument in the town of Krivoi Rog, when the policeman ordered the soldier to stop smoking on the local bus. The argument ended with the policeman shooting the soldier to death. When the soldier's comrades found out about it they rushed into the city and killed seven policemen. The military authorities then assumed control, imposed martial law, and imposed a curfew.[281]

In this period protest meetings and demonstrations took place in Grozny,

Krasnodar, Donetsk, Yaroslavl, Murom, Gorky, and even in Moscow at the Moskvich Auto Plant.[282]

## THE FALL OF KHRUSHCHEV

The musical chairs of administrative reorganization, the crisis in agriculture, complications in Sino–Soviet relations and in those with the United States all fed the neo-Stalinist tendencies within the Soviet ruling circles. It was said almost openly that the leaders of the Malenkov–Molotov "anti-party group" were right when they warned against rash and impulsive actions.

The "Ryazan miracle" (described in a previous section) and the Cuban missile crisis dealt heavy blows to Khrushchev's reputation as a leader. It was under these conditions that he decided to resume the struggle against the consequences of the personality cult, because in this sphere he held the trump cards against Malenkov, Molotov, and Kaganovich.

In October 1961 the Twenty-Second Party Congress called renewed attention not only to the crimes of Stalin but also to the complicity of Molotov, Kaganovich, Malenkov, and Voroshilov. The newspapers published the texts of death penalties handed down not only against "enemies of the people" but against their wives as well, documents bearing the signatures of Molotov, Kaganovich, and the others. At the congress, itself, speeches denouncing Zhdanov were made. On a motion by the Moscow party organization, Stalin's body was removed from the Lenin Mausoleum,[283] to be buried in a separate grave at the base of the Kremlin wall. For most of the congress delegates this came as a complete surprise. Among those whose careers had been made in the 1930s, that is, who had benefited from Stalin's terror, dissatisfaction was rampant and barely concealed. The party apparatchiks did not know what Khrushchev's intentions were, or how far he would go in this new phase of de-Stalinization. It was in the corridors of the Twenty-second Party Congress that the groundwork was laid for the conspiracy against Khrushchev, a plot involving a fairly influential segment of party officialdom. Its inspirer was Mikhail Suslov, the Central Committee secretary responsible for party ideology. De facto sabotage of de-Stalinization measures began.

At the Twenty-second Party Congress Khrushchev decided to institutionalize the "return to Leninst norms," obviously remembering what had happened after the Twentieth Congress. At his suggestion, the party rules and program were changed. Under the new rules, in all subsequent elections of leading party bodies, their composition had to be changed by one-third.

Thus Khrushchev acquired a weapon that allowed him to manipulate the party apparatus so as to remove undesirables in legal ways.

Generally speaking, Khrushchev, like the majority of Soviet leaders, overestimated his individual power to influence the course of events. While verbally recognizing the existence of objective processes in society, Soviet leaders in practice have constantly intervened in the natural course of events with crude attempts to gain quick successes. Such efforts only produce crises in one area after another, and these cannot be resolved by administrative reshufflings or the erection of new bureaucratic structures. However, such methods were the only ones Khrushchev knew. Seeing that the economy, after a slight upturn in 1958–1959 was running into problems again despite his reforms, he decreed that all party organizations be divided into two parts: one to direct agriculture, the other industry.[284] In late 1962 the party organizations of all provinces (oblasts) and districts (raiony) were split up on this basis, as were government bodies on the province level.

On the district level the district party committees (raikomy) were abolished. Territorial kolkhoz-sovkhoz administrations were set up and each administration's party committee took up the functions of the old raikom.

On the republic and all-union levels separate Central Committee bureaus were established, one for industry, one for agriculture.

In effect Khrushchev divided the party in two.

The party apparatus at all levels was dissatisfied with this arrangement. In provinces rivalries sprang up between leaders of party organizations and those of government bodies, which threatened to cause a disintegration of all authority before long.

The secretaries of party provincial committees (obkomy), who were against reforms in general, were especially opposed to this reform. Khrushchev, with his restless temperament and mania for reform, would not leave them in peace; yet all they wanted was stability and calm.

The top party officials had reconciled themselves to the abolition of the system of special tax-free salary supplements (pakety), but they could not and would not accept instability.

It was not only the top party bureaucracy that was dissatisfied with Khrushchev's policies. He had aroused feelings of protest and resistance in the most varied strata of society, among all who had been pressured or hurt in any way by his mania for reform. This included the industrial workers, whose interests were affected by the school reform and by the moratorium or repayment to citizens for loans made to the government, as well as peasants, collective farmers, blue collar and white collar workers of small cities and towns, who were deprived of the right to cultivate a small plot of land around their homes. Officers in the armed forces were affected by substantial staff reductions and reductions in real earnings. The same was true for state security personnel when bonuses for rank (the number of "stars" on one's shoulders) were abolished.

In virtually every social stratum there was deep dissatisfaction over the unrestrained glorification of Khrushchev as government, military, and party leader.

A kind of court camarilla had taken shape around Khrushchev, headed by his son-in-law Aleksei Adzhubei, who was made editor-in-chief of *Izvestia* and a member of the party's Central Committee. This group controlled the mass media. The Adzhubei clique tried to take over foreign affairs as well. These ambitions alarmed and alienated the minister of foreign affairs and the apparatus of the ministry as a whole. They too found themselves in the anti-Khrushchev camp.

The intelligentsia, Khrushchev's most reliable base of support in his de-Stalinization drive, were increasingly restricted and harassed. A major blow to them was Khrushchev's speech, timed to coincide with the tenth anniversary of Stalin's death, lavishly praising the late dictator for his uncompromising struggle against all opposition elements, explaining Stalin's mistakes to be the result of his overly suspicious nature and the persecution mania that afflicted him especially in his final years.[285]

This speech did not, however, result in a rehabilitation of Stalin. That was not what Khrushchev wanted. In all likelihood he was attempting to "clear himself" of accusations of revisionism brought against him by Mao Tse-tung and circulated by "pro-Chinese" (Stalinist) elements in the Soviet leadership.

Through his frequent public appearances, speeches, interviews with foreign correspondents (sometimes granted after a few drinks), and inappropriate remarks, Khrushchev succeeded in undermining not only his own prestige but also the authority of the government in the eyes of the people, who began to snicker at Khrushchev's speeches. They stopped taking him seriously. All his errors of commission and omission, his antics and buffoonery, were carefully noted by the Stalinists and magnified out of all proportion. It was as though his positive accomplishments, particularly during the war with Germany, were purposely inflated and exaggerated to make him more laughable in the public eye.

By the fall of 1964 the psychological groundwork had been laid for a move against Khrushchev. The party hierarchy, in the overwhelming majority, had reached agreement on the necessity for his removal.

As at the time of Marshal Zhukov's removal, the Presidium of the Central Committee convened in Khrushchev's absence, while he was vacationing at the Black Sea. The support of army and state security leaders had been assured in advance. With everything in readiness, Khrushchev was summoned to Moscow for an expanded session of the Central Committee Presidium. On October 13 the organizer of the conspiracy, Suslov, presented a report to the Presidium with a long list of accusations against Khrushchev. At first Khrushchev tried to put up a fight but finally realizing that he was isolated, was compelled to agree to resign "for reasons of health." The next day a Central Committee plenum convened. It passed a resolution removing Khrushchev from the position of first secretary of the Central Committee and chairman of the Council of Ministers and dropping him from membership in the Central Committee.[286] The resolution was approved without any discussion. No full or alternate member of the Central Committee who might have opposed Khrushchev's removal had been admitted to the session.

The plenum resolved that the posts of first secretary and chairman of the Council of Ministers no longer be held by one person. In light of the experience with Khrushchev, the Presidium decided to fill the post of first secretary with the most calm and even-tempered person possible, one who would not aspire to the role of Leader. That person was Leonid Brezhnev. Aleksei Kosygin became the new chairman of the Council of Ministers.

The years of hope for a democratization of Soviet society were over, and with them, the years of disarray and uncertainty on the part of the regime. The era of Soviet conformism was beginning.

Khrushchev's removal from power marked the end of a "glorious decade." Those years were like a bridge in time between the Stalin era of unlimited terror and the dictatorship of Soviet conformism.

It would be a mistake to call Khrushchev liberal or conservative, progressive or reactionary. He contained hints of each of these. Sometimes these conflicting impulses were at war within him; sometimes they "peacefully coexisted." Khrushchev was a contradictory figure, and the times during which he chanced to rule were contradictory. It is possible that Khrushchev sincerely wished to break with the Stalinist past, both his own and that of the Soviet system. By some miracle, purely human feelings and values survived in Khrushchev, feelings which for the overwhelming majority of Stalin's comrades-in-arms had been completely cast aside or effaced by the passage of time. It cannot be ruled out that the tragic events of the terror in the 1930s and famine in the Ukraine in the 1940s (events in which he bore direct responsibility) played a considerable part in the fact that Khrushchev retained a "human face." During the war years while he was at the front he probably had occasion more than once to reflect on the course of human destiny.

Whatever the reason, it fell to Khrushchev's lot to carry out the truly great mission (it is no exaggeration to call it that) of exposing the crimes of the Stalin regime, that is, of the Soviet system, freeing millions of prisoners from the camps, and posthumously rehabilitating millions of others. The return of non-Russian populations of the Northern Caucasus who had been exiled to Siberia and Central Asia during the war is also to Khrushchev's credit. Under Khrushchev, antilabor legislation was abolished (although not entirely, since the work books were maintained), the tax burden was lightened, the social security system was improved, the construction of housing was expanded, and obligatory loans to the state were dropped.

It would be fair to say that the only reforms of Khrushchev that took hold were the ones that did not undermine the foundations of the regime, for the foundations remained unchanged. Among these were the retention of complete power by the party bureaucracy, preservation of the state security apparatus (though with reduced powers), and the censorship (with the same "protective" functions it had been charged with under Lenin and Stalin). Reforms in the legal code carried out during the Khrushchev era kept alive the possibility that people could be prosecuted for political reasons and for dissent. Under Khrushchev the use of psychiatric measures against dissenters became more widespread.

Khrushchev's reforms aimed at improving the food situation in Soviet society as well as bettering conditions for the most deprived part of that society, the peasantry, were convulsive and inconsistent. They could not have been otherwise because the collective farm system was and remained an insuperable obstacle to economic recovery; yet it was one of the cornerstones of the regime. Khrushchev's attempts to decentralize control of the Soviet economy ran up against the existing practices of the centralized state and naturally failed.

Every time Khrushchev tried to put through a positive reform it proved to be in irreconcilable contradiction to the existing social order and a direct challenge to the interests of the elite, who had acquired a sense of security after Stalin's death. The upper echelons of Soviet society felt that governmental continuity and consistency were essential. Any threat to this was a dangerous challenge. With his reforming zeal, Khrushchev not only irritated the party bureaucracy; he frightened it, in particular by dividing the party administration into separate industrial and agricultural sections.

Khrushchev often frightened himself by what he did. He later admitted that he had feared the "thaw" in 1954 lest it become a flood that would sweep away the regime. This fear was manifested in the suppression of the Hungarian revolution and the bloody reprisals against protesters at Temir-

Tau, Karaganda, and Novocherkassk. Khrushchev underwent a considerable evolution during his years in power. The removal of Stalin's embalmed remains from the Mausoleum on Red Square in 1961, unlike Khrushchev's secret speech of 1956, was not an act of supreme justice but a tactical move in Khrushchev's fight against a growing opposition.

He cut a hole in the iron curtain, but he also built the Berlin Wall. He proclaimed peaceful coexistence, but came very close to provoking nuclear war by placing Soviet missiles in Cuba.

Like every Soviet leader who held supreme power, Khrushchev considered it his duty to express his opinion and pass judgment in all fields without exception, in all areas of social and cultural life. His opinions, especially on literature and art, were remarkably superficial. He accepted only that which in his opinion could be "useful to the people." Here he was the supreme judge. His social intuition warned him of danger in the spread of ideas outside the accustomed framework of party ideology. Anything that would not fit within this narrow framework or in the limits of his understanding of the world drove him to an emotional outburst. Only once did his keen social intuition fail him seriously, when he allowed publication of *One Day in the Life of Ivan Denisovich*.

Khrushchev was the only Soviet leader who tried to adjust to the times. But sometimes he was in a hurry and prodded others to hurry; at other times he would pull back. It was said of him that he tried to leap over an abyss by making two leaps in a row. Probably that is why he was not buried near the Kremlin wall, but in Novodevichy cemetery.

CHAPTER

# 11

# "REAL SOCIALISM": THE BREZHNEV ERA, 1965–1982

## COLLECTIVE LEADERSHIP

The ouster of Khrushchev brought the post-Stalin era to an end. The eleven years that had followed the death of Lenin's heir, Stalin, had been a time of struggle for his mantle, a time for the Soviet system to adapt to its new existence without Stalin and his dictatorship.

The system demonstrated its stability despite the struggle at the top and despite the often ruthless and bloody suppression of the centrifugal forces that emerged after the denunciation of the "personality cult"—both within the heart of the empire and, most significantly, at its outer reaches, in East Berlin, Hungary, and Poland. During this period the regime sought to counteract these centrifugal forces not solely by repression, but also by coopting the reformist tendencies that made their appearance during the era of confusion and uncertainty which is sometimes called The Thaw.

In the post-Stalin era, the main features of the interregnum of the 1920s reappeared under new conditions, more favorable for the Soviet system. These included the rise of a single figure within the collective leadership

603

who gradually subordinated the others to himself, accompanied by an easing of repression in all areas—largely due to the absence of one central leader. Incidentally, all the ins and outs of the struggle in the Soviet Union for a "Stalinism without Stalin" were repeated in China after the death of Mao.

The fight to see who would don Stalin's uniform was a test of the stability of the Soviet system's foundation. It was at the same time a struggle of the party apparatus against all those who wished to enlarge their personal positions at its expense. The unique feature of the Soviet system is that the party controls and monitors everything but is responsible for nothing; it only provides its own "overall leadership." The party makes all the decisions and gives all the orders, including unwritten ones over the phone or in person, and keeps no records. When failures result, it is the government departments or heads of enterprises and institutions which are held responsible.

The party is always right. It corrects the errors of others; it punishes and pardons. Khrushchev had wanted to "bring the party closer to practice," to make it responsible for the day-to-day business of running the country. But the party was wedded to theory, not practice. It was the fountainhead of ideology, the guardian of truth. Khrushchev was challenging the essential feature of the Communist state—a structure unique in human history.

Khrushchev's twofold division of the party had frightened the party apparatus, although perhaps not everyone understood the revolutionary implications of that reform. It was his second reform, however, that frightened the apparatus and lost him its support. At the Twenty-second Party Congress, Khrushchev introduced into the party rules a provision for the obligatory rotation of offices. In all future party elections, one-third of each party committee, from the Presidium to the district committees, would have to be replaced. New people had to be nominated and elected. Exceptions were made only for the first secretary and a handful of "tried and tested officials with long experience." This introduced a principle of instability which would affect every officeholder in the party, something the apparatus would not and could not accept. The apparatchiks had submitted to Stalin's rotation-through-terror, a kind of lottery in which one could cling to the illusory hope of drawing a lucky number, but inevitable rotation "according to law" was more than they could stomach. After Khrushchev's removal the rotation rule was immediately revoked.

The revolt of the apparatchiks against the first secretary, who personified the party's power in general, was an act of self-defense aimed at protecting the power and privileges of each individual bureaucrat. According to one version of the events, given by Solzhenitsyn in *The Oak and the Calf*, as well as by others, the party conspirators originally wanted to award the post of first secretary to Aleksandr Shelepin, the former secretary of the Komsomol Central Committee who had risen to the chairmanship of the KGB and to membership in the party Presidium.[1] But the apparatus was leery of Shelepin's pro-Stalin radicalism. It was said that he intended to seek reconciliation with China, to "tighten the screws" in the economy and public administration, and to strike out energetically at all deviations from orthodox ideology. The apparatus preferred a quieter man, a conservative to be sure, but not one given to extremes. There was something too oppressive about Shelepin the ascetic and purist. Moscow intellectuals jokingly nicknamed him "Iron Shurik" (Shurik being a diminutive of Aleksandr), a play on the nickname of the first head of the Cheka, "Iron Felix" Dzerzhinsky.

The apparatus longed for tranquility. It chose Brezhnev to be its first secretary.

Brezhnev's biography was a model one for the apparatchik, a perfect example of a party functionary's quiet, steady rise through the apparatus to the heights of power. It was perfect especially for its dullness, the absence of any sudden "flights," the constancy with which he ascended step by step, accumulating both sponsors and protégés along the way.

Brezhnev was born in 1906 in the small factory town of Kamenskoe (later renamed Dneprodzerzhinsk), not far from Ekaterinoslav (now Dnepropetrovsk, the provincial capital). Although the son of a worker, he was accepted into the Kamenskoe classic gymnasium, which by the time he graduated had become a vocational school under the Soviet regime. The American journalist John Dornberg, author of the first more or less complete biography of the Soviet leader, was able to gather some information from Brezhnev's former schoolmates, but many details of the chief of state's life remain obscure and unexplained.[2] After secondary school, Brezhnev completed a course of study at a land surveying college, then worked for several years at agricultural agencies in Byelorussia, Kursk, and Sverdlovsk. Suddenly he returned to his home region and changed professions, entering a metallurgical institute, and at the age of twenty-five he joined the party. His career had begun.

A major turning point in Brezhnev's career coincided with one in the history of the Soviet Union itself: the great purges of 1936–1938. In May 1937 he was elected deputy chairman of the Dneprodzerzhinsk city soviet; in May 1938 he was transfered to Dnepropetrovsk to fill the slot of Agitprop head in the provincewide committee of the party. It was here that he truly joined the apparatus and here that he found the teammates who would accompany him to the Kremlin.

Brezhnev's rise began under the wing of Nikita Khrushchev, the new first secretary of the Ukrainian party's Central Committee who had been sent to the Ukraine in 1938 to "put things in order." Khrushchev ruthlessly purged the republic, starting with the party apparatus. Stalin insisted in all earnestness that every party leader train "two or three deputies"—that is, potential replacements. Brezhnev was one of those who were "third in line" and who came in after the first two rows had been eliminated by the purges. He displayed the ideal array of qualities necessary for deliberate and steady advancement without a snap. Completely colorless but reliable, he benefited from Khrushchev's favor both in the province committee and, during the war, in military service, first as head of the political section of one of the armies and then as deputy chief of the political directorate of an entire front. By the end of the war he was the chief of this directorate, and had advanced in rank from lieutenant colonel to major general. He even attracted the attention of Lev Mekhlis, one of Stalin's righthand men.

Brezhnev had the one talent indispensable for a party leader, the ability to lead: to issue orders on virtually every subject, without being a specialist in anything. As secretary of a province committee, first in Zaporozhye, then in Dnepropetrovsk, he oversaw the reconstruction of enterprises and urban areas destroyed during the war. In 1950 Khrushchev, having been made a secretary of the Central Committee by Stalin, brought Brezhnev to Moscow. In July of that year, Brezhnev was sent to Kishinev, capital of Moldavia, to be first secretary of the Moldavian Central Committee, thus becoming boss of one of the fifteen Soviet republics. He transferred a group of close friends from Dnepropetrovsk to Kishinev. Later they formed the core of his innermost circle, those who in the future would be known as the Dnepropetrovsk mafia. To this nucleus he added "reliable people" from Kishinev, for example, Konstantin Chernenko, then head of the propaganda and agitation department of the Moldavia Central Committee. (Chernenko later became head of Brezhnev's private cabinet and the closest adviser to the new first secretary of the party. He was made a Politburo member and in 1979 he assumed the role of "crown prince.")

In 1952, at the Nineteenth Party Congress, Brezhnev became a candidate (or alternate) member of the newly formed Central Committee Presidium. Stalin may well have intended, after the next purge, to fill the place of some full member with this young candidate from Kishinev. During the reorganization of the organs of power after Stalin's death, Brezhnev was put in charge of the political directorate of the Soviet navy, a second-rate post which nevertheless allowed him to establish solid friendships with marshals and admirals.

As Khrushchev rose, Brezhnev automatically rose with him. He held the successive posts of secretary of the Kazakhstan Central Committee, president of the Supreme Soviet of the USSR, and a secretary of the CPSU Central Committee. In October 1964 he turned against his benefactor and ascended to the highest rank. However, according to the usual practice, the new leadership was said to be collective. More than ten years would pass before it became clear that the "collective" leadership had been transformed into one-man rule, just as it had under Stalin and Khrushchev. Under Brezhnev this process was carried out more slowly and prudently, almost imperceptibly. He pursued a painstaking policy of quietly removing the supporters of others and replacing them with his own people. By the end of the 1970s they occupied all the key posts. The Dnepropetrovsk mafia controlled the Politburo and Secretariat and held positions at all lower levels of the hierarchy.

Thus, in the late 1970s, the process was once again complete. After Lenin, after Stalin, and after Khrushchev, each time the system moved inexorably from "collective" to individual leadership, following the most important law of socialist society which Lenin had noted in 1918, the need for "one-man leadership" (*edinolichnoe rukovodstvo*). An inseparable part of this process was the elaboration of a cult around the new leader. Just a year and a half after replacing Khrushchev, who was accused of promoting a "personality cult," Brezhnev took the first step toward creating his own cult. At the Twenty-third Party Congress he proposed that the Presidium resume the name it had had under Stalin (Politburo) and that the title of first secretary likewise be changed. From then on he would be called general secretary, the title Stalin had used.

It took Brezhnev about ten years to acquire all the attributes of the socialist leader, but he did not become a new Stalin. Nevertheless he occupied Stalin's position. "One-man leadership" means that all decisions are made by the narrow circle around the man at the top. So it had been under Lenin, Stalin, and Khrushchev. So it would be under Brezhnev. The leader is the incarnation of the party's power.

## THE PARTY LONGS FOR TRANQUILITY

The removal of Khrushchev was a revolt of the priesthood against the high priest, who had threatened their caste.

Lenin was the first to raise the question of who really holds the power in the Soviet state. His formula, "a workers' state with bureaucratic deformations," was carried further by Trotsky, who after losing power argued that a privileged bureaucratic caste had taken over in the Soviet Union. Milovan Djilas reworked Trotsky's theory and made the concept of "the new class" famous in his book of the same name. The importance of Djilas's book was that it demonstrated, by the example of Yugoslavia, that an identical process was occurring in all the countries where Communist parties had taken power.

The Soviet constitution refers to the Communist party as the "leading force" in Soviet society. At the Twenty-sixth Party Congress in 1981, the party had 17,480,000 members (full and provisional), slightly more than 9 percent of the population.[3] However, it cannot be said that political power is held by the party as a whole.

George Orwell in *1984* spoke of the "outer party" and the "inner party." In 1969 two citizens of Leningrad, a teacher named S. Zorin and an engineer, N. Alekseev, wrote an essay which in *samizdat* came to be known as the Leningrad Program. Analyzing soviet society at the end of the 1960s, they argued as follows:

> The party and the government apparatus constitute a genuine and decisive political force in our country. It is a pyramid whose upper part consists of the party officials belonging to the *nomenklatura*, with the CPSU Central Committee, its Politburo, Secretariat, and departments, at the peak. To this uppermost segment should be added the top military leaders, the apparatus of the KGB and that of the Ministry of Internal Affairs, and all higher-ranking government officials.[4]

The authors of the Leningrad Program saw the *nomenklatura* as an authentic ruling class, what Orwell called the "inner party."

In the first half of the 1920s the term *nomenklatura* referred to a list of key positions that could be filled only by the Central Committee department in charge of personnel assignments and transfers. The list quickly grew to include all leading positions in the party and government and in the trade union, military, and cultural establishments. An elaborate hierarchical structure arose, with *nomenklatura* lists for the CPSU Central Committee, for the central committees of the union republics, and for provincial and district committees.

According to the 1970 census, the number of persons in "leading positions" (i.e., the *nomenklatura*), including the secretaries of base-level party organizations and the chairmen and secretaries of village soviets, was 405,784, or 0.35 percent of the population.[5]

The *nomenklatura* officials, who possess power proportionate to the level on the list in which their office appears, constitute an oligarchy of a particular type, a group defined by its role in the administration of the country.

Aristotle regarded oligarchy as one of the "bad" forms of government and defined it as power for its own sake. The *nomenklatura* is an oligarchy which conceals its power behind an ideological screen, claiming that what exists is "people's power." The *nomenklatura* reproduces itself by selecting people with the necessary attributes, inducting them into the oligarchy, and rewarding them generously. Andrei Sakharov has described the selection process this way:

> Recently a large group of students who had been graduated with honors from various colleges in the country were brought together for a month in Leningrad. . . . (Naturally they were Komsomol members. . . . ) They were lavishly wined and dined at the best restaurants, and entertained in every way—all at no expense to themselves. In short, they lived off the fat of the land. Then they were asked: "Would you like to live like this the rest of your life? If so, go to the VPSh [the Higher Party School]" upon graduation, from which even a minimally gifted person can become at least second secretary of a regional committee.[6]

The *nomenklatura* is a composite of groups that, within the framework of mutual support, engage in shifting alliances and conflicts. It is comparable to the lord and vassal system of feudal society. Each official belonging to the *nomenklatura* has his own vassals and is in turn the vassal of a higher-ranking leader. The general secretary has the greatest number of vassals and there is no one above him; yet he cannot disregard the wishes and interests of his subordinates.

The program of the *nomenklatura* can be summed up in three points: to increase its power, to increase its privileges, and to enjoy both in tranquility. Khrushchev violated these rules.

The collective leadership elected by the October 1964 plenum set about reassuring and calming the *nomenklatura*. In the first major speech of his administration, Brezhnev talked incessantly about problems—"unsolved problems," "new problems," "countless problems," and "problems in need of resolution." He mentioned numerous "shortcomings," "inadequacies," "demands," and tasks that should be completed. Apparently forgetting that he had been second secretary under Khrushchev, he painted a somber picture of the recent past, when "subjectivism and voluntarism" had reigned. The prescription the new first secretary offered was this: "objective evaluation," "proper utilization," the application of "scientific methods," the taking of "necessary measures," but above all, "harmonious development."[7]

The first action of the new leadership was to retract Khrushchev's reforms. The industrial–agricultural division of the party was ended, along with the rotation rule. Khrushchev's economic councils (*sovnarkhozy*) were abolished, and the traditional ministries they had superseded were restored. Also restored was the traditional ten-year school curriculum, which Khrushchev had tried to replace with an eleven-year program of "polytechnical" education. To reassure the population, the leadership restored the right of peasants to cultivate the areas around their homes as private plots whose produce they could sell on the market and halted religious persecution. Most of all, the leadership wished to show what it did not intend to do.

Its positive program was presented at the first post-Khrushchev plenum of the Central Committee, in May 1965, which was especially devoted to the question of agriculture. As Khrushchev had done after Stalin's death, Brezhnev laid the blame for the failures in agriculture on his predecessor, "Tsar Nikita." The new first secretary proposed certain measures that, he claimed, would at last solve the agricultural problem.

Since the first days of the revolution the Communist party had searched for the philosopher's stone that would enable it to perform the miracle of supplying the country with farm products. There had been Lenin's plan for cooperatives, then Stalin's collectivization. After collectivization, a vast array of magic tricks had been tried: Lysenko's charlatanry; fantastic forestation and desert irrigation projects; innovations such as "deep plowing"; cultivating the "virgin lands"; and planting maize throughout the country. All these plans were based on extensive rather than intensive methods. Brezhnev's program was to free the farmers from their obligations to deliver fixed amounts of maize, and to shift the focus back from the virgin lands to the central agricultural regions. Compulsory deliveries of all kinds were reduced until by the end of 1970 quotas were quite low. In theory this meant that the government would buy more from the collective farmers at higher prices after paying low fixed prices for the compulsory deliveries. Brezhnev's program also stressed structural improvements, significant increases in land reclamation projects, the construction of more canals, and increased production of fertilizers and farm machinery and envisioned the allocation of large sums for capital investment to agriculture. Certain long-awaited social measures were included in the program: pensions for collective farmers, and the introduction of a minimum monthly salary, although it was still much lower than wages at factories or state farms.

This "new program" was not new at all. For the most part it continued policies Khrushchev had initiated in 1958.[8] But now these policies were stripped of Khrushchev's promotional rhetoric, his unbelievable promises and unabashed bombast. They were presented as a "scientific plan," guaranteeing "the ascent of agriculture."

Other reforms were announced to correct the "voluntarist errors" in industry. They were presented by Kosygin, approved by the Central Committee plenum of September 1965, and confirmed by the Twenty-third Party Congress in March 1966. They too had been initiated by Khrushchev. The central conception behind the reforms was outlined in an article in *Pravda* on September 9, 1962, by Professor Evsei Liberman of the Kharkov Engineering and Economics Institute. He proposed that profitability be made the central criterion for judging the economic performance of an enterprise. This implied recognition of a principle previously unknown to Soviet economics, the law of supply and demand, and the use of material incentives to raise the productivity of workers and enterprises. A necessary condition for the success of such a reform was the granting of broad autonomy to individual enterprises, freeing them from petty tutelage by the central planning bodies and the agencies of "state control."

Khrushchev, with his restless desire for change, had wished to make use of Liberman's proposals, which enjoyed the support of such prominent Soviet economists as Kantorovich, Nemchinov, and Novozhilov. In August 1964, shortly before his downfall, he allowed the Liberman system to be applied on a trial basis at two textile plants, the Bolshevichka in Moscow and the Mayak in Gorky. Two days after Khrushchev's ouster, Kosygin extended the experiment to several other plants and announced that a reform program for all of Soviet industry was in preparation.

The economic reform finally adopted by the Central Committee plenum and confirmed by the Twenty-third Party Congress was doomed before it began. It sought to reconcile the irreconcilable: to enlarge the rights of individual enterprises—and to restore the central economic ministries abolished under Khrushchev. The Russian historian Klyuchevsky, writing about the reforms of Peter the Great, described a similar attempt to square the circle centuries earlier: "He hoped to use the menace of his authority to instill initiative in an enslaved population.... He wanted the slave to act consciously and freely while remaining a slave."[9]

## DISTURBERS OF THE PEACE

During the 1960s stormy youth protests developed in the West. In France, the United States, and West Germany students were rebelling against their conditions of life and lack of prospects. They had grown up in a consumer society which has raised material prosperity to levels never before seen in history. Society, however, had suffered a loss of spirituality that could not be compensated for.

The Soviet press gave coverage to the student unrest in the capitalist world, enjoying it to the fullest and comparing it unfavorably to the calm among Soviet youth, who were sure of themselves and their future and were always willing to sacrifice for the Communist cause. Behind this facade of familiar boasting, however, hid a different reality. For Soviet youth, too, the 1960s were years of search, accompanied by controversy, overt displays of dissatisfaction with the regime, and active protests against it. In the summer of 1966 G. S. Pavlov, a secretary of the Komsomol Central Committee, wrote somewhat nervously in the periodical *Kommunist* of the younger generation's heightened interest in the history and theory of the Communist movement. Like every new generation, the one born in the late 1940s wanted to learn the truth about its country. The party was confronting the same problem as in the past: it was necessary again to falsify the collective memory of the people and create a legend about the past. Pavlov proposed to bring young people together with Old Bolsheviks who had witnessed the past, to enable the young to hear the "truth" from the lips of those who had witnessed the past.[10] Such meetings were organized everywhere— between young people and those who, by chance, had survived or had taken an active part in the terror. Either type was only too happy to tell the "truth."

But the youth, especially the students, derived no satisfaction from these meetings. They called for public discussions, debate, a free exchange of opinions. Within the student milieu, especially in Moscow, Leningrad, Kiev, and Gorky, the desire to put an end to the cynicism pervading society from top to bottom was increasing and gathering strength. The academic authorities, the Komsomol and party district committees, and local activists tried to limit the composition and number of participants in these public discussions, but to no avail. During a discussion organized by the students of the Physics and Mathematics Department of Moscow University on the topic "Cynicism and Social Ideals" in March 1965, several speakers fiercely denounced the false information being carried by the official press and demanded the full truth about the crimes of the Stalin era. The party was blamed for the lack of faith, skepticism, and cynicism spreading among the youth, because the party had been hiding the truth. During the debate, one of the speakers proposed changing the name of *Pravda* ("Truth") to *Lozh* ("Lie"). Other students demanded that Stalin's accomplices be brought to justice, naming Shvernik, Suslov, and Mikoyan.[11] The alarm evoked in the authorities by the debate soon found its expression in a tightening of the screws at institutions of higher education: the teaching of Marxism-Leninism ("scientific communism") was reinforced, and it was decided that those students who did not pass this subject would not be allowed to take other exams.

Disenchantment began to spread from the universities to the high schools. Posters defending Sinyavsky and Daniel were pasted at night on the walls of Moscow's School No. 16. Members of the group that did it were dispersed to various other schools. The school's principal and a teacher named Baral were reprimanded. Baral was accused of having organized two evening meetings in commemoration of Tukhachevsky and Yakir, two of the military leaders shot in 1937.[12] According to some sources, in 1967 the country had roughly 400 unofficial youth groups that in effect stood in opposition to the regime. The members of these groups held a wide range of opinions, from populism to fascism. "Prophylactic" measures were applied to them: individual talks with officials; lectures on morality; time spent in industrial production for "reeducation" purposes; reassignment to other schools; meetings with parents; and denunciation meetings. More vigorous measures were applied against the most active figures: arrests, trials, and imprisonment.

In September 1965 the writers Andrei Sinyavsky and Yuli Daniel were arrested. They were tried in February 1966 and sentenced—seven years for Sinyavsky, five for Daniel. The trial showed that the government wanted to get rid of its biggest headache: the hopes for liberalization that had arisen under Khrushchev.

The condemnation of the "personality cult" at the Twentieth Party Congress, the liberation of thousands of prisoners and the rehabilitation of some, the relaxation of censorship, which some writers had taken advantage of to raise questions about the terror, the military defeats at the beginning of the war with Germany, the structure of Soviet society, and above all, Khrushchev's behavior and policies which increasingly lurched from one extreme to the next—all these factors had given rise to hopes that the system might be able to reform itself, that a genuine public opinion could develop. Khrushchev had allowed publication of *One Day in the Life of Ivan Denisovich* and, in so doing, had allowed the birth of the Solzhenitsyn phenomenon. Even Solzhenitsyn's genius could not have given this work and his other works, especially *The Gulag Archipelago*, the power that shook the world's conscience if the authenticity of his narrative had not been confirmed by the "official" publication of his first book. In denouncing some of Stalin's crimes and authorizing publication of Solzhenitsyn's works, Khrushchev was not abandoning repression. In *My Testimony*, the first book about the camps to appear under Khrushchev, distributed of course in *samizdat* form, Anatoly Marchenko showed that while the number of inmates had decreased from the days of Stalin, the nature of the camps themselves remained unchanged.

Khrushchev's repressive policies could not stop the social ferment. In addition, this repression had a "confidential" character: trials were held behind closed doors. The crushing of the Novocherkassk revolt in 1962, as of other workers' demonstrations, was kept secret for a long time.

The trial of Sinyavsky and Daniel was the first show trial of the post-Stalin era. Its importance lay in the fact that the defendants were writers, guilty of "agitation or propaganda seeking to undermine or weaken the Soviet power" and of "disseminating, for the same purpose, slanderous statements against the Soviet state and social system." Article 70 of the penal code, adopted under Khrushchev, was used against the defendants. "Agitation and propaganda" and "anti-Soviet slander" referred to the literary work of the authors Sinyavsky and Daniel—their stories, poems, and literary criticism. Their literary works were used as evidence. The authors were tried for the characters they invented. This was perhaps an unprecedented case in the annals of the world's legal practice. Up until then, no one could have envisioned that Dostoevsky might be charged because Raskolnikov committed an act of premeditated murder.

The Sinyavsky–Daniel trial marked the end of the era of "confusion and disarray." The "Thaw" was over. After Stalin's death, writers had been the first to ask questions. Pomerantsev's article "On Sincerity in Literature" had been the first public condemnation of the lies that had impregnated the social fabric and the first public expression of the need for honesty and truth.[13] In various forms and with varying intensity writers were expressing ideas and feelings that had seemingly forever been eradicated in the years following the revolution. Unable to express themselves because of the censorship in literature, the writers found a vehicle in *samizdat*. As Anna Akhmatova put it, "a pre-Gutenberg period" had begun in Soviet literature. Poetry and later prose were being copied and circulated freely in uncensored form. *Samizdat* made possible the discovery of writers shunned by the official literary authorities: Bulgakov, Tsvetaeva, Platonov, Mandelstam, and new writers. The awarding of the Nobel Prize in Literature to Pasternak in 1958 spurred *samizdat*. Uncensored literature found its way to the West, where it was published; this written material was then returned to the Soviet Union and disseminated unofficially. *Tamizdat* (*samizdat* published abroad) was born.

In the Sinyavsky–Daniel trial two forms of free literature were being attacked: on the one hand, the defendants had evaded the confines of the censorship, and, on the other, they had sent their manuscripts abroad to be published. Even worse was the fact that the authors had used pseudonyms. The harsh verdicts against them were a warning to all other *samizdat* and *tamizdat* authors, as well as an indisputable victory for the pro-Stalinist wing of the party. In fact, here and there, voices praising Stalin could be heard.[14]

The Stalinists were actively preparing themselves for a battle at the Twenty-third Party Congress. For example, one week before the opening session four "seditious" plays being performed at Moscow theaters were banned. Also the name of Tvardovsky, the chief editor of the magazine *Novy mir*, was crossed off the list of candidates to be elected delegates from the Moscow party organization to the congress.[15]

The threat of official rehabilitation of Stalin briefly solidified the ranks of the incipient and still amorphous opposition among the intelligentsia. The sentencing of Daniel and Sinyavsky, while sowing confusion and disarray among the "progressives," also sparked a resistance on their part. Sixty-three members of the Writers' Union, soon joined by an additional 200 intellectuals, addressed a letter to the Twenty-third Party Congress and the presidia of both the RSFSR and USSR supreme soviets (each of the latter two possessing the authority to grant a pardon). This letter requested the release of Sinyavsky and Daniel, with the intellectuals' guarantee of their good behavior.[16]

Academician Aksel Berg, one of the foremost Soviet experts on cybernetics, having learned of the plan for Stalin's rehabilitation, announced that if it were to happen, he would resign from the USSR Academy of Sciences in protest.[17]

This period witnessed the birth of a new Russian word, *podpisant* (signer), referring to those who agreed to express their opinions publicly on government actions. This neologism was subsequently followed by others: *inakomyslyashchy* (one who thinks differently), and *dissident*. The "signers" operated within the strict limits of Soviet legality and demanded only that the laws be observed. In the letter by the sixty-three writers, the request for the release of the condemned writers was based on the following arguments: "Our country's interests demand it. The interests of peace demand it. The interests of the international Communist movement demand it."[18]

These protests brought on renewed repression. In 1966–1967 political trials were staged all over the country, in Moscow, Leningrad, Kiev, Lvov, Gorky, Riga, Tashkent, and Omsk. The trial of Sinyavsky and Daniel was met by protests in the West, where no one wanted to believe in the immutable nature of the Soviet system. *Pravda*'s reply was clear and to the point:

> The campaign of unprecedented scope orchestrated in the West in defense of the two literary saboteurs has misled some honest individuals. Evidently, lacking adequate information and taking the word of the bourgeois press, which shamelessly compares Sinyavsky and Daniel to Gogol and Dostoevsky and pretends that during the trial questions of literature and artistic freedom were discussed, some progressive people have expressed their concern.[19]

To the Soviet intelligentsia, the Sinyavsky–Daniel trial seemed to threaten a return to Stalinism. Their protests were explicitly nonoppositional in character; the "signers" did not want to be seen as an opposition faction and did not consider themselves as such. On December 5, 1965, on the anniversary of the Stalin constitution, nearly a hundred people demonstrated on Pushkin Square, asking that the constitution be respected. All these collective protests stressed the appeal to legality.

For the Soviet leaders this call to respect the law constituted open opposition and threatened the system. To demand that the law be placed between citizen and state and that it be made binding for both was viewed as a crime punishable with a term in labor camp. A spiral of chain reactions began. Trials sparked protests, which in turn led to more arrests and more protests. Aleksandr Ginzburg, who in 1960 had founded one of the first samizdat magazines (Syntax), was arrested in 1967. He had compiled a white paper on the Sinyavsky–Daniel trial. Pavel Litvinov, a grandson of Maxim Litvinov, for his part published The Trial of the Four, a compilation of all documents relating to the trial of Ginzburg and his friend Yuri Galanskov, founder of the samizdat magazine Phoenix. Both were sentenced to seven years in the camps; in 1968, Litvinov was sentenced to five years in internal exile.

The movement that formed after the fall of Khrushchev called itself democratic. Andrei Amalrik, one of its participants, and the first to analyze it, pointed out that the democratic movement consisted of representatives of three ideological currents that took shape in the post-Stalin period: "genuine Marxism-Leninism," "liberal ideology," and "Christian ideology."[20] The program of the first tendency started from the assumption that Stalin had deformed Marxist-Leninist ideology and that a return to orthodoxy would allow a thorough cleansing of society. The second tendency suggested that the gradual transition toward a Western-style democracy was possible, while still maintaining the principles of socialized state property. The third tendency advocated traditional Christian moral and spiritual values as the foundation of social life and, following the Slavophile tradition, stressed Russia's unique character. Each of these tendencies became identified with a prominent personality. Andrei Sakharov personified the democratic-minded liberal opposition; Aleksandr Solzhenitsyn became the symbol of "Christian ideology"; and Roy and Zhores Medvedev became the best-known exponents of "authentic Marxism-Leninism."

In 1968 Amalrik noted, "The number of supporters of the movement is almost as indeterminable as its aim. They amount to several dozen active participants and several hundred who sympathize with the movement and are prepared to lend it their support."[21] Given the impossibility of providing exact figures on the number of participants, Amalrik attempted to analyze the movement's social composition. Among the 738 signers of collective and individual letters protesting the trial of Galanskov and Ginzburg, 45 percent were scientists, 22 percent artists, 13 percent engineers and technicians, 9 percent editors, doctors, or lawyers, 6 percent workers, and 5 percent students. Amalrik estimates that from 1966 to 1969 more than a thousand individuals signed various declarations and letters calling for observance of the law.[22]

The protests against arbitrariness, against trials that violated the law and the defense of human rights, nurtured social consciousness and awakened civic sentiments that had been subject to ruthless eradication for long decades. The protests also undermined the state monopoly on secrecy and publicized its repressive activities. *The Chronicle of Current Events*, which began publication in 1968, played an important role in this. Remaining strictly within the limits of legality, it reported on all violations of the law carried out by the organs of the state. The influence of "genuine Marxist-Leninist" ideology showed in the proliferation of the conviction that the democratic movement's principal goal was to prevent the rehabilitation of Stalin and a return to Stalinism.

The absence of any profound theoretical study of Soviet society and the Soviet system led people to believe that the replacement of mass terror with selective terror was in itself an advance, one that had to be maintained and defended. The fear of a rebirth of Stalinism was so great that the existing regime seemed soft, liberal, and weak by comparison. In 1969 Amalrik reached the conclusion that the regime was "not on the attack but on the defensive. Its motto is, 'Don't touch us and we won't touch you.'" But Amalrik had been mistaken. This defensive posture was only temporary.[23]

During the second half of the 1950s and during the 1960s, for the first time in long decades, the Soviet system encountered the phenomenon of internal opposition. Yet this was no true opposition, but rather one still in its embryonic stages. The very appearance of Soviet citizens questioning the functioning of the regime, however, evoked fear in the authorities. The loyal request that the law be respected not only appeared to be an encroachment on the foundations of the Soviet state; this is in fact what it was, for it revealed the law to be a fiction and exposed the reality hidden behind the illusion of words.

Repression did not stop after the death of Stalin; it merely assumed a different character and was reduced in scale. The "liberal" Khrushchev, who had emptied out Stalin's camps, very rapidly began to fill them up again, adding a new weapon to the repressive arsenal: the psychiatric hospital, as a place of confinement for those holding different views. The best illustration of Khrushchev's policies was the arrest of young people at

Mayakovsky Square (among them Galanskov, Bukovsky, and Eduard Kuznetsov) in October 1961, three days before the Twenty-second Party Congress, where Stalin's crimes were openly denounced. The Congress voted to remove Stalin's body from the Mausoleum, but his spirit presided over the arrests conducted at the same time.

The monstrousness of Stalin's crimes went beyond anything one could imagine and gave birth to the idea that mass terror was the essential feature of the Stalinist system. The possibility of getting along without mass terror and without altering the foundations of the Stalinist socialist state was demonstrated during Khrushchev's years. Khrushchev also showed that terror could be focused. Through the force of inertia Stalinist terror had spread mercilessly to all segments of society, stopping only at the feet of the Great Helmsman; Khrushchev made it stop at the doors of the Central Committee.

As Abdurakhman Avtorkhanov has written,

> From the moment when Khrushchev liquidated the "antiparty" grouping of Molotov, Malenkov, and Kaganovich, he committed a fatal error in the system, an error that in the last analysis determined his own fall: he left at large the actors of the first plot against him. If he had physically liquidated the 1957 plotters, the 1964 coup would never have taken place. The October plotters knew very well that, if they failed, what awaited them was a pension, not a bullet.[24]

The terror had not been given up; it merely became more selective. Its nature had not changed, though its appearance was transformed. The fact that terror could be applied selectively bore witness to the stability of the regime; it further evidenced that the mass terror of the Lenin and Stalin eras had been successful. Mass terror had permitted the destruction of the opposition, change in the composition of society, and the creation of a state—a state based on fear. Since Stalin's death, total, outright terror had become undesirable and dangerous for the *nomenklatura*. It is only in comparison with Stalinist repression that the terror in the Khrushchev era, and later in Brezhnev's, seemed mild, insignificant, liberal. The terms of five and seven years in the camps to which Daniel and Sinyavsky were sentenced for publishing literary works abroad would have evoked outrage had they been pronounced on writers of any capitalist country. In comparison with Stalin's times, such terms seemed like an act of charity. At the Twenty-third Party Congress, Nobel laureate Mikhail Sholokhov remembered with nostalgia the days when "people were tried without having to rely on particular articles in the penal code, but guided by the instinct of the revolutionary concept of justice," a time when the "werewolves"

Sinyavsky and Daniel would undoubtedly have been shot. Any sentence seemed milder than the death penalty. For this reason the Brezhnev era seems pale when compared to that of Stalin. This would be true as long as the Stalinist terror was used as a measure, as it continued to be by the Soviet leaders, who believed that in not executing people with dissenting views they were demonstrating their leniency. It was also the norm for participants in the democratic movement, who uneasily anticipated a rehabilitation of Stalin, followed in turn by the appearance of a new Stalin.

Vladimir Bukovsky, one of the most visible and representative activists, made a distinction between two currents within the growing movement: the "clandestine" and the "overt" oppositions. Bukovsky saw in the two forms an expression of two different psychologies, of "two different ways of life: one, secret, underground, and dichotomous; the other open, directed with regard to the law, and actively defending civil rights."[25] He recalled that "all through the 1950s and 1960s organizations, unions, groups, even parties of the most varied shades were growing like mushrooms in all walks of life."[26] Some of them, predominantly in Leningrad, were conspiratorial and attempted to operate clandestinely.

As Bukovsky aptly remarked, the "underground" organizations, many of which had only a handful of members, were attempting to "repeat the history of the CPSU." The history of the "underground movement" of the time is vivid proof of the force exerted by a myth invented by the CPSU, a force that still affected those who no longer believed in the myth. These "clandestine militants" were trying to create an organization which, by distributing literature, would win recruits of like views and then go on to achieve its objectives. The myth that the Bolshevik party had made the revolution through these methods had been believed even by the Bolsheviks themselves.

Clandestine organizations were persecuted with particular brutality, without regard to their programs, ranging from Kolokol, the organization of underground Marxists (tried in 1965) to the clandestine "social Christians" (tried in 1967–68). The latter group—the All-Russia Social Christian Union for the Liberation of the People (Russian initials, VSKhSON)—was founded in February 1964 by four graduates of Leningrad University. The organization survived for three years. The VSKhSON had twenty-eight members (and thirty others who were ready to join).[27] Thus it was the largest of all the clandestine organizations discovered by the police. Based on Berdyaev's "Russian idea," its program rejected the Soviet regime, seeing it as a "variety of state monopoly capitalism," from an economic point of view, and "an extreme totalitarianism, degenerating into despotism," from a political point of view. Rejecting the Communist system and criticizing all of the shortcomings of capitalism, it proposed a "theocratic, social, representative, and popular" state.[28]

For members of the union, this program, which linked personalism, corporatism, and Christian socialism, was seen as a long-term objective. On the more immediate and practical level, its goals were self-education and the numerical growth of the organization. But the program contained one clause that allowed the KGB to cast the organization as a terrorist group. "The liberation of all peoples from the Communist yoke can only be achieved by armed struggle. To achieve total victory, it is essential that the people have their own clandestine liberation army, which will overthrow the dictatorship and smash the oligarchy's security detachments."[29]

The history of the VSKhSON is a clear example of the thinking of the "underground" groups that were inspired by Bolshevik mythology. The organization had been structured like an actual Communist party, with a "leader," an "ideological section director," and an "archivist." Its leader, Igor Ogurtsov, was condemned to fifteen years, of which seven were in the notoriously harsh Vladimir prison. The government, frightened by this clandestine organization that had managed to survive unnoticed for three years, mercilessly repressed these "terrorists," whose sole weapon was a rusty old handgun.

The clandestine character of the VSKhSON, and the fact that its trial took place behind closed doors, meant that the organization's program and activity remained virtually unknown for years.

A particularly significant event in Soviet life was Solzhenitsyn's letter to the Fourth Congress of the Writer's Union in May 1967. None of the 300 delegates who received it read it from the podium. But eighty writers, later joined by nine others, demanded that the problems raised by Solzhenitsyn be discussed. The author of *One Day in the Life of Ivan Denisovich* spoke out against the censorship:

> Under the obfuscating label of Glavlit, this censorship—which is not provided for in the [Soviet] constitution and is therefore illegal, and which is nowhere publicly labeled as censorship—imposes a yoke on our literature and gives people unversed in literature arbitrary control over writers. A survival of the Middle Ages, the censorship has managed, Methuselah-like, to drag out its existence almost to the twenty-first century.[30]

Cautiously, in a veiled manner, Solzhenitsyn suggested that censorship was fundamental to the Soviet system, which feeds on lies and forbids the truth. Three years later, in 1970, in his Nobel Prize acceptance speech, he would express the same idea in a formula more like an epitaph. "One word of truth will outweigh the whole world."[31]

## THE PRAGUE SPRING

Although not read at the writers' congress in Moscow in 1967, Solzhenitsyn's letter was read at the writers' congress in Prague the same year and approved by the overwhelming majority of the Czech and Slovak delegates.

The Prague Spring, as the events of 1967–68 in Czechoslovakia came to be known, has many features resembling those of the Hungarian events of 1956. A similar process had occurred in Poland in 1956 and 1968.[32] The dissent which had grown throughout the population found its expression above all among the intellectuals: writers became the spokesmen for the feelings and demands of the population; the reform programs put forward found supporters among rank-and-file party members and even among the leaderships; leaders appeared, who promised to eliminate all defects in communism, retaining the system: they promised "socialism with a human face."

The events of 1956 and 1968 showed that latent discontent in the socialist countries could lead to mass rebellions at times when power was weakened in the central metropolis, the Soviet Union. Stalin's death and the Twentieth Party Congress were the signal for the Polish October and the Hungarian revolution. The removal of Khrushchev and the rise of oppositionist attitudes in the Soviet Union helped unleash the Prague Spring and the 1968 events in Poland.

The birth of an opposition movement in the Soviet Union in the years 1964–1968 and the emergence of an embryonic public opinion were accompanied by rising nationalist feelings in the non-Russian Soviet republics. The government's nationalities policy of the time was ambiguous. The year 1967 marks the high point in the struggles of the peoples deported during the war; they were rehabilitated and everything seemed to be returning to normal. The Crimean Tatars, however, were not allowed to return to their homeland, nor were the Georgian Muslims (the Meskhetians) or the Volga Germans.

In the middle of the 1960s nationalist movements reappeared in the Ukraine, Lithuania, and the Transcaucasus.

In 1965 the Ukraine suffered a wave of arrests. The main target was the intelligentsia, particularly those of the younger generation. Ivan Dzyuba, a literary critic, addressed a long memorandum entitled "Internationalism or Russification?" to Petr Shelest, first secretary of the Central Committee of the Ukrainian Communist party and Vladimir Shcherbitsky, the chairman of the Ukrainian Council of Ministers. Dzyuba explained the reasons behind the unrest on the part of the Ukrainian intelligentsia and especially protested against "Russification," which he saw as a threat to the existence of the

Ukrainian people. He accused the Ukrainian government of violating "Leninist principles of nationalities policy and nation-building."[33]

In 1965 Vyacheslav Chornovil, a successful Ukrainian journalist of the younger generation, was summoned as a witness at the trial of another writer, Mikola Osadchy, arrested because of an uncensored book he had written; *Belmo* (*Eyesore*), describing life in the prison camps. Chornovil protested the violations of Soviet law at the trial and afterward addressed a complaint about the persecution of the Ukrainian intelligentsia to the prosecutor of the republic. He was arrested.[34] The history teacher Valentyn Moroz met a similar fate in 1965 because of his emphatic protests against Russification. The fate of these engineers of the Ukrainian nationalist movement during the mid-1960s paralleled that of the movement as a whole. After their first arrests they were sentenced again to terms in the camps. In 1980 Chornovil and Osadchy were serving new sentences. In 1979, after thirteen years of imprisonment, Moroz was exchanged, along with Aleksandr Ginzburg, Eduard Kuznetsov, and Petr Vins, for two Soviet spies who had been arrested in the United States. Dzyuba, sentenced in 1973 to five years in the camps, recanted first in the newspaper *Literaturna Ukraina*, and then in the book *Facets of the Crystal*. He renounced his earlier views and expressed regret that they had been "seized upon by hostile, bourgeois nationalist propaganda abroad."[35]

In Lithuania the opposition during the 1960s was inseparably linked to resistance to the persecution of the Catholic church. Even according to official figures, no less than half the population of the republic consists of Lithuanians who are practicing Catholics. During the second half of the 1960s, the Lithuanian Supreme Soviet issued several decrees seeking to prevent young people from going to church. Since 1968 dozens of petitions protesting religious persecution have been directed to government agencies. The trial of two priests accused of teaching the catechism to children sparked a street demonstration.

Following the example of the Russian-language *Chronicle of Current Events*, which began to circulate unofficially in 1968, a similar Ukrainian-language journal, the *Ukrainian Herald*, appeared in 1970, and in 1972 the *Chronicle of the Lithuanian Catholic Church*, in Lithuanian. Thus an uncensored press emerged in *samizdat*, with the sole aim of recording and making known all instances of repression. This tended to undermine one of the pillars of the Soviet system, the secrecy which allowed the government to commit its crimes with impunity. At the same time this type of information was essential for the existence of an independent public opinion.

In January 1968 a political crisis in Czechoslovakia, caused by a number of economic, social, and national factors, led to the replacement of the old

Stalinist Antonin Novotny by the forty-six-year-old Alexander Dubček as first secretary of the Central Committee of the Czechoslovak Communist party. A graduate of the Higher Party School in Moscow and son of a Communist who had gone to the Soviet Union before World War II to help "build socialism," Alexander Dubček seemed to the Soviet leaders, who were on familiar terms with him, a reliable guarantor of stability in Czechoslovakia.

The activities of Dubček and his followers between January and August 1968—following the pattern of Poland, Hungary, and Khrushchev's USSR— added up to one more attempt to improve and reform the system without touching its foundations. As in all other instances, the introduction of reforms began in the wake of personnel changes in the party leadership. By the mere force of inertia, the struggle for power, combined with obviously critical problems in the country and the opportunity on the part of the new leadership to blame all the failures on its predecessors, steadily escalated to the point where the reforms threatened the foundations of the regime. Nikita Khrushchev perfectly expressed the feelings of a Communist leader who is forced to grant some reforms: "The leadership was consciously moving toward a relaxation, and just as consciously it feared a thaw. It could turn into a flood, which would threaten us and be difficult to surmount. At the time we feared that the leadership would not be able to meet its tasks, and keep all this within Soviet channels." As usual, Khrushchev concluded his thoughts with a popular saying: "You want it so badly, but Mama says no."[36]

In each of the socialist countries undergoing crisis, the system set the limits at different points. In Hungary, the reasons for the invasion were the establishment of workers councils and the demands for withdrawal of Soviet troops. Khrushchev sealed his own fate by splitting the party in two. In Czechoslovakia, the limit of tolerable reforms was reached with the abolition of censorship. On July 14, 1968, at the meeting of Communist parties convened in Warsaw, Gomulka demanded an end to the "Czechoslovak experiment." His argument: "The lifting of censorship means that the party is refusing to exert the slightest influence on the country's general evolution."[37] For Gomulka, who was supported by all present at the meeting, the lifting of censorship was equivalent to an abdication of power. The Soviet press declared the abolition of censorship to be a counterrevolution which, after "seizing the mass media would demoralize the country's population and poison the consciousness of the workers with the venom of antisocialist ideas."[38]

Gomulka's interpreter, who had accompanied him at the Warsaw meeting, tells of the fear of "the venom of antisocialist ideas" which resounded in all the speeches of all the Communist leaders. "We are dealing with a counterrevolution, with an enemy who does not shoot," Gomulka explained to those present. "If they were shooting at us, things would be a lot simpler for us, because then we could react in a totally different manner."[39]

Alexander Dubček and his supporters tried their best to convince the representatives of the "fraternal countries" of their ability to implement successfully all reforms, reforms which would bring the crisis to an end, leaving the foundations of socialism untouched. A series of meetings between the Czechoslovak reformers and the leaders of their fraternal countries did not produce any results. Nevertheless, Joseph Smrkovsky, one of the people who had inspired the Prague Spring, an ardent supporter of "socialism with a human face," Politburo member, and president of the Czechoslovak parliament in 1968, wrote a letter to Brezhnev in 1973 asserting that his "socialist ideas had not changed" and that he "would gladly follow the Soviet policy of detente."[40] Thus, five years after the intervention by Warsaw Pact troops in Prague, Smrkovsky still believed that Brezhnev might follow his advice and "begin talks between representatives of the USSR, the politicians of 1968 and the current political leaders," to make Czechoslovakia "a reliable ally of the USSR."[41] Until his death in February 1974, Smrkovsky believed that "in the coming months we can expect some sort of concrete measures."[42] Thus, to the end of his life, Smrkovsky kept his illusions regarding Soviet intentions and the struggle between "hawks and doves" in the Soviet Politburo.

It was upon these same illusions that Dubček and his supporters built their policies in the summer of 1968. Materials relating to the negotiations between Soviet and Czechoslovak leaders and to the conferences of the "fraternal countries" that have come to light indicate that the decision to intervene was made following the June publication of an appeal to the people known as the Two Thousand Words. The manifesto, signed by tens of thousands of Czechoslovaks, noted that "the apparatus of power has escaped from the hands of the people," that the Czechoslovak Communist party "from being a political party and an organization of ideas, has become an organ of power, and a magnet for the ambitious and the greedy, the lazy, and those whose consciences are not clear."[43]

Following publication of the manifesto, the question of intervention was reduced to a question of tactics. Among the leaders of socialist countries were some who advocated an immediate intervention: Gomulka, Ulbricht, and Zhivkov. Kadar, on the other hand, preferred to wait. All, however, agreed to intervention in principle. Likewise, inside the Politburo of the CPSU, as far as can be established, only the timetable of the invasion was at issue. Czechoslovakia's neighbor, first secretary of the Ukrainian Communist party Shelest, demanded the immediate elimination of the "Prague Spring," which threatened to spread the "poison of antisocialist ideas" to the Ukrainians. Brezhnev, who was still consolidating his power at the time, was prepared to wait.

Having learned the lessons of the Hungarian experience, the Soviet leaders decided to intervene in Czechoslovakia using the forces of all Eastern European socialist states. Tito and Ceaussescu asserted their support for Dubček's policies, and Romania refused to join the expeditionary corps.

During the night of August 20–21, 1968, Soviet military aircraft dropped paratroopers on the Prague airport. Military forces from the Soviet Union, East Germany, Poland, Hungary, and Bulgaria drove into Czechoslovak territory. Some troops were there already, taking part in "maneuvers." Czechoslovak Politburo members were seized and delivered to Moscow, in handcuffs. The Czechoslovak leaders could not withstand the pressure of the CPSU Politburo and with the exception of František Kriegel, signed an agreement with the Soviet Union regarding the stationing of troops on Czechoslovakian territory. They also pledged to reimpose censorship and nullify all the reforms that were giving socialism a "human face."

Thirty years before, in 1938, the Czechoslovak president, democrat Gakha, in tears, had signed an accord forced on him by Hitler under which his country was annexed to the Third Reich. The Nazis had shattered his will. In 1968, the Soviet Communists shattered the will of the Czechoslovak Communists who, in trying to reform their socialist system, had breached the discipline required of all Communists.

"All we wish to do," Dubček once said, "is create a socialism that has not lost its human character."[44] This was the utmost in sedition, a direct accusation hurled in the face of real Soviet socialism. The new Czechoslovak leaders set to the task of "normalizing" the country: all expressions of discontent were suppressed with harsh repression.

The invasion of Czechoslovakia was not a fortuitous act by "hawks" imposed on "doves" in the Soviet Politburo. It was the expression of the principles of Soviet "proletarian internationalism" and of Soviet foreign policy, upon which Lenin had laid the foundations of the socialist state. The invasion of Poland in 1920 and the installation of Soviet governments in Transcaucasia in 1920–1921, all of which Lenin engineered, were the first applications of these principles. If the Soviet state did not always apply them, this was because it was too weak.

Leninist principles were recalled, after the intervention in Czechoslovakia, in a *Pravda* article which gave a clear and unambiguous theoretical justification for the invasion of Czechoslovakia: "Every Communist party is responsible not only to its people, but also to all socialist countries and to the world Communist movement. . . . A socialist state forms part of the socialist community and cannot ignore the overall interests of this community." Proceeding from general principles to the concrete example of Czechoslovakia, *Pravda* noted, "Communists in the fraternal countries could not allow themselves to remain inactive in the name of an abstract principle of sovereignty while watching one of their number fall into the process of antisocialist degeneration." *Pravda* concluded: "Those who speak of the action of the allied socialist nations in Czechoslovakia in terms of 'violations of rights' forget that in class society there is not and there has never been a classless law. Laws and legal procedures obey the class struggle, the laws of social development. . . . Formal legal considerations should not lose the class point of view."[45]

Since the socialist countries are classless societies, such considerations as "class rights," "class morality," "formal rights," and "abstract sovereignty" could only have relevance on the planetary scale. This "class struggle" was that of real socialism against capitalism. On the eve of the entry of armies from the fraternal countries into Czechoslovakia, *Pravda* solemnly declared: "Marxist-Leninists cannot be, and never will be, indifferent to the fate of socialist construction in other nations, the common Communist cause on this earth." The article was entitled "The Front of Uncompromising Struggle."[46]

Western journalists termed the principles put forward in *Pravda* the "Brezhnev doctrine." This is one more example of their ignorance of Soviet history. On September 2, 1920, after the fall of Bukhara, the commander of the Red Army units that were implanting a Soviet government in Central Asia sent a telegram to Lenin with the following message, "The last bastion of Bukharan obscurantism . . . has fallen. The red banner of world revolution flies victoriously over the Registan."[47] In 1948 the commander of the troops occupying Czechoslovakia could have written Lenin's heirs that the "red banner of world revolution" had advanced to the West.

The crushing of the Hungarian revolution by Soviet troops had shocked many Soviet young people. Vladimir Bukovsky recalled in his memoirs the tragedy of his generation.

> After the tanks with the red star, dream and pride of our childhood, had crushed our peers in the streets of Budapest, everything we saw was stained with blood. The entire world had betrayed us, and we no longer believed anyone. Our parents turned out to have been agents and informers, our military leaders were butchers, and even the games and fantasies of our childhood seemed to be tainted with fraud.[48]

Twelve years later a significant part of the population accepted the invasion in Czechoslovakia as necessary and just. Soviet propaganda put forward as its main justification the alleged threat posed by West Germany to Czechoslovakia and consequently to all the socialist countries. The Soviet propaganda machine succeeded in executing a masterwork of disinformation. The broad coalition government in West Germany, in which the Social Democrat Willy Brandt was foreign minister and vice-chancellor and which had just come to power in the FRG shortly before the events in Czechoslovakia, was portrayed as a direct successor to Hitler. Bitter memories of the war were utilized to justify Soviet actions. The propaganda machine also availed itself of the feeling diligently nurtured in the Soviet people that the world should be grateful to the Soviet Union for the sacrifices it had suffered in the process of constructing socialism, during the war with Nazi Germany, and for the assistance it had rendered, was now providing, and would continue to give to the "fraternal countries." The press harped incessantly on the "ingratitude" of the Czechs and Slovaks, who had supposedly forgotten who had liberated them in 1945. And this argument struck a chord in many Soviet citizens.

But the Soviet government could not completely crush the element of independent public opinion that had emerged. Voices of protest made themselves heard at meetings and gatherings organized to gain approval for the invasion of Czechoslovakia. Newspapers received letters along the same lines. On August 25, 1968, the student Tatyana Baeva, the linguist Konstantin Babitsky, the philologist Larisa Bogoraz, the poet Vadim Delone, the worker Vladimir Dremlyuga, the physicist Pavel Litvinov, the poet Natalya Gorbanevskaya, and the art critic Viktor Fainberg appeared at Red Square. Gorbanevskaya was carrying her three-month-old baby. The demonstrators unfurled banners with the inscriptions "Long live free and independent Czechoslovakia," "Shame on occupiers," "Hands off the CSSR," and "For your freedom and for ours."[49] Immediately arrested by the KGB, the demonstrators were tried and sentenced to long terms. Ninety-five persons prominent in Soviet culture addressed a protest letter to the Supreme Soviet of the USSR.

In the summer of 1968, at the time when the Soviet government was preparing to crush the Prague Spring, the voice of Andrei Sakharov rang out. His book, *Progress, Peaceful Coexistence, and Intellectual Freedom*, appeared in *samizdat*. His program was based on the concept of convergence: socialism and capitalism would merge as each lost its negative aspects in the process. Very rapidly Sakharov reached the conclusion that the socialist system rejected the idea of convergence, which it viewed as a deadly peril to its existence. His main field of activity became the struggle in defense of human rights. In 1970, with two other physicists, Andrei Tverdokhlebov and Valery Chalidze, he founded the Human Rights Committee. Despite the committee's overt character and its adherence to Soviet law, it was subjected to harsh persecution. The voice of Sakharov, however, could not be stilled.

Solzhenitsyn explained the importance of the "Sakharov phenomenon" this way:

> When Lenin conceived and initiated, and Stalin developed and made safe, their brilliant scheme for a totalitarian state, they thought of everything, did everything to ensure that the system would stand firm to all eternity, changing only when the leader waved his wand. . . . They foresaw all eventualities but one—a miracle, an irrational manifestation whose cause could not be anticipated, predicted, and thwarted. . . . Just such a miracle was the appearance of Andrei Dmitrievich Sakharov in the Soviet state, amid the throngs of bribed, corrupt, unprincipled technical intelligentsia, and what is more, in one of their most important, most secret, and most lavishly favored nests— in the vicinity of the hydrogen bomb.[50]

The appearance of Solzhenitsyn was a similar miracle.

After fifty years of existence of the totalitarian Soviet state, where all efforts had been invested in the creation of a new man, Homo Sovieticus, the appearance of a Solzhenitsyn, of a Sakharov, and of the demonstrators at Red Square protesting the invasion of Czechoslovakia, and of the "signers" demanding freedom for Sinyavsky and Daniel, as well as the emergence of *samizdat* and the formation of semilegal and illegal groups, all bore witness to the extraordinary force of the human spirit.

With very few exceptions, these "dissidents" (as all those who questioned the divine wisdom of the state were soon labeled) did not constitute an organized opposition, armed with a program and a plan of action. They simply demanded that the state respect both its own laws and civil rights, including national and religious rights. The dissidents were few in number, an indication of the extreme difficulty of casting off the fear in which Soviet citizens had been steeped over the last half century. The appearance of dissidents showed that such actions were possible, that the state was not omnipotent. Attitudes toward the dissidents on the part of the general population varied. Some viewed them with hatred; others feared them; still others sympathized with them. Dissident activity made some educated people of liberal inclination uncomfortable. They themselves led a dual existence: on the one hand, Soviet reality oppressed them; on the other, their material circumstances were far from bad by Soviet standards: they had apartments, stable salaries, perhaps a car and a country house (dacha). They feared for their children's future and their own. They disagreed with the government on many issues but choose "not to get involved," well aware of what getting involved might cost them. What's more, their "opposition" was only skin deep. These liberals were ready to give financial aid to dissidents secretly or give clothing to the families of those who had been arrested, willing secretly to read *samizdat* writings and listen to foreign broadcasts in Russian. (They preferred the BBC to Radio Liberty; the former's moderation was to their liking.) Seeking to justify their position, which largely coincided with that of the government (they always voted "yes"), these liberals developed a justification, the "theory" of Galileo and Giordano Bruno. Galileo renounced his ideas under the threat of torture by the Inquisition and lived; Bruno defended his and died. Before his death, Galileo exclaimed, "Eppur, si muove" ("And still it moves"), thus showing that in publicly renouncing his views he was only submitting to violence. The liberals preferred Galileo's way, even though they were not being tortured, and they tried to inculate this, their own caution, into their children, turning them into cynics, conformists, and pragmatists.

## DETENTE

The invasion of Czechoslovakia by Warsaw Pact troops was regarded in the West as a normal measure aimed at restoring order in this part of the Soviet bloc. President Johnson said on September 10, 1968, three weeks after the invasion "We hope—and we shall strive—to make this setback a temporary one."[51] Echoing Johnson's tactfulness, the French foreign minister, Michel Debré, called the invasion an "unpleasant incident along the road." West German Foreign Minister Willy Brandt met with Gromyko in New York several weeks after the incident. Gromyko declared that the negotiations on an agreement to refrain from the use of force which had already been begun would be extended. "What could we do?" sighed Helmut Allard, the German ambassador to Moscow. "In the USA, Richard Nixon was in more of a hurry to forget the episode than Georges Pompidou."[52] Henry Kissinger, who was in charge of U.S. foreign policy, cited in his memoirs a myriad of reasons for the haste with which the West, forgetting Czechoslovakia, returned to the policy of "international detente." He said that the Western European governments pressured the United States, insisting on an agreement with the Soviet Union. Among other reasons, Kissinger mentions the hope that the Soviet Union would help the

United States find a way out of the Vietnam war, and pressure from business circles, who had not ceased to hope for the magical "Soviet market," and from Soviet experts like Averell Harriman, Llewellyn Thompson, George Kennan, and Charles Bohlen, who wanted the Russian proposals for a "relaxation of tensions" accepted as quickly as possible "lest the balance of forces within the Kremlin shift again to a hard line."[53]

The lack of understanding of Soviet policy on the part of Westerners is best seen in their definition of terms. "Detente," in the West, really means "a relaxation of tensions." However, the Soviet *Short Political Dictionary*, the party's propaganda encyclopedia, states that "detente" (*razryadka*, in Russian) is the "steady strengthening of the position of the countries of the socialist camp" and a defeat for the "imperialist forces."[54]

Detente was thus another name for a policy whose basics had been envisioned in Lenin's time: "Once we are strong enough to defeat imperialism as a whole, we will immediately grab it by the scruff of its neck." Using that time a subjunctive mood, Lenin expressed his hope of grabbing imperialism by the neck, but at the same time stated that this objective was impossible at the moment. As long as it was impossible, Lenin thought temporary agreements must be sought, for an "agreement is a method for gathering forces."[55] At the birth of Soviet power, the Seventh (Extraordinary) Party Congress arrived at a decision that became a central principle of Soviet foreign policy. "The congress especially underscores that it empowers the Central Committee to break at any time peace agreements with imperialist and bourgeois states, and to declare war upon them if necessary."[56]

The period of disarray following Stalin's death, which was aggravated by the deep economic crisis that arose in the midst of the struggle for power, forced the new leadership to abandon cold war policies. The resolution of the Twentieth Party Congress stated that the "general line of the foreign policy of the Soviet Union has been and remains the Leninist principle of peaceful coexistence with states of differing social systems."[57] Following Khrushchev's fall the foreign policy of the Soviet Union changed its name but not its substance. At the first post-Khrushchev assembly, in 1966, at the Twenty-third Party Congress, Brezhnev declared, "The Soviet Union considers the coexistence of states a form of the class struggle between socialism and capitalism."[58] At the Twenty-fourth Party Congress, in 1971, during the honeymoon of detente, Brezhnev praised the victories of the international Communist movement, spoke of the "unwaning ideological struggle," and stressed that "total victory for the socialist cause in the entire world is inevitable. And we will not spare efforts to achieve that triumph."[59] The *Short Political Dictionary* explains in language clear to every party member,

In the conditions of detente the ideological struggle between socialism and capitalism does not diminish but becomes more complex, taking on the most varied forms. Detente creates favorable conditions for the wide dissemination of the appeal of communist ideology and socialist values; it facilitates the development of an offensive ideological struggle within the framework of peaceful coexistence between states with differing social systems.[60]

"Peaceful coexistence" or "detente" was, according to one of Lenin's favorite expressions (reversing the famous saying by Clausewitz), the continuation of war by other means. The West considered detente as an opportunity to obtain a "lasting peace [which] depended on the settlement of the political issues that were dividing the two nuclear superpowers."[61] In Soviet political jargon, "lasting peace" only exists in the sense used by Stalin, when he named the journal of the postwar international Communist movement *For Lasting Peace, for People's Democracy*. Thus, "lasting peace" is conceived of merely as a step toward "people's democracy."

The West's strong desire for detente stemmed above all from its extraordinary economic growth. The "consumer society" wanted to consume more than ever and was afraid of losing its prosperity. Never before had such a high standard of living been accessible to such broad segments of a population. The concessions indispensable for reaching an agreement with the Soviet Union seemed a small price to pay for detente and "lasting peace." Another cause for the West's aspiration for detente was the sharply weakened position of the United States in the world resulting from the catastrophic war in Vietnam. This war, the first in history to take place before television cameras, was at the same time a classic example of an attempt to win an ideological war by military means.

The Soviet policy of detente was mainly inspired by the need for a "breathing spell." In the late 1960s and early 1970s the Soviet Union was suffering another crisis, a political crisis. "In 1968," wrote Bukovsky, "[this crisis] reached its peak. Just a bit more, it seemed, and the authorities would be driven back, abandoning their self-destructive rigidity. Entire nationalities threatened to rise in revolt, challenging the very existence of the last colonial empire."[62]

There was also an economic crisis: in the late 1960s economic growth had decreased sharply, even according to official figures. It became obvious that the extensive period of growth, made possible by major reserves of labor, had come to an end. The thoroughgoing economic reform solemnly proclaimed after the replacement of Khrushchev remained purely on paper. It was impossible to modify the Soviet economic system by firing part of the labor force and the broad introduction of new technology. Soviet citizens—workers, engineers, and technical managerial leaders—were told that economic reform would require independence, individual initiative, and brave decisions. Simultaneously it was underscored that all such activity could be undertaken only on the directions of the central agencies and under the control of the party.

Complaining about the economic problems, Brezhnev said at a plenum of the Central Committee, "Comrades, the question we face is, How will we explain this inability to rid ourselves of these bottlenecks that hinder us from advancing even faster?"[63] But Stalin had already found the formula to straighten out such problems. "Night was Stalin's most fruitful time. His mistrustful mind unwound slowly in the morning. With his gloomy morning mind he would remove people from their positions, cut back expenditures, order two or three ministries consolidated into one. With his sharp and supple nighttime mind he would decide how to dissolve ministries, divide them up, and what to call the new ones."[64] Brezhnev followed this prescription in his own way.

The cause of the Soviet economic crisis was not the bureaucratic apparatus but rather the party's ideological control. The party led and controlled everything; any manifestation of independent initiative was seen as a challenge to its authority, a blow against the official ideology.

In this chronic crisis, agriculture was the most backward sector. Abandoning Khrushchev's proposed panaceas for agriculture (maize, expansion into arid zones), Brezhnev's administration found other magic formulas, mainly heavy investment and the use of chemicals. The bad harvest of 1963 blamed on Khrushchev was followed by those of 1965, 1967, and 1972, and the most serious, 1975. To prevent more failures, vast sums were channeled into agriculture: in 1973, 26.5 percent of all investments were allocated to agriculture, a sharp increase from the 23 percent at the beginning of the 1960s. By 1975 the percentage has risen to 27.[65] These investments were used mainly to build chemical enterprises, so that after 1970 Soviet fertilizer consumption exceeded that of the United States.

Nonetheless, the crisis in Soviet agriculture was not overcome. It remained the Achilles' heel of the Soviet Union, which everywhere was being called the second economic power in the world.

One of the most important arguments advanced under Stalin to justify collectivization had been the need to mechanize agriculture, since machinery was more productive than manual labor. An individual farmer could not afford machinery, nor did he have enough land to use machinery efficiently. In the Soviet Union in 1973 a seventy-horsepower tractor was plowing an average of 114 hectares of land, and a combine, harvesting an average of 185 hectares. In the United States, at the same time, these figures were 35 and 85 hectares, respectively. According to the Soviet economic plan, assuming it would be carried out, Soviet industry would need between ten and thirty years to supply an adequate amount of machinery. Labor productivity is by far the best index of the efficiency of any economic system. In the period 1971–1973, grain yield in the USSR was 14.7 quintals per hectare, as it had been in Greece and Yugoslavia during the period 1956–1959. In 1970, a Soviet agricultural worker harvested 4.5 tones of grain per year; in the United States 54.7 tons. The figures for meat are, respectively, 320 and 4,570 kilos; for milk, 2.8 and 11.8 tons. A Soviet agricultural worker tilled an average of 5.4 hectares, a figure equal to that of the Russian peasant of 1913, when on the average a peasant family owned 15 hectares.[66]

The Soviet rulers had long ago tacitly admitted that the collective farm system was not profitable. The consolidation of numerous "weak" kolkhozes into one large farm, a process which began soon after the war, gradually turned into the liquidation of the kolkhozes and their replacement with sovkhozes (state farms). The following figures speak for themselves: in 1965, kolkhozes worked 44.7 percent of all land under cultivation; in 1970, they worked only 34.7 percent, and in 1973, 24.2 percent. At the same time the percentage of sovkhoz land went up from 55.1 in 1956 to 65.6 in 1970 and 75.2 in 1978.[67] The work force employed by the kolkhoz declined by one-fourth, while that of the sovkhoz rose by 39 percent. All this points toward the disappearance of the kolkhoz system in the near future. It also means increased centralization of the administration of agriculture, with all the negative consequences that entails.

At the end of the 1960s it was difficult to hide the gap between the triumphant statistics and reality. "The USSR over the past thirty years has grown faster than the United States," wrote British economist Alec Nove.[68] Statistics showed that between 1928 and 1969 the Soviet Union had graduated more engineers than the United States.[69] Such figures amazed Western statesmen and scholars. Nevertheless, official Soviet statistics were forced to recognize that in 1979 the Soviet economy was producing no more than 65 percent as much as the U.S. economy.[70]

The history of Ivan Khudenko's "social and economic experiment" demonstrated the impossibility of any fundamental reforms in the Soviet Union. On November 12, 1960, the USSR Council of Ministers authorized Ivan Khudenko, a high official in an agency under the Council of Ministers, to carry out an experiment with a new system of labor and wages at a state farm. At that time Khrushchev was in power and seeking magical cure-alls for the ailing Soviet system. Khudenko suggested that all work be shared among small teams (zvenya) of workers, which would have full economic autonomy. Their main goal was to produce a certain quantity of goods within a certain time. The payment they would receive for the results of their work would not be restricted to any certain wage. The results were astounding. The cost of grain production fell to one-fourth of its former level and wages quadrupled, but profits per worker increased sevenfold. The workers had begun to produce as if they were working for themselves. Khudenko presented calculations which indicated that if his system were introduced throughout the country, grain production would rise by a factor of four, while the agricultural work force of 35 million could be reduced to a little over 5 million, i.e., by a factor of six.

The experiment was initially well received by the Soviet press. Even a movie (*Man of the Soil*) was dedicated to the experiment. But when it became obvious that if the use of Khudenko's "social and economic experiment" were spread it would result in a radical reform of the Soviet economy (increase local economic initiative and reduced central planning), the experiment was ended. Khudenko was arrested and sentenced to a long term in the camps on charges of "attempting to damage state property on an especially large scale." He died in prison on November 12, 1974.[71]

The Soviet Union's chronic inability to produce food supplies adequate for even its domestic needs is not only indicative of fundamental defects in the Soviet system; it further suggests the system's low level of social advancement. In the United States, which is endlessly attacked by Soviet propaganda, agriculture employs between 2.5 and 3 percent of the labor force. In the Soviet Union the figure is 25 percent.[72] These are the facts, and as Stalin used to say, facts are stubborn things.

Nevertheless, in spite of its difficulties and erratic performance, the Soviet economy continues to function. And this for a variety of reasons. The natural wealth of the country is used to pay for huge losses, although this means that the inheritance of future generations is being used to pay today's food bill. Also, a "second economy" comes to the aid of the "first," the state economy. No law provides for this second economy, nor is it planned by anyone. It is an unofficial system governed by the laws of the market. In Moscow, Leningrad, the Baltic countries, Transcaucasia, and Central Asia, there are private factories and shops and clandestine restaurants and taxis. There is a brisk business in hard foreign currencies and items produced in the West. This second economy provides the consumer with items the first cannot. Trials were held everywhere in the Soviet Union during the 1960s and 1970s on charges related to such underground businesses and to illegal trafficking in diamonds and foreign currency. These trials revealed that the "second economy" was closely linked to the state distribution network, that the clandestine enterprises were receiving necessary equipment on the orders of high-ranking officials of different ministries, and that they were often purchasing directly from state enterprises. But that was only one aspect of the matter. In many cases state enterprises were producing goods in quantities greater than provided for under the economic plan. This was because the enterprise had used raw materials other than those they usually used, or the quality of the goods had been lowered. These surpluses were then sold through state stores.

These were sizable financial and commercial operations, on the scale of hundreds of millions of rubles, with the full and profitable participation of the ministerial bureaucracy. These clever businessmen paid for the protection of the police, the justice department, and district or provincial party leadership. Among those guilty were such highly placed people as Mzhavanadze, first party secretary in Georgia and candidate member of the Politburo, and Nasreddinova, chairman of the Council of Nationalities of the USSR.[73] They were removed from their posts, but not one of them was tried or sentenced.

Bribery became one of the most widespread forms of corruption in the Soviet Union, reaching disastrous proportions. At institutions of higher learning bribes were taken during admissions and sometimes even during routine examinations; at medical facilities they were taken for operations and good nursing care in hospitals. In the trade and distribution network everyone was on the take. The spiral went all the way to the ministries of the republics and the central ministries. The trade was not only in merchandise; state and party posts could be bought, too, along with academic and honorific titles, and so on.

To reinforce the existing system, the party allowed the use, within fixed limits, of certain fashionable Western theories, such as management systems theory, marketing theory, and systems research. The Polish satirist Stanislaw Lec warned his readers, "Don't tell your dreams; Freudians may come to power." The writers of "socialist realism" have revealed the dreams of the Soviet leadership. A three-volume saga by Mikhail Kolesnikov about Sergei Altunin, a Siberian blacksmith and the exemplary Soviet man who becomes a deputy minister (because in the Soviet Union personal advancement is possible for everyone), provides an example of the decision-making mechanism at the uppermost levels of Soviet leadership. Sergei Altunin, a cultured person ("I love Rembrandt," he tells his wife, "and I love *Swan Lake*, too") has the opportunity to go abroad: "I will have to visit the London and Manchester schools of business. ... Then I should go to the United States to take advantage of the management training at Harvard and Sloane. ... Then there is Sweden and the European management centers." Sergei Altunin succeeds in making a brilliant career, for he knows very well that all Western managerial training is merely for decoration. Real power is in the hands of the party committee. "The party's committee was the active organ. It controlled the work of the apparatus (the ministry) all the time, and with extreme vigilance."[74] The party organizers had never studied at Harvard or London. They had studied at the party's higher school and they were more servile than anyone, but they had the weapon of Marxism-Leninism, the only victorious doctrine because it is real, and the only real doctrine because it is victorious.

Thus at the end of the 1960s the Brezhnev government decided to use the West in an attempt to eliminate the "bottlenecks" affecting the Soviet economy and to obtain a breathing spell.

In the West the Soviet initiatives were welcomed. "Detente" was seen as a true "relaxation of tensions." Joy was natural for Communist parties the world over and for left-leaning public opinion when, in 1967, at the Karlovy Vary conference of Communist parties, Brezhnev did not conceal that "these last years have clearly shown that, in the situation of international detente, the needle of the political barometer is moving to the left."[75]

Further impetus toward detente was provided by the general public's fear of nuclear war. Problems of nuclear arms limitation and nonproliferation were at the center of international relations during the 1960s and 1970s. The Soviet Union set itself the goal of preventing the transfer of nuclear weapons to the Germans and succeeded in this aim to a large extent. Agreement was reached on a nonproliferation treaty. The United States was interested in maintaining a monopoly in this field. The danger posed by the possible spread of nuclear weapons to the "hot spots" (the Middle East and Southeast Asia) was quite obvious. The superpowers wanted to keep from being pushed directly into armed conflict and could not ignore the possibility of a nuclear weapon in the hands of a terrorist organization. In 1968, at the initiative of the Soviet Union and the United States, the nonproliferation treaty was signed.[76] In 1970 a new treaty was concluded, prohibiting the installation of any kind of weapons of mass destruction on the ocean floor.

In the 1970's the United States and the Soviet Union signed agreements on strategic arms limitation. The first strategic arms limitation agreement, SALT I (1973) confirmed the fact that the Soviet Union had already achieved parity with the United States in strategic weapons. SALT II, in 1979, suggested a certain Soviet superiority. Both were in effect accords on new stages of the arms race. The SALT II agreement was reached, after seven years of talks, at a time when both of the superpowers were facing the problem of developing a new kind of weapon—laser weapons.

Each of the superpowers had a nuclear stockpile large enough to reduce the planet to dust. The SALT agreements signified only an insignificant reduction iun the immediate threat; they could not alter the dangerous overall situation in which the world found itself.

Historians in the twenty-first century (if censorship allows them) will undoubtedly cite as the greatest paradox of the twentieth century the fact that the capitalist states showed a strong desire to help the Communist states, which made no secret of their desire to overthrow capitalism. In the sixty years that the Soviet Union has existed, the capitalists have constantly dreamed about the transformation of communism into a capitalist state of a higher order—one with a stable regime where there is no right to strike and thus profit-making possibilities are unlimited. As early as the beginning of the 1930s, the American historian Michael Florinsky was convinced that "the former crusaders of world revolution at any cost have exchanged their swords for machine tools, and now rely more on the results of their labor than on direct action to achieve the ultimate victory of the proletariat."[77]

World War II had strengthened such hopes. After Yalta, Harry Hopkins, Roosevelt's closest adviser and the most ardent admirer of Stalin in the American president's immediate entourage, expressed no doubts: "The Russians had proved that they could be reasonable and farseeing and there wasn't any doubt in the mind of the President or any of us that we could live with them and get along with them peacefully for as far into the future as any of us could imagine."[78] A poll by *Fortune* magazine in 1945 showed that of all segments of the U.S. population, it was businessmen who were most optimistic about the Soviet Union's postwar intentions. They believed that no less than one-third of American exports would go to the USSR.[79] The fact that at the end of the war exports to the USSR were no more than 1 percent of all U.S. exports did not lessen the hopes of Western businessmen and politicians. The only thing that frightened them was the prospect that Stalin would die and be replaced by a "real Communist." Harry Hopkins warned that all such hopes for cooperation could be shattered if anything happened to Stalin. "We felt sure that we could count on him to be reasonable and sensible and understanding."[80]

Charles Bohlen, the American ambassador in Moscow, reassured Washington on the question of Malenkov as Stalin's likely successor. Malenkov, he said, "impressed me as a man with a more Western-oriented mind than other Soviet leaders. He at least seemed to perceive our position and, while he did not agree with it, I felt he understood it." Bohlen placed serious hopes in Malenkov for another reason: "He... stood out from other Soviet leaders of the period in that he did not drink."[81] Bohlen's optimism still remained high when Malenkov was replaced by Khrushchev, who drank even during diplomatic meetings. Averell Harriman wrote in 1959: "I think that Mr. Khrushchev is keenly anxious to improve Soviet living standards. I believe that he looks upon the current Seven-Year Plan as the crowning success of the Communist revolution and a historic turning point in the lives of the Soviet people."[82]

Khrushchev's exuberance, his tendency to say whatever he felt ("We will bury you," he said, and shocked the West), his eccentricity (pounding the table with his shoe at the UN General Assembly), explains to some degree the indifference shown in the West to his fate and their renewed hopes in Brezhnev and his "collective leadership." This time there were no doubts. After all, the new men in power were engineers. It was unimportant that the majority of the Politburo members with engineering degrees obtained in their distant youth had never worked in their fields: they had always worked for the party. The German ambassador could not find the words to express his delight at these "technocrats in the best sense of the word." He was referring to Kosygin and Gromyko.[83] Technocrats, managers, conservatives—this was how the West saw the Brezhnev administration.

In the opinion of the West, the intentions of the Brezhnev administration were peaceful. Henry Kissinger, in guiding President Nixon's foreign policy, believed that Soviet foreign policy

> was being pulled in two directions. There were pressures for conciliation with the West, coming from a rising desire for consumer goods [and] from the fear of war. . . . At the same time there were pressures for continued confrontation with the United States arising our of Communist ideology, the suspiciousness of the leaders, the Party apparatus, and the military, and those who feared that any relaxation of tensions could only encourage the satellites to try once again to loosen Moscow's apron strings.[84]

Kissinger was a political scientist who had taught at the university level for years before taking charge of U.S. foreign policy for the Nixon administration. He was convinced, as were most heads of state, that the Soviet Union was torn between two directions in its foreign policy, one political, the other nonpolitical, and that there was a struggle between the supporters of these two lines. Consequently, it was important to support the "technocrats" against the "ideologists." On the basis of this schematic conception, which is widely accepted in the West, Kissinger developed a plan to sign a multitude of agreements on cooperation in various fields with the Soviet Union. The aim was to weave a web of common interests to defuse expansionist impulses. In 1978 Kissenger, already removed from power, acknowledged that his policy had failed.[85] His explanation was that "in 1972 we were in the middle of Vietnam and in 1974 in the middle of Watergate."[86]

The fundamental reason for the failure of detente, however, became evident to the West at the end of the 1970s: failure to understand the fact that chief characteristic of the Soviet state is that every act is a political one. On the eve of the Moscow Olympics in 1980, the opponents of the boycott argued that sports should not be mixed with politics. Likewise, Western business circles argued that commerce should not be mixed with politics and that all possible economic aid should be provided to the Soviet Union. Less than a year after the invasion of Czechoslovakia, the *New York Times* warned: "Few cold war policies have proved more self-defeating than the imposition by the United States of curbs on trade with the Soviet Union and other Communist countries."[87]

Samuel Pisar, an international lawyer and the most eloquent spokesman for pro-detente business circles, wrote: "If they are prepared to build automobiles, highways, filling stations, parking lots, motels, and roadside restaurants, it is in our interest to help them along."[88] The American Soviet specialist Theodore Shabad said that Soviet Union should be helped to explore and develop its energy resources.[89] At the same time, "arms control has a value and urgency," according to the *Washington Post*, "entirely apart from the status of political issues."[90]

One of the factors that led the Soviet rulers to propose "detente" to the West was their conflict with China. The break in relations between the two countries was blamed on Khrushchev, as were so many other problems. After his fall, the new leadership attempted to improve relations with China, at the very moment that Mao was directing a fierce struggle for power called the cultural revolution. He rebuffed all of Moscow's offers. The cultural revolution was strikingly similar to the Great Terror of the 1930s in the USSR, not only in its objectives (the transformation of the country according to the designs of the deified "Great Helmsman") but also in its methods— (total terror, sparing no one),[91] and the need for a foreign enemy as a factor unifying the people. The "hate demonstrations" held in China, with many millions taking part, were similar to those organized periodically in the Soviet Union and to the "days of hate" described so eloquently by Orwell in *1984*. The demonstrations in China were against the "revisionists," the "new tsars," and the like. Tensions also rose on the Sino-Soviet border.

On March 2, 1969, 300 Chinese troops fired on a Soviet border patrol that had landed on the uninhabited island of Damansky, in the Ussuri River. The Chinese call the Island Cherpad and consider it to be their territory. Soviet maps dispute this contention. The Soviet troops retreated after suffering twenty-three killed and fourteen wounded. On March 15, the two sides, after building up their forces, fought two major battles over the uninhabited island, one square kilometer in size. Artillery, rockets and tanks were used in the 9-hour battle, and each side suffered heavy losses. For the first time since the Hungarian events of 1956 and armed clash had taken place between two Communist states.

The Soviet Union and China each used the conflict for its own political needs, domestic and foreign. For many weeks the Soviet embassy in Peking was besieged. At the Chinese embassy in Moscow thousands of demonstrators were authorized to smash all the windows and spill ink on the walls. The leaderships of both countries filled their propaganda with nationalist themes. The Chinese accused Moscow of a "tsarist foreign policy." Evtushenko epitomized the Soviet propaganda with his poem "Red Snow on the Ussuri." He called on the reader to fight "for Russia and for the faith" against the "new Batu Khan."[92]

At the same time that armed clashes with China were occuring on the Sino-Soviet border (after the Ussuri there were clashes in Sinkiang and on the Amur), the Soviet leaders sought to reap the first dividends from the policy of "detente." Moscow's main argument was that the "yellow peril" was also a threat to the West. A commentator for the Soviet press agency Novosti used a page provided by *Le Monde* to warn the Europeans that the Chinese were a threat not only to Russia but to Europe as well. He argued that the territory Russia annexed in 1858–1860 did not belong to China any more than anyone else; thus Peking had no right to it. He also pointed out that the Great Wall of China was not located on the Ussuri, and not even in Manchuria.[93] The Soviet ambassador to Washington heatedly tried to convince Kissinger that "China was everybody's problem."[94]

On August 18 a Soviet diplomat in Washington asked a State Department official he was having lunch with what the U.S. government's reaction would be if Soviet planes destroyed China's nuclear installations.[95] One month later, Victor Louis, the only "independent Soviet journalist," who fulfills various delicate missions for the Soviet security "organs," published an article on London claiming that "Marxist theoreticians" foresaw a "Sino-Soviet war," including an air strike against Chinese installations at Loo Nor and the appeal of "anti-Maoist forces" in China for "fraternal help" from the other socialist countries.[96]

This scenario had already been tested—except for the destruction of nuclear installations—in Hungary in 1956, in Czechoslovakia in 1968— and would be used again twelve years later in Afghanistan. Its execution, however, always required the consent of the West. The green light for Soviet action had been given by the West in 1956 and again in 1968. Zdenek Mlynar, who in 1968 had been a member of the Czechoslovak Politburo, said that at the end of August 1968 Brezhnev told the leaders of the Prague

Spring that he had been assured by the United States that they would not intervene in Czechoslovak affairs.[97]

In 1969 the United States refused to give its blessings to preventive war against China. To this day it is uncertain whether the Soviet Union would have carried out its plan of attack or was spreading these rumors only to exert pressure on China and the West.

The Chinese government took the Soviet threats seriously and in 1969 said it was willing to reopen talks with the USSR. In the fall of 1970 the Chinese and Soviet ambassadors, who had been recalled some years before, returned to their posts. The volume of trade between the two countries began to increase.[98] After Mao's death (1976) the Chinese government gradually abandoned its openly anti-Soviet tone, and in 1979 border talks were initiated. It is not to be excluded that in the future relations between China and the Soviet Union may gradually improve.

Also during the 1970s, China took steps to improve relations with the United States. During the 1970s a threeway Moscow-Peking-Washington axis emerged and began to play a determining role in international affairs. The fact that two points in this triangle were Communist powers showed the new configuration of forces in the world. The capitalist world, above all the United States, tried to take advantage of the Sino-soviet rivalry by supporting first one adversary, then the other. The result, however, was the strengthening of the ideology whose ultimate objective was to destroy all other systems and ideologies.

## THE ROAD TO HELSINKI

The first half of the 1970s should be viewed as a self-contained period. The first decade of the Brezhnev era was coming to an end, as was the Ninth Five-Year Plan, which had been under heavy pressure due to the worldwide economic crisis. The final act of the European accord—the long-awaited fruit of detente—was signed in Helsinki.

An event which represents a turning point in world politics also took place in the first half of the 1970s. The Soviet Union reached military parity with the United States in the strict sense of numerical equality in strategic launchers. American superiority in the field of nuclear weapons, which had lasted throughout the entire postwar period, came to an end. In 1969 the number of Soviet missiles capable of reaching American territory equaled the number of American missiles and continued to increase steadily.[99] In an article on the world situation and the Soviet Union written on

May 4, 1980 in exile in Gorky, Andrei Sakharov cites as the most important fact that "in the 1960s and 1970s, the Soviet Union . . . carried out a fundamental reequipping and expansion of its weaponry."[100] at the Twenty-fourth Party Congress, Marshal Grechko, the Soviet defense minister, announced: "The Soviet Union is capable of responding to force with superior force."[101]

According to American and English sources (reliable Soviet data do not exist), the defense budget of the Soviet Union showed an annual increase of at least 4.5 percent between 1965 and 1977 and represented between 11 and 13 percent of the gross national product. During this same period the United States allocated 6 percent of its gross national product for military spending, although the GNP of the United States was twice that of the Soviet Union.[102] Characteristically, the Soviet Union spent 16 percent of its defense budget on military personnel, and the United States 56 percent.[103]

Figures can provide eloquent testimony to the changed balance of power. In 1967 the United States had 1,054 intercontinental ballistic missiles at its disposal, and the Soviet Union no more than 570. In 1979 the number of American missiles remained unchanged, while the Soviets had increased theirs to 1,409.[104] The number of American servicemen was reduced from 3.5 million to 2.06 million in one decade, 1969–1979, while the Soviet forces grew from 3.68 million to 4.19 million.[105]

Even more striking was the ratio of NATO and Warsaw Pact forces in the European theater: tanks 1:2; armored vehicles 1:2; antitank rockets 2:1, and cannons and mortars 1:2, respectively.[106]

Contributing to the strategic advantage of the Soviet Union was the fact that the United States, Western Europe's ally, was located far across the ocean, whereas the main force of the Warsaw Pact, the Soviet army, was within striking distance.

In the 1960s and 1970s the Soviet navy was rapidly enlarged. One of the initiators of this development, Admiral Gorshkov, defined the naval force of the Soviet Union as "the real capability of the state to use the oceans effectively in the interest of Comminist construction.[107] Citing Lenin as a leader who "paid serious attention to . . . the problem of naval supremacy," the commander-in-chief of the Soviet navy admitted that "the goal of achieving naval supremacy still remains in force."[108] He added, "The Soviet art of naval warfare flatly rejects any attempt to equate the term 'naval supremacy' with the term 'world supremacy.'"[109] The Soviet navy had become an important element in Soviet global strategy, an "important instrument of policy in time of peace, because it serves to protect Soviet interests and to suppport friendly countries."[110]

The dream of Lenin, who believed that the Red Army would bring "happiness and peace" to Europe by invading Poland in 1920 under the command of Tukhachevsky, the caution of Stalin, who rejected the idea of building a "large navy" in the 1930s because "we will not fight near American shores," looked naive to the heirs of the Soviet state's founders. By the middle of the 1970s they finally had the means to realize their utopia.

The U.S. secretary of defense, Harold Brown, admitted: "We don't understand why the Soviet Union seeks so persistently to increase its strategic nuclear potential."[111] The Soviet military theorist M. Skirdo gave an answer: "Most important today is not a country's economic potential, which could be used to tip the scales during a war, but the proportion of forces and resources available to each side in the case of an emergency even before military actions begin."[112]

The Soviet leadership was anxious to create a huge arms advantage before the beginning of military actions because it was very well aware of the economic weakness of the USSR. This weakness induces the Soviet leadership to expand the ever increasing amounts of the country's resources required to fulfill plans for armaments and the armed forces. These inordinate expenditures, in turn, continue to weaken the Soviet economy.

At the end of November 1961 the Twenty-second Party Congress endorsed a new program, which promised great things on the basis of the most advanced findings of "science." It predicted:

> In the coming decade (1961–1970) the Soviet Union will create the material and technical basis for communism and will surpass the most powerful and richest capitalist country, the United States, in per capita production. The material well-being of the working people and their cultural and technical standards will increase substantially. Everyone will be assured material abundance, while all kolkhozes and sovkhozes will become highly productive and highly profitable enterprises. The basic needs of the population for housing will be satisfied; hard physical labor will disappear and the USSR will become the country with the shortest working day in the world.

In January 1970 an editorial in *Pravda* presented the main outlines of a report by Brezhnev to a Central Committee plenum held in December 1969. The general secretary explained that the promises of the 1961 program could not be kept, that the golden age had to be postponed: "In a number of republics and oblasts an unjustified reduction in the numbers of livestock and poultry and in the production of meat, milk, and eggs has been permitted, and as a result difficulties have begun to appear in the supply of animal products to the population, especially in the large industrial centers." The article also noted a "drag in the rate of growth in a number of branches of industry" and only a "slow rise in the labor productivity and efficiency of social production."[113]

The Ninth Five-Year Plan (1971–1975) was supposed to be the first in Soviet history to bring faster growth in the production of consumer goods (group B) than the means of production (group A). The fantastic promises of Khrushchev now had given way to the unkept promises of Brezhnev. But more importantly, it was announced the the Soviet Union had entered the stage of "real socialism"—a new and higher stage in the direction of their ultimate Goal.

The choice of adjective was faultless. The word "real" effectively concealed the unreality of the economy, of Soviet society in its entirety, and of the Goal itself.

The plan was fulfilled, or overfulfilled, or slightly underfulfilled. The Central Statistical Bureau published the figures. At the same time it was necessary to stand in line for food. The incorrigible authors of Soviet political jokes suggested that the improvement in the standard of living of Soviet citizens could be seen by the fact that people waiting in lines were better dressed than before. For the great holiday, the hundredth anniversary of Lenin's birth, it was promised that supplies of thread would be rushed to the stores.

The paradoxes of the Soviet economy rendered it a unique phenomenon that is impossible to understand by traditional methods of economic analysis. Summing up the results of the Ninth Five-Year Plan at the Twenty-fifth Party Congress in 1976, Brezhnev spoke of the remarkable success of industry and a growth in the output of goods. (He was to repeat these same things at the Twenty-sixth Congress in 1981.) But before the Twenty-fifth Congress, Shevarnadze, first secretary of the Georgian party, who was at that time restoring order (after a purge) in his republic, let the truth slip out: "One out of every four consumer goods articles is of unsatisfactory quality. . . . For the first four years of the Ninth Five-Year Plan, an average of fifty apartments per 10,000 inhabitants were built in Georgia each year; for the whole of the USSR, this figures was ninety-one per 10,000." At the congress, Brezhnev said that in the new five-year plan 172 billion rubles would be allocated to agriculture.[114] Shevarnadze admitted: "For every ruble invested in agriculture, we get back 39 kopeks."[115]

In Soviet industry, according to the economist Academician Khachaturov, labor producticity was 50 percent lower than in the United States, and in agriculture 75–80 percent lower.[116] The Soviet planning and accounting system is set up in such a way that increasing productivity is extraordinarily disadvantageous to enterprises. The higher the productivity, the smaller the number of workers needed, resulting in increased plan targets and reduction in the wage fund allotted to that enterprise. "There is a threshold in labor productivity," Khachaturov acknowledged. "The enterprise has no interest in exceeding planned growth, because that would result in an enormous increase in the targets (or quotas) assigned by the plan for the next year."[117] Thus, "the majority of machine-building plants in the USSR have 1.3 or 1.4 times more workers than similar industries in other countries."[118] The utilization of unnecessary workers allows full employment; however, it is also one of the reasons for low wages.

The calculations of Soviets wages often made by Western economists provide a fine example of the unreality of the Soviet economy. Basile Kerblay, the best Soviet economic specialist in France, meticulously calculated the average wage received in the Soviet Union, the United States, and France in 1973, the third year of the Ninth Five-Year Plan, using both Soviet and Western sources. In the USSR, the average net salary was 121.90 rubles; in France, 1496.61 francs; in the United States, 606.51 dollars. Changing rubles and francs into dollars at the official rates, Kerblay found the average salaries to be $168.14, $361.61, and $606.51, respectively.[119] At the same time, Academician Sakharov, basing his calculations on observations inside the country, arrived at the conclusion that the average Soviet monthly wage was 110 rubles, which "in terms of purchasing power ... amounts to about $55 or 275 francs."[120] However, even this calculation does not reflect the entire reality. Sakharov took the dollar at 1 dollar to 2 rubles (slightly raising the dollar's value), on the assumption that this better corresponded to the real buying power of the ruble. Apparently, Sakharov did not want to complicate his analysis by trying to calculate the real value of the ruble, the most amazing money in the world.

The ruble's value is fixed by the party and the government. In the Soviet Union there are several varieties of exchange rates for the ruble, which allow goods to be purchased in special stores not accessible to ordinary people. In 1930 these stores had the stern and mysterious name *Torgsin*, meaning "commerce with foreigners." In the era of "real socialism" they are poetically called *Beryozka* (little birch tree) stores. In the Beryozka stores, the ruble has no value—a peculiar situation, when a country will not accept its own currency. Aside from the Beryozkas, there is a whole network of special stores reserved for the *nomenklatura*, where the price of merchandise varies in accordance wth the customer's position in the hierarchy. Lastly, in practice the chronic shortage of all goods made the ruble an illusory money, for it could not buy any merchandise.

The insubstantial character of workers' wages in the Soviet Union contributed to absenteeism, lower labor productivity, and poorer quality in the work performed. In August 19790, *Pravda* triumphantly reported on an "outstanding achievement of the space program, the longest manned space flight in history—175 days—has been successfully completed."[121] At the same time, *Komsomolskaya pravda* published a selection of letters from readers who complained about the railroads: the Krasnoyarsk–Moscow train arrived fourteen hours late; the Novokuznetsk–Chelyabinsk, seventeen hours, 30 minutes late; the Voronezh–Moscow, four hours late.[122]

Interplanetary flights are part of the USSR's military sector; success in this domain is undeniable. Military industry occupies a special place in the Soviet ecomomy, not only because it is the object of special attention but also because it is the only industrial branch that genuinely competes with the West. This does not mean that the military industry does not suffer from the general inadequacies plaguing the Soviet economy overall. It does mean, however, that in this industry these problems are given special attention.

The two-volume set of speeches and interviews with Brezhnev, prepared as a gift to the Twenty-fifth Party Congress, summed up the Brezhnev leadership's thinking after ten years in power and indicated how the country would be developed in the stage of "mature socialism." Brezhnev put it openly and clearly: no reforms, no scientific and technological revolution: "Only the party, armed with Marxist-Leninist doctrine and the experience of political organization of the masses, is capable of determining the main lines of social development." The chief qualities required of managers were "great ideological firmness and competence."[123] First ideology, then competence.

The failure of the Ninth Five-Year plan (Soviet statistics recognized it indirectly in declaring that contrary to the promise that had been made Group A, producer goods, had developed more rapidly than Group B, consumer goods) was explained officially by two bad harvests, in 1972 and 1975. The results could have been disastrous for the country as well as the government, especially after the poor harvest of 1975, had it not been for immediate aid from the West, in particular the United States.

The practice of buying foreign wheat was inaugurated by Khrushchev in 1962. Since then, the USSR has bought grain year in and year out from the United States, Canada, Australia, Argentina, and Brazil. Political considerations played a major part in this. The shortages of foodstuffs led to the greatest worker unrest after the Novocherkassk revolt in 1962 and at the Togliatti automobile factory in 1980. Enterprises in Central Russia (Yaroslavl, Murom) were also affected by strikes. The reasons were always the same: food shortages and the low standard of living. Nor did agitation cease in the most vulnerable spot in the Soviet empire—Poland. In 1970, worker revolts led to the replacement of Gomulka by Gierek and ten years later, in 1980, the replacement of Gierek by Kanya and then Jaruzelski. The lesson was clear: economic difficulties are fraught with political complications. Moreover, purchases of meat and other foodstuffs have steadily increased. In 1972 the USSR brought 18 million metric tons of grain from the United States, but this record amount was exceeded in 1979, when 25 million metric of grain were bought, again from the United States.[124] Under an agreement concluded earier, the USSR could buy 15 million metric tons of grain annually for five years without having to get special authorization from the U.S. government.

The signing of this agreement, the first of its kind, was frank acknowledgment of the failure of the Soviet agricultural policy. One-fourth of the economically active population in the USSR was employed in agriculture in 1978. In the United States the figure was 2.5–3 percent.[125] Neither the size of the work force, nor the use of technology and chemical pesticides and fertilizers could help the situation. One fact speaks louder than words: the hourly wage of a Soviet agricultural worker was 44 kopeks (59 cents at the offical exchange rate), as opposed to $2.35 in the United Staes.[126] A ton of grain could be purchased from the United States at half the cost of a ton of grain produced in the USSR. For the USSR, it was cheaper to buy grain from other countries than to produce it at home. Under detente the credits necessary to make these purchases could also be found in the West.

This is what Senator Henry Jackson said on the subject: "A relaxation of controls on strategic trade with the Soviet Union has been a central principle of the policy of detente." He continued, "A purported benefit to be achieved was greater cooperation from the Soviets. But they have exploited detente to acquire the West's latest technology to fortify their military industrial complex."[127]

The difficult dilemma between guns and butter was resolved. Detente allowed the Soviet Union to dedicate itself to the production of "guns" while purchasing "butter" in case of extreme need under favorable conditions, from the West. And it was not only butter. The West also helped, as it has always done, in the production of "guns." It was during detente that the embargo on the sale of strategic materials to the Soviet Union was virtually abandoned. On February 25, 1976, the State Department admitted that since 1972 the USSR had produced, under American license, the miniature ball bearings absolutely necessary for the construction of guidance systems for long-range nuclear missiles with multiple warheads (MIRVs).[128] American computers are the basis for the air defense system of the Warsaw Pact countries.[129] After having given $500 million for the construction of a huge automobile factory on the Kama River, the Americans "discovered" that this factory was producing motors for military vehicles.[130] This kind of assistance and cooperation was developed in all domains. During the Vietnam war, the United States shared its experience with the Soviet Union, sending them manuals with such titles as *Training for Operations in the Jungle*, *The Terrorist Tactics of the Vietcong in South Vietnam*, *Systems of Air-to-Surface Operations*, and *Use of Chemical and Biological Warfare*.[131]

A Senate investigation during the summer of 1980 revealed that American and Western European firms were providing the USSR with chemical equipment and expertise that assisted the Soviet Union in developing chemical and biological weapons: 80 percent of the Soviet production of polyethlylene and 75 percent of the chemical fertilizers came from equipment provided by the West.[132]

Western leaders have sufficient proof of concrete cooperation between the USSR and Western firms that manufacture materials and equipment that may be readily used for military purposes. It has also become known that the Soviet Union has obtained other equipment of strategic importance from the United States through third countries.

A comparison of scientific exchange programs between the United States and the Soviet Union leaves no doubt that the Soviets have used this exchange to improve their military technology and to expand their military potential. Soviet scientists who come to the United States study research in the fields of plasma, physics, metallurgy, computer-based control systems (for industry), ferroelectric ceramics, photoelectrics, and semiconductors. American scientists travels to the Soviet Union to do research in sociology, history, literature, Russian poetry, archaeology.[133]

The provision of "butter" and assistance in producing "guns" are only elements of the system of economic linkages between the USSR, other socialist countries, and the West. During the years of detente, the nature of these interconnections assumed a new character. The cooperation without which the USSR could not have survived became a relation between "partners," as the director of a large London bank explained: "If you give someone a small loan he becomes your debtor. If you give him a large loan, you make him your partner. In spite of its ideology, the Soviet bloc is currently a very important partner for us."[134]

During the 1960s, the socialist bloc obtained very few Western credits. By 1974 such credits existed on a large scale—$13 billion worth. In 1978 they reached $50 billion and continued to grow. British banks loaned 30 percent of this amount to the USSR and the other socialist countries; 20

percent each was provided by French and German banks, and 13 percent by American banks. In 1975 Western bankers thought that if a debtor nation was devoting 20 percent of its income to interest payments, it should be given no more credits or loans. In 1978 the USSR was paying 28 percent of its income to service its debts.[135] But one Swiss banker admitted, "Only the Kremlin knows the exact amound of this debt. We're navigating in the fog, because Western banks keeps their relations with the Soviet bloc secret. So we don't know exactly the conditions for repayment of these debts, nor do we know the reasons for these new Russian loans."[136]

After awarding huge credits to the "real socialist" part of the world, the Western banks found themselves loaning still more to help pay the interest on the original loans. In this way, the capitalist world has continued to bind itself to the socialist one by innumerable economic links. The West's main concern thus became preserving the stability of the socialist world (and hence its capacity to pay). The interests of "real socialism" became those of the West. The Soviet Union cannot solve all its economic problems with the help of the "butter," "guns," and credits supplied by the West, but it does solve the most important ones, i.e., those that are unsolvable under the conditions of the socialist system, such as the introduction of the latest technology. At the same time, the Soviet Union gains understanding, cooperation, and help from its enemy.

In 1978 the American businessman Armand Hammer, one of the initiators and promoters of Western cooperation with the USSR, was decorated with the Soviet Order of Friendship Among the Peoples. "I was very moved by such high recognition and by the letter from Leonid Ilyich Brezhnev," the head of Occidental Petroleum confided. Occidental ranks as the twenty-sixth largest corporation in the United States. "He is an outstanding leader and at the same time a man of heart, warm and simple."[137] Hammer for more than sixty years has served a model of how Western businessmen can collaborate with the USSR. He crowned his record of collaboration, begun under Lenin, by the signing of a $20 billion contract with Brezhnev in 1973 for the construction of a chemical enterprise. In 1980 after invasion of Afghanistan by Soviet troops, when President Carter proclaimed an embargo on the export of certain chemical products to the Soviet Union, an exception was made for Occidental Petroleum. The invasion of Afghanistan, an "unforeseen difficulty," another "temporary detour" or "incident along the road," could not break the ties between Western business and the Soviet Union.

The first half of the 1970s was a time of intense diplomatic activity. Detente facilitated the conclusion of treaties validating the new balance of forces in the world. Most important were the Soviet treaty with West Germany in 1970 and the agreement limiting strategic weapons with the United States—SALT I (1972–1974).

The treaty with West Germany was "drafted in haste by Egon Bahr, the West German secretary of state, and Andrei Gromyko, the Soviet foreign minister, then signed just as hastily, in the Kremlin, by Chancellor Brandt and Kosygin," Helmut Allard tells us in his memoirs.[138] The treaty acknowledged Soviet hegemony over the socialist camp and confirmed the existing borders of the Soviet zone. As Allard puts it, the treaty provided the Soviet Union with "the key to carrying further its far-reaching plans in foreign and domestic policy."[139] Key economic agreements with the United States were also signed in the Kremlin. On May 23, 1972, all the Soviet newspapers carried a photograph on the center of the first page, showing a huge table with many chairs along both sides with Nixon and Brezhnev in the foreground smiling benevolently at one another. No one else was seated at the table. The two were presented as joint masters of the world. Nixon's visit to Moscow underlined the significance of the agreements that were signed. The United States recognized the USSR as an equal partner with which it wished to collaborate. Soviet commentators stressed, above all, the importance of the agreement on scientific and technical cooperation. "In our century of impetuous development of the scientific and technological revolution," wrote *Izvestia*, "no country can develop its science and technology alone, no matter how strong and developed it may be, without participating in international cooperation."[140] The meaning of this comment is clear: the powerful Soviet Union would receive aid from the United States and could soon "catch up with and surpass America."

All during the Nixon visit the Soviets were careful to emphasize that the rapprochement with the United States was "party policy." This was underscored by Brezhnev, who signed the most important agreements in his capacity as general secretary of the Central Committee. It was explained to the surprised American journalists that the USSR Supreme Soviet has the right to empower the person of its choice to sign state documents.

The policy of detente transformed the character of Western diplomacy. The French historian Alain Besançon noted: "A reversal has taken place in the traditional relations between politics and diplomacy. Normally, diplomacy is an instrument serving politics. A visit by chief of state, for example, is a means to achieving a political accord. . . . Now we are doing the opposite, putting politics at the service of diplomacy. We make a political arrangement in order to justify an official visit."[141] Nixon's trip to Moscow, and his summit meeting there with the Soviet leaders, had become a political goal in and of itself. Kissinger tells us that from 1970 on Nixon had been trying to arrange such a "summit meeting."

On August 1, 1975, thirty-two European heads of state, together with those of Canada and the United States, took part in another summit meeting with Brezhnev. On that day, the Final Act of the Conference of European Security and Cooperation was signed at Helsinki. The idea of a Europe-wide conference that would confirm the results of World War II had been proposed by Khrushchev in the early 1960s. In 1975 the Helsinki confer-ence above all codified the results of detente.

During the Helsinki conference, in July 1975, the Soviet and American spaceships *Soyuz* and *Apollo* met in space. This event was portrayed by the Soviet press as a triumph of detente and of Soviet advanced technology, a triumph that was meant to cover over the defeat in the "race to the moon" and to show the full equality of the two partners.

The Soviet–American meeting in space had determined the character of the meeting on earth, at Helsinki. The final act of the conference consisted of agreements in three problem areas, three "baskets" as they were called in Helsinki. There was first the political problem. The borders established after World War II were confirmed, not only those of the Soviet Union, the only state to enlarge its territory after the war, but also those of an inviolable zone of "real socialism" in Europe. The second "basket" was economic, an agreement to expand economic relations between the two parts of the world. In other words, the West promised to help the Soviet Union and its satellites to modernize their economies. Lastly, the third" basket" expressed the West's hope that the USSR and the other countries of "real socialism" would lift the iron curtain a bit, that is, would respect the rights of their citizens and allow the free exchange of ideas.

The Thiry Years' war culminated in the Treaty of Westphalia in 1648, which established the principle by which the war between Catholics and Protestants would be ended: *cuius regio, eius religio*. The religion of the subjects was determined by that of their ruler. The Helsinki conference adopted the same principle, but for one side only. The West agreed to respect the "religion" of Eastern Europe, the "Soviet" religion; the Soviet Union refused to consider itself bound by any obligations whatsoever: in-sofar as "the interests of humanity coincide with the interests of the inter-national working class and of socialism... the policy of detente... does not in any way contradict the revolutionary strategy of the struggle for the liberation of peoples from national and class oppression and for social progress."[142]

In a speech given to American trade union leaders during the Helsinki conference, Solzhenitsyn asked, "is detente necessary or not?" "Not only is it necessary;" he replied, "it is as vital as air! It is the only solution for the planet." However, he argued, detente could be real only on three conditions, which he went on to list: that disarmament be applied not only to war but to violence as well, eliminating not only the weapons that are used to destroy neighbors but also those that are used to oppress compatriots; that the "other side" be subjected to the control of public opinion, the press, and a free parliament; and that it reject the use of "misanthropic propaganda," that which in the Soviet Union "is proudly called ideological war."[143]

Thirty years earlier, Arthur Koestler had said:

A state which constructs a Maginot Line of censorship, then fires off its propaganda from behind the shelter of this line, is committing psychological aggression. The Western powers . . . should demand: (1) free circulation of foreign newspapers, periodicals, books, and films in the Soviet Union: (2) reforms in the Soviet system of censorship (if it must remain in existence) that would allow information about the outside world to circulate freely in the USSR; (3) free access by accredited journalists, parliamentarians, and others to the territory occupied by the Soviet Union; (4) an end to restrictions on the entry of foreigners to the USSR and the departure of Soviet citizens from the USSR; and (5) active cooperation between the USSR and the Western powers in organizing travel abroad through exchange programs for students, teachers, writers, workers, etc.[144]

Koestler believed that this "demand for the free circulation of ideas across borders, to revive the damaged flow of the world's circulatory system," should be put forward at the United Nations, at the Security Council, and at every summit meeting. It should be made a precondition for any and all negotiations between East and West.

On the fifth anniversary of the Helsinki conference, Brezhnev found the results "absolutely positive."[145] So they were: having obtained recognition of its hegemony in Europe and economic aid, the Soviet Union dismissed the agreement on "so-called humanitarian matters," that is, increased contacts between individuals, broader exchange of information, and greater respect for human rights, labeling it "interference in the internal affairs of the socialist countries."[146] Aleksandr Chakovsky, Brezhnev's court scribe, dedicated an "epic novel" to the Helsinki conference. It was called *Victory*. Describing two conferences, Potsdam in 1945 and Helsinki in 1975, and two Soviet leaders, Stalin and Brezhnev, Chakovsky developed the theme of the great Soviet victory: Stalin shattered Hitler, despite the fact that Roosevelt, Truman, and above all Churchill tried to prevent this to the best of their ability, and at Potsdam laid the foundations for peace and a new order in the world; Brezhnev completed this work and achieved final Victory. Helsinki only served to confirm it.

In 1975, the postwar period in European and world history came to an end and the next stage in the history began: the history of the Soviet Union and the world. In his speech at the Twenty-fifth Party Congress in February 1976, Brezhnev spoke of plans for the future, plans whose realization became possible after Helsinki. He talked of victories in Vietnam, Laos, Cambodia, and Angola. "Detente," he insisted, "does not in any way rescind, nor can it rescind or alter, the laws of class struggle. We do not conceal the fact that we see in detente a path toward the creation of more favorable conditions for the peaceful construction of socialism and communism."[147]

## ORDINARY SOCIALISM

In 1939 Churchill, a master of the bon mot, defined the Soviet Union as "a riddle wrapped in a mystery inside an enigma." By the early 1970s the first socialist state in the world, having become the strongest military power in the world, still remained an enigma to the West. Failing to find the means to understand this new phenomenon in the history of mankind, Western Sovietologists tended to view the Soviet Union as a country like any other and to evaluate its achievements "objectively."

"The orientation of Brezhnev's policy" was judged "liberal." To one American Sovietologist, the 1970s were a time of "expansion of individual freedoms" and "increased egalitarianism," which was particularly evident in the fact that the disparity between the salaries of the best paid and least paid white and blue collar workers went from 3.7 percent in 1964 to 3.2 percent in 1970.[148] Another American Sovietologist agreed:

> I see the 1960s and 1970s as a very benign period in Soviet history. It is quite possible that future historians will say this was the greatest, the best period in their history. It was a society that for the first time was able to provide both guns and butter, to raise the standard of living a bit, and to reach military equality with the West.[149]

In 1975 Andrei Sakharov, a member of the Soviet and the American Academy of Sciences, had this to say:

> Today the world press is full of items about inflation, the energy crisis, and growing unemployment in the capitalist countries. . . . I would nonetheless

like to say: You are not dying of hunger...and even if you reduced your standard of living to one-fifth of what it is, you would still be better off than citizens of the world's wealthiest socialist country.[150]

Five years later, from exile in Gorky, he noted a worsening of the situation in the Soviet Union: "A country living for decades under conditions in which all means of production belong to the state is suffering serious economic and social hardship. It cannot feed itself without outside assistance; and it cannot make progress in science and technology on the contemporary level without using the benefits of detente.[151]

Andrei Amalrik began his essay, "Will the Soviet Union Survive Until 1984?"—one of the first free reflections on his country and the world—by expressing the hope that it would have the same interest for Western Sovietologists "that a fish would have for ichthyologists if it suddenly began to talk."[152] The decade that followed the publication of this essay was an era in which the Soviet Union was made wide open for examination: the books, articles, reflections, and testimonies of Solzhenitsyn, Sakharov, Aleksandr Zinoviev, Vladimir Maksimov, Sinyavsky, Bukovsky, and many other writers, social activists, and witnesses revealed the nature of the socialist state that had built its utopia.

But the "talking fish" made little impression on the "ichthyologists." Many Western specialists, Sovietologists, statesmen, and businessmen who dealt with the socialist world wanted to remain deaf. Even the shock produced by *The Gulag Archipelago*, the strongest blow ever to the prestige of the Soviet Union, had little effect on those who made the Soviet Union their business. In time, Solzhenitsyn too was classed among the "reactionaries," which made it possible to ignore his words.

For the West, the Soviet "tsardom of shams" remained a reality that differed only slightly from that of the non-Communist states. Its distinctive features were attributed to Russia's unusual history and the national peculiarities of the Russian people. But for the most part, it was considered a country like any other with an economy (including powerful industry and a somewhat backward agriculture, in need only of capital, machinery, and fertilizer); a culture, with its famous ballet—the best in the world: universal literacy; free medicine; mass organizations (unions, the Komsomol, the CPSU); general elections; and a constitution which granted the citizenry broad democratic rights.

The mystery of the Soviet system lies in its exceptional simplicity. Rejecting what they call the obsolete model of "totalitarianism," some American political scientists and Sovietologists prefer to use the term "institutional pluralism" to analyze the Soviet Union and refer to it as a "pluralistic system."[153] In 1980 Sakharov defined the Soviet system as totalitarian:

A totalitarian system that conducts its policies through control from a single center. Diplomacy, information, and disinformation services inside and outside the country, foreign trade, tourism, academic and scientific exchange, economic and military assistance to liberation movements (a term that in some cases must be placed in quotation marks), the foreign policy of satellite countries—all these are coordinated from a single center.[154]

The foundation of the totalitarian system is ideology.

Ideology is the most mysterious element of the Soviet system. Some deny its importance: "Probably most analysts would agree," one British economist writes, "that ideology (i.e., Marxism-Leninism) is not a powerful force in the Soviet Union today."[155] Others assert that ideology is dead, since no one believes in Marxism-Leninism anymore. Aleksandr Solzhenitsyn, who does not doubt the vitality of this doctrine, hsa tried to persuade the Soviet leaders to abandon it: "Pull and shake off from all of us, the filthy, sweaty shirt of Ideology which is now so covered with blood that it prevents the living body of the nation from breathing."[156] Solzhenitsyn has insisted that it is essential to abandon the ideology of Marxism-Leninism because it is a "false doctrine" and a "worn out ideology" that "has nothing with which to answer objections and protests other than weapons and prison bars."[157] Logical arguments refuting the doctrine seldom harm it. Moreover, it is particularly difficult to regard an ideology as "beaten" when it is spreading over the world with the speed of a forest fire.

The failure to comprehend the essence of Soviet ideology can be explained specifically by the fact that it is treated as a religion that requires "faith." In fact, however, Soviet ideology exterminated all the "believers" and declared "faith" to be a dangerous deviation from the "general line" during the Stalin era. When Ivan Yakhimovich, a confirmed Communist, sent a letter to the Central Committee in 1968 protesting the invasion of Czechoslovakia and the trials of the dissidents, events which, in his opinion, had seriously damaged the cause of communism, Soviet psychiatrists declared him mentally ill. "He claims," said an expert report,

that never and under no circumstances would he betray the idea of the struggle for a Communist order, for socialism. On the basis of the foregoing the commission concludes that Yakhimovich displays the paranoid development symptomatic of a psychopathic personality. The patient's condition should be equated with a mental illness and therefore, with regard to the actions for which he has been charged, I. A. Yakhimovich should be considered not responsible. He must be placed in a special hospital for compulsory treatment.[158]

Soviet ideology has long since ceased to be a philosophical doctrine or even a system of views. It has become a technique for conditioning human consciousness and spirit and for transforming man into Soviet man. As Solzhenitsyn asserted:

> The stock phrases of required thinking, not even thinking but rather dictated argument, dinned into us daily from the magnetic gullets of radios, reproduced by the thousands in different newspapers that are really all identical to one another, and condensed into weekly surveys for political study groups, have maimed us all, leaving almost no undamaged minds.[159]

The hero of Aleksandr Zinoviev's *The Yellow House*, himself a worker on the ideological front, enumerates the forms of ideological work: evening university courses in Marxism-Leninism; the Komsomol schools; newspapers; magazines; grade school lessons; radio; and television. He draws this conclusion.

> It doesn't at all matter what people think to themselves or in private conversations. The only thing that matters is that they are constantly in a powerful field of ideological influence and no matter what their attitude toward it, they are still only particles in this field, and from it they receive a certain charge, disposition, orientation, and the like.[160]

Ideology never lets go of Soviet man, from the cradle to the grave. *Pravda*, noting that "man spends one-third of his time at work," rejected the idea that the rest of a man's time is his own: "The use of free time, behavior in public places or in private life, is not only a question involving the individual and him alone. As already mentioned several times, it is an issue involving the state as a whole, demanding the most serious attention of party, government, trade union, and Komsomol organizations."[161]

In the Soviet Union, the ideological army surpasses the army, navy, and air force in number. The secretary of the Kazakhstan Central Committee announced proudly at a routine ideological meeting that besides the kolkhoz workers, "a great number of ideological workers—more than 140,000 political propagandists, lecturers, political educators, and organizers of cultural and artistic activities—participated in the harvest of 1979."[162] This number—140,000—equals approximately ten full-strength divisions. Suslov, the leader of the "ideological front," in an address to all his "soldiers" (a conference of ideological workers), referred to the "army of millions and millions of ideological cadres" whose duty was "to encompass the entire mass of the people with their influence and at the same time to reach every individual." The secretary of the Komsomol declared at the same conference that the process of ideological upbringing "must be uninterrupted" and occur everywhere—in the home, at work, and on the streets.[163]

Ideology regulates the behavior of Soviet citizens and, through a refined system of techniques, arouses the emotions and reflexes essential to the party at any given moment. Belief is not required of Soviet citizens. They are supposed to repeat the standard slogans without believing them, even sometimes mocking them (to themselves). They do not even have to repeat them, but merely listen to them. Participation in the ritual alone is adequate for the ideology to penetrate the brain and the blood.

There are two pillars on which this ideology rests: (1) the party is always right because it is leading the way to communism, the bright future; and (2) hatred of the enemy is a quality "Soviet man" cannot do without. "Hatred has become your barren atmosphere," wrote Solzhenitsyn, "a hatred second not even to racism."[164] As though wishing to demonstrate the truth of Solzhenitsyn's words, a Soviet lieutenant colonel Demin teaches his soldiers: "Even today a just and noble hatred of the imperialist aggressors serves as a bright expression of one's love for the motherland."[165] The party, of course, chooses when and whom to hate.

Ideological education begins at a very early age, when the child is in kindergarten. Every summer, 16 million young Pioneers, ten to fifteen years old, take part in a war game called "lightning" (*Zarnitsa*) at military camps.[166] Every year another military game—"Eaglet" (*Orlenok*)—is organized for teenagers fifteen to eighteen.

Ideology has a most important function in Soviet society, the infantilization of Soviet citizens. Just like the stern father of a lazy and disobedient child, ideology teaches Soviet citizens how to understand events in the world around them, how to behave, how to relate to their families, neighbors, and strangers. At the 1979 ideological conference mentioned above, Suslov presented his army of ideologues with a new mission, as a result of the economic crisis: "to work out an arrangement for meeting people's real needs."[167]

Hegel's formula "All that is real is reasonable, and all that is reasonable is real," found a new meaning: "zeal" is what the party considers real, whether it is reasonable or not. This means that without ideology life is impossible. Ideology permits the transformation of fiction into reality and nourishes the population with words.

The first half of the 1970s witnessed the birth of the cult of the general secretary. No decisions made in the feverishness after the ouster of Khrushchev nor any talk of "collective leadership" could halt the irrepressible rise of one general secretary. The ideology requires a Leader, a Priest, in whom it can find a formal, tangible incarnation.

The career of Brezhnev, which in its most essential features repeated the careers of his predecessors, Stalin and Khrushchev, allows us to conclude that it is impossible for a state of the Soviet type to manage without a Leader. The experience of China after the death of Mao, who fulfilled the function of Lenin and Stalin simultaneously, confirms the universality of this system: deified during his life, Mao, several months after his death, began to get in the way of the new leaders, who were involved in a bitter struggle for power. They proceeded with "de-Maoization," all the while selecting the quotes from his works and the examples of his creations they needed in order to eliminate their rivals and take his place.

The struggle against "the rehabilitation of Stalin," which was one of the most important concerns of newly awakened public opinion from the end of the 1950s to the mid-1960s, played a significant educational role. At the same time, it created the illusion of a victory that was never won.

The rehabilitation of Stalin did take place, for he was cleared of all criminal accusations: discarded were accusations of "subjective and unilateral judgment" concerning preparation for war with Germany and the course of the war. Brezhnev said solemnly: "Our party had foreseen the possibility of a military confrontation with the forces of imperialism and prepared the country and its people for defense."[168]

At the same time, Stalin could not be fully rehabilitated, for his place was occupied by another. The first general secretary was included in the small iconostasis of Leaders, but he took third place behind Lenin and Brezhnev. Brezhnev's rise proceeded in two directions, both leading to the same goal. The first was the consolidation of his personal power. In the course of a fifteen-year "creeping purge," Brezhnev got rid of all his actual and potential rivals in the Politburo and the Secretariat of the Central Committee. This gradual transformation of the leadership bodies was limited to political, not physical, elimination. By 1980 power had been concentrated in the names of Brezhnev's inner cabinet, headed by Konstantin Chernenko, who was made a member of the Politburo. The members of this "Dnepropetrovsk mafia," Brezhnev's vassals, owed their power to him alone and occupied the key posts in the central apparatus. The first and second deputies to the chairman of the KGB, the minister of the interior, and four deputies to the chairman of the Council of Ministers were all Dnepropetrovsk men. In 1978 a special law was passed on "collectivity in the work of the USSR Council of Ministers,"[169] leaving Kosygin, the head of the government, with only nominal power.

By the fifteenth anniversary of his advent to power, Brezhnev held the posts of general secretary of the General Committee, chairman of the Presidium of the Supreme Soviet of the USSR, chairman of the Council of Defense, and commander-in-chief of the armed forces. Khrushchev had violated the rule, accepted after Stalin's death, that one person could not simultaneously hold both the post of first secretary of the Central Committee and that of chairman of the Council of Ministers. After Khrushchev's death Brezhnev circumvented this rule by combining the posts of general secretary and head of state (chairman of the USSR Supreme Soviet Presidium.

The second part of Brezhnev's rise to power which occurred simultaneously with the consolidation of power, was the transformation of the general secretary into the Leader, and the creation of a Brezhnev cult. The model for the true Leader was sketched by the writer Vsevolod Kochetov, a loyal Stalinist and editor of the magazine *October*. After Khrushchev's removal, Kochetov wrote a novel portraying a Leader who had failed to justify the power the party had placed in him, and a contrasting figure, a Leader of the required type. Delving into history, Kochetov compared two Russian tsars: Ivan the Terrible and Vasily Shuisky.[170]

> In order to govern our Mother Russia, one must have, oh, oh, such a great held on one's shoulders! Insolence alone is not enough; wisdom is needed; and unhurried statesmanship. And tremendous erudition. But what was Shuisky like? Nothing special. An upstart, that's all. He puffed himself up and played at being the tsar of Russia, but soon went flying off the throne without a shred of glory.[171]

The image of Brezhnev as Leader was created on this model: unhurried, reasonable, wise, with "tremendous erudition." Above all, he was credited with an eminent military career and the title of Marshal of the Soviet Union. In 1979 his dress uniform bore sixty decorations, while Zhukov, the most prominent military leader of World War II, had only forty-six.[172] Brezhnev was now said to have played a decisive role in the victory over Hitler. He was awarded the Gold Medal of Karl Marx for his "outstanding contribution to the development of the theory of Marxism-Leninism and the scientific study of current problems in the development of socialism and the historic world-wide struggle for communist ideals."[173] He received the Lenin Peace Prize. Uncovering a bronze bust of Brezhnev sent to his native village, the first secretary of the Ukraine attested: "We are fully justified in saying: lasting peace, just peace in the world, and the name of Leonid Ilyich Brezhnev are inseparable."[174]

In 1933, responding to a member of the party who had decided to send his decoration to Stalin as an expression of his admiration for the Leader, the general secretary who was known for his modesty, wrote: "Decorations are not made for those who are already famous but for the little-known heroes.... Moreover, I must tell you that I already have two decorations. That is more than I need, I assure you."[175] At the end of his life, Stalin changed his view on this question. And not only, it seems, because he felt that two medals were a beggarly reward for what he had done, but also because he understood the magical power of medals and uniforms.

The mystical and ritualistic aspect of Soviet ideology still awaits an analyst. Rationally inexplicable phenomena are interpreted by the party as natural phenomena. The Old Bolshevik Lazurkina, who was a prisoner for many years in the Stalinist camps, appeared before the Twenty-second Party Congress and related a dream she had had about Lenin. Lenin asked her to remove his tiresome successor from the Mausoleum. And the congress fulfilled the wish of the deceased Leader: it removed Stalin from the Mausoleum. A Byelorussian poet published a poem in a Minsk journal in which he wrote of a telephone call to Lenin: "We have the right: wake him up! We have the right: call him!"[176]

On March 2, 1973, all Soviet newspapers announced that Brezhnev had begun a routine purge of the party—an exchange of membership cards—on March 1, in the presence of the Politburo and the secretaries of the Central Committee. He gave a sample of the new party card, bearing the number 00000001, to Vladimir Ilyich Lenin. Leonid Ilyich Brezhnev received 00000002. The mystical transfer of the symbol of power was complete.

On April 21, 1979, "at the request of the workers," Brezhnev was awarded the Lenin Prize for Literature for his three books: *The Little Land*, *The Rebirth*, and *The Virgin Lands*, which told in the first person of Brezhnev's exploits during the war, on the industrial front, and in agriculture. The general secretary was declared the best writer in the country. Stalin, who had a profound belief in the magic of words, dreamed his whole life of being recognized as a poet. But it was Brezhnev who realized this dream. Markov, chairman of the Union of Soviet Writers, described Brezhnev's books as embodying "the science of victory" and asserted that "in their popularity, in their influence on the reading masses, and in their creativity the books of Leonid Ilyich have no equal."[177] Thus, party propaganda was officially proclaimed to be literature, and the party's high priest became the guardian of the written word.

When receiving his prize, the winner promised: "If I find the time, if I am able, I will continue my memoirs."[178] In 1964 the cult of Brezhnev seemed impossible, just as the cult of Khrushchev had seemed impossible in 1954, and that of Stalin in 1924. Historical experience shows that the qualities necessary to the general secretary are revealed only in the harshest struggle for power. Until he achieves victory, the general secretary-to-be develops the qualities he has and acquires those he lacks. He is forged until he assumes the necessary form, having demonstrated outstanding talents: cunning, dexterity, prudence, ruthlessness, and a total contempt for all dogma.

Boris Souvarine, a preeminent specialist on bolshevism, explains the origin of the Soviet state in the following way. Lenin was obsessed with two historical precedents: first, the Jacobins, who were defeated because they did not guillotine enough people; and second, the Paris Commune, which was defeated because its leaders did not shoot enough people. Lenin saw it necessary to avoid these errors, and terror surged in a crescendo.

Since October 1917 terror has become an essential element in constructing the socialist utopia. In every country that embarks on the path of building the best world, based on the Soviet model, from Cuba to Cambodia, from Albania to Ethiopia, from Czechoslovakia to China, resistance to the Communist party is suppressed in the cruelest manner. Terror is considered the sole means of imposing the power of a minority on the majority. In comparison with the Stalinist terror, the persecutions of the Khrushchev era seemed extremely mild. They came to be called repression.

Soviet citizens, including those directly subjected to persecution and imprisonment, and Western observers alike were so accustomed to the scale of Stalin's terror that they considered its replacement with "repression" to be a change in the system.

The German psychologist Bruno Bettelheim, who spent time in the Nazi concentration camps and later emigrated to the United States, analyzed the behavior of the SS guards and the prisoners. He noted that an essential part in the process of psychologically destroying the individual is played by ruthless, senseless, and total cruelty to the prisoner immediately after his arrest. Solzhenitsyn wrote a classic description of this process in his novel *The First Circle* (the chapter entitled "The Arrest of Volodin"). The psychological shock of the prolonged terror under Stalin, something the entire population experienced, left profound traces: the Great Fear substituted for the Great Terror. The heirs of Lenin and Stalin are capable of applying a selective terror whenever it becomes apparent that the Great Fear is beginning to diminish.

The repressions of the Khrushchev–Brezhnev era became a real reflection of significant processes underway in society, processes that exposed the fiction of total subordination to ideology. Repression trampled the young shoots of resistance that broke through the crust of an earth scorched by terror.

The primary object of these repressions was the dissident movement. In 1978, the *Soviet Small Political Dictionary* for the first time included a definition for the term *dissidents*: "those who deviate from the doctrine of the church (heterodox)." Imperialist propaganda, the dictionary explains, uses the term "to designate isolated renegades, people who have broken away from socialist society and who actually come out against the socialist system, engage in anti-Soviet activity, violate the law, and, lacking any support from within the country, look for support from abroad, from the subversive centers of imperialist propaganda and espionage."[179] This definition is broad enough to encompass all who "deviate from the doctrine of the ruling church"—Soviet ideology. The entry, "Dissidents," which sounds more like an accusation, concludes with a verdict formulated by Brezhnev: "Our people demand that these activists, if you will, be treated as opponents of socialism, as people who have turned against their own Motherland, and moreover, as agents of imperialism. Naturally, we are taking and will continue to take measures against them as prescribed by law."[180]

Andropov, at that time chairman of the KGB and the number one specialist on dissent, deciphering the general secretary's message, considered dissidents to be people "stirred up by political or ideological errors, religious fanaticism, nationalist deviations, personal grudges and failures, . . . and finally, in a number of cases, by mental instability." Andropov reminded his listeners that "socialist democracy has a class character." Consequently, "all Soviet citizens whose interests coincide with those of society as a whole enjoy the highest democratic liberties. It is an entirely different matter for those whose interests do not so coincide." In this case: "Let no one lecture us about humanism."[181] On the sixtieth anniversary of the October revolution, the chairman of the KGB solemnly proclaimed the law of socialist democracy: those who agree with us are totally free to agree with us.

The early 1970s saw the culmination of the first period of the dissident movement, which took as its primary slogan the defense of civil rights and respect for the law. The courage of the dissidents, who made public facts about repression and violations of the law, impressed the world. Solzhenitsyn and Sakharov gave press conferences to foreign correspondents. An American journalist signed up Vladimir Bukovsky, Aleksandr Ginzburg, Andrei Amalrik, and Petr Yakir for television interviews, and Ginzburg sent tape recording with his comments from his camp. Yakir defined the new situation in the USSR: "Under Stalin there was always an iron curtain and no one knew what was going on here. Now we are trying to publicize every arrest, every dismissal from work, i.e., we are trying to inform people of what is going on in our country." In 1970 Sakharov, Tverdokhlebov, and

Chalidze founded the Human Rights Committee, the first open dissident group. The awarding of the Nobel prize to Solzhenitsyn in October 1970 was perceived as a victory for the dissidents and a challenge to the authorities. The open activities of the dissidents were regarded as a display of weakness by the authorities and a concession to the West, as the price of detente. Struck by their courage, Western public opinion came to their defense. "The force of the West's enraged reaction was unexpected for everyone and for the West itself, which had long not put up such staunch and massive opposition to the land of communism. The reaction was even more unexpected for our rulers, who simply lost their heads."[182]

The arrest of Petr Yakir in June 1972 illustrated that the KGB had devised tactics for those of dissenting opinion. These tactics remained unchanged throughout the 1970s. Every dissident became the object of vigilant scrutiny, surrounded by agents—secret and open. This period of incubation ended when all the dissident's friends, sympathizers, and accomplices had become known. Then one or several arrests were made, and a trial arranged. The commotion created by the trial of a known dissident was concentrated on by the West. Under the cover of this commotion other, lesser-known dissidents were arrested; repression spread in concentric circles, like ripples from a stone thrown into the water. The fear returned.

The trial of Yakir and Krasin, organized in August 1973, was the first post-Stalin political trial in which the accused pleaded guilty and repented. The Soviet organs of repression once again used recantation as a means of struggle. The majority of dissidents, however, refused to plead guilty and used their trials as a platform to express their opinions. *Samizdat* circulated the court speeches of Bukovsky, Amalrik, Orlov, Tverdokhlebov, and others. Conversely, the press and television gave publicity to the "repenting dissidents": Yakir (in 1973), the Ukrainian Ivan Dzyuba (in 1976), the Georgian Z. Gamsakhurdia (in 1978), and the Orthodox priest Dmitry Dudko (in 1980).

In the late 1970s the KGB destroyed the human rights movements, arresting members of the Helsinki Watch Group created in Moscow in 1975 on the initiative of Yuri Orlov. Then it broke up similar groups in the Ukraine, Lithuania, Georgia, and Armenia (1976–1977) and arrested the organizers of free unions (1978–1980), believers, and participants in nationalist movements. An Amnesty International report, *Political Prisoners in the USSR: How They Are Treated and the Conditions of Their Imprisonment*, enumerated the most widespread forms of repression: "Camps, prisons, psychiatric hospitals, in which the prisoners have fewer rights than their comrades in the camps, internal exile, and deportation from the country."[183]

The persecutions to which the dissidents were subjected for their "freedom of thought" was only one aspect of the state's repressive policy. "The goal of communism is the harmonious and fully rounded development of the individual," Soviet philosophers contend. However, "this goal cannot be reached without active regulation and organization by the state."[184] The repressive policy of the USSR is explained as a pedagogical necessity, a struggle against "remnants of the past." The primary defects in the society of "real socialism" were "theft of state property, absenteeism, and the abuse of alcoholic beverages."[185]

Theft and corruption had become so common that a Soviet lawyer was able to conclude that in the 1960s and 1970s the USSR was being transformed into a "Kleptocratic state."[186]Alcoholism reached monstrous proportions. At a plenum of the Supreme Soviet, the results of an investigation conducted in a region of Lithuania were cited. In 1963, an average of 8 liters of vodka were consumed for every inhabitant; in 1973 the figure was 28.5 liters. The average resident of this region (note that Lithuania is one of the most culturally advanced republics of the USSR) spent 330 rubles on vodka and 3 rubles on books.[187]

One of the consequences of alcoholism was a sharp increase in the number of prisoners. In 1974, 600,000 drivers were brought to trial for driving while intoxicated. Each one did a term in the camps.[188]

The government, preparing to fight alcoholism, actually encouraged it, because a significant part of its budget comes from profit on the production and sale of alcoholic beverages and also because intoxication stupefied the population, distracting them from their troubles. Likewise, the government went on a campaign against theft and corruption but at the same time closed its eyes to them, since they served as the grease that allowed the wheels of the socialist economy to turn. In the end, general corruption and rampant intoxication strengthened the government: all citizens were guilty and the government was free to punish or forgive them as it chose. In the former case, the government was just, in the latter, it was good; and always, it was right.

Drinking was called a "serious problem" by Brezhnev in his report to the Twenty-sixth Party Congress.[189] But this was the least of the problems plaguing Soviet society.

Since 1975 the Soviet Union has published no figures concerning infant mortality. And for a reason. The last figures published by the Central Statistical Bureau showed that between 1970 and 1975 infant mortality increased by more than one-third. Using various statistics, Western researchers have established that the official figures left out some 14 percent of all infant mortality cases. According to their calculations, infant mortality in the USSR reached 40 per thousand, compared to 13 per thousand in the United States and Western Europe. Life expectancy in the USSR has also declined since the early 1960s. It is now six years lower than in the other developed countries.[190] No European country has experienced such a decline. As for infant mortality and life expectancy, the situation in the Soviet Union is now being compared to that in the developing countries of Latin America or Asia (Costa Rica, Jamaica, Malaysia, Sri Lanka, and Mexico). This condition can be explained, but only in part, by worsening nutrition, the increase in alcoholism, pollution, the destruction of nature, an increased number of accidents at the work place, automobile accidents, and the consequences of frequent abortions. But it is also known that mortality has increased among the metallurgical workers of Kharkov, among middle-aged women kolkhozniks, and so on. In 1975 almost every age group in the USSR had a higher mortality rate than in 1960. In the group over fifty, it increased almost 20 percent; for those in their forties, more than 40 percent. Since 1956 male life expectancy has declined by four years.[191]

To a large extent this phenomenon is the result of a decrease in the quality of medical service. Researchers have concluded that expenditures for health care have decreased (from 6.6 percent of the budget in 1965 to 5.2 percent in 1978). Funds are spent, not on the improvement of medical service, but on its expansion. Meanwhile, influenza alone kills tens of thousands of infants each year. The USSR has two medical personnel for every one in the United States, but their training is far inferior. Health care professionals are among the lowest-paid categories of workers in the Soviet Union, and the profession of physician is not a prestigious one. The poor training of Soviet medical personnel contributes to a sharp increase in postoperative complications and deaths.

In the Soviet Union medical care is officially free. Here, however, as in other sectors of the economy, corruption flourishes. If you want a good doctor, you pay for it; good care, pay a nurse or companion. The USSR is effectively undergoing a health care crisis. Yet this is but one manifestation of the permanent state of crisis in the economy.

In his memoirs Vladimir Bukovsky records calculations he made concerning the total number of prisoners in the Soviet Union: "According to our most careful calculations, the number of prisoners was never less than 2.5 million: 1 percent of the population, one person out of every hundred."[192] The official figures (divulged illegally in the West) cited 976,090 persons sentenced in 1976. On January 1, 1977, Soviet camps and prisons contained 1,612,378 prisoners. Moreover, 495,711 people were serving terms "building the national economy."[193] Yuri Orlov, sentenced on May 18, 1978, to seven years in the camps and five in exile for helping to found the Helsinki Watch Group, and his friends prepared a report on the number of prisoners in 1979. According to their calculations, in the late 1970s the prison and camp population comprised no less than 3 million. To this should be added the approximately 2 million people sentenced to "lesser terms" (up to three years), whose terms are spent "building the economy."[194]

The state maintains this high prison population for political, educational, and economic reasons. The law against "parasites" is analogous to England's notorious medieval vagrancy laws. Article 209 of the penal code provides for "deprivation of liberty for up to two years or corrective labor for a term of six months to one year" for "systematic vagrant or begging activity." In November 1970 a resolution of the Central Committee "on the improvement of work to maintain order and to intensify the struggle against crime" signaled a renewal of repression; a "parasite" is defined as one who "does not work for a prolonged period (four months, plus one month's warning)." Following the Central Committee's November 1979 decree, article 209 also applies to those who have a home and do not beg but are in good health and did not work.[195] A new army of convict laborers was thus sent off to toil upon the building sites of communism.

The nature of a state can be defined by various criteria. The number of prisoners is one. Even according to the official figures of February 8, 1977, Soviet inmates numbered 1.7 million. Given an overall population of 260 million in the country in 1979, this is undeniable progress compared to the 15 million prisoners out of a population of 180 million in Stalin's time. If we recall that in the United States in 1979 there were 263,000 prisoners and 140,000 juvenile delinquents in municipal prisons or a total of 400,000 prisoners, and that in Russia in 1912 the number of prisoners was 183,000 out of 140 million inhabitants, the results obtained after sixty years of building a new world speak rather eloquently for themselves.

The October revolution solemnly promised to eliminate the "national problem" in the former Russian empire, which had become the first socialist state. In the age of "real socialism" a formula was found that expresses the past, present, and future of this problem. The past, capitalism, had divided and alienated nations, but socialism had "created new and higher forms of human community." As for the present and future, "the development of the Soviet people is the guarantee of the future creation of a human community that is qualitatively new, excompassing all the people of the earth who will have embarked on the path to socialism and communism."[196]

In commemoration of the fortieth anniversary of the Soviet constitution

(formerly the Stalin constitution), the president of the Council of Nationalities of the Supreme Soviet of the USSR recalled, "In previous times,
too, there were many attempts to create vast empires, beginning with Alexander the Great and ending with Hitler's Reich." Assuming, apparently,
that multinational empires has always been the dream of mankind, the
speaker concluded, "Only with the birth of the socialist state . . . has the
age-old dream of mankind found true embodiment."[197]

The creation of the "ideal empire" has deepened national conflicts and
complicated the national question, which has turned into a most convoluted
dilemma involving not only the national problems within the USSR but also
those of the peoples on the periphery of the Soviet empire, as well.

The awakening of national consciousness among the nations of the USSR
has assumed various forms. In the Ukraine there have been calls for "a
struggle for national liberation and for democracy."[198] In Armenia in 1968
a clandestine Unified National party was founded "to create an independent
Armenian state."[199] Independence slogans acquired widespread popularity
in Lithuania. On May 14, 1972, a young worker named Romas Kalenta
immolated himself in the center of Kaunas after announcing that he was
dying for the freedom of Lithuania. His funeral became the occasion for a
demonstration by thousands, which the police dispersed.[200] The seaman
Simon Kudirka, who in 1972 jumped ship from a Soviet vessel in the
United States and was subsequently extradited to the Soviet authorities by
the Americans, concluded his trial speech with the words, "I ask that my
homeland Lithuania be given independence." In Georgia, the Ukraine, and
the Baltic republics there has been mounting resistance to the more vigorous
inculcation of the Russian language and the "Russification" of the educational system.

Rome never forced the peoples it conquered to learn Latin. The language
of the center of the empire was adopted by all who wanted to make a career
in the Roman world. Russian is indispensable to anyone who wants to make
a career in the Soviet world or to assimilate Russian culture, but at the
same time it is imposed on all Soviet subjects, for it is an essential tool of
the ideology. Russian nationalism is a special phenomenon. Vladimir Osipov,
editor of the *samizdat* magazine *Veche*, which describes itself as "the first
organ of a Russian nationalist orientation to appear in the USSR," warned
in 1972 that "the Russian nation could disappear" and declared: "There
is no way out of the moral and cultural impasse in which Russia finds itself
other than reliance on Russian national self-awareness." For Osipov called
the nationalism he advocated in *Veche* "protective," an expression of "the
self-preservation instinct of a vanishing nation."[201] This call to preserve
the Russian nation, which is the dominant nation in the largest empire of

the twentieth century, and the fear that the Russian nation might disappear, is necessitated by the danger posed by Soviet ideology, which treats Russian national values with the same ruthlessness it does the national values of other peoples.

The Soviet state uses diverse methods in the struggle against nationalist movements, which not only refuse to die out but also display as irrepressible a tendency to grow. The first tried and true method of the authorities is repression: arrests, the camps, and psychiatric hospitals. The stronger the national movement, the more severe the repression: nationalists, particularly in the Ukraine, Lithuania, and Romania, are subjected to especially harsh persecution. On January 30, 1979, the Soviet news agency TASS reported that three Armenian nationalists, Stepan Zatikyan, Akop Stepanyan, and Zaven Bagdassaryan, had been shot. Arrested in November 1977 and accused of exploding a bomb in a Moscow subway station on January 8, 1977, they were sentenced to death in a closed session in spite of the fact that many witnesses had corroborated their alibis. Their execution, the first resulting from a political trial since the death of Stalin, was an unambiguous warning to all nationalists.

In the arsenal of combat techniques against nationalism, the idea of "Soviet patriotism" is of utmost significance because it represents a further elaboration of the old notion of national bolshevism. In the Soviet Union in the late 1960s there were articles in Soviet journals which actually advocated the ideas of national bolshevism.[202] But they were served up with a new sauce: "neo-Slavophilism." The notion of the special mission of Russia which was brought into being through the socialist revolution was promoted and supported. This "authorized" nationalism swept through literature, the fine arts, and other cultural areas. In cases where it assumed the hysterical forms of Black Hundred-style Russian chauvinism, the guardians of Soviet ideology applied the brakes, warning: "The realm of relations between nationalities... in a multinational state like ours is one of the most complicated areas of social life." An overemphasized Russian nationalism, if too strong, could provoke a reaction in the form of "local nationalisms."[203]

The Soviet Communist party uses Russian nationalism to enlarge the sphere of activity of Soviet ideology. The recantation of the priest Dmitry Dudko was composed in the spirit of "Soviet patriotism":

> I realize that I have yielded to the voices of the propagandists who strive to undermine our way of life.... My activities have acquired an even more anti-Soviet character because they were initially stimulated, and lately also directed from abroad.... I regret that my actions have brought harm to my country, to my people, as well as to the Orthodox church.[204]

The clergyman thus confesses that he has caused damage—first to the country, then to the people, and only then does he acknowledge damage to the church.

Those who express nationalist views exceeding the bounds permitted by Soviet ideology are subjected to repression. Vladimir Osipov himself, who sincerely believed in Russian nationalism, was able to publish nine issues of *Veche* between January 1971 and March 1974. He was then arrested and sentenced to seven years in camp and five years of internal exile. Nor do authorities encourage the open adherents of nazism, who have called for anti-Semitic pogroms and reproached the party for excessive lenience. Soviet ideology began to absorb Russian nationalist ideas as early as the 1920s, adapting them to its own needs. But Soviet ideology could not become nationalistic, the way nazism did, for then it would lose its essence and cease to be open to multiple interpretations. Not having principles— except the absence of principle—it cannot really adopt the principle of nationalism.

Punishment was meted out when signs of nationalism appeared in the Communist parties of the non-Russian republics. As a rule this was the nationalism of local satraps who wished to grab a larger chunk of the power for themselves, to become a little more independent of the central government. In 1972, for example, there occurred the fall of Petr Shelest, first secretary of the Ukranian Central Committee. One of the initiators of the intervention in Czechoslovakia and an advocate of the harshest of measures and reprisals against all displays of dissent in the Ukraine, the USSR, or the Warsaw Pact countries, Shelest showed himself to be excessively independent in the eyes of the rest of the Politburo—and his career ended.

The system by which the non-Russian republics are governed from Moscow is based on certain administrative guarantees. The second party secretary of each republics's central committee is a Russian. As a rule, the head of the KGB in each republic and the commander of the military district are also Russian. But the most reliable guarantee of the republic's loyalty to Moscow is the fact that the first secretary of the republic's central committee and all the other party and government leaders devotedly serve the cause of Soviet power. With few exceptions—and such exceptions are quickly discovered and eliminated—the *nomenklatura* in the national republics is firmly committed to Moscow, for that is the source of their power. Russians who live in Georgia, Latvia, Uzbekistan, and other republics do not perceive themselves as representatives of a colonizing master race, as Englishmen did in India. Likewise, in Moscow, in the Politburo, some key positions were held by Ukrainians in the late 1970s. Those Russians who settle in the national republics do not bring Russian culture with them; they bring Soviet culture. And the Ukrainians in the Politburo pursue not Ukrainian but Soviet policies.

In Isaac Babel's *Tales from Odessa* the cavalryman Leva Krik gave the following reply to a rabbi who had reproached him, saying that a Jew should not ride horseback: "A Jew on a horse ceases to be a Jew." By the same token, a Ukrainian, Georgian, Armenian, or Kazakh who becomes a Central Committee secretary loses his nationality and becomes a component of the party's power. Every blow against that power is a blow against him personally. This same system supports the CPSU in its relations with the Communist parties of the "fraternal socialist countries."

In the struggle against nationalism a very important part is played by official anti-Semitism. The first openly anti-Semitic book officially published in the Soviet Union was *Iudaizm bez Prikras* (*Judaism Without Embellishment*), by T. Kichko, published by the Ukrainian Academy of Sciences in 1964. This booklet, with its vulgar tone and crude illustrations lifted from the Nazi periodical *Der Stürmer* (*The Stormtrooper*), aroused protest and dismay in the West. Khrushchev, shortly before his fall from power, felt obliged to disavow the booklet and remove it from circulation for the time being. When it was reprinted in the 1970s, it seemed even mild in comparison with the most recent anti-Semitic literature. The Six Day War in 1967 opened a new chapter in the history of Soviet anti-Semitism. After that, the authorities ceased to be ashamed of anti-Semitism, and it acquired full rights. Zionism became the latest approved and authorized object of hatred, just as Nepmen, wreckers, and kulaks had once been. In books and periodicals, published in millions of copies, and in movies and television broadcasts, Zionism was depicted as a most serious threat to the Soviet state. A Permanent Commission was established under the Social Sciences Section of the USSR Academy of Sciences "to coordinate research dedicated to the exposure and criticism of the history, ideology, and practical activity of Zionism."

The model and primary inspiration for anti-Semitic publications was a book by Yuri Ivanov, an official of the party's Central Committee, entitled *Danger, Zionism!* It was published in the late 1970s in an edition of 400,000 copies. Anti-Semitic novels also appeared by such authors as Shevtsov, Pikul, and Kolesnikov. The "struggle against Zionism" is an outstanding example of the omnipotence of Soviet ideology. With the aid of quotations from Marx and Lenin anti-Zionism is presented as a form of class struggle. Soviet ideologists have added a new chapter to Lenin's theory of imperialism as the last stage of capitalism: Zionism as the last stage of imperialism.

Within the USSR anti-Zionism is used to mobilize the country's peoples against a common enemy: the Jews. One of the greatest victories of Soviet ideology during the 1970s was the United Nations resolution pronouncing Zionism to be a form of racism. In the repertoire of Soviet propaganda, "racism" used to be one of the rare terms that had but a single meaning. Following the resolution, its meaning became manifold, like the terms "formal democracy," "real freedom," "bourgeois democracy," "social democracy," "pseudo-humanism," and "proletarian humanism." Soviet ideologues managed to complete Hitler's work: anti-Zionism (equated with anti-Semitism) ceased to be the property of reactionaries and fascists. It became a Marxist, i.e., scientifically justified form of the national liberation struggle. "Anti-Zionism" has become the proletarian internationalism of the epoch of "real socialism."

In the last quarter of the twentieth century, the national question in the USSR has acquired particular importance in connection with the demographic changes occurring in the country. The 1970 census bore testimony to a regressive trend in Soviet population statistics. Between the census of 1959 and that of 1970 the growth of the population was approximately equal to the growth between 1925 and 1939. But the 1930s were a time of upheaval—collectivization, famine, and terror—while the 1960s were a period of peace and of a relative rise in the standard of living. Based on the results of the 1959 census, demographers expected a population of 250 million in 1970: there turned out to be 10 million fewer than that.

The most unexpected aspect of the 1959 census were the figures showing the dropping birthrate of the Russian population. Conversely, the republics of Central Asia experienced a demographic explosion among the peoples traditionally classified as Muslim, although the exact number of those practicing Islam remains far from clear. Islam in the USSR is for the most part a cultural tradition, rather than a religion per se. In 1970, the Russian Republic (the RSFSR) accounted for 53.7 percent of the population of the USSR; Central Asia, 13.7 percent; and the Caucasus, 5.1 percent. The figures for 1980 were 52 percent, 15.9 percent, and 5.5 percent, respectively. The forecasts for the year 2000 are 47.2 percent, 23 percent, and 6.6 percent.[205] In absolute figures this means that by the beginning of the twenty-first century the Soviet Union will have 310–320 million inhabitants, nearly 100 million of whom will be indigenous to Central Asia and the Caucasus.[206] It is especially significant that the age structure of the population will shift to the advantage of the so-called Muslim population. If this prediction proves accurate, by the end of the century the population of the RSFSR will consist of 21.8 percent children under fifteen years and 21.8 percent people over sixty. In Uzbekistan, the respective proportions will be 40 percent and 8 percent; in Tadzhikistan, 45.6 percent and 7.4 percent; in Turkmenistan, 39.5 percent and 7.9 percent.[207]

The rapid growth of the indigenous populations of Central Asia during the 1970s refutes all the demographers' predictions. The forecast was for 10 percent growth between 1971 and 1980; in fact, the increase was 27 percent. Instead of the expected 6 percent increase, the population of Kazakhstan grew 13 percent, and in Azerbaijan the disparity between the projected and actual figures was even more spectacular: instead of the 5.5 percent anticipated by 1980, the population had grown by 18 percent already in 1979.[208] (In the period between the 1970 and 1979 censuses, the Uzbek and Tadzhik populations increased 36 percent, the Turkmen 33 percent, the Kirghiz 31 percent, the Kazakh 24 percent, and the Azerbaijani 25 percent.[209]) Those Soviet peoples designated as Muslim inhabiting regions other than Central Asia and Azerbaijan have shown a significantly smaller growth: 6.5 percent for the Volga Tatar population, for example.[210]

The demographic explosion in Central Asia is partly explained by the traditional inertia of the indigenous population, who migrate little, and by the traditional life of the family clan particularly; whether an increase in the population of Central Asia will lead to a change in the political balance in the federal structure of the USSR, and to a change in the systematic policy of Russification, is a rather controversial question. It depends, in part, on how long the Muslim community can continue to prevent intrusion into its traditional way of life by passive and sometimes purely instinctive resistance. For example, the census of 1979 showed that the young generation in the republics of Central Asia has a better and better command of the Russian language, which, for them, is an indispensable condition for a future career.[211]

Demography confronts the Soviet state with two difficult problems. The first is that of manpower; this dilemma was officially acknowledged as such at the Twenty-sixth Party Congress.[212] The projections were that the Soviet population would grow from 243 million (the 1970 census) to 267 million in 1980. In 1979 it was barely above 262 million.[213] The drop in the birthrate especially affected the Russian and Ukrainian populations. In 1979 the Russians comprised 52.4 percent of the entire Soviet population.[214] The Russians as a proportion of the total Soviet populations had decreased by 1 percent in this brief ten-year period. All the Soviet republics, with the exception of those in Central Asia, suffered a decline in the growth of the labor force. The principal industrial regions are located in the western part of the Soviet Union and in Siberia. This problem is exceptionally complex. Actually, workers from Central Asia are continually imported to the European part of the country. They constitute the majority of the working class in the new industrial centers of Uzbekistan. Whether Central Asia can be used as a labor reserve and if so, how, remain to be seen.

The other problem to which the drop in the birthrate among the Slavic peoples contributes is that of the national composition of the armed forces, especially of the officer corps.

At the Twenty-fifth Congress of the CPSU (1976) Brezhnev defined Soviet society as "a society where a scientific and materialistic concept of the world dominates." Nevertheless, Soviet ideologues recognize the persistence of "religious survivals under socialism." Sociological research conducted by the Pskovsky party committee showed that "approximately 12–13 percent of the city's residents consider themselves believers."[215] We may assume that this is the official figure for the percentage of Russian orthodox believers in the Soviet population as a whole.

Pilot and Cosmonaut O. Makarov, who has been in space and thus is considered a specialist on philosophical problems, wrote: "The word 'faith' is often associated with 'religious faith.' But I am profoundly convinced that we cannot live without faith. The only problem is: What should we believe in?" And he explains: "Like millions of other Soviet citizens, I have faith in science, which is all penetrating and knowing. I believe in the moral strength of human reason."[216] Pskov's believers were seeking a "universal source of moral education" in religion rather than science.[217]

Six decades of atheistic propaganda have been unable to eradicate the human need for faith in God, for religion. On the contrary, there is some indication of a growing interest in religion. This can be judged above all by the intensifying waves of repression crashing down on believers. Numerous cases of such repression have been documented by the Christian Committee for the Defense of Believers' Rights in the USSR, founded in Moscow in 1976, by the *Chronicle of the Catholic Church of Lithuania*, which began publication in 1972, as well as by the *samizdat* periodical *Jews in the USSR* and by other *samizdat* publications. Many churches have been closed; in two years, from 1959 to 1961, the number of active Orthodox churches went from 20,000 to 7,000.[218] Raising children in a religious manner remains strictly forbidden and is punished severely. The government jealously guards its monopoly on matters of the upbringing of Soviet man. A specialist on atheist propaganda explained that "two diametrically opposed influences" result in "an inner struggle that is harmful to a child's mental health ... causing nervous exhaustion and may possibly lead to serious illnesses."[219]

Persecuting believers is only one method of combatting religion. A second is control over the church, which is exercised by the Council for Church Affairs, whose task is to eliminate religion little by little and to make use of it while it still exists, in the interests of the state. A secret report to the council, recently published in Paris, gives an idea of its objectives and forms of control over the Orthodox church. There is no reason to think that the council deals with other religious bodies, those of the Catholics or Muslims, any differently.

The theoretical basis for the council's functioning, it seems from the report, is the conviction that "religion has always adhered and will always adhere to positions alien to Marxism," but that "as a result of constant political work with the high clergy, they ... are increasingly taking a patriotic stand." Control over the church takes the form of control over the clergy, from the patriarch to the humblest lay brother. Admission to the three seminaries (in Moscow, Leningrad, and Odessa) and the two church academies (in Moscow and Leningrad) is strictly controlled. Each candidate is selected by the "local authorities," that is, the local committees of the KGB, guided by the principle that there should be as few clergymen as possible, and each of those that does exist should not only demonstrate "loyalty and patriotism toward socialist society ... but also be truly conscious of the fact that our state is not interested in raising the role of religion and the church in society and, understanding this, should not be especially active in spreading Orthodoxy among the population."[220] As a result of a steady reduction in the number of clergymen, on January 1, 1975, there were 7,062 operating churches and 5,954 clergymen.[221] A good number of priests and bishops were evaluated positively in the report: they did not proselytize. As an example of a "good pastor" they cite Bishop Jonas: "He does not demonstrate particular zeal in Mass. ... He preaches regularly, but his services are very brief, not very expressive, and without enthusiasm. Almost every sermon ends with an appeal to the believers to live in peace, to struggle for peace in the world, to work well and produce.[222] The work of Bishop Viktorin is also evaluated favorably, because he "educates the flock entrusted to him in the spirit of love for our beloved homeland."[223]

The "good pastors" are trained in church institutions, for example, at the Odessa Seminary, where the future priests hear lectures on the following subjects: "The Success of the CPSU and the Soviet government in the struggle to Realize the Program of Peace, Elaborated at the Twenty-fifth Party Congress," "V. I. Lenin and the Cultural Revolution," "Lenin's Teachings on Communist Morality and the Fundamental Principles of Moral Education," "Educating the New Man: The Most Important Task in the Construction of Communism," and the like.

The report proudly emphasized the successes achieved by the Council on Church Affairs in its endeavor to transform the Russian Orthodox Church into an instrument to educate Soviet citizens in the spirit of "Soviet patriotism" and love for the socialist homeland.

Decades of control and efforts to demoralize the Orthodox church led Father Dmitry Dudko, not long before his arrest and "recantation," to refer to the church hierarchy as "protégés of the godless." He asked, "But what do they believe in?" He could not answer. Dudko explained that the KGB manipulates the church, playing on "Russianness: You are Russian, we are Russian, we should be together."[224] In *The Gulag Archipelago.* Solzhenitsyn recalls that in 1922, at the trial of the SRs, the defendants were urged to confess with the argument, "After all, you and we are revolutionaries!" In 1924 Savinkov was given the same argument at his trial: "After all, we are all Russians." In 1937, the same bewitching melody was played: "After all, you and we are Communists!"[225]

This "tamed" religion allows Soviet ideology to enlarge its vocabulary and its sphere of activity. The album *The Madonna of the Don* was published with a preface explaining that "the deeply emotional image of the Don Madonna is the embodiment of the progressive ideas of the Russian people formed in the course of their struggle for independence."[226]

On the sixtieth anniversary of the October revolution, the poet Smirnov sang the glories of the "remarkable Soviet people" and concluded his poem with these words: "May god plus Soviet Power preserve them."[227] The Soviet poet wrote "god" with a small letter and "Soviet Power" in capitals. His formula is a paraphrase of Lenin's famous statement: Communism is Soviet power plus electrification. For Smirnov, "god" plays the role of electricity in this new stage, in which Soviet power is stronger than ever before.

In April 1933 Hitler declared to the Reichstag. "You can be Christian or German, but you can't be both at the same time." The Soviet citizen could be a believer only if his faith did not hinder him from being, above all, a Soviet patriot.

Soviet power has encountered the greatest difficulties in Lithuania, where the majority of the population is Catholic. To the Lithuanians, religion and national identity are inseparable. The number of Catholic churches has continually diminished in Lithuania, as is true of all other churches in the USSR. In 1974, there were 629 churches and 554 priests in Lithuania.[228] But if it is considered that the population of the Republic was 2.8 million in 1979, then, comparatively, Catholic churches are far more numerous than Orthodox in Lithuania. The Lithuanian Catholic Council of Bishops "demonstrates a tendency to submit to the pressure of the authorities, but it is not a blind instrument of the Communist leaders."[229] The example of the Catholic church in neighboring Poland and the selection of the Polish

Cardinal Wojtyla to become Pope John Paul II, strengthened the position of the Lithuanian Catholics.

The second largest religion in the Soviet Union, in order of importance, is Islam. With its Muslim population of 50 million, the USSR is the fifth largest Muslim state after India, Bangladesh, Pakistan, and Indonesia. The Soviet government's relations with Islam are similar to its relations with all other churches. The government seeks to eliminate Islam but in the meantime uses it for its own interests.

In 1959, before Khrushchev's antireligious campaign, there were some 1,200 mosques. By 1977 the number had diminished to 300.[230] The two Islamic universities (in Bukhara and Tashkent) turn out about fifty clerics a year. Soviet policy toward Islam, adopted in the 1930s, envisaged a first phase (*sblizhenie*), in which the Muslim peoples would be brought closer to the other Soviet nationalities, and a second stage (*sliyanie*), in which they would be assimilated biologically, culturally, and linguistically with their "big brothers," the Russians. The vitality of Islam outside the Soviet Union in the 1960s and 1970s needs no commentary. The distractiveness of Islam as a religion enables the clergy to affirm the unity of all Muslims, whether they are believers or not. The Muslim clergy found new ways of observing rites that did not lead to conflicts with the authorities but permitted the Muslims to feel their ties with the rest of the Islamic world.

The most important element of Islamic ideology in the USSR is based on the thesis of "peaceful coexistence" between Islam and communism. At the Congress of Soviet Muslims in Tashkent in 1970 it was said: "Soviet leaders believe neither in Allah nor his Prophet. . . . Nevertheless, they carry out the laws dictated by God and explained by his Prophet." Or: "I admire the genius of the Prophet, who proclaimed the social laws of socialism. I am happy that a large number of the socialist principles are realizations of Muhammad's commandments!!"[231] The Muslim clergy actively promote Soviet foreign policy. Alexandre Bennigsen, a leading specialist on Soviet Islam, described Mufti Zia ud-Din Babakhan, head of the clergy of Central Asia and Kazakhstan, as one of "the most efficient representatives of the Soviet establishment in the non-Soviet Muslim world." The mufti travels widely in the Islamic countries, "testifying by his presence that Islam in the Soviet Union prospers and is free."[232]

The uniqueness of Soviet Islam is that side by side with the "official" religion, controlled by the Council on Religious Affairs, there exists a "parallel" Islam, secret Sufi brotherhoods called the Tarikat. They are well organized, dynamic, and hostile to the Soviet regime. Thanks to them, Islam has been able to survive as a religion and a "way of life."

The combination of these two forms of religious life allows "social" Islam to make compromises, to perform its propaganda functions for the Soviet government, and to obtain certain concessions in return. The Muslim clergy orient their policy toward "eternity"; the Soviet government's policy is aimed at immediate gain. In the 1960s and 1970s there were no dissidents in the Muslim republics. It was reported in the Western press that the first wave of Soviet troops entering Afghanistan was composed of units from the Central Asian military district containing large numbers of native Central Asians. After the invasion of Afghanistan Soviet Muslim representatives were sent to other Islamic states to seek support for Soviet actions. At the Twenty-sixth Congress of the CPSU in February 1981, Brezhnev spoke openly of Soviet willingness to support those Islamic movements that contributed to the expansion of "the national liberation struggle," but he immediately warned that Islam might just as easily bear the banner of counterrevolution.[233]

The Soviet leaders themselves decide when Islamic movements are to be considered progressive and when they are reactionary. In this regard, Soviet leaders have already much experience.

The symbiosis of Islam and Marxism in the Soviet Union leaves for the future to decide which will come first: the Islamization of Marxism or the Marxization of Islam.

"A third method of combatting religion, which supplements persecution and 'adaptation'—is the creation of new rites." Convinced that people are attracted not so much by faith as by religious rituals and celebrations, the spokesmen for "scientific atheism" have decided to try to influence not only reason but emotions as well. In 1979, the second all-union seminar conference on socialist ceremonies (the first took place in 1964) assumed the task of "extinguishing the illusory sun in the minds of believers," as Marx called religion, and turning on the "Soviet sun" in their minds instead.[234] The conference summed up the "theory of Soviet rites" and the effects on Soviet citizens of monuments (chiefly—Lenin's Mausoleum), wedding palaces, Red Saturdays, and the like. The work of existing commissions on rites and holidays in other republics, akin to the Vatican's Congregation of Rites, was also reviewed at the conference.

The most important ceremony is "political education." In 1978 more than 22 million people (nearly 12 percent of the population, including infants) "were taking courses within the system of party education." Noting this, Suslov, the country's chief ideologist, recommended organizing special "unified political days" (*edinie politdni*) once a month or once a week. On such days the entire population of a city or region, including those groups of the population who do not receive sufficient attention,[235] can get a "concentrated dose of ideology" by carrying out the ritual.

• • •

Soviet culture in the era of "mature," or "real," socialism is both a product of the system and the most important means of its formation. As in all other areas of Soviet life, the upheavals of the Stalin era and the zigzags of the Khrushchev era had come to an end. Socialist culture was established, and its forms have become permanent and its monstrous weight rests heavily on society, preserving it in the state achieved thus far. From the past it takes whatever it needs. Above all, the merits of Zhdanov are highly valued. "His speeches on the problems of science, literature, and the arts," wrote *Pravda*, "have made a significant contribution to the ideological education of the Soviet people and to the development of their spiritual culture."[236] The idea that there was a cultural renaissance after Stalin's death and the Twentieth Congress was rejected: "The start of the renewal should be dated earlier than the usual date of 1956." As this historian of Soviet literature sees it, the "renewal" began during Stalin's lifetime. Hence the Brezhnev era began—under Stalin.[237]

The results are plain to see. Soviet ideology sociologists studied high school graduates in both rural and urban areas and concluded, "A comparison between graduates of the 1950s and 1970s with high school graduates of the 1920s has shown that, on the whole, students today have reached a level of political and social maturity which in the 1920s was characteristic only of the finest representatives of the young workers and peasants."[238]

Georgy Markov, head of the Soviet Writers' Union, defined the dualities required of the creators of Soviet culture today: "correct ideological orientation, enthusiasm for the party, maturity in socialist thought, the penetrating insights of the writer," and, at the very end, "great professional mastery."[239] It is perfectly clear that not one of the great Russian writers or artists, who possessed only "professional mastery," would have passed the test for a master of socialist culture.

"Correct ideological orientation," named first among the most important criteria, constitutes the foundation of Soviet culture and makes it a unique phenomenon in history. One of the guardians of the ideological purity of Soviet writers, while acknowledging that, as is well known, "truth is the highest artistic criterion in literature," nevertheless rejected the traditional bourgeois conception of the truth: "The whole problem is in knowing what the truth must serve."[240] Marietta Shaginyan, a writer from the old guard, explained the superiority of the new society using a historical example and its culture: "Two thousand years ago, a certain Roman dignitary named

Pilate asked a popular leader, a simple fisherman, preacher, 'What is truth?' The man could not answer, he was silent. . . . In our time, a new man had come who organized society in a new way. . . . He has answered the question, What is truth? The truth is specific."[241]

"The truth is specific." Consequently, only the party knows the truth, and the "correct ideological orientation" is therefore to follow the party.

Censorship in socialist society begins with self-censorship. It operates in the heads of writers, historians, and philosophers. "The truth is specific." Therefore, one must know what can be written without fear and what things are better left unsaid. In selecting a research topic or a novel theme, it is essential not only to clarify a given theme's chances of "passing" at a specific historical moment but also to anticipate all possible objections by the ideological authorities. That is where censorship begins. The rest of the work is completed by the "competent" authorities, the censors, whose duty is to supervise the press and protect readers and authors alike from deviations from the truths of real socialism. Any who deviate from self-censorship and official censorship face serious difficulties.

We have only rare and fragmentary bits of information on how the censorship works in practice. Several works by Soviet writers have been published in the West in their complete form and can be compared with their censored editions. A much fuller picture of the principles and methods used by the agency that allows the "necessary" truth to pass and withholds the "unnecessary" truth can be found in *The Black Book of Censorship in the PPR*,[242] which consists of documents from the Polish censorial offices—a "book of prohibitions and recommendations," instructional materials, and annotations and comments by censors. It makes clear the technique by which human consciousness is deliberately worked upon. There is every reason to assume that the Soviet censorship served, and still serves, as the model for the Polish censorship.

The idea behind censorship is not to distinguish between correct and incorrect information. The censor intervenes to prohibit the publication or broadcast of texts not because they are false but because some truths are "harmful," while others are "useful." The censorship attempts to block any access for the real world to information. Books, newspapers, magazines, radio, and television should present the fictitious world of socialism.

For example, an informational note of the Polish censorship on materials censored December 1–15, 1974, contains the reminder that it is forbidden to "publish information on food supplies to the population (including meat) and on the standard of living."[243] Meat will not appear as a result of not writing about its absence, yet the implication is that the absence of information about the absence of meat is supposed to create the illusion that the meat exists.

The first demand of literature, awakening after the death of Stalin, was for sincerity.[244] The illusion that it was possible to have a literature based "not on a sermon, but on confession" continued even after *Doctor Zhivago* was denied publication. The publication of Solzhenitsyn's stories and novellas gave birth to hopes for a "thaw," but the trial of Sinyavsky and Daniel dealt a fresh blow. Fifteen years later, a group of writers who had not lost hope of publishing uncensored literature, tried unsuccessfully to publish in Moscow the literary anthology *Metropol*, "an attempt at a cultural compromise, an attempt to improve the climate, to infuse some new blood into an increasingly decrepit body."[245]

The history of Soviet literature in the Brezhnev era—and literature can serve here as the model for Soviet culture in general—was marked by a constantly recurring phenomenon. A talented writer would appear, his first works would be published, but as soon as he began to present a true picture of reality his work would no longer be printed. Then he would begin either to write for "his desk drawer" in the hope of being published later or outside the USSR, or he would censor himself and becomes a genuine Soviet writer. The first path was chosen by such writers as Vladimir Maksimov, V. Voinovich, Georgy Vladimov, Yuri Dombrovsky, and Andrei Sinyavsky. Solzhenitsyn, too, tried at first to publish his novels in Moscow. The second path was chosen, for example, by Sergei Zalygin, author of the novel *On the Irtysh*, the best book about collectivization written in the post-Stalin era.

Two literatures and two cultures came into existence—one officially authorized, the other not. In 1974 it suddenly became possible to measure the relative merits of these two bodies of literature. In connection with the paper shortage the book-selling network announced that it would sell some real works of literature—fairy tales by Hans Christian Andersen and Lev Tolstoy and Alexandre Dumas's *Queen Margot*—in exchange for twenty kilos of "junk literature" (*makulatura*), in order to recycle the paper. So much "junk literature" turned up (officially published works that people didn't really want) that the offer had to be withdrawn. There wasn't enough "real" literature to trade for the "junk."

Since the early 1970s, Soviet culture has undergone a general purge. Writers who lost all hope of being published felt obliged to emigrate, along with artists who could not exhibit their work and musicians who did not have the right to play the music they wished. Emigration was a different kind of purge. Stalin used to kill the artists, writers, and musicians who had the misfortune to displease him, so that the survivors would understand that "truth is specific." For an artist, exile is a heavy blow. For the culture, the loss of its most talented representatives is a death sentence. Thirty-five years after the end of the war, Germany still feels the loss of leading figures in German culture as a result of Hitler's twelve-year rule. Defending the authorized culture against its rival, KGB agents and the police used bulldozers to destroy an outdoor exhibit in Moscow on September 3, 1974. Most of the organizers and participants in that exhibit have since been forced to emigrate.[246]

A key component of Soviet culture is the obligatory ten-year public school education, whose principal task is "to instill a scientific and materialist world view and Communist convictions in its students."[247] Another is the publication of millions of books, among which first place is occupied by the works of Lenin, of which there were 15 million copies in print in 1980,[248] and the "remarkable works of Leonid Brezhnev," of which there were 17 million copies in print by early 1980, "but the number continues to grow; these books are printed virtually non-stop."[249]

The number of clubs, theaters, and schools may serve to define the level of culture. But it was defined just as well in a speech by Valentin Kataev, a prominent writer who has authorized numerous books and who has been active in literature for some sixty years. Thanking the author of the new constitution on behalf of the intelligentsia, Kataev declared:

> We have all been accorded the greatest honor and confidence, and I would like to thank with all my heart the Soviet people, the Communist party, its Central Committee, and the chairman of the Constitution Commission, our dear comrade and friend, Leonid Ilyich Brezhnev. He has accomplished a truly titanic job in the creation of the new Soviet constitution. History will never forget his feat.[250]

Arkady Belinkov defined art as a "dynamometer of the vileness of a tyrannical regime."[251] In the Brezhnev era, culture sank to a level significantly lower than that reached in the preceding period. The death of Aleksandr Galich, the King of the Bards, in 1978 (in exile) and of Vladimir Vysotsky in 1980 in Moscow were a kind of symbol of the silence that would ensue: the "unauthorized voices" that sang about real life were stilled.

The October revolution was the cause of the first mass Russian emigration of the twentieth century. The second wave occurred as a result of the Soviet–German war. A third wave rose in the early 1970s. The origin of this emigration differentiates it from its predecessors.

The crack that opened up during the NEP was sealed tight in the last half of the 1920s; thereafter the Soviet Union was totally isolated from the world. Khrushchev, reflecting in retirement on the nature of the state he had ruled for ten years, marveled: "It is incredible, after fifty years, to keep a paradise under lock and key."[252] The former general secretary's reasoning was logical: "Our social organization is undoubtedly the most progressive in the world . . . in this phase of human development. . . . Our people live and build socialism because of their convictions, not because they are forced to. . . . We must therefore make it possible for them to leave."[253]

Khrushchev began to think logically only after he was removed from power. The turning point in the official attitude toward the emigration path was the trial of a group of Jews in 1970 who were arrested at the Leningrad airport and accused of trying to hijack an airplane in order to leave the Soviet Union. The unusually severe sentences (two death sentences, nine long sentences in the camps) aroused the indignation of world public opinion, which was already high, as it occurred at the very moment that Spanish terrorists were sentenced to death in Burgos. In December 1970 even the Communist parties of the West were compelled to protest the death sentences in the socialist USSR as well as in Franco's Spain.

The harsh sentences did not inspire fear, as the authorities had anticipated, but rather an upsurge in the movement of Soviet Jews seeking the right to emigrate to Israel. The Soviet government decided to permit emigration. Like every decision of this type, however, the authorization was ambiguous: "It is not the Soviet citizen's right to leave and return to his homeland: it is a gift from the state, which first grants the right, then revokes it, only to grant it again later."

Those applying to emigrate became pariahs; they were fired from their jobs, defamed in the press, attacked and beaten in the streets, and sometimes forced to wait for their exit visas for years or to pay "ransom" in the form of an exorbitant fee.[254] But emigration increased steadily. In 1970 there were 1,000 emigrants; in 1973, 34,783. The number fell to 13,222 in 1975,[255] and rose again to 43,000 in 1979.[256] The Volga Germans also rushed toward the open door: from 1970 to 1976, 30,000 of them left for West Germany or other countries in the West.[257]

Permission to emigrate was a very important concession won from the authorities by the pressure of a mass movement of Soviet Jews and dissidents and supported by world public opinion. However, the Soviet government wished to turn this defeat into victory.

By the beginning of the 1970s the world already had some experience with "socialist emigration." Any country where a Communist party came to power immediately put its "paradise" under lock and key. Opportunities for emigration, however, varied from country to country in the socialist bloc. In the years 1946–48, Poland and Czechoslovakia allowed the exit of Jews to the new state of Israel, for at that time the Soviet Union thought of making Israel its outpost in the Middle East. In 1956 the Jews were again allowed to leave Poland during a wave of liberalization generated by the "Polish October." The events in Hungary in 1956 forced hundreds of thousands of Hungarians to flee. Many Czechs and Slovaks did the same after the occupation of their country in 1968. The most numerous was the emigration from East Germany, for up until the construction of the Berlin Wall in 1961 emigration could have hardly been easier—it sufficed just to cross the street and be in a free country with the same language. In 1968, for the first time an exodus was deliberately organized in Poland: Jews were forced to leave the country. Gomulka's government wanted to find a scapegoat for the country's difficulties. Moreover, the Jews had played an important role in the prewar Communist party; they occupied very high posts after the war. When exile opened up these posts, apartments, and so on, the Soviet government learned from all these experiences.

There was a further consideration. In allowing Jews to emigrate, the government could also name a concrete enemy which would come to embody everything hostile to the USSR, its people, and socialism. Emigration singled the Jews out from other peoples of the USSR and gave them a right that was possessed by no one else; it turned them into potential "traitors," a "fifth column." That is how Gomulka characterized them in 1968.

Emigration, as in the time of Lenin, made it possible to purge the country of its malcontents by forcibly expelling them or compelling them to leave "voluntarily." In February 1974 Aleksandr Solzhenitsyn was arrested, placed on an airplane and flown to Germany. This was the first case of deportation abroad since that of Trotsky in 1929. Solzhenitsyn's exile occurred within the framework of "Jewish emigration," and although Europe greeted the exile as no other since Garibaldi, it was not difficult to spread a rumor through official channels in the Soviet Union that Solzhenitsyn was a Jew.

The traditional distrust of Russians toward the West and the hostility toward emigrés that was carefully cultivated by the state, which portrayed them as mortal enemies—all this was reinforced by the government's anti-Semitism. Jews were equated with dissidents, dissidents with Jews, and both were said to be spies for foreign intelligence services. A *White Book* published in Moscow in late 1978, dedicated to the dissidents and emigrés and intended for propagandists, KGB agents, and the police, placed an official equals sign between all these "enemies of the USSR." This *White Book* was the work of the Association of Soviet Jurists and was supplied with a foreword by L. Smirnov, chairman of the Supreme Court of the USSR.

Allowing people to emigrate served certain practical purposes as well.

In 1977 Bukovsky was sent to the West in exchange for Luis Corvalan, head of the Communist Party of Chile. In 1979 five Soviet dissidents were freed from camps and prisons and deported to the West in exchange for two Soviet spies seized in the United States. The GDR converted the trade in dissidents into an important source of revenue: they were sold to West Germany for hard currency or goods in short supply. Thus far the Soviet Union has used dissidents as bartering chips only sporadically. There is also the very real possibility that the KGB might use emigration as a vivarium for its agents.

The "third emigration" is composed primarily of Jews, but it also includes members of other Soviet nationalities. The common feature of the "third wave" is that it consists of people educated and raised on the Soviet regime: they breathed Soviet air from birth. In comparing the third wave to the first, a difference can be discovered in their attitudes toward the world, reality, their homeland, and each other. Emigrés recreate the milieu they leave behind. It is typical, for example, that the Russian emigrés of the early 1920s immediately reconstituted the rainbow of political parties that had existed in Russia before the revolution, while the third emigration has not created any political organizations. The only political organization functioning in emigration is the NTS, established in the 1930s.

But the absence of political organizations does not signify an absence of political discussion. This goes on among the representatives of the three views that were born with the dissident movement.

Aleksandr Solzhenitsyn bases his hopes on a moral and religious revival among the Russian people. He criticizes the democratic system, believing that it is powerless before totalitarianism, unjust, and founded on chance, because it has replaced general consensus with the law of the mathematical majority. He also considers it hollow, because it lacks any transcendent principle. Solzhenitsyn has proposed a "a slow, even descent from the cliff of chilling totalitarianism ... [a] slow and smooth descent via an authoritarian system (because for an unprepared people, a jump directly from that cliff into democracy would mean a fatal slam into an anarchistic pulp)." Critics have paid no attention to the writer's qualifying statements. The authoritarian system he conceives of is based on "love of one's fellow man," with a "solid basis in laws that reflect the will of the people, a calm and stable system" that would not "degenerate into arbitrariness and tyranny." It would renounce "secret trials, psychiatric violence," and "the brutal, immoral trap of the camps." It would include "the toleration of all religions, without oppression," "free publication and free literature and art."[258]

Many share the views most persuasively elucidated by Andrei Sakharov, the Nobel Peace prize laureate who has been subject to persecution in the Soviet Union. Sakharov believes in the coming of a "moral movement which would instill in human consciousness the foundations of the democratic and pluralistic transformations that are essential for the country [the USSR] and necessary to all mankind for the sake of peace on Earth." He is convinced that nationalist ideology is dangerous and destructive even in its "dissident" forms, which at first glance may seem most humane.[259]

Finally, there are the supporters of Marxist historian Roy Medvedev, who continues to write in Moscow. For him, "the situation in Moscow could be changed by nondogmatic Marxists, who would be capable of giving socialism a new look." He believes that "if younger and more intelligent men came to power," the situation could change. "Perhaps even Andropov understands the problems of the intelligentsia better than Suslov or Kirilenko."[260]

Writers play a leading role in the third emigration. It is they who produce the magazines containing fiction, poetry, and political and social commentary. *Kontinent*, whose editor-in-chief is Vladimir Maksimov, is a traditional Russian "thick journal." It tries to make available a broad platform to unify all the enemies of "red and black fascism" and devotes much space to literature and the intellectual life in the countries of Eastern Europe. Among the numerous other emigré periodicals, two should be mentioned: the polemical journal *Syntax*, whose editors are Andrei Sinyavsky and M. Rozanova, and the literary magazine *Echo*, edited by V. Maramzin and A. Khvostenko. Also, the oldest emigré publication, founded in 1925: *Bulletin of the Russian Christian Movement*, which has many readers in the USSR. With the third wave of emigration, the *Bulletin* has had an infusion of new blood.

The emigré literature is interesting not only in itself but because it is beginning to influence the literature produced inside the USSR. This free literature is becoming the measure by which the quality of what is written in the Soviet Union can be judged.

Among the carefully cultivated myths in the USSR, one of the most important is that a Russian writer cannot write if he leaves his native soil. This myth is refuted by the books written by Ivan Bunin, Mark Aldanov, Vladimir Nabokov, and other writers from the first emigration, as well as by outstanding works from the third wave.

At the Twenty-second Party Congress in 1961, which adopted a new party program promising to complete the construction of communism in the near future and announcing that the Soviet state was "a state of the people as a whole," Khrushchev announced it was necessary to prepare a new constitution. A commission was formed in 1962. It took fifteen years to write the new constitution, the fourth since the revolution. It was adopted in 1977.

The essential core of the Brezhnev constitution (the anniversary of which is celebrated every year on October 5) was taken from the Stalin constitution of 1936 (whose anniversary was celebrated every December 5). The changes the country had undergone in forty years are expressed in the accentuated role of the party.

The preamble of the 1977 constitution asserts: "In the USSR a developed socialist society has been built." Furthermore, "developed socialist society is yet another step forward on the road to communism. The supreme objective of the Soviet state is to build a classless society." The first two constitutions only implied the leading role of the party. By the Stalin constitution, article 126 stated that the CPSU was "the vanguard of the workers in their struggle to build a Communist society" and represents "the guiding nucleus in all the workers' organizations, both social and governmental." In the Brezhnev constitution, article 6 of the first chapter is devoted to the party; it states

The Communist Party of the Soviet Union is the leading and guiding force of Soviet society and the nucleus of its political system and of all state and public organizations. The CPSU exists for one people and serves the people. Armed with the teachings of Marxism-Leninism, the Communist party determines the general perspectives of society's development and the course of domestic and foreign policy of the USSR, directs the great constructive activity of the Soviet people, and imparts a planned, systematic, and scientifically substantiated character to their struggle for the victory of communism.

Thus the Brezhnev constitution codified the party's total power over the country.

Like its Stalinist counterpart, the Brezhnev constitution grants broad rights to the workers, but there is a qualifying clause: "The exercise of rights and liberties by citizens must not be detrimental to the interests of society and the state or to the rights of other citizens" (article 39). Freedom of speech, the press, assembly, meetings, and public demonstrations is guaranteed in cases where such liberties are "in accordance with the interests of the workers and the aims of building communism" (article 47). The right to education is assured, but article 25 declares: "In the Soviet Union, there is a single educational system, which serves Communist education."

For the first time a chapter on foreign policy was included in a Soviet constitution. The first paragraph of article 28 asserts: "The Soviet state consistently conducts the Leninist policy of peace and supports the reinforcement of the security of the peoples of the world and broad cooperation." The second paragraph of the same article states in part: "The foreign policy of the USSR is aimed at assuring international conditions favorable for building communism in the USSR, reinforcing the position of world socialism, and supporting the struggle for national liberation and social progress."

The changes introduced into the Soviet anthem are very illustrative of the type of changes instituted in the new constitution. Stalin's hymn, which in 1944 replaced the Internationale, became a "song without words" after 1956, for it mentioned the leader by name. Since September 1, 1977, the Soviet anthem once again has its words. The refrain has been modified: instead of the lines, "The party of Lenin, the party of Stalin / Leads us from victory to victory," the new anthem has: "The party of Lenin, the strength of the people, leads us toward the triumph of communism."

The innovations were minor: the elimination of Stalin's name and an elaboration on the glorious ultimate goal. "From victory to victory" means, of course, to the victory of communism.

## FROM HELSINKI TO KABUL

The five years following the Soviet victory at Helsinki was a time of increasing economic difficulties. The innate flaws of the Soviet system were aggravated by the economic crisis in the West which was felt immediately in the USSR. There was a statistical decline in the growth rates, which was important because statistics are used as an element of ideology. Of more immediate practical importance, the food situation, which was already unsatisfactory, became worse.

A new attempt to "resolve the food problem," in other words, to provide the population with a minimum of food, merely confirmed once again the catastrophic situation in Soviet agriculture. In 1977 V. A. Tikhonov, a member of the USSR Academy of Agricultural Sciences, admitted, "the private plots (of collective farmers and urban dwellers) supply approximately 28 percent of our country's gross agricultural product."[261] On the kolkhozes and sovkhozes such individual plots measure 0.25 hectares, while the urban plots are smaller—0.06–0.09 hectares. All together, these plots account for only about 1 percent of all cultivated land. According to official figures published in 1978, private plots supplied the country with 61 percent of its potatoes, 29 percent of its vegetables, 29 percent of its meat, 29 percent of its milk, and 34 percent of its eggs.[262]

Since the era of collectivization the attitude of the Soviet state toward private plots has been hostile. Theoretically, this hostility is explained by the fact that a private economy generates bourgeois instincts. Practically, it is because by providing for themselves, Soviet citizens become, at least in one area, less dependent on the government. In particularly difficult periods, the private plots have been authorized, only to be prohibited and then again permitted later on. In the early 1970s an active campaign was waged against the spread of private farming. In 1978 the CPSU Central Committee and the Council of Ministers issued a decree permitting the development of private plots in both rural and urban areas. Particular attention was paid to the development of auxiliary farming at enterprises and other institutions, which were urged to feed their own employees. The army was given the same task.

The desperate food situation forced Brezhnev to make an appeal at the Twenty-sixth Party Congress for the rural private plots and the auxiliary farming at industrial enterprises to be used more efficiently.[263]

The five years following Helsinki were a period of a systematic offensive against dissidence: any manifestation of dissent was harshly suppressed. Certain observers, in assessing the results of the Helsinki accords, saw a positive gain in the emergence of several Helsinki Watch groups. By 1980 nearly all the members of these groups had been arrested. In 1982 the few remaining members announced the disbandment of the Moscow Helsinki Group.

Despite the censorship, actions by workers in various parts of the country in defense of their economic rights became increasingly well known. The workers movement in the USSR gained new impetus from the struggle of Polish workers in 1970, 1976, and particularly in 1980–81.

Twice, in 1970 and 1976, Polish workers in Baltic ports came out in defense of their rights. These movements were suppressed by the authorities, but the strike committees continued to exist. In 1980, in connection with a severe worsening of the economic situation in Poland and the attempts by the authorities to get out of the crisis by lowering the already low standard of living, the workers of the Gdansk shipyards went on strike. The movement spread to other regions and culminated in the formation of a network of free trade unions called Solidarity. Lech Walesa, an electrician, became its head. Ten million Polish workers were organized into free unions. Their example was followed by the peasants, who demanded recognition of their own union. The movement to renovate Poland also seized the intelligentsia.

Students demanded and partially achieved academic freedom. In certain regions, the population called for the replacement of corrupt local leaders. The Catholic church showed cautious support for the movement.

Gierek, the first secretary of the Central Committee of the United Polish Workers' party, who had come to power on a wave of a worker movement in 1970, was forced to step down. He was replaced by Stanislaw Kania and, in March 1981, the minister of defense, General Jaruzelski, was appointed head of the government. For the first time in the history of the Soviet empire, a career general was heading the government. The Polish government was forced to acknowledge the legality of the new unions and their right to strike.

The victory of Solidarity became a turning point not only in the history of Poland, but in the entire Soviet empire as well. Soviet leaders made undisguised threats of military intervention and demanded that the new Polish leadership repress the workers' movement. Polish dissidents, who had already won the right to a semilegal existence, worked hand in hand with Solidarity. Acting on orders from Moscow, the Polish authorities began police persecution of the dissidents' leaders, Kuron and Michnik. Solidarity quickly demanded an immediate halt to these persecutions.

The Soviet leaders preferred that the workers' movement be repressed by the Poles themselves. An armed intervention into a country of 37 million, which had proved on many occasions in its history that it was ready to sacrifice anything for the sake of independence, could have had unpredictable consequences. That is why the Soviets primarily used political demands, whose aim was to isolate the free Polish unions from the dissidents, then to create disputes between the workers and the rest of the population, and thus destroy the forces of opposition one by one. When this failed—when it became obvious that the reforms proposed by Solidarity could cause the Polish economy to recuperate—General Jaruzelski introduced martial law on December 13, 1981. There were mass arrests of Solidarity members, workers, scientists, scholars, writers, and artists. The party realized that as a result of the reforms it would lose its power in the country, would cease to be the "leading force," and would be reduced to a merely political party; it thus resorted to armed force and declared war on the people.

Martial law did not resolve even one of the problems Poland was facing. However, it was the only way for the party to retain its power.

In February 1978 a group of workers who had gathered in Moscow announced the formation of a free union of Soviet workers. In an open letter "to world opinion," on the eve of the sixtieth anniversary of the formation of the USSR, they wrote: "We believe we number in the tens of thousands, the hundreds of thousands....We are the numerous army of the Soviet unemployed, thrown out of our jobs for demanding our right to lodge a complaint, the right to criticize, and the right to speak freely."[264] The main organizer of the group, Vladimir Klebanov, was arrested and sent to a psychiatric hospital.[265] After the first attempt, another followed. A new free union was formed using the name Free Interprofessional Association of Workers (Russian acronym, SMOT). Many of its members were arrested, and one of them, Vladimir Borisov, was deported from the Soviet Union in June 1980.

One of the prominent figures in the Soviet free trade union movement was Aleksei Nikitin, who gained popularity among the miners of Donetsk by standing up for their rights. Since 1969, Nikitin had repeatedly defended the rights of workers in conflicts between the management of the Butovka mine and the miners. In 1970 he was fired. On December 22, 1971, there was an accidental explosion at the mine where he had previously worked in which several miners were killed and more than one hundred injured. Nikitin had repeatedly warned the management of the dangers of such an explosion. He was soon arrested, and his ordeal in the prisons and psychiatric hospitals began. In December 1980 he managed to organize a meeting between Donetsk workers and the Moscow correspondents of the London *Financial Times* and the *Washington Post*, David Setter and Kevin Klose, respectively. The workers and inhabitants of Donetsk spoke frankly to the foreign journalists of their difficult living conditions. The journalists concluded that the causes of industrial unrest in Poland were present to an even greater degree in the Soviet Union.[266]

By the end of 1980 and early 1981, workers' unrest had surfaced at enterprises in Moscow, Kiev, Leningrad, Voronezh, Minsk, Petrozavodsk, and Vilnius. These workers expressed their solidarity with the workers of Gdansk.[267]

The five years that followed Helsinki were a time of spectacular Soviet expansion. In the Khrushchev era the Soviet Union began to extend its influence beyond the bounds set by the Yalta agreement, primarily in the direction of the Middle East. Castro's advent to power enlarged the zone of Soviet interests to the Western hemisphere. In the 1950s and 1960s the USSR did suffer defeats from time to time. The Soviet Union was forced to remove its missiles from Cuba, for example, and to recall its advisers from Egypt, and it lost its influence in Ghana. But these failures were always far from the Soviet Union's own territory. In certain parts of the globe the offensive has slowed, but not stopped.

As soon as the final act of the Helsinki accords was signed, the Soviet

Union achieved victory in Angola. Commenting on the establishment of a pro-Soviet regime in Angola, *Pravda* wrote: "The entire world knows that in Angola the Soviet Union seeks not economic profit, not military profit, nor profit of any other kind. There is not a single Soviet man bearing a weapon on Angolan territory."[268] This phrase was an application of Lenin's famous prescription: true in form, but in essence a mockery. The men who were fighting on Angolan territory with Soviet arms were Cuban. The Cuban expeditionary corps was then used to support the pro-Soviet government in Ethiopia and in other regions that had become the object of Soviet attention. The Cubans became the Soviet foreign legion.

Rejecting the timid objections of the U.S. secretary of state, who expressed the opinion that the Soviet–Cuban expansion expansion affected regions "where neither the USSR nor Cuba had any historical interests," *Pravda* explained: "Concerning expansion, this is untrue. As for historical interests, they are not what the U.S. secretary of state has in mind. They consist rather in the Soviet Union's full and permanent support for the struggle of the peoples for liberty and independence."[269]

In 1977 this obligation to "support the struggle of the peoples" was to be inscribed in the Soviet constitution. In 1978 a new edition of the *Small Political Dictionary* added two entries, "Ideological Struggle" and "Class Struggle."

Henry Kissinger writes in his memoirs that he did not believe that Brezhnev had a plan under his pillow to establish world hegemony. "The Kremlinologists often tend to interpret the acts of Soviet leaders as part of an elaborate plan in which each detail flows inexorably from the preceding one."[270] The former U.S secretary of state is correct. There is no carefully detailed plan. There is, however, a view of the world as an object for expansion, as mere plunder.

In a speech at a conference of "ideological workers" in October 1979, Boris Ponomarev listed the successes of the "peoples' struggles": Vietnam, Laos, Cambodia, Angola, Mozambique, Guinea-Bissau, Ethiopia, and Afghanistan. "There is an inexorable process of replacing outmoded reactionary regimes with progressive regimes that are more and more of a socialist orientation."[271] Ponomarev divided the world into four zones, setting forth a modernized version of the "Lenin–Brezhnev" doctrine. The first zone is the zone of developed socialism—the Soviet Union. The second consists of the "fraternal countries," the world socialist commonwealth. In the third zone are the "progressive regimes," notably Iran and Nicaragua. The fourth zone is the capitalist world.[272] Three of these zones make up the Soviet Union's legitimate sphere of activity, defined by historical laws. The time had long passed since the first socialist state considered itself to be a "besieged fortress." At the end of the 1970s it was the fourth zone, the capitalist world, that became the besieged fortress. "Today the global problems that face mankind, as well as the obvious necessity of finding urgent solutions for them, constitute some of the even more weighty arguments in favor of socialism and communism, for the full social and national liberation of mankind."[273]

The strategic mission was set: socialism for all of mankind, as a means of resolving the "global problems." The tactics—complete the mission to strike at the weakest links of the fourth zone.

The invasion of Afghanistan in December 1979 was a practical application of the right that the USSR had conferred on itself. After the coup in April 1978, which brought the Afghan Communist party to power, Afghanistan became part of the third zone. The operation was conducted on the Czechoslovak model: "an invitation," occupation of the capital's airport, an assault landing of the tank-borne infantry, then the invasion of the army.

The first surprise for the Soviet Union was the reaction of the United States. After the April coup in Kabul, the *New York Times* wrote: "United now, the Carter administration has remained completely calm regarding the coup in Afghanistan, where the leaders of a small Communist Party took power in Kabul. . . . Ten years ago, every Communist victory was considered a clear defeat for the United States. Today, the majority of Americans believe the world is more complex."[274] For the Soviet leaders, the passing of Afghanistan from the third zone to the second was indisputable grounds for intervention, including military. Carter's decision to place an embargo on any further grain sales to the Soviet Union (beyond the quota stipulated by the five-year accord) and the call to boycott the Olympic Games were perceived as hostile acts.

Carter's policy was criticized by American supporters of detente at any price. George Kennan supported the Soviet thesis that "the introduction of a limited Soviet military contingent in Afghanistan was a necessary measure for the government of the USSR, and was not an easy decision." "The events in Afghanistan," said the former American ambassador to Moscow, "concern two countries above all, the USSR and Afghanistan."[275] The Western European nations, with the exception of Great Britain, refused to support Carter's policy. The scenario of 1956 and 1968 was repeated: after some anxious misgivings and hesitations, France and West Germany resumed the diplomatic dialogue with Moscow. Western Europe began to forget the "incident along the road."

Soviet strategists had correctly estimated the Western reaction to the invasion of Afghanistan, which one American commentator described concisely as business as usual, adding: "Afghanistan had not been attached to the West, and the Soviet occupation did not in itself affect the world strategic balance."[276] On the other hand, Soviet strategists made a mistake in their estimation of the Afghan reaction.

Their first error was their underestimation of the weakness of the Communist party, which had been formed on the eve of the April 1978 coup by the fusion of two factions, the Khalk (The People) and the Parcham (The Flag), which were closely connected with Moscow. The union did not last long, however. The Khalk monopolized power and initiated a rapid Sovietization of the country, eliminating all its opponents, including even members of the Parcham. Under the authority of Taraki and then Amin, a regime of bloody terror was established in Afghanistan. As is usual in conflicts among Communist groups, it was not ideological disagreements but the struggle for power that was of importance. In Afghanistan this struggle was intensified by national divisions. The Khalk recruited partisans principally from the Pushtu tribes, the Parcham from the Tadzhik tribes. Among the Soviet advisers were many Tadzhiks who spoke Farsi, one of Afghanistan's languages. In spite of the fact that it was the Khalk who tried to impose a Soviet-type regime on Afghanistan, a hostile attitude toward the Tadzhiks spread among the advisers from the USSR.

The first action by the Soviet troops, after occupying Kabul and installing Babrak Karmal as president (Karmal was a member of the Parcham), was to kill President Amin, a head of the Khalk. This resulted in a mystery that continues to puzzle the world. According to the official explanation, Soviet troops had been invited by the Afghan government, but their first act was to kill their host.

Once in power, Karmal and his supporters began to persecute the Khalk. The social base as well as the membership of the Communist party were reduced to practically nothing.

The principal error made by the Soviet strategists was to underestimate the Afghan people's desire for independence. The Soviet press depicted the entry of Soviet troops into Afghanistan using the model of 1968. The newspapers could not restrain their desire to describe the joy of the local population. First place goes without doubt to *Izvestia*, which reported that an Afghan peasant, on seeing the Soviet soldiers, "prostrated himself to a tank and kissed its dust-covered armor."[277]

It took eight months to "normalize" Czechoslovakia, whose population put up only passive resistance. Eight months after the invasion of Afghanistan, close to 1 million inhabitants of a population of 17–18 million had fled the country to escape the bombardments. The Afghan army had collapsed.

Numerous partisan detachments battled the occupying forces, taking advantage of geographical conditions in their country, which were extraordinarly favorable for this type of resistance. The Soviet army, numbering 80,000, controlled a few large cities and the principal roads with difficulty. The use of the most modern arms, which could inflict heavy losses on the guerrillas and the civilian population, did not save Soviet troops from steadily growing losses.

Outwardly the situation is reminiscent of the situation of the American army in Vietnam. A huge, heavy military machine, equipped with the latest technology, faces an enemy that maneuvers freely on its own territory, thus compensating for the weakness of its weaponry. On the one hand are soldiers sent to a foreign country; on the other, people fighting on home territory and for their own homes. But the essential difference between the two situations is that the Americans were fighting a television war in Vietnam. It was the first war in history that the public could follow every day and every hour. The U.S. army suffered defeat in Vietnam because the American people did not want to continue the war; the government could not continue fighting against the will of the people. The Soviet army is conducting a war about which the Soviet people know nothing; except for rumors and funeral announcements received by the families of Soviet soldiers killed in Afghanistan. Afghanistan is closed to all foreign journalists (with the exception of some Communist newspapers).

Like their American counterparts, Soviet generals have a vested interest in continuing a war that has given them the opportunity to test new types of weapons, to perfect their tactics, and to give their soldiers and officers combat experience. In contrast to the United States, however, where the government is responsible for everything the army does, in the Soviet Union the party, which provides the political leadership of the army, always denies responsibility for the military's failures. The credit for victory is claimed by the party; the blame for defeat falls on the military.

The difficulties encountered in Afghanistan prompted the Soviet government to request Western aid, particularly American. "If the United States wanted peace in this region (i.e., Afghanistan)," wrote a representative of the Central Committee just two months after the invasion, "then it would be sufficient for the president of the United States to give the command to stop the invasion of the territory of Afghanistan, stop the delivery of arms, and eradicate the bases of mercenaries; in short, to cease all forms of interference directed against the government and the people of Afghanistan."[278]

Six months later, he repeated more clearly and with even more insistence: "The key to the political normalization of the Afghan situation can be found in Washington."[279] The Soviet leadership anticipated that the West, above all the United States, would help the Soviet Union find a favorable political solution to the "Afghan problem," which would in fact mean assisting the USSR in suppressing the Afghan resistance. The same theme was heard distinctly in Brezhnev's report to the Twenty-sixth Party Congress in February 1981. All the blame was laid on the United States.[280]

The invasion of Afghanistan compelled the U.S. government and several of the Western powers to take a firmer position against the Soviet Union's expansionist policy. The United States imposed an embargo on the sale of grain to the USSR (but lifted it in April 1981). Washington called for a boycott of the Olympic Games in Moscow and put a freeze on projected economic agreements with the Soviet Union. At the United Nations, 104 nations condemned this armed intervention by a foreign country in Afghanistan. Historical experience nevertheless suggested to the Soviet leaders that they could expect forgetfulness and myopia from the West. Hardly had the new U.S. President, Ronald Reagan, come to power, however, than he revoked the embargo on grain deliveries. By skillfully exploiting the fear of nuclear war, the Soviet Union showed the world once again that detente was divisible.

## THE END OF THE BREZHNEV ERA

By the end of Brezhnev's eighteen-year rule everything was on the decline. More and more the upper echelons of the party felt the need to "tighten the screws," to strengthen discipline and "restore order." But first it was necessary to find a successor to Brezhnev.

Aleksei Kosygin, chairman of the USSR Council of Ministers, whose name at one time had been closely linked with unwarranted expectations of economic reform, was retired in 1979. He died a year later. The effective withdrawal from activity of Kirilenko, the second secretary of the Central Committee, due to illness, and the death of Suslov, the party's chief ideologist, in January 1982 intensified the struggle among the possible candidates for the post of general secretary. The leading figure in this competition was Yuri Andropov, who in May 1982 at the age of sixty-eight returned to the Secretariat of the Central Committee from the KGB just one year and three months after the Twenty-sixth Party Congress delegates had unanimously reelected Brezhnev—who was growing senile—as general secretary. The other candidate was seventy-one-year-old Konstantin Chernenko, who with the help of his patron, Brezhnev, had moved with dizzying speed from head of the secretariat of the Presidium of the Supreme Soviet

(1964) to secretary of the Central Committee of the CPSU (1976) and member of the Politburo (1978). He was also in charge of the Leader's personal secretariat.

The ruling class had never experienced such good times as under Brezhnev. Besides a sense of personal security and confidence, which it had been denied in the Stalin era and, to an admittedly lesser extent, during Khrushchev's "glorious decade," it had acquired a sense of stability and, consequently, growing self-esteem. The bestowing of every possible privilege upon its members resulted in an unusually high standard of living in all areas: work conditions, vacation and recreation facilities, supplies of food and other essentials, living quarters, educational opportunities, and influence over the fate of those beneath them. All this greatly strengthened their innate or acquired feelings of envy, greed, self-indulgence, and contempt for the law and stirred up hatred for anyone who might disrupt this stable and well-favored way of life, whether dissidents, "hostile voices" from abroad, fault-finding writers and artists, or simply anyone who complained, not to mention, of course, the Jews.

During these years, the Soviet elite built themselves special apartment blocks according to the most modern Western models, with swimming pools, saunas, underground garages, special shops, and even two bathrooms (something they had not dared to dream of earlier). The country wide standard for housing space in Soviet cities, nine square meters per person, did not apply to high-ranking officials. What counted was the post one held. One's housing became a matter of social status and prestige. In Moscow, Leningrad, and other major cities homes were built for the top bureaucracy in areas isolated from the rest of the city's residents. The centers of the cities were rebuilt along new lines and became the homogeneous preserve of the elite and of a few foreigners. The primary example, of course, is Moscow. The streets and narrow lanes of the Arbat were revamped, many old buildings were torn down, and new ones "of the highest quality" were erected in their places. The Kremlin hospital had already been there for many years, along with the Central Committee hotel that accommodates high-level functionaries of the world Communist movement.

The former residents of the Arbat (blue collar and white collar workers and writers, artists, and similar professionals) were forced to relocate to new "microdistricts" (*mikroraiony*) on the city's outer edges. Thus, the top-ranking officials, both civilian and military, who took over the center of the city, were spared the hostile atmosphere often found when rich and poor live side by side.

Bulat Okudzhava, a native of the Arbat, poet, singer, writer, and sometime "Frondeur," commented on these social changes:

*Evicted from the Arbat, I'm an Arbat emigrant.*
*On Bezbozhny Lane today my talent shrivels.*
*Around me—alien faces, hostile places.*
*Across the way a sauna, but not the same fauna.*

. . . . . . . . . . . . . . . . . . . . . . . . . . . . . . . . . . . . . . . . . . . . . . . . . . . . . . . . .

*The imperious walk. The haughty set of the mouth.*
*Ah, the flora's still the same, but not the fauna.*
*I live and bear my cross, an Arbat emigrant. . . .*
*But the rose has frozen and all its leaves are gone.*

In the reconstructed New Arbat there was a nightclub for foreigners. On the Krasnopresnenskaya Embankment a whole complex was built for these representatives of the hostile capitalist world. It was a true colonial-style foreign settlement, with the one difference that its residents did not enjoy the right of extraterritoriality and were constantly under the watchful eye of the KGB. One block contained the offices of foreign banks and corporations. Next door were apartments and a hotel for foreigners, as well as bars, restaurants, and the nightclub. Only foreigners and their invited guests were allowed there, as well as high-class prostitutes. Prostitution is forbidden by law in the USSR, but the authorities made concessions in this case, not only for the entertainment of their valued foreign guests but also, if things went well, for the extraction of useful information. Thus, to a limited extent, the Soviet elite allowed foreigners into its native habitat. Nonetheless, that did not protect the foreigners from being reminded from time to time of their proper place—that is, slightly below the Soviet bureaucrat.

David Shipler, a *New York Times* correspondent in Moscow, noted:

What is so enervating is that the danger comes in large measure from inside your own mind. Enveloped in official lies, swathed in *vranyo* (hokum) and ironic smiles, smothered in warm and generous friendliness that can turn cold at an order from above, you exist in the knowledge that at any moment of the state's choosing, it can manipulate your surrounding environment gradually or dramatically to cause slight discomfort or excruciating pain.[281]

Social barriers were reinforced in the field of education as well. In the late 1950s special schools, with instruction in foreign languages from the second grade on, had been established in a number of major Soviet cities. Gradually the system of special schools expanded in accordance with the growth of the ruling class and its needs. The percentage of workers' children in these schools was minimal. Associating constantly with one another, the children breathed in an atmosphere of exclusivity; a feeling of privilege "by right of birth" entered the bloodstream, and later the bonds of exclusive association would be made fast through marriage. Dynasties of a certain kind were thus established. The CPSU is not against dynasties. Time and again in the pages of Soviet newspapers there have been stories about "workers' dynasties"—generations of steelworkers, miners, machinists. Sometimes they even write about dynasties of scientists. The government called upon the children of workers and collective farmers to accept the baton of their fathers and grandfathers. There has been no mention, however, of the political dynasties of those at the helm of power. The most noteworthy example was the Brezhnev family. Brezhnev's son was the deputy minister of foreign trade; Brezhnev's daughter, the wife of the deputy minister of internal affairs; the sister of Brezhnev's wife was the wife of Shchelokov, the minister of internal affairs. The family of Foreign Minister Gromyko provides another example: his son is a corresponding member of the USSR Academy of Sciences and director of its Institute of Africa, while his son-in-law is a law professor at the Diplomatic Academy. The same holds true in the republics. For example, the Sturua family: the head of the family, now deceased, was chairman of the Presidium of the Georgian Supreme Soviet. One of his sons was first a secretary of the Central Committee of the Georgian Communist party, then director of the Institute of Marxism-Leninism in Tbilisi. The second son is an international journalist, a correspondent for *Izvestia* in the United States, England, and France.

A special form of nestalgia was typical of the Soviet ruling class in the Brezhnev era—a nostalgia for the past, for illustrious genealogies. Many were busily searching for distinguished ancestors. Worker or peasant origin was useful only to put on official questionnaires. While insisting on ideological purity in the line of duty, quite a few high-ranking party officials were surreptitiously buying up paintings by artists who were branded or not officially acknowledged, such as abstractionists and primitives.

The pursuit of pleasure in all its forms became a way of Soviet life at the upper levels: hunting and fishing in specially set aside areas; travel abroad, paid for, as a rule, either by the government or by foreign firms trading with the USSR; shopping in the network of exclusive stores; seeing foreign films not shown to audiences at large; and privileged access to theaters and concert halls.

The *nomenklatura* has a keenly developed social sense—those who belong to it seldom associate with workers or collective farmers, even in their own country, not to mention abroad. "Proletarian internationalism" has its own distinctive meaning. While outside the boundaries of the USSR on official business or special visits, Soviet representatives and delegates meet, as a rule, only with the upper crust; after all, these are their class brothers and sisters. For example, a delegation of the Committee of Soviet Women visiting the United States in December 1983, headed by the committee's vice-president, Eliseeva, was received by the upper-middle-class ladies of New York and Boston. The life of the American working class did not interest them.

Members of the *nomenklatura* also lead the "sweet life" in the union republics, where rank is valued even more highly, where the chain of dependence upon one's superiors is firmer, and where corruption is simply a fact of everyday life.

Over the eighteen years of Brezhnev's rule the annual growth in the country's national income dropped from 9.0 percent to 2.6 percent, while industrial growth slowed from 7.3 percent to 2.8 percent. Growth rates for labor productivity in industry also declined sharply, and in agriculture turned negative.[282] Despite enormous capital investments, reaching the level of 27 percent of all capital investments in 1975, agriculture continued to stagnate.[283] The land was no longer fertile, owing to soil exhaustion, and the collective farmers did not want to work because of the poor compensation for their labor. In order to keep food prices in state stores fairly low, the government constantly resorted to subsidies. The population had to adapt itself to the specific conditions of a system in which famine is warded off only by imported agricultural products or by those grown on the miniscule private plots and "auxiliary farms" at large industrial enterprises.

Seven decades after the revolution, after eleven five-year plans, the creation of an industrial base, significant achievements in space and thermonuclear weaponry, and the organization of a powerful ocean-going navy, the Soviet superpower is still a backward country, where mining and the extraction of fuels predominate over manufacturing and machine building. The extraction and processing of raw materials and fuel "consumes up to 40 percent of all fixed capital and labor resources,"[284] yet output of these raw materials fell by 8 percent between 1950 and 1980.[285] In an age of precipitous technological progress even in recently colonial countries the share of manual, unmechanized labor in Soviet industry remains as high as 40 percent.[286]

During the Brezhnev period, the amount of freight handled by the transport system decreased, and there was a shortage of loading and unloading equipment; the country's transport system generally is in a state of technological and organizational decline.[287] G. Marchuk, chairman of the State Committee on Science and Technology, stated that "quite a few of today's enterprises are in need of radical reconstruction. Transport and communications are lagging behind the growing demands of the economy. Capital construction is also in need of better organization."[288]

Several months before Brezhnev's death, the deplorable condition of the economy and its causes were subjected to criticism by none other than *Pravda*, which published an article by Academician Vadim Trapeznikov, head of the Institute of Automation and Control Processes of the USSR Academy of Sciences. Trapeznikov not only rejected the official reasons for the decline in the national income, such as poor climatic conditions, exhaustion of several sources of raw materials, and the high cost of opening up new territories; he gave more plausible, though still insufficient, explanations—the unsuitability of the rigid system of centralized planning, the lack of material incentives and suppression of initiative on the part of workers and staff, and the fact that managers themselves were not affected by the consequences of their management.[289]

A document written by some Soviet economists was being passed around in scholarly and academic circles in Moscow in early 1983, not long after Brezhnev's death. It sharply criticized social relations in the Soviet Union and emphasized that "the centralized-administrative form of management" of the economy had "exhausted its possibilities."[290] In the opinion of the document's authors, the existing system of production relations was "being transformed more and more into a brake on forward motion."[291] Reorganization of the economy was encountering "hidden resistance"; "the social mechanism for the development of the economy" was not ensuring "satisfactory results"; and "the mechanism" was inclined toward "the suppression of the useful economic activity of the population."[292] The thinking of these economists, though veiled somewhat by sociological terminology, was clear enough: the existing system of economic relations was doing nothing but harm. However, under both Andropov and Chernenko the system remained as before.

This was understandable, however. No one leader could bring about structural changes without exposing the Soviet system itself to mortal danger and jeopardizing the provisional balance between social groups that has existed historically and is artificially maintained in order to keep all the levers of control, without exception, in the hands of the top leaders.

Therefore the leaders, both present and future, have little choice. They can either limit the power of the party oligarchy at the top (i.e., their own) and of the party machinery at the lower level and take irreversible measures to improve the health of the state and its economic system (in the Soviet state, as we have shown, all problems are political), or they can do nothing, make some noise about the need for change, threaten someone with a "big stick," make a few minor repairs in the facade, and stick to essentially the same course as before, trusting in the long-suffering spirit of the population, which has been demonstrated over the decades, trust to luck and the chance of finding new sources of raw materials, and of course trust in help from the West, which is interested in long-term investments and in preserving the equilibrum of the Soviet system (the very thought of the possible collapse of the Soviet empire arouses horror in the West).

In the near future the center of gravity for locating and exploring new sources of raw materials and energy will shift to Siberia, but this will require enormous investments of capital and time. It was natural, then, that Brezhnev's successors should look to both West and East in the hope of attracting West German and Japanese capital. Negotiations with West Germany on constructing factories for converting deposits of lignite in Achinsk-Kansk (southern Siberia) into synthetic oil began as early as the late 1970s. In 1981 a Soviet–German commission was organized for cooperation in the development of energy sources. The project, in which the Deutsche Bank and the giant Mannesman A. G. steel corporation participated, was expected to last almost to the end of the century. The value of the contracts was estimated at $16.5 billion.[293] This is the second major project in which Western Europe has provided assistance to the Soviet economy. The first was the agreement on the participation of Western European capital in the construction of a gas pipeline from the USSR to Western Europe, bringing a yearly profit of 5–8 billion to the Soviet Union.[294]

# 12

# AFTER BREZHNEV,
# 1982–1985

## ANDROPOV: FROM KGB CHAIRMAN TO GENERAL SECRETARY

Brezhnev died in early November 1982. The mechanism for the transfer of power from the dead general secretary to the new one was well oiled and apparently ran smoothly, without any significant hitches.

For the first time in the history of the CPSU and the Soviet government a principle of orderly succession operated. There was no disagreement over major policy alternatives, as after Lenin's death, nor any dramatic struggle within the ruling clique, with arrests, executions, and the use of armed force, as there was shortly after Stalin's death, nor any conspiracy to remove the Leader while he was still alive, as happened with Khrushchev in the "bloodless coup" of October 1964. The backstage battle for the top post ended in victory for Yuri Andropov, who was elected general secretary of the Central Committee on the very next day after Brezhnev's death. His candidacy was put forward by his closest rival, Konstantin Chernenko.

Born in 1914, Andropov like other Soviet leaders of the middle generation, began his political career in the late 1930s, when Komsomol activists on the district (*raion*) and provincial (*oblast'*) level were being promoted hastily to replace the party veterans destroyed in the purges.

These young activists enthusiastically helped to find and unmask "enemies of the people." Andropov, who was secretary of the Yaroslavl oblast committee of the Komsomol in the late 1930s and leader of the Komsomol in the Karelo-Finnish SSR after the Soviet–Finnish war of 1939–40, took part in the organization of the partisan movement during the German–Soviet war and became second secretary of the Central Committee of the Karelo-Finnish SSR in the late 1940s. He advanced quickly in Stalin's last years, when a constant demonstration of devotion to Stalin, not simply loyalty to the regime, was the sole guarantee of safety and, with good luck, a successful career. Andropov was lucky: during the postwar purge the first secretary of the Central Committee of the Karelo-Finnish SSR was arrested, but Andropov, the second secretary, was spared.[1] In fact, he was chosen for work in the apparatus of the Central Committee in 1951.

From 1954 to 1957 Andropov was ambassador to Hungary. At the height of the Hungarian revolution in 1956 he skillfully misled the government of Imre Nagy about Soviet intentions.[2] His successful handling of this mission—suppression of the revolution—was rewarded by his appointment as head of the CPSU Central Committee's department on the socialist countries. In 1962 he became a secretary of the Central Committee, thus mounting the necessary step on the ladder leading to the highest power. In 1967 Andropov accepted the traditionally dangerous post of chairman of the state security apparatus (KGB), thereby becoming the thirteenth leader of the Soviet secret police. Five of his predecessors had been shot as "enemies of the people," and three others had fallen into disgrace. Probably as a reward for agreeing to become the "party's sword" in the struggle against "internal and external enemies," Andropov was made a candidate member of the Politburo in 1967. He was elected a full member of the Politburo in 1973 in recognition of his service in crushing the dissident movement.

The importance of the KGB increased under Andropov. Andropov's fifteen years as its chairman were marked by success in demoralizing and suppressing the dissident movement inside the country and by a substantial strengthening of Soviet espionage abroad. The post, which in earlier times had seemed a moral impediment to reaching positions of the highest power, served Andropov as a springboard for the decisive leap. There was a historical precedent, however. Joseph Fouché, the all-powerful minister of the police during the French revolution and the Napoleonic era, became chief of the Directory immediately after Napoleon's defeat at Waterloo. Fouché ruled France for a total of five days. Andropov's days were also numbered—he had fifteen months.

Andropov's advent to power was facilitated not only by his personal qualities and his painstaking effort to instill in top party circles a sense of immunity from domestic turmoil as long as he, Andropov, was on the job, but also by the fact that in the preceding years the KGB had absorbed the most enterprising cadres of Komsomol and young party activists, which become an important part of the establishment.

The rehabilitation of the organs of state security, which began even under Khrushchev (with the appointment of Shelepin, first secretary of the Komsomol Central Committee, to head the KGB), was completed under Brezhnev, when the State Security Committee (KGB) under the Council of Ministers of the USSR was reorganized as the KGB of the USSR. The committee head was first made a candidate member of the Politburo, then a Politburo member. Andropov, and Chernenko after him, reaffirmed the status of the KGB as one of the cornerstones of the Soviet system. When Geidar Aliev, former chairman of the Azerbaijan KGB, was elected to the Politburo, Andropov also made Viktor Chebrikov, the new leader of the KGB, a candidate member. Chernenko subsequently promoted Chebrikov to four-star general and awarded him a marshal's star.

It is natural, then, that a sense of confidence and special destiny grew strong among the KGB's operatives. They felt they were rightly represented on the party's highest body.

In his book *The Trial*, Viktor Krasin presents a conversation with Colonel Volodin, head of the investigative branch of the KGB. The subject of the conversation was investigator Aleksandrov, who conducted the Krasin and Yakir case. "Pavel Ivanovich," said Volodin, "he has the mind of the statesman. He is even cramped here in the center (of the KGB). His place is in the Central Committee (of the party)."[3]

Under Andropov, the KGB did not remain merely an instrument of the party but, to a certain extent, became an interpreter of the party's will. When Andropov became general secretary, he became the embodiment of the Leninist principle that a good Communist is simultaneously a good Chekist. Andropov succeeded where Beria and Shelepin had not. The old-fashioned prejudice that the head of the secret police should not be general secretary of the Communist party was abandoned. When Andropov died, the KGB published a moving obituary that noted, "Under his direct leadership, an action program—scientifically based and adjusted in practice— was elaborated and successfully effected in conditions of developed socialism."[4]

While Brezhnev had been seen as a moderate by Western observers at the start of his career as general secretary, Andropov was portrayed as a statesman of the new school long before he became top leader. Andropov's staff—which included consultants in the International Department of the CPSU Central Committee, in Soviet academic circles, and in the KGB apparatus—worked for many years creating an image for the future general secretary. There were even some dissidents who contributed to this effort by spreading stories about Andropov's alleged liberalism. In the end there emerged the image of a serious and energetic statesman who, although fairly tough-minded, was capable of ruling without falling into warlike rhetoric or conservative extremism, who had a good grasp of the intricacies of international politics and the world Communist movement, who was an expert on the psychology of the West, and who even had a taste for Western culture.

The Western media and acknowledged experts on Soviet affairs tried to present the man who crushed the dissident movement and sent KGB torture teams to Afghanistan as a kind host who spent hours talking with dissidents in his own home and then had them driven home in his car. Thus wrote the *Washington Post*, for example.[5] The *New York Times* did likewise, spreading fables about a highly educated grandee with a splendid command of the English language who spent his leisure time drinking French cognac, reading American novels, and listening to the Voice of America.[6]

Usually reliable American Sovietologists predicted that Andropov would withdraw troops from Afghanistan, recall Sakharov from exile, and do good in general. Professor Jerry Hough, blessing the selection of Andropov as secretary of the Central Committee of the CPSU in May 1982, called this "one of the most propitious events to take place in the USSR in recent years."[7] True, not everyone agreed that Andropov was a liberal. For example, the London *Economist* declared him to be an "enlightened conservative."

When the euphoria abated a little, it became clear that the real educational background of this "enlightened grandee" consisted of a diploma from the Rybinsk Technical College of Water Transport and two years at Petrozavodsk University. On the other hand, he also had to his credit a full course of study at the Central Committee's Higher Party School. He did not speak English, however, nor did he listen to Glen Miller records as the Western press had reported. The intervention in Afghanistan intensified. Sakharov not only was not recalled from exile; his isolation from the outside world was increased.

The myth about Andropov as a "secretly liberal apparatchik in blue jeans" quickly evaporated after the first contact with reality.[8]

Andropov assumed his duties as general secretary on November 10,

1982, and later (June 1983), relatively quickly, also became chairman of the Presidium of the Supreme Soviet of the USSR. He died on February 9, 1984, after being in power for fifteen months.


## DISCIPLINE—THE MOTHER OF ORDER

Like other Soviet leaders, Andropov borrowed a great deal from his predecessors. Although slightly disguised, as usual, by talk about preserving peace, the main goal remained the same as before: the ultimate spread of the socialist system throughout the world. That is, the goal of Sovietizing the world was reconfirmed.

The party's main concern was also the same—creating the "Soviet man," but with an essential change. The new Soviet man was supposed to understand at long last that his primary need was to work, while the satisfaction of his material needs was a secondary matter. Thus, there was a change in the party's orientation in regard to the fullest satisfaction of material and spiritual needs. The accent shifted: spiritual needs were to come first, material second. Soviet man was urged to tighten his discipline and resolutely struggle against his consumer instincts. The basic law of developed socialist society was reaffirmed: before all else, one must meet one's obligations to the government. (In the Stalin era the same principle had been called "the first commandment of the collective farmer.")

The measures adopted by Andropov for normalizing the country's economy were intended to squeeze the fat out of the system without altering its foundations—to tighten discipline, strengthen the "agro-industrial complexes," and broaden the powers of the managers of industrial enterprises. This was accompanied by promises of greater consideration for regional economic interests and new incentives to encourage fulfillment of the "food program" adopted under Brezhnev. There was nothing new in any of this. The need for similar measures, including a struggle against theft and bribe taking, had been announced many times by Andropov's predecessors, but each time such efforts had sunk gradually into the stagnant waters of the Soviet bureaucratic system. Andropov did not carry out a single reform; he never intended to. Right at the start, on his assumption of the post of general secretary in November 1982, Andropov stated that he had no ready-made prescriptions for solving the Soviet Union's pressing problems and that he would act together with the party's Central Committee, i.e., the responsibility would be collective. He thus made clear that he was not suffering from the itch for reform.

Andropov attempted to remove those leaders whose incompetence exceeded all permissible limits and who were involved in corruption. The word "corruption" (*korruptsiya*) is not used in reference to the Soviet system. The *Great Soviet Encyclopedia* states this quite definitely: "Corruption is well known in all types of exploitative states, but the especially widespread occurrence of corruption is intrinsic to an imperialistic state."[9] Everyone knows that the Soviet state is not exploitative.

In the Soviet lexicon the word "corruption" is replaced by more ordinary terms, such as bribe taking (*vzyatochnichestvo*), graft (*podkup*), and embezzlement or misappropriation of funds (*raskhititel'stvo*). The existence of large-scale abuses in all spheres of Soviet life are well known. Corruption is an integral part of the system. All of Soviet society, from top to bottom, is involved in it to some extent. Only the degree of involvement varies. Therefore, the struggle against corruption in the USSR has been and is conducted solely against those who "take more than befits their rank" (*berut ne po chinu*), who go beyond certain bounds that have been established by custom and are tacitly recognized, and who thereby disturb the equilibrium of the system, endangering everyone.

Andropov, while still the chief of the KGB, assembled an enormous amount of material on the grafters, bribe takers, and extortionists. In consolidating his power, he aimed his first blow at the KGB's rival, the USSR Ministry of Internal Affairs (MVD), headed by Brezhnev's relative Shchelokov, who had protected embezzlers and speculators, apparently in return for due compensation. The pretext for Andropov's move was a case involving speculation in jewelry, an affair in which Brezhnev's daughter, Galina, was apparently implicated. Disclosure of this affair led to the suicide of S. K. Tsvigun, the first deputy chairman of the KGB and a Brezhnev protégé. It is rumored that he tried to prevent the investigation.[10]

Among other widely publicized investigations undertaken by Andropov was one involving bribery and abuse of power in the Krasnodar region. Local officials and militia were involved in corruption on a scale that makes the nineteenth-century abuses satirized by Gogol seem like a cheerful musical comedy.[11] The extortion had gone on under the very noses of the regional party committee, and with its full protection. At the CPSU Central Committee plenum in June 1983, the secretary of the Krasnodar regional committee, S. F. Medunov, was removed from the Central Committee, as was former Interior Minister Shchelokov.[12] Leaders were replaced in a number of provinces, cities, and ministries. A purge of MVD and police personnel was carried out, and political sections were established within the MVD and the police that were staffed with people from the party apparatus and the KGB. Fedorchuk, who had replaced Andropov as head of the KGB, became the new minister of internal affairs.

For the edification of all, bribe takers from various ministries, including the Ministry of Foreign Trade, were put on trial.[13] Several heads of main departments (*glavnye upravleniya*) were convicted, and even a few deputy ministers suffered.

The fifteen months of Andropov's rule attracted much attention because of his campaign against corruption. At the same time, however, arrests of dissidents, Baptists, Russian Orthodox activists, Jews, and supporters of free trade unions continued on a large scale. Those arrested were usually known only to small groups of friends and to the "organs." The symbol of this new wave of repression organized by General Secretary Andropov was the arrest of the twenty-eight-year-old poet Irina Ratushinskaya, who was sentenced in March 1983 to seven years in a strict-regime prison camp and five years' internal exile on account of several lyrical poems that had been sent abroad. In a preface to a collection of her verse, a trilingual edition in Russian, English, and French, Joseph Brodsky wrote:

> The sentencing of a poet is not only a criminal offense but above all an anthropological one. It is a crime against the language, which distinguishes man from beast. As the second millennium after the birth of Christ draws to a close, the sentencing of a twenty-eight-year-old woman for writing and circulating poetry whose content the state finds displeasing gives one the impression of a savage Neanderthal cry, or more exactly, it testifies to the degree of bestialization achieved under the first socialist state in the world.[14]

In the brief span of Andropov's rule, all the peculiarities of the Soviet system seemed to stand out in sharp profile, reflecting everything that had happened in the country during the sixty-six years of the system's existence. Andropov tried to mitigate the negative aspects of the system, but all he could see as the key to success was the same tired old formula, "imposing order." Discipline was the general secretary's motto in all areas—labor, public life, the military. After announcing a universal campaign to tighten up discipline, Andropov immediately began to use the familiar methods of violence and coercion: patrols were sent into the streets, stores, and restaurants to check whether Soviet citizens were skipping work or making purchases during work hours. The indomitable spirit of the people was expressed in the immediate addition of a new word to the Soviet Russian vocabulary—*zaandropit*, which meant the same as the old word *zaarkanit* (to lasso or ensnare).

The measures applied to ordinary violators of labor discipline were not new: wage and salary cuts, loss of bonuses, or applications for apartments put at the bottom of the pile. The penalty, in other words, was a worsening of the material position of the violator and his family. Permission to leave a job or change the place where one worked required a preliminary discussion by the collective. This was all vividly reminiscent of the antilabor legislation of 1940, with its broad range of punishments for absenteeism and lateness. In 1983 regulations concerning suspended sentences were amended, making the suspension of a sentence dependent on the opinion of the labor collective, to whom the one at fault was entrusted for correction. On June 17, 1983, a law was passed "on labor collectives and increasing their role in the management of enterprises, offices, and organizations."[15] In August of the same year there came a series of decrees aimed at strengthening control over and increasing responsibility for breaches of discipline at enterprises.[16]

The draft of the law was submitted for nationwide discussion. According to the official figures, 110 million Soviet citizens discussed it; 5 million people spoke about it at 1,230,000 meetings, and 130,000 amendments were proposed. The result: seventy amendments were accepted, i.e., 129,930 amendments proposed by "ordinary Soviet citizens" were rejected. Such is Soviet socialist democracy in action.

Geidar Aliev, a Politburo member and career officer in the KGB, presenting the draft of the law to the Supreme Soviet of the USSR, called the worker collective "the basic cell of Soviet society." But like all other "cells," the worker collective is headed by the party organization. Speaking and acting in the name of the collective is a "quartet" made up of one representative each from the management, the party bureau, the trade union committee, and the Komsomol bureau. The main aim of the law is to strengthen control over the workers.[17]

Formally, the law provides for worker participation in discussions on production plans and other matters. In fact, under the existing system, management decisions do not depend on them at all. The workers were given the right to voice their opinions on the matter of the assignment of apartments, an issue on which passions run particularly high. The events in Poland were taken into account—a safety valve was opened slightly so that workers could vent their discontent. The Soviet leadership regarded the disorders in Poland as the result of weakened discipline and unwarranted measures for raising the population's living standards. Regulating the standard of living, maintaining it at a tolerable but fairly low level, became the most important social problem. In his first and only discussion with the workers (at the Sergo Ordzhonikidze Machine Tool Plant in Moscow on January 31, 1983), Andropov made it clear that prices for essential goods could be increased.[18]

The people were urged to think more about production and the satisfaction of their spiritual needs, but the party did not forget to stress from time to time that owing to its efforts the standard of living was constantly rising.

At the end of 1983 prices were lowered for carpets and sheepskin coats. The chairman of the committee on prices declared that this reduction, carried out despite the underhanded plotting of American imperialism, was "convincing evidence of the USSR's economic might."[19]

The crusade to tighten up labor discipline began to lose steam after several months. It was regarded in some places as a routine campaign. The uneasy general secretary appealed to the leaders: "The main thing is not to let the impulse of the masses die down."[20] But the "impulse" was giving out nonetheless.

It gradually became clear that the drop in production could not be attributed to absenteeism. Research conducted by the Central Statistical Agency in the metalworking and machine-building industries showed that absenteeism was responsible for less than 2 percent of lost work time.[21] The long-established truth was confirmed once again: the Soviet economy needs serious structural changes. Matters can't be improved just by plugging up the holes.

Through tremendous exertions Andropov managed barely to budge the economy from its standstill. In 1983, according to official data, the national income increased by 3.1 percent, industrial production rose 4 percent, and "social production" in agriculture (as opposed to output from private plots) rose 6 percent.[22]

However, a comparative analysis by economist Boris Rumer of the average annual rates of growth in industrial production for several branches of industry in a three-year period from the Tenth Five-Year Plan (1976–1978) and a three-year period from the Eleventh (1981–1983) testifies to the economy's continued downhill slide. Let us cite some of the figures: the annual rate of growth in the production of electrical energy (in kilowatt hours) was 5 percent in 1976–1978, but 3 percent in 1981–1983; for crude oil it was 5 percent and 0.8 percent; for steel, 2.4 percent and 1.1 percent; for automobiles, 3.1 percent and 0.0 percent; and cement, 1.4 percent and 0.8 percent *respectively*.[23]

The "law on labor collectives" was Andropov's second law. His first had been issued on November 24, 1982, immediately after his election as general secretary; it concerned "the state borders of the USSR."[24] Its aim was to raise the level of discipline, vigilance, and intolerance. The inviolability of the USSR's borders was confirmed once again.

Border troops were ordered to prevent the penetration of any kind of printed matter, photographs, manuscripts, microfilm, or tape recordings whose contents might be detrimental to the Soviet Union's economic and political interests, security and social order, as well as to the spiritual health and moral status of its people (article 28). All Soviet citizens were assigned the duty of actively assisting in the protection of Soviet borders. The law also served as a reminder that foreigners are to be feared, as the Soviet Union is under constant threat from external enemies.

It is important that there always be someone and something to fear. This is one of the cornerstones of the system—the troublesome Poles, the crafty Chinese, American spies. The law fully fit in with the basic slogan of Andropov's period, "tighten up discipline," and with the Stalinist behest to keep the border "under lock and key." This is virtually straight out of Pushkin's *Boris Godunov*:

> *That not a hare run o'er to us from Poland,*
> *Nor crow fly here from Cracow.*[25]

A number of additions and corrections to already existing legislation which were adopted a month before Andropov's death (January 11, 1984) were in accord with the campaign to tighten up "discipline and self-discipline." The law "On criminal responsibility for state crimes" of December 25, 1958, was changed and supplemented: imprisonment for up to ten years threatened citizens for "activities carried out by using monetary means or other material valuables received from foreign organizations."[26] This was a heavy blow administered by Andropov to political prisoners and their families. During the preceding decade and a half, the KGB had done its best to cut off the activities of philanthropic organizations operating from abroad, such as the Russian Social Fund to Aid the Persecuted and Their Families (whose president is Natalya Solzhenitsyn), Amnesty International, Aid to Russian Christians, various Baptist organizations, international human rights organizations, and a large number of private individuals who render aid to Soviet political prisoners and their families. Those responsible for such funds in the USSR have been systematically persecuted and arrested, but new volunteers have taken their places. The threat of prison was intended to intimidate political prisoners and their families and thus undermine the very existence of the funds.

An article was added to the law of 1958 which would punish with two to eight years' imprisonment anyone who transmits to "foreign organizations or their representatives" information considered to be a trade secret, or industrial secret (*sluzhebnaya taina*). The term "industrial secret" has not been defined, however. The interpretation, as in other cases, is left to the authorities.

The preservation of order in cities and towns by the citizens themselves is included in the notion of social discipline. Hooliganism and drunkenness are constant companions of the Soviet way of life. The protection of the citizens is declared to be a matter for the citizens themselves. The government is unable to guarantee citizens peace and security with the forces of many thousands of militia and internal troops. (Of course, the chief responsibility of the internal troops is to put down popular unrest, should it arise anywhere.) The so-called people's patrols (*druzhiny*) were organized all over the country under Khrushchev. Now their numbers have grown considerably. *Pravda* reports that every day the streets of Soviet cities are patrolled by "hundreds of thousands of *druzhinniki*."[27] In Moscow, in one neighborhood (*mikroraion*) alone, order was maintained by 2,500 *druzhinniki* from the First State Ball-Bearing Factory.[28] From this it is easy to imagine the scope of hooliganism in the USSR. The *druzhinniki* have been proclaimed the bearers of social discipline. Like the forces of "order," they may be used in cases that require the suppression of popular unrest.

## STRAIGHT FROM THE SCHOOL DESK TO AFGHANISTAN

Khrushchev placed his successors in a difficult position, having promised in 1961 that the construction of communism would be fundamentally complete in twenty years, that is, by 1981.[29] Khrushchev did not have to pay for this thoughtless remark, because he died ten years before it was supposed to come true. Many had belived Khrushchev, though. To Soviet citizens, communism meant distribution of material goods, chiefly public facilities and services, such as housing and transportation without charge. (In *Problems of Economics*, Stalin had even spoken of the distribution of bread without charge, but being a cautious man he did not specify a date.)

Khrushchev's successors had to reformulate his frivolous promise. They announced that the advent of communism was indefinitely postponed. The period of developed, or mature socialism ("real socialism") would continue for an unspecified period. The USSR, they said, was only at the beginning of this prolonged historical stage. "Full equality in the sense of equal access to material goods," Andropov confirmed, "will be possible only under communism."[30]

But movement toward the Goal continues. (At one time, Eduard Bernstein, who devised the brilliant formula, "The goal is nothing; the movement everything," was branded a revisionist and an apostate from Marxism by Lenin.) Renovation of the official ideology, the adaptation of its dogmas to the requirements of the moment, was especially typical of the late 1970s and early 1980s. The concept of "the historically prolonged stage of developed socialism" is included in the everyday political lexicon, but the term "communism" has almost disappeared, for it is associated with the concept of the advent of an era of abundance. An unforgettable contribution from the 1930s to the "treasure-trove of Marxism-Leninism"—the theory that the state will wither away by being strengthened and reinforced—has in fact been revived. Today the promise is made that at some unspecified future date the Soviet state system will be transformed into one of socialist self-management closer to utopia in terminology if not in fact.

In the course of this movement toward the Goal the formation of the "new man" will proceed apace, which in fact means the establishment of a total control over man. Lest anyone harbor doubts on this point, Defense Minister Dmitry Ustinov asserted: "We are moving along a broad front toward that end, using every resource of developed socialist society, the entire arsenal of means—organizational, political, educational."[31]

The militarization of schools, and of the consciousness of the younger generation have become the party's main instrument in the post-Khrushchev era. Of course, the term "militarization" is never used in reference to socialist society; the expression "military-patriotic education" is used instead.

Military training in the schools, introduced under Brezhnev, was strengthened even more under Andropov and Chernenko. The newspapers and journals of the post-Brezhnev period are full of articles and speeches on the theme of military-patriotic education. It is discussed at conferences of various groups: army, party, and Komsomol officials, teachers, veterans, and CPSU Central Committee plenums. Aleksei Epishev, head of the Chief Political Directorate of the Soviet army, who in effect directed this activity, reported at the June 1983 Central Committee plenum that 4,000 servicemen were working as nonstaff Pioneer leaders in the Moscow military district.[32]

The Central Committee's resolution calling for additional measures to promote Russian language learning in the union republics has a special purpose: the Russian language is essential for the mastering of military technology. The same Epishev stressed, "Increasing the level of mastery of the Russian language, which is used to direct troops and naval forces in battle as well as complex modern weapon systems, will make it possible to carry out military training more effectively."[33] He was echoed by A. A. Voss, first secretary of the Communist Party of Latvia, who in enumerating the achievements of his republic at the June 1983 plenum of the CPSU Central Committee, did not fail to note that "all Latvians called up for duty are fluent in the Russian language." He added that this was of no small importance—for increasing the fighting efficiency of the Soviet army and navy.[34] The militarization of the rising generation is proceeding at full force. "We are doing everything," said V. I. Golovchenko, director of the Azovsky State Farm, at a USSR Ministry of Defense meeting with veterans, "to implant the heroic spirit in our children so that the young people are well prepared for service in the army."[35]

Defense Minister Ustinov made his own demands: "To shape a young person's understanding of the essence of conscious battle discipline, initial military training should begin in secondary school."[36]

The job of training good soldiers is one of the primary tasks of the schools. This was stated with the utmost clarity by *Pravda*, the central party organ, in June 1984:

> Their job is to awaken the aspiration to become an exemplary soldier, to develop the psychological readiness to maintain the strictest discipline and order in their units and on board ship. In the general system of military-patriotic work, important emphasis is placed on orienting those leaving the secondary schools to enter military schools.[37]

It turns out that not everything is going quite so smoothly. At the June 1983 plenum Chernenko pointed to the "belated coming to civic awareness and political naiveté of some young people."[38] V. M. Mishin, first secretary of the Komsomol Central Committee, noted anxiously: "Unfortunately, we are encountering both apathy and pacifist attitudes." Ustinov referred to the political naiveté (isolated instances, of course!) of "young people who have just put on a military uniform," and he noted "elements of complacency and carelessness in their behavior."[39]

How to combat this? First of all, seal every crack through which free thought, doubt, or curiosity about the past might creep in. Epishev called for the prohibition, "even in isolated instances . . . of books, films, or plays that are based on material about the war (or having to do with war) but are imprecise in thought content or are notable for narrowness of vision and an undemanding attitude in regard to our view of the world."

The concept of the educational role of the Soviet armed forces as a special arm of the government is deepening. Moreover, the role of the army has been enhanced, transformed from an instrument of the government to an integral part of it. The army has been entrusted with the function of educating young people during their transition from youth to maturity. "It is as though the army," wrote one of its political leaders in early 1984, "at a certain stage takes the 'baton' from the family or the labor or educational collectives, and later, after active duty as a fighting man has been completed, the army returns it—now with a higher level of breeding—to the same or other collectives of the types mentioned above."[40] From collective to collective, discipline in every form, discipline above all!

Soviet military discipline is proclaimed to be "one of the facets of socialist state discipliine. . . . It is discipline of the highest order."[41] It is of precisely this discipline—the unconditional obedience of subordinates to their superiors—that the party dreams. But an important obstacle has arisen on this path, one that will likely be difficult to overcome: human nature, with its unpredictability. And this upsets the party leadership most of all.

Under Andropov, the negative factors that influence the formation of the new Soviet man were at last revealed. It turns out that the "new man" not only has the usual "birthmarks of capitalism" but also a scanty record of work and social activity and "because of this, a limited development of class and professional characteristics."[42] School reform, a project that was drawn up in Andropov's time and became law in April 1984, was called on to correct the situation: it is planned that up to half of those graduating from secondary school will work in the productive sphere.[43]

The army has a serious interest in the quality of education in the secondary school and the state of industry and agriculture. If order cannot be established in the schools or in the populace at large, it is impossible to expect high quality performance from the army.

The government minister who, it would seem, should be trying to counteract the invasion of the military spirit into the schools, has stipulated greater attention to military training. "We must consider questions of providing the schools with experienced military instructors," declared M. A. Prokofiev, the USSR minister of education.[44] He assured the Central Committee that the Ministry of Education was working in close contact with the Ministry of Defense. The fruit of this cooperation is evident.

A *New York Times* correspondent visited a celebration of the anniversary of the Bolshevik revolution at a Moscow kindergarten. This is how he described their festivities:

> First the girls skipped in, wearing red skirts, red ribbons in their hair, and holding a red flag in each hand. Then came the boys in olive drab helmets with big red stars on the fronts, reciting and singing songs about the revolution, the "glorious holiday." Other children were dressed in blue and yellow, holding bunches of plastic autumn leaves, chanting: "Glory to our great motherland, let her future be stronger and redder." Then the whole group broke into song as a teacher played the piano: "Our motherland guards the peace,/Victorious Red Army,/Our motherland is strong,/She guards the peace."
>
> "Long live Great October!" shouted a teacher. "Hoorah!" yelled the tiny voices. "Long live our great motherland!" the teacher shouted. "Hoorah!"[45]

And this is the result: in Ashkhabad, in a school whose director is Sanarmet Khodzhaev, Hero of the Soviet Union, seven seniors were honored for taking part in the war against the Afghan people.[46]

Changes in the country's ethnic balance alarm the military leaders. "The armed forces are already considering a possible negative effect from the complex demographic situation beginning in the mid-1980s."[47] The first problem is filling the sergeant and junior officer rosters. In the national republics there are not many who are willing to become professional soldiers. The Komsomol was given a goal: to overcome this negative trend. "We consider it our important task," declared Mishin, "to raise the prestige of the profession of Soviet officer, particularly among the youth of the indigenous nationalities of the republics of Central Asia, Transcaucasia, and the Baltic region."[48] These are the sore spots because these young people are not overjoyed at the prospect of becoming a career officer.

Arkady Belinkov, an extraordinary scholar on the Soviet era, wrote in his book about Yuri Olesha:

> Heroes, heroism, brave exploits, military glory, progress, and remarkable successes were definitely supposed to make our hearts beat faster and more joyfully. But this is only half of it. The second half is that the heroes, heroism, brave exploits, and other amazing things should be used in strictly limited amounts so that they do not exceed the average percentage of casualties from automobile and train disasters.[49]

Brezhnev was still able to make himself a Hero of the Soviet Union four times and was even awarded the Order of Victory. After all, he had fought in the war. His successor Andropov's part in the war effort was sporadic, and with the arrival of Chernenko, it might have seemed that the connection with the heroic war had been broken completely. But was that so?

During his youthful years (1930–1939) Chernenko served as a volunteer in the OGPU border guard. Here he joined the party and was elected to his first party post, secretary of the party cell at his outpost. "From that point," Chernenko says, "party work became the meaning and content of my entire life." He went on to suggest to today's young frontier guards: "The main thing was and remains to have a tremendous sense of responsibility, to be at top readiness, and of course, to maintain vigilance."[50]

The appearance of a biographical sketch on Chernenko as a frontier guard with his photograph in the organ of the armed forces seemed to lay the groundwork for a military biography of the general secretary, something he desperately needed. The foundation for Brezhnev's glorification was laid down in the journal *Novoe vremya* (*New Times*), which published an essay entitled "This Small Earth," by the then young journalist Andropov. The times make their own demands on the biographies of Soviet leaders. Only Lenin had no military rank—there simply weren't any in his day.

Stalin became a marshal, then generalissimo during the war against Hitler's Germany. At that time Khrushchev and Brezhnev received their military ranks. Khrushchev was made a lieutenant general and Brezhnev a major general. Finally, Brezhnev awarded himself the rank of marshal. Andropov received the rank of four-star general for his position as head of the KGB.

But the party leadership is running into a serious problem. Memory of the war against fascist Germany is fading into the past, and with it the romance of military service. The chain forged between the younger generation and its elders by memories of a common suffering has also weakened with the natural disappearance of the war's survivors. Young people have turned their attention to new and more immediate practical matters. In the process, one of the most important components of the CPSU's magic power has begun to disintegrate. It matters increasingly little whether or not general secretaries have the rank of marshal of the Soviet Union.

## WAR IS PEACE

The end of the Brezhnev era was accompanied by serious complications for the Soviet Union in the world political arena. Among them were worsening relations with the United States, the drawn out war in Afghanistan, the aggravated situation in the Middle East, and instability in Southeast Asia, complicated by the Sino–Vietnamese conflict over Kampuchea. Within the Soviet bloc a critical situation arose in Poland, where the population of 37 million withdrew psychologically from a government that was dependent on and controlled by the Soviet Union.

To his successors, Brezhnev left the state of "real socialism" with an economy in continuous crisis. It was a superpower drained by the arms race, an empire whose tentacles were extended far beyond its own borders but which was incapable of solving a single problem either in its own center or at its outer reaches. At the same time, the process of Sovietizing the planet, begun in 1917, continued. By the early 1980s, regimes of the Soviet or similar type had been established in many countries of Europe, Asia, Africa, and Latin America. Their territories occupied 41 million square kilometers, or 27.5 percent of the earth's land area. Their populations numbered 1,783 million (including China's 1,035 million), or 39.7 percent of the earth's entire population.

Andropov became the head of the Soviet state at a time when the military balance in Europe between the NATO countries and those of the Warsaw Pact had shifted in favor of the latter. Actually the Soviet Union had had military superiority in conventional (nonnuclear) forces ever since the end of World War II. In the mid-1970s it began a program to increase its nuclear strength and eventually equipped its armed forces with more than 300 SS-20 ballistic missiles, each having a range of up to 5,000 kilometers. The military balance in Europe shifted decidedly in favor of the USSR. NATO could do nothing except warn the Soviet Union that in response it would be forced to install similar intermediate-range nuclear weapons in Europe, such as the Pershing 2 and the cruise missile. In this way the balance of nuclear forces in Europe would be restored. The European countries had no desire to station American missiles on their territory, but the USSR's bellicose policy left them no other choice.

The Soviet Union was warned in advance of the impending placement of new missiles in West Germany, Great Britain, and other countries. After refusing to settle the dispute by diplomatic means, the Soviet Union began a noisy propaganda war. The deployment of the missiles was accompanied not only by sharp debates in the NATO countries, including the United States, but also by numerous demonstrations throughout Europe, particularly in West Germany, organized by the opponents of such deployment and supports of a "nuclear freeze," as well as by threats and direct pressure from the Soviet Union. However, the deployment of American missiles could not be averted or even delayed. The danger of the Soviet Union's increased nuclear potential, especially with medium-range missiles directed at Western Europe, Asia, and Japan, was too great.

The crude pressure exerted by the Soviet Union on the eve of the general elections in West Germany (Foreign Minister Gromyko, who was in West Germany, openly declared the USSR's desire to see the Social Democratic party in power) caused a reaction the USSR did not expect: the Christian Democrats won and, together with their allies, the Free Democrats, formed a coalition government under Chancellor Kohl. All types of antiwar and pacifist movements in the West, which had been supported by the USSR and objectively played into the hands of Soviet policy, quieted down for the time being. There came a second menacing warning, this time from Andropov himself to Kohl in July 1983, on the consequences if more American missiles were deployed in West Germany.[51] This too accomplished nothing. The deployment proceeded according to schedule. For effect, the Soviet delegation in Geneva walked out of the talks on limiting nuclear weapons, but this only underscored the interim setback the Soviet Union had suffered.

At the same time, however, the Soviet leadership managed to persuade West German political and business circles of the need to cultivate better relations with the Soviet Union. The prospect of developing economic ties, on the one hand, and fear of nuclear war, on the other, would bring long-term pressure to bear on West German policy.[52]

The USSR answered the placement of American missiles in Western Europe with a declaration of its intention to install its own missiles (SS-21s, SS-22s, and SS-23s) on the territory of its allies East Germany and Czechoslovakia.[53] The announcement did not mean, however, that it would really be carried out. One of the principles of long-term Soviet policy in the Warsaw Pact countries was, whenever possible, not to keep weapons of the most recent generation on satellite territory. This does not mean, of course, that plans of this type do not exist, since all the changing factors in the military-political situation are considered in military planning. However, the danger of such a policy change immediately became evident. In Czechoslovakia a petition campaign against the installation of missiles began among students in the city of Brno, near which—it was rumored—the Soviet missiles would be placed. The campaign reached such proportions that *Rude pravo*, the central organ of the Czechoslovak Communist party, had to issue a reassuring explanation.[54]

In relation to Poland, Andropov, and Chernenko after him, continued to adhere to the political course taken under Brezhnev: to exert constant pressure on Jaruzelski's government to liquidate the Solidarity movement and to suppress all opposition in the country, but to avoid direct Soviet intervention, which might only enflame the situation.

Negotiations on normalization of relations with China, which began successfully enough, turned into protracted talks that produced no political results. The stumbling block, as before, was the Soviet Union's support of China's enemy, Vietnam, and the conflict over Kampuchea.[55]

Relations with Japan worsened as a result of the installation of new Soviet missiles in the Asiatic part of the USSR close to Hokkaido on the island of Etorofu (Iturup) and the USSR's refusal to negotiate on the question of returning four of the Kurile islands, which had passed to the USSR as a result of Japan's defeat in World War II.[56]

The USSR's bad relations with the non-Soviet world unexpectedly almost developed into a crisis situation with the Soviets' shooting down of a South Korean passenger plane, KAL-007, on the night of August 31–September 1, 1983. The airliner, on a regularly scheduled flight from New York to Seoul, strayed from its course and, while flying over Soviet territory, was shot down by a Soviet interceptor over the Sea of Japan. The crew and 269 passengers on board were lost. At first the Soviet government concealed the very fact of the airplane's destruction.[57] Later it declared that the airplane had been on a spy mission for the CIA and was shot down for violating the "sacred Soviet borders."[58] The investigation conducted by an independent international organization of civilian pilots repudiated the Soviet claim of a "spy mission" and established that the deviation from its course was caused by a malfunction of the automatic instruments.[59]

The Soviet government brushed aside the facts. It was important to show once and for all that the USSR is unshakable—regardless of the facts.

Marshal Nikolai Ogarkov, chief of the Soviet general staff, announced at a press conference in Moscow that the protection of the "sacred, inviolable borders of our country and our political system" was more important than the lives of the airliner's passengers. The destruction of the aircraft and the passengers on board was officially declared an example for imitation and placed on a par with the shooting down of the American (U-2) reconnaissance plane flown by Captain Gary Powers in 1960.[60] However, the borders of other countries are not quite as sacred to the USSR: Soviet submarines constantly conduct reconnaissance in the territorial waters of Sweden and Norway. (A Soviet submarine was detained in Sweden in 1982, then peacefully released, although Swedish authorities had the right to confiscate and destroy it.[61]) Soviet fighter planes constantly invade Pakistan's air space from Afghanistan. Pakistan limits its response to protests, which is the normal procedure in peacetime. In the incident with the Korean airliner, the Soviet Union demonstrated that it is fully resolved to thrust its own rules of behavior on the rest of the world. The United Nations was unable to pass a resolution condemning the destruction of the airliner, since the Soviet representative exercised his veto.[62] The international organization of civil aviation pilots called for a boycott of Aeroflot. Several countries banned the landing of Soviet aircraft, but the boycott did not last long.[63]

According to one of the tales spread about Andropov before his advent to power, the KGB chairman objected to the invasion of Afghanistan. It was predicted that under Andropov the conflict would be settled and Soviet troops withdrawn. In fact, the war against the Afghan people became more brutal, with the resort to scorched earth tactics, the slaughter of civilians, and torture and murder under the direction and supervision of Soviet military instructors and KGB torture teams.[64]

In 1983 the number of Afghan refugees forced to abandon their homeland reached 4 million, one-fourth the population of Afghanistan. Soviet policy in Afghanistan under Andropov became more systematic and refined. No fewer than 10,000 Afghan youths were sent to the USSR to be educated in the proper spirit.[65] Bribery and attempts to demoralize tribal leaders and sow discord among the Afghan resistance groups became more persistent. The extremely limited aid rendered to the Afghan resistance by the free world enables the USSR to carry out its policy. Constant pressure is exerted on Pakistan, which finds itself between two fires: the Soviet Union and India, with whom the USSR has a military pact. Although the Afghan resistance has become better organized and the various groups have began to coordinate their military actions, the situation remains extremely serious for the people of Afghanistan.

Soviet dissidents have spoken out in support of Afghanistan's struggle for freedom. They have also undertaken an effort to explain to Soviet soldiers in Afghanistan the real aim of Soviet aggression. Bukovsky, Maksimov, and others helped to establish Radio Free Kabul, a station broadcasting directly to Soviet soldiers in Afghanistan. The station achieved its main aim, according to Bukovsky: the provision of free and uncensored information to the Afghan population and Soviet troops.[66]

The Soviet people have remained indifferent to the war in Afghanistan, probably because Soviet losses are relatively minor—approximately 2,000 killed per year,[67] thus enabling the leaders to pursue this unjust war of aggression against the Afghan people.

The situation in Afghanistan remains unresolved: the Soviet Union is unable to secure victory over the Afghans, and the Afghans are not strong enough to expel the Soviet aggressors from their territory and not united enough politically to create a genuinely national government as a counterweight to Kabul.

In Central America, the activization of a U.S. policy aimed at stopping attempts to Sovietize a number of countries bore fruit. Soviet policy in this region had been notable earlier for a certain caution and inclination to maneuver, because the USSR had only Cuba upon which to rely. The Soviet Union and Cuba tried to exploit for their own purposes the Sandinista revolution in Nicaragua and the rebel movement in El Salvador, which were the results of internal developments and the necessity for and inevitability of change. Serious gaps in U.S. policy in Central America and the widespread anti-Americanism in the region helped the USSR and Cuba in this effort, although only to a limited extent, because suspicion had spread among Latin Americans in regard to Soviet intentions, particularly in view of the extremely insignificant aid the USSR renders to developing countries. At the same time in Cuba, Nicaragua, and El Salvador the "leftists" eagerly imitated Soviet techniques for manipulating the masses.

On the island of Grenada in the early 1980s, Cuba and the Soviet Union managed to begin building a bridgehead. (A Marxist regime under Maurice Bishop had been established there in 1979.) Very soon the Grenadian government entered into secret agreements with Cuba, the USSR, and North Korea on the delivery of weapons, war material, equipment, and training for the Grenadian army.[68] Marshal Ogarkov confided to Major Lewison, chief of staff of the Grenadian army, the Soviet Union's growing hopes in relation to Central America: "For more than twenty years there was only Cuba in Latin America. Today there is Nicaragua, Grenada, and a serious battle going on in El Salvador. . . . The Soviet Union will facilitate an increase in the battle readiness and fighting capacity of Grenada's armed forces."[69]

A sharp factional struggle among the top leaders of the ruling New Jewel party flared up in Grenada in 1983. As is the custom in a Marxist-Leninist party, the leaders began to accuse each other of "right opportunism," "lack of ideological principles," "backsliding," and other sins, just as the "big" parties do. Even the finale was similar: Maurice Bishop, the head of the party and government, was killed by his rivals (on October 19, 1983). The bloody events on the island led to armed intervention by the United States and neighboring Caribbean countries. The overwhelming majority of the island's residents (population, 112,000) welcomed deliverance from the rule of the new dictator, Bernard Coard. Large stocks of arms and ammunition, which many times exceeded the needs of the small Grenadian army, were discovered on the island.

Andropov did not prove to be a skillful, flexible politician in his relations with the West. It cannot be ruled out, however, that Foreign Minister Gromyko, who was made deputy chairman of the Council of Ministers of the USSR, continued to exert great influence on foreign affairs. Andropov overrated the significance of the antiwar and pacifist movements in the West. His European policy and its manifestation at the time of the general elections in Germany helped Europeans to understand Soviet intentions— to separate Europe from the United States, Germany from NATO, and peoples from their governments. The Soviet Union's refusal to negotiate on limiting nuclear weapons until the American missiles were removed from Europe demonstrated the Soviet political leadership's confusion and could not be offset by its numerous new initiatives in foreign policy.

Disappointment struck Andropov in another more professional sphere of his activity: the massive dispatch of Soviet spies to the West, which occurred during Andropov's tenure as chief of the KGB, turned into a massive expulsion during his term as general secretary. By the end of January 1984, 135 Soviet spies had been expelled from twenty-one nations (compared to 27 in 1981 and 49 in 1982).[70] It is highly probable, however, that the tactic of sending large numbers of Soviet agents to the West allowed the Soviets to camouflage the intrusion of their ace spies into the Western structure.

The attempt to create a Cuban–Soviet strongpoint in Grenada was proof once again that the USSR's basic foreign policy, as before, is to spread the Soviet system wherever favorable circumstances arise. Moscow had learned how to take advantage of the errors and omissions of its opponents, to fan and exploit anti-Americanism and the discontent of people in the developing countries with their social conditions.

The 660 battleships of the Soviet ocean fleet constantly plowing the seas demonstrate the USSR's readiness at any moment to extend its expansionist tentacles further.

In the early 1980s Soviet ideologists, in conformity with the changing conditions and needs of Soviet foreign policy, perfected the concept of the peaceful coexistence of governments with different social systems. A "philosophy of peace" was worked out, and the tasks of the Soviet armed forces were defined in accordance with it. Western statesmen proceed from the premise that the world consists of the Soviet bloc, the free world, and the Third World. The Soviet conception is different: there is no Third World between the Soviet and capitalist worlds. Instead there are former colonial countries whose fate is to align themselves with either one system or the other. Each system seeks to extend itself to these countries. Thus any independent role for these states is out of the question. For the USSR, this is a kind of buffer zone in which it is conducting an offensive.

The Soviet Union is for peace, but against "appeasement." It is for peace inasmuch as the historic victory of socialism is already assured, and socialism means peace. The USSR is not simply for any peace, however, it wants a "just" peace. A new distinction has been introduced: "just" peace and "unjust" peace. Earlier, in Marxist phraseology the only such distinction was drawn between "just" and "unjust" wars. "Unjust peace" is simply the absence of war. Soviet ideology rejects this as an ideal, "for preserving such a peace has its price, which oppressed nations and classes have a right to reject."[71] The Soviet Union is struggling, by means that do not exclude military means, for a "just peace," that is, for the victory of socialism throughout the world.

"We are certain," declared Mikhail Gorbachev, at that time one of the candidates for the post of general secretary and at fifty-two years of age in 1984 the youngest member of the Politburo, "that social progress cannot be stopped, that it is impossible to impede the historical process of mankind's transition to socialism. And socialism means peace."[72] But "peace," according to the party's new concepts, turns out to be war! While rejecting thermonuclear war as a means for attaining its global aims, the USSR has by no means abandoned any of those aims. As Admiral Sorokin, deputy director of the Main Political Directorate of the Soviet army and navy, declared, one of the most important missions of the Soviet armed forces is "to defend peace throughout the world."[73] This is in fact a legitimization of the Soviet right to military intervention wherever the interests of a "just peace," as interpreted by the Soviets, require it.

The very principle of the peaceful coexistence of the two systems, according to the blunt admission of Soviet ideologists, creates "maximally favorable conditions for bringing about progressive changes in the world."[74]

From this it is perfectly logical for Soviet military doctrine to postulate the existence of two fronts for the capitalist world: the external front, which consists of the USSR, its allies and satellites, and the internal front, made up of members of antiwar movements. The united efforts of the two fronts is the most effective means of action against the "aggressive aspirations of imperialism."[75] In other words, against the free world.

## LAST OF THE HONOR GUARD

Yuri Andropov, in his carefully worked out plan for attaining supreme power, failed to take into account one factor—his own health. It is not known whether he was fatally ill at the time of his selection as general secretary or whether the stress connected with his new position hastened the progress of his disease. What is known is that on February 9, 1984, as TASS reported the next day, Yuri Vladimirovich Andropov, general secretary of the Central Committee of the CPSU and president of the Supreme Soviet of the USSR, passed away after a serious illness.

It may be debated whether fifteen months in power is a sufficient length of time for making one's mark on the substance of policy in the Soviet Union, or even for leaving the imprint of one's personality on the forms of administration. It is indisputable that Andropov did not realize the great expectations many had of him. Except for insignificant details, everything remained unchanged.

On February 13, 1984, Konstantin Chernenko (three years older than his predecessor) was chosen to be the new general secretary. After Andropov's death there were three "legitimate" pretenders, that is, two others besides Chernenko (born 1911) who were members of the Politburo and secretaries of the Central Committee: Mikhail Gorbachev (born 1931); and Georgy Romanov (born 1923), who was added to the Secretariat in June 1983. The question was whether to prolong the transitional period or to open the way for the new generation of leaders. The second alternative provided certain advantages from the standpoint of the interests of the state, but it also contained one colossal disadvantage: if the "young" were to come to power, that would inevitably deprive the "not so young" of their share of the power. Chernenko's candidacy was proposed by the oldest member of the Politburo, Nikolai Tikhonov (born 1905), who was chairman of the Council of Ministers. Behind him stood a group of four "not so young" leaders: Foreign Minister Andrei Gromyko (born 1909), Defense Minister Dmitry Ustinov (born 1908), Dinmukhamed Kunaev (born 1912), and Viktor Grishin (born 1914).

The selection of Chernenko was the logical result of the party's total power over the country. Since the party ran everything, it was natural that those who ran the party should seek to preserve their power to their biological end. It is also quite natural that when the party's power was still young, in the first decades after the revolution, its leadership was also young. As the party's power aged, so did those who held the power.

The Brezhnev constitution of 1977, which legally institutionalized the supreme, indivisible power of the party in the Soviet Union, also became the basis for the automatic selection of the general secretary as chairman of the Supreme Soviet of the USSR. The party chief now also took the formal title of chief of state, chairman of the institution that functions as the collective presidency of the country.

Following the lead of Brezhnev and Andropov, Chernenko was elected chairman of the Supreme Soviet on April 11, 1984. He was the first general secretary who had no experience outside of party work. Chernenko, as his official biography states, was born in a Siberian village. Although his last name sounds Ukrainian, the nationality inscribed in his passport is Russian. In his youth he served as a Komsomol official, then was transferred to the party apparatus. During the war he worked as secretary of a number of regional (oblast) party committees and thus did not even see the front. In 1950 a meeting took place that was decisive for his career. While working in the Central Committee apparatus of the Moldavian Communist party, he met Brezhnev. By that time Chernenko had graduated from the higher school of the party organizers under the CPSU Central Committee and had earned a diploma from the pedagogical institute in Kishinev, where he was an important party functionary. From 1950 on, Chernenko was constantly at Brezhnev's side. When Brezhnev became general secretary in 1964, the career of his loyal associate began an irresistible upward course. Chernenko became head of a Central Committee department, then a secretary of the Central Committee, and in 1978 a member of the Politburo.

The one year of Chernenko's activity as general secretary of the Central Committee of the CPSU was marked by the adoption of two laws important to the internal life of the Soviet Union. In April 1984 the draft of a law on reform of general education and professional schools, which had been published in January under Andropov, was finally confirmed and adopted. This law on "the school under conditions of developed socialism" stressed the unchanging nature of the final goal: "The unshakable foundation of Communist education for schoolchildren is the formation in their minds of a Marxist-Leninist world outlook."[76] Practical measures aimed at carrying out this goal included: lowering the age at which children enter school, from seven to six, thus strengthening the ideological education of children;

assigning a significant number of schoolchildren to the network for vocational education, in order to reduce the number going to university-level institutions and thus helping to overcome the labor shortage; and lastly, improving the teaching of the Russian language. This third goal was clarified by Marshal Ogarkov: "In the armed forces, as everyone knows, all the regulations, instructions, textbooks, and manuals on military technology and weaponry are written in Russian. Orders and instructions issued by the command are also in Russian."[77] The necessity for improved instruction in the language of the military high command was self-evident.

The second major law of Chernenko's year of rule was connected with the chronic problem of agriculture. Chernenko came up with yet another wonderworking method for solving the problem. Speaking at a Central Committee plenum in October 1984, he stressed that the Soviet Union "had to engage in agricultural production . . . under circumstances that were not at all easy."[78] He meant by this that the land of mature socialism, extending all the way from the Pacific Ocean to the Hindu Kush, was located in an unfavorable climatic zone. Chernenko proposed several "genuinely innovative and creative approaches" for a long-term program of land improvement-and-reclamation: irrigating land or reclaiming wetlands amounting to millions of hectares; building canals; and diverting "part of the flow of some northern and Siberian rivers, as well as the Danube, in order to irrigate lands in the central and southern parts of the country, beyond the Urals, and in western Siberia."[79]

In presenting this program, Chernenko proudly announced: "Earlier we could not even dream of posing or resolving such tasks in the countryside."[80] This was not exactly true. On November 6, 1951, at an observance of the thirty-fourth anniversary of the October revolution, Beria had proposed an even more grandiose program of land improvement.[81] Chernenko was right in only one respect, namely, that in the Stalin era it was impossible to dream of carrying out the project of redirecting southward the northerly flow of the Ob, Irtytsh, and Lena rivers. The project had become technically possible as a result of the harnessing of nuclear power. Bitter disagreements have raged for a quarter of a century over this project. The realization of Stalin's program for "the transformation of nature," including the building of giant dams, canals, and power plants, followed by Khrushchev's virgin lands program, have dealt terrible blows to the environment. The ecological consequences of redirecting the Siberian rivers to the south, which would reduce the amount of water flowing into the Arctic Ocean and raise its temperature, could affect the entire planet more seriously than a nuclear war.

This program of new labors in the style of the pharaohs serves a number of functions. It acts as a substitute for reform while giving the appearance of solving the agricultural problem. And it is the type of project that ideally corresponds to the Soviet model of economic planning, one for which "the enthusiasm of the masses" can be whipped up and in which unskilled labor can be utilized on a large scale, above all, prisoner labor. No small part in all this is played by the desire of the general secretary to link his name with some "great construction project of communism." That is what Stalin and Khrushchev did, and Brezhnev followed the same pattern, seeking to immortalize his name through the construction of the Baikal-Amur Mainline (BAM), a railway that makes little sense economically, although it may have some limited military-strategic value.

Chernenko's year in power in fact differed little from preceding years. Rhetoric about the "struggle against corruption" persisted in the mass media, but this campaign ceased to affect even middle-level officials. It descended to the level of the masses. The organs of the judiciary carried out a plan of arrests for alleged corruption, jailing everyone against whom a case could be made, mainly with the help of informers' denunciations. There was a sharp turn for the worse in the penal system, evidenced by the greater stringency introduced into the criminal code under Andropov. This was accompanied by greater cruelty on the part of prison and camp authorities. Torture became an everyday affair, including inhuman beatings of those arrested and special "pressure cells" in which political prisoners were left completely at the mercy of hardened criminals. During the second half of 1984 alone, five prominent dissidents were killed or died from improper medical treatment: the engineer Aleksei Nikitin, one of the founders of the free trade union groups in the USSR; Oleks Tikhy, a teacher and one of the founders of the Ukrainian Helsinki Watch Group; the writer and poet Yuri Litvin, also a member of this group; the journalist Valery Marchenko; and the poet Valentin Sokolov, who wrote under the name Valentin Zeka (Valentin the Prison Camp Inmate) because he had spent thirty-four years in the Gulag.

Chernenko inherited from his predecessors a key foreign policy task: to fight American missiles in Western Europe and Reagan's reelection. In November 1984, speaking to leaders of the youth organizations of the socialist countries, Chernenko stated his position:

> If the world situation gives cause for alarm, the responsibility falls entirely and completely on imperialist reaction, headed by the United States. It is the United States and its allies who have set themselves the insane goal of attaining military superiority over the socialist states. It is understandable that we cannot allow this, and we will not allow it.[82]

Exactly one month later Chernenko received that "prominent represen-tative of American business circles" Armand Hammer and in meeting with him "stressed that the Soviet Union consistently holds to the line of estab-lishing equal and good relations with the United States . . . and favors the development of mutually advantageous ties in all fields, including trade and economic matters, as long as the obstacles artificially placed in the way are removed."[83]

One may assume that the "artificial obstacles" were removed, for on February 7–8, 1985, a meeting was held in Geneva between Soviet Foreign Minister Gromyko and U.S. Secretary of State Shultz. The Geneva meeting ended with an agreement to resume the disarmament talks which the Soviet Union had walked out of fourteen months earler. While the secret nego-tiations were going on in Geneva, a U.S. government delegation arrived in Moscow to discuss an expansion of U.S.–Soviet trade, the first since 1978. Simultaneously, the U.S. government had been considering proposing to Moscow another joint space flight like the Apollo–Soyuz mission, which had marked the high point of detente in July 1975.[84]

Five years had passed since the invasion of Afghanistan by Soviet troops, but that seemed to have been forgotten by the United States, as were the suppression of Solidarity in Poland and the shooting down of the South Korean airliner. One more new cycle of "detente" was setting in.

The honor guard of "iron old men," the nucleus controlling the Politburo, had decided to defend its power to the very last breath.

Chernenko breathed his last in March 1985. His death brought to an end the rule of the second generation of Soviet leaders. The third generation irresistibly moved into power, for even the Politburo cannot grant immor-tality. A new era had begun, the era of general secretaries who had been born, grown up, and reached the heights of power entirely under the Soviet system. The incurable optimists now link their hopes with this third gen-eration. Great expectations are placed on their presumed liberalism, de-mocratism, and technocratic bent, especially in the West. Mikhail Gorbachev, one of this generation, was elected the new general secretary. His visit to Britain in December 1984 eloquently demonstrated how easy it is to charm Westerners. It was enough for Gorbachev, then the number two man in the Kremlin, to bring with him a wife who differed little in outward appearance from Western women for the conclusion to be drawn that, since Gorbachev did not have a fat wife, all the talk about Soviet totalitarianism must be false.

In the late 1920s Bukharin called Stalin Genghis Khan with a telephone. The Soviet Union has come a long way in the past half century: the new leaders have computers.

# CONCLUSION

After celebrating its sixty-fifth anniversary, the state born in October 1917 entered the eighth decade of the twentieth century in the form of the last world empire. From Cuba to Vietnam, from Czechoslovakia to Angola, the sun never sets on the zones of Soviet control.

Nearly seventy years is a rather short time compared with the thousand-year history of Russia. However, it was within these terrible, bloody, and difficult years—Lenin's half-decade, Stalin's three decades, Khrushchev's ten years, Brezhnev's eighteen, and the three-year interlude under Andropov and Chernenko—that a system previously unknown to humanity was formed. During its first thirty years, when the world knew only one socialist state, history, geography, and the Russian national character were claimed for the peculiar shape taken by the Soviet utopia.

After World War II history performed a monstrously cruel experiment: countries were cut in two in such a way that each half lived a totally different life, one in utopia, the other in reality. The experiment succeeded. Regardless of historical traditions, geography, or national character, each country where a Soviet-style socialist system was installed produced identical results. Tolstoy began *Anna Karenina* with the observation: "All happy families are alike: every unhappy family is unhappy in its own way." All the socialist countries resemble one another in having only one political party, which runs everything and is responsible to no one, a police network that penetrates every fiber of the social fabric, and a low standard of living.

The Soviet Union, the heart of the socialist system, is also its model. The countries which join or are embraced by the Soviet bloc imitate the Soviet model perfectly, just as every human fetus in the mother's womb repeats the biological evolution of the human race. That is why the history of Soviet Union is of such importance.

729

Nearly seventy years of history, eighteen of which, under Brezhnev, were a time of detente and good relations with the West, have determined the nature of the USSR and have brought out all the inherent traits of utopia in power. Significant successes in foreign policy have not contributed to the resolution of a single problem within the country. The Soviet system has shown itself incapable of resolving economic, social, or nationality problems.

The second greatest industrial power in the world, as it is often called, is unable to feed its population or maintain a system of foreign trade comparable to that of prerevolutionary Russia: it exports mainly raw materials and imports industrial equipment. Instead of moving toward the proclaimed goal of constructing a classless society, the Soviet state has given birth to an extremely hierarchical caste system. This multinational empire, ruled from Moscow, has not resolved any of the nationality problems in the USSR itself or in the "fraternal" countries. The changing demographic balance could only complicate and aggravate national conflicts.

The eighteen "calm" years under Brezhnev showed that the Soviet Union is incapable of overcoming its internal crisis. Every shift in relation to the median line, whether toward reform or increased repression, disrupted the system's equilibrium and threatened its foundations. It became obvious that the system was blocking and defeating itself, which is especially apparent in the economic sphere. Every reform proved to be unworkable because, on the one hand, decentralization threatened to undermine the system, while on the other hand, excessive centralization ran the risk of total paralysis. The KGB managed to contain the political ferment that developed after Stalin's death, during the years of confusion and hesitation; the mass terror of the Stalin era gave way to a selective, creeping terror under Brezhnev. Psychiatric hospitals and emigration were used to supplement the prisons and camp system: the regime had become more flexible.

The past seventy years of the history of the USSR suggest a question of central importance: is Soviet society a "dead-end" society, incapable of overcoming a natural tendency to inertia and stagnation? Perhaps this is why the Soviet Union finds life-giving energy only in expansionism and an aggressive foreign policy. Thus expansion is becoming the only form of life for mature socialism.

The Soviet leaders are congenitally hostile to the West and reject its right to exist in its present form. They need the West as an object of hatred, however, as potential prey, and at the same time, as the only source of aid in overcoming chronic "temporary" difficulties. Marx's concept of the interdependence between the base and the superstructure has found strange application in the socialist utopia, which builds its superstructure partly on a base outside of itself, in the West.

The founding fathers of the October revolution took upon themselves the task of creating a "new man," Homo sovieticus. At the Twenty-fifth Party Congress, in 1976, Brezhnev called Soviet man the "most important result of the last sixty years." The general secretary of the CPSU was exactly right. During those sixty years the party's main efforts were concentrated on the Sovietization of its people. At first this process meant that citizens were pressured into believing the official doctrine. Later they were taught to regard their condition as natural and to believe that change would only make matters worse. "The moral enslavement of a population is achieved," wrote Leszek Kolakowski, "not when people, or a substantial part of them, give credence to official ideology, but when they are plunged into despair."[1] In 1980, after the invasion of Afghanistan, Andrei Sakharov wrote bitterly:

> The people of our country submit uncomplainingly to all the shortages of meat, butter, and much else. They put up with the gross social inequality between the elite and the ordinary citizens. They endure the arbitrary behavior and cruelty of the authorities. . . . They do not speak out—sometimes they even gloat—about the unjust retribution against dissidents. They are silent about any and all foreign policy actions.[2]

This is the portrait of Soviet man, the product of seventy years. A population that has lost hope for a better future and lives in fear of tomorrow is an essential factor in the stability of the Soviet system.

A new human community has come into existence in which no one has rights, but each possesses a tiny share of power: he can work poorly, mock the customer if he is a sales clerk, denounce his neighbor, and be arrogant toward little people if he is a civil servant. He can steal, and give and take bribes. This bit of power is always gained by an abuse or infraction of official legislation, to which the state closes its eye.

Mikhail Suslov, who rose to the top during the Great Terror of the 1930s and was the leading ideologist for thirty years, enumerates the characteristic features of Soviet life (although he called them "alien phenomena") in the following order: "drunkenness, hooliganism, parasitism, the desire to take from society as much as possible without giving anything in return, abuse of power, corruption and venality, fraud and waste, bureaucratism, and a soulless attitude toward people."[3] The Central Committee secretary placed a "soulless attitude toward people" in last place.

The regime's stability is explained by a new kind of "social contract"; the citizens surrender their freedom to the state, and in exchange the state gives them the right (under its supervision) to abuse their positions and violate the law. At the same time the state guarantees minimal conditions for survival.

Another factor behind the stability of the system is that it rests on a privileged stratum—the party and state bureaucracy, the military brass, the KGB, the corrupt elite of the working class, and an array of dignitaries in science and culture, along with the families and servants of all these people. Those belonging to the Soviet elite enjoy various privileges, but like other Soviet citizens, they have no rights.

The system's stability and its successes in foreign policy are increased because the process of Sovietization is not limited to the USSR and the socialist countries. The Soviet language has spread over the entire world. Political parties far removed from communism imitate it with "central committees" and "politburos." The world sees this political system only in its outer manifestations and concludes that it has been successful, especially in the last ten years. A victor is both frightening and attractive. The Soviet mentality is starting to spread throughout the globe, the idea that one should accept whatever is happening today as one's due, for tomorrow can only be worse. This defeatist attitude, which has already sunk deep roots in Western Europe, is also gaining in Asia. This, for example, was what a Japanese economist, Professor Michio Morishima, had to say about the prospect of a Soviet invasion of Japan: "If the Russians come, let us welcome them calmly with a white flag in one hand and a red flag in the other. Undoubtedly, even under Soviet power, a viable, though socialist, economy could be built if we accepted our defeat with dignity."[4]

A final reason for the stability of the Soviet system is that the Western conception of a world balance of power requires it.

Nevertheless, the past, present, and future depend on the human individual. The Soviet Union's future, like that of all humanity, very largely depends on success or failure in the effort to "Sovietize" man. The inhabitants of the utopia imagined by Zamyatin in We are happy, but the process of their total "Sovietization," their definitive transformation into little cogs in the state machine, cannot be completed without a small operation on the brain.

The history of the Soviet Union is one of a society and state subjugated to a party, that of a state which has enslaved society, and that of a party which seized state power in order to create a human type that would allow it to keep power forever. It is also, however, a history of eloquent human resistance to that enslavement.

The system's successes are evident. But history has not yet come to a halt. To remember the past is to keep hope alive.

# CHRONOLOGY

*1914*

August               Beginning of World War I.

*1917*

February 23*     Workers' demonstrations and protests begin in Petrograd.

February 28      Formation of the Soviet of Workers' and Soldiers' Deputies, and of the Duma Committee (later reorganized as the Provisional Government).

March 2           Abdication of Tsar Nicholas II.

April 3            Lenin arrives in Petrograd.

July 3             Armed demonstration of workers and sailors in Petrograd (a dress rehearsal for the *coup d'état*).

August 26        Collapse of the Kornilov rebellion.

October 21–25    Bolsheviks seize power in Petrograd. Left SR party joins the new government, the Council of People's Commissars.

December 7      Birth of the Cheka.

*1918*

January 5        Convocation of the Constituent Assembly.

January 6        Constituent Assembly dispersed.

February 8      New style (Gregorian) calendar adopted.

March 3           Brest-Litovsk peace treaty with Germany.

*Old style (until February 9, 1918).

733

| | |
|---|---|
| April–May | Beginning of civil war in Russia. |
| June | Organization of first Soviet concentration camps. |
| July 1 | British and French forces landed in Murmarsk. |
| July 5 | Constitution of the Russian Soviet Federated Socialist Republic (RSFSR). |
| July | Unsuccessful left SR attempt to overthrow Lenin. They are ousted from the government. Beginning of one-party rule by the Bolsheviks (Communists). |
| July 17 | Nicholas II and his family executed in Ekateriuburg. |
| Summer | Beginning of "war communism": confiscation of grain, prohibition of private trade, total nationalization of the economy. |
| August 30 | Attempt on Lenin's life. |
| August 31 | Beginning of Red Terror. |
| Autumn | Disintegration of former Russian empire: borderlands oppose Soviet power. Uprisings in Central Russia. |
| September 10 | Red Army, organized by Trotsky, wins Battle of Kazan. |
| September 18 | First Soviet law code, on marriage and the family. |

## 1919

| | |
|---|---|
| March 4 | Founding of the Third (Communist) International (Comintern). |
| Autumn | Red Army proves superior on all fronts of the civil war. |

## 1920

| | |
|---|---|
| January | The Entente lifts its blockade of the Soviet Republic. |
| February 2 | Signing of peace treaty with Estonia (soon followed by similar treaties with Latvia and Lithuania). |
| April 26 | Poland goes to war against Soviet Ukraine. |
| May 7 | Polish troops capture Kiev. |
| June 12 | Soviet troops liberate Kiev. |
| July | Red Army enters Polish territory. |
| | Trade treaty between Soviet Russia and Great Britain. |
| August 16–17 | Defeat of Red Army near Warsaw. |
| September | Congress of the Peoples of the East in Baku: proclamation of a "holy war against British imperialism." |

| | |
|---|---|
| October 12 | Signing of armistice with Poland. |
| November 9–10 | Defeat of Wrangel's army in the Crimea—factual end of civil war. |

## 1921

| | |
|---|---|
| February–March | Red Army intervenes in Georgia; the Menshevik government of the Georgian Republic surrenders. Bolshevization of Transcaucasia completed. |
| | Adoption of the New Economic Policy (NEP) at the Tenth Party Congress. The prohibition of factious inside of the Party. |
| March 8–16 | Revolt of Kronstadt sailors—highest point of the peasant war, extending throughout Soviet territory. |
| March 18 | Bloody suppression of the Kronstadt revolt. |
| | Peace treaty with Poland signed in Riga. |
| Summer | Famine over an area embracing 20 percent of the population. |
| July 21 | Formation of the nongovernmental All-Russia Famine Relief Committee. |
| August 7 | Death of the poet Alexander Blok. |
| August 21 | Agreement between the Soviet government and the philanthropic American Relief Administration for delivery of food to those suffering from the famine. |
| August 31 | Dissolution of the nongovernmental All-Russian Famine Relief Committee and arrest of its members. |
| | Trial of the so-called St. Petersburg Combat Organization—the last major trial organized by the Cheka. Among those shot are prominent Russian scholars and the poet Nikolai Gumilev. |

## 1922

| | |
|---|---|
| February 6 | Cheka reorganized as GPU. |
| April 2 | Joseph Stalin elected general secretary of the Central Committee of the Russian Communist party. |
| May 26 | Lenin's first stroke. |
| April 16 | Rapallo treaty with Germany. |
| June | Trial of the Socialist Revolutionaries. First show trial organized by the GPU, successor to the Cheka. |

June 8    The Council of People's Commissars established Glavlit-Main Literature and Art Administration, under whose authority "all varieties of censorship" are placed.

August    Decision to deport intellectuals from the Soviet Republic.

October    Beginning of currency reform. The State Bank is authorized to issue the "chervonets," a banknote supposedly equal in value to ten prerevolutionary gold rubles.

December 16    Lenin's second stroke.

December 30    The foundation of the USSR.


*1923*

January    Introduction of the Soviet government monopoly on vodka and other distilled alcoholic beverages.

March 3    Lenin's third stroke, effectively removing him from the government.

July    Adoption of the Constitution of the USSR.


*1924*

January 21    Death of Lenin.

January 31    Constitution of USSR goes into effect.

February–March    Currency reform completed: the stable ruble helps revive the economy.

The "Lenin levy"—200,000 new members accepted by the Soviet Communist party.

Leadership of the party and country in the hands of a triumvirate—Zinoviev, Kamenev, and Stalin.

October    France recognizes the Soviet Republic. During 1924 recognition won from Great Britain, Norway, Italy, Austria, Greece, Sweden, China, and Denmark.


*1925*

April    Bukharin calls on the peasants to "enrich themselves," expressing the agrarian policy favored by Stalin at that period.

August    The CPSU Central Committee adopts its first resolution "in the area of imaginative literature."

| November 28 | Suicide of the poet Sergei Esenin. |

### 1926

| July 14–23 | Zinoviev expelled from the Politburo and removed from leadership of Comintern. Stalin begins his rise to one-man rule. |
| October | A new code of family law is approved, putting an end to the "bourgeois family" once and for all. |
| October 23 | Trotsky and Kamenev expelled from the Politburo. |

### 1927

| July 29–August 9 | Discussion by the Central Committee and the Central Control Commission of the letter submitted by the United Opposition (led by Trotsky, Zinoviev, and Kamenev) criticizing Stalin's policies. |
| Autumn | Peasants reduce grain sales to the state, protesting low government procurement prices. |
| November 12 | Trotsky and Zinoviev expelled from the party. |

### 1928

| January | Stalin's trip to Siberia. He orders the use of "extraordinary measures" to obtain grain forcibly. |
| January 16 | Trotsky banished to Alma-Ata. |
| May–July | Shakhty trail. |
| May–October | Gorky's first visit to the USSR. |
| July 11 | Bukharin's secret meeting with Kamenev. |
| July | Sixth Congress of the Comintern: Social Democrats are proclaimed the main enemy ("social fascists"). |

### 1929

| January–February | Trotsky expelled from the USSR. |
| April | Sixteenth Party Conference approves the First Five-Year Plan, supposed to have begun in October 1928. |
| September–December | Armed conflict with China over the Chinese Eastern Railway in Manchuria. |
| November | Bukharin removed from the Politburo. The "right danger" declared the main one. |
| December 21 | Stalin's fiftieth birthday—beginning of his cult. |

| | |
|---|---|
| December 27 | At a conference of Marxist students of the agrarian question Stalin announced the end of NEP and the changeover to collectivization and "liquidation of the kulak as a class." |

### 1930

| | |
|---|---|
| March 2 | *Pravda* publishes Stalin's "Dizziness from Success," temporarily suspending "total collectivization." |
| April 14 | Suicide of the poet Vladimir Mayakovsky. |
| August | Closed trial of a group of bacteriologists headed by Professor Karatygin, accused of infecting horses with the plague. Defendants convicted and sentenced to be shot. |
| September | Closed trial of officials of the food industry, headed by Professor Ryazanov, accused of organizing famine. Forty-eight defendants sentenced to be shot. |
| November 15 | *Pravda* and *Izvestia* publish Gorky's article, "If the Enemy Does Not Surrender, He Must Be Destroyed." |
| November– December | Trial of the so-called Industrial party, a group of engineers and technicians accused of "wrecking" and conspiring to overthrow the Soviet government. |

### 1931

| | |
|---|---|
| March | Trial of Mensheviks accused of wrecking activities in the planning sphere. |
| August | Central Committee decree on elementary and secondary schools. All educational reforms in the schools since the revolution are reversed. |
| September | Collectivization reaches the level of approximately 60 percent of peasant households. |
| October | *Proletarskaya revolutsiya* publishes Stalin's article, "Some Questions Concerning the History of Bolshevism." This marks the establishment of Stalin's ideological autocracy. |

### 1932

| | |
|---|---|
| April 23 | Central Committee resolution on the reorganization of literary and artistic organizations abolishes all groups, associations, and trends in literature, painting, music, architecture, etc. |

| | |
|---|---|
| May 15 | Announcement of an "antireligious five-year plan" providing for the elimination of all houses of worship in the USSR by May 1, 1937, and "banishment of the very concept of God." |
| August 7 | Law on protection of state property at factories, collective farms, and cooperatives, reinforcing the principle of public (socialist) ownership. It provides for the death penalty in cases of theft of state property or, under mitigating circumstances, ten years in prison camp. |
| December | Introduction of an internal passport system of a kind abolished by the revolution. Only urban residents are given the right to a passport. Collective farmers are thus bound to their home villages. |

## 1933

| | |
|---|---|
| January | Stalin announces fulfillment of the First Five-Year Plan in four years in all fundamental respects. |
| April | The last major trial of "wreckers," including seven British engineers. |
| November 16 | Diplomatic relations established between the USSR and the United States. |

## 1934

| | |
|---|---|
| January | Seventeenth Party Congress, the "Congress of Victors." |
| June 8 | Adoption of a law on "betrayal of the fatherland," providing for the death penalty as the only punishment and making family members collectively responsible for any violations. |
| August | First Congress of Soviet Writers. |
| September 18 | The USSR joins the League of Nations. |
| December 1 | Assassination of Sergei Kirov. |

## 1935

| | |
|---|---|
| January 1 | Ration cards for food, introduced in 1930, are withdrawn. |
| February 1 | An "exchange of party cards" is begun, continuing a purge of the party underway since 1931. |

| | |
|---|---|
| March 23 | Conclusion of an agreement selling the Soviet-controlled Chinese Eastern Railway to Japan. |
| May 2 | Signing of a treaty with France of mutual assistance in the event of aggression. |
| May 16 | Signing of a similar treaty with Czechoslovakia. |
| July | First parade of Soviet gymnasts on Red Square. "Life has become better, comrades; life has become more joyous." |
| July–August | Seventh Congress of the Comintern. Adoption of a new line favoring unification of "all democratic forces" into a "popular front" against fascism. |
| August 30 | Beginning of Stakhanovism. (A. Stakhanov cuts 102 tons of coal in a day instead of the usual 7 tons.) |
| September | New ranks are introduced into the Red Army (lieutenant, captain, major, colonel, and marshal). |

### 1936

| | |
|---|---|
| January 27 | Publication of notes on proposed history textbooks by Stalin, Zhdanov, and Kirov (written in 1934), completing the process of state takeover of all spiritual life in the USSR. |
| January 28 | *Pravda* publishes "Chaos Instead of Music," blasting Shostakovich's opera *Yekaterina Izmailova*. |
| June 27 | Anti-abortion law introduced, along with a new family and marriage code. |
| July 4 | Central Committee resolution on distortions in the field of pedagogy, pedology is abolished. |
| August 19–24 | First Moscow trial, with Zinoviev, Kamenev, and fourteen "accomplices" as defendants. All sentenced to death. |
| October 4 | Stalin's telegram to the leader of the Spanish Communist party, José Diaz, expressing support for the Spanish Republic in its struggle against General Franco (whose rightist rebellion began on July 18). |
| December 5 | Adoption of a new Soviet constitution. |

### 1937

| | |
|---|---|
| January 23–30 | Second Moscow trial. The seventeen defendants include Pyatakov and Radek; thirteen executed. |

| | |
|---|---|
| March | Stalin's speech at the "February–March plenum" calling for intensified struggle against "enemies of the people." |
| April 1 | Announcement of fulfillment of the Second Five-Year Plan in four years and three months. |
| June 13 | Publication of an order by the Commissariat of Defense on the arrest of a group of top military leaders, including Marshal Tukhachevsky. The order states that all the arrested men were tried and shot. |
| September 25 | Telegram from Stalin and Zhdanov on the need for Yagoda to be replaced as people's commissar of internal affairs (head of the NKVD). He is replaced by Ezhov. |
| December 12 | First elections to the Supreme Soviet of the USSR. The vote for the "bloc of Communists and nonparty people" is 98.6 percent. |

*1938*

| | |
|---|---|
| March 13 | The Russian language becomes a required subject in the schools of all national republics and autonomous regions. |
| March | Third Moscow trial, with Bukharin and Rykov as the chief defendants. Eighteen executed, Bukharin and Rykov among them. |
| July | Fighting with Japanese forces at Lake Khasan. |
| September | Publication of the *Short Course* history of the party. |
| December | Ezhov removed as head of the NKVD. Beria appointed head of the NKVD. |

*1939*

| | |
|---|---|
| March 15 | German occupation of Czechoslovakia (following the Munich pact of September 30, 1938). |
| April–August | Negotiations among the Soviet Union, Great Britain, and France on an alliance against Hitler's Germany. |
| April 17 | Soviet ambassador in Berlin tells the German Foreign Ministry that ideological differences are not an obstacle to an improvement in German–Soviet relations. |
| May 3 | Litvinov replaced by Molotov as people's commissar of foreign affairs. |

| | |
|---|---|
| May 20 | Molotov announces to the German ambassador that the USSR desires a better political foundation for German–Soviet relations. |
| May 11–August 31 | Soviet–Japanese battles at Khalkin-Gol. |
| August 23 | The signing of the nonaggression pact between Germany and the USSR and a secret clause on the partition of Poland and spheres of interest in Eastern Europe. |
| September 1 | German invasion of Poland. Beginning of World War II. |
| September 17 | Red Army enters eastern Poland. |
| September 28 | The signing of the Friendship and Border treaty between Germany and the USSR, fixing the border between the two countries, with secret clauses on territorial questions and joint struggle against Polish resistance. |
| November 1–2 | The Soviet Union annexes the western Ukraine and western Byelorusia. |
| November 30, 1939–March 12, 1940 | Soviet–Finnish war. |
| December 14 | Expulsion of the USSR from the League of Nations because of Soviet aggression against Finland. |

### 1940

| | |
|---|---|
| February 11 | Soviet–German trade agreement: the USSR agrees to supply agricultural products and raw materials to Germany. |
| March 12 | Soviet–Finnish peace treaty. |
| April 8–11 | The Katyn massacre (near Smolensk) of Polish prisoners of war by NKVD. |
| June 26 | Antilabor laws in the USSR, increasing the workday to eight hours, establishing a seven-day week, prohibiting workers from changing jobs on their own initiative, and making absenteeism and lateness criminal offenses. |
| June 28 | The USSR recovers Bessarabia and annexes Northern Bukovina. |
| August 3–6 | Annexation of Lithuania, Latvia, and Estonia. |
| August 20 | Assassination of Trotsky by a Soviet agent in Mexico. |

| | |
|---|---|
| October 2 | The founding of the state reserves labor system. |
| November 12–14 | Molotov negotiates with Hitler in Berlin. |
| November 26 | Note from the Soviet government to the German government: the USSR agrees to adhere to the Tripartite Pact under certain conditions. |

*1941*

| | |
|---|---|
| April 5 | Soviet–Yugoslav friendship and nonaggression treaty. |
| April 6 | Germany attacks Yugoslavia. |
| April 13 | Soviet–Japanese neutrality pact. |
| May 6 | Stalin assumes the post of chairman of the Council of People's Commissars of the USSR. |
| December 1940–<br>June 1941 | Numerous warnings to the Soviet government that Germany is preparing to attack the USSR. |
| June 14 | TASS communiqué stating that rumors of Soviet preparations for war against Germany are false and provocative. |
| June 22 | German invades the Soviet Union. Beginning of the German–Soviet war. |
| June 24 | President Roosevelt's statement about readiness of the United States of America to assist the Soviet Union in its war against Nazi Germany. |
| June 27 | British military and economic missions arrive in Moscow. |
| June 28 | The fall of Minsk. |
| June 30 | Formation of the State Committee of Defense. |
| July 3 | Stalin appeals to the people to defend the fatherland. |
| July 12 | Agreement between the USSR and Great Britain on joint actions in the war with Germany. |
| August 25 | Soviet and British troops enter Iran. |
| September 29–<br>October 1 | Conference of Soviet, British, and U.S. representatives on questions of supplying the Soviet Union with arms and strategic materials. |
| September 30 | Beginning of the German offensive against Moscow. |
| October 2–13 | Defeat of the Soviet armies near Vyazma. |
| October 15–16 | Mass exodus from Moscow. |
| November 7 | Lend-lease for the Soviet Union. |
| November 15–<br>December 5 | Second phase of the German drive on Moscow. |

| | |
|---|---|
| December 5/6–<br>January 7, 1942 | Soviet counteroffensive in the Battle of Moscow. |
| December 7 | Japan attacks U.S. and British possession in the Pacific. |
| December 11 | Germany declares war on the United States. |

## 1942

| | |
|---|---|
| January 8–April 20 | Soviet army offensive on various fronts. |
| Spring–Summer | Soviet attempts fail to relieve siege of Leningrad. |
| May 8–15 | Loss of Soviet forces on the Kerch peninsula. |
| May 17–28 | Defeat of the Red Army at Kharkov. |
| May 26 | Treaty between the USSR and Great Britain agreeing to a military alliance against Germany and its European allies and cooperation and mutual aid after the war. |
| June 11 | Soviet–American agreement on principles applicable to mutual aid in waging war against aggression. |
| June 28 | Beginning of a new German offensive on the Soviet front.<br>German breakthrough in drive toward the Volga and Caucasus. |
| July 17–<br>February 2, 1943 | Battle of Stalingrad. |
| August 21 | German army reaches the Greater Caucasus Range. |
| December 27 | Creation in Germany of the "Russian National Committee" and the Russian Liberation Army (ROA), commanded by General Vlasov. |

## 1943

| | |
|---|---|
| January 12–18 | Partial lifting of the siege of Leningrad. |
| February 2 | Surrender of the German forces surrounded at Stalingrad. |
| May 15 | Dissolution of the Comintern. |
| July 5–August 23 | Battle of Kursk. |
| July 25 | Anglo-American troops land in Italy. |
| September | Soviet government authorizes the Russian Orthodox church to elect a patriarch. |
| November 28–<br>December 1 | Teheran conference (Roosevelt, Stalin, and Churchill). |

| | |
|---|---|
| November | Dissolution of the Karachai Autonomous Region. Karachais deported to eastern parts of the USSR. |
| December 27–30 | Dissolution of the Kalmyk Autonomous Republic. Kalmyks deported to the east. |

*1944*

| | |
|---|---|
| January 27 | Final raising of the siege of Leningrad, which lasted 870 days. |
| February 23 | Dissolution of the Chechen-Ingush Republic. The Chechens and Ingush deported to eastern parts of the USSR. |
| March 8 | The Kabardino-Balkar Autonomous Republic becomes the Kabardinian Autonomous Republic. Balkars deported to eastern parts of USSR. |
| April 8–May 12 | Liberation of the Crimea. |
| May 17–18 | Dissolution of the Crimean Tatar Autonomous Republic. Crimean Tatars deported to eastern parts of USSR. |
| June 6 | Anglo-American troops land in France. Establishment of a second front in Europe. |
| July 3 | Liberation of Minsk. |
| July 8 | A new Soviet family law revives the concept of illegitimate children. |
| July–August | Soviet offensive in Poland. Creation in Lublin of a pro-Soviet *rada* (council). |
| August 1–October 2 | Warsaw uprising against German occupation. |
| August 31 | Soviet army enters Bucharest. |
| September 16 | Soviet army enters Sofia. |
| October 11–13 | USSR annexes Tuva. |
| October 20 | Soviet army enters Belgrade. |
| November 14 | Formation in Prague of the Committee for the Liberation of the Peoples of Russia and its armed forces under the command of General Vlasov. The "Prague Manifesto" is issued. |
| December 10 | Franco-Soviet treaty of cooperation and mutual aid. |
| 1944–1950 | Armed resistance against Soviet authority in the western Ukraine and Byelorussia, as well as Poland and Czechoslovakia. Deportation of 300,000 western Ukrainians and Byelorussians to the interior of the USSR. |

## 1945

| | |
|---|---|
| January 12– February 3 | Soviet offensive through Poland, the "Vistula-Oder operation." |
| February 4–11 | Yalta conference (Roosevelt, Stalin, and Churchill). |
| February 13 | Soviet army takes Budapest. |
| April 4 | Fighting ends in Hungary. |
| April 13 | Soviet army enters Vienna. |
| April 16–May 8 | Final Soviet·offensive, the "Berlin operation." |
| May 2 | Capitulation of German forces in Berlin. |
| May 7–8 | Troops of the First Division of the ROA, commanded by General Bunyachenko, save Prague from SS troops. |
| May 8 | Nazi Germany signs in Karlshorst the official document of unconditional surrender. |
| July 17–August 2 | Potsdam conference (Truman, Stalin, and Churchill, then Attlee.) |
| August 6 | The United States drops an atomic bomb on Hiroshima. |
| August 8 | The Soviet Union declares war on Japan. |
| August 9 | A second American atomic bomb is dropped on Nagasaki. |
| August 9– September 2 | Soviet offensive in Manchuria. |
| August 14 | Japanese emperor orders his forces to stop fighting. |
| September 2 | Japan signs the final instrument of unconditional surrender. |
| September 3 | End of World War II. |
| October 24 | Founding of the United Nations. |
| November 20, 1945–October 1, 1946 | Nuremberg trials. |

## 1946

| | |
|---|---|
| February 9 | Stalin's speech to voters for the USSR Supreme Soviet, considered by some to mark the beginning of the cold war. |
| March 15 | Churchill's "iron curtain" speech at Fulton, Missouri, also considered as marking the start of the cold war. Prison uprisings at Kolyma, Ust-Vym, and Dzhezkazgan. |
| August 2 | Vlasov and his associates are executed in Moscow. |

| | |
|---|---|
| December | The USSR builds its first nuclear reactor. |
| | The USSR seeks trusteeship over the former Italian colony of Libya. |
| 1946–1948 | Ideological campaign against Western cultural influences and relations with the West. "Zhdanovism." |

## 1947

| | |
|---|---|
| | Famine in the Ukraine and in the central and southern parts of the USSR. |
| September | Founding of the Cominform (dissolved in April 1956). |
| December 14 | Ration card system, introduced during the war, is abolished and a reform of Soviet currency is introduced. |

## 1948

| | |
|---|---|
| January 13 | Assassination in Minsk of Mikhoels, president of the Jewish Antifascist Committee, by agents of the secret police. |
| July 31–August 7 | Session of the Academy of Agricultural Science at which Soviet agrobiology and genetics are condemned. Lysenko's theories and influence imposed. "Special regime" camps instituted. Revolt of prisoners in the Pechora and Salekhard camps. |
| | The "Leningrad affair." |
| October 10 | Launching of the first Soviet guided ballistic missile. |

## 1949

| | |
|---|---|
| January 5–10 | A session of the USSR Academy of Sciences in Lengingrad calls for a struggle against "kowtowing to the West" and for affirmation of the primacy of Russian science. |
| January 25 | Formation of the Council for Mutual Economic Assistance (Comecon). |
| | Campaign against persons of Jewish origin in science and culture, under the guise of a struggle against "rootless cosmopolitanism." |
| April 4 | Signing of the North Atlantic Treaty (NATO). |
| September 25 | TASS communiqué on testing of an atomic bomb in the USSR. |

| | |
|---|---|
| October 1 | Formation of the People's Republic of China. |

*1950*

Mass executions of prisoners in the camps of the Gulag. Second revolt of prisoners at Salekhard and revolt at Taishet.

Political trials in socialist countries.

June 26 — North Korea attacks South Korea. Korean war begins (lasting until July 27, 1954).

November 30 — Truman threatens to use atomic weapons in the Korean war.

*1951*

At a conference of leaders of socialist countries in the Kremlin, Stalin poses the task of preparing for seizure of power in Western Europe during the next three or four years.

More political trials in socialist countries.

Prison revolts in Dzhezkazgan and on Sakhalin Island.

*1952*

Prison revolts in Vozhel and the Krasnoyarsk Region.

Execution of the members of the Jewish Antifascist Committee arrested in 1948.

October 5–14 — Nineteenth Party Congress.

Stalin's speech on tactics by which the Western Communist parties can seize power.

*1953*

January 13 — Beginning of the "doctors' plot."

January 21 — Presidium of the Supreme Soviet of the USSR awards L. Timashuk, provocateur in the "doctors' plot," the Order of Lenin.

March 5 — Stalin's death.

March 15 — Reorganization of power. Malenkov-Beria-Molotov triumvirate.

| | |
|---|---|
| April 4 | Communiqué from the Ministry of Internal Affairs: the "doctors' plot" was a provocation and the doctors were innocent. |
| June 17 | Soviet tanks suppress an open revolt of workers in Berlin. |
| July 9 | Arrest and execution of Beria. Second triumvirate: Malenkov, Molotov, and Khrushchev. |
| July 27 | Signing of the armistice in Korea. |
| August 20 | Soviet government announces its first hydrogen bomb test. |
| September | Khrushchev is elected first secretary of the Central Committee. |
| September 7 | Laws reducing agricultural taxes, writing off arrears, and encouraging agricultural development. |
| 1953–54 | Beginning of the rehabilitation of the victims of Stalin's terror. |

## 1954

| | |
|---|---|
| April | Prison uprising at Kengir, under the leadership of Kuznetsov (lasting forty-two days). |
| June 27 | The first nuclear power plant in the world goes into operation in the USSR. |

## 1955

| | |
|---|---|
| February 8 | Malenkov is retired from his post as chairman of the Council of Ministers. Replaced by Bulganin. |
| May 14 | Signing of the Warsaw Pact. |
| May 26–June 2 | Formal reconciliation between the USSR and Yugoslavia. Khrushchev visits Belgrade. |
| September 9–14 | Negotiations with Chancellor Adenauer in Moscow. Agreement on establishment of diplomatic relations between the Soviet Union and West Germany. |

## 1956

| | |
|---|---|
| February 14–25 | Twentieth Party Congress. |
| February 25 | Khrushchev's secret report on the crimes of Stalin. |
| April 25 | Abrogation of the antilabor legislation of 1940. |

| | |
|---|---|
| June 30 | Resolution by the CPSU Central Committee on "overcoming the personality cult and its consequences." |
| July 14 | Law on government pensions. |
| September 8 | Establishment of minimum wage. |
| October–November | Repression of Hungarian revolution by Soviet troops. |
| 1956–57 | "Union of Russian Patriots" (Krasnopevtsev group) at Moscow University. |

## 1957

| | |
|---|---|
| July 4 | Elimination of so-called antiparty opposition (Malenkov, Molotov, Kaganovich, Shepilov). |
| October 4 | The Soviet Union launches *Sputnik*, the earth's first artificial satellite. |
| October 26 | Marshal Zhukov is relieved of all his duties and retired. |

## 1958

| | |
|---|---|
| February 26 | Abolition of the machine and tractor stations (MTSs). Massive antireligious campaign in the USSR. |
| March 27 | Khrushchev becomes chairman of the Council of Ministers. |
| June | Execution of Imre Nagy. |
| August 24–27 | Race riots against Chechens and Ingush in Grozny. |
| October 23 | Pasternak awarded Nobel Prize for Literature for his novel *Doctor Zhivago*. |
| October.–November | Officially sanctioned persecution of Pasternak. |
| December 24 | School reform. Sakharov's first appeal to Khrushchev to end H-bomb testing. |

## 1959

| | |
|---|---|
| | Poetry readings begin at the statue of Mayakovsky in Moscow. Appearance of the *samizdat* journal *Syntax*. |

*1960*

| | |
|---|---|
| April | Polemic begins between Communist parties of the Soviet Union and China. |
| May 7 | Law establishing the seven-hour workday. |
| May 30 | Death of the poet Boris Pasternak. |
| August | Soviet specialists recalled from China. |

*1961*

| | |
|---|---|
| | Trial of members of the Ukrainian Union of Workers and Peasants, in Lvov. |
| April 12 | *Vostok*, the first manned space vessel in the world, is launched with Cosmonaut Yuri Gagarin on board. |
| July | Talks between Khrushchev and Kennedy in Vienna. |
| August | Construction of the Berlin Wall. |
| September 7 | General Grigorenko warns against a new "personality cult." |
| | Appearance of the *samizdat* journal *Phoenix-61*. |
| October 17–31 | Twenty-second Party Congress. |
| | Adoption of a new party program and new party rules. |
| | Stalin's body is removed from the Mausoleum. |

*1962*

| | |
|---|---|
| | Trial of the "Baltic Federation," in Riga. |
| June 2 | Workers protesting against cuts in the standard of living were fired on in Novocherkassk. |
| October | Soviet Union installs missiles in Cuba, resulting in the Cuban missile crisis. After thirteen days the missiles are removed under U.S. pressure. |
| November | *Novy mir* publishes Solzhenitsyn's *One Day in the Life of Ivan Denisovich.* |

*1963*

| | |
|---|---|
| August 5 | Treaty to end nuclear testing in the atmosphere, in space, and under water signed by the USSR, Great Britain, and the United States. |
| | Unrest, strikes, and street demonstrations in Krivoi Rog, Grozny, Krasnodar, Donetsk, Murom, and Yaroslavl. |
| | Worker unrest at the Moskvich Auto Plant in Moscow. |
| | Drought and a poor harvest. |

| | |
|---|---|
| November 23 | Completion of the Unified Energy System of Siberia. |
| November 19–23 | Plenum of the CPSU Central Committee decides to divide the party into industrial and agricultural sections. |

## 1964

| | |
|---|---|
| May 24 | Arson in the library of the Ukrainian National Academy of Sciences, destroying some treasures of Ukrainian culture. |
| October 14 | Khrushchev is removed from power and forced to retire. |
| | Leonid Brezhnev is elected first secretary of the CPSU Central Committee. |

## 1965

| | |
|---|---|
| February 15 | Formation of a provisional organizing committee near Tashkent for the return of the deported Meskhi people to their homeland. |
| August 28 | Decree exonerating the Volga Germans. |

## 1966

| | |
|---|---|
| February 10–14 | Sinyavsky–Daniel trial. |
| March | Numerous protests from prominent scientific and cultural personalities against legalized forms of arbitrary justice and attempts to rehabilitate Stalin. |
| March 29–April 8 | Twenty-third Party Congress: the Politburo is restored, replacing the Presidium of the Central Committee; the post of general secretary is also restored, replacing the "first secretary," and is filled by Brezhnev. |
| | Trial of Ukrainian teacher Valentyn Moroz. |
| September 11 | Decree of the Presidium of the Supreme Soviet amends the penal code in such a way as to facilitate judicial reprisals against dissidents (articles 190-1 and 190-3). |

## 1967

| | |
|---|---|
| April | Svetlana Alliluyeva, Stalin's daughter, refuses to return to the USSR. |

| | |
|---|---|
| May 16 | Solzhenitsyn's letter to the Fourth Congress of Soviet Writers opposing censorship. |
| June | A decree of the Presidium of the Supreme Soviet exonerates the Soviet Kurds, Turks, and Islamic Armenians (Khemshins), accused of treason during the war. |
| September 11 | Decree of the Presidium of the Supreme Soviet exonerating the Crimean Tatars accused of treason during the war. |

## 1968

| | |
|---|---|
| February | Galanskov—Ginzburg trial. |
| March—April | Trial in Leningrad of the members of the VSKhSON (All-Russia Social Christian Union for the Liberation of the People), organized in 1964. |
| April 21 | Crimean Tatar celebration in Chirchik (Uzbek republic) dispersed by police and troops. |
| April 30 | First issue of the *Chronicle of Current Events*. |
| June | Publication, in *samizdat*, of Sakharov's *Progress, Coexistence, and Intellectual Freedom*. |
| June 27 | A new family code abolishes laws concerning illegitimate children. |
| August 21 | The Soviet Union and Warsaw Pact countries invade Czechoslovakia. |
| August 25 | Demonstration in Moscow's Red Square by a group of dissidents protesting Soviet intervention in Czechoslovakia. |
| October 9–11 | Trial of the Red Square demonstrators. |

## 1969

| | |
|---|---|
| March 2–15 | Bloody skirmishes on the Sino—Soviet border. |
| April—June | Andrei Amalrik's book *Will the Soviet Union Survive Until 1984?* begins to circulate in *samizdat*. |
| May | Formation of an action group for the defense of civil rights in the USSR. |
| | Arrest and imprisonment of Grigorenko in a psychiatric hospital. |
| June 6 | Demonstration by Crimean Tatars in Moscow. |

*1970*

|  | First issue of *The Ukrainian Herald*. |
| March 5 | Sakharov's second letter to the Soviet leadership. |
| June | Beginning of the Soviet Jewish movement for the right to emigrate to Israel. |
| October | Nobel Prize for Literature awarded to Solzhenitsyn. |
| December 15–31 | Trial of Soviet Jewish dissidents who attempted to hijack an airplane in Leningrad. Worldwide protest against death sentences for two of them, Dymshits and Kuznetsov. Their sentences are commuted to fifteen years' imprisonment. |

*1971*

| September 11 | Death of Nikita Khrushchev. |

*1972*

| January 11–15 | Massive searches and arrests in Moscow and the Ukraine, aimed at stopping publication and circulation of the *Chronicle of Current Events*. |
| May 14 | Self-immolation in Kaunas of a twenty-year-old Lithuanian worker, Romas Kalenta, to protest persecution of the Lithuanian Catholic church. |
| May 18 | Protest demonstration in the wake of Kalenta's funeral is bloodily put down by troops. |
| May 22–30 | President Nixon visits Moscow. Signing of the first Soviet–American agreement on strategic nuclear arms limitation (SALT I). |

*1973*

| June 22 | Soviet–American agreement on prevention of nuclear war. |
| August | Yakir–Krasin trial. |
| September | Solzhenitsyn's *Letter to the Soviet Leaders*. |

*1974*

| February 11–17 | Demonstration by Volga Germans in Moscow and Tallin, calling for permission to emigrate to West Germany. |

| February 12–13 | Arrest and expulsion of Solzhenitsyn after the publication in Paris of his *Gulag Archipelago* (in Russian). |

## 1975

| | Soviet–Cuban intervention in Angola. |
| August 1 | Signing of the Helsinki accords. |
| December | Nobel Peace Prize awarded to Sakharov. |

## 1976

| May 13–15 | Formation of groups to monitor observance of the Helsinki accords (in Moscow, the Ukraine, Lithuania, Georgia, and Armenia). |

## 1977

| February | Arrest of members of the Helsinki Group, led by Yuri Orlov. |
| June 16 | Brezhnev becomes chairman of the Presidium of the Supreme Soviet (head of state), while remaining general secretary of the party's Central Committee. |
| June–July | Belgrade conference for verification of progress on the Helsinki accords. |
| August 28– September 1 | World Psychiatric Congress in Honolulu votes to condemn Soviet abuse of psychiatry for political purposes. |
| September 6 | Inhabitants of Gorky call for churches to be reopened. Soviet dissident Vladimir Bukovsky is exchanged for Chilean Communist leader Luis Corvalan. |
| | Mass hunger strike by prisoners in the camps of Perm. |
| October 7 | Adoption of the new Constitution of the USSR. |

## 1978

| February 1 | Organization of a free trade union of Soviet workers, in Moscow. |
| May 18 | Trial of members of the Moscow Helsinki Group. |
| September 20 | Joint Soviet–Ethiopian communiqué: "The Soviet Union considers the Ethiopian revolution an integral part of the world revolutionary process." |

*1979*

April 27        Exchange of five Soviet dissident prisoners in the USSR for two Soviet spies arrested in the United States.

December 24–26      Soviet troops invade Afghanistan.

*1980*

January        After an open protest against the Soviet invasion of Afghanistan, Sakharov is exiled to Gorky.

August        Strikes in Gdansk and other Polish cities result in the signing of an agreement between the strikers and a Polish government delegation. Formation of the independent self-governing trade union Solidarity.

*1981*

February 24–
March 3        Twenty-sixth Party Congress. Start of a new Soviet "peace offensive."

December 13        Declaration of martial law in Poland, mass arrests, suppression of Solidarity. The "re-Stalinization" process begins.

*1982*

January 25        Death of Mikhail Suslov (born 1902).

May        CPSU Central Committee adopts a ten-year Agricultural Program, with the goal of guaranteeing the population a stable supply of all types of foodstuffs.

November 10        Death of Leonid Brezhnev (born 1906).

November 12        Election of Yuri Andropov as general secretary of the CPSU Central Committee.

November 24        Law "On the State Border of the USSR."

*1983*

June 17        Law "On Labor Collectives and Their Increased Role in the Management of Enterprises, Institutes, and Organizations."

September 1        Soviet jet fighter shoots down Korean Air Lines jet 007 over Sea of Japan, killing 269.

## 1984

| | |
|---|---|
| February 9 | Death of Yuri Andropov (born 1914). |
| February 13 | Election of Konstanin Chernenko as general secretary of the CPSU Central Committee. |
| April 12 | Resolution of the Supreme Soviet of the USSR "On Fundamental Directions for Reform of the General Education and Professional School." |
| November | CPSU Central Committee adopts a Program for Land Improvement, with the goal of decisively resolving the problems of agriculture. The program envisions reversing the course of rivers from north to south. |

## 1985

| | |
|---|---|
| January | Soviet Foreign Minister Gromyko meets with U.S. Secretary of State Shultz. |
| March 10 | Death of Konstanin Chernenko (born 1911). |
| March 11 | Election of Mikhail Gorbachev as general secretary of the CPSU Central Committee. |

# NOTES

## CHAPTER ONE

1. Edmond Théry, *La transformation économique de la Russie*, Paris, 1914, p. xiii.
2. S. N. Prokopovich, *Narodnoe khoziaistvo SSSR* (The economy of the USSR), vol. 1, New York, 1952, p. 381.
3. N. A. Bazili, *Rossiia pod sovetskoi vlast'iu* (Russia under Soviet rule), Paris, 1937, p. 10.
4. *Istoriia SSR. Epokha sotsializma* (History of the USSR: Age of socialism), Moscow, 1975, p. 16.
5. L. M. Spirin, *Klassy i partii v grazhdanskoi voine v Rossii* (Classes and parties in the Russian civil war), Moscow, 1968, p. 36.
6. Norman Stone, *The Eastern Front, 1914–1917*, London, 1975, p. 18.
7. Théry, *La transformation*, p. xii.
8. Ibid., p. xix.
9. See Iu. A Poliakov and I. N. Kiselev, "Naselenie Rossii v 1917 g." (The population of Russia in 1917), *Voprosy istorii* (Problems of history), no. 6, 1980.
10. Vasily V. Shulgin, *Dni* (Days), Belgrade, 1925, p. 59.
11. Théry, *La transformation*, p. xii.
12. Basile Kerblay, *La société soviétique contemporaine*, Paris, 1977, p. 146.
13. Leon Trotsky, *The History of the Russian Revolution*, London, 1967, p. 64.
14. Byloe (The past), no. 19, 1922, pp. 101–176.
15. *Materialy po istorii franko-russkikh otnoshenii za 1910–14 gody* (Materials on the history of Franco-Russian relations, 1910–1914), Moscow, 1922, p. 698.
16. Ibid., p. 700 ff.
17. A. L. Sidorov, *Ekonomicheskoe polozhenie Rossii v gody Pervoi mirovoi voiny* (Economic conditions in Russia during World War I), Moscow, 1973, pp. 5–6.
18. Shulgin, *Dni*, p. 63.
19. Ibid., p. 85.
20. Ibid., p. 96. M M. Bok, in *Vospominaniia o moem ottse P. A. Stolypine* (Reminiscences of my father, P. A. Stolypin) (New York, 1953, p. 331), states that Nicholas II made this remark during a conversation with his prime minister.
21. Sidorov, *Ekonomicheskoe polozhenie*, p. 350.

22. Stone, *Eastern Front*, pp. 208–211.
23. Shulgin, *Dni*, p. 101.
24. Spirin, *Klassy i partii*, p. 38.
25. William G. Rosenberg, *Liberals in the Russian Revolution: The Constitutional Democratic Party, 1917–1921*, Princeton, 1974, p. 18.
26. *Proletarskaia revoliutsiia* (Proletarian revolution), no. 4, 1928, p. 67.
27. Indicative of Lenin's warm attitude toward Malinovsky were the words he wrote to Gorky in January 1913: "Malinovsky, Petrovsky, and Badaev send you warm greetings and best wishes. They are [fine] fellows, especially the first." See Vladimir Lenin, *Collected Works*, Moscow, 196– , 35:70. (Hereafter cited as *CW*.)
28. Aleksandr Shliapnikov, *Semnadtsatyi god* (The year 1917), 4 vols., Moscow, 1925, 3:187.
29. Quoted in Mark Aldanov, *Sovremenniki* (Contemporaries), Paris, 1928, p. 244. The *otzovisty* were a Bolshevik splinter group which in 1918 demanded the recall (*otzyv*) of Social Democratic representatives from the Duma.
30. Aleksandr Spiridovich, *Istoriia bol'shevizma v Rossii* (History of bolshevism in Russia), Paris, 1922, p. 229.
31. A. E. Badaev, *Bol'sheviki v Gosudarstvennoi Dume* (The Bolsheviks in the Duma), Moscow, 1930, pp. 228–229.
32. Aleksandr A. Blok, *Poslednie dni imperatorskoi vlasti* (The last days of imperial rule), Petrograd, 1921, p. 8.
33. A. M. Anfimov, *Rossiiskaia derevnia v gody Pervoi mirovoi voiny* (The Russian countryside during World War I), Moscow, 1962, p. 290.
34. Stone, *Eastern Front*, pp. 298–299.
35. Blok, *Poslednie dni*, p. 28.
36. Quoted in Bazili, *Rossiia*, p. 35.
37. Lenin, "Lecture on the 1905 Revolution," *CW*, 23:253.
38. Shliapnikov, *Semnadtsatyi god*, 1:40.
39. Blok, *Poslednie dni*, pp. 45–46.
40. Ibid., pp. 63, 64.
41. Nikolai N. Sukhanov, *Zapiski o revoliutsii* (Notes on the revolution), 7 vols., Berlin-Petrograd-Moscow, 1922–1923, 3:48.
42. V. Kaiurov, "Shest' dnei revoliutsii" (Six days of revolution), *Proletarskaia revoliutsiia*, no. 1, 1923, pp. 157–170.
43. Shulgin, *Dni*, p. 150.
44. Shliapnikov, *Semnadtsatyi god*, 1:119.
45. *Okitabr'skoe vooruzhennoe vosstanie*, (The armed October uprising), vol. 1, Moscow, 1957, p. 65.
46. See the first of Lenin's "Letter's from Afar," *CW*, 23:302.
47. Lenin, *CW*, 23:292.
48. Shliapnikov, *Semnadtsatyi god*, 2:183–184.
49. Vladimir D. Bonch-Bruevich, *Na boevykh postakh fevral'skoi i oktiabr'skoi revoliutsii* (At combat posts in the February and October revolutions), Moscow, 1931, p. 21.
50. V. I. Lenin, *Polnoe sobrarie sochinerii* (Complete collected works), 5th ed., Moscow, 1958–1959, 29:199. (Hereafter cited as *PSS*.)
51. Erich Ludendorff, *Meine Kriegserrinerungen*, Berlin, 1919.
52. Bonch-Bruevich, *Na boevykh*, pp. 23–24.
53. Sukhanov, *Zapiski*, 3:57.
54. Marc Ferro, *La révolution de 1917*, vol. 1, Paris, 1967, pp. 174–190.

55. *Malaia sovetskaia entsiklopediia* (Small Soviet encyclopedia), vol. 2, Moscow, 1930, p. 176. The information comes from the article on the All-Union Communist Party (Bolshevik).

56. Shliapnikov, *Semnadtsatyi god*, 3:107.

57. Maksim Gor'kii, *Zametki iz dnevnika. Vospominaniia* (Notes from a diary: Reminiscences), Berlin, 1924, p. 198.

58. Leon Trotsky, *Lenin*, Paris, 1925, p. 117.

59. *History of the Communist Party of the Soviet Union (Bolsheviks): Short Course*, New York, 1939, p. 194.

60. *Istoriia KPSS* (History of the CPSU), Moscow, 1959, p. 218.

61. Grigorii Zinoviev, *N. Lenin. Vladimir Il'ich Ul'ianov* (Lenin: Vladimir Ilyich Ulyanov), Petrograd, 1917, p. 56.

62. Bonch-Bruevich, *Na boevykh*, p. 77.

63. Leon Trotsky, *My Life*, New York, 1970, p. 313.

64. Lenin, *CW*, 25:167.

65. Ibid., p. 179.

66. Ibid., p. 216.

67. Ibid., 35:321.

68. Mark Aldanov, "Kartiny oktiabr'skoi revoliutsii" (Scenes of the October revolution), *Poslednie novosti* (Latest news), September 7, 1935.

69. Shliapnikov, *Semnadtsatyi god*, 1:50.

70. Ibid., p. 116.

71. Aldanov, "Kartiny."

72. W. S. Woytinsky, *Stormy Passage: A Personal History Through Two Revolutions to Democracy and Freedom*, New York, 1969, pp. 347–349.

73. William Henry Chamberlin, *The Russian Revolution, 1917–1921*, 2 vols., New York, 1935, 1:236.

74. Lenin, *CW*, 25:289.

75. *History of the CPSU, Short Course*, p. 205.

76. *Vsesoiuznoe soveshchanie istorikov* (All-Union Conference of Historians), Moscow, 1964, p. 281.

77. Lenin, *CW*, 26:84.

78. *Proletarskaia revoliutsiia*, no. 10, 1922.

79. Ibid.

80. Pierre Pascal, *Mon journal de Russie, 1916–1918*, Paris, 1975, pp. 214, 239. Putilov was one of Russia's leading industrialists.

81. Lenin, *CW*, 26:235.

82. *Pravda*, November 6, 1918.

83. In July 1917, when the press was full of articles denouncing the Bolsheviks as German collaborators, Lenin appealed to the editors of *Novaya zhizn* for help, asking them to publish a letter by himself, which began: "Permit us, comrades, to turn to your hospitality on account of the forced suspension of our Party paper." Lenin, *CW*, 25:179.

84. David R. Francis, *Russia from the American Embassy*, New York, 1921, pp. 177–178.

85. Trotsky, *History of the Russian Revolution*, 3:345.

86. N. Podvoisky, in *Vospominaniia o V. I. Lenine v 5 tomakh* (Recollections of Lenin in 5 volumes), Moscow, 1969, 2:449–450.

87. Leon Trotsky, *On Lenin*, London, 1971, pp. 91–92. Pereverzev was minister of justice

in the Provisional Government; his regime could hardly be considered "tyrannical."

88. Podvoisky, in *Vospominaniia o V. I. Lenine*, 2:449–450.

89. See Lenin's speech of February 28, 1921, in Lenin, *CW*, 32:153.

90. Ibid., 26:258–259.

91. Ibid., 25:281.

92. Sukhanov, *Zapiski*, 7:257.

93. S. P. Melgunov, *Kak bol'sheviki zakhvatili vlast'* (How the Bolsheviks seized power), Paris, 1953, p. 158.

94. Leon Trotskii, "Vospominaniia ob oktiabr'skoi revoliutsii" (Recollections of the October revolution), *Proletarskaia revoliutsiia*, no. 10, 1922, pp. 61–62.

95. An———skii, *Arkhiv russkoi revoliutsii*, vol. 1, pp. 48–49.

96. *Protokoly TsK RSDRP(b): Avgust 1917–fevral' 1918* (Minutes of the Central Committee of the Bolshevik party, August 1917–February 1918), Moscow, 1958, p. 136.

97. *Pravda*, October 26, 1917.

98. Trotsky, *History of the Russian Revolution*, 3:279.

99. A. Ia. Grunt, *Moskva 1917, revoliutsiia i kontrrevoliutsiia* (Moscow 1917, revolution and counterrevolution), Moscow, 1976.

100. Maksim Gor'kii, "Nesvoevremennye mysli" (Untimely thoughts), *Novaia zhizn'*, January 9, 1918.

101. Vladimir I. Nevskii, *Istoriia RKP* (History of the Russian Communist party), pt. 1, Moscow, 1926, p. 448.

102. Spirin, *Klassy i partii*, p. 59.

103. Bonch-Bruevich, *Na boevykh*, p. 245. (Lenin's biographers have not paid sufficient attention to the fact that Lenin often discussed the most serious questions while "laughing." Apparently he was a very cheerful person, although his was a most peculiar sense of humor.)

104. Ibid., pp. 243, 245, 249.

105. Ibid., p. 189.

106. *Novaia zhizn'*, January 9, 1918.

# CHAPTER TWO

1. Nicholas Berdyaev, *The Origins of Russian Communism*, Ann Arbor, 1960, p. 93.

2. Lenin, *CW*, 25:424–426, 462.

3. Ibid., 26:522.

4. Bonch-Bruevich, *Na boevykh*, p. 254.

5. *Malaia sovetskaia entsiklopediia*, vol. 1. See the article on the Brest-Litovsk treaty.

6. *Novaia zhizn'*, January 19, 1918.

7. Ibid., January 17, 1918.

8. Bonch-Bruevich, *Na boevykh*, p. 262.

9. Ibid., p. 296.

10. Ibid., p. 302.

11. *Izvestiia*, December 8, 1917.

12. Bonch-Bruevich, *Na boevykh*, p. 190.

13. Ibid., pp. 191–192.

14. Aleksandr Ia. Tairov, "V poiskakh stilia" (In search of style), *Teatr i dramaturgiia* (Theater and dramaturgy), no. 4, 1936, p. 202.

15. Evgenii Zamiatin, "Ia boius'" (I am afraid), in *Litsa* (Persons), New York, 1955, p. 186.

16. *Sobranie uzakonenii i rasporiazhenii rabochego i krest'ianskogo pravitel'stva* (Collected laws and decrees of the workers' and peasants' government), Petrograd, 1917, vol. 3.

17. Lenin, *CW*, 26:468.

18. *Novaia zhizn'*, May 21, 1918.

19. *Vestnik truda* (Herald of Labor), no. 3, 1920, p. 91.

20. *Professional'nyi vestnik* (Trade union herald), no. 7–8, 1918, p. 7.

21. A. Vol'skii, *Umstvennyi rabochii* (Intellectual worker), New York, 1968, p. 359.

22. *Kontinent* (Continent), no. 2, p. 387. An account of the "emergency conference" was published in pamphlet form in March 1918. Aleksandr Solzhenitsyn reprinted it in *Kontinent*, no. 2, 1975.

23. Ibid., pp. 415–416.

24. *Trudy I Vserossiiskogo s"ezda sovnarkhozov* (Proceedings of the First All-Russia Congress of Economic Councils), Moscow, 1918, p. 380.

25. Lenin, *Sobranie sochinenii* (Collected works), 2d ed., 1926, vols., 16, 19; 133–134.

26. B. Knipovich, *Ocherki deiatel'nosti Narodnogo komissariata zemledeliia za tri goda, 1917–1920* (Essays on the activities of the People's Commissariat of Agriculture for the three years 1917–1920), Moscow, 1920, p. 9.

27. Nikolai D. Kondratiev, *Rynok khlebov i ego regulirovanie vo vremia voiny i revoliutsii* (The grain market and its regulation during the war and revolution), Moscow, 1922, pp. 238–245.

28. Lenin, *CW*, 27:242, 245.

29. Ibid., 33:62.

30. Ibid., 27:253.

31. From the original version of "Immediate Tasks of the Soviet Government," published in Russian in the magazine *Kommunist* (Communist), no. 14, 1962, p. 13.

32. Lenin, *Sobranie sochinenii*, 2d ed., Moscow, 1926–1932, 24:569–570.

33. Lenin, *CW*, 36:529.

34. Ibid., 28:143.

35. Bonch-Bruevich, *Na boevykh*, p. 356.

36. Lenin, *PSS*, 27:150.

37. Ibid., 24:441.

38. Ibid., 24:443.

39. Ibid., 25:212.

40. Ibid., 27:268–269.

41. Ibid., 36:200.

42. Bonch-Bruevich, *Na boevykh*, p. 153.

43. Hermann Rauschning, *Gespräche mit Hitler*, 1940, p. 143.

44. *Khleb i revoliutsiia. Prodovol'stvennaia politika Kommunisticheskoi partii i sovetskogo pravitel'stva v 1917–22 gg.* (Bread and revolution: The food policy of the Communist party and Soviet government, 1917–22), Moscow, 1972, p. 41.

45. Lenin, *CW*, 35:558.

46. Trotsky, *On Lenin*, p. 115.

47. Martyn I. Latsis (Sudrabs), *ChK v bor'be s kontrrevoliutsiei* (The Cheka in the struggle against the counterrevolution), Moscow, 1921, p. 8.

48. Pavel Malkov, *Zapiski komendanta moskovskogo kremlia* (Memoirs of the commandant

of the Moscow Kremlin), Moscow, 1962, p. 163. Malkov writes with pride that he personally shot Kaplan.

49. Yakov Kh. Peters, "Vospominaniia o rabote v VChK v pervyi god revoliutsii" (Recollections of Cheka work in the first year of the revolution), *Byloe*, no. 47, 1933, p. 123.

50. *Ezhenedel'nik VChK* (Cheka weekly), no. 1, 1918, p. 11.

51. Latsis, *ChK v bor'be*, p. 54.

52. Leon Trotskii, *Kak vooruzhalas' revoliutsiia* (How the revolution armed), vol. 1, Moscow, 1923, p. 216.

53. Leon Trotskii, *Sochineniia* (Works), vol. 17, Moscow, 1926, pt. 1, pp. 290–291.

54. Trotskii, *Kak vooruzhalas'*, vol. 1, pp. 232–233.

55. Cf. Lenin, *CW*, 36:489. (My rendering of Lenin's Russian differs here from the rather inadequate official translation, which gives, for example, "suspects" for "suspicious elements." The Russian text is in Lenin, *PSS*, 5th ed., 50:143–144—Tr.)

56. *Ezhenedel'nik VChK*, no. 1, p. 11.

57. *Iz istorii VChK, 1917–1921* (From the history of the Cheka, 1917–1921), Moscow, 1958, p. 58.

58. Lenin, *CW*, 27:33.

59. *Sobranie uzakonenii* (Collected statutes), no. 44, 1918, p. 536.

60. Latsis, *ChK v bor'be*, p. 56.

61. *Izvestiia*, July 19, 1918.

62. *Dekrety sovetskoi vlasti* (Decrees of the Soviet government), vol. 4, Moscow, 1968, p. 627.

63. "Stenogramma vystupleniia F. E. Dzerzhinskogo na 8-m zasendanii VTsIK 17 fevralia 1919 g." (Stenogram of F. E. Dzerzhinsky's speech at the eighth session of the All-Russia Central Executive Committee, February 17, 1919), in *Istoricheskii arkhiv* (Historical archive), no. 1, 1958, pp. 6–11.

64. *Ezhenedel'nik VChK*, no. 2, p. 11.

65. Central Committee resolution of December 12, 1918, in reference to a report by Dzerzhinsky on "malicious articles about the Cheka that have appeared in the press."

66. *Krasnaia kniga VChK* (Red book of the Cheka), ed. P. Makintsian, vol. 1, Moscow, 1920, p. 111.

67. Ibid., p. 208.

68. Ibid., p. 210.

69. I. I. Vatsetis, "Miatezh levykh eserov" (The left SR revolt) in *Prometei* (Prometheus) (Moscow), no. 4, 1967, p. 250. Also, *Krasnaia kniga VChK*, p. 211.

70. Vatsetis, *Miatezh*, p. 253.

71. *Krasnaia kniga VChK*, p. 231.

72. *Pravda*, July 8, 1918.

73. Andrei Belyi, *Peterburg* (Petersburg), Moscow, 1978, p. 23.

74. Decree of March 20, 1917, in *Sbornik ukazov i postanovlenii Vremennogo Pravitel'stva* (Collected laws and decrees of the Provisional Government), vol. 1, Petrograd, 1917, pp. 46–49.

75. Joseph Stalin, (*Sochneniia*) (Works), Moscow, 1947, 4:5.

76. D. Doroshenko, *Istoriia Ukrainy 1917–1923* (History of the Ukraine, 1917–1923), Uzhgorod, 1932, pp. 44–45.

77. See S. A. Piontkovskii, *Grazhdanskaia voina v Rossii: Khrestomatiia* (The civil war in Russia: Readings), Moscow, 1925, p. 344.

78. Quoted by Ivan Koshelivets', in "Mykola Skrypnik," *Suchasnist'* (Present day), 1972, p. 21.
79. Ibid., p. 20.
80. *Dekrety sovetskoi vlasti* (Decrees of the Soviet government), vol. 1, Moscow, 1957, p. 40.
81. I. L. Groshev and O. I. Chechenkina, *Kritika burzhuaznoi fal'tsifikatsii natsional'noi politiki KPSS* (Critique of the bourgeois falsification of CPSU nationalities policy), Moscow, 1974, p. 89.
82. Richard Pipes, *The Formation of the Soviet Union*, Cambridge, 1964, p. 90.
83. Ibid., p. 16.
84. Spirin, *Klassy i partii*, p. 418.
85. A. Stavrovskii, *Zakavkaz's posle oktiabria* (Transcaucasia after October), Moscow-Leningrad, 1925, p. 38.
86. V. I. Lenin, *Sochineniia* (Works), 4th ed. Moscow, 1941–1967, vol. 17.
87. Ibid., 20:29.
88. S. Gililov, *V. I. Lenin — organizator sovetskogo mnogonatsional'nogo gosudarstva* (V. I. Lenin, organizer of the Soviet multinational state), Moscow, 1960, p. 25.
89. Stalin, *Sochineniia*, 4:85–89.
90. Ibid., p. 32.
91. A. A. Gordeev, *Istoriia kazakov* (History of the Cossacks), pt. 3, Paris, 1970, p. 271.
92. *Znamia truda* (Banner of labor), May 16, 1918.
93. F. Popov, *Chekho-slovatskii miatezh i samarskaia uchredilka* (The Czechoslovak uprising and the Samara constituent assembly government), Samara, 1939, pp. 44–46.
94. See, for example, Izvestiia, April 9, May 11, and May 19, 1918, for coverage of revolts prompted by hunger in Pavlov-Posad, Rybinsk, Zvenigorod, and Kolpino.
95. *Krasnaia kniga VChK*, pp. 101–115, 123.
96. Leon Trotsky, *Terrorism and Communism*, Ann Arbor, 1961, p. 58.
97. Trotskii, *Kak vooruzhalas'*, 1:123–124.
98. E. Gorodetskii, "O zapiskakh N. M. Potapova" (On N. M. Potapov's Memoirs), *Voenno-istoricheskii zhurnal* (Military-historical journal), 1968, no. 1.
99. *Petrogradskaia pravda* (Petrograd truth), April 21, 22, 1918.
100. Trotskii, *Kak vooruzhalas'*, 1:135.
101. Isaac Deutscher, *The Prophet Armed*, London, 1954, pp. 429–430.
102. Anton I. Denikin, *Ocherki russkoi smuty* (Sketches of the Russian turmoil), vol. 3, Berlin, 1926, p. 146.
103. Mikhail V. Frunze, *Izbrannye proizvedeniia* (Selected works), Moscow, 1934. p. 228.
104. Leon Trotskii, *Sochineniia* (Works), 21 vols., Moscow-Leningrad, 1926, 17(2):326.
105. Leon Trotsky, *Stalin: An Appraisal of the Man and His Influence*, New York, 1941, p. 284.
106. Robert Bruce Lockhart, *Memoirs of a British Agent*, London, 1952, p. 287.
107. Denikin, *Ocherki*, 5:146.
108. Ibid., p. 118.
109. G. K. Gins, "Sibir', soiuzniki i Kolchak" (Siberia, the Allies, and Kolchak), in *Kolchakovshchina. Iz belykh memuarov* (The Kolchak regime: From White memoirs), Leningrad, 1930, p. 29.
110. This decree of the Workers' and Peasants' Government of the Ukraine, dated February 11, 1919, is quoted by M. Kubanin, *Makhnovshchina* (The Makhno movement), Leningrad, 1928, p. 54.

111. Vladimir P. Muliutin, *Sotsializm i sel'skoe khoziaistvo* (Socialism and agriculture), quoted in Kubanin, *Makhnovshchina*, p. 59.

112. Joachim I. Vatsetis, "Vospominaniia" (Memoirs), *Pamiat'. Istoricheskii sbornik* (Memory: A historical anthology), no. 2, Moscow, 1977; Paris, 1979, p. 69.

113. See Deutscher, *Prophet Armed*, p. 436.

114. Stalin, *Sochineniia*, 4:118.

115. *Pravda*, September 20, 1963.

116. "Tsirkuliarnoe pis'mo Orgbiuro TsK RKP(b) vsem otvetstvennym rabotnikam v kazach'ikh voiskakh" (Circular letter of the Orgburo of the Bolshevik party Central Committee to all responsible officials in Cossack regions), quoted in M. Bernshtam, "Storony v grazhdanskoi voine 1917–1921 gg." (The sides in the civil war, 1917–1921), *Vestnik russkogo khristianskogo dvizheniia* (Herald of the Russian Christian movement) (Paris, New York, Moscow), no. 128, 1979, p. 301.

117. Ibid., p. 317.

118. See Vatsetis, "Vospominaniia," p. 72.

119. Lenin, *CW*, 44:166.

120. Vladimir G. Korolenko, "Iz dnevnikov 1917–1921 gg." (From diaries of 1917–1921), *Pamiat'*, no. 2, p. 392.

121. See *Internatsionalisty. Trudiashchiesia zarubezhnykh stran—uchastniki bor'by za vlast' Sovetov na iuge i vostoke respubliki* (Internationalists: Laborers from foreign countries who helped fight for Soviet power in the southern and eastern parts of the republic), Moscow, 1971; L. I. Zharov and V. M. Ustinov, *Internatsional'nye chasti Krasnoi armii v boiakh za vlast' Sovetov v gody inostrannoi voennoi interventsii i grazhdanskoi voiny v SSSR* (The international units of the Red Army in the battles for Soviet power during the foreign military intervention and civil war in the USSR), Moscow, 1960; *Latyshskie strelki v bor'be za sovetskuiu vlast' v 1917–1920 gg. Vospominaniia i dokumenty* (The Latvian rifles in the struggle for Soviet power, 1917–1920: Memoirs and documents), Riga, 1962.

122. Adolf Jozwienko, "Misja Marchlewskiego w 1919 roku na tle stosunkow polsko-radziechich" (Marchlewski's 1919 mission against the background of Polish–Soviet relations), in *Z badan nad wplywem i znaczeniem rewolucji rosyjskich 1917 roku* (Research on the influence and significance of the Russian revolutions of 1917), Wroclaw, 1968.

123. *L'internationale communiste*, December 25, 1919.

124. Trotskii, *Kak vooruzhalas'*, 3:165.

125. Karl Radek, "O kharaktere voiny s beloi Pol'shei" (The nature of the war with White Poland), *Pravda*, December 11, 12, 1920.

126. N. E. Kakurin and V. A. Melikov, *Voina s belopoliakami* (War with the White Poles), Moscow, 1925, p. 475.

127. Lenin, *CW*, 25:238.

128. See Adolf Jozwienko, *Polska a "biala" Rosja (od listopada 1918 do kwietnia 1920)* (Poland and "White" Russia, November 1918 to April 1920), Wroclaw, 1979, p. 235.

129. Trotskii, *Kak vooruzhalas'*, 2(2):166.

130. L. O. Frossard, *De Jaurès à Lenine. Notes et souvenirs d'un militant*, Paris, 1930, p. 137.

131. G. V. Kuz'min, *Razgrom interventov i belogvardeitsev v 1917–22* (The smashing of the interventionists and White Guards, 1917–22), Moscow, 1977.

132. Ibid., p. 357.

133. Sergei S. Kamenev, *Zapiski o grazhdanskoi voine i voennom stroitel'stve* (Notes on the civil war and on building the military), Moscow, 1963, p. 167.

134. Compare Norman Davies, *White Eagle, Red Star: The Polish–Soviet War*, London, 1972, p. 92. According to this British historian's estimates, the French loans to Poland during its war with the USSR (375 million francs) were comparable to the amount the French army had spent in a single day during World War I.

135. Karl Radek, *Vneshniaia politika sovetskoi Rossii* (Foreign policy of Soviet Russia), Moscow-Leningrad, 1923, p. 61.

136. Davies, *White Eagle*, p. 174.

137. Ibid., p. 169.

138. Maxime Weygand, *Mémoires*, vol. 2, Paris, 1957, p. 166.

139. Lord D'Abernon, *The Eighteenth Decisive Battle of World History*, London, 1931, pp. 8–9, 11.

140. See Peter Arshinov, *History of the Makhnovist Movement*, Detroit and Chicago, 1974.

141. Kuz'min, *Razgrom*, p. 366.

142. *Kommunisty Urala v gody grazhdanskoi voiny* (The Communists of the Urals during the civil war), Sverdlovsk, 1959, p. 172.

143. Spirin, *Klassy i partii*, p. 262.

144. I. Ia. Trifonov, *Klassy i klassovaia bor'ba v SSSR*, (Classes and the class struggle in the USSR), Leningrad, 1964, p. 73.

145. A. I. Khriashcheva, *Gruppy i klassy v krest'ianstve* (Groups and classes within the peasantry), Moscow, 1924, p. 62.

146. Trifonov, *Klassy*, p. 54.

147. Lenin, *CW*, 28:56.

148. Ibid., 30:482–483.

149. P. G. Sofinov, *Ocherki istorii VChK* (Essays in the history of the Cheka), Moscow, 1960, p. 82.

150. Mikhail I. Kalinin, *Za eti gody* (During these years), vol. 2, Moscow, 1926, p. 92.

151. The text of Mironov's letter has not been published in Russian. It is quoted in French in Roy Medvedev, *La Révolution d'octobre était-elle inéluctable?* Paris, 1976, pp. 134–180. Lengthy excerpts in English may be found in Sergei Starikov and Roy Medvedev, *Philip Mironov and the Russian Civil War*, New York, 1978, pp. 145–153.

152. M. Kubanin, *Makhnovshchina*, p. 61.

153. Report by Iakov A. Iakovlev on "The Struggle Against Banditry," to the Fifth Ukraine-wide Party Conference in 1920, quoted in ibid., p. 61.

154. G. Lelevich, *Strekopytovshchina* (The Strekopytov revolt), Moscow, 1923, p. 36.

155. *Chapan* was the term for the type of peasant's smock or blouse worn in this region.

156. B. Chistov, "Chapannoe vosstanie. Istoricheskaia spravka" (The Chapan revolt: A historical review), in A. Veselyi, *Chapany* (The Chapan rebels), Kuibyshev, 1936.

157. The Muslim peasants who fought the Soviet authorities from 1918 to 1927 were labeled *basmachi* ("bandits"). The peasant rebels referred to themselves as *beklar kharekati* ("freedom fighters movement").

158. Mikhail V. Pokrovskii, *Kontrrevoliutsiia za 4 goda* (Four years of counterrevolution), Moscow, 1922, p. 4.

159. Trifonov, *Klassy*, pp. 3–4, 259.

160. N. Kakurin, *Kak srazhalas' revoliutsiia* (How the revolution fought), 2 vols., Moscow-Leningrad, 1925–1926, 2 vols., 2:137.

161. From a leaflet issued by the Political Directorate of the Red Army's Western Front, quoted in Trifonov, *Klassy*, p. 112.

162. Trifonov, *Klassy*, p. 260.

163. Ibid., p. 265.

164. Leonidov, "Esero-banditizm v Tambovskoi gubernii i bor'ba s nim" (SR banditry in Tambov Province and the struggle against it), *Revoliutsiia i voina* (Revolution and war), no. 14–15, 1922, p. 168.

165. Trifonov, *Klassy*, pp. 215–216.

166. *Antonovshchina: Sbornik statei i vospominanii* (The Antonov revolt: Collected articles and memoirs, published by the Bureau of Party History of the Tambov Province Committee of the Bolshevik party), Tambov, 1923, p. 24.

167. On February 6, 1921, Lenin sent Sklyansky a note suggesting he use armored trains, armored cars, and airplanes against the "bandits." Lenin, *CW*, 35:474.

168. D. Smirnov, *Zapiski chekista* (Notes of a Cheka agent), Minsk, 1972.

169. *Antonovshchina*, pp. 45–46.

170. Trifonov, *Klassy*, pp. 94, 212, 219. The Soviet historian Trifonov had access to party archives that are rarely made available. In Siberia, by order of the Siberian Revolutionary Committee (*revkom*) of February 12, 1921, the local population was made responsible for the protection of railroad tracks. Hostages were taken who, in the event of repeated attacks on the rail lines, could be shot and their property confiscated.

171. Mikhail Tukhachevskii, *Voina i revoliutsiia* (War and revolution), no. 7, 1927, p. 16.

172. *Iz istorii VChK. Sbornik dokumentov* (From the history of the Cheka: Collected documents), Moscow, 1957, p. 437.

173. Lenin, *CW*, 30:483.

174. G. V. Sharapov, *Razreshenie agrarnogo voprosa v Rossii posle pobedy Oktiabr'skoi revoliutsii* (Resolution of the agrarian problem in Russia after the victory of the October revolution), Moscow, 1961, p. 165.

175. Trifonov, *Klassy*, pp. 96–97.

176. Ibid., p. 98.

177. Trifonov, *Klassy*, p. 110.

178. Kubanin, *Makhnovshchina*, p. 63.

179. Nestor Makhno, *Pod udarami kontrrevoliutsii* (Under the blows of the counterrevolution), vol. 2, Paris, 1936, pp. 125–126.

180. Fedor Dan, *Dva goda skitanii (1919–1921)* (Two years of wandering, 1919–1921), Berlin, 1922, p. 122.

181. The decree is in *Pravda*, January 22, 1921.

182. Dan, *Dva goda*, p. 107.

183. The full text of the *Petropavlovsk* resolution is in English in Paul Avrich, *Kronstadt 1921*, New York, 1974, pp. 73–74. For the Russian text, see *Pravda o Kronshtadte* (The truth about Kronstadt), Prague, 1921, p. 9.

184. The text of the March 2 order is in the documentary collection of writings by Lenin and Trotsky entitled *Kronstadt*, New York, 1979, pp. 65–66. See also *Pravda o Kronshtadte*, p. 13.

185. The text of Trotsky's order of March 5 is in English in *Kronstadt*, p. 67.

186. The English text of this proclamation is in Avrich, *Kronstadt 1921*, pp. 241–243. For the Russian, see *Pravda o Kronshtadte*, p. 23.

187. I. A. Shchetnikov, *Sorvannyi zagovor* (The foiled plot), Moscow, 1978, p. 93.

188. *Krasnyi mech* (Kiev), August 18, 1919.

189. Avrich, *Kronstadt 1921*, p. 217.
190. See, for example, Shcetinikov, *Sorvannyi zagovor*, p. 102; Avrich, *Kronstadt 1921*, p. 231.

## CHAPTER THREE

1. *Istorik-marksist* (Marxist historian), no. 2, 1940, p. 12.
2. S. I. Iakubovskii, *Ob"edinitel'noe dvizhenie za obrazovanie SSSR, 1917–1922* (The unification movement for the founding of the USSR, 1917–1922), Moscow, 1947, p. 99.
3. Filipp Makharadze, *Sovety i bor'ba za sovetskuiu vlast' v Gruzii, 1917–1921* (The Soviets and the struggle for Soviet power in Georgia, 1917–1921), Tiflis, 1928, p. 223.
4. See Pipes, *Formation*, p. 236. S. S. Kamenev's February 17, 1921, letter discussing this matter was addressed to Sklyansky, then transmitted to Lenin; it is reproduced in *The Trotsky Papers, 1917–1922*, ed. by Jan. M. Meijer, 2 vols., The Hague, 1964–1971, 2:378–379.
5. G. Zhvaniia, "V. I. Lenin i partiinaia organizatsiia Gruzii v period bor'by za sovetskuiu vlast'" (V. I. Lenin and the Georgian party organization during the struggle for Soviet power), *Zaria vostoka* (Dawn of the East) (Tiflis), April 21, 1961.
6. Noi Zhordania, *Moia zhizn'* (My life), Stanford, 1968, p. 109.
7. Lenin, *CW*, 33:62.
8. Ibid., 32:215–216.
9. Statement by Aleksandr D. Tsiurupa, commissar of food supply, *Pravda*, April 30, 1925.
10. Piontkovskii, *Grazhdanskaia voina*, p. 456.
11. Lenin, *CW*, 33:96.
12. Yuri Larin, "Proizvodstvennaia propaganda i sovetskoe khoziaistvo na rubezhe chetvertogo goda. Doklad na s"ezde politprosvetov, 4.11.1920" (Production propaganda and the Soviet economy at the beginning of the fourth year: Report to the Congress of Political Education Workers, November 4, 1920).
13. Trotsky, "Report on the Organization of Labor" (presented to the Third All-Russia Congress of Trade Unions, April 4, 1920), quoted in his *Terrorism and Communism*, Ann Arbor, 1961, pp. 132–176.
14. Ibid., p. 144.
15. Ibid., p. 142.
16. Iu. A. Poliakov, *1921: Pobeda nad golodom* (1921: Victory over famine), Moscow, 1975, pp. 14, 19–20.
17. Mikhail Osorgin, *Vremena* (Times), Paris, 1955, p. 159.
18. *Poslednie novosti*, April 19, 1930.
19. A. Beliakov, *Iunost' vozhdia* (The Great Leader's youth), Moscow, 1960, p. 82.
20. Lenin, Letter to Nikolai Semashko, July 12, 1921, *CW*, 45:208–209.
21. Elizaveta Kuskova, "Mesiats soglashatel'stva" (A month of collaborationism), *Volia Rossii* (The will of Russia), nos. 3–5, 1928.
22. Lenin, *PSS*, 52:80, 322–323.
23. Lenin, *CW*, 45:89.
24. Quoted in Kuskova, "Mesiats soglashatel'stva."
25. *Great Soviet Encyclopedia*, English ed. New York, 1973, 1:338.
26. Prokopovich, *Narodnoe khoziaistvo SSSR*, 1:59.

27. M. Maksudov, "Losses Suffered by the Population of the USSR, 1918–1958," in *Samizdat Register II*, New York, 1981, pp. 220–276.
28. *Poslednie novosti*, November 11, 1921.
29. Maksim Gor'kii, *O russkom krest'ianstve* (On the Russian peasantry), Berlin, 1922, pp. 43–44.
30. Ibid., pp. 40–41.
31. *Krasnaia gazeta* (Red gazette), September 6, 1921.
32. Quoted in Elizaveta Drabkina, "Zimnii pereval" (Winter crossing), *Novyi mir* (New world), no. 10, 1968, p. 62.
33. G. Z. Besedovskii, *Na putiakh k termidoru* (On the road to Thermidor), Paris, 1930, pp. 121–122.
34. Radek, *Vneshniaia politika Sovetskoi Rossii*, pp. 76–77.
35. Karl Radek, *Piat' let Kominterna* (Five years of the Comintern), 2 vols., Moscow, 1924, 1:228.
36. Lev Kamenev, "Leninizm ili trotskizm" (Leninism or Trotskyism), in *Ob "Urokakh oktiabria"* (On [Trotsky's] "Lessons of October"), Leningrad, 1924, p. 3.
37. Lenin, *PSS*, 31:465.
38. Ibid., 27:112.
39. Stalin, *Sochineniia*, 6:37.
40. Nikolai Aseev, *Stikhotvoreniia i poemy* (Verse and narrative poems), Leningrad, 1967, p. 465.
41. Andrei Platonov, *Chevengur*, Ann Arbor, 1978, pp. 135, 137.
42. I. S. Kondurushkin, *Chastnyi kapital pered sovetskim sudom* (Private capital before the Soviet court of justice), Moscow-Leningrad, 1927, p. 48.
43. Mikhail Bulgakov, *Ranniaia neizdannaia proza* (Early unpublished prose), Munich, 1976, p. 53.
44. *Pravda*, April 17, 1921.
45. *Dvenadtsatyi s"ezd RKP(b). Stenograficheskii otchet* (Twelfth Party Congress: Stenographic record), pp. 144–145.
46. Lenin, *CW*, 33:287–288.
47. Ibid., p. 274–275.
48. S. I. Liberman, *Dela i liudi* (Deeds and people), New York, 1944, p. 115.
49. Aleksandra Kollontai, "Rabochaia oppozitsiia" (The Workers' opposition), quoted in Emelian Iaroslavskii, *Kratkaia istoriia VKP(b)* (Brief history of the All-Union Communist party [Bolshevik]), Moscow, 1930, p. 348.
50. Lenin, *CW*, 33:309.
51. Trotskii, *Sochineniia* (Works), 17(2):325.
52. Stalin, *Sochineniia*, 5:71.
53. Yurii Libedinskii, *Nedelia*, in *Nashi dni* (Our days), vol. 2, Moscow, 1922, pp. 108–109.
54. Ibid, p. 111.
55. Ibid., pp. 110–111. In later editions, Libedinskii expurgated his novel of all such realistic details from the Soviet life of the early 1920s.
56. Gor'kii, "Nesvoevremennye mysli" *Novaia zhizn'*, November 7 (20), 1917.
57. *Pravda*, November 12, 1921.
58. Ibid., March 21, 1926.
59. Rosa Luxemburg, *The Russian Revolution*, Ann Arbor, 1961, pp. 71–72.
60. Lenin, *CW*, 33:279.
61. Ibid., 31:49.

62. Ibid.
63. Stalin, *Sochineniia*, 5:386.
64. Merle Fainsod, *Smolensk Under Soviet Rule*, Cambridge, 1958, pp. 42–43.
65. See, for example, E. E. Kruze, *Polozhenie rabochego klassa v Rossii v 1900–1914* (The condition of the working class in Russia, 1900–1914), Leningrad, 1976.
66. *Pravda*, November 15, 1923.
67. Ibid., November 22, 1923.
68. Anastas Mikoian, *V nachale dvadtsatykh* (The early twenties), Moscow, 1975, p. 250.
69. Fainsod, *Smolensk*, p. 43.
70. Nikita Struve, *Les chrétiens en U.R.S.S.*, Paris, 1963, p. 20.
71. *Voprosy istorii religii i ateizma* (Problems in the history of religion and atheism), Vol. 5, Moscow, 1968, pp. 16–20.
72. Kuskova, "Mesiats soglashatel'stva."
73. *Pravda*, November 17, 1922.
74. *Vestnik RSKhD* (RSKhD Herald) (Paris, New York), no, 98, 1970, p. 57. Cf. *Uncensored Russia*, New York, 1970, pp. 319–320.
75. *Vestnik RSKhD*, no. 98, 1970, p. 56.
76. Struve, *Les chrétiens*, p. 32.
77. Anatolii Levitin and Vadim Shavrov, *Ocherki po istorii russkoi tserkovnoi smuty* (Essays in the history of the turmoil in the Russian church), 3 vols., 1977, 1:54. [r86]
78. Mikhail Gorev, "Agoniia tserkovnoi kontrrevoliutsii" (Death agony of the clerical counterrevolution), *Izvestiia*, June 2, 1922.
79. Lenin, *PSS*, 51:48.
80. Ibid., p. 52.
81. D. L. Golinkov, *Krushenie antisovetskogo podpol'ia v SSSR* (The downfall of the anti-Soviet underground in the USSR), vol. 2, Moscow, 1980, p. 115.
82. Compare the accounts in Sofinov, *Ocherki*; Golinkov, *Krushenie*; and the collection of documents, *V. I. Lenin i VChK* (Lenin and the Cheka), Moscow, 1975, p. 640.
83. Liberman, *Dela*, p. 93.
84. Lenin, *PSS*, 53:169.
85. Victor Serge, *Memoirs of a Revolutionary*, London, 1967, p. 150.
86. Il'ia Erenburg; "Rvach" (Self-seeker), in *Sobranie sochinenii* (Collected works), vol. 2, Moscow, 1964, p. 79.
87. *Pravda*, March 1, 1923.
88. Golinkov, *Krushenie*, pp. 156–157.
89. Lenin, *CW*, 45:555.
90. I. Voznesenskii, "Imena i sud'by. Nad iubileinom spiskom AN" (Names and destinies: On the anniversary listing of members of the Academy of Sciences), in *Pamiat'*, no. 1 (circulated in Moscow in 1976; reprinted in New York, 1978), p. 377.
91. Lenin, *CW*, 45:555.
92. Ibid., 33:358.
93. Ibid., 42:418.
94. Ibid., 33:358–359.
95. Leszek, Kolakowski, *Glowne nurty marksizmu* (Main currents of Marxism), vol. 2, Paris, 1977, p. 518.
96. G. Fediukin, *Velikii oktiabr' i intelligentsiia* (Great October and the intelligentsia), Moscow, 1972, p. 287.
97. Lenin, *CW*, 32:455.
98. P. E. Kovalevskii, *Zarubezhnaia Rossiia* (Russia abroad), Paris, 1972, p. 12.

99. I. Ia. Trifonov, *Likvidatsiia ekspluatatorskikh klassov v SSSR* (The elimination of the exploiting classes in the USSR), Moscow, 1975, p. 169.
100. Fediukin, *Velikii oktiabr'*, p. 233.
101. Ibid., p. 271.
102. I. Gurovich, *Zapiski emigranta* (Notes of an emigré), Petrograd-Moscow, 1923, p. 166.
103. D. Aminado, *Poezd na tret'em puti* (Train on track three), New York, 1954, pp. 282–283.
104. Ibid.
105. N. Ustrialov, *V bor'be za Rossiiu* (In the struggle for Russia), Harbin, 1920, p. 63.
106. Ibid., p. 21.
107. Ibid., p. 47.
108. Ibid., p. 34.
109. Ibid., p. 55.
110. Ibid., p. 36.
111. Ibid., p. 69.
112. Ibid., p. 48.
113. Ibid., p. 36.
114. Ibid., p. 55.
115. Vasilii Shulgin, *1920 god* (The year 1920), Sofia, 1922, pp. 275–276.
116. N. Ustrialov, *Pod znakom revoliutsii* (Under the sign of revolution), Harbin, 1927, p. 26.
117. Ibid., p. 15.
118. Ibid., p. 28.
119. Ibid.
120. *Bol'shaia sovetskaia entsiklopediia*, 1st ed., Moscow, 1926–1947, 64:162.
121. Ustrialov, *Pod znakom*, p. 70.
122. *Izvestiia*, October 13, 1921.
123. *Pravda*, October 14, 1921.
124. Ustrialov, *Pod znakom* p. 70.
125. Ibid., p. 102.
126. Ibid., p. 142.
127. *Pravda*, September 3, 1922.
128. Ustrialov, *Pod znakom*, p. 111.
129. Stalin, *Sochineniia*, 5:244, 245.
130. I. P. Trainin, *SSSR i natsional'nye problemy* (The USSR and nationality problems), Moscow, 1924, p. 26.
131. Lenin, *CW*, 36:606.
132. Mariia Skrypnik, *Vospominaniia ob Il'iche* (Memories of Ilyich [Lenin]), Moscow, 1965, pp. 68–69.
133. Stalin, *Sochineniia*, 5:301–312.
134. V. V. Pentkovskaia, "Rol' V. I. Lenina v obrazovanii SSSR" (Lenin's role in the formation of the USSR), *Voprosy istorii*, no. 3, 1956, p. 17.
135. *Kommunist*, no. 10, 1956, p. 37.
136. Zh. L. Zlatopol'skii, *Obrazovanie i razvitie SSSR kak soiuznogo gosudarstva* (The formation and development of the USSR as a state based on union), Moscow, 1954, pp. 132–133.
137. Lenin's "Letter to the Congress" in the official Soviet-approved English translation, is in Lenin, *CW*, 36:593ff.

138. Lenin, *CW*, 32:61.

139. Ibid., 30:476.

140. Ibid., 33:315.

141. Boris Souvarine, "Staline: Pourquoi et comment," *Est et Ouest*, no. 602, November 1–15, 1977.

142. Leon Trotskii, *Uroki oktiabria* (Lessons of October), Moscow, 1924, p. 28.

143. Quoted in Iaroslavskii, *Kratkaia istoriia*, pp. 391–393. Cf. the English version in E. H. Carr, *The Interregnum, 1923–1924*, Baltimore, 1969, pp. 375–376.

144. Boris Souvarine, *Staline: Aperçu historique du bolchevisme*, Paris, 1977, p. 352.

145. Liberman, *Dela*, p. 80.

146. Iaroslavskii, *Kratkaia istoriia*, p. 387.

147. See Leon Trotsky, *Challenge of the Left Opposition, 1923–1925*, New York, 1975, p. 161.

148. V. Kolbanovskii, "Izuchenie mozga Lenina" (The study of Lenin's brain), *Molodaia gvardiia*, (Young guard), no. 2, 1929, p. 81.

149. Marietta Shaginian, *Dnevniki* (Diaries), Leningrad, 1930, p. 39.

150. *Bol'shevik* (Bolshevik), no. 8, 1925.

151. *Leningradskaia pravda* (Leningrad truth), July 26, 1925.

152. M. Larsons, *Na sovetskoi sluzhbe Zapiski spetsa* (In the Soviet service: Notes of a specialist), Paris, 1930, p. 70.

153. Kondurushkin, *Chastnyi kapital*, p. 220.

154. *Pravda*, September 4, 1922.

155. Stalin, *Sochineniia*, 9:192.

156. Quoted in G. Furman, "Antialkogol'naia nedelia" (Anti-alcohol week), *Revoliutsiia i kul'tura* (Revolution and culture), no. 18, 1929, p. 72.

157. Ibid., p. 73.

158. Kondurushkin, *Chastnyi kapital*, p. 221.

159. Clara Zetkin, *Lenin on the Emancipation of Women*, Moscow, n.d., p. 102.

160. Lev Gumilevskii, *Sobachii pereulok* (Dogs' alley), Riga, 1928, pp. 204–205.

161. Nikolai Bukharin and Evgeny Preobrazhenskii, *Azbuka kommunizma* (The ABCs of communism), Moscow, 1928, p. 126.

162. A. Goikhberg, *Zakon o brake* (Marriage law), Moscow, 1922, p. 63.

163. *Malaia sovetskaia entsiklopedia*, vol. 10.

164. V. N. Shulgin, *Pedagogika perekhodnogo perioda* (Pedagogy in the transitional period), Moscow, 1927, p. 97.

165. V. Katan'ian, "Protokoly o nesostoiatel'nosti" (Record of Bankruptcy), *Molodaia gvardiia*, no. 17, 1930, p. 103.

166. *Malaia sovetskaia entsiklopediia*, vol. 1.

167. *Pravda*, December 2, 1925.

168. Lenin, *PSS*, 33:55.

169. *Narodnoe obrazovanie v SSSR (sbornik dokumentov) 1917–1973*, (Popular education in the USSR [collected documents] 1917–1973), Moscow, 1974, p. 377.

170. Mikhail Koltsov, *Izbrannye proizvedeniia v 3 tomakh* (Selected works in 3 volumes), Moscow, 1957, 1:578.

171. Struve, *Les chrétiens*, p. 39.

172. Lev Regel'son, *Tragediia russkoi tserkvi, 1917–1945* (Tragedy of the Russian church, 1917–1945), Paris, 1977, p. 118.

173. Stalin, *Sochineniia*, 10:133.

174. *Za rubezhom. Khronika sem'i Zernovykh* (Abroad: The Zernov family's chronicle), Paris, 1926, p. 72.

175. Pavel Miliukov, *Emigratsiia na pereput'e* (The emigration at the crossroads), Paris, 1926, p. 72.

176. *Iskhod k vostoku* (Exodus to the East), Sofia, 1921, p. iv.

177. Ibid., p. 1.

178. Ibid., p. 2.

179. Ibid., p. vii.

180. Ibid., p. 83.

181. V. S. Varshavskii, *Nezamechennoe pokolenie* (The unnoticed generation), New York, 1966, p. 53.

182. *Evraziistvo (opyt sistematicheskogo izlozheniia)* (Eurasianism—an attempt at a systematic exposition), n.p., 1926, p. 47.

183. G. Fedotov, *I est' i budet* (That which is shall be), Paris, 1932, p. 133.

184. Vladimir Nabokov, "Godovshchina" (Anniversary), *Rul'* (The helm) (Paris), November 18, 1927.

185. Stalin, *Sochineniia*, 9:192.

186. The speaker was Glebov-Avilov, of the oppositional Leningrad delegation. See the stenographic record of the Fourteenth Congress: *Chetyrnadtsatyi s"ezd VKP(b). Stenograficheskii otchet*, Moscow, 1926, p. 791.

187. "Letter of the Thirteen," L. Trotskii, in *Challenge of the Left Opposition, 1926–1927*, New York, 1980, p. 761.

188. *Pravda*, November 28, 1923.

189. Ibid., December 5, 1923.

190. Ibid., November 22, 1923.

191. Ibid., November 18, 1923.

192. *Chetyrnadtsatyi s"ezd*, p. 570.

193. Ibid., pp. 600–601.

194. *Izvestiia*, October 22, 1923.

195. *Partiia v tsifrovom otnoshenii. Materialy po statistike lichnogo sostava partii* (The party in figures: Statistical material on the composition of the party's personnel), Moscow, 1925, pp. 93–94.

196. Stalin, *Sochineniia*, 7:379–380.

197. Ibid., 5:382.

198. Ibid., 6:275.

199. *Severnaia kommuna* (Northern Commune), March, 14, 1919. (This passage was not included in Lenin's collected works.)

200. This passage was included in the second and third Russian editions of Lenin's works, but omitted from the fourth and fifth.

201. *Writings of Leon Trotsky, 1930–31*, p. 57.

202. *Writings of Leon Trotsky, 1932*, p. 336.

203. *Writings of Leon Trotsky, 1932–33*, p. 279.

204. Leon Trotsky, *Their Morals and Ours*, New York, 1973.

205. This contradiction was noted by Kolakowski, *Glowne nurty marksizmu*, 3:204.

206. E. H. Carr, *Socialism in One Country, 1924–1926*, vol. 1, Baltimore, 1970, p. 263.

207. *Pravda*, November 28, 1925.

208. E. A. Preobrazhenskii, *Novaia ekonomika* (New economics), vol. 1, pt. 1, Moscow, 1924, pp. 101–140.

209. *Chetyrnadtsatyi s"ezd*, pp. 150–151.
210. Stalin, *Voprosy leninizma* (Problems of Leninism), 9th Russ. ed., Moscow, 1933, p. 160. This text was deleted from later editions.
211. *Bol'shevik*, no. 8, 1925.
212. Ustrialov, *Pod znakom*, p. 194.
213. Ibid., pp. 234–235.
214. Ibid., p. 239.
215. Ibid., p. 236.
216. Ibid., pp. 268–269.
217. *Pravda*, November 14, 1922.
218. Stalin, *Sochineniia*, 7:250.
219. *Piatnadtsatyi s"ezd VKP(b). Stenograficheskii otchet* (Fifteenth Party Congress: Stenographic record), Moscow, 1928, pp. 251–252.
220. *Piatradtsatyi s"ezd*, p. 261.
221. Stalin, *Sochineniia*, 10:190.
222. Souvarine, *Staline*, p. 352.
223. *Novaia zhizn'*, April 26, 1918.
224. *Izvestiia*, August 14, 1922.
225. V. V. Gorbunov, *V. I. Lenin i Proletkul't* (Lenin and Proletcult), Moscow, 1974, p. 5.
226. Quoted in Ibid., p. 146.
227. *Voprosy istorii KPSS* (Problems in CPSU history), no. 1, 1958, p. 33.
228. *Proletarskaia kul'tura* (Proletarian culture), no. 20–21, 1921, p. 33.
229. A. Blok, *Dnevnik* (Diary), ed. P. N. Medvedev, vols. 1–2, Leningrad, 1928.
230. A. Blok, *Sobranie sochinenii v 8 tomakh* (Collected works in 8 volumes), Moscow, 1962, 6:166.
231. *Arkhiv A. M. Gor'kogo. Neizdannaia perepiska* (The Gorky archive: Unpublished correspondence), vol. 14, Moscow, 1976.
232. Quoted in Marietta Shaginian, *Literaturnyi dhevnik* (Literary diary), Moscow-Petrograd, 1923, p. 168.
233. *Vospominaniia o V. I. Lenine v 5 tomakh* (Recollections of Lenin in 5 volumes), Moscow, 1969, 5:13.
234. Viktor Shklovskii, Khod konia (sbornik statei) (Knight's move [collection of essays]), Moscow-Berlin, 1923, p. 16.
235. *Pravda*, November 8, 1921.
236. "Za glubokuiu razrabotku istorii sovetskoi literatury" (For profound research work on the history of Soviet literature), *Kommunist*, no. 12, 1956.
237. E. Zamyatin, *A Soviet Heretic*, Chicago, 1970, pp. 51–52.
238. E. Zamyatin, *We*, New York, 1972.
239. Zamyatin, *Soviet Heretic*, p. 57.
240. Quoted in *Malevich*, Amsterdam, 1970, p. 51.
241. Quoted in a denunciatory speech by I. Lezhnev in the stenographic record of the First Soviet Writers' Congress, *Pervyi s"ezd sovetskikh pisatelei. Stenograficheskii otchet*, (First Soviet Writers' Congress: Stenographic record), Moscow, 1934, p. 174.
242. A. Blok, *Sobranie sochinenii*, 6:166.
243. Petr S. Kogan, *Literatura etikh let, 1917–1923* (The literature of these years, 1917–1923), Ivanovo-Voznesensk, 1924, p. 79.
244. Zamyatin, *We*, p. 5.
245. Compare the analysis of "Chekist literature" in Michael Heller, *Kontsentratsionnyi*

*mir i sovetskaia literatura* (The concentration camp world and Soviet literature), London, 1974.

246. Kogan, *Literatura etikh let*, p. 73.

247. *Sud'by sovremennoi intelligenstii* (Fates of the modern intelligentsia), Moscow, 1925, p. 3.

248. Ibid., p. 7.

249. Ibid.

250. Ibid., p. 17.

251. See the Central Committee statement addressed to the intelligentsia in the newspaper *Kommunisticheskii trud* (Communist labor), December 14, 1920.

252. *Sud'by*, pp. 18–19.

253. Ibid., p. 31.

254. Ibid., p. 34.

255. Ibid., p. 24.

256. Ibid., p. 25.

257. Ibid.

258. Ibid., p. 24.

259. Ibid., p. 27.

260. Fediukin, *Velikii oktiabr'*, p. 357.

261. *Pravda*, August 1, 1925.

262. *Zhurnalist* (Journalist), no. 8–9, 1925.

263. *Literaturnoe nasledstvo* (Literary heritage), vol. 65, Moscow, 1958, p. 40.

# CHAPTER FOUR

1. N. Valentinov (Volsky), *Doktrina pravogo kommunizma* (The doctrine of right-wing communism), Munich, 1960, p. 44.

2. Ibid., p. 67.

3. *Ekonomicheskaia zhizn'* (Economic life), November 2, 1926.

4. Ibid.

5. *Bol'shevik*, September 13, 1926.

6. Boris Pilniak, "Krasnoe derevo" (Mahogany), in *Opal'nye povesti* (Frowned-upon tales), New York, 1955, p. 185.

7. *Molodaia gvardiia*, no. 5, 1929, pp. 2–6.

8. Ibid., no. 10, 1929, pp. 83–92.

9. *Pravda*, January 12, 1923.

10. Mikoian, *V nachale dvadtsatykh* (The early twenties).

11. *Kratkaia istoriia sovetskogo kino* (Brief history of the Soviet cinema), Moscow, 1969, p. 132.

12. A. Tishkov, *Pervyi chekist* (The first Chekist), Moscow, 1968, p. 128.

13. *Kommunist*, no. 5, 1957, p. 23.

14. Tishkov, *Pervyi*, p. 126.

15. N. Valentinov (Volsky), *NEP i krizis partii posle smerti Lenina* (NEP and the party crisis after Lenin's death), Stanford, 1971, p. 101.

16. Ibid., p. 102.

17. According to the magazine *Planovoe khoziaistvo* (Planned economy) (no. 2, 1926, p. 132), the number of unemployed in the USSR was 1,728,364.

18. Quoted in Valentinov (Volsky), *Doktrina*, p. 74.
19. *Bol'shevik*, no. 14, 1926.
20. *Pravda*, August 14, 1926.
21. Ibid., October 7, 1926.
22. Ante Ciliga, *The Russian Enigma*, London, 1979, p. 22.
23. *Izvestiia*, March 22, 1925.
24. Quoted in Valentinov (Volsky), *Doktrina*, p. 79.
25. Stalin, *Sochineniia*, 11:171.
26. Pilniak, *Opal'nye povesti*, pp. 208–209.
27. Ciliga, *Russian Enigma*, p. 60.
28. Stalin, *Sochineniia*, 11:63.
29. Robert Conquest, *The Great Terror: Stalin's Purge of the Thirties*, rev. ed., New York, 1973, pp. 730–731.
30. Alexander Orlov, *The Secret History of Stalin's Crimes*, London, 1954, p. 21.
31. *Pravda*, May 19, 1920.
32. Ibid., May 18, 1928.
33. Iaroslavskii, *Kratkaia istoriia*, pp. 355–356.
34. Walter Krivitsky, *I Was Stalin's Agent*, London, 1939, p. 39.
35. Ibid., p. 65.
36. G. S. Agabekov, *Zapiski chekista* (Notes of a Cheka agent), Berlin, 1930, p. 104.
37. Anthony C. Sutton, *Western Technology and Soviet Economic Development, 1917–1930*, Stanford, 1972, p. 320.
38. Ibid., pp. 263–265.
39. Ibid., pp. 325–326, 347–348.
40. Sutton, *Western Technology*, p. 348.
41. *Ekonomicheskaia zhizn'*, August 29, 1929.
42. Ivy Lee, *USSR: A World Enigma*, London, 1927.
43. Bob Considine, *An American in Moscow: The Extraordinary Life of Doctor Armand Hammer*, New York, 1975, p. 82.
44. Quoted in Robert C. Tucker, "The Emergence of Stalin's Foreign Policy," *Slavic Review*, vol. 36, no. 4, 1977, p. 567.
45. Rene Fulop-Miller, *The Mind and Face of Bolshevism*, New York, 1927, p. 243.
46. Ruth Epperson-Kennel, *Theodore Dreisier and the Soviet Union*, New York, 1969, pp. 69–70.
47. Stalin, *Sochineniia*, 12:112.
48. *Sud'by sovremennoi intelligentsii*, p. 41.
49. *Itogi desiatiletiia sovetskoi vlasti v tsifrakh* (Statistical balance sheet of a decade of Soviet power), Moscow, 1927, p. 116.
50. M. N. Gernet, *Istoriia tsarskoi tiur'my* (History of the tsarist prison), 5 vols., Moscow, 1960–1963, 4:23.
51. Lenin, *CW*, 4:23.
52. Fulop-Miller, *Mind*, p. 270.
53. Boris Cederholm, *Au pays du Nep et de la Tscheka*, Paris, 1928.
54. George Popov, *La Tscheka*, Paris, 1926.
55. Il'ia Erenburg, *Zhizn' i gibel' Nikolaia Kurbova* (The life and death of Nikolai Kurbov), Berlin, 1923, p. 98.
56. *Istoriia sovetskogo gosudarstva i prava* (History of the Soviet state and Soviet law), vol. 2, Moscow, 1968, p. 575.
57. *Pravda*, December 18, 1927.

58. *Izvestiia*, June 9, 1927.
59. Nikolai Bukharin, "Lenin i problema kul'turnoi revoliutsii" (Lenin and the problem of the cultural revolution), in *Put' k sotsializmu v Rossii* (The road to socialism in Russia), New York, 1967, p. 375.
60. Alfred Fabre-Luce, *Russie 1927*, Paris, 1927, p. 264.

## CHAPTER FIVE

1. *KPSS v rezoliutsiiakh* (The CPSU in resolutions), vol. 4, Moscow, 1970, p. 227.
2. Agabekov, *Zapiski*, p. 152.
3. Lev Kassil', *"Na zlobu dnia sed'mogo"* (On the topic of the seventh day), *Molodaia gvardiia*, no. 1, 1930, p. 99.
4. Alec Nove, *An Economic History of the USSR*, London, 1972, p. 145.
5. Ibid., p. 146.
6. *Biulleten' oppozitsii* (Bulletin of the opposition), no. 29–30, 1932, p. 34. Cf. *Writings of Leon Trotsky, 1932*, New York, 1973, p. 208.
7. *Problemy ekonomiki* (Problems of economics), no. 10–11, 1929, p. 27.
8. Fainsod, *Smolensk*, p. 315.
9. Fedor Gladkov, *Energiia* (Energy), Moscow, 1936, p. 375.
10. Fainsod, *Smolensk*, p. 315.
11. Margaret Buber-Neumann, *Vom Potsdam nach Moskau. Stationen eines Irrwegs*, Stuttgart, 1957, p. 322.
12. See Fainsod, *Smolensk*, pp. 311–313.
13. Ciliga, *Russian Enigma*, p. 108.
14. Fainsod, *Smolensk*, pp. 311–312.
15. Stalin, *Sochineniia*, 12:14.
16. Ibid., p. 12.
17. Solzhenitsyn gives a profound analysis of the Moscow show trials—political, sociological, and psychological— in *The Gulag Archipelago*, 3 vols., New York, 1973–1978.
18. Emelian Iaroslavskii, "Mechty Chaianovykh i sovetskoi deistvitel'nosti" (The dreams of the Chayanovs and Soviet reality), *Pravda*, October 18, 1930.
19. S. Krylov, "Kondrat'evshchina i pravyi uklon" (The Kondratievites and right-wing deviation), *Pravda*, October 10, 1930.
20. *Planovoe khoziaistvo*, no. 5–6, 1933, p. 15.
21. Krivitsky, *Stalin's Agent*, p. 187.
22. In 1966 Solzhenitsyn spent eight hours along the canal and found that there was virtually no traffic on it. See *The Gulag Archipelago* 2:100–102.
23. Stalin, *Sochineniia*, 13:183.
24. *Piatiletnii plan* (The five-year plan), vol. 1, Moscow, 1928, pp. 104–105.
25. Josif Stalin, "Report to the Seventeenth Congress," January 26, 1934.
26. *Ekonomicheskaia gazeta*, (Economic Gazette), June 18, 1932.
27. Krivitsky, *Stalin's Agent*, pp. 135–158.
28. Sutton, *Western Technology*, vol. 2, p. 249.
29. *Pravda*, February 2, 1935.
30. Stalin, *Sochineniia*, 12:125–126.
31. Ibid., p. 140.
32. Ibid., p. 146.

33. Ibid., p. 169.
34. Ibid., p. 170.
35. *Istoriia SSSR v 10 tomakh*, 8:551.
36. *Voprosy istorii KPSS*, no. 4, 1962, pp. 61–65.
37. Quoted in Stalin, *Sochineniia*, 12:134.
38. *Istoriia KPSS* (History of the CPSU), Moscow, 1960, p. 423.
39. *Istoriia SSSR*, 8:550.
40. Ibid., p. 571.
41. Krivitsky, *Stalin's Agent*, p. 11.
42. Maksim Gor'kii, *Sobranie sochinenii v 30 tomakh* (Collected works in 30 volumes), Moscow, 1949–1956, 25:228.
43. *Istoricheskie zapiski* (Historical notes), no. 76, p. 20.
44. *Sel'skoe khoziaistvo SSSR. Ezhegodnik* (USSR Agriculture: Yearbook), Moscow, 1935, p. 217.
45. *Narodnoe khoziaistvo Kazakhskoi SSR* (Economy of the Kazakh SSR), Alma-Ata, 1957, p. 141.
46. *Pravda*, May 26, 1964.
47. Nikita Khrushchev, *Khrushchev Remembers: The Last Testament*, Boston, 1974, p. 112. (Hereafer cited as *The Last Testament*.)
48. S. Dmitrievskii, *Sovetskie portrety* (Soviet portraits), Berlin, 1932, p. 57.
49. Krivitsky, *Stalin's Agent*, pp. 10–11.
50. Stalin, *Problems of Leninism*, Moscow, 1953, p. 530.
51. *Pravda*, October 2, 1932.
52. Stalin, "Report to the Seventeenth Congress of the CPSU," in *Problems of Leninism*, p. 637.
53. *Istoricheskie zapiski*, no. 76, p. 52.
54. Fainsod, *Smolensk*, p. 187.
55. William Henry Chamberlin, *Russia's Iron Age*, Boston, 1934, p. 157.
56. *Istoriia SSSR*, 8:587–588.
57. Ibid., p. 594.
58. Stalin, *Sochineniia*, 13:191.
59. Winston S. Churchill, *The Second World War*, vol. 4, London, 1951, pp. 447–448.
60. *Pravda*, January 29, 1935.
61. Orlov, *Stalin's Crimes*, p. 42.
62. B. Ts. Urlanis, *Problemy dinamiki naseleniia* (Problems of population dynamics), Moscow, 1974.
63. Conquest, *Great Terror*, p. 46.
64. I. G. Diadkin, *Otsenka neestestvennoi smertnosti naseleniia SSSR v 1927–1958 gg.* (An estimate of the nonnatural mortality rate in the USSR, 1927–1958), Moscow, 1976–1978.
65. Mikhail Bakunin, *Narodnoe delo* (The people's cause), London, 1862, p. 19.
66. Ivan Bunin, *Okaiannye dni* (Accursed days), London, 1973, pp. 71–72.
67. S. Dmitrievskii, *Stalin*, Berlin, 1931, p. 312.
68. Ibid., p. 313.
69. Dmitrievskii, *Sovetskie portrety*, p. 106.
70. Robert C. Tucker, "The Rise of Stalin's Personality Cult," *American Historical Review*, vol. 84, no. 2, 1979, pp. 348–349.
71. Dmitrievskii, *Sovetskie portrety*, p. 142.
72. Ibid., p. 143.

73. Ibid.
74. Ciliga, *Russian Enigma*, p. 217
75. Krivitsky, *Stalin's Agent*, p. 203.
76. "Stalin kak teoretik," *Biulleten' oppozitsii* (Paris), no. 14, August 1930, pp. 24–37. Cf. "Stalin as Theoretician," in *Writings of Leon Trotsky, 1930*, New York, 1975, pp. 308 ff.
77. *Biulleten' oppozitsii*, no. 14, 1930, p. 16.
78. Quoted in Isaac Deutscher, *The Prophet Outcast: Trotsky, 1929–1940*, London, 1963, p. 175.
79. *Pravda*, February 4, 1931.
80. Dmitrievskii, *Stalin*, p. 8.
81. Ibid., p. 281.
82. Ibid., p. 297.
83. Ibid.
84. Ibid., p. 304.
85. Ibid., p. 335.
86. Dmitrievskii, *Sovetskie portrety*, p. 128.
87. Dmitrievskii, *Stalin*, p. 312.
88. Stalin, *Problems of Leninism*, p. 629.
89. Henri Barbusse, *Stalin: A New World Seen Through One Man*, New York-London, 1935, pp. 282–283.
90. Dmitrievskii, *Stalin*, p. 335.
91. Barbusse, *Stalin*, p. 283.
92. Agabekov, *Zapiski*, pp. 178–179.
93. Alexander Barmine, *One Who Survived*, New York, 1945.
94. Ibid.
95. Buber-Neumann, *Von Potsdam nach Moskau*, p. 284.
96. *Communist International*, vol. 10, no. 11, June 15, 1933, p. 367.
97. *Writings of Leon Trotsky, 1938–39*, New York, 1974, p. 20–21.
98. *Writings of Leon Trotsky, 1939–40*, New York, 1973, p. 190.
99. Quoted in Warren Lerner, *Karl Radek: The Last Internationalist*, Stanford, 1970, p. 121.
100. Popov, *La Tscheka*, p. iv.
101. Koestler, *Arrow in the Blue*, p. 345.
102. Vasilli Rozanov, *Izbrannoe* (Selections), Munich, 1970, p. 494.
103. *Literaturnaia gazeta* (Literary gazette), January 13, 1930.
104. Arthur Koestler, "The Initiates," in *The God That Failed*, New York, 1954, p. 61.
105. A Russian edition of the Webbs' book was published in Moscow in 1937.
106. See George Bernard Shaw, *The Rationalization of Russia*, ed. Harry M. Geduld, Bloomington, 1964, p. 31.
107. Ella Winter, *Red Virtue: Human Relationships in the New Russia*, New York, 1933, p. 39.
108. *Nation*, July 1934, quoted in David Caute, *Les compagnons de route, 1917–1968*, Paris, 1979.
109. Peter G. Filene, *Americans and the Soviet Experiment, 1917–1933*, Cambridge, 1967, p. 197.
110. Caute, *Compagnons*, p. 85.
111. Filene, *Americans*, p. 141.
112. Margaret Buber-Neumann, *La révolution mondiale*, Paris, 1970, p. 301.

113. Caute, *Compagnons*, p. 86.
114. Serge, *Memoirs*, p. 301.
115. Stalin, *Sochineniia*, 13:104–105.
116. Ibid., p. 109.
117. Ibid., pp. 111–112.
118. *Istoriia sovetskopo gosudarstva i prava*, vol. 2, Moscow, 1968, p. 494.
119. *Svod zakonov* (Register of laws), no. 62, 1932, p. 360.
120. *Istoriia sovetskogo gosudarstva i prava*, 2:588.
121. *Istoriia SSSR*, 8:584.
122. *Malaia sovetskaia entsiklopediia*, vol. 6.
123. *Pravda*, October 2, 1932.
124. Ibid., July 7, 1932.
125. Boris Souvarine, "Derniers entretiens avec Babel," *Contrepoint*, no. 30, 1979.
126. *Svod zakonov*, no. 22, 1930, p. 248.
127. See Mikhail Heller, "Poet i vozhd'" (The Poet and the Leader), *Kontinent*, no. 16, 1978.
128. People's Commissariat of Defense, *Stenograficheskii otchet* (Stenographic record), Moscow, 1937, p. 384.
129. A. Karaganov, "Istoriia odnoi p'esy" (History of a certain play), *Znamia*, (Banner), no. 1, 1963.
130. Voznesenskii, "Imena i sud'by," p. 386.
131. Ibid., p. 397.
132. Tucker, "Rise of Stalin's Personality Cult," p. 364.
133. *Pravda*, January 12, 1932.
134. Gor'kii, *Sobranie sochinenii*, 27:333.
135. Arthur Koestler, *The Invisible Writing*, London, 1969, p. 329.
136. Stalin, *Problems of Leninism*, p. 455.
137. *Spravochnik partiinogo rabotnika* (Party worker's handbook), no. 7, 1930, pp. 410–422.
138. *Literaturnaia gazeta*, June 10, 1929.
139. *Proletarskaia revoliutsiia*, no. 1, 1929, pp. 61–62.
140. *Literaturnaia gazeta*, September 2, 1929.
141. The resolution was written in red pencil on the back of a letter dated February 24, 1935, from Lily Brik. See *Pamiat'*, no. 1, p. 310.
142. Souvarine, "Derniers entretiens."
143. Gor'kii, *Sobranie sochinenii*, 25:230.
144. Ibid., p. 235.
145. Ibid.
146. Orlov, *Stalin's Crimes*, p. 275.
147. Gor'kii, *Sobranie sochinenii*, 25:453.
148. Ibid.
149. Stalin, *Sochineniia*, 12:173.
150. Gor'kii, *Sobranie sochinenii*, 28:238.
151. Ibid., p. 460.
152. *Pervyi s"ezd sovetskikh pisatelei*, p. 550.
153. Ibid., p. 277.
154. Ibid.
155. See Solzhenitsyn, *Gulag Archipelago*, vol. 2, ch. 3.
156. *Pervyi s"ezd sovetskikh pisatelei*, p. 234.

157. Ibid., p. 277.

158. Ibid., p. 16.

159. Ibid., p. 681.

160. "Dokument ideologicheskoi bor'by" (Document of the ideological struggle), *Iskusstvo kino* (Art of the cinema), no. 4, 1964, pp. 14–15.

161. "Vsesoiuznoe tvorcheskoe soveshchanie rabotnikov sovetskoi kinematografii" (All-Union Creative Conference of Soviet Cinematographers), in *Za bol'shoe kinoiskusstvo* (For a great cinematic art), Moscow, 1935, p. 65.

162. Gor'kii, *Sobranie sochinenii*, 27:434.

163. *Pervyi s"ezd sovetskikh pisatelei*, p. 1.

164. Gor'kii, *Sobranie sochinenii*, 27:434.

165. Ibid., p. 509.

166. Ibid.

167. Ibid., p. 422.

# CHAPTER SIX

1. Elisabeth Lermolo, *Face of a Victim*, New York, 1955.

2. Krivitsky, *Stalin's Agent*, p. 19.

3. Conquest, *Great Terror*, p. 72.

4. *Pravda*, December 6, 18, 1934.

5. Lermolo, *Face*, pp. 264–265.

6. Ciliga, *Russian Enigma*, p. 296.

7. *Pravda*, August 29, 1929.

8. Dmitrii Manuilskii, *Itogi sotsialisticheskogo stroitel'stva v SSSR* (Results of socialist construction in the USSR), Moscow, 1935, p. 4.

9. Stalin, *Problems of Leninism*, pp. 688–689.

10. *Lenin i Stalin o sovetskoi konstitutsii. Sbornik statei, rechei i dokumentov* (Lenin and Stalin on the Soviet constitution: Collected articles, speeches, and documents), Moscow, 1936, pp. 176–177.

11. *Pravda*, May 4, 1935.

12. Ibid., August 1, 1935.

13. Ibid., August 2, 1935.

14. Caute, *Compagnons*, pp. 85, 127.

15. *Pravda*, May 8, 1936.

16. Lenin's figures were published in 1899 in his book *The Development of Capitalism in Russia* (Lenin, *CW*, vol. 3).

17. *Narodno-khoziaistvennyi plan na 1935 god* (The Soviet economic plan for 1935), 2d ed., Moscow, 1935, p. 533.

18. *Legkaia industriia* (Light industry), May 9, 1937.

19. See Bazili, *Rossiia pod sovetskoi vlast'iu*, p. 284.

20. Ibid., p. 286.

21. Kléber Legay, *Un mineur français chez les russes*, Paris, 1937, p. 79.

22. The October 1935 and May 1936 issues of the magazine *Za industrializatsiiu* (For industrialization) contain material on the wages of Stakhanovites.

23. *Pravda*, September 23, 1935.

24. *Biulleten' oppozitsii*, no. 52–53, October 1936.

25. *Izvestiia*, May 1, 1936.

26. Ibid., January 1, 1936.
27. Quotes in Joachim Fest, *Hitler: Eine Biographie*, vol. 2, Frankfurt, 1976, p. 973.
28. *Pravda*, May 28, 1936.
29. See A. S. Makarenko, *Sochineniia* (Works), vol. 5, Moscow, 1951, p. 112.
30. Gor'kii, *Sobranie sochinenii*, 27:440.
31. Boris I. Nicolaevsky, *Power and the Soviet Elite*, Ann Arbor, 1975, p. 22.
32. *Pravda*, June 22, 1936.
33. Ibid., November 26, 1936.
34. Nicolaevsky, *Power*, pp. 16–17.
35. Ibid, p. 20.
36. Kolakowski, *Glownye nurty*, 2:527.
37. N. Valentinov (Volsky), "Piatakov o bol'shevizme" (Pyatakov on bolshevism), *Novyi; zhurnal* (New York), no. 52, 1958, p. 149.
38. Nicolaevsky, *Power*, p. 25.
39. *Pravda*, June 18, 1936.
40. Mark Popovskii, *Upravliaemaia nauka* (Controlled science), London, 1978, p. 25.
41. Ibid., p. 26.
42. Ibid., p. 28.
43. Ibid., p. 267.
44. Bukharin, *Put' k sotsializmu*, p. 213.
45. Nicolaevsky, *Power*, p. 17.
46. L. O. Tsederbaum-Dan, "Vospominaniia" (Memoirs), *Novyi zhurnal*, no. 75, 1964.
47. *Pravda*, December 30, 1936.
48. Ibid., July 5, 1936.
49. *Malaia sovetskaia entsiklopediia*, vol. 6.
50. *Rabochii i teatr* (The worker and the theater), no. 1, 1932, pp. 6–7.
51. *Pravda*, January 28, 1936.
52. Arkady Belinkov, *Sdacha i gibel' sovetskogo intelligenta: Iurii Olesha* (The surrender and destruction of a Soviet intellectual: Yurii Olesha), Madrid, 1976, p. 172.
53. Leon Trotsky, *The Stalin School of Falsification*, New York, 1972, p. xxxiii.
54. *Pravda*, January 27, 1936.
55. André Gide, *Retour de l'URSS*, Paris, 1936, p. 49.
56. *Rabochii i teatr*, no. 1, 1934, p. 14.
57. "O p'ese 'Bogatyri' Dem'iana Bednogo" (On Demian Bednyi's play *Bogatyri*), in *Protiv fal'tsifikatsii narodnogo proshlogo* (Against the falsification of the national past), Moscow-Leningrad, 1937, pp. 3–4.
58. *Vsesoiuznoe soveshchanie istorikov* (All-Union Conference of Historians), Moscow, 1964, p. 338.
59. George Orwell, *1984*, New York, 1962, p. 128.
60. Adolf Hitler, *Mein Kampf*, Munich, 1927, p. 468.
61. Mikhail N. Pokrovskii, *Marksizm i osobennosti istoricheskogo razvitiia Rossii* (Marxism and the peculiarities of Russia's historical development), Leningrad, 1925, p. 82.
62. Mikhail N. Pokrovskii, "K voprosu ob istoricheskom razvitii Rossii" (On the question of Russia's historical development), *Pod znamenem marksizma* (Under the banner of Marxism), no. 5–6, 1924, p. 93.
63. Pokrovskii, *Marksizm i osobennosti*, pp. 78–79.
64. *Pravda*, August 22, 1937.
65. Stalin, *Sochineniia*, 13:104.
66. *Pravda*, June 26, 1937.

67. Sergei Eizenshtein, *Izbrannye proizvedeniia v 6 tomakh* (Selected works in six volumes), Moscow, 1964–1971, 6:159.

68. Ibid., p. 500.

69. *Iskusstvo kino*, no. 3, 1964, pp. 4–9.

70. Petr Pavlenko, *Na vostoke* (In the East), Moscow, 1937, pp. 438–439.

71. Francis Courtade and Pierre Cadars, *Histoire du cinéma nazi*, Paris, 1972, p. 62.

72. Stalin, *Sochineniia*, 8:152.

73. *Natsional'no-gosudarstvennoe stroitel'stvo v SSSR v perekhodnyi period ot kapitalizma k sotsializmu, 1917–1936* (Nation-state building in the USSR in the period of transition from capitalism to socialism, 1917–1936), Moscow, 1968, p. 447.

74. Ibid., p. 450.

75. *Partiinoe stroitel'stvo* (Party building), no. 5, 1933, p. 16.

76. Koshelivets', "Mykola Skrypnik," p. 195.

77. Stalin, *Sochineniia*, 13:361.

78. *Pravda*, January 2, 1934.

79. *Malaia sovetskaia entsiklopediia*, Moscow, 1940, vol. 9.

80. *Istoriia SSSR. Epokha sotsializma* (History of the USSR: Age of socialism), 3rd enl. ed., Moscow, 1974, p. 321.

81. *Pravda*, August 2, 1940.

82. Nikita Khrushchev, *Khrushchev Remembers*, Boston, 1970, p. 89.

83. See "Un Caligula au Kremlin," *Bulletin d'études et d'informations politiques internationale* (Paris), no. 102, January 16–31, 1954.

84. Souvarine, *Staline*, p. 488.

85. Krivitsky, *Stalin's Agent*, p. 168.

86. S. Uranov, *O nekotorykh priemakh verbochnoi raboty inostrannykh razvedok* (On some recruiting techniques of foreign intelligence agencies), Moscow, 1937, p. 8. This work was published by the Central Committee's "Party Press" (Partizdat) in a run of 1,050,000 copies.

87. Vladimir and Evdokiia Petrov, *The Empire of Fear*, London, 1956, p. 71.

88. Krivitsky, *Stalin's Agent*, pp. 166–168.

89. Souvarine, "Derniers entretiens."

90. *Istoriia Velikoi otechestvennoi voiny Sovetskogo Soiuza 1941–45 v 6 tomakh* (History of the Great Patriotic War of the Soviet Union, 1941–45, in 6 volumes), Moscow, 1960–1965, 6:124.

91. Gunter Peis, *Naujocks, l'homme qui déclencha la guerre*, Paris, 1961, p. 88.

92. *Pravda*, August 24, 1936.

93. Orlov, *Stalin's Crimes*, p. 164.

94. Ibid., pp. 129–130.

95. Conquest, *Great Terror*, p. 705.

96. Solzhenitsyn, *Gulag Archipelago*, 1:439.

97. Robert Conquest, *Kolyma: The Arctic Death Camps*, New York, 1978, pp. 226–229.

98. John Toland, *Adolf Hitler*, Paris, 1978, vol. 1, pp. 363–64.

99. Khrushchev, *Khrushchev Remembers*, pp. 88–89.

100. Lidiia Libedinskaia, *Zelenaia lampa* (Green light), Moscow, 1966, p. 374.

101. Guy Hentsch, *Staline negociateur*, Neuchâtel, 1967, pp. 42–43.

102. Khrushchev, *Khrushchev Remembers*, p. 99.

103. Stalin, *Problems of Leninism*, pp. 778–779.

104. Fitzroy Maclean, *Eastern Approaches*, London, 1965, p. 96.

105. Stalin, *Sochineniia*, 7:14.

106. *Le Figaro*, May 7, 1939. Cf. *Est et Ouest*, no. 628, 1979.

107. Krivitsky, *Stalin's Agent*, p. 39.

108. *Seventh Congress of the Comintern: Stenographic Report of the Proceedings*, Moscow, 1939, p. 588.

109. Evgeny Gnedin, *Iz istorii otnoshenii mezhdu SSSR i fashistskoi Germanii. Dokumenty i sovremennye kommentarii* (From the history of relations between the USSR and fascist Germany: Documents and contemporary commentary), New York, 1977, pp. 22–27.

110. Gustav Hilger and Alfred Meyer, *The Incompatible Allies: A Memoir-History of German–Soviet Relations, 1918–1941*, New York, 1953, p. 262.

111. Krivitsky, *Stalin's Agent*, p. 38.

112. *Novyi grad* (New town), no. 10, 1935, p. 129.

113. Ibid., p. 131.

114. Krivitsky, *Stalin's Agent*, p. 254.

115. *Krasnaia zvezda*, (Red star), October 22, 1965.

116. A. Shneider, *Zapiski starogo moskvicha* (Notes of an old Muscovite), Moscow, 1966, pp. 118–119.

117. Georgii Fedotov, *Rossiia, Evropa i my* (Russia, Europe, and ourselves), vol. 2, Paris, 1973, pp. 288–289.

118. Kirill Khenkin, "Ispanskii bloknot" (Spanish notebook), *Kontinent*, no. 16, pp. 266–267.

119. Elisabeth K. Poretsky, *Our Own People*, Ann Arbor, 1970, pp. 238–240.

120. A copy of the letter is in the Russian Museum in San Francisco. It is quoted in Petr Balakshin, *Final v Kitae. Vozniknovenie, razvitie i ischeznovenie Beloi emigratsii na Dal'nem Vostoke* (Finale in China: Rise, development, and disappearance of the White emigré community in the Far East), 2 vols., San Francisco, 1955, 2:125–126.

# CHAPTER SEVEN

1. Estimates on the number of prisoners in Soviet camps in 1939 vary from 8 million to 17 million. We have taken the lower figure, which is probably too low but quite eloquent nevertheless.

2. *Nardnoe khoziaistvo SSSR v 1962 g. Statisticheskii sbornik* (The Soviet economy in 1962: Collected statistics), Moscow, 1963, p. 52; G. S. Kravchenko, *Voennaia ekonomika SSSR, 1941–1945* (The war economy of the USSR, 1941–1945), Moscow, 1963, pp. 21–22.

3. *Narodnoe khoziaistvo SSSR v 1962 g.*, p. 71.

4. Kravchenko, *Voennaia ekonomika*, p. 36.

5. Aleksandr Nekrich, *1941, 22 iiunia* (June 22, 1941), Moscow, 1965, p. 70.

6. Ibid.

7. Kravchenko, *Voennaia ekonomika*, pp. 63–64.

8. Ibid.

9. *Voenno-istoricheskii zhurnal* (Military-history journal), no. 2, 1962, p. 81.

10. Ibid.

11. Ibid., p. 84.

12. G. A. Ozerov, *Tupolevskaia sharaga* (The Tupolev Prison Institute), Frankfurt, 1973.

13. Conquest, *Great Terror*, p. 706.

14. The text of the "State Plan for the Economic Development of the USSR in 1941," never published in the USSR, was found in the Smolensk archives in the form of a supplement attached to a decree of the Sovnarkom and Central Committee, dated January 17, 1941. The Russian text has been published in the United States as *Gosudarstvennyi plan razvitiia narodnogo khoziaistva SSSR na 1941 god* (State plan for the development of Soviet agriculture for 1941), American Council of Learned Societies Reprints, no. 30, Baltimore, Md., n.d. (Hereafter cited as *Gosudarstvennyi plan.*)

15. *Gosudarstvennyi plan*, pp. 141–147.

16. Ibid., pp. 727, 15.

17. Ibid., p. 17.

18. Ibid., pp. 44, 49, 61, 67, 69, 71, 86, 89, 93, 136.

19. Vladimir Petrov, *Soviet Gold*, New York, 1949.

20. *Gosudarstvennyi plan*, pp. 483–484.

21. Ibid., p. 546.

22. S. Swianiewicz, *Forced Labour and Economic Development*, London, 1965, p. 39.

23. *Izvestiia*, August 2, 1940.

24. *Vneshniaia politika SSSR* (Foreign policy of the USSR), vol. 18, Moscow, 1973, pp. 249–250, doc. no. 148: transcript of conversation between Stalin, Molotov, and Eden.

25. See the papers of the British Foreign Office, file 24845, p. 47, doc. 371: N. Butler to O. Sargeant, Washington, D.C., September 13, 1940.

26. Hilger and Meyer, *Incompatible Allies*, p. 256.

27. Ibid., p. 257.

28. Karlheinz Niclauss, *Die Sowjetunion und Hitlers Machtergreifung*, Bonn, 1966, pp. 120–121.

29. *Documents on German Foreign Policy*, (hereafter *DGFP*), series C., vol. 2, p. 83, doc. no. 47.

30. *Vneshniaia politika SSSR*, vol. 16, p. 714, doc. 405.

31. Ibid., p. 743, doc. 424.

32. Ibid., p. 793.

33. *Istoriia KPSS*, p. 453.

34. *DGFP*, series C., vol. 2, pp. 338–339, 352–353, docs. 176, 181.

35. Stalin, *Problems of Leninism*, p. 585.

36. Ibid., p. 592.

37. Foreign Office, file 24845, doc. 371, p. 47.

38. Walter Krivitsky, *In Stalin's Secret Service*, New York, 1939, p. 2.

39. Ibid., p. 10.

40. *DGFP*, series C., vol. 3, p. 455, doc. 299: Schulenburg to the German Foreign Ministry, October 3, 1934.

41. *Vneshniaia politika SSSR*, 18:249.

42. *DGFP*, series C, vol. 5, pp. 453–454, doc. 211: Schacht's notes on his meeting with Kandelaki and Friedrichsohn, July 15, 1935.

43. *DGFP*, series C, vol. 4, pp. 931–933, doc. 472: memorandum by Roedinger, Berlin, December 21, 1935.

44. Gnedin, *Iz istorii otnoshenii mezhdu SSSR i fashistskoi Germaniei*, Akhronika, N.Y., 1977, p. 37.

45. Krivitsky, *In Stalin's Secret Service*, p. 15.

46. Ibid.

47. According to a letter by Herbert Goering about his uncle Hermann's meeting on May 28, 1936, with Kandelaki and Friedrichsohn, in J. W. Bruegel, ed., *Stalin und Hitler: Pact gegen Europa*, Vienna, 1973, pp. 37–38.

48. Hencke's notes on his meeting with Bessonov, July 3, 1936, in Bruegel, *Stalin und Hitler*, p. 38.

49. Schacht's notes on his meeting with Kandelaki and Friedrichsohn, Berlin, February 6, 1937, in Bruegel, *Stalin und Hitler*, pp. 39–40.

50. Krivitsky, *In Stalin's Secret Service*, pp. 214–215.

51. Neurath to Schacht, February 11, 1937, in Bruegel, *Stalin und Hitler*.

52. Foreign Office, no. 371, file 20346, 1936, Soviet Union, doc. 4771g: Collier to Chilston, January 29, 1936.

53. See, for example, *The Guardian* (Manchester), February 7, 1936.

54. Foreign Office, no. 371, file 20346, 1936, Soviet Union, doc. 90/6/36: February 11, 1936.

55. *Vneshniaia politika SSSR*, vol. 10, p. 164, doc. 98; pp. 174–176, doc. 110.

56. *Le livre jaune français*, Paris, 1939, p. 38, doc. 28.

57. Stalin, *Problems of Leninism*, p. 756.

58. *Nazi–Soviet Relations 1939–1941: Documents from the Archives of the German Foreign Office*, ed., Raymond James Sontag and James Stuart Beddie, Washington, D.C., 1948, p. 76.

59. *Izvestiia*, September 1, 1939.

60. *Times* (London), April 1, 1939; Parliamentary Debates, House of Commons, vol. 346, col. 13, and vol. 347, cols. 952–953.

61. *Izvestiia*, March 22, 1939.

62. *Documents on British Foreign Policy* (hereafter *DBFP*), series 3, vol. 6, pp. 12–15, doc. 9: British Ambassador Henderson to Lord Halifax, the foreign minister, Berlin, June 9, 1939; ibid., pp. 389–391, 407–410, docs. 354, 370: transcript of conversation between British Minister of Trade Hudson and Wohltat, July 20, 1939. See also, *Dokumenty i materialy kanuna Vtoroi mirovoi voiny* (Documents and materials from the eve of World War II), vol. 2: The Dirksen Archive (1938–1939), Moscow, 1948.

63. *DBFP*, series 3, vol. 6.

64. *Fal'tsifikatory istorii* (Falsifiers of history), Moscow, 1948, p. 43.

65. Peter Kleist, *Zwischen Hitler und Stalin, 1939–1945*. Bonn, 1950, p. 28.

66 *Akten zur deutschen auswärtigen Politik 1918–1945* (hereafter *ADAP*), series D (1937–1945), vol. 6, p. 222, doc. 215: Weizsaecker's memorandum of April 17, 1939.

67. Ibid., p. 346, doc. 325: Tippelskirch to Weizsaecker, Moscow, May 4, 1939.

68. Ibid., p. 464, doc. 424: memorandum by Schulenburg, Moscow, May 20, 1939.

69. Ibid., p. 502, doc. 450: memorandum of the German Foreign Ministry, Berlin, May 29, 1939.

70. Ibid., pp. 607–608, doc. 529: Notes by Wermann, head of the political department of the German Foreign Ministry, Berlin, June 15, 1939.

71. *Izvestiia*, June 16, 1939.

72. *DBFP*, series 3, vol. 6, pp. 12–15, doc. 9: Henderson to Halifax, Berlin, June 9, 1939.

73. Ibid., pp. 387–391, 407–410, docs. 354, 370. See also *Dokumenty i materialy kanuna Vtoroi mirovoi voiny*, vol. 2, docs. 13, 24, 29.

74. *ADAP*, series D, vol. 6, pp. 673–674, doc. 579: Schulenburg to the German Foreign Office, Moscow, June 29, 1939.

75. Ibid., pp. 698–699, doc. 607: Schulenburg to the German Foreign Office, July 3, 1939.
76. *DBFP*, series 3, vol. 6, app. 5, pp. 763–764, 777.
77. Ibid., p. 628, doc. 647: Seeds to Halifax, August 13, 1939.
78. *ADAP*, series D, vol. 6, pp. 846–849, doc. 729: Schnurre's memorandum on his conversation with Astakhov and Babarin, Berlin, July 27, 1939.
79. Ibid., pp. 854–855, doc. 736: Weizsaecker to Schulenburg, Berlin, July 29, 1939.
80. Ibid., pp. 883–884, doc. 760: Ribbentrop to Schulenburg, August 3, 1939.
81. Ibid., pp. 892–893, doc. 766: Schulenburg to the German Foreign Office, Moscow, August 4, 1939.
82. *ADAP*, series D, vol. 7, pp. 14–16, doc. 18: Schnurre's memorandum on his meeting with Astakhov, Berlin, August 10, 1939.
83. Ibid., p. 48, doc. 50: Schnurre to Schulenburg, Berlin, August 14, 1939.
84. Ibid., pp. 51–52, doc. 56: Ribbentrop to Schulenburg, Berlin, August 14, 1939.
85. Ibid., pp. 63–64, doc. 70: Schulenburg to the German Foreign Office, Moscow, August 16, 1939; pp. 72–76, doc. 79: Schulenburg's memorandum, Moscow, August 16, 1939; pp. 82–83, doc. 88: Schulenburg to Weizsaecker, Moscow, August 16, 1939.
86. Ibid., p. 70, doc. 75: Ribbentrop to Schulenburg, Berlin, August 16, 1939.
87. Ibid., pp. 95–96, doc. 105: Schulenburg to the German Foreign Ministry, Moscow, August 18, 1939.
88. Ibid., pp. 124–125, doc. 132: Schulenburg to the German Foreign Ministry, Moscow, August 19, 1939.
89. *Pravda*, August 21, 1939.
90. *ADAP*, series D, vol. 7, p. 31, doc. 142: Hitler to Stalin, Berlin, August 20, 1939.
91. Ibid., pp. 140–141, doc. 159: Stalin to Hitler, Moscow, August 21, 1939.
92. Ibid., pp. 206–207, doc. 229: text of the additional secret protocol signed in Moscow by Molotov and Ribbentrop, August 23, 1939.
93. *Nazi–Soviet Relations*, p. 76.
94. Ibid., p. 74.
95. *Pravda*, September 1, 1939.
96. Ibid., August 24, 1939.
97. *ADAP*, series D, vol. 8, pp. 3–4, doc. 5: Schulenburg to the German Foreign Ministry, Moscow, September 5, 1939.
98. *Izvestiia*, September 18, 1939.
99. *ADAP*, series D, vol. 8, pp. 34–35, doc. 46: Schulenburg to German Foreign Ministry, Moscow, September 10, 1939.
100. Ibid., pp. 53–54, doc. 70: Ribbentrop to Schulenburg, Berlin, September 15, 1939.
101. Ibid., p. 60, doc. 78: Schulenburg to German Foreign Ministry, Moscow, September 16, 1939.
102. Ibid.
103. Ibid., pp. 74–76, doc. 94: memorandum by Gustav Hilger, counselor at the German Embassy, Moscow, September 18, 1939.
104. Photos of this parade appeared in the book *Deutschlands Sieg in Polen* (Germany's victory in Poland), Berlin, 1940.
105. For the texts of the Soviet-German Border and Friendship Treaty and the secret protocol, see *ADAP*, series D, vol. 8, pp. 127–130, docs. 157–161.
106. *Izvestiia*, November 1, 1939.
107. Ibid.

108. Ibid., December 25, 1939.
109. *Istoriia Estonskoi SSR* (History of the Estonian Soviet Socialist Republic), ed. G. I. Naan, 2d ed., Tallin, 1958, pp. 595–597.
110. *ADAP*, series D, vol. 10, p. 19, doc. 20: Schulenburg to German Foreign Ministry, Moscow, July 26, 1940.
111. Ibid., series D, vol. 8, pp. 151–152, doc. 178: memorandum by Weizsaecker, Berlin, October 2, 1939.
112. *Izvestiia*, November 29, 1939.
113 Ibid., December 3, 1939.
114. C. Leonard Lundin, *Finland in the Second World War*, Bloomington, 1957, p. 58.
115. Khrushchev, *Khrushchev Remembers*, p. 155.
116. Anthony F. Upton, *Finland in Crisis, 1940–1941*, Ithaca, 1964, pp. 22, 24.
117. Khrushchev, *Khrushchev Remembers*, p. 156.
118. Nekrich, *1941, 22 iiunia*, p. 84.
119. *Istoriia Velikoi otechestvennoi voiny*, 6:125.
120. Vasilii Morozov, "Soviet–German Pact of 1939 Seen in Retrospect," *Soviet News*, June 5, 1979; *Istoriia vneshnei politiki SSSR* (History of USSR foreign policy), ed. Andrei Gromyko and Boris Ponomarev, vol. 1, Moscow, 1975, p. 393.
121. *Trial of the Major War Criminals Before the International Military Tribunal* (hereafter *IMT*), vol. 39, Nuremburg, 1947, doc. 090-TC, p. 107.
122. *ADAP*, series D, vol. 6, pp. 607–608, doc. 529.
123. D. M. Proektor, *Voina v Evrope, 1939–1941* (The War in Europe, 1939–1941), Moscow, 1963, p. 30.
124. *Istoriia vneshnei politiki SSSR*, 1:374.
125. *Istoriia Velikoi otechestvennoi voiny*, 1:480.
126. *Fal'tsifikatory istorii*, p. 53.
127. See for example Stalin's remarks to the Eighteenth Party Congress, *Problems of Leninism*, p. 754.
128. *Izvestiia*, August 2, 1940.
129. Ibid., August 23, 1940.
130. *ADAP*, series D, vol. 9, p. 257, doc. 226: Schulenburg to the German Foreign Ministry, Moscow, May 10, 1940.
131. Ibid., pp. 495–496, doc. 471: Schulenburg to the German Foreign Ministry, Moscow, June 18, 1940.
132. Churchill, *The Second World War*, 2:134–135.
133. I. M. Faingar, *Ocherk razvitiia germanskogo monopolisticheskogo kapitala* (Outline of the development of German monopoly capital), Moscow, 1958, p. 26.
134. F. Friedensberg, "Die sowjetischen Kriegslieferungen an das Hitler reich," *Vierteljahrsheft zur Wirtschaftsforschung*, no. 4, 1962, pp. 331–338.
135. Gerhard L. Weinberg, *Germany and the Soviet Union, 1939–1941*, London, 1954, p. 74.
136. Ibid., p. 78.
137. *ADAP*, series D, vol. 11, bk. 1, p. 25, doc. 22: Wermann to Schulenberg, Berlin, September 5, 1940.
138. *IMT*, 34:679.
139. Ibid., pp. 680–681.
140. Weinberg, *Germany*, p. 84.
141. *DGFP*, series D, vol. 8, docs. 74, 87, 138, 142, 203, 318; also, *Foreign Relations*

*of the United States: Diplomatic Papers* (hereafter *FR*), 1939, 1:519–521, 529, 535–537.

142. Franz Halder, *Kriegstagebuch*, vol. 2, Stuttgart, 1963, p. 32; Walter Warlimont, *Im Hauptquartier der deutschen Wehrmacht, 1939–1945*, Frankfurt, 1962, p. 126.

143. Halder, *Kriegstagebuch*, p. 80.

144. *ADAP*, series D, vol. 11, bk. 2, pp. 889–890, doc. 638.

145. Ibid., bk. 1, p. 235, doc. 166: Ribbentrop to Schulenburg, Berlin, October 9, 1940.

146. Ibid., pp. 248–253, doc. 176: Ribbentrop to Stalin, Berlin, October 13, 1940.

147. Ibid., pp. 455–461, doc. 326: memorandum on the conversation between Hitler and Molotov, Berlin, November 12, 1940.

148. *ADAP*, series D, vol. 11, bk. 2, pp. 597–598, doc. 404: Schulenburg to the German Foreign Ministry, Moscow, November 26, 1940.

149. *FR*, 1941, 1:714, 723.

150. E. L. Woodward, *British Foreign Policy in the Second World War*, London, 1962, p. 148.

151. Churchill, *Second World War*, 3:320.

152. *Istoriia Velikoi otechestvennoi voiny*, 1:478.

153. Ibid., p. 479.

154. Hilger and Meyer, *Incompatible Allies*, p. 328.

155. Otto von Bismarck, *Mysli i vospominaniia* (Thoughts and recollections), vol. 1, Moscow, 1940, pp. xvi–xvii.

156. *ADAP*, series D, vol. 12, pt. 2, p. 467, doc. 351: Tippelskirch, chargé d'affaires at the German embassy in Moscow, to the German Foreign Ministry, April 15, 1941.

157. Ibid., pp. 502–503, doc. 381: Tippelskirch to the German Foreign Ministry, Moscow, April 22, 1941.

158. Ibid., pp. 447–448, doc. 333: Schulenburg to the German Foreign Ministry, Moscow, April 13, 1941.

159. Ibid., pp. 688–689, doc. 521: Schnurre's memorandum on the state of Soviet–German trade relations, Berlin, May 15, 1941.

160. *Izvestiia*, June 14, 1941.

161. Barton Whaley, *Codeword Barbarossa*, Cambridge, 1973, pp. 24–129.

162. A. Nikitin, "Perestroika raboty voennoi promyshlennosti SSSR v pervom periode Velikoi otechestvennoi voiny" (The Reorganization of the Soviet war industry in the first phase of the Great Patriotic War), *Voenno-istoricheskii zhurnal*, no. 1, 1963, p. 61.

163. Georgii Zhukov, *Vospominaniia i razmyshleniia* (Recollections and reflections), Moscow, 1969, p. 219.

# CHAPTER EIGHT

1. Zhukov, *Vospominaniia*, p. 243.

2. Ibid.

3. *Istoriia Velikoi otechestvennoi voiny*, 2:14.

4. Rodion Malinovskii, "Dvadtsatiletie nachala Velikoi otechestvennoi voiny," (Twentieth anniversary of the start of the Great Patriotic War), *Voenno-istoricheskii zhurnal*, no. 6, 1961, pp. 6–7.

5. I. V. Boldin, *Stranitsy zhizni* (Pages from a life), Moscow, 1961, p. 86.

6. M. Zakharov, "Nachal'nyi period Velikoi otechestvennoi voiny i ego uroki" (The opening phase of the Great Patriotic War and its lessons), *Voenno-istoricheskii zhurnal*, no. 7, 1961, p. 9.

7. *Istoriia Velikoi otechestvennoi voiny*, 6:25.

8. V. A. Anfilov, *Bessmertnyi podvig* (The immortal feast), Moscow, 1971, p. 122.

9. For details, see Nekrich, *1941, 22 iiunia*, p. 154.

10. Anfilov, *Bessmertnyi podvig*, p. 191.

11. Zhukov, *Vospominaniia*, p. 382.

12. Anfilov, *Bessmertnyi podvig*, p. 199.

13. Halder, *Kriegstagebuch*, 3:148.

14. Leonid Volynskii, "Skvoz' noch'" (Through the night), *Novyi mir*, no. 1, 1963, p. 117. The same version of events appears in the book by R. G. Umanskii, *Na boevykh rubezhakh* (On the fighting lines), Moscow, 1960, pp. 60–61. The death of the commander of a front is no small matter. In the Soviet army it is not customary or acceptable for a commander to take his own life. Consequently the September 1964 issue of *Voenno-istoricheskii zhurnal* ran an unsigned article entitled, "The Truth About the Death of General Kirponos" (pp. 61–69), asserting that he died from battle wounds that proved fatal.

15. *Vneshniaia politika Sovetskogo Soiuza v period Otechestvennoi voiny* (Foreign policy of the Soviet Union during the Patriotic war), 3 vols., Moscow, 1946–1947, 1:29.

16. N. A. Kirsanov, *Po zovu rodiny. Dobrovol'cheskie formirovaniia Krasnoi armii v period Velikoi otechestvennoi voiny* (At the call of the homeland: Volunteer formations in the Red army during the Great Patriotic War), Moscow, 1974, pp. 15, 22, 25. The author of this study of the popular militia asserts that no less than 4 million persons served in such units during the war, nearly 2 million of them fighting at the front in the summer and fall of 1941. These figures seem inflated.

17. Khrushchev, *Khrushchev Remembers*, pp. 168–169.

18. On the work of the State Committee for Defense, see Sanford R. Lieberman, "The Party Under Stress: The Experience of World War II," in *Soviet Society and the Communist Party*, ed. Karl W. Ryavec, Amherst, 1978, pp. 108–133.

19. Nikolai Voznesenskii, *Voennaia ekonomika SSSR v period otechestvennoi voiny* (The war economy of the USSR during the Patriotic War), Moscow, 1947, pp. 42–43.

20. *Istoriia Velikoi otechestvennoi voiny*, 2:160.

21. For further details, see Aleksandr Nekrich, *The Punished Peoples*, New York, 1978; and Robert Conquest, *The Soviet Deportation of Nationalities*, London, 1960.

22. Kh. Salimov, *Naselenie Srednei Azii* (The Population of Central Asia), Tashkent, 1975, p. 92.

23. David J. Dallin and Boris I. Nikolaevsky, *Forced Labor in Soviet Russia*, New Haven, 1947, pp. 263–264.

24. For a detailed account, see Solzhenitsyn, *Gulag Archipelago*, 3:7–36.

25. Conquest, *Great Terror*, pp. 478–480.

26. *Velikaia otechestvennaia voina Sovetskogo Soiuza, 1941–45. Kratkaia istoriia* (The Great Patriotic War of the Soviet Union, 1941–45: A brief history), Moscow, 1970, p. 115. (Hereafter *Kratkaia istoriia.*)

27. *Istoriia Velikoi otechestvennoi voiny*, 2:240.

28. Kurt von Tippelskirch, *Geschichte des zweiten Weltkriegs*, Bonn, 1951; the statistics are cited from the Russian translation, *Istoriia Vtoroi mirovoi voiny*, Moscow, 1956, p. 200.

29. *Kratkaia istoriia*, p. 120.

30. Zhukov, *Vospominaniia*, 1974, 2:35.
31. Walther Hubatsch, ed., *Hitlers Weisungen fur die Kriegsführung 1939–1945: Dokumente des Oberkommandos der Wehrmacht*, Frankfurt am Main, 1962, p. 171, doc. 39.
32. Zhukov, *Vospominaniia*, 1974, 2:46–47.
33. Kirill Meretskov, *Na sluzhbe narodu* (Serving the people), Moscow, 1971, p. 259.
34. Ibid., pp. 260–261.
35. *Kratkaia istoriia*, p. 158.
36. Franz Halder, *War Diaries*, Russ. ed., vol. 3, pt. 2, Moscow, 1971, p. 250, entry for May 19, 1942.
37. Zhukov, *Vospominaniia*, 1974, 2:66–67.
38. Ibid., p. 69.
39. A. M. Vasilevskii, *Delo vsei zhizni* (A whole life's work), Moscow, 1974.
40. Khrushchev, *Khrushchev Remembers*, pp. 185–186.
41. Zhukov, *Vospominaniia*, 1974, 2:69.
42. Tippelskirch, *Geschichte*, p. 232.
43. Ibid., pp. 178, 184, 194, 200.
44. Alexander Dallin, *German Rule in Russia, 1941–1945*, London, 1957, p. 424, n.2.
45. K. Kromiadi, "Sovetskie voennoplennye v Germanii v 1941 godu" (Soviet prisoners of war in Germany in 1941), *Novyi zhurnal*, no. 32, 1953, p. 194.
46. Dallin, *German Rule*, pp. 427, 424.
47. *Kratkaia istoriia*, pp. 155–157.
48. *Istoriia Velikoi otechestevennoi voiny*, 2:430.
49. Conquest, *Great Terror*, p. 655.
50. *Kratkaia istoriia*, pp. 594–595.
51. Voznesenskii, *Voennaia ekonomika SSSR*, p. 42.
52. *Niurnbergskii protsess* (The Nuremburg Trial), vol. 5, Moscow, 1958, p. 30.
53. *IMT*, 26:622, doc. 1058–PS.
54. *Hitler's Table Talk, 1941–1944*, trans. Norman Caneron and R. H. Stevens, London, 1953, p. 424.
55. Reuben Ainsztein, *Jewish Resistance in Nazi-Occupied Eastern Europe*, London, 1974, p. 239. See also, *Chernaia kniga (Black book)*, ed. Vasilii Grossman and Il'ia Erenburg, Jerusalem, 1980.
56. Ainsztein, p. 239.
57. *Istoriia SSSR*, 10:390.
58. Joachim Hoffmann, *Deutsche und Kalmyken, 1942–1945*, Freiburg, 1974, p. 136.
59. M. Luther, "Die Krim unter deutscher Besatzung im zweiten Weltkriegs," Studies in East European History, vol. 3, Berlin, 1956, p. 61; E. Kirimal, *Der nationale Kampf der Krimturken*, Emsdetten, 1952, p. 311.
60. Dallin, *German Rule*, p. 143.
61. Nekrich, *Punished Peoples*, pp. 28–31.
62. *Kratkaia istoriia*, p. 595.
63. Ibid. pp. 598–599.
64. These are approximate figures. Cf. ibid., p. 579.
65. J. K. Zawodny, *Death in the Forest*, South Bend, 1962, p. 10.
66. *Izvestiia*, April 16, 1943.
67. *Vneshniaia politika Sovetskogo Soiuza v period Otechestvennoi voiny*, 1:346–359.
68. Churchchill, *Second World War*, 4:760–761.
69. *Vneshniaia politika Sovetskogo Soiuza v period Otechestvennoi voiny*, 1:397–400.

70. *Izvestiia*, January 24, 1944.
71. Churchill, *Second World War*, 4:761.
72. Jan Abramski and Ryszard Zywiecki, *Katyn*, Warsaw, 1977, p. 14.
73. Zawodny, *Death*, p. 109.
74. Ibid., p. 158.
75. Harvey Fireside, *Icon and Swastika*, Cambridge, 1971, p. 166.
76. Dallin, *German Rule*, p. 424, n. 2.
77. *Zhurnal Moskovskoi Patriarkhii* (Journal of the Moscow Patriarchate), no. 1, September 12, 1943, p. 7.
78. William C. Fletcher, *The Russian Orthodox Church Underground, 1917–1970*, London, 1971, pp. 161–164.
79. Fireside, *Icon*, p. 87.
80. Dallin, *German Rule*, p. 480.
81. Fireside, *Icon*, p. 112.
82. Wilfried Strik-Strikfeldt, *Against Stalin and Hitler*, London, 1970, p. 30.
83. Fireside, *Icon*, p. 119.
84. William C. Fletcher, *A Study in Survival: The Church in Russia, 1927–1943*, New York, 1965, p. 115.
85. *Vneshniaia politika Sovetskogo Soiuza v period Otechestvennoi voiny*, 1:729.
86. Fletcher, *Study in Survival*, p. 107.
87. *Zhurnal Moskovskoi Patriarkhii*, no. 1, 1943, p. 16.
88. Ibid., no. 3, 1943, pp. 22–25.
89. Metropolitan Nikolai, "Verkhovnyi vozhd' strany i Krasnoi armii" (Supreme leader of the country and the Red army), *Zhurnal Moskovskoi Patriarkhii*, no. 1, 1944, p. 14.
90. Franz von Papen, *Memoirs*, London, 1952, p. 479.
91. For details, see A. M. Nekrich, *Vneshniaia politika Anglii 1939–1941*, (England's Foreign Policy, 1939–1941), Moscow, 1963.
92. Harvey Cantril, *Public Opinion 1935–1946*, Princeton, 1956, p. 276.
93. Winston Churchill, *The Unrelenting Struggle*, Boston, 1942, pp. 171–174.
94. H. Nicolson, *Diaries, 1939–1945*, London, 1970, pp. 173–174.
95. For the text of the agreement, see *Vneshniaia politika Sovetskogo Soiuza v period Otechestvennoi voiny*, 1:131–132.
96. Ibid., pp. 139–144.
97. Ibid., pp. 176–178.
98. Basil K. Liddell Hart, ed., *History of the Second World War*, London, 1970, vol. 3, no. 6, pp. 1057–1058.
99. *Istoriia Velikoi otechestvennoi voiny*, 6:48, 62.
100. The abundance of works, both Soviet and Western, on the history of the "second front" is so great that only the essential aspects need be included here. The official positions of the U.S., British, and Soviet governments are presented in the State Department publication *Foreign Relations* for the appropriate years, and in a two-volume documentary collection issued by the Soviet Foreign Ministry, *Perepiska predsedatelia Soveta Ministrov SSSR s prezidentami SShA i prem'er-ministrami Velikobritanii vo vremia Velikoi otechestvennoi voiny 1941–1945 gg.* (Correspondence of the chairman of the USSR Council of Ministers with the presidents of the U.S.A. and the prime ministers of Britain during the Great Patriotic War, 1941–1945), Moscow, 1957. (Hereafter *Perepiska*.) See also Churchill's memoirs, *Second World War*, vols. 2–4.

Questions of strategy are analyzed in detail in the multivolume official British publication *Grand Strategy*, by J. R. M. Butler, John Ehrman, and I. M. A. Gwyer,

London, 1957–1964. An abridged translation of this work was published in the USSR by Voenizdat (Military Publishing House), 1959–1967.

101. *Kratkaia istoriia*, p. 566.
102. Josif Stalin, "26-aia godovshchina Velikoi oktiabr'skoi sotsialisticheskoi revoliutsii" (26th anniversary of the Great October Socialist revolution ), in *Vneshniaia politika Sovetskogo Soiuza v period Otechestvennoi voiny*, 1:118.
103. *Kratkaia istoriia*, p. 318.
104. *Perepiska*, 1:258, doc. 323: Stalin to Churchill and Roosevelt, August 22, 1944.
105. "Sprava Polska w czasie drugiej wojny światowej na arenie międzynarodowej." Zbior Dokumentow. Warszawa 1965, N54, S. 613–621.
106. *Foreign Relations*, 1944, 3:1335: Roosevelt to Mikolajczyk, November 17, 1944.
107. Churchill, *The Second World War*, vol. 6, London, 1954, p. 198.
108. Ibid., p. 442. See also George Ehrman, *Bol'shaia strategiia oktiabr' 1944–avgust 1945* [The Grand Strategy, October 1944–August 1945], Moscow, 1958, pp. 161–162.
109. E.R. Stettinius, *Roosevelt and the Russians: The Yalta Conference*, New York, 1949, p. 25.
110. *Krymskaia konferentsiia rukovoditelei trekh soiuznykh derzhav—Sovetskogo Soiuza, Soedinennykh Shtatov Ameriki i Velikobritanii (4-11 fevralia 1945 g.)* (The Crimean Conference of the Leaders of the Three Allied Powers—The Soviet Union, the United States of America, and Great Britain), Moscow, 1979, p. 47. (Hereafter cited as *Krymskaia konferentsiia*).
111. *The Conferences at Malta and Yalta, 1945*, Washington, D.C., U.S. Government Printing Office, 1955, p. 668.
112. Ibid.
113. Ibid., pp. 669–670.
114. Stettinius, p. 113.
115. *Sotsialistickeskii vestnik*, No. 1–2, January 10, 1944, p. 2.
116. *The Conferences at Malta and Yalta*, p. 720.
117. *Krymskaia konferentsiia*, p. 93.
118. Stettinius, p. 220.
119. *Krymskaia konferentsiia*, p. 83.
120. Ibid., p. 211.
121. Ibid., p. 64.
122. *The Conferences at Malta and Yalta*, p. 589; Stettinius, p. 112.
123. *The Conferences at Malta and Yalta*, p. 589.
124. Stettinius, p. 112.
125. Ibid., pp. 112–113.
126. Churchill, p. 392; *The Conferences at Malta and Yalta*, p. 923.
127. *Kratkaia istoriia*, p. 460.
128. Ibid., p. 466.
129. V. I. Iukshinskii, *Sovetskie kontsentratsionnye Iageri v 1945–1955 gg.* (Soviet concentration camps, 1945–1955), Munich, 1958, pp. 29–30.
130. Dallin, *German Rule*, p. 531.
131. *IMT*, vol. 38, p. 88, doc. 221-L.
132. Gerald Reitlinger, *The House Built on Sand*, New York, 1960, pp. 310–311.
133. Sven Steenberg, *Wlassow, Verräter oder Patriot?* Cologne, 1968, p. 80.
134. Patrik von zur Mühlen, *Zwischen Hackenkreuz und Sowjetstern*, Dusseldorf, 1971, p. 60.

135. According to Western sources, no less than 8,000 Russians from German units joined the French Resistance. See Nikolai Tolstoy, *Victims of Yalta*, London, 1977, p. 57.

136. Ibid.

137. For a detailed account, see Strik-Strikfeldt, *Against Stalin and Hitler*.

138. For material on Vlasov's biography, see Strik-Strikfeldt, *Against Stalin and Hitler*; and V. M. Shatov, *Materialy i dokumenty osvoboditel'nogo dvizheniia narodov Rossii v gody Vtoroi mirovoi voiny, 1941–1945* (Materials and documents of the liberation movement of the peoples of Russia during World War II, 1941–1945), New York, 1966.

139. Khrushchev, *Khrushchev Remembers*, p. 181.

140. *Parizhskii vestnik*, (Paris herald), June 12, 1943.

141. Dallin, *German Rule*, p. 558.

142. *Parizhskii vestnik*, July 31, 1943.

143. The text of the manifesto is in V. Osokin, *Andrei Andreevich Vlasov*, New York, 1966, p. 28.

144. Boris Nikolaevskii, "O 'staroi' i 'novoi' emigratsii" (On the 'old' and 'new' emigrations), pt. 2, *Sotsialisticheskii vestnik* (Paris), no. 2, 1948, p. 33.

145. See, for example, *Parizhskii vestnik*, June 5, 1943.

146. George Fischer, *Soviet Opposition to Stalin*, Cambridge, 1952, app. 3, pp. 188–193.

147. Iu. Pis'mennyi, "Ob odnom voprose, sviazannom s Manifestom" (On one question concerning the manifesto), in Shatov, *Materialy*, pp. 151–154.

148. Nikolaevskii, "O 'staroi,'" p. 35.

149. Fischer, *Soviet Opposition*, pp. 96–97.

150. Iu. Koreiskii, "Poezdka v Verkhniuiu Sileziiu" (Journey to Upper Silesia), in Shatov, *Materialy*, p. 69.

151. Fischer, *Soviet Opposition*, pp. 100–103.

152. Petro Grigorenko, *Memoirs*, New York, 1982, p. 94.

153. See Petro Grigorenko, *V podpol'e mozhno vstretit' tol'ko krys* (In the underground you meet only rats), New York, 1981, p. 216.

154. *Foreign Relations of the United States: "The Conference of Berlin" (The Potsdam Conference)*, vol. 1, Washington, D.C., 1945, pp. 41–42.

155. Arthur Bryant, *Triumph in the West*, London, 1959, p. 478.

156. *Vneshniaia politika Sovetskogo Soiuza. 1946 god* (Foreign policy of the Soviet Union: 1946), Moscow, 1952, p. 40.

157. *Kratkaia istoriia*, p. 542.

158. Ibid., p. 553.

159. *Vneshniaia politika Sovetskogo Soiuza v period Otechestvennoi voiny*, 3:458–475.

160. These figures were first made public by Khrushchev in 1961.

161. *Istoriia SSSR*, 10:390.

162. All figures on losses in World War II are taken from Liddell Hart, *History of the Second World War*, vol. 6, no. 16, pp. 2682–2683.

163. *Sovetskaia voennaia entsiklopediia* (Soviet military encyclopedia), vol. 8, Moscow, 1980. p. 539.

164. N. N. Voronov, *Na sluzhbe voennoi* (In military service), Moscow, 1963, p. 174.

165. *Voenno-istoricheskii zhurnal*, no. 6, 1965, pp. 7–8.

166. *Vneshniaia politika Sovetskogo Soiuza v period Otechestvennoi voiny*, 1:43.

167. *Vneshniaia politika SSSR, 1949* (Foreign policy of the USSR, 1949), Moscow, 1953, p. 28.

168. Svetlana Alliluyeva, *Only One Year*, New York, 1970, p. 392.

## CHAPTER NINE

1. "Agreement Between the USA and the Soviet Union Concerning Liberated Prisoners of War and Civilians," in *Foreign Relations of the United States: Diplomatic Papers: The Conferences of Malta and Yalta, 1945*, Washington, D.C., 1955, pp. 985–987, also pp. 694–696, 946.
2. Nicholas W. Bethell, *The Last Secret*, New York, 1974.
3. Tolstoy, *Victims*, p. 185.
4. N N. Krasnov-mladshii, *Nezabyvaemoe 1945–1956. Russkaid zhizn'* (Unforgettable times, 1945–1956: Russian life), San Francisco, 1958, p. 79.
5. *Sotsialisticheskii vestnik*, no. 8, 1946, pp. 186–188; V. Novikov, "Vstrechi s sovetskimi poddannymi vo Frantsii" (Meetings with Soviet citizens in France), *Novyi zhurnal*, no. 12, 1946, pp. 207–222.
6. *Izvestiia*, December 9, 10, 1947.
7. Tolstoy, *Victims*, p. 409.
8. Fischer, *Soviet Opposition*, pp. 114–115.
9. *Istoriia Velikoi otechestvennoi voiny*, 5:107.
10. V. Kubijovic, "Ukraine During World War II," in V. Kubijovic, ed., *Ukraine: A Concise Encyclopedia*, vol. 1, Toronto, 1963, pp. 872–873.
11. Ibid., pp. 879, 886.
12. For details, see John A. Armstrong, *Ukrainian Nationalism, 1939–1945*, New York, 1955, pp. 77–102.
13. Yaroslav Bilinsky, *The Second Soviet Republic: The Ukraine After World War II*, New Brunswick, 1964, pp. 130–132.
14. M. Prokop, "The Ukrainian Insurgent Army," in Kubijovic, *Ukraine*, vol. 2, 1971, pp. 1089–1090.
15. Bilinsky, *Second Soviet Republic*, pp. 101–109.
16. V. Holubnichy, "Ukraine Since World War II, 1945–1962," in Kubijovic, *Ukraine*, 1:903.
17. Bilinsky, *Second Soviet Republic*, p. 132.
18. *FR*, 1947, 3:224–225, 237–238.
19. Harry S. Truman, *Public Papers, 1948*, Washington, D.C., 1964, pp. 178–179.
20. *Istoriia vneshnei politika SSSR 1945–1975* (History of Soviet foreign policy, 1945–1975) vol. 2, Moscow, 1976, pp. 137–141.
21. *Mirnyi dogover s Italiei* (The Peace Treaty with Italy), Moscow, 1947.
22. *Istoriia vneshnei politiki SSSR*, pp. 38–39; Daniel Yergin, *Shattered Peace*, Boston, 1977, pp. 143, 150.
23. *Vneshniaia politika SSSR, 1948 god*, pt. 1, Moscow, 1950, p. 203.
24. *Freundschaft DDR-UdSSR. Dokumenten und Materialen*, Berlin, 1965; *Obrazovanie GDR. Dokumenty i materialy* (The formation of the GDR: Documents and materials), Moscow, 1950, pp. 13–16.
25. *Documents on American Foreign Relations*, vol. 13, Princeton, 1953, p. 483.
26. For details, see Vladimir Dedijer, *The Battle Stalin Lost*, New York, 1972.
27. Ibid., pp. 190–191; see also Milovan Djilas, *Conversations with Stalin*, New York, 1962, pp. 178–186.
28. Khrushchev, *Khrushchev Remembers*, app. 4, p. 600.

29. *Soveshchanie Informatsionnogo biuro kommunisticheskikh partii v Varshave, iiun' 1948* (Conference of the Information Bureau of the Communist parties, June 1948), Moscow, 1948.

30. Lenin, *PSS*, 40:43.

31. *Times*, March 6, 1946.

32. *Vneshniaia politika Sovetskogo Soiuza, 1946*, pp. 167–170.

33. Walter Bedell Smith, *My Three Years in Moscow*, New York, 1950, pp. 52–54.

34. Ministerstvo Inostrannykh Del SSSR (USSR Ministry of Foreign Affairs), *Sovetskii Soiuz i berlinskii vopros. Dokumenty* (The Soviet Union and the Berlin question: Documents), Moscow, 1948.

35. See, for example, *Istoriia vneshnei politiki SSSR, 1945–1975*, vol. 2, pp. 156–160.

36. Khrushchev, *Khrushchev Remembers*, p. 368.

37. Ibid., p. 369.

38. Ibid., p. 370.

39. *Vneshniaia politika SSSR, 1950 god* (Foreign policy of the USSR, 1950), 1953, p. 189.

40. *Istoriia vneshnei politiki SSSR, 1945–1975*, vol. 2, p. 165.

41. Ibid.

42. Truman, *Public Papers, 1950*, p. 727.

43. *Naselenie SSSR. Spravochnik* (Population of the USSR: Statistical handbook), Moscow, 1974, p. 8.

44. Ibid., p. 11.

45. *Vedomosti Verkhovnogo Soveta SSSR*, (Gazette of the Supreme Council of the USSR), September 9, 1945.

46. Report of a special government commission, quoted in *Vneshniaia politika Sovetskogo Soiuza, 1945 god* (Foreign policy of the Soviet Union, 1946), Moscow, 1949, p. 36.

47. *Istoriia SSSR. Epokha sotsializma* (History of the USSR: Age of socialism), Moscow, 1957, p. 653.

48. *Narodnoe khoziaistvo SSSR. Statisticheskii sbornik* (Economy of the USSR: Collected Statistics), Moscow, 1956, pp. 63, 65.

49. Ibid., p. 75.

50. Ibid., p. 46.

51. Ibid.

52. *Izvestiia*, September 25, 1949.

53. For details, see Zhores A. Medvedev, *Soviet Science*, New York, 1978, p. 52.

54. Alec Nove, *An Economic History of the USSR*, London, 1972, p. 319.

55. *Narodnoe khoziaistvo SSSR*, pp. 62–69.

56. B. Nosik, *Po Rusi iaroslavskoi* (Through the Old Russian Yaroslavl region), Moscow, 1968, pp. 164–178.

57. *Sbornik zakonov SSSR 1938–1967* (Registry of laws of the USSR, 1938–1967), vol. 2, Moscow, 1968, pp. 165–173.

58. Ibid., pp. 409–418.

59. Khrushchev, *Khrushchev Remembers*, p. 233.

60. Ibid., p. 235.

61. Akademiia nauk Latviiskoi SSR, Institut istorii (Latvian Academy of Sciences, Institute of History), *Istoriia Latviiskoi SSR. Sokrashchennyi kurs* (History of the Latvian SSR: Abridged course), 2d rev. and enl. ed., Riga, 1971, pp. 706–707.

62. *Istoriia SSSR. Epokha sotsializma*, 1974, p. 413.

63. Akademiia nauk Latviiskoi SSR, Institut istorii i material'noi kul'tury (Latvian Acad-

emy of Sciences, Institute of History and Material Culture), *Istoriia Latviiskoi SSR* (History of the Latvian SSR), vol. 3, Riga, 1958, p. 644.

64. Ibid.

65. J. Zhiugzhdyi, ed., *Istoriia Litovskoi SSR. Uchebnik dlia VII-VIII klassov* (History of the Lithuanian SSR: Textbook for grades 7 and 8), Kaunas, 1963, p. 116.

66. Akademiia nauk Belorusskoi SSR, Institut istorii (Academy of Sciences of the Belorussian SSR, Institute of History), *Istoriia Belorusskoi SSR* (History of the Belorussian SSR), vol. 2, Minsk, 1961, p. 532.

67. *Istoriia SSSR. Epokha sotsializma*, 1974, p. 411.

68. Ibid.

69. Ibid.

70. *Vneshniaia politika Sovetskogo Soiuza, 1945 god*, p. 36.

71. *Naselenie SSSR. Statisticheskii sbornik* (Population of the USSR: Collected statistics), Moscow, 1974, p. 53.

72. *KPSS v rezoliutsiiakh*, 6:176.

73. Robert Conquest, *Power and Policy in the USSR*, New York, 1961, p. 113.

74. *Istoriia Uzbekskoi SSR* (History of the Uzbek SSR), 4 vols., Tashkent, 1967–1968, 4:171.

75. Quoted in *Sotsialisticheskaia zakonnost'* (Socialist legality), no. 9, 1950, p. 3.

76. *Istoriia Sibiri* (History of Siberia), vol. 5, Leningrad, 1969, p. 185.

77. N. S. Khrushchev, "Doklad na plenume TsK KPSS 15 dekabria 1958 g." (Report at the December 15, 1958, plenum of the Central Committee of the CPSU), in *Stroitel'stvo kommunizma v SSSR i razvitie sel'skogo khoziaistva* (The building of communism in the USSR and agricultural development), vol. 2, Moscow, 1962, p. 344.

78. Ibid., p. 345.

79. Iu. B. Arutiunian, "Osobennosti i znachenie novogo etapa razvitiia sel'skogo khoziaistva SSSR" (Specific features and significance of the new stage of development of agriculture of the USSR), in *Istoriia sovetskogo krest'ianstva i kolkhoznogo stroitel'stva v SSSR. Materialy nauchnoi sessii, 18–21 aprelia 1961 g.* (History of the Soviet peasantry and collective farm construction in the USSR: Materials form a scholarly conference, April 18–21, 1961), Moscow, 1963, p. 409.

80. Ibid.

81. *Narodnoe khoziaistvo SSSR*, p. 123.

82. Ibid., p. 124.

83. *Istoriia SSSR. Epokha sotsializma*, 1974, p. 681. In subsequent editions these figures were deleted. See also Khrushchev, *Stroitel'stvo kommunizma*, 1:20.

84. See Nove, *Economic History*, p. 300.

85. *Narodnoe khoziaistvo SSSR*, p. 100.

86. Greorgii Malenkov, *Otchetnyi doklad XIX s"ezdu partii o rabote Tsentral'nogo Komiteta VKP(b)* (Report to the Nineteenth Party Congress on the work of the Central Committee), Moscow, 1952, p. 48.

87. Abram Bergson, *The Real National Income of Soviet Russia Since 1928*, Cambridge, 1961, table H-1, p. 422.

88. Janet G. Chapman, *Real Wages in Soviet Russia Since 1928*, Cambridge, 1963, p. 139.

89. Ibid., p. 145.

90. Ibid., pp. 145–147.

91. Ibid., p. 176.

92. Ibid., pp. 55–57.

93. Khrushchev, *Stroitel'stvo kommunizma*, 2:344.
94. Naum Jasny, *The Soviet 1956 Statistical Handbook: A Commentary*, East Lansing, 1957, p. 149.
95. Arvid Brodersen, *The Soviet Worker*, New York, 1966, p. 132.
96. *Vo glave zashchity sovetskoi rodiny. Ocherk deiatel'nosti KPSS v gody Velikoi otechestvennoi voiny* (Heading the defense of the Soviet homeland: Outline of the activities of the CPSU during the Great Patriotic War), Moscow, 1975, p. 362.
97. *Istoriia Velikoi otechestvennoi voiny Sovetskogo Soiuza*, 6:366.
98. Ibid., p. 365.
99. Leonard Schapiro, *The Communist Party of the Soviet Union*, New York: 1960, p. 440.
100. Brodersen, *Soviet Worker*, p. 228.
101. Rigby, *Communist Party Membership in the USSR 1917–1967*, p. 453. According to Professor Rigby's estimates, 32.1 percent of those joining the party during the war could be classified as blue collar workers, 25.3 percent as peasants, and 42.6 percent as white collar workers (p. 239).
102. Brodersen, *Soviet Worker*, p. 234.
103. *Vneshniaia politika Sovetskogo Soiuza v period otechestvennoi voiny*, 2:45.
104. *Pravda*, June 27, 1945.
105. For details, see Mark Popovskii, *Upravliaemaia nauka*, pp. 29–30; and Zhores A. Medvedev, The Rise and Fall of T. D. Lysenko, New York, 1969.
106. For details, see *O polozhenii v biologicheskoi nauke. Stenograficheskii otchet sessii Vsesoiuznoi Akademii sel'skokhoziaistvennykh nauk imeni V. I. Lenina, 31 iiulia–7 avgusta 1948 g.* (On the situation in biological science: Stenographic record of the session of the V. I. Lenin All-Union Academy of Agricultural Sciences, July 31–August 7, 1948), Moscow, 1948.
107 *Kul'tura i zhizn'* (Culture and life), September 11, 1948.
108. Ibid., July 17, 1950.
109. Ibid.
110. Ibid.
111. Ibid., August 21, 1948.
112. *Vestnik Akademii Nauk SSSR* (Bulletin of the USSR Academy of Sciences), no. 2, 1949, pp. 99–102, 130–134.
113. Khrushchev, *The Last Testament*, pp. 63–67.
114. See *Documents on Polish–Soviet Relations, 1939–1945*, vol. 1, 1939–1943, London, 1961, doc. 298, pp. 503–504; and *The Case of Henry Erlich and Victor Alter*, New York, 1943.
115. *Ivzestiia*, February 19, 1946.
116. Mikhail Zoshchenko, *Izbrannoe* (A Selection), Ann Arbor, 1960, pp. 316–324.
117. *Pravda*, August 22, 1946.
118. *Literaturnaia gazeta*, December 22, 1948.
119. *Kul'tura i zhizn'*, January 11, 1951.
120. *Pravda*, December 28, 1947.
121. *Kul'tura i zhizn'*, February 21, 1948.
122. Ibid., February 29, April 19, April 21, 1948.
123. *Pravda*, January 28, 1949.
124. *Literaturnaia gazeta*, February 26, 1949.
125. *Voprosy istorii*, no. 11, 1947.
126. Ibid., no. 4, 1951.

127. Conquest, *Great Terror*.
128. R. Roeder, *Katorga*, (Forced Labor), London, 1958, p. xiii.
129. Swianiewicz, *Forced Labour*, p. 44.
130. B. Iakovlev (in collaboration with A. Burtsov), *Kontsentratsionnye lageri SSSR* (The concentration camps of the USSR), Munich, 1955, pp. 65–68.
131. Ibid., p. 80.
132. Ibid., p. 92.
133. Ibid., p. 96.
134. Ibid., p. 167.
135. Ibid., p. 185. Iukshinskii, (*Sovetskie lageri*, p. 52) gives the figure 70,000.
136. V. P. Artem'ev, *Rezhim i okhrana ispravitel'no-trudovykh lagerei MVD* (The regimen and guard system in the corrective labor camps of the MVD), Munich, 1956, p. 11.
137. Ibid.
138. Ibid., pp. 38–39.
139. Iakovlev, *Kontsentratsionnye*, p. 37.
140. Ibid., p. 36.
141. Ibid., p. 38.
142. Artem'ev, *Rezhim*, p. 78.
143. Ibid., p. 69.
144. Iakovlev, *Kontsentratsionnye*, p. 38.
145. Aleksandr Solzhenitsyn, *The Gulag Archipelago*, 3 vols., New York, 1973–1975, 3:108.
146. Ibid., pp. 222–223.
147. Ibid., p. 65.
148. U.S. Senate, *USSR Labour Camps*. Hearings Before the Subcommittee to Investigate the Administration of the Internal Security Act and Other Internal Security Laws of the Committee on the Judiciary, 93rd Cong., 1st Sess., pt. 3, February 2, 1973, Washington, D.C., p. 175.
149. Solzhenitsyn, *Arkhipelag Gulag, 1918–1956*, V-VI-VII, pp. 244–245. Gulag, 3:233–234.
150. Joseph Schomler, *Vorkuta*, London, 1954, pp. 166–167.
151. Ibid., p. 96.
152. Ibid.
153. Paul Barton, *L'institution concentrationnaire en Russe (1930–1957)*, Paris, 1959, p. 287.
154. Solzhenitsyn, *Gulag*, 3:230.
155. Iakovlev, *Kontsentratsionnye*, p. 166.
156. Solzhenitsyn, *Gulag*, 3:230.
157. Ibid., p. 230.
158. Ibid., pp. 229–230.
159. Ibid.
160. Ibid., p. 265 ff.
161. Khrushchev, *Khrushchev Remembers*, pp. 308–309.
162. See Aleksandr Nekrich, "The Arrest and Trial of I. M. Maisky," *Survey*, no. 100–101, 1976, pp. 313–320.
163. Schapiro, *The CPSU*, p. 723.
164. Khrushchev, *Khrushchev Remembers*, p. 246.
165. Ibid., p. 262.
166. Ibid., p. 264.

167. Ibid., p. 263.
168. Ibid.
169. Yehoshua A. Gilboa, *The Black Years of Soviet Jewry, 1939–1953*, Boston, 1971, pp. 52–53.
170. Author's personal archive.
171. Khrushchev, *Khrushchev Remembers*, p. 261.
172. *Pravda*, January 13 and 18, 1953.
173. Ibid., January 21, 1953.
174. *Literaturnaia gazeta*, January 13, 1953.
175. Aleksandr Nekrich, *Otreshis' ot strakha. Vospominaniia istorika* (Forsake fear: Memoirs of a historian), London, 1979, p. 115.
176. Karel Kaplan, *Dans les archives du Comité central. Trente ans de secrets du bloc sovietique*, Paris, 1973, pp. 165–167. The information reported by Kaplan was confirmed by Michal Reiman, another Czech historian, in conversation with the author.
177. Josif Stalin, *Rech' na XIX s"ezde partii, 14 oktiabria 1952* (Speech at the Nineteenth Party Congress, October 14, 1952), Moscow, 1952, p. 6.
178. Ibid., p. 8.
179. Ibid.
180. Ibid., p. 9.
181. Ibid., p. 12.
182. Ibid., p. 13.
183. Ibid.
184. Khrushchev, *Khrushchev Remembers*, pp. 306–315.
185. *Pravda*, March 7, 1953.
186. Krushchev, *Krushchev Remembers*, pp. 317–319.
187. *Pravda*, March 10, 1953.
188. *Kommunist*, no. 4, 1953.
189. Ibid.
190. Robert C. Tucker, ed. *Stalinism: Essays in Historical Interpretation*, New York, 1977.

## CHAPTER TEN

1. *Pravda*, March 12, 1953.
2. Khrushchev, *Khrushchev Remembers*, p. 323.
3. *Pravda*, March 21, 1953.
4. Ibid., March 16, 1953.
5. *Izvestiia*, April 1, 1953.
6. Ibid., March 16, 1953.
7. *Kommunist*, no. 12, 1953, p. 17.
8. Ibid.
9. *Sbornik zakonov SSSR*, 2:285–294.
10. *Kommunist*, no. 1, 1953, p. 5.
11. Ibid., no. 13.
12. Nikita Khrushchev, *O merakh dal'neishego razvitiia sel'skogo khoziaistva SSSR* (On measures for the further development of Soviet agriculture), Moscow, 1953, p. 28.
13. *Pravda*, June 25, 1953.
14. *Izvestiia*, April 4, 1953.
15. Khrushchev, *Khrushchev Remembers*, p. 261.

16. Alliluyeva, *Only One Year*, p. 371.
17. *Izvestiia*, March 28, 1953.
18. K. Nefedov and M. Tiurin, "Druzhba narodov SSSR—istochnik sily sovetskogo go-sudarstva" (Friendship of the Peoples of the USSR—a source of strength for the Soviet state), *Izvestiia*, June 19, 1953.
19. Khrushchev, *Khrushchev Remembers*, p. 330.
20. Ibid.
21. *Izvestiia*, July 12, 1953; see the lead editorial "Osnovy prochnosti mnogonatsional'nogo sovetskogo gosudarstva" (The foundations of the stability of the multinational Soviet state).
22. Ibid., March 16, 1953.
23. *Public Papers of the Presidents: Dwight D. Eisenhower*, Washington, D.C., 1960, p. 184.
24. Ibid., pp. 184–185.
25. *Pravda*, April 25, 1953.
26. *Times*, April 27, 1953.
27. United Kingdom House of Commons, *Parliamentary Debates*, vol. 515, col. 895, May 11, 1953.
28. This account of the events at Kengir is based on information published in the following works: Barton, *L'institution concentrationnaire*, pp. 323–340; U.S. Senate, *USSR Labour Camps*. pp. 169–175; Solzhenitsyn, *Gulag*, 3:290–331; Alexander Dolgun and Patrick Watson, *An American in the Gulag*, New York, 1975, pp. 283–292; Liubov' Bershadskaia, *Rastoptannye zhizni* (Trampled lives), Paris, 1975, pp. 82–100; and Krasnov-mladshii, *Nezabyvaemoe*, pp. 216–217.
29. Zdenek Suda, *The Czechoslovak Socialist Republic*, Baltimore, 1969, p. 66.
30. Walther Hubatsch, ed., *The German Question*, New York, 1967, p. 156.
31. Ibid.
32. Philip Windsor, *City on Leave: A History of Berlin, 1945–1962*, New York, 1963, p. 154; Hubatsch, *German Question*, p. 157.
33. Windsor, *City on Leave*, p. 155; for details, see *Der Volksaufstand vom 17. Juni, 1953*, Bonn, 1963.
34. Hubatsch, *German Question*, p. 157.
35. Paul Kecskemeti, *The Unexpected Revolution*, Stanford, 1961, p. 42.
36. Imre Nagy, *On Communism: In Defense of the New Course*, New York, 1957, pp. 80–86.
37. Kecskemeti, *Unexpected Revolution*, p. 51.
38. Ferenc A. Vali, *Rift and Revolt in Hungary*, Cambridge, 1961, pp. 200–210.
39. *Pravda*, July 16, 1953.
40. *Izvestiia*, December 17 and 24, 1953.
41. *Pravda*, July 23, 1954.
42. Ibid., December 24, 1954.
43. See, for example, the economic plan for 1941 found in the Smolensk archives, cited earlier.
44. Roy and Zhores Medvedev, *N. S. Khrushchev. Gody u vlasti* (N. S. Khrushchev: The years in power), New York, 1975, p. 33.
45. Conquest, *Great Terror*.
46. Roy and Zhores Medvedev, *Khrushchev: The Years in Power*, New York, 1975, p. 63.
47. *Sbornik zakonov*, 2:629–632.

48. Peter Raina, *Political Opposition in Poland, 1954–1977*, London, 1978, pp. 30–31.

49. Khrushchev, *Khrushchev Remembers*, pp. 254, 256.

50. *Izvestiia*, February 9, 1955.

51. Khrushchev, *Khrushchev Remembers*, p. 343.

52. Ibid.

53. Ibid., p. 344.

54. *Dvadtsatyi s"ezd Kommunisticheskoi partii Sovetskogo Soiuza, 14–25 fevralia 1956 g. Stenograficheskii otchet* (Twentieth Congress of the CPSU, February 14–25, 1956: Stenographic record), vol. 1, Moscow, 1956, pp. 102, 115, 116.

55. Ibid., pp. 99–100.

56. Ibid., p. 326.

57. Khrushchev, *Khrushchev Remembers*, pp. 347–348.

58. Ibid., p. 349.

59. Ibid., p. 353.

60. Khrushchev's "secret speech" at the Twentieth Congress was never published in the official Soviet press. Its contents became known in the West almost immediately, however, and the full text of the speech was soon translated into all main languages of the world. It is included as an appendix to Khrushchev, *Khrushchev Remembers*.

61. *Dvadtsatyi s"ezd*, pp. 89–91.

62. See, for example, Nekrich, *Otreshis' ot strakha*, pp. 141–143.

63. See, for example, Arthur Gerard London, *On Trial*, London, 1970.

64. *KPSS v rezoliutsiiakh*, 7:199–218.

65. For details, see Nekrich, *Nakazannye narody*; and Conquest, *The Soviet Deportation of Nationalities*.

66. Kh. I. Khutuev, *Balkarskii narod v gody Velikoi otechestvennoi voiny i poslevoennyi period* (The Balkar people during the Great Patriotic War and in the postwar period), Manuscript at the Lenin Library in Moscow, reg. Dk 67–7/513, pp. 164–171.

67. The decrees restoring autonomy to these populations were published in *Vedomosti Verkhovnogo Soveta SSSR* (News of the Supreme Soviet of the USSR), February 24, 1957, no. 4 (871), p. 134.

68. "Obrashchenie krymsko-tatarskogo naroda k belgradskomu soveshchaniiu po bezopasnosti i sotrudnichestvu v Evrope" (Appeal of the Crimean Tatar people to the Belgrade Conference on Security and Cooperation in Europe), in Nekrich, *Nakazannye narody*, p. 155.

69. S. Sul'kevich, *Naselenie SSSR* (The Population of the USSR), Moscow, 1939, p. 30.

70. R. Muzafarcy, *Vdali ot krymskikh gor* (Far from the Crimean mountains), Manuscript, p. 67.

71. Nekrich, *Nakazannye narody*, p. 116.

72. Ibid., pp. 126–128.

73. *Zasedaniia Verkhovnogo Soveta Kalmykskoi ASSR, 2-go sozyva. Stenograficheskii otchet* (Proceedings of the Second Supreme Soviet of the Kalmyk ASSR: Stenographic record), Elista, 1958, p. 120.

74. Raina, *Political Opposition in Poland*, pp. 44–45.

75. Khrushchev, *The Last Testament*, p. 203.

76. Ibid.

77. Ibid., pp. 203–204.

78. Ibid., p. 205.

79. Kecskemeti, *Unexpected Revolution*, p. 71.

80. Ibid., p. 76.
81. Stephen D. Kertesz, *East Central Europe and the World: Developments in the Post-Stalin Era*, South Bend, 1962, p. 125.
82. Vali, *Rift and Revolt*, p. 321.
83. Ibid., p. 285.
84. François Fejto, *Behind the Rape of Hungary*, New York, 1957, pp. 237–238.
85. Ibid., pp. 223–224.
86. For details, see Tibor Meray, *Thirteen Days That Shook the Kremlin*, New York, 1959; and Hungarian Committee, *Facts About Hungary*, comp. and ed. Imre Kovac, New York, 1958.
87. *Pravda*, October 28, 1956; see the lead article, "Proval antinarodnoi avantiury v Vengrii" (Collapse of the anti-people's adventure iin Hungary).
88. Khrushchev, *Khrushchev Remembers*, p. 417.
89. Ibid.
90. Ibid.
91. Khrushchev, *Khrushchev Remembers*, p. 419.
92. Ibid.
93. Khrushchev, *Khrushchev Remembers*, p. 421; see also Richard Lowenthal, "Tito's Affair with Khrushchev," *New Leader*, October 6, 1958.
94. Vali, *Rift and Revolt*, pp. 368–369.
95. Ibid., p. 371.
96. For details on the discussion of the Hungarian question at the United Nations, see Kertesz, *East Central Europe*, pp. 146–152.
97. Vali, *Rift and Revolt*, p. 375.
98. *Pravda*, June 16, 1958.
99. *Narodnoe khoziaistvo SSSR v 1959 godu. Statisticheskii sbornik* (Economy of the USSR in 1959: Collected statistics), Moscow, 1960, pp. 329–333; and *Narodnoe khoziaistvo SSSR v 1964 godu. Statisticheskii sbornik* (Economy of the USSR in 1964: Collected statistics), Moscow, 1965, pp. 272–273.
100. "Postanovlenie plenuma TsK KPSS o merakh dal'neishego razvitiia sel'skogo khoziaistva SSSR, 7 sentiabria 1953 g." (Resolutiion of the Central Committee plenum on measures for the further development of agriculture in the USSR, September 7, 1953), in *KPSS v rezoliutsiiakh*, vol. 6 (1951–1954), Moscow, 1971, pp. 385–429.
101. *Dvadtsatyi s"ezd*, 1:55.
102. "Postanovlenie plenuma TsK KPSS o dal'neishem uvelichenii proizvodstva zerna v strane i ob osvoenii tselinnykh i zalezhnykh zemel', 2 marta 1954 g." (Resolution of the Central Committee plenum on further increasing the production of grain in the country and cultivating virgin and fallow lands, March 2, 1954), in *KPSS v rezoliutsiiakh*, 6:437–442.
103. Khrushchev, *Stroitel'stvo kommunizma*, 2:243.
104. Martin McCauley, *Khrushchev and the Development of Soviet Agriculture*, London, 1976, p. 88.
105. Nazodnoe khoziaistro SSSR v 1958 godu, p. 436; nazodnoe khoziaistro SSSR v 1965 godu, p. 311.
106. "Postanovlenie TsK KPSS i Soveta Ministrov SSSR ob izmenenii praktiki planirovaniia sel'skogo khoziaistva, 9 marta 1955 g." (Resolution of the Central Committee and Council of Ministers on changes in agricultural planning, March 9, 1955), in *KPSS v rezoliutsiiakh*, vol. 7 (1955–1959), Moscow, 1971, pp. 52–70. See also the March 6, 1956 resolution, pp. 183–200.

107. For a detailed analysis of the policy on maize, se Naum Jasny, *Khrushchev's Crop Policy*, Glasgow, 1965, pp. 100–114.

108. Khrushchev, *Stroitel'stvo kommunizma*, 2:57.

109. Jasny, *Crop Policy*, p. 88; Nazodnoe khoziaistro SSSR v 1965 godu, p. 311.

110. Khrushchev, *Stroitel'stvo kommunizma*, 2:444–449.

111. Ibid., p. 446.

112. *Narodnoe khoziaistvo SSSR v 1960, godu: Statisticheskii sbornik* (Economy of the USSR in 1960: Collected statistics), Moscow, 1961, pp. 440–441.

113. *Narodnoe khoziaistvo SSSR v 1958 godu: Statisticheskii sbornik* (Economy of the USSR in 1958: Collected statistics), Moscow, 1959, p. 469; *Narodnoe khoziaistvo SSSR v 1964 godu*, p. 362.

114. Khrushchev, *Stroitel'stvo kommunizma*, 4:61.

115. Ibid., pp. 364, 497. Admissions of deception occur here and in several other works and statements by Khrushchev.

116. *Narodnoe khoziaistvo SSSR v 1964 godu*, p. 362.

117. Ibid., p. 250.

118. "Postanovlenie plenuma TsK KPSS o dal'neishem razvitii kolkhoznogo stroia i reorganizatsii mashinno-traktornykh stantsii" (Resolution of the Central Committee plenum on the further development of the kolkhoz system and reorganization of the machine and tractor stations), *KPSS v rezoliutsiiakh*, 7:316–322.

119. R. and Zh. Medvedev, *Khrushchev*, p. 101.

120. Sidney I. Ploss, *Conflict and Decision-Making in Soviet Russia: A Case Study of Agricultural Policy, 1953–1963*, Princeton, 1965, p. 209.

121. *Narodnoe khoziaistvo SSSR v 1964 godu*, p. 261.

122. Ibid., p. 353.

123. Ibid., p. 245.

124. Khrushchev, *Stroitel'stvo kommunizma*, 8:304.

125. *Narodnoe khoziaistvo SSSR v 1965 godu. Statisticheskii sbornik* (Economy of the USSR in 1965: Collected statistics), Moscow, 1966, p. 188; *Narodnoe khoziaistvo SSSR v 1972 godu. Statisticheskii sbornik* (Economy of the USSR in 1972: Collected statistics), Moscow, 1973, p. 219; *Narodnoe khoziaistvo SSSR v 1977 godu. Statisticheskii sbornik* (Economy of the USSR in 1977: Collected statistics), Moscow, 1978, p. 155.

126. L. I. Brezhnev, *Leninskim kursom* (By the Leninist course), Moscow, 1970, pp. 68–93.

127. John A. Armstrong, *The Politics of Totalitarianism*, New York, 1961, p. 309.

128. *KPSS v rezoliutsiiakh*, 7:232.

129. Ibid., pp. 249–256.

130. *Zakonodatel'nye akty po voprosam narodnogo khoziaistva SSSR* (Legislative acts concerning questions of the USSR economy), vol. 1, Moscow, 1961, pp. 361–365.

131. *KPSS v rezoliutsiiakh*, 7:267–273.

132. Ibid., pp. 295–297; see also Khrushchev, *The Last Testament*, pp. 11–18; and Timothy J. Colton, *Commissars, Commanders and Civilian Authority*, Cambridge, 1979, pp. 175–195.

133. *Narodnoe khoziaistvo SSSR*, p. 71.

134. *Narodnoe khoziaistvo SSSR v 1965, godu*, p. 162.

135. *Narodnoe khoziaistvo SSSR*, p. 69.

136. *Narodnoe khoziaistvo SSSR v 1965 godu*, p. 174.

137. Narodnoe khoziaistvo SSSR, p. 64.

138. *Narodnoe khoziaistvo SSSR v 1965 godu*, p. 181.

139. *Narodnoe khoziaistvo SSSR*, p. 67.

140. *Narodnoe khoziaistvo SSSR v 1965 godu*, p. 178.

141. *Sbornik zakonov SSSR, 1938–1967*, 1:367–383.

142. Ibid., 2:183–184.

143. *KPSS v rezoliutsiiakh*, 7:222–223.

144. *Sbornik zakonov SSSR*, 2:217–241.

145. Ibid., pp. 241–248.

146. Ibid., p. 185.

147. Ibid., p. 195.

148. *KPSS v rezoliutsiiakh*, 7:278–294.

149. Ibid., p. 283.

150. *Narodnoe khoziaistvo SSSR*, p. 177; *Narodnoe khoziaistvo SSSR v 1964 godu*, p. 610.

151. *Sbornik zakonov SSSR*, 2:328.

152. Ibid.

153. Ibid., p. 327.

154. Ibid., pp. 418–419, 196–197.

155. For details, see *Protsess nad Iosifom Brodskim v Leningrade, 18 fevralia, 1964 g.* (The trial of Joseph Brodsky in Leningrad, February 18, 1964), *Arkhiv samizdata* (Samizdat archive), vol. 4, doc. 236.

156. *Istoriia vneshnei politiki SSSR*, 2:410.

157. *KPSS v rezoliutsiiakh*, 7:270.

158. *Dvadtsatyi s"ezd*, 2:410.

159. Khrushchev, *Khrushchev Remembers*, p. 380.

160. *Dvadtsatyi s"ezd*, 1:35–38.

161. Adam B. Ulam, *Expansion and Coexistence: Soviet Foreign Policy 1917–1973*, New York, 1974.

162. For details, see Robert M. Slusser, *The Berlin Crisis of 1961*, Baltimore, 1973.

163. *Istoriia vneshnei politiki SSSR*, 2:333.

164. Molotov's retirement was timed to coincide with Tito's visit to the USSR. See Conquest, *Power and Policy in the USSR*, p. 291.

165. *Istoriia vneshnei politiki SSSR*, 2:374.

166. See document 7, "Letter of the Central Committee of the CCP of February 29, 1964, to the Central Committee of the CPSU," in William E. Griffith, *Sino-Soviet Relations, 1964–1965*, Cambridge, 1967, p. 183.

167. Walter C. Clemens, Jr., *The Arms Race and Sino-Soviet Relations*, Stanford, 1968, p. 258, n. 41.

168. Ibid.

169. Klaus Mehnert, *Peking and Moscow*, New York, 1963, p. 299.

170. Ibid., p. 339.

171. Griffith, *Sino-Soviet Relations*, doc. 7, p. 183.

172. Ibid., doc. 3, p. 162.

173. Khrushchev, *Khrushchev Remembers*, pp. 463–464.

174. Ibid. p. 470.

175. Ibid., pp. 472–474.

176. Donald Z. Zagoria, *The Sino-Soviet Conflict, 1956–1961*, Princeton, 1962, pp. 93–94.

177. Mehnert, *Peking and Moscow*, p. 339.

178. *Istoriia vneshnei politiki SSSR*, 2:379.

179. *Pravda*, April 3, 1964.

180. Ibid.

181. Mehnert, *Peking and Moscow*, p. 300.

182. Ibid., p. 304; for details, see also Clemens, *Arms Race*, p. 37.

183. Clemens, *Arms Race*, p. 255, n. 5.

184. See, for example, Griffith, *Sino-Soviet Relations*, doc. 7, pp. 181–182.

185. Khrushchev, *Khrushchev Remembers*, p. 474.

186. "Letter of the Central Committee of the CPSU of November 29, 1963, to the Central Committee of the CCP," in Griffith, *Sino-Soviet Relations*, p. 151.

187. The discussion of a possible "preventive strike" against China was also related to the atom bomb testing in China in the fall of 1964; see Clemens, *Arms Race*, pp. 273–274, n. 2.

188. Khrushchev, *Khrushchev Remembers*, p. 474.

189. Ibid., p. 475.

190. An entire brigade of Soviet journalists and writers accompanied Khrushchev on his U.S. trip. The result was the book *Litsom k litsu s Amerikoi* (Face to Face with America), Moscow, 1960, 675 pages long and published in a very large edition. The authors were awarded the Lenin Prize.

191. *Zhit' v mire i druzhbe! Prebyvanie predsedatelia Soveta Ministrov SSSR N. S. Khrushcheva v SShA 15–27 sentiabria 1959 g.* (Live in peace and friendship! The U.S. Tour of N. S. Khrushchev, Chairman of the USSR Council of Ministers, September 15–27, 1959), Moscow, 1959, pp. 82–83.

192. Ulam, *Expansion*, p. 628.

193. Ibid., p. 631.

194. Harold Macmillan, *Pointing the Way (1959–1961*, New York, 1962, p. 279.

195. Ulam, *Expansion*, pp. 666–667.

196. L. Iu. Slezkin, *Istoriia Kubinskoi respubliki* (History of the Cuban Republic), Moscow, 1966, pp. 404–405.

197. Ibid.

198. Ibid., p. 423.

199. *Vneshniaia politika Sovetskogo Soiuza i mezhdunarodnye otnosheniia, 1962 god* (Soviet foreign policy and international relations, 1962), Moscow, 1963, pp. 340–342.

200. G. T. Allison, *Essence of Decision: Explaining the Cuban Missile Crisis*, Boston, 1971, pp. 103–105; A. Chayes, *The Cuban Missile Crisis*, New York, 1974, p. 8.

201. Robert F. Kennedy, *Thirteen Days: A Memoir of the Cuban Missile Crisis*, New York, 1969, p. 27.

202. Ibid.

203. Chayes, *Cuban Missile Crisis*, p. 13.

204. Kennedy, *Thirteen Days*, pp. 28–29.

205. Ibid., p. 35.

206. Ibid., p. 36.

207. Khrushchev, *Khrushchev Remembers*, p. 496.

208. For details, see Elie Abel, *The Missile Crisis*, Philadelphia, 1966, p. 44; Kennedy, *Thirteen Days*, pp. 36–37.

209. Khrushchev, *Khrushchev Remembers*, p. 493.

210. Ibid., p. 494.

211. Ibid., p. 496.

212. Kennedy, *Thirteen Days*, p. 40.

213. *Public Papers of the Presidents, John F. Kennedy, 1962*, Washington, D.C., p. 807.

214. Ibid., p. 808.

215. Ibid., pp. 809–810.
216. Ibid., p. 812.
217. Ibid., p. 811.
218. Kennedy, *Thirteen Days*, pp. 93–94.
219. *Public Papers of JFK*, pp. 813–814.
220. Kennedy, *Thirteen Days*, pp. 107–108.
221. *Public Papers of JFK*, pp. 814–815.
222. *Istoriia vneshnei politiki SSSR*, 2:361.
223. Ibid., pp. 416–417.
224. For the texts of these communiqués, see Griffith, *Sino-Soviet Relations*, pp. 326–329, 340–353, 371–387.
225. *Novyi mir*, no. 12, 1953, pp. 218–245.
226. *Znamia*, no. 5, 1954, pp. 14–87.
227. *Novyi mir*, nos. 8–10, 1956.
228. Ibid., no. 4, 1956, pp. 18–58.
229. *Voprosy istorii*, no. 4, 1956, pp. 38–56, no. 8, 1956, pp. 109–114.
230. Ol'ga Ivinskaia, *V plenu vremeni* (A Captive of time), Paris, 1978, pp. 232–233.
231. Ibid., p. 243.
232. See the stenographic record of the meeting of the Moscow branch of the Soviet Writers' Union on the Pasternak case, in *Novyi zhurnal*, no. 83, 1966, pp. 185–227.
233. Ibid., p. 226.
234. *Pravda*, November 1, 1958.
235. Ibid., November 6, 1958; see also, Ivinskaia, *V plenu*, p. 319.
236. Ivinskaia, *V plenu*, pp. 298–299.
237. Lydia Chukovskaya gives a powerful and moving description of the Pasternak affair, the poet's last days, his death, and the events at his funeral in *Zapiski ob Anne Akhmatovoi* (Notes on Anna Akhmatova), vol. 2, Paris, 1980, pp. 323–335.
238. "Delo F. F. Shul'tsa" (The Case of F. F. Shults), *Arkhiv samizdata*, doc. 589, pp. 1, 2, 5.
239. Petr Grigorenko, *Sbornik statei* (Collected essays), New York, 1977, pp. 64–65.
240. Petr Grigorenko, *Mysli sumashedshego* (Thoughts of a madman), Amsterdam, 1973, p. 203.
241. Ibid., p. 204.
242. Vladimir Bukovskii, *I vozvrashchaetsia veter...* (To build a castle...), New York, 1978, pp. 100–106.
243. L. Rendel', *Podborka dokumentov, otnosiashchikhsia k pokaiannoi stat'e L. Krasno-pevtseva, napechatannoi v lagernoi gazete "Za otlichnyi trud," 20 avgusta 1971* (A selection of documents on the statement of recantation by L. Krasnopevtsev printed in the labor camp newspaper "For outstanding labor," August 20, 1971), *Arkhiv samizdata*, vol. 22, doc. 1073.
244. V. N. Osipov, *Biograficheskaia spravka Valentiny Mashkovoi* (Biographical note on Valentina Mashkova), *Arkhiv samizdata*, vol. 29, doc. 1611a, pp. 5–6.
245. On the events at Mayakovsky Square, see Bukovskii, *I vozvrashchaetsia*, pp. 133–139.
246. Pavel Litvinov, comp, *The Trial of the Four*, New York, 1972, p. 6.
247. *Vestnik Russkogo Khristianskogo Dvizheniia* (Bulletin of the Russian Christian Movement) (Paris), no. 117, 1976, p. 285.
248. George Lucky, "Turmoil in the Ukraine," in Abraham Brumberg, ed., *In Quest of Justice*, New York, 1970, pp. 54–55.

249. Ibid., p. 55.
250. *Pravda*, October 21, 1962.
251. *Izvestiia*, August 18, 1963.
252. *Novyi mir*, nos. 3–5, 1962.
253. Ibid., no. 11, 1962.
254. *Novyi mir*, no. 1, 1963.
255. Vasilii Grossman, *Za pravoe delo* (For the right cause), Moscow, 1964. For a detailed discussion of post-Stalin Soviet literature, see Heller, *Kontsentratsionnyi mir i sovetskaia literatura.*
256. This second part was nevertheless published abroad in 1980, by the Swiss publisher L'Age d'Homme, under the title *Zhizn' i sud'ba* (Life and destiny), edited by Simon Markish and Efim Etkind, the latter contributing an introduction.
257. For details, see Aleksandr Podrabinek, *Karatel'naia meditsina* (Punitive medicine), New York, 1979.
258. For details, see Valery Chalidze, *To Defend These Rights: Human Rights and the Soviet Union*, New York, 1974.
259. Andrei Sakharov, *My Country and the World*, New York, 1975, p. vii.
260. Ibid.
261. Ibid., p. viii.
262. Ibid.; see also Khrushchev, *The Last Testament*, pp. 68–71.
263. *Pravda*, June 1, 1962.
264. Albert Boiter, "When the Kettle Boils Over," *Problems of Communism*, no. 1, 1964, p. 37.
265. *Pravda*, April 6, 1962.
266. Boiter, "When the Kettle," p. 37.
267. Ibid.
268. Solzhenitsyn, *Gulag*, 3:509.
269. Ibid., p. 508.
270. Ibid.
271. Ibid., p. 509.
272. Boiter, "When the Kettle," p. 36.
273. Ibid., p. 37; Solzhenitsyn, p. 510.
274. Boiter, "When the Kettle," p. 37; Solzhenitsyn, pp. 510–11.
275. Solzhenitsyn, p. 512.
276. Ibid., pp. 513–514.
277. Boiter, "When the Kettle," p. 38.
278. Ibid.
279. Ibid., p. 39.
280. Ibid., p. 41.
281. Ibid., p. 42.
282. Ibid., p. 38.
283. *KPSS v rezoliutsiiakh*, 8:325.
284. Ibid., pp. 390–392.
285. *Pravda*, March 10, 1963.
286. *KPSS v rezoliutsiiakh*, 8:494.

## CHAPTER ELEVEN

1. Aleksandr I. Solzhenitsyn, *Bodalsia telenok c dubom* (The Oak and the Calf), Paris, 1975, pp. 98–99.

2. John Dornberg, *Brezhnev: The Masks of Power*, London, 1974.

3. *Pravda*, February 24, 1981.

4. S. Zorin and N. Alekseev, *Vremia ne zhdet. Nasha strana nakhoditsia na povorotnom punkte istorii* (Time does not wait: Our country stands at a turning point in history), Frankfurt, 1970, p. 4.

5. Tsentral'noe statisticheskoe upravlenie SSSR (Central Statistical Agency of the USSR—TsSU SSSR), *Itogi vsesoiuznoi perepisi naseleniia 1970 g.* (Findings of the 1970 All-Union Census), vol. 4, Moscow, 1973, pp. 19–20.

6. Sakharov, *My Country*, pp. 26–27.

7. *Pravda*, November 7, 1964.

8. Khrushchev, *Stroitel'stvo kommunizma*, pp. 91–107.

9. V. Kliuchevskii, *Kurs russkoi istorii* (A course in Russian history), vol. 4, Moscow, 1910, p. 293.

10. *Politicheskii dnevnik 1964–1970* (Political diary 1964–1970), vol. 1, Amsterdam, 1972, p. 128.

11. Ibid., 2:154.

12. Ibid., p. 153.

13. *Novyi mir*, no. 12, 1953.

14. *Arkhiv samizdata*, vol. 9, doc. 667, p. 6.

15. Ibid., p. 8.

16. Ibid., pp. 6–7.

17. Ibid., p. 8.

18. *Grani* (Facets), no. 62, 1966, p. 127.

19. *Pravda*, February 22, 1966.

20. Andrei Amal'rik, *Will The Soviet Union Survive Until 1984?*, New York, 1970, p. 11.

21. Ibid., p. 10.

22. Ibid., pp. 15–16.

23. Ibid., p. 19.

24. A. Avtorkhanov, *Sila i bessilie Brezhneva* (Brezhnev's Power and Impotence), Frankfurt, 1979, pp. 11–12.

25. Bukovskii, *I vozvrashchaetsia*, p. 271.

26. Ibid., p. 106.

27. VSKhSON, *Programma. Sud. V tiur'makh i lageriakh*, (Program. Trial. In prisons and camps), Paris, 1975, p. 7.

28. Ibid., p. 74.

29. Ibid., p. 34.

30. Aleksandr Solzhenitsyn, *Sobranie sochinenii v 6 tomakh* (Collected works in 6 volumes), Frankfurt, 1973, 6:9.

31. Ibid., p. 368.

32. The discontent in Poland, although suppressed in 1968, reappeared in 1970, when strikes by workers forced Gomulka to transfer power to Gierek; worker unrest continued, with major strike struggles in 1976 and in 1980.

33. Ivan Dzyuba, *Internatsionalizm ili russifikatsiia?* (Internationalism or Russification?), Amsterdam, 1968, p. 277.

34. Vyacheslav Chornovil, comp. *The Chornovil Papers*, Toronto, 1968, pp. 2–76.

35. Ivan Dzyuba, *Grani kristala* (Facets of a crystal), Kiev, 1976, p. 5.

36. Nikita Khrushchev, *Vospominaniia Izbrannye otryvki* (Memoirs: Selected passages), New York, 1979, pp. 275–276.

37. Erwin Weit, *Dans l'ombre de Gomulka*, Paris, 1971, p. 277.

38. *K sobytiiam v Chekhoslovakii. Fakty, dokumenty, svidetel'stva pressy i ochevidtsev, vypusk pervyi, press-gruppa sovetskikh zhurnalistov* (The events in Czechoslovakia: Facts, documents, press accounts, and eyewitness reports, issue no. 1, by a group of Soviet journalists), Moscow, 1968, p. 51.

39. Weit, *Gomulka*, p. 277.

40. *Sem' pisem iz Pragi. Pis'ma cheshskogo intelligenta, otpravlennye im svoemu drugu na Zapade v dekabre 1973–fevrale 1974 gg.*, (Seven letters from Prague: Letters from a Czech intellectual to a friend in the West, December 1973–February 1974), Rome, 1975, p. 33.

41. Ibid., p. 34.

42. Ibid., p. 36.

43. Robin Alison Remington, ed., *Winter in Prague: Documents on Czechoslovak Communism in Crisis*, Cambridge, 1969, p. 196.

44. Vojtech Mastny, ed., *East European Dissent*, vol. 2, *1965–1970*, New York, 1972, p. 81.

45. *Pravda*, September 26, 1968.

46. Ibid., August 20, 1968.

47. M. V. Frunze, *Na frontakh grazhdanskoi voiny* (On the fronts of the civil war), Moscow, 1941, p. 330.

48. Bukovskii, *I vozvrashchaetsia*, p. 103.

49. Natalia Gorbanevskaya, *Red Square at Noon*, New York, 1970, pp. 31–41.

50. Solzhenitsyn, *Oak and Calf*, p. 367.

51. Henry Kissinger, *White House Years*, Boston, 1979, p. 132.

52. Helmut Allard, *Moskauer Tagebuch. Beobachtungen, Notizen, Erlebnisse*, Dusseldorf, 1973, p. 49.

53. Kissinger, *White House Years*, p. 135.

54. *Kratkii politicheskii slovar'* (Short political dictionary), Moscow, 1978, p. 321.

55. *KPSS v rezoliutsiiakh*, 8th ed., vol. 8, Moscow, 1970, p. 27.

57. *Dvadtsatzi s"ezd KPSS*, pt. 2, p. 413.

58. *Materialy XXIII s"ezda KPSS* (Materials of the Twenty-third CPSU Congress), Moscow, 1966, p. 29.

59. *Materialy XXIV s"ezda KPSS* (Materials of the Twenty-fourth CPSU Congress), Moscow, 1971, p. 22.

60. *Kratkii politicheskii slovar'*, p. 127.

61. Kissinger, *White House Years*, p. 127.

62. Bukovskii, *I vozvrashchaetsia*, p. 303.

63. *Pravda*, November 28, 1979.

64. Solzhenitsyn, translated as *The First Circle*, New York, 1968, 1969, p. 94.

65. Gregory Grossman, "An Economy at Middle Age," *Problems of Communism*, March-April 1976, p. 20.

66. See Basile Kerblay, "Les enseignements de l'experience soviétique d'agriculture collectiviste," *Revue d'études comparatives Est-Ouest*, September 1979, pp. 18–19.

67. *Narodnoe khoziaistvo SSSR*, 1965, pp. 277, 405, 422, 424; Ibid., 1970, pp. 290, 382, 396; Ibid., 1978, pp. 211, 261, 275, 278; for details, see Boris Rumer, "The 'Second' Agriculture in the USSR," *Soviet Studies*, vol. 33, no. 4, October 1981, pp. 560–572.
68. Alec Nove, *The Soviet Economic System*, London, 1977, p. 360.
69. Kerblay, *La société soviétique contemporaine*, p. 185.
70. *Time*, special issue "Inside the USSR," April-June 1980, p. 57.
71. Cf. Sakharov, *My Country*, pp. 46–47; Bukovskii, *I vozrashchaetsia*, pp. 168–169.
72. *SSSR v tsifrakh v 1978 g.*, p. 7.
73. Konstantin Simis, "The Machinery of Corruption in the Soviet Union," *Survey*, vol. 23, no. 4 (105), Autumn 1977–78, p. 39.
74. Mikhail Kolesnikov, "Shkola ministrov" (School of ministers), *Znamia*, no. 10, 1977, p. 113.
75. *Pravda*, April 24, 1967.
76. *Istoriia vneshnei politiki SSSR*, 2:422–424.
77. Michael T. Florinsky, *World Revolution and the USSR*, New York, 1933, p. 216.
78. Robert E. Sherwood, *Roosevelt and Hopkins: An Intimate History*, New York, 1948, p. 870.
79. See Robert Conquest, *Present Danger: Towards a Foreign Policy*, Oxford, 1978, p. 42.
80. Sherwood, *Roosevelt*, p. 870.
81. Charles E. Bohlen, *Witness to History, 1929–1969*, New York, 1973, p. 370.
82. Averell Harriman, *Peace with Russia?* New York, 1959, p. 168.
83. Allard, *Moskauer Tagebuch*, p. 207.
84. Kissinger, *White House Years*, pp. 126–127.
85. Solzhenitsyn has coined a term, the "Kissinger syndrome," for the process by which Western statesmen come to their senses after retiring. Only then do the scales fall from their eyes. See Solzhenitsyn, "Chem grozit Zapadu neponimanie Rossii" (How a lack of understanding of Russia threatens the West), *Vestnik RKhD*, no. 131, 1980, p. 191.
86. *International Herald Tribune*, December 6, 1978.
87. *New York Times*, June 3, 1969.
88. Samuel Pisar, "Let's Put Detente Back on the Rail," *New York Times Magazine*, September 25, 1977.
89. *New York Times*, April 5, 1969.
90. *Washington Post*, April 5, 1969.
91. Unlike Stalin, Mao relied on fanatical youth, the Red Guards, rather than the security police—although Stalin also made wide use of young people in battle against "enemies of the people."
92. *Literaturnaia gazeta*, March 19, 1969.
93. *Le monde*, March 2, 1969.
94. Kissinger, *White House Years*, p. 172.
95. Ibid., p. 183.
96. *London Evening News*, September 16, 1969.
97. Zdenek Mlynar, *Nachtfrost*, Cologne-Frankfurt, 1978, p. 301.
98. *Istoriia vneshnei politiki SSSR*, 2:383; *Vneshniaia torgovlia SSSR v 1978 g.* (Soviet foreign trade, 1978), 1979, p. 11.
99. Kissinger, *White House Years*, p. 124.
100. *Novoe russkoe slovo* (New Russian word), June 13, 1980.

101. *Pravda*, April 3, 1971.
102. International Institute for Strategic Studies, *The Military Balance, 1978–1979*, London, 1978, p. 88. (Hereafter cited as *The Military Balance*.)
103. *International Herald Tribune*, June 30, 1979.
104. *USSR Facts & Figures Annual*, ed., John L. Scherer, vol. 4, 1980, p. 125. (Hereafter cited as *Facts and Figures*.)
105. *The Military Balance*, p. 86; *Facts and Figures*, p. 121; *Le point*, September 3, 1979.
106. *Facts and Figures*, pp. 121–122.
107. S. G. Gorshkov, *Morskaia moshch' gosudarstva* (The naval power of the state), Moscow, 1979, p. 408.
108. Ibid., pp. 342, 346.
109. Ibid., p. 342.
110. Ibid., p. 412.
111. *International Herald Tribune*, May 29, 1979.
112. M. P. Skirdo, *Narod, armiia, polkovodets* (The people, the army, the military leader), Moscow, 1970, p. 97.
113. *Pravda*, January 13, 1970.
114. Ibid., February 27, 1976.
115. *Zaria vostoka*, January 23, 1976.
116. *Planovoe khoziaistvo*, no. 6, 1976, p. 13.
117. *Literaturnaia gazeta*, no. 25, 1979.
118. *Trud* (Labor), July 17, 1979.
119. Kerblay, *La société soviétique*, p. 132.
120. Sakharov, *My Country*, pp. 15–16.
121. *Pravda*, August 20, 1979.
122. *Komsomol'skaia pravda* (Komsomol truth), August 15, 1979.
123. Brezhnev, *Ob osnovnykh voprosakh ekonomicheskoi politiki KPSS na sovremennom etape*. (On basic questions of CPSU economic policy at the contemporary stage), vol. 1, Moscow, 1975, p. 118.
124. *International Herald Tribune*, October 5, 1979.
125. *SSSR v tsifrakh v 1978* (The USSR in figures in 1978), Moscow, 1979, p. 7.
126. Kerblay, "Les enseignements," p. 20.
127. Ted Agres, "U.S. Builds Soviet War Machine," *Industrial Research and Development*, July 1980, p. 51.
128. Charles Levinson, *Vodka-Cola*, Paris, 1977, p. 312.
129. *International Herald Tribune*, September 9, 1979.
130. Ibid., May 24, 1979.
131. Ibid., June 20, 1979.
132. Agres, "U.S. Builds," p. 53.
133. Ibid., p. 54.
134. *Le point*, March 14, 1977.
135. *Le monde*, September 30, 1979.
136. *Le point*, March 14, 1977.
137. *Literaturnaia gazeta*, August 9, 1978.
138. Allard, *Moskauer Tagebuch*, p. 12.
139. Ibid.
140. *Izvestiia*, June 5, 1972.
141. *Le Figaro*, April 25, 1979.
142. *Pravda*, September 24, 1976.

143. Solzhenitsyn, *Amerikanskie rechi* (American speeches), Paris, 1975, p. 42.

144. *New York Times*, March 10, 1946.

145. *Pravda*, July 30, 1980.

146. *Novoe vremia* [New times], no. 31, 1976.

147. *Pravda*, February 25, 1976.

148. Jerry F. Hough and Merle Fainsod, *How the Soviet Union Is Governed*, Cambridge, 1979, p. 265.

149. Seweryn Bialer in *Time*, June 23, 1980, p. 29.

150. Sakharov, *My Country*, pp. 16–17.

151. Sakharov, "Trevozhnoe vremia," *Novoe russkoe slovo*, June 14, 1980.

152. Amalrik, *Will the Soviet Union Survive*, p. 6.

153. Hough and Fainsod, *How the Soviet Union*, pp. 237, 526.

154. Sakharov, "Trevozhnoe vremia," *Novoe russkoe slovo*, June 13, 1980.

155. Nove, *Soviet Economic System*, p. 10.

156. Aleksandr Solzhenitsyn, "Pis'mo vozhdiam Sovetskogo Soiuza" (Letter to the Soviet Leaders), Paris, 1974, p. 41.

157. Ibid.

158. Quoted in Bukovskii, *I vozvrashchaetsia*, p. 322.

159. Aleksandr Solzhenitsyn, ed., (From Under the Rubble), Boston, 1975, p. 2.

160. Aleksandr Zinov'ev, *Zheltyi dom* (The Yellow House), pt. 1, Lausanne, 1980, p. 48.

161. *Pravda*, August 13, 1975.

162. *Pravda*, October 18, 1979.

163. Ibid.

164. Solzhenitsyn, *Sobranie sochinenii*, 6:202.

165. B. Demin, "Nenavist' k vragu—neot"emlemaia storona patriotizma sovetskikh voinov" (Hatred for the enemy—an inseparable part of the patriotism of Soviet soldiers), *Kommunist vooruzhennykh sil* (Communist of the armed forces), no. 3, 1969, p. 63.

166. *Sovetskii patriot* (Soviet patriot), November 29, 1972, p. 2.

167. *Pravda*, October 18, 1979.

168. Ibid., April 13, 1970.

169. Ibid., July 6, 1978.

170. Vasily Shuisky occupied the Russian throne from 1606 to 1610, when he was overthrown. He fled to Poland and died in Warsaw in 1612.

171. Vsevolod Kochetov, "Zapisi voennykh let" (Notes from the war years), *Oktiabr'* (October), no. 5, 1965, p. 97.

172. Avtorkhanov, *Sila i bessilie Brezhneva*, p. 61.

173. *Pravda*, November 17, 1977.

174. Ibid., May 9, 1976.

175. Stalin, *Sochineniia*, vol. 13, Moscow, 1952, p. 235.

176. Maksim Luzhanin, "Bessonnyi telefon" (The sleepless telephone), *Belarus'*, no. 4, 1977, p. 8.

177. *Izvestiia*, September 1, 1980.

178. Ibid.

179. *Kratkii politicheskii slovar'*, p. 108.

180. Ibid., p. 109.

181. *Izvestiia*, October 10, 1977.

182. Solzhenitsyn, *Oak and Calf*, p. 354.

183. See *Le monde*, April 30, 1980.

184. *Izvestiia*, January 15, 1972.

185. *Pravda*, January 11, 1970.
186. Simis, "Machinery of Corruption," p. 55.
187. *Literaturnaia gazeta*, October 15, 1975.
188. Ibid.
189. *Pravda*, February 24, 1981.
190. Nick Eberstadt, "The Health Crisis in the USSR," *New York Review of Books*, February 19, 1981, p. 23.
191. Ibid., p. 25.
192. Bukovskii, *I vozvrashchaetsia*, p. 285.
193. Fridrikh Neznanskii, "Statistika prestupnosti v SSSR" (Crime statistics in the USSR), *Posev*, no. 5, 1979.
194. A system of early or conditional release of prisoners was introduced in the mid-1960s for those who would go to work on remote construction sites, usually chemical plants at that time. Thus, prisoners' slang for this system was "to work in chemistry" (*na khimii*) and such prisoners were called "chemists" (*khimiki*).
195. *Nedelia* (The week), no. 38, 1979.
196. *Voprosy istorii* no. 10, 1972.
197. *Literaturnaia gazeta*, December 1, 1976.
198. *Ukrains'kii vysnik* (Ukrainian herald), Spring 1974 (Baltimore, 1975), p. 7.
199. *Delo Airikiana* (The Airikian case), New York, 1977, p. 42.
200. V. Stanley Vardys, *The Catholic Church, Dissent, and Nationality in Soviet Lithuania*, Boulder, 1978, p. 174.
201. "Interv'iu V. Osipova amerikanskim zhurnalistam" (Interview of Osipov to American journalists), *Vestnik RKhD* (RKhD herald), no. 106, 1972, p. 295.
202. See Chapter 3, under "The Emigrés."
203. A. Iakovlev, "Protiv antiistorizma" (Against antihistoricism), *Literaturnaia gazeta*, October 15, 1972.
204. *Izvestiia*, July 5, 1980.
205. Hélène Carrère d'Encausse, *L'empire éclaté*, Paris, 1978, p. 88.
206. G. A. Bondarskaia, *Rozhdaemost' v SSSR. Etnograficheskii aspekt* (The birthrate in the USSR: The ethnographic aspect), Moscow, 1977, pp. 92–93.
207. Alexandre Bennigsen, "Islam in the USSR," *Soviet Jewish Affairs*, no. 2, 1979, p. 5.
208. TsU SSSR, *O predvaritel'nykh itogakh Vsesoiuznoi perepisi naseleniia 1979 g.* (Preliminary results of the 1979 All-Union Census), Moscow, 1979, p. 3.
209. Ibid.
210. Ibid.
211. Ibid. The possibility that these figures have been significantly exaggerated cannot be ruled out.
212. *Pravda*, February 24, 1981.
213. *Naselenie SSSR. Po dannym Vsesoiuznoi perepisi naseleniia 1979 goda* (Population of the USSR: Based on data from the 1979 All-Union Census), Moscow, 1980, p. 3.
214. Ibid., p. 23.
215. *Pravda*, September 5, 1970.
216. *Nauka i religiia* (Science and religion), no. 4, 1979.
217. *Pravda*, September 5, 1970.
218. *Vestnik RKhD*, no. 130, 1979, p. 275.
219. *Nauka i religiia*, no. 6, 1979, pp. 14–15.
220. *Vestnik RKhD*, no. 130, p. 278.

221. Ibid., p. 298.
222. Ibid., p. 282.
223. Ibid., p. 281.
224. D. Dudko, "Na segodniashnii den'" (Unto this day), *Posev*, no. 7, 1979, p. 37.
225. Solzhenitsyn, *Gulag*, 3:346, 356, 400–401.
226. *Novye knigi* (New books), no. 25, 1976, p. 58. The album was timed to commemorate the five hundredth anniversary of the Battle of Kulikovo (1380), in which the Grand Duke of Vladimir and Moscow, Dmitry Ivanovich, defeated the Mongols and the Tatars for the first time.
227. *Molodaia gvardiia*, no. 11, 1977, p. 38.
228. Carrère d'Encausse, *L'empire*, p. 229.
229. *SSSR v tsifrakh v 1980 godu*, Moscow, 1981.
230. Bennigsen, "Islam," p. 9.
231. Quoted in Carrère d'Encausse, *L'empire*, p. 245.
232. Bennigsen, "Islam," p. 12.
233. *Pravda*, February 24, 1981.
234. *Nauka i religiia*, no. 2, 1979, p. 62.
235. *Pravda*, October 18, 1979.
236. *Pravda*, March 10, 1976.
237. L. Ershov, "Dvizhenie literatury—dvizhenie kritiki" (As literature moves—so moves criticism), *Nash sovremennik* (Our contemporary), no. 7, 1978, p. 177.
238. *Literaturnaia gazeta*, July 12, 1978.
239. See Markov's speech at the Sixth Congress of Soviet Writers, in *Literaturnaia gazeta*, July 7, 1976.
240. Feliks Kuznetsov, "Glavnoe nashe bogatstvo" (What we are richest in), *Literaturnaia gazeta*, October 24, 1979.
241. Marietta Shaginian, "Chelovek i vremia" (Man and the times), *Novyi mir*, no. 11, 1978, p. 228.
242. *Czarna ksiega cenzury PRL* (The black book of censorship in the Polish People's Republic), vols. 1–2, London, 1977–1978.
243. Ibid., 2:200.
244. Vladimir Pomerantsev, "Ob iskrennosti v literature" (On sincerity in literature), *Novyi mir*, no. 12, 1953.
245. From an interview with Vasily Aksyonov, the moving spirit behind *Metropol'*, in the newspaper *Russkaia mysl'* (Russian thought), Paris, August 14, 1980.
246. *Iskusstvo pod bul'dozrom. Siniaia kniga* (Art under the bulldozer: A blue book), comp. Aleksandr Glezer, London, 1979.
247. *Kommunist Litvy* (Communist of Lithuania), no. 6, 1978, pp. 87–92.
248. *Nedelia*, no. 6, 1980.
249. B. Stukalin and L. Gvishiani, "Dialog o zhizni, professii i iskusstve" (A Dialogue on life, professions, and art), *Moskva* (Moscow), no. 1, 1980, p. 7.
250. *Literaturnaia gazeta*, October 26, 1977.
251. Belinkov, *Sdacha i gibel'*, p. 172.
252. Khrushchev, *Vospominaniia*, p. 288.
253. Ibid., pp. 289–290.
254. After the mid-1970s, when it became known and widely publicized in the West that there were official instructions in the Soviet Union for Jews to be required to pay a ransom-type fee in order to obtain exit visas, the practice was temporarily suspended.
255. *New York Times*, April 6, 1979.

256. *International Herald Tribune*, January 1, 1980.

257. Carrère d'Encausse, *L'empire*, p. 206.

258. Solzhenitsyn, "Chem grozit Zapadu," p. 210.

259. Sakharov, "Trevozhnoe vremia," *Novoe Russkoe slovo*, June 14, 1980.

260. See the interview with Roy Medvedev in *The Observer* (London), June 15, 1975.

261. *Literaturnaia gazeta*, August 24, 1977.

262. *Narodnoe khoziaistvo SSSR v 1978 godu. Statisticheskii sbornik* (Economy of the USSR in 1978: Collected statistics). Moscow, 1979, p. 196.

263. *Pravda*, February 24, 1980.

264. Valery Chalidze, comp., *SSSR—rabochee dvizhenie?* (The USSR—a workers' movement?), New York, 1978, p. 35.

265. *Arkhiv samizdata*, no. 4218, p. 12.

266. Quoted in M. Korti, "Aleksei Nikitin i dvizhenie za prava rabochikh v SSSR" (Aleksei Nikitin and the workers' rights movement in the USSR), manuscript, pp. 2–3.

267. *Corriere della sera*, March 8, 1981.

268. *Pravda*, February 1, 1976.

269. Ibid.

270. Kissinger, *White House Years*, pp. 161–162.

271. *Pravda*, October 18, 1979.

272. Ibid.

273. V. Zagladin and I. Frolov, "Global'nye problemy sovremennosti. Poiski reshenii" (Global problems of the present day: In search of solutions), *Pravda*, May 7, 1979.

274. *New York Times*, May 10, 1978.

275. *Izvestiia*, February 12, 1980.

276. Anthony Lewis, "After Afghanistan, Business as Usual?" *International Herald Tribune*, January 8, 1980.

277. *Izvestiia*, March 19, 1980.

278. Leonid Zamiatin, "Vosstanovit' klimat razriadki i doveriia" (Restore the climate of detente and trust), *Literaturnaia gazeta*, February 27, 1980.

279. Zamyatin's statement on the signing of the treaty between the Soviet Union and West Germany on August 12, 1980, was quoted in the *International Herald Tribune*, August 13, 1980.

280. *Pravda*, February 24, 1981.

281. David K. Shipler, *Russia: Broken Idols, Solemn Dreams*, New York, 1983, p. 38.

282. Boris Rumer, "Structural Imbalance in the Soviet Economy," *Problems of Communism*, July-August 1984, p. 24.

283. *Narodnoe khoziaistvo SSSR v 1982 godu. Statisticheskii sbornik* (Economy of the USSR in 1982: Collected statistics), Moscow, 1983, p. 372.

284. Rumer, "Structural Imbalance," p. 26.

285. Ibid.

286. Yuri Andropov, "Uchenie Karla Marksa i nekotorye voprosy sotsialistcheskogo stroitel'stva v SSSR" (The teachings of Karl Marx and some problems of socialist construction in the USSR), *Kommunist*, no. 3, 1983, p. 17.

287. V. Dolgikh, "Uluchshit' partiinoe rukovodstvo rabotoi zheleznodorozhnogo transporta" (Improve party supervision of rail transport), *Partiinaia zhizn'* (Party life), no. 7, April 1983, p. 10.

288. *Kommunist*, no. 4, 1983, p. 63.

289. *Pravda*, May 7, 1982.

290. *Arkhiv samizdata*, doc. 5042, p. 7. This work, entitled "On the Need for More Intensive

Study of the Social Mechanism of Economic Development in the USSR," was probably crafted in Novosibirsk, at the Institute of the Economics and Organization of Industrial Production (IZiOPP) of the Siberian Branch of the USSR Academy of Sciences, for a scientific seminar in Moscow. The *Archive of Samizdat* attributes authorship to T. I. Zaslavskaya, who heads the institute's department of social problems, and dates it April 1983.

291. Ibid., p. 10.
292. Ibid., pp. 30–31.
293. *New York Times*, May 27, 1983.
294. Ibid.

# CHAPTER TWELVE

1. Viktor Krasin, *Sud* (The Trial), New York, 1983, p. 73.
2. Meray, *Thirteen Days That Shook the Kremlin*, pp. 188–189, 191, 193–194.
3. Krasin, *Sud*, p. 83.
4. *Pravda*, February 11, 1984.
5. *Washington Post*, May 30, 1982.
6. *New York Times*, November 16, 1982.
7. *Time*, November 22, 1982.
8. T. H. Rigby, "Pervyi god Andropova" (Andropov's first year), *Obozrenie* (Survey), no. 7, November 1983, p. 10.
9. *Bol'shaia sovetskaia entsiklopediia*, 13:216.
10. Zhores Medvedev, *Andropov*, New York, 1983, p. 93.
11. *Sovetskaia Rossiia* (Soviet Russia), March 22, 1983.
12. *Plenum Tsentral'nogo Komiteta KPSS. 14–15 iiunia 1983 goda. Stenograficheskii otchet* (Plenum of the CPSU Central Committee: June 14–15, 1983: Stenographic record), Moscow, 1983, p. 5. (Hereafter cited as *Plenum Tsentral'nogo Komiteta.*)
13. *Pravda*, February 19, 1983.
14. Irina Ratushinskaia, *Stikhi. Poems. Poéms*. Ann Arbor, 1984, p. 8.
15. *Vedomosti Verkhovnogo Soveta SSSR* (Register of the USSR Supreme Soviet), no. 25 (2203), June 22, 1983, pp. 396–408.
16. *Pravda*, August 7, 1983.
17. Mikhail Heller, "Andropov: A Retrospective View," *Survey*, vol. 28, no. 1 (120), Spring 1984, p. 53.
18. *Pravda*, February 1, 1983.
19. Ibid., December 1, 1983.
20. Ibid., June 18, 1983.
21. Mark Beissinger, "Ekonomicheskaia strategiia Andropova i ee lovushki" (Andropov's economic strategy and its pitfalls), *Obozrenie*, no. 7, November 1983, p. 5.
22. *Pravda*, January 29, 1984.
23. Rumer, "Structural Imbalance," p. 25.
24. *Vedomosti Verkhovnogo Soveta SSSR*, no. 48 (2174), December 1, 1982, pp. 872–889.
25. *The Poems, Prose, and Plays of Alexander Pushkin*, New York, Modern Library, p. 368.
26. *Vedomosti Verkhovnogo Soveta SSSR*, no. 3 (2233), January 18, 1984, pp. 91–93.
27. *Pravda*, January 30, 1983.

28. Ibid., March 15, 1984.
29. *Dvadtsat' vtoroi s"ezd KPSS. 17–31 oktobria 1961 goda. Stenograficheskii otchet* (Twenty-second CPSU Congress: October 17–31, 1961: Stenographic record), vol. 1, Moscow, 1962, p. 167.
30. Andropov, "Uchenie Karla Marksa," p. 20.
31. *KPSS o formirovanii novogo cheloveka. Sbornik dokumentov i materialov 1965–1981* (The CPSU on the formation of the new man: Collected documents and materials, 1965–1981), Moscow, 1982, p. 625.
32. *Plenum Tsentral'nogo Komiteta*, p. 102.
33. Ibid., p. 103.
34. Ibid., p. 109.
35. *Kommunist vooruzhennykh sil*, no. 1, January 1984, p. 5.
36. Ibid., p. 14.
37. *Pravda*, June 9, 1984.
38. *Plenum Tsentral'nogo Komiteta*, p. 33.
39. Ibid., p. 186.
40. B. P. Utkin, "Vospitatel'naia rol' Sovetskikh vooruzhennykh sil v usloviiakh razvitogo sotsializma" (The educational role of the Soviet armed forces under developed socialism), *Voprosy filosofii* (Problems of philosophy), no. 1, 1984, p. 28.
41. Ibid., p. 36.
42. Ibid., p. 37.
43. *Pravda*, January 4, 1984.
44. *Plenum Tsentral'nogo Komiteta*, p. 168.
45. Shipler, *Russia*, p. 102.
46. *Kommunist vooruzhenykh sil*, January 1984, p. 7.
47. *Voprosy filosofii* (Problems of philosophy), no. 1, 1984, p. 37.
48. *Plenum Tsentral'nogo Komiteta*, p. 186.
49. Belinkov, *Sdacha i gibel'*, p. 113.
50. *Krasnaia zvezda*, April 10, 1984.
51. *Newsweek*, July 18, 1983, pp. 34–36.
52. Heller, "Andropov," p. 55.
53. *Pravda*, October 25, 1983.
54. *U.S. News and World Report*, April 4, 1984.
55. *Pravda*, February 11, 1984.
56. *Japan Times*, March 11, 1983.
57. *Pravda*, September 3, 1983.
58. Ibid., September 8, 1983.
59. *New York Times*, September 10, 1983.
60. Ibid., April 8, 1984.
61. Ibid., April 27, 1983.
62. Ibid., September 13, 1983.
63. Ibid., September 7, 1983.
64. *Evidence of Mohammed Ayob Assil*. U.S. House of Representatives, Foreign Affairs Committee, Subcommittee on Human Rights, Washington, D.C., October 9, 1983.
65. *New York Times*, April 9, 1984.
66. *Novoe russkoe slovo*, June 22, 1982.
67. *New York Times*, April 9, 1984.
68. Ibid., November 7, 1983.
69. Ibid., November 15, 1983.

70. *U.S. News and World Report*, February 6, 1984.
71. F. M. Burlatskii, "Filosofiia mira" (The philosophy of peace), *Voprosy filosofii*, no. 12, 1982, p. 62.
72. *Pravda*, April 23, 1983.
73. A. I. Sorokin, "Vooruzhennye sily razvitogo sotsializma" (The armed forces of developed socialism), *Voprosy filosofii*, no. 2, 1983, p. 6.
74. *Voprosy filosofii*, no. 1, 1984, p. 22.
75. *Voenno-istoricheskii zhurnal*, no. 4, 1983, p. 10.
76. *Pravda*, April 14, 1984.
77. N. V. Ogarkov, *Vsegda v gotovnosti k zashchite otechestva* (Ever ready to defend the fatherland), Moscow, 1982, p. 64.
78. *Pravda*, October 24, 1984.
79. Ibid., October, 27, 1984.
80. Ibid., October 24, 1984.
81. Ibid., November 7, 1951.
82. Ibid., November 6, 1984.
83. Ibid., December 5, 1984.
84. *Le monde*, January 9, 1985.

# CONCLUSION

1. *Survey*, no. 4, 1979, p. 3.
2. Sakharov, "Trevozhnoe vremia," *Novoe russkoe slovo*, June 13, 1980.
3. *Pravda*, October 18, 1979.
4. *International Herald Tribune*, September 5, 1979.

# BIBLIOGRAPHY

Abel, Elie. *The Missile Crisis*. Philadelphia, 1966.

Abramskii, Jan and Ryszard Zywiecki. *Katyn*. Warsaw, 1977.

Agabekov, G. S. *Zapiski chekista* (Notes of a Cheka agent). Berlin, 1930.

Agres, Ted. "U.S. Builds Soviet War Machine." *Industrial Research and Development*, July 1980.

Ainsztein, Reuben. *Jewish Resistance in Nazi-Occupied Eastern Europe*. London, 1974.

Akademiia nauk Belorusskoi SSR. Institut istorii (Academy of Sciences of the Belorussian SSR. Institute of History). *Istoriia Belorusskoi SSR* (History of the Belorussian SSR). Vol. 2. Minsk, 1961.

Akademiia nauk Latviiskoi SSR. Institut istorii (Academy of Sciences of the Latvian SSR. Institute of History). *Istoriia Latviiskoi SSR. Sokrashchennyi kurs* (History of the Latvian SSR: Abridged course). 2d rev. and enl. ed. Riga, 1971.

Akademiia nauk Latviiskoi SSR. Institut istorii i material'noi kul'tury (Academy of Sciences of the Latvian SSR. Institute of History and Material Culture). *Istoriia Latviiskoi SSR* (History of the Latvian SSR). Vol. 3. Riga, 1958.

*Akten zur deutschen auswärtigen Politik 1918–1945*. Series D (1937–1945).

Aldanov, Mark. "Kartiny oktiabr'skoi revoliutsii" (Scenes of the October revolution). *Poslednie novosti*, September 7, 1935.

———. *Sovremenniki* (Contemporaries). Paris, 1928.

*Aleksandr Solzhenitsyn: Critical Essays and Documentary Materials*. Edited by John B. Dunlop, Richard Haugh, and Alexis Klimoff. New York, 1975.

Allard, Helmut. *Moskauer Tagebuch. Beobachtungen, Notizen, Erlebnisse*. Dusseldorf, 1973.

Alliluyeva, Svetlana. *Only One Year*. New York, 1970.

Allison, G. T. *Essence of Decision: Explaining the Cuban Missile Crisis*. Boston, 1971.

Amal'rik, Andrei. *Prosushchestvuet li Sovetskii Soiuz do 1984 g.?* Amsterdam, 1969. English translation: *Will the Soviet Union Survive Until 1984?* New York, 1970.

Aminado, D. *Poezd na tret'em puti* (Train on track three). New York, 1954.

Andropov, Iurii. "Uchenie Karla Marksa i nekotorye voprosy sotsialisticheskogo stroitel'stva v SSSR" (The teachings of Karl Marx and some problems of socialist construction in the USSR). *Kommunist*, no. 3, 1983.

Anfilov, V. A. *Bessmertnyi podvig* (The immortal feat). Moscow. 1971.

820

Anfimov, A. M. *Rossiiskaia derevnia v gody Pervoi mirovoi voiny* (The Russian countryside during World War I). Moscow, 1962.

*Antonovshchina. Sbornik statei i vospominanii* (The Antonov revolt: Collected articles and memoirs). Published by the Bureau of Party History of the Tambov Province Committee of the Bolshevik party. Tambov, 1923.

*Arkhiv A. M. Gor'kogo. Neizdannaia perepiska* (The Gorky archives: Unpublished correspondence). Vol. 14. Moscow, 1976.

Armstrong, John A. *The Politics of Totalitarianism.* New York, 1961.

————. *Ukrainian Nationalism, 1939–1945.* New York, 1955.

Arshinov, Peter. *History of the Makhnovist Movement.* Translated by Black & Red and Solidarity. Detroit and Chicago, 1974.

Artem'ev, V. P. *Rezhim i okhrana ispravitel'no-trudovykh lagerei MVD* (The regimen and guard system in the corrective labor camps of the MVD). Munich, 1956.

Arutiunian, Iu. B. "Osobennosti i znachenie novogo etapa razvitiia sel'skogo khoziaistva SSSR" (Specific features and significance of the new stage of development in Soviet agriculture). In *Istoriia sovetskogo krest'ianstva i kolkhoznogo stroitel'stva v SSSR. Materialy nauchnoi sessii, 18–21 aprelia 1961 g.* (History of the Soviet peasantry and kolkhoz construction in the USSR: Materials from a scholarly conference, April 18–21, 1961). Moscow, 1963.

Aseev, Nikolai. *Stikhotvoreniia i poemy* (Verse and narrative poems). Leningrad, 1967.

Avrich, Paul. *Kronstadt 1921.* New York, 1974.

Avtorkhanov, Abdurrakhman. *Sila i bessilie Brezhneva* (Brezhnev's power and importance). Frankfurt, 1979.

Badaev, A. E. *Bol'sheviki v Gosudarstvernoi Dune* (The Bolsheviks in the tsarist Duma). Moscow, 1930. English edition: *The Bolsheviks in the Tsarist Duma.* New York, 1929.

Bakunin, Mikhail. *Narodroe delo* (The people's cause). London, 1862.

Balakshin, Petr. *Final v Kitae. Vozniknovenie, razvitie i ischeznovenie Beloi emigratsii na Dal'nem Vostoke* (Finale in China: Rise, development, and disappearance of the White emigré community in the Far East). 2 vols. San Francisco, 1955.

Barbusse, Henri. *Stalin: A New World Seen Through One Man.* New York-London, 1935.

Barmine, Alexander. *One Who Survived.* New York, 1945.

Barton, Paul. *L'institution concentrationnaire en Russie (1930–1957).* Paris, 1959.

Bazili, N. A. *Rossiia pod sovetskoi vlast'iu* (Russia under Soviet rule). Paris, 1937.

Beissinger, Mark. "Ekonomicheskaia strategiia Andropova i ee lovushki" (Andropov's economic strategy and its pitfalls). *Obozrenie,* no. 7, November 1983.

Beliakov, A. *Iunost' vozhdia* (The Great Leader's youth). Moscow, 1960.

Belinkov, Arkadii. *Sdacha i gibel' sovetskogo intelligenta: Iurii Olesha* (The surrender and destruction of a Soviet intellectual: Yuri Olesha). Madrid, 1976.

Belyi, Andrei. *Peterburg* (Petersburg). Moscow, 1978. English translation: *Petersburg.* New York, 1959.

Bennigsen, Alexandre. "Islam in the USSR." *Soviet Jewish Affairs,* no. 2, 1979.

Berdyaev, Nicholas. *The Origins of Russian Communism.* Ann Arbor, 1960.

Bergson, Abram. *The Real National Income of Soviet Russia Since 1928.* Cambridge, 1961.

Bernshtam, M. "Storony v grazhdanskoi voine 1917–1921 gg." (The sides in the civil war, 1917–1921). *Vestnik russkogo khristianskogo dvizheniia,* no. 128, 1979.

Bershadskaia, Liubov'. *Rastoptannye zhizni* (Trampled lives). Paris, 1975.

Besedovskii, G. Z. *Na putiakh k termidoru* (On the road to Thermidor). Paris, 1930.

Bethell, Nicholas W. *The Last Secret.* New York, 1974.

Bilinsky, Yaroslav. *The Second Soviet Republic: The Ukraine After World War II*. New Brunswick, 1964.

Bismarck, Otto von. *Mysli i vospominaniia* (Thoughts and recollections). Moscow, 1940.

Blok, Aleksandr A. *Poslednie dni imperatorskoi vlasti* (The last days of imperial rule). Petrograd, 1921.

———. *Sobranie sochinenii v 8 tomakh* (Collected works in 8 volumes). Moscow, 1962.

Bohlen, Charles E. *Witness to History, 1929–1969*. New York, 1973.

Boiter, Albert. "When the Kettle Boils Over," *Problems of Communism*, no. 1, 1964.

Bok, M. M. *Vospominaniia o moem ottse P. A. Stolypine* (Reminiscences of my father, P. A. Stolypin). New York, 1953.

Boldin, I. V. *Stranitsy zhizni* (Pages from a life). Moscow, 1961.

*Bol'shaia sovetskaia entsiklopediia* (Great Soviet encyclopedia). 1st ed. Moscow, 1926–1947.

Bonch-Bruevich, Vladimir D. *Na boevykh postakh fevral'skoi i oktiabr'skoi revoliutsii* (At combat posts in the February and October revolutions). Moscow, 1931.

Bondarskaia, G. A. *Rozhdaemost' v SSSR. Etnograficheskii aspekt* (The birthrate in the USSR: Ethnographic aspect). Moscow, 1977.

Brezhnev, Leonid I. *Leninskim kursom* (By the Leninist course). Moscow, 1970.

———. *Ob osnovnykh voprosakh ekonomicheskoi politiki KPSS na sovremennom etape* (On basic questions of CPSU economic policy at the contemporary stage). 2 vols. Moscow, 1975.

———. "Rech' na torzhestvennom zasedanii po sluchaiu 47-oi godovshchiny Oktiabr'skoi revoliutsii" (Speech at the ceremonial session on the 47th anniversary of the October revolution). *Pravda*, November 7, 1964.

Broderson, Arvid. *The Soviet Worker*. New York, 1966.

Bruegel, J. W., ed. *Stalin und Hitler: Pact gegen Europa*. Vienna, 1973.

Brumbert, Abraham, ed. *In Quest of Justice*. New York, 1970.

Bryant, Arthur. *Triumph in the West*. London, 1959.

Buber-Neumann, Margarete. *Kriegsschauplatze der Weltrevolution*. Stuttgart, 1967.

———. *La révolution mondiale*. Paris, 1970.

———. *Vom Potsdam nach Moskau. Stationen eines Irrwegs*. Stuttgart, 1957.

Bukharin, Nikolai. "Lenin i problema kul'turnoi revoliutsii" (Lenin and the problem of cultural revolution). In *Put' k sotsializmu v Rossii* (The road to socialism in Russia). New York, 1967.

Bukharin, Nikolai and Evgenii Preobrazhenskii. *Azbuka kommunizma* (The ABCs of communism). Moscow, 1928.

Bukovskii, Vladimir. *I vozvrashchaetsia veter* (And the wind returns). New York, 1978. English translation: *To Build a Castle*. New York, 1978.

Bulgakov, Mikhail. *Ranniaia neizdannaia proza* (Early unpublished prose). Munich, 1976.

Bunin, Ivan. *Okaiannye dni* (Accursed days). London, 1973.

Burlatskii, F. M. "Filosofiia mira" (The philosophy of peace). *Voprosy filosofii*, no. 12, 1982.

Butler, J.R.M., Ehrman, John and I.M.A. Gwyer. *Grand Strategy*. London, 1957–1964.

"Un Caligula au Kremlin." *Bulletin d'études et d'informations politiques internationale* (Paris), no. 102, January 16–31, 1954.

Cantril, Hadley. *Public Opinion 1935–1946*. Princeton, 1956.

Carr, E. H. *Foundations of a Planned Economy, 1926–1929*. 2 vols. (Vol. 1 with R. W. Davies). New York, 1969–1971.

———. *The Interregnum, 1923–1924*. Baltimore, 1969.

————. *Socialism in One Country, 1924–1926.* 3 vols. Baltimore, 1970–1972.

Carrère d'Encausse, Hélène. *L'empire éclaté* (Decline of an empire). Paris, 1978. English translation: *Decline of an Empire.* New York, 1979.

*The Case of Henry Erlich and Victor Alter.* Foreword by Camille Huysmans. New York, 1943.

Caute, David. *Les compagnons de route, 1917–1968.* Paris, 1979.

Cederholm, Boris. *Au pays du NEP et de la Tscheka.* Paris, 1928.

Chalidze, Valery. *To Defend These Rights: Human Rights and the Soviet Union.* New York, 1974.

Chalidze, Valerii, comp. *SSSR—rabochee dvizhenie?* (The USSR—a workers' movement?). New York, 1978.

Chamberlin, William Henry. *The Russian Revolution, 1917–1921.* 2 vols. New York, 1935; paperback ed. New York, 1965.

————. *Russia's Iron Age.* Boston, 1934.

Chapman, Janet G. *Real Wages in Soviet Russia Since 1928.* Cambridge, 1963.

Chayes, A. *The Cuban Missile Crisis.* New York, 1974.

*Chernaia kniga* (Black book). Edited by Vasilii Grossman and Il'ia Erenburg. Jerusalem, 1980.

*Chetyrnadtsatyi s'ezd VKP(b). Stenograficheskii otchet* (Fourteenth Party Congress: Stenographic record). Moscow, 1926.

Chistov, B. "Chapannoe vosstanie. Istoricheskaia spravka" (The Chapan revolt: A historical review). In *Chapany* (The Chapan rebels). Edited by A. Veselyi. Kuibyshev, 1936.

Chornovil, Vyacheslav, comp. *The Chornovil Papers.* Toronto, 1968.

Chukovskaia, Lidiia. *Zapiski ob Anne Akhmatovoi* (Notes on Anna Akhmatova). 2 vols. Paris, 1980.

Churchill, Winston S. *The Second World War.* 6 vols. Boston, 1948–1953.

————. *The Unrelenting Struggle.* Boston, 1942.

Ciliga, Ante. *The Russian Enigma.* London, 1979.

Clemens, Walter C., Jr. *The Arms Race and Sino-Soviet Relations.* Stanford, 1968.

Colton, Timothy J. *Commissars, Commanders, and Civilian Authority.* Cambridge, 1979.

Conquest, Robert. *The Great Terror: Stalin's Purge of the Thirties.* Rev. ed. New York, 1973.

————. *Kolyma: The Arctic Death Camps.* New York, 1978.

————. *Power and Policy in the USSR.* New York, 1961.

————. *Present Danger: Towards a Foreign Policy.* Oxford, 1978.

————. *The Soviet Deportation of Nationalities.* London, 1960.

Considine, Bob. *An American in Moscow: The Extraordinary Life of Doctor Armand Hammer.* New York, 1975.

Courtade, Francis and Pierre Cadars. *Histoire du cinéma nazi.* Paris, 1972.

Czarna ksiega cenzury PRL (The black book of censorship in the Polish People's Republic). 2 vols. London, 1977–1978.

D'Abernon, Lord. *The Eighteenth Decisive Battle of World History.* London, 1931.

Dallin, Alexander. *German Rule in Russia, 1941–1945.* London, 1957.

Dallin, David G. and Boris I. Nikolaevsky. *Forced Labor in Soviet Russia.* New Haven, 1947.

Dan, Fedor. *Dva goda skitanii (1919–1921)* (Two years of wanderings, 1919–1921). Berlin, 1922.

Davies, Norman. *White Eagle, Red Star: The Polish–Soviet War.* London, 1972.

Dedijer, Vladimir. *The Battle Stalin Lost.* New York, 1972.

*Dekrety sovetskoi vlasti* (Decrees of the Soviet government). Moscow, 1957.

Dekrety sovetskoi vlasti (Decrees of the Soviet government). Moscow, 1968.

*Delo Airikiana* (The Airikian case). New York, 1977.

"Delo F. F. Shul'tsa" (The F. F. Shults case). *Arkhiv samizdata*, doc. 589.

Demin, B. "Nenavist' k vragu—neot"emlemaia storona patriotizma sovetskikh voinov" (Hatred for the enemy—an inseparable part of the patriotism of Soviet soldiers). *Kommunist vooruzhennykh sil*, no. 3. 1969.

Denikin, Anton I. *Ocherki russkoi smuty* (Sketches of the Russian turmoil). Berlin, 1926.

Deutscher, Isaac. *The Prophet Armed*. London, 1954.

———. *The Prophet Outcast: Trotsky, 1929–1940*. London, 1963.

*Deutschlands Sieg in Polen*. Berlin, 1940.

Diadkin, I. G. *Otsenka neestestvennoi smertnosti naseleniia SSSR v 1927–1958 gg*. (An estimate of the nonnatural mortality rate in the USSR, 1927–1958). Moscow, 1976–1978.

Djilas, Milovan. *Conversations with Stalin*. New York, 1962.

Dmitrievskii, S. *Sovetskie portrety* (Soviet portraits). Berlin, 1932.

———. *Stalin*. Berlin, 1931.

*Documents on American Foreign Relations*. Vol. 13. Princeton, 1953.

*Documents on British Foreign Policy*.

*Documents on German Foreign Policy*.

*Documents on Polish–Soviet Relations, 1939–45*. Vol. 1. London, 1961.

"Doklad na torzhestvennom zasedanii po sluchaiu stoletiia so dnia rozhdeniia F. E. Dzerzhinskogo" (Report at a commemorative meeting on the hundredth birthday of F. E. Dzerzhinsky). *Izvestiia*, October 10, 1977.

"Dokument ideologicheskoi bor'by" (Document of the ideological struggle). *Iskusstvo kino*, no. 4. 1964.

*Dokumenty i materialy kanuna Vtoroi mirovoi voiny* (Documents and materials from the eve of World War II). Vol. 2: The Dirksen Archive (1938–1939), Moscow, 1948.

Dolgikh, V. "Uluchshit' partiinoe rukovodstvo rabotoi zheleznodorozhnogo transporta" (Improve party supervision of rail transport). *Partiinaia zhizn'*, no. 7, April 1983.

Dolgun, Alexander and Patrick Watson. *An American in the Gulag*. New York, 1975.

Dornberg, John. *Brezhnev: The Masks of Power*. London, 1974.

Doroshenko, D. *Istoriia Ukrainy 1917–1923* (History of the Ukraine, 1917–1923). Uzhgorod, 1932.

Drabkina, Elizaveta, "Zimnii pereval" (Winter crossing). *Novyi mir*, no. 10, 1968.

Dudko, D. "Na segodniashnii der'" (Unto this day). *Posev*, no. 7, 1979.

*Dvadtsat' vtoroi s"ezd KPSS, 17–31 oktiabria 1961 god. Stenograficheskii otchet* (Twenty-second CPSU Congress, October 17–31, 1961: Stenographic record). Moscow, 1962.

*Dvadtsatyi s"ezd Kommunisticheskoi partii Sovetskogo Soiuza, 14–25 fevralia 1956 god. Stenograficheskii otchet* (Twentieth Congress of the CPSU, February 14–25, 1956: Stenographic record). 2 vols. Moscow, 1956.

Dzyuba, Ivan. *Grani kristala* (Facets of a crystal). Kiev, 1976.

———. *Internatsionalizm ili russifikatsiia?* Amsterdam, 1968.

Eberstadt, Nick. "The Health Crisis in the USSR." *New York Review of Books*, February 19, 1981.

Eizenshtein, Sergei, *Izbrannye proizvedeniia v 6 tomakh* (Selected works in 6 volumes). Moscow, 1964–1971.

Epperson-Kennel, Ruth. *Theodore Dreiser and the Soviet Union*. New York, 1969.

Erenburg, Il'ia. "Rvach" (Self-seeker). In *Sobranie sochinenii* (Collected works), vol. 2. Moscow, 1964.

————. *Zhizn' i gibel' Nikolaia Kurbova* (The life and death of Nikolai Kurbov). Berlin, 1923.

Erickson, John. *The Soviet High Command.* New York, 1962.

Ershov, L. "Dvizhenie literatury—dvizhenie kritiki" (As literature moves, so moves criticism). *Nash sovremennik,* no. 7, 1978.

*Evraziistvo (opyt sistematicheskogo izlozheniia)* (Eurasianism—an attempt at a systematic exposition). N.p., 1926.

Fabre-Luce, Alfred. *Russie 1927.* Paris, 1927.

Faingar, I. M. *Ocherk razvitiia germanskogo monopolisticheskogo kapitala* (Outline of the development of German monopoly capital). Moscow, 1958.

Fainsod, Merle. *Smolensk Under Soviet Rule.* Cambridge, 1958.

*Fal'sifikatory istorii* (Falsifiers of history). Moscow, 1948.

Fediukin, G. *Velikii oktiabr' i intelligentsia* (Great October and the intelligentsia). Moscow, 1972.

Fedotov, G. *I est' i budet* (That which is shall be). Paris, 1932.

Fedotov, Georgii. *Rossiia, Evropa i my* (Russia, Europe, and ourselves). Paris, 1973.

Fejto, Francois. *Behind the Rape of Hungary.* New York, 1957.

Ferro, Marc. *La révolution de 1917.* Paris, 1967.

Fest, Joachim. *Hitler: Eine Biographie.* 2 vols. Frankfurt, 1976.

Filene, Peter G. *Americans and the Soviet Experiment, 1917–1933.* Cambridge, 1967.

Fireside, Harvey. *Icon and Swastika.* Cambridge, 1971.

Fischer, George. *Soviet Opposition to Stalin.* Cambridge, 1952.

Fischer, Louis. *Russia's Road from Peace to War.* New York, 1969.

Fletcher, William C. *The Russian Orthodox Church Underground, 1917–1970.* London, 1971.

————. *A Study in Survival: The Church in Russia, 1927–1943.* New York, 1965.

Florinsky, Michael T. *World Revolution and the USSR.* New York, 1933.

*Foreign Relations of the United States: Diplomatic Papers.*

*Foreign Relations of the United States: Diplomatic Papers. The Conferences at Malta and Yalta, 1945.* Washington, D.C., 1955.

*Foreign Relations of the United States: "The Conference of Berlin" (The Potsdam Conference).* Washington, D.C., 1945.

Francis, David R. *Russia from the American Embassy.* New York, 1921.

*Freundschaft DDR-UdSSR. Documenten und Materialen.* Berlin, 1965.

Friedensberg, F. "Die sowjetischen Kriegslieferungen an das Hitler reich." *Vierteljahrsheft zur Wirtschaftsforschung,* no. 4, 1962.

Frossard, L.-O. *De Jaurès à Lenine. Notes et souvenirs d'un militant.* Paris, 1930.

Frunze, Mikhail V. *Izbrannye proizvedeniia* (Selected works). Moscow, 1934.

————. *Na frontakh grazhdarskoi voiny* (On the fronts of the civil war). Moscow, 1941.

Fulop-Miller, Rene. *The Mind and Face of Bolshevism.* New York, 1927.

Furman, G. "Antialkogol'naia nedelia" (Anti-alcohol week). *Revoliutsiia i kul'tura,* no. 18, 1929.

Geller, Mikhail. *See* Heller, Mikhail.

Gernet, M. N. *Istoriia tsarskoi tiur'my* (History of the tsarist prison). 5 vols. Moscow, 1960–1963.

Gide, Andre. *Retour de l'URSS.* Paris, 1936.

Gilboa, Yehoshua A. *The Black Years of Soviet Jewry, 1939–1953.* Boston, 1971.

Gililov, S. *V. I. Lenin—organizator sovetskogo mnogonatsional'nogo gosudarstva* (V. I. Lenin, organizer of the Soviet multinational state). Moscow, 1960.

Gins, G. K. "Sibir', soiuzniki i Kolchak" (Siberia, the Allies, and Kolchak). In *Kolchak-ovshchina. Iz belykh memuarov* (The Kolchak regime: From White memoirs). Leningrad, 1930.

Gladkov, Fedor. *Energiia* (Energy). Moscow, 1936.

Gnedin, Evgenii. *Iz istorii otnoshenii mezhdu SSSR i fashistskoi Germaniei. Dokumenty i sovremennye kommentarii* (From the history of relations between the USSR and fascist Germany: Documents and contemporary commentary). New York, 1977.

Goikhberg, A. *Zakon o brake* (Marriage law). Moscow, 1922.

Golinkov, D. L. *Krushenie antisovetskogo podpol'ia v SSSR* (The downfall of the anti-Soviet underground in the USSR). Moscow, 1980.

Gorbanevskaia, Natalia. *Polder'* (Noon). Frankfurt, 1970. English translation: *Red Square at Noon.* New York, 1970.

Gorbunov, V. V. *V. I. Lenin i Proletkul't* (V. I. Lenin and Proletcult). Moscow, 1974.

Gordeev, A. A. *Istoriia kazakov* (History of the Cossacks). Paris, 1970.

Gorev, Mikhail. "Agoniia tserkovnoi kontrrevoliutsii" (Death agony of the clerical counterrevolution). *Izvestiia,* June 2. 1922.

Gor'kii, Maksim. *O russkom krest'ianstve* (On the Russian peasantry). Berlin, 1922.

——. *Sobranie sochinenii v 30 tomakh* (Collected works in 30 volumes). Moscow, 1949–1956.

——. *Zametki iz dnevnika. Vospominaniia* (Notes from a diary: Reminiscences). Berlin, 1924.

Gorodetskii, E. "O zapiskakh N. M. Potapova" (On N. M. Potapov's memoirs). *Voenno-istoricheskii zhurnal,* no. 1. 1968.

Gorshkov, S. G. *Morskaia moshch' gosudarstva* (The naval power of the state). Moscow, 1979. English translation: *The Sea Power of the State.* Oxford, 1979.

*Gosudarstvennyi plan razvitiia narodnogo khoziaistva SSSR na 1941 god* (State plan for the development of Soviet agriculture for 1941). American Council of Learned Societies Reprints, no. 30, Baltimore, n.d.

*Great Soviet Encyclopedia.* English translation of 3d Russ. ed. 30 vols. New York, 1973–

Griffith, William E. *Sino-Soviet Relations, 1964–1965.* Cambridge, 1967.

Grigorenko, Petro. *Memoirs.* New York, 1982.

——. *Mysli sumashedshego* (Thoughts of a madman). Amsterdam, 1973.

——. *Sbornik statei* (Collected essays). New York, 1977.

——. *V podpol'e mozhno vstretit' tol'ko krys* (In the underground you meet only rats). New York, 1981.

Groshev, I. I. and O. I. Chechenkina. *Kritika burzhuaznoi fal'tsifikatsii natsional'noi politiki KPSS* (Critique of the bourgeois falsification of CPSU nationalities policy). Moscow, 1974.

*Der grosse Feldzug gegen Polen.* Vienna, 1940.

Grossman, Gregory. "An Economy at Middle Age." *Problems of Communism, March–April 1976.*

Grossman, Vasilii. *Za pravoe delo* (For the right cause). Moscow, 1964.

Grunt, A. Ia. *Moskva 1917, revoliutsiia i kontrrevoliutsiia* (Moscow 1917: Revolution and counterrevolution). Moscow, 1976.

Gumilevskii, Lev. *Sobachii pereulok* (Dog's alley). Riga, 1928.

Gurovich, I. *Zapiski emigranta* (Notes of an emigré). Petrograd-Moscow, 1923.

Halder, Franz. *Kriegstagebuch.* 2 vols. Stuttgart, 1963.

Harman, Chris. *Bureaucracy and Revolution in Eastern Europe.* London, 1974.

Harriman, Averell. *Peace with Russia?* New York, 1959.

Heller [Geller], Mikhail. "Andropov: A Retrospective View." *Survey*, vol. 28, no. 1 (120), Spring 1984.

———. *Kontsentratsionnyi mir i sovetskaia literatura* (The concentration camp world and Soviet literature). London, 1974.

———. "Poet i vozhd'" (Poet and leader). *Kontinent*, no. 16, 1978.

Hentsch, Guy. *Staline negociateur.* Neuchâtel, 1967.

Hilger, Gustav and Alfred Meyer. *The Incompatible Allies: A Memoir-History of German–Soviet Relations, 1918–1941.* New York, 1953.

*History of the Communist Party of the Soviet Union (Bolsheviks): Short Course.* New York, 1939.

Hitler, Adolf. *Mein Kampf.* Munich, 1927.

*Hitler's Table Talk, 1941–1944.* Translated by Norman Cameron and R. H. Stevens. London, 1953.

Hoffman, Joachim. *Deutsche und Kalmyken, 1942–1945.* Monograph Series on the Military History of World War II, no. 14. Freiburg, 1974.

Holubnichy, V. "Ukraine Since World War II, 1945–1962." In *Ukraine: A Concise Encyclopedia.* Edited by V. Kubijovic. Vol. 1. Toronto, 1963.

Hough, Jerry and Merle Fainsod. *How the Soviet Union Is Governed.* Cambridge, 1979.

Hubatsch, Walther, ed. *The German Question.* New York, 1967.

———. *Hitlers Weisungen fur die Kriegsführung 1939–1945. Dokumente des Oberkommandos der Wehrmacht.* Frankfurt am Main, 1962.

Hungarian Committee. *Facts About Hungary.* Compiled and edited by Imre Kovac. New York, 1958.

Iakovlev, A. "Protiv antiistorizma" (Against antihistoricism). *Literaturnaia gazeta*, October 15, 1972.

Iakovlev, B. (with A. Burtsov). *Kontsentratsionnye lageri SSSR* (The concentration camps of the USSR). Munich, 1955.

Iakubovskii, S. I. *Ob"edinitel'noe dvizhenie za obrazovanie SSSR, 1917–1922* (The unification movement for the founding of the USSR, 1917–1922). Moscow, 1947.

Iaroslavskii, Emelian. *Kratkaia istoriia VKP(b)* (Brief history of the All-Union Communist party [Bolshevik]). Moscow, 1930.

———. "Mechty Chaianovykh i sovetskoi deistvitel'nosti" (Dreams of the Chayanovs and Soviet reality). *Pravda*, October 18, 1930.

"Inside the USSR." *Time*, June 23, 1980.

International Institute for Strategic Studies. *The Military Balance, 1978–1979.* London, 1978.

*Internatsionalisty. Trudiashchiesia zarubezhnykh stran—uchastniki bor'by za vlast' Sovetov na iuge i vostoke respubliki* (Internationalists: Laborers from foreign countries who helped fight for Soviet power in the southern and eastern parts of the republic). Moscow, 1971.

"Interv'iu V. Osipova amerikanskim zhurnalistam" (V. Osipov's interview with American journalists). *Vestnik RKhD*, no. 106, 1972.

*Iskhod k vostoku* (Exodus to the East). Sofia, 1921.

*Iskusstvo pod bul'dozerom. Siniaia kniga* (Art under the bulldozer: A blue book). Compiled by Aleksandr Glezer. London, 1979.

*Istoriia Estonskoi SSR* (History of the Estonian SSR). Edited by G. I. Naan, Tallin, 1958.

*Istoriia KPSS* (History of the CPSU). Moscow, 1959.

*Istoriia KPSS* (History of the CPSU). Moscow, 1960.

*Istoriia Sibiri* (History of Siberia). Vol. 5. Leningrad, 1969.

*Istoriia sovetskogo gosudarstva i prava* (History of the Soviet state and Soviet law). Moscow, 1968.

*Istoriia sovetskogo krest'ianstva i kolkhoznogo stroitel'stva v SSSR. Materialy nauchnoi sessii, 18–21 aprelia 1961 g.* (History of the Soviet peasantry and kolkhoz construction in the USSR. Materials from a scholarly session, April 18–21, 1961). Moscow, 1963.

*Istoriia SSSR. Epokha sotsializma* (History of the USSR: Age of socialism). Moscow, 1957.

*Istoriia SSSR. Epokha sotsializma* (History of the USSR: Age of socialism). 3rd enl. ed. Moscow, 1974.

*Istoriia SSSR. Epokha sotsializma* (History of the USSR: Age of socialism). Moscow, 1975.

*Istoriia Uzbekskoi SSR* (History of the Uzbek SSR). 4 vols. Tashkent, 1967–1968.

*Istoriia Velikoi otechestvennoi voiny Sovetskogo Soiuza 1941–45 v 6 tomakh* (History of the Great Patriotic War of the Soviet Union, 1941–45, in 6 volumes). Moscow, 1960–1965.

*Istoriia vneshnei politiki SSSR* (History of USSR foreign policy). 2d rev. and enl. ed. Edited by Andrei Gromyko and Boris Ponomarev. 2 vols. Moscow, 1975–1976.

*Itogi desiatiletiia sovetskoi vlasti v tsifrakh* (Statistical balance sheet of a decade of Soviet power). Moscow, 1927.

Iukshinskii, V. I. *Sovetskie kontsentratsionnye lageri v 1945–1955 gg.* (Soviet concentration camps, 1945–1955). Munich, 1958.

Ivinskaia, Ol'ga. *V plenu vremeni* (Captive of time). Paris, 1978. English translation: *Captive of Time.* New York, 1978.

*Iz istorii VChK, 1917–1921* (From the history of the Cheka, 1917–1921). Moscow, 1958.

*Iz istorii VChK. Sbornik dokumentov* (From the history of the Cheka: Collected documents). Moscow, 1957.

Jasny, Naum. *Khrushchev's Crop Policy.* Glasgow, 1965.

———. *The Soviet 1956 Statistical Handbook: A Commentary.* East Lansing, 1957.

Jozwienko, Adolf. "Misja Marchlewskiego w 1919 roku na tle stosunkow polsko-radziechich" (Marchlewski's 1919 mission against the background of Polish–Soviet relations). In *Z badan nad wplywem i znaczeniem rewolucji rosyjskich 1917 roku* (Research on the influence and significance of the Russian revolutions of 1917). Wroclaw, 1968.

———. *Polski a "biala" Rosja (od listopada 1918 do kwietnia 1920)* (Poland and "White" Russia, November 1918 to April 1920). Wroclaw, 1979.

Kaiurov, V. "Shest' dnei revoliutsii" (Seven days of revolution). *Proletarskaia revoliutsiia*, no. 1, 1923.

Kakurin, Nikolai E. *Kak srazhalas' revoliutsiia* (How the revolution fought). 2 vols. Moscow-Leningrad, 1925–1926.

Kakurin, N. E. and V. A. Melikov. *Voina s belopoliakami* (War with the White Poles). Moscow, 1925.

Kalinin, Mikhail. *Za eti gody* (During these years). Vol. 2. Moscow, 1926.

Kamenev, Lev. "Leninizm ili trotskizm" (Leninism or Trotskyism). In *Ob "Urokakh oktiabria"* (On [Trotsky's] "Lessons of October"). Leningrad, 1924.

Kamenev, Sergei S. *Zapiski o grazhdanskoi voine i voennom stroitel'stve* (Notes on the civil war and the building of the military). Moscow, 1963.

Kaplan, Karel. *Dans les archives du Comité central. Trente ans de secrets du bloc soviétique.* Paris, 1973.

Karaganov, A. "Istoriia odnoi p'esy" (History of a certain play). *Znamia*, no. 1, 1963.

Kassil', Lev. "Na zlobu dnia sed'mogo" (On the topic of the seventh day). *Molodaia gvardiia*, no. 1, 1930.

Katan'ian, v. "Protokoly o nesostoiatel'nosti" (Record of bankruptcy). *Molodaia gvardiia*, no. 17, 1930.

Kecskemeti, Paul. *The Unexpected Revolution*. Stanford, 1961.

Kennedy, Robert F. *Thirteen Days: A Memoir of the Cuban Missile Crisis*. New York, 1969.

Kerblay, Basile. "Les enseignements de l'experience soviétique d'agriculture collectiviste." *Revue d'études comparatives Est-Ouest*, September 1979.

———. *La société soviétique contemporaine*. Paris, 1977.

Kertesz, Stephen D. *East Central Europe and the World: Developments in the Post-Stalin Era*. South Bend, 1962.

Khenkin, Kirill. "Ispanskii bloknot" (Spanish notebook). *Kontinent*, no. 16.

*Khleb i revoliutsiia. Prodovol'stvennaia politika Kommunisticheskoi partii i sovetskogo pravitel'stva v 1917–22 gg.* (Bread and revolution: The food policy of the Communist party and Soviet government, 1917–22). Moscow, 1972.

Khriashcheva, A. I. *Gruppy i klassy v krest'ianstve* (Groups and classes within the peasantry). Moscow, 1924.

Khrushchev, Nikita. *Khrushchev Remembers*. Boston, 1970.

———. *Khrushchev Remembers: The Last Testament*. Boston, 1974.

———. *O merakh dal'neishego razvitiia sel'skogo khoziaistva SSSR* (On measures for the further development of Soviet agriculture). Moscow, 1953.

———. *Stroitel'stvo kommunizma v SSSR i razvitie sel'skogo khoziaistva* (The building of communism in the USSR and agricultural development). 2 vols. Moscow, 1962.

———. *Vospominaniia. Izbrannye otryvki* (Memoirs: Selected passages). New York, 1979.

Khutuev, Kh. I. *Balkarskii narod v gody Velikoi otechestvennoi voiny i poslevoennyi period* (The Balkar people during the Great Patriotic War and in the postwar period). Manuscript at the Lenin Library in Moscow, registration no. Dk 67–7/513.

Kirimal, E. *Der nationale Kampf der Krimturken*. Emsdetten, 1952.

Kirsanov, N. A. *Po zovu rodiny. Dobrovol'cheskie formirovaniia Krasnoi armii v period Velikoi otechestvennoi voiny* (At the call of the homeland: Volunteer formations in the Red army during the Great Patriotic War). Moscow, 1974.

Kissinger, Henry. *The White House Years*. Boston, 1979.

Kleist, Peter. *Zwischen Hitler und Stalin, 1939–1945*. Bonn, 1950.

Kliuchevskii, V. *Kurs russkoi istorii* (A course in Russian history). Vol. 4. Moscow, 1910.

Knipovich, B. *Ocherki deiatel'nosti narodnogo komissariata zemledeliia za tri goda, 1917–1920* (Essays on the activities of the People's Commissariat of Agriculture for the three years 1917–1920). Moscow, 1920.

Kochetov, Vsevolod. "Zapisi voennykh let" (Notes from the war years). *Oktiabr'*, no. 5, 1965.

Koestler, Arthur. "The Initiates." In *The God That Failed*. New York, 1954.

———. *The Invisible Writing*. London, 1969.

Kogan, Petr S. *Literatura etikh let, 1917–1923* (The literature of those years, 1917–1923). Ivanovo-Voznesensk, 1924.

Kokovtsev, V. N. *Iz moego proshlogo* (From my past). Paris, 1933.

Kolakowski, Leszek. *Glownye nurty marksizmu* (Main currents of Marxism). Paris, 1977.

Kolbanovskii, V. "Izuchenie mozga Lenina" (The study of Lenin's brain). *Molodaia gvardiia*, no. 2, 1929.

Kolesnikov, Mikhail. "Shkola ministrov" (School of ministers). *Znamia*, no. 10, 1977.

Kollontai, Alexandra. *The Workers' Opposition in Russia*. London, 1923.

Koltsov, Mikhail. *Izbrannye proizvedeniia v 3 tomakh* (Selected works in 3 volumes). Moscow, 1957.

*Kommunisticheskaia partiia Sovetskogo Soiuza v rezoliutsiiakh i resheniiakh s"ezdov, konferentsii i plenumov TsK* (The Communist party of the Soviet Union in resolutions and decisions of congresses, conferences, and Central Committee plenums). Vol. 4. Moscow, 1970. (Cited as *KPSS v rezoliutsiiakh.*)

*Kommunisty Urala v gody grazhdanskoi voiny* (The Communists of the Urals during the civil war). Sverdlovsk, 1959.

Kondratiev, Nikolai D. *Rynok khlebov i ego regulirovanie vo vremia voiny i revoliutsii* (The grain market and its regulation during the war and revolution). Moscow, 1922.

Kondurushkin, I. S. *Chastnyi kapital pered sovetskim sudom* (Private capital before the Soviet court of justice). Moscow-Leningrad, 1927.

Korolenko, Vladimir G. "Iz dnevnikov 1917–1921 gg." (From diaries of 1917–1921). *Pamiat'*, no. 2, 1977.

Korti, M. "Aleksei Nikitin i dvizhenie za prava rabochikh v SSSR" (Aleksei Nikitin and the workers' rights movement in the USSR). Manuscript.

Koshelivets', I. "Mykola Skrypnik." *Suchasnist'*, 1972.

Kovalev, S. "Suverenitet i internatsional'nye obiazannosti sotsialisticheskikh stran" (Sovereignty and the international obligations of socialist countries). *Pravda*, September 26, 1968.

Kovalevskii, P. E. *Zarubezhnaia Rossiia* (Russia abroad). Paris, 1972.

*KPSS o formirovanie novogo cheloveka. Sbornik dokumentov i materialov, 1965–1981.* (The CPSU and the formation of the new man: Collected documents and materials, 1965–1981). Moscow, 1982.

Krasin, Victor, *Sud* (The trial). New York, 1983.

*Krasnaia kniga VChK* (Red book of the Cheka). Edited by P. Makinstian. Moscow, 1920.

Krasnov-mladshii, N. N. *Nezabyvaemoe, 1945–1956. Russkaia zhizn'* (Unforgettable times, 1945–1956: Russian life). San Francisco, 1958.

*Kratkaia istoriia sovetskogo kino* (Brief history of the Soviet cinema). Moscow, 1969.

*Kratkii politicheskii slovar'* (Short political dictionary). Moscow, 1978.

Kravchenko, G. S. *Voennaia ekonomika SSSR, 1941–1945* (The war economy of the USSR, 1941–1945). Moscow, 1963.

Krivitsky, Walter. *In Stalin's Secret Service*. New York, 1939.

———. *I Was Stalin's Agent*. London, 1939.

Kromiadi, K. "Sovetskie voennoplennye v Germanii v 1941 godu" (Soviet prisoners of war in Germany in 1941). *Novyi zhurnal*, no. 32, 1953.

Kruze, E. E. *Polozhenie robochego klassa v Rossii v 1900–1914* (The condition of the working class in Russia, 1900–1914). Leningrad, 1976.

Krylov, S. "Kondrat'evshchina i pravyi uklon" (The Kondratievites and right-wing deviation). *Pravda*, October 10, 1930.

*K sobytiiam v Chekhoslovakii. Fakty, dokumenty, svidetel'stva pressy i ochevidtsev. Vypusk pervyi. Press-gruppa sovetskikh zhurnalistov* (The events in Czechoslovakia: Facts, documents, press accounts, and eyewitness reports, issue no. 1, by a group of Soviet journalists). Moscow, 1968.

Kubanin, M. *Makhnovshchina* (The Makhno movement). Leningrad, 1928.

Kubijovic, V. "Ukraine During World War II." In *Ukraine: A Concise Encyclopedia*. Edited by V. Kubijovic. Vol. 1. Toronto, 1963.

Kubijovic, V., ed. *Ukraine: A Concise Encyclopedia*. Toronto, 1963.

Kuskova, Elizaveta. "Mesiats soglashatel'stva" (A month of collaborationism). *Volia Rossii*, nos. 3–5, 1928.

Kuz'min, G. V. *Razgrom interventov i belogvardeitsev v 1917–22* (The rout of the interventionists and White Guards in 1917–22). Moscow, 1977.

Kuznetsov, Feliks. "Glavnoe nashe bogatstvo" (What we are richest in). *Literaturnaia gazeta*, October 24, 1979.

Larin, Iurii. "Proizvodstvennaia propaganda i sovetskoe khoziaistvo na rubezhe chetvertogo goda. Doklad na s"ezde politprosvetov, 4.11.1920" (Production propaganda and the Soviet economy at the beginning of the fourth year: Report to the Congress of Political Education Workers, November 4, 1920).

Larsons, M. *Na sovetskoi sluzhbe. Zapiski spetsa* (In the Soviet service: Notes of a specialist). Paris, 1930.

Latsis (Sudrabs), Martyn I. *ChK v bor'be s kontrrevoliutsiei* (The Cheka in the struggle against the counterrevolution). Moscow, 1921.

*Latyshski strelki v bor'be za sovetskuiu vlast' v 1917–1920 gg. Vospominaniia i dokumentov* (The Latvian rifles in the struggle for Soviet power in 1917–1920: Memoirs and documents). Riga, 1962.

Lee, Ivy. *USSR: A World Enigma*. London, 1927.

Legay, Kléber. *Un mineur français chez les russes*. Paris, 1937.

Lelevich, G. *Strekopytovshchina* (The Strekopytov revolt). Moscow, 1923.

Lenin, V. I. *Collected Works*. Moscow, 1960– .

———. *Polnoe sobranie sochinenii* (Completed collected works). 5th ed. Moscow, 1958–1959.

———. *Sobranie sochinenii*. (Collected works). 2d ed. Moscow, 1926–1932.

———. *Sochineniia* (Works). 4th ed. Moscow, 1941–1967.

Lenin, V. I. and Leon Trotsky. *Kronstadt*. New York, 1979.

*Lenin i Stalin o sovetskoi konstitutsii. Sbornik statei, rechei i dokumentov* (Lenin and Stalin on the Soviet constitution: Collected articles, speeches, and documents). Moscow, 1936.

Leonidov. "Esero-banditizm v Tambovskoi gubernii i bor'ba s nim" (SR banditry in Tambov Province and the struggle against it). *Revoliutsiia i voina* (Moscow), no. 14–15, 1922.

Lermolo, Elisabeth. *Face of a Victim*. New York, 1955.

Lerner, Warren. *Karl Radek: The Last Internationalist*. Stanford, 1970.

Levinson, Charles. *Vodka-Cola*. Paris, 1980.

Levitin, Anatolii and Vadim Shavrov. *Ocherki po istorii russkoi tserkovnoi smuty* (Essays on the history of the turmoil in the Russian church). 3 vols. 1977.

Lewis, Anthony. "After Afghanistan, Business as Usual?" *International Herald Tribune*, January 8, 1980.

Libedinskaia, Lidiia. *Zelenaia lampa* (Green light). Moscow, 1966.

Liberman, S. I. *Dela i liudi* (Deeds and people). New York, 1944.

Liddell Hart, Basil H., ed. *History of the Second World War*. London, 1970.

Lieberman, Sanford R. "The Party Under Stress: The Experience of World War II." In *Soviet Society and the Communist Party*. Edited by Karl W. Ryavec. Amherst, 1978.

*Litsom k litsu s Amerikoi* (Face to face with America). Moscow, 1960.

Litvinov, Pavel, comp. *The Trial of the Four*. New York, 1972.

*Le livre jaune français*. Paris, 1939.

Lockhart, Robert Bruce. *Memoirs of a British Agent*. London, 1952.

London, Arthur Gerard. *On Trial*. London, 1970.

Lowenthal, Richard. "Tito's Affair with Khrushchev." *New Leader*, October 6, 1958.

Lucky, George. "Turmoil in the Ukraine." In *In Quest of Justice*, ed. Abraham Brumberg. New York, 1970.

Ludendorff, Erich. *Meine Kriegserinnerungen*. Berlin, 1919.

Lundin, C. Leonard. *Finland in the Second World War*. Bloomington, 1957.

Luther, M. "Die Krim unter deutscher Besatzung im zweiten Weltkriegs." Studies in East European History, vol. 3. Berlin, 1956.

Luxemburg, Rosa. *The Russian Revolution*. Ann Arbor, 1961.

Luzhanin, Maksim, "Bessonyi telefon" (The sleepless telephone). *Belarus'*, no. 4, 1977.

Maclean, Fitzroy. *Eastern Approaches*. London, 1965.

Macmillan, Harold. *Pointing the Way (1959–1961)*. New York, 1962.

Makarenko, A. S. *Sochineniia* (Works). Moscow, 1951.

Makharadze, Filipp. *Sovety i bor'ba za sovetskuiu vlast' v Gruzii, 1917–1921* (The Soviets and the struggle for Soviet power in Georgia, 1917–1921). Tiflis, 1928.

Makhno, Nestor. *Pod udarami kontrrevoliutsii* (Under the blows of the counterrevolution). Vol. 2. Paris, 1936.

Maksudov, M. "Losses Suffered by the Population of the USSR, 1918–1958." In *Samizdat Register II*. New York, 1981.

*Malaia sovetskaia entsiklopediia* (Small Soviet encyclopedia). 1st ed. Moscow, 1920.

*Malaia sovetskaia entsiklopediia* (Small Soviet encyclopedia). Moscow, 1930.

Malenkov, Georgii. *Otchetnyi doklad XIX s"ezdu partii o rabote Tsentral'nogo komiteta VKP(b)* (Report to the Nineteenth Party Congress on the work of the Central Committee). Moscow, 1952.

*Malevich*. Amsterdam, 1970.

Malinovskii, Rodion. "Dvadtsatiletie nachala Velikoi otechestvennoi voiny" (Twentieth anniversary of the start of the Great Patriotic War). *Voenno-istoricheskii zhurnal*, no. 6, 1961.

Malkov, Pavel. *Zapiski komendanta moskovskogo kremlia* (Memoirs of the commandant of the Moscow Kremlin). Moscow, 1962.

Manuilskii, Dmitrii. *Itogi sotsialisticheskogo stroitel'stva v SSSR* (Results of socialist construction in the USSR). Moscow, 1935.

Mastny, Vojtech, ed. *East European Dissent*. Vol. 2, 1965–1970. New York, 1972.

*Materialy XXIII s"ezda KPSS* (Materials of the Twenty-third CPSU Congress). Moscow, 1966.

*Materialy XXIV s"ezda KPSS* (Materials of the Twenty-fourth CPSU Congress). Moscow, 1971.

*Materialy po istorii franko-russkikh otnoshenii za 1910–14 gody* (Materials on the history of Franco-Russian relations, 1910–14). Moscow, 1922.

McCauley, Martin. *Khrushchev and the Development of Soviet Agriculture*. London, 1976.

Medvedev, Roy. *La révolution d'octobre était-elle inéluctable?* Paris, 1976.

Medvedev, Roy and Zhores. *Khrushchev: The Years in Power*. New York, 1975.

Medvedev, Zhores A. *Andropov*. New York, 1983.

———. *The Rise and Fall of T. D. Lysenko*. New York, 1969.

———. *Soviet Science*. New York, 1978.

Mehnert, Klaus. *Peking and Moscow*. New York, 1963.

Melgunov, S. P. *Kak bol'sheviki zakhvatili vlast'* (How the Bolsheviks seized power). Paris, 1953.

Meray, Tibor. *Thirteen Days That Shook the Kremlin*. New York, 1959.

Meretskov, Kirill. *Na sluzhbe narodu* (Serving the people). Moscow, 1971.

*Metropol: A Literary Almanac*. Edited by Vasily Aksyonov et al. New York, 1982.

Mikoian, Anastas. *V nachale dvadtsatykh* (The early twenties). Moscow, 1975.

Miliukov, Pavel. *Emigratsiia na pereput'e* (The emigration at the crossroads). Paris, 1926.

*Mirnyi dogovor s Italiei* (The Peace treaty with Italy). Moscow, 1947.

Mlynar, Zdenek. *Nachtfrost.* Cologne-Frankfurt, 1978.

Morozov, Vasilii. "Soviet–German Pact of 1939 Seen in Retrospect." *Soviet News*, June 5, 1979.

Mühlen, Patrik von zur. *Zwischen Hackenkreuz und Sowjetstern.* Dusseldorf, 1971.

Muzafarcy, R. *Vdali ot krymskikh gor* (Far from the Crimean mountains). Manuscript.

Nabokov, Vladimir. "Godovshchina" (Anniversary). *Rul'*, November 18, 1927.

Nagy, Imre. *On Communism: In Defense of the New Course.* New York, 1957.

*Narodnoe khoziaistvo Kazakhskoi SSR* (Economy of the Kazakh SSR). Alma-Ata, 1957.

*Narodnoe khoziaistvo SSSR. Statisticheskii sbornik* (Economy of the USSR: Collected statistics). Moscow, 1956.

*Narodnoe khoziaistvo SSSR v 1958 godu. Statisticheskii sbornik* (Economy of the USSR in 1958. Collected statistics). Moscow, 1959.

*Narodnoe khoziaistvo SSSR v 1959 godu. Statisticheskii sbornik* (Economy of the USSR in 1959. Collected statistics). Moscow, 1960.

*Narodnoe khoziaistvo SSSR v 1960 godu. Statisticheskii sbornik* (Economy of the USSR in 1960. Collected statistics). Moscow, 1961.

*Narodnoe khoziaistvo SSSR v 1961 godu. Statisticheskii sbornik* (Economy of the USSR in 1961. Collected statistics). Moscow, 1962.

*Narodnoe khoziaistvo SSSR v 1962 godu. Statisticheskii sbornik* (Economy of the USSR in 1962. Collected statistics). Moscow, 1963.

*Narodnoe khoziaistvo SSSR v 1963 godu. Statisticheskii sbornik* (Economy of the USSR in 1963. Collected statistics). Moscow, 1964.

*Narodnoe khoziaistvo SSSR v 1964 godu. Statisticheskii sbornik* (Economy of the USSR in 1964. Collected statistics). Moscow, 1965.

*Narodnoe khoziaistvo SSSR v 1965 godu. Statisticheskii sbornik* (Economy of the USSR in 1965. Collected statistics). Moscow, 1966.

*Narodnoe khoziaistvo SSSR v 1972 godu. Statisticheskii sbornik* (Economy of the USSR in 1972: Collected statistics). Moscow, 1973.

*Narodnoe khoziaistvo SSSR v 1977 godu. Statisticheskii sbornik* (Economy of the USSR in 1977: Collected statistics). Moscow, 1978.

*Narodnoe khoziaistvo SSSR v 1978 godu. Statisticheskii sbornik* (Economy of the USSR in 1978: Collected statistics). Moscow, 1979.

*Narodnoe khoziaistvo SSSR v 1982 godu. Statisticheskii sbornik* (Economy of the USSR in 1982: Collected statistics). Moscow, 1983.

*Narodnoe obrazovarie v SSSR (sbornik dokumentov) 1917–1973* (Popular education in the USSR (collected documents, 1917–1973). Moscow, 1974.

*Narodno-khoziaistvennyi plan na 1935 god* (Economic plan for 1935). Moscow, 1935.

*Naselenie SSSR. Po dannym Vsesoiuznoi perepisi naseleniia 1979 goda* (Population of the USSR: Based on data from the 1979 All-Union Census). Moscow, 1980.

*Naselenie SSSR. Spravochnik* (Population of the USSR: Statistical handbook). Moscow, 1974.

*Naselenie SSSR. Statisticheskii sbornik* (Population of the USSR: Collected statistics). Moscow, 1974.

*Natsional'no-gosudarstvennoe stroitel'stvo v SSSR v perekhodnyi period ot kapitalizma k sotsializmu, 1917–1936* (Nation-state building in the USSR in the transitional period from capitalism to socialism, 1917–1936). Moscow, 1968.

*Nazi–Soviet Relations 1939–1941: Documents from the Archives of the German Foreign Office.* Edited by Raymond James Sontag and James Stuart Beddie. Washington, D.C., 1948.

Nefedov, K. and M. Tiurin. "Druzhba narodov SSSR—istochnik sily sovetskogo gosudarstva" (Friendship of the peoples of the USSR: A source of strength for the Soviet state). *Izvestiia*, June 19, 1953.

Nekrich, Aleksandr M. "The Arrest and Trial of I. M. Maisky." *Survey*, no. 100–101, 1976.

———. *Nakazannye narody* (The punished peoples). New York, 1978. English translation: *The Punished Peoples.* New York, 1978.

———. *Otreshis' ot strakha. Vospominaniia istorika* (Forsake fear: Memoirs of a historian). London, 1979.

———. *1941, 22 iiunia* (June 22, 1941). Moscow, 1965.

———. *Vneshniaia politika Anglii, 1939–1941* (England's foreign policy, 1939–1941). Moscow, 1963.

Nevskii, Vladimir I. *Istoriia RKP* (History of the Russian Communist party). Moscow, 1926.

Neznanskii, Fridrikh. "Statistika prestupnosti v SSSR" (Crime statistics in the USSR). *Posev*, no. 5, 1979.

Niclauss, Karlheinz. *Die Sowjetunion und Hitlers Machtergreifung.* Bonn, 1966.

Nicolaevsky, Boris I. *Power and the Soviet Elite.* Paperback ed. Ann Arbor, 1975. *See also* Nikolaevskii, Boris.

Nicolson, H. *Diaries, 1939–1945.* London, 1970.

Nikitin, A. "Perestroika raboti voennoi promyshlennosti SSSR v pervom periode Velikoi otechestvennoi voiny" (The reorganization of the Soviet war industry in the first phase of the Great Patriotic War). *Voenno-istoricheskii zhurnal*, no. 1, 1963.

Nikolaevskii, Boris. "O 'staroi' i 'novoi' emigratsii" (On the "old" and "new" emigrations). *Sotsialisticheskii vestnik*, no. 2, 1948. *See also* Nicolaevsky, Boris I.

Metropolitan Nikolai. "Verkhovnyi vozhd' strany i Krasnoi armii" (Supreme leader of the country and the Red Army). *Zhurnal Moskovskoi Patriarkhii*, no. 1, 1944.

*Niurnbergskii protsess* (The Nuremburg trial). Vol. 5. Moscow, 1958.

Nosik, B. *Po Rusi Iaroslavskoi* (Through the Old Russian Yaroslavl region). Moscow, 1968.

Nove, Alec. *An Economic History of the USSR.* London, 1972.

———. *The Soviet Economic System.* London, 1977.

Novikov, V. "Vstrechi s sovetskimi poddanymi vo Frantsii" (Meetings with Soviet citizens in France). *Novyi zhurnal*, no. 12. 1946.

*Obrazovanie GDR. Dokumenty i materialy* (The formation of the GDR: Documents and materials). Moscow, 1950.

Ogarkov, N. V. *Vsegda v gotovnosti k zashchite otechestva* (Ever ready to defend the fatherland). Moscow, 1982.

*Oktiabr'skoe vooruzhennoe vosstanie* (The armed October uprising). Moscow, 1957.

"O p'ese 'Bogatyri' Dem'iana Bednogo" (On Demyan Bedny's play *Bogatyri*). In *Protiv fal'tsifikatsii narodnogo proshlogo* (Against the falsification of the national past). Moscow-Leningrad, 1937.

*O polozhenii v biologicheskoi nauke. Stenograficheskii otchet sessii Vsesoiuznoi Akademii sel'skokhoziaistvennykh nauk imeni V. I. Lenina, 31 iiulia–7 avgusta 1948 g.* (On the situation in biological science: Stenographic record of the sessions of the V. I. Lenin All-Union Academy of Agricultural Sciences, July 31–August 7, 1948). Moscow, 1948.

Orlov, Alexander. *The Secret History of Stalin's Crimes.* London, 1954.

Orwell, George, *1984.* Paperback ed. New York, 1962.

Osipov, V. N. *Biograficheskaia spravka Valentiny Mashkovoi* (Biographical note on Valentina Mashkova). *Arkhiv samizdata*, vol. 29, doc. 1611a.

"Osnovy prochnosti mnogonatsional'nogo sovetskogo gosudarstva" (Foundations for the stability of the multinational Soviet state). *Izvestiia*, July 12, 1953.

Osokin, V. *Andrei Andreevich Vlasov.* New York, 1966.

Osorgin, Mikhail. *Vremena* (Times). Paris, 1955.

Ozerov, G. A. *Tupolevskaia sharaga* (The Tupolev Prison Institute). Frankfurt, 1973.

Papen, Franz von. *Memoirs.* London, 1952.

*Partiia v tsifrovom otnoshenii. Materialy po statistike lichnogo sostava partii* (The party in figures: Statistical materials on the composition of the party's personnel). Moscow, 1925.

Pascal, Pierre. *Mon journal de Russie, 1916–1918.* Paris, 1975.

Pavlenko, Petr. *Na vostoke* (In the East). Moscow, 1937.

Peis, Gunter. *Naujocks, l'homme qui déclencha la guerre.* Paris, 1961.

Pentkovskaia, V. V. "Rol' V. I. Lenina v obrazovanii SSSR" (Lenin's role in the formation of the USSR). *Voprosy istorii*, no. 3, 1956.

*Perepiska predsedatelia Soveta Ministrov SSSR s prezidentami SShA i prem'er-ministrami Velikobritanii vo vremia Velikoi otechestvennoi voiny 1941–1945 gg.* (Correspondence of the chairman of the USSR Council of Ministers with the president of the U.S.A. and the prime ministers of Great Britain during the Great Patriotic War 1941–1945). 2 vols. Moscow, 1957.

*Pervyi s"ezd sovetskikh pisatelei. Stenograficheskii otchet* (First Soviet Writers' Congress: Stenographic record). Moscow, 1934.

Peters, Yakov Kh. "Vospominaniia o rabote v VChK v pervyi god revoliutsii" (Recollections of Cheka work in the first year of the revolution). *Byloe*, no. 47, 1933.

Petrov, Vladimir. *Soviet Gold.* New York, 1949.

Petrov, Vladimir and Evdokia. *The Empire of Fear.* London, 1956.

*Piatiletnii plan* (The five-year plan). Moscow, 1928.

*Piatnadtsatyi s"ezd VKP(b). Stenograficheskii otchet* (Fifteenth Party Congress: Stenographic record). Moscow, 1928.

Pilniak, Boris. "Krasnoe derevo" (Mahogany). In *Opal'nye povesti* (Frowned-upon tales). New York, 1955.

Piontkovskii, S. A. *Grazhdanskaia voina v Rossii. Khrestomatiia* (Civil war in Russia: Readings). Moscow, 1925.

Pipes, Richard. *The Formation of the Soviet Union.* Cambridge, 1964.

Pisar, Samuel. "Let's Put Detente Back on the Rails." *New York Times Magazine*, September 25, 1977.

Platonov, Andrei. *Chevengur.* Ann Arbor, 1978.

*Plenum Tsentral'nogo Komiteta KPSS. 14–15 iiunia 1983 goda. Stenograficheskii otchet* (Plenum of the CPSU Central Committee, June 14–15, 1983: Stenographic Record). Moscow, 1983.

Ploss, Sidney I. *Conflict and Decision-Making in Soviet Russia: A Case Study of Agricultural Policy, 1953–1963.* Princeton, 1965.

Podrabinek, Aleksandr. *Karatel'naia meditsina* (Punitive medicine). New York, 1979.

Pokrovskii, Mikhail N. *Kontrrevoliutsiia za 4 goda* (Four years of counterrevolution). Moscow, 1922.

———. "K voprosu ob istoricheskom razvitii Rossii" (On the question of Russia's historical development). *Pod znamenem marksizma*, no. 5–6, 1924.

———. *Marksizm i osobennosti istoricheskogo razvitiia Rossii* (Marxism and the peculiarities of Russia's historical development). Leningrad, 1925.

Poliakov, Iu. A. *1921. Pobeda nad golodom* (1921: Victory over famine). Moscow, 1975.

Poliakov, Iu. A. and I. N. Kiselev. "Naselenie Rossii v 1917 g." (The population of Russia in 1917). *Voprosy istorii*, no. 6, 1980.

*Politicheskii dnevnik, 1964–1970* (Political diary, 1964–1970). 2 vols. Amsterdam, 1972–75.

Pomerantsev, Vladimir. "Ob iskrennosti v literature" (On sincerity in literature). *Novyi mir*, no. 12, 1953.

Popov, F. *Chekho-slovatskii miatezh i samarskaia uchredilka* (The Czechoslovak uprising and the Samara constituent assembly government). Samara, 1939.

Popov, George. *La Tscheka*. Paris, 1926.

Popovskii, Mark. *Upravlaemaia nauka* (Controlled science). London, 1978.

Poretsky, Elisabeth K. *Our Own People*. Ann Arbor, 1970.

"Pravda o gibeli generala M. P. Kirponosa" (The truth about the death of General M. P. Kirponos). *Voenno-istoricheskii zhurnal*, no. 9, 1964.

*Pravda o Kronshtadte* (The truth about Kronstadt). Prague, 1921.

Preobrazhenskii, E. A. *Novaia ekonomika* (New economics). Moscow, 1924.

Proektor, D. M. *Voina v Evrope, 1939–1941* (The war in Europe, 1939–1941). Moscow, 1963.

Prokopovich, S. N. *Narodnoe khoziaistvo SSSR* (The economy of the USSR). Vol. 1. New York, 1952.

*Protokoly Tsk RSDRP(b): August 1917–fevral' 1918* (Minutes of the Central Committee of the Bolshevik party, August 1917–February 1918). Moscow, 1958.

*Protsess nad Iosifom Brodskim v Leningrade, 18 fevralia 1964* (The trial of Joseph Brodsky in Leningrad, February 18, 1964). *Arkhiv samizdata*, vol. 4, doc. 236.

"Proval antinarodnoi avantiury v Vengrii" (Collapse of the anti-people's adventure in Hungary). *Pravda*, October 28, 1956.

*Public Papers of the Presidents: Dwight D. Eisenhower*. Washington, D.C., 1960.

*Public Papers of the Presidents: John F. Kennedy, 1962*. Washington, D.C.

Radek, Karl. "O kharaktere voiny s beloi Pol'shei" (On the nature of the war with White Poland). *Pravda*, December 11, 12, 1920.

———. *Piat' let Kominterna* (Five years of the Comintern). 2 vols. Moscow, 1924.

———. *Vneshniaia politika sovetskoi Rossii* (Foreign policy of Soviet Russia). Moscow-Leningrad, 1923.

Raina, Peter. *Political Opposition in Poland, 1954–1977*. London, 1978.

Ratushinskaia, Irina. *Stikhi. Poems. Poèmes*. Ann Arbor, 1984.

Rauschning, Hermann. *Gespräche mit Hitler*. 1940.

Reddaway, Peter, ed. *Uncensored Russia: Protest and Dissent in the Soviet Union—The Unofficial Moscow Journal "A Chronicle of Current Events."* New York, 1972.

Regel'son, Lev. *Tragediia russkoi tserkvi, 1917–1945* (Tragedy of the Russian church, 1917–1945). Paris, 1977.

Reitlinger, Gerald. *The House Built on Sand*. New York, 1960.

Remington, Robin Alison, ed. *Winter in Prague: Documents on Czechoslovak Communism in Crisis*. Cambridge, 1969.

Rendel', Leonid. *Podborka dokumentov, otnosiashchikhsia k pokaiannoi stat'e L. Krasnopevtseva, napechatannoi v lagernoi gazete "Za otlichnyi trud," 20 avgusta 1971* (Selection of documents on the statement of recantation by L. Krasnopevtsev printed in the labor camp newspaper "For outstanding labor," August 20, 1971) *Arkhiv samizdata*, vol. 22, doc. 1073.

Rigby, T. H. "Pervyi god Andropova" (Andropov's first year). *Obozrenie*, no. 7, November 1983.

Roeder, R. *Katorga*. London, 1958.

Rosenberg, William G. *Liberals in the Russian Revolution: The Constitutional Democratic Party, 1917–1921*. Princeton, 1974.

Rozanov, Vasilii. *Izbrannoe* (Selections). Munich, 1970.

Rumer, Boris. "The 'Second' Agriculture in the USSR." *Soviet Studies*, vol. 33, no. 4, October 1981.

———. "Structural Imbalance in the Soviet Economy." *Problems of Communism*, July-August 1984.

Sakharov, Andrei D. "A Letter from Exile." *New York Times Magazine*, June 8, 1980.

———. *O strane i mire* (My country and the world). New York, 1976. English translation: *My Country and the World*. New York, 1975.

———. *Sakharov Speaks*. New York, 1974.

Salimov, Kh. *Naselenie Srednei Azii* (The population of Central Asia). Tashkent, 1975.

*Sbornik ukazov i postanovlenii Vrenennogo Pravitel'stva* (Collected laws and decrees of the Provisional Government). Vol. 1. Petrograd, 1917.

*Sbornik zakonov SSSR, 1938–1967* (Registry of laws of the USSR, 1938–1967). Moscow, 1968.

Schapiro, Leonard. *The Communist Party of the Soviet Union*. New York, 1960.

Schomler, Joseph. *Vorkuta*. London, 1954.

Selikson-Bobrovskaia, Z. *Zapiski riadovogo podpolshchika* (Notes of a rank-and-file underground activist). Moscow, 1924.

*Sel'skoe khoziaistvo SSSR. Ezhegodnik* (USSR agriculture: Yearbook). Moscow, 1935.

*Sem' pisem iz Pragi. Pis'ma cheshskogo intelligenta, otpravlennye im svoemu drugu na Zapade v dekabre 1973–febrale 1974 gg.* (Seven letters from Prague: Letters from a Czech intellectual to a friend in the West, December 1973–February 1974). Rome, 1975.

Serge, Victor. *Memoirs of a Revolutionary*. London, 1967.

*Seventh Congress of the Comintern: Stenographic Report of the Proceedings*. Moscow, 1939.

Shaginian, Marietta. "Chelovek i vremia" (Man and the times). *Novyi mir*, no. 11, 1978.

———. *Dnevniki* (Diaries). Leningrad, 1930.

———. *Literaturnyi dnevnik* (Literary diary). Moscow-Petrograd, 1923.

Sharapov, G. V. *Razreshenie agrarnogo voprosa v Rossii posle pobedy Oktiabr'skoi revoliutsii* (Resolution of the agrarian problem in Russia after the victory of the October revolution). Moscow, 1961.

Shatov, V. M. *Materialy i dokumenty osvoboditel'nogo dvizheniia narodov Rossii v gody Vtoroi mirovoi voiny, 1941–1945* (Materials and documents of the liberation movement of the peoples of Russia during World War II, 1941–1945). New York, 1966.

Shaw, George Bernard. *The Rationalization of Russia*. Edited by Harry M. Geduld. Bloomington, 1964.

Shchetnikov, I. A. *Sorvannyi zagovor* (The foiled plot). Moscow, 1978.

Sherwood, Robert E. *Roosevelt and Hopkins: An Intimate Journey*. New York, 1948.

Shipler, David K. *Russia: Broken Idols, Solemn Dreams*. New York, 1983.

Shklsovskii, Viktor. *Khod konia* (Knight's move). Moscow-Berlin, 1923.

Shliapnikov, Aleksandr. *Semnadsatyi god* (The year 1917). 4 vols. Moscow, 1925.

Shneider, A. *Zapiski starogo moskvicha* (Notes of an Old Muscovite). Moscow, 1966.

Shulgin, Vasily V. *Dni* (Days). Belgrade, 1925.

———. *1920 god* (The year 1920). Sofia, 1922.

Shulgin, V. N. *Pedagogika perekhodnogo perioda* (Pedagogy in the transitional period). Moscow, 1927.

Sidorov, A. L. *Ekonomicheskoe polozhenie Rossii v gody Pervoi mirovoi voiny* (Economic conditions in Russia during World War I). Moscow, 1973.

Simis, Konstantin. "The Machinery of Corruption in the Soviet Union." *Survey*, vol. 23, no. 4 (105), Autumn 1977–78.

Skirdo, M. P. *Narod, armiia, polkovodets* (The people, the army, the military leader). Moscow, 1970.

Skrypnik, Mariia. *Vospominaniia ob Il'iche* (Memories of Ilyich [Lenin]). Moscow, 1965.

Slezkin, L. Iu. *Istoriia Kubinskoi respubliki* (History of the Cuban republic), Moscow, 1966.

Slusser, Robert M. *The Berlin Crisis of 1961*. Baltimore, 1973.

Smirnov, D. *Zapiski chekista* (Notes of a Cheka agent). Minsk, 1972.

Smith, Walter Bedell. *My Three Years in Moscow.* New York, 1950.

Sofinov, P. G. *Ocherki istorii VChK* (Essays in the history of the Cheka). Moscow, 1960.

*Solzhenitsyn: A Documentary Record.* Edited by Leopold Labedz. New York, 1971.

Solzhenitsyn, Aleksandr I. *Amerikanskie rechi* (American speeches). Paris, 1975.

———. *Arkhipelag GULag*. Vol. 3. Paris, 1975. English translation: *Gulag Archipelago.* 3 vols. New York, 1973–1978.

———. *Bodalsia telenok s dubom* (The oak and the calf). Paris, 1975. English translation: *The Oak and the Calf.* New York, 1980.

———. "Chem grozit Zapadu neponimanie Rossii" (How a lack of understanding of Russia threatens the West). *Vestnik RKhD*, no. 131, 1980.

———. *Sobranie sochinenii v 6 tomakh* (Collected works in 6 volumes). Frankfurt, 1973.

———. *V pervom kruge* (In the first circle). Paris, 1969. English translation: *The First Circle.* New York, 1968.

Solzhenitsyn, Aleksandr I., ed. *Iz-pod glyb* (From under the rubble). Paris, 1974. English translation: *From Under the Rubble.* Boston, 1975.

Sorokin, A. I. "Vooruzhennye sily razvitogo sotsializma" ((The armed forces of developed socialism). *Voprosy filosofii*, no. 2, 1983.

Souvarine, Boris. "Derniers entretiens avec Babel." *Contrepoint*, no. 30, 1979.

———. *Staline: Aperçu historique du bolchevisme.* Paris, 1977.

———. "Staline: pourquoi et comment." *Est et Ouest*, no. 602, November 1–15, 1977.

*Soveshchanie Informatsionnogo biuro Kommunisticheskikh partii v Varshave, iiun' 1948* (Conference of the Information Bureau of the Communist parties, Warsaw, June 1948). Moscow, 1948.

*Sovetskaia voennaia entsiklopediia* (Soviet military encyclopedia). Moscow, 1980.

Spiridovich, Aleksandr. *Istoriia bol'shevizma v Rossii* (History of bolshevism in Russia). Paris, 1922.

Spirin, L. M. *Klassy i partii v grazhdanskoi voine v Rossii* (Classes and parties in the Russian civil war). Moscow, 1968.

SSSR. Ministerstvo inostrannykh del (USSR. Ministry of Foreign Affairs). *Sovetskii Soiuz i Berlinskii vopros. Dokumenty* (The Soviet Union and the Berlin Crisis: Documents). Moscow, 1948.

*SSSR v tsifrakh v 1978 g.* (The USSR in figures, 1978). Moscow, 1979.

*SSSR v tsifrakh v 1980 g.* (The USSR in figures, 1980). Moscow, 1981.

Stalin, Iosif. *Rech' na XIX s"ezde partii, 14 oktiabria 1952* (Speech at the Nineteenth Party Congress, October 14, 1952). Moscow, 1952.

———. *Sochineriia* (Works). Moscow, 1947.

———. Sochineriia (Works). Vol. 13. Moscow, 1952.

————. *Voprosy leninizma* (Problems of Leninism). 9th Russ. ed. Moscow, 1933. English translation: *Problems of Leninism*. Moscow, 1953.

Starikov, Sergei and Roy Medvedev. *Philip Mironov and the Russian Civil War*. New York, 1978.

Stavrovskii, A. *Zakavkaz'e posle oktiabria* (Transcaucasia after October). Moscow-Leningrad, 1925.

Steenberg, Sven. *Wlassow, Verräter oder Patriot?* Cologne, 1968.

"Stenogramma vystupleniia F. E. Dzerzhinskogo na 8-m zasedanii VTsIK 17 fevralia 1919 g." (Stenogram of F. E. Dzerzhinsky's speech at the 8th session of the All-Russian Central Executive Committee, February 17, 1919). *Istoricheskii arkhiv*, no. 1, 1958.

Stone, Norman. *The Eastern Front, 1914–1917*. London, 1975.

Strik-Strikfeldt, Wilfried. *Against Stalin and Hitler*. London, 1970.

Struve, Nikita. *Les chrétiens en URSS*. Paris, 1963.

————. *Christians in Contemporary Russia*. London, 1967.

Stukalin, B. and L. Gvishiani. "Dialog o zhizni, professii i iskusstve" (A dialogue on life, professions, and art). *Moskva*, no. 1, 1980.

Suda, Zdenek. *The Czechoslovak Socialist Republic*. Baltimore, 1969.

*Sud'by sovremennoi intelligentsii* (Fates of the modern intelligentsia). Moscow, 1925.

Sukhanov, Nikolai N. *Zapiski o revoliutsii* (Notes on the revolution). 7 vols. Berlin-Petrograd-Moscow, 1922–1923.

Sul'kevich, S. *Naselenie SSSR* (The Population of the USSR). Moscow, 1939.

Sutton, Anthony C. *Western Technology and Soviet Economic Development, 1917–1930*. Stanford, 1972.

Swianiewicz, S. *Forced Labour and Economic Development*. London, 1965.

Tairov, Aleksandr Ia. "V poiskakh stilia" (In search of a style). *Teatr i dramaturgiia*, no. 4, 1936.

Théry, Edmond. *La transformation économique de la Russie*. Paris, 1914.

Tippelskirch, Kurt von. *Geschichte des zweiten Weltkriegs*. Bonn, 1951. Russian translation: *Istoriia Vtoroi mirovoi voiny*. Moscow, 1956.

Tishkov, A. *Pervyi chekist* (The first Chekist). Moscow, 1968.

Toland, John. *Adolf Hitler*. Paris, 1978.

Tolstoy, Nikolai, *Victims of Yalta*. London, 1977.

Trainin, I. P. *SSSR i natsional'nye problemy* (The USSR and nationality problems). Moscow, 1924.

*Trial of the Major War Criminals Before the International Military Tribunal*. Vol. 39. Nuremburg, 1947.

Trifonov, I. Ia. *Klassy i klassovaia bor'ba v SSSR* (Classes and the class struggle in the USSR). Leningrad, 1964.

————. *Likvidatsiia ekspluatatorskikh klassov v SSSR* (The elimination of the exploiting classes in the USSR). Moscow, 1975.

Trotsky [Trotskii], Leon. *Challenge of the Left Opposition, 1923–1925*. New York, 1975.

————. *Challenge of the Left Opposition, 1926–1927*. New York, 1980.

————. *The History of the Russian Revolution*. London, 1967.

————. *Kak vooruzhalas' revoliutsiia* (How the revolution armed). Moscow, 1923.

————. *Lenin*. Paris, 1925.

————. *My Life*. New York, 1970.

————. *On Lenin*. London, 1971.

————. *Sochineniia* (Works). 21 vols. Moscow, 1925–1927.

————. *Stalin: An Appraisal of the Man and His Influence*. New York, 1941.

————. *The Stalin School of Falsification.* New York, 1972.

————. *Terrorism and Communism.* Ann Arbor, 1961.

————. *Their Morals and Ours.* New York, 1973.

————. *The Trotsky Papers, 1917–1922.* Edited by Jan M. Meijer. 2 vols. The Hague, 1964–1971.

————. *Uroki oktiabria* (Lessons of October). Moscow, 1924.

————. "Vospominaniia ob oktiabr'skoi revoliutsii" (Recollections of the October revolution). *Proletarskaia revoliutsiia,* no. 10, 1922.

————. *Writings of Leon Trotsky, 1929–1940.* 14 vols. New York, 1969–1979.

Truman, Harry S. *Public Papers, 1945–50.* Washington, D.C., 1964–1965.

Tsederbaum-Dan, L. O. "Vospominaniia" (Memoirs). *Novyi zhurnal,* no. 75, 1964.

Tsentral'noe statisticheskoe upravlenie (TsSU) SSSR (Central Statistical Agency of the USSR). *Itogi Vsesoiuznoi perepisi naseleniia 1970 g.* (Results of the 1970 All-Union Census). Vol. 4. Moscow, 1973.

————. *O predvaritel'nykh itogakh Vsesoiuznoi perepisi naseleniia 1979 g.* (Preliminary results of the 1979 All-Union Census). Moscow, 1979.

Tucker, Robert C. "The Emergence of Stalin's Foreign Policy." *Slavic Review,* vol. 36, no. 4, 1977.

————. "The Rise of Stalin's Personality Cult." *American Historical Review,* vol. 84, no. 2, 1979.

Tucker, Robert C., ed. *Stalinism: Essays in Historical Interpretation.* New York, 1977.

*Ukrainskii vysnik,* no. 7–8, Spring 1974. Baltimore, 1975.

Ulam, Adam B. *Expansion and Coexistence: Soviet Foreign Policy 1917–1973.* New York, 1974.

Umanskii, R. G. *Na boevykh rubezhakh* (On the fighting lines). Moscow, 1960.

United Kingdom. House of Commons. *Parliamentary Debates.*

Upton, Anthony F. *Finland in Crisis, 1940–1941.* Ithaca, 1964.

Uranov, S. *O nekotorykh priemakh verbochnoi raboty inostrannykh razvedok* (On some recruiting techniques of foreign intelligence agencies). Moscow, 1937.

Urlanis, B. Ts. *Problemy dinamiki naseleniia* (Problems of population dynamics). Moscow, 1974.

U.S. House of Representatives. *Evidence of Mohammed Ayob Assil.* Hearings Before the Subcommittee on Human Rights of the Foreign Affairs Committee. October 9, 1983.

U.S. Senate. *USSR Labour Camps.* Hearings Before the Subcommittee to Investigate the Administration of the Internal Security Act and Other Internal Security Laws of the Committee of the Judiciary. February 2, 1973.

*USSR Facts & Figures Annual.* Editec by John L. Scherer. Vol. 4, 1980.

Ustrialov, N. *Pod znakom revoliutsii* (Under the sign of revolution). Harbin, 1927.

————. *V. bor'be za Rossiiu* (In the struggle for Russia). Harbin, 1920.

Utkin, B. P. "Vospitatel'naia rol' sovetskikh vooruzhennykh sil v usloviiakh razvitogo sotsializma" (The educational role of the Soviet armed forces under developed socialism). *Voprosy filosofii,* no. 1, 1984.

Valentinov (Volskii), N. *Doktrina pravogo kommunizma* (The doctrine of right-wing communism). Munich, 1960.

————. *NEP i krizis partii posle smerti Lenina* (NEP and the party crisis after Lenin's death). Stanford, 1971.

————. "Piatakov o bol'shevizm" (Pyatakov on bolshevism). *Novyi zhurnal,* no. 52, 1958.

Vali, Ferenc A. *Rift and Revolt in Hungary.* Cambridge, 1961.

Vardys, V. Stanley. *The Catholic Church, Dissent, and Nationality in Soviet Lithuania.* Boulder, 1978.

Varshavskii, V. S. *Nezamechennoe pokolenie* (The unnoticed generation). New York, 1966.

Vasilevskii, A. M. *Delo vsei zhizni* (A whole life's work). Moscow, 1974.

Vatsetis, Joachim I. "Miatezh levykh eserov" (The Left SR revolt). *Prometei,* no. 4, 1967.

————. "Vospominaniia" (Reminiscences). *Pamiat'. Istoricheskii sbornik* (Memory: A historical anthology), no. 8, Moscow, 1977; Paris, 1979.

*Velikaia otechestvennaia voina Sovetskogo Soiuza, 1941–45. Kratkaia istoriia* (The Great Patriotic War of the Soviet Union, 1941–45: A brief history). Moscow, 1970.

*Vneshniaia politika Sovetskogo Soiuza i mezhdunarodnye otnosheniia, 1962 god* (Foreign policy of the Soviet Union and international relations, 1962). Moscow, 1963.

*Vneshniaia politika Sovetskogo Soiuza, 1945 god* (Foreign policy of the Soviet Union, 1945). Moscow, 1949.

*Vneshniaia politika Sovetskogo Soiuza, 1946 god* (Foreign policy of the Soviet Union, 1946). Moscow, 1952.

*Vneshniaia politika Sovetskogo Soiuza v period Otechestvennoi voiny* (Foreign policy of the Soviet Union during the Patriotic War). 3 vols. Moscow, 1946–1947.

*Vneshniaia politika SSSR* (Foreign policy of the USSR). Vol. 18. Moscow, 1973.

*Vneshniaii politika SSSR, 1948 god.* (Foreign policy of the USSR, 1948). Moscow, 1950.

*Vneshniaia politika SSSR, 1949 god* (Foreign policy of the USSR, 1949). Moscow, 1953.

*Vneshniaia politika SSSR, 1950 god* (Foreign policy of the USSR, 1950). Moscow, 1953.

*Vneshniaia torgovlia SSSR v 1978 g.* (Soviet foreign trade, 1978). Moscow, 1979.

*Vo glave zashchity sovetskoi rodiny. Ocherk deiatel'nosti KPSS v gody Velikoi otechestvennoi voiny* (Heading the defense of the Soviet homeland: Outline of the activities of the CPSU during the Great Patriotic War). Moscow, 1975.

*Der Volksaufstand vom Juni 17, 1953.* Bonn, 1963.

Volskii, A. *Umstvennyi rabochii* (Intellectual worker). New York, 1968.

Volynskii, Leonid. "Skvoz' noch'" (Through the night). *Novyi mir,* no. 1, 1963.

Voronov, N. N. *Na sluzhbe voennoi* (In military service). Moscow, 1963.

Voslenskii, Mikhail S. *Nomenklatura* (Nomenklatura). Paris, 1980; Vienna, 1980.

*Vospominaniia o V. I. Lenine v 5 tomakh* (Recollections of V. I. Lenin in 5 volumes). Moscow, 1969.

Voznesenskii, I. "Imena i sud'by. Nad iubileinom spiskom AN" (Names and destinies: On the anniversary listing of members of the Academy of Sciences). *Pamiat',* no. 1, Moscow, 1976; New York, 1978.

Voznesenskii, Nikolai. *Voennaia ekonomika SSSR v period Otechestvennoi voiny* (The war economy of the USSR during the Patriotic War). Moscow, 1947.

*Vsesoiuznoe soveshchanie istorikov* (All-Union Conference of Historians). Moscow, 1964.

"Vsesoiuznoe tvorcheskoe soveshchanie rabotnikov sovetskoi kinematografii" (All-Union Creative Conference of Soviet Cinematographers). In *Za bol'shoe kinoiskusstvo* (For a great cinematic art). Moscow, 1935.

VSKhSON. *Programma.* (All-Russia Social Christian Union for the Liberation of the People). *Sud. V tiur'makh i lageriakh* (Program; trial; in prisons and camps). Paris, 1975.

Warlimont, Walter. *Im Hauptquartier der deutschen Wehrmacht, 1939–1945.* Frankfurt, 1962.

Webb, Sidney and Beatrice. *Soviet Communism: A New Civilization?* 2 vols. London, 1936.

Weinberg, Gerhard L. *Germany and the Soviet Union, 1939–1941.* London, 1954.

Weit, Erwin. *Dans l'ombre de Gomulka.* Paris, 1971.

Weygand, Maxime. *Mémoires*. Vol. 2. Paris, 1957.

Whaley, Barton. *Codeword Barbarossa*. Cambridge, 1973.

Windsor, Philip. *City on Leave: A History of Berlin, 1945–1962*. New York, 1963.

Winter, Ella. *Red Virtue: Human Relationships in the New Russia*. New York, 1933.

Woodward E. L. *British Foreign Policy in the Second World War*. London, 1962.

Woytinsky, W. S. *Stormy Passage: A Personal History Through Two Revolutions to Democracy and Freedom*. New York, 1969.

Yergin, Daniel. *Shattered Peace*. Boston, 1977.

Zagladin, V. and I. Frolov. "Global'nye problemy sovremennosti. Poiski reshenii" (Global problems of the present day: In search of solutions). *Pravda*, May 7, 1979.

*Za glubokuiu razrabotku istorii sovetskoi literatury* (For a profound elaboration of the history of Soviet literature). *Kommunist*, no. 12, 1956.

Zagoria, Donald Z. *The Sino-Soviet Conflict, 1956–1961*. Princeton, 1962.

Zakharov, M . "Nachal'nyi period Velikoi otechestvennoi voiny i ego uroki" (The opening phase of the Great Patriotic War and its lessons). *Voenno-istoricheskii zhurnal*, no. 7, 1961.

*Zakonodatel'nye akty po voprosam narodnogo khoziaistva SSSR* (Legislative acts concerning questions of the Soviet economy). Vol. 1. Moscow, 1961.

Zamiatin [Zamyatin], Evgenii. "Ia boius'" (I am afraid). *Litsa* (Persons). New York, 1955. English translation: "I Am Afraid." In *A Soviet Heretic: Essays by Yevgeny Zamyatin*. Edited and translated by Mirra Ginsburg. Chicago, 1970.

———. *We*. Translated by Mirra Ginsburg, New York, 1972.

Zamiatin, Leonid. "Vosstanovit' klimat razriadki i doveriia" (Restore the climate of detente and trust). *Literaturnaia gazeta*, February 27, 1980.

*Za rubezhom. Khronika sem'i Zernovykh* (Abroad: The Zernov family's chronicle). Paris, 1926.

*Zasedaniia Verkhovnogo Soveta Kalmykskoi ASSR, 2-go sozyva. Stenograficheskii otchet* (Proceedings of the Second Supreme Soviet of the Kalmyk ASSR: Stenographic record). Elista, 1958.

Zaslavskaia, T. I. "O neobkhodimosti bolee uglublennogo izucheniia v SSSR sotsial'nogo mekhanizma razvitiia ekonomiki" (On the necessity for more intensive study of the social mechanism of economic development in the USSR). April 1983. *Arkhiv samizdata*, doc. 5042.

Zawodny J. K. *Death in the Forest*. South Bend, 1962.

Zetkin, Clara. *Lenin on the Emancipation of Women*. Moscow, n.d.

Zharov, L. I. and V. M. Ustinov. *Internatsional'nye chasti Krasnoi armii v boiakh za vlast' Sovetov v gody inostrannoi voennoi interventsii i grazhdanskoi voiny v SSSR* (The international units of the Red Army in the battles for Soviet power during the foreign military intervention and civil war in the USSR). Moscow, 1960.

*Zhit' v mire i druzhbe! Prebyvanie predsedatelia Soveta Ministrov SSSR N. S. Khrushcheva v SShA 15–27 sentiabria 1959 g.* (Live in peace and friendship! The U.S. tour of N. S. Khrushchev, chairman of the USSR Council of Ministers, September 15–27, 1959). Moscow, 1959.

Zhordaniia, Noi. *Moia zhizn'* (My life). Stanford, 1968.

Zhukov, Georgii. *Vospominaniia i razmyshleniia* (Recollections and reflections). Moscow, 1969.

———. *Vospominaniia i razmyshleniia* (Recollections and reflections). Moscow, 1974.

Zhvaniia, G. "V. I. Lenin i partiinaia organizatsiia Gruzii v period bor'by za sovetskuiu vlast'" (V. I. Lenin and the Georgian party organization during the struggle for Soviet power). *Zaria vostoka*, April 21, 1961.

Zinoviev, Aleksandr. *Zheltyi dom* (Yellow house). Lausanne, 1980.

Zinoviev, Grigorii. *N. Lenin. Vladimir Il'ich Ul'ianov* (Lenin: Vladimir Ilyich Ulyanov). Petrograd, 1917.

Zlatopol'skii, Zh. L. *Obrazovanie i razvitie SSSR kak soiuznogo gosudarstva* (The formation and development of the USSR as a state based on union). Moscow, 1954.

Zorin, S. and N. Alekseev. *Vremia ne zhdet. Nasha strana nakhoditsia na povorotnom punkte istorii* (Time does not wait: Our country stands at a turning point in history). Frankfurt, 1970.

Zoshchenko, Mikhail. *Izbrannoe* (A selection). Ann Arbor, 1960.

# PERIODICALS

*Arkhiv samizdata* (Samizdat archive).

*Belarus'* (Belorussia).

*Biulleten' oppozitsii* (Bulletin of the opposition).

*Bol'shevik* (Bolshevik). Theoretical organ of the Central Committee of the Communist party. Name changed to *Kommunist* in 1952.

*Byloe* (The past).

*Communist International.*

*Corriere della sera.*

*Ekonomicheskaia gazeta* (Economic gazette).

*Ekonomicheskaia zhizn'* (Economic life).

*Est et Ouest.*

*Ezhenedel'nik VChK* (Cheka weekly).

*Le Figaro.*

*Grani* (Facets).

*L'internationale communiste.*

*International Herald Tribune.*

*Iskusstvo kino* (Art of the cinema).

*Istoricheskie zapiski* (Historical notes).

*Istoricheskii arkhiv* (Historical archive).

*Istorik-marksist* (Marxist historian).

*Izvestiia* (News).

*Japan Times.*

*Kommunist* (Communist). See *Bol'shevik.*

*Kommunisticheskii trud* (Communist labor).

*Kommunist Litvy* (Communist of Lithuania).

*Kommunist vooruzhennykh sil* (Communist of the armed forces).

*Komsomol'skaia pravda* (Komsomol truth).

*Kontinent* (Continent).

*Krasnaia gazeta* (Red gazette).

*Krasnaia zvezda* (Red star).

*Krasnyi mech* (Red sword). Kiev.

*Kul'tura i zhizn'* (Culture and life).

*Legkaia industriia* (Light industry).

*Leningradskaia pravda* (Leningrad truth).
*Literaturnaia gazeta* (Literary gazette).
*Literaturnoe nasledstvo* (Literary heritage).
*London Evening News.*
*Manchester Guardian.*
*Molodaia gvardiia* (Young guard).
*Le monde.*
*Moskva* (Moscow).
*Nash sovremennik* (Our contemporary).
*Nauka i religiia* (Science and religion).
*Nedelia* (The week).
*Newsweek.*
*New York Times.*
*Novaia zhizn'* (New life).
*Novoe vremia* (New times).
*Novoe russkoe slovo* (New Russian word).
*Novye knigi* (New books).
*Novy grad* (New town).
*Novyi mir* (New world).
*Novyi zhurnal* (New journal). New York.
*Oktiabr'* (October).
*Pamiat'* (Memory).
*Parizhskii vestnik* (Paris herald).
*Partiinaia zhizn'* (Party life).
*Partiinoe stroitel'stvo* (Party building).
*Petrogradskaia pravda* (Petrograd truth).
*Planovoe khoziaistvo* (Planned economy).
*Pod znamerem marksizma* (Under Marxism's banner).
*Le point.*
*Posev* (The sowing).
*Poslednie novosti* (Latest news). Paris.
*Pravda* (Truth).
*Problemy ekonomiki* (Problems of economics).
*Professional'nyi vestnik* (Trade union herald).
*Proletarskaia kul'tura* (Proletarian culture).
*Proletarskaia revoliutsiia* (Proletarian revolution).
*Prometei* (Prometheus).
*Rabochii i teatr* (The worker and the theater).
*Revoliutsiia i kul'tura* (Revolution and culture).
*Revoliutsiia i voina* (Revolution and war).
*Rul'* (The helm). Paris.
*Russkaia mysl'* (Russian thought).
*Severnaia kommuna* (Northern commune).
*Sobranie uzakonenii* (Collected statutes).
*Sotsialisticheskaia zakonnost'* (Socialist legality).
*Sotsialisticheskii vestnik* (Socialist herald).
*Sovetskaia Rossiia* (Soviet Russia).
*Sovetskii patriot* (Soviet patriot).
*Soviet Jewish Affairs.*

*Soviet News.*

*Soviet Studies.*

*Suchasnist'* (Present day).

*Survey.*

*Svod zakonov* (Register of laws).

*Teatr i dramaturgiia* (Theater and playwrighting).

*Time.*

*Times.* London.

*Trud* (Labor).

*Ukrainskii vysnik* (Ukrainian herald).

*U.S. News and World Report.*

*Vedomosti Verkhovnogo Soveta SSSR* (News of the USSR Supreme Soviet).

*Vestnik Akademii Nauk SSSR* (Bulletin of the USSR Academy of Sciences).

*Vestnik RSKhD* (Bulletin of the Russian Student Christian Movement). Paris and New York.

*Vestnik truda* (Labor herald).

*Voenno-istoricheskii zhurnal* (Military-historical journal).

*Voina i revoliutsiia* (War and revolution).

*Volia Rossii* (Russia's will).

*Voprosy filosofii* (Problems of philosophy).

*Voprosy istorii* (Problems of history).

*Voprosy istorii KPSS* (Problems of CPSU history).

*Washington Post.*

*Za industrializatsiiu* (For industrialization).

*Zaria vostoka* (Dawn of the East).

*Zhurnalist* (Journalist).

*Zhurnal Moskovskoi Patriarkhii* (Journal of the Moscow Patriarchate).

*Znamia* (Banner).

*Znamia truda* (Banner of labor). The Left SR newspaper.

# INDEX

# ABOUT THE AUTHORS

Mikhail Heller was born in 1922 and is a historian by profession, having received his Ph.D. and post-doctoral degrees in Historical Sciences. Since 1969 he has lived in Paris, where he teaches at the Sorbonne. Mikhail Heller's books include: *The World of Concentration Camps and Soviet Literature* (London: Overseas Publications, 1974) and *Andrei Platonov in Search of Happiness* (Paris: IMCA Press, 1982). He has authored numerous articles on literary as well as historical topics.

Aleksandr M. Nekrich was born in 1920 and completed his doctoral and post-doctoral education in Historical Sciences. From 1950 to 1976, A. Nekrich was a Senior Scholar at the USSR Academy of Sciences Institute of History. Since 1976 he has been at Harvard's Russian Research Center. His works include: *British Foreign Policy 1939–1941* (Moscow: Academy of Sciences Publishing House, 1964); *June 22, 1941* (Moscow: Nauka Publishers, 1965); *The Punished Peoples* (New York: W.W. Norton, 1979); and *Forsake Fear* (London: Overseas Publications, 1979). Currently A. Nekrich is Editor-in-Chief of the analytical journal *Obozrenie* (Paris).